Historical Periodicals

AN ANNOTATED WORLD LIST
OF
HISTORICAL AND RELATED SERIAL PUBLICATIONS

Historical Periodicals

AN ANNOTATED WORLD LIST OF HISTORICAL AND RELATED SERIAL PUBLICATIONS

Publicaciones Periódicas de Carácter Histórico

Периодические издания по истории

Periodici di Argomento Storico

Périodiques Historiques

Historische Periodica

历史定期刊物

EDITORS:

ERIC H. BOEHM and LALIT ADOLPHUS

Editor, Historical Abstracts

Assistant Editor, Historical Abstracts

CLIO PRESS

Santa Barbara, California · Munich, Germany

1961

Clio Reference Publications

Historical Periodicals

CLIO PRESS

800 East Micheltorena Street, Santa Barbara, California

München-Solln, Emil-Dittler-Strasse 12, Germany

Library of Congress Catalog Card Number 59-87 83

Price $ 27.50

Contents

WORLD LIST OF HISTORICAL AND RELATED SERIAL PUBLICATIONS

Acknowledgments

The editors acknowledge with thanks the contributions made by:

Vetilio Alfau Duran, Director, Library of the University of Santo Domingo, Ciudad Trujillo
Dirk van Arkel, Leiden
Paula Armstrong, Editorial Department, University of Toronto Press, Toronto
Ino Arndt, Munich
A. G. Bagnall, Librarian, National Library Centre, National Library Service, Wellington
D. L. Banerjee, Assistant Librarian, National Library, Calcutta
Robert-Henri Bautier, *Archivum*, Paris
Charles R. Bawden, Lecturer in Mongolian, School of Oriental and African Studies, University of London
Eloy Benito Ruano, Consejo Superior de Investigaciones Científicas, Escuela de Estudios Medievales, Madrid
Nils Berndtson, Chief Librarian, Library of Scientific Societies, Helsinki
Todor Borov, Director, Bulgarian Bibliographical Institute, Sofia
W. T. Brandhorst, General Reference and Bibliography Division, Library of Congress, Washington, D. C.
Juan F. Cabestany Fort, *Indice Histórico Español*, Barcelona
Guillermo Céspedes del Castillo, University of Seville
Chaoying Fang, Berkeley, California
Chen Tsu-lung, Librarian, Institut des Hautes Etudes Chinoises, University of Paris
Hilary Conroy, Tokyo
Carmen Cook de Leonard, Editor, *El Mexico Antiguo*, Mexico, D. F.
Antony Croghan, Colonial Office Library, London
J. C. Currie, South African Public Library, Cape Town
Else Dahl, Département des Périodiques, Bibliothèque Nationale, Paris
Ricardo Donoso, Director, Sociedad Chilena de Historia y Geografía, Santiago
Alexander F. Dygnas, London
Sylvia L. England, North Library, British Museum, London
H. B. Fant, National Historical Publications Commission, Bethesda, Maryland
Fritz Fellner, University of Vienna
Maxima M. Ferrer, Library Coordinator, Inter-Departmental Reference Service, Institute of Public Administration, University of the Philippines, Manila
A. M. C. Field, Institute of Historical Research, University of London
Zora Gregorich, Berkeley, California
John A. S. Grenville, University of Nottingham
Leo Gruliow, Editor, *The Current Digest of the Soviet Press*, Columbia University, New York
A. Halim, Professor of History, University of Dacca
Philip M. Hamer, Executive Director, National Historical Publications Commission, Bethesda, Maryland
Abdul Hamid, Professor of History, Government College, Lahore
Kentaro Hayashi, Professor of Western History, University of Tokyo

Cecil Hobbs, Head, South Asia Section, Library of Congress, Washington, D. C.
José Honorio Rodrigues, Director, Arquivo Nacional, Rio de Janeiro
Janina Hoskins, Slavic and Central European Division, Library of Congress, Washington, D. C.
Marilyn M. Houston, Washington, D. C.
U San Htwar, Sarpay Beikman Institute, Rangoon
Josef M. A. Janssen, Editor, Annual Bibliography of the International Association of Egyptologists, Leiden
Ruth Jones, Librarian, International African Institute, London
Karin Kaut, Munich
Charles Kecskemeti, Archivum, Paris
Catherine Koumarianoû, Neohellenic Research Center, Athens
Melvin Kranzberg, Case Institute of Technology, Cleveland, Ohio
Girja Kumar, Librarian, Indian Council of World Affairs Library, New Delhi
P. Michael Lacko, S. J., Pontificium Institutum Orientalium Studiorum, Rome
Trüong Bửu Lâm, Director, Institut National des Recherches Historiques, Département de l'Education Nationale, Republic du Viêt-Nam, Saigon
David Large, Trinity College, Dublin
G. Level, Administrateur, Bibliothèque Nationale d'Alger, Algiers
Madeleine Ly-Tio-Fane, Assistant Librarian, Mauritius Institute, Port Louis
Ann E. Macara, Munich
A. M. Magee, Editorial Department, The Canadian Historical Review, Calgary, Alberta
Luis Martínez Delgado, Director, Sección de Coordinación de Estudios Historicós, Ministerio de Educación Nacional, República de Colombia, Bogotá
James R. Masterson, Editor, Writings on American History, National Historical Publications Commission, Bethesda, Maryland
D. Matthews, India Office Library, London
Oswald F. A. Menghin, Centro Argentino de Estudios Prehistóricos, Buenos Aires
Haakon Falck Myckland, Librarian, Royal University Library, Oslo
Nils Palmborg, Librarian, Universitetsbiblioteket, Lund
J. D. Pearson, Librarian, School of Oriental and African Studies, University of London
E. Pfeffermann, Jewish National and University Library, Jerusalem
Armando D. Pirotto, President, Comité Uruguay de Ciencias Históricas, Montevideo
Paul Podjed, Munich
Herbert E. Reed, Associate Editor, Historical Abstracts
Lore Reed-Wymar, Munich
Benvenuto Reghini, Vice Director, Biblioteca Nazionale Centrale, Florence
Ina Renner, Munich
Veronica Roberts, London
A. M. Lewin Robinson, Assistant Chief Librarian, South African Public Library, Cape Town
Leo E. Rose, Indian Press Digests, Center for South Asia Studies, Institute of International Studies, University of California, Berkeley
Jorge Rubió Loís, Indice Histórico Español, Barcelona
Ursula Schmidt-Tausendfreund, Munich
Robert Schumacher, Bibliothèque Nationale, Luxembourg
Dorothea Scott, University of Hong Kong Library, Hong Kong
Karl Selber, Historisches Institut, University of Vienna
M. Shuja-ud-Din, Professor of History, Dyal Singh College, Lahore
C. R. Spurgin, Chicago, Illinois
Irene A. Stachura, Library, University of California, Berkeley

Eugen Stănescu, Chief Editor, Studii, Bucharest
The Rev. James D. M. Stuart, Librarian, Cambridge Brotherhood House, Delhi
Pamela H. Sutton, Rome
Margit Szekeres, Librarian, Országos Széchényi Könyvtar, Budapest
Angelo Tamborra, Biblioteca, Ministero degli Affari Esteri, Rome
A. Toussaint, Chief Archivist, Archives Department, Colony of Mauritius, Port Louis
Frank N. Trager, Center for International Affairs and Development, New York University
Harald L. Tveteras, Director, Universitetsbiblioteket, Oslo
Trailokya Nath Upraity, Principal, College of Education, and Deputy Secretary of Education, Kathmandu
Ramón Valdés del Toro, Centro de Enseñanza Media y Profesional, Tapia del Casariego, Asturias
J. Van Hove, Conservateur, Bibliothèque Royale de Belgique, Brussels
Michelle Villoing, Département des Périodiques, Bibliothèque Nationale, Paris
Thilo Vogelsang, Head of the Library, Institut für Zeitgeschichte, Munich
W. Vontobel, Schweizerische Landesbibliothek, Bern
Francis S. Wagner, Library of Congress, Washington, D. C.
Wang Gungwa, University of Malaya, Kuala Lumpur
Paul Wheatley, University of California, Berkeley
A. W. Willemsen, wetenschappelijk ambtenaar, Koninklijke Bibliotheek, The Hague
Erna Wollert, Munich
Hugh B. Wood, Professor of Education, University of Oregon, Eugene, Oregon
Joseph G. Zakhour, Director, Damascus University Library
Costi K. Zurayk, American University of Beirut
A. A. Zvorykin, Editor, Bol'shaia Sovetskaia Entsiklopediia, Moscow

The collaboration of the following institutions is gratefully acknowledged:

Academia Portuguesa da História, Lisbon
American University of Beirut (Arab Studies Program)
Arquivo Histórico Ultramarino, Lisbon
Asiatic Research Center, Korea University, Seoul
Australian National Library, Canberra
Bayerische Staatsbibliothek, Munich
Bibliografski institut FNRJ [Bibliographical Institute of the Federal People's Republic of Yugoslavia], Belgrade
Biblioteca Academiei Republicii Populare Romîne, Bucharest
Biblioteca Nazionale Centrale, Florence
Bibliothèque Generale et Archives, Rabat
Burma Historical Commission, Rangoon
Commonwealth National Library, Canberra
Deutsche Akademie der Wissenschaften zu Berlin, Berlin
Fine Arts Department, Bangkok
Gennadius Library, American School of Classical Studies, Athens
Ghana Library Board, Accra
Gregg M. Sinclair Library, University of Hawaii, Honolulu
Historický ústav, Československá akademie věd [Historical Institute, Czechoslovak Academy of Sciences], Prague

Indice Historico Español, Barcelona
Institute for the Study of the U.S.S.R., Munich
Instituto Brasiliero de Bibliografia e Documentação, Rio de Janeiro
Instytut Istorii, Polska Akademia Nauk [Historical Institute, Polish Academy of Sciences], Cracow
Istoriski institut Srpske akademije nauka [Historical Institute of the Serbian Academy of Sciences], Belgrade
Library of Congress (Serial Division and General Reference and Bibliography Division), Washington, D. C.
Library of the Royal University of Malta, Valletta
Madjelis Ilmu Pengetahuan Indonesia (Council for Sciences of Indonesia), Djakarta
Milli Kütüphane, Bibliyografya Enstitüsü [National Library, Bibliographical Institute], Ankara
Ministry of Education of the Hashemite Kingdom of Jordan, Amman
Ministry of Guidance, Republic of Iraq, Baghdad
National Diet Library, Tokyo
National Historical Publications Commission, Bethesda, Maryland
National Information Service, Poona
National Library, Calcutta
National Library, Tehran
National Library of Canada, Ottawa
National Library of Ireland, Dublin
National Library Service, Wellington
New Zealand High Commissioner's Office, London
Office of the High Commissioner for Australia, London
Office of the Registrar of Books and Newspapers, Nuwara Eliya, Ceylon
Public Archives of Canada, Ottawa
Rigsbibliotekarembedet [The Office of the National Librarian], Copenhagen
Royal University Library, Oslo
Sarpay Beikman Institute, Rangoon
Schweizerische Landesbibliothek, Bern
Société d'Histoire des Colonies Françaises, Paris
Zeitschrift für Geschichtswissenschaften, Berlin

Indroduction

Scope. Genesis, Sources and Methods.
Acknowledgments. Plans for the Future.

SCOPE

This book is an annotated directory of serial publications which contain articles on historical topics. The term history has been interpreted in its broadest sense as the study of the past. The editors therefore also included many periodicals which fall outside the discipline of history as it is usually taught in universities. For instance, a student of the history of such fields as music or the fine arts will find periodicals thereon listed here.

The editors have attempted to satisfy a need for an all-inclusive rather than an evaluative inventory. We included periodicals from fields other than history if only one article in five was considered to be historical. We have, further, cited periodicals which were recommended for inclusion even though their historical content did not reach that proportion. Of approximately ten thousand periodicals examined by the staff of HISTORICAL ABSTRACTS and by our collaborators, about five thousand periodicals have been listed.

The following fields of history and related subjects are included in this work:

A. HISTORY: all periods, and prehistory.

B. AUXILIARY HISTORICAL DISCIPLINES:

chronology, diplomatics, filigranology, genealogy, heraldry, iconography, numismatics, paleography, sphragistics, toponymy.

C. LOCAL HISTORY.

D. RELATED FIELDS AND GENERAL PUBLICATIONS (if they contain more than 20 per cent historical material or are otherwise recommended as worthy of inclusion):

academy and university publications,
anthropology,
archaeology,
archives,
art,
behavioral sciences,
bibliography,
cartography,
demography,
economics,
education
ethnology,
exploration,
folklore,
geography,
government publications,
international affairs and relations,
international law,
library publications,
linguistics,
literature,
museum publications,
music,
philately,
philology,
philosophy,
political science,
printing,
religion,
natural sciences,
sociology,

and others which contain historical articles.

The type of publications included in HISTORICAL PERIODICALS go beyond the normal definition of "periodical." Annual publications and those published at less frequent or at irregular or rare intervals have all been listed. The editors have also incorporated such publications as Acta, Transactions, Proceedings and Mitteilungen unless they clearly fall outside the definition of a serial publication and can be deemed to be series. As a rule HISTORICAL PERIODICALS does not contain series, that is, publications appearing as separate monographs under a common title and often at irregular intervals, unless the contributors on a particular country list felt that a distinction between serial publications and series would be meaningless.

HISTORICAL PERIODICALS does not include publications which do not contain articles, such as abstracts publications, bibliographies, calendars and directories, nor does it include newspapers, almanacs, publications by press services, advertising publications or company organs and customer bulletins.

This is a list of current periodicals, but periodicals which ceased publication in or after 1957 are cited, with a notation as to the year of termination.

In view of the large number of entries to be included the editors could not provide equally detailed information for all the periodicals in the book. The distinction between the more detailed entries ("long entries") and the briefer entries ("short entries") has been explained on page XV. This differentiation does not, however, imply any judgment as to the quality of the periodical. While all contributors were requested to bear in mind general rules as a guide to the preparation of their lists, each contributor, an expert in his own country, was left some discretion as to whether a long or short entry should be supplied for a periodical. Consequently there has been a slight difference of emphasis between one country list and another on periodicals deemed peripheral to the study of history.

GENESIS, SOURCES AND METHODS

Two considerations have stimulated the preparation of this book. The historian finds frequently that it is difficult to trace periodicals which are not purely historical, or which are not issued by members of the historical profession. Furthermore, geographic and linguistic barriers often tend to impede research seriously. A reference tool such as this book will, we trust, be of aid in reducing these difficulties.

World War II made the thorough work by Pierre Caron and Marc Jaryc (eds.), World List of Historical Periodicals and Bibliographies (Oxford: International Committee of Historical Sciences, 1939) of retrospective interest more quickly than we would have wished. HISTORICAL ABSTRACTS, under whose auspices HISTORICAL PERIODICALS has been prepared, therefore had to start anew in 1953. Volume 1, No. 1 (1955) of HISTORICAL ABSTRACTS included as a supplementary part the beginning of a World List of Historical Periodicals. Although HISTORICAL ABSTRACTS has been limited to articles on the period 1775-1945, these lists have always included periodicals on all historical periods. The demands which publication of the lists made on our staff, while we endeavored to maintain pace with the articles published, and the realization that we would not be able to complete this project for many years more, led us to decide in 1958 on a separate publication. The response of historians and librarians to the country lists in HISTORICAL ABSTRACTS encouraged us, and their comments and evaluations of our published lists have also been valuable in the preparation of this work.

Most of the information for HISTORICAL PERIODICALS has been collected during the years 1958 to 1960, and some data and supplements were received early in 1961. The date of the most recent available information is evident from the volume and year listed in the long entries. These are also a clue as to the date of information on the short entries, as all the information on one country was normally gathered at the same time. Entries which were received too late for inclusion in the body of a country list, usually in the first few months of 1961, have been added as supplements at the end of a list, where necessary. Complete coverage of all new periodicals appearing in 1960 can not be guaranteed, although efforts were made to include all applicable ones.

The material for this book has been collected from four different sources. The first comprised libraries, history departments and bibliographical institutes. The editorial office of HISTORICAL ABSTRACTS had established what was probably the most extensive, although still incomplete, international file on historical periodicals. The scope for a comprehensive directory, it was felt, should be much broader than anything we had undertaken. We therefore examined the extensive holdings of the Library of Congress, the British Museum and the Bayerische Staatsbibliothek, and our collaborators made use of libraries with special holdings in certain fields, such as East Asia, Africa or Latin America. Institutions which made contributions are cited with the individual country lists and in the general acknowledgment section.

The second source consisted of publications from which information on titles of periodicals could be gathered: 1) periodicals with bibliographies, 2) the national bibliographies and subject bibliographies, national periodicals lists and postal lists issued by some countries, and 3) lists issued by publishers and booksellers.

Historians, librarians, archivists and teachers in various branches of the social sciences and the humanities constituted the third source. They are identified at the head of the individual sections and on the acknowledgment pages of this book. The work of preparing country lists, suggesting titles, collecting information which was difficult to obtain, detecting errors and answering questions fell on their shoulders. They performed this task with devotion, although they were all engaged in university teaching and other work at the same time. The completed lists were examined with great care by specialists in various fields and areas, and changes were made as late as May 1961 to reflect their suggestions.

And, finally, the periodical itself provided the fourth source. As a rule the two most recent complete volumes and the most recent numbers were used for the long entries, but we also resorted to cumulative indices and cumulative tables of contents in order to assure ourselves of full and accurate information for Points 8 and 9 of our long entries, the description of contents of the periodicals, and the remark section. The publishers or editors were, for the most part, responsive to our requests, and we wish to express our appreciation here. They answered our questionnaires, sent us sample copies of their periodicals and occasionally also lent us complete volumes.

With the exception of international periodicals, those published by international societies or institutes, all titles are listed under the country of publication. Cross-references are inserted where several countries may be involved, and liberal cross-referencing within individual lists will, we hope, facilitate search. The Index would be the first place to look if the user does not know the country of publication.

ACKNOWLEDGMENTS

This book is a monument to international cooperation. The editors wish to express deep appreciation to all who have collaborated and rendered such valuable assistance. They are listed in a separate acknowledgment section.

The dedicated service rendered by some editorial contributors and members of the immediate staff of HISTORICAL ABSTRACTS deserves special recognition, and our gratitude is expressed to Karin Kaut for the extraordinary devotion with which she has assisted during the past three years, to Ino Arndt, Marilyn M. Houston, Paul Podjed and Ina Renner for their outstanding editorial collaboration, to Guillermo Céspedes del Castillo, Chen Tsu-lung, Alexander F. Dygnas, Fritz Fellner, John A. S. Grenville, Ann E. Macara, Herbert E. Reed and Ursula Schmidt-Tausendfreund for their valuable contributions, and to Lore Reed-Wymar for her graphical work.

PLANS FOR THE FUTURE

The user of this book may be interested to hear of plans for bringing the lists up-to-date. We are considering the publication of a much enlarged revised edition, which would cite, in each country section, not only periodicals, as in this book, but also monographic series and bibliographical publications. In order to avoid publication delays resulting from simultaneous collection of such a large amount of material, we hope to publish separate fascicles, possibly twice a year, each to include information on one geographical area. Over a period of four to five years all fascicles would together form one new and enhanced edition of this book. Meanwhile, persons who are searching for information on predominantly historical periodicals are referred to the Index Numbers of HISTORICAL ABSTRACTS, beginning with Volume 8 (1962). New or defunct historical periodicals would be cited therein with the relevant information.

This book, the inaugural publication of Clio Press, was designed to be of service to many different users. We hope that it will be of assistance in their various fields of research. Although we went to great length to avoid or eliminate errors, some may have been overlooked. We invite users to write us to point out any they detect. Your comments and suggestions will be very much appreciated and carefully considered in the preparation of a revised edition.

Eric H. Boehm and Lalit Adolphus

May 1961

Explanation

Information on periodicals is cited in the order indicated below. Some entries ("long entries") have deliberately been made in greater detail, while others ("short entries") are cited without certain data (points 4, 5, 7 and 8 of the items of information listed below).

Long Entries

Long entries are given for periodicals dealing with history (all periods and fields) and prehistory, auxiliary historical disciplines (chronology, diplomatics, filigranology, genealogy, heraldry, iconography, numismatics, paleography, sphragistics, toponymy), local history - if of broader than local scope -, and periodicals concerned with related fields, or general publications if they have more than 40 per cent historical content.

INFORMATION SUPPLIED	ILLUSTRATION
1. Title [and translation into English]	ELLINIKÁ [Matters pertaining to Greece].
2. Subtitle [and translation into English]	Philologikón, Istorikón ké Laographikón Sýngramma [Philological, historical and folkloric journal].
3. Frequency of publication	S-A (Irr.).
4. First (starting) year of publication	1928
5. Most recent volume examined	(1959: vol. 16).
6. Publisher or sponsoring institution [and translation into English, if not in a Romance language or German]	Etaireía Makedonikôn Spoudôn [Soc. of Macedonian Studies], Odós Vasilíssis Sophias 2, Salonika.
7. Editor(s) or editorial board and address (if different from the publishing address)	Stílpon P. Kyriakídis, Línos N. Polítis.
8. Description of contents	Art. on Greek hist., literature and culture from antiquity to the present; doc.; bk. rev.; biblio.; news and notes;
9. Remarks (such as language of articles, summaries, indices and cumulative table of contents)	art. also in languages other than Greek.
10. Annual subscription: domestic rate/foreign rate	Drs 80 / $5

Short Entries

Short entries are given for periodicals dealing purely with local history, with fields related to history, and for general publications if they contain between 20 and 40 per cent historical material or have for other reasons been recommended for inclusion. These entries contain information on points 1, 2, 3, 6 and 10, and sometimes on point 9. The editor is sometimes cited, if he is also the publisher, or if no other publisher could be ascertained. See illustration below:

1. VĂN-HOÁ NGUYỆT-SAN [Monthly cultural review].
2. Co'quan nghiên-cứ'u và phô-thông [Organ of researches and popularization].
3. M.
6. Direction of Cultural Affairs, Dept. of National Education, 266 rue Công-lý, Saigon.
10. VN $240

Further Explanation of Entries

1. TITLE [AND TRANSLATION INTO ENGLISH]:

For the convenience of the general user, diacritical marks are disregarded in the alphabetization of titles in foreign languages.

Example: In the section on Denmark Årbogen for Skjerk og Omega is alphabetized after Acta Philologica Scandinavica rather than at the end of the list where it belongs.

Titles in Latin are not translated, nor are proper names unless the latter have an equivalent in English.

Titles beginning with words such as "Bulletin," "Journal," "Proceedings," "Review," "Transactions," etc., or their equivalents in foreign languages, followed by the name of the publishing or sponsoring institution or society, are listed under the names of the respective institutions or societies. Relevant cross-references have been inserted, wherever necessary, to facilitate search.

Example: In the section on Great Britain, the title, Transactions of the Honourable Society of Cymmrodorion, has been inverted and listed under Honourable Society of Cymmrodorion, Transactions of the. A cross-reference appears under "Transactions," to guide the user.

In cases where the inversion requires alteration of the title (due to the change from genitive to nominative case), the full original title has been added in parentheses after the inverted title.

Example: Moskovskii Universitet, Vestnik... (Vestnik Moskovskogo Universiteta) [Review of the University of Moscow].

2. SUBTITLE [AND TRANSLATION INTO ENGLISH]:

A subtitle which only repeats information contained elsewhere in an entry (such as frequency of publication or name of publishing institution) is not cited.

Example: The Biannual Journal of the Delhi School of Economics.

3. FREQUENCY OF PUBLICATION:

The actual frequency of publication is stated in parentheses if it differs from the announced frequency.

Examples: Q (S-A), or A. (Irr.).

4. FIRST (STARTING) YEAR OF PUBLICATION.

5. MOST RECENT VOLUME NUMBER EXAMINED:

If a periodical uses a continuous numbering system instead of volume numbers, the numbers of all the issues of the most recent known year of publication of the periodical are given.

Example: (1960: no. 138-141).

In the event of a discrepancy between the scheduled and actual dates of publication of a volume, the actual date of publication is given in brackets after the scheduled date.

Example: (1959 [1960]: vol. 14).

6. PUBLISHER OR SPONSORING INSTITUTION AND ADDRESS:

The name of the publishing or sponsoring institution or society is translated into English unless it is in a Romance language or in German or if its meaning is obvious from the title of the periodical, or if it is a proper name or the name of a firm. Occasional exceptions to this general rule have been made to suit individual cases.

The publisher's address contains the name of the town in the original language (e.g., München, not Munich, Buçuresti, not Bucharest), except when a town is not widely known by its original name (e.g., Cairo, not al-Qahirah). This rule applies also to the address of the editor or editorial board.

7. EDITOR(S) OR EDITORIAL BOARD AND ADDRESS:

If there is an editorial board and the number of its members exceeds five, the name of the chief editor or managing editor only is given.

The address of the editor or editorial board is given only if it differs from the publishing address.

8. DESCRIPTION OF CONTENTS:

This description includes the subject matter and period and area concentration of articles and information on supplementary sections such as documents, book reviews, bibliographies and professional news. The scope of the supplementary sections corresponds to that of the articles, unless stated otherwise. Obituaries are not cited.

9. REMARKS (Language of articles, summaries, indices, cumulative table of contents, etc.):

A periodical is published in the language in which its title appears, unless specified otherwise.

Former titles of a periodical and titles of the supplements and special sections, if any, are translated into English, unless they are in a Romance language or in German.

Tables of contents are cited only if they are cumulative for more than a year or appear in a language other than that of the periodical.

10. ANNUAL SUBSCRIPTION: DOMESTIC RATE / FOREIGN RATE:

Price is always per annum, unless otherwise stipulated.

If two different subscription rates are given, the rate for libraries is indicated first and that for individuals in parentheses thereafter.

If a special subscription rate is offered to members of the sponsoring society, this is indicated, but it may or may not include the membership fee of the society.

CROSS-REFERENCES are inserted to aid the user

a) whenever a title is inverted (see point 1 above),
b) whenever a periodical has more than one title,
c) whenever a periodical has changed its previous title(s),
d) whenever a periodical is printed in a country other than that in which its publishing institution is located, and
e) whenever a periodical, published in a given country, deals with, and appears in the language of, another country.

NOTE

Readers searching for a periodical are also advised to see the Addenda sections included at the end of some lists

Abbreviations

GENERAL

abstr.	abstract (s)
acad.	academy (-ies)
art.	article (s)
assoc.	association(s)
biblio.	bibliography (-ies), bibliographical
bk.	book (s)
c.	circa
cent.	century (-ies)
cum.	cumulative
dept.	department (s)
doc.	document (s)
ed.	editor (s), editorial
govt.	government (s)
graph	graphic material, charts, diagrams, tables
hist.	history (-ies), historic, historical
illus.	illustrated, illustration (s)
inst.	institute (s), institution (s)
illus.	illustrated, illustration (s)
manag. ed.	managing editor
memb.	member (s)
mri	most recent information
nfs	not for sale
no vol. indic.	no volume numbers indicated on the periodical
p (1)	price for 1 number
p.a.	per annum
pni	price not indicated
pub.	publisher (s), publish (-es, -ed), publications (s)
pv	price varies
rev.	review (s), reviewed
soc.	society (-ies)
sum.	summary (-ies)
univ.	university (-ies)
vol.	volume (s)

FREQUENCY OF PUBLICATION

A	annual
B	biennial
B-M	bi-monthly
B-W	bi-weekly
Irr.	irregular
M	monthly
Q	quarterly
S-A	semi-annual
S-M	semi-monthly
3 x y	3 times a year
T	triennial
W	weekly

Other frequencies of publication are indicated by number, similar to:
" 3 x y. "

MONEY SYMBOLS

Bfr	Belgian francs
Bs	bolivars (Venezuela)
C $	Canadian dollars
CFr	Congo francs
Cr	cruzeiros (Brazil)
d	pence (U.K., Eire)
Dcr	Danish crowns
Din	dinars (Yugoslavia)
DJ	Jordanian dinars
DM	German marks
$	dollars (U.S.A., Uruguay)
Drs	drachmas (Greece)
Esc.	escudos (Portugal)
f	guilder (Netherlands)
F.	gourde (Haiti)
Fmk	Finnish markka
Fr	francs (Morocco)
Ft	forint (Hungary)
HK $	Hong Kong dollars
ID	Tunisian, Iraqi dinars
IL	Israeli pounds
K	kyat (Burma)
Kčs	Czech crowns
L	lire (Italy)
Lfr	Luxembourg francs
LL	Lebanese, Libyan pounds
LS	Syrian pounds
M $	Malayan dollars
M$N	moneda nacional (Argentina, Cuba, Mexico)
Ncr	Norwegian crowns
N.Fr.	new French francs
N.Fr. CFA	new French francs of the Communauté Française Africaine
NT $	new Taiwan dollars
P	pesos (Philippines)
PRs	Pakistan rupees
PT	Egyptian, Sudanese pounds
ptas	pesetas (Spain)
Q	quetzals (Guatemala)
Rls	rials (Iran)
Rps	rupiahs (Indonesia)
Rs	rupees (India, Ceylon)
rub.	rubles (U.S.S.R.)
s	shillings (U.K., Eire)
s EA	East African shillings
S	schillings (Austria)
Scr.	Swedish crowns
Sfr	Swiss francs
TKr	Turkish kurns
TL	Turkish pounds
VN $	Vietnamese dollars
Y	Chinese yen
¥	Japanese yen
zł	złoty (Poland)

This list does not include money symbols which are written out in full.

WORLD LIST OF

HISTORICAL AND RELATED SERIAL PUBLICATIONS

INTERNATIONAL PERIODICALS

International Periodicals

Note: This section includes only periodicals published by international organizations. For other periodicals which are international in character, see the sections on the respective countries in which they are published.

1. ACTA MUSICOLOGICA. Q. 1928 (1959: vol. 31). Bärenreiter-Verlag, Basel, for Société Internationale de Musicologie, Stapfelberg 9, Basel. **Ed: Hans Albrecht, Neue Universität, Haus 11, Kiel. Art. on the hist. of music and on present-day musicology; reports on research in the field of music; in German or French and occasionally in English or Italian.**
Sfr 25 / DM 25

2. ACTUALITES EUROPEENNES [European news]. 10 x y. Centre Européen de la Culture, villa Moynier, 122 rue de Lausanne, Genève. A separate edition appears in German under the title: Europäische Mitteilungen.

3. AFRICA. Q. Institut international africain, St. Dunstan's Chambers, 10-11 Fetter Lane, Fleet St., London, E.C. 4. Art. on sociology and linguistics and on administrative and economic questions pertaining to Africa; bk. rev.; biblio.; in English and French.

4. AMERICA INDIGENA [Indian America]. Q. Inter-American Indian Inst., Niños Héroes, 139, México 7, D.F. In English, Portuguese and Spanish. Includes supplement entitled: Boletín indigenista.

ANNUAIRE DE LA COMMISSION DU DROIT INTERNATIONAL see COMMISSION DU DROIT INTERNATIONAL, ANNUAIRE DE LA...

5. ANNUAIRE EUROPEEN [European yearbook]. A. 1955 (1959: vol. 5). Martinus Nijhoff, P.O.B. 269, Den Haag, for Conseil de l'Europe, Strasbourg. Ed. board: C. Pisanelli, B. Landheer, Lord Layton, M. Sørensen. Art. on European politics, with emphasis on European integration; doc.; biblio.; bk. rev; in English and French. **pv (c. f 37.50 / $ 9.90)**

ANNUAIRE JURIDIQUE INTERAMERICAIN see ANUARIO JURIDICO INTERAMERICANO

6. ANUARIO JURIDICO INTERAMERICANO. INTER-AMERICAN JURIDICAL YEARBOOK. ANNUAIRE JURIDIQUE INTERAMERICAIN. A. (Irr.). Pan American Union, 18th and Constitution Ave. NW, Washington, D.C. Survey of the development of Inter-American regional law; records and interpretations of all significant legal events affecting the Americas; in English, French, Portuguese and Spanish.

ARCHIV FÜR ORDENSKUNDE see RECORDER OF ORDER RESEARCHES

7. ARCHIVES INTERNATIONALES DE SOCIOLOGIE DE LA COOPERATION. ARCHIVIO INTERNAZIONALE DI SOCIOLOGIA DELLA COOPERAZIONE. INTERNATIONAL ARCHIVES OF SOCIOLOGY OF COOPERATION. S-A. Bureau d'Etudes Coopératives et Communautaires, 18 bis ave. Hoche, Paris 8e, for Conseil international pour la recherche en sociologie de la coopération. Art. on sociology, social hist., and international cooperation; in English, French and Italian. Formerly pub. under the title : Communauté et Vie Coopérative.

ARCHIVIO INTERNAZIONALE DI SOCIOLOGIA DELLA COOPERAZIONE see ARCHIVES INTERNATIONALES DE SOCIOLOGIE DE LA COOPERATION

8. ARCHIVUM. Revue Internationale des Archives [International review of archives]. A. 1951 (1957 : vol. 7). Conseil International des Archives, pl. de Fontenoy, Paris 7e. Ed : Pierre Marot (chief ed.), Robert-Henri Bautier, 60 rue des Francs-Bourgeois, Paris 3e. Reports on international archival congresses; investigations of archival problems; A. international analytical biblio. of archival pub. ; in English, French, German, Italian or Spanish; English, French or Spanish sum. ; illus. N. Fr. 15/$ 3.60

9. ARKIV FÖR NORDISK FILOLOGI [Archives for Scandinavian philology]. S-A. Ed : K.G. Ljunggren, L. Fiskaregatan 2, Lund. Pub. with grants from the Swedish, Norwegian and Danish govt. Scr. 24/$ 4.66

10. BOLETIN AEREO [Aerial bulletin]. M. Pan American Inst. of Geography and Hist., Ex-Arzobispado 29, México 18, D.F.

BOLETIN DEL COMITE DE ARCHIVOS see COMITE DE ARCHIVOS, BOLETIN DEL...

BOLETIN ECONOMICO DE AMERICA LATINA see ECONOMIC BULLETIN FOR LATIN AMERICA

11. BOLETIN INDIGENISTA [Indian bulletin]. Q. Inter-American Indian Inst., Niños Héroes, 139, México 7, D.F. In English, Spanish and Portuguese. Supplement of America indigena.

BULLETIN DU CENTRE EUROPEEN DE LA CULTURE see CENTRE EUROPEEN DE LA CULTURE, BULLETIN DU...

12. BULLETIN ECONOMIQUE POUR L'EUROPE [Economic bulletin for Europe]. 3xy. Section des Ventes de l'Office Européen des Nations Unies, Palais des Nations, Genève. Separate editions also appear in English (Economic Bulletin for Europe) and Russian.

13. BULLETIN INTERNATIONAL DES SCIENCES SOCIALES [International bulletin of social sciences]. Q. UNESCO, pl. de Fontenoy, Paris 7e. A separate edition appears in English under the title : International Social Science Bulletin.

BULLETIN OFFICIEL see UNESCO, CHRONIQUE DE L'...

BULLETIN TRIMESTRIEL see UNESCO, CHRONIQUE DE L'...

14. CAHIERS D'HISTOIRE MONDIALE. JOURNAL OF WORLD HISTORY. CUADERNOS DE HISTORIA MUNDIAL. Irr. (Q). 1953 (1958 : vol. 4).

Editions de la Baconnière, Neuchâtel, for UNESCO, Commission internationale pour une histoire du développment scientifique et culturel de l'humanité. Ed: François Crouzet, bureau A307, UNESCO, 19 ave. Kléber, Paris 16e. Art. on hist., not confined to any area or period, with emphasis on cultural hist.; in French, English and Spanish. Sfr 34.40/$ 8

15. CENTRE EUROPEEN DE LA CULTURE, BULLETIN DU... [Bulletin of the European Cultural Center]. M. Centre Européen de la Culture, Villa Moynier, 122 rue de Lausanne, Genève. In French, German, English, Italian and Greek.

CHRONIQUE DE L'UNESCO see UNESCO, CHRONIQUE DE L'...

16. COMITE DE ARCHIVOS, BOLETIN DEL... [Bulletin of the Committee on Archives]. S-A. Pan American Inst. of Geography and Hist., Committee on Archives, Archivo Nacional, Compostela y Velasco, La Habana. In Spanish, Portuguese, English and French.

17. COMITE INTERNATIONAL DES SCIENCES HISTORIQUES. BULLETIN D'INFORMATION [International Committee of Historical Sciences. Bulletin of information]. Irr. 1953 (1956/57). Imprimerie Protat Frères, Macon, for Comité international des sciences historiques. Ed: Michele François, 270 bd. Raspail, Paris 14e. Extracts and reprints of papers read at the congresses on hist. and auxiliary sciences; bk. rev.; in several languages. pni

18. COMMISSION DU DROIT INTERNATIONAL, ANNUAIRE DE LA... [Yearbook of the International Law Commission]. A. (2 vol. p.a.). Nations Unies, Section des Ventes et de la Distribution, New York, N.Y. Separate editions also appear in English and Spanish.

19. COMMISSION INTERNATIONALE DE NUMISMATIQUE. COMPTE-RENDU [International Commission of Numismatics. Reports]. A. Commission international de numismatique, Zeestraat 71b, Den Haag.

COMMUNAUTE ET VIE COOPERATIVE see ARCHIVES INTERNATIONALES DE SOCIOLOGIE DE LA COOPERATION

20. COMPRENDRE [Understanding]. Revue de politique de la culture [Review of cultural policy]. 2-3 x y. Société Européenne de Culture, piazza S. Marco 52, Venezia.

21. CONGRESO POR LA LIBERTAD DE LA CULTURA, CUADERNOS DEL... [Review of the Congress for Cultural Freedom]. B-M. Congrès pour la Liberté de la Culture, 23 rue de la Pépinière, Paris 8e. N.Fr. 11/$ 4

22. CONSEIL DE L'EUROPE, NOUVELLES DU... [News from the Council of Europe]. M. 1951 (1959: vol. 9). Conseil de l'Europe, Direction de l'information, Strasbourg. Ed: Paul M.-G. Lévy. Art. on the activities of the Council of Europe. Separate editions appear in English, German and Italian. pni

EL CORREO DE LA UNESCO see UNESCO, LE COURRIER DE L'...

23. COUNCIL OF EUROPE NEWS. Direction of Information. M. 1951 (1959: new series, no. 2). Maison de l'Europe, Strasbourg. Ed: Paul M.-G.

Lévy. Art. on hist. and political problems; maps, illus. A separate edition appears in French under the title: Nouvelles du Conseil de l'Europe. pni

LE COURRIER DE L'UNESCO see UNESCO, LE COURRIER DE L'...

CRONICA DE LA UNESCO see UNESCO, CRONICA DE LA...

CUADERNOS DE HISTORIA MUNDIAL see CAHIERS D'HISTOIRE MONDIALE

CUADERNOS DEL CONGRESO POR LA LIBERTAD DE LA CULTURA see CONGRESO POR LA LIBERTAD DE LA CULTURA, CUADERNOS DEL...

24. DIOGENES. Q. 1952 (1960: no. 30). Univ. of Chicago Press, 5759 Ellis Ave., Chicago 37, Ill. Ed: Roger Caillois, c/o International Council for Philosophy and Humanistic Studies, 19 av. Kléber, Paris 16e. Art. on philosophy, humanistic studies and the hist. of ideas; bk. rev.; cum. index. Separate editions also appear in Arabic, French, German and Spanish.
$ 4/$ 5

25. ECONOMIC BULLETIN FOR ASIA AND THE FAR EAST. 3xy. Nations Unies, Section des Ventes et de la Distribution, New York, N.Y.

ECONOMIC BULLETIN FOR EUROPE see BULLETIN ECONOMIQUE DE L'EUROPE

26. ECONOMIC BULLETIN FOR LATIN AMERICA. S-A. Section des Ventes de l'Office Européen des Nations Unies, Palais des Nations, Genève. A separate edition appears in Spanish under the title: Boletín Económico de América Latina.

ETUDES DE CONSERVATION see STUDIES IN CONSERVATION

27. EUROPA ETHNICA. B-M. (1958: vol. 18). Wilhelm Braumüller Universitäts-Verlagsbuchhandlung G.m.b.H., Servitengasse 5, Wien IX, for Union Fédéraliste des Communautés Ethniques Européennes (UFCE). Art. on various aspects of the hist. and policies of national minorities in Europe; news and notes; in English, French and German. Formerly pub. under the title: Nation und Staat. S 120 (memb. S 100)/$ 4.80 (memb. $ 4)

EUROPÄISCHE MITTEILUNGEN see ACTUALITES EUROPEENNES

28. FOLKLORE AMERICANO [American folklore]. A. Committee on Folklore, Pan American Inst. of Geography and Hist., Aptdo. 3048, Lima. Art. on American folklore; bk. rev.; biblio.; in English, French, Portuguese and Spanish.

29. FORUM. M. Congrès pour la Liberté de la Culture, Museumstr. 5, Wien VII.

30. GEOGRAFIA REVUO [Geographic review]. Irr. Association internationale geographique, c/o Marinko Gjivoje, Gornji trg. 31/II, Ljubljana. Art. on geography, anthropology, archaeology and related subjects; in Esperanto.

31. ICOM NEWS - NOUVELLES DE L'ICOM. B-M. Conseil international des musées, pl. de Fontenoy, Paris 7e. In English and French.

32. I I C NEWS LETTER - I I C NOTES D'ACTUALITE. Irr. International Inst. for the Conservation of Museum Objects, c/o Brooklyn Museum, Eastern Parkway, Brooklyn 38, N.Y. In English and French.

I I C NOTES D'ACTUALITE see I I C NEWS LETTER

IMPACT OF SCIENCE ON SOCIETY see IMPACT - SCIENCE ET SOCIETE

33. IMPACT - SCIENCE ET SOCIETE [Impact - science and society]. Q. Unesco, pl. de Fontenoy, Paris 7e. A separate editon appears in English under the title : Impact of Science on Society.

34. INFORMACIONES ECONOMICAS [Economic information]. M. Pan American Union, 18th and Constitution Ave. NW, Washington, D.C.

INTER-AMERICAN JURIDICAL YEARBOOK see ANUARIO JURIDICO INTERAMERICANO

INTERNATIONAL ARCHIVES OF SOCIOLOGY OF COOPERATION see ARCHIVES INTERNATIONALES DE SOCIOLOGIE DE LA COOPERATION

INTERNATIONAL LAW COMMISSION, YEARBOOK OF THE see COMMISSION DU DROIT INTERNATIONALE, ANNUAIRE DE LA...

35. INTERNATIONAL REVIEW OF SOCIAL HISTORY. 3xy. Internationaal Instituut voor Sociale Geschiedenis, Amsterdam. In French, English and German. f 23/$ 6

36. INTERNATIONAL SOCIAL SCIENCE BULLETIN. Q. UNESCO, pl. de Fontenoy, Paris 7e. A separate edition appears in French under the title : Bulletin international des sciences sociales. N.Fr. 20

JOURNAL OF WORLD HISTORY see CAHIERS D'HISTOIRE MONDIALE

37. MEDAILLES [Medals]. S-A. Fédération internationale des éditeurs de Médailles, 15 bd. Péreire, Paris 17e. N.Fr. 10 (for 4 no.)

MUSEION see MUSEUM

38. MUSEUM. Q. UNESCO, pl. de Fontenoy, Paris 7e. In English and French; Spanish and Russian sum.; index; illus. Formerly pub. under the title: Museion. N.Fr. 20/$ 6.50

NATION UND STAAT see EUROPA ETHNICA

NOUVELLES DE L'ICOM see ICOM NEWS

NOUVELLES DU CONSEIL DE L'EUROPE see CONSEIL DE L'EUROPE, NOUVELLES DU...

39. NOVUM TESTAMENTUM. An International Quarterly for New Testament and Related Studies Based on International Cooperation. Irr. E.J. Brill, Leiden. In English and occasionally in French or German. f 26

40. NUMEN. International Review for the History of Religions. 3 xy. 1954 (1958 : vol. 5). E.J. Brill, Leiden, for International Assoc. for the Hist. of Religions, Churchill-laan 290, Amsterdam. Ed : Raffaele Pettazzoni, via Crescenzio 63, Roma. Art. on the hist. and phenomenology of religion; bk. rev.; index. f 20/$6.30

OFFICIAL BULLETIN see UNESCO CHRONICLE

41. ORBIS. Bulletin international de documentation linguistique [International bulletin of linguistic documentation]. A. Centre international de dialectologie générale, 185 ave. des Alliés, Louvain. Hist. of dialects; in French, English and German. Bfr 500

42. POLITIQUE [Politics]. Revue internationale des doctrines et des institutions [International review of doctrines and institutions]. Q. Compagnie d'Editions Libres, Sociales et Economiques, 3, Fbg. St. Honoré, Paris, for Académie internationale de science politique et d'histoire constitutionelle. From 1936 to 1957 pub. under the title : Revue Internationale d'Histoire Politique et Constitutionelle.

43. PREUVES [Proofs]. M. Congrès pour la Liberté de la Culture, 23 rue de la Pépinière, Paris 8e.

44. RECHERCHES. RESEARCHES. Q. Conseil de l'Europe, pl. de l'Europe, Strasbourg. In English, French, German and Italian.

45. RECORDER OF ORDER RESEARCHES. ARCHIV FÜR ORDENSKUNDE. Irr. International Orders Research Soc., Leibnizstr. 48, Charlottenburg 4, Berlin W. Texts about orders, decorations, and medals; biblio.; in English, French and German.

RESEARCHES see RECHERCHES

46. REVISTA CARTOGRAFICA [Cartographic review]. A. Commission on Cartography, Pan American Inst. of Geography and Hist., Cabildo 381, Buenos Aires. In Spanish, Portuguese, French and English.

47. REVISTA DE HISTORIA DE AMERICA [Review of the history of America]. S-A. Commission on Hist., Pan American Inst. of Geography and Hist., Ex-Arzobispado 29, México 18, D.F. Art. on American hist.; bk. rev.; biblio.; news and notes; in Spanish, Portuguese, French and English.

48. REVISTA DE LA HISTORIA DE LAS IDEAS [Review of the history of ideas]. A. Committee on the Hist. of Ideas, Pan American Inst. of Geography and Hist., Casa de la Cultura Ecuatoriana, Quito. In Spanish, Portuguese, English and French.

49. REVISTA GEOGRAFICA [Geographical review]. S-A. Commission on Geography, Pan American Inst. of Geography and Hist., Av. Churchill 129, Sala 1204, Rio de Janeiro. Geography of the Western Hemisphere; bk. rev.; news and notes; in Spanish, Portuguese, English and French.

REVUE INTERNATIONALE D'HISTOIRE POLITIQUE ET CONSTITUTIONELLE see POLITIQUE

50. SOCIAL SCIENCE PROJECTS IN SOUTHERN ASIA. Research Information Bulletin. Irr. UNESCO Research Center on the Social Implications of Industrialization in Southern Asia, P.O.B. 242, Calcutta. Name and subject index; list of research organizations supplying information for the issue concerned.

SOVIET CULTURE see SOVIET SURVEY

51. SOVIET SURVEY. A Quarterly Review of Cultural Trends. Q. Congrès pour la Liberté de la Culture, 25 Haymarket, London, S.W. 1. Former titles: Soviet Culture and Survey.

52. STUDIES IN CONSERVATION. ETUDES DE CONSERVATION. S-A. Aberdeen Univ. Press Ltd., 6 Upper Kirkgate, Aberdeen, for International Inst. for the Conservation of Museum Objects. In English and French.

SURVEY see SOVIET SURVEY

UNESCO BULLETIN see UNESCO CHRONICLE

53. UNESCO CHRONICLE. M. UNESCO, pl. de Fontenoy, Paris 7e. Supersedes Official Bulletin (1948-1953) and Unesco Bulletin (1954-1955). Separate editions also appear in French and Spanish under the titles: Chronique de l'Unesco and Crónica de la Unesco, respectively.

54. UNESCO, CHRONIQUE DE L'... [Unesco chronicle]. M. UNESCO, pl. de Fontenoy, Paris 7e. Supersedes Bulletin Officiel (1948-1953) and Bulletin Trimestriel (1954-1955). Separate editons also appear in English and Spanish under the titles: Unesco Chronicle, and Crónica de la Unesco, respectively.

THE UNESCO COURIER see UNESCO, LE COURRIER DE L'...

55. UNESCO, CRONICA DE LA... [Unesco chronicle]. M. UNESCO, pl. de Fontenoy, Paris 7e. Separate editions also appear in English and French under the titles : Unesco Chronicle and Chronique de l'Unesco, respectively.

56. UNESCO, LE COURRIER DE L'... [The Unesco courier]. M. UNESCO, pl. de Fontenoy, Paris 7e. Separate editons also appear in English and Spanish under the titles : The Unesco Courier and El Correo de la Unesco respectively. An edition in Russian is pub. by Commission nationale de l'U.R.S.S., Ul. imeni Kalinina 9, Moskva.

57. UNION ACADEMIQUE INTERNATIONALE. COMPTES RENDUS [International Academic Union. Reports]. A. Secrétariat administratif de l'Union académique internationale, Palais des Académies, 1 rue Ducale, Bruxelles.

58. VETUS TESTAMENTUM. Q. E.J. Brill, Leiden, for International Organization of Old Testament Scholars. Ed : P.A.H. de Boer, 35 Hofdyk, Oegstgeest, Leiden. In English, French and German. 53s

YEARBOOK OF THE INTERNATIONAL LAW COMMISSION see COMMISSION DU DROIT INTERNATIONALE, ANNUAIRE DE LA...

For information on HISTORICAL ABSTRACTS please see page 620.

AFRICA AND ISLANDS OFF THE AFRICAN COAST

(Political subdivisions and designations used in this section are those in existence on 1 January 1961.

For Egypt see the section on the Near and Middle East.)

East and East Central Africa

Prepared with the assistance of

J.D. Pearson, Librarian, School of Oriental and African Studies, University of London, and

Arquivo Histórico Ultramarino, Lisbon

BRITISH EAST AFRICA

1. TANGANYIKA NOTES AND RECORDS. S-A. 1936 (1960: no. 54). Tanganyika Soc., P.O.B. 511, Dar-es-Salaam, Tanganyika. Ed: Mrs. E.H. Leslie. Art. on the hist. and cultural patterns of East Africa, with emphasis on anthropology and ethnology; bk. rev.; biblio.; index; illus. (memb.) 20s EA

2. THE UGANDA JOURNAL. S-A. 1934 (1960: vol. 24). Uganda Soc., Private Bag, Kampala, Uganda. Ed: A.W. Southall, J.W. Pallister. Aims at the "publication of historical, literary and scientific matters of local interest"; bk. rev.; in English and vernacular languages; maps, illus.; index; cum. index for vol. 1-4. (memb.) 20s EA

ETHIOPIA

1. ANNALES D'ETHIOPIE [Annals of Ethiopia]. A. 1955 (1957: vol. 2). Bibliothèque nationale d'Ethiopie, B.P. 717, Addis Ababa. Art. on excavations and archaeological explorations in Ethiopia; reports on and studies of monuments; bk. rev.

MOZAMBIQUE

(Portuguese East Africa)

BOLETIM DA SOCIEDADE DE ESTUDOS DE MOÇAMBIQUE see SOCIEDADE DE ESTUDOS DE MOÇAMBIQUE, BOLETIM DA...

1. ITINERARIO [Itinerary]. Publicação Mensal de Letras, Arte, Ciencia e Critica [Monthly publication of letters, art, science and criticism]. M. Pub. in Lourenço Marques.

2. MOÇAMBIQUE [Mozambique]. Documentário trimestral [Quarterly documentary]. Q. Repartição Técnica de Estatística, Caixa Postal 493, Lourenço Marques. 60 Esc.

3. SOCIEDADE DE ESTUDOS DE MOÇAMBIQUE, BOLETIM DA... [Bulletin of the Society for Studies of Mozambique]. B-M. Sociedade de Estudos da Provincia de Moçambique, Avenida Pinheiro Chagas 137, Lourenço Marques. Charts, statistics, illus.; index. pni

SOMALILAND

1. SOMALIA D'OGGI [Somaliland of today]. Revista Independente di Interessi Somali [Independent review of Somali affairs]. B-M. Pub. address: P.O.B. 315, Piazzale Garesa, Mogadishu. pni

2. SOMALILAND JOURNAL. A. 1954 (mri 1955: vol. 1). Somaliland Soc., P.O.B. 39, Hargeisa. Ed: J.G.S. Drysdale, Ali Mirreh. Art. mainly on hist. and sociology; some art. also on literature; in English; mimeographed; illus. A supplement appeared in Arabic in 1954. p (1) 3s 6d

SUDAN

1. KUSH. Journal of the Sudan Antiquities Service. A. 1953 (1959: vol. 7). Sudan Antiquities Service, Khartoum. Ed: J. Vercoutter, P.O.B. 178, Karthoum. Art. on the archaeology of the Sudan; bk. rev.; notes and news; in English or French; maps, illus. PT 75 / $ 2.18

2. SUDAN ANTIQUITIES SERVICE. REPORT. A. 1938 (1957/58: no vol. indic.). Sudan Antiquities Service, P.O.B. 178, Khartoum. Ed: J. Vercoutter. Report on the Antiquities Service and museums, including an account of archaeological field work; biblio. of bk. and art. on the archaeology, ancient hist. and ethnology of the Sudan; in English and Arabic. PT 5

3. SUDAN NOTES AND RECORDS. Incorporating Proceedings of the Philosophical Society of the Sudan. S-A. 1918 (1957: vol. 38). Pub. address: P.O.B. 555, Khartoum. Ed: G.N. Sanderson. Art. on the Sudan, "showing every aspect of the country - its history, people, institutions including not only the social but also the natural sciences"; rev. of bk. and new periodicals on the Sudan. PT 75

Monographic series

and

bibliographical and abstracts publications

are not included in this book

North Africa

Prepared with the assistance of

J.D. Pearson, Librarian, School of Oriental and African Studies, London,

G. Level, Administrateur, Bibliothèque Nationale d'Alger, Algiers, and

Bibliothèque Generale et Archives, Rabat

ALGERIA

ANNALES DE L'INSTITUT D'ETUDES ORIENTALES see INSTITUT D'ETUDES ORIENTALES, ANNALES DE L'...

1. BULLETIN DE LIAISON SAHARIENNE [Bulletin of information on the Sahara]. Irr. Inspection Generale des Territoires du Sud. Immeuble Mauretania, Alger. Illus.; index. pni

2. INSTITUT D'ETUDES ORIENTALES, ANNALES DE L'... [Annals of the Institute of Oriental Studies]. A. 1934 (1958: vol. 16). Faculté des Lettres de l'Université d'Alger, Alger. N.Fr 2.20

3. LIBYCA. Anthropologie, archéologie, préhistoriques [Prehistoric, anthropology and archaeology]. S-A. Délégation générale du Gouvernement en Algerie, Service des Antiquités, Alger. N.Fr. 16

4. LIBYCA. Archéologie, epigraphie [Archaeology, epigraphy]. S-A. Délégation générale du Gouvernement en Algérie, Service des Antiquités, Alger. N.Fr. 16

5. REVUE AFRICAINE [African review]. Q (2 double no. p.a.). 1856 (1959: vol. 103). Société Historique Algérienne, 5 rue Eugèn-Deshayes, Alger. Art. on hist. and related subjects with reference to North Africa; reports of the meetings of the soc.; doc.; bk. rev.; notes; illus. N.Fr. 12/N.Fr. 15

6. REVUE DE LA MEDITERRANEE [Review of the Mediterranean]. Revue de pensée et d'information françaises [Review of French thought and news]. B-M. Université d'Alger, Alger. N.Fr. 7/N.Fr. 10

LIBYA

LIBIA see addenda at the end of the section on Italy

MOROCCO

1. BULLETIN D'ARCHEOLOGIE MAROCAINE [Bulletin of Moroccan archaeology]. A. 1956 (1957 [1959]: vol. 2). Centre national de la Recherche Scientifique (CNRS), Mission culturelle et universitaire française au Maroc, and Service des Antiquités du Maroc, 38 rue Lapérouse, Casablanca. Ed. address: B. P. 503 Rabat-Chellah. Art. on prehist. and classical archaeology; reports on archaeological activities in Morocco; memoirs; biblio. A supplement to vol. 2 (1957) appeared under the title: Bibliographie des applications archéologiques de la photographie aérienne. pv

BULLETIN DE LA SOCIETE DE PREHISTOIRE DU MAROC see SOCIETE DE PREHISTOIRE DU MAROC, BULLETIN DE LA...

BULLETIN DU COMITE MAROCAIN DE DOCUMENTATION HISTORIQUE DE LA MARINE see COMITE MAROCAIN DE DOCUMENTATION HISTORIQUE DE LA MARINE, BULLETIN DU...

2. COMITE MAROCAIN DE DOCUMENTATION HISTORIQUE DE LA MARINE, BULLETIN DU... [Bulletin of the Moroccan Committee of Historical Documentation of the Navy]. Irr. 1956 (1958: no. 7). Comité marocain de documentation historique de la marine, 225 bd. Mohamed V, Casablanca. Art. on the hist. of Morocco. pni

3. HESPERIS. Q. 1920 (1958: vol. 45). Librairie Larose, 11 rue Victor-Cousin, Paris 5e, for Institut des Hautes Etudes Marocaines, Rabat. Art. on the hist., languages, civilization and demography of Morocco; bk. rev.; biblio. of bk. and periodicals. Merged with Tamuda in 1960 under the title: Hespéris-Tamuda. Fr. 2,500/Fr. 3,000

HESPERIS-TAMUDA see HESPERIS and TAMUDA

4. MAURITANIA. Revista de Cultura Marroqui [Review of Moroccan culture]. M. (Irr.). Misiones Franciscano-Españolas de Marruecos, 55 San Francisco, Tanger. Includes art. on the hist. of Spanish missionary activity in Morocco. pta 40

5. SOCIETE DE PREHISTOIRE DU MAROC, BULLETIN DE LA... [Bulletin of the Moroccan Prehistoric Society]. Irr. Société de Prehistoire du Maroc, Lycée Lyantey, Casablanca. Abstr.; illus. pni

6. TAMUDA. Revista de Investigaciones Marroquies [Review of Moroccan studies]. S-A. 1953 (1959: 7th year). Art. on the hist. and culture of Morocco; in Spanish. Bibliografía marroquí pub. as supplements, 1953-1958. Merged with Hespéris in 1960 under the title: Hespéris-Tamuda. Fr. 1,000/$ 4

7. TATWAN [Tetuan]. Majallat al-Abhāth al-Maghribiyyah wa al-Andalusiyyah [Bulletin of Moroccan and Andalusian studies]. A. (Irr.). Wizārat al tarbīyat al-watnīya wa'l-shabība wa'l-riyāda [Ministry of Education], Rabat. Only one issue pub. so far, in 1956, together with a supplement entitled: al-Bibliyoghrāfīyā al-Maghribīya li-sanat 1956 (Moroccan biblio. for 1956). Fr. 1,250/$ 4

TUNISIA

1. LES CAHIERS DE TUNISIE [Journal of Tunisia]. Revue de Sciences Humaines [Review of the humanities]. Q. 1953 (1959: no. 25). Institut des Hautes Etudes à Tunis, 8 rue de Rome, Tunis. Ed. board: J. Pignon (hon. secretary), P. Marthelot, R. Mantran. Art. on the hist. (including military hist.) of Tunisia; doc.; bk. rev.; charts, illus. ID 500/ID 700

2. IBLA. Q. 1938 (1959: no. 88). Institut des Belles Lettres Arabes, 12 rue Jamaã El Haoua, Tunis. Ed: A. Demeerseman. Art. on Arabic culture; bk. rev.; biblio.; in Arabic and English. ID 200/ID 400

South and South Central Africa

FEDERATION OF RHODESIA AND NYASALAND

Prepared with the assistance of

J.D. Pearson, Librarian, School of Oriental and African Studies, University of London

1. CENTRAL AFRICAN ARCHIVES. REPORTS. Irr. Central African Archives, Salisbury, Southern Rhodesia.

2. HUMAN PROBLEMS IN BRITISH CENTRAL AFRICA. THE RHODES-LIVINGSTONE JOURNAL. S-A. 1944 (1959: no. 26). Rhodes-Livingstone Inst. for Social Research, P.O.B. 900, Lusaka, Northern Rhodesia. Ed: H.A. Fosbrooke. Art. and bk. rev. on hist. and sociological subjects and their sources, with special reference to British Central Africa in the 19th cent.; illus. The title of the journal varies. 10s / **$ 1.50**

3. NADA. A. 1923 (1958: no. 35). Southern Rhodesia Native Dept., P.O.B. 8030, Causeway, Southern Rhodesia. Ed: J.H. Farquhar. Art. on the hist., ethnology and linguistics of Southern Rhodesia. No. 35 contains a cum. index to vol. 31-35 (1954-1958). 5s

4. THE NORTHERN RHODESIA JOURNAL. S-A. 1950 (1960: vol. 4). Northern Rhodesia Soc., c/o Rhodes-Livingstone Museum, P.O.B. 124, Livingstone, Northern Rhodesia. Ed: W.V. Brelsford, P.O.B. 8140, Causeway, Salisbury, Northern Rhodesia. Art. on Rhodesian hist., ethnology, geography, natural hist. and related sciences; bk. rev.; news of the soc.; maps, illus. 10s

5. THE NYASALAND JOURNAL. S-A. 1948 (1960: vol. 13). Nyasaland Soc., P.O.B. 125, Blantyre, Nyasaland. Ed: G.D. Hayes, P.O.B. 135, Limbe, Nyasaland. Art. on all periods of the hist. of Nyasaland; letters and diaries; reports; maps, statistics. 10s

PROCEEDINGS AND TRANSACTIONS OF THE RHODESIA SCIENTIFIC ASSOCIATION see RHODESIA SCIENTIFIC ASSOCIATION, PROCEEDINGS AND TRANSACTIONS OF THE

THE RHODES-LIVINGSTONE JOURNAL see HUMAN PROBLEMS IN BRITISH CENTRAL AFRICA

6. RHODESIA SCIENTIFIC ASSOCIATION, PROCEEDINGS AND TRANSACTIONS OF THE. Irr. A.S. Boughey, Univ. College of Rhodesia and Nyasaland, P.O.B. 167, Salisbury, Southern Rhodesia, for Rhodesia Scientific Assoc. 15s

UNION OF SOUTH AFRICA

Prepared with the assistance of

A.M.Lewin Robinson, Assistant Chief Librarian, and
Miss J.C.Currie,
South African Public Library, Cape Town

1. AFRICA SOUTH. Q. Africa South Pub., New Bridge Court, Koeberg Rd., Maitland, Cape Town. Ed: Ronald M. Segal, P.O.B. 1039, Cape Town. Since July 1960 pub. in London under the title: Africa South in Exile. See addenda at the end of the section on Great Britain. 15s / $3

2. AFRICAN STUDIES. A Quarterly Journal Devoted to the Study of African Administration, Cultures and Languages. Q. Witwatersrand Univ. Press, Univ. of the Witwatersrand, Milner Park, Johannesburg. 30s

AFRICANA AANTEKENINGE EN NUUS see AFRICANA NOTES AND NEWS

3. AFRICANA NOTES AND NEWS. AFRICANA AANTEKENINGE EN NUUS. Q. 1943 (1959: vol. 13). Africana Soc., Africana Museum, Public Library, Market Sq., Johannesburg. Ed: R.F.Kennedy, Miss A. H. Smith. Art. on South African hist. since the first European settlement, with emphasis on local and personal hist.; doc.; notes and queries regarding hist. information and anecdotes supplied by correspondents and / or the ed.; rev. of bk. pub. in South Africa and elsewhere on South African hist. and related subjects; in English and occasionally in Afrikaans; separately pub. author and subject index to vol. 1-10. 20s

ARCHIVES YEARBOOK FOR SOUTH AFRICAN HISTORY see ARGIEF-JAARBOEK VIR SUID-AFRIKAANSE GESKIEDENIS

4. ARGIEF-JAARBOEK VIR SUID-AFRIKAANSE GESKIEDENIS. ARCHIVES YEARBOOK FOR SOUTH AFRICAN HISTORY. A. (2 vol. together). 1938 (1957: 20th year). Union Archives, Union Bldgs., Pretoria, Transvaal. Ed: A. Kieser. Art., univ. theses, and monographs on the hist. of South and Southwest Africa since the earliest European settlement, with emphasis on political hist.; doc.; in Afrikaans, Dutch or English; indices and biblio. included with individual works. One of the 2 A. vol. is usually a monograph, the other a collection of art. and / or theses. pv (c. 40s / $2

5. ARMA. Q. 1958 (1959: vol. 1). Heraldry Soc. of Southern Africa, c/o Foyles Bookshop, P.O.B. 3427, Cape Town. Ed: L.S.Rood "Arma," P.O.B. 1, Observatory, Cape Town. Art. on heraldry, chiefly South African and European, and on genealogy; in English and occasionally in Afrikaans. nfs

6. BONDGENOOT [Confederate]. Amptelike maandelikse kultuurblad van die Afrikaanse Taal-en Kultuurbond [Official monthly cultural journal of the Afrikaans Language and Cultural Association]. M. Afrikaanse Taal-en Kultuurbond, 78 Saambou Bldgs., Andries St., P.O.B. 2047, Pretoria. In Afrikaans. 10s

7. THE 1820. The Settler's Magazine on Southern Africa. M. 1929 (1959: vol. 30). The 1820 Memorial, Settlers' Assoc. of Southern Africa, P.O.B. 1754, Cape Town. Ed: Alan Lennox-Short. Art. on the hist. of Southern Africa since the beginning of European settlement, with emphasis on local Cape hist. and the hist. of Rhodesia, as well as on existing conditions and modern developments in Southern Africa likely to be of interest to prospective immigrants; illus. 6s / 7s 6d

8. HISTORIA. Q (3 xy. prior to vol. 2, no. 3, 1957). 1956 (1958: vol. 3). Historiese Genootskap van Suid-Afrika [Hist. Assoc. of South Africa], P.O.B. 508, Germiston, Transvaal. Ed: A.N. Pelzer, c/o Univ. of Pretoria, Pretoria. Art. on South African hist. from the earliest European occupation to modern times, and on methods of teaching hist.; rev. of bk., pub. in South Africa and elsewhere, on South African and world hist. and related subjects; list of bk. received for rev.; A. international biblio. of pub. on the hist. of South Africa; in Afrikaans and occasionally in English, Dutch, French or German. 20s

JOURNAL. For titles beginning with "Journal," followed by the name of the publishing or sponsoring institution or society, see the respective institution or society.

KWARTAALBLAD VAN DIE SUID-AFRIKAANSE BIBLIOTEEK see SOUTH AFRICAN LIBRARY, QUARTERLY BULLETIN OF THE

9. LANTERN. Tydskrif vir kennis en kultuur. Journal of Knowledge and Culture. Q. South African Assoc. for the Advancement of Knowledge and Culture, P.O.B. 1758, Pretoria. In English and in Afrikaans; English sum of art. in Afrikaans. 17s

10. METHODIST HISTORICAL SOCIETY, JOURNAL OF THE. S-A (Irr. prior to 1956). 1952 (1958: vol. 3). Principal, Indaleni Missionary Inst., Indaleni via Richmond, Natal. Ed: Rev. L.A. Hewson, 2 Gilbert St., Grahamstown, C.P. Art. relating to all periods of the hist. of Methodism and Methodist missionaries in South Africa; doc. (letters, diaries, etc.); notes and news concerning the activities of the soc. and its memb. and Methodist churches and missions in South Africa; lists of acquisitions to the archives of the soc.; in English. (memb.) 10s

11. PRETORIANA. 3 xy. (Q until no. 23, 1957). Genootskap Oud-Pretoria [Assoc. of Old Pretoria], P.O.B. 1442, Pretoria. Local hist. of Pretoria; in English or Afrikaans. p (1) 1s (April 1955)

QUARTERLY BULLETIN OF THE SOUTH AFRICAN LIBRARY see SOUTH AFRICAN LIBRARY, QUARTERLY BULLETIN OF THE

12. RACE RELATIONS JOURNAL. Q. South African Inst. of Race Relations, P.O.B. 97, Johannesburg. In English. p(1) 2s 6d (memb. free)

13. SAMAB. South African Museums Association. Bulletin. Suid-Afrikaanse Museums-Assosiasie. Bulletin. Q. South African Museums Assoc., 103 Musgrave Rd., Durban. Illus. p (1) 5s (memb. free)

14. SOUTH AFRICAN ARCHAEOLOGICAL BULLETIN. DIE SUID-AFRIKAANSE ARGEOLOGIESE BULLETIN. Q. 1945 (1959: vol. 14). South African Archaeological Soc., P.O.B. 31, Claremont, Cape Town. Ed: A.J.H. Goodwin.

Art. on the archaeology of Africa, especially Southern Africa; rev. of bk. and art., mainly in English, pub. in all parts of the world; in English. 20s

15. S.A. ARCHIVES JOURNAL. S.A. ARGIEFBLAD. A. 1959 (1959: no. 1). Union Archives, Union Bldgs., Pretoria, Transvaal. Ed: A. Kieser. Art. on the hist., holdings and organization of the Union Archives Dept. pni

S.A. ARGIEFBLAD see S.A. ARCHIVES JOURNAL

16. SOUTH AFRICAN LAW JOURNAL. Q. Juta and Co. Ltd., Regis House, Church St., Cape Town. 42s

17. SOUTH AFRICAN LIBRARY, QUARTERLY BULLETIN OF THE. KWARTAALBLAD VAN DIE SUID-AFRIKAANSE BIBLIOTEEK. Q. 1946 (1958: vol. 13). South African Library, Queen Victoria St., Cape Town. Ed: D. H. Varley. Art. and notes on printed and manuscript material in the library, chiefly Africana, but also of general interest, with emphasis on local Cape hist. of the 17th-19th cent.; reprints of works or parts of works in the library, usually of hist. interest; news of South African periodicals and govt. pub.; supplement to the Bibliography of African Bibliographies; in English and occasionally in Afrikaans; illus. 15s

18. SOUTH AFRICAN PHILATELIST. M. Philatelic Federation of Southern Africa, P O.B. 375, Johannesburg. A. subject index.
12s / 12s 6d (USA and Canada $2)

19. SPRINGBOK. M. South African Legion, B.C.E.S.L., Duncan House, 11 De Villiers St., Johannesburg. Art. on military hist.; in English and occasionally Afrikaans. 5s

DIE SUID-AFRIKAANSE ARGEOLOGIESE BULLETIN see SOUTH AFRICAN ARCHAEOLOGICAL BULLETIN

SUID-AFRIKAANSE BIBLIOTEEK, KWARTAALBLAD VAN DIE... see SOUTH AFRICAN LIBRARY, QUARTERLY BULLETIN OF THE

20. TYDSKRIF VIR HEDENDAAGSE ROMEINS-HOLLANDSE REG [Journal of present-day Roman-Dutch law]. Kwartaalblad vir die regspraktisyn en die regstudent in Suid-Afrika [Quarterly bulletin for the lawyer and law student in South Africa]. Q. Butterworth and Co. (Africa) Ltd., 33-35 Beach Grove Rd., Durban, for the Hugo de Groot Assoc. In Afrikaans and occasionally English.
35s

21. TYDSKRIF VIR RASSE-AANGELEETHEDE. JOURNAL OF RACIAL AFFAIRS. Q. S.A.B.R.A. [South African Bureau of Racial Affairs], P.O.B. 238, Stellenbosch, C.P. In Afrikaans and occasionally English.
p (1) 2s (memb.free)

22. TYDSKRIF VIR VOLKSKUNDE EN VOLKSTAAL [Journal of folklore and language]. Kwartaalblad van die Genootskap vir Afrikaanse Volkskunde gewy aan die Kennis van die Afrikaanse Volkslewe [Quarterly bulletin of the Society for Afrikaans Folklore and the study of the Afrikaans' way of life]. Q. Assoc. of African Folklore, P.O.B. 1176, Johannesburg. 15s

West and West Central Africa

Prepared with the assistance of

J.D. Pearson, Librarian, School of Oriental and African Studies, University of London,

Arquivo Histórico Ultramarino, Lisbon, and the

Ghana Library Board, Accra

ANGOLA

(Portuguese West Africa)

1. ARQUIVO HISTORICO E DA BIBLIOTECA DO MUSEU DE ANGOLA, BOLETIM DO... [Bulletin of the Historical Archives and the Library of the Museum of Angola]. Q. 1949 (1957: no. 32). Museu de Angola, Caixa Postal 1267-C, Luanda. Art. on museum holdings; list of periodicals received; abstr. of art. pni

2. ARQUIVOS DE ANGOLA [Archives of Angola]. Q (Irr.). 1943 (1955: 2nd series, vol. 12). Museu de Angola, Luanda. Ed: Carlos Dias Coimbra, Caixa Postal 1267-C, Luanda. Art. and doc. on the hist. of Angola; indices. Esc. 160

BOLETIM. For titles beginning with "Boletim," followed by the name of the publishing or sponsoring institution or society, see the respective institution or society.

3. INSTITUTO DE ANGOLA, BOLETIM DO... [Bulletin of the Institute of Angola]. Irr. Calçada de Santo Antônio 23, Caixa Postal 2767, Luanda. Biblio.; English and French sum.; illus. Esc. 120 / Esc. 150

4. MENSARIO ADMINISTRATIVO [Administrative monthly]. Publicação de assuntes de interesse Ultramarino [Publication of subjects of overseas interest]. M. Direcção dos Serviços de Administração Civil, Caixa Postal 1237, Luanda. Includes art. on regional ethnology and anthropology. Esc. 120

5. REVISTA ANGOLA [Angola review]. M. Pub. address: Rua Conde de Ficalho, Caixa Postal 931, Luanda.

CAMEROONS

1. ETUDES CAMEROUNAISES [Cameroon studies]. Q. 1935 (1958: no. 56). Institut Français d'Afrique Noire, Centre Cameroun, B.P. 339, Douala. Art. on hist., ethnography and economics with special reference to the Cameroons. Ceased pub. in 1958; succeeded by Recherches et Etudes Camerounaises, founded in 1960. N.Fr. CFA 4 / N.Fr. CFA 5

RECHERCHES ET ETUDES CAMEROUNAISES see ETUDES CAMEROUNAISES

CONGO REPUBLIC (Brazzaville)

BULLETIN DE L'INSTITUT D'ETUDES CENTRAFRICAINES see INSTITUT D'ETUDES CENTRAFRICAINES, BULLETIN DE L'...

1. INSTITUT D'ETUDES CENTRAFRICAINES, BULLETIN DE L'... [Bulletin of the Institute of Central African Studies]. S-A. 1955 (1959: no. 17-18). Institut d'études centrafricaines, B.P. 181, Brazzaville, Congo Republic. Art. on hist., ethnography, economics and geography with special reference to Central Africa; bk. rev.; index, charts, illus. N.Fr. 15 CFA

CONGO REPUBLIC (Léopoldville)

1. AEQUATORIA. Q. 1937 (1960: 23rd year). Ed: G. Hulstraert, B.P. 276, Coquilhatville. Art. on explorations and travel, ethnology and native law and customs pertaining to equatorial Africa; notes on hist. and contemporary subjects; doc.; bk. rev.; biblio.; in French or Flemish. CFr 190

2. BAND [Union]. Tijdschrift voor Vlaams kultuurleven [Journal for Flemish cultural life]. M. Ed. board: H.A. Cornelis, O.V. Spitaels, O.J.L. De Munck (secretary), B.P. 3007, Léopoldville-Kalina. In Flemish. CFr 200 / CFr 250

3. BROUSSE [Bush]. S-A. 1939 (1959: no. 12). Amis de l'Art Indigène du Congo Belge, c/o Musée de la Vie Indigène, B.P. 587, Léopoldville. Ed: Jean Van Den Bossche. Art. on ethnology and cultural hist., with emphasis on native arts and crafts in the Congo; illus. (memb.) CFr 100

BULLETIN TRIMESTRIEL DU CENTRE D'ETUDES DES PROBLEMES SOCIAUX INDIGENES see PROBLEMS SOCIAUX CONGOLAIS

CENTRE D'ETUDES DES PROBLEMES SOCIAUX INDIGENES, BULLETIN TRIMESTRIEL DU... see PROBLEMES SOCIAUX CONGOLAIS

4. FOLIA SCIENTIFICA AFRICAE CENTRALIS. Q. 1955 (1959: vol. 5). Institut pour la recherche scientifique en Afrique Centrale, Bukavu. Ed: C. Derein. Includes brief sum. of works in the humanities; in French; sum. in English of literature pub. recently in the field of African studies. CFr 100

5. JEUNE AFRIQUE [Young Africa]. Q. Secrétariat général de l'Union Africaine des Arts et des Lettres, B.P. 523, Elisabethville. CFr 200

6. LOVANIA. Tendances du temps. Revue universitaire catholique d'Afrique belge [Trends of the times. The Catholic University review of the Belgian Congo]. Q. Association des anciens étudiants de l'Université Catholique de Louvain, B.P. 3020, Léopoldville-Kalina, and B.P. 1259, Elisabethville. In French and occasionally in Flemish. CFr 250 / $ 7

7. PROBLEMES D'AFRIQUE CENTRALE [Problems of Central Africa]. Q. 1931 (1959: 13th year, no. 44). Association des anciens étudiants de l'Institut Universitaire des Territoires d'Outre Mer, B.P. 3071, Léopoldville-Kalina. Ed:

André Gascht, 34 rue de Stassart, Bruxelles, Belgium. Art. on administration, anthropology, ethnology, law and related subjects pertaining to the Congo; rev. art.; bk. rev.; in French or Flemish; English sum. CFr 150

8. PROBLEMES SOCIAUX CONGOLAIS [Congolese social problems]. Q. (1960: no. 48). Association des anciens étudiants de l'Université Catholique de Louvain, groupement du Katanga, and Office Central du Travail du Katanga, Elisabethville, for Centre d'Etudes des Problemes Sociaux. Ed. address: B.P. 1873, Elisabethville. Art. on Congolese social problems; doc.; bk. rev. Prior to 1958 pub. under the title: Bulletin trimestriel du Centre d'Etude des Problèmes sociaux indigènes. CFr 150 / CFr 250

9. LA VOIX DU CONGOLAIS [The voice of the Congolese]. Pour les Congolais par les Congolais [By the Congolese for the Congolese]. B-M. Commissariat de l'Information du Gouvernement Général, Léopoldville. Ceased pub. with no. 165 (December 1959). CFr 80 / BFr 200

DAHOMEY REPUBLIC

1. ETUDES DAHOMEENNES [Dahomey studies]. Irr. 1948 (1959: vol. 22). Institut Français d'Afrique Noire, Centre IFAN, B.P. 6, Porto Novo. Ed: J. Lombard. Art. on the hist., ethnography and economy of Dahomey, and on African settlers in other areas from prehist. times to the present; doc.; charts, maps, illus. N.Fr. 5 CFA

GHANA

1. HISTORICAL SOCIETY OF GHANA, TRANSACTIONS OF THE. S-A. 1952 (1959: vol. 4). Hist. Soc. of Ghana, Dept. of Hist., Univ. College of Ghana, Legon. Ed: J.D. Fage. Art. on the hist. of Ghana and the adjacent West African territories; biblio.; news of the soc.; maps. Formerly appeared under the title: Transactions of the Gold Coast and Togoland Historical Society. (memb.) 40s

TRANSACTIONS OF THE HISTORICAL SOCIETY OF GHANA see HISTORICAL SOCIETY OF GHANA, TRANSACTIONS OF THE

2. UNIVERSITAS. 3 x y. 1953 (1960: vol. 4). Univ. College of Ghana, Legon. Ed: T.A. Dunn. Art. on the hist. and economy of Ghana, and on related subjects; bk. rev.; biblio.; index; illus. 5s / 5s 6d

NIGERIA

BULLETIN OF NEWS OF THE HISTORICAL SOCIETY OF NIGERIA see HISTORICAL SOCIETY OF NIGERIA, BULLETIN OF NEWS OF THE

1. HISTORICAL SOCIETY OF NIGERIA, BULLETIN OF NEWS OF THE. Q. 1956 (1960: vol. 5). Hist. Soc. of Nigeria, Arts Bldg., Univ. College, Ibadan. Ed: H.F.C. Smith, P.O.B. 916, Ibadan. News of the soc.; biblio. of bk. and art. on West African hist. in African and European languages; list of periodicals. Mimeographed. memb. free

2. HISTORICAL SOCIETY OF NIGERIA, JOURNAL OF THE. A. 1956 (1959: vol. 1, no. 4). Hist. Soc. of Nigeria, Arts Bldg., Univ. College, Ibadan. Ed: J.D. Omer-Cooper. Art. on various aspects of the hist. of West Africa; bk. rev.; research notes. 20s / $2.80 (memb. only)

JOURNAL OF THE HISTORICAL SOCIETY OF NIGERIA see HISTORICAL SOCIETY OF NIGERIA, JOURNAL OF THE

3. NIGERIA MAGAZINE. A Quarterly Publication for Everyone Interested in the Country and Its People. Q. (1960: no. 65). Govt. of Nigeria, Lagos. Ed: Michael Crowder. Includes anthropological and hist. art.; bk. rev.; readers' letters. 10s 10d / $2

4. ODU [One of the significant patterns of kernels or pods which are used in the Ifa system of divination, a well-known element in the old Yoruba culture -- ed.]. Journal of Yoruba and Related Studies. Irr. (A. or S-A). 1955 (1959: no. 7). General Pub. Section, Ministry of Education, Ibadan. Ed: S.O. Biobaku, H. U. Beier. Art. on Yoruba and West African hist. and occasionally on Yoruba literature; bk. rev.; in English (except for occasional Yoruba poems); illus. pni

PORTUGUESE GUINEA

1. BOLETIM CULTURAL DA GUINE PORTUGUESA [Cultural bulletin of Portuguese Guinea]. Q. Centro de Estudos da Guiné Portuguesa, Caixa Postal 37, Bissau. Biblio.; index; graph, illus. Esc. 55

SENEGAL REPUBLIC

1. ANNALES AFRICAINES [African annals]. A. 1954 (1959). Imprimerie Guillemot et de Lamothe, 35 rue des Petits-Champs, Paris, for Faculté de Droit et des Sciences Economiques de Dakar. Art. on legal studies and the constitutional and legislative hist. of French West and Equatorial Africa; doc. pni

BULLETIN DE L'INSTITUT FRANÇAIS D'AFRIQUE NOIRE see INSTITUT FRANÇAIS D'AFRIQUE NOIRE, BULLETIN DE L'...

2. INSTITUT FRANÇAIS D'AFRIQUE NOIRE, BULLETIN DE L'...[Bulletin of the French Institute of Negro Africa]. Serié B: Sciences Humaines [Series B: Humanities]. Q. 1939 (1960: vol. 22). Institut Français d'Afrique Noire (IFAN), B.P. 206, Dakar. Art. on the hist. and ethnography of Africa; bk. rev.; biblio.; index; illus. Supplement to vol. 14, with cum. table of contents for the years 1939-49, pub. in 1952. N.Fr. 36 CFA

3. NOTES AFRICAINES [African notes]. Bulletin d'information et de correspondance de l'Institut français d'Afrique Noire [Information and correspondence

bulletin of the French Institute of Negro Africa]. Q. Institut français d'Afrique Noire, Service Pub., B.P. 206, Dakar. N.Fr. 5 CFA

SIERRA LEONE

1. SIERRA LEONE STUDIES. S-A. 1919 (1960: new series, no. 13). Sierra Leone Soc., Fourah Bay College, Freetown, Sierra Leone. Ed: A.P. Kup. Art. on the hist. of Sierra Leone and Africa and on Africans in other parts of the world, covering all periods; biblio. art.; doc.; occasional bk. rev.; news of the soc.; correspondence; illus.; graph. 5s (memb. free)

Islands off the African Coast

Prepared with the assistance of

A. Toussaint, Chief Archivist, Archives Department, Colony of Mauritius, Port Louis, and

Miss Madeleine Ly-Tio-Fane, Assistant Librarian, Mauritius Institute, Port Louis

MADAGASCAR

1. ACADEMIE MALGACHE, BULLETIN DE L'... [Bulletin of the Academy of Madagascar]. A. 1902 (1957: vol. 35). Académie Malgache, Tsimbazaza, Tananarive. Ed: R. Paulian. Art. on sociology, philology, genealogy, ethnography and natural sciences. pni

BULLETIN DE L'ACADEMIE MALGACHE see ACADEMIE MALGACHE, BULLETIN DE L'...

2. INSTITUT SCIENTIFIQUE DE MADAGASCAR, MEMOIRES DE L'... [Memoirs of the Institue of Science of Madagascar]. Series C. Sciences Humaines. Irr. 1952 (1957: vol. 4). Institut Scientifique de Madagascar, B.P. 434, Tsimbazaza, Tananarive. Ed: J. Millot, 55 rue de Buffon, Paris 5e, M.R. Paulian (secretary-general), Tsimbazaza, Tananarive. Art. on the ethnography, demography, economy and sociology of the people of Madagascar. N.Fr. 40 CFA

MEMOIRES DE L'INSTITUT SCIENTIFIQUE DE MADAGASCAR see INSTITUT SCIENTIFIQUE DE MADAGASCAR, MEMOIRES DE L'...

3. LE NATURALISTE MALGACHE [The Madagascar naturopathist]. A. Institut de Recherche Scientifique de Madagascar, and Société des Amis du Parc de Tsimbazaza, Parc Zoologique et Botanique, Tsimbazaza, Tananarive. N.Fr. 5 CFA / N.Fr. 7.50 CFA

4. REVUE DE MADAGASCAR [Madagascar review]. Q. Service Général de l'information, place Colbert, B.P. 271, Tananarive. N.Fr. 11 CFA/ N.Fr. 15 CFA

MAURITIUS

ANNUAL REPORT OF THE ARCHIVES DEPARTMENT (OF MAURITIUS) see ARCHIVES DEPARTMENT (OF MAURITIUS), ANNUAL REPORT OF THE

1. ARCHIVES DEPARTMENT (OF MAURITIUS), ANNUAL REPORT OF THE. A. Mauritius Archives Dept., 52 Sir William Newton St., Port Louis. Includes a current biblio. of pub. issued in and dealing with Mauritius. Rs 0.50

BULLETIN DE LA SOCIETE DE L'HISTOIRE DE L'ILE MAURICE see SOCIETE DE L'HISTOIRE DE L'ILE MAURICE, BULLETIN DE LA...

2. DICTIONARY OF MAURITIAN BIOGRAPHY. Irr. 1941. Société de l'Histoire de l'Ile Maurice, Curepipe. Ed: A. Toussaint. Biographical notices on famous Mauritians or persons identified with Mauritius; in English and French. p (1) Rs 3

3. LA REVUE RETROSPECTIVE DE L'ILE MAURICE [Retrospective review of Mauritius Island]. B-M. 1950 (mri 1955: vol. 6). Ed: L. Noel Regnard, rue Pierre de Sornay, Curepipe Rd., Ile Maurice. Art. on exploration and travel, and on the economic and cultural hist. and toponymy of the Mascarene Islands since their discovery by the Europeans; doc.; A. name index. Pub. suspended in November 1955. Rs 30

4. SOCIETE DE L'HISTOIRE DE L'ILE MAURICE, BULLETIN DE LA... [Bulletin of the Society for the History of Mauritius Island]. Irr. 1939 (mri 1948-53: vol. 4). Société de l'Histoire de L'Ile Maurice, Curepipe. Art. on Mauritian local hist.; bk. rev.; in French and English. p (1) Rs 5

REUNION

1. RECUEIL DE DOCUMENTS ET TRAVAUX INEDITS POUR SERVIR A L'HISTOIRE DE LA REUNION (ANCIENNE ILE BOURBON) [Collection of unpublished documents and papers devoted to the history of Réunion (Ancient island of Bourbon)]. Irr. 1954 (1959: vol. 3). Archives Departementales de la Réunion, P.B. 289, Saint Denis, Réunion. Art. on the local hist. and local archives of Réunion; reproductions of doc.; biblio. pni

EAST AND EAST CENTRAL ASIA

China
(MAINLAND)

Prepared with the assistance of

Chen Tsu-lung, Institut des Hautes
Etudes Chinoises, University of Paris

Note: The Wade-Giles system has been used below for the transliteration of Chinese words. But whenever a title has been transcribed on the periodical itself, the Romanized title as cited on the periodical is given first, with a transliteration according to the Wade-Giles system in parentheses thereafter.

1. BEIJING SHIFAN DAXUE XUEBAO (Pei-ching Shih-fan Ta-hsüeh Hsüeh-pao) [Journal of the Peking Normal University]. Shê-hui K'o-hsüeh [Social sciences]. B-M (beginning 1959). Pei-ching Shih-fan Ta-hsüeh, Peking. p(1) Y 0.50

2. CHÊ-HSÜEH YEN-CHIU [Philosophical research]. B-M (M in 1958/59). K'o-hsüeh Ch'u-pan Shê [Science Press], Ch'ao-yang Mên Ta-chieh, Peking. Y 4.80

3. CHÊNG-CHIH HSÜEH-HSI [Political study]. M. T'ung-su Tu-wu Ch'u-pan Shê [Popular Literature Pub. Co.], Peking. Y 2

4. CHÊNG-FA YEN-CHIU [Political and legal research]. B-M (M up to 1958). Chêng-fa Yen-chiu Ch'u-pan Shê [Political and Legal Research Press], P.O.B. 399, Peking. Y 1.80

5. CHÊNG-MING [Contention]. M. Pub. in Peking. Y 2

CHI-HUA CHING-CHI see CHING-CHI YEN-CHIU

6. CHIANG-HAI HSÜEH-K'AN [Chiang-hai journal of learning]. M. Chiang-hai Journal of Learning, P.O.B. 399, Peking. Y 5

7. CHIANG-HUAI WÊN-HSÜEH [Chiang-huai literature]. M. Jên-min Ch'u-pan Shê [People's Pub. House], Hofei. Y 4

CHIAO-HSÜEH YÜ YEN-CHIU see JIAOXUE YU YANJIU

8. CH'IAO-WU PAO [Overseas Chinese report]. M. Ch'iao-wu-pao Shê [Overseas Chinese Report Press], Wang-Ta-jên Hu-t'ung, Peking. Y 2.40

9. CHIAO-YÜ I-PAO [Journal of translations pertaining to education]. B-M. Jên-min Chiao-yü Ch'u-pan Shê [People's Education Press], Peking. Y 1.80

10. CHIEN-CHU [Architecture]. B-W. Chung-kuo Chien-chu Hsüeh-hui [Chinese Architectural Soc.], Pai-wan Chuang, Hsi-chiao, Peking. Chien-chu Chi-shu T'ung-hsün [Architectural arts bulletin] has been combined with this periodical since 1957.

CHIEN-CHU CHI-SHU T'UNG-HSÜN see CHIEN-CHU

11. CHIEN-CHU HSÜEH-PAO [Architectural journal]. M. Chung-kuo Chien-chu Hsüeh-hui [Chinese Architecture Soc.], Pai-wan Chuang, Hsi-chiao, Peking. Y 16

12. CHIEN-CHU I-TS'UNG [Journal of translations pertaining to architecture]. B-W. Chien-chu Kung-chêng Ch'u-pan Shê [Architectural Engineering Press], Hsi-chiao, Peking. Y 8

13. CHIH-SHIH CHIU-SHIH LI-LIANG [Knowledge is power]. M. K'o-hsüeh chi-shu Ch'u-pan Shê [Science and Technique Press], Peking. Y 6

14. CHIN-TAI SHIH TZU-LIAO [Materials on recent history]. B-M. 1955 (1957: no. 5). Third Bureau of the Inst. of Hist., Academia Sinica, 1 Tung-ch'ang Hu-t'ung, Peking. Art. on modern Chinese hist.; doc.; source material for the study of modern Chinese civilization; rev. art.; bk. rev.; illus. Y 5

15. CHIN-YUNG YEN-CHIU [Financial research]. Q. Pub. in Peking. Y 2.40

16. CHINA RECONSTRUCTS. M. Chian Welfare Inst., 40A East Huang-ch'êng Kên, Peking. Sometimes carries reproductions of speeches by govt. leaders or, as supplements, political doc.; in English. Y 9

17. CHINESE LITERATURE. M (1959); B-M (1958); Q (1957). Foreign Languages Press, Pai-wan Chuang, Peking. In English. Y 7 / $2.50

18. CHING-CHI I-TS'UNG [Translations pertaining to economics]. M. Pub. address: P.O.B. 399, Peking. Y 6

19. CHING-CHI YEN-CHIU [Economic research]. M (1958); B-M (1955-57). 1955 (1959: no. 1-2). Inst. of Economics, Academia Sinica, San-li Ho, Fu-hsing Mên Wai, Peking. Art. on Chinese socio-economic studies, with emphasis on the economic hist. of modern China; fresh interpretations (mostly by New China's leading economists and historians) of Marx-Lenin's materialism; reports and critiques on capitalist economic systems; biographies; translations of foreign (predominantly Russian) socio-economic papers; bk. rev.; tables of contents in Chinese, English and Russian; illus. Chi-hua Ching-chi [Planned economy] has been combined with this periodical since 1959. Y 9

20. CHÜ-PÊN [Drama]. M. Chung-kuo Hsi chü Ch'u-pan Shê [Chinese Drama Press], 64 Wang-fu Ta-chieh, Peking. Y 6

21. CHUANG-SHIH [Decoration]. B-M. Jên-min Mei-shu Ch'u-pan Shê [People's Art Press], 10 Tung Tsung-pu Hu-t'ung, Peking. Y 9

22. CHUNG-HSÜEH CHIAO-SHIH [Middle-school teacher]. M. Jên-min Ch'u-pan Shê [People's Pub. House], Nanking. Y 1.80

CHUNG-HSÜEH LI-SHIH CHIAO-HSÜEH see ZHONGXUE LISHI JIAOXUE

23. CHUNG-I TSA-CHIH [Journal of Chinese medicine]. M. Jên-min Wei-shêng Ch'u-pan Shê [Public Health Press], Peking. Y 3.60

CHUNG-KUO CH'ING-NIEN see ZHONGGUO QINGNIAN

24. CHUNG-KUO FU-NÜ [Chinese women]. B-W. Chung-hua Chüan-Kuo-Min-chü Fu-nü Lien-ho Hui [All-China Women's Assoc.], Peking. Formerly pub. under the title: Hsin Chung-kuo Fu-nüe [New China's women]. Y 3.60

25. CHUNG-KUO HUA [Chinese painting]. M(Irr.). Chung-Kuo-hua Pien-chi Wei-yüan-hui [Chinese Painting Ed. Board], Peking. p(1) Y 1

26. CHUNG-KUO K'O-HSÜEH [Chinese science]. Irr. Academia Sinica, 3 Wên-chin Chieh, Peking. p(1) Y 1.80

27. CHUNG-KUO K'O-HSÜEH YÜAN LI-SHIH YEN-CHIU SO TI-SAN SO CHI-K'AN [Bulletin of the Third Bureau of the Institute of History, Academia Sinica]. A. 1954 (mri 1955: no. 2). Third Bureau of the Inst. of Hist., Academia Sinica, 1 Tung-ch'ang Hu-t'ung, Peking. Art. on modern Chinese hist. and cultural movements; bk. rev.; illus. Y 1.40

CHUNG-KUO KUNG-JÊN see ZHONGGUO GONGREN

CHUNG-KUO YÜ-WÊN see ZHONGGUE YUWEN

CHUNG-SHAN TA-HSÜEH HSÜEH-PAO see ZHONGSHAN DAXUE XUEBAO

28. FU-CHIEN CHUNG I-YAO [Fu-chien journal of Chinese medicine]. B-M. Pub. in Fuchow. Y 1.80

29. FU-CHIEN NUNG-HSÜEH YÜAN HSÜEH-PAO [Journal of the Fu-chien College of Agriculture]. S-A. College Press, Fuchow, for Fu-chien Nung-hsüeh Yüan. Y 1.80

30. FU-TAN [(Journal of the) Fu-tan (University)]. M. Univ. Press, Shanghai, for Fu-tan Univ. Y 1.20

GEOGRAPHICAL SOCIETY OF CHINA, JOURNAL OF THE see TI-LI HSÜEH-PAO

31. HA-ERH-PIN KUNG-YEH TA-HSÜEH HSÜEH-PAO [Journal of the Harbin Industrial University]. Q. Univ. Press, Harbin, for Ha-erh-pin Kung-yeh Ta-hsüeh. Y 4.80

32. HO-FEI K'UANG-YEH HSÜEH-YÜAN HSÜEH-PAO [Journal of the Hofei College of Mineralogy]. Q. College Press, Hofei, for Ho-fei K'uang-yeh Hsüeh-yüan, Hofei. pni

33. HO-NAN I-HSÜEH YÜAN HSÜEH-PAO [Ho-nan Medical College journal]. Q. 1957 (1957: no. 1). College Press, Chengchow, for Ho-nan I-hsüeh Yüan, Chengchow. Art. on the hist. of Chinese medical science and all fields of the study of medicine; notes and news. pni

34. HO-P'ING HO SHÊ-HUI-CHU-I WÊN-T'I [Questions relating to peace and socialism]. M. Peace and Socialism Press, Peking. pni

HSI-CHÜ LUN-TS'UNG see HSI-CHÜ YEN-CHIU

35. HSI-CHÜ PAO [Theater journal]. B-W (1957); M (1954/56). Pub. address: 64 Wang-fu Ta-chieh, Peking. Combined with Hsi-chü Yen-chiu since 1959. See next entry. Y 7.20

36. HSI-CHÜ YEN-CHIU [Studies on the theater]. B-M. Pub. address: P.O.B. 399, Peking. Combined with Hsi-chü Pao since 1959. See preceding entry. pni

37. HSI-NAN SHIH-FAN HSÜEH-YÜAN HSÜEH-PAO [Southwest (China) Normal College journal]. Irr. 1957 (1957: no. 1). College Press, Chungking, for Hsi-nan Shih-fan Hsüeh-yüan, Chungking. Art. on hist., social, political, and economic studies of China; bk. rev. pni

38. HSI-PEI NUNG-HSÜEH YÜAN HSÜEH-PAO [Northwest (China) Agriculture College journal]. Q. Jên-min Ch'u-pan Shê [People's Pub. House], Sian, for Hsi-pei Nung-hsüeh Yüan. Y 8.40

39. HSI-PEI NUNG-YEH K'O-HSÜEH [Northwest (China) agricultural science]. B-M. Pub. in Sian. Y 2.70

40. HSI-PEI TA-HSÜEH HSÜEH-PAO [Northwest (China) University journal]. Jên-wên K'o-hsüeh [Humanities]. Q. 1957 (1957: no. 1-4). Univ. Press, Hsiao Nan-mên Wai, Sian, for Hsi-pei Ta-hsüeh, Sian. Art. on Chinese hist. (of all periods), language, literature, philosophy, religion, archaeology, and sociology; notes and news on academic activities and organizations; bk. rev. Y 3.30

41. HSIA-MÊN TA-HSÜEH HSÜEH-PAO [Hsia-mên University journal]. Shê-hui K'o-hsüeh [Social sciences]. S-A. 1957 (1958: no. 1). Univ. Press, Amoy, for Hsia-mên Ta-hsüeh, Amoy. Art. on Chinese hist. (ancient and modern) and on all branches of the study of social science; occasional art. on inter-Asian cultural relations; bk. rev.; art. and table of contents in Chinese or English; English sum. of Chinese-language art. Y 2.40

42. HSIN CHIEN-SHÊ [New construction]. M. Kuang-ming Daily Pub. Co., Peking. Y 4.80

HSIN CHUNG-KUO FU NÜ see CHUNG-KUO FU NÜ

43. HSIN-HUA PAN-YÜEH-K'AN [The New China biweekly]. B-W. 1953 (1958: no. 1-12). Pub. address: 320 Ch'ao-yang Mên Ta-chieh, Peking. Art. on Chinese politics (mostly modern), international relations and the world situation; reproductions of political, diplomatic and economic doc.; news and notes. Y 21.60

44. HSIN KUAN-CH'A [New observer]. B-W. Chung-kuo Tso-chia Hsieh-hui [Chinese Writers' Assoc.], Peking. Y 7.20

45. HSIN KUNG-SHANG [New industry and commerce]. B-W. Pub. in Peking. Y 6

46. HSIN-WÊN CHAN-HSIEN [News front]. M. 1957 (1957: no. 1). All-China Journalists' Assoc., Peking. Art. on newspaper editing and production; papers on the hist. of the press; doc.; translations and abstr. of news and notes from the foreign press; rev. art. Y 3.60

47. HSÜEH-HSI [Study]. B-W (1957); M (1949-56). Hsüeh-hsi Tsa-chih Shê [The Study Magazine], Peking. Illus. Y 3.60

48. HSÜEH-HSI I-TS'UNG [Journal of translations pertaining to studies]. M. Pub. in Peking. Y 6

49. HSÜEH K'O-HSÜEH [Learning science]. B-W (1958); M (1956/57). Pub. address: P.O.B. 399, Peking. Y 3.60

50. HSÜEH-SHU LUN-T'AN [Learning forum]. Q. Pub. address: P.O.B. 399, Peking. Y 1.50

51. HSÜEH-SHU YÜEH-K'AN [Learning monthly]. M. 1957 (1957: no. 1-12). Jên-min Ch'u-pan Shê [People's Pub. House], 54 Shao-hsing Rd., Shanghai. Art. on Chinese hist. (ancient and modern), politics, philosophy, religion, language, literature, and other socio-economic topics; reproductions of current political doc.; news of literary activities (from China and other countries); occasional rev. art. or notes on the study of Russian civilization (predominantly modern); bk. rev. Y 3.60

52. HUA-CHUNG SHIH-FAN HSÜEH-YÜAN HSÜEH-PAO [Central China Normal College journal]. Q. College Press, Wuchang, for Hua-chung Shih-fan Hsüeh-yüan. Y 4

53. HUA-NAN NUNG-YEH K'O-HSÜEH [South China agricultural science]. Q. Jên-min Ch'u-pan Shê [People's Pub. House], Canton. Y 2.40

54. HUA-TUNG NUNG-YEH K'O-HSÜEH T'UNG-PAO [East China agricultural science journal]. M. Jên-min Ch'u-pan Shê [People's Pub. House], Shanghai. Y 5.40

55. HUA-TUNG SHIH-FAN TA-HSÜEH HSÜEH-PAO [East China Normal University journal]. Jên-wên K'o-hsüeh [Humanities]. Q. Hua-tung Shih-ta [East China Normal Univ.], Shanghai. Y 3

56. HUNG-CH'I [Red flag]. B-W. Pub. in Peking. Y 4.50

57. HUO-CHIEN [Rocket]. M. Dept. of Chinese Language, Nanking Univ., Nanking. Y 1.44

58. I-HSÜEH SHIH YÜ PAO-CHIEN TSU-CHIH [History of medicine and health (services) organization]. Q. Pub. address: P.O.B. 399, Peking. Y 3

I-WÊN see SHIH-CHIEH WÊN-HSÜEH

59. JÊN-MIN CHIAO-YÜ [People's education]. B-W (since May 1958); M (1950-April 1958). Jên-min Chiao-yü Ch'u-pan Shê [People's Education Press], Peking. Pub. suspended from November 1957 to March 1958. Y 3.60

60. JÊN-MIN WÊN-HSÜEH [People's literature]. M. Jên-min Wên-hsüeh Ch'u-pan Shê [People's Literature Pub. Co.], 320 Ch'ao-nui Ta-chieh, Peking. Y 6.90

61. JÊN-MIN YIN-YÜEH [People's music]. M. Yin-yüeh Ch'u-pan Shê [People's Music Pub. Co.], West Liu-li Ch'ang, Ho-p'ing Mên Wai, Peking.
Y 2.40

62. JÊN-WÊN K'O-HSÜEH TSA-CHIH [The humanities journal]. B-M. 1957 (1957: no. 1). Dept. of the Humanities, Yün-nan Univ., Kunming. Art. on all branches of the study of Chinese culture, with emphasis on the hist. of modern cultural advancement of the Chinese tribes; bk. rev.; notes and news on literary activities in China. Y 1.80

63. JÊN-WÊN TSA-CHIH [The humanities journal]. B-M. Jên-wên tsa-chih Shê [Humanities Press], Sian. Y 1.80

64. JIAOXUE YU YANJIU (Chiao-hsüeh Yü Yen-chiu) [Journal of education and research]. M. Chung-kuo Jên-min Ta-hsüeh [Chinese People's Univ.], Hsi-chiao, Peking. Y 4.60

JOURNAL OF THE GEOGRAPHICAL SOCIETY OF CHINA see TI-LI HSÜEH-PAO

65. K'AI-FÊNG SHIH-FAN HSÜEH-YÜAN HSÜEH-PAO [K'ai-fêng Normal College journal]. Irr. 1956 (mri 1956: no. 1). College Press, Kaifeng, for K'ai-fêng Shih-fan Hsüeh-yüan. Art. on the socio-hist., political and cultural aspects of China; rev. art.; doc.; notes and news on organizations of the college.
pni

66. K'AO-KU [Archaeology]. M. 1959 (1959: no. 1-2). Science Press, 117 Ch'ao-yang Mên Ta-chieh, Peking. Ed. address: 9 Wang-fu Ta-chieh, Peking. Art. on Chinese archaeology and hist.; essays on the teaching of hist. and archaeology in different countries; notes on materials for the study of hist.; news items; correspondence; discussions; bk. rev.; illus. Formerly pub. under the title: T'ung-hsün [Archaeological bulletin]. Y 5.52

67. K'AO-KU HSÜEH-PAO [Journal of archaeology]. Q. 1951 (1958: no. 19-22). K'o hsüeh Ch'u-pan Shê [Science Press], 117 Ch'ao-yang Mên Ta-chieh, Peking. Ed. address: 9 Wang-fu Ta-chieh, Peking. Art. on archaeological discoveries, Chinese cultural hist. and the hist. of antiquity, art, epigraphy and anthropology as well as archival studies; sometimes translations of foreign (predominantly Russian) archaeological studies; occasional bk. rev.; in Chinese, with English sum.; tables of contents in Chinese, Russian and English; illus.
Y 12 / $ 4.80

K'AO-KU T'UNG-HSÜN see K'AO-KU

68. K'O-HSÜEH CHI-LU [Science record]. M. 1957 (1957: no. 1). K'o-hsüeh Ch'u-pan Shê [Science Press], 117 Ch'ao-yang Mên Ta-chieh, Peking. Art. on all fields of the study of sciences; information concerning international scientific activities; notes and reports; rev. art. Y 19.80

69. K'O-HSÜEH CHI-SHU KUNG-TSO [Scientific and technical works]. M. Science and Arts Press, Peking. Y 1.20

70. K'O-HSÜEH TA-CHUNG [Popular science]. M. Science and Arts Press, Peking. Y 3.60

71. K'O-HSÜEH T'UNG-PAO [Science journal]. B-W (1957); M (1950-56). K'o-hsüeh Ch'u-pan Shê [Science Press], 117 Chao-yang Mên Ta-chieh, Peking. Y 12

72. K'O-HSÜEH YÜ CHI-SHU [Science and technology]. Q. Jên-min Ch'u-pan Shê [People's Pub. House], Sian. pni

73. KU-TIEN WÊN-HSÜEH YEN-CHIU HUI-K'AN [Classical literature research journal]. Irr. Ku-tien Wên-hsüeh Ch'u-pan Shê [Classical Literature Pub. Co.], 755 K'ang-p'ing Rd., Shanghai. pv (p (1) Y 0.62 - 1.20)

74. KUANG-TUNG LI-SHIH TZŬ-LIAO [Kwantung history materials]. Q. 1959 (1959: no. 1). Jên-min ch'u-pan Shê [People's Pub. Co.], 43 Ta-nan Rd., Canton. Ed. address: 222 North Yüeh-hsiu Rd., Canton. Art. on relics, archaeological remains and other materials relating to the hist. of Kwantung; discussions on the cultural relations between Kwantung and its surrounding provinces; doc. (official and private); rev. art.; notes and news on hist. organizations in China. Y 2.10

75. KUO-CHI WÊN-T'I I-TS'UNG [Journal of translations pertaining to international questions]. B-W (1958); M (1952-57). Pub. address: 27 Kan-mien Hu-t'ung, Peking. Y 8

76. LAN-CHOU TA-HSÜEH HSÜEH-PAO [Lanchow University journal]. Jên-wên K'o-hsüeh [Humanities]. Q. Univ. Press, Lanchow, for Lan-chou Ta-hsüeh. Y 1.20

77. LI-LUN CHAN-HSIEN [Theoretical front]. M. Jên-min Ch'u-pan Shê [People's Pub. House], 332 Chieh-fang Ta-tao, Hankow. Y 2.40

78. LI-LUN YÜ SHIH-CHI EN [Theory and practice]. M. Pub. in Peking. Y 3

79. LI-SHIH CHIAO-HSÜEH [History teaching]. M. Jên-min Ch'u-pan Shê [People's Pub. House], Tientsin. pni

80. LI-SHIH CHIAO-HSÜEH WÊN-T'I [Questions relating to history teaching]. M (1958); B-M (1957). 1957 (1958: no. 1). Hsin Chih-shih Ch'u-pan Shê [New Knowledge Pub. Co.], Shanghai. Art. on all aspects of the teaching of hist. in China; discussions and critiques on Chinese historiography; rev. art.; news and notes. Y 3.60

81. LI-SHIH YEN-CHIU [Historical research]. M (since 1956); B-M (1954/55). 1954 (1958: no. 1-12). K'o-hsüeh Ch'u-pan Shê [Science Press], 117 Ch'ao-yang Mên Ta-chieh, Peking. Ed. address: 1 East Ssŭ-tou T'iao, Peking. Art. on all aspects of the study of hist.; discussions and critiques on ancient and modern hist. topics; rev. art. on Chinese historiography; news and notes on important source materials; information concerning hist. research in China; bk. rev.; table of contents in Chinese, Russian and English; illus. Y 9

LI-SHIH YEN-CHIU SO TI-SAN SO CHI-K'AN see CHUNG-KUO K'O-HSÜEH YÜAN LI-SHIH YEN-CHIU SO TI-SAN SO CHI-K'AN

82. LIN-NUNG I-PAO [Journal of translations pertaining to forestry and agriculture]. Q. Lin-nung Pu Lin-nung K'o-hsüeh Yen-chiu So [Ministry of Forestry and Agriculture, Forestry and Agricultural Sciences Research Bureau], Peking. pni

83. LIN-YEH K'O-HSÜEH [Science of forestry]. Q. K'o-hsüeh Ch'u-pan Shê [Science Press], 117 Ch'ao-yang Mên Ta-chieh, Peking. Y 9

84. MEI-SHU [Art]. M. Jên-min Mei-shu Ch'u-pan Shê [People's Art Press], Shanghai. Y 8 / $2.40

85. MEI-SHU TSO-P'IN [Works of art]. Q. Jên-min Mei-shu Ch'u-pan Shê [People's Art Press], Shanghai. Y 10

86. MEI-SHU YEN-CHIU [Research on art]. Q. Jên-min Mei-shu Ch'u-pan Shê [People's Art Press], Shanghai. Y 2.40

87. MIN-CHIEN WÊN-HSÜEH [Folk literature]. M. Jên-min Wên-hsüeh Ch'u-pan Shê [People's Literature Pub. Co.], 320 Ch'ao-nui Ta-chieh, Peking. Y 4

88. MIN-TSU T'UAN-CHIEH ["All-People's" (national) solidarity]. M. Min-tsu Ch'u-pan Shê [National Press], Ho-ping Rd., Peking. Y 2.52

MIN-TSU WÊN-T'I I-TS'UNG see next entry

89. MIN-TSU YEN-CHIU ["All-People's" (national) research]. M. Min-tsu Ch'u-pan Shê [National Press], Ho-ping Rd., Peking. Up to September 1958 pub. under the title: Min-tsu Wên-t'i I-ts'ung [Journal of translations pertaining to national questions]. Y 3

90. NAN-CHING NUNG-HSÜEH YÜAN HSÜEH-PAO [Journal of the Nanking College of Agriculture]. Q. College Press, Nanking, for Nan-ching Nung-hsüeh Yüan. pni

91. NUNG-YEH HSÜEH-PAO [Agricultural journal]. Q. K'o-hsüeh Ch'u-pan Shê [Science Press], 117 Ch'ao-yang Mên Ta-chieh, Peking. Y 9.36

92. PEI-CHING K'UANG-YEH HSÜEH-YÜAN HSÜEH-PAO [Journal of the Peking Mining College]. Q. Pei-ching K'uang-yeh Hsüeh-yüan, Peking. Y 2

PEI-CHING SHIH-FAN TA-HSÜEH HSÜEH-PAO see BEIJING SHIFAN DAXUE XUEBAO

93. PEI-CHING TA-HSÜEH HSÜEH-PAO [Peking University journal]. Jên-wên K'o-hsüeh [Humanities]. Q. 1955 (1958: no. 1-2). Peking Univ. Press, Hai-ting, Hsi-chiao, Peking, for Pei-ching Ta-hsüeh. Art. on all periods of Chinese cultural hist., mostly from a Marxist viewpoint; papers on all branches of the study of social science; translations; rev. art.; notes and news on academic activities of the univ.; bk. rev.; table of contents in Chinese, Russian and English. Y 19.20

94. PIEN-CHIANG WÊN-I [Frontier literature and art]. M. Pub. in Kunming. pni

P'IN-YIN see WÊN-TZŬ KAI-KÊ

PINJIN see WÊN-TZŬ KAI-KÊ

95. PO-WU KUAN I-TS'UNG [Journal of translations pertaining to museums]. Irr. Cultural Remains Press, Peking. p (1) 0.60

96. SHAN-HSI SHIH-FAN HSÜEH-YÜAN HSÜEH-PAO [Shan-hsi Normal College journal]. Q. 1957 (1957: no. 1). Jên-min Ch'u-pan Shê [People's Pub. House], Taiyuan, for Shan-hsi Shih-fan Hsüeh-yüan. Art. on Chinese hist. (ancient and modern), archaeology, language, literature, politics and economics; rev. art.; notes and news on literary activities of the college. Y 3

97. SHAN-TUNG CHIAO-YÜ [Shantung education]. B-W. Jên-min Ch'u-pan Shê [People's Pub. House], Chinan. pni

98. SHANG-HAI CHIAO-YÜ [Shanghai education]. B-W. Education Press, Shanghai. Two editions, one for elementary schools, another for middle schools. Y 3.36

99. SHANG-HAI KUNG-SHANG [Shanghai industry and commerce]. B-W. Pub. in Shanghai. Y 3

100. SHANG-HAI KUNG-YEH CHIAO-YÜ [Shanghai industrial education]. B-W. Education Press, Shanghai. Y 2.40

101. SHIH-CHIEH CHIH-SHIH [World knowledge]. B-W. Pub. address: 27 Kan-mien Hu-t'ung, Peking. Y 6

102. SHIH-CHIEH KUNG-HUI YÜN-TUNG [World trade union movement]. M. Shih-chieh Kung-hui Lien-ho-hui [World Trade Union Assoc.], Peking. Y 3.60

103. SHIH-CHIEH WÊN-HSÜEH [World literature]. M. Pub. address: 64 Wang-fu Ta-chieh, Peking. Formerly pub. under the title: I-wên [Translations]. Y 7.20

104. SHIH-HSÜEH CHI-K'AN [Historical papers]. S-A. Tung pei Jên-min Ta-hsüeh [Northeast People's Univ.], Peking. Ceased pub. in 1958.

105. SHIH-HSÜEH I-TS'UNG [Journal of translations pertaining to history]. B-M. 1954 (1957: no. 1). K'o hsüeh Ch'u-pan Shê [Science Press], 117 Ch'ao-yang Mên Ta-chieh, Peking. Translations of foreign art. on hist. and historiography (ancient and modern); news and notes on the study of hist. in China and abroad; bk. rev. p (1) Y 0.60

106. SHIH-HSÜEH YÜEH-K'AN [Monthly of historical studies]. M. K'ai-fêng Shih-fan Hsüeh-yüan [Kaifeng Normal College], Kaifeng. Y 2.40

107. SHIH-K'AN [Journal of poetry]. M. Jên-min Wên-hsüeh Ch'u-pan Shê [People's Literature Pub. Co.], 320 Ch'ao-nui Ta-chieh, Peking. Y 5.66

108. SICHUAN DAXUE XUEBAO (Ssŭ-ch'uan Ta-hsüeh Hsüeh-pao) [Szechwan University journal]. Shehui-kexue (Shê-hui K'o-hsüeh) [Social sciences]. Q. 1955 (1959: no. 4). Ssŭ-ch'uan Ta-hsüeh, Chengtu. Art. on all periods of Chinese cultural hist.; research reports on the study of the Chinese social structure; bk. rev.; correspondence; notes and news; table of contents in Chinese, Russian and English. pv (p (1) Y 0.60)

SSŬ-CH'UAN TA-HSÜEH HSÜEH-PAO see SICHUAN DAXUE XUEBAO

109. TANG-AN KUNG-TSO [Archival work]. M. Tang-an Kung-tso Shê [Archival Work Press], Feng-sheng Hu-t'ung 8, Peking. Y 1.68

110. TI-LI CHIH-SHIH [Geographical knowledge]. M. K'o hsüeh Ch'u-pan Shê [Science Press], 117 Ch'ao-yang Mên Ta-chieh, Peking. Y 3

111. TI-LI HSÜEH-PAO [Geographical journal]. Q. Pub. address: c/o P.O.B. 399, Peking. Former English title: Journal of the Geographical Society of China. Y 9.60

112. TIAO-SHUO [Sculpture]. Irr. Jên-min Mei-shu Ch'u-pan Shê [People's Art Press], Peking. pni

113. TS'AI-CHÊNG [Finance]. M. Ts'ai-chêng Ch'u-pan Shê [Finance Pub. Co.], P.O.B. 399, Peking. Y 3.60

114. TS'AI-CHING K'O-HSÜEH [Financial and economic science]. B-M. Ssŭ ch'uan Ts'ai Ching hsüeh-yüan [Szechwan College of Finance and Economics], Chengtu. Y 1.80

115. TS'AI-CHING YEN-CHIU [Financial and economic research]. M (1958); Q (1957). 1957 (1958: no. 1). Hsin Chih-shih Ch'u-pan Shê [New Knowledge Pub. Co.], Shanghai. Art. on socio-economic studies, with emphasis on the economic hist. of modern China; reports and critiques on capitalist economic systems; biblio.; notes and news; bk. rev. Y 5.88

116. T'U-SHU-KUAN-HSÜEH T'UNG-HSÜN [Library science bulletin]. Irr. Pei-ching T'u-shu-kuan [Peking Library], Wên-tsin Chieh, Peking. pni

117. T'U-SHU KUAN KUNG-TSO [Library work]. M. Pei-ching T'u-shu-kuan [Peking Library], Peking. Y 1.80

118. T'UNG-CHI KUNG-TSO [Statistical work]. B-W. T'ung-Chi Kung-tso Tsa chih Shê [Statistical Work Press], Peking. Y 6

119. TUNG-CHI TA-HSÜEH HSÜEH-PAO [Tungchi University journal]. Q. Tung-Chi Ta-hsüeh, Shanghai.

120. TUNG-PEI JÊN-MIN TA-HSÜEH JÊN-WÊN K'O-HSÜEH [Journal of the Northeast (China) People's University]. Hsüeh-pao [Humanities]. Q. 1955 (1958). Tung-pei Jên-min Ta-hsüeh [Northeast People's Univ.], Changchun, for Tung-pei Jên-min Ta-hsüeh. Art. on Chinese hist., language, literature, politics, economics, philosophy and religion; notes and news on general cultural events (in China and abroad); rev. art.; table of contents in Chinese, Russian and English. Y 2.80

121. TUNG-PEI NUNG-HSÜEH YÜAN HSÜEH-PAO [Northeast (China) Agricultural College journal]. Irr. Northeast Agricultural College Press, Harbin, for Tung-pei Nung-hsüeh Yüan. pni

122. WÊN-HSÜEH P'ING-LUN [Literary critic]. B-M. 1959 (1959: no. 1). Jên-min Wên-hsüeh Ch'u-pan Shê [People's Literature Pub. Co.], 320 Ch'ao-nui Ta-chieh, Peking. Ed. address: Chien-kuo Mên Nui, Peking. Art. on the hist. of literature, language and art; discussions on the varying styles of writing in modern times; notes and news on literary activities; rev. of international writers and artists and their chief works; bk. rev.; illus. Formerly pub. under the title: Wên-hsüeh Yen-chiu [Research on literature]. Y 2.88

WÊN-HSÜEH YEN-CHIU see WÊN-HSÜEH P'ING-LUN

123. WÊN-I HSÜEH-HSI [Studies in literature and art]. M. Chung-kuo Ch'ing-nien Ch'u-pan Shê [China Youth Pub. Co.], 1 West Kung-yüan Chieh, Tung-tan, Peking. Y 3

124. WÊN-I PAO [Journal of literature and art]. B-W (1958); W (1957); B-W (1949-56). Jên-min Wên-hsüeh Ch'u-pan Shê [People's Literature Pub. Co.], 320 Ch'ao-nui Ta-chieh, Peking. Y 4.80

125. WÊN-I YÜEH-PAO [Monthly of literature and art]. M. Chinese Writers' Assoc., Shanghai. Y 5.40

126. WÊN SHIH CHÊ [Literature, history, philosophy]. M. 1951 (1958: no. 65-76). Shantung Univ., 5 Yu-shan Rd., Tsingtao, Shantung. Art. on the humanities, with some emphasis on language, literature and Chinese social and cultural hist. of all periods, and on current domestic and foreign affairs; many of the art. express criticism of non-Marxist views in specific pub. works. Ceased pub. with the December 1958 issue. Y 3.60

WÊN-TZŬ KAI-KÊ see WENZI GAIGE

127. WÊN-WU [Cultural artifacts]. M. 1959 (1959: no. 1-12). Wên-wu Ch'u-pan Shê [Cultural Remains Press], Peking. Ed. address: Imperial (National) Palace, Ching-shan Ch'ien-chieh, Peking. Art. on archaeology, epigraphy, Chinese hist. and anthropology; doc.; rev. art.; notes, news and reports on explorations and excavations; illus. Formerly pub. under the title: Wên-wu Ts'an-K'ao Tzu-Liao [Materials for the study of cultural remains]. Y 6

WÊN-WU TS'AN-K'AO TZU-LIAO see WÊN-WU

128. WENZI GAIGE (Wên-tzu Kai-kê) [Script reform]. B-W. Wên-tzu Kai-kê Wei-yüan-hui [Script Reform Assoc.], 45 Ching-shan Tung-chieh, Peking. Formerly pub. under the title: P'in-yin (Pinjin) [Phonetic spelling]. Y 2.88

WU-HAN TA-HSÜEH HSÜEH-PAO see WUHAN DAXUE XUEBAO

129. WUHAN DAXUE XUEBAO (Wuhan Ta-hsüeh Hsüeh-pao) [Wuhan University journal]. Renwen Kexue (Jên-wên K'o-hsüeh) [Humanities]. M. Wuhan Univ. Press, Wuchang, for Wuhan Univ. Table of contents in Chinese and Russian. Y 3.60

130. YÜ-WÊN [Language]. M. Dept. of Chinese Language, Southwest China Normal College, Chungking. Y 1.92

131. YÜ-WÊN CHIAO-HSÜEH [Language teaching]. M. Hua tung Ta-hsüeh [East China Univ.], Shanghai. Y 3

132. YÜ-WÊN CHIH-SHIH [Language knowledge]. M. Hsin Chih-Shih Ch'u-pan Shê [New knowledge Pub. Co.], Shanghai. Y 4

133. YÜ-WÊN HSÜEH-HSI [Linguistic studies]. M. Jên-min Chiao yu Ch'u-pan Shê [People's Education Pub. Co.], Peking. Y 4

YÜ-YEN YEN-CHIU see YŬYÁN YÁNJIU

134. YÜN-NAN TA-HSÜEH HSÜEH-PAO [Yunnan University journal]. Jên-wên K'o-hsüeh [Humanities]. S-A. 1956 (1957: no. 2). Univ. Press, Kunming,

for Yün-nan Ta-hsüeh. Art. on Chinese hist., literature, philosophy, archaeology and sociology; bk. rev.; inquiries concerning general cultural topics of all periods; notes and news on academic activities. Y 1

135. YŬYÁN YÁNJIU (Yü-Yen Yen-chiu) [Linguistic research]. A. 1956 (1959: vol. 4). K'o-hsüeh Ch'u-pan Shê [Science Press], 117 Ch'ao-yang Mên Ta-chieh, Peking. Art. embodying the results of original investigation by Chinese scholars in the fields of language, literature, hist. and philology (mainly Chinese); inquiries concerning Chinese language reform problems; translations of foreign literary works; bk. rev.; news on the study of philology in China and abroad; English sum.; table of contents in Chinese, English and Russian. pv

136. ZHONGGUE YUWEN (Chung-kuo Yü-wên) [Chinese language]. M. 1952 (1959: no. 79-90). Jên-min Chiao-yü Ch'u-pan Shê [People's Education Press], Peking. Art. on the hist. of Chinese philology and literature; bk. rev.; inquiries concerning Chinese grammar, composition and rhetoric; biographies; notes and news on current literary movements; correspondence. Y 2.88

137. ZHONGGUO GONGREN (Chung-kuo Kung-jên) [The Chinese worker]. B-M. Chung-kuo Kung-jên Shê [Chinese Worker Soc.], Peking. p (1) Y 0.15

138. ZHONGGUO QINGNIAN (Chung-kuo Ch'ing-nien) [Chinese youth]. B-W. Chung-kuo Ch'ing-nien Shê [Chinese Youth Soc.], 3 Yü-ho Ch-iao, Peking. Y 7.20

139. ZHONGSHAN DAXUE XUEBAO (Chung-shan Ta-hsüeh Hsüeh-pao) [Sun Yat-sen University journal]. Shê-hui K'o-hsüeh [Social sciences]. Irr. 1956 (1959: no. 1-2). Univ. Press, Canton, for Chung-shan Ta-hsüeh. Art. on all periods of Chinese cultural hist. and other branches of the social sciences; translations of foreign papers on all branches of the study of the social sciences; bk. rev.; correspondence; news and notes; table of contents in Chinese, Russian and English; illus. Y 4

140. ZHONGXUE LISHI JIAOXUE (Chung-hsüeh Li-shih Chiao-hsüeh) [Middle-school history teaching]. M. Jên-min Ch'u-pan Shê [People's Pub. House], Canton.

Hong Kong

Prepared with the assistance of

Chen Tsu-lung, Institut des Hautes Etudes Chinoises, University of Paris, and

Mrs. Dorothea Scott, University of Hong Kong Library, Hong Kong

Note: The Wade-Giles system has been used below for the transliteration of Chinese words.

1. CONTEMPORARY CHINA. TANG-TAI CHUNG-KUO. A. Hong Kong Univ. Press, Hong Kong, for Research Seminar on Problems of Contemporary China, Dept. of Economics and Political Science, Univ. of Hong Kong, Hong Kong B.C.C. Selected doc.; current biblio.; subject, name and geographical index. HK $25/$5

2. HSIN-YA HSÜEH-PAO [New Asia journal]. S-A. 1955 (1957/58: vol. 3). New Asia Research Inst., Kowloon. Ed: Ch'ien Mu. Art. on Chinese hist., literature, philosophy, religion and art; English sum.; table of contents in Chinese and English; illus. HK $10/$2

3. JÊN-SHÊNG [Life]. B-W. The "Life," 155 B Church Rd., Diamond Hill, Kowloon. HK $10/ $3

JOURNAL OF ORIENTAL STUDIES see TUNG-FANG WÊN-HUA

4. TA-HSÜEH SHÊNG-HUO [College life]. M. Union Press, 110 Waterloo Rd., Kowloon. HK $5/$1

TANG-TAI CHUNG-KUO see CONTEMPORARY CHINA

5. TÊNG-T'A [Lighthouse]. M. Asia Press, P.O.B. 5364, Kowloon. HK $6/$1.50

6. TSU-KUO CHOU-K'AN [China weekly]. W. 1953 (1957: vol. 20). Union Press, 110 Waterloo Rd., Kowloon. Ed. address: 110 Waterloo Rd., Kowloon. Art. on international politics and cultural intercourse, Chinese hist. and civilization (ancient and modern), philosophy and sociology; reports; correspondence; news and notes on cultural events in Communist countries; bk. rev.; illus. HK $6/$1.50

7. TUNG-FANG WÊN-HUA. JOURNAL OF ORIENTAL STUDIES. S-A. 1954 (mri 1956: vol. 3). Inst. of Oriental Studies, Univ. of Hong Kong, Hong Kong. Ed: F.S. Drake. Art. on the hist., geography, fine arts, language, literature, philosophy, architecture, archaeology, economics and politics of China, Japan, Korea, Southeast Asia and the Philippines; rev. art.; bk. rev.; in Chinese, with English sum., or in English; "Far Eastern Bibliography": 1) tables of contents of periodicals dealing with Asia pub. throughout the world, but mainly in Asia (in English or in Japanese or Chinese with English translation); 2) list of bk. received for rev.; biblio. in English and in Chinese with Romanization of the titles. HK $36/$8

Japan

Prepared with the assistance of the
National Diet Library, Tokyo, and
Kentaro Hayashi, Professor of Western History, University of Tokyo

Note: The Hepburn system has been used below for the transliteration of Japanese words.

ACADEMIC ASSOCIATION OF KOREANOLOGY IN JAPAN, JOURNAL OF THE see CHOSEN GAKUHO

1. AIZU SHIDAN KAISHI [Aizu historical journal]. Irr. 1952 (1958: no. 33-34). Aizu Shidankai [Aizu Hist. Soc.], c/o Aizu Toshokan [Aizu Library], 231 Sakae-machi, Aizu-Wakamatsu-shi, Fukushima-ken. Ed: Shigeo Suzuki. Art. on the hist. and archaeology of the district of Aizu, Fukushima prefecture; illus. p(1) ¥ 300 (memb.)

2. AJIA KENKYU [Asiatic studies]. Q. Ajia Seikei Gakkai [Soc. for Asian Political and Economic Studies], c/o Tokyo Daigaku Fuzoku Toshokan [Tokyo Univ. Library], Motofuji-cho, Bunkyo-ku, Tokyo. Art. on the economic analysis of present-day China and the modern hist. of China; bk. rev.; table of contents also in English. p(1) ¥ 200-250

ANCIENT CULTURE see JODAI BUNKA

ANTHROPOLOGICAL SOCIETY OF NIPPON, THE JOURNAL OF THE see JINRUIGAKU ZASSHI

ARCHAEOLOGIA JAPONICA see NIHON KOKOGAKU NENPO

3. ASIAN AFFAIRS. Q. Asia Kyokai ["Soc. for Economic Co-operation in Asia"], 1, 3-chome, Kyobashi, Chuo-ku, Tokyo. Statistics; graph. $ 5

4. ASIATIC SOCIETY OF JAPAN, THE TRANSACTIONS OF THE. A. Asiatic Soc. of Japan, P.O.B. 592, Tokyo Central, Tokyo. Hist., language, literature, arts and folklore of Japan; illus. ¥ 1200

5. BIJITSUSHI [Art history]. Journal of the Japan Art History Society. Q. 1952 (mri 1956: vol. 5). Bijutsushi Gakkai [Japan Art Hist. Soc.], c/o Tokyo National Research Inst. of Cultural Properties, Ueno Koen, Taito-ku, Tokyo. Ed: Nobuo Kumagai. Art. mainly on the hist. of Japanese art; description of plates; notes and news; report of the soc.; in Japanese. p(1) ¥ 150

6. BUKKYO SHIGAKU [History of Buddhism]. Q. 1949 (1958: vol. 7). Bukkyoshi Gakkai [Soc. for the Hist. of Buddhism], c/o Heirakuji Shoten, Higashi-no-toin, 3-jo iru, Nakakyo-ku, Kyoto. Art. on the hist. of Buddhism in Japan, China and India; bk. rev.; reports on the activities of the soc. ¥ 500

7. BUNGAKU [Literature]. M. Iwanami Shoten [Iwanami Pub. Co.], 2-3 Kanda Hitotsubashi, Chiyoda-ku, Tokyo. p(1) ¥ 90

8. BUNKA [Culture]. B-M. (1959: vol. 23). Tohoku Daigaku Bungakkai [Literary Soc., Tohoku Univ.], Katahira-cho, Sendai. Ed: Susumu Muraoka, c/o Faculty of Literature, Tohoku Univ., Katahira-cho, Sendai. Art. on philosophy, religion, hist. and literature; bk. rev.; professional news; English sum. p (1) ¥ 150

9. BUNKA SHIGAKU [Studies in cultural history]. 3 x y. 1950 (1958: no. 14). Bunka Shigakkai [Inst. for Studies in Cultural Hist.], c/o Doshisha Daigaku Bungakubu [Faculty of Letters, Doshisha Univ.], Karasuma Imadegawa, Kamikyo-ku, Kyoto. Ed: Ichiro Ishida. Art. on the hist. of Japanese culture and thought; bk. rev.; table of contents also in English. p(1) ¥ 120-130

10. BUNKASHI KENKYU [Cultural history]. Irr. 1955 (1959: no. 9-10). Doshisha Daigaku Nihon Bunkashi Kenkyukai [Soc. for the Study of Cultural Hist., Doshisha Univ.], c/o Doshisha Daigaku Bungakubu [Faculty of Letters, Doshisha Univ.], Karasuma Imadegawa, Kamikyo-ku, Kyoto. Ed: Masayuki Annen. Art. on the hist. of Japanese culture and thought; bk. rev.; professional news; illus. p(1) ¥ 120

CHINESE (ORIENTAL) CULTURE AND SOCIETY see TOYO NO BUNKA TO SHAKAI

11. CHOSEN GAKUHO [Korean studies]. JOURNAL OF THE ACADEMIC ASSOCIATION OF KOREANOLOGY IN JAPAN. S-A. 1951 (1958: no vol. indic.). Chosen Gakkai [Assoc. of Koreanology], Tenri Daigaku, Tenri-shi, Nara-ken. Ed: Toro Takahashi. Art. on all periods of Korean hist., and occasionally on philology, literature, anthropology and archaeology; bk. rev.; professional news; reports of meetings; list of new bk. received; in Korean and, occasionally, Japanese and English; table of contents also in English; English sum. of art. in a mimeographed supplement. nfs

12. CHUO DAIGAKU BUNGAKU-BU KIYO [Journal of the Faculty of Literature, Chuo University]. 3 x y. 1955 (1959: no. 15-17). Chuo Daigaku Bungaku-bu, Koishikawa, Bunkyo-ku, Tokyo. Ed: Kyutaro Takase, 3-9 Kanda Surugadai, Chiyoda-ku, Tokyo. Art. on the hist. of Japan, Asia and the West, with emphasis on political and local hist. nfs

COMPARATIVE STUDIES OF CULTURE see HIKAKU BUNKA

13. DOTAKU [Copper hand-bell]. Journal of the Archaeological Society of Rissho University. Q. 1951 (1957: no vol. indic.). Rissho Univ., 4 Higashi Osaki, Shinagawa-ku, Tokyo. Ed: Tsuneharu Kubo. Art. on archaeological research in Japan, with emphasis on Buddhistic archaeology; bk. rev.; illus. Suspended pub. in 1957.

14. EHIME DAIGAKU REKISHIGAKU KIYO [Ehime University studies in history]. A. 1953 (1959: no. 6). Ehime Daigaku Bunrigakubu Rekishigaku Kenkyushitsu [Inst. of Hist. Science, Faculty of Science and Literature, Ehime Univ.], Mochita-machi, Matsuyama. Ed: Shigemi Tatsuma. Art. on the political, cultural and economic hist. of Japan, Asia and the West. nfs

15. FUKUSHIMA SHIGAKU KENKYU [Fukushima historical studies]. A. 1951 (mri 1955: no. 6). Fukushima-ken Shigakkai [Fukushima Hist. Soc.], c/o

Fukushima Daigaku Keizai Gakubu [Faculty of Economics, Fukushima Univ.], Moriai, Fukushima. Art. on the local hist. of Fukushima. pv

16. GEIRIN [Literally, a library of classical books, but used figuratively for art and culture -- ed.]. The Journal of Cultural Sciences. B-M. Geirin-kai [Cultural Sciences Committee], 17 Koyama Shimofusa-machi, Kita-ku, Kyoto. English sum.; illus. ¥ 480

17. GIFU DAIGAKU GAKUGEI GAKUBU KENKYU HOKOKU JINBUN KAGAKU [Science report of the Faculty of Liberal Arts and Education, Gifu University]. A. 1953 (1958: no. 6-7). Gifu Daigaku Gakugei Gakubu, Nagara, Gifu. Ed: Hideichi Hattori. Art. on Japanese hist., with emphasis on socio-economic hist. nfs

18. GIFU SHIGAKU [Gifu historical studies]. Q. 1951 (1959: no. 25-27). Gifu Shigakkai [Gifu Hist. Soc.], c/o Gifu Daigaku Gakugei Gakubu [Faculty of Liberal Arts and Education, Gifu Univ.], Nagara, Gifu. Ed: Koshiro Nakano. Art. on the hist. of industrial development in the Chubu district of Japan. nfs

19. GUNMA DAIGAKU KIYO. JINBUN KAGAKU [Report of the Gunma University. Cultural science series]. A. Gunma Daigaku [Gunma Univ.], 146 Seioji-machi, Maebashi-shi, Gunma-ken. nfs

20. HAKUSAN SHIGAKU [Historical science]. THE HISTORICAL STUDIES OF THE TOYO UNIVERSITY. Irr. 1953 (1957: no. 3). Toyo Daigaku Hakusan Shigakkai [Hist. Assoc. of Toyo Univ.], 17, Hara-machi, Bunkyo-ku, Tokyo. Ed: Masao Toba. Art. on general hist., not confined to any period or country or aspect; bk. rev.; professional news and notes; table of contents also in English. Suspended pub. in 1957. nfs

21. HANDAI HOGAKU [Journal of jurisprudence of Osaka University]. Q. Osaka Daigaku Hogakubu [Faculty of Law, National Osaku Univ.], Shibahara, Toyonaka-shi, Osaka-fu. p (1) ¥ 130

22. HIKAKU BUNKA. COMPARATIVE STUDIES OF CULTURE. A. 1954 (1958: vol. 5). Tokyo Joshi Daigaku Fuzoku Hikaku Bunka Kenkyusho [Inst. for Comparative Studies of Culture, affiliated to Tokyo Women's Christian College], Iogi 3- chome, Suginami-ku, Tokyo, and Harvard Yenching Inst., 2 Divinity Ave., Cambridge 38, Mass., U.S.A. Ed: President, Tokyo Joshi Daigaku Fuzoku Hikaku Bunka Kenkyusho. Art. on cultural intercourse between Japan and China; in Japanese and English; doc.; graph., illus. pv (c. $ 1)

23. HIKAKU BUNKA KENKYUSHO KIYO. PUBLICATIONS OF THE INSTITUTE FOR COMPARATIVE STUDIES OF CULTURE. S-A. 1955 (1958: vol. 6). Tokyo Joshi Daigaku Fuzoku Bunka Kenkyusho [Inst. for Comparative Studies of Culture, affiliated to Tokyo Women's Christian College], Iogi, 3-chome, Suginami-ku, Tokyo, and Harvard Yenching Inst., 2 Divinity Ave., Cambridge 38, Mass., U.S.A. Ed: President, Tokyo Joshi Daigaku Fuzoku Bunka Kenkyusho. Art. on the hist. of cultural intercourse among Japan, China and India; English sum.; table of contents also in English. pv (c. $ 2)

THE HISTORICAL STUDIES OF THE TOYO UNIVERSITY see HAKUSAN SHIGAKU

24. HISUTORIA [History]. Q. 1951 (1957: no. 17-20). Osaka Rekishi Gakkai [Hist. Soc. of Osaka], c/o Kansai Daigaku Uozumi Kenkyushitsu [Uozumi

Inst., Kansai Univ.], Senriyama, Suita-shi, Osaka-fu. Ed: Sogoro Uozumi. Art. mainly on the political, cultural and intellectual hist. of Japan; bk. rev.; in Japanese; news of professional interest; notes on source-material. Suspended pub. in 1957. p(1) ¥ 100

25. HOGAKU KENKYU [Legal studies]. Horitsu, Seiji, Shakai [Law, politics, sociology]. Journal of Law, Politics and Sociology. M. Keio Gijuku Daigaku Hogaku Kenkyukai [Assoc. for the Study of Law and Politics, Keio Gijuku Univ.], Shiba Mita, Minatoku, Tokyo. Doc.; graph, statistics. p(1) ¥ 80

26. HOGAKU KYOKAI ZASSHI ["The Journal of the Jurisprudence Association"]. M. Hogaku Kyokai [Jurisprudence Assoc.], c/o Tokyo Daigaku Hogakubu Kenkyushitsu [Law School, Tokyo Univ.], Motofuji-cho, Bunkyo-ku, Tokyo. ¥ 1500 /$ 4

27. HOGAKU SHIRIN [History of law]. Q. Hogaku Shirin Kyokai [Hosei Univ. Law and Political Science Soc.], 3-1 Fujimi-cho, Chiyoda-ku, Tokyo. p(1) ¥ 220

28. HOKKAIDO CHIHOSHI KENKYU [Studies on the local history of Hokkaido]. Q. Hokkaido Chihoshi Kenkyukai [Soc. for Hist. Studies of Hokkaido], c/o Sapporo Kogyo Kotogakko [Sapporo Technical High School], Minami 14-jo, Nishi 12-chome, Sapporo, Hokkaido. Mimeographed. ¥ 500 /$ 1.5

29. HOKUDAI SHIGAKU [Historical studies at Hokkaido University]. Journal of the Historical Association of Hokkaido University. Irr. 1951 (1959: no. 5). Hokudai Shigakkai [Hist. Assoc. of Hokkaido Univ.], c/o Hokkaido Daigaku Bungakubu [Faculty of Literature, Hokkaido Univ.], Nishi 5, Kita 8-jo, Sapporo. Ed: Hideo Nagai. Art. on various aspects of the hist. of Japan, Asia and the West; bk. rev.; professional news. Cum. table of contents for the years 1951-1959 appeared in no. 5. p(1) ¥ 150

30. HOKURIKU SHIGAKU [Hokuriku historical studies]. S-A. 1953 (1959: no. 8). Ishikawa Shigakkai [Ishikawa Hist. Assoc.], c/o Kanazawa Daigaku Hobungakubu [Department of Law and Letters, Kanazawa Univ.], Ote-machi, Kanazawa. Ed: Katsumi Nishii. Art. on various aspects of the hist. of Japan, Asia and the West; bk. rev. p(1) ¥ 150

HOSEI HISTORICAL SOCIETY, JOURNAL OF THE see HOSEI SHIGAKU

31. HOSEI SHIGAKU [Hosei historical studies]. JOURNAL OF THE HOSEI HISTORICAL SOCIETY. S-A. 1950 (1959: no. 12). Hosei Shigakkai [Hosei Hist. Soc.], c/o Hosei Daigaku Bungakubu [Faculty of Literature, Hosei Univ.], 3-1 Fujimi-cho, Chiyoda-ku, Tokyo. Ed: Takeo Itazawa. Art. on various aspects of the hist. of Japan and the West, with emphasis on Japan; bk. rev.; table of contents also in English. nfs

32. HOSEISHI KENKYU [Studies in legal history]. LEGAL HISTORY REVIEW. A. 1952 (1958: no. 9). Hoseishi Gakkai, ["Japan Legal History Assoc."], c/o Tokyo Daigaku Hogakubu [Faculty of Law, Tokyo Univ.], Motofuji-cho, Bunkyo-ku, Tokyo. Ed: Masahata Kubo. Art. on the ancient and modern legal hist. of Japan and Europe, covering both public and private law; rev. art.; bk. rev.; reports on the activities of the soc.; English sum. ¥ 800

HUMAN GEOGRAPHY see JINBUN CHIRI

HUMANITIES REVIEW see JINBUN RONKYU

33. HYOGO SHIGAKU [Hyogo historical studies]. Q. 1954 (1959: no. 19-21). Hyogo Shigakkai [Hyogo Hist. Soc.], c/o Kobe Daigaku Bungakubu Nihonshi Kenkyushitsu [Inst. of Japanese Hist., Faculty of Literature, Kobe Univ.], Mikagemachi, Higashinada-ku, Kobe. Ed: Rintaro Imai. Art. on Japanese hist. with special reference to political and socio-economic hist. and hist. geography; bk. rev. p (1) ¥ 100

34. IBARAGI DAIGAKU BUNRIGAKUBU KIYO. SHAKAI KAGAKU [Bulletin of the Faculty of Liberal Arts, Ibaragi University. Social Science]. A. 1953 Ibaraki Daigaku Bunrigakubu [Faculty of Liberal Arts, Ibaraki Univ.], Watarimachi, Mito, Ibaragi-ken. nfs

35. INA. M. Ina Kyodo Shigakkai [Ina Local Hist. Soc.], 7 Suwa-machi, Iida-shi, Nagano-ken. nfs

36. INDOGAKU BUKKYOGAKU KENKYU [Indian and Buddhist studies]. JOURNAL OF INDIAN AND BUDDHIST STUDIES. S-A. Nihon Indogaku Bukkyo Gakkai [Japanese Assoc. of Indian and Buddhist Studies], c/o Tokyo Daigaku Bungakubu Indo Tetsugaku Kenkyushitsu [Seminar of Indian Philosophy, Faculty of Letters, Tokyo Univ.], Motofuji-cho, Bunkyo-ku, Tokyo. In Japanese and English. p (1) ¥ 480 (memb.)

INSTITUTE FOR COMPARATIVE STUDIES OF CULTURE, PUBLICATIONS OF THE see HIKAKU BUNKA KENKYUSHO KIYO

INSTITUTE OF ORIENTAL CULTURE, MEMOIRS OF THE see TOYO BUNKA KENKYUSHO KIYO

37. INTERNATIONAL CONFERENCE OF ORIENTALISTS IN JAPAN, TRANSACTIONS OF THE. KOKUSAI TOHO GAKUSHA KAIGI KIYO. A. 1956 (1959: no. 4). Toho Gakkai ["Inst. of Eastern Culture"], 2, Nishi-Kanda 2-chome, Chiyoda-ku, Tokyo. Ed: Hideo Aoyama. Research reports dealing with Oriental hist., religion, philosophy, politics, economics and folklore, presented at international conferences of Orientalists in Japan; sum. of other reports delivered; list of scholars attending the conferences; in English; statistics; graph; illus. ¥ 200

38. ITARIA GAKKAISHI [Journal of the Association of Italian Studies]. STUDI ITALICI [Italian studies]. A. 1952 (1958: no. 7). Itaria Gakkai ["Associazione degli Studi Italiani"], Nihon Dante Gakkai ["Società Dante Alighieri in Giappone"], c/o Kyoto Daigaku Bungakubu [Faculty of Letters, Kyoto Univ.], Yoshidahon-machi Sakyo-ku, Kyoto. Ed: Motoichi Nogami. Art. on Italian hist., literature, philosophy and art, with emphasis on cultural and art hist.; bk. rev.; professional news and notes; table of contents also in Italian; Italian sum. p (1) ¥ 100 / $ 2

39. IWATE SHIGAKU KENKYU [Iwate historical studies]. Q. 1948 (1959: no. 30-32). Iwate Shigakkai [Iwate Hist. Assoc.], c/o Iwate Daigaku Gakugei Gakubu [Gakugei Faculty, Iwate Univ.], Ueda, Morioka. Ed: Kahei Mori. Art. on the hist. of Japan and the Orient, with emphasis on the local hist. of the northeastern districts of Japan. p (1) ¥ 130

40. IYO SHIDAN [Iyo local history]. Q. Iyo Shidankai [Iyo Local Hist. Soc.] c/o Ehime Kenritsu Toshokan [Ehime Prefectural Library], Niban-cho, Matsuyama. p (1) ¥ 500

THE JAPANESE ANCIENT CULTURE see JODAI BUNKA

THE JAPANESE JOURNAL OF ETHNOLOGY see MINZOKUGAKU KENKYU

41. JINBUN CHIRI. HUMAN GEOGRAPHY. B-M. Jinbun Chiri Gakkai [Assoc. for Human Geography], c/o Kyoto Daigaku Bungakubu Chirigaku Kyoshitsu [Inst. of Human Geography, Faculty of Letters, Kyoto Univ.], Yoshidahon-machi, Sakyo-ku, Kyoto. English sum. ¥ 600

42. JINBUN GAKUHO [Journal of humanistic studies]. THE JOURNAL OF SOCIAL SCIENCES AND HUMANITIES. Irr. (A. or S-A). Kyoto Daigaku Jinbun Kagaku Kenkyusho [Research Inst. for Humanistic Studies, Kyoto Univ.], 50 Ogura-cho, Kitashirakawa, Sakyo-ku, Kyoto. Table of contents also in English; English title varies: vol. 1-6 entitled Journal of Humanistic Science. nfs

43. JINBUN KENKYU ["Studies in the Humanities"]. M. Osaka Shiritsu Daigaku Bungakkai [Literary Assoc. of Osaka City Univ.], Utsubo Nakadori, Nishi-ku, Osaka. Table of contents also in English. ¥ 1200

44. JINBUN RONKYU [Studies in the humanities]. Journal of the Society of Liberal Arts. Q. Hakodate Jinbun Gakkai [Soc. of Liberal Arts, Hakodate], c/o Hokkaido Gakugei Daigaku Hakodate Bunko [Hakodate School, Hokkaido Gakugei Univ.], 153 Hachiman-cho, Hakodate. Table of contents also in English. p (1) ¥ 150

45. JINBUN RONKYU [Studies in the humanities]. HUMANITIES REVIEW. B-M. Kwansai Gakuin Daigaku Jinbun Gakkai [Literary Assoc. of Kwansai Gakuin Univ.], Uegahara, Nishinomiya-shi, Hyogo-ken. Table of contents also in English. p (1) ¥ 150

JINBUN SHAKAI KAGAKU KENKYU HOKOKU see SHAKAI KAGAKU RONSO

46. JINRUIGAKU ZASSHI [Journal of anthropology]. THE JOURNAL OF THE ANTHROPOLOGICAL SOCIETY OF NIPPON. Q (occasionally 3 or 5 x y). Nippon Jinruigaku-Kai [Anthropological Soc. of Japan], Anthropological Inst., Faculty of Science, Univ. of Tokyo, Bunkyo-Ku, Tokyo. In Japanese; table of contents also in English; English or German sum. ¥ 800 / $ 6

47. JODAI BUNKA [Ancient culture]. THE JAPANESE ANCIENT CULTURE. A. 1928 (1959: no. 29). Kokugakuin Daigaku Koko Gakkai [Archaeological Soc. of Kokugakuin Univ.], 9 Wakagi-cho, Shibuya-ku, Tokyo. Ed: Yoshinobu Zennyu. Art. on Japanese archaeology; professional news and notes; illus. English title varies: no. 24 entitled Ancient Culture. p (1) ¥ 250

JOURNAL OF AGRARIAN HISTORY see TOCHI SEIDO SHIGAKU

JOURNAL OF HISTORY see SHIRIN

JOURNAL OF HUMANISTIC SCIENCE see JINBUN GAKUHO

JOURNAL OF INDIAN AND BUDDHIST STUDIES see INDOGAKU BUKKYOGAKU KENKYU

THE JOURNAL OF ORIENTAL RESEARCHES see TOYOSHI KENKYU

JOURNAL OF POLITICAL ECONOMY see KEIZAIGAKU KENKYU

JOURNAL OF SINOLOGICAL STUDIES see SINAGAKU KENKYU

THE JOURNAL OF SOCIAL SCIENCES AND HUMANITIES see JINBUN GAKUHO

JOURNAL OF THE ACADEMIC ASSOCIATION OF KOREANOLOGY IN JAPAN see CHOSEN GAKUHO

THE JOURNAL OF THE ANTHROPOLOGICAL SOCIETY OF NIPPON see JINRUIGAKU ZASSHI

JOURNAL OF THE HOSEI HISTORICAL SOCIETY see HOSEI SHIGAKU

48. KADAI SHIGAKU [Kadai (Kagoshima University) historical studies]. A. 1953 (1958: vol. 6). Kagoshima Daigaku Bunri Gakubu [Faculty of Literature and Science, Kagoshima Univ.], 201 Kamoike-cho, Kagoshima. Ed: Eshin Momozono, 221 Yakushi cho, Kagoshima. Art. on hist., with emphasis on Japan and China; bk. rev.; graph; table of contents also in English. ¥ 200 /$ 0.65

49. KAGAKUSHI KENKYU [Studies in the history of science]. Q. 1941 (1959: no. 49-52). Nihon Kagakushi Gakkai [Hist. of Science Soc. of Japan], c/o Tokyo Kogyo Daigaku [Tokyo Inst. of Technology], Ookayama, Meguro-ku, Tokyo. Ed: Suketoshi Yajima. Art. on the hist. of science and scientific thought in Japan and other countries; bk. rev.; news about new pub.; reports of the soc.; general table of contents covering no. 1-30. p (1) ¥ 100

50. KAGOSHIMA SHIGAKU [Kagoshima historical studies]. S-A. Kagoshima-ken Koto Gakko Rekishi Bukai [Section for Hist. Studies, High Schools Assoc. in Kagoshima Prefecture], c/o Tsurumaru Koto Gakko [Tsurumaru High School], Kajiya-machi, Kagoshima. Art. on the local hist. and archaeology of the southern part of Kyushu district. nfs

51. KANAZAWA DAIGAKU HOBUN GAKUBU RONSHU, HO-KEI-HEN ["Studies and Essays by the Faculty of Law and Literature, Kanazawa University, Law and Economics"]. A. Kanazawa Daigaku Hobun Gakubu [Faculty of Law and Economics, Kanazawa Univ.], Ote-machi, Kanazawa, Ishikawa-ken. Table of contents also in English; English sum. nfs

52. KANAZAWA DAIGAKU HOBUN GAKUBU RONSHU, TETSUGAKU-SHIGAKU-HEN [Journal of the Faculty of Law and Literature, Kanazawa University, Philosophy and History]. Irr. 1956 (1958: no. 6). Kanazawa Daigaku Hobun Gakubu, Ote-machi, Kanazawa, Ishikawa-ken. Ed: Ryuji Jimbo. Art. on the hist. of Japan, Asia and the West, not confined to any period or aspect. nfs

53. KANSAI DAIGAKU BUNGAKU RONSHU [Journal of the Faculty of Literature, Kansai University]. Essays and Studies by Members of the Literary Faculty, Kansai University. B-M. Kansai Daigaku Bungaku-kai [Literary Soc., Kansai Univ.], Senriyama, Suita-shi, Osaka-fu. In Japanese.

54. KEIZAI RIRON [Economic theory]. B-M. Wakayama Daigaku Keizai Gakkai [Economic Soc., Hokkai Gakuen College], 278 Sekito, Wakayama-shi. Art. on economic theory, including some of hist. interest; bk. rev. ¥ 600 /$ 1.66

55. KEIZAIGAKU [Economics]. Annual Report of the Economic Faculty, Tohoku University. Q. Department of Economics, Tohoku Univ., Katahiracho, Sendai, Miyagi-ken. Art. on economics and economic hist., with emphasis on Japan; table of contents also in English. ¥ 550/$ 1.5

56. KEIZAIGAKU KENKYU [Studies in economics]. JOURNAL OF POLITICAL ECONOMY. Q. Kyushu Daigaku Keizai Gakkai [Economics Soc. of Kyushu Univ.], Hakozaki, Fukuoka. Contents page also in English. (memb.) ¥ 600

57. KEIZAIGAKU RONSHU [Studies in economics]. The Journal of Economics. Q. Tokyo Daigaku Keizai Gakubu Keizai Gakkai [Tokyo Univ. Economics Soc.], c/o Tokyo Daigaku Keizai Gakubu [Faculty of Economics, Tokyo Univ.], Motofuji-cho, Bunkyo-ku, Tokyo. p (1) ¥ 250

58. KEIZAIGAKU ZASSHI ["Journal of Economics"]. M. Osaka Shiritsu Daigaku Keizai Kenkyukai [Economics Soc. of Osaka City Univ.], 2-6 Awaza Nakadori, Nishi-ku, Osaka. p (1) ¥ 100

59. KENCHIKUSHI KENKYU [Studies in architectural history]. B-M. 1950 (1959: no. 19-21). Kenchikushi Kenkyukai [Architectural Hist. Soc. of Japan], c/o Tokyo Daigaku Kogakubu Kenchiku Gakkai [Inst. of Architecture, Faculty of Engineering, Univ. of Tokyo], Motofuji-cho, Bunkyo-ku, Tokyo. Art. on the hist. of Japanese architecture; bk. rev. p (1) ¥ 150

60. KINDAI NIHONSHI KENKYU [Studies in modern Japanese history]. Q. 1955 (1958: no. 5-6). Kindai Nihonshi Kenkyukai [Soc. for the Study of Modern Japanese Hist.], c/o Waseda Daigaku Kokushi Kenkyushitsu [Inst. of Japanese Hist., Waseda Univ.], Totsuka-machi, Shinjuku-ku, Tokyo. Art. on modern Japanese hist. since the Meiji Restoration (1868); maps, statistics. p (1) ¥ 40

61. KINSEISHI KENKYU [Studies in modern history]. M. 1954 (1959: no. 27-28). Osaka Rekishi Gakkai Kinseishi-bukai [Modern Hist. Section, Hist. Soc. of Osaka], c/o Kansai Daigaku Shigaku-ka [Inst. of Hist., Kansai Univ.], Suita-shi, Osaka-fu. Ed: Shigeru Kobayashi, 20-13 Kon'yo Kita-no-tsuji, Itami, Osaka-fu. Art. on modern Japanese hist., with emphasis on political and economic hist.; mimeographed. (memb.) ¥ 500

62. KOBUNKAZAI NO KAGAKU [Science of ancient cultural properties]. SCIENTIFIC PAPERS ON JAPANESE ANTIQUES AND ART CRAFTS. Irr. 1952 (1958: no. 15). Kobunka Shiryo Shizen Kagaku Kenkyukai [Assoc. of Scientific Research of Antiques], c/o Kokuritsu Hakubutsukan [Tokyo National Museum], Ueno Koen, Taito-ku, Tokyo. Ed: Ichiro Oga. Art. on Japanese antiquities; contents page also in English. ¥ 500

63. KODAI [Ancient ages]. The Journal of the Archaeological Society of Waseda University. B-M. 1950 (1959: no. 31-33). Waseda Daigaku Koko Gakkai [Archaeological Soc. of Waseda Univ.], Totsuka-machi, Shinjuku-ku, Tokyo. Ed: Hiroshi Takiguchi. Art. on Japanese archaeology; contents page also in English. ¥ 300

64. KODAIGAKU KENKYU [Paleolithic studies]. Q. 1954 (1959: no. 20-22). Kodaigaku Kenkyukai [Soc. for Paleolithic Studies (in Japan)], c/o Sansei Byoin [Sansei Hospital], 15 Hon-machi, Higashimaya-ku, Kyoto. Ed: Koichi Mori. Art. on the paleolithic age of Japanese hist.; bk. rev.; professional news. ¥ 500

65. KOKKA GAKKAI ZASSHI [Journal of the Association of Political and Social Sciences]. M. Kokka Gakkai, c/o Inst. of Law, Tokyo Univ., Motofujicho, Bunkyo-ku, Tokyo. p (1) ¥ 120

66. KOKOGAKU ZASSHI [Journal of archaeology]. Journal of the Archaeological Society of Nippon. B-M. 1896 (1958: vol. 44). Nihon Koko Gakkai [Archaeological Soc. of Japan], c/o Tokyo Kokuritsu Hakubutsukan [National Museum], Ueno Koen, Taito-ku, Tokyo. Ed: Yoshito Harada. Art. on Japanese hist. monuments; occasionally English sum. of some art.; bk. rev.; maps, graph, illus. (memb.) ¥ 800

KOKUSAI TOHO GAKUSHA KAIGI KIYO see INTERNATIONAL CONFERENCE OF ORIENTALISTS IN JAPAN, TRANSACTIONS OF THE

67. KOKUSHIGAKU [Study of Japanese history]. Q. 1929 (1958: no. 70). Kokushi Gakkai [Soc. of Japanese Hist. Research], c/o Kokugakuin Daigaku [Kokugakuin Univ.], 9 Wakagicho, Shibuya-ku, Tokyo. Ed: Koyata Iwahashi. Art. on Japanese hist., with emphasis on political, economic and legal hist.; bk. rev.; professional news. p (1) ¥ 95

68. KOMAZAWA DAIGAKU KENKYU KIYO ["Journal of the Komazawa University"]. Irr. Komazawa Daigaku, 1-3408 Fukazawa-machi, Setagaya-ku, Tokyo.

69. KOMAZAWA SHIGAKU [Komazawa historical studies]. The Journal of the Historical Association of Komazawa University. S-A. 1953 (1959: no. 9). Komazawa Daigaku Shigakkai [Hist. Assoc., Komazawa Univ.], 1 Fukazawa-cho, Setagaya-ku, Tokyo. Ed: Taikei Iwai. Art. on the hist. of Japan and Asia, with emphasis on the hist. of Zen Buddhism in Japan and China; table of contents also in English. nfs

70. KUMAMOTO SHIGAKU [Kumamoto historical studies]. 3 x y. 1952 (1959: no. 17). Kumamoto Shigakkai [Hist. Soc. of Kumamoto], c/o Kumamoto Daigaku Hobun Gakubu [Faculty of Law and Literature, Kumamoto Univ.], Kurokami-machi, Kumamoto. Ed: Toshiaki Harada. Art. on the hist. of Japan, with emphasis on the local hist. of the Kyushu district; bk. rev. pv

71. KWANSEI GAKUIN SHIGAKU ["The Historical Studies of the Kwansei Gakuin University"]. Irr. 1952 (1959: no. 5). Kwansei Gakuin Daigaku Shigakkai [Hist. Assoc., Kwansei Gakuin Univ.], Uegahara-machi, Nishinomiya. Ed: Rainosuke Awano. Art. on the hist. of Japan, Asia and the West, with emphasis on the hist. of Christianity in Japan, and on archaeology and hist. geography; in Japanese; table of contents also in English; illus. (memb.) ¥ 600

72. KYUSHU BUNKASHI KENKYUSHO KIYO ["The Bulletin of the Institute of Research in Kyushu Cultural History"]. A. Kyushu Bunkashi Kenkyusho [Inst. of Research in Kyushu Cultural Hist.], c/o Kyushu Daigaku Bungakubu [Faculty of Literature, Kyushu Univ.], Hakozaki, Fukuoka. Art. on the cultural hist. of the Kyushu district with special reference to the use of new source materials; table of contents also in English. nfs

LEGAL HISTORY REVIEW see HOSEISHI KENKYU

73. LES MANUELS DE L'INSTITUT FRANCO-JAPONAIS DE TOKYO [The manuals of the Franco-Japanese Institute of Tokyo]. Irr. Tokyo Nichifutsu

Gakuin ["L'Institut Franco-Japonais de Tokyo"], 15 Ichigaya Funakawara-cho, Shinjuku-ku, Tokyo. Separate Japanese and French editions. nfs

MEMOIRS OF THE INSTITUTE OF ORIENTAL CULTURE see TOYO BUNKA KENKYUSHO KIYO

MEMOIRS OF THE RESEARCH DEPARTMENT OF THE TOYO BUNKO see TOYO BUNKO, MEMOIRS OF THE RESEARCH DEPARTMENT OF THE

74. MINZOKUGAKU KENKYU [Ethnological studies]. THE JAPANESE JOURNAL OF ETHNOLOGY. Q. 1935 (1958: vol. 22). Nippon Minzokugaku Kyokai [Japanese Ethnological Soc.], 132 Shimo Hoya, Hoya-machi, Kitatama-gun, Tokyo. Ed: Nobuhiro Matsumoto. Art. on Japanese ethnology and folklore; bk. rev.; report of the soc. and of affiliated soc.; contents page also in English; English sum.; illus. p (1) ¥ 200 / $ 6 (annual foreign subscription)

75. MITA GAKKAI ZASSHI. MITA JOURNAL OF ECONOMICS. M. Keio Gijuku Keizai Gakkai [Keio Economic Soc.], c/o Keio Gijuku Daigaku [Keio Gijuku Univ.], Shiba Mita, Minato-ku, Tokyo. English sum.; graph. p(1) ¥ 90

MITA JOURNAL OF ECONOMICS see MITA GAKKAI ZASSHI

76. MONUMENTA NIPPONICA. Studies of Japanese Culture, Past and Present. Q. 1938 (1958: vol. 14). Sophia Univ., 7, Kioi-cho, Chiyoda-ku, Tokyo. Ed: Wilhelm Schiffer, S.J. Art. on Japanese culture, past and present, with original texts quoted wherever necessary; bk. rev.; in English, French and German; translations of Japanese texts; graph, illus. ¥ 2160 / $ 6

77. MONUMENTA SERICA. Journal of Oriental Studies. S-A. 1935 (1958: vol. 17). S.V.D. Research Inst., c/o Nanzan Daigaku [Nanzan Univ. (Catholic Univ. of Nagoya)], Goken'ya-chō, Showa-ku, Nagoya. Tokyo office: 20 Honshio-cho, Shinjuku-ku, Tokyo. Ed. board: Heinrich Busch, S.V.D. (chief ed.), Eugen Feifel, Gerhard Schreiber, Harrie Vanderstappen. Art. on various aspects of Chinese social, economic and cultural hist.; bk. rev.; in English and German; illus. nfs

78. MUSASHI DAIGAKU RONSHU [Musashi University journal]. Q. 1953 (1959: vol. 7). Musashi Daigaku Gakkai [Soc. for Social Sciences, Musashi Univ.], 1-26 Toyotama-kami, Nerima-ku, Tokyo. Ed: Ryôichi Hanawa. Art. on economics and general hist. relating to the modern period, not confined to any country; notes. ¥ 100

79. MUSASHINO [Name of a district in Japan - - ed.]. B. Musashino Bunka Kyokai [Musashino Cultural Assoc.], Musashino Kyodokan, Koganei Koen, Koganei-machi, Kitatama-gun, Tokyo-to. (memb.) ¥ 300

80. MUSASHINO SHIDAN [Discourses on Musashino history]. Title varies: vol. 4 was entitled Saitama Shidan [Discourses on Saitama history]. Q. Saitama Kaikan Urawa-shi Kenshi Hensanshitsu [Editorial Office for the Hist. of Saitama (Urawa) Prefecture], c/o Saitama Kenritsu Toshokan [Saitama Prefectural Library], 3173 Takasago-cho, Urawa. Illus. (memb.) ¥ 500

81. MUSEUM. Tokyo Kokuritsu Hakubutsukan Bijutsu-shi [Art magazine of the Tokyo National Museum]. M. 1951 (1959: no. 94-105). Tokyo Kokuritsu Hakubutsukan, Ueno Park, Taito-ku, Tokyo. Art. on the hist. of Japan, China and India; in Japanese; illus. ¥ 1800

82. NICHI - I BUNKA KENKYU. STUDI DI CULTURA ITALO-GIAPPONESE [Italian-Japanese cultural studies]. A. Nichi-I Kyokai ["Istituto Italo-Giapponese"], 4 Sanban-cho, Chiyoda-ku, Tokyo. Gravures. p (1) ¥ 200

83. NIHON JOKOSHI KENKYU [Studies in ancient Japanese history]. M. 1957 (1959: vol. 34). Nihon Jôkoshi Kenkyûkai [Soc. for the Study of Ancient Japanese Hist.], cho-me Zuiko-dori Higashi Yodogawa-ku, Osaka. Ed: Takashi Tanaka. Art. on ancient Japanese hist.; rev. art.; bk. rev.; English sum. p (1) ¥ 60

84. NIHON KOKOGAKU NENPO [Annual report on Japanese archaeology]. ARCHAEOLOGIA JAPONICA. A. 1951. Nihon Kokogaku Kyokai [Japanese Archaeologists' Assoc.], c/o Tokyo Daigaku Bungakubu Kokogaku Kenkyushitsu [Inst. of Archaeology, Faculty of Letters, Tokyo Univ.], Motofuji-cho, Bunkyo-ku, Tokyo. p (1) ¥ 550

85. NIHON MINZOKUGAKU [Japanese folklore]. Q. 1950 (1957: vol. 5). Nihon Minzokugakkai [Folklore Soc. of Japan], 1-3 Ginza-nishi, Chûôku, Tokyo. Ed: Tarô Wakamori. General art. on Japanese folklore; bk. rev.; reports and notes. Suspended pub. in 1957. p (1) ¥ 150

86. NIHON MINZOKUGAKU KAIHO [Bulletin of Japanese folklore]. Bulletin of the Folklore Society of Japan. B-M. 1958 (1959: no. 5-10). Nihon Minzoku Gakkai [Folklore Soc. of Japan], c/o Mrs. T. Noda, 12, 2-chome, Nishiogikubo, Suginami-ku, Tokyo. Ed: Takayoshi Mogami. Art. on Japanese folklore; bk. rev.; biblio. of art.; professional news; table of contents also in English; graph, illus. Supersedes Nihon Minzokugaku [Japanese folklore], founded in 1950. ¥ 600

87. NIHON NO TOKUSHU BURAKU [Special communities of Japan]. Tokyo Shidan-kai [Tokyo Hist. Soc.], 2140 Hebikubo Fuchushi, Tokyo. Ed: S. Kikuchi. Art. of sociological, hist., geographical and archaeological interest on different Japanese social communities from early times (c. 8th cent.) to the present; maps, graph, illus. p (1) ¥ 200

88. NIHON ORIENTO GAKKAI GEPPO [Monthly report of the Society for Near Eastern Studies in Japan]. M. 1955 (1957: no. 8). Nihon Oriento Gakkai, c/o Kunaicho Shoryobu Mikasanomiya Kenkyushitsu [Mikasanomiya Laboratory, Archives and Mausolea Division, Imperial Household Agency], Chiyoda-ku, Tokyo. Ed: Takahito Mikasanomiya. Art. on hist., archaeological and linguistic studies of the Near East. ¥ 500

89. NIHON REKISHI [Japanese history]. M. 1946 (1958: no. 115-126). Nihon Rekishi Gakkai [Inst. of Japanese Hist.], 45 Shiroyama-machi, Nakano-ku, Tokyo. Ed: Mitsutoshi Takayanagi. Art. on the political, economic, cultural and intellectual hist. of Japan; bk. rev.; biblio.; graph, illus. ¥ 1000 /$ 2.77

90. NIHONSHI KENKYU [Studies in Japanese history]. Q. 1946 (1959: no. 45). Nihonshi Kenkyukai [Japanese Hist. Soc.], 89 Sakuradai-cho, Shishigatani, Sakyo-ku, Kyoto. Art. on the political, economic and cultural hist. of Japan; bk. rev.; biblio. p (1) ¥ 100

91. NOGYO SOGO KENKYU [Synthetic studies in agricultural economy]. Q. Norinsho Nogyo Sogo Kenkyusho [National Research Inst. of Agriculture, Ministry of Agriculture and Forestry], 8 Azabu Shinryudo-cho, Minato-ku, Tokyo. Ed: Seiichi Tobata. nfs

92. OCHANOMIZU JOSHI DAIGAKU JIMBUN KAGAKU KIYO [Memoirs of the Research Institute of Cultural Science, Ochanomizu-Joshi University]. STUDIES IN ARTS AND CULTURE. S-A. 1952 (1958: vol. 11). Ochanomizu Joshi Univ., 35 Otsuka-machi, Bunkyo-ku, Tokyo. Ed: Kenji Fujita. Art. on cultural subjects, with emphasis on the Far East; in Japanese and occasionally in English; quotations from English and German texts; English sum.; graph. nfs

93. OITA-KEN CHIHOSHI [Local history of Oita prefecture]. Q. Oita-ken Chihôshi Kenkyûkai [Oita Local Hist. Soc.], c/o Oita Daigaku Gakugei Gakubu [Liberal Arts Faculty of Oita Univ.], Nakano Danohara, Oita. (memb.) ¥ 300

94. OKAYAMA SHIGAKU [Okayama historical studies]. Journal of History and Geography. A. 1955 (1959: no vol. indic.). Okayama Shigakkai [Okayama Soc. of Hist. Research], c/o Okayama Daigaku Hobun Gakubu [Faculty of Law and Letters, Okayama Univ.], Tsushima, Okayama. Ed: Taneyuki Hara. Art. on political and economic hist. and geography, with emphasis on the Far East; bk. rev.; professional news and notes. p (1) ¥ 150

95. OKURAYAMA RONSHU [Okuraya journal]. Irr. Okurayama Seishin Bunka [Okuraya Research Inst. of Cultural Studies], 406 Futoo-cho, Kohoku-ku, Yokohama. In Japanese and English. p (1) c. ¥ 500

ORIENTAL CULTURE see TOYO BUNKA

96. OSAKA SHIDAN [Osaka local history]. Irr. Osaka Shidankai [Osaka Local Hist. Soc.], 158 Mikunihon-machi, Higashi Yodogawa-ku, Osaka. p (1) ¥ 120

97. OTANI SHIGAKU [Otani historical studies]. A. 1951 (1959: no. 7). Otani Daigaku Shigakkai [Hist. Soc., Otani Univ.], Koyama Kamifusa-cho, Kamikyo-ku, Kyoto. Ed: Toshishizu Nogami. Art. on the social and cultural hist. of Asia, with emphasis on Japan. nfs

98. OU SHIDAN [Ou historical studies]. Q. 1950 (1959: no. 26). Ou Shidankai [Ou Hist. Soc.], Morioka-shi Sangyo Bunkakan, Shimokoji, Morioka. Ed: Sadayuki Fuchizawa. Art. on the local hist., including archaeology and folklore, of the Ou district of Japan, consisting of the Akita, Iwate and Aomori prefectures. (memb.) ¥ 300

99. PALAEOLOGIA. Q. Palaeological Assoc. of Japan, Osaka Fine Arts Museum, Osaka. In English, French, German and Japanese; illus. $ 3

PUBLICATIONS OF THE INSTITUTE FOR COMPARATIVE STUDIES OF CULTURE see HIKAKU BUNKA KENKYUSHO KIYO

100. REKISHI [History]. Irr. 1956 (1959: no. 11). Fukushima Daigaku Rekishigaku Kenkyukai [Soc. for Hist. Studies, Fukushima Univ.], 84 Hamada-cho, Fukushima. Ed: Kiyomitsu Monoe. Art. on the political and economic hist. of modern Japan; bk. rev.; professional news; mimeographed. nfs

101. REKISHI [History]. TOHOKU HISTORICAL REVIEW. S-A. 1949 (1958: no. 17). Tohoku Shigakkai [Tohoku Hist. Soc.], c/o Tohoku Daigaku Bungakubu [Faculty of Arts and Letters, Tohoku Univ.], Katahira-cho, Sendai. Ed: Ryoichi Furuta. Art. on the hist. of Japan, China and the West, with emphasis on socio-economic hist.; bk. rev.; notes on hist. materials; in Japanese. p (1) ¥ 100

102. REKISHI CHIRI [History and geography]. Q. 1899 (1959: vol. 89). Nihon Chiri Rekishi Gakkai [Japanese Soc. of Hist. Geography], c/o Okada, Akio 3-14-2 Shimura-cho, Itabashi-ku, Tokyo. Ed: Takeo Itazawa. Art. on the hist. of Japan and China and on hist. geography; news of new pub. p(1) ¥ 100

103. REKISHI CHIRI KYOIKU [Historical and geographical education]. M. Pub. address: 3-274 Hyakunin-cho, Chiyoda-ku, Tokyo. pv

104. REKISHI HYORON [Historical review]. M. 1947 (1959: no. 101-112). Minshu Shugi Kagakusha Kyokai [Democratic Scientists' Soc. in Japan], 2-4 Kanda Jinbo-cho, Chiyoda-ku, Tokyo. Ed: Shiro Nohara. Art. on the hist. of Japan, Asia and the West, and on hist. education, from the Marxist viewpoint; rev. art.; bk. rev.; news of new pub. p (1) ¥ 70

105. REKISHI HYORON [Historical review]. B-M. 1955 (1958: no. 9-11). Waseda Daigaku Kyoiku Gakubu Rekishigaku Kenkyukai [Soc. for the Study of Hist., Faculty of Education, Waseda Univ.], Totsuka-machi, Shinjuku-ku, Tokyo. Art. on the socio-economic hist. of villages in modern Japan; mimeographed. nfs

106. REKISHI KENKYU [Study of history]. Irr. 1957 (1959: no. 4). Osaka Furitsu Daigaku Rekishi Kenkyukai [Hist. Soc., Univ. of Osaka Prefecture], Mozu Higashino-cho, Sakai-shi, Osaka-fu. Art. on Japanese cultural hist. and on the economic hist. of Japan and the West; bk. rev.; illus. (memb.) ¥ 600

107. REKISHI KYOIKU [Historical education]. M. 1935 (1959: vol. 7). Rekishi Kyoiku Kenkyukai [Inst. of Hist. Education], c/o Nihon Shoin, 1-12 Shin Ogawa-machi, Shinjuku-ku, Tokyo. Ed: Toshiharu Hirata. Art. on various aspects of the hist. of Japan, Asia and the West; rev. of bk. and art.; professional news; notes on hist. education. p (1) ¥ 100

108. REKISHI NO KENKYU [Study of history]. A. 1952 (1958: no. 6). Yamagata Rekishi Gakkai [Yamagata Hist. Soc.], c/o Yamagata Daigaku Bunri Gakubu [Faculty of Literature and Science, Yamagata Univ.], Koshirakawa-machi, Yamagata. Art. on the economic, political and social hist. of Japan and China. nfs

109. REKISHIGAKU KENKYU [Journal of historical studies]. M. 1933 (1959: no. 227-235). Rekishigaku Kenkyukai [Hist. Science Soc.], c/o Auki Shoten, 1-60 Kanda Jinbo-cho, Chiyoda-ku, Tokyo. Ed: Bokuro Eguchi. Art. on the hist. of Japan, Asia and the West, mainly from the Marxist viewpoint; bk. rev.; professional news. p (1) ¥ 80

110. RISSHO SHIGAKU [Rissho historical studies]. A. 1933 (1959: no. 33). Rissho Daigaku Shigakkai [Soc. of Hist. Research, Rissho Univ.], 4 Higashi Osaki, Shinagawa-ku, Tokyo. Ed: Iwao Aritaka. Art. on various aspects of the hist. of Japan, China and the West; bk. rev.; notes on materials. nfs

111. RITSUMEIKAN DAIGAKU JINBUN KAGAKU KENKYUSHO KIYO [Memoirs of the Research Institute of the Cultural Sciences of Ritsumeikan University]. A. Ritsumeikan Daigaku Jinbun Kagaku Kenkyusho, Tera-machi, Higashiiru, Hirokoji-dori, Kamikyo-ku, Kyoto. In Japanese and English. p (1) ¥ 200

112. RITSUMEIKAN HOGAKU [Ritsumeikan law]. A Quarterly Review of the Ritsumeikan University Law Association. Q. Ritsumeikan Daigaku Jinbun Kagaku Kenkyusho [Research Inst. of Cultural Sciences, Ritsumeikan Univ.], Hirokoji-Teramachi, Kamikyo-ku, Kyoto. ¥ 600 / $ 65

113. RYUKOKU SHIDAN [Ryukoku historical review]. The Journal of History of Ryukoku University. S-A. 1929 (1959: no. 45). Ryukoku Daigaku Shigakkai [Hist. Soc. of Ryukoku Univ.], Inokuma, 7-jo Kado, Shimokyo-ku, Kyoto. Ed: Enjun Miyazaki. Art. on the hist. of Japan and Asia with special reference to Buddhism; reports on the activities of the soc. nfs

SAITAMA SHIDAN see MUSASHINO SHIDAN

SCIENTIFIC PAPERS ON JAPANESE ANTIQUES AND ART CRAFTS see KOBUNKAZAI NO KAGAKU

114. SEIKO BUNKA [Culture in the western suburbs]. The Culture in the Western Suburbs of Tokyo. Irr. Suginami Kushi Hensan Iinkai [Suginami-ku Hist. Compilation Committee], c/o Suginami Kuyakusho, 1-715 Asagaya, Suginami-ku, Tokyo. In Japanese; illus. nfs

115. SEIYO SHIGAKU ["Studies in Western History"]. Q. 1949 (1959: no. 40-43). Nihon Seiyoshi Gakkai [Japanese Soc. of Western Hist.], c/o Kyoto Daigaku Bungakubu Seiyoshi Kenkyushitsu [Dept. of Western Hist., Faculty of Letters, Kyoto Univ.], Yoshidahon-machi, Sakyo-ku, Kyoto. Ed: Takashi Toyoda. Art. on the hist. of Europe and America, with emphasis on cultural hist.; bk. rev.; news of new pub.; professional news. p (1) ¥ 140

116. SEIYOSHI GAKUHO [Studies in western history]. Irr. 1953 (mri 1954: no. 2). Seiho Shigaku Kenkyukai [Soc. of Occidental Hist.], c/o Kyushu Daigaku Bungakubu [Faculty of Literature, Kyushu Univ.], Hakozaki, Fukuoka. Ed: Kazuto Takayama, c/o Inst. of Western Hist., Hiroshima Univ., Higashi Sendamachi, Hiroshima. Outlines of hist. works and art. by western scholars; mimeographed. nfs

117. SEIYOSHI KENKYU [Studies in western history]. A. 1932 (1959: no. 5). Seiyoshi Kenkyukai [Soc. for the Study of Western Hist.], c/o Tohoku Daigaku Bungakubu Seiyoshi Kenkyushitsu [Dept. of Western Hist., Faculty of Literature, Tohoku Univ.], Katahira-cho, Sendai. Ed: Nobuhiko Gionji. Art. on various aspects of European and American hist.; bk. rev.; news of new pub. p (1) ¥ 160

118. SEKAISHI KENKYU [Studies in world history]. Q. 1952 (1959: vol. 8). Sekaishi Kenkyukai [Japanese Soc. of World Hist.], c/o Kumamoto Daigaku Hobun Gakubu Seiyoshi Kenkyushitsu [Dept. of Western Hist., Faculty of Law and Literature, Kumamoto Univ.], Kurokami-machi, Kumamoto. Ed: Saburo Sakai. Art. on various aspects of world hist., with emphasis on western hist.; bk. rev.; biblio. in no. 1 of each vol.; illus. p (1) ¥ 150

119. SEKKI JIDAI ["The Stone Age"]. 3 x y. 1955. Sekki Jidai Kenkyukai [Stone Age Culture Research Assoc.], c/o Noguchi, Yoshimaro, 4-1, 131 Matsubara-cho, Setagaya-ku, Tokyo. English sum. p (1) ¥ 350

120. SENSHI JIDAI [Prehistoric age]. S-A. 1955 (1959: vol. 8). Pub. and ed: Toshio Oba, Higashi 8, Odori, Sapporo. Essays, reports and art. on the prehist. age in Hokkaido; mimeographed; illus. nfs

121. SHAKAI KAGAKU KENKYU [Studies in social sciences]. Q. Shakai Kagaku Kyokai [Soc. of Social Sciences], c/o Tokyo Daigaku Shakai Kagaku Kenkyusho [Inst. of Social Sciences, Tokyo Univ.], Motofuji-cho, Bunkyo-ku, Tokyo.
pv

122. SHAKAI KAGAKU KIYO [Journal of social sciences]. The Proceedings of the Department of Social Sciences, College of General Education, University of Tokyo. A. Tokyo Daigaku Kyoyo Gakubu [College of General Education, Tokyo Univ.], Komaba, Meguro-ku, Tokyo. Art. on politics, economics and hist. with special reference to Japan; English sum. nfs

123. SHAKAI KAGAKU RONSHU [Journal of social sciences]. Irr. Kashiwazaki Tanki Daigaku [Kashiwazaki Junior College], Hisumi, Kashiwazakishi, Niigata-ken. nfs

124. SHAKAI KAGAKU RONSHU [Journal of social sciences]. Irr. Tokyo Kyoiku Daigaku Shakai Gakkai [Social Science Soc., Tokyo Univ. of Education], Otsuka Kubo-machi, Bunkyo-ku, Tokyo. One of several separately pub. no. which form the Bulletin of the Tokyo Kyoiku University Literature Department.
p (1) ¥ 200

125. SHAKAI KAGAKU RONSO [Researches in the social sciences]. Title varies: no. 1-4 entitled Jinbun Shakai Kagaku Kenkyu Hokoku [Researches in the humanities and social sciences]. A. Nagasaki Daigaku Gakugei Gakubu [Faculty of Liberal Arts and Education, Nagasaki Univ.], Ohashi-machi, Nagasaki. nfs

126. SHAKAI KEIZAI SHIGAKU ["Socio-Economic History"]. Q. 1930 (1958: vol. 24). Shakai Keizai Shigakkai [Socio-Economic Hist. Soc.], c/o Waseda Daigaku Jinbun Shakai Kagaku Kenkyushitsu [Graduate School for the Social Sciences and Humanities, Waseda Univ.], Totsuka-machi, Shinjuku-ku, Tokyo. Ed: Kentaro Nomura. Art. on the social and economic hist. of Japan and other countries; bk. rev.; contents page also in English; maps, graph.
p (1) ¥ 140 / $ 6.50 (annual foreign subscription)

127. SHAKAIGAKU KENKYU. THE STUDY OF SOCIOLOGY. Q. Tohoku Shakaigaku Kenkyukai [Tohoku Soc. for the Study of Sociology], c/o Department of Sociology, Tohoku Univ., Katahira-cho, Sendai. In Japanese; contents page also in English; statistics; graph. ¥ 100 / $ 0.25

128. SHICHO [The trend of history]. Q. 1931 (mri 1954: no. 2). Otsuka Shigakkai [Otsuka Hist. Science Soc.], c/o Tokyo Kyoiku Daigaku [Tokyo Univ. of Education], Otsuka Kubo-machi, Bunkyo-ku, Tokyo. Ed: Kazuo Hattori. Art. on the hist. of Japan, Asia and the West, and on hist. education; bk. rev.; news of new pub.; reports on the activities of the soc.; selected biblio. of art.
p (1) ¥ 100

129. SHIEN [The garden of history]. The Journal of Historical Studies. S-A. 1928 (1958: vol. 19). Rikkyo Daigaku Shigaku Kenkyu-shitsu [Inst. of Hist., Rikkyo Univ.], Ikebukuro 3 chome, Toshima-ku, Tokyo. Ed: Shimizu. Art. on various aspects of the hist. of Japan, Asia and the West; bk. rev.; biblio. of art. on American hist.; statistics, graph. ¥ 150 / $ 0.42

130. SHIEN [The abyss of history]. The Journal of History. 4-5 x y. 1929 (1958: vol. 77). Kyushu Shigakkai [Kyushu Hist. Soc.], c/o Kyushu Daigaku Bungakubu [Faculty of Literature, Kyushu Univ.], Hakozaki, Fukuoka. Ed: Kaizaburo Hino. Art. on various aspects of the hist. of Japan, Asia and the

West; reports on the activities of the soc.; bk. rev.; general tables of contents covering vol. 16-18; English and French sum. nfs

131. SHIGAKU ["The Historical Science"]. Q. 1923 (1958: vol. 31). Mita Shigakukai [Mita Hist. Soc.], Keio Univ., 2-2 Shiba-Mita, Minatoku, Tokyo. Ed: Yoshio Matsumoto. Art. on all periods of the hist. of Japan, Asia and the West, and on anthropology, geography and archaeology; bk. rev.; cum. index no.; occasional special no.; maps, graph, illus. p (1) ¥ 170

132. SHIGAKU KENKYU ["Review of Historical Studies"]. Q. 1929 (1959: no. 71-74). Hiroshima Shigaku Kenkyukai [Soc. for Hist. Studies], c/o Hiroshima Daigaku Bungakubu [Literature Department, Hiroshima Univ.], Higashi Senda-machi, Hiroshima. Ed: Ken Chiyoda. Art. on hist. with special reference to Japan and the Far East; rev. of bk. and art.; professional news. p (1) ¥ 100

133. SHIGAKU ZASSHI [Historical review]. Historical Journal of Japan. M. 1889 (1958: vol. 67). Tokyo Daigaku Bungakubu Shigakukai [Hist. Soc., Faculty of Letters, Tokyo Univ.], 1 chome, Motofuji-cho, Bunkyo-ku, Tokyo. Ed: Seiichi Iwao. Art. on world hist., predominantly Asian and Japanese; rev. art. and bk. rev.; news on the meetings of the soc. with sum. of papers; news of new pub.; professional news; selected list of periodical art.; general index covering vol. 1-50. ¥ 1200 / $ 3.30

134. SHIKAI [Sea of history]. A. 1954 (1959: no. 6). Tokyo Gakugei Daigaku Shigakkai [Inst. of Hist. Research, Tokyo Gakugei Univ.], 3 Shimouma-cho, Setagaya-ku, Tokyo. Ed: Minoru Chijiwa. Art. on Far Eastern hist., and on hist. education; bk. rev.; sum. of theses prepared at the univ.; professional news. nfs

135. SHIKAN [Historical view]. Q. 1908 (mri 1956: no. 46-47). Waseda Daigaku Shigakkai [Hist. Soc. of Waseda Univ.], Totsuka-machi, Shinjuku-ku, Tokyo. Ed: Ugenji Sadakane. Art. on various aspects of the hist. of Japan, Asia and the West; rev. of bk. and art.; reports on the activities of the soc. p (1) ¥ 100 - 130

136. SHIMOTSUKE SHIGAKU [Shimotsuke historical studies]. Irr. Shimotsuke Shigakkai [Shimotsuke Hist. Soc.], c/o Utsunomiya Daigaku Shigaku Kenkyushitsu [Dept. of Hist., Utsunomiya Univ.], Mine-machi, Utsunomiya. nfs

137. SHINA GAKUHO [Studies in Sinology]. A. Otani Daigaku Shina Gakkai [Sinological Soc., Otani Univ.], Koyama Kamifusa-cho, Kamikyo-ku, Kyoto. Mimeographed. nfs

THE SHINTO HISTORY REVIEW see SHINTOSHI KENKYU

138. SHINTOGAKU [Shintoism]. The Journal of Shinto Studies. Q. 1954 (1959: no. 21-24). Shinto Gakkai [Soc. of Shintoism], 1 Azabu Kasumi-cho, minato-ku, Tokyo. Ed: Takanobu Senge, Taisha-machi, Shimane-ken. Art. on theoretical, religious and hist. studies of Shintoism; bk. rev.; biblio.; in Japanese; illus. ¥ 300

139. SHINTOSHI KENKYU. THE SHINTO HISTORY REVIEW. B-M. 1953 (1959: vol. 7). Shintoshi Gakkai [Shinto Hist. Assoc.], c/o Yasaka Jinsha [Yasaka Shrine], Gion-machi, Higashiyama-ku, Kyoto. Ed: Osamu Kubota, 17

Koyama Shimofusa-machi, Kita-ku, Kyoto. Art. on Japanese hist. with special reference to Shintoism; bk. rev.; biblio. in vol. 1; in Japanese; illus. ¥ 500

140. SHIRIN [The forest of history]. JOURNAL OF HISTORY. B-M. 1916 (1959: vol. 42). Shigaku Kenkyukai [Soc. of Hist. Research], c/o Kyoto Daigaku Bungakubu [Faculty of Letters, Kyoto Univ.], Yoshidahon-machi, Sakyo-ku, Kyoto. Ed: Nakamura Insatsu Kabushiki Kaisha, 39 Higashi-machi, 7 Jogo-sho No Uchi, Shimokyo-ku, Kyoto. Art. on the hist., geography and archaeology of Japan, Asia and the West; rev. of bk. and art.; professional news; English and, occasionally, German sum.; cum. table of contents covering vol. 1-40 issued separately in 1958. ¥ 900

141. SHIRON [Historical essays]. Historica. A. 1953 (1959: no. 7). Tokyo Joshi Daigaku Rekishigaku Kenkyushitsu [Hist. Seminar, Tokyo Women's Christian College], 3-124 Iogi, Suginami-ku, Tokyo. Art. on Japanese hist. and folklore, with emphasis on intellectual and cultural hist.; cum. table of contents for no. 1-7 pub. in no. 7; sum. in a European language. p (1) ¥ 200

142. SHISEKI TO BIJUTSU [Historic spots and fine arts]. M. 1930 (1959: vol. 29). Shiseki Bijutsu Dokokai [Japanese Soc. of Hist. Spots and Ancient Arts], 14 Shimoyanagi-cho, Murasakino, Kamikyo-ku, Kyoto. Ed: Masataro Kawakatsu. Art. on Japanese hist. remains and the hist. of fine arts and religion in Japan; catalogues of national treasures and important cultural properties; news of new pub. ¥ 960

143. SHISEN [Journal of history]. Irr. 1951 (1959: no. 15-17). Kansai Daigaku [Kansai Univ.], 17 Senriyama, Suita-shi, Osaka-fu. Ed: Teicho Mikami. Art. on the hist. of Japan and the West, with emphasis on intellectual and cultural hist.; bk. rev.; biblio.; cum. table of contents for no. 1-10 pub. in no. 10 and for no. 11-17 in no. 17. p (1) ¥ 80

144. SHISO [The window of history]. S-A. Kyoto Joshi Daigaku Shigakkai [Soc. for Hist. Studies, Kyoto Women's Univ.], 7-jo, Higashiyama, Higashiyama-ku, Kyoto. nfs

145. SHISO [Thought]. M. 1921 (1959: no. 415-426). Iwanami Shoten, 2-3 Kanda Hitotsubashi, Chiyoda-ku, Tokyo. Ed: Z. Inanuma. Art. on hist., politics, economics and philosophy with special reference to Japan; bk. rev. p (1) ¥ 100

146. SHIYO [Journal of history]. S-A. Chiba Daigaku Bunri Gakubu Shigaku Kenkyukai [Hist. Soc., College of Arts and Sciences, Chiba Univ.], Konakadai-machi, Chiba. Mimeographed. nfs

147. SHOGAKU RONSHU [Journal of commercial sciences]. Journal of commerce, economics and economic history. Q. Fukushima Daigaku Keizai Gakkai [Economic Soc. of Fukushima Univ.], Moriai, Fukushima. In Japanese. (memb.) ¥ 600

148. SHORYOBU KIYO [Journal of the Archives and Mausolea Division (Imperial Household Agency)]. Bulletin: The Study on the Japanese Culture in Relation to the Imperial Family and Court. A. Kunaicho Shoryobu [Archives and Mausolea Division, Imperial Household Agency], Tokyo. Cum. table of contents for no. 1-10 pub. in no. 10. p (1) ¥ 230

149. SHUDAI SHIGAKU [Shudai (Akita University) historical studies]. S-A. 1952 (1959: no vol. indic.). Akita Daigaku Shigakkai [Hist. Science Soc., Akita Univ.], 1 Fukada, Tegata-machi, Akita. Ed: Yoshitaka Imamura. Art. on Japanese hist. and archaeology, with emphasis on the ancient period. p (1) ¥ 100

150. SINAGAKU KENKYU. JOURNAL OF SINOLOGICAL STUDIES. S-A. 1948 (1958: vol. 21). Hiroshima Shinagakkai [Sinological Soc. of Hiroshima], Literature Department, Hiroshima Univ., Hiroshima. Ed: T. Nishitani. Art. on Chinese classics, literature and epigraphy; bk. rev.; biblio.; professional news; contents page also in English; English sum.; cum. index; graph.
¥ 300 / $ 1

151. SOPHIA. Tozai Bunka narabini Tozai Bunka Koryu no Kenkyu ["Studies in Western Civilization and the Cultural Interaction of West and East"]. Q. 1952 (1958: vol. 7). Sophia Univ., Kioicho, Chiyoda-ku, Tokyo. Ed: J. Roggendorf. Art. on Western hist., culture and philosophy and on the cultural interaction of West and East; bk. rev.; in Japanese; contents page also in English; English sum. of main art. ¥ 600 / $ 2

STUDI DI CULTURA ITALO - GIAPPONESE see NICH - I BUNKA KENKYU

STUDI ITALICI see ITARIA GAKKAISHI

STUDIES IN ARTS AND CULTURE see OCHANOMIZU JOSHI DAIGAKU JIMBUN KAGAKU KIYO

THE STUDY OF SOCIOLOGY see SHAKAIGAKU KENKYU

SUNDAI HISTORICAL REVIEW see SUNDAI SHIGAKU

152. SUNDAI SHIGAKU. SUNDAI HISTORICAL REVIEW. A. 1951 (1959: no. 9). Meiji Daigaku Shigakkai [(Sundai) Hist. Assoc. of Meiji Univ.], Kanda Surugadai, Chiyoda-ku, Tokyo. Art. on the political, economic and cultural hist. and historiography of the Far East; bk. rev.; report of the A. meeting of the soc.; English sum.; no. 1-3 issued by the soc. under its earlier name : Meiji Daigaku Rekishi Chiri Gakkai [Historico-Geographical Assoc. of Meiji Univ.].
p (1) ¥ 150

153. TOCHI SEIDO SHIGAKU. JOURNAL OF AGRARIAN HISTORY. Q. 1958 (1959: no. 2-5). Tochi Seido Shigakkai [Agrarian Hist. Soc.], c/o Tokyo Daigaku Fuzoku Toshokan [Tokyo Univ. Library], Motofuji-cho, Bunkyo-ku, Tokyo. Ed: Moritaro Yamada. Art. on economic theory, economic hist. and agricultural analysis with special reference to Japan; in Japanese. Supersedes Tochi Seido Shigaku. Bulletin of Agrarian History founded in 1954. p (1) ¥ 180

154. TOHO GAKUHO [Report of Oriental studies]. Journal of Oriental Studies. A. 1931 (1959: no. 29). Kyoto Daigaku Jinbun Kagaku Kenkyusho [Research Inst. for Humanistic Studies, Kyoto Univ.], 50 Ogura-cho, Kitashirakawa, Sakyo-ku, Kyoto. Ed: Keishiro Miyatani. Art. on the hist. and thought of the Orient, with emphasis on China; miscellaneous reports; in Japanese.
nfs

155. TOHO KODAI KENKYU [Journal of Oriental antiquities]. S-A. 1952 (1958: no. 8). Toho Kodai Kenkyukai [Soc. of Oriental Antiquities], c/o Kumamoto Daigaku Hobun Gakubu [Faculty of Law and Literature, Kumamoto Univ.],

Kurokami-machi, Kumamoto. Ed: Masaaki Matsumoto. Art. on Chinese classics, epigraphy and hist.; in Japanese. p (1) ¥ 80

156. TOHOGAKU [Eastern studies]. S-A. Toho Gakkai [Inst. of Eastern Culture], 2-2 Nishi Kanda, Chiyoda-ku, Tokyo. English sum. p (1) ¥ 200

157. TOHOKU KEIZAI [Economy of the North-East]. Q. Fukushima Daigaku Fuzoku Tohoku Keizai Kenkyusho [Tohoku Economic Research Inst., Faculty of Economics, Fukushima Univ.], Moriai, Fukushima. nfs

158. TOKYO SHIDAN [Local history of Tokyo]. Q. Tokyo Shidan-kai [Tokyo Local Hist. Soc.], 2140 Hebikubodai, Fuchu-shi, Tokyo. ¥ 400 /$1.10

159. TOKYO SHINA GAKUHO [Tokyo Sinological bulletin]. Bulletin of the Tokyo Sinological Society]. S-A. Tokyo Shina Gakkai [Tokyo Sinological Soc.], c/o Tokyo Daigaku Bungakubu [Faculty of Letters, Tokyo Univ.], Motofuji-cho, Bunkyo-ku, Tokyo. In Japanese. p (1) c. ¥ 300 (memb.)

160. TOYO BUNKA [Oriental culture]. A. Toyo Bunka Shinkokai [Soc. for the Promotion of Oriental Culture], Dept. of General Education, Nagoya Univ., Mizuho-cho, Mizuho-ku, Nagoya. free

TOYO BUNKA KENKYU see TOYO BUNKA. ORIENTAL CULTURE

161. TOYO BUNKA KENKYUSHO KIYO. MEMOIRS OF THE INSTITUTE OF ORIENTAL CULTURE. Irr. 1943 (1959: no. 17-18). Toyobunka Kenkyusho [Inst. for Oriental Culture], Univ. of Tokyo, 56 Otsuka-machi, Bunkyo-ku, Tokyo. Art. on the hist. and culture of the Far East with emphasis on China; English sum. nfs

162. TOYO BUNKA. ORIENTAL CULTURE. Q. 1950 (1959: no. 27-28). Toyobunka Kenkyujo [Inst. for Oriental Culture], Univ. of Tokyo, 56 Otsuka-machi, Bunkyo-ku, Tokyo. Ed: Masao Fukushima. Art. on the hist., politics and economy of the Far East; in Japanese and English; illus. Formerly entitled Toyo Bunka Kenkyu [Studies in Oriental culture]. p (1) ¥ 180

163. TOYO BUNKO [Oriental Library], MEMOIRS OF THE RESEARCH DEPARTMENT OF THE. Irr. 1926 (1959: no. 18). Research Department of the Toyo Bunko, 147 Kamifujimae-cho Bunkyo-ku, Tokyo. Ed: Kiyoshi Wada. Art. on all aspects and periods of the cultural hist. of Asia (with emphasis on China and Chinese sources) including political and economic hist., art, religion, philology, archaeology, geography, and the relationship of Asian culture with the West; in English; cum. table of contents in no. 16 and 17; illus. Appears as "Series B" of the Toyo Bunko Publications.

164. TOYO GAKUHO [Oriental studies]. Reports of the Oriental Society. Q. 1911 (1958: vol. 41). Toyo Gakujutsu Kyokai [Oriental Sciences and Arts Soc.], c/o Toyo Bunko, 147 Komagome Kamifujimae-cho, Bunkyo-ku, Tokyo. Ed: Kiyoshi Wada. Art. on Oriental hist., with emphasis on China; occasional bk. rev.; biblio.; English sum. p (1) ¥ 130

165. TOYO NO BUNKA TO SHAKAI. CHINESE (ORIENTAL) CULTURE AND SOCIETY. A. 1952 (no. 2) (1958: no. 7). Kyoto Daigaku Bungakubu Shina Tetsugakushi Kenkyushitsu [Department of Chinese Philosophy, Faculty of Letters, Kyoto Univ.], Yoshidahon-machi, Sakyo-ku, Kyoto. Ed: Toshio Shigesawa.

Art. on the hist. of Chinese philosophy and literature; in Japanese and English; Chinese sum. ¥ 150

TOYO UNIVERSITY, THE HISTORICAL STUDIES OF THE see HAKUSAN SHIGAKU

166. TOYOSHI KENKYU [Studies in Oriental history]. THE JOURNAL OF ORIENTAL RESEARCHES. Q. 1935 (1958: vol. 17). Toyoshi Kenkyukai [Soc. of Oriental Researches], c/o Kyoto Daigaku Bungakubu Toyoshi Kenkyushitsu [Inst. of Oriental Researches, Faculty of Letters, Kyoto Univ.], Yoshidahon-machi, Sakyo-ku, Kyoto. Ed: Ichisada Miyazaki. Art. on the political, economic, cultural and intellectual hist. of China; bk. rev.; biblio.; news of new pub.; reports of the soc.; in Japanese and English; English sum.; maps. p (1) ¥ 130

TRANSACTIONS OF THE ASIATIC SOCIETY OF JAPAN see ASIATIC SOCIETY OF JAPAN, TRANSACTIONS OF THE

TRANSACTIONS OF THE INTERNATIONAL CONFERENCE OF ORIENTALISTS IN JAPAN see INTERNATIONAL CONFERENCE OF ORIENTALISTS IN JAPAN, TRANSACTIONS OF THE

167. WAKAGI KOKO [Wakagi archaeology]. 10 x y. 1950 (1958: no. 1-3). Kokugakuin Daigaku Koko Gakkai [Archaeological Soc. of Kokugakuin Univ.], 9 Wakagi-cho, Shibuya-ku, Tokyo. Ed: Iwao Oba. Art. on Japanese archaeology; illus. p (1) ¥ 50 (memb.)

168. YAMATO BUNKA KENKYU [Studies of ancient Japanese culture]. The Bulletin of the Cultural Association of the Survey of Ancient Japan. B-M. 1953 (1957: vol. 4). Yamato Bunka Kenkyukai [Cultural Assoc. of the Survey of Ancient Japan], c/o Nara Kokuritsu Hakubutsukan [Nara National Museum], Nobori Oji-machi, Nara. Ed: Akio Koizumi. Art. on the ancient hist. and archaeology of Japan; bk. rev.; in Japanese; illus. nfs

Korea

Note: The McCune-Reischauer system has been used below for the transliteration of Korean words.

PEOPLE'S DEMOCRATIC REPUBLIC OF KOREA (NORTH KOREA)

Prepared with the assistance of

Chaoying Fang, Berkeley, California

1. CHOSŎN CHUNGANG YŎNGAM [Korean central yearbook]. A. (1959). Chosŏn Chungang T'ongsinsa [Korean Central News], Pyŏngyang. Art. on Korean and international affairs; in Korean. 360 wŏn

2. MUNHWA YUSAN [Cultural heritage]. B-M. (1960: no. 3). Kogohak mit Minsokhak Yonguso, Kwahagwon, Chosŏn Minjujuŭi Inmin Konghwaguk [Archaeological and Folkloric Research Inst., Acad. of Sciences, Korean Democratic People's Republic], Pyŏngyang. Art. on the prehist. and ancient hist. of Korea and on Korean archaeology, art, culture and folklore; bk. rev.; in Korean; table of contents also in Russian and Chinese; illus. p (1) 80 chŏn

3. YOKSA KWAHAK [Historical sciences]. B-M. (1960: no. 3). Yŏksa Yŏnguso, Kwahagwŏn, Chosŏn Minjujuŭi Inmin Konghwaguk [Hist. Research Inst., Acad. of Sciences, Korean Democratic People's Republic], Pyŏngyang. Art. on Korean political, economic and social hist., with emphasis on the modern period; in Korean. p (1) 70 chŏn

REPUBLIC OF KOREA (SOUTH KOREA)

Prepared with the assistance of the

Asiatic Research Center, Korea University, Seoul

1. ASEA YŎN'GU [Asiatic studies]. THE JOURNAL OF ASIATIC STUDIES. S-A. 1958 (1959: vol. 2). Asiatic Research Center, Korea Univ., 1 Anam-dong, Sŏngbuk-ku, Seoul. Ed: Sang-eun Lee. Art. on the hist., politics, language, culture and soc. of Korea and its neighbors; in Korean and English; English sum.; doc.; statistics; graph. Hwan 3000

2. ASIATIC RESEARCH BULLETIN. M. Asiatic Research Center, Korea Univ., Seoul. Each issue contains one hist. art.; news of the center; news of academic activities in South Korea; biblio. nfs / $ 4

3. CHINDAN HAKPO [Chindan (Korea) journal]. A. 1934 (1959: vol. 20). Chindan Soc., National Museum of Korea, Chŏngdong, Sŏdaemun-gu, Seoul. Ed:

Kim Chae-wŏn. Art. on the culture, hist., language, literature and folklore of Korea and its neighbors; English sum.; illus. Hwan 900 / $ 3

4. CH'ULP'AN YŎN'GAM [Publishing yearbook]. A. Korean Pub. Yearbk. Co., 109 1st St., Inhyŏn-dong, Chung-gu, Seoul. Hwan 3500

5. CHUNGANG ECONOMIC REVIEW. KYŎNGSANG HAKPO. S-A. Students' Research Club of Economics and Commerce, Chungang Univ., Seoul. In English and Korean. nfs

6. CHUNGDALE NONMUNJIP [Collections of Chungang University theses]. A. Chungang Univ., Seoul. In Korean, English and German; illus. available on exchange basis

7. HAN' GŬL [The Korean language]. Q. Korean Language Acad., 58 1st St., Sinmun-no, Chongno-gu, Seoul. Hwan 300

8. HAPTONG YŎN'GAM [Haptong yearbook]. A. Haptong News Agency, 101, 1-ka, Ulchiro, Seoul. Art. on Korean and world affairs; calendar of Korean and world events; doc.; statistics. Hwan 8000 / $ 16

9. HYANGT'O SEOUL [Hometown Seoul]. Q. Committee for the Compilation of the Hist. of Seoul City, City Hall, Seoul. nfs

10. INMUN KWAHAK [The humanitics]. A. College of Literature, Yonsei Univ., 134 Sinch'on-dong, Sŏdaemun-gu, Seoul. nfs

THE JOURNAL OF ASIATIC STUDIES see ASEA YŎN'GU

THE KOREAN HISTORICAL REVIEW see YOKSA HAKPO

11. KOREANA QUARTERLY. S-A. International Research Center, 282 Nagwŏn-dong, Chongno-gu, Seoul. In English and German. Hwan 2000/$2

12. KORYŎ TAEHAKKYO KYŎNGSANG NONCH'ONG [Korea University collection of theses on economics and commerce]. A. College of Commerce, Korea Univ., 1 Anam-dong, Sŏngbuk-ku, Seoul. nfs

13. KORYŎ TAEHAKKYO MULLI NONJIP [Korea University collection of theses on the humanities and sciences]. A. College of Liberal Arts and Sciences, Korea Univ., 1 Anam-dong, Sŏngbuk-ku, Seoul. nfs

14. KUGŎ KUNGMUNHAK [National language and literature]. Q. National Language and Literature Acad., 18 Kwanhun-dong, Chongno-gu, Seoul. Hwan 300

15. KYŎNGJE YŎN'GAM [Economic yearbook]. A. Bank of Korea Research Dept., 110 2nd St., Namdaemun-no, Chung-gu, Seoul. Hwan 3000

16. KYŎNGJEHAK NONJIP ["Journal of Economics and Business Administration"]. S-A. Inst. of Economic Research, Chungyang Univ., Seoul. In Korean; English sum.; illus. nfs

KYŎNGSANG HAKPO see CHUNGANG ECONOMIC REVIEW

17. MUYŎK YŎN'GAM [Trade yearbook]. A. Korean Trade Assoc., 123 2nd St., Namdaemun-no, Chung-gu, Seoul. Hwan 5000

18. NONGŎP YŎN'GAM [Yearbook of agriculture]. A. Agricultural Bank Research Dept., 75 1st St., Ch'ungjŏng-no, Sŏdaemun-gu, Seoul. Hwan 3500

19. PŎPCHŎNG NONCH'ONG [Review of law and political science]. S-A. Students' Assoc., College of Law and Political Science, Chungang Univ., Seoul. Illus. nfs

20. ROYAL ASIATIC SOCIETY, TRANSACTIONS OF THE KOREA BRANCH OF THE. A. 1900 (1958: vol. 34). Council of the Korea Branch, Royal Asiatic Soc., c/o British Embassy, Seoul. Ed: Horace G. Underwood. Art. on Koreanology; quotations from original Korean texts; report of the council; occasionally illus. Hwan 1000 / $ 2

SAHAK' YONGU see next entry

21. SAHAK YUENKU (Sahak Yongu) ["The Study of History"]. Q. 1958 (1959: no vol. indic.). Hankuk Sahak Hoe [Hist. Soc. of Korea], 1 Sechong-no Chongno-Ku, Seoul. Ed: Sin Sŏk-ho. Art. on hist., with emphasis on Korea; biblio.; doc.; professional news; English sum.; graph; statistics. Hwan 500

22. SAHOE KWAHAK [Journal of social sciences]. S-A. 1958 (1958: no. 1-2). Korean Social Sciences Research Soc., c/o Social Sciences Research Library, 198 Kwanhun Dong, Chongno-Ku, Seoul. Ed: Yi Pyŏng-do, Graduate School, Seoul National Univ., Seoul. Art. on the humanities and social sciences; bk. rev.; professional news; in Korean and occasionally English; English sum.; table of contents also in English; illus. Hwan 800

23. SEOUL TAEHAKKYO NONMUNJIP [Seoul National University journal]. Inmun Sahoe Kwahak [Humanities and social sciences]. S-A. 1954 (1959: no. 8). Research Committee, Graduate School, Seoul National Univ., Tongsung-dong, Chongno-Ku, Seoul. Ed. board: Yi Pyŏngdo, Yi Sungnyŏng, Chang Pal, Kim Chŭnghan, Yun T'aerim. Art. on the humanities and social sciences, not restricted to Korea; in Korean and English; illus. nfs

24. TONGBANG HAKCHI [Journal of Far Eastern studies]. A. 1954 (1959: vol. 4). Inst. of Far Eastern Studies, Yonsei Univ., 134 Sinchon, Sodaimun-ku, Seoul. Ed: George L. Paik. Art. on the hist. and culture of the Far East, with emphasis on Korea. Hwan 3000 / $ 5

TRANSACTIONS OF THE KOREA BRANCH OF THE ROYAL ASIATIC SOCIETY see ROYAL ASIATIC SOCIETY, TRANSACTIONS OF THE KOREA BRANCH OF THE

25. YOKSA HAKPO [Historical journal]. THE KOREAN HISTORICAL REVIEW. Irr. (A. or S-A). 1952 (1958: no. 10). Yŏksa Hakhoe Hist. Soc., c/o Sasang Ge Sa, Chongno-Ku, Seoul. Ed: Hong I-Sŏp. Art. on all periods of Korean and Chinese hist. and occasionally on the hist. of other countries; bk. rev., primarily of Korean, Japanese, English and American bk. dealing with Korean hist.; professional news; list of pub. received by the soc.; biblio. of art.; table of contents also in English. Hwan 1200 / $ 2

Mongolian People's Republic

Prepared with the assistance of

C.R. Bawden, Lecturer in Mongolian, School of Oriental and African Studies, University of London

Note: As Mongolian now uses the Cyrillic alphabet, Mongolian words in this list have been transcribed according to the system used by the Library of Congress, Washington, D.C., for the transliteration of Russian. The two special Mongol letters θ and Y have been transcribed as ö and ü respectively.

1. EDIĬN ZASAG [Economics]. 5 - 6 x y. BNMA Ulsyn Tölövlögöönii Komiss [State Planning Commission of the People's Republic of Mongolia], Ulan Bator. In Mongolian. Up to 1959, no. 2, pub. under the title: Ediĭn Zasgiĭn Asuudluud [Questions of economics]. p (1) Tugrik 2.50 / DM 15 (p.a.)

EDIĬN ZASGIĬN ASUUDLUUD see EDIĬN ZASAG

2. SHINZHLEKH UKHAAN [Science]. B-M. Deed Bolovsrolyn Khüreelen [Committee of Sciences and Higher Education], Ulan Bator. All fields of learning, including hist. and archaeology; in Mongolian; table of contents also in Russian. p (1) Tugrik 3 / DM 12 (p.a.)

3. SOVREMENNAIA MONGOLIIA [Contemporary Mongolia]. M. Information and Broadcasting Dept. of the Mongolian People's Republic, ul. Stalina 59, Ulan Bator. Includes hist. art. of popular interest; in Russian; illus. DM 7.20

Taiwan

(FORMOSA)

Prepared with the assistance of

Chen Tsu-lung, Institut des Hautes Etudes Chinoises, University of Paris

Note: The Wade-Giles system has been used below for the transliteration of Chinese words.

ACADEMIA SINICA, ANNALS OF see CHUNG-YANG YEN-CHIU YÜAN YÜAN-K'AN

ANNALS OF ACADEMIA SINICA see CHUNG-YANG YEN-CHIU YÜAN YÜAN-K'AN

BULLETIN OF THE CHINESE ASSOCIATION FOR THE ADVANCEMENT OF SCIENCE see CHINESE ASSOCIATION FOR THE ADVANCEMENT OF SCIENCE, BULLETIN OF THE

BULLETIN OF THE RESEARCH INSTITUTE OF EDUCATION OF TAIWAN NORMAL UNIVERSITY see T'AI-WAN SHÊNG-LI SHIH-FAN TA-HSÜEH CHIAO-YÜ YEN-CHIU SO CHI-K'AN

1. CHÊNG-CHIH P'ING-LUN [Political critic]. B-W. Nan-ching chêng-chih p'ing-lun Shê [Nanking Political Critic Soc.], 26 West Ning-po Chieh, Taipeh. NT $48

2. CHÊNG-LUN CHOU-K'AN [Political weekly]. China Critic. W. 1956 (1957: no. 105-129). Chung-kuo Hsin-wên Ch'u-pan Kung-ssŭ [China News Press], 25 Lane 16, Section 2, North Chung-shan Rd., Taipeh. Art. on world hist., literature, language, politics, economics and sociology, with emphasis on the cultural problems; biographies; bk. rev.; news and notes on world events; table of contents in Chinese and English; photographs of and notes on the writers and artists. Former titles: San-min Chu-i Pan-yüeh-k'an [The three people's principles, a fortnightly] and Chu-i Yü Kuo-ts'ê [Dogma and national strategy]. p (1) NT $3 / p (1) $0.15

CHIAO-YÜ T'UNG-HSÜN see CHIAO-YÜ YÜ WÊN-HUA

CHIAO-YÜ YEN-CHIU SO CHI-K'AN see T'AI WAN SHÊNG-LI SHIH-FAN TA-HSÜEH CHIAO-YÜ YEN-CHIU SO CHI-K'AN

3. CHIAO-YÜ YÜ WÊN-HUA [Education and culture]. B-W (W up to end of 1958). 1955 (1957/58: no. 138-158). T'ai-wan Shu-tien [Taiwan Bk. Co.], 14, Section 1, South Ch'ung-ch'ing Rd., Taipeh. Ed. address: 11 South Chung-shan Rd., Taipeh. Art. on general hist. and cultural studies; doc. and reports on the intellectual hist. of modern China; news and notes on Chinese cultural activities (at home and abroad); rev. art.; illus.; every 5th vol. contains a cum. index of art. From 1949 to 1954 (vol. 1-5) pub. under the title: Chiao-yü T'ung-hsün [Bulletin of education]. NT $5

CHIN-JIH CHUNG-KUO see CHINA TODAY

CHINA NEWSWEEK see CHUNG-KUO I-CHOU

4. CHINA TODAY. CHIN-JIH CHUNG-KUO. An English Language Monthly. M. 1958 (1958: no vol. indic.). China Today Soc., in collaboration with Chinese Inst. of Translation and Research, 11 Lane 44, Chin-mên Rd., Taipeh. Art. on hist. (mostly modern), education, philosophy, religion, language, literature, agriculture, economics, politics, sociology, international relations and local hist.; bk. rev.; illus. NT $ 90

5. CHINESE ASSOCIATION FOR THE ADVANCEMENT OF SCIENCE, BULLETIN OF THE. M. Chinese Assoc. for the Advancement of Science, 59 Kuan-ch'ien Rd., Taipeh. NT $ 84 / $ 4

6. CHINESE CULTURE. CHUNG-KUO WÊN-HUA. Q. 1957 (1957/58: vol. 1). Chinese Culture Research Inst., Ministry of Education, Taipeh. Ed: Chang Ch'i-yün, 11 South Chung-shan Rd., Taipeh. Art. on Chinese civilization from ancient times to the present; bk. rev.; doc. NT $ 170

7. THE CHINESE MAGAZINE. M. Hengtse Tu, P.O.B. 270, Taipeh. In English. NT $ 36 / $ 3

8. CH'ING-HUA HSÜEH-PAO [Tsing Hua journal]. TSING-HUA JOURNAL OF CHINESE STUDIES. S-A. 1956 (new series) (1956/57: vol. 1). Pub. address: 77 Chung-hua Rd., Taipeh. Ed: Franklin L. Ho (Ed. address in the U.S.A.: P.O.B. 661, New Haven, Conn.). Art. on all fields of the study of social and natural sciences, with emphasis on Chinese cultural hist.; rev. art.; bk. rev.; in Chinese, with English sum., or in English; table of contents in Chinese and English. Formerly pub. in Peking. $ 3

CHU-I YÜ KUO-TS'Ê see CHÊNG-LUN CHOU-K'AN

9. CHUNG-HUA K'O-HSÜEH HSIEH-CHIN HUI NIEN-HUI LUN-WÊN CHUAN-CHI [Transactions of the Chinese Association for the Advancement of Science]. Irr. Chung-hua K'o-hsüeh Hsieh-chin Hui, 59 Kuan-ch'ien Rd., Taipeh. pni

10. CHUNG-HUA K'O-HSÜEH HUA-PAO [Chinese science illustrated]. CHUNG-HUA POPULAR SCIENCE. M. Chung-hua K'o-hsüeh Kung-ssŭ [China Scientific Co.], 1618 Chung-chêng Rd., Taipeh. NT $ 40

11. CHUNG-HUA NIEN-PAO [Chinese yearbook]. 4-5 x y. 1953 (1957: vol. 4). Chung-kuo Hsin-wên Ch'u-pan Shê [China News Press], 25 Lane 16, Section 2, North Chung-shan Rd., Taipeh. Ed. board: Chiao-yü yü Wên-hua Shê [Educational and Cultural Assoc.], 11 South Chung-shan Rd., Taipeh. Art. on all periods and aspects of Chinese cultural hist.; hist. papers on international politics, economics, literature and art subjects; doc. and rev. art.; tables of contents in Chinese and English. Vol. 1 (1953) appeared under the title: Chung-kuo Nien-pao [Chinese yearbook]. NT $ 120

CHUNG-HUA POPULAR SCIENCE see CHUNG-HUA K'O-HSÜEH HUA-PAO

12. CHUNG-KUO I-CHOU [China weekly]. CHINA NEWSWEEK. W. Chung-kuo Hsin-wên Ch'u-pan Shê [China News Press], 25 Lane 16, Section 2,

North Chung-shan Rd., Taipeh. Table of contents in Chinese and English; notes on the contributors; illus. p (1) NT$3 / p (1) $0.10

CHUNG-KUO NIEN-PAO see CHUNG-HUA NIEN-PAO

CHUNG-KUO WÊN-HUA see CHINESE CULTURE

13. CHUNG-KUO YÜ-WÊN YÜEH-K'AN [Chinese language monthly]. M. Taiwan Provincial Normal Univ., East Ho-p'ing Rd., Taipeh. NT $60

14. CHUNG-YANG YEN-CHIU YÜAN LI-SHIH YÜ-YEN YEN-CHIU SO CHI-K'AN [Bulletin of the Institute of History and Philology, Academia Sinica]. Irr. 1928 (1957/58: vol. 29). Chung-yang Yen-chiu Yüan Li-shih Yü-yen Yen-chiu So, Nan Kang, Taipeh. Well-documented art. on the hist. and philology of China, ancient and modern; reports on archaeological findings; dissertations on international cultural relations; rev. art.; bk. rev.; biographies; in Chinese and occasionally in English; table of contents in Chinese and English; illus. Formerly pub. under the title: Kuo-li Chung-yang Yen-chiu Yüan Li-shih Yü-yen Yen-chiu So Chi-k'an [Bulletin of the National Institute of History and Philology, Academia Sinica]. pv (p (1) NT $30-50)

15. CHUNG-YANG YEN-CHIU YÜAN MIN-TSU-HSÜEH YEN-CHIU SO CHI-K'AN [Bulletin of the Institute of Ethnology, Academia Sinica]. S-A. Chung-yang Yen-chiu Yüan Min-tsu-hsüeh Yen-chiu So, Nan Kang, Taipeh. Art. in Chinese or English; English sum. of Chinese-language art.; table of contents in Chinese and English; illus. $ 4

16. CHUNG-YANG YEN-CHIU YÜAN YÜAN-K'AN. ANNALS OF ACADEMIA SINICA. A. 1954 (mri 1956: no. 3). Chung-yang Yen-chiu Yüan, Taipeh. Ed: Li Chi. Art. on all fields of research, chiefly concerning the cultural hist. of East Asian countries; rev. art.; occasional English sum. of Chinese-language art.; in Chinese or English; table of contents in Chinese and English; illus. In 1954 pub. under the title: Kuo-li Chung-yang Yen-chiu Yüan Yüan-k'an [Annals of the National Academia Sinica]. p (1) NT $50

17. THE FREE CHINA FORTNIGHTLY. B-W. Ed: Lei Chin, No. 1, Lane 18, Ho Ping Tung Rd. (Section II), Taipeh. NT $96 / $10

HSIN SHÊNG-LI see THE LIVING FORCE

18. HSIN SSŬ-CH'AO [New tide]. M. Chung-hua Wên-hua Ch'u-pan Shih-yeh Wei-yüan Hui [China Cultural Pub. Foundation], 1730 Chung Cheng Rd., 2nd floor, Taipeh. Ceased pub. in 1958. NT $ 90

19. HSÜEH-SHU CHI-K'AN ["Academic Quarterly"]. Q. 1952 (1957/58: vol. 6). Chung-hua Wên-hua Ch'u-pan Shih-yeh Wei-yüan Hui [China Cultural Pub. Foundation], Taipeh, for Hsüeh-shu Chi-k'an Shê [Academic Quarterly Soc.], 1730 Chung-chêng Rd., Taipeh. Art. on Chinese hist. (ancient and modern), language, literature, archaeology, geography, architecture, art, philosophy, religion, politics, local hist. and other socio-economic topics; notes and reports on international cultural relations; bk. rev.; tables of contents in Chinese and English; occasional notes on museums and libraries (at home and abroad). NT $45

JOURNAL OF THE RESEARCH INSTITUTE OF CHINESE LITERATURE OF TAIWAN NORMAL UNIVERSITY see T'AI-WAN SHÊNG-LI SHIH-FAN TA-HSÜEH KUO-WÊN YEN-CHIU SO CHI-K'AN

K'AO-KU JÊN-LEI HSÜEH-K'AN see KUO LI T'AI-WAN TA-HSÜEH K'AO-KU JÊN-LEI HSÜEH-K'AN

20. K'O-HSÜEH CHIAO-YÜ ["Science Education"]. B-M. 1955 (1959: vol. 5). Chung-kuo Tzu-jan K'o-hsüeh Ts'u-chin Hui [Chinese Assoc. for the Advancement of Natural Science], P.O.B. 143, Taipeh. Ed: Chang I-tsun. Art. on science and the hist. of science, scientific education and development in China and international scientific research works; translations; extracts; biographies; news and notes on the assoc.; illus. NT $ 25

21. K'O-HSÜEH HUI-PAO [Science reports]. M (2 vol. p.a.). Chung-hua K'o-hsüeh Hsieh-chin-hui [Chinese Assoc. for the Advancement of Science], 59 Kuan-ch'ien Rd., Taipeh. Address in U.S.A.: Mei Tai-chi, 125 East 65th St., New York 21, N.Y. Humanities and natural and applied sciences. NT $ 42 / $ 3

KUO-LI CHUNG-YANG YEN-CHIU YÜAN LI-SHIH YÜ-YEN YEN-CHIU SO CHI-K'AN see CHUNG-YANG YEN-CHIU YÜAN LI-SHIH YÜ-YEN YEN-CHIU SO CHI-K'AN

KUO-LI CHUNG-YANG YEN-CHIU YÜAN YÜAN-K'AN see CHUNG-YANG YEN-CHIU YÜAN YÜAN-K'AN

22. KUO-LI T'AI-WAN TA-HSÜEH K'AO-KU JÊN-LEI HSÜEH-K'AN [Archaeological and anthropological bulletin of the Taiwan National University]. Bulletin of the Department of Archaeology and Anthropology. S-A. 1953 (1958: no. 11-12). Kuo-li T'ai-wan Ta-hsüeh, Wên-hsüeh Yüan [Faculty of Letters, Taiwan National Univ.], Taipeh. Ed: Li Chi. Art. on archaeology and cultural anthropology, pertaining mostly to Taiwan, but dealing also with China and other parts of Asia; "Frontispiece," "Original Articles," "Field Notes," "Illustrated Description of Department Collections," "Miscellaneous Notes" (short art.); bk. rev.; professional and academic news; list of pub. received; in Chinese and English; occasional English sum.; illus. NT $ 60 / $ 3

KUO-WÊN YEN-CHIU SO CHI-K'AN see T'AI-WAN SHÊNG-LI SHIH-FAN TA-HSÜEH KUO-WÊN YEN-CHIU SO CHI-K'AN

LI-SHIH YÜ-YEN YEN-CHIU SO CHI-K'AN see CHUNG-YANG YEN-CHIU YÜAN LI-SHIH YÜ-YEN YEN-CHIU SO CHI-K'AN

23. THE LIVING FORCE. HSIN SHÊNG-LI. The Leading English Language Pictorial in Free China. M. Pub. address: P.O.B. 470, Taipeh. In English; Chinese abstr. NT $ 100

MIN-TSU-HSÜEH YEN-CHIU SO CHI-K'AN see CHUNG-YANG YEN-CHIU YÜAN MIN-TSU-HSÜEH YEN-CHIU SO CHI-K'AN

24. NUNG-LIN HSÜEH-PAO ["Agriculture and Forestry Journal"]. A. T'ai-wan Shêng-li Nung-hsüeh Yüan [Taiwan Provincial College of Agriculture], 1 Kuo-kuang Rd., Taichung. In Chinese; English sum.; table of contents in Chinese and English; illus. NT $ 20

RESEARCH INSTITUTE OF CHINESE LITERATURE OF TAIWAN NORMAL UNIVERSITY, JOURNAL OF THE see T'AI-WAN SHÊNG-LI SHIH-FAN TA-HSËUH, KUO-WÊN YEN-CHIU SO CHI-K'AN

RESEARCH INSTITUTE OF EDUCATION OF TAIWAN NORMAL UNIVERSITY, BULLETIN OF THE see T'AI-WAN SHÊNG-LI SHIH-FAN TA-HSÜEH CHIAO-YÜ YEN-CHIU SO CHI-K'AN

SAN-MIN CHU-I PAN-YÜEH-K'AN see CHÊNG-LUN CHOU-K'AN

25. SHE HUI K'O-HSÜEH LUN T'SUNG [Social science collected papers]. Journal of Social Science. A. (no vol. in 1957). 1950 (1959: vol. 9). Kuo-li T'ai-wan Ta-hsüeh Fa-hsüeh Yüan [College of Law, Taiwan National Univ.], 1 Hsü-chou Rd., Taipeh. Art. on the social sciences, including hist. (dealing with all areas and periods, mostly recent), with emphasis on law, govt. and economics; commercial statistics; table of contents also in English; cum. table of contents (in Chinese) for vol. 1-7 in vol. 8. NT $ 40

26. SHIH-TA HSÜEH-PAO [Normal University journal]. Bulletin of Taiwan Normal University. A. 1956 (1959: vol. 4). T'ai-wan Shêng-li Shih-fan Ta-hsüeh [Taiwan Provincial Normal Univ.], East Ho-p'ing Rd., Taipeh. Art. on Chinese hist., literature, philosophy, archaeology, art, linguistics, geography and other social sciences; rev. art.; table of contents in Chinese and English; illus. NT $ 30

STUDIA TAIWANICA see T'AI-WAN YEN-CHIU

27. TA-LU TSA-CHIH ["Continent Magazine"]. B-W. 1950 (1958: vol. 17). Pub. address: 13 Ch'üan Chou St., Taipeh. Ed: Tung Tso-pin. Art. on the social sciences, with emphasis on Chinese hist. and culture; bk. rev.; news; accounts of travels; biographies; research reports on the hist. of Taiwan; correspondence; every 6th issue of the vol. carries a general subject index; occasional special issues; illus. NT $ 100

TA-LU TSA-CHIH T'Ê-K'AN see TA-LU TSA-CHIH

28. T'AI-WAN SHÊNG-LI SHIH-FAN TA-HSÜEH CHIAO-YÜ YEN-CHIU SO CHI-K'AN. BULLETIN OF THE RESEARCH INSTITUTE OF EDUCATION OF TAIWAN NORMAL UNIVERSITY. Irr. 1958 (1959: vol. 2). T'ai-wan Sheng-li Shih-fan Ta-hsüeh, East Ho-p'ing Rd., Taipeh. Art. on the hist., soc., education, politics, economy, language and literature of ancient and modern China; table of contents in Chinese and English. p (1) NT $ 20

29. T'AI-WAN SHÊNG-LI SHIH-FAN TA-HSÜEH KUO-WÊN YEN-CHIU SO CHI-K'AN. JOURNAL OF THE RESEARCH INSTITUTE OF CHINESE LITERATURE OF TAIWAN NORMAL UNIVERSITY. A. 1957 (1959: no. 3). T'ai-wan Shêng-li Shih-fan Ta-hsüeh, East Ho-p'ing Rd., Taipeh. Art. on all fields and periods of the culture of China, with emphasis on hist., philosophy, literature and art; table of contents in Chinese and English. NT $ 30 / $ 0.70

30. T'AI-WAN YEN-CHIU [Studies on Formosa]. STUDIA TAIWANICA. S-A. 1956 (mri 1956: no. 1). Assoc. for the Advancement of Taiwan Culture, 54 Nan-hai Rd., Taipeh. Ed. address: 2 Lane 76, Section 3, South Hsin-shêng Rd., Taipeh. Art. on all fields and periods of the hist. of Taiwan, with emphasis on archaeology, geography, anthropology and archival hist.; in Chinese with English sum., or in English, with Chinese abstr.; table of contents in Chinese and English. NT $ 30

TSING HUA JOURNAL OF CHINESE STUDIES see CH'ING-HUA HSÜEH-PAO

31. TZU-YŬ CHUNG-KUO ["Free China"]. B-W. 1949 (1960: vol. 22). Tzŭ-yu Chung-kuo Shê [Free China Soc.], 1 Lane 18, Section 2, East Ho-p'ing Rd., Taipeh. Art. on Chinese hist., sociology, literature, philosophy, domestic and international politics, economics, and law, and occasionally on diplomatic, political and economic hist.; bk. rev.; correspondence; notes and news. p (1) NT $4 / $0.30 (airmail); $0.15 (surface mail)

32. WÊN-HSIEN CHUAN-K'AN [Documentary papers]. T'ai-Wan Wên-hsien. Report of Historico-Geographical Studies of Taiwan. S-A (2 double no.). 1950 (mri 1954: vol. 5). T'ai-wan Shêng Wên-hsien Wêi-yüan Hui [Hist. Research Commission of Taiwan Province], 111 Yien Ping Rd., South, Taipeh. Ed: Lin Hsiung-hsiang. Art. on all fields and periods of the hist. of Taiwan, with emphasis on the cultural relations between Taiwan and surrounding countries; notes and reports on archaeological findings; bk. rev.; correspondence; annotated translations of important papers on the hist. of Taiwan; table of contents in Chinese and English; occasional special issues or separate brochures. pni

33. WÊN-SHIH-CHÊ HSÜEH-PAO [Journal of literature, history, philosophy]. Bulletin of the College of Arts, National Taiwan University. Irr. 1950 (1958: vol. 8). Kuo-li T'ai-wan Ta'hsüeh Wên-hsüeh Yüan [Arts College, National Taiwan Univ.], Taipeh. Art. on Chinese hist., philosophy, sociology, literature, archaeology and art; annotated translations of papers on international cultural relations; bk. rev.; table of contents in Chinese and English; illus. NT $60 / $4

Readers searching for a periodical are also advised to see the ADDENDA sections included at the end of some lists

EUROPE

Albania

Prepared with the assistance of

Francis S. Wagner, Library of Congress, Washington, D. C.

BULETIN I UNIVERSITETIT SHTETËROR TË TIRANËS see UNIVERSITETITI SHTETËROR TË TIRANËS, BULETIN I ...

1. BULETIN PËR SHKENCAT SHOQERORE [Bulletin for social sciences]. Q. 1947 (1959: no. vol. indic.). Institut i Shkencave [Inst. of Sciences], Tirana. Ed. board: Stefanaq Pollo (chief ed.), Aleksander Xhuvani, Aleks Buda, Androkli Kostallari. Art. on hist. and the social sciences, with emphasis on Albania, neighboring countries, and the "people's democratic republics"; doc.; bk. rev. and biblio. survey; French sum.; table of contents in Albanian and French. p(1) Leks 50

2. UNIVERSITETI SHTETËROR TË TIRANËS, BULETIN I... [Bulletin of the Tirana State University]. Seria Shkencat Shoqerore [Social science series]. Q. 1947 (1959: vol. 13). Universiteti Shtetëror i Tiranës [Tirana State Univ.], Tirana. Ed. board: Petro Lalaj (chief ed.), Aleks Buda, Alfred Uçi, Androkli Kostallari. Art. on social and hist. sciences, with emphasis on Albania, neighboring countries and the "people's democratic republics"; discussions; news and notes of scholarly interest; French sum.; table of contents in Albanian and French. p (1) Leks 50

Austria

Prepared with the assistance of
Karl Selber, Historisches Institut,
University of Vienna

1. ADLER [Eagle]. Zeitschrift für Genealogie und Heraldik [Journal of genealogy and heraldry]. B-M. 1871 (1956-58: vol. 4 [18], 74th-76th year). Heraldisch-Genealogische Gesellschaft "Adler," Haarhof 4a, Wien I. Ed: Franz Gall, Dr. Karl-Lueger-Ring 1, Wien I. Art. on genealogy and heraldry, almost exclusively of the Habsburg Empire and Germany; bk. rev.; supplement: Austrian genealogical list. S 60 / $ 5

ALMANACH. For titles beginning with "Almanach," followed by the name of the publishing or sponsoring institution or society, see the respective institution or society.

2. ANTHROPOLOGISCHE GESELLSCHAFT IN WIEN, MITTEILUNGEN DER... (Mitteilungen der Anthropologischen Gesellschaft in Wien) [Communications of the Anthropological Society of Vienna]. 1-3 x y. Ferdinand Berger, Horn, for Anthropologische Gesellschaft in Wien, Burgring 7, Wien I. Art. on anthropology, prehist. and cultural hist.; bk. rev.; professional news; minutes of meetings; illus. S 150

ANZEIGER. For titles beginning with "Anzeiger," followed by the name of the publishing or sponsoring institution or society, see the respective institution or society.

3. ANZEIGER FÜR DIE ALTERTUMSWISSENSCHAFT [News on the study of antiquity]. Q. Universitätsverlag Wagner, Innrain 27/29, Innsbruck, for Österreichische Humanistische Gesellschaft, Innsbruck. Philology, philosophy and literature. S 92 / S 116

4. ARCHAEOLOGIA AUSTRIACA. Beiträge zur Paläanthropologie, Ur- und Frühgeschichte Österreichs [Contributions on pale-anthropology, the prehistory and early history of Austria]. S-A. 1948 (1958: no. 23 and 24). Franz Deuticke, Helferstorferstr. 4, Wien I, for Urgeschichtliches Institut, Universität Wien, Hanuschgasse 3/1, Wien. Ed: Richard Pittioni. Art. on Austrian prehist., early hist. and pale-anthropology; special section on research in mining in prehist. and early hist. times; bk. rev.; illus., maps. p(1) S 72 / DM 12

5. ARCHIV FÜR ORIENTFORSCHUNG [Archives for Oriental research]. Internationale Zeitschrift für die Wissenschaft vom Vorderen Orient [International journal for studies of the Near East]. A. (1 part p.a., 2 parts constituting a vol.). 1923 (1957/58: vol. 18). Pub. and ed: Ernst F. Weidner, Goethestr. 43, Graz. Art. on all fields of the study of antiquity (including archaeology and the hist. of art), pertaining to Mesopotamia, Egypt, Iran and Arabia; reports on explorations and excavations; professional news; bk. rev.; detailed biblio. of bk. and art., classified by area; in English, French or German; illus.; reproductions of papyri. S 420 / DM 70

6. ARCHIV FÜR ÖSTERREICHISCHE GESCHICHTE [Archives for Austrian history]. Irr. 1848 (1955-57: vol. 121). R.M. Rohrer, Singerstr. 12, Wien I, for Historische Kommission, Österreichische Akademie der Wissenschaften, Dr. Ignaz Seipelplatz 2, Wien I. Ed: Leo Santifaller. Art. on the hist. of Austria from the Middle Ages to the present. pv (c. S 70-174 / $ 2.80-6.80)

7. ARCHIV FÜR VÖLKERKUNDE [Archives of ethnology]. A. 1946 (1957: vol. 12). Wilhelm Braumüller, Wien, for Museum für Völkerkunde, Wien, and the soc. "Freunde der Völkerkunde," Wien. Ed: Etta Becker-Donner, Annemarie Schweeger-Hefel. Art. on ethnology, past and present, and related fields; bk. rev.; illus., maps. pv (e.g., S 70 / $2.80; S 174 / $ 6.80)

8. BIBLOS. Österreichische Zeitschrift für Buch- und Bibliothekswesen, Dokumentation, Bibliographie und Bibliophilie [Austrian journal for book and library science, documentation, bibliography and bibliophily]. Q. Gesellschaft der Freunde der Österreichischen Nationalbibliothek, Josefsplatz 1, Wien I, Vereinigung österreichischer Bibliothekare, and Österreichische Gesellschaft für Dokumentation und Bibliographie. S 40 / $ 2.50

9. BLÄTTER FÜR HEIMATKUNDE [Bulletin for local history]. Q. Historischer Verein für Steiermark, Hamerlinggasse 3, Graz. S 40

10. BLÄTTER FÜR TECHNIKGESCHICHTE [Bulletin for the history of technology]. A. 1932 (1958: vol. 20). Technisches Museum für Industrie und Gewerbe, Forschungsinstitut für Technikgeschichte, Mariahilferstr. 212, Wien XIV. Ed: Josef Nagler. Art. on the hist. of technology in Austria; notes and news; bk. rev. pv (S 40 / $ 1.55 - S 60 / $ 2.40

11. BURGENLÄNDISCHE HEIMATBLÄTTER [Burgenland regional bulletin]. Q. Volksbildungswerk für das Burgenland, Josef Haydngasse 11, Eisenstadt. S 35

12. CARINTHIA I. Geschichtliche und volkskundliche Beiträge zur Heimatkunde Kärntens [Historical and folkloric contributions to Carinthian local studies]. Q. Geschichtsverein für Kärnten, Museumgasse 2, Klagenfurt. Many art. of more than local importance; subject and name indices pub. for vol. 1-100 (1811-1910) in 1911, for vol. 101-125 (1911-1935) in 1936 and for vol. 126-145 (1936-1955) in 1958, each index including the Archiv für Vaterländische Geschichte und Topographie. S 50 / 2

13. CISTERCIENSERCHRONIK [Chronicle of the Cistercians]. Q. Cistercienserkloster Mehrerau, Bregenz. S 42

14. DER DONAURAUM [The Danube area]. Q. 1956 (1960: vol. 5.). Verlag Hermann Böhlaus Nachfolger GmbH, Wien, for Forschungsinstitut für den Donauraum, Schottengasse 10, Wien I. Ed: Peter Berger. Art. on all aspects and problems of the Danube area; rev. of bk. and periodicals; biblio.; reports on the meetings of the inst.; news and notes; list of bk. received. S 96 / $ 4

EUROPA ETHNICA see section on International Periodicals

15. FORUM. Österreichische Monatsblätter für kulturelle Freiheit [Austrian monthly bulletin for cultural freedom]. M. "Schriften zur Zeit," Museumstr. 5, Wien VII. S 60 / $4

16. GESELLSCHAFT FÜR DIE GESCHICHTE DES PROTESTANTISMUS IN ÖSTERREICH, JAHRBUCH DER... [Yearbook of the Society for the History of Protestantism in Austria]. A. 1880 (1958: vol. 74). Gesellschaft für die Geschichte des Protestantismus in Österreich. Ed: Wilhelm Kühnert, Sieveringerstr. 22, Wien XIX. Art. on the hist. of Protestantism in Austria; bk. rev.; place and name index; illus. pv (S 48-72)

17. GESELLSCHAFT FÜR SALZBURGER LANDESKUNDE, MITTEILUNGEN DER... [Communications of the Society for Studies of Salzburg]. A. Gesellschaft für Salzburger Landeskunde, Salzburg. S 76

18. HERALDISCH-GENEALOGISCHE GESELLSCHAFT "ADLER," NEUES JAHRBUCH DER... (Neues Jahrbuch der Heraldisch-Genealogischen Gesellschaft "Adler") [New yearbook of the Heraldic-Genealogical Society "Adler"]. Irr. 1945/46 (mri 1951-54: 3rd series, vol. 3). Heraldisch-Genealogische Gesellschaft "Adler," Haarhof 4a, Wien I. Ed: Heinz Schöny. Art. on heraldry, genealogy and general hist.; genealogical tables; reproductions of coats-of-arms. S 80 / DM 16 (memb. S 60 / DM 12)

19. HISTORISCHER VEREIN FÜR STEIERMARK, ZEITSCHRIFT DES... (Zeitschrift des Historischen Vereins für Steiermark) [Journal of the Historical Society of Styria]. A. Historischer Verein für Steiermark, Hamerlinggasse 3, Graz. S 63 / S 72 (memb. free)

20. HISTORISCHES JAHRBUCH DER STADT LINZ [Historical yearbook of the city of Linz]. A. Stadtarchiv, Stadt Linz. pv (S 60-80)

21. INSTITUT FÜR ÖSTERREICHISCHE GESCHICHTSFORSCHUNG, MITTEILUNGEN DES... (Mitteilungen des Instituts für Österreichische Geschichtsforschung) [Communications of the Institute for Austrian Historical Research]. A. (2 double or 4 single no.). 1880 (1958: vol. 66). Hermann Böhlaus Nachfolger, Frankgasse 4, Wien IX, for Institut für Österreichische Geschichtsforschung an der Universität Wien, Dr. Karl-Lueger-Ring 1, Wien I. Ed: Leo Santifaller, Heinrich Fichtenau. For the "fostering of the so-called historical auxiliary sciences in the broadest sense, with special emphasis on paleography and diplomatics as well as Austrian history and history of the Middle Ages including source study, legal, constitutional and economic history"; doc.; detailed bk. rev.; biblio. of art.; professional news; 18 supplementary vol. pub. S 150

JAHRBUCH. For titles beginning with "Jahrbuch," followed by the name of the publishing or sponsoring institution or society, see the respective institution or society.

22. JAHRBUCH FÜR LANDESKUNDE VON NIEDERÖSTERREICH [Yearbook for studies of Lower Austria]. Irr. Verein für Landeskunde von Niederösterreich und Wien, Herrengasse 13, Wien I. pv (S 35-60)

JAHRBUCH FÜR VOLKSKUNDE DER HEIMATVERTRIEBENEN see section on the Federal Republic of Germany

JAHRESHEFTE. For titles beginning with "Jahreshefte," followed by the name of the publishing or sponsoring institution or society, see the respective institution or society.

MITTEILUNGEN. For titles beginning with "Mitteilungen," followed by the name of the publishing or sponsoring institution or society, see the respective institution or society.

23. MONTFORT. Zeitschrift für Geschichte, Heimat- und Volkskunde Vorarlbergs [Journal for the history, local studies and folklore of Vorarlberg]. S-A. Vorarlberger Verlagsanstalt GmbH, Marktplatz 16, Dornbirn. S 60

24. MUSEALVEREIN WELS, JAHRBUCH DES... (Jahrbuch des Musealvereins Wels) [Yearbook of the Museum Society of Wels]. A. Musealverein Wels. S 78

25. "MUSEUM FERDINANDEUM," VERÖFFENTLICHUNGEN DES... [Publications of the "Museum Ferdinandeum"]. A. Verein Tiroler Landesmuseum Ferdinandeum, Innsbruck. pv (S 98-120)

26. NACHRICHTENBLATT FÜR DIE ÖSTERREICHISCHE UR- UND FRÜHGESCHICHTSFORSCHUNG [News bulletin for Austrian research in prehistory and early history]. B-M (3 double no. p.a.). 1952 (1958: vol. 7). Österreichische Arbeitsgemeinschaft für Ur- und Frühgeschichte and Urgeschichtliches Institut der Universität Wien, Hanuschgasse 3, Wien I. Ed: Josef Reitinger. Reports on excavations and research, new findings and congresses; chronicle of events; rev. of bk. and periodicals. S 10

NEUES JAHRBUCH DER HERALDISCH-GENEALOGISCHEN GESELLSCHAFT "ADLER" see HERALDISCH-GENEALOGISCHE GESELLSCHAFT "ADLER," NEUES JAHRBUCH DER...

27. NUMISMATISCHE ZEITSCHRIFT [Numismatic review]. B. 1869 (1957: vol. 77). Österreichische Numismatische Gesellschaft, Burgring 5, Wien I. Art. on the hist. of coins, money and finance, with emphasis on Austria and the Roman and Byzantine empires; occasional art. on economic and commercial hist.; bk. rev.; reproductions of coins. S 90

28. OBERÖSTERREICHISCHE HEIMATBLÄTTER [Upper Austrian regional bulletin]. Q. Institut für Landeskunde von Oberösterreich, Bahnhofstr. 16, Linz/D. p (1) S 20

29. OBERÖSTERREICHISCHER MUSEALVEREIN, JAHRBUCH DES... (Jahrbuch des Oberösterreichischen Musealvereins) [Yearbook of the Upper Austrian Museum Society]. A. 1840 (1958: vol. 103). Oberösterreichischer Musealverein, Museumstr. 14, Linz. Ed: Eduard Strassmayr (hist.), Wilhelm Freh (natural sciences). Art. on prehist., archaeology, hist., geography, geology and botany; rev. art.; reports of the soc. and cultural reports from Upper Austria; illus. S 40

30. OBERÖSTERREICHISCHES LANDESARCHIV, MITTEILUNGEN DES... (Mitteilungen des Oberösterreichischen Landesarchivs) [Communications of the Upper Austrian Regional Archives]. Irr. 1950 (1957: vol. 5). Hermann Böhlaus Nachfolger, Frankgasse 4, Wien IX, for Oberösterreichisches Landesarchiv, Promenade 33, Linz. Ed: Alfred Hoffmann, Hans Sturmberger. Art. on Upper Austrian hist., archival science and auxiliary sciences, of broader than local scope; maps. pv (1955: S 60; 1957: S 98)

31. ÖSTERREICH IN GESCHICHTE UND LITERATUR [Austria in history and literature]. Q. 1957 (1958: vol. 2). Arbeitskreis für österreichische Geschichte, Proschkogasse 1, Wien VI. Ed: Walter Jambor, Fuhrmanngasse 18a, Wien VIII. Art. on the hist. of Austrian literature and politics; news and notes; bk. rev. S 50

32. ÖSTERREICHISCHE AKADEMIE DER WISSENSCHAFTEN, ALMANACH DER... (Almanach der Österreichischen Akademie der Wissenschaften) [Almanac of the Austrian Academy of Sciences]. A. Österreichische Akademie der Wissenschaften, Ignaz Seipelplatz 2, Wien I. pv (S 114.30-148)

33. ÖSTERREICHISCHE AKADEMIE DER WISSENSCHAFTEN, ANZEIGER DER... (Anzeiger der Österreichischen Akademie der Wissenschaften) [News of the Austrian Academy of Sciences]. Philosophisch-historische Klasse [Section on philosophy and history]. A. 1864 (1959: vol. 96, with 25 no., also available separately). Verlag R.M. Rohrer, Singerstr. 12, Wien I, for Österreichische Akademie der Wissenschaften, Ignaz Seipelplatz 2, Wien I. Extracts and reprints of papers on hist. (including the hist. of art) and auxiliary sciences, philosophy, music, literature and philology, read at the meetings of the acad.; professional news and news of the acad.; name and subject index; illus. pv

34. ÖSTERREICHISCHE AKADEMIE DER WISSENSCHAFTEN. SITZUNGSBERICHTE [Austrian Academy of Sciences. Proceedings]. Philosophisch-historische Klasse [Section on philosophy and history]. Irr. 1848 (1959: vol. 233). Rudolf M. Rohrer, Wien, for Österreichische Akademie der Wissenschaften, Ignaz Seipelplatz 2, Wien I. Art. on all aspects of hist. and the humanities pertaining to ancient and medieval Europe; charts, maps, illus.; index. pni

35. ÖSTERREICHISCHE ARBEITSGEMEINSCHAFT FÜR UR- UND FRÜHGESCHICHTE, MITTEILUNGEN DER... (Mitteilungen der Österreichischen Arbeitsgemeinschaft für Ur- und Frühgeschichte) [Communications of the Austrian Study Group for Prehistory and Early History]. A. (3 double no. p.a.). 1950 (1958: vol. 9). Österreichische Arbeitsgemeinschaft für Ur- und Frühgeschichte, Urgeschichtliches Institut der Universität Wien, Hanuschgasse 3, Wien I. Ed: Franz Kalliany. Art. on prehist.; reports of research and reports from other countries; news of the study group. Title till 1957: Mitteilungen der Urgeschichtlichen Arbeitsgemeinschaft in der Anthropologischen Gesellschaft in Wien. S 25 / DM 6

36. ÖSTERREICHISCHE BYZANTINISCHE GESELLSCHAFT, JAHRBUCH DER... (Jahrbuch der Österreichischen Byzantinischen Gesellschaft) [Yearbook of the Austrian Byzantine Society]. A. 1951 (1957: vol. 6). Österreichische Byzantinische Gesellschaft, Wien. Ed: Herbert Hunger, Österreichische Nationalbibliothek, Josefsplatz 1, Wien I. Art. on Byzantine hist. (including art hist.); bk. rev.; biblio.; A. report of the soc.; in German, English, French or Italian; illus. pv

37. ÖSTERREICHISCHE MONATSHEFTE [Austrian monthly]. M. Österreichischer Verlag, Strozzigasse 2, Wien VIII. S 26.40

38. ÖSTERREICHISCHE NUMISMATISCHE GESELLSCHAFT, MITTEILUNGEN DER... (Mitteilungen der Österreichischen Numismatischen Gesellschaft) [News of the Austrian Numismatic Society]. B-M (1 vol. with 12 no.). 1937 (1957/58: old series, vol. 26; new series, vol. 10). Österreichische Numismatische Gesellschaft, Burgring 5, Wien I. Ed: Josef Beisser, Linke Wienzeile 64, Wien VI. Art. on Austrian coins; professional news. S 24

39. ÖSTERREICHISCHE OSTHEFTE [Austrian journal for Eastern Europe]. B-M. 1959 (1960: vol. 2). Stiasny Verlag, Josefsplatz 6, Wien I, for Arbeitsgemeinschaft Ost. Ed. board: Otto Liess, Thorvi Eckhardt, Gunnar Hering. Art. on problems of research on Eastern Europe; bk. rev.; research reports.

40. ÖSTERREICHISCHE ZEITSCHRIFT FÜR VOLKSKUNDE [Austrian journal of folklore]. A. 1947 (1958: vol. 61, new series, vol. 12). Verein für Volkskunde, Laudongasse 19, Wien VIII. Ed: Leopold Schmidt. Art. on folklore, with emphasis on Austria; news of the soc. and of meetings; bk. rev.; list of bk. and periodicals received; illus. S 96 (memb. s 72)

41. ÖSTERREICHISCHES ARCHÄOLOGISCHES INSTITUT IN WIEN, JAHRESHEFTE DES... (Jahreshefte des Österreichischen Archäologischen Instituts in Wien) [Annual publications of the Austrian Archaeological Institute in Vienna]. S-A. 1898 (1956-58: vol. 43). Österreichisches Archäologisches Institut, Universität Wien, Dr. Karl-Lueger-Ring 1, Wien I. Art. on archaeology, epigraphy and the hist. of antiquity; reports on research and excavations; news from the inst.; subject and epigraphical indices; illus.; each vol. consists of 2 no.: a "Hauptblatt" and a "Beiblatt." pv (Hauptblatt S 190-230; Beiblatt S 120-230)

42. ÖSTERREICHISCHES ARCHIV FÜR KIRCHENRECHT [Austrian archives of church law]. Q. 1950 (1958: vol. 9). Herder, Wien, for Österreichische Gesellschaft für Kirchenrecht, Rechts- und Staatswissenschaftliche Fakultät der Universität Wien. Ed: Franz Arnold, Willibald M. Plöchl, Universität Wien, Dr. Karl-Lueger-Ring 1, Wien I. Interpretations of church laws; bk. rev.; biblio. of art.; personal news, confined to Austria. p (1) S 35 / DM 6.50

43. ÖSTERREICHISCHES STAATSARCHIV, MITTEILUNGEN DES... (Mitteilungen des Österreichischen Staatsarchivs) [Communications of the Austrian National Archives]. A. 1948 (1957: vol. 10). Ferdinand Berger, Wienerstr. 21/23, Horn, for Generaldirektion des Österreichischen Staatsarchivs, Minoritenplatz 1, Wien I. Art. on archival science and the science of doc. in the late Middle Ages and modern times and the hist. of the same period, with emphasis on Austria; rev. art.; bk. rev.; reports of the archives; research reports; illus. 5 supplementary issues appeared till 1957.
pv (1957: vol. 10: S 220 / $ 9)

44. OSTTIROLER HEIMATBLÄTTER [Local bulletins of East Tyrol]. Heimatkundliche Beilage des "Osttiroler Boten" [Supplement of the "Osttiroler Bote" for local studies]. M. Osttiroler Bezirkslandwirtschaftskammer, Schweizergasse 30, Lienz. Q. subscription for "Osttiroler Bote" including the supplement: S 12.50

45. PRÄHISTORISCHE KOMMISSION DER ÖSTERREICHISCHEN AKADEMIE DER WISSENSCHAFTEN, MITTEILUNGEN DER... (Mitteilungen der Prähistorischen Kommission der Österreichischen Akademie der Wissenschaften) [Communications of the Prehistoric Commission of the Austrian Academy of Sciences]. Irr. 1903 (1954/55: vol. 7). Prähistorische Kommission, Österreichische Akademie der Wissenschaften, Ignaz Seipelplatz 2, Wien I. Art. on Austrian prehist. pv

46. PRO AUSTRIA ROMANA. Nachrichtenblatt für die Forschungsergebnisse über die Römerzeit Österreichs [News bulletin for the results of research on Austria's Roman period]. M (6 double no. p.a.). 1951 (1958: vol. 8). Österreichische Arbeitsgemeinschaft für Ur- und Frühgeschichte, Hanuschgasse 3, Wien I. Ed: Rudolf Noll. Reports on excavations and research; news of congresses; biblio. of bk. and art. S 10

47. RELIGION, WISSENSCHAFT, KULTUR [Religion, science, culture]. Q. Wiener Katholische Akademie, Freyung 6, Wien I. S 32

48. RÖMISCHE HISTORISCHE MITTEILUNGEN [Roman historical communications]. A. 1956/57. Abteilung für Historische Studien des Österreichischen Kulturinstituts in Rom und der Österreichischen Akademie der Wissenschaften. Ed: Leo Santifaller, Universität Wien, Dr. Karl-Lueger-Ring 1, Wien I. Art. on Austrian hist. S 72

DER SCHLERN see section on Italy

49. SENFTENEGGER MONATSBLATT FÜR GENEALOGIE UND HERALDIK [Senftenegg monthly bulletin for genealogy and heraldry]. M. K. Friedrich, V. Frank, Schloss Senftenegg, Post Ferschnitz. Genealogical lists and tables of Austrian families; occasional art.; bk. rev. S 15

SITZUNGSBERICHTE DER ÖSTERREICHISCHEN AKADEMIE DER WISSENSCHAFTEN see ÖSTERREICHISCHE AKADEMIE DER WISSENSCHAFTEN. SITZUNGSBERICHTE

50. STEIERMÄRKISCHES LANDESARCHIV, MITTEILUNGEN DES... (Mitteilungen des Steiermärkischen Landesarchivs) [News of the Styrian Provincial Archives]. A. 1951 (1958: vol. 8). Steiermärkisches Landesarchiv, Bürgergasse 2a, Graz. Ed: Fritz Posch. Art. on the holdings of the archives; commemorative art. on Styrian archivists, with biblio. of their pub.; doc.; occasional bk. rev.; report on the activities of the archives; illus.
pv (1955: S 10; 1956: S 15)

51. STEIRISCHER BURGENVEREIN, MITTEILUNGEN DES... (Mitteilungen des Steirischen Burgenvereins) [News of the Styrian Castle Society]. A. 1951 (1958: vol. 7). Steirischer Burgenverein, Bürgergasse 2a, Graz. S 10

SÜDTIROL IN WORT UND BILD see section on the Federal Republic of Germany

52. TIROLER HEIMAT [Tyrolean homeland]. Jahrbuch für Geschichte und Volkskunde [Yearbook for history and folklore]. A. Tyrolia-Verlag, Innsbruck.
pv (S 90-120)

53. TIROLER HEIMATBLÄTTER [Tyrolean local bulletin]. Zeitschrift für Geschichte, Natur- und Volkskunde [Journal for history, natural science and folklore]. M (Q). Verein für Heimatschutz und Heimatpflege in Tirol, Innsbruck.
p (1) S 7.50

54. UNSER NEUSTADT [Our Neustadt]. Q. Wiener-Neustädter Denkmalschutzverein, Hauptplatz 15, Wiener Neustadt. p (1) S 1.50

55. UNSERE HEIMAT [Our homeland]. B-M. Verein für Landeskunde von Niederösterreich und Wien, Herrengasse 13, Wien I. (memb.) S 30

URGESCHICHTLICHE ARBEITSGEMEINSCHAFT IN DER ANTHROPOLOGISCHEN GESELLSCHAFT IN WIEN, MITTEILUNGEN DER... see ÖSTERREICHISCHE ARBEITSGEMEINSCHAFT FÜR UR- UND FRÜHGESCHICHTE, MITTEILUNGEN DER...

56. VEREIN DER FREUNDE CARNUNTUMS, MITTEILUNGEN DES... (Mitteilungen des Vereins der Freunde Carnuntums) [Communications of the Society of the Friends of Carnuntum]. Irr. 1948 (1956: no. 9). Verein der Freunde Carnuntums, Antikensammlung, Burgring 5, Wien I. Ed: Rudolf Sunkowsky. Art. on excavations and research in Carnuntum. pv

57. VEREIN FÜR DIE GESCHICHTE DER STADT WIEN, JAHRBUCH DES... (Jahrbuch des Vereins für die Geschichte der Stadt Wien) [Yearbook of the Society for the History of the City of Vienna]. A. (last 2 vol. B). 1939 (1957/58: new series, vol. 13). Verein für Geschichte der Stadt Wien, Neues Rathaus (Stadtarchiv), Wien I. Ed: Rudolph Geyer. Art. on the hist. of the city of Vienna; illus.; maps. pv (S 54 - S 114 / DM 9 - DM 19)

VERÖFFENTLICHUNGEN. For titles beginning with "Veröffentlichungen," followed by the name of the publishing or sponsoring institution or society, see the respective institution or society.

58. VORARLBERGER LANDESMUSEUMSVEREIN, JAHRBUCH DES... (Jahrbuch des Vorarlberger Landesmuseumsvereins) [Yearbook of the Vorarlberg Provincial Museum Society]. A. Vorarlberger Landesmuseumsverein Bregenz, Kornmarkt 1, Bregenz. pv (S 40-60)

59. DER WÄCHTER [The watchman]. Zeitschrift für alle Zweige der Kultur [Journal for all branches of culture]. 3 x y. Wächter-Verlag, Herrengasse 5, Wien I. p (1) S 15 / DM 3

60. DAS WALDVIERTEL. Zeitschrift für Heimatkunde und Heimatpflege [Journal for the study and cultivation of the homeland]. B-M. Waldviertler Heimatbund, Obere Landstrasse 12, Krems/D. S 36

61. WIENER GESCHICHTSBLÄTTER [Viennese historical publications]. Q. 1946 (1958: old series, vol. 73; new series, vol. 13). Verlag für Jugend und Volk, Tiefer Graben 7/9, Wien, for Verein für Geschichte der Stadt Wien, Neues Rathaus, Stadtarchiv, Wien I. Ed: Rudolf Till. Art. on the hist. of the city of Vienna; bk. rev.; news of the soc. S 25

62. WIENER VÖLKERKUNDLICHE MITTEILUNGEN [Vienna ethnological communications]. S-A. Österreichische Ethnologische Expeditions- und Forschungsgesellschaft, Reitschulgasse 2, Wien I. Art. on ethnology, hist. and archaeology; in German or English. S 72 / DM 12

63. WIENER ZEITSCHRIFT FÜR DIE KUNDE DES MORGENLANDES [Viennese journal for the study of the Orient]. Irr. (1 vol. with several no.). 1887 (1957: vol. 54). Orientalisches Institut, Universität Wien, Hanuschgasse 3, Wien I. Ed: Herbert W. Duda. Art. on the legal and cultural hist. and the hist. of art (predominantly ancient) of the Orient; bk. rev.; in English, French or German; reproductions. pv (c. S 180-264)

64. WISSENSCHAFT UND WELTBILD [Science and conception of the world]. Zeitschrift für die Grundfragen der Forschung [Journal for basic research problems]. Q. Österreichischer Bundesverlag, Schwarzenbergstr. 5, Wien I. S 52 / DM 8.80

ZEITSCHRIFT. For titles beginning with "Zeitschrift," followed by the name of the publishing or sponsoring institution or society, see the respective institution or society.

Belgium

Prepared with the assistance of

J. Van Hove, Conservateur,
Bibliothèque Royale de Belgique, Brussels

1. ACADEMIE ROYALE DE BELGIQUE. ANNUAIRE. KONINKLIJKE ACADEMIE VAN BELGIË. JAARBOEK [Royal Academy of Belgium. Yearbook]. A. Sécrétariat de l'Académie Royale, Palais des Académies, 1 rue Ducale, Bruxelles. Bfr 100

2. ACADEMIE ROYALE DE BELGIQUE. BULLETIN DE LA CLASSE DES LETTRES ET DES SCIENCES MORALES ET POLITIQUES. KONINKLIJKE ACADEMIE VAN BELGIË. MEDEDELINGEN VAN DE KLASSE DER LETTEREN EN DER MORELE EN STAATKUNDIGE WETENSCHAPPEN [Royal Academy of Belgium. Bulletin of the Section of Letters, Philosophy and Political Science]. Irr. 1899 (1958: 5th series, vol. 44). Académie Royale de Belgique, Palais des Académies, 1 rue Ducale, Bruxelles. Art. and papers read by memb. of the acad. on general and cultural hist., literature, archaeology and philosophy; reports on the monthly meetings; rev. of bk. and periodicals; in Dutch or French; illus.; A. subject and author indices. Bfr 100 / Bfr 120

3. ACADEMIE ROYALE DES SCIENCES COLONIALES. BULLETIN DES SEANCES. KONINKLIJKE ACADEMIE VOOR KOLONIALE WETENSCHAPPEN. MEDEDELINGEN DER ZITTINGEN [Royal Academy of Colonial Sciences. Bulletin of the meetings]. 7 x y. 1929 (1959: new series, vol. 5). Académie Royale des Sciences Coloniales, 80 A rue de Livourne, Bruxelles 5. Reports of the sections of the acad. on Congo problems; reports of the Classe des Sciences Morales et Politiques on the hist. of the Congo; reports on the archives and the activities of the acad.; lists of bk. and periodicals received. Bfr 840

ALLIANCE NUMISMATIQUE DE BELGIQUE, BULLETIN DE L'... see ALLIANCE NUMISMATIQUE EUROPEENNE

4. ALLIANCE NUMISMATIQUE EUROPEENNE. EUROPEES GENOOTSCHAP VOOR MUNT- EN PENNINGKUNDE [European Numismatic Association]. M. 1950 (1960: no vol. indic.). Alliance Numismatique Européenne, rue des Capucines, Anvers. Ed: René de Martelaere, Antoine Vanden Brande. Art. on numismatics, medals and paper money in Europe and North Africa; catalogues; news and notes about numismatics; in Dutch or French. Up to 1949 appeared under the title Bulletin de l'Alliance numismatique de Belgique. Bfr 100

5. AMIS BELGES DU VIEUX LAON, ANNALES DES... [Annals of the Friends of Old Laon]. A. Pub. address: 11 rue Montoyer, Bruxelles. Bfr 50

6. ANALECTA BOLLANDIANA. Q. 1882 (1960: vol. 78). Société des Bollandistes, 24 bd. Saint-Michel, Bruxelles. Ed: Mauritius Coens S.J. Studies on the lives of the saints (hagiography, martyrology and legends); doc.; rev. art.; bk. rev.; biblio. of bk. and periodicals; in French and occasionally in German or Italian; A. subject and author index. Bfr 250 / $5

7. ANALECTA LOVANIENSIA BIBLICA ET ORIENTALIA. A. Université de Louvain, 2 place Cardinal Mercier, Louvain. Art. on Biblical and Oriental hist.; in Dutch, English or French. Bfr 20

8. ANALECTA PRAEMONSTRATENSIA. Q (2 double no. p.a.). 1925 (1959: vol. 35). Commissio Historica Ordinis Praemonstratensis, Abbaye Averbode. Ed: J.B. Valvekens. Art. on ecclesiastical hist. and literature, with emphasis on the Premonstratensian Order, and on theology, canon law, liturgy and art hist.; doc.; bk. rev.; in Dutch, English, French, German or Latin; index of places and authors. Bfr 220 / $5

9. ANCIENS PAYS ET ASSEMBLEES D'ETAT. STANDEN EN LANDEN [Old countries and institutions]. Irr. 1950(1959). Section Belge de la Commission Internationale pour l'Histoire des Assemblées d'Etats, Louvain. Ed: E. Nauwelaerts, 41 rue de Neufchâteau, Arlon. Art. on the hist., general and cultural, of the old Belgian provinces and representative and parliamentary institutions, with stress on the period before the French Revolution; reports of historians in this field; doc.; in Dutch or French with French sum.; A. author index.
pv (p (1) Bfr 100)

ANNALEN. For titles beginning with "Annalen," followed by the name of the publishing or sponsoring institution or society, see the respective institution or society.

ANNALES. For titles beginning with "Annales," followed by the name of the publishing or sponsoring institution or society, see the respective institution or society.

ANNUAIRE. For titles beginning with "Annuaire," followed by the name of the publishing or sponsoring institution or society, see the respective institution or society.

10. ANNUAIRE D'HISTOIRE LIEGEOISE [Annals of the history of Liège]. A. Imprimerie Vaillant-Carmanne, 4 place Saint-Michel, Liège, for Commission Communale de l'Histoire de l'Ancien Pays de Liège. Formerly pub. under the title Annuaire de la Commission Communale de l'Histoire de l'Ancien Pays de Liège. Bfr 50

11. L'ANTIQUITE CLASSIQUE [Classical antiquity]. Revue Semestrielle de Philologie Classique, d'Histoire Ancienne, d'Archéologie Classique et Nationale [Bimonthly review of classical philology, ancient history, classical and national archaeology]. S-A. 1935 (1958: vol. 27). Pub. address: 4 place Smolders, Louvain. Ed. board: A. Carnoy, A Delatte, H. Grégoire, P. van de Woestijne. Art. on linguistics, literature, hist. (including religious hist.), archaeology, art, and the auxiliary hist. disciplines; bk. rev.; biblio. of bk. and periodicals; news and notes; in Dutch, English or French. Bfr 360 / $9

12. ARCHIVES, BIBLIOTHEQUES ET MUSEES DE BELGIQUE [Archives, libraries and museums of Belgium]. S-A. 1923 (1958: vol. 29). Association des Conservateurs d'Archives, de Bibliothèques et de Musées, 1 rue du Musée, Bruxelles. Ed. address: 18 rue Ravenstein, Bruxelles. Art. on Belgian hist. (including art hist.), archaeology, libraries, library science, and the archives and museums of Belgium and the Congo; reports on the meetings of the assoc. and its activities; biblio. of bk. and periodicals; in Dutch and French.
Bfr 150 / Bfr 175

13. ARCHIVES VERVIETOISES [Archives of Verviers]. Q. Ed: Math. G. Fisher, Heusy-Verviers. Art. on genealogy. Bfr 150

14. ARDENNE ET FAMENNE. Art, Archéologie, Histoire, Folklore [Art, archaeology, history, folklore]. Q. Pub. address: 19 rue de la Gendarmerie, Marche-en-Famenne. Local hist., folklore, archaeology. Bfr 100

15. ASSOCIATION DES CLASSIQUES DE L'UNIVERSITE DE LIEGE, BULLETIN DE L'... [Bulletin of the Association of Classical Philologists of the University of Liége]. S-A. 1953 (1959: vol. 7). Association des Classiques de l'Université de Liége. Ed: F. Dusinix, 59 rue Neuve, Stavelot. Art. on the teaching of Greek and Latin and on classical studies, including hist.; notes and news; bk. rev.; cum. table of contents for the years 1953-57 in vol. 4. Bfr 125

16. AUGUSTINIANA. Tijdschrift voor de Studie van Sint Augustinus en de Augustijnenorde. Revue pour l'Etude de Saint Augustin et de l'Ordre des Augustins [Journal for the study of St. Augustine and the Augustinian Order]. Q (frequently as combined no.). 1951 (1959: vol. 9). Institutum Historicum Augustinianum Lovanii, Pakenstraat 109, Héverlé-Louvain. Art. on the hist. of the Augustinian Order and its missionary activity, and on the hist. of theology; doc.; in Dutch, English, French, German, Latin or Spanish. Bfr 150 / $ 4

BELGISCH TIJDSCHRIFT VOOR KUNSTGESCHIEDENIS EN OUDHEIDKUNDE see REVUE BELGE D'ARCHEOLOGIE ET D'HISTOIRE DE L'ART

17. BIJDRAGEN TOT DE GESCHIEDENIS DE STAD DEINZE EN VAN HET LAND AAN LEIE EN SCHELDE [Studies in the history of the city of Deinze and the region of the Lys and Schelde]. A. Kunst- en Oudheidkundige Kring [Soc. for Art and Archaeology], Deinze. Bfr 100

18. BIJDRAGEN TOT DE GESCHIEDENIS, INZONDERHEID VAN HET OUD HERTOGDOM BRABANT [Contributions to history, especially of the old duchy of Brabant]. Q. Pub. address: St. Willibrordusstraat 27, Antwerpen. Bfr 110

BIJDRAGEN TOT DE PRIJZEN GESCHIEDENIS see CAHIERS D'HISTOIRE DES PRIX

BIJDRAGEN VOOR DE GESCHIEDENIS DER NEDERLANDEN see section on the Netherlands

19. LE BLASON [The Blazon]. Revue Mensuelle Belge de Généalogie, d'Héraldique et de Sigillographie [Monthly Belgian review of genealogy, heraldry and sigillography]. M. 1946 (mri 1956: vol. 10). Ed: F. Koller, 55 rue de l'Alliance, Bruxelles. Art. on blazonry, heraldry, genealogy, biography and sigillography. Bfr 200

20. DE BRABANTS FOLKLORE. LE FOLKLORE BRABANCON [Folklore of Brabant]. Q. Dienst voor Geschiedkundige en Folkloristische Opzoekingen van Brabant [Office for Hist. and Folkloric Research of Brabant], Bruxelles. Bfr 125

BULLETIN. For titles beginning with "Bulletin," followed by the name of the publishing or sponsoring institution or society, see the respective institution or society.

21. BULLETIN DE THEOLOGIE ANCIENNE ET MEDIEVALE [Bulletin of ancient and medieval theology]. Q. Abbaye du Mont César, Louvain. Rev. of bk. and periodicals on ancient and medieval theology; subject and author index in each no. Bfr 160

22. BYZANTION. 1924 (1958: vol. 28). Fondation Byzantine et Neogrecque, 10 Petite rue du Musée, Bruxelles. Ed: H. Grégoire. Art. on the hist. and civilization of the Byzantine Empire; news and notes on research, congresses and important new pub. in the field of Byzantine studies; bk. rev. pv (c. Bfr 500)

23. CAHIERS D'HISTOIRE DES PRIX [Journal of the history of prices]. A. 1956 (1958 [1959]: vol. 3). Centre Interuniversitaire pour l'Histoire des Prix et Salaires en Belgique, Etablissements Ceuterick, s.c., 66 rue Vital Decoster, Leuven. Ed. board: P. Harsin, J. de Sturler, J.A. van Houtte, C. Verlinden. Art. on the hist. of prices, wages and production in industrialized countries, mostly in Western Europe, and on the methodology of economic research; list of research projects in progress. A separate edition appears in Dutch under the title Bijdragen tot de Prijzengeschiedenis [Contributions to the history of prices]. Bfr 100

24. CAHIERS DE BRUGES [Bruges journal]. Recherches Européennes [European researches]. Q. Ed. address: College of Europe, 11 Dyver, Bruges. Bfr 180 / Bfr 200

25. CALMPTHOUTANIA. Driemaandelijks tijdschrift voor geschiedenis, folklore en streekkunde [Quarterly for history, folklore and regional studies]. Q. Oudheidkundige Kring van Kalmthout [Archaeological Soc. of Calmpthout], 34 Kapellensteenweg, Kalmthout. Bfr 75

26. CERCLE ARCHEOLOGIQUE D'ENGHIEN, ANNALES DU... [Annals of the Archaeological Society of Enghien]. Q. Imprimerie E. Delwarde, Enghien, for Cercle Archéologique d'Enghien. Illus. Bfr 200

CERCLE ARCHEOLOGIQUE DE LA VILLE ET DE L'ANCIEN PAYS DE TERMONDE, ANNALES DU... see OUDHEIDKUNDIGE KRING VAN HET LAND VAN DENDERMONDE, GEDENKSCHRIFTEN VAN DE...

CERCLE ARCHEOLOGIQUE DU PAYS DE WAES, ANNALES DU... see OUDHEIDKUNDIGE KRING VAN HET LAND VAN WAAS, ANNALEN VAN DEN...

27. CERCLE ARCHEOLOGIQUE, LITTERAIRE ET ARTISTIQUE DE MALINES, BULLETIN DU... HANDELINGEN VAN DEN KONINKLIJKEN KRING VOOR OUDHEIDKUNDE, LETTEREN EN KUNST TE MECHELEN [Proceedings of the Society for Archaeology, Literature and Arts of Mechelen]. A. Cercle Archéologique, Littéraire et Artistique de Malines, 137 Koningin Astridlaan, Mechelen. In Dutch or French. Bfr 130

28. CERCLE HUTOIS DES SCIENCES ET BEAUX-ARTS, ANNALES DU... [Journal of the Society of Sciences and Arts of Huy]. Q. Ed: Nicolas Rouche, Lonys Thiers, Huy. Art. on local hist. pni

29. CERCLE ROYALE ARCHEOLOGIQUE D'ATH ET DE LA REGION, ANNALES DU... [Annals of the Royal Society of Ath and Environs]. A. Cercle Royal d'Archéologie d'Ath et de la région, c/o R. Crombain, 17 sq. Saint-Julien, Ath. Bfr 150

CERCLE ROYAL HISTORIQUE ET ARCHEOLOGIQUE DE COURTRAI, MEMOIRES DU... see KONINKLIJKE GESCHIED- EN OUDHEIDKUNDIGE KRING VAN KORTRIJK, HANDELINGEN VAN DE...

30. CHRONIQUE D'EGYPTE [Chronicle of Egypt]. S-A. 1935 (1958: vol. 33). Fondation Egyptologique Reine Elisabeth, Musées Royaux d'Art et d'Histoire, Parc du Cinquantenaire, Bruxelles. Ed: M. Werbrouck, Pierre Gilbert. Art. on the hist. and civilization of Egypt, mostly under the Pharaos and during Greek and Roman times; doc.; bk. rev.; professional news; biblio. of bk. and periodicals; list of memb. of the soc.; in English, French, German or Italian; illus. Bfr 300 / $6

CHRONIQUE DU MUSEE GAUMAIS see MUSEE GAUMAIS, CHRONIQUE DU...

31. CITEAUX IN DE NEDERLANDEN [Cîteaux in the Low Countries]. Q. 1950 (1959: vol. 10). Cisterciënzer abdij, Westmalle. Ed: Roger de Ganck. Art. on aspects of Cistercian life (theology, spirituality, liturgy, monastic life, hist., canon law, economy, sociology, architecture and the arts), with emphasis on the period from the founding of the Order up to the French Revolution; in Dutch and occasionally French, English or German; illus.; A. index of personal and place names. Bfr 125 / $3

32. CIVILISATIONS. Q. Institut National des Civilisations Différentes, 11 bd. de Waterloo, Bruxelles. Bfr 250 / $5

33. CLAIR-LIEU. Tijdschrift gewijd aan de Geschiedenis der Kruisheren [Journal devoted to the history of the Crosier Fathers]. S-A. 1943 (1957/58: vol. 15/16). Geschiedkundige Kring "Clair-Lieu" ["Clair-Lieu" Hist. Soc.], 12 H. Verstappenplein, Diest. Ed: A. Ramaekers, Kruisherenklooster, Diest; A. Van Asseldonk. Art. on the hist. of the Order of the Holy Cross; doc.; biblio.; in Dutch or French; illus. Bfr 60 / $2

COLLECTANEA ORDINIS CISTERCIENSIUM REFORMATORUM see ORDO CISTERCIENSIUM REFORMATORUM, COLLECTANEA

COMMISSIE VOOR NAAMKUNDE TE AMSTERDAM, MEDEDELINGEN VAN DE... see VERENIGING VOOR NAAMKUNDE TE LEUVEN EN DE COMMISSIE VOOR NAAMKUNDE TE AMSTERDAM, MEDEDELINGEN VAN DE... in section on the Netherlands

COMMISSION COMMUNALE DE L'HISTOIRE DE L'ANCIENS PAYS DE LIEGE, ANNUAIRE DE LA... see ANNUAIRE D'HISTOIRE LIEGEOISE

34. COMMISSION ROYALE D'HISTOIRE. BULLETIN. HANDELINGEN VAN DE KONINKLIJKE COMMISSIE VOOR GESCHIEDENIS [Bulletin of the Royal Historical Commission]. Q. 1834 (1957: vol. 122). Société Royale d'Histoire, Palais des Académies, 1 rue Ducale, Bruxelles. Art. on Belgian hist. (including church hist.); doc.; bk. rev.; biblio. and cum. indices; news of archives and pub.; reports on meetings of the commission, printed separately; in Dutch, French or Latin. Bfr 120 / Bfr 160

35. COMMISSION ROYALE DE TOPONYMIE ET DE DIALECTOLOGIE. BULLETIN [Royal Commission of Toponymy and Dialectology. Bulletin]. A. 1927 (1958: vol. 32). Commission Royale de Toponymie et de Dialectologie, Ministère de l'Instruction Publique, 155 rue de la Loi, Bruxelles. Art. on

Belgian place names, personal names and dialects, with emphasis on Wallonian Belgium and Flanders; extensive biblio.; in Dutch or French; index of vol. 1-15 pub. in 1942, and of the French part of vol. 1-25 in 1956. A separate edition in Dutch appears under the title Handelingen van de Koninklijke Commissie voor Toponymie en Dialectologie. Bfr 200

36. COMMISSION ROYALE DES ANCIENNES LOIS ET ORDONNANCES DE LA BELGIQUE. BULLETIN. KONINKLIJKE COMMISSIE VOOR DE UITGAVE DER OUDE WETTEN EN VERORDENINGEN VAN BELGIE. HANDELINGEN [Bulletin of the Royal Commission of Old Laws and Ordinances in Belgium]. A. (1 vol. comprises several A. no.). 1848 (1956-58: vol. 19). Ministère de la Justice en Belgique, Commission Royale des Anciennes Lois et Ordonnances de Belgique, place Poelaert, Bruxelles. Ed: John Gilissen (secretary), 155 av. des Statuaires, Bruxelles 18. Doc., with introductions, on old laws and ordinances in Belgium from the Middle Ages to the 18th cent.; reports on the meetings of the commission; in Dutch or French. pv

DOCUMENTS ET RAPPORTS DE LA SOCIETE ROYALE D'ARCHEOLOGIE ET DE PALEONTOLOGIE DE L'ARRONDISSEMENT JUDICIAIRE DE CHARLEROI see SOCIETE ROYALE D'ARCHEOLOGIE ET DE PALEONTOLOGIE DE L'ARRONDISSEMENT JUDICIAIRE DE CHARLEROI, DOCUMENTS ET RAPPORTS DE LA...

37. EIGEN SCHOON EN DE BRABANDER [The Brabantine and his region's beauty]. M. J. Verbesselt, Ransbeekstraat, Neder-over-Heembeek, for Geschied- en Oudheidkundige Genootschap van Vlaams-Brabant [Hist. and Archaeological Soc. of Flemish Brabant]. Art. on local hist., archaeology and folklore. Bfr 180

ENQUETES DU MUSEE DE LA VIE WALLONNE see MUSEE DE LA VIE WALLONNE, ENQUETES DU...

38. LES ETUDES CLASSIQUES [Classical studies]. Q. Facultés Universitaires Notre-Dame de la Paix, Namur. Bfr 125 / Bfr 150

39. EUPENER GESCHICHTSVEREIN, ZEITSCHRIFT DES... (Zeitschrift des Eupener Geschichtsvereins). JOURNAL DE LA SOCIETE HISTORIQUE D'EUPEN [Journal of the Eupen Historical Society]. 3 x y. Martin Schlembach A.G., Aachener Str. 46, Eupen, for Eupener Geschichtsverein. Bk. rev.; in French and German. Bfr 20

EUROPEES GENOOTSCHAP VOOR MUNT- EN PENNINGKUNDE see ALLIANCE NUMISMATIQUE EUROPEENNE

40. FEDERATION HISTORIQUE ET ARCHEOLOGIQUE DE BELGIQUE, ANNALES DE LA... [Annals of the Belgian Historical and Archaeological Federation]. Irr. 1886 (1955 [1959]: vol. 36). J. Duculot, Gembloux, for Fédération Historique et Archéologique de Belgique, Anvers. Ed: Baron Jean de Béthun. Art. on hist., archaeology, folklore, art, numismatics, sigillography and epigraphy, with emphasis on medieval Belgium. A separate edition appears in Dutch under the title Handelingen van het Verbond der geschiedkundige en oudheidkundige Kringen van Belgie. Bfr 200

LE FOLKLORE BRABANCON see DE BRABANS FOLKLORE

41. FRANCISCANA. Tijdschrift voor Franciscaanse geschiedenis en bibliografie [Journal of Franciscan history and bibliography]. 3 x y. 1946 (1959: vol. 14). Archief der Paters Minderbroeders [Archives of the Minorite Fathers], Minderbroedersstraat 5, St-Truiden. Ed. board: Archangelus Houbaert, O.F.M., Hugolinus Lippens, O.F.M., Matthaeus Verjans, O.F.M., Herwig Ooms, O.F.M. Art. on Franciscan hist. and biblio., with emphasis on Belgium and the Netherlands, from 1226 to the present; rev. art.; doc.; biblio. of bk. and periodicals, classified by area and author, with short evaluations for Dutch pub.; chronicle of events and news from the Franciscan Order; in Dutch and occasionally French or Latin; cum. indices of names and subjects, and of art., biblio., chronicles and news pub. every five years (in 1956 for the years 1952-56). Bfr 60

GENOOTSCHAP VOOR GESCHIEDENIS, HANDELINGEN VAN HET... see SOCIETE D'EMULATION DE BRUGES, ANNALES DE LA...

42. GESCHIED- EN OUDHEIDKUNDIGE KRING VAN OUDENAARDE, VAN ZIJNE KASTELNIJ EN VAN DEN LANDE TUSSEN MAERCKE EN RONNE, HANDELINGEN VAN DE... [Proceedings of the Historical and Archaeological Society of Oudenaarde, of its castles and of the country between Maercke and Ronne]. S-A. Geschied- en Oudheidkundige Kring, Oudenaarde. pni

43. GESCHIEDENIS IN HET ONDERWIJS [History in teaching]. M. Belgische Federatie de leraars in de geschiedenis [Belgian Federation of Hist. Teachers], Brusselstraat 1, Dendermonde. A separate French edition appears under the title Histoire et Enseignement. Bfr 240

HANDELINGEN. For titles beginning with "Handelingen," followed by the name of the publishing or sponsoring institution or society, see the respective institution or society.

44. HISTOIRE ET ENSEIGNEMENT [History and teaching]. A. 1951 (1957/58 [1959]: vol. 7/8). Fédération Belge des Professeurs d'Histoire, 24 rue des Moissonneurs, Bruxelles IV. Art. on the hist. of Belgium, general hist. and the teaching of hist.; rev. art.; biblio. of bk. and periodicals; news and notes. A separate edition appears in Dutch under the title Geschiedenis in het Onderwijs. Bfr 100

45. H.O.K. A. E.H. Lamverys, Hoogstraten, for Hoogstraten's Oudheidkundige Kring [Archaeological Soc. of Hoogstraten]. Bfr 75

HOOGSTRATEN'S OUDHEIDKUNDIGE KRING, JAARBOEK VAN... see H.O.K.

46. INSTITUT ARCHEOLOGIQUE DU LUXEMBOURG, ANNALES DE L'... [Annals of the Archaeological Institute of Luxembourg]. A. Institut Archéologique du Luxembourg, 16 rue des Martyrs, Arlon. Art. on the hist. of the province of Luxembourg. Bfr 150 / Bfr 175

47. INSTITUT ARCHEOLOGIQUE DU LUXEMBOURG. BULLETIN TRIMESTRIEL [Archaeological Institute of Luxembourg. Quarterly Bulletin]. Q. Bibliothéque de l'Institut Archéologique du Luxembourg, 13 rue des Martyrs, Arlon. Bfr 175 (memb. free)

48. INSTITUT ARCHEOLOGIQUE LIEGOIS, BULLETIN DE L'... [Bulletin of the Archaeological Institute of Liège]. A. 1852. Institut Archéologique Liègeois, 13 quai de Maestricht, Liège. pni

49. INSTITUT DE PHILOLOGIE ET D'HISTOIRE ORIENTALES DE L'UNIVERSITE LIBRE DE BRUXELLES, ANNUAIRE DE L'... [Annual of the Institute of Philology and Oriental History of the Free University of Bruxelles]. A. 1932 (1954-57 [1959]: vol. 14). Institut de Philologie et d'Histoire Orientales, Université Libre de Bruxelles, 219 av. Louise, Bruxelles. Art. on Oriental hist. and on philology; in English, French or German. pv

50. INSTITUT DE SOCIOLOGIE, REVUE DE L'... [Review of the Institute of Sociology]. Q. 1920 (1960). Librairie encyclopédique, S.P.R.L., Université Libre de Bruxelles, 7 rue du Luxembourg, Bruxelles, for Institut de Sociologie Solvay, parc Léopold, Bruxelles. Art. on sociology, political science, economics and legal and cultural hist.; rev. art. and bk. rev.; notes and news on the activities of the inst. and other news of interest to scholars. Bfr 400 / Bfr 450

51. INSTITUT HISTORIQUE BELGE DE ROME, BULLETIN DE L'... [Bulletin of the Belgian Institute of History in Rome]. Irr. 1919 (1957: vol. 30). Institut Historique Belge de Rome, 78 galerie Ravenstein, Bruxelles, and Academia Belgica, 8 Via Omero, Roma. Ed: Leopold Kumps. Art. on cultural and political relations between Belgium and Italy from the early Middle Ages to the 18th cent., and occasionally on ancient Greek and Roman hist.; doc.; reports on the activities of the inst.; illus. pv (Bfr 250 / $5)

52. L'INTERMEDIAIRE DES GENEALOGISTES [The medium of the genealogists]. B-M. 1946 (1960: vol. 15). Service de Centralisation des Etudes Généalogiques et Démographiques de Belgique, 30 bd. de Waterloo, Bruxelles. Ed: P.E. Claessens (chief ed.). Art. on genealogy and demography; rev. art. Bfr 275

JAARBOEK. For titles beginning with "Jaarboek," followed by the name of the publishing or sponsoring institution or society, see the respective institution or society.

JOURNAL. For titles beginning with "Journal," followed by the name of the publishing or sponsoring institution or society, see the respective institution or society.

KEESINGS HISTORISCH ARCHIEF see section on the Netherlands

53. KONGO-OVERZEE [Congo overseas areas]. Tijdschrift voor en over Belgisch-Kongo en andere overzeese gewesten [Journal for and about Belgian Congo and other overseas areas]. S-A. De Sikkel, Lamorinierestraat 116, Antwerpen. Bfr 225

KONINKLIJKE ACADEMIE VAN BELGIË. JAARBOEK see ACADEMIE ROYALE DE BELGIQUE. ANNUAIRE

KONINKLIJKE ACADEMIE VAN BELGIË. MEDEDELINGEN VAN DE KLASSE DER LETTEREN EN DER MORELE EN STAATKUNDIGE WETENSCHAPPEN see ACADEMIE ROYALE DE BELGIQUE. BULLETIN DE LA CLASSE DES LETTRES ET DES SCIENCES MORALES ET POLITIQUES

KONINKLIJKE ACADEMIE VOOR KOLONIALE WETENSCHAPPEN. MEDEDELINGEN DER ZITTINGEN see ACADEMIE ROYALE DES SCIENCES COLONIALES. BULLETIN DES SEANCES

KONINKLIJKE COMMISSIE VOOR DE UITGAVE DER OUDE WETTEN EN VERORDENINGEN VAN BELGIË. HANDELINGEN see COMMISSION ROYALE DES ANCIENNES LOIS ET ORDONNANCES DE LA BELGIQUE. BULLETIN

KONINKLIJKE COMMISSIE VOOR GESCHIEDENIS, HANDELINGEN VAN DE... see COMMISSION ROYALE D'HISTOIRE, BULLETIN DE LA...

KONINKLIJKE COMMISSIE VOOR TOPONYMIE EN DIALECTOLOGIE, HANDELINGEN VAN DE... see COMMISSION ROYALE DE TOPONYMIE ET DIALECTOLOGIE, BULLETIN DE LA...

54. KONINKLIJKE GESCHIED- EN OUDHEIDKUNDIGE KRING VAN KORTRIJK, HANDELINGEN VAN DE... MEMOIRES DU CERCLE ROYAL HISTORIQUE ET ARCHEOLOGIQUE DE COURTRAI [Proceedings of the Royal Historical and Archaeological Society of Kortrijk]. A. Koninklijke Geschied- en Oudheidkundige Kring, Toekomststraat 1, Kortrijk. In Dutch or French; illus. pni

KONINKLIJKE KRING VOOR OUDHEIDKUNDE, LETTEREN EN KUNST TE MECHELEN, HANDELINGEN VAN HET... see CERCLE ARCHEOLOGIQUE, LITTERAIRE ET ARTISTIQUE DE MALINES, BULLETIN DU...

KONINKLIJKE MUSEA VOOR KUNST EN GESCHIEDENIS, BULLETIN VAN DE... see MUSEES ROYAUX D'ART ET D'HISTOIRE, BULLETIN DES...

KONINKLIJKE MUSEA VOOR SCHONE KUNSTEN, BULLETIN DER... see MUSEES ROYAUX DES BEAUX-ARTS, BULLETIN DES...

55. KONINKLIJKE VLAAMSE ACADEMIE VOOR WETENSCHAPPEN, LETTEREN EN SCHONE KUNSTEN VAN BELGIË. MEDEDELINGEN VAN DE KLASSE DER LETTEREN [Royal Flemish Academy of Sciences, Letters and Fine Arts of Belgium. Communications of the Section of Letters]. Irr. 1939 (1959: vol. 21, no. 4). Koninklijke Vlaamse Academie voor Wetenschappen, Letteren en Schone Kunsten van België, Paleis der Academiën, Hertogstraat 1, Bruxelles. Short monographs on linguistics, literature, hist. and related subjects, presented at meetings of the section; in Dutch; occasional French sum. pv

56. HET LAND VAN AALST [The district of Aalst]. B-M. Ed: A. van Lul, Naeyerlaan 51, Forest-Bruxelles, for Heemkundige Vereniging "Het Land von Aalst" [Local Studies Soc. "The District of Aalst"]. Bfr 100

57. LATOMUS. Revue d'Etudes Latines [Review of Latin studies]. Q. 1937 (1959: vol. 18). Collection Latomus, 61 av. Laure, Berchem-Bruxelles. Ed: M. Renard, 262 bd. d'Avroy, Liège. Art. on ancient Rome, pertaining primarily to its philology, philosophy, archaeology, hist. and literature; rev. art.; rev. of bk. and periodicals; in French and occasionally English, Italian or Latin; illus. Bfr 300 / $6

58. LEODIUM. M. Ed: R. Forgeur, 39 bd. d'Avroy, Liège, for Société d'Art et d'Histoire du Diocèse de Liège. pni

59. LEUVENSE BIJDRAGEN [Leuven contributions]. Tijdschrift voor Moderne Filologie [Review of modern philology]. Q. 1896. Pub. and ed: J.L. Pauwels, Naamse Vest 48, Leuven. In Dutch, English or German. Bfr 100 / $ 12

60. LIMBURG. Maandelijks Tijdschrift voor Limburgse Geschiedenis, Oudheidkunde, Kunst en Folklore [Monthly review of the history, archaeology, art and folklore of Limburg]. M. E.H.A. Remans, Normaalschool, Mechelen-aan-de-Maas. Bfr 100

61. MAATSCHAPPIJ VOOR GESCHIEDENIS EN OUDHEIDKUNDE TE GENT, HANDELINGEN DER... [Proceedings of the Gent Society of History and Archaeology]. 1894 (1960: new series, vol. 14). Maatschappij voor Geschiedenis en Oudheidkunde te Gent, Abrahamstraat 13, Gent. Ed: J. Dhondt, Universiteitsstraat 16, Gent. Art. on the hist. of Flanders; in Dutch or French. Bfr 150

MEDEDELINGEN. For titles beginning with "Mededelingen," followed by the name of the publishing or sponsoring institution or society, see the respective institution or society.

MEMOIRES. For titles beginning with "Mémoires," followed by the name of the publishing or sponsoring institution or society, see the respective institution or society.

62. LE MOYEN AGE [The Middle Ages]. Revue d'Histoire et de Philologie [Review of history and philology]. Q. 1888 (1959: new series, vol. 14). La Renaissance du Livre, 12 place du Petit Sablon, Bruxelles. Ed. board: R. Bossuat, E. Perroy, M. Delbouille, F. Vercauteren. Art. on medieval hist. and inst., early ecclesiastical hist., medieval art and music, philology and biography; bk. rev.; biblio. Bfr 250 / Bfr 300

63. MUSEE DE LA VIE WALLONNE, ENQUETES DU... [Investigations of the Museum of Walloon Life]. M. Musée de la Vie Wallonne, 136 rue Féronstrée, Liège. Art. on folklore and hist. Bfr 100

64. MUSEE GAUMAIS, CHRONIQUE DU... [Chronicle of the Museum of Gaumais]. 8 x y. Musée Gaumais, Virton. Art. on folklore and archaeology. pni

65. MUSEES ROYAUX D'ART ET D'HISTOIRE, BULLETIN DES... BULLETIN VAN DE KONINKLIJKE MUSEA VOOR KUNST EN GESCHIEDENIS [Bulletin of the Royal Museums of Art and History]. Irr. 1901 (mri 1955: 4th series, vol. 27). Musées Royaux d'Art et d'Histoire, 10 parc du Cinquantenaire, Bruxelles. Ed: Comte J. de Borchgrave d'Altena. Art. on archaeology; bk. rev.; illus.; cum. index for the years 1928-1938 and 1947-1952; in Dutch or French. Bfr 100 / Bfr 125

66. MUSEES ROYAUX DES BEAUX-ARTS, BULLETIN DES... [Bulletin of the Galleries of Fine Arts]. Q. Musées Royaux des Beaux-Arts, 9 rue du Musée, Bruxelles. Illus. A separate edition appears in Dutch under the title Bulletin der Koninklijke Musea voor Schone Kunsten. Bfr 160

67. LE MUSEON. Revue d'Etudes Orientales. Tijdschrift voor Orientalisme [Review of Oriental studies]. S-A (2 double no.). 1882 (1958: vol. 71). L. Th. Lefort, 9 rue des Poissoniers, Louvain. Ed: G. Garitte, 9 av. des Hêtres, Louvain. Art. on culture, hist., literature, folklore, philology and art pertaining to peoples of Asia and the Near and Middle East, with emphasis on the ancient period; bk. rev.; in English, French and German; illus. Bfr 300

68. NAMURCUM. Chronique de la Société Archéologique de Namur [Bulletin of the Society of Archaeology of Namur]. Q. Société Archéologique, rue Joseph Saintraint, Namur. pni

NEERLANDS VOLKSLEVEN see section on the Netherlands

69. ONS GEESTELIJK ERF [Our spiritual inheritance]. Driemaandelijks Tijdschrift gewijd aan de Studie der Nederlandse Vroomheid vanaf de Bekering tot circa 1750 [Quarterly devoted to the study of Dutch piety from the Conversion to circa 1750]. Q. 1927 (1960: vol. 34). Ruusbroec-Vereniging [Ruusbroec Soc.], Prinsstraat 17, Antwerpen, with the assistance of Universitaire Stichting van België [Univ. Foundation of Belgium]. Ed: L. Moereels, S.J., Prinsstraat 17, Antwerpen (for the Southern Netherlands); H.J. Scheerman, O.S.B., Priory H. Graf, Doornbergh, Maarssen, the Netherlands (for the Northern Netherlands). Art. on the subject indicated in the subtitle; bk. rev.; index for vol. 1-25 (1927-1951/52). Bfr 250 (for Belgium and Holland) / Bfr 300

ORBIS see section on International Periodicals

70. ORDO CISTERCIENSIUM REFORMATORUM, COLLECTANEA... Q. 1934 (1960: vol. 18). Order of the Cistercians, Cistercian Abbey, Westmalle. Ed: R.P. André Fracheboud, Abbaye de Tamié, Mercury-Gemilly (Savoie), France. Art. on spirituality, monastic life, liturgy, hist. and other branches of monastic studies; rev. art.; bk. rev.; doc.; notes and news on the Cistercian Order; biblio. of bk. and periodicals; in English, French, German or Spanish.
Bfr 110 / Bfr 120

71. OSIRIS. Commentationes de Scientiarium et Eruditionis Historia Rationeque. Irr. 1936 (mri 1956: vol. 12). "De Tempel," Tempelhof 37, Bruges. Ed: A. Rome, J. Mogenet, 32 Vieux-Marché, Louvain. Art. on the hist. of science; in the languages of the authors; illus. Bfr 400 / 8

72. OSTBELGISCHE CHRONIK [Chronicle of East Belgium]. A. Ed: B. Willems, 19 rue Abbé Peters, Malmedy. Art. on local hist.; in German.
Bfr 140

73. HET OUDE LAND VAN LOON [The ancient region of Loon]. A. Federatie der Geschied- en Oudheidkundige Kringen van Limburg [Federation of the Hist. and Archaeological Soc. of Limburg], Bampslaan 8, Hasselt. Bfr 100

74. OUDHEIDKUNDIGE KRING VAN HET LAND VAN DENDERMONDE, GEDENKSCHRIFTEN VAN DE... ANNALES DU CERCLE ARCHEOLOGIQUE DE LA VILLE ET DE L'ANCIEN PAYS DE TERMONDE [Annals of the Archaeological Society of the City and the Region of Termonde]. A. Oudheidkundige Kring van het Land van Dendermonde, Sint-Gillis. pni

75. OUDHEIDKUNDIGE KRING VAN HET LAND VAN WAAS, ANNALEN VAN DEN... ANNALES DU CERCLE ARCHEOLOGIQUE DU PAYS DE WAES [Annals of the Archaeological Society of the Region of Waas]. S-A. Oudheidkundige Kring van het Land van Waas, Museum, Sint-Niklaas. pni

76. LE PAYS GAUMAIS [The region of Gaume]. La terre et les hommes [The country and the people]. Q. Editions du Musée Gaumais, Virton. Bfr 100

77. PHOIBOS. S-A. Cercle de Philologie Classique et Orientale, Université Libre de Bruxelles, 50 av. F.D. Roosevelt. Bk. rev.; biblio.; maps; illus. Bfr 175

78. RECHERCHES DE THEOLOGIE ANCIENNE ET MEDIEVALE [Research on ancient and medieval theology]. Q (2 double no.). 1929 (1958: vol. 25).

Abbaye du Mont César, 202 rue de Malines, Louvain. Art. on ancient and medieval theology and philosophy and such subjects as ecclesiastical hist., literature, early church music, liturgy, architecture and the hist. of art; doc.; biblio. of bk. and periodicals; in English, French, German or Latin; A. vol. index. Bfr 260

79. REVUE BELGE D'ARCHEOLOGIE ET D'HISTOIRE DE L'ART. BELGISCH TIJDSCHRIFT VOOR KUNSTGESCHIEDENIS EN OUDHEIDKUNDE [Belgian journal of archaeology and the history of art]. Q. 1931 (1958 [1960]: vol. 27). Académie Royale d'Archéologie de Belgique, 10 parc du Cinquantenaire, Bruxelles. Ed: Ad. Jansen, 79 rue van Schoonbeke, Anvers. Art. on archaeology and Belgian art hist.; rev. art.; bk. rev.; in Dutch or French. Bfr 225

80. REVUE BELGE DE NUMISMATIQUE ET DE SIGILLOGRAPHIE [Belgian review of numismatics and sigillography]. A. 1841 (1959: vol. 105). Société Royale de Numismatique de Belgique, 5 rue du Musée, Bruxelles. Art. on numismatics and discoveries of coins and signets; notes and news on numismatic events and exhibitions; rev. art.; bk. rev.; doc.; biblio. of bk. and periodicals. Bfr 275

81. REVUE BELGE DE PHILOLOGIE ET D'HISTOIRE [Belgian review of philology and history]. Q. 1922 (1960: vol. 38). Société pour le Progrès des Etudes Philologiques et Historiques, 3 av. Saint Augustin, Bruxelles. Ed. board: M. Renard (chief ed.), J. Stengers, M. De Grève. Art. on hist., philology, art and the hist. of literature, with emphasis on the Middle Ages; bk. rev.; notes and news; biblio. of art.; in Dutch, English, French, German, Italian or Latin. Bfr 400 / Bfr 450

82. REVUE BENEDICTINE DE CRITIQUE, D'HISTOIRE ET DE LITTERATURE RELIGIEUSES [Benedictine review of religious criticism, history and literature]. Q (2 double no.). 1884 (1958: vol. 68). Abbaye de Maredsous. Ed: Cyrille Lambot. Art. on religious hist., literature, liturgy, church hist., theology, and canon law, with emphasis on the Benedictine Order; doc.; bk. rev.; contains 2 supplements with separately numbered pages: Bulletin d'Histoire Bénédictine, an annotated biblio. of bk. and art., and Bulletin d'Ancienne Littérature Chrétienne Latine, a biblio. of studies; in French and occasionally English, German or Italian. Bfr 300 / $ 6.50

83. REVUE D'HISTOIRE ECCLESIASTIQUE [Review of church history]. Q. 1900 (1959: vol. 54). Université Catholique de Louvain, Bibliothèque de l'Université, place Ladeuze, Louvain. Ed: R. Aubert. Art. on church hist.; bk. rev.; doc.; news and notes classified by country, including short descriptions of source pub. and studies; extensive biblio. containing sections dealing with 1) auxiliary disciplines; 2) source pub. and rev. of sources; 3) hist. studies, classified by subject; 4) list of bk. rev., by author; alphabetical list of authors; cum. tables of contents pub. for the years 1900-1926 and 1927-1940. Bfr 450 / Bfr 500

84. REVUE DE DOCUMENTATION MILITAIRE. TIJDSCHRIFT VOOR MILITAIRE DOCUMENTATIE [Review of military documentation]. M. Institut Géographique Militaire, 2 allée du Cloître, Bruxelles. Bk. rev.; biblio.; illus.; in Dutch and French. pni

REVUE DE L'INSTITUT DE SOCIOLOGIE see INSTITUT DE SOCIOLOGIE, REVUE DE L'...

REVUE DU NORD see section on France

85. REVUE INTERNATIONALE DES DROITS DE L'ANTIQUITE [International review of ancient law]. Q. 1948 (1959: 3rd series, vol. 6). Office International de Librairie, 30 av. Marnix, Bruxelles. Ed: Fernand De Visscher and Jacques Pirenne. Art. on law in ancient Asia Minor, Greece and Rome; bk. rev.; news and notes; in English, French, German or Italian. Bfr 400

86. SACRIS ERUDIRI. Jaarboek voor Godsdienstwetenschapen [Yearbook of religious studies]. A. 1948 (1957: vol. 9). St. Pietersabdij, Steenbrugge. Art. on religion and religious hist., with emphasis on liturgy; doc.; index of personal names; in Dutch, English, French, German, Latin or Spanish; sum. in Latin. Bfr 320 / $ 6.50

87. SCRIPTORIUM. Revue Internationale des Etudes Relatives aux Manuscrits. "International Review of Manuscript Studies." S-A. 1946 (1958: vol. 12). Standaard Boekhandel, 151 av. de Belgique, Anvers. Ed: F. Lyma, F. Masai, 5 rue du Musée, Bruxelles. Art. on paleography and all aspects of manuscript studies; rev. art. and rev. of new pub.; biblio. of manuscript copies; in English, French, German or Latin; A. index of places and collections; reproductions of manuscript pages. Bfr 500 / $12

88. SOCIETE ARCHEOLOGIQUE DE NAMUR, ANNALES DE LA... [Annals of the Archaeological Society of Namur]. S-A. 1849 (1958: vol. 49). Société Archéologique de Namur, c/o J. Bovesse (secretary), 86 Ch. de Dinant, Wépion. Art. on archaeology; illus. Bfr 225

89. SOCIETE BELGE D'ETUDES NAPOLEONIENNES, BULLETIN DE LA ... [Bulletin of the Belgian Society of Napoleonic Studies]. Q. 1950 (1959: no. 29-32). Société Belge d'Etudes Napoléoniennes, 43 av. Hamoir, Uccle-Bruxelles. Ed: Théo Fleischman. Art. on the life of Napoleon Bonaparte and his time, with emphasis on Belgium; rev. of bk. and periodicals; news and notes; illus. Bfr 150

90. SOCIETE D'ART ET D'HISTOIRE DU DIOCESE DE LIEGE, BULLETIN DE LA... [Bulletin of the Society for Art and History of the Diocese of Liège]. A. 1881 (1960: vol. 41). Société d'Art et d'Histoire du Diocèse de Liège. Ed: R. Forgeur, 39 bd. d'Avroy, Liège. Art. on hist., including the hist. of art. Bfr 100

91. SOCIETE D'EMULATION DE BRUGES, ANNALES DE LA... [Annals of the "Society of Emulation" of Bruges]. Revue trimestrielle pour l'étude de l'histoire et des antiquités de la Flandre. Driemaandelijks Tijdschrift voor de Studie van Geschiedenis en Oudheden van Vlaanderen [Quarterly for the study of history and antiquities of Flanders]. Q. 1839 (1959 [1960]: vol. 96). "Société d'Emulation": Genootschap voor Geschiedenis te Brugge [Hist. Soc. in Bruges], 22 Komvest, Bruges. Ed. address: 10 Sint-Gilliskerkstraat, Bruges. Art. on the hist. and culture of Flanders; doc.; chronicle containing information on new pub. and personal news; bk. rev.; biblio.; in Dutch and occasionally in French; indices for the years 1839-1939. Bfr 150

92. SOCIETE D'HISTOIRE DU PROTESTANTISME BELGE, ANNALES DE LA... [Annals of the Society for the History of Belgian Protestantism]. Irr. 1904 (1955-57 [1959]: 4th series, vol. 4). Société d'Histoire du Protestantisme Belge, 84 av. du Parc, Bruxelles. Art. and biographical sketches relating to

the hist. of Protestantism in Belgium and to the Reformation. A separate edition appears in Dutch under the title Annalen van de Vereniging voor de Geschiedenis van het Belgisch Protestantisme.

93. SOCIETE ROYALE BELGE D'ANTHROPOLOGIE ET DE PREHISTOIRE, BULLETIN DE LA... [Bulletin of the Royal Belgian Society of Anthropology and Prehistory]. A. 1883 (1957 [1959]: vol. 68). Société Royale Belge d'Anthropologie et de Préhistoire, 20 rue Baron de Castro, Bruxelles. Reports of papers read at meetings of the soc. on anthropology, geography, folklore, prehist. art, research and discoveries, medicine, biology and paleontology. pni

94. SOCIETE ROYALE BELGE D'ETUDES GEOLOGIQUES ET ARCHEOLOGIQUES "LES CHERCHEURS DE LA WALLONIE," BULLETIN ILLUSTRE DE LA... [Illustrated bulletin of the Royal Belgian Society for Geological and Archaeological Studies "The Walloon Inquirers"]. A. (1957: vol. 16). Société Royale Belge d'Etudes Géologiques et Archéologiques "Les Chercheurs de la Wallonie," 9 rue du Corbeau, Seraing. Art. on archaeology and geology. Bfr 150

95. SOCIETE ROYALE D'ARCHEOLOGIE DE BRUXELLES, ANNALES DE LA... [Annals of the Royal Archaeological Society of Brussels]. Irr. (1957: vol. 49). Société Royale d'Archéologie de Bruxelles, Musée de la Porte de Hal. Ed: Comte J. de Borchgrave d'Altena. Art. on archaeology, the hist. of art and the hist. of Belgium. pni

96. SOCIETE ROYALE D'ARCHEOLOGIE ET DE PALEONTOLOGIE DE L'ARRONDISSEMENT JUDICIAIRE DE CHARLEROI, DOCUMENTS ET RAPPORTS DE LA... [Documents and reports of the Royal Archaeological and Paleontological Society of the Judicial District of Charleroi]. A. V. Rosquin, Musée Archéologique, bd. J. Bertrand, Charleroi, for Société Royale d'Archéologie et de Paleontologie de l'Arrondissement Judiciaire de Charleroi. pni

97. SOCIETE ROYALE "LE VIEUX-LIEGE," BULLETIN DE LA...[Bulletin of "The Old Liège" Royal Society]. Q. Comité d'Etudes Archéologiques, Historiques et Folkloriques au Pays de Liège. Bfr 125

98. SOCIETE ROYALE PALEONTOLOGIQUE ET ARCHEOLOGIQUE DE L'ARRONDISSEMENT JUDICIAIRE DE CHARLEROI, BULLETIN DE LA... [Bulletin of the Royal Society for Paleontology and Archaeology of the Judicial District of Charleroi]. Q. Notaire Delentre, Thuin, for Société Royale Paleontologique et Archéologique de l'Arrondissement Judiciaire de Charleroi. pni

99. SOCIETE VERVIETOISE D'ARCHEOLOGIE ET D'HISTOIRE, BULLETIN DE LA... [Bulletin of the Archaeological and Historical Society of Verviers]. A. Société d'Archéologie et d'Histoire, Verviers. Bfr 100

STANDEN EN LANDEN see ANCIENS PAYS ET ASSEMBLEES D'ETAT

100. SYNTHESES [Syntheses]. Revue Internationale [International review]. M. Editions "Synthèses," 230 rue J. -Fr. de Becker, Woluwe-St-Lambert, Bruxelles. Bfr 400

101. TABLETTES DES FLANDRES [Surveys of Flanders]. Généalogie, Histoire, Héraldique [Genealogy, history, heraldry]. A. Ch. van Renynghe de Voxvrie, 1 rue de l'Outre, Bruxelles. Pub. in 2 parts: "Documents" and "Recueil." Bfr 225 ("Documents"), Bfr 250 ("Recueil")

102. TAXANDRIA. Q. Fr. de Vel, Merodelei 117, Turnhout, for Koninklijke Geschied- en Oudheidkundigen Kring van de Antwerpsche Kempen [Royal Hist. and Archaeological Soc. of Antwerp-Kempen]. pni

TIJDSCHRIFT VOOR GESCHIEDENIS see section on the Netherlands

103. TIJDSCHRIFT VOOR GESCHIEDENIS EN FOLKLORE [Journal for history and folklore]. Q. 1938 (1958: vol. 21). Commissie voor Geschiedkundige en Folkloristische Opzoekingen der Provincie Antwerpen [Commission for Research on Hist. and Folklore of the Province of Antwerp], Antwerpen. Art. on hist. and folklore. Bfr 50

TIJDSCHRIFT VOOR MILITAIRE DOCUMENTATIE see REVUE DE DOCUMENTATION MILITAIRE

TIJDSCHRIFT VOOR RECHTSGESCHIEDENIS see section on the Netherlands

VERBOND DER GESCHIEDKUNDIGE EN OUDHEIDKUNDIGE KRINGEN VAN BELGIË, HANDELINGEN VAN HET... see FEDERATION HISTORIQUE ET ARCHEOLOGIQUE DE BELGIQUE, ANNALES DE LA...

VEREENIGING VOOR NAAMKUNDE TE LEUVEN EN DE COMMISSIE VOOR NAAMKUNDE TE AMSTERDAM, MEDEDELINGEN VAN DE... see section on the Netherlands

VERENIGING VOOR DE GESCHIEDENIS VAN HET BELGISCH PROTESTANTISME, ANNALEN VAN DE... see SOCIETE D'HISTOIRE DU PROTESTANTISME BELGE, ANNALES DE LA...

104. LA VIE WALLONNE [Walloon life]. Q. 1920 (1959: vol. 33). Editions de la Revue "La Vie Wallonne," Soc. Coop., 13 rue Wiertz, Liège. Ed: Jean Servais, R. van der Made (secretary), 206 rue des Vennes, Liège. Art. on Walloon hist., with emphasis on cultural hist. and folklore; news of exhibitions and congresses; bk. rev.; illus. Bfr 150 / $3

VOLKSKUNDE see section on the Netherlands

105. WAVRIENSIA. B-M. Cercle Historique et Archéologique de Wavre et de la Région, 14 rue du Ruhaux, Ottignies. Bfr 75

106. ZAÏRE. Revue Congolaise. Congolees Tijdschrift. "Belgian African Review." 10 x y. 1947 (1959: vol. 13). Editions Universitaires, 163 rue du Thrône, Bruxelles. Ed: N. De Cleene and G. Malengreau. Studies on various aspects of life in the Congo, past and present; bk. rev.; biblio.; news and notes; in French, Dutch or English. Bfr 350 / Bfr 400

ZEITSCHRIFT DES EUPENER GESCHICHTSVEREIN see EUPENER GESCHICHTSVEREIN, ZEITSCHRIFT DES...

107. ZUIDNEDERLANDSE MAATSCHAPPIJ VOOR TAAL- EN LETTERKUNDE EN GESCHIEDENIS, HANDELINGEN DER... [Proceedings of the Society for Linguistics and History of the South Netherlands]. A. (1959: vol. 13). Gilbert Degroote, Herderinlaan 22, St.-Agatha-Berchem, for Zuidnederlandse Maatschappij voor Taal- en Letterkunde en Geschiedenis. Art. on hist. and linguistics. Bfr 100

Bulgaria

Prepared with the assistance of

Todor Borov, Director, Bulgarian Bibliographical Institute, Sofia

Note: Bulgarian words have been transliterated below according to the system used by the Library of Congress, Washington, D.C.

1. ARKHEOLOGICHESKI INSTITUT, IZVESTIIA NA... (Izvestiia na Arkheologicheskiia institut) [Proceedings of the Institute of Archaeology]. Irr. 1921 (1957: vol. 21). Otdelenie za filosofiia, istoriia i arkheologiia, B"lgarska akademiia na naukite [Section for Philosophy, Hist. and Archaeology, Bulgarian Acad. of Sciences], Ruski 15, Sofiya. Ed: Kr. Miiatev. Art. on archaeology in Bulgaria; bk. rev.; biblio.; German or French sum. (earlier vol. contained sum. also in Russian); subject index. pv (vol. 21: Leva 38.10)

2. ARKHEOLOGICHESKO DRUZHESTVO, GRAD VARNA, IZVESTIIA NA... (Izvestiia na Arkheologicheskoto druzhestvo, grad Varna) [Proceedings of the Archaeological Society in Varna]. Irr. 1908 (mri 1956: vol. 10). DI Nauka i izkustvo, Varna, for Arkheologichesko druzhestvo. Ed: Ek. Peeva, M. Cvetanova. Art. on the hist., archaeology, numismatics and epigraphy of Varna and surrounding towns and villages; news and notes; French or German sum.; general subject and epigraphical index. Leva 15.45

3. ARKHIVEN INSTITUT, IZVESTIIA NA... (Izvestiia na Arkhivniia institut) [Proceedings of the Institute for Archives]. 1957 (1957: vol. 1). Arkhiven institut, B"lgarska akademiia na naukite [Inst. for Archives, Bulgarian Acad. of Sciences], Ruski 15, Sofiya. Ed. board: Iv. Snegarov, P. Miiatev, Hr. Hristov, G. Dimov, J. Jotsov. Art. on Bulgarian archives and on the activities of the inst.; doc.; bk. rev.; research news; Russian and French sum. Leva 24

4. D"RZHAVNI ARKHIVI, IZVESTIIA NA... (Izvestiia na D"rzhavnite arkhivi) [Proceedings of the Public Record Office]. A. 1957 (1958: vol. 2). Arkhiven otdel, Ministerstvo na v"treshnite raboti [Dept. of Archives, Ministry of the Interior], Slavianska 4, Sofiya. Ed. board: M. Aleksiev, V. Hadzhinikolov, N. Nedialkov, L. Dimitrov, K. Georgiev. Art. and doc. on the theory and practice of archives; doc. on the hist. of Bulgaria (including literary hist., the hist. of the labor movement and that of the Bulgarian Communist Party); bk. rev.; Bulgarian and foreign archival news. Leva 6.30

5. DUKHOVNA AKADEMIIA "SV. KLIMENT OKHRIDSKI," GODISHNIK NA... (Godishnik na Dukhovnata akademiia "Sv. Kliment Okhridski") [Yearbook of the "Sv. Kliment Okhridski" Theological Academy]. A. 1924 (1957/58: vol. 7; old series, vol. 33). Izdatelstvo, Sofiya, for Dukhovna akademiia "Sv. Kliment Okhridski," Sofiya. Ed: P. Todorov. Art. on the hist. of Christianity in Bulgaria, on religious art and on Old Bulgarian literature; sum. of some art. in Russian, German, French or English. Leva 96

6. ETNOGRAFSKI INSTITUT S MUZEI, IZVESTIIA NA... (Izvestiia na Etnografskiia institut s muzei) [Proceedings of the Ethnographical Institute and Museum]. Irr. 1953 (1958: vol. 3). Otdelenie za ezikoznanie, ethnografiia i literatura, B"lgarska akademiia na naukite [Section for Linguistics, Ethnography and Literature, Bulgarian Acad. of Sciences], Rakovski 108, Sofiya, for Etnografski institut s muzei. Ed: St. Romanski. Art. on ethnography and folklore in Bulgaria; biblio. of Bulgarian ethnography for the years 1943-52 pub. in vol. 2 (1955); sum. in Russian and French or German. Leva 24.70

GODISHNIK. For titles beginning with "Godishnik," followed by the name of the publishing or sponsoring institution or society, see the respective institution or society.

7. INSTITUT BOTEV-LEVSKI, IZVESTIIA NA... (Izvestiia na Instituta Botev-Levski) [Proceedings of the Botev-Levski Institute]. Irr. 1954 (mri 1956: vol. 2). Institut Botev-Levski, B"lgarska akademiia na naukite [Botev-Levski Inst., Bulgarian Acad. of Sciences], Shipka 23, Sofiya. Ed: M. Dimitrov, Iv. Undzhiev. Art. on the hist. of Bulgaria, pertaining mainly to the national-revolutionary movement during the 19th cent. and the role played in it by the two ideologists and leaders, Hristo Botev and Vasil Levski; doc. and research notes; bk. rev.; news; Russian and French sum.; author and geographical index in vol. 1. Leva 23.20

8. INSTITUT PO ISTORIIA NA BKP, IZVESTIIA NA... (Izvestiia na Instituta po istoriia na BKP) [Proceedings of the Institute for the History of the Bulgarian Communist Party]. Irr. 1957 (1958: vol. 5). Izdatelstvo na BKP [Pub. House of the Bulgarian Communist Party], Lenin 47, Sofiya, for Institut po istoriia na BKP. Ed: P. Georgiev. Art. and information on the hist. of the Bulgarian Communist Party; biographies of Party workers; doc.; bk. rev.; biblio.; notes on lectures; news of the activities of the inst. and of similar inst. in other countries; materials on the Great Socialist October Revolution in vol. 5. Leva 20.50

9. INSTITUT ZA B"LGARSKA ISTORIIA, IZVESTIIA NA... (Izvestiia na Instituta za b"lgarska istoriia) [Proceedings of the Institute for Bulgarian History]. A. 1951 (1957: vol. 7). Otdelenie za istoriia, arkheologiia i filosofiia, B"lgarska akademiia na naukite [Section for Hist., Archaeology and Philosophy, Bulgarian Acad. of Sciences], Ruski 15, Sofiya, for Institut za b"lgarska istoriia. Ed: Dimitur Kosev. Art. on Bulgarian hist., including the Byzantine and Ottoman periods; doc.; bk. rev.; Russian and French sum.; table of contents also in Russian and French. pv (vol. 6: Leva 49.40; vol. 7: Leva 32.45)

10. ISTORICHESKI PREGLED [Historical review]. B-M. 1945 (1959: vol. 15). Institut za b"lgarska istoriia, B"lgarska akademiia na naukite [Inst. for Bulgarian Hist., Bulgarian Acad. of Sciences], Benkovski 3, Sofiya. Ed: J. Natan. Art. on the general, economic and cultural hist. of Bulgaria, on the hist. of the relations between Bulgaria and other countries and on Marxist historiography in Bulgaria; bk. rev.; biblio.; news and reports of conferences. Leva 25 / $2

11. ISTORIIA I GEOGRAFIIA [History and geography]. B-M. 1958 (1958: vol. 1). DI Narodna prosveta, Vasil Drumev 37, Sofiya, for Ministerstvo na prosvetata i kulturata [Ministry of Education and Culture]. Ed: N. Popova. Research and popular art. on hist. and geography with the purpose of aiding teachers; bk. rev.; biblio. of new pub.; news. Leva 36

IZVESTIIA. For titles beginning with "Izvestiia," followed by the name of the publishing or sponsoring institution or society, see the respective institution or society.

12. MUZEI V PLOVDIVSKI OKR˝G, GODISHNIK NA... (Godishnik na Muzeite v Plovdivski okr˝g) [Yearbook of the museums in the Plovdic district]. Irr. 1954 (mri 1954/55 [1956]: vol. 2). "Nauka i izkustvo" ["Science and Arts"], Ruski 6, Sofiya, for the museums in the Plovdic district (Revolutionary Movement Museum, National Ethnographical Museum, National Archaeological Museum and Angel Bukoreshtliev Museum). Ed: I. Gocheva. Art., by the collaborators of the above-named museums, on the revolutionary movement of the Bulgarian people, the development of socialism, and on Bulgarian folklore, ethnography, archaeology and cultural hist.; archaeological news; French sum. Leva 27.60

13. NOVO VREME [New time]. Teoretichen organ na Tsentralniia komitet na B˝lgarskata komunisticheska partiia [Theoretical organ of the Central Committee of the Bulgarian Communist Party]. M. TsK, BKP [Central Committee, Bulgarian Communist Party], Sofiya. Leva 20

14. PAMETNITSI NA KULTURATA I MUZEI [Monuments of culture and museums]. Q (Irr.). 1956 (1957: vol. 2). Upravlenie izkustvo i kulturno-prosvetni uchrezhdeniia [Dept. of Arts and Cultural Institutions, Ministry of Education and Culture], Sofiya. Ed: B.M. Markov. Art. on the theory, practice and methodology of museum expositions, on the maintenance and restoration of cultural monuments (with the aim of popularizing museum expositions and cultural monuments) and on Bulgarian cultural hist., archaeology, ethnography, numismatics and related fields; news; A. author index. Temporarily suspended. Leva 14.40

15. SLAVIANI [Slavs]. M (B-M until 1958). Slavianski komitet v B˝lgariia [Slavonic Committee of Bulgaria], Kalojan 1, Sofiya. Leva 20 / Leva 40

16. SOFIISKI UNIVERSITET, GODISHNIK NA... (Godishnik na Sofiiskiia universitet) [Yearbook of the University of Sofia]. Filosofskogo-istoricheski fakultet [Faculty of Philosophy and History]. A. 1904 (1958: vol. 51). DI Nauka i izkustvo, Ruski 6, Sofiya, for Filosofsko-istoricheski fakultet, Sofiiski universitet. Ed. board: St. Conevski, G. Hrusanov, An. B'nkov, Al. Burmov. Art. on philosophy, pedagogy, archaeology, Bulgarian hist. (with emphasis on the hist. of the Bulgarian Communist Party and the development of socialism in Bulgaria) and on general hist.; sum. in Russian and German or French. pni

17. VISSHA PARTIINA SHKOLA "STANKE DIMITROV" PRI TSK NA BKP, IZVESTIIA NA... (Izvestiia na Visshata partiina shkola "Stanke Dimitrov" pri TsK na BKP) [Proceedings of the "Stanke Dimitrov" High Party School attached to the Central Committee of the Bulgarian Communist Party]. Irr. Vissha partiina shkola "Stanke Dimitrov" pri TsK na BKP, An. Ivanov 5, Sofiya. Leva 31.50

18. VOENNO-ISTORICHESKI SBORNIK [Annals of military history]. Q. 1927 (1958: vol. 27). Voenno-istoricheski otdel, MNO [Section of Military Hist., Ministry of National Defense], Skobelev 23, Sofiya. Ed: V. Popov. Art. on military hist. and the art of war (with emphasis on Bulgaria), pertaining mostly to the modern period; doc.; bk. rev. Leva 15

Cyprus

Prepared with the assistance of

Mrs. Catherine Koumarianoû, Neohellenic Research Center, Athens

Note: Greek words in this list have been transliterated according to the method followed in the section on Greece. See note at the beginning of the section on Greece.

ANNUAL REPORT OF THE DIRECTOR OF ANTIQUITIES see DIRECTOR OF ANTIQUITIES, ANNUAL REPORT OF THE

1. DIRECTOR OF ANTIQUITIES, ANNUAL REPORT OF THE. A. 1949 (1958). Director of Antiquities, Govt. of Cyprus, c/o Dept. of Antiquities, Nicosia. Administrative report of the director, including an account of archaeological research and discoveries during the year and a record of conservation work carried out at ancient monuments and archaeological sites in Cyprus; illus. 150 mils / 3s

2. KYPRIAKA GRAMMATA [Cypriot letters]. M. Ed: N. Kranidiotis, Palace of the Archbishop, Nicosia.

3. KYPRIAKAÍ SPOUDAÍ [Cypriot studies]. A. 1937 (1959: vol. 23). Etaireias Kypriakôn Spoudôn, P.O.B. 34, Nicosia. Ed. board: G. Papacharalambous, K. Spyridakis, Th. Sophokléous, K. Hadjipsaltis. Ed. address: Pan-Cyprian Gymnasium, Nicosia. Art. on the hist., archaeology, literature, art, folklore and religion of Cyprus from antiquity to the present; doc.; news of the activities of the soc.; in Greek, English and French; combined subject and author indices. 30s / 30s

Czechoslovakia

Prepared with the assistance of the

Historický ústav, Československá akademie věd [Historical Institute, Czechoslovak Academy of Sciences], Prague, and

Francis S. Wagner, Library of Congress, Washington, D.C.

1. ACTA COMENIANA. Archiv pro bádání o životě a díle Jana Amose Komenského [Archives for research on the life and work of Jan Amos Comenius]. S-A. 1910 (1960: vol. 19). Pedagogický ústav Jana Amose Komenského Československé akademie věd [Jan Amos Comenius Inst. of Pedagogy of the Czechoslovak Acad. of Sciences], Mikulandská 5, Praha 11. Chief ed: Josef Brambora, Hřbitovní 15, Praha 16. Art. on the life and work of Jan Amos Comenius; doc.; biblio.; research news; English, German or Russian sum. Kčs 20 / $2.40

ACTA UNIVERSITATIS CAROLINAE see UNIVERSITAS CAROLINAE, ACTA...

ACTA UNIVERSITATIS PALACKIANAE OLOMUCENSIS see UNIVERSITAS PALACKIANAE OLOMUCENSIS, ACTA...

2. ARCHEOLOGICKÉ ROZHLEDY [Archaeological review]. Informační orgán archeologických a příbuzných vědeckých ústavů v ČSR [Information bulletin of the archaeological and similar scientific institutes of the Czechoslovak Republic]. B-M. 1949 (1960: vol. 12). Nakladatelství Československé akademie věd [Pub. House of the Czechoslovak Acad. of Sciences], Vodičkova 40, Praha 2, for Préhistorický ústav Karlovy University [Prehist. Inst. of Charles Univ.], Pařížská 27, Praha 1. Ed: J. Filip. Art. on the European primeval age, on research and discoveries in Czechoslovakia and on museum exhibitions; archaeological reports; rev. of bk. and periodicals; German or French sum.; indices, of 1) authors of art., 2) authors of bk. rev., 3) new bk. and periodicals, 4) personal news, 5) places, 6) discoveries, and 7) museums and expositions, for vol. 1-10, pub. in 1958: vol. 10, no. 6. Kčs 39 / $5.80

3. ARCHIV ORIENTÁLNÍ [Oriental archives]. Q. 1929 (1960: vol. 28). Orientální ústav Československé akademie věd [Oriental Inst. of the Czechoslovak Acad. of Sciences], Lázeňská 4, Praha 1. Ed: L. Matouš. Art. on Oriental linguistic, literary, religious and art hist.; bk. rev.; in English, French, German or Russian; A. supplement containing a biblio. of Czechoslovak studies on the Orient; A. author index. Kčs 80 / $8.60

4. ARCHIVNÍ ČASOPIS [Review of archives]. Q. 1951 (1960: no vol. indic.). Archivní správa ministerstva vnitra [Archival Section of the Ministry of the Interior], Obránců míru 133, Praha 6. Ed: Gabriela Čechová. Description of the holdings of Czech archives; art. on Soviet archival practice and hist.; detailed rev. of periodieals (on archival science) and bk. pub. in Eastern Europe; archival and related news; illus. Kčs 23.20 / $1.05

5. BYZANTINOSLAVICA. Mezdunarodnyi zurnal po vizantinovedeniju. International Journal of Byzantine Studies. Revue internationale des études byzantines. S-A. 1929 (1960: vol. 21). Slovanský ústav Československé akademie věd [Slavonic Inst. of the Czechoslovak Acad. of Sciences], Valentinská 1, Praha 1.

Ed: Antonín Dostál, Zborovská 24, Praha 16. Art. on Byzantine hist. and Slav-Byzantine relations; bk. rev.; annotated international biblio. of bk. and art., classified by subject, with short rev.; in English, French, German or Russian.
Kčs 50 / $ 3.50

ČASOPIS. For titles beginning with "Časopis," followed by the name of the publishing or sponsoring institution or society, see the respective institution or society.

6. ČASOPIS PRO MODERNÍ FILOLOGII [Review of modern philology]. Germánskou, Anglickou, Románskou [German, English and Romance languages]. Q. Kabinet pro moderní filologii, Československé akademie věd [Section of Modern Philology, Czechoslovak Acad. of Sciences], Liliová 13, Praha 1.
Kčs 16 / $ 3.70

7. ČESKÁ LITERATURA [Czech literature]. Q. Ústav pro českou literaturu Československé akademie věd [Inst. of Czech Literature of the Czechoslovak Acad. of Sciences], Strahovské nádvoří 132, Praha 1. Table of contents also in English, French, German and Russian. Kčs 26 / $ 2.80

8. ČESKOSLOVENSKÁ AKADEMIE VĚD, VĚSTNÍK... (Věstník Československé akademie věd) [Journal of the Czechoslovak Academy of Sciences]. 10 xy. 1892 (1960: vol. 69). Nakladatelství Československé akademie věd [Pub. House of the Czechoslovak Acad. of Sciences], Národní třída 5, Praha 1. Ed: L. Khás. Art. on the development of all branches of science in Czechoslovakia.
Kčs 50 / $ 5.20

9. ČESKOSLOVENSKÁ ETNOGRAFIE [Czechoslovak ethnography]. Q. Nakladatelství Československé akademie věd [Pub. House of the Czechoslovak Acad. of Sciences], Vodičkova 40, Praha 2, for Ústav pro etnografii a folkloristiku Československé akademie věd [Inst. of Ethnography and Folklore of the Czechoslovak Acad. of Sciences], Praha, with the collaboration of branch inst. in Brno and Bratislava. Kčs 58 / $ 5

10. ČESKOSLOVENSKÁ HISTORICKÉ SPOLEČNOST PŘI ČESKOSLOVENSKÉ AKADEMII VĚD, ZPRÁVY... (Zprávy Československá historické společnost při Československé akademii věd) [Reports of the Czechoslovak Historical Society attached to the Czechoslovak Academy of Sciences]. Q. 1958 (1960: vol. 3). Československé Historické společnost při Československé akademie věd, Jiřská 3, Praha 4-Hrad. Chief ed: Pavel Oliva. Reports on hist. conferences in Czechoslovakia and on the activities of the soc. and of Czechoslovak historians.
(memb.) Kčs 10

11. ČESKOSLOVENSKÁ RUSISTIKA [Czechoslovak Russian studies]. Q. Československo-sovětský institut Československé akademie věd [Czechoslovak-Soviet Inst. of the Czechoslovak Acad. of Sciences], Thunovska 22/I, Praha 1.
Kčs 16 / $1.80

12. ČESKOSLOVENSKÁ SPOLEČNOST ARCHEOLOGICKÁ PŘI ČESKOSLOVENSKÉ AKADEMII VĚD, ZPRÁVY... (Zprávy Československé společnosti archeologické při Československé akademii věd) [Reports of the Czechoslovak Archaeological Society attached to the Czechoslovak Academy of Sciences]. Informační orgán Čs. společnosti archeologické, archeologických institucí a pracovišt [Information bulletin for the Czechoslovak Archaeological Society and archaeological institutions and sections]. S-A. 1957 (1958: vol. 2). Československá společnost archeologická, Grohova 7, Brno. Ed. board: F. Kalousek

(manag. ed.), M. Buchvaldek, Vil. Hrubý, M. Novotná. Art. and information on archaeological problems and research; reports about the memb. of the soc.; French sum. pni

13. ČESKOSLOVENSKÁ SPOLEČNOST ZEMĚPISNÁ, SBORNÍK... (Sborník Československé společnosti zeměpisné) [Journal of the Czechoslovak Geographical Society]. Q. Československá Společnost zeměpisná, Albertov 6, Nové Město, Praha 2. Kčs 28 / $ 3

14. ČESKOSLOVENSKÝ ČASOPIS HISTORICKÝ [Czechoslovak historical review]. B-M. 1953 (1960: vol. 8). Historický ústav Československé akademie věd [Hist. Inst. of the Czechoslovak Acad. of Sciences], Jiřská 3, Praha 4 - Hrad. Ed: František Graus. Art. predominantly on modern Czech hist.; discussions; doc.; rev. of bk. and art.; professional notes and news; Russian and French sum.; A. subject and author indices. Kčs 51 / $ 5.40

15. ČESKÝ LID [The Czech people]. B-M. 1891 (1960: vol. 47). Ústav pro etnografii a folkloristiku Československé akademie věd [Inst. of Ethnography and Folklore of the Czechoslovak Acad. of Sciences], Lazarská 8, Praha 2. Ed: O. Skalníková. Art. on ethnography and hist. (including the hist. of art); bk. rev.; biblio. of current bk. on ethnography and folklore; news of exhibitions, conferences and museums. Kčs 42 / $ 4.50

16. COMMUNIO VIATORUM. Q. 1958 (1960: vol. 3). Ekumenický ústav Komenského evangelické bohoslovecké fakulty [Ecumenical Inst. of the Comenius Evangelical Theological Faculty], Jungmanova 9, Praha 2. Ed. board: J. L. Hromádka (chief ed.), J. B. Souček, L. Brož. Art. on the hist. of Protestant Christianity; doc. from the Hussite period and the period of the Bohemian Brethren; rev. of bk. and periodicals; in English, French, German or Latin. Kčs 40 / $ 3

17. DĚJINY A SOUČASNOT [History and presence]. M. 1959 (1960: vol. 2). Orbis, Valdaštejnská 14, Praha, for Czechoslovak Soc. for the Promotion of Political and Scientific Knowledge, and the Board of Education. Chief ed: Z. Šolle. Art. of popular interest on hist. and geographical subjects. Kčs 42

18. EIRENE. Studia Greca et Latina. A. 1960 (1960: vol. 1). Kabinet pro studia řecká, římská a latinská, Československá akademie věd [Section for the Study of Greek, Roman and Latin, Czechoslovak Acad. of Sciences], Lazerská 8, Praha 2. Art. and essays on all aspects of antique culture; in English, German, Russian or French; illus. Kčs 21

19. EKONOMICKÝ ČASOPIS [Economic review]. B-M. Ekonomický ústav Slovenské akadémie věd [Economic Inst. of the Slovak Acad. of Sciences], Vajanského Nábr. 2, Bratislava. Table of contents also in German and Russian. Kčs 30 / $ 6.30

EUNOMIA see LISTY FILOLOGICKÉ

20. FILOSOFICKÝ ČASOPIS [Review of philosophy]. B-M. Filosofický ústav Československé akademie věd [Inst. of Philosophy of the Czechoslovak Acad. of Sciences], Na příkopě 29, Praha 1. Table of contents also in English, French, German and Russian. Kčs 45 / $ 4.80

21. HISTORICA. A. (S-A from 1961). 1959 (1960: vol. 2). Nakladatelství Československé akademie věd [Pub. House of the Czechoslovak Acad. of Sciences],

Vodičkova 40, Praha 2. Ed: Josef Macek, Jiřská 3, Praha 4. Art. on world hist., with strong emphasis on Czechoslovakia; in English, French, German or Russian; illus. Kčs 57

22. HISTORICKÉ ŠTUDIE [Historical studies]. A. 1955 (1959: vol. 5). Historický ústav, Sekcia spoločenských vied, Slovenská akadémia vied [Hist. Inst., Dept. of Social Sciences, Slovak Acad. of Sciences], Klemensova ul. 27, Bratislava. Ed: A. Húščava. Monographs on Slovak hist. and on Slovak-Czech relations. pv (1958: Kčs 31)

23. HISTORICKÝ ČASOPIS [Historical review]. Q. 1953 (1960: vol. 8). Vydavateľstvo Slovenskej akadémie vied [Pub. House of the Slovak Acad. of Sciences], Klemensova ul. 27, Bratislava, for Historický ústav Slovenskej akadémie vied [Hist. Inst. of the Slovak Acad. of Sciences], Bratislava. Ed: Ľudovít Holotík. Art. on the political, economic and cultural hist. of Slovakia, pertaining almost exclusively to the modern period, and on European hist., with emphasis on the Habsburg Empire; rev. art.; doc.; rev. of bk. and periodicals; notes and news; in Slovak; graph; A. table of contents also in French, German and Russian. Kčs 40 / $ 5

24. HISTORIE A VOJENSTVÍ [History and military science]. Q. 1952 (1958: no vol. indic.). Vojenský historický ústav [Inst. of Military Hist.], U Památníku 2, Praha 3. Ed: J. Beránek. Art. on modern military hist., with emphasis on Czechoslovakia; bk. rev.; biblio. of new bk. on military science. Kčs 30.40 / $ 3.90

25. JIHOČESKÝ SBORNÍK HISTORICKÝ [Historical collection of South Bohemia]. Q. 1928 (1960: vol. 29). Krajské vlastivědné museum [Regional Hist. and Ethnographical Museum], Dukelská 1, České Budějovice. Ed: B. Janoušek. Art. on South Bohemian hist., mainly from the Hussite period on; bk. rev.; classified subject, author, biographical and geographical indices for vol. 1-25 (1928-56) pub. in 1958. Kčs 15 / $ 1.20

26. KATEDRA ČESKOSLOVENSKÝCH DĚJIN A ARCHIVNÍHO STUDIA, ZÁPISKY... (Zápisky Katedry československých dějin a archivního studia) [Transactions of the Chair of Czechoslovak History and Archival Studies]. Q. 1956 (1958: vol. 3/4). Katedra československých dějin a archivního studia filosoficko-historické fakulty Karlovy University [Chair of Czechoslovak Hist. and Archival Studies at the Philosophical-Hist. Faculty of Charles Univ.], Náměsti Krásnoarmějců 2, Praha 1. Ed: Václav Husa. Art. on Czechoslovak hist.; bk. rev. pv (Kčs 6-7.20)

27. KATEDRY DĚJIN KSČ A DĚJIN SSSR A KSSS, ZPRÁVY... (Zprávy Kateder dějin KSČ a dějin SSSR a KSSS) [Reports of the Chairs of the History of the Communist Party of Czechoslovakia and of the History of the U.S.S.R. and the Communist Party of the U.S.S.R.]. S-A. 1958 (1960). Katedry dějin KSČ a dějin SSSR a KSSS, filosófické fakulty, Karlovy University [Chairs of the Hist. of the Communist Party of Czechoslovakia and of the Hist. of the U.S.S.R. and the Communist Party of the U.S.S.R. at the Faculty of Philosophy, Charles Univ.], Náměstí Krásnoarmějců 2, Praha 1. Ed: L. Vebr, F. Hrbata. Reports on the pedagogical and academic activities of teachers and students in the hist. dept. named above. p(1) Kčs 12

28. LISTY FILOLOGICKÉ [Philological papers]. S-A. 1874 (1960: vol. 8). Kabinet pro studia řecká, římská a latinská, Československá akademie věd [Section for the Study of Greek, Roman and Latin, Czechoslovak Acad. of Sciences]

Lazarská ul. 8, Praha 2. Ed: Antonín Salač (chief ed.), František Ryšánek (Bohemica), Václav Machek (comparative linguistics). Art. on classical philology and hist.; "Archiv pro dějiny filologie" [Archives for the hist. of philology]: reports on the work of Czechoslovak univ. in the field of classical studies and reprints of lectures; rev. of bk. and art.; A. name, word and papyri indices; German, English, French or Latin sum.; illus.; includes a supplement pub. under the title: Eunomia. Kčs 52 / $5.40

MATICE MORAVSKÁ, ČASOPIS... see next entry

29. MATICE MORAVSKÁ, SBORNÍK... (Sborník Matice Moravské) [Journal of the Moravian "Matice"]. A. 1869 (1960: vol. 79). Matice Moravská, Gorkého 14, Brno. Ed: Šindelář. Art. on Moravian hist. from the Middle Ages to the present; doc.; rev. art.; bk. rev. and detailed rev. of Czechoslovak hist. periodicals. Formerly pub. under the title: Časopis Matice Moravské [Review of the Moravian "Matice"]. Kčs 23.40 / $ 3.20

30. MORAVSKÉ MUSEUM V BRNĚ, ČASOPIS...(Časopis Moravského musea v Brně) [Review of the Moravian Museum, Brno]. Acta Musei Moraviae. Scientiae sociales. A. 1901 (1959: vol. 44). Moravské museum, Náměstí 25, února 8, Brno. Ed: J. Stehlík. Art. on the hist. (including literary and art hist.), archaeology and ethnography of Moravia; German or French sum.
pv (1959: Kčs 50 /$ 4)

MOST see section on U.S.A.

31. NÁRODNÍ MUSEUM V PRAZE, ČASOPIS... (Časopis Národního musea v Praze) [Review of the National Museum at Prague]. Oddíl věd společenských [Section of Social sciences]. S-A. 1827 (1960: vol. 129). Národní museum, Václavské náměstí 1700, Praha 2. Ed: Z. Drobná, R. Turek. Art. on archaeology, hist. and museum work; information on museums in Czechoslovakia and other countries and on different sections of the Národní museum; Russian and German sum. of main art. Kčs 18 / $3.80

32. NÁRODNÍ MUSEUM V PRAZE, SBORNÍK... (Sborník Národního musea v Praze) [Journal of the National Museum at Prague]. Acta Musei Nationalis Pragae. Řada A - Historie [Series A - History]. 5xy. 1938 (1960: vol. 14). Národní museum v Praze, Václavské náměstí 68, Praha 2. Ed: V. Denkstein. Art. on hist. (including the hist. of art), archaeology and numismatics; in Czech and occasionally in English; English, French, German or Russian sum. pv

33. NÁRODNÍ MUSEUM V PRAZE, SBORNÍK... (Sborník Národního musea v Praze) [Journal of the National Museum at Prague]. Acta Musei Nationalis Pragae. Rada C-Literární historie [Series C-Literary history]. Q. Národní museum, Václavské náměstí 68, Praha 2. Russian and German sum.
Kčs 26 / $3.80

34. NAŠA VEDA [Our science]. M. Slovenská akadémie vied [Slovak Acad. of Sciences], ul. Obrancov mieru 41, Bratislava. Reports on the work of the acad. and on the past and present state of the social and natural sciences; rev. of the pub. of Czechoslovak and foreign acad. Kčs 36 / $4.20

35. NAŠE ŘEČ [Our language]. 10xy (5 double no. p.a.). Nakladatelství Československé akademie věd [Pub. House of the Czechoslovak Acad. of Sciences], for Ústav pro jazyk český Československé akademie věd [Inst. for the Czech Language of the Czechoslovak Acad. of Sciences], Letenská 4, Praha 1. A. subject index. Kčs 15 / $ 2

36. NOVÁ MYSL [New thought]. Teoretický a politický časopis ústředního výboru Komunistické strany Československa [Theoretical and political review of the Central Committee of the Communist Party of Czechoslovakia]. M. Pub. address: Na poříčí 30, Praha 3. Kčs 24 / $3

37. NOVINÁŘSKÝ SBORNÍK [Journalists' magazine]. Teoretický časopis Svazu Československých novinářů [Theoretical review of the Federation of Czechoslovak Journalists]. Q. Svaz Československých novinářů, Vinohrady, Stalinova 3, Praha 12. Kčs 48 / $5

38. NOVÝ ORIENT [New Orient]. 10 xy. Orientální ústav Československé akademie věd [Oriental Inst. of the Czechoslovak Acad. of Sciences], Lázeňská 4, Praha 1. Kčs 40 / $3.30

39. NUMISMATICKÁ SPOLEČNOST ČESKOSLOVENSKÁ V PRAZE, NUMISMATICKÉ LISTY... (Numismatické listy Numismatické společnosti Československé v Praze) [Numismatic papers of the Numismatic Society of Czechoslovakia at Prague]. B-M. 1945/46 (1960: vol. 15). Numismatická společnost Československá, Belehradská 130, Praha 2. Ed: K. Castelin. Art. on numismatics, mint law and prices; information about newly found coins; bk. rev.; reports on the activities of the soc. Kčs 30 / $3.90

NUMISMATICKÉ LISTY NUMISMATICKÉ SPOLEČNOSTI ČESKOSLOVENSKÉ V PRAZE see preceding entry

40. NUMISMATICKÝ SBORNÍK [Numismatic journal]. A. 1953 (1960: vol. 6). Numismatická komise, Historický ústav Československé akademie věd [Numismatic Committee, Hist. Inst. of the Czechoslovak Acad. of Sciences], Jiřská 3, Praha 4-Hrad. Ed: E. Nohejlová-Prátová. Art. on numismatics pertaining to all periods; reports on discoveries of coins of Czechoslovak and foreign origin; Russian and French sum. Kčs 50.50

41. PAMÁTKY ARCHEOLOGICKÉ [Archaeological treasures]. S-A. 1855 (1960: vol. 51). Archeologický ústav Československé akademie věd [Archaeological Inst. of the Czechoslovak Acad. of Sciences], Letenská 4, Praha 3. Ed: J. Böhm. Art. on archaeology (prehist. and hist.), based on newly acquired material and on the latest results of archaeological excavations in Czechoslovakia; German or French sum. Kčs 134 / $12.20

42. PAMIATKY A MÚZEÁ [Relics and museums]. Časopis pre ochranu pamiatok a problémy múzeí [Review for the preservation of historical treasures and problems of museums]. Q. 1952 (1960: vol. 9). Nakladatelstvi Martin [Martin pub. House], Osveta. Ed: S. Pisoň. Art. on archaeology, art hist. ethnography, local hist., museum work and hist. relics and their preservation, pertaining mostly to Slovakia; bk. rev.; Russian or German sum. Kčs 24 / $2.40

43. PHILOLOGICA PRAGENSIA. Q. Kabinet pro moderní filologii, Československá akademie věd [Section of Modern Philology, Czechoslovak Acad. of Sciences], Liliová 13, Praha 1. In English, French, German, Italian or Spanish. Kčs 20 / $2.20

44. POLITICKÁ EKONOMIE [Political economy]. 10 xy. Ekonomický ústav Československé akademie věd [Inst. of Economics of the Czechoslovak Acad. of Sciences], Třída Politických vězňů 7, Praha 1. Kčs 45 / $4.30

45. PRÁVNĚHISTORICKÉ STUDIE [Studies on the history of law]. A. 1955 (1960: vol. 6). Oddělení dějin státu a práva ČSR, Ústav práva Československé akademie věd [Section of the Hist. of the State and Law in the Czechoslovak Republic, Inst. of Law of the Czechoslovak Acad. of Sciences], Opletalova 57, Praha 3. Ed: J. Houser and J. Kejř. Art. on the hist. of law in Czechoslovakia and other countries; bk. rev.; reports of hist. and legal conferences; German and Russian sum. pv (1960: Kčs 23.20)

46. PRÁVNÍK [Lawyer]. Teoretický časopis pro otázky státu a práva [Theoretical review on the problems of state and law]. 10 xy. Nakladatelství Československé akademie věd [Pub. House of the Czechoslovak Acad. of Sciences], Vodičkova 40, Praha 2, for Ústav práva Československé akademie věd [Inst. of Law of the Czechoslovak Acad. of Sciences], Praha. Kčs 55 / $5.80

47. PRÁVNY OBZOR [Law review]. 10 xy. Slovenská akadémia vied [Slovak Acad. of Sciences], Klemensova 27, Bratislava. Czechoslovak law; table of contents also in Russian. Kčs 30

48. PŘÍSPĚVKY K DĚJINÁM KSČ [Essays on the history of the Communist Party of Czechoslovakia]. Irr. 1957 (1960). Ústav dějin Komunistické strany Československa [Inst. of the Hist. of the Communist Party of Czechoslovakia], Rytířská 31, Praha 1. Ed: J. Pachta. Art. on the hist. of the Communist Party and the labor movement in Czechoslovakia; doc. on recent hist. p (1) Kčs 6 / $ 1

SBORNÍK. For titles beginning with "Sborník," followed by the name of the publishing or sponsoring institution or society, see the respective institution or society.

49. SBORNÍK ARCHIVNÍCH PRACÍ [Journal of archival studies]. S-A. 1951 (1960: vol. 10). Archivní správa ministerstva vnitra [Archival Dept. of the Ministry of the Interior], Praha. Ed: Zdeněk Šamberger, Obránců míru 133, Praha 6. Art. on archival management and the holdings of Czech and other archives and on Czech hist. and the hist. of the Czech provinces in the Habsburg Empire, from the Middle Ages to the present; doc.; rev. of bk. and periodicals; professional news. Kčs 34 / $2.30

50. SBORNÍK HISTORICKÝ [Historical journal]. A. 1953 (1960: vol. 7). Historický ústav Československé akademie věd [Inst. of Hist. of the Czechoslovak Acad. of Sciences], Jiřská 3, Praha 4. Ed: V. Vojtíšek. Art. on Czechoslovak and international hist., predominantly medieval and modern; Russian and French sum. Kčs 26.50

51. SBORNÍK PRO DĚJINY PŘÍRODNÍCH VĚD A TECHNIKY [Journal on the history of natural sciences and technology]. Acta Historiae Rerum Naturalium necnon Technicarum. A. 1954 (1960: vol. 5). Komise pro dějiny přírodních věd lekařských a technických, Historický ústav Československé akademie věd [Committee for the Hist. of Natural Sciences and Technology, Inst. of Hist. of the Czechoslovak Acad. of Sciences], Jiřská 3, Praha 4-Hrad. Ed: J. Kořán. Art. on the hist. of natural sciences and technology; rev. of bk. and periodicals; biblio. of Czechoslovak pub.; English, French, German or Russian sum. pv (1960: Kčs 32)

SBORNÍK ŠTÚDII A PRÁC VYSOKEJ ŠKOLY PEDAGOGICKEJ V BRATISLAVĚ see VYSOKÁ ŠKOLA PEDAGOGICKÁ V BRATISLAVĚ, SBORNÍK ŠTÚDII A PRÁC...

52. SLAVIA. Časopis pro slovanskou filologii [Review of Slavic philology]. Q. 1922 (1960: vol. 29). Slovanský ústav Československé akademie věd [Slavic Inst. of the Czechoslovak Acad. of Sciences], Valentinská 1, Praha 1. Ed: K. Krejčí. Art. on Slavic philology and hist.; doc.; bk. rev.; news of interest to students of Slavic philology; in Czech, Slovak, Russian, Polish or French. Kčs 80 / $ 8.20

53. SLEZSKÝ MUSEUM, ČASOPIS... (Časopis Slezského musea) [Review of the Silesian Museum]. Vědy společenské [Social sciences]. Acta Musei Silesiae. Scientiae Sociales. S-A. 1951 (1960: vol. 9). Slezský muzeum, Tyršova 1, Opava. Ed: B. Sobotík. Art. on archaeology, hist., art and numismatics pertaining to Silesia; reports of the museum; occasional German or Russian sum. Kčs 12 / $ 5.10

54. SLEZSKÝ SBORNÍK [Silesian review]. Acta Silesiaca. Q. 1878 (1960: vol. 58). Slezský studijní ústav [Soc. for Silesian Studies], Nádražní Okruh 31, Opava. Ed: Andělín Grobelný. Art. on the culture and social hist. of Czechoslovak Silesia and adjoining areas, with emphasis on the 19th cent.; doc.; rev. art.; rev. of bk. and periodicals; German and Polish sum. Kčs 36 / $1.75

55. SLOVANSKÉ HISTORICKÉ STUDIE [Slavic historical studies]. Irr. 1955 (1960: vol. 3). Slovanský ústav Československé akademie věd [Slavic Inst. of the Czechoslovak Acad. of Sciences], Valentinská 1, Praha 1. Ed: O. Říha, Letohradská 38, Praha 7. Art. on Slavic hist. from the earliest times to the present; French and Russian sum. pv (1960: Kčs 43.50)

56. SLOVANSKÉ ŠTÚDIE [Slavic studies]. Irr. 1957 (1960: vol. 3). Vydavatel'stvo Slovenskej akadémie vied [Pub. House of the Slovak Acad. of Sciences], Bratislava. Ed: J. Hrozienčik. Art. and doc. on Slavic hist. pv (1960: Kčs 51)

57. SLOVANSKÝ PŘEHLED [Slavic review]. B-M. Slovanský výbor Československa [Slavic Committee of Czechoslovakia], Loretánská 9, Praha 1. Kčs 18 / $1.75

58. SLOVENSKÁ ARCHEOLÓGIA [Slovak archaeology]. S-A. 1953 (1960: vol. 8). Archeologický ústav Slovenskej akadémie vied [Archaeological Inst. of the Slovak Acad. of Sciences], Hrad, Nitra. Ed: A. Točník. Monographs on archaeological research and theoretical studies on the Slovak primeval age; English, French, German or Russian sum. Kčs 120 / $ 12.20

59. SLOVENSKÁ LITERATÚRA [Slovak literature]. Q. Ústav slovenskej literatúry Slovenskej akadémie vied [Inst. of Slovak Literature of the Slovak Acad. of Sciences], Klemensova 27, Bratislava. Kčs 28 / $ 3.20

60. SLOVENSKÝ FILOZOFICKÝ ČASOPIS [Slovak philosophical review]. Q. Vydavatel'stvo Slovenskej akadémie vied [Pub. House of the Slovak Acad. of Sciences], Klemensova 27, Bratislava. Kčs 24 / $2.50

61. SLOVENSKÝ NÁRODOPIS [Slovak ethnography]. Q. Vydavatel'stvo Slovenskej akadémie vied [Pub. House of the Slovak Acad. of Sciences], Klemensova 27, Bratislava. German, Russian, English or French sum. Kčs 54 / $ 6

62. SPOLEČNOST PŘÁTEL STAROŽITNOSTÍ, ČASOPIS... (Časopis Společnosti přátel starožitností) [Review of the Society of Friends of Antiquities]. Orgán historické vlastivědy České [Journal of the history and geography of Bohemia]. Q. 1893 (1960: vol. 68). Společnost přátel starožitností, Praha. Ed: J. Klik, Bubeneč, Puškinovo náměstí 7, Praha 6. Art. on the hist. and geography of Bohemia; notes on doc.; bk. rev.; author and topographical index. (memb.) Kčs 16 / $2.10

63. UMĚNÍ [Art]. Q. Nakladatelství Československé akademie věd [Pub. House of the Czechoslovak Acad. of Sciences], Praha, for Ústav pro teorii a dějiny umění, Československé akademie věd [Inst. for the Theory and Hist. of Art, Czechoslovak Acad. of Sciences], Haštalská 6, Praha 1. Hist. of art in Czechoslovakia; Russian, French or English sum. Kčs 138 / $14

64. UNIVERSITAS CAROLINAE, ACTA... (Acta Universitatis Carolinae). Philosophica et Historica. Sectio A, Seria 3: Historica. Irr. 1954 (1960). Universita Karlova [Charles Univ.], Staré Město, Pařížská 27, Praha 1. Ed: J. Kladira. Art. on Czechoslovak and world hist.; Russian and German sum. Kčs 12.20

65. UNIVERSITAS PALACKIANAE OLOMUCENSIS, ACTA... (Acta Universitatis Palackianae Olomucensis). Facultas Philosophica. Historica. A. 1960 (1960: vol. 1). Státní pedagogické nakladatelství [State Pedagogical Pub. House], Ostrovní 30, Praha 2, for Vysoka škola pedagogicka v Olomouci [Pedagogical Univ. of Olomouc]. Ed: D. Krandžalov. Art. on Czechoslovak hist.; Russian or German sum. From 1954 to 1959 pub. under the title: Sborník Vysoké školy pedagogické v Olomouci. Historie [Journal of the Pedagogical Univ. of Olomouc. Hist.]. Kčs 31

66. ÚSTAV DEJÍN KSS, SBORNÍK... (Sborník Ústavu dejín KSS) [Journal of the Institute of the History of the Slovak Communist Pary]. Irr. 1959 (1960: vol. 3). Slovenské vydavatelstvo politickej literaratúry [Slovak Pub. House of Political Literature], Bratislava, for Ústav dejín KSS. Ed: B. Graca. Art. on the hist. of the Communist Party and the labor movement in Slovakia. pv (vol. 3: Kčs 9.90)

VĚSTNÍK. For titles beginning with "Věstník," followed by the name of the publishing or sponsoring institution or society, see the respective institution or society.

67. VLASTIVĚDNÝ VĚSTNÍK MORAVSKÝ [Moravian historical-geographical journal]. A. 1946 (1960: vol. 15). Krajské nakladatelství [Regional Pub. House], Brno. Ed: A. Gregor. Art. on the hist. and geography of Moravia; bk. rev.; reports of museums and hist.-geographical soc.; index for vol. 1-10 pub. separately. Kčs 16.50 / $1.30

68. VYSOKÁ ŠKOLA PEDAGOGICKÁ V BRATISLAVĚ, SBORNÍK ŠTÚDII A PRÁC... (Sborník štúdii a prác Vysokej školy pedagogickej v Bratislavě) [Collection of studies and papers of the Pedagogical University at Bratislava]. Spoločenské vedy. Slovenský jazyk a literatúra [Social sciences. Slovak language and literature]. Irr. 1957 (1957: vol. 1). Slovenské pedagogické nakladatelstvo [Slovak Pedagogical Pub. House], Sasinkova 5, Bratislava. Ed: M. Gašparík. Art. on social sciences pertaining to Slovakia and on Slovak language and literature. Kčs 60

VYSOKÁ ŠKOLA PEDAGOGICKÁ V OLOMOUCI, SBORNÍK... Historie see UNIVERSITAS PALACKIANAE OLOMUCENSIS, ACTA...

69. VYSOKÁ ŠKOLA PEDAGOGICKÁ V OLOMOUCI, SBORNÍK... (Sborník Vysoké školy pedagogické v Olomouci) [Journal of the Pedagogical University at Olomouc]. Jazyk a literature [Language and literature]. A. Státní pedagogické nakladatelství [State Pedagogical Pub. House], Ostrovní 30, Praha 2, for Vysoká škola pedagogická v Olomouc. Kčs 22.90

70. VYSOKÁ ŠKOLA PEDAGOGICKÁ V PRAZE, SBORNÍK... (Sborník Vysoké školy pedagogické v Praze) [Journal of the Pedagogical University at Prague]. Historie [History]. Irr. 1957 (1959: vol. 2). Státní pedagogické nakladatelství [State Pedagogical Pub. House], Ostrovní 30, Praha 2. Ed: A. Klíma. Art. on Czechoslovak hist. and its relation to European hist. and on methods of teaching hist. and philosophy; Russian and German, English or French sum. Kčs 19.30

71. VYSOKÁ ŠKOLA PEDAGOGICKÁ V PRAZE, SBORNÍK... (Sborník Vysoké školy pedagogické v Praze)[Journal of the Pedagogical University at Prague]. Jazyk-literature [Language-literature]. Irr. Státní pedagogické nakladatelství [State Pedagogical Pub. House], Ostrovní 30, Praha 2, for Vysoká škola pedagogická v Praze. Russian or German sum. p (1) Kčs 22.90

ZÁPISKY. For titles beginning with "Zápisky," followed by the name of the publishing or sponsoring institution or society, see the respective institution or society.

ZPRÁVY. For titles beginning with "Zprávy," followed by the name of the publishing or sponsoring institution or society, see the respective institution or society.

Denmark

Prepared with the assistance of

Rigsbibliotekarembedet [The Office of the National Librarian], Copenhagen

1. ACTA ARCHAEOLOGICA. A. 1930 (1957 [1958]: vol. 28). Ejnar Munksgaards forlag, Nørregade 6, København K, for Nationalmuseet [National Museum], Frederiksholms kanal 12, København K. Ed: C.J. Becker. Well-documented art. on the archaeology, prehist. and anthropology of Europe, particularly Scandinavia, with emphasis on the prehist., ancient and medieval periods; news of excavations; in English, French or German; subject index; illus. Dcr 45 / $ 7

2. ACTA PHILOLOGICA SCANDINAVICA. Tidsskrift for nordisk sprogforskning [Journal of Scandinavian philology]. Q. Ed: Johs. Brøndum-Nielsen, Rungstedvej 9, Rungsted Kyst. Dcr 40

ÅRBOG, ÅRBØGER. For titles beginning with "Årbog" or "Årbøger," followed by the name of the publishing or sponsoring institution or society, see the respective institution or society.

3. ÅRBØGER FOR NORDISK OLDKYNDIGHED OG HISTORIE [Yearbooks of Scandinavian antiquities and history]. A. 1836 (1957: no vol. indic.). Det kongelige nordiske oldskriftselskab [Royal Soc. of Scandinavian Antiquaries], Frederiksholms kanal 12, København K. Art. on the archaeology and anthropology of Scandinavia, with emphasis on the prehist., ancient and medieval periods; English sum. Dcr 20

4. ARKAEOLOGISK-KUNSTHISTORISKE SKRIFTER [Archaeology and art history papers]. Irr. 1942 (1957: vol. 2). Ejnar Munksgaard forlag, for Det kongelige danske videnskabernes selskab [Royal Danish Acad. of Sciences and Letters], Dantes plads 5, København V. Art. on archaeology and art hist.; in Danish, English, French or German. Ceased pub. Dcr 120

5. ARV OG EJE [Inheritance and possession]. A. 1950 (1958: vol. 7). Dansk kulturhistorisk museumsforening [Soc. of Danish Museums of Cultural Hist.], Frederiksholms kanal 12, København K. Ed: Holger Rasmussen. Art. on Danish cultural and local hist., predominantly based on the collections of the museums of cultural hist.; bk. rev. Prior to 1956 pub. under the title Danske Museer [Danish museums]. Dcr 10

6. AVISÅRBOGEN [Press yearbook]. A. Ed: B. V. Elberling, Sandbyvej 43, København. Dcr 38

7. BIBLIOTEK FOR LÆGER [Medical library]. B-M. Ed: Poul Bonnevie and Mogens Fog, Kristianiagade 12, København Ø. Dcr 20

8. BOGVENNEN [Book-lover]. Årbog for bogkunst and boghistorie [Yearbook of art and history of books]. A. Forening for boghaandværk [Soc. for bookcraft], Hostrups Have 27, København V. Illus. Dcr 20

9. BORNHOLMSKE SAMLINGER [Collections from Bornholm]. A. Bornholmsk samfund [Soc. of Bornholm], Rønne. Dcr 7

10. BUDSTIKKEN [Messenger]. A. 1953 (mri 1956: vol. 3). Dansk folkemuseum [Danish Public Museum], Nationalmuseet 3. afdeling, Frederiksholms kanal 12, København K. Ed: Peter Michelsen. Art. on Danish and, occasionally, European cultural hist., with emphasis on the medieval and modern periods; reports on the activities, personnel and literature of the Dansk folkemuseum, and on museum science. Dcr 20

11. CATHOLICA. Q. Ed: L.B. Fabricius, Havrevej 11, København Brh. Dcr 18

12. CENTAURUS. International Magazine of the History of Science and Medicine. Irr. 1950 (1956-58: vol. 5). Ejnar Munksgaard forlag, Nørregade 6, København K. Ed: A.G. Drachmann, Mogen's Pihl, Edv. Gotfredsen. Art. on the hist. of science and medicine; bk. rev.; in English, French or German. Dcr 60

13. CLASSICA ET MEDIAEVALIA. Revue danoise de philologie et d'histoire [Danish review of philology and history]. A. 1938 (1958: vol. 19). Societas Danica indagationis antiqvitatis et mediiaevi, Klareboderne 3, København. Ed: Franz Blatt, Århus Universitet, Århus. Art. on general, legal and ecclesiastical hist., and the hist. of philosophy, literature and philology, pertaining to ancient and medieval Europe; in English, French, German or Italian. Dcr 40

14. DANSK TEOLOGISK TIDSSKRIFT [Danish theological journal]. Q. G.E.C. Gads forlag, København. Dcr 15

15. DANSK UDSYN [Danish outlook]. B-M. Askov Højskole, Askov pr. Vejen. Dcr 15

16. DANSKE FOLKEMÅL [Danish dialects]. Irr. Ed: Poul Andersen, Fiolstræde 1, København K. Dcr 5

17. DET DANSKE MAGASIN [The Danish review]. 10 x y. Ed: Terkel M. Terkelsen, Pilestræde 34, København K. Ceased pub. in 1957.

18. DANSKE MAGAZIN [Danish magazine]. Indeholdende bidrag til den danske histories oplysning [Containing contributions to Danish history]. Irr. 1745 (1958: 8th series, vol. 1). Det kongelige danske selskab for fædrelandets historie [The Royal Danish Soc. for National Hist.], Nationalmuseet, Frederiksholms kanal 12, København K. Ed: Georg Galster. Annotated pub. of Danish and foreign source material pertaining to Danish hist., with emphasis on the modern period. Vol. subject index. p (1) Dcr 6

DANSKE MUSEER see ARV OG EJE

19. DANSKE STUDIER [Danish studies]. A. Ed: Aage Hansen, Erik Dal, Amaliegade 21 C, København K. Dcr 15

20. ERHVERVSHISTORISK ÅRBOG [Yearbook of business history]. A. 1949 (1957: vol. 9). Universitetsforlaget i Århus, for Erhvervsarkivet [Business Archives], Carl Blochsgade 18, Århus. Ed: Vagn Dybdahl. Art. on Danish business and industrial hist., and archival problems, mainly based on the collec-

tions of the archives; doc.; reports on the activities of the archives; statistics; illus. pv (c. Dcr 14-16)

21. FOLKEMINDER [Folklore]. Irr. "Danmarks Folkeminder" ["Folklore of Denmark"], Dansk folkemindesamling, Det kgl. Bibliotek [Inst. of Folklore, the Royal Library], Christians Brygge 8, København K. Dcr 12

22. FORTID OG NUTID [Past and present]. Tidsskrift for kulturhistorie og lokalhistorie [Journal of cultural and local history]. Irr. (1-2 x y). 1914 (1958: vol. 20). Dansk historisk fællesforening [Danish Hist. Assoc.], Frederiksborg slot, Hillerød. Ed: P. Michelsen, Nationalmuseets 3. afdeling, Frederiksholms kanal 12, København K. Art. on the local and cultural hist. of Denmark, with emphasis on the medieval and modern periods; bk. rev.; biblio. of bk. and periodicals; news and notes on the work of Danish museums, archives and hist. soc. in the field of local and cultural hist.; vol. subject index. Dcr 16

23. FRA ALS OG SUNDEVED [From Als and Sundeved]. Irr. Historisk samfund for Als og Sundeved [Hist. Soc. of Als and Sundeved], Sønderborg. Dcr 8

24. FRA DET GAMLE GILLELEJE [From the old Gilleleje]. Nordsjællands-Kystens årbog [Yearbook of the North Zealand coast]. A. (vol. 26 and 27 [1958/59]pub. in 1 vol.). Gilleleje museums forlag, Gilleleje. Dcr 8/$ 1.15

25. FRA FREDERIKSBORG AMT. ÅRBOG [From the county of Frederiksborg. Yearbook]. A. Frederiksborg amts historiske samfund [Hist. Soc. of the County of Frederiksborg], Frederiksborg museet, Hillerød. Statistics, maps; illus. Cum. index. Dcr 15

26. FRA HIMMERLAND OG KJÆR HERRED [From the districts of Himmerland and Kjær]. A. Historisk samfund for Ålborg amt [Hist. Soc. of the County of Ålborg], Ålborg. Dcr 7

27. FRA HOLBÆK AMT [From the county of Holbæk]. A. Historisk samfund for Holbæk amt [Hist. Soc. of the County of Holbæk], Holbæk. Dcr 5

28. FRA KØBENHAVNS AMT [From the district of Copenhagen]. A. Historisk samfund for Københavns amt [Hist. Soc. of the County of Copenhagen], Roskilde. Dcr 10

29. FRA RANDERS AMT [From the district of Randers]. Historisk årbog fra Randers amt [Historical yearbook from the County of Randers]. A. Randers. Dcr 10

30. FRA RIBE AMT [From the district of Ribe]. A. Historisk samfund for Ribe amt [Hist. Soc. of the County of Ribe], København. Dcr 10

31. FRA VIBORG AMT [From the district of Viborg]. A. Historisk samfund for Viborg amt [Hist. Soc. of the County of Viborg], Viborg. Dcr 14

32. FREDERIKSBERG GENNEM TIDERNE [Frederiksberg through the ages]. Irr. Historisk-topografisk selskab for Frederiksberg [Hist.-topographical Soc. of Frederiksberg], Solbjergvej 25, København F. Dcr 16

33. FREMTIDEN [Future]. International orientering [International orientation]. 10 x y. Det undenrigspolitiske selskab [Foreign Policy Assoc.], Frederiksholms kanal 18, København K. Dcr 20

34. FUND OG FORSKNING I DET KGL. BIBLIOTEKS SAMLINGER [Finds and research in the Collections of the Royal Library]. A. Det kgl. Bibliotek, Christians Brygge 8, København K. Dcr 16

35. FYNSKE ÅRBØGER [Yearbooks of Funen]. A. Historisk samfund før Fyns stift [Hist. Soc. of the Diocese of Funen], Odense. Dcr 11

36. FYNSKE MINDER [Memories of Funen]. A. Odense bys museer [Museums of Odense], Odense. Dcr 9

37. GEOGRAFISK TIDSSKRIFT [Geographical journal]. A. Det Kgl. danske geografiske selskab [Royal Danish Geographical Soc.], Nationalmuseet, Frederiksholms kanal 12, København K. Dcr 25

38. GLOSTRUP BOGEN [Glostrup-Book]. A. Historisk selskab for Glostrup og omegn [Hist. Soc. of Glostrup and its vicinity], Glostrup. Dcr 5

39. GRØNLAND [Greenland]. M. Det grønlandske selskab [Greenland Soc.], L.E. Bruuns Vej 10, Charlottenlund. Dcr 48

40. HANDELS- OG SØFARTSMUSEET PÅ KRONBORG. ÅRBOG [Museum of Commerce and Shipping at Kronborg. Yearbook]. A. Handels- og søfartsmuseets venner [Friends of the museum of commerce and shipping], Helsingør. Dcr 12

41. HARDSYSSELS ÅRBOG [The yearbook of Hardsyssel]. A. Historisk samfund før Ringkøbing amt [Hist. Soc. of the County of Ringkøbing], København. Dcr 10

42. HISTORISK ÅRBOG FOR THISTED AMT [Historical yearbook for the County of Thisted]. A. Historisk samfund før Thy og Hanherred [Hist. Soc. of Thy and Hanherred], København. Dcr 4

HISTORISK-FILOLOGISKE MEDDELELSER see HISTORISK-FILOSOFISKE MEDDELELSER

43. HISTORISK-FILOLOGISKE SKRIFTER [Historical-philological writings]. Irr. 1940 (1951-58: vol. 3). Ejnar Munksgaard forlag for Det kongelige danske videnskabernes selskab [Royal Danish Acad. of Sciences and Letters], Dantes plads 5, København V. Art. on hist. (including art hist.), philology, philosophy and archaeology; in Danish, English, French or German. The title will be changed to <u>Historisk-filosofiske skrifter</u> [Hist.- philosophical writings], beginning with vol. 4 pv

44. HISTORISK-FILOSOFISKE MEDDELELSER [Historical-philosophical reports]. Irr. 1917 (1957/58: vol. 37). Ejnar Munksgaard forlag for Det kongelige danske videnskabernes selskab [Royal Danish Acad. of Sciences and Letters Dantes plads 5, København V. Art. on hist. (including art hist.), philology, philosophy and archaeology; in Danish, English, French or German. Prior to 195 pub. under the title <u>Historisk-filologiske meddelelser</u> [Hist.- philological reports] pv

HISTORISK-FILOSOFISKE SKRIFTER see HISTORISK-FILOLOGISKE SKRIFTER

45. HISTORISK SAMFUND FOR ÅRHUS STIFT, ÅRBØGER UDG. AF... [Yearbooks published by the Historical Society of the Diocese of Århus]. A. Historisk samfund for Århus stift, Århus. Dcr 10 / $ 1.50

46. HISTORISK SAMFUND FOR PRÆSTØ AMT. ÅRBOG [Historical society of the county of Præstø. Yearbook]. A. Historisk samfund før Præstø amt, Næstved. Dcr 7

47. HISTORISK SAMFUND FOR SORØ AMT, ÅRBOG FOR... [Yearbook of the Historical Society of the County of Sorø]. A. Historisk samfund før Sorø amt, Slagelse. Dcr 6

48. HISTORISK TIDSSKRIFT [Historical review]. Irr. 1840 (1956-58: 11th series, vol. 5). Den danske historiske forening [Danish Hist. Soc.], Kristian Zahrtmanns plads 83, København. Ed: Astrid Friis, Povl Bagge. Art. on Danish medieval and modern hist.; rev. art.; bk. rev. of most of the works of Danish historians; biblio.; English and German sum. Dcr 12

49. HISTORISK-TOPOGRAFISK SELSKAB FOR GJENTOFTE KOMMUNE, MEDDELELSER FRA... [Reports of the Historical-Topographical Society of the Municipality of Gjentofte]. A. Historisk-topografisk selskab for Gjentofte kommune, Hellerup. Dcr 6

50. HISTORISKE MEDDELELSER OM KØBENHAVN [Historical notes on Copenhagen]. Irr. 1907/08 (1957-59: vol 5). E. C. Gad, København K., for Selskabet for staden Københavns historie [Soc. for the Hist. of the City of Copenhagen], Stadsarkivet, Rådhuset, København V. Ed: Sigurd Jensen. Art. on the hist. of Copenhagen. p (1) Dcr 1.50

51. HØJSKOLEBLADET [Folk high school journal]. Tidende for folkeoplysning [Organ for popular education]. W. Ed: Poul Dam, Slotsgade 6-8, Kolding. Dcr 48

JØDISK FAMILIEBLAD see JØDISK SAMFUND

52. JØDISK SAMFUND [Jewish society]. M. Ed: Max Arnheim, Krystalgade 11, København K. Supersedes Jødisk Familieblad [Jewish family bulletin]. Dcr 10

53. JYSKE SAMLINGER [Jutland collections]. Tidsskrift for Danmarks historie [Journal for the history of Denmark]. S-A. 1868 (1958: new series, vol. 4). Jysk selskab for historie, sprog og litteratur [Jutland Soc. for Hist., Language and Literature], Erhvervsarkivet, Carl Blochsgade 28, Århus. Ed. board: Troels Fink, Johan Hvidtfeldt, Vagn Dybdahl (secretary), Harald Jensens plads 21, Århus. Art. on the hist., language and literature of Jutland and Denmark in general, with emphasis on the medieval and modern periods; bk. rev.; news of the soc.; vol. subject index. pv (p(1) Dcr 7-16)

54. KIRKEHISTORISKE SAMLINGER [Church history collections]. A. (1 vol. for 3 years). 1849 (1957/58: 7th series, vol. 3). Selskabet for Danmarks kirkehistorie [Soc. for Danish Church Hist.], Rahbeks allé 23, København V. Ed: N.K. Anderson, Knud Banning. Art. on general Danish church hist.; biographies; vol. subject index. Dcr 12 / $ 2

55. KØBSTADMUSEET "DEN GAMLE BY" (I ÅRHUS) ÅRBOG [Yearbook of "The Old Town" Museum (in Århus)]. A. Købstadmuseet "Den gamle By," Århus. Dcr 20

56. DET KGL. DANSKE VIDENSKABERNES SELSKAB. OVERSIGT OVER SELSKABETS VIRKSOMHED [Royal Danish Academy of Sciences and Letters. Report on the Academy's activities]. A. Ejnar Munksgaard, for Det kongelige danske videnskabernes selskab, Dantes plads 5, København V. Dcr 16

57. KULTUR OG FOLKEMINDER [Culture and folklore]. A. Nordsjællands museumsforening [Museum Assoc. of North Zealand], Hillerød. Dcr 8

58. KULTURGEOGRAFI [Cultural geography]. Tidsskrift for befolkningsgeografi, bebyggelsesgeografi, erhvervsgeografi, politisk geografi, historisk geografi [Journal of population geography, ecological geography, industrial geography, political geography, historical geography]. B-M. Ed: Johannes Humlum, Vanløsevej, Århus. Dcr 15

59. KULTURMINDER [Cultural history]. A. (Irr.). 1939 (1957: new series vol. 2). Nyt nordisk forlag, for Selskabet for dansk kulturhistorie [Soc. for Danish Cultural Hist.]. Ed: K. F. Plesner, Henrik Steffensvej 1, København V. Art. on Danish cultural hist. after 1536; biographies. pv

60. KUML. A. 1951 (1958 [1959]: vol. 8). Jysk arkæologisk selskab [Jutland Archaeological Soc.], Forhistorisk museum [Prehist. Museum], Århus. Ed: P.V. Glob Vester allé, Århus. Art. on archaeology, from the prehist. to medieval periods, with emphasis on Jutland, and reports on expeditions organized by Forhistorisk museum and Århus Univ.; reports of the soc.; English and German sum. Dcr 12 /$ 2

61. KUNSTMUSEETS ÅRSSKRIFT [Yearbook of the Museum of Art]. A. Statens museum for kunst [State Museum of Art], Sølvgade, København K. Dcr 27

62. LOLLANDS-FALSTERS HISTORISKE SAMFUNDS AARBOG [Yearbook of the Historical Society of Lolland-Falster]. A. Lollands-Falsters historiske samfund, Nykøbing F. Dcr 10

63. LYNGBY-BOGEN [Lyngby bulletin]. A. (Irr.). Historisk-topografisk selskab for Lyngby-Taarbæk Kommune [Hist.-Topographical Soc. of the Municipality of Lyngby-Taarbæk], c/o Stadsingeniør J.A.C. Rastrup, Rådhuset, Kongens Lyngby. Maps; illus. Dcr 6 /$ 1

MEDDELELSER. For titles beginning with "Meddelelser," followed by the name of the publishing or sponsoring institution or society, see the respective institution or society.

64. MEDICINSK FORUM [Medical forum]. B-M. MEFA, Foreningen af danske medicinfabrikker [Assoc. of Danish Medicine Manufacturers], Buen 266, Vester Farimagsgade 3, København V. Illus. Dcr 9

65. MILITÆRT TIDSSKRIFT [Military journal]. M. Det krigsvidenskabelige selskab [Soc. for Military Science], Hærens arkiv, Slotsholmsgade 10, København K. Statistics; graph. Dcr 24

66. NATIONALMUSEETS ARBEJDSMARK [Field of activities of the National Museum]. A. 1928 (1958: no vol.indic.). Nationalmuseet [National Museum], Frederiksholms kanal 12, København K. Art. on archaeological, hist. and ethnographical subjects related to the collections, excavations and expeditions of the museum. Dcr 18

67. NATIONALØKONOMISK TIDSSKRIFT [Economic review]. For samfundsspørgsmål, økonomi og handel [On social problems, economics and trade]. B-M. 1873 (1959: vol. 97). Danske boghandleres kommissionsanstact, København, for Nationaløkonomisk forening [Economic Soc.], Frederiksholms kanal 27, opgang F, København K. Ed. board: Poul Milhøj, K. Hansen, C. Iversen, V. Kampmann. Art. on economic theory, world economy, Danish economy and social statistics, and occasionally economic hist.; bk. rev.; news of the soc.; in Danish and occasionally in other languages; statistics; graph. Dcr 20

68. NORDISK ADMINISTRATIVT TIDSSKRIT [Scandinavian journal of administration]. Q. Scandinavian Administrative Assoc., Christiansborg Slotsplads 1, København K. Dcr 12

69. NORDISK ARKIVNYT [News from Scandinavian archives]. Q. Rigsarkivet [National Archives], Rigsdagsgården, København K. Illus. Dcr 12

70. NORDISK NUMISMATISK UNIONS MEDLEMSBLAD [Membership journal of the Scandinavian Numismatic Union]. 10xy. 1936 (1958: no vol.indic.). Nordisk numismatisk union, Nationalmuseet, Frederiksholms kanal 12, København K. Ed: P. Proschowsky. Art. on numismatics pertaining to Scandinavia; in Scandinavian languages; illus. Dcr 15

71. NORDISK TIDSSKRIFT FOR INTERNATIONAL RET OG JUS GENTIUM [Scandinavian journal of international law and jus gentium]. Acta scandinavica juris gentium. Q. Ed: Erik Brüel, Nikolaj plads 26, København K. Dcr 20

72. NYT FRA HISTORIEN [Historical news]. Q. 1950 (1958: vol. 9). Ejnar Munksgaard forlag, Nørregade 6, København K. Ed. board: V. Dybdahl (chief ed.), E. Reske-Nielsen, R. Thomsen, Erhvervsarkivet, Carl Blochsgade 28, Århus. Rev. by Danish hist. of Danish and foreign literature on hist. and ancillary subjects; S-A author index. Dcr 16

73. ØKONOMI OG POLITIK [Economics and politics]. Q. 1926 (1958: vol. 32). Samfundet for historie og samfundsøkonomi [Assoc. for Hist. and Economics], Sct. Pederstræde 5, København K. Ed: Jørgen L. Halck. Art. on modern hist. and economics; surveys of the international economic situation abroad and at home; political chronicle; reports of the inst.; vol. subject index. Dcr 15

74. ORBIS LITTERARUM. Revue internationale d'études littéraires [International review of literary studies]. Q. Ed: Steffen Steffensen, Hans Sørensen, Ved Lindevangen 30, København F. Dcr 65

75. ØSTJYDSK HJEMSTAVN [Region of eastern Jutland]. A. Østjydsk hjemstavnsforening [Regional Soc. of Eastern Jutland], Skanderborg. Dcr 16

76. PERSONALHISTORISK TIDSSKRIFT [Biographical journal]. Q. 1880 (1958: vol. 78). Samfundet for dansk genealogi og personalhistorie [Assoc. for Danish Genealogy and Biography], Søndre Fasanvej 46, København, Valby. Ed:

Sven Houmøller. Art. on Danish genealogy and cultural hist.; bk. rev.; biblio. of genealogical and biographical literature; news of the soc.; index of persons.
Dcr 20

77. RINGKJØBING ÅRBOG [Yearbook of Ringkjøbing]. A. Bollerups boghandel, Jens Holm, Ringkjøbing. Dcr 4.50

78. SKIVEBOGEN [Book on Skive]. Historisk årbog for Skive og omegn [Historical yearbook of Skive and its vicinity]. A. Historisk Samfund for Skive og Omegn [Hist. Assoc. for Skive and environments], Skive. Dcr 6

79. SOCIALT TIDSSKRIFT [Social welfare journal]. 8xy. Ed. board: E. Dreyer, J. Bonnesen, G. Drachmann, A. Skalts, Slotsholmsgade 6, København K. Dcr 25

80. SØNDERJYDSK ÅRBØGER [South Jutland yearbooks]. S-A. 1889 (1958: no vol. indic.). Historisk samfund for Sønderjylland [Hist. Soc. of South Jutland], Åbenrå. Ed. board: Knud Fanø, J. Hvidtfeldt, P.K. Iversen. Art. on the medieval and modern hist. of South Jutland; bk. rev.; biblio. of periodicals; news of the soc.; statistics; illus. Dcr 10

81. SØNDERJYDSK MAANEDSSKRIFT [South Jutland monthly]. M. Ed: W. Christiansen, Brorsonsvej 37, Tønder. Dcr 16

82. SPROG OG KULTUR [Language and culture]. Irr. 1932 (1958: vol. 21) Institut for jysk sprog-og kulturforskning [Inst. for Research in Jutland Language and Culture], Universitetsforlaget, Århus. Ed: P. Skautrup, P. Hansen, Niels Åge Nielsen. Art. on the cultural and linguistic hist. of Jutland, with emphasis on the medieval and modern periods. Dcr 10 / c. $ 1.50

83. TIDSSKRIFT FOR SØVAESEN [Maritime journal]. M. Ed: S. S. Thostrup, Kaptajn Grundtvig, Edelslundsvej 5, Klampenborg. Dcr 30

84. VÅBENHISTORISKE ÅRBØGER [Yearbooks of the history of arms and armor]. Irr. Våbenhistorisk selskab [Soc. for the Hist. of Arms and Armor], Frederiksborg Slot, Hillerød. Sum. in Danish, English, German or French.
Dcr 25

85. VEJLE AMTS ÅRBOG [Yearbook from the district of Vejle]. A. Vejle amts historiske samfund [Hist. Soc. of the County of Vejle], Kolding.
Dcr 8

86. VENDSYSSELSKE ÅRBØGER [Yearbooks from Vendsyssel]. A. Historisk samfund for Hjørring amt [Hist. Soc. of the County of Hjørring], Hjørring.
Dcr 9

87. VOR VIDEN [Modern knowledge]. B-W. Ed: Frithiof Hansen, Amagertorv 1, København K. Dcr 10

Finland

Prepared with the assistance of

Nils Berndtson, Chief Librarian, Library of Scientific Societies, Helsinki

1. ÅBO STADS HISTORISKA MUSEUM. ÅRSSKRIFT [Yearbook of the Historical Museum of Turku City]. A. Åbo stads historiska museum, Turku. pv

2. ÅLÄNDSK ODLING [Alandian culture]. A. Ålands Folkminnesförbund [Folklore Soc. of Åland], Mariehamn. Fmk 200

3. ANALECTA ARCHAEOLOGICA FENNICA. Irr. 1890 (1957: vol. 15). Muinaistieteellinen Toimikunta [Archaeological Board], Kansallismuseo, Helsinki. A. reports on the work of the board; reports on discussions at museum conferences; in Finnish or Scandinavian languages. free

4. ANKKAPURHA. Kymenlaakson Osakunnan Kotiseutujulkaisu [Regional research publication of the Student Association of Kymenlaakso]. Irr. Kymenlaakson Osakunta, Mannerheimintie 5A5, Helsinki. pv (p (1) c. Fmk 600)

ANNUAIRE DES HISTORIENS DE LA LITTERATURE see KIRJALLISUUDENTUTKIJAIN SEURAN VUOSIKIRJA

5. BUDKAVLEN [Fiery cross]. Organ för Brages Folklivsforskning och Institutet för Nordisk Etnologi vid Åbo Akademi [Organ of Ethnological Research of Brage and the Institute of Northern Ethnology at Åbo Academy]. Q (A.). Förlaget Bro, Kaskisgaten 2, Turku. Fmk 300

6. ENTISAIKAIN HELSINKI [Helsinki of olden times]. Irr. Helsinki-Seura [Helsinki Soc.], Pohjois-Esplanaadikatu 25, Helsinki. pv (p (1) c. Fmk 600)

7. FINNISCHE AKADEMIE DER WISSENSCHAFTEN, SITZUNGSBERICHTE DER... PROCEEDINGS OF THE FINNISH ACADEMY OF SCIENCE AND LETTERS. A. Suomalainen Tiedeakatemia [Finnish Acad. of Science and Letters], Säätytalo, Snellmaninkaut 9-11, Helsinki. Fmk 400

FINNISH ACADEMY OF SCIENCE AND LETTERS, PROCEEDINGS OF THE see FINNISCHE AKADEMIE DER WISSENSCHAFTEN, SITZUNGESBERICHTE DER...

8. FINSK TIDSKRIFT [Finnish review]. Kultur, Ekonomi, Politik [Culture, Economics, Politics]. 8 x y. Föreningen Granskaren [Examiner Soc.], (Erik Bergh), Konstmuseet, Turku. Fmk 1000 / Fmk 1100

FINSKA FORNMINNESFÖRENINGENS TIDSKRIFT see SUOMENT MUINAISMUISTOYHDISTYKSEN AIKAKAUSKIRJA

FINSKA KYRKOHISTORISKA SAMFUNDETS ÅRSSKRIFT see SUOMEN KIRKKOHISTORIALLISEN SEURAN VUOSIKIRJA

9. FINSKT MUSEUM [Finnish Museum]. A. 1894 (1959: vol. 65). Suomen Muinaismuistoyhdistys (Finska Fornminnesföreningen) [Archaeological Soc. of Finland], Kansallismuseo, Helsinki. Ed: C.F.Meinander. Art. on all periods of archaeology, ethnography and cultural hist., with emphasis on Finland; bk. rev.; in Swedish and German; German sum. See also Suomen Museo. Fmk 500

10. FOLKLIVSSTUDIER [Ethnological studies]. Irr. 1945 (1959: vol. 5). Folkkultursarkivet [Ethnological Archives], Svenska Litteratursällskapet i Finland [Swedish Literary Soc. of Finland], Regeringsgatan 11-13, Helsinki. Studies on the cultural hist. and ethnology of Swedish Finland; in Swedish. pv (p(1) c. Fmk 1400)

GENEALOGISKA SAMFUNDETS I FINLAND ÅRSSKRIFT see SUOMEN SUKUTUTKIMUSSEURAN VUOSIKIRJA

11. GENOS. Q. 1930 (1960: vol. 31). Suomen Sukututkimusseura [Genealogical Soc. of Finland], Säätytalo, Snellmaninkatu 9-11, Helsinki. Ed: Heikki Soininvaara, Laajalahdentie 20 A, Helsinki. Art. on Finnish genealogy and on the theory of genealogy; bk. rev.; notes and news; reports of discoveries and on the activities of the soc.; in Finnish and Swedish; German sum. of art. on the theory of genealogy. Fmk 700

12. HÄMEENMAA. Irr. Hämeen Heimoliitto [Tribal Assoc. of Häme], Hämeenlinna. pv (p (1) c. Fmk 500)

13. HISTORIALLINEN AIKAKAUSKIRJA [Historical review]. Q. 1903 (1960: vol. 58). Suomen Historiallinen Seura [Finnish Hist. Soc.], Säätytalo, Snellmaninkatu 9-11, Helsinki. Ed: Pentti Renvall, Jaakko Numminen, Albertinkatu 19 A 1, Helsinki. Art. on the ancient and modern hist. of Europe, with emphasis on Finland, on the philosophy of hist., and on problems of research; rev. art.; biblio.; news and notes on persons and inst. and on new hist. pub.; in Finnish; sum. in German or English. Fmk 750

14. HISTORIALLINEN ARKISTO [Historical archives]. Irr. 1866 (1958: vol. 56). Suomen Historiallinen Seura [Finnish Hist. Soc.], Säätytalo, Snellmaninkatu 9-11, Helsinki. Ed: Veikko Kerkkonen. Art. on the medieval and modern hist. of Finland; reports of the proceedings of the soc.; in Finnish and occasionally in Swedish; German sum. pv

15. HISTORIAN AITTA [Historical magazine]. Tutkielmia. Kuvauksia. Muistelmia [Essays. Descriptions. Memoirs]. Irr. 1929 (mri 1956: vol. 13). Historian Ystäväian Liitto [Assoc. of the Friends of Hist.], Portimonpolku 14 A 43, Helsinki. Art. on the hist. of Finland and other countries. pv

HISTORIENS DE LA LITTERATURE, ANNUAIRE DES... see KIRJALLISUUDENTUTKIJAIN SEURAN VUOSIKIRJA

16. HISTORISK TIDSKRIFT FÖR FINLAND [Historical review of Finland]. Q. 1916 (1960: vol. 45). Pub. and ed: Eric Anthoni, Brändö, Brädövägen 6, Helsinki. Art. on the medieval and modern hist. of Finland and on toponymy; rev. art.; bk. rev.; doc.; notes and news; information on new hist. pub.; in Swedish. Fmk 450 / Fmk 550

17. HISTORISKA OCH LITTERATURHISTORISKA STUDIER [Studies on history and literary history]. A. 1925 (1960: vol. 35). Svenska Litteratursällskapet i Finland [Swedish Literary Soc. of Finland], Säätytalo, Snellmaninkatu 9-11, Helsinki. Ed: Torsten Steinby. Art. on the hist. (including literary hist.) of Finland and on the general hist. of ideas; in Swedish. pv

18. HISTORISKA SAMFUNDET I ÅBO, SKRIFTER UTGIVNA AV... [Publications of the (Swedish) Historical Society of Åbo (Turku)]. Irr. 1942 (mri 1954: vol. 5). Historiska Samfundet i Åbo, Turku. Art. on the cultural hist. of Finland; list of authors. pv

19. JATULI. Irr. Kemin Kotiseutu-ja Museoyhdistys [Regional and Museum Soc. of Kemi]. pv

20. JOUKO. Pohjois-Pohjalaisen Osakunnan Kotiseutujulkaisu [Regional research publication of the Student Association of Northern Ostrobothnia]. Irr. Pohjois-Pohjalainen Osakunta, Töölönkatu 3, Helsinki. pv (p (1) Fmk 600)

21. KAIKUJA HÄMEESTÄ [Echoes from Häme]. Irr. Hämäläis-Osakunta [Student Assoc. of Häme], Kampinkatu 4-6. D, Helsinki. pv (p (1) Fmk 800)

22. KALEVALASEURAN VUOSIKIRJA [Yearbook of the Kalevala Society]. A. Kalevalaseura, Kluuvikatu 8, Helsinki. Fmk 1250, bound 1500

23. KANSATIETEELLINEN ARKISTO [Ethnological journal]. Irr. 1934 (1957: vol. 13). Suomen Muinaismuistoyhdistys [Archaeological Soc. of Finland], Kansallismuseo, Helsinki. Ed: T.I.Itkonen, Kustaa Vilkuna. Art. on ethnology, with emphasis on Finland; in Finnish and German; German sum. pv

24. KESKI-POHJANMAA. MAAKUNTAJULKAISU [Central Ostrobothnia. Provincial publication]. Irr. Keski-Pohjanmaan Maakuntaliitto [Provincial Union of Central Ostrobothnia], Kokkola. pv (p (1) c. Fmk 300)

25. KESKI-SUOMI [Central Finland]. Irr. Keski-Suomen Museoyhdistys [Museum Soc. of Central Finland], Jyväskylä. pv (p (1) c. Fmk 600)

26. KIRJALLISUUDENTUTKIJAIN SEURAN VUOSIKIRJA. ANNUAIRE DES HISTORIENS DE LA LITTERATURE [Yearbook of the Society of Historians of Literature]. Irr. 1929 (1959: vol. 17). Kirjallisuudentutkijain Seura, Hallituskatu 1, Helsinki. Art. mainly on Finnish literary hist.; biblio.; in Finnish; French sum. pv

27. KOTISEUTU [Regional research]. 8 x y. 1910 (1960: no vol. indic.). Kotiseutuliitto [Union of Regional Research], Hallituskatu 1, Helsinki. Ed: Toivo Vuorela, Veikko Anttila. Art. on Finnish ethnology and hist.; bk. rev.; reports on regional research. Fmk 700

28. KOULU JA MENNEISYYS [School and history]. Irr. 1935 (1959: vol. 11). Suomen Kouluhistoriallinen Seura [Soc. of School Hist. of Finland], Etelä-Esplanaadikatu 16, Helsinki. Ed. board: Urho Somerkivi, E.O.Kuujo, Santeri Liikkanen, Eino Viitasaari, Sven Gladh. Art. on Finnish school hist. pv (p (1) c. Fmk 350)

29. KYMENLAAKSO. Irr. Kymenlaakson Maakuntaliitto [Provincial Union of Kymenlaakso], Kouvola. pv (p (1) c. Fmk 450)

30. KYRÖNMAA. Irr. Etelä-Pohjalainen Osakunta [Student Assoc. of Southern Ostrobothnia], Töölönkatu 3 A, Helsinki. pv (p (1) c. Fmk 1100)

31. KYTÖSAVUT [Smoke from burning turf]. Irr. Etelä-Pohjanmaan Maakuntaliitto [Provincial Union of Southern Ostrobothnia], Seinäjoki. pv

32. LOUNAIS-HÄMEEN KOTISEUTU-JA MUSEOYHDISTYKSEN VUOSIKIRJA [Yearbook of the Regional and Museum Society of South-west Häme]. A. Lounais-Hämeen Kotiseutu-ja Museoyhdistys, Teatteritalo, Forssa. pv

33. MISCELLANEA BIBLIOGRAPHICA. Irr. 1925 (1959: vol. 7). Helsinki Univ. Library, Unioninkatu 36, Helsinki. Art. mainly on Finnish bk. hist.; biblio. of Finnish bk.; list of authors; in Finnish or Swedish; English, German or French sum. pv

34. NORDENSKIÖLD-SAMFUNDETS TIDSKRIFT [Review of the Nordenskiöld Society]. A. Nordenskiöld-Samfundet i Finland, Säätytalo, Snellmanninkatu 9-11, Helsinki. Fmk 500

35. OSMA. A. Suomen Museoliitto [Finnish Museum Assoc.], Cygnaeuksenkatu 14, Helsinki. pv

36. ÖSTERBOTTNISK ÅRSBOK [Yearbook of Ostrobothnia]. A. Svensk-Österbottniska Samfundet [Soc. of the Swedish Ostrobothnia], Vasa. pv

37. POHJOIS-POHJANMAAN MAAKUNTALIITTO. VUOSIKIRJA [Yearbook of the Provincial Union of Northern Ostrobothnia]. A. Pojhois-Pohjanmaan Maakuntaliitto, Hallituskatu 11, Oulu. Fmk 350

PROCEEDINGS OF THE FINNISH ACADEMY OF SCIENCE AND LETTERS see FINNISCHE AKADEMIE DER WISSENSCHAFTEN, SITZUNGSBERICHTE DER...

38. PYHÄJÄRVI. Kotiseutujulaisu [Regional research publication]. Irr. Pyhäjärvi-Seura [Pyhäjärvi Soc.], Pyhäjärvi Ol. pv

39. SATAKUNTA. Kotiseutututkimuksia [Regional researches]. Irr. Satakuntalainen Osakunta [Student Assoc. of Satakunta], Lapinrinne 1 A, Helsinki. pv (p (1) c. Fmk 1000)

SITZUNGSBERICHTE DER FINNISCHEN AKADEMIE DER WISSENSCHAFTEN see FINNISCHE AKADEMIE DER WISSENSCHAFTEN, SITZUNGSBERICHTE DER...

40. SKOLHISTORISKT ARKIV [Archives of school history]. Irr. 1952 (1959: vol. 5). Svenska Skolhistoriska Föreningen i Finland [Soc. of Swedish School Hist. of Finland], Kouluhallitus, Etelä-Esplanaadikatu 16, Helsinki. Ed. board: Gösta Cavonius, Einar Pontán, Konst. Sjöström, Kurt Thodén. Art. on Swedish school hist. in Finland; doc.; in Swedish. pv (p (1) c. Fmk 380)

SKRIFTER UTGIVNA AV HISTORISKA SAMFUNDET I ÅBO see HISTORISKA SAMFUNDET I ÅBO, SKRIFTER UTGIVNA AV...

41. SOCIETAS SCIENTIARUM FENNICA. ÅRSBOK. VUOSIKIRJA [Yearbook of the Finnish Scientific Society]. A. Societas Scientiarum Fennica, Säätytalo, Snellmaninkatu 9-11, Helsinki. Fmk 1500

42. SOTAMUSEO [War Museum]. Irr. 1948 (mri 1955: vol. 6). Sotamuseo, Maurinkatu 3, Helsinki. Art. on Finnish and general war hist.; in Finnish or Swedish; English sum. Fmk 400

43. STUDIA FENNICA. Revue de Linguistique et d'Ethnologie Finnoises [Review of Finnish linguistics and ethnology]. Irr. 1933 (1959: vol. 8). Suomalaisen Kirjallisuuden Seura [Finnish Literary Soc.], Hallituskatu 1, Helsinki. Ed: Martti Haavio, Lauri Hakulinen, Jouko Hautala. Art. on the ethnology, linguistics and cultural hist. of Finland and the Baltic area; biblio. on linguistics and folklore; in English, French and German. pv

44. SUOMALAINEN SUOMI [Finnish Finland]. Suomalaisuuden Liiton Kultuuripoliittinen Aikakauskirja [Cultural-political review of the Society of Finnish Nationalism]. 9xy. Valiolehdet Oy., Hietalahdenranta 13, Helsinki, for Suomalaisuuden Liiton. Fmk 1400 / Fmk 1500 (Scandinavian countries); Fmk 1800 (other foreign countries)

45. SUOMALAINEN TIEDEAKATEMIA. ESITELMÄT JA PÖYTÄKIRJAT [Finnish Academy of Science and Letters, Proceedings]. A. Suomalainen Tiedeakatemia, Säätytalo, Snellmaninkatu 9-11, Helsinki. Fmk 400

46. SUOMEN KIRKKOHISTORIALLISEN SEURAN VUOSIKIRJA. FINSKA KYRKOHISTORISKA SAMFUNDETS ÅRSSKRIFT [Yearbook of the Finnish Society of Church History]. A. (double no.). 1912 (1959: vol. 45-47). Suomen Kirkkohistoriallinen Seura, Säätytalo, Snellmaninkatu 9-11, Helsinki. Ed: Kauko Pirinen, Vuorimiehenkatu 23 b A, Helsinki. Art. on the ecclesiastical hist. of Finland; notes and news; reports of the proceedings of the soc.; in Finnish and occasionally in Swedish; Swedish or German sum. Fmk 500

47. SUOMEN MUINAISMUISTOYHDISTYKSEN AIKAKAUSKIRJA. FINSKA FORNMINNESFÖRENINGENS TIDSKRIFT [Journal of the Archaeological Society of Finland]. Irr. 1874 (1959: vol. 60). Suomen Muinaismuistoyhdistys, Kansallismuseo, Helsinki. Ed: Lars Pettersson. Art. on the prehist. period and on the hist. of culture and art in northern Europe; in Finnish, Swedish, German and English; German or English sum. pv

48. SUOMEN MUSEO [Finnish Museum]. A. 1894 (1959: vol. 66). Suomen Muinaismuistoyhdistys [Archaeological Soc. of Finland], Kansallismuseo, Helsinki. Ed: Ella Kivikoski. Art. on all periods of archaeology, ethnography and cultural hist., with emphasis on Finland; bk. rev.; biblio. on Finnish archaeology; reports of the activities of the soc.; in Finnish and German; German sum. See also Finskt Museum. Fmk 500

49. SUOMEN SUKUTUTKIMUSSEURAN VUOSIKIRJA. GENEALOGISKA SAMFUNDETS I FINLAND ÅRSSKRIFT [Yearbook of the Genealogical Society of Finland]. 3xy. 1917 (1957: vol. 36). Suomen Sukututkimusseura, Snellmaninkatu 9-11, Helsinki. Ed: Heikki Soininvaara, Laajalahdentie 20 A, Helsinki. Art. on Finnish genealogy; biblio. of genealogical literature pub. outside the soc.; A. report of the soc.; in Finnish or Swedish; indices of persons. pv

50. TAMMERKOSKI. Tampereen Kotiseutulehti [Regional journal of Tampere]. M. Tampere-Seura [Tampere Soc.], Hatanpäänvaltatie 6. A, Tampere. Fmk 900 / Fmk 1200

51. TIEDE JA ASE [Science and weapon]. A. Suomen Sotatieteellinen Seura [Finnish Soc. of Military Science], Sotakorkeakoulu, Liisankatu 1, Helsinki. pv

52. TURUN HISTORIALLINEN ARKISTO [Historical archives of Turku]. Irr. 1924 (1958: vol. 14). Turun Historiallinen Yhdistys [Hist. Soc. of Turku], Turun Yliopisto, Turku. Art. primarily on the economic and cultural hist. of Finland, with emphasis on southwestern Finland; German sum. pv

53. TURUN KAUPUNGIN HISTORIALLINEN MUSEO. VUOSIJULKAISU [Yearbook of the Historical Museum of Turku]. A. Turun Kaupungin Historiallinen Museo, Turku. pv

54. VALVOJA [Guardian]. B-M. Valvoja-Ajan Kannatusyhdistys [Patrons' Assoc. of Valvoja-Aika], Kluuvikatu 8, Helsinki. Fmk 800 / Fmk 1100

55. VARSINAIS-SUOMEN MAAKUNTAKIRJA [Provincial book of Finland proper]. Irr. Varsinais-Suomen Maakuntaliitto [Provincial Union of Finland Proper], Turku. Fmk 500

56. YHTEISKUNTA [Society]. Yhteiskunnallisen Korkeakoulun Vuosikirja [Yearbook of the School of Social Sciences]. Irr. Yhteiskunnallinen Korkeakoulu, Tampere. Fmk 400

Monographic series

and

bibliographical and abstracts publications

are not included in this book

France

Prepared with the assistance of

Michelle Villoing and Else Dahl,
Département des Périodiques, Bibliothèque nationale, Paris

1. ACADEMIE D'ARLES, BULLETIN SEMESTRIEL DE L'... [Semi-annual bulletin of the Academy of Arles]. S-A. J. Rossi, Musée Arlaten, Arles, for Académie d'Arles. pni

2. ACADEMIE DE MACON, ANNALES DE L'... [Annals of the Academy of Macon]. B. Académie de Mâcon, Société des arts, sciences, belles-lettres, archéologie, agriculture et encouragement au bien de Saône-et-Loire, Hôtel Senecé, Mâcon. memb. free

3. ACADEMIE DE MOUSTIERS. BULLETIN [Academy of Moustiers. Bulletin]. A. Académie de Moustiers, Basses-Alpes. pni

4. ACADEMIE DE NIMES, BULLETIN DES SEANCES DE L'... [Bulletin of the meetings of the Academy of Nîmes]. Q. Imprimerie Chastanier Frères et Bertrand, 12 rue Pradier, Nîmes, for Académie de Nîmes. pni

5. ACADEMIE DE STANISLAS, MEMOIRES DE L'... [Transactions of the Academy of Stanislas]. A. Académie de Stanislas, 43 rue Stanislas, Nancy. pni

6. ACADEMIE DE VERSAILLES, BULLETIN MENSUEL DE L'... [Monthly bulletin of the Academy of Versailles]. M. Académie de Versailles, Société des sciences morales, lettres et arts de Seine-et-Oise, Hôtel de la Bibliothèque, 5 rue de l'Indépendance-américaine, Versailles. pni

7. ACADEMIE DELPHINALE, BULLETIN DE L'... [Bulletin of the Delphian Academy]. A. 1846 (1953-55 [1957]: 6th series, vol. 24-26). Allier, 26 cours Jean-Jaurès, Grenoble, for Académie Delphinale. Art. on French culture and general hist., with emphasis on the 18th and 19th cent.; reports on the meetings of the acad. N.Fr. 6

8. ACADEMIE DES INSCRIPTIONS ET BELLES-LETTRES. COMPTES RENDUS DES SEANCES DE L'ANNEE [Academy of Inscriptions and Letters. Reports on the meetings of the year]. Q. 1857 (1958: no vol. indic.). Académie des inscriptions et belles-lettres, Librairie C. Klincksieck, 11 rue de Lille, Paris 7e. Art. on archaeology and numismatics; extracts and reprints of papers read at the meetings of the acad. on hist. and auxiliary hist. sciences. N.Fr. 45

9. ACADEMIE DES INSCRIPTIONS ET BELLES-LETTRES, MONUMENTS ET MEMOIRES PUBLIES PAR L'... [Monuments and memoirs published by the Academy of Inscriptions and Letters]. Fondation Eugène Piot [Eugène Piot Foundation]. A. 1894 (1958: vol. 50). Presses universitaires de France, 108 bd. Saint Germain, Paris 6e, for Institut de France, Académie des inscriptions et belles-lettres. Art. on archaeology, hist. and auxiliary hist. sciences; name index; illus. pv (vol. 49: N.Fr. 22; vol. 50: N.Fr. 24)

10. ACADEMIE DES SCIENCES, BELLES-LETTRES ET ARTS D'ANGERS, BULLETIN MENSUEL DE L'... [Monthly bulletin of the Academy of Sciences, Humanities and Arts of Angers]. M. H. Siraudeau, 46 rue Fulton, Angers, for Académie des sciences, belles-lettres et arts d'Angers. N.Fr. 4

11. ACADEMIE DES SCIENCES D'OUTRE-MER, COMPTES RENDUS MENSUELS DES SEANCES DE L'... [Monthly reports on the meetings of the Academy for the Study of the (French) Overseas (Departments and Territories)]. M. Académie des sciences d'Outre-Mer, 15 rue Lapérouse, Paris 16e. N.Fr. 12 / N.Fr. 15

12. ACADEMIE DES SCIENCES, LETTRES ET ARTS D'ARRAS, MEMOIRES DE L'... [Transactions of the Academy of Sciences, Letters and Arts of Arras]. Q. Imprimerie de P. et O. Lussaud, 9 rue des Loges, Fontenay-le-Comte, for Académie d'Arras, 9 rue des Capucines, Arras, Pas-de-Calais. pni

13. ACADEMIE DES SCIENCES MORALES ET POLITIQUES, REVUE DES TRAVAUX DE L'... ET COMPTES RENDUS DE SES SEANCES [Review of the activities of the Academy of Moral and Political Sciences and reports on its meetings]. S-A. Librairie Sirey, 22 rue Soufflot, Paris 5e, for Académie des sciences morales et politiques. pni

14. ACADEMIE DU CENTRE, REVUE DE L'... [Review of the Academy of Central France]. A. Académie du Centre, 33 av. de la Gare, Châteauroux. N.Fr. 5

15. ACADEMIE DU VAR, BULLETIN DE L'... [Bulletin of the Academy of Var]. A. Académie du Var, 9 place de la Liberté, Toulon. pni

16. ACADEMIE NATIONALE DE METZ, MEMOIRES DE L'... [Memoirs of the National Academy of Metz]. B (A. till 1939). Académie Nationale de Metz, Archives départementales, Préfecture, Metz, Moselle. N.Fr. 18

17. ACTA GEOGRAPHICA. Q. Société de géographie, 184 bd. Saint Germain, Paris 6e. N.Fr. 20

18. L'ACTION REGIONALISTE [Regionalist action]. Q. 1902 (1959: vol. 59). Fédération régionaliste française, 36 rue de Naples, Paris 8e. Ed: Bernard Appert. Art. on the hist. and geography of the various provinces of France. p (1) N.Fr. 1.25

19. L'ACTUALITE DE L'HISTOIRE [The reality of history]. Q. 1951 (1958: no. 22-25). Institut français d'histoire sociale, 117 bis, rue Armand-Silvestre, Courbevoie, Seine. Ed: J. Maitron. Short art. mostly on the hist. of the labor movement and socialism in France; bk. rev.; news of the inst. N.Fr. 10 / N.Fr. 12

20. L'AFRIQUE ET L'ASIE [Africa and Asia]. Revue politique, sociale et économique et Bulletin des anciens du Centre des hautes études d'administration musulmane [Political, social and economic review and bulletin of the alumni of the School of Moslem Administration]. Q. I.A.C., 8 rue de Furstenberg, Paris 6e. N.Fr. 10 / N.Fr. 12

21. AFRIQUE FRANÇAISE [French Africa]. B-M. Comité de l'Afrique française and Comité du Maroc, 21 rue Cassette, Paris 6e. N.Fr. 7 / N.Fr. 9

22. ALLEMAGNE D'AUJOURD'HUI [Present-day Germany]. Revue française d'information [French review of information]. B-M. Presses universitaires de France, 1 place Paul Painlevé, Paris 5e. N.Fr. 8

ALLIANCE FRANÇAISE, BULLETIN DE L'... see LE MERCURY DE FRANCE

23. LES ALPES DE LUMIERE [The Alps of light]. Bulletin culturel de la Provence intérieure [Cultural bulletin of the interior Provence]. Q. Centre de recherches "Alpes de Lumière," Mane, Basses-Alpes. N.Fr. 5

24. AMIS DE CARENTOIR, BULLETIN DES... [Bulletin of the Friends of Carentoir]. M. Les Amis de Carentoir, 8 rue Gratinière, Carentoir, Morbihan. N.Fr. 3

25. AMIS DE CLUNY, BULLETIN ANNUEL DES... [Annual bulletin of the Friends of Cluny]. A. Les Amis de Cluny, Cluny, Saône-et-Loire. pni

26. LES AMIS DE DOUAI [The Friends of Douai]. Q. Marcel Lévêque, 21 rue Morel, Lille, for Syndicat d'initiative "Les Amis de Douai." N.Fr. 5

27. AMIS DE L'AVALLONNAIS, REVUE DES... [Review of the Friends of the Avallonnais]. Irr. R. Picon, 4 place Edouard-Renard, Paris 12e, for Société amicale des amis de l'Avallonnais. pni

28. LES AMIS DE LYON ET DE GUIGNOL [The Friends of Lyons and Guignol]. Q. Société des Amis de Lyon et de Guignol, Mairie du 1er arrondissement, Lyon. N.Fr. 3

29. LES AMIS DE NISSAN [The Friends of Nissan]. Irr. Nissan-lez-Ensérune, Hérault, for Société des Amis de Nissan. pni

30. LES AMIS DE SAINT-CLOUD [The Friends of Saint-Cloud]. Irr. Imprimerie Girault, 11 rue Gaston-Latouche, Saint-Cloud. (memb.) N.Fr. 3

31. AMIS DES MONUMENTS ET SITES DE L'EURE [Friends of the monuments and sites of the province of Eure]. Irr. Amis des monuments et sites de l'Eure, Tourville-la-Campagne, Eure. pni

32. LES AMIS DU MONT-ST.-MICHEL. BULLETIN ANNUEL [The Friends of Mont-St.-Michel. Annual bulletin]. A. Les Amis du Mont-St.-Michel, 79 bd. Saint-Germain, Paris 6e. N.Fr. 5

33. LES AMIS DU VIEUX CHINON [The Friends of old Chinon]. Irr. Société d'histoire locale de Chinon et de ses environs, Musée, 81 rue Voltaire, Chinon. p (1) N.Fr. 3

34. LES AMIS DU VIEUX DIEPPE [The Friends of old Dieppe]. Amis du Musée et de la Bibliothèque [Friends of the Museum and the Library]. A. Amis de Vieux Dieppe, 1 bd. de la Libération, Dieppe. N.Fr. 5

35. LES AMIS DU VIEUX SAINT-ETIENNE [The Friends of old Saint-Etienne]. Q. Société historique, archéologique, littéraire, 13 bis, rue Gambetta, Saint-Etienne, Loire. pni

36. L'AMITIE FRANÇAISE DU MIDI [French friendship of the South]. M. Syrlan-Gueynard, 1 rue d'Austerlitz, Toulouse. N.Fr. 1.50

ANNALES. For titles beginning with "Annales," followed by the name of the publishing or sponsoring institution or society, see the respective institution or society.

ANNALES AFRICAINES see section on West and West-Central Africa (Senegal Republic)

37. ANNALES DE BOURGOGNE [Annals of Bourgogne]. Q. 1929 (1958: vol. 30). Centre d'études bourguignonnes, 36 rue Chabot-Charny, Dijon. Ed: Pierre Gras, Jean Richard, 8 rue Jeannin, Dijon. Art. on the hist. of Burgundy; discussions; doc.; biblio.; reports on research; notes and news on the soc. and other news of interest to scholars; illus. N.Fr. 10 / N.Fr. 11

38. ANNALES DE BRETAGNE [Annals of Bretagne]. Q. Librairie universitaire J. Plihon, 5 rue Motte-Fablet, Rennes. N.Fr. 17

39. ANNALES DE GEOGRAPHIE [Annals of geography]. B-M. Armand Colin, 103 bd. Saint-Michel, Paris, for Société de géographie.
N.Fr. 15 / N.Fr. 18

40. ANNALES DE L'EST [Annals of Eastern France]. Q. 1887 (1959: 5th series, vol. 10). Annales de l'Est, Editions Berger-Levrault, for Faculté des lettres de l'Université de Nancy and Fédération historique lorraine, 13 place Carnot, Nancy. Art. on the religious hist. of Eastern France, with emphasis on Lorraine; biographies of important hist. personalities; bk. rev.; illus.
N.Fr. 7.50 / N.Fr. 10

41. LES ANNALES DE NANTES [Annals of Nantes]. Q. Société académique de Nantes et de la Loire-Atlantique, Château des Ducs, Nantes. N.Fr. 4

42. ANNALES DE NORMANDIE [Annals of Normandy]. Revue trimestrielle d'études régionales [Quarterly review of local studies]. Q. Laboratoire d'ethnographie régionale, place Guillouard, Caen. N.Fr. 6 / N.Fr. 9

43. ANNALES DU MIDI [Annals of the South]. Revue de la France méridionale [Review of Southern France]. Q. Librairie Edouard Privat, 14 rue des Arts, Toulouse. N.Fr. 15 / N.Fr. 18

44. ANNALES: ECONOMIES, SOCIETES, CIVILISATIONS [Annals: Economies, societies, civilizations]. Q. 1946 (1959: vol. 14). Armand Colin, 103 bd. Saint-Michel, Paris 5e. Ed: Fernand Brodel, Georges Friedmann, Charles Morazé, Paul Leuilliot, Robert Mandrou. Art. on economic, social and cultural hist., with some emphasis on methodological problems; discussions; rev. art.; rev. of bk. and periodicals; reports on research in progress; news of interest to scholars; classified list of bk. received; graph; classified index for the Annales and its predecessors for the years 1929-51; illus. N.Fr. 20 / N.Fr.23

45. ANNALES HISTORIQUES DE LA REVOLUTION FRANÇAISE [Historical annals of the French Revolution]. Q. 1924 (1959: vol. 31). Société des études Robespierristes, 304 rue de Belleville, Paris 20e. Ed: Georges Lefèbvre, 86 bd. Jean-Jaurès, Boulogne-sur-Seine. Art. on the French Revolution; short contributions by readers; bk. rev.; biblio. of art.; news of hist. conferences.
N.Fr. 11 / N.Fr. 14.50

ANNALES LITTERAIRES DE L'UNIVERSITE DE BESANCON see UNIVERSITE DE BESANCON, ANNALES LITTERAIRES DE L'...

46. ANNALES SEDANAISES D'HISTOIRE ET D'ARCHEOLOGIE [Sedan annals of history and archaeology]. Q. Société des Amis du vieux Sedan, 13 bd. Fabert, Sedan. N.Fr. 5

47. L'ANNEE POLITIQUE ET ECONOMIQUE [The year in politics and economics]. B-M (Irr.). Presses Universitaires, 49 bd. Saint-Michel, Paris 7e. N.Fr. 18 / N.Fr. 21

48. ANNESCI. A. Société des Amis du Vieil Annecy, 1 rue Camille Dunant, Annecy. N.Fr. 6

ANNUAIRE-BULLETIN DE LA SOCIETE DE L'HISTOIRE DE FRANCE see SOCIETE DE L'HISTOIRE DE FRANCE, ANNUAIRE-BULLETIN DE LA...

ANNUAIRE DE LA SOCIETE HISTORIQUE ET LITTERAIRE DE COLMAR see SOCIETE HISTORIQUE ET LITTERAIRE DE COLMAR, ANNUAIRE DE LA...

ANNUAIRE EUROPEEN see section on International Periodicals

49. L'ANTHROPOLOGIE [Anthropology]. B-M. 1890 (1958: vol. 62). Masson et Cie, Editeurs, 120 bd. Saint-Germain, Paris 6e. Ed: H. Vallois, R. Vaufrey. Art. on anthropology including hist. aspects, and on prehist. and geology; bk. rev.; biblio.; illus. N.Fr. 60 / $17

50. ARCHIVES D'ANCHOINA [Archives of Anchoine]. Q. "Anchoina" Société historique, scientifique et artistique en Charente-Maritime, Ronce-les-Bains. Art. on the legendary city of Anchoine and the south-west of Charente-Maritime. (memb.) N.Fr. 5

51. ARCHIVES D'HISTOIRE DOCTRINALE ET LITTERAIRE DU MOYEN AGE [Archives on the doctrinal and literary history of the Middle Ages]. A. Librairie philosophique J. Vrin, 6 place de la Sorbonne, Paris 5e. Includes biblio. in German, French or Latin on various medieval manuscripts. pni

52. ARCHIVES DE L'EGLISE D'ALSACE [Archives of the Alsatian Church]. Irr. F.X. Le Roux, 34 rue des Hallebardes, Strasbourg, for Société d'histoire de l'Eglise d'Alsace. Biblio. of manuscripts; in German, French and Latin. pni

ARCHIVES DU DIOCESE DE LUÇON see DIOCESE DE LUÇON, ARCHIVES DU...

53. ARCHIVES INTERNATIONALES D'HISTOIRE DES SCIENCES [International archives of the history of sciences]. Q. 1947/48 (1958: vol. 11). Division d'histoire des sciences de l'Union internationale d'histoire et de philosophie des sciences, c/o Hermann et Cie., 115 bd. Saint-Germain, Paris 6e. Ed: Maurice Daumas, 12 rue Colbert, Paris 2e. Art. on the hist. of sciences and on museum holdings; doc.; reports on the activities of the union; bk. rev., classified by subject; tables of contents of selected rev. on the hist. of sciences; in the native languages of the authors. N.Fr. 25 / $6

ARCHIVES INTERNATIONALES DE SOCIOLOGIE DE LA COOPERATION see section on International Periodicals

ARCHIVIO INTERNAZIONALE DI SOCIOLOGIA DELLA COOPERAZIONE see section on International Periodicals

ARCHIVUM see section on International Periodicals

54. L'ART CHRETIEN [Christian art]. Q. Pichard, 38 av. de Chatillon, Paris 14e. N.Fr. 16.50

55. ART DE BASSE-NORMANDIE [Art in Lower Normandy]. Q. J. Pougheol, 49 rue Canchy, Caen, Calvados. N.Fr. 9 / N.Fr. 12

56. ART ET STYLE [Art and style]. Q. Robert Lang, Art et style, 14 rue Marignan, Paris 8e. N.Fr. 46 / N.Fr. 54

57. L'ART SACRE [Sacred art]. M. Editions du Cerf, 29 bd. Latour-Maubourg, Paris 7e. N.Fr. 10 / N.Fr. 12

58. ARTS ASIATIQUES [Asiatic arts]. Q. 1954 (1958: vol. 5). Presses universitaires de France, 108 bd. Saint-Germain, Paris 6e. Ed: Jeannine Auboyer, Musée Guimet, 6 place d'Iéna, Paris 16e, and Georges A. Salles. Art. on the hist. (including art hist.) and archaeology of Asia; bk. rev.; illus. N.Fr. 28 / $6.70

59. ARTS ET TRADITIONS POPULAIRES [Folk art and traditions]. Q. 1953 (1958 [1959]: vol. 6). Editions des Quatre Jeudis, Paris, for Société d'ethnographie française, Musée national des arts et traditions populaires, Palais de Chaillot, Paris 16e. Ed: Marie-Louise Tenèze. Art. on the folk art, traditions and folklore of France; doc.; rev. of bk. and art.; biblio. of films, phonograph records and pub. on French ethnography, classified by subject; news of the soc. and other relevant news; illus. N.Fr. 15 / N.Fr. 18

60. ASSOCIATION BRETONNE ET UNION REGIONALISTE BRETONNE. ARCHEOLOGIE, HISTOIRE, AGRICULTURE, COMPTES RENDUS, PROCES-VERBAUX, MEMOIRES [Breton Association and Regionalist Union of Britanny. Archaeology, history, agriculture. Reports, minutes, transactions]. Irr. Les Presses bretonnes, Saint-Brieuc, for Association bretonne et union regionaliste Bretonne. N.Fr. 4

61. ASSOCIATION DE GEOGRAPHES FRANÇAIS, BULLETIN DE L'... [Bulletin of the Association of French Geographers]. B-M. A. Libault, 121 bd. Saint-Michel, Paris 5e, for Association de géographes français. N.Fr. 12 / N.Fr. 14

62. ASSOCIATION GUILLAUME BUDE, BULLETIN DE L'... [Bulletin of the Guillaume Budé Association]. Revue de culture générale [General cultural review]. Q. Société d'édition "Les Belles-Lettres," 95 bd. Raspail, Paris 6e, for Association Guillaume Budé. Includes art. on Greek and Roman antiquity. N.Fr. 10

63. ASSOCIATION INTERNATIONALE DES ETUDES FRANÇAISES, CAHIERS DE L'... [Publications of the International Association for French Studies]. Irr. 1951 (1959: no vol. indic.). Société d'édition "Les Belles-Lettres," 95 bd. Raspail, Paris 6e. Extracts and reprints of papers on the hist. of art and literature read at the congresses of the assoc.; lists of memb. of the assoc. N.Fr. 15 / $4

64. ASSOCIATION POUR L'HISTOIRE DE LA CIVILISATION. ASSOCIATION MARC BLOC. SEANCE [Association for the History of Civilization. Marc Bloc Association. Meeting]. S-A. 1949/50 (mri 1953/55 [1956]: no. 5/6). Centre régional de documentation pédagogique, 4 rue Albert-Lautman, Toulouse, for Association pour l'histoire de la civilisation. Ed: D. Faucher. Art. on the general hist. of civilization; extracts and reprints of papers on hist. read at the meetings of the assoc. pni

65. L'AUVERGNE LITTERAIRE, ARTISTIQUE ET HISTORIQUE [Literary, artistic and historical Auvergne]. Q. P.-A. Hauvette, 7 place Michel-de-l'Hospital, Clermont-Ferrand. N.Fr. 8

66. BARR-HEOL [Sunbeam]. Feiz ha Breiz [Faith and Britanny]. Q. Abbé Le Clerc, Buhulien, Côtes-du-Nord. In Breton. N.Fr. 5.50

67. AR BED KELTIEK [The Celtic world]. M. Skourr Breizh ar C'hend-alc'h keltiek [Britanny Section of the International Celtic Congress], c/o Y. Martin, 21 rue de Dixmude, Brest. N.Fr. 7 / $1.60

68. BIBLIOTHEQUE DE L'ECOLE DES CHARTES [Library of the "Ecole des chartes"]. Revue d'Erudition [Review of learning]. A. 1839 (1957: vol. 115). Société de l'Ecole des Chartes, 19 rue de la Sorbonne, Paris 5e. Art. on the manuscripts and hist. of the Middle Ages; doc.; bk. rev.; reports on the activities of the soc. and on congresses and meetings; index of authors, place-names and subjects; reproductions. N.Fr. 20

69. BIBLIOTHEQUES DE FRANCE, BULLETIN DES... [Bulletin of the libraries of France]. M. 1956 (1959: 4th year). Direction des bibliothèques de France, 55 rue Saint-Dominique, Paris 7e. Art. on library science, new catalogues and acquisitions and on the hist. of libraries and bk.; bk. rev.; descriptive biblio.; library news. N.Fr. 25 / N.Fr. 30

70. BLEUN-BRUG [Heather]. M. Pub. address: 21 rue Jos. Doury, Nantes, Loire-Atlantique. In Breton and French. N.Fr. 5

71. LE BOUSSET. Irr. Aimé Coulaudon, 20 rue Bonnabaud, Clermont-Ferrand, for confréries d'Auvergne. pni

72. BREIZ SANTEL [Holy Britanny]. M. Mouvement pour la protection des monuments religieux bretons, c/o Hôtel de Ville, Vannes, Morbihan. N.Fr. 3

73. LE BUGEY. A. Société scientifique, historique et littéraire, c/o M.F. Berlioz, 34 Grande-Rue, Belley. Hist. of the region of Bugey. N.Fr. 5

BULLETIN. For titles beginning with "Bulletin," followed by the name of the publishing or sponsoring institution or society, see the respective institution or society.

BULLETIN ARCHEOLOGIQUE DU COMITE DES TRAVAUX HISTORIQUE ET SCIENTIFIQUES see COMITE DES TRAVAUX HISTORIQUE ET SCIENTIFIQUES, BULLETIN ARCHEOLOGIQUE DU...

BULLETIN BIBLIOGRAPHIQUE DE LA SOCIETE INTERNATIONALE ARTHURIENNE see SOCIETE INTERNATIONALE ARTHURIENNE, BULLETIN BIBLIOGRAPHIQUE DE LA...

BULLETIN D'HISTOIRE ET D'ARCHEOLOGIE DU DIOCESE DE BELLEY see DIOCESE DE BELLEY, BULLETIN D'HISTOIRE ET D'ARCHEOLOGIE DU...

BULLETIN D'HISTOIRE MODERNE ET CONTEMPORAINE (DEPUIS 1715) DU COMITE DES TRAVAUX HISTORIQUES ET SCIENTIFIQUES see COMITE DES TRAVAUX HISTORIQUES ET SCIENTIFIQUES, BULLETIN D'HISTOIRE MODERNE ET CONTEMPORAINE (DEPUIS 1715) DU...

74. BULLETIN DE GEOGRAPHIE D'AIX-MARSEILLE [Geographical bulletin of Aix-Marseille]. Irr. Secrétariat de la Société de géographie de Marseille, 40 Allées Léon-Gambetta, Marseille, and Laboratoire de géographie de la Faculté des lettres d'Aix-en-Provence, rue Benjamin-Abram, Aix-en-Provence. pni

75. BULLETIN DU BIBLIOPHILE ET DU BIBLIOTHECAIRE [Bulletin of the bibliophile and the librarian]. B-M. 1834 (1959: no vol. indic., no. 1-2). Librairie Giraud-Badin, 128 bd. Saint-Germain, Paris 7e. Art. on important bk. collections; supplement included with each no. N.Fr. 18 / N.Fr. 18

76. BULLETIN FOLKLORIQUE D'ILE-DE-FRANCE [Bulletin of folklore of the Ile-de-France]. Q. Fédération folklorique d'Ile-de-France, 38 rue Truffaut, Paris 17e. N.Fr. 5

77. BULLETIN GENEALOGIQUE D'INFORMATION [Genealogical bulletin of information]. B-M. Centre généalogique de Paris, 64 rue de Richelieu, Paris 2e. Genealogical tables. N.Fr. 10 / N.Fr. 11

78. BULLETIN HISTORIQUE ET SCIENTIFIQUE DE L'AUVERGNE [Historical and scientific bulletin of Auvergne]. Q. Académie des sciences, belles-lettres et arts de Clermont-Ferrand, 1 bd. Lafayette, Clermont-Ferrand, Puy-de-Dôme. N.Fr. 6

BULLETIN INTERNATIONAL DES SCIENCES SOCIALES see section on International Periodicals

79. BUTTERFLY. English-French magazine. Revue mensuelle destinée à faciliter l'étude comparée des langues anglaise et française [Monthly review intended to facilitate the comparative study of the English and French languages]. M. E.-H. Massein, 14 rue Vauguelin, Le Hâvre. In English and French. N.Fr. 8.50 / $ 2

CAHIERS. For titles beginning with "Cahiers," followed by the name of the publishing or sponsoring institution or society, see the respective institution or society.

80. CAHIERS ALSACIENS D'ARCHEOLOGIE, D'ART ET D'HISTOIRE [Alsatian review of archaeology, art and history]. Irr. 1909 (1957: new series, no. 1). Société pour la conservation des monuments historiques d'Alsace, 2 place du Château, Strasbourg. Ed. board: Jean-Jacques Hatt (prehist.), Victor Beyer (Middle Ages), René Metz (modern hist.). Art. on the hist. of Alsace; doc.; report of the activities of the soc.; illus. pni

81. CAHIERS ARCHEOLOGIQUES [Archaeological journal]. Fin de l'Antiquité et Moyen Age [End of antiquity and the Middle Ages]. Irr. 1945 (1957: vol. 9). Librairie C. Klincksieck, 11 rue de Lille, Paris 7e. Ed: André Grabar 2 av. Dode de la Brunerie, Paris 16e, and Jean Hubert, 94 bd. Flandrin, Paris 16e

Art. on archaeology, exploration and excavations and on the hist. of ancient and medieval art; bk. rev.; illus.; graph. pni

82. CAHIERS D'ART [Art journal]. A. Editions "Cahiers d'Art," 14 rue du Dragon, Paris 6e. pni

83. CAHIERS D'ETUDES AFRICAINES [Journal of African studies]. Q. Mouton et Co., 68 quai des Orfèvres, Paris 1er, for Ecole pratique des hautes etudes, VIe Section, Division des Aires Culturelle, 20 rue de la Baume, Paris 8e. N.Fr. 33 / N.Fr. 40

84. CAHIERS D'ETUDES CATHARES [Journal of Cathari studies]. Q. Pub. address: Arques, Aude. N.Fr. 10

85. CAHIERS D'HISTOIRE [Journal of history]. Q. 1956 (1959: vol. 4). Comité historique des régions lyonnaise, stéphanoise, dauphinoise et savoyarde, 72 rue Pasteur, Lyon 7e, for Univ. of Clermont, Lyon and Grenoble. Ed: Richard Gascon, 31 bis rue Pasteur, Caluire, Rhône. Art. on French hist., with emphasis on South-East France; rev. of bk. and art.; biblio. on the south-eastern departments of France; news of local learned soc.; graph. N.Fr. 10 / N.Fr. 12

LES CAHIERS D'HISTOIRE ET DE FOLKLORE see VISAGES DE L'HOMME

LES CAHIERS D'HISTOIRE MONDIALE see section on International Periodicals

CAHIERS D'HISTOIRE PUBLIES PAR LES UNIVERSITES DE CLERMONT-LYON-GRENOBLE see UNIVERSITES DE CLERMONT-LYON-GRENOBLE, CAHIERS D'HISTOIRE PUBLIES PAR LES...

86. CAHIERS DE CIVILISATION MEDIEVALE [Journal on medieval civilization]. Q. 1958 (1959: 2nd year). Centre d'études supérieures de civilisation médiévale, Société d'études médiévale, 36 rue de la Chaînes, Poitiers, Vienne. Ed: René Crozet, E.-R. Labande. Art. on medieval hist.; bk. rev.; biblio.; graph. N.Fr. 30 / N.Fr. 36

87. LES CAHIERS DE L'IROISE [Journal of the Iroise district]. Q. G.M. Thomas, 5 rue Portzmoguer, Brest, for Société d'études de Brest et de Léon. In Breton and French. N.Fr. 10 / N.Fr. 12

88. CAHIERS DE L'ORIENT CONTEMPORAIN [Journal of the contemporary East]. Irr. Documentation française, 16 rue Lord-Byron, Paris 8e, for Centre d'études de l'Orient contemporain and Direction de la documentation de l'Institut d'études islamiques, Université de Paris. N.Fr. 19.50 / N.Fr. 21

CAHIERS DE LA ROUMANIE OUVRIERE see ROMÂNIA MUNCITOARE

89. LES CAHIERS DU REOLAIS [Review of Réolais]. Q. Société "Les Amis du Vieux Réolais," 78 rue Armand Caduc, La Réole, Gironde. (memb.) N.Fr. 2.50

90. CAHIERS DU SUD [Journal of the South]. B-M. Jean Ballard, 10 Cours d'Estienne-d'Orves, Marseille 1er. Art. on literature, hist. and auxiliary hist. sciences; bk. rev. N.Fr. 15 / N.Fr. 18

91. LES CAHIERS HAUT-MARNAIS [Review of Haut-Marne]. Q. Service des archives de la Haute-Marne, B.P. 167, Chaumont, Haute-Marne. N.Fr. 5

92. CAHIERS INTERNATIONAUX [International journal]. Revue internationale du monde du travail [International review of the labor world]. M. J.M. Hermann, 66 rue J.J. Rousseau, Paris 1er. N.Fr. 20 / N.Fr. 27.50

93. CAHIERS LEOPOLD DELISLE [Léopold Delisle journal]. Q. Société parisienne d'histoire et d'archéologie normandes, c/o Michel Nortier, 14 bis rue Charles-VII, Nogent-sur-Marne, Seine. Includes biblio. on the hist. and prehist. of Normandy; author index. N.Fr. 6

94. LES CAHIERS LORRAINS [The Lorraine journal]. Q. Société d'histoire et d'archéologie de la Lorraine, Archives departementales, Metz. N.Fr. 7.50 (including Annuaire pub. by the soc.)

95. CAHIERS LYONNAIS D'HISTOIRE DE LA MEDECINE [Lyonese journal on the history of medicine]. Q. Société française d'histoire de la médecine, filiale lyonnaise, 11 rue d'Algérie, Lyon. Art. on the hist. of medicine in the Lyon area. N.Fr. 6

CAHIERS PEDAGOGIQUES DE L'INSTITUT D'ETUDES OCCITANES see INSTITUT D'ETUDES OCCITANES, CAHIERS PEDAGOGIQUES DE L'...

96. CAHIERS PEDAGOGIQUES POUR L'ENSEIGNEMENT DU SECOND DEGRE [Pedagogical review for teaching in secondary schools]. 8xy. Service d'édition et de vente des publications de l'Education nationale, 13 rue du Four, Paris 6e. Includes art. on the teaching of hist. N.Fr. 10 / N.Fr. 14

97. LES CAHIERS TECHNIQUES DE L'ART [Technical journal of art]. Irr. Editions le Tilleul, 23 rue Wimpfeling, Strasbourg. Hist. of art in Strasbourg and vicinity; in German and French. p (1) N.Fr. 12

98. CARNET DE LA SABRETACHE [Journal of the Sabretache]. Revue d'histoire militaire... [Review of military history...]. Irr. 1893 (1957: vol. 5, no. 416). Société "La Sabretache," 24 bd. des Capucines, Paris 9e. Art. on French military hist., with emphasis on the Napoleonic period; illus. N.Fr. 20 / N.Fr. 25

CENTRE D'ENTR'AIDE GENEALOGIQUE, BULLETIN DU... see LA FRANCE GENEALOGIQUE

99. CENTRE INTERNATIONAL D'ETUDE DES TEXTILES ANCIENS, BULLETIN DE LIAISON DU... [Liaison bulletin of the International Center for the Study of Old Textiles]. S-A. 1955 (1959: no vol. indic.). Centre international d'étude des Textiles Anciens, 34 rue de la Charité, Lyon. Art. on the hist., preservation and restoration of textile museum exhibits; information and studies in the field of old textiles; reports on the activities of the center; biblio. pni

100. CENTRE UNIVERSITAIRE MEDITERRANEEN, ANNALES DU... [Annals of the Mediterranean University Center]. A. 1946 (1958/59: vol. 11). Société des amis du Centre universitaire méditerranéen, 65 Promenade des Anglais, Nice. Extracts or reprints of papers on hist., literature and auxiliary hist. sciences, read at the meeting of the Center. pni

101. CERCA. Q. 1958. Archives des Pyrénées Orientales, 11 rue du Bastion St. Dominique, Perpignan, for Centre d'Etudes et de Recherches Catalanes des Archives. Ed: J.G. Gigot. Art. on the archaeology and hist. of the region of Perpignan and Catalonia, on the auxiliary hist. sciences and on archives, libraries and museums. N.Fr. 8 / N.Fr. 12

102. CERCLE D'ETUDES SAVANTES, ARTISTIQUES, ARCHEOLOGIQUES, FOLKLORIQUES, BULLETIN INTERIEUR DU... [Internal bulletin of the Club for Studies on Science, Arts, Archaeology, Folklore]. Irr. Voie normande, Bâtiment H, Villeneuve-le-Roi, Seine-et-Oise. p (1) N.Fr. 0.75

103. CERCLE ERNEST RENAN, BULLETIN DU... [Bulletin of the Ernest Renan Circle]. M (Irr.). 1952 (1958: no. 50-58). Cercle Ernest Renan, 3 rue Récamier, Paris 7e. Short art. on the hist. of Christianity and contemporary topics related to Christianity; bk. rev.; supplement to Cahiers du Cercle Ernest Renan. p (1) N.Fr. 0.30 (memb. N.Fr. 8 / N.Fr. 14)

104. CERCLE ERNEST RENAN, CAHIERS DU... [Review of the Ernest Renan Circle]. Pour libres recherches d'histoire du christianisme [For free research on the history of Christianity]. Q. 1952 (1959: vol. 6). Cercle Ernest Renan, 3 rue Récamier, Paris 7e. One art. per no. on the origins and hist. of Christianity, on questions of interest to Christians today and the role of Christianity in the modern world; supplemented by Bulletin du Cercle Ernest Renan. (memb.) N.Fr. 8 / N.Fr. 14; p (1) N.Fr. 1.30

105. LA CHATAIGNE [The chestnut]. Q. Georges Dauzonne, 16 av. Emile-Zola, Paris 15e, for Société amicale du canton de Montsalvy. N.Fr. 1.50

CHRONIQUE DE LA UNESCO see section on International Periodicals

CHRONIQUES D'OUTRE-MER see next entry

106. CHRONIQUES DE LA COMMUNAUTE [Chronicles of the community]. M. Documentation française, 14-16 rue Lord Byron, Paris 8e. Prior to October 1959 pub. under the title Chroniques d'Outre-Mer. N.Fr. 19

COLLECTANEA ORDINIS CISTERCIENSUM REFORMATORUM see ORDO CISTERCIENSUM REFORMATORUM, COLLECTANEA... in the section on Belgium

107. COMITE D'HISTOIRE DE LA DEUXIEME GUERRE MONDIALE. BULLETIN [Committee of the History of the Second World War. Bulletin]. M. 1952 (1960: no. 84). Pub. address: 22 rue d'Athènes, Paris 9e. Gen. Secretary: Henri Michel. Art. on the hist. of the Second World War, the French resistance movement, the concentration camps and related subjects; bk. rev. pni

108. COMITE DES TRAVAUX HISTORIQUES ET SCIENTIFIQUES, BULLETIN ARCHEOLOGIQUE DU... [Archaeological bulletin of the Committee of Historical and Scientific Studies]. A. 1863 (1957 [1959]: no vol. indic.). Presses universitaires de France, 108 bd. Saint-Germain, Paris 6e, for Comité des travaux historiques et scientifiques, Ministère de l'Education nationale. Reports on archaeological excavations and exploration; proceedings of archaeological soc.; descriptive biblio. of important archaeological and hist. works; illus. pni

109. COMITE DES TRAVAUX HISTORIQUES ET SCIENTIFIQUES, BULLETIN D'HISTOIRE MODERNE ET CONTEMPORAINE (DEPUIS 1715) DU... [Bulletin of modern and contemporary history (since 1715) of the Committee of Historical and Scientific Works]. A. 1956 (1957: vol. 1, no. 2). Presses universitaires de France, 108 bd. Saint-Germain, Paris 6e, for Comité des travaux historiques et scientifiques, Ministère de l'Education nationale. Art. on social hist. since 1715. pni

COMITE INTERNATIONAL DES SCIENCES HISTORIQUES see section on International Periodicals

110. COMMISSION HISTORIQUE ET ARCHEOLOGIQUE DE LA MAYENNE, BULLETIN DE LA... [Bulletin of the Historical and Archaeological Commission of the District of Mayenne]. A. Commission historique et archéologique de la Mayenne, 43 rue des Fossés, Laval. (memb.) N.Fr. 5

COMPTES RENDUS. For titles beginning with "Comptes Rendus," followed by the name of the publishing or sponsoring institution or society, see the respective institution or society.

CONFERENCES DE L'INSTITUT HISTORIQUE DE PROVENCE see INSTITUT HISTORIQUES DE PROVENCE, CONFERENCES DE L'...

CONGRESO POR LA LIBERTAD DE LA CULTURA, CUADERNOS DEL... see section on International Periodicals

111. CONNAISSANCE DES ARTS [Knowledge of the arts]. M. Ed: Didier W. Rémen, Humbert Frèrejean, 13 rue Saint-Georges, Paris 9e. Art. on the arts and on art hist.; bk. rev. N.Fr. 84.50 / $ 18

CONSEIL DE L'EUROPE, NOUVELLES DU... see section on International Periodicals

112. LE CONTRAT SOCIAL [The Social Contract]. Revue historique et critiques des faits et des idées [Historical and critical review of facts and ideas]. B-M. 1957 (1958: vol. 2). Institut d'histoire sociale, 199 bd. Saint-Germain, Paris 7e. Ed. address: 165 rue de l'Université, Paris 7e. Art. on the hist. of socialist ideas, with emphasis on recent hist. and Communism; doc.; bk. rev. N.Fr. 9 / N.Fr. 10.50

COUNCIL OF EUROPE NEWS see section on International Periodicals

LE COURRIER DE LA UNESCO see section on International Periodicals

CRONICA DE LA UNESCO see section on International Periodicals

CUADERNOS DEL CONGRESO POR LA LIBERTAD DE LA CULTURA see section on International Periodicals

113. "LA DIANA," BULLETIN DE... [Bulletin of "La Diana"]. Q. "La Diana," Société Historique et Archéologique du Forez, rue Florimond-Robertet, Montbrison. N.Fr. 10

114. DIOCESE DE BELLEY, BULLETIN D'HISTOIRE ET D'ARCHEOLOGIE DU... [Bulletin of history and archaeology of the Diocese of Belley].

Irr. Société Gorini, 25 rue Bourgmayer, Bourg. Art. on the religious hist. and archaeology of the diocese and on ecclesiastical topics. N.Fr. 3

115. DIOCESE DE LUÇON, ARCHIVES DU... [Archives of the Diocese of Luçon]. Bulletin d'histoire ecclésiastique et d'archéologie religieuse [Bulletin of ecclesiastical history and religious archaeology]. Q. Chanoine Buchou, Evêché de Luçon, Vendée. N.Fr. 3 / N.Fr. 3.25

DIOGENES see section on International Periodicals

116. DIX-SEPTIEME SIECLE (XVIIe siècle) [Seventeenth century]. Q. 1949 (1959: no. 40-43). Société d'étude du XVIIe siècle, 24 bd. Poissonière, Paris 9e. Ed: P. Jaillet, 105 rue de l'Abbé-Groult, Paris 15e. Art. on hist., literature, philosophy, law and science relating to 17th cent. France. N.Fr. 10 / N.Fr. 15

117. DOCUMENTS [Documents]. Revue des questions allemandes [Review of German questions]. B-M. Pub. address: 3 rue Bourdaloue, Paris 9e. N.Fr. 12 / N.Fr. 13.50

118. DOCUMENTS ET RECHERCHES [Documents and research]. Q. Société archéologique, historique et géographique de Creil, Hôtel de Ville, Creil, Oise. N.Fr. 5 / N.Fr. 6

119. DOKUMENTI O JUGOSLAVIJI [Documents of Yugoslavia]. Irr. Ed: J. Cvetkovic, 20 rue de Boulainvilliers, Paris 17e. Art. on the hist. and political problems of Yugoslavia; in Serbo-Croatian. pni

120. ECOLE FRANÇAISE D'EXTREME-ORIENT, BULLETIN DE L'... [Bulletin of the French School of the Far East]. S-A. 1901 (1958/59: vol. 49). Adrien Maisonneuve, 11 rue Saint Sulpice, Paris 6e, for Ecole Française d'Extrême Orient, c/o Collège de France, 11 place Marcelin Berthelot, Paris 5e. Art. on Southeast Asian culture, ethnography, hist. and related fields, with emphasis on Indochina and Indonesia; rev. art.; bk. rev.; illus. pv

121. ECRITS DE PARIS [Writings from Paris]. Revue des questions actuelles [Review of current questions]. M. Centre d'études des questions actuelles, 354 rue Saint-Honoré, Paris 1er. N.Fr. 19 / N.Fr. 22

ENCYCLOPEDIE MENSUELLE D'OUTRE-MER see next entry

122. ENCYCLOPEDIE MENSUELLE DE L'AFRIQUE [Monthly encyclopedia of Africa]. Politique, économique, sociale, culturelle et scientifique [Political, economic, social, cultural and scientific]. M. Pub. address: 18 rue de la Chaussée d'Antin, Paris 2e. From 1951 to 1957 pub. under the title: Encyclopédie mensuelle d'outre-mer. N.Fr. 50 / N.Fr. 56

123. L'ETHNOGRAPHIE [Ethnography]. S-A. 1913 (1958/59: new series, no. 53). Société d'ethnographie de Paris, c/o Librairie orientaliste Paul Geuthner, 12 rue Vavin, Paris 6e. Art. on Oriental hist., ethnology and ethnography; illus. pni

124. ETUDES ANGLAISES [English studies]. Grande-Bretagne. Etats Unis [Great Britain. United States]. Q. Librairie Marcel Didier, 6 rue de la Sorbonne, Paris 5e. Literary subjects; bk. rev.; biblio.; in English or French. N.Fr. 20

125. ETUDES ARDENNAISES [Ardennes studies]. Q. Société d'études Ardennaises, Archives départementales, Mézières. N.Fr. 8

126. ETUDES CORSES [Corsican studies]. Q. Société des sciences historiques et naturelles de la Corse, Lycée de Bastia, Corse. N.Fr. 9 / N.Fr. 12

127. ETUDES D'OUTRE-MER [Oversea studies]. Irr. Institut français d'outre-mer, Palais de la Bourse, Marseille. N.Fr. 30 / N.Fr. 35

128. ETUDES DE PRESSE [Studies of the press]. Q. Institut français de presse, 27 rue Saint-Guillaume, Paris 7e. Includes art. on the hist. of the press in France. N.Fr. 10 / N.Fr. 12.50

129. ETUDES GERMANIQUES [Germanic studies]. Allemagne, Autriche, Suisse, Pays scandinaves et néerlandais [Germany, Austria, Switzerland, the Scandinavian countries and the Netherlands]. Q. Librairie Marcel Didier, 6 rue de la Sorbonne, Paris 5e, for Société des études germaniques. Art. on literary and philological subjects; bk. rev.; biblio. of periodicals; in English or French. N.Fr. 18 / N.Fr. 20

130. ETUDES HAGUENOVIENNES [Studies of Haguenau]. Irr. Editions du Musée, Haguenau, for Société d'histoire et d'archéologie de Haguenau. pni

131. ETUDES NORMANDES [Norman studies]. Q. Association d'études normandes, 21 rue de Crosne, Rouen. Art. on hist. and related subjects concerning Normandy; bk. rev. N.Fr. 20

132. ETUDES ROUSSILLONNAISES [Studies of Roussillon]. Revue d'histoire et d'archéologic méditerranéennes [Review of Mediterranean history and archaeology]. Q. Pub. address: 2 rue des Abreuvoirs, Perpignan. Art. on the hist. and archaeology of the province of Roussillon.
N.Fr. 15 / N.Fr. 17.50

133. ETUDES TSIGANES [Gypsy studies]. Q. 1955 (1959: 5th year). Association des études tsiganes, 5 rue Las-Cases, Paris 7e. Art. on the hist. and ethnography of the gypsies in Europe; bk. rev. N.Fr. 5

134. EVOCATIONS. M. Groupe d'études historiques, géographiques et folkloriques du Bas-Dauphiné, Cremieu, Isère. p(1) N.Fr. 1

135. FACULTE DES LETTRES D'AIX, ANNALES DE LA... [Annals of the Faculty of Letters of Aix]. Irr. 1907 (1958: vol. 32). Faculté des Lettres d'Aix, place de l'Université, Aix. Art. on general hist. (not confined to any period or area), geography and literature; maps; graph. pni

136. FACULTE DES LETTRES DE BORDEAUX, ANNALES DE LA... [Annals of the Faculty of Letters of Bordeaux]. Bulletin hispanique [Hispanic bulletin]. Q. 1898/99 (1958: vol. 60). Féret et Fils, éditeurs, 9 rue de Grassi, Bordeaux. Art. on Spanish hist. and art; bk. rev.; in Spanish and French. N.Fr. 15 / N.Fr. 20

137. FACULTE DES LETTRES DE STRASBOURG, BULLETIN DE LA... [Bulletin of the Faculty of Letters of Strasbourg]. M. 1922 (1959: 38th year, no. 1). Association des publications de la Faculté des lettres de l'Université de Strasbourg, place de l'Université, Strasbourg, Bas-Rhin. N.Fr. 10 / N.Fr. 14

138. FACULTE DES LETTRES DE TOULOUSE, ANNALES PUBLIEES PAR LA... [Annals published by the Faculty of Letters of Toulouse]. Irr. 1951 (1958: 7th year). Faculté des lettres, 4 rue Albert-Lautman, Toulouse. Art. relating to work on literature and hist. done under the auspices of the faculty; each no. contains 4 sections; Littératures, Pallas, Via Domitia and Homo. N.Fr. 12

139. AR FALZ [The sickle]. B-M. Mouvement de la culture bretonne, "ar Falz," 6 rue Neptune, Brest. Bk. rev.; biblio.; in Breton and English. pni

140. FE [Belief]. Caièr de presènci prouvençalo [Review of current Provence]. Q. M.T.Jouveau, 28 rue Maréchal-Joffre, Aix-en-Provence. In Provençal and French. N.Fr. 4 / N.Fr. 5

141. FEDERATION DES SOCIETES SAVANTES DE MAINE-ET-LOIRE, BULLETIN DE LA... [Bulletin of the Federation of the Learned Societies of Maine-et-Loire]. Irr. Librairie H. Siraudeau, Angers. pni

142. FOLKLORE. B-M. 1950 (1961: no vol. indic.). Confédération nationale des groupes folkloriques français. Ed: L. Buyret, 11 bd. Vieussens, Montpellier, Hérault. Art. on the hist. of various branches of folklore; bk. rev.; biblio.; illus. pni

143. FOLKLORE. Q. Centre de documentation and Musée audois des arts et traditions populaires, 75/77 rue Trivalle, Carcassonne. N.Fr. 5

144. FONTAINES DE BROCELIANDE [Fountains of Brocéliande]. Artistiques, littéraires, touristiques [Artistic, literary, tourist]. Q. Pub. address: 54 rue Poullain-Duparc, Rennes. In Breton and French. N.Fr. 5

145. LE FRANÇAIS MODERNE [Modern French]. Revue consacrée à l'étude de la langue française [Review devoted to the study of the French language]. Q. Editions d'Artrey, 17 rue de la Rochefoucauld, Paris 9e. Bk. rev.; biblio. of periodicals. N.Fr. 15 / N.Fr. 20

146. FRANCE-AMERIQUE MAGAZINE [France-America magazine]. Revue des nations américaines... [Review of the American nations...]. Q. Institut des études américaines, Comité France-Amérique, 9-11 av. Franklin-Roosevelt, Paris 8e. N.Fr. 15

147. LA FRANCE GENEALOGIQUE [French genealogy]. B-M. 1959 (1959: no. 1-6). Centre d'entr'aide généalogique. Ed: du Chalard, Villaines-la-Juhel, Mayenne. Art. on the genealogy of French families and on heraldry and local hist.; genealogical tables; questions and answers; biblio. Formerly pub. under the title: Bulletin du Centre d'entr'aide généalogique. N.Fr. 18 / N.Fr. 20

148. LA FRANCE LATINE [Latin France]. M. Union des écrivains et artistes latins, 8 Impasse Truillot, Paris 11e. N.Fr. 5

149. FRANCE-MIDI [South-France]. Organe des régions et pays sous-développés et du Comité international des pays latins [Organ of the under-developed areas and countries and of the International Committee for Latin Countries]. M. Ed: E.Martinez, 39 rue des Acacias, Paris 17e. Prior to 1958 pub. under the title: Quercy-Midi-France. N.Fr. 4.50

150. FRANCE-U.S.A. [France-U.S.A.]. Organe mensuel des relations franco-américaines [Monthly organ of French-American relations]. M. Pub. address: 24 rue Eugène-Flachat, Paris 17e. p(1) N.Fr. 0.40

151. GALLIA. Fouilles et monuments archéologiques en France métropolitaine [Excavations and archaeological monuments in metropolitan France]. Tri-annual. 1943 (1958: vol. 16). Comité technique de la recherche archéologique en France, Centre national de la recherche scientifique, 155 rue de Sèvres, Paris 15e. Ed: Albert Grenier, Paul-Marie Duval. Art. on the archaeology of metropolitan France from classical antiquity to the 7th cent. A.D.; doc.; rev. art. on recently pub. literature; archaeological reports; illus. pv (N.Fr. 11-32)

152. GALLIA. PREHISTOIRE [Gallia. Prehistory]. Fouilles et monuments archéologiques en France métropolitaine [Excavations and archaeological monuments in metropolitan France]. A. 1958. Comité technique de la recherche archéologique en France, Centre national de recherche scientifique, 155 rue de Sèvres, Paris 15e. Ed: Albert Grenier, Paul-Marie Duval. Art. on French prehist.; rev. art. on recently pub. literature; archaeological reports; illus. Longer memoirs are pub. as separate supplements. pv (c. N.Fr. 30)

153. GAUCHE EUROPEENNE [European Left]. Revue de l'actualité démocratique et sociale [Review of democratic and social events]. M. Pub. address: 19 rue de Lille, Paris 7e. Pub. suspended in 1958. N.Fr. 9 / N.Fr. 12

154. LA GAZETTE DES ARCHIVES [The review of archives]. S-A. 1947 (1958: no. 23-24). Association amicale et professionnelle des Archivistes français. Ed. secretary: Michel Duchein, 60 rue des Francs-Bourgeois, Paris 3e. Art. on the organization and activities of French archives, archival problems and the holdings of archives; bk. rev.; biblio. of archival inventories, repertories and guides; reports of congresses; archival news. N.Fr. 5

155. GEOGRAPHIA. M. Henri Gauber, Editions Chaix, 126 rue des Rosiers, Saint-Ouen. N.Fr. 19.50 / $ 4.50

156. GROUPE LINGUISTIQUE D'ETUDES CHAMITOE-SEMITIQUES. COMPTES RENDUS DES SEANCES [Linguistic Group of Hamito-Semitic Studies. Reports of the meetings]. Irr. Imprimerie nationale, 27 rue de la Convention, Paris 16e. pni

157. GURE HERRIA [Our people]. Irr. Louis Dassance, Ustaritz, Basses-Pyrénées, for Association Gure Herria. In Basque and French. N.Fr. 8 / N.Fr. 10

HESPERIS see section on North Africa (Morocco)

158. HISTOIRE DE LA MEDECINE [History of medicine]. M. 1951 (1959: vol. 9). Société française d'histoire de la médecine, 61 rue de Vaugirard, Paris 6e. Ed: A. Manoury. Art. on the hist. of medicine; and biographical art.; bk. rev.; illus. N.Fr. 15 / N.Fr. 20

159. HISTOIRE DES ENTREPRISES [Business history]. S-A. 1958 (1959: no. 3-4). Centre de recherches historiques, 54 rue de Varenne, Paris 7e. Art. on business hist.; doc.; inventories of business archives; biblio. N.Fr. 8 / N.Fr. 11

160. HISTOIRE LOCALE [Local history]. Q. 1949 (1957: vol. 9, no. 29-32). Société française des historiens locaux, Ecole pratique des Hautes Etudes, 47 rue des Ecoles, Paris 5e. Ed: P. Fortier Beaulieu. Art. on French local hist. research; maps; biblio. N.Fr. 3

161. HISTORIA. La revue vivante du passé [The living review of the past]. M. 1956 (1959: no. 146-157). Editions Tallandier, 17 rue Rémy-Dumoncel, Paris 19e. Ed: Chr. Melchior-Bonnet. Art. on all aspects of hist.; bk. rev.; illus. N.Fr. 13.50 / N.Fr. 18 / $5

ICOM NEWS see section on International Periodicals

IMPACT - SCIENCE ET SOCIETE see section on International Periodicals

162. L'INFORMATION ARCHEOLOGIQUE [Archaeological information]. Q. 1959. Pub. and ed: André Perraud, 25 rue du Faubourg-du-Temple, Paris 10e. Art. on methodological problems of archaeology; news and notes of interest to scholars. N.Fr. 2

163. L'INFORMATION D'HISTOIRE DE L'ART [Information on the history of art]. B-M. 1955 (1959: 4th year). J.B. Baillière et fils, 19 rue Hautefeuille, Paris 6e. Art. on the hist. of art; bk. rev.; illus.; graph. N.Fr. 16 / N.Fr. 18

164. L'INFORMATION HISTORIQUE [Historical information]. 5xy. 1938 (1958: vol. 20). J.B. Baillière et fils, 19 rue Hautefeuille, Paris 6e. Ed: Albert Troux (chief ed.), Emile Coornaert, Robert Schnerb. Art. on French hist., rev. art.; rev. of bk. and art., arranged by period; extracts from doc. (annotated), bk. and memoirs, primarily for use in schools; illus.; charts. N.Fr. 16 / N.Fr. 18

165. INFORMATIONS ET DOCUMENTS [Information and documents]. S-M. Centre culturel américain, 4 av. Gabriel, Paris 8e. pni

166. INSTITUT D'ETUDES CENTRAFRICAINES. BULLETIN [Institute of Central African Studies. Bulletin]. S-A. Office de la recherche scientifique et technique outre-mer, 47 bd. des Invalides, Paris. N.Fr. 15

167. INSTITUT D'ETUDES OCCITANES, ANNALES DE L'... [Annals of the Institute of Occitan Studies]. A. Institut d'études occitanes, 1 rue Lafaille, Toulouse. N.Fr. 2

168. INSTITUT D'ETUDES OCCITANES, CAHIERS PEDAGOGIQUES DE L'... [Pedagogical publications of the Institute of Occitan Studies]. Irr. Institut d'études occitanes, 1 rue Lafaille, Toulouse. In French and Occitan. N.Fr. 2

169. INSTITUT DE RECHERCHE ET D'HISTOIRE DES TEXTES, BULLETIN D'INFORMATION DE L'... [News bulletin of the Institute for Research and History of Texts]. Irr. (1958 [1959]: no. 7). Editions du Centre national de la recherche scientifique, 13 Quai Anatole-France, Paris 7e, for Institut de recherche et d'histoire des textes. Art. on Latin and Oriental manuscripts. pni

170. INSTITUT HISTORIQUE DE PROVENCE, CONFERENCES DE L'... [Meetings of the Provence Historical Institute]. Q. Institut Historique de Provence, c/o Archives municipales, Hôtel de ville, Marseille. p (1) N.Fr. 0.15

171. INSTITUT NAPOLEON, REVUE DE L'... [Review of the Napoleon Institute]. Q. 1938 (1959: no vol. indic.). Institut Napoléon, 82 rue Bonaparte, Paris 6e. Art. on all subjects relating to Napoleon I and Napoleon III; bk. rev.; biblio.; illus. N.Fr. 15 / N.Fr. 20

172. L'INTERMEDIAIRE DES CHERCHEURS ET CURIEUX [The intermediary of investigators and those interested in curiosities]. Mensuel de questions et réponses historiques, litteraires, artistiques et sur toutes autres curiosités [Monthly of questions and answers in the fields of history, literature, arts and on all other curiosities]. M. Pub. address: 16 rue de Montpensier, Paris 1er. N.Fr. 30 / N.Fr. 34

INTERNATIONAL ARCHIVES OF SOCIOLOGY OF COOPERATION see section on International Periodicals

INTERNATIONAL SOCIAL SCIENCE BULLETIN see section on International Periodicals

JOURNAL. For titles beginning with "Journal," followed by the name of the publishing or sponsoring institution or society, see the respective institution or society.

173. JOURNAL ASIATIQUE [Asiatic review]. Q. 1822 (1958: vol. 246). Société asiatique, 1 rue de Seine, Paris 6e. Ed: Marcel Lalou. Art. on the hist., culture, philology and literature of Asian civilizations, with emphasis on the ancient and medieval periods; bk. rev.; reports on the meetings of the soc. pni

JOURNAL OF ECONOMIC AND SOCIAL HISTORY OF THE ORIENT see section on the Netherlands

174. LE JURA FRANÇAIS [The French Jura]. Q. Pub. address: 84 rue de Varenne, Paris 7e. N.Fr. 5 / $ 1

175. KULTURA [Culture]. Skice - Opowiadania - Sprawozdania [Sketches - short stories - reports]. M. Edition Libella, 12 rue Saint-Louis-en-l'Ile, Paris 4e, for Instytut Literacki [(Polish) Literary Inst.], Paris. In Polish; French and English sum.; A. author and subject index. N.Fr. 22 / $ 6

176. LATITUDES. S-A. Association des anciens élèves et élèves de l'Ecole nationale de la France d'Outre-mer, 2 av. de l'Observatoire, Paris 6e. N.Fr. 4 / N.Fr. 6

177. LA LEGITIMITE [Legitimacy]. Revue historique indépendante [Independent historical review]. A. 1955 (1958: no. 4). "Les Chartriers de la légitimité," Hôtel des Sociétés savantes, 28 rue Serpente, Paris 6e. Studies on the monarchy in France, with emphasis on constitutional aspects. pni

178. AL LIAMM [The bond]. Q. P. Le Bihan, 6 Domaine des Hocquettes, Suresnes, Seine. p (1) N.Fr. 3

179. LIGUE MARITIME ET D'OUTRE-MER, BULLETIN DE LA... [Bulletin of the Maritime and Overseas League]. Q. Ligue maritime et d'outre-mer, Section locale d'Amiens, 67 rue des Jacobins, Amiens.
(memb.) N.Fr. 4 / N.Fr. 8

MEMOIRES. For titles beginning with "Memoires," followed by the name of the publishing or sponsoring institution or society, see the respective institution or society.

180. MER OUTRE-MER [The sea and overseas areas]. Q. Ligue maritime et d'outre-mer, 41 rue de la Bienfaisance, Paris 8e.
(memb.) N.Fr. 5 / N.Fr. 10

181. LE MERCURE DE FRANCE [The Mercury of France]. M. 1890 (1958: vol. 335). Editions du Mercure de France, 26 rue de Condé, Paris 6e. Ed: S. de Sacy. Art. on literature, hist. and philosophy; bk. rev. Supplement to each no.: Bulletin de l'Alliance française. N.Fr. 27 / N.Fr. 32

182. MINISTERE DE L'EDUCATION NATIONALE. COMITE DES TRAVAUX HISTORIQUES ET SCIENTIFIQUES. SECTION DE GEOGRAPHIE. BULLETIN [Ministry of National Education. Committee for Historical and Scientific Studies. Geographical section. Bulletin]. A. Presses universitaires de France, 108 bd. Saint-Germain, Paris 5e, for Comité des travaux historiques et scientifiques. pv

183. MIROIR DE L'HISTOIRE [Mirror of history]. M. 1950 (1959: no. 109-120). Nouvelle librairie de France, 61 rue de Vaugirard, Paris 6e. Ed: L. H. Parias. Art. of popular interest on hist. from the Middle Ages to the present; rev. of bk. and phonographic records; correspondence section; illus.
N.Fr. 12 / N.Fr. 16

184. LE MONDE NON CHRETIEN [The non-Christian world]. Q. Pub. address: 17 rue Saint-Antoine, Paris 4e. Art. (including some of hist. interest) on Protestant missions; subject index for the first 5 years (1947-52) pub. separately. N.Fr. 8 / N.Fr. 10

MONUMENTS ET MEMOIRES PUBLIES PAR L'ACADEMIE DES INSCRIPTIONS ET BELLES-LETTRES see ACADEMIE DES INSCRIPTIONS ET BELLES-LETTRES, MONUMENTS ET MEMOIRES PUBLIES PAR L'...

185. MUSEE BERNADOTTE, BULLETIN DU... [Bulletin of the Bernadotte Museum]. A. Société des amis du Musée Bernadotte, 8 rue Tran, Pau.
(memb.) N.Fr. 5

186. MUSEE CARNAVALET, BULLETIN DU... [Bulletin of the Carnavalet Museum]. Collections historiques de la ville de Paris [Historical collections of the city of Paris]. S-A. Société des amis de Carnavalet, 23 rue de Sévigné, Paris 3e. (memb.) N.Fr. 7

187. MUSEE HISTORIQUE DE MULHOUSE, BULLETIN DU... [Bulletin of the Historical Museum of Mulhouse]. A. Musée historique, Mulhouse. pni

188. MUSEES ET COLLECTIONS PUBLIQUES DE FRANCE ET DE LA COMMUNAUTE FRANÇAISE [Museums and public collections of France and the French Community]. Q. 1927 (1959: new series, no. 18-21). Association générale des conservateurs des collections publiques de France et de la commu-

nauté française, 107 rue de Rivoli, Paris 1er. Ed: Michel Florisoone. Art. on the museums and public collections of France and the French Community; analyses of museum catalogues; biblio. of newly pub. bk.; biblio. of art. pub. in French museum bulletins; news and notes from museums; list of museum exhibitions; illus. N.Fr. 10 / N.Fr. 10.50

MUSEUM see section on International Periodicals

189. LA NATION GEORGIENNE [The Georgian nation]. M. Ed: M. Kerhuel, B.P. 3, Issy-les-Moulineaux, Seine. N.Fr. 5 / $ 3

190. LA NATION ROUMAINE [The Rumanian nation]. M. Société roumaine d'éditions, 35 bd. de Strasbourg, Paris 10e. N.Fr. 20 / N.Fr. 35

191. NEPTUNIA. Q. 1946 (1959: no. 53-56). Amis du Musée de la Marine, Musée de la Marine, Palais de Chaillot, Paris 16e. Art. on maritime hist. and navigation; doc.; bk. rev.; museum news; philatelic chronicle; illus.; supplement: Le Triton. N.Fr. 14 / N.Fr. 16

192. THE NEW BRITON. M. Publications Butterfly, 4 rue Vauquelin, Le Havre. In English. Ceased pub. with no. 57, 1957. N.Fr. 4.30

193. NICE HISTORIQUE [Historical Nice]. Q. Académia Nissarda, 65 rue de France, Nice. N.Fr. 10

194. NOROIS [Northwesterner]. Revue géographique de l'Ouest et des pays de l'Atlantique nord [Geographical review of the West and the North-Atlantic districts]. Q. S.F.I.L., 8 rue Descartes, Poitiers, for Instituts de géographie des Facultés des lettres de Caen, Poitiers, Rennes. N.Fr. 8.50 / N.Fr. 12

195. NOROIT [Northwest]. M. Société des conférences littéraires et artistiques, 9 rue des Capucins, Arras. N.Fr. 5

NOTICES, MEMOIRES ET DOCUMENTS PUBLIES PAR LA SOCIETE D'ARCHEOLOGIE ET D'HISTOIRE NATURELLE DU DEPARTMENT DE LA MANCHE see REVUE DU DEPARTMENT DE LA MANCHE

196. NOTRE BOURBONNAIS [Our Bourbonnais]. Revue de vulgarisation et d'action régionaliste [Review of popularization and regionalist action]. Q. Société bourbonnaise des études locales. Ed: Delaunay, 21 rue Léopold Maupas, Moulins. Hist. of Bourbonnais; doc. N.Fr. 2.50

NOTRE CANTON see REVUE DE MORET

197. NOTRE CONTREE [Our region]. A. E.Soitel, 8 bis rue des Perriers Montfermeil, Seine-et-Oise. N.Fr. 0.60

198. NOTRE FLANDRE [Our Flanders]. Q. Ed: L. Hoex, 60 rue du Calvaire, Lille. In Flemish and French. N.Fr. 6.50

199. NOTRE SEIZIEME (Notre XVIe) [Our sixteenth (arrondissement)]. Politique, littéraire, financier [Political, literary, financial]. M. S. Sicé, 148 av. Malakoff, Paris 16e. N.Fr. 3

200. LA NOUVELLE REVUE FRANC-COMTOISE [The new review of Franche-Comté]. Q. Pub. address: 4 rue du Parlement, Dôle, Jura. N.Fr. 10 / N.Fr. 12

NOUVELLES DU CONSEIL DE L'EUROPE see section on International Periodicals

NOUVELLES DE L'ICOM see section on International Periodicals

201. OC. Revista trimestrala de las letras occitanas [A quarterly review of Occitan letters]. Q. Institut d'études occitanes, 1 rue Lafaille, Toulouse. In Languedoc. N.Fr. 5 / N.Fr. 6

202. OCCITANIA. Q. Institut d'études occitanes, 1 rue Lafaille, Toulouse. N.Fr. 2 / N.Fr. 4

203. L'OEIL [The eye]. Revue d'art mensuelle [Monthly art review]. M. G. et R. Bernier, 67 rue des Saints Pères, Paris 6e. N.Fr. 44 / $ 10

204. OGAM. Tradition celtique: histoire - langue, archéologie - religion, numismatique - folklore [The Celtic tradition: history - language, archaeology - religion, numismatics - folklore]. B-M. 1948 (1959: vol. 11). Société des amis de la tradition celtique, 2 rue Léonard-de-Vinci, Rennes. Ed: Pierre Leroux. Art. on the aspects of Celtic studies named in the sub-title; doc.; bk. rev.; dictionary of old-Celtic pub. in installments; illus. Includes Bulletin de Numismatique Celtique. N.Fr. 20 / N.Fr. 40

ORDO CISTERCIENSUM REFORMATORUM, COLLECTANEA... see section on Belgium

205. ORIENT. Q. Orient, Société d'études et des publications, 114 av. des Champs-Elysées, Paris 8e. Art. on the evolution of the states of the Middle East, their problems, and the policies of Great Britain, France, the U.S.A. and the Soviet Union in the area. N.Fr. 30 / N.Fr. 32

ORIENT-OCCIDENT see section on International Periodicals

206. L'ORIENT SYRIEN [The Syrian Orient]. Revue d'études et de recherches sur les églises de langue syriaque [Review of studies and researches on Syriac language churches]. Q. 1956 (1959: vol. 4). Centre national de la recherche scientifique, 93 av. Paul Doumer, Paris 16e. Ed: Gabriel Khouri-Sarkis. Art. on the early hist., theology and liturgy of the Syriac, or Aramaic-speaking churches of Eastern and Western Syria. N.Fr. 17.75 / $ 3.60

207. OVERLAND. Revue d'études bardiques [Review of bardic studies]. Q. Ed: R. Tauzin, 21 rue Charles-Floquet, Talence, Gironde. N.Fr. 2

208. PACIFIC. Revue des Asiatiques [Asiatic review]. Q. Ed: Ley Hian, 82 bd. Saint-Michel, Paris 6e. In English and French; name and subject index. N.Fr. 5

209. PARIS ET ILE-DE-FRANCE [Paris and Ile-de-France]. A. 1949 (1957/58: vol. 9). Librairie des Méridiens Klincksieck, 11 rue de Lille, Paris 7e, for Fédération des Sociétés de Paris et de l'Ile-de-France, 29 rue de Sévigné, Paris 3e. Art. and memoirs on the hist., archaeology and folklore of Paris and Ile-de-France; illus. pni

210. LE PAYS BAS-NORMAND [The district of Lower Normandy]. B-M. Société historique et archéologique, 6 rue de Mayenne, Domfront, Orne. N.Fr. 7

211. LE PAYS D'AUGE [The Auge district]. M. Association "Le Pays d'Auge," 14 rue Duhamel, Lisieux. N.Fr. 10 / N.Fr. 13

212. PAYS DE BOURGOGNE [District of Bourgogne]. Q. Pub. address: 35 bd. Paul-Doumer, Dijon. N.Fr. 2.50

213. LE PAYS LORRAIN [The Lorraine district]. Q. Editions Berger-Levrault, 18 rue des Glacis, Nancy, for Société d'archéologie lorraine and Musée historique lorrain, 64 Grande-Rue, Nancy. N.Fr. 10 / N.Fr. 16

214. LA PENSEE [Thought]. Revue du rationalisme moderne. Arts-sciences-philosophie [Review of modern rationalism. Arts-sciences-philosophy]. B-M. Ed: René Maublanc, 95-97 bd. de Sébastopol, Paris 2e. Rev. of bk. and art. N.Fr. 12 / N.Fr. 14

215. LA PENSEE FRANÇAISE [French thought]. M. Pub. address: 35 rue Gayet, Saint-Etienne. N.Fr. 6

216. PHY-ELEC. La Gazette des arts [The arts gazette]. M. Ed: S. Pourcel, 28 rue Serpente, Paris 6e. pni

POLITIQUE see section on International Periodicals

217. POLITIQUE ETRANGERE [Foreign policy]. B-M. Centre d'études de politique étrangère, 54 rue de Varenne, Paris 7e. N.Fr. 18 / N.Fr. 22.50

218. PREHISTOIRE [Prehistory]. Recueil périodique de mémoires [Periodic collection of memoirs]. Irr. 1932 (mri 1956: vol. 12). Presses universitaires de France, 108 bd. Saint-Germain, Paris 6e. Ed: Raymond Lantier. Memoirs pertaining to excavations of objects or groups of objects of general art, archaeological, prehist. or protohist. interest; graph. pv (c. N.Fr. 10)

219. PREHISTOIRE-SPELEOLOGIE ARIEGEOISES [Prehistory-spelaeology of Ariège]. A. Société préhistorique de l'Ariège, Mairie, Tarascon-sur-Ariège. (memb.) N.Fr. 5

220. PRESENCE AFRICAINE [Africa to-day]. B-M. Pub. address: 42 rue Descartes, Paris. Ethnographic and political studies. N.Fr. 20 / N.Fr. 23

221. PRESENCES NAPOLEONIENNES [Napoleonic presence]. Revue trimestrielle du fait français dans le monde des origines à nos jours [Quarterly review of the French role in the world from the beginning to the present]. Q. 1957 (1957: vol. 1). Ed: P. Dargent, Centre Napoléon, 57 bd. Lefebvre, Paris 15e. Art. on all subjects relating to Napoleon I and Napoleon III and their influence in the world. pni

PREUVES see section on International Periodicals

PROCES VERBAUX. For titles beginning with "Procès Verbaux," followed by the name of the publishing or sponsoring institution or society, see the respective institution or society.

222. PROSPECTIVE. Irr. 1958 (1959: 2nd year). Presses universitaires de France, 108 bd. Saint-Germain, Paris 6e, for Centre international de prospective, 173 bd. Saint-Germain, Paris 6e. Essays on the evolution of humanity, chiefly in cultural, economic, social and technical fields. pv (c. N.Fr. 4.50-6)

223. PROVENCE HISTORIQUE [Historical Provence]. Q. La Pensée universitaire, 12 bis, rue Nazareth, Aix-en-Provence, for Fédération historique de Provence. N.Fr. 10

224. PROVINCE DE NAVARRE [Province of Navarre]. 3xy. Imprimerie Moulia, Orthez. pni

225. LA PROVINCE DU MAINE [The province of Maine]. Q. Société historique de la province du Maine, Hôtel Cardinal Dubois, 26 rue des Chanoines, Le Mans. N.Fr. 10 / N.Fr. 13

226. PROVINCIA. Revue mensuelle d'histoire et d'archéologie provençales... [Monthly review of history and archaeology of Provence...]. B-M. Société de statistique, d'histoire et d'archéologie de Marseille et de Provence, Palais de la Bourse, Marseille. Extracts and reprints of papers on hist., auxiliary hist. sciences and archaeology, pertaining to Provence, read at the meetings of the soc. N.Fr. 8

227. PYRENEES. Q. Société des amis du Musée pyrénéen de Lourdes, Chambre de commerce, Tarbes. N.Fr. 8 / N.Fr. 10

QUERCY-MIDI FRANCE see FRANCE-MIDI

RECHERCHES see section on International Periodicals

228. RESONANCES LYONNAISES [Echoes of Lyon]. Revue bi-mensuelle des arts [Bimonthly review of arts]. B-M. S.M.E., 26 place Tolozan, Lyon. N.Fr. 12

REVUE. For titles beginning with "Revue," followed by the name of the publishing or sponsoring institution or society, see the respective institution or society.

229. LA REVUE [The review]. Littérature, histoire, art et sciences des deux mondes [Literature, history, art and sciences of the two worlds]. B-W. 1829 (1959: no vol. indic.). Pub. address: 15 rue de l'Université, Paris 7e. Art. of general interest on literature, hist., art and science; world-wide news on cultural activities; bk. rev. N.Fr. 42 / N.Fr. 55

230. REVUE ARCHEOLOGIQUE [Archaeological review]. Q. 1844 (1959: vol. 63). Presses universitaires de France, 108 bd. Saint-Germain, Paris 6e. Ed: R. Lautier, Ch. Picard, 90 bd. Saint-Germain, Paris 5e. Art. on archaeology, epigraphy, numismatics and paleography, with emphasis on prehist. and antiquity; reports on explorations and excavations; bk. rev.; name index; illus. N.Fr. 26 / N.Fr. 29

231. REVUE ARCHEOLOGIQUE DE L'EST ET DU CENTRE-EST [Archaeological review of the East and Central East (France)]. Q. Pub. address: 12 rue Pelletier-de-Chambure, Dijon. N.Fr. 12 / N.Fr. 17.50

232. REVUE D'ALSACE [Review of Alsace]. Q. Institut des Hautes études alsaciennes, Université, Strasbourg, and Fédération des Sociétés d'histoire et d'archéologie d'Alsace. Bk. rev.; biblio. on Alsace. N.Fr. 8.50 / N.Fr. 10

233. REVUE D'ASSYRIOLOGIE ET D'ARCHEOLOGIE ORIENTALE [Review of Assyriology and Eastern archaeology]. Q. 1884 (1959: vol. 53). Presses universitaires de France, 108 bd. Saint-Germain, Paris 6e. Ed: G. Contenau, E. Dhorme, A. Parrot, 90 bd. Saint-Germain, Paris 6e. Art. on all fields of Assyriology and on the archaeology and hist. of Oriental countries; rev. of bk. and art. N.Fr. 26 / N.Fr. 29

234. REVUE D'AUVERGNE [Review of the Auvergne]. B-M. Société des amis de l'Université de Clermont, 3 av. Vercingetorix, Clermont-Ferrand. N.Fr. 8

235. REVUE D'ECONOMIE POLITIQUE [Review of political economy]. B-M. Librairie Sirey, 22 rue Soufflot, Paris 5e. N.Fr. 50 / N.Fr. 55

236. REVUE D'EGYPTOLOGIE [Review of Egyptology]. Irr. 1933 (1957: vol. 11). Société française d'égyptologie, Collège de France, 11 place Marcelin Berthelot, Paris, 5e. Ed: J.J. Clère, 34 rue du Cotentin, Paris 15e. Art. on all fields of the study of ancient Egypt; bk. rev.; in English and French; illus. pni

237. REVUE D'HISTOIRE DE L'EGLISE DE FRANCE [Review of the history of the French Church]. S-A. 1910 (1957: vol. 43). Société d'histoire ecclésiastique de la France, 52 av. de Breteuil, Paris 7e. Ed: Pierre Marot, 32 rue Cassette, Paris 6e. Art. on the hist. of the French Church and of Roman Catholicism; bk. rev. N.Fr. 16

238. REVUE D'HISTOIRE DE LA DEUXIEME GUERRE MONDIALE [Review of the history of the Second World War]. Q. 1950 (1959: vol. 9). Presse universitaires de France, 108 bd. Saint-Germain, Paris 6e. Ed: Henri Michel, 22 rue d'Athènes, Paris 8e. Art. on the hist. of the Second World War; bk. rev.; biblio., classified by period and area, with short descriptions of contents. N.Fr. 13 / N.Fr. 15

239. REVUE D'HISTOIRE DE LA MEDECINE HEBRAÏQUE [Review of the history of Hebrew medicine]. Q. 1948 (1959: vol. 12). Société d'histoire de la médecine hébraïque, 177 bd. Malesherbes, Paris 17e. Ed: I. Simon. Art. on the hist. of Hebrew medicine; bk. rev.; Hebrew sum.; illus.; author and subject indices for the years 1956-58 and tables of contents for the years 1948-58 pub. together in 1959. N.Fr. 12.50 / N.Fr. 18

REVUE D'HISTOIRE DES COLONIES see REVUE FRANÇAISE D'HISTOIRE D'OUTRE-MER

240. REVUE D'HISTOIRE DES SCIENCES ET DE LEURS APPLICATIONS [Review of the history of the sciences and their applications]. Q. 1948 (1959: vol. 12). Centre international de synthèse, section d'histoire des sciences, 12 rue Colbert, Paris 2e. Ed: Suzanne Delorme, René Taton. Art. on the hist. of science from antiquity to the present; bk. rev.; news of interest to scholars. N.Fr. 10 / N.Fr. 12

241. REVUE D'HISTOIRE DIPLOMATIQUE [Review of diplomatic history]. Q. 1887 (1958: vol. 72). A.Pedone, 13 rue Soufflot, Paris, for Société d'histoire générale et d'histoire diplomatique. Ed: René Dollot, 26 rue Martignac, Paris 7e. Art. on modern French diplomatic hist.; bk. rev. N.Fr. 30 / N.Fr. 36

242. REVUE D'HISTOIRE DU THEATRE [Review of the history of the theater]. Q. 1948 (1958: vol. 10). Michel Brient, 64 rue de Saintonge, Paris 3e, for Société d'histoire du théâtre, 55 rue Saint Dominique, Paris 7e. Art. on the hist. of the theater; biographies of authors and actors; bk. rev.; biblio.; illus. N.Fr. 15 / N.Fr. 17

243. REVUE D'HISTOIRE ECONOMIQUE ET SOCIALE [Review of social and economic history]. Q. 1908 (1959: vol. 37). Marcel Rivière et Cie., 31 rue Jacob, Paris 6e. Ed: Jean Vidalenc. Art. on economic and social hist., with strong emphasis on France, pertaining mostly to the modern period; bk. rev. N.Fr. 12 / N.Fr. 14

244. REVUE D'HISTOIRE ET DE PHILOSOPHIE RELIGIEUSES [Review of religious history and philosophy]. Q. Presses universitaires de France, 108 bd. Saint-Germain, Paris 6e, for Faculté de théologie protestante de l'Université de Strasbourg. Art. on Protestant hist., philosophy and religion; bk. rev. N.Fr. 10 / N.Fr. 12

245. REVUE D'HISTOIRE MODERNE ET CONTEMPORAINE [Review of modern and recent history]. Q. 1954 (1958: vol. 5). Presses universitaires de France, 108 bd. Saint-Germain, Paris 6e, for Société d'histoire moderne, 22 av. de la Bourdonnais, Paris 7e. Ed: board. Charles H. Pouthas (chief ed.), Roger Portal, René Rémond, 90 bd. Saint-Germain, Paris 5e. Art. on modern and recent European hist., with emphasis on France; doc.; reports of important international hist. meetings; professional news; supplement: Bulletin de la Société d'histoire moderne. N.Fr. 13 / N.Fr. 15

246. REVUE DE BOULOGNE ET DE SA REGION [Review of Boulogne and its surroundings]. B-M. Hôtel de la Chambre de commerce, quai Gambetta, Boulogne. p (1) N.Fr. 2.50

247. REVUE DE COMMINGES [Comminges review]. Pyrénées centrales [Central Pyrenees]. Q. Société des études du Comminges, 2 rue Thiers, Saint Gaudens, and Société Julien Sacaze, Château Lafont-Lasalle, Luchon. N.Fr. 10 / N.Fr. 14

248. REVUE DE DEFENSE NATIONALE [Review of national defense]. M. Comité d'études de défense nationale, 1 place Joffre, Paris 7e. N.Fr. 20 / N.Fr. 25

249. REVUE DE GEOGRAPHIE ALPINE [Review of Alpine geography]. Q. Institut de géographie alpine de l'Université de Grenoble, 2 rue Très-Cloître, Grenoble. Rev. of bk. and art.; name and subject index. N.Fr. 12 / N.Fr. 15

250. REVUE DE GEOGRAPHIE DE LYON [Geographical review of Lyon]. Q. Institut des études rhodaniennes de l'Université et Institut de géographie, 72 rue Pasteur, Lyon. N.Fr. 10

251. REVUE DE L'AGENAIS [Review of Agenais]. Q. Société des sciences, lettres et arts, 9 bd. de la République, Agen. N.Fr. 5 / N.Fr. 7

252. REVUE DE L'AVRANCHIN ET DU PAYS DE GRANVILLE [Review of Avranches and the Granville district]. Q. Société d'archéologie, de littérature, sciences et arts d'Avranches, Mortain et Granville, 40 bd. du Maréchal Foch, Avranches. N.Fr. 7

253. REVUE DE L'HISTOIRE DES RELIGIONS [Review of the history of religions]. Q. 1880 (1959: vol. 155). Presses universitaires de France, 108 bd. Saint-Germain, Paris 6e. Ed: E.Dhorme, H.C.Puech, 90 bd. Saint-Germain, Paris 5e. Art. on the hist. of religions and religious philosophy; bk. rev. N.Fr. 17 / N.Fr. 19

254. LA REVUE DE MORET ET SA REGION [Review of Moret and its surroundings]. Q. Ed: Max Brezol, 26 bd. Poissonnière, Paris 9e. Superseded Notre Canton in 1959. (memb.) N.Fr. 2

255. LA REVUE DE PARIS [The review of Paris]. M. Pub. address: 114 av. de Champs-Elysées, Paris 8e. N.Fr. 25 / N.Fr. 29

256. REVUE DE PHILOLOGIE, LITTERATURE ET HISTOIRE ANCIENNE [Review of ancient philology, literature and history]. S-A. Librairie Klincksieck, 11 rue de Lille, Paris 7e. Bk. rev. N.Fr. 25 / $ 6

257. REVUE DE SAVOIE [Review of Savoy]. Q. Librairie Dardel, 6 rue de Boigne, Chambéry. Art. on the hist. of, and cultural and economic topics relating to, Savoy; rev. of bk. and art.; illus. N.Fr. 12 / N.Fr. 13

258. REVUE DE SYNTHESE [Synthetic review]. Q. 1931 (1958: vol. 79). Editions Albin Michel, 22 rue Huyghens, Paris 14e, for Centre international de synthèse, 12 rue Colbert, Paris 2e. Art. on general and cultural hist. and the hist. of philosophy; rev. art.; bk. rev., classified by subject. N.Fr. 17

259. REVUE DES ETUDES ANCIENNES [Review of ancient studies]. S-A. 1899 (1959: vol. 61). Feret et Fils, 9 rue de Grassi, Bordeaux, for Faculté des lettres de Bordeaux. Ed: J.Audiat, 20 Cours Pasteur, Bordeaux. Art. on all fields of the study of antiquity, with emphasis on hist., linguistics and literature; bk. rev.; author and subject index; author index of bk. reviewed; illus. N.Fr. 15 / N.Fr. 20

260. REVUE DES ETUDES BYZANTINES [Review of Byzantine studies]. A. 1943 (1958: vol. 16). Institut français d'études byzantines, 8 rue François Ier, Paris 8e. Art. on Byzantine studies, with emphasis on archaeology, hist. and its auxiliary sciences and philology; doc.; bk. rev.; illus. N.Fr. 20 / $ 5

261. REVUE DES ETUDES GRECQUES [Review of Greek studies]. Q. 1888 (1958: vol. 71). Société d'édition "Les Belles Lettres," 95 bd. Raspail, Paris 6e, for Association pour l'encouragement des études grecques. Ed: A. Plassart, 129 bd. du Montparnasse, Paris 6e. Art. on the archaeology, epigraphy, hist., linguistics, literature and philosophy of ancient Greece; proceedings of the meetings of the assoc.; rev. of bk. and art. N.Fr. 25 / N.Fr. 30

262. REVUE DES ETUDES ISLAMIQUES [Review of Islamic studies]. A. 1927 (1958: vol. 26). Librairie orientaliste Paul Geuthner, 12 rue Vavin, Paris 6^{e}. Ed: L.Massignon, H.Laoust, 21 rue Monsieur, Paris 7e. Art. on all aspects of the study of Islam, past and present, with emphasis on hist., philosoph literature and religion. pni

263. REVUE DES ETUDES ITALIENNES [Review of Italian studies]. Q. 1919 (1958: new series, vol. 5). Librairie Marcel Didier, 4-6 rue de la Sorbonn Paris 5e, for Société d'études italiennes, 5 rue de l'Ecole de médecin, Paris 6e. Art. on Italian hist. and literature; biographies; rev. of bk. and art.; in French and Italian; illus. N.Fr. 15 / N.Fr. 18

264. REVUE DES ETUDES LATINES [Review of Latin studies]. A. 1923 (1958: vol. 36). Société d'édition "Les Belles Lettres," 95 bd. Raspail, Paris 6e, for Société des études latines, Ecole des Hautes Etudes, Sorbonne, Paris 5e. Ed: J. Marouzeau, 270 bd. Raspail, Paris 14e. Art. on all aspects of Latin studies and teaching, particularly on archaeology, hist., paleography, literature, linguistics, including classical and medieval Latin; bk. rev.; critical biblio. of Latin studies; proceedings of the meetings of the soc. N.Fr. 12 / N.Fr. 15

265. REVUE DES ETUDES SLAVES [Review of Slavic studies]. Q. 1921 (1958: vol. 35). Institut des études slaves, 9 rue Michelet, Paris 6e. Ed: A. Mazon, 140 av. de Suffron, Paris 15e. Art. on Slavic linguistics, literature, hist. and ethnography; general index for the years 1945-54. N.Fr. 18 / N.Fr. 22

266. REVUE DES FORCES TERRESTRES [Review of the ground forces]. Q. 1955 (1959: no. 15-18). Editions Ozanne, 56 rue de Verneuil, Paris 7e. Ed: Colonel Brusaut, 17 place Joffre, Paris 7e. Art. on the strategy and tactics of the modern army, and on military hist., with emphasis on France; bk. rev.; illus. N.Fr. 12.50 / N.Fr. 14

267. LA REVUE DU BAS-POITOU [The review of Lower Poitou]. B-M. Société des amis du Bas-Poitou, 74 rue Alsace-Lorraine, Niort, Deux-Sèvres. N.Fr. 10

268. REVUE DU DEPARTEMENT DE LA MANCHE [Review of the department of La Manche]. Q. Société d'archéologie et d'histoire de la Manche, Hôtel de Ville, Saint-Lô, Manche. Prior to 1959 pub. under the title: Notices, Mémoires et documents publiés par la Société d'archéologie et d'histoire naturelle du département de la Manche. N.Fr. 10

269. REVUE DU GEVAUDAN [Review of Gevaudan]. A. Société des lettres, science et arts de la Lozère, Musée de Mende, Mende. N.Fr. 5

270. REVUE DU MOYEN-AGE LATIN [Review of the Latin Middle Ages]. Etudes, textes, chronique, bibliographie [Studies, texts, chronicle, bibliography]. Q. 1945 (1955 [1959]: vol. 11). Pub. address: Palais de l'Université, Strasbourg. Ed: F. Chatillon. Art. on all fields of the study of the Latin Middle Ages, particularly philosophy, literature, linguistics, hist., epigraphy and paleography; doc.; bk. rev.; biblio. N.Fr. 15 / $6

271. REVUE DU NORD [Northern review]. Q. 1910 (1958: vol. 40). Faculté des lettres, Université de Lille, 9 rue Auguste-Angellier, Lille. Art. on the hist. and archaeology of northern France, Belgium and the Netherlands; doc.; rev. art.; bk. rev.; extensive biblio. rev. of hist. studies by area; professional news; 3rd no. of each vol. devoted to geography. N.Fr. 10 / N.Fr. 13

272. REVUE DU ROUERGUE [Review of the Rouergue]. Q. Société des lettres, sciences et arts de l'Aveyron, place de la Cité, Rodez. N.Fr. 10

273. REVUE DU SOUVENIR VENDEEN [Review devoted to the memory of the Vendée]. Q. Souvenir Vendéen, 6 rue Barjot, Cholet. N.Fr. 3 / N.Fr. 5

274. REVUE DU VIVARAIS [Review of Vivarais]. Q. Jean Messié, Bourg-Saint-Andéol, Ardèche. N.Fr. 9

275. REVUE ECONOMIQUE [Economic review]. B-M. Armand Colin, 103 bd. Saint-Michel, Paris 5e. N.Fr. 25 / N.Fr. 29

276. REVUE ECONOMIQUE FRANÇAISE [French economic review]. Q. Société de géographie commerciale de Paris, 20 rue de Tournon, Paris 6e. N.Fr. 8

276. REVUE FRANÇAISE D'HERALDIQUE ET DE SIGILLOGRAPHIE [French review of heraldry and sphragistics]. 3-4xy. 1938 (1958: vol. 12). Société française d'héraldique et de sigillographie, 113 rue de Courcelles, Paris 17e. Art. on coats-of-arms, heraldry and seals, with emphasis on France; biblio. (occasionally with brief descriptions of contents), classified by country; reports of sessions of the soc.; news of interest to scholars; illus. (memb.) N.Fr. 10

278. REVUE FRANÇAISE D'HISTOIRE D'OUTRE-MER [French review of overseas history]. Q. 1913 (1958: vol. 45). Larose, 11 rue Victor Cousin, Paris 5, for Société de l'histoire des colonies françaises, 43 rue Cambon, Paris 1er. Art. on French colonial and related hist.; doc.; biblio. reports on colonial areas. Prior to 1959 pub. under the title: Revue d'histoire des colonies. N.Fr. 12 / N.Fr. 15

279. REVUE FRANÇAISE DE SCIENCE POLITIQUE [French review of political science]. Q. Fondation nationale des sciences politiques, 27 rue Saint-Guillaume, Paris. N.Fr. 23 / N.Fr. 25

280. REVUE GEOGRAPHIQUE DES PYRENEES ET DU SUD-OUEST [Geographical review of the Pyrenees and the Southeast]. Q. Institut de Géographie, 4 rue Albert Lautman, Toulouse. N.Fr. 12 / $ 2.50

281. REVUE HISTORIQUE [Historical review]. Q. 1876 (1958: vol. 221/222, no. 449-452). Presses universitaires de France, 108 bd. Saint-Germain, Paris 6e. Ed: Pierre Renouvin, 90 bd. Saint-Germain, Paris 6e. Art. on all aspects of hist., with emphasis on modern France; rev. art.; bk. rev.; biblio. of art. in the major hist. rev., classified by subject and area; news and notes of interest to scholars. N.Fr. 23 / N.Fr. 26

282. REVUE HISTORIQUE DE BORDEAUX ET DU DEPARTEMENT DE LA GIRONDE [Historical review of Bordeaux and the department of Gironde]. Q. 1908 (1959: new series, vol. 8). Pub. address: Hôtel des Sociétés savantes, 71 rue du Loup, Bordeaux. Art. on the hist. and folklore of Southwestern France, with emphasis on Bordeaux and the dept. of Gironde; biographies of local personalities of national or international importance; bk. rev.; biblio.; index; charts, maps, illus.; cum. index for vol. 1-25 (1908-32) and vol. 26-34 (1933-45). N.Fr. 8 / N.Fr. 10

283. REVUE HISTORIQUE DE DROIT FRANÇAIS ET ETRANGER [Historical review of French and foreign law]. Q. 1922 (1958: 4th series, vol. 36). Editions Sirey, 22 rue Soufflot, Paris 5e. Ed. secretary: Ch. Perrat. Art. on the hist. of law; bk. rev.; news of interest to scholars. N.Fr. 25 / N.Fr. 28

284. REVUE HISTORIQUE DE L'ARMEE [Historical review of the army]. Q. 1945 (1959: vol. 15). Ministère de la Guerre, Service historique de l'armée, 231 bd. Saint-Germain, Paris 7e. Ed: P. Lyet. Art. on French military hist., mostly modern; rev. of bk. and art.; maps, illus. N.Fr. 28 / N.Fr. 32

285. REVUE HISTORIQUE ET ARCHEOLOGIQUE DU LIBOURNAIS [Historical and archaeological review of the Libournais]. Q. Société historique et archéologique, B.P. 75, Libourne. N.Fr. 6

286. REVUE HITTITE ET ASIANIQUE [Hittite and Asian review]. S-A. 1930 (1959: vol. 17). Librairie Klincksieck, 11 rue de Lille, Paris 7e. Ed: E. Laroche, 5 rue Grandidier, Strasbourg. Art. on hist., auxiliary hist. sciences, archaeology and linguistics pertaining to ancient Asia Minor; bk. rev.; in English, French and German; illus. pni

287. REVUE INTERNATIONALE D'ONOMASTIQUE [International review of onomastics]. Noms de lieux, noms de personnes [Place names, persons' names]. Q. 1949 (1959: 11th year). Editions d'Artrey, 17 rue de la Rochefoucauld, Paris 9e. Art. on personal and place names and on linguistics; rev. of bk. and art. N.Fr. 15 / N.Fr. 20

288. REVUE JURIDIQUE ET POLITIQUE D'OUTRE-MER [Overseas judicial and political review]. Q. Librairie générale de droit et de jurisprudence, 20 rue Soufflot, Paris 5e. Prior to 1959 pub. under the title: Revue juridique et politique de l'Union Française. N.Fr. 45

REVUE JURIDIQUE ET POLITIQUE DE L'UNION FRANÇAISE see preceding entry

289. LA REVUE LIBERALE [The liberal review]. Revue trimestrielle scientifique, philosophique, économique [Quarterly review of science, philosophy, economy]. Pub. address: 1 rue François Ier, Paris 8e. N.Fr. 6 / N.Fr. 7

290. LA REVUE MARITIME [Naval review]. M. Ozanne, 56 rue de Verneuil, Paris 7e. N.Fr. 25 / N.Fr. 30

291. REVUE NUMISMATIQUE [Numismatic review]. A. 1836 (1958: 6th series, vol. 1). Société d'éditions "Les Belles Lettres," 95 bd. Raspail, Paris 6e. Ed. secretary: J. Lafaurie, Cabinet des Médailles, Bibliothèque nationale, 58 rue de Richelieu, Paris 2e. Art. on numismatics; notes on recent finds; bk. rev.; illus.; subject and general index for the years 1916-56.
N.Fr. 30 / N.Fr. 32

292. REVUE POLITIQUE DES IDEES ET DES INSTITUTIONS [Political review of ideas and institutions]. B-M. Pub. address: 22 rue de Chateaudun, Paris 9e. N.Fr. 18 / N.Fr. 23

293. REVUE POLITIQUE ET PARLEMENTAIRE [Political and parliamentary review]. M. Pub. address: 10 rue Auber, Paris 9e. N.Fr. 20 / N.Fr. 25

294. REVUE REGIONALISTE DES PYRENEES [District review of the Pyrenees]. Q. Association régionaliste de Béarn, du Pays Basque, des contrées de l'Adour et de l'académie des lettres Pyrénéennes, 2 place de la Libération, Pau, Basses-Pyrénées. N.Fr. 5

295. REVUE SAVOISIENNE [Savoy review]. Q. 1860 (1957: 98th year). Académie florimontane, Hôtel de Ville, Annecy. Art. on the art, hist., archaeology, literature and folklore of Savoy; biographies of hist. and literary personalities; proceedings of the meetings of the Académie Savoyard; biblio.; illus. N.Fr. 5

296. REVUE SOCIALISTE [Socialist review]. Revue mensuelle de culture politique et sociale publiée par le Parti socialiste et le Cercle d'études Jean Jaurès [Monthtly review of political and social culture published by the Socialist Party and the "Jean Jaurès" study group]. M. Pub. address: 61 rue La Fayette, Paris 9e. N.Fr. 18.50 / N.Fr. 21

297. RHODANIA. A. Société archéologique du Bassin du Rhône, Rousset, Drôme. Illus. N.Fr. 5

298. ROMANIA. Revue trimestrielle consacrée à l'étude des langues et littératures romanes [Quarterly review devoted to the study of Romance languages and literatures]. Q. Ed: Mario Roques, 2 rue Poissy, Paris 5e. Rev. of bk. and art. pni

299. ROMÂNIA MUNCITOARE [Working Rumania]. Revista socială şi polică a sindicatelor în exil [Social and political review of trade-unionists in exile]. M. Ed: Eftimie Gherman, 198 av. du Maine, Paris. Irr. supplement pub. in French under the title: Cahiers de la Roumanie ouvrière.

300. RYTHMES DU MONDE [Rythms of the world]. Q. Pub. address: 5 rue de la Source, Paris. N.Fr. 10 / Bfr. 120

301. LES SAPINS VERTS A TRAVERS LES VILLAGES D'AURE [The green firs in the villages of Aure]. Bulletin folklorique mensuel [Monthly folklore bulletin]. M. Ed: O. Redon, Guchan, Hautes-Pyrénées. N.Fr. 2

302. LA SCIENCE HISTORIQUE [Historical science]. 3xy. 1921 (1958: vol. 37). Institut des sciences historiques, Société archéologique de France, 169 rue Saint-Jacques, Paris 5e. Ed: Jean-Pascal Romain. Art. on hist., with emphasis on French hist. from the 18th cent. on, particularly on Napoleon I and his age, on social hist. and on dynastic problems; section devoted to archaeology; doc.; rev. of bk. and art.; letters to the ed.; news and notes from French hist. soc. N.Fr. 9

303. SEMITICA. A. 1948 (1958: vol. 8). Librairie d'Amérique et d'Orient, Adrien-Maisonneuve, 11 rue Saint-Sulpice, Paris 5e, for Institut d'études sémitiques, Université de Paris. Art. on Semitic studies, dealing largely with cultural hist., linguistics, the hist. of ideas, mythology, archaeology, epigraphy and related subjects, from ancient times to the modern period; doc. and texts; illus. pni

304. SKOL [School]. Revue trimestrielle de pédagogie [Quarterly review of pedagogy]. Q. Ed: Abbé Armand Le Calvez, Rundavid, Plouezec, Côtes du Nord. In Breton. N.Fr. 8

305. SOCIALISME OU BARBARIE [Socialism or barbarism]. Organe de critique et d'orientation révolutionnaire [Organ of criticism and revolutionary orientation]. Q. Pub. address: 42 rue René-Boulanger, Paris 10e. N.Fr. 10/N.Fr. 1

306. SOCIETE ACADEMIQUE D'AGRICULTURE, DES SCIENCES, ARTS ET BELLES-LETTRES DU DEPARTEMENT DE L'AUBE, BULLETIN MENSUEL DE LA... [Monthly bulletin of the Academic Society of Agriculture, Sciences, Arts and Letters of the Department of Aube]. M. Sciété académique d'agriculture, des sciences, arts et belles-lettres du département de l'Aube, 21 rue Chrestien-de-Troyes. pni

307. SOCIETE ACADEMIQUE D'AGRICULTURE, DES SCIENCES, ARTS ET BELLES-LETTRES DU DEPARTEMENT DE L'AUBE, PROCES VERBAUX DES SEANCES DE LA... [Minutes of the meetings of the Academic Society for Agriculture, Sciences, Arts and Letters of the Department of Aube]. A. 1957 [1958]. Les Imprimeries Paton, 27-29 rue Général Saussier, Troyes, for Société d'agriculture, des sciences, arts et belles-lettres du Département de l'Aube. pni

308. SOCIETE ACADEMIQUE D'ARCHEOLOGIE, SCIENCES ET ARTS DU DEPARTEMENT DE L'OISE. BULLETIN [Academic Society of Archaeology, Sciences and Arts of the Department of Oise. Bulletin]. 5xy. Société académique d'archéologie, sciences et arts du département de l'Oise, Hôtel de Ville, Beauvais. N.Fr. 1

309. SOCIETE ACADEMIQUE DE BAS-RHIN POUR LE PROGRES DES SCIENCES, DES LETTRES, DES ARTS ET DE LA VIE ECONOMIQUE. BULLETIN [Academic Society of Lower Rhine for the Advancement of Sciences, Letters, Arts and Economic Life. Bulletin]. Irr. Société académique, Palais universitaire, place de l'Université, Strasbourg. pni

310. SOCIETE ACADEMIQUE DES ANTIQUAIRES DE LA MORINIE, BULLETIN TRIMESTRIEL DE LA... [Quarterly bulletin of the Academic Society of Antiquarians of La Morinie]. Q. Société académique des antiquaires de la Morinie, 42 bis, place Foch, Saint-Omer, P.d.C. Index of authors, places and art. for the years 1833-1957 pub. in 1957. N.Fr. 5

311. SOCIETE AGRICOLE, SCIENTIFIQUE ET LITTERAIRE DES PYRENEES-ORIENTALES [Agricultural, Scientific and Literary Society of Eastern Pyrenees]. A. Société agricole, scientifique et littéraire, Hôtel Pams, rue Emile Zola, Perpignan. pni

312. SOCIETE ARCHEOLOGIQUE CHAMPENOISE, BULLETIN DE LA... [Bulletin of the Archaeological Society of Champagne]. S-A. Société archéologique champenoise, 13 rue Nanteuil, Reims. N.Fr. 8

313. SOCIETE ARCHEOLOGIQUE DE FINISTERE, BULLETIN DE LA... [Bulletin of the Archaeological Society of Finistère]. A. Société archéologique du Finistère, Archives départementales, Quimper. N.Fr. 8

314. SOCIETE ARCHEOLOGIQUE DE TARN-ET-GARONNE, BULLETIN ARCHEOLOGIQUE, HISTORIQUE ET ARTISTIQUE DE LA... [Bulletin on archaeology, history and arts of the Archaeological Society of Tarn-et-Garonne]. A. Société archéologique de Tarn-et-Garonne, Hôtel de la Chambre de commerce, Allées de Mortarieu, Montauban. N.Fr. 6

315. SOCIETE ARCHEOLOGIQUE DE TOURAINE, BULLETIN TRIMESTRIEL DE LA... [Quarterly bulletin of the Archaeological Society of Touraine]. Q. Société archéologique de Touraine, 8 place Foire-le-Roi, Tours. pni

316. SOCIETE ARCHEOLOGIQUE DU MIDI DE LA FRANCE, MEMOIRES DE LA... [Memoirs of the Archaeological Society of Southern France]. B. 1832/33 (1957: vol. 26). Librairie E.Privat, 14 rue des arts, Toulouse, for Société archéologique du Midi de la France. Art. on the archaeology and hist. of Southern France, not confined to any period; biblio.; illus. pni

317. SOCIETE ARCHEOLOGIQUE ET HISTORIQUE DE CHELLES, BULLETIN DE LA... [Bulletin of the Archaeological and Historical Society of Chelles]. B-M. Société archéologique et historique, Mairie, Chelles, Seine et Marne. pni

318. SOCIETE ARCHEOLOGIQUE ET HISTORIQUE DE CLERMONT-EN-BEAUVAISIS, COMPTES RENDUS ET MEMOIRES DE LA... [Reports and memoirs of the Archaeological and Historical Society of Clermont-en-Beauvaisis]. A. Société archéologique et historique de Clermont-en-Beauvaisis, 9 rue Fernet, Clermont, Oise. N.Fr. 5

319. SOCIETE ARCHEOLOGIQUE ET HISTORIQUE DE L'ORLEANAIS. BULLETIN PROVISOIRE DE LIAISON [Archaeological and Historical Society of Orléanais. Provisional bulletin of communication]. 5xy. Ed: P. Hamel, 2 bis rue d'Angleterre, Orléans. N.Fr. 6.50

• 320. SOCIETE ARCHEOLOGIQUE ET HISTORIQUE DE LA CHARENTE, BULLETIN MENSUEL DE LA... [Monthly bulletin of the Archaeological and Historical Society of Charente]. M. Société archéologique et historique, 44 rue de Montmoreau, Angoulème. pni

321. SOCIETE ARCHEOLOGIQUE ET HISTORIQUE DE LA CHARENTE, MEMOIRES DE LA... [Memoirs of the Archaeological and Historical Society of Charente]. A. Société archéologique et historique de la Charente, 44 rue de Montmoreau, Angoulème. pni

322. SOCIETE ARCHEOLOGIQUE ET HISTORIQUE DE NANTES ET DE LOIRE-ATLANTIQUE, BULLETIN DE LA... [Bulletin of the Archaeological and Historical Society of Nantes and the Loire-Atlantique District]. A. Société archéologique et historique de Nantes et de Loire-Atlantique, place Jean V, Nantes. N.Fr. 8

323. SOCIETE ARCHEOLOGIQUE ET HISTORIQUE DU CHATILLONNAIS, BULLETIN DE LA... [Bulletin of the Archaeological and Historical Society of Châtillonnais]. A. Ed: R. Paris, 11 rue de Seine, Châtillon-sur-Seine, Seine. N.Fr. 2

324. SOCIETE ARCHEOLOGIQUE ET HISTORIQUE DU LIMOUSIN, BULLETIN DE LA... [Bulletin of the Archaeological and Historical Society of Limousin]. A. Société archéologique et historique, Archives départementales de la Haute-Vienne, 2 rue des Combes, Limoges. N.Fr. 7

325. SOCIETE ARCHEOLOGIQUE, HISTORIQUE ET ARTISTIQUE "LE VIEUX PAPIER" POUR L'ETUDE DE LA VIE ET DES MOEURS D'AUTREFOIS, BULLETIN DE LA... [Bulletin of "Le Vieux Papier" Society of Archaeology, History and Art for the Study of the Life and Customs of the Past]. Q. 1900 (1958: vol. 22). Association "Le Vieux Papier," c/o André Desfeuilles (gen. secretary), 24 rue de Verneuil, Paris 7e. Art. on old French customs and the old French way of life; bk. rev.; illus. N.Fr. 10

326. SOCIETE ARCHEOLOGIQUE, HISTORIQUE ET SCIENTIFIQUE DE NOYON, BULLETIN DE LA... [Bulletin of the Archaeological, Historical and Scientific Society of Noyon]. B-M. Société archéologique, historique et scientifique, Noyon, Oise. (memb.) N.Fr. 3

327. SOCIETE ARCHEOLOGIQUE, HISTORIQUE, LITTERAIRE ET SCIENTIFIQUE DE GERS, BULLETIN DE LA... [Bulletin of the Archaeological, Historical, Literary and Scientific Society of Gers]. Q. Société archéologique, historique, littéraire et scientifique du Gers, 13 place Saluste-du-Barthas, Auch. N.Fr. 3.50 / N.Fr. 5

328. SOCIETE ARCHEOLOGIQUE, SCIENTIFIQUE ET LITTERAIRE DU VENDOMOIS, BULLETIN DE LA... [Bulletin of the Archaeological, Scientific and Literary Society of Vendômois]. A. Société archéologique, scientifique et littéraire du Vendômois, Cloître de l'Abbaye, Vendôme, Loir-et-Cher. N.Fr. 3

329. SOCIETE D'AGRICULTURE, COMMERCE, SCIENCE ET ARTS DU DEPARTEMENT DE LA MARNE, MEMOIRES DE LA... [Transactions of the Society of Agriculture, Trade, Science and Arts of the Department of Marne]. A. Société d'agriculture, commerce, science et arts du département de la Marne, 1 rue des Buttes, Châlons-sur-Marne. N.Fr. 10

330. SOCIETE D'AGRICULTURE, SCIENCES, ARTS ET COMMERCE DU DEPARTEMENT DE LA CHARENTE. BULLETIN MENSUEL [Society of Agriculture, Sciences, Arts and Trade of the Department of Charente. Monthly bulletin]. M. Société d'agriculture, sciences, arts et commerce du département de la Charente, Hôtel de Ville, Angoulème. pni

331. SOCIETE D'AGRICULTURE, SCIENCES ET ARTS DE LA SARTHE, BULLETIN DE LA... [Bulletin of the Society of Agriculture, Sciences and Arts of Sarthe]. A. Société d'agriculture, sciences et arts de la Sarthe, Hôtel de Tessé, 2 rue de Tessé, Le Mans. pni

332. SOCIETE D'ARCHEOLOGIE ET D'HISTOIRE DU TONNERROIS, BULLETIN ANNUEL DE LA... [Annual bulletin of the Society of Archaeology and History of Tonnerrois]. A. Société d'archéologie et d'histoire du Tonnerrois, rue Rougemont, Hôtel Coeurderoy, Tonnerre, Yonne. N.Fr. 2

SOCIETE D'ARCHEOLOGIE ET D'HISTOIRE NATURELLE DU DEPARTEMENT DE LA MANCHE, NOTICES, MEMOIRES ET DOCUMENTS PUBLIES PAR LA... see REVUE DU DEPARTEMENT DE LA MANCHE

333. SOCIETE D'ARCHEOLOGIE ET DE STATISTIQUE DE LA DRÔME, BULLETIN DE LA... [Bulletin of the Society of Archaeology and Statistics of Drôme]. Q. Société d'archéologie et de statistique de la Drôme, 4 place des Ormeaux, Valence. N.Fr. 4

334. SOCIETE D'EMULATION DES CÔTES-DU-NORD. BULLETINS ET MEMOIRES [Society of Emulation of Côtes-du-Nord. Bulletins and memoirs]. A. Société d'émulation, 8 rue Saint Guoueno, Saint Brieuc. N.Fr. 10 / N.Fr. 12

335. SOCIETE D'ETUDES D'AVALLON, BULLETIN D'INFORMATION DE LA... [News bulletin of the Society for Studies of Avallon]. Histoire, sciences, lettres et arts [History, sciences, letters and arts]. B-M. Imprimerie générale de la Nièvre, Clamecy, for Société d'études d'Avallon. pni

336. SOCIETE D'ETUDES DE LA PROVINCE DE CAMBRAI. BULLETIN [Society for Studies of the Province of Cambrai. Bulletin]. 3xy. Société d'études de la province de Cambrai, 24 rue Esquermoise, Lille. N.Fr. 5 / N.Fr. 5.75

337. SOCIETE D'ETUDES ET DE RECHERCHES PREHISTORIQUES ET INSTITUT PRATIQUE DE PREHISTOIRE, LES EYZIES. BULLETIN [Society of Prehistoric Studies and Research and Practical Institute for Prehistory, Les Eyzies. Bulletin]. A. 1952 (1957: no. 7). Société d'études et de recherches préhistoriques and Institut pratique de préhistoire, Les Eyzies. Ed: L. Coulonges, Sauveterre-la-Lémance, Lot-et-Garonne; E. Peyrony (secretary), Musée, Les Eyzies, Dordogne. Art. on all aspects of prehist.; graph, maps, illus. (memb.) N.Fr. 8

338. SOCIETE D'ETUDES HISTORIQUES, GEOGRAPHIQUES ET SCIENTIFIQUES DE LA REGION PARISIENNE, BULLETIN DE LA... [Bulletin of the Society of Historical, Geographical and Scientific Studies of the District of Paris]. Q. 1927 (1958: vol. 32). Société d'études historiques, géographiques et scientifiques de la region Parisienne, 191 rue Saint Jacques, Paris 5e. Ed. board: A. Perpillou, A. Chatelain, A. Delcourt. Art. on the hist. and geography of Paris and its surroundings; general index for the years 1927-57. N.Fr. 5 / N.Fr. 6

339. SOCIETE D'ETUDES HISTORIQUES, SCIENTIFIQUES, ARTISTIQUES ET LITTERAIRES DES HAUTES-ALPES, BULLETIN DE LA... [Bulletin of the Society for Historical, Scientific, Art and Literary Studies of Hautes-Alpes]. A. Société d'études historiques, scientifiques, artistiques et littéraires des Hautes-Alpes, 23 rue Carnot, Gap. Alphabetical table of contents for the years 1912-53 pub. separately in 1953. N.Fr. 8

340. SOCIETE D'ETUDES SCIENTIFIQUES ET ARCHEOLOGIQUES DE DRAGUIGNAN ET DU VAR, BULLETIN DE LA... [Bulletin of the Society of Scientific and Archaeological Studies of Draguignan and Var]. A. Société d'études scientifiques et archéologique de Draguignan et du Var, 21 Allées d'Azémar, Draguignan, Var. N.Fr. 5

341. SOCIETE D'HISTOIRE ET D'ARCHEOLOGIE DE BRETAGNE, BULLETIN DE LA... [Bulletin of the Historical and Archaeological Society of Bretagne]. A. Société d'histoire et d'archéologie de Bretagne, 2 place Saint-Melaine, Rennes. (memb.) N.Fr. 0.80, N.Fr. 1.20

342. SOCIETE D'HISTOIRE ET D'ARCHEOLOGIE DE BRETAGNE, MEMOIRES DE LA... [Memoirs of the Historical and Archaeological Society of Bretagne]. A. Société d'histoire et d'archéologie de Bretagne, 2 place Saint-Melaine, Rennes. Indices of art., authors and subjects for the years 1920-43 pub. separately. (memb.) N.Fr. 8, N.Fr. 10

343. SOCIETE D'HISTOIRE ET D'ARCHEOLOGIE DE CHALON-SUR-SAÔNE, MEMOIRES DE LA... [Memoirs of the Historical and Archaeological Society of Chalon-sur-Saône]. A. Imprimerie de Buguet-Comptour, 1 rue Senecé, Mâcon, for Société d'histoire et d'archéologie de Chalon-sur-Saône. pni

344. SOCIETE D'HISTOIRE ET D'ARCHEOLOGIE DE L'ARRONDISSEMENT DE PROVINS, BULLETIN DE LA... [Bulletin of the Historical and Archaeological Society of the District of Provins]. A. Société d'histoire et d'archéologie de l'arrondissement de Provins, Hôtel de Ville, Provins, Seine-et-Marne. N.Fr. 3

345. SOCIETE D'HISTOIRE ET D'ARCHEOLOGIE DE L'ARRONDISSEMENT DE SAINT-MALO, ANNALES DE LA... [Annals of the Historical and Archaeological Society of the District of Saint-Malo]. A. Société d'histoire

et d'archéologie de l'arrondissement de Saint-Malo, c/o Chambre de commerce, rue de Toulouse, Saint-Malo. pni

346. SOCIETE D'HISTOIRE ET D'ARCHEOLOGIE DE LA LORRAINE, ANNUAIRE DE LA... [Yearbook of the Historical and Archaeological Society of Lorraine]. A. Editions Le Lorrain, 14 rue des Clercs, Metz, for Société d'histoire et d'archéologie de la Lorraine, Archives de la Moselle, Metz. pni

347. SOCIETE D'HISTOIRE ET D'ARCHEOLOGIE DE MAURIENNE, TRAVAUX DE LA... [Works of the Historical and Archaeological Society of Maurienne]. A. Société d'histoire et d'archéologie, Saint-Jean-de-Maurienne. pni

348. SOCIETE D'HISTOIRE ET D'ARCHEOLOGIE DE RIBEAUVILLE. BULLETIN [Historical and Archaeological Society of Ribeauville. Bulletin]. A. Société d'histoire et d'archéologie de Ribeauville, Haut-Rhin. In French or German. N.Fr. 5

349. SOCIETE D'HISTOIRE ET D'ARCHEOLOGIE DE SAVERNE ET ENVIRONS. BULLETIN [Historical and Archaeological Society of Saverne and Its Surroundings. Bulletin]. Q. Société d'histoire et d'archéologie de Saverne et environs, Saverne, Bas-Rhin. In French and occasionally in German. N.Fr. 5

350. SOCIETE D'HISTOIRE ET D'ARCHEOLOGIE DE VICHY ET DES ENVIRONS, BULLETIN DE LA... [Bulletin of the Historical and Archaeological Society of Vichy and Its Surroundings]. S-A. Société d'histoire et d'archéologie de Vichy et des environs, 1 av. Thermale, Vichy. (memb.) N.Fr. 4

351. SOCIETE D'HISTOIRE ET D'ARCHEOLOGIE DES VIIe ET XVe ARRONDISSEMENTS DE PARIS. BULLETIN [Historical and Archaeological Society of the VIIe and XVe Districts of Paris. Bulletin]. M. Société d'histoire et d'archéologie des VIIe et XVe arrondissements de Paris, Mairie du 7e, 116 rue de Grenelle, Paris 7e. pni

352. SOCIETE D'HISTOIRE ET D'ART DU DIOCESE DE MEAUX, BULLETIN DE LA... [Bulletin of the Historical and Art Society of the Diocese of Meaux]. A. Société d'histoire et d'art du diocèse de Meaux, 8 rue de Châge, Meaux, Seine-et-Marne. N.Fr. 5

353. SOCIETE D'HISTOIRE ET DU MUSEE D'HUNINGUE ET DU CANTON D'HUNINGUE. BULLETIN [Society of History and of the Huningue Museum and the Canton of Huningue. Bulletin]. A. Ed: L.Kiechel, Musée, Huningue, Haut-Rhin. pni

354. SOCIETE D'HISTOIRE MODERNE, BULLETIN DE LA... [Bulletin of the Society for Modern History]. Q. 1901/02 (1958: 12th series, vol. 57). Société d'histoire moderne, 22 av. de La Bourdonnais, Paris 7e. Ed: Lucien Genet. Reports on the meetings of the soc. and reprints of papers read; rev. of bk. and art.; news of the soc. Supplement to: Revue d'histoire moderne et contemporaine. (memb.) N.Fr. 13 / (memb.) N.Fr. 15

355. SOCIETE DAUPHINOISE D'ETHNOLOGIE ET D'ARCHEOLOGIE PROCES-VERBAUX MENSUELS DE LA... [Monthly minutes of the Society of Dauphiné for Ethnology and Archaeology]. M. Société dauphinoise d'ethnologie et d'archéologie, Ecole de Médecine, Grenoble. pni

356. SOCIETE DE BIOGEOGRAPHIE, COMPTE RENDU SOMMAIRE DES SEANCES DE LA... [Summary report of the meetings of the Society of Biogeography]. Q. Société de biogéographie, 61 rue Buffon, Paris 5e.
N.Fr. 10 / N.Fr. 12

357. SOCIETE DE BORDA, BULLETIN DE LA... [Bulletin of the Society of Borda]. Q. Société de Borda, 17 av. Victor-Hugo, Dax, Landes.
N.Fr. 5.50 / N.Fr.7

358. SOCIETE DE GEOGRAPHIE DE TOULOUSE, BULLETIN DE LA... [Bulletin of the Geographical Society of Toulouse]. M. G.de Montsabert, 34 rue Bayard, Toulouse, for Société de géographie de Toulouse. p(1) N.Fr. 1.50

359. SOCIETE DE L'HISTOIRE DE FRANCE, ANNUAIRE-BULLETIN DE LA... [Yearbook-Bulletin of the Society of the History of France]. A. 1834 (1956/57: no vol. indic.). Librairie C. Klincksieck, 11 rue de Lille, Paris 7e, for Société de l'histoire de France, 60 rue des Francs-Bourgeois, Paris 3e. Art. on the general hist. of France; correspondence of famous hist. personalities; bk. rev. pni

360. SOCIETE DE L'HISTOIRE DE L'ART FRANÇAISE, BULLETIN DE LA... [Bulletin of the Society for the History of French Art]. A. 1875 (1957 [1958]: no vol. indic.). Librairie Armand Colin, 103 bd. Saint-Michel, Paris 5e, for Société de l'histoire de l'art française, Paris. Art. on all periods of the hist. of French art; illus.; index of authors, subjects and illus. pni

361. SOCIETE DE L'HISTOIRE DU PROTESTANTISME FRANÇAIS, BULLETIN DE LA... [Bulletin of the Society of the History of French Protestantism]. Q. 1852 (1959: vol. 105). Société d'histoire du protestantisme français, 54 rue des Saints-Pères, Paris 7e. Art. on the hist. of Protestantism in France and on literature relating to French Protestantism; biographies of Protestant personalities; doc.; bk. rev.; name index. N.Fr. 18

362. SOCIETE DE LINGUISTIQUE DE PARIS, BULLETIN DE LA... [Bulletin of the Society of Linguistics of Paris]. S-A. Librairie C. Klincksieck, 11 rue de Lille, Paris 7e, for Société de linguistique, Ecole des Hautes Etudes, Sorbonne, Paris 5e. Name index. N.Fr. 15

363. SOCIETE DE MYTHOLOGIE FRANÇAISE, BULLETIN DE LA... [Bulletin of the Society for French Mythology]. Q. Société de mythologie française, Lycée Charlemagne, Paris. N.Fr. 5 / N.Fr. 7.50

364. SOCIETE DE SAINT JEAN POUR L'ENCOURAGEMENT DE L'ART CHRETIEN, BULLETIN DE LA... [Bulletin of the Saint Jean Society for the Promotion of Christian Art]. Q. Société de Saint Jean pour l'encouragement de l'art Chrétien, 8 rue de Furstenberg, Paris 6e. p(1) N.Fr. 0.20

365. SOCIETE DE SCIENCES NATURELLES ET D'ARCHEOLOGIE DE LA HAUTE-MARNE, BULLETIN DE LA... [Bulletin of the Society of Natural Sciences and Archaeology of Haute-Marne]. S-A. Société de sciences naturelles et d'archéologie de la Haute-Marne, 26 rue Adonais, Chaumont.
(memb.) N.Fr. 5

366. SOCIETE DES AFRICANISTES, JOURNAL DE LA... [Journal of the Society of Africanists]. A. 1931 (1957: vol. 27). Société des africanistes, Musée de l'homme, place du Trocadéro, Paris 16e. Ed: G. Dieterlen (gen.

secretary). Art. on the ethnography and ethnology of the African aborigines and on African prehist., archaeology, paleontology, linguistics, hist., geography and demography; biblio. of bk. and art. limited to territories under French influence and classified by subject and area; illus. N.Fr. 16 / N.Fr. 19

367. SOCIETE DES AMERICANISTES, JOURNAL DE LA... [Journal of the Society of Americanists]. A. 1896 (1957: new series, vol. 46). Société des americanistes, Musée de l'homme, place du Trocadéro, Paris 16e. Ed: R. d'Harcourt (gen. secretary). Art. on the ethnography of the aborigines of North and South America (including anthropology, archaeology, sociology, folklore, linguistics, hist. and geography); bk. rev.; biblio. classified by subject and area; reports on the meetings of the soc.; illus.; author index for the years 1896-1946. N.Fr. 17 / N.Fr. 22

368. SOCIETE DES AMIS D'ANET, BULLETIN DE LA... [Bulletin of the Society of the Friends of Anet]. Irr. Ed: C. de Yturbe, 14 rue Jean-Goujon, Anet, Eure-et-Loire. p(1) N.Fr. 3

369. SOCIETE DES AMIS DE MEUDON-BELLEVUE, BULLETIN DE LA... [Bulletin of the Society of the Friends of Meudon-Bellevue]. Q. Ed: F. Roux-Devillas, 1 rue des Fougères, Fleury-Meudon, Seine-et-Oise.
p(1) N.Fr. 0.50

370. SOCIETE DES AMIS DE VILLEFRANCHE ET DU BAS-ROUERGUE, MEMOIRES DE LA... [Memoirs of the Society of the Friends of Villefranche and Bas-Rouergue]. A. Imprimerie Salingardes, Villefranche-de-Rouergue, for Société des amis de Villefranche et du Bas-Rouergue.
pv (no. 7: N.Fr. 3; no. 8: N.Fr. 4.50)

371. SOCIETE DES AMIS DES ARTS ET DES SCIENCES DE TOURNUS [Society of the Friends of Arts and Sciences of Tournus]. A. Imprimerie Buguet-Comptour, Mâcon, for Société des amis des arts et des sciences, Tournus.
pni

372. SOCIETE DES AMIS DU MUSEE DE L'ARMEE, BULLETIN DE LA... [Bulletin of the Society of the Friends of the Army Museum]. S-A. 1909 (1958: no vol. indic.). Société des amis du Musée de l'armée, Hôtel des Invalides, Paris 7e. Art. on the hist. of the French army; biographies of military personalities; sum. of the meetings of the soc.; illus. (memb.) N.Fr. 5 / N.Fr. 6

373. SOCIETE DES ANTIQUAIRES DE L'OUEST ET DES MUSEES DE POITIERS, BULLETIN DE LA... [Bulletin of the Society of Antiquarians of the West and of the Museums of Poitiers]. Q. Société des antiquaires de l'Ouest et des Musées de Poitiers, Passage de l'Echevinage, Poitiers.
(memb.) N.Fr. 5, N.Fr. 8

374. SOCIETE DES ANTIQUAIRES DE PICARDIE, BULLETIN TRIMESTRIEL DE LA... [Quarterly bulletin of the Society of Antiquarians of Picardy]. Q. Société des antiquaires de Picardie, Musée de Picardie, Amiens.
(memb.) N.Fr. 5

375. SOCIETE DES ETUDES LITTERAIRES, SCIENTIFIQUES ET ARTISTIQUES DU LOT, BULLETIN DE LA... [Bulletin of the Society for the Study of Literature, Science and Art of Lot]. Q. Société des études littéraires, scientifiques et artistiques du Lot, 54 rue Emile Zola, Cahors, Lot.
(memb.) N.Fr. 5, N.Fr. 7

376. SOCIETE DES LETTRES, SCIENCES ET ARTS DE LA CORREZE, BULLETIN DE LA... [Bulletin of the Society of Letters, Sciences and Arts of Corrèze]. Q. Société des lettres, sciences et arts de la Corrèze, Musée du Cloître, Tulle. N.Fr. 7.50

377. SOCIETE DES LETTRES, SCIENCES ET ARTS DES ALPES-MARITIMES, ANNALES DE LA... [Annals of the Society of Letters, Sciences and Arts of Alpes-Maritimes]. A. Imprimerie Don-Bosco, 40 place du XVe Corps, Nice, for Société des lettres, sciences et arts des Alpes-Maritimes. pni

378. SOCIETE DES LETTRES, SCIENCES ET ARTS DU SAUMUROIS [Society of Letters, Sciences and Arts of Saumurois]. Q. Ed: P.Sénéchal, 1 rue d'Alsace, Saumur. N.Fr. 3

379. SOCIETE DES NATURALISTES ET ARCHEOLOGUES DU NORD DE LA MEUSE, BULLETIN DE LA... [Bulletin of the Society of Naturalists and Archaeologists of the North of the Meuse]. A. Imprimerie Huguet, Verdun, for Société des naturalistes et archéologues du Nord de la Meuse. (memb.) N.Fr. 4

380. SOCIETE DES NATURALISTES ET DES ARCHEOLOGUES DE L'AIN, BULLETIN DE LA... [Bulletin of the Society of Naturalists and Archaeologists of Ain]. A. Société des naturalistes et archéologues de l'Ain, Salle Alphonse Mas, rue Alphonse Mas, Bourg-en-Bresse. N.Fr. 5

381. SOCIETE DES OCEANISTES, JOURNAL DE LA... [Journal of the Society of Students of Oceania]. A. 1945 (1958: vol. 14). Société des Océanistes, Musée de l'homme, Paris 14e. Art. on Oceania, pertaining mainly to hist., geography, anthropology, ethnography, economics and linguistics; bk. rev.; biblio.; news of the soc.; illus. N.Fr. 30

382. SOCIETE DES PROFESSEURS D'HISTOIRE ET DE GEOGRAPHIE DE L'ENSEIGNEMENT PUBLIC, BULLETIN DE LA... [Bulletin of the Society of Teachers of History and Geography in Public Instruction]. 5xy. Société des professeurs d'histoire et de géographie de l'enseignement public, 75 cours de Vincennes, Paris 20e. N.Fr. 10

383. SOCIETE DES SCIENCES, LETTRES ET ARTS DE BAYONNE. BULLETIN TRIMESTRIEL [Society of Sciences, Letters and Arts of Bayonne. Quarterly bulletin]. Q. Société des sciences, lettres et arts, Musée basque, Bayonne. N.Fr. 3.50

384. SOCIETE DES SCIENCES, LETTRES ET ARTS DE PAU, BULLETIN DE LA... [Bulletin of the Society of Sciences, Letters and Arts of Pau]. A. Imprimerie commerciale des Pyrénées, 11 rue du Maréchal Joffre, Pau, for Société des sciences, lettres et arts de Pau. pni

385. SOCIETE DES SCIENCES, LETTRES ET BEAUX-ARTS DE CHOLET ET DE SA REGION, BULLETIN DE LA... [Bulletin of the Society of Sciences, Letters and Arts of Cholet and Its Surroundings]. A. Société des sciences, lettres et beaux-arts, Musée, bd. Gustave-Richard, Cholet. pni

386. SOCIETE FRANÇAISE D'ARCHEOLOGIE. BULLETIN MONUMENTAL [French Society of Archaeology. Bulletin concerning monuments]. Q. 1834 (1958: vol. 116). M. Pillault, 37 rue du Pot-de-Fer, Orléans, for Société française d'archéologie. Ed: M. Aubert, F. Salet. Art. on local hist. monuments; bk. rev.; biblio.; graph, illus. pni

387. SOCIETE FRANÇAISE DE NUMISMATIQUE, BULLETIN DE LA... [Bulletin of the French Numismatic Society]. 10 xy. 1945 (1958: vol. 13). Société française de numismatique, Bibliothèque nationale, Cabinet des medailles, 58 rue de Richelieu, Paris 2e. Reports on the meetings of the soc. and short sum. of lectures given; includes also reports on the meetings of the Cercle lyonnais de numismatique and Société d'étude et documentation pour l'histoire du papier-monnaie; news and notes of interest to scholars; subject index every 5 years; list of memb. of the soc. pub. every 3 years. (memb.) N.Fr. 27

388. SOCIETE FRANÇAISE DE PHILOSOPHIE, BULLETIN DE LA... [Bulletin of the French Philosophical Society]. Q. Armand Colin, 103 bd. Saint-Michel, Paris 5e, for Société française de philosophie. N.Fr. 8.50 / N.Fr. 10

389. SOCIETE HISTORIQUE DE SURESNES, BULLETIN DE LA... [Bulletin of the Historical Society of Suresnes]. Q. Société historique de Suresnes, 34 av. Franklin Roosevelt, Suresnes, Seine. memb. free

390. SOCIETE HISTORIQUE DE VILLIERS-SUR-MARNE. BULLETIN [Historical Society of Villiers-sur-Marne. Bulletin]. Irr. Société historique de Villiers-sur-Marne, Hôtel de Ville, Villiers-sur-Marne, Seine-et-Oise. Illus. pni

391. SOCIETE HISTORIQUE DU RAINCY ET DU PAYS D'AULNOYE. BULLETIN [Historical Society of Raincy and the District of Aulnoye. Bulletin]. A. Société historique du Raincy et du pays d'Aulnoye, Hôtel de Ville, Raincy, Seine-et-Oise. N.Fr. 5

392. SOCIETE HISTORIQUE ET ARCHEOLOGIQUE D'ARGENTEUIL ET DU PARISIS "LE VIEIL ARGENTEUIL," MEMOIRES DE LA... [Memoirs of the Historical and Archaeological Society of Argenteuil and Parisis "The Old Argenteuil"]. B. Société "Le Vieil Argenteuil," Musée communal, rue Pierre-Guienne, Argenteuil. pni

393. SOCIETE HISTORIQUE ET ARCHEOLOGIQUE DE CORBEIL, D'ETAMPES ET DU HUREPOIX, BULLETIN DE LA... [Bulletin of the Historical and Archaeological Society of Corbeil, Etampes and Hurepoix]. A. Société historique et archéologique de Corbeil, d'Etampes et du Hurepoix, Hôtel de Ville, Corbeil-Essonnes. N.Fr. 5

394. SOCIETE HISTORIQUE ET ARCHEOLOGIQUE DE L'ORNE [Historical and Archaeological Society of Orne]. Q. Société historique et archéologique, Hôtel Libert, 18 rue de Cygne, Alençon. N.Fr. 6

395. SOCIETE HISTORIQUE ET ARCHEOLOGIQUE DE LANGRES, BULLETIN DE LA... [Bulletin of the Historical and Archaeological Society of Langres]. Q. Société historique et archéologique de Langres, Musée, place Saint Didier, Langres. pni

396. SOCIETE HISTORIQUE ET ARCHEOLOGIQUE DE NOGENT-SUR-MARNE ET DU CANTON DE NOGENT, BULLETIN DE LA... [Bulletin of the Historical and Archaeological Society of Nogent-sur-Marne and the Canton of Nogent]. S-A. Société historique et archéologique de Nogent-sur-Marne et de canton de Nogent, 30 bd. Gallieni, Nogent-sur-Marne, Seine. (memb.) N.Fr. 2

397. SOCIETE HISTORIQUE ET ARCHEOLOGIQUE DU PERIGORD, BULLETIN DE LA... [Bulletin of the Historical and Archaeological Society of

Périgord]. Q. Société historique et archéologique du Périgord, 18 rue du Plautier, Périgueux. (memb.) N.Fr. 5 / N.Fr. 7

398. SOCIETE HISTORIQUE ET ARCHEOLOGIQUE "LES AMIS DES ANTIQUITES DE PARTHENAY," BULLETIN DE LA... [Bulletin of the Historical and Archaeological Society "The Friends of Antiquities of Parthenay"]. A. Amis des antiquites de Parthenay, 37 rue Alsace-Lorraine, Parthenay. (memb.) N.Fr. 2.50

399. SOCIETE HISTORIQUE ET LITTERAIRE DE COLMAR, ANNUAIRE DE LA... [Yearbook of the Historical and Literary Society of Colmar]. A. Imprimerie Alsatia, 10 rue Bartholdi, Colmar, for Société historique et littéraire de Colmar. pni

400. SOCIETE HISTORIQUE ET SCIENTIFIQUE DES DEUX-SEVRES, BULLETIN DE LA... [Bulletin of the Historical and Scientific Society of Deux-Sèvres]. Q. Société historique et scientifique des Deux-Sèvres, Bibliothèque municipale, Niort. N.Fr. 5 (memb. N.Fr. 3)

401. SOCIETE HISTORIQUE, LITTERAIRE ET SCIENTIFIQUE DU CHER. BULLETIN MENSUEL [Historical, Literary and Scientific Society of Cher. Monthly bulletin]. M. Société historique, littéraire et scientifique du Cher, 9 rue Joyeuse, Bourges. pni

402. SOCIETE INTERNATIONALE ARTHURIENNE, BULLETIN BIBLIOGRAPHIQUE DE LA... [Bibliographical bulletin of the International Arthurian Society]. A. 1949 (1958: no. 10). Société internationale arthurienne. Ed: Ch. Foulon, 165 rue des Fougères, Rennes. Art. and biblio. on all fields of Arthurian studies; in English and French; author, title and subject index for the biblio. section. $3.75

403. SOCIETE LANGUEDOCIENNE DE GEOGRAPHIE. BULLETIN TRIMESTRIEL [Languedoc Society of Geography. Quarterly bulletin]. Q. Institut de géographie de la Faculté des Lettres, 14 rue du Cardinal de Cabrières, Montpellier, for Société Languedoc de géographie. N.Fr. 15

404. SOCIETE NIEDERBRONNOISE D'HISTOIRE ET D'ARCHEOLOGIE, BULLETIN DE LA... [Bulletin of the Niederbronn Society for History and Archaeology]. Irr. Société Niederbronnoise d'histoire et d'archéologie, Groupe Scolaire, Niederbronn-les-Bains, Bas-Rhin. pv (N.Fr. 1 - N.Fr. 5

405. SOCIETE NORMANDE D'ETUDES PREHISTORIQUES, BULLETIN DE LA... [Bulletin of the Norman Society of Prehistoric Studies]. A. Société normande d'études préhistoriques, Musée d'histoire naturelle et de préhistoire, rue Beauvoisine, Rouen. Papers and extracts of papers on the prehist. and hist. of Normandy read at the meetings of the soc.; bk. rev.; subject index for vol. 1-36. (memb.) N.Fr. 2

406. SOCIETE PHILOMATIQUE VOSGIENNE, BULLETIN DE LA... [Bulletin of the Vosges Philomathical Society]. A. Société philomatique Vosgienne, Bibliothèque municipale, Saint-Dié. N.Fr. 5

407. SOCIETE POUR L'HISTOIRE DU DROIT ET DES INSTITUTIONS DES ANCIENS PAYS BOURGUIGNONS, COMTOIS ET ROMANDS, BULLETIN DE LIAISON DE LA... [Bulletin of communication of the Society for the History

of Law and Institutions of the Old Regions of Bourgogne, Franche-Comté and French Switzerland]. Irr. Faculté de Droit, 5 rue de l'Ecole de Droit, Dijon, for Société pour l'histoire du droit et des institutions des anciens pays Bourguignons, Comtois et Romands. pin

408. SOCIETE POUR L'HISTOIRE DU DROIT ET DES INSTITUTIONS DES ANCIENS PAYS BOURGUIGNONS, COMTOIS ET ROMANDS, MEMOIRES DE LA... [Memoirs of the Society for the History of Law and Institutions of the Old Regions of Bourgogne, Franche-Comté and French Switzerland]. A. Faculté de Droit, 5 rue de l'Ecole de Droit, Dijon, for Société pour l'histoire du droit et des institutions des anciens pays Bourguignons, Comtois et Romands.
N.Fr. 8 / N.Fr. 10

409. SOCIETE POUR LA CONSERVATION DES MONUMENTS HISTORIQUES D'ALSACE, BULLETIN DE LA... [Bulletin of the Society for the Preservation of the Historical Monuments of Alsace]. Irr. Imprimerie des Dernières nouvelles de Strasbourg, 17-19 rue de la Nuée bleue, Strasbourg, for Société pour la conservation des monuments historiques d'Alsace. pni

410. SOCIETE PREHISTORIQUE FRANÇAISE, BULLETIN DE LA... [Bulletin of the French Prehistoric Society]. 7xy. 1904 (1958: vol. 55). Société prehistorique française, 250 rue Saint Jacques, Paris 5e. Ed: G. Gaudron (gen. secretary), 2 rue du Pas-de-la-Mule, Paris 3e. Art. on prehist., mostly of France and French territories in Africa, confined to the period immediately preceding the beginning of the Christian era; reports on excavations; list of bk. and periodicals received; illus.; A. index of authors and place-names.
(memb.) N.Fr. 12 / N.Fr. 20

411. SOCIETE SCIENTIFIQUE ET ARTISTIQUE DE CLAMECY, BULLETIN DE LA... [Bulletin of the Scientific and Artistic Society of Clamecy]. A. Société scientifique et artistique, Musée, Clamecy. (memb.) N.Fr. 3

412. SOCIETE SCIENTIFIQUE, HISTORIQUE ET ARCHEOLOGIQUE DE LA CORREZE, BULLETIN DE LA... [Bulletin of the Scientific, Historical and Archaeological Society of Corrèze]. A. Société scientifique, historique et archéologique de la Corrèze, Hôtel de La Banche, Brive, Corrèze. N.Fr. 6

413. SOCIETE TOULOUSAINE D'ETUDES CLASSIQUES, BULLETIN DE LA... [Bulletin of the Toulouse Society of Classical Studies]. M. Société d'études classiques, Faculté des Lettres, Toulouse. pni

414. SOCIETES SAVANTES DE HAUTE-NORMANDIE, REVUE DES... [Review of the scientific societies of Upper Normandy]. Q. Consortium des sociétés savantes de Haute-Normandie, 16 rue Dufay, Rouen. N.Fr. 15

415. AR SONER [The bagpipe player]. La revue du folklore vivant de Bretagne [The review of living folklore in Britanny]. B-M. "Bodadeg ar sonerion" (Assemblée des Sonneurs de Biniou de Bretagne), c/o Polig Montjarret, 18 bd. Joffre, Lorient. N.Fr. 10

416. SOUVENIR NAPOLEONIEN [Memory of Napoleon]. M. Société d'histoire Napoléonienne, 3 av. Georges-Clémenceau, Nice, Alpes-Maritimes.
N.Fr. 8 / N.Fr. 10

417. STUDIA ISLAMICA. Irr. 1953 (1959: no. 10). Edition Larose, 11 rue Victor-Cousin, Paris 5e. Ed: R. Brunschwig, 10 av. de Clamart, Vanves,

Seine, J. Schacht, Cronesteinkade 8 A, Leiden, Netherlands. Art. on all fields of the study of Islam, chiefly hist., literature, law and religion; in English and French. pni

418. LE SUBIET. Journal littéraire et folklorique du Pays d'Ouest [Journal of literature and folklore of the Western country]. B-M. 168 rue du Tondu, Bordeaux. Ceased pub. in December 1959. N.Fr. 6.50

419. SYRIA. Revue d'art oriental et d'archéologie... [Review of Eastern art and archaeology...]. Q. 1920 (1958: vol. 35). Librairie orientaliste Paul Geuthner, 12 rue Vavin, Paris 6e, for Institut français d'archéologie de Beyrouth. Ed. board: R.Dussaud, H.Seyrig, A.Parrot. Art. on archaeology, art, hist., literature and religion of the Near and Middle East in antiquity; bk. rev.; illus. pni

420. LES TEMPS MODERNES [Modern times]. M. Editions Julliard, 30 rue de l'Université, Paris 7e. N.Fr. 38 / $8.40

421. THALES. Recueil des travaux de l'Institut d'histoire des sciences et des techniques de l'Université de Paris [Collection of the works of the Institute for the History of Sciences and Technology of the University of Paris]. Irr. 1934 (1952-58: vol. 9). Presses universitaires de France, 108 bd. Saint-Germain, Paris 6e, for Institut d'histoire des sciences et des techniques, 13 rue du Four, Paris 6e. Art. on the hist. of ideas and civilizations, with emphasis on the hist. of sciences and technology. p(1) N.Fr. 6

422. LA TOUR D'ARGENT [The silver tower]. Cahiers d'art et de littérature héraldiques, de généalogie et d'anthroponymie [Journal of heraldic art and literature, genealogy and the study of persons' names]. Q. 1957. Librairie de Massol, 1 rue de Cerisoles, Paris 8e. Art. on subjects named in the subtitle. N.Fr. 4

423. LA TRAMONTANE [The north wind]. Revue mensuelle du Roussillon [Monthly review of Roussillon]. M. Ed: Ch. Bauby, 2 rue Font-Na-Pincarda, Perpignan. In Catalan and French. N.Fr. 14 / N.Fr. 15

424. TRANSMONDIA. Economie et transport [Economy and transport]. M. Editions Chaix, 126 rue des Rosiers, Saint Ouen, Seine. N.Fr. 19.50 / Sfr 20 or Bfr 230

TRAVAUX. For titles beginning with "Travaux," followed by the name of the publishing or sponsoring institution or society, see the respective institution or society.

425. AN TRIBANN [The three rays]. Q. Collège des Druides, Bardes et Ovates de Bretagne, "Gorsedd," 70 av. du Plessis-Tison, Nantes. In French and Breton. N.Fr. 7.50

426. LE TRITON [The Triton]. Supplément trimestriel de documentation maritime au Neptunia [Quarterly supplement of maritime documentation of Neptunia]. Q. 1948 (1959: no. 48-51). Association des Amis des musées de la marine, Palais de Chaillot, Paris 16e. Art. on the hist. of navigation and related subjects; doc.; illus. (memb.) N.Fr. 8 / N.Fr. 10

427. TROPIQUES [Tropics]. Revue des Troupes d'Outre-Mer [Review of oversea forces]. M. Presses modernes, 10 rue Saint-Roch, Paris 1er. N.Fr. 25 / N.Fr. 28.50

UNESCO CHRONICLE see section on International Periodicals

UNESCO, CHRONIQUE DE L'... see section on International Periodicals

UNESCO, CRONICA DE LA... see section on International Periodicals

UNESCO, LE COURRIER DE L'... see section on International Periodicals

428. UNIVERSITE DE BESANÇON, ANNALES LITTERAIRES DE L'... [Literary annals of the University of Besançon]. Irr. "Les Belles-Lettres," 95 bd. Raspail, Paris 6e, for Université de Besançon. pni

429. UNIVERSITE DE PARIS, ANNALES DE L'... [Annals of the University of Paris]. Q. Sorbonne, 47 rue des Ecoles, Paris 5e. N.Fr. 14

430. UNIVERSITES DE CLERMONT-LYON-GRENOBLE, CAHIERS D'HISTOIRE PUBLIES PAR LES... [Historical journal published by the Universities of Clermont-Lyons-Grenoble]. Q. Faculté des lettres, 71 rue Pasteur, Lyon. Local hist.; biographical art.; bk. rev.; illus. N.Fr. 10 / N.Fr. 12

431. LE VIEIL ARGENTEUIL [The old Argenteuil]. Q. Société historique et archéologique d'Argenteuil et du Parisis, 5 rue Pierre Guienne, Argenteuil, Seine-et-Oise. pni

432. LE VIEUX MONTFERMEIL [The old Montfermeil]. Q. Syndicat d'initiative and société historique de Montfermeil et de la région, 71 rue Général de Gaulle, Montfermeil, Seine-et-Oise. N.Fr. 3

433. LE VIEUX MONTMARTRE [The old Montmartre]. A. Société d'histoire et d'archéologie des IXe et XVIIIe arrondissements, 22 rue Tourlaque, Paris 18e. (memb.) N.Fr. 2

434. LE VIEUX SAINT-MAUR [The old Saint-Maur]. Irr. Société historique et archéologique de Saint-Maur-des-Fossés et des localités avoisinantes, Bibliothèque, Musée local, 23 av. Henri-Martin, Saint-Maur-des-Fossés, Seine. (memb.) N.Fr. 2

435. VISAGES DE L'HOMME [Visages of man]. Revue de culture et d'étude [Review of culture and study]. Q (Irr.). 1955 (1959: new series, no. 3). Association François Duine, 13 Grande Rue, Dol en Bretagne, Ille-et-Vilaine. Ed: Claude Henry Galocher. Art. on the hist. of Celtic art; bk. rev.; illus. Formerly pub. under the title: Les cahiers d'histoire et de folklore. N.Fr. 12

436. LA VOIX DE LA RESISTANCE [The voice of the Resistance]. M. Comité d'action de la Résistance, 5 rue Lamartine, Paris 9e. Illus. N.Fr. 5

437. YAOUANKIZ [Youth]. S-A. Ed: P. Le Bihan, 6 domaine des Hocquettes, Suresnes, Seine. In Breton and French. p(1) N.Fr. 0.90

Germany

Prepared with the assistance of
Paul Podjed, Munich

THE DEMOCRATIC REPUBLIC OF GERMANY (EAST GERMANY)

1. DAS ALTERTUM [Antiquity]. Q. 1955 (1960: vol. 6). Akademie-Verlag, Leipziger Str. 3-4, Berlin W 1. Ed: J.Irmscher, Otto-Nuschke-Str. 22-23, Berlin W 8. Art. on Greek and Roman antiquity and the ancient Orient as well as on their influence on the culture of the modern world; reports on the remains of ancient civilizations; illus. DM 12

2. ARCHIVMITTEILUNGEN [Archival communications]. Zeitschrift für Theorie und Praxis des Archivwesens [Journal for the theory and practice of archival systems]. B-M. 1951 (1960: vol. 10). Staatliche Archivverwaltung der Deutschen Demokratischen Republik, Stalinallee 98-101, Potsdam. Ed: Eberhard Schetelich. Art. on the theory, practice and technique of maintaining archives, on the hist. of archives, particularly East German, and on archival holdings; rev. of bk. and periodicals; professional news and notes. DM 6

3. AUSGRABUNGEN UND FUNDE [Excavations and finds]. Nachrichtenblatt für Vor- und Frühgeschichte [News bulletin for prehistory and early history]. B-M. 1956 (1960: vol. 5). Akademie-Verlag, Leipziger Str. 3-4, Berlin W 1, for Sektion für Vor- und Frühgeschichte bei der Deutschen Akademie der Wissenschaften zu Berlin. Ed: P.Grimm. Art. on methodology; reports on excavations in East Germany; biblio. of art. pub. in East Germany (each no. devoted to one particular area); professional news and notes; illus. p (1) DM 2

4. BEITRÄGE ZUR GESCHICHTE DER DEUTSCHEN ARBEITERBEWEGUNG [Contributions to the history of the German labor movement]. M. 1959 (1960: vol. 2). Dietz-Verlag, Wallstr. 76-79, Berlin C 2, for Institut für Marxismus-Leninismus beim Zentralkomittee der Sozialistischen Einheitspartei Deutschlands, Wilhelm-Pieck-Str. 1, Berlin N 54. p (1) DM 2

BEITRÄGE ZUR ZEITGESCHICHTE see DOKUMENTATION DER ZEIT

5. BERLINER HEIMAT [Berlin homeland]. Zeitschrift für die Geschichte Berlins [Journal for the history of Berlin]. Q. Berliner Verlag, Otto-Nuschke-Str. 10-11, Berlin W 8. Reproductions of hist. interest included as supplements. p (1) DM 1

6. BIBLIOTHECA CLASSICA ORIENTALIS. Dokumentation der altertumswissenschaftlichen Literatur der Sowjetunion und der Länder der Volksdemokratie [Documentation of the literature on studies of antiquity in the Soviet Union and the people's democracies]. B-M. Akademie-Verlag, Leipziger-Str. 3-4, Berlin W 1, for Institut für griechisch-römische Altertumskunde bei der Deutschen Akademie der Wissenschaften zu Berlin, Otto-Nuschke-Str. 22-23, Berlin W 8. Rev. of East European pub. (bk. and art.) on classical antiquity, classified by subject. p (1) DM 4

7. DEUTSCHE AUSSENPOLITIK [German foreign policy]. M. Rütten und Loening, Taubenstr. 1-2, Berlin W 8, for Gesellschaft zur Verbreitung wissenschaftlicher Kenntnisse. DM 30

8. DEUTSCHE LITERATURZEITUNG FÜR KRITIK DER INTERNATIONALEN WISSENSCHAFT [German literary gazette for the critical review of international scholarship]. M. Akademie-Verlag, Leipziger Str. 3-4, Berlin W 1, for Deutsche Akademie der Wissenschaften zu Berlin, Otto-Nuschke-Str. 22-23, Berlin W 8. Bk. rev., arranged by subject, including the following sections on hist.: general hist., prehist., hist. of culture, art, law, religion and economy; reports of the sessions of the various German acad. (in East and West Germany) and personal news; list of new bk. DM 12

9. DEUTSCHES INSTITUT FÜR LÄNDERKUNDE, WISSENSCHAFTLICHE VERÖFFENTLICHUNGEN DES... (Wissenschaftliche Veröffentlichungen des Deutschen Instituts für Länderkunde) [Academic publications of the German Institute of Geography]. A. 1896 (1958: new series, no. 15/16). Deutsches Institut für Länderkunde, Georgi-Dimitroff-Platz 1, Leipzig C. 1. Ed: E. Lehmann. Art. on geography (including agricultural geography), and demography, past and present; illus.

10. DEUTSCHES JAHRBUCH FÜR VOLKSKUNDE [German yearbook for folklore]. A. 1955 (1959: vol. 5). Akademie-Verlag, Leipziger Str. 3-4, Berlin W 1, for Institut für deutsche Volkskunde an der Deutschen Akademie der Wissenschaften zu Berlin, Unter den Linden 8, Berlin W 8. Ed: W. Fraenger. Art. on German folklore and ethnography as well as on museum holdings, with emphasis on East Germany; reports on conferences and congresses; bk. rev.; biblio. of pub. on specific subjects and of particular countries; illus. DM 14

11. DOKUMENTATION DER ZEIT [Contemporary documentation]. Informations-Archiv [Archives of information]. S-M. Deutsches Institut für Zeitgeschichte, Hessische Str. 12, Berlin N 4. Current affairs; chronicle of events; Q. subject index; Q. supplement: Beiträge zur Zeitgeschichte. p (1) DM 1.75

12. EINHEIT [Unity]. Zeitschrift für Theorie und Praxis des wissenschaftlichen Sozialismus [Journal for the theory and practice of scientific socialism]. M. (1960: vol. 15). Dietz-Verlag, Wallstr. 76-79, Berlin C 2, for Zentralkomittee der Sozialistischen Einheitspartei Deutschlands, Werderscher Markt, Berlin C 2. Art. on the theory and practice of socialism and Communism and on the hist. of the labor movement in Germany and other countries. p (1) DM 0.50

13. ERNST MORITZ ARNDT UNIVERSITÄT GREIFSWALD, WISSENSCHAFTLICHE ZEITSCHRIFT DER... [Academic journal of the Ernst Moritz Arndt University of Greifswald]. Gesellschafts- und sprachwissenschaftliche Reihe [Social and linguistic series]. Irr. 1951 (1958/59: vol. 8). Ernst Moritz Arndt Universität, Greifswald. Art. on prehist., hist., archaeology, art, literature, philology, the social sciences, pedagogy and theology; A. author index. nfs

14. ETHNOGRAPHISCH-ARCHÄOLOGISCHE FORSCHUNGEN [Ethnographical-archaeological researches]. A. 1953 (1959: vol. 6). VEB Deutscher Verlag der Wissenschaften, Berlin. Ed: K.-H. Otto. Art. on ethnography and archaeology; bk. rev.; illus. p (1) DM 13.60

15. FORSCHUNGEN UND FORTSCHRITTE [Researches and advances]. Nachrichtenblatt der deutschen Wissenschaft und Technik [News bulletin of German

scholarship and technology]. M. Deutsche Akademie der Wissenschaften zu Berlin, Otto Nuschke Str. 22-23, Berlin W 8. DM 12

16. FRIEDRICH SCHILLER UNIVERSITÄT JENA, WISSENSCHAFTLICHE ZEITSCHRIFT DER... [Academic journal of the Friedrich Schiller University of Jena]. Gesellschafts- und sprachwissenschaftliche Reihe [Social and linguistic series]. Irr. 1951 (1958/59: vol. 8). Friedrich Schiller Universität, Jena. Art. on the social sciences, philosophy, law, culture, hist. (mainly local and German), education, philology, voice and speech training, library science, and theology; A. subject indices. nfs

17. HUMBOLDT UNIVERSITÄT BERLIN, WISSENSCHAFTLICHE ZEITSCHRIFT DER... [Academic journal of the Humboldt University of Berlin]. Gesellschafts- und sprachwissenschaftliche Reihe [Social and linguistic series]. Irr. 1951 (1958/59: vol. 8). Humboldt Universität, Berlin. Art. on various aspects of the social sciences. nfs

18. INSTITUT FÜR ORIENTFORSCHUNG, MITTEILUNGEN DES...(Mitteilungen des Instituts für Orientforschung) [Communications of the Institute for Oriental Research]. 3 x y. 1953 (1959: vol. 7). Akademie-Verlag, Leipziger Str. 3-4, Berlin W 1. Ed: F. Hintze, Unter den Linden 8, Berlin W 8. Art. on Oriental studies; illus. p (1) DM 18

19. INSTITUT SERBSKI LUDOSPYT, LETOPIS... (Letopis instituta serbski ludospyt) [Annals of the Institute for the Study of the Sorb People]. Rjad B [Series B]. A. (1960: vol. 7). Domowina-Verlag, Bautzen, for Institut für sorbische Volksforschung, Ernst-Thälmann-Str. 6, Bautzen. Art. on the hist. of the Sorbs and Slavs. pv

JAHRBUCH. For titles beginning with "Jahrbuch," followed by the name of the publishing or sponsoring institution or society, see the respective institution or society.

JAHRBUCH FÜR GESCHICHTE DER DEUTSCH-SLAWISCHEN BEZIEHUNGEN UND GESCHICHTE OST- UND MITTELEUROPAS see JAHRBUCH FÜR GESCHICHTE DER UDSSR UND DER VOLKSDEMOKRATISCHEN LÄNDER EUROPAS

20. JAHRBUCH FÜR GESCHICHTE DER UDSSR UND DER VOLKSDEMOKRATISCHEN LÄNDER EUROPAS [Yearbook for the history of the U.S.S.R. and the people's democracies of Europe]. A. 1956 (1959: vol. 3). Rütten und Loening, Taubenstr. 1-2, Berlin W 8. Ed: E. Donnert, Historisches Institut der Friedrich Schiller Universität, Goetheallee 1, Jena. Art. on the hist. of German relations with East European countries, particularly in the modern period, with emphasis on Russia and Poland; rev. art. on Russian hist. periodicals; bk. rev.; biblio. of miscellaneous pub. Vol. 1 and 2 pub. under the title: Jahrbuch für Geschichte der deutsch-slawischen Beziehungen und Geschichte Ost- und Mitteleuropas. pv

21. JAHRBUCH FÜR WIRTSCHAFTSGESCHICHTE [Yearbook for economic history]. A. Akademie-Verlag, Leipziger Str. 3-5, Berlin W 1, for Institut für Geschichte an der Deutschen Akademie der Wissenschaften zu Berlin, Clara-Zetkin-Str. 26, Berlin W 8. part one: DM 18; part two: DM 18.50

22. JAHRESSCHRIFT FÜR MITTELDEUTSCHE VORGESCHICHTE [Yearbook for Central German prehistory]. A. VEB Max Niemeyer, Halle/Saale, for Institut für Vor- und Frühgeschichte, Richard-Wagner-Str. 9-10, Halle/Saale. pv (c. DM 30)

23. KARL MARX UNIVERSITÄT LEIPZIG, WISSENSCHAFTLICHE ZEITSCHRIFT DER... [Academic journal of the Karl Marx University of Leipzig]. Gesellschafts- und sprachwissenschaftliche Reihe [Social and linguistic series]. 5 x y. 1951 (1959/60: vol. 9). Karl Marx Universität, Leipzig. Art. on various aspects of the social sciences. nfs

LETOPIS INSTITUTA SERBSKI LUDOSPYT see INSTITUT SERBSKI LUDOSPYT, LETOPIS...

24. MARTIN LUTHER UNIVERSITÄT HALLE-WITTENBERG, WISSENSCHAFTLICHE ZEITSCHRIFT DER... [Academic journal of the Martin Luther University of Halle-Wittenberg]. Gesellschafts- und sprachwissenschaftliche Reihe [Social and linguistic series]. B-M. 1952 (1958/59: vol. 8). Martin Luther Universität, Halle-Wittenberg. Art. on economics, hist. (including prehist. and archaeology), law, politics, literature, linguistics, art and theology; list of dissertations submitted to the univ.; illus.; A. author index. DM 25

MITTEILUNGEN DES INSTITUTS FÜR ORIENTFORSCHUNG see INSTITUT FÜR ORIENTFORSCHUNG, MITTEILUNGEN DES...

25. MUSEUM FÜR VÖLKERKUNDE ZU LEIPZIG, JAHRBUCH DES... (Jahrbuch des Museums für Völkerkunde zu Leipzig) [Yearbook of the Museum of Ethnology at Leipzig]. A. Akademie-Verlag, Leipziger Str. 3-4, Berlin W 1, for Museum für Völkerkunde, Leipzig.

26. ORIENTALISTISCHE LITERATURZEITUNG [Literary gazette for Oriental studies]. Monatsschrift für die Wissenschaft vom ganzen Orient und seinen Beziehungen zu den angrenzenden Kulturkreisen [Monthly for studies of the entire Orient and its relations with the adjoining cultural areas]. B-M (3 double no. p.a.). 1898 (1960: vol. 55). Akademie-Verlag, Leipziger Str. 3-4, Berlin W 1, in collaboration with J.C. Hinrichs Verlag, Scherlstr. 2, Leipzig C. 1. Ed: R. Hartmann, Unter den Linden 8, Berlin W 8. Every no. contains one art. on Oriental studies; rev. of bk. and art., classified by subject; illus. DM 72

27. PÄDAGOGISCHE HOCHSCHULE POTSDAM, WISSENSCHAFTLICHE ZEITSCHRIFT DER... (Wissenschaftliche Zeitschrift der Pädagogischen Hochschule Potsdam) [Academic journal of the Pedagogical College of Potsdam]. Gesellschafts- und sprachwissenschaftliche Reihe [Social and linguistic series]. Irr. 1954/55 (1959-60: vol. 5). Pädagogische Hochschule, Potsdam. Art. on pedagogy, linguistics and the social sciences, including Marxist theory and its applications, and also on hist., predominantly of modern Germany; A. subject index. nfs

SAVIGNY-STIFTUNG FÜR RECHTSGESCHICHTE, ZEITSCHRIFT DER... see section on the Federal Republic of Germany

28. SOWJETWISSENSCHAFT [Soviet scholarship]. Gesellschaftswissenschaftliche Beiträge [Social science contributions]. M. Gesellschaft für deutsch-sowjetische Freundschaft, c/o Verlag Kultur und Fortschritt, Taubenstr. 10, Berlin W 8. DM 21.60

29. THÜRINGER HEIMAT [Thüringen homeland]. Q. Volksverlag, Weimar. Illus. p (1) DM 1.50

30. UNIVERSITÄT ROSTOCK, WISSENSCHAFTLICHE ZEITSCHRIFT DER ... [Academic journal of Rostock University]. Gesellschafts- und sprachwissenschaftliche Reihe [Social and linguistic series]. Irr. 1951 (1959: vol. 8). Universität Rostock, Rostock. Art. on the social sciences, philosophy, education, law, art, linguistics, hist., and theology; A. author index. nfs

31. VORGESCHICHTLICHE MUSEUMSARBEIT UND BODENDENKMALPFLEGE [Museum work in the field of prehistory and the preservation of prehistoric monuments]. A. (Irr.). Landesmuseum für Vorgeschichte, Halle/Saale.

WISSENSCHAFTLICHE VERÖFFENTLICHUNGEN DES DEUTSCHEN INSTITUTS FÜR LÄNDERKUNDE see DEUTSCHES INSTITUT FÜR LÄNDERKUNDE, WISSENSCHAFTLICHE VERÖFFENTLICHUNGEN DES...

WISSENSCHAFTLICHE ZEITSCHRIFT. For titles beginning with "Wissenschaftliche Zeitschrift," followed by the name of the publishing or sponsoring institution or society, see the respective institution or society.

ZEITSCHRIFT DER SAVIGNY-STIFTUNG FÜR RECHTSGESCHICHTE see section on the Federal Republic of Germany

32. ZEITSCHRIFT FÜR ÄGYPTISCHE SPRACHE UND ALTERTUMSKUNDE [Journal for Egyptian language and antiquity]. S-A. 1863 (1959: vol. 84). Akademie-Verlag, Leipziger Str. 3-4, Berlin W 1, in collaboration with J. C. Hinrichs Verlag, Leipzig. Ed: F. Hintze, Institut für Orientforschung, Unter den Linden 8, Berlin W 8, and S. Morenz, Ägyptologisches Institut der Karl Marx Universität, Schillerstr. 6, Leipzig C 1. Art. on Egyptian linguistics, hist., religion, art and general culture; illus. DM 64

33. ZEITSCHRIFT FÜR GESCHICHTSWISSENSCHAFT [Journal for historical sciences]. 8 x y. 1953 (1960: vol. 8). Rütten und Loening, Taubenstr. 1-2, Berlin W 8. Ed: Rolf Rudolph. Art. predominantly on modern German hist.; rev. of bk. and art.; discussions; professional news and notes; A. biblio. of art. on German and general hist., classified by period; A. special no.; table of contents also in English, French and Russian. DM 28

THE FEDERAL REPUBLIC OF GERMANY
(WEST GERMANY)
and
WEST BERLIN

1. AACHENER GESCHICHTSVEREIN, ZEITSCHRIFT DES... (Zeitschrift des Aachener Geschichtsvereins) [Journal of the Aachen Historical Society]. A. Aachener Geschichtsverein, Fischmarkt 3, Stadtarchiv, Aachen.
DM 6 (memb. free)

2. AFRIKA UND ÜBERSEE [Africa and overseas]. Sprachen - Kulturen [Languages - cultures]. Q. Seminar für Sprachen und Kulturen der Universität Hamburg, Hamburg. DM 32

3. ALBERTUS-UNIVERSITÄT ZU KÖNIGSBERG/PR., JAHRBUCH DER... [Yearbook of the Albertus University at Königsberg/Pr.]. A. Holzner Verlag, Neubaustr. 22, Würzburg, for Göttinger Arbeitskreis, Sternstr. 2, Göttingen. pv

4. ALEMANNISCHES JAHRBUCH [Alemannic yearbook]. A. Moritz Schauenburg KG, Schillerstr. 13, Lahr (Schwarzwald), for Alemannisches Institut, Lahr (Schwarzwald). DM 30

5. ALLGÄUER GESCHICHTSFREUND [Allgäu friend of history]. Blätter für Heimatforschung und Heimatpflege [Bulletin for local research and conservation]. A. Heimatverein Kempten e.V. im Heimatbund Allgäu e.V., Königstr. 25/II, Kempten. memb. free

6. ALT-HILDESHEIM [Old Hildesheim]. Eine Zeitschrift für Stadt und Stift Hildesheim [A periodical for the city and the bishopric of Hildesheim]. A. A. Lax Verlagsbuchhandlung, Weinberg 56, Hildesheim. DM 2.40

7. ALTNÜRNBERGER LANDSCHAFT [The country of old Nuremberg]. Irr. Arbeitsgemeinschaft für Heimatpflege und Heimatforschung in den Landkreisen Erlangen, Hersbruck, Lauf und Nürnberg-Land, Wiesenstr. 12, Hersbruck.
DM 4

8. ALTPREUSSISCHE GESCHLECHTERKUNDE [Old Prussian genealogy]. Irr. Verein für Familienforschung in Ost- und Westpreussen e.V., c/o R. Farnsteiner, Sierichstr. 145, Hamburg 39. for memb. only

9. ANGLER HEIMATVEREIN, JAHRBUCH DES... (Jahrbuch des Angler Heimatvereins) [Yearbook of the Angeln Local Society]. A. Angler Heimatverein, Kappeln (Schlei). nfs

ANNALEN DES HISTORISCHEN VEREINS FÜR DEN NIEDERRHEIN see HISTORISCHER VEREIN FÜR DEN NIEDERRHEIN, ANNALEN DES...

ANNALES UNIVERSITATIS SARAVIENSIS see UNIVERSITAS SARAVIENSIS, ANNALES...

10. ARABIC REVIEW. Q. Inst. for the Study of the USSR, Mannhardtstr. 6, München 22. In Arabic. DM 12

11. ARCHAEOLOGIA GEOGRAPHICA. Beiträge zur vergleichenden geographisch-kartographischen Methode in der Urgeschichtsforschung [Contributions to the comparative geographic-cartographic method in researches in primeval history]. A. 1950 (1958: no. 7). Flemmings-Verlag, Kartographisches Institut, Leinpfad 75, Hamburg 39, for Vorgeschichtliche Abteilung des Hamburgischen Museums für Völkerkunde und Vorgeschichte. Ed. board: H.J. Eggers, R. Hachmann, H. Jankuhn. Art. on the hist. of European settlements and their description on maps, with emphasis on Germany, from prehist. times to the late Middle Ages; maps. DM 12

12. ARCHIV DES VÖLKERRECHTS [Archives for international law]. Q. J.C.B. Mohr (Paul Siebeck) Verlag, Wilhelmstr. 18, Tübingen. DM 56

13. ARCHIV FÜR DEUTSCHE POSTGESCHICHTE [Archives for German postal history]. S-A. 1953 (1960: no vol. indic.). Gesellschaft für deutsche Postgeschichte e.V., Koblenzerstr. 81, Bonn. Ed: H. Hartmann, Oberpostdirektion München. Art. on German postal hist. from Roman times to the present; illus.; subject indices of art. pub. in the local periodicals of the sponsoring soc. DM 3.60

14. ARCHIV FÜR DIPLOMATIK, SCHRIFTGESCHICHTE, SIEGEL- UND WAPPENKUNDE [Archives for diplomatics, history of palaeography, knowledge of seals and heraldics]. A. 1955 (1958: vol. 4). Böhlau-Verlag, Riehler Str. 86, Köln 16. Ed: E.E. Stengel, Renthof 20, Marburg. Critical evaluations of official doc. and charters, and art. on their importance and on the development of script, both during the Middle Ages; reproductions of doc. DM 34 / 8.10

15. ARCHIV FÜR DRUCK UND PAPIER. ARCHIVES FOR PRINTING, PAPER AND KINDRED TRADES. Buchgewerbe, Graphik, Werbung [Book-craft, graphic arts, advertizing]. Q. 1863 (1960: vol. 97, new series, vol. 6). Buch- und Druckgewerbe Verlag F.X. Oettl und Co., KG, Kiepertstr. 19, Berlin-Marienfelde. Ed: F.X. Oettl. Art. on all aspects of the printing and paper trades, particularly their hist. and that of libraries and collections, as well as modern technical problems, with many illus.; news of bk. and printing exhibitions, conferences, courses and other trade news; in English and German. DM 30 / 8

16. ARCHIV FÜR FRANKFURTS GESCHICHTE UND KUNST [Archives for the history and art of Frankfurt]. A. Verlag W. Kramer, Bornheimer Landstr. 57a, Frankfurt (Main), for Frankfurter Verein für Geschichte und Landeskunde. DM 4.50

17. ARCHIV FÜR GESCHICHTE VON OBERFRANKEN [Archives for the history of Upper Franconia]. A. Historischer Verein für Oberfranken, Bayreuth. pni

18. ARCHIV FÜR HESSISCHE GESCHICHTE UND ALTERTUMSKUNDE [Archives for the history and archaeology of Hesse]. A. Historischer Verein für Hessen, Schloss, Darmstadt. DM 10

19. ARCHIV FÜR KATHOLISCHES KIRCHENRECHT [Archives for Catholic canon law]. S-A. Kirchheim und Co. GmbH, Kaiserstr. 41, Mainz. DM 20

20. ARCHIV FÜR KULTURGESCHICHTE [Archives for cultural history]. 3 x y. 1910 (1959: vol. 41). Böhlau Verlag, Riehler Str. 86, Köln 16. Ed. board: Herbert Grundmann, Kolbergerstr. 11, München 27; Fritz Wagner, Georg-

Voigt-Str. 1, Marburg (Lahn); Arno Borst, Gertrudenstr. 3, Münster. Art. on cultural hist. from the Middle Ages to the present, with emphasis on Europe; rev. art. DM 22.50

21. ARCHIV FÜR MITTELRHEINISCHE KIRCHENGESCHICHTE [Archives for the church history of the Middle Rhine]. A. Jaeger Verlag, Kirngasse 28, Speyer. DM 12

ARCHIV FÜR ORDENSKUNDE see section on International Periodicals

22. ARCHIV FÜR POSTGESCHICHTE IN BAYERN [Archives for postal history in Bavaria]. A. Gesellschaft zur Erforschung der Postgeschichte in Bayern, Oberpostdirektion, München 2. DM 3.60

23. ARCHIV FÜR REFORMATIONSGESCHICHTE [Archives for the history of the Reformation]. Internationale Zeitschrift zur Erforschung der Reformation und ihrer Weltwirkungen. "An International Journal Concerned with the History of the Reformation and its Significance in World Affairs." S-A. 1903/04 (1960: vol. 51). Gütersloher Verlagshaus Gerd Mohn, Gütersloh, for Verein für Reformationsgeschichte and American Soc. for Reformation Research. Ed. board: G. Ritter, Mozartstr. 48, Freiburg i. Br., H.J. Grimm, Dept. of Hist., 216 North Oval Drive, Ohio State Univ., Columbus 10, O., R.H. Bainton, H. Bornkamm, E. Hassinger. Art. on the hist. of the Reformation and its significance; bk. rev.; reports on research; sum. of art. from other periodicals; in German or English; German sum. of art. in English. DM 26 / $6 (memb. DM 20.80 / $5)

24. ARCHIV FÜR SCHLESISCHE KIRCHENGESCHICHTE [Archives for Silesian church history]. A. Verlag A. Lax, Hildesheim, for Institut für ostdeutsche Kultur- und Kirchengeschichte, Kreuzstr. 21, Hildesheim. DM 11

25. ARCHIV OSTDEUTSCHER FAMILIENFORSCHER [Archives of East German genealogists]. Irr. Arbeitsgemeinschaft ostdeutscher Familienforscher e.V., c/o C. Liebich, Salzdahlumerstr. 61, Wolfenbüttel. pni

26. ARCHIVALISCHE ZEITSCHRIFT [Archival review]. A. 1876 (1959: vol. 55). Bayerisches Hauptstaatsarchiv, Arcisstr. 12, München 2. Ed: Otto Schottenloher, Geheimes Staatsarchiv, Leonrodstr. 57, München 19. Art. on archival theory and practice, auxiliary hist. sciences, archival holdings and biographies of archivists; rev. of bk. and periodicals; illus. DM 22.50

27. DER ARCHIVAR [The archivist]. Mitteilungsblatt für deutsches Archivwesen [News bulletin on German archives]. Q. 1947 (1959: vol. 12). Verein Deutscher Archivare, Staatsarchiv Düsseldorf, Prinz Georgstr. 78, Düsseldorf. Ed. board: F.W. Oediger, H. Dahm, G. Vollmer. Art. on the theory, practice and technique of maintaining archives, on the hist. of archives and on auxiliary hist. sciences; reports on congresses; rev. of bk. and periodicals; biblio. classified by country. p (1) DM 2.50

ARCHIVES FOR PRINTING, PAPER AND KINDRED TRADES see ARCHIV FÜR DRUCK UND PAPIER

28. AUSSENPOLITIK [Foreign policy]. Zeitschrift für internationale Fragen [Journal for international questions]. M. 1950 (1960: vol. 11). Deutsche Verlags-Anstalt, Neckarstr. 121, Stuttgart O. Ed: Herbert v. Borch, Wilhelm Wolfgang Schütz, Schüllerweg 8, Bonn. Art. on international politics, with emphasis on current problems and recent hist.; each issue contains a leading art.

on current events; "Aussenpolitische Chronik": an informative rev. of significant world news, with emphasis on personnel changes; diplomatic news; bk. rev. DM 27.50 / Sfr. 30.25

29. BADISCHE FUNDBERICHTE [Reports on findings in Baden]. Amtliches Jahrbuch für ur- und frühgeschichtliche Forschung Badens [Official yearbook for prehistorical and early historical research on Baden]. A. Staatliches Amt für Ur- und Frühgeschichte, Freiburg, and Staatliches Amt für Denkmalpflege, Abteilung Ur- und Frühgeschichte, Karlsruhe. pni

30. BADISCHE HEIMAT [Homeland Baden]. Mein Heimatland [My homeland]. Q. Landesverein Badische Heimat e.V., Hansjakobstr. 12, Freiburg i. Br. DM 12

31. BAESSLER-ARCHIV [Baessler-Archives]. Beiträge zur Völkerkunde [Contributions on ethnology]. S-A. 1911 (1959: new series, vol. 7). Dietrich Reimer, Marienplatz 8, Berlin-Lichterfelde. Ed: H.D. Disselhoff, K. Krieger, Museum für Völkerkunde, Arnim-Allee 23, Berlin-Dahlem. Art. on ethnology; bk. rev.; illus. pv (DM 12-22)

32. BALTISCHE AHNEN- UND STAMMTAFELN [Baltic family charts and genealogical trees]. Q. Verlag H. von Hirschheydt, Wichmannstr. 20, Hannover-Döhren. Appears also as supplement to Baltische Hefte. DM 6

33. BALTISCHE HEFTE [Baltic journals]. Vierteljahresschrift für Gegenwartsfragen, Kultur und Wissenschaft des Baltikums [Quarterly journal for the contemporary questions, culture and scholarship of the Baltikum]. Q. H. von Hirschheydt, Wichmannstr. 20, Hannover-Döhren. Includes: "Baltische Familiengeschichtliche Nachrichten," and a supplement entitled: Baltische Ahnen- und Stammtafeln. DM 7.80

34. BAYERISCHER LANDESVEREIN FÜR FAMILIENKUNDE, BLÄTTER DES... (Blätter des Bayerischen Landesvereins für Familienkunde) [Bulletins of the Bavarian Provincial Society for Genealogy]. 3 x y. Bayerischer Landesverein für Familienkunde e.V., Stadtarchiv, Winzererstr. 68, München 13. DM 8

35. BAYERISCHES JAHRBUCH FÜR VOLKSKUNDE [Bavarian yearbook for folklore]. A. Josef Habbel, Gutenbergstr. 17, Regensburg, for Bayerische Landesstelle für Volkskunde, Ludwigstr. 23, München 22. pv

36. DER BAYERWALD [The Bavarian forest]. Q. Kulturausschuss des Bayerischen Waldvereins e.V., Rennbahnstr. 35, Straubing. DM 3

37. BEITRÄGE ZUR DEUTSCHEN VOLKS- UND ALTERTUMSKUNDE [Contributions to German ethnography and antiquity]. A. 1954 (1959: vol. 4). Hamburger Museumsverein e.V., Holstenwall 24, Hamburg 36, for Museum für Hamburgische Geschichte. Ed: H. Freudenthal. Art. on German ethnography and cultural hist., with emphasis on modern times; bk. rev.; report on the activities of the Niederdeutscher Verband für Volks- und Altertumskunde e.V. pni

38. BEITRÄGE ZUR GESCHICHTE DORTMUNDS UND DER GRAFSCHAFT MARK [Contributions to the history of Dortmund and the county of Mark]. Irr. Historischer Verein für Dortmund und die Grafschaft Mark, Dortmund. pv (c. DM 9.50)

39. BEITRÄGE ZUR GESCHICHTE VON STADT UND STIFT ESSEN [Contributions to the history of the town and chapter of Essen]. A. Fredebeuel und Koennen KG, Kibbelstr. 9-15, Essen, for Historischer Verein für Stadt und Stift Essen. pv

40. BEITRÄGE ZUR NAMENSFORSCHUNG [Contributions to onomastics]. 3 x y. 1949 (1959: vol. 10). Carl Winter, Universitätsverlag, Lutherstr. 59, Heidelberg. Ed: Hans Krahe, Indogermanisches Seminar, Universität Tübingen, Tübingen. Art. on place and personal names; rev. of bk. and periodicals; news and notes of scholarly interest; index. DM 36 / $8.57

41. BEITRÄGE ZUR SCHLESWIGER STADTGESCHICHTE [Contributions to the history of the town of Schleswig]. Irr. Gesellschaft für Schleswiger Stadtgeschichte, Schleswig.

42. BEITRÄGE ZUR WESTFÄLISCHEN FAMILIENFORSCHUNG [Contributions to Westphalian genealogical research]. 3 x y. Aschendorffsche Verlagsbuchhandlung, Gallitzinstr. 13, Münster (Westf.), for Westfälische Gesellschaft für Genealogie und Familienforschung. DM 5 (memb. free)

43. BELORUSSIAN REVIEW. A. Inst. for the Study of the U.S.S.R., Mannhardtstr. 6, München 22. Superseded in 1961 by Studies on the Soviet Union. DM 4

44. DAS BENTHEIMER LAND [The Bentheim country]. A. Walter Dorn Verlag, Bremen-Horn, for Heimatverein der Grafschaft Bentheim. pv

45. DER BERGFRIED [The watch-tower]. Rothenburger Blätter für Heimatforschung, Heimatkunde und Heimatpflege [Rothenburg bulletins for local research, topography and preservation]. M. H. Giessberger, Jahnstr. 1, Rothenburg o.d.T. p (1) DM 0.20

46. BERICHTE ZUR DEUTSCHEN LANDESKUNDE [Reports on German geography]. Irr. (S-A). Bundesanstalt für Landeskunde, Zentralarchiv für Landeskunde von Deutschland, Bergstr. 38, Remagen a. Rh. p (1) DM 10

47. BERLINER BLÄTTER FÜR VOR- UND FRÜHGESCHICHTE [Berlin bulletins for prehistory and early history]. M. H. Lehmann Verlag, Hildburghauserstr. 107, Berlin-Lichterfelde. DM 1

48. BERLINER MUSEEN [Berlin museums]. Irr. G. Grotesche Verlagsbuchhandlung, Hamm, and Gebr. Mann Verlag, Berlin. p (1) DM 3

49. BERLINER NUMISMATISCHE ZEITSCHRIFT [Berlin numismatic journal]. Irr. (3-4 x y). 1949 (1959: no. 25). Numismatische Gesellschaft zu Berlin e.V. Ed: W. Wruck, Niebuhrstr. 78, Berlin-Charlottenburg 2. Art. on coins; information on findings; reports on the activities of the soc.; illus. p (1) DM 3

50. BEZIRKSGRUPPE KIEL DER "GESELLSCHAFT FÜR DEUTSCHE POSTGESCHICHTE" E. V., MITTEILUNGEN DER... [Communications of the Kiel district group of the "Society for German Postal History"]. Q. Bezirksgruppe Kiel der Gesellschaft für deutsche Postgeschichte e.V., Oberpostdirektion Kiel. DM 3.60

51. BIBLISCHE ZEITSCHRIFT [Biblical journal]. S-A. 1957 (1960: vol. 4). F. Schöningh Verlag, Paderborn. Ed: V. Hamp, Karl-Theodorstr. 47/I, München 13 (for Old Testament), R. Schnackenburg, Sonnenstr. 15, Würzburg (for New Testament). Art. on the hist. of the Old and New Testaments; reports on congresses; list of unprinted doctoral dissertations and "Habilitationsschriften"; bk. rev. p (1) DM 15

52. BIELARUSKI ZBORNIK [Belorussian review]. A. Inst. for the Study of the U.S.S.R., Mannhardtstr. 6, München 22. Ceased pub. in 1961. DM 3

BLÄTTER DES BAYERISCHEN LANDESVEREINS FÜR FAMILIENKUNDE see BAYERISCHER LANDESVEREIN FÜR FAMILIENKUNDE, BLÄTTER DES...

53. BLÄTTER FÜR DEUTSCHE LANDESGESCHICHTE [Bulletins for German provincial history]. A. 1852 (1960: vol. 96). Selbstverlag des Gesamtvereins der deutschen Geschichts- und Altertumsvereine Wiesbaden, Mainzerstr. 80, Wiesbaden. Ed: G.W. Saute, O. Renckhoff. Art. on German provincial hist., including Austria and Switzerland; reports on German hist. inst., listing their pub. and special fields of studies, arranged by subject; exhaustive list of German provincial hist. periodicals with titles of art., arranged by geographical area, including Austria and Switzerland; bk. rev. divided into a general part, arranged by subject, and a provincial part, arranged by area; list of new pub.; author and geographical indices of bk. rev. pni

54. BLÄTTER FÜR FRÄNKISCHE FAMILIENKUNDE [Bulletins for Franconian genealogical studies]. Irr. Verlag Degener und Co., Neustadt a.d. Aisch, for Gesellschaft für Familienforschung in Franken e.V. p (1) DM 2

55. BLÄTTER FÜR PFÄLZISCHE KIRCHENGESCHICHTE UND RELIGIÖSE VOLKSKUNDE [Bulletins for the church history of the Palatinate and religious ethnography]. Q. Emil Sommer Verlag, Grünstadt. (memb.) DM 8

56. BLÄTTER FÜR WÜRTTEMBERGISCHE KIRCHENGESCHICHTE [Bulletins for Württemberg church history]. A. Verlag Chr. Scheufele, Christophstr. 26, Stuttgart S, for Verein für Württembergische Kirchengeschichte. DM 19.60

57. BODENSEE-HEFTE [Lake Constance publications]. Zeitschrift für Geschichte, Kunst und Literatur. Monatsschrift der Landschaft um den Bodensee [Periodical for history, art and literature. Monthly journal for the country around Lake Constance]. M. Verlag R.W. Schwarz, Rosgartenstr. 18, Konstanz, for Internationaler Bodensee-Verkehrsverein. DM 16

58. BONNER GESCHICHTSBLÄTTER [Bonn historical bulletins]. A. Verein Alt-Bonn, Kurfürstenstr. 23a, Bonn, for Bonner Heimat- und Geschichtsverein, Bonn. pni

BONNER JAHRBÜCHER DES RHEINISCHEN LANDESMUSEUMS IN BONN UND DES VEREINS VON ALTERTUMSFREUNDEN IM RHEINLANDE see RHEINISCHES LANDESMUSEUM IN BONN UND DER VEREIN VON ALTERTUMSFREUNDEN IM RHEINLANDE, BONNER JAHRBÜCHER DES...

59. BRAUNSCHWEIGER POSTGESCHICHTLICHE BLÄTTER [Brunswick bulletins of postal history]. Irr. Bezirksgruppe Braunschweig der Gesellschaft für deutsche Postgeschichte e.V., Oberpostdirektion, Braunschweig. (memb.) DM 3.60

60. BRAUNSCHWEIGISCHE HEIMAT [Brunswick homeland]. Zeitschrift für Natur- und Heimatpflege, Geschichte, Kunst und Schrifttum Ostfalens [Journal for the preservation of nature and the homeland, history, art and literature of Eastphalia]. Q. Braunschweigischer Landesverein für Heimatkunde e. V., Mönchstr. 1, Braunschweig. (memb.) DM 6

61. BRAUNSCHWEIGISCHES JAHRBUCH [Brunswick yearbook]. A. G. Kallmeyer Verlag, Wilhelm-Busch-Str. 6, Wolfenbüttel, for Braunschweiger Geschichtsverein, Braunschweig. DM 4.50

62. BREMISCHE WEIHNACHTSBLÄTTER [Bremen Christmas bulletins]. Irr. Historische Gesellschaft, Wätjenstr. 39, Bremen. memb. free

63. BREMISCHES JAHRBUCH [Bremen yearbook]. A. (Irr). Historische Gesellschaft, Wätjenstr. 39, Bremen. pni

BULLETINO DELL' ISTITUTO ARCHEOLOGICO GERMANICO, SEZIONE ROMANA see DEUTSCHES ARCHAEOLOGISCHES INSTITUT, ROEMISCHE ABTEILUNG, MITTEILUNGEN DES...

64. BURGEN UND SCHLÖSSER. CASTLES AND HISTORIC HOUSES. Zeitschrift für Burgenkunde und Burgenpflege, für Wehrbau, für Schloss- und Landhausbau [Journal for the study and preservation of castles, for the building of bulwarks, palaces and country houses]. S-A. Deutsche Burgenvereinigung e.V. zum Schutze historischer Wehrbauten, Schlösser und Wohnbauten, Marksburg ob Braubach (Rhein). Title also in French and Italian. DM 8

65. BYZANTINISCHE ZEITSCHRIFT [Byzantine journal]. S-A. 1892 (1960: vol. 53). C.H. Becksche Verlagsbuchhandlung, Wilhelmstr. 9, München 23. Ed: F. Dölger. Art. on Byzantine hist. and related fields; bk. rev.; critical biblio. of recently pub. studies; reports on excavations; professional news; in German and English, French, Greek or Latin. DM 45

66. DAS CAROLINUM. Blätter für Kultur und Heimat [Bulletins for culture and the homeland]. S-A. G. Piehler, Guldenhagen 19, Göttingen. DM 12

CASTLES AND HISTORIC HOUSES see BURGEN UND SCHLÖSSER

67. CAUCASIAN REVIEW. A. Inst. for the Study of the U.S.S.R., Mannhardtstr. 6, München 22. Superseded in 1961 by Studies on the Soviet Union. DM 4

68. COBURGER LANDESSTIFTUNG, JAHRBUCH DER... [Yearbook of the Coburg Country Foundation]. A. Coburger Landesstiftung, Schloss Ehrenburg, Coburg. pni

69. COMMENTATIONES BALTICAE. A. (Irr.). Baltisches Forschungsinstitut e.V., Universität, Hauptgebäude, Zimmer 376, Bonn. DM 30

70. DAUGAVAS VANAGI [The hawks of Daugava]. B-M. Pub. address: Gravenstr. 69, Münster (Westf.).

71. DERGI [Review]. Q. Inst. for the Study of the U.S.S.R., Mannhardtstr. 6, München 22. In Turkish. DM 12

72. DEUTSCHE GAUE [German districts]. Zeitschrift für Gesellschaftswissenschaft und Landeskunde [Journal for social science and country studies]. Irr. M. Weikmann, Postfach 50, Kaufbeuren. DM 3.40

73. DER DEUTSCHE HUGENOTT [The German Huguenot]. Q. R. Fouquet Verlag, Friesische Str. 76, Flensburg. memb. free

74. DEUTSCHE MORGENLÄNDISCHE GESELLSCHAFT, ZEITSCHRIFT DER... (Zeitschrift der Deutschen Morgenländischen Gesellschaft) [Journal of the German Oriental Society]. S-A. F. Steiner Verlag, Bahnhofstr. 39, Wiesbaden, for Deutsche Morgenländische Gesellschaft. Literature and all aspects of the culture of Asia and the Islamic countries. p (1) DM 30

75. DEUTSCHE RUNDSCHAU [German review]. M. Rudolf Pechel, Haussmannstr. 38, Stuttgart O. DM 18

76. DEUTSCHER PALÄSTINA-VEREIN, ZEITSCHRIFT DES... (Zeitschrift des Deutschen Palästina-Vereins) [Journal of the German Palestine Society]. S-A. 1878 (1959: vol. 75). O. Harrassowitz, Taunusstr. 5, Wiesbaden, for Deutscher Verein zur Erforschung Palästinas. Ed: D.M. Noth, Lennestr. 24, Bonn. Art. on the Biblical hist. of Palestine; bk. rev.; illus. (memb.) DM 15

77. DEUTSCHES ADELSARCHIV [Archives of German nobility]. M. Verlag Deutsches Adelsarchiv, c/o v. Flotow, Westerbrak über Vorwohle, Kreis Holzminden. DM 18

78. DEUTSCHES ARCHAEOLOGISCHES INSTITUT, ROEMISCHE ABTEILUNG, MITTEILUNGEN DES... (Mitteilungen des Deutschen Archaeologischen Instituts, Roemische Abteilung). BULLETINO DELL' ISTITUTO ARCHEOLOGICO GERMANICO, SEZIONE ROMANA [Communications of the Roman Department of the German Archaeological Institute]. A. 1886 (1959: vol. 66). F.H. Kerle Verlag, Heidelberg, für Deutsches Archäologisches Institut, Römische Abteilung. Art. on archaeological excavations and findings in Italy; in German and Italian and occasionally in English; illus. pv (c. DM 42-61)

79. DEUTSCHES ARCHÄOLOGISCHES INSTITUT, ATHENISCHE ABTEILUNG, MITTEILUNGEN DES... (Mitteilungen des Deutschen Archäologischen Instituts, Athenische Abteilung) [Communications of the Athenian Department of the German Archaeological Institute]. Irr. 1876 (1957: vol. 72). Gebr. Mann Verlag, Hauptstr. 26, Berlin-Schöneberg, for Deutsches Archäologisches Institut, Athenische Abteilung. Art. on archaeological excavations and findings in Greece; illus. Pub. suspended from 1943 to 1955. pv (c. DM 40)

80. DEUTSCHES ARCHÄOLOGISCHES INSTITUT, JAHRBUCH DES... (Jahrbuch des Deutschen Archäologischen Instituts) [Yearbook of the German Archaeological Institute]. A. 1886 (1958: vol. 73). W. de Gruyter, Genthinerstr. 13, Berlin W 35, for Deutsches Archäologisches Institut, Maienstr. 1, Berlin W 30. Art. on all aspects of the culture of classical antiquity, usually based on excavations, findings or museum holdings; illus. Includes: "Archäologischer Anzeiger": shorter art. on the same subjects and A. reports of the Archäologische Gesellschaft zu Berlin. DM 44

81. DEUTSCHES ARCHIV FÜR ERFORSCHUNG DES MITTELALTERS [German archives for research on the Middle Ages]. S-A. 1937 (1960: vol. 61). Böhlau Verlag, Riehlerstr. 86, Köln 16, for Monumenta Germaniae Historica, München. Ed.board: F.Baethgen, W.Holtzmann, H.Grundmann, Meiserstr. 10,

München 2. Art. on all aspects of the hist. of the Middle Ages, covering the period from 400 to 1500 and on its sources; reports on the activities of the Monumenta Germaniae Historica; rev. of bk. and art., arranged by subject as follows: general, auxiliary sciences and source studies, political and church hist. of the Middle Ages, legal and constitutional hist., social and economic hist., general provincial hist., cultural and intellectual hist.; illus. DM 39.60

DIOGENES see section on International Periodicals

82. DOKUMENTE [Documents]. Zeitschrift für übernationale Zusammenarbeit [Journal for supranational co-operation]. B-M. Gesellschaft für übernationale Zusammenarbeit, Hohenstaufenring 11, Köln. DM 12

83. DUISBURGER FORSCHUNGEN [Duisburg researches]. Schriftenreihe für Geschichte und Heimatkunde Duisburgs [Series of publications for the history and local studies of Duisburg]. A. (Irr.). Verlag für Wirtschaft und Kultur, Duisburg-Ruhrort, for Stadtarchiv and Mercator-Gesellschaft, Duisburg. DM 7.50

84. DÜRENER GESCHICHTSBLÄTTER [Düren historical bulletins]. Q. Dürener Geschichtsverein, Bergstr. 66, Düren. p (1) DM 0.50

85. DÜSSELDORFER JAHRBUCH [Düsseldorf yearbook]. Beiträge zur Geschichte des Niederrheins [Contributions to the history of the Lower Rhine]. A. (Irr.). Ed. Lintz, Düsseldorf, for Düsseldorfer Geschichtsverein. pv

86. THE EAST TURKIC REVIEW. S-A. Inst. for the Study of the U.S.S.R., Mannhardtstr. 6, München 22. Superseded in 1961 by Studies on the Soviet Union. DM 8

87. ELLWANGER JAHRBUCH [Ellwangen yearbook]. Ein Volksbuch für Heimatpflege im Virngrund und Ries [A people's book for the preservation of the homeland in Virngrund and Ries]. Irr. Bucher in Komm., Ellwangen, for Geschichts- und Altertumsverein Ellwangen. pv (c. DM 7.50)

88. ERLANGER BAUSTEINE ZUR FRÄNKISCHEN HEIMATFORSCHUNG [Erlangen contributions to Franconian local research]. Q (Irr.). Heimatverein Erlangen und Umgebung e.V., Henkestr. 12, Erlangen. DM 7

89. ESZLINGER STUDIEN [Esslingen studies]. A. Kulturamt der Stadt Esslingen, Stadtarchiv, Marktplatz 20, Esslingen (Neckar). pni

90. EUROPA ARCHIV [Europe Archives]. S-M. Wilhelm Cornides (Co.), for Deutsche Gesellschaft für Auswärtige Politik, Myliusstr. 20, Frankfurt (Main). DM 43.50

91. DER EUROPÄISCHE OSTEN [The European East]. Politische Monatsschrift für neue Ordung [Political monthly for a new order]. M. Fides-Verlagsgesellschaft mbH, Bayerstr. 57-59, München. DM 30

92. EVANGELISCHE THEOLOGIE [Evangelical theology]. M. Chr. Kaiser Verlag, Isabellastr. 20, München. DM 19.20

93. FAMILIE UND VOLK [Family and nation]. Zeitschrift für Genealogie und Bevölkerungskunde [Journal for genealogy and population studies]. B-M. 1952 (1960: vol. 9). Arbeitsgemeinschaft genealogischer Verlage, Nürnberger

Str. 27-29, Neustadt a.d. Aisch, for Deutsche Arbeitsgemeinschaft genealogischer Verbände and Abteilung Genealogie und Heraldik im Gesamtverein der deutschen Geschichts- und Altertumsvereine. Ed: Gottfried Roesler, Plattlingerstr. 10, Osterhofen (Ndb.). Art. on German genealogy; reports on the activities of the soc.; rev. of bk. and periodicals. DM 15

FAMILIENBLATT DER LUTHERIDEN-VEREINIGUNG see LUTHERIDEN-VEREINIGUNG, FAMILIENBLATT DER...

94. DER FAMILIENFORSCHER IN BAYERN, FRANKEN UND SCHWABEN [The genealogist in Bavaria, Franconia and Swabia]. Q. R. Pflaum Verlag, Lazarettstr. 2-6, München 2, for Bayerischer Landesverein für Familienkunde. p (1) DM 2

95. FAMILIENGESCHICHTLICHE QUELLEN [Genealogical sources]. Zeitschrift familiengeschichtlicher Quellennachweise [Journal of genealogical source information]. B-M. Verlag Degener und Co., Neustadt a.d. Aisch. DM 6

96. FAMILIENKUNDLICHE NACHRICHTEN [Genealogical news]. Mitteilungen - Literatur - Rundfragen - Empfehlungen [Information - literature - questions - recommendations]. Q. Arbeitsgemeinschaft genealogischer Verlage, Nürnberger Str. 27-29, Neustadt a.d. Aisch. Appears as supplement to most genealogical periodicals. free

97. FRANKENLAND [Franconia]. Zeitschrift für das Frankenvolk und seine Freunde [Journal for the people of Franconia and their friends]. B-M. "Frankenland," Kroatenstr. 10, Würzburg. memb. free

98. FRANKENWALD [Franconian forest]. B-M. Frankenwaldverein e.V., c/o H. Seiffert, Ottostr. 5, Helmbrechts (Obf.). memb. free

99. FRANKFURTER HEFTE [Frankfurt reviews]. Zeitschrift für Kultur und Politik [Journal for culture and politics]. M. Pub. address: Leipzigerstr. Frankfurt (Main). p (1) DM 2

100. FRÄNKISCHE POSTGESCHICHTSBLÄTTER [Franconian bulletins of postal history]. Irr. Gesellschaft für deutsche Postgeschichte e.V., Bezirksgruppe Nürnberg, Oberpostdirektion Nürnberg. (memb.) DM 3.60

101. FRANZISKANISCHE STUDIEN [Franciscan studies]. Q. 1914 (1960: vol. 42). Dietrich-Coelde-Verlag, Werl (Westf.). Ed: Julian Kaup, O.F.M., Westernstr. 19, Paderborn. Art. on the hist. and attitudes of the Franciscan Order and on theological questions; bk. rev.; in German and occasionally in English or French. DM 16

102. FREIBURGER DIÖZESAN-ARCHIV [Archives of the diocese of Freiburg]. A. Herder Verlag, Freiburg i. Br., for Kirchengeschichtlicher Verein für Geschichte, christliche Kunst, Altertums- und Literaturkunde des Erzbistums Freiburg mit Berücksichtigung der angrenzenden Gebiete. (memb.) DM 8

103. F R H R L. SCHENCK ZU SCHWEINSBERGSCHES SAMTARCHIV, MITTEILUNGEN AUS DEM... (Mitteilungen aus dem F r h r l. Schenck zu Schweinsbergschen Samtarchiv) [Communications from the Baronial United Archives Schenck zu Schweinsberg]. Irr. Schencksches Samtarchiv, Schweinsberg, Kreis Marburg. DM 2.50

104. FULDAER GESCHICHTSBLÄTTER [Fulda historical bulletins]. M. Fuldaer Geschichtsverein, Im Stadtschloss, Fulda. pni

FUNDBERICHT DES LANDESAMTES FÜR KULTURGESCHICHTLICHE BODENALTERTÜMER see NASSAUISCHE HEIMATBLÄTTER

105. FUNDBERICHTE AUS SCHWABEN [Reports on finds from Swabia]. Irr. 1893 (1959: new series, vol. 15). Schweizerbartsche Verlagsbuchhandlung, Johannesstr. 3, Stuttgart W, for Württembergischer Geschichts- und Altertumsverein, Stuttgart, and Staatliche Ämter der Denkmalspflege in Stuttgart und Tübingen. Ed: Hartwig Zürn. Art. on excavations and findings in Swabia from the Stone Age to the Middle Ages; bk. rev.; biblio.; index, illus., maps. pv

106. FÜRTHER HEIMATBLÄTTER [Fürth local bulletins]. M. Verein für Heimatforschung Alt-Fürth, c/o A. Schwamberger, Blumenstr. 22, Fürth. pni

107. GEOGRAPHISCHE RUNDSCHAU [Geographical survey]. Zeitschrift für Schulgeographie [Journal for school geography]. M. Georg Westermann Verlag, Georg-Westermann-Allee 66, Braunschweig. DM 24

108. GERMANIA. A. 1917 (1959: vol. 37). W. de Gruyter und Co., Genthinerstr. 13, Berlin W 35, for Römisch-Germanische Kommission des Deutschen Archäologischen Instituts, Palmengartenstr. 10-12, Frankfurt (Main). Ed. board: G. Bersu, W. Schleiermacher, W. Wagner, Bockenheimer Landstr. 97, Frankfurt (Main). Art. on European archaeology, prehist. and ancient hist. and on ancient culture and art, with emphasis on Germany; bk. rev.; list of acquisitions of bk. and periodicals; reports on excavations; illus.
DM 16 (memb. DM 8)

109. GESCHICHTE IN WISSENSCHAFT UND UNTERRICHT [History in scholarship and teaching]. M. 1950 (1960: vol. 11). Ernst Klett Verlag, Postfach 809, Stuttgart W, for Verband der Geschichtslehrer Deutschlands. Ed: Karl Dietrich Erdmann, Ernestinenweg 7, Mönkeberg b. Kiel, Felix Messerschmid, Akademie für Politische Bildung, Tutzing (Obb.). Art. on hist., with emphasis on historiographical questions and the methods and problems of teaching hist., with reference to the West German school system; rev. art.; rev. of hist. films; news of conferences and courses for professional historians and hist. teachers.
DM 32 (memb. DM 28)

110. GESCHICHTSBLÄTTER FÜR WALDECK [Historical bulletins for Waldeck]. A. Waldeckischer Geschichtsverein, Arolsen. (memb.) DM 6

111. GESELLSCHAFT FÜR BILDENDE KUNST UND VATERLÄNDISCHE ALTERTÜMER ZU EMDEN, JAHRBUCH DER... [Yearbook of the Society for Plastic Arts and National Relics at Emden]. A. Verlag Ostfriesische Landschaft, Aurich. DM 7.50

112. GESELLSCHAFT FÜR DEUTSCHE POSTGESCHICHTE E.V., BEZIRKSGRUPPE DORTMUND, POSTGESCHICHTLICHE BLÄTTER DER... [Postal history bulletins of the Society for German postal history, District Group Dortmund]. Irr. Gesellschaft für deutsche Postgeschichte e.V., Bezirksgruppe Dortmund, Postamt, Dortmund-Hörde.

"GESELLSCHAFT FÜR DEUTSCHE POSTGESCHICHTE" E.V., MITTEILUNGEN DER BEZIRKSGRUPPE KIEL DER... see BEZIRKSGRUPPE KIEL DER "GESELLSCHAFT FÜR DEUTSCHE POSTGESCHICHTE" E.V., MITTEILUNGEN DER...

113. GESELLSCHAFT FÜR KIELER STADTGESCHICHTE, MITTEILUNGEN DER... [Communications of the Society for the History of the Town of Kiel]. Q (Irr.). Gesellschaft für Kieler Stadtgeschichte, Stadtarchiv, Kiel.
p (1) 0.50 (memb. free)

114. GESELLSCHAFT FÜR NATUR- UND VOLKSKUNDE OSTASIENS, NACHRICHTEN DER... [News of the Society for the Geography and Ethnography of East Asia]. Zeitschrift für Kultur und Geschichte Ostasiens [Journal for the culture and history of East Asia]. S-A. Verlag O. Harassowitz, Friedrichstr. 14, Wiesbaden. DM 4

115. GESELLSCHAFT FÜR NIEDERSÄCHSISCHE KIRCHENGESCHICHTE, JAHRBUCH DER... [Yearbook of the Society for the Church History of Lower Saxony]. A. Gesellschaft für niedersächsische Kirchengeschichte, Klopstockstr. 11, Göttingen. DM 9

116. GESELLSCHAFT FÜR SCHLESWIG-HOLSTEINISCHE GESCHICHTE, ZEITSCHRIFT DER... [Journal for the history of Schleswig-Holstein]. Irr. K. Wachholtz Verlag, Gänsemarkt 1-3, Neumünster. pv

117. GIESSENER HOCHSCHULGESELLSCHAFT, NACHRICHTEN DER... [News of the Giessen University Society]. A. W. Schmitz Verlag, Giessen.

118. GNOMON. Kritische Zeitschrift für die gesamte klassische Altertumswissenschaft [Critical journal for all fields of classical antiquity]. 8 x y. 1925 (1960: vol. 32). C.W. Becksche Verlagsbuchhandlung, Wilhelmstr. 9, München 23. Ed: Walter Marg, Seminar für klassische Philologie, Universität Mainz, Mainz. Bk. rev. in German, English, French and Italian; news and notes.
DM 56

119. GÖTTINGER JAHRBUCH [Göttingen yearbook]. A. Heinz Reise Verlag, Hainholzweg 7, Göttingen. DM 11.50

120. GÖTTINGISCHE GELEHRTE ANZEIGEN UNTER AUFSICHT DER AKADEMIE DER WISSENSCHAFTEN [Göttingen learned reviews under the supervision of the Academy of Sciences]. Q (S-A). 1939 (1958: vol. 212). Vandenhoeck und Ruprecht, Göttingen. Ed: G. Patzig, Calsowstr. 23a, Göttingen. Rev. art. and bk. rev. pertaining to classical and modern philology, Oriental and Indo-German studies, hist., auxiliary hist. disciplines and philosophy. DM 20

121. GYMNASIUM. Zeitschrift für Kultur der Antike und humanistische Bildung [Journal for the culture of antiquity and humanistic learning]. B-M. C. Winter Universitätsverlag, Lutherstr. 59, Heidelberg. DM 21

122. HAMBURGER BEITRÄGE ZUR NUMISMATIK [Hamburg contributions to numismatics]. A. 1947 (1960: no. 14). Hamburger Museumsverein e.V., Holstenwall 24, Hamburg 36, for Museum für Hamburgische Geschichte, Abteilung Münzkabinett, Hamburg. Ed. board: W. Hävernick, G. Hatz, P. Berghaus, V. Hatz, G. Albrecht. Art. on coins and numismatic finds, with emphasis on Germany; reports on finds; rev. of bk. and art., arranged by area and period; in German and occasionally in English; illus. pv (c. DM 14)

123. HAMBURGISCHE GESCHICHTS- UND HEIMATBLÄTTER [Hamburg historical and local bulletins]. S-A (4 no. constitute a vol.). Verein für Hamburgische Geschichte, c/o G. Bolland, Himmelstr. 28, Hamburg 39.
p (1) DM 1.50

124. HAMMABURG. Vor- und frühgeschichtliche Forschungen aus dem niederelbischen Raum [Prehistorical and early historical researches from the Lower Elbe area]. Irr. Hamburger Museumsverein e.V., Museum für Hamburgische Geschichte, Abteilung Bodendenkmalpflege, Holstenwall 24, Hamburg 36. DM 4

125. HANNOVERSCHE GESCHICHTSBLÄTTER [Hanover historical bulletins]. Q. Verlag Hahnsche Buchhandlung, Leinstr. 32, Hannover, for Historischer Verein für Niedersachsen, Hannover. for memb. only

126. HANSISCHE GESCHICHTSBLÄTTER [Hanse historical bulletins]. A. 1872 (1959: vol. 77). Böhlau Verlag, Riehler Str. 86, Köln 16, for Hansischer Geschichtsverein, St. Annenstr. 2, Lübeck. DM 14.80

127. HARZER ZEITSCHRIFT [Harz journal]. A. Harz-Verein für Geschichte und Altertumskunde e.V., Markt 1, Stadtarchiv, Goslar. DM 6 (memb. free)

128. HEGAU. Zeitschrift für Geschichte, Volkskunde und Naturgeschichte des Gebietes zwischen Rhein, Donau und Bodensee [Journal for the history, folklore and natural history of the area between the Rhine, the Danube and Lake Constance]. S-A. Verein für die Geschichte des Hegaus, Hohgarten 1, Singen (Hohentwiel). DM 5 (memb. DM 1.80)

129. HEIDELBERGER JAHRBÜCHER [Heidelberg yearbooks]. A. 1957 (1958: vol. 2). Springer Verlag, Berlin, for Universitätsgesellschaft Heidelberg. Ed. address: Universitätsgesellschaft Heidelberg, Plöck 107-109, Heidelberg. Art. by memb. of the faculties of Heidelberg Univ. on their respective fields; biblio. of pub. by memb. of the univ. faculties; illus. DM 18

130. DAS HEILIGE LAND [The holy land]. Q (S-A). Deutscher Verein vom Heiligen Land, Steinfeldergasse 17, Köln. (memb.) DM 6

* 131. DIE HEIMAT [The homeland]. M. Verein zur Pflege der Natur- und Landeskunde in Schleswig-Holstein und Hamburg, c/o W. Christiansen, Eckernförder Allee 18, Kiel. (memb.) DM 15

132. DIE HEIMAT [The homeland]. Zeitschrift für niederrheinische Heimatpflege [Journal for the preservation of the Lower Rhine homeland]. A. Verein für Heimatkunde, Krefeld-Uerdingen. (memb.) DM 10

133. HEIMATBLÄTTER DES SIEGKREISES [Homeland bulletins of the Sieg district]. S-A. Geschichts- und Altertumsverein für Siegburg und den Siegkreis e.V., Rathaus, Stadt-Kulturamt, Siegburg. DM 2.50

134. HEIMATBLÄTTER FÜR DEN SÜD-WESTLICHEN HARZRAND [Local bulletins for the south-western border of the Harz]. Irr. Heimat- und Geschichtsverein Osterode (Harz) und Umgebung, Osterode (Harz). p (1) DM 1.50

135. HEIMATKUNDLICHE LESEBOGEN FÜR DAS COBURGER LAND [Local topographical bulletin for the country of Coburg]. M. Verlag K. Ihl und Co., Postfach 683, Coburg. p (1) DM 0.15

136. DIE HEIMATSTADT ESSEN [The hometown Essen]. A. Heimat-Verlag A. Müller, Essen.

137. DER HEROLD [The herald]. Vierteljahresschrift für Heraldik, Genealogie und verwandte Wissenschaften [Quarterly for heraldry, genealogy and related disciplines]. Q. 1939 (1959: vol. 4). Pub. address: Westfälische Str. 38, Berlin-Halensee. Ed: H. Schulz-Blochwitz, Gutzmannstr. 40, Berlin-Zehlendorf. Art. on genealogy, heraldry and related fields; rev. of bk. and periodical literature; biblio. and lists of archival holdings. (memb.) DM 6

138. HESSISCHE BLÄTTER FÜR VOLKSKUNDE [Hesse bulletins for folklore]. A. Hessische Vereinigung für Volkskunde, Eichgartenweg 1-3, Giessen. pv (c. DM 11)

139. HESSISCHE FAMILIENKUNDE [Hessian genealogy]. Q. H.T. Friederichs, Dehnhardtstr. 32, Frankfurt-Eschersheim. DM 8 (memb. free)

140. HESSISCHE KIRCHENGESCHICHTLICHE VEREINIGUNG, JAHRBUCH DER... (Jahrbuch der Hessischen Kirchengeschichtlichen Vereinigung) [Yearbook of the Hesse Church History Society]. A. Verlag der Hessischen Kirchengeschichtlichen Vereinigung, c/o F.H. Herrmann, Kaiserstr. 72, Friedberg (Hessen). (memb.) DM 9

141. HESSISCHE POSTGESCHICHTE [Hesse postal history]. Irr. Gesellschaft für deutsche Postgeschichte e.V., Bezirksgruppe Hessen, Friedrich-Ebert-Anlage 58-72, Frankfurt (Main). (memb.) DM 3.60

142. HISTORIA [History]. Zeitschrift für Alte Geschichte. Revue d'Histoire Ancienne. Journal of Ancient History. Rivista di Storia Antica. Q. 1952 (1960: vol. 9). Franz Steiner Verlag, Bahnhofstr. 39, Wiesbaden. Ed: Hermann Bengtson, Karl Strohecker, Gerold Walser. Art. on the ancient hist. of the Mediterranean world; rev. art.; bk. rev.; occasional short abstr. of the contents of 2 or 3 selected periodicals; list of bk. and periodicals received; in German, French, English or Italian. DM 40 / $ 9.60

143. DAS HISTORISCH-POLITISCHE BUCH [The historical-political book]. Ein Wegweiser durch das Schrifttum [A guide through the literature]. M. 1953 (1960: vol. 8). Ranke Gesellschaft, Vereinigung für Geschichte im öffentlichen Leben, Arnimstr. 1, Hamburg-Hochkamp. Ed: Günther Franz, Schloss, Stuttgart-Hohenheim. Bk. rev.; A. author index; author index for the years 1953-1958 scheduled to be pub. soon. DM 12

144. HISTORISCHE ZEITSCHRIFT [Historical review]. B-M (3 no. constitute a vol.). 1859 (1961: vol. 92). R.Oldenbourg, Rosenheimerstr. 145, München 8. Ed: Theodor Schieder, Gyrhofstr. 21, Köln-Lindenthal; Walther Kienast, Zimmer 232, Universität, Mertonstr. 17, Frankfurt (Main). Art. on hist.; rev. of art., printed lectures and shorter studies; bk. rev. and biblio. of new bk., both classified by period and area; vol. indices of authors of bk. and art. rev. DM 40 (S-A subscription)

145. HISTORISCHER VEREIN DER PFALZ, MITTEILUNGEN DES... (Mitteilungen des Historischen Vereins der Pfalz) [Communications of the Palatinate Historical Society]. A. Verlag des Historischen Vereins der Pfalz e.V., Gr. Pfaffengasse 7, Speyer. DM 8

146. HISTORISCHER VEREIN DILLINGEN AN DER DONAU, JAHRBUCH DES... (Jahrbuch des Historischen Vereins Dillingen an der Donau) [Yearbook of the Historical Society of Dillingen on the Danube]. A. Historischer Verein, Kardinal-von-Waldburgstr. 7, Dillingen a.d. Donau. DM 10 (memb. DM 3)

147. HISTORISCHER VEREIN FÜR DEN NIEDERRHEIN, ANNALEN DES... (Annalen des Historischen Vereins für den Niederrhein) [Annals of the Historical Society for the Lower Rhine]. A. Historischer Verein für den Niederrhein, Charlottenstr. 80-86, Düsseldorf. (memb.) DM 8

148. HISTORISCHER VEREIN FÜR DIE GRAFSCHAFT RAVENSBERG, JAHRESBERICHTE DES... (Jahresberichte des Historischen Vereins für die Grafschaft Ravensberg) [Yearbook of the Historical Society for Ravensberg County]. A. Historischer Verein für die Grafschaft Ravensberg, Wertherstr. 8, Bielefeld. pv

149. HISTORISCHER VEREIN FÜR HESSEN, MITTEILUNGSBLÄTTER DES... (Mitteilungsblätter des Historischen Vereins für Hessen) [Information bulletins of the Historical Society for Hesse]. A. Historischer Verein für Hessen, Schloss, Darmstadt. DM 2

150. HISTORISCHER VEREIN FÜR NIEDERBAYERN, VERHANDLUNGEN DES... (Verhandlungen des Historischen Vereins für Niederbayern) [Communications of the Lower Bavaria Historical Society]. A. or S-A. Historischer Verein für Niederbayern, Landshut. p (1) DM 6 (memb. DM 5)

151. HISTORISCHER VEREIN FÜR OBERPFALZ UND REGENSBURG, VERHANDLUNGEN DES... (Verhandlungen des Historischen Vereins für Oberpfalz und Regensburg) [Transactions of the Historical Society for the Upper Palatinate and Regensburg]. A. Historischer Verein für Oberpfalz und Regensburg, Dachauplatz 4, Regensburg. DM 10 (memb. free)

152. HISTORISCHER VEREIN FÜR STRAUBING UND UMGEBUNG, JAHRESBERICHT DES... (Jahresbericht des Historischen Vereins für Straubing und Umgebung) [Annual report of the Historical Society of Straubing and its vicinity]. A. Historischer Verein für Straubing und Umgebung, Straubing.

153. HISTORISCHER VEREIN INGOLSTADT, SAMMELBLATT DES... (Sammelblatt des Historischen Vereins Ingolstadt) [Collections of the Historical Society of Ingolstadt]. A. Historischer Verein Ingolstadt, Ingolstadt.

154. HISTORISCHES JAHRBUCH [Historical yearbook]. A. 1880 (1959 [1960]: vol. 79). Verlag Karl Alber, München, for Görres-Gesellschaft, Sektion für Geschichte. Ed: J. Spörl, Kaiserstr. 59, München 23. Art. on hist. (pertaining largely to the medieval period), with emphasis on Germany; rev. art.; rev. of bk. and art. (not confined to the Middle Ages), classified by subject and period. pv (c. DM 40)

155. HOCHLAND [Highlands]. Zeitschrift für alle Gebiete des Wissens und der schönen Künste [Journal for all fields of knowledge and of the fine arts]. B-M. Kösel-Verlag, Kaiser-Ludwig-Platz 6, München 15. DM 15

156. HOHENZOLLERISCHE HEIMAT [Hohenzollern homeland]. Q. Verein für Geschichte, Kultur- und Landeskunde Hohenzollerns, c/o Hohenzollerische Heimatbücherei, Heiligkreuzstr. 17, Hechingen. DM 1.60

157. HOHENZOLLERISCHE JAHRESHEFTE [Hohenzollern yearbooks]. A. Verein für Geschichte, Kultur- und Landeskunde Hohenzollerns, c/o Hohenzollerische Heimatbücherei, Heiligkreuzstr. 17, Hechingen. (memb.) DM 6

158. HUMANISMUS UND TECHNIK [Humanism and technology]. Zeitschrift zur Erforschung und Pflege der Menschlichkeit [Journal for the research and preservation of humanity]. Irr. Gesellschaft von Freunden der technischen Universität Berlin-Charlottenburg. DM 8.25

159. INSTITUT FÜR GESCHICHTE DER MEDIZIN AN DER UNIVERSITÄT WÜRZBURG, MITTEILUNGEN AUS DEM... [Communications from the Institute for the History of Medicine at Würzburg University]. Irr. Georg-Sticker-Institut für Geschichte der Medizin, Medizinische Fakultät der Universität Würzburg, Würzburg.

160. INSTITUTE FOR THE STUDY OF THE U.S.S.R. BULLETIN. M. Inst. for the Study of the U.S.S.R., Mannhardtstr. 6, München 22. DM 24

INTERNATIONAL LAW AND DIPLOMACY see INTERNATIONALES RECHT UND DIPLOMATIE

161. INTERNATIONALES JAHRBUCH FÜR GESCHICHTSUNTERRICHT [International yearbook for the teaching of history]. A. 1951 (1957/58: vol. 6). Albert Limbach Verlag, Braunschweig. Ed: Georg Eckert, Otto-Ernst Schüddekopf, Internationales Schulbuchinstitut, Okerstr. 8b, Braunschweig. Art. on the teaching of hist. in different countries and on ways and means of overcoming nationalist biases; international rev. of textbk.; communications and reports on hist. conferences; in German, English and French. pv (c. DM 5)

162. INTERNATIONALES RECHT UND DIPLOMATIE. INTERNATIONAL LAW AND DIPLOMACY. Q. Verlag Girardet und Co., Gänsemarkt 21-23, Hamburg 36. Title also in French and Russian. DM 35

163. DER ISLAM. Zeitschrift für Geschichte und Kultur des islamischen Orients [Journal for the history and culture of the Islamic Orient]. 3 x y. 1910 (1959: vol. 34). Walter de Gruyter und Co., Genthiner Str. 13, Berlin W 35, for Deutsche Morgenländische Gesellschaft. Ed: R. Strothmann, B. Spuler, Seminar für Geschichte und Kultur des Vorderen Orients, Grindelhof 38, Hamburg 13. Art. on the hist. and culture of Islamic countries, with emphasis on early Islamic hist. and classical Arabic literature; bk. rev. pv (1958: DM 32)

ISTITUTO ARCHEOLOGICO GERMANICO, SEZIONE ROMANA, BULLETTINO DELL'... see DEUTSCHES ARCHAEOLOGISCHES INSTITUT, ROEMISCHE ABTEILUNG, MITTEILUNGEN DES...

JAHRBUCH. For titles beginning with "Jahrbuch," followed by the name of the publishing or sponsoring institution or society, see the respective institution or society.

164. JAHRBUCH FÜR AMERIKASTUDIEN [Yearbook for American studies]. A. 1956 (1958: vol. 3). Carl Winter, Universitätsverlag, Lutherstr. 59, Heidelberg. Ed: Walther Fischer, Am Plan 1, Marburg. Art. in the field of American studies; bk. rev.; A. biblio. of German bk. and art., classified by subject; in German and occasionally in English. pv (c. DM 25)

165. JAHRBUCH FÜR BRANDENBURGISCHE LANDESGESCHICHTE [Yearbook for Brandenburg provincial history]. A. Landesgeschichtliche Vereinigung für die Mark Brandenburg, Berlin.

166. JAHRBUCH FÜR DIE GESCHICHTE MITTEL- UND OSTDEUTSCHLANDS [Yearbook for the history of Central and East Germany]. A. 1952 (1958: vol. 7). Friedrich-Meinecke-Institut der Freien Universität Berlin, Altensteinstr. 40, Berlin-Dahlem. Ed: Wilhelm Berges, Carl Hinrichs. Art. on the hist. of Central and Eastern Germany, with emphasis on Prussia, from the Middle Ages to the present. pv (1957: DM 24; 1958: DM 35)

167. JAHRBUCH FÜR FRÄNKISCHE LANDESFORSCHUNG [Yearbook for Franconian country research]. A. Institut für fränkische Landesforschung, Universität Erlangen, Erlangen. pv

168. JAHRBUCH FÜR GESCHICHTE UND KUNST DES MITTELRHEINS UND SEINER NACHBARGEBIETE [Yearbook for the history and art of the Middle Rhine and its neighboring areas]. A. Verein für Geschichte und Kunst des Mittelrheins in collaboration with Nassauische Kulturstiftung and Landesamt für Denkmalspflege, Staatsarchiv, Karmeliterstr. 1-3, Koblenz. DM 10

169. JAHRBUCH FÜR SCHLESISCHE KIRCHE UND KIRCHENGESCHICHTE [Yearbook for the Silesian Church and church history]. A. Verlag der Schlesischen Evangelischen Zentralstelle, Am Hetzenbäumle 156, Ulm (Donau).

170. JAHRBUCH FÜR VOLKSKUNDE DER HEIMATVERTRIEBENEN [Yearbook for the folklore of the "Heimatvertriebene" (Germans evacuated or expelled since 1945 from German territories east of the Oder-Neisse Line or from other parts of Central and Eastern Europe -- ed.)]. A. O. Müller Verlag, Salzburg, Austria, for Kommission der Heimatvertriebenen im Verband der Vereine für Volkskunde, Dillmannstr. 3, Stuttgart W.

171. JAHRBÜCHER FÜR GESCHICHTE OSTEUROPAS [Yearbooks for the history of Eastern Europe]. Q. 1953 (1960: new series, vol. 8). Isar Verlag, Thierschstr. 11, München, for Osteuropa-Institut, Maximilianstr. 41, München 22. Ed: E. Kubaschek. Art. on the hist. of Eastern Europe, with emphasis on Russia; rev. of bk. and periodicals; classified biblio. of post-war dissertations on Eastern Europe, with name and subject indices; professional news. DM 40

172. JAHRBÜCHER FÜR STATISTIK UND LANDESKUNDE VON BADEN-WÜRTTEMBERG [Yearbooks for statistics and provincial studies of Baden-Württemberg]. A. (2 no. p.a.). Statistisches Landesamt für Baden-Württemberg, Neckarstr. 18 B, Stuttgart. Formerly pub. under the title: Württembergische Jahrbücher für Statistik und Landeskunde. pv (c. DM 16)

JAHRESBERICHTE. For titles beginning with "Jahresberichte," followed by the name of the publishing or sponsoring institution or society, see the respective institution or society.

173. KÖLNER JAHRBUCH FÜR VOR- UND FRÜHGESCHICHTE [Cologne yearbook for pre-history and early history]. A. Verlag Gebr. Mann, Berlin, for Römisch-Germanisches Museum, Zeppelinstr. 8, and Archäologische Gesellschaft, Köln.

174. KÖLNISCHER GESCHICHTSVEREIN, JAHRBUCH DES... (Jahrbuch des Kölnischen Geschichtsvereins) [Yearbook of the Cologne Historical Society].

A. Kölnischer Geschichtsverein e.V., Gereonskloster 12, Stadtarchiv, Köln. DM 14

175. DIE KUNDE [Tidings]. A. Niedersächsischer Landesverein für Urgeschichte, Niedersächsisches Landesmuseum, Urgeschichtliche Abteilung, Am Maschpark 5, Hannover. (memb.) DM 10

176. KURPFALZ. Q. Verein Kurpfalz e.V., Ludwigstr. 67-69, Ludwigshafen. (memb.) DM 4

177. LÄNDERKUNDLICHE NACHRICHTEN [Geographical news]. A. May und Co., Am Stift 14, Dortmund-Hörde, for Länderkundliche Arbeitsgemeinschaft. (memb.) DM 5

178. LAUENBURGISCHE HEIMAT [Lauenburg homeland]. B-M. Heimatbund und Geschichtsverein Herzogtum Lauenburg e.V., Domhof 13, Ratzeburg, Kreis Lauenburg.

179. LÜNEBURGER BLÄTTER [Lüneburg bulletins]. A. Museumsverein für das Fürstentum Lüneburg, Wandrahmstr. 10, Lüneburg. DM 10 (memb. DM 5)

180. LUTHER. Mitteilungen der Luthergesellschaft [Communications of the Luther Society]. 3 x y. Lutherisches Verlagshaus H. Renner, Königsallee 40, Berlin-Grunewald, for Luthergesellschaft. DM 6

181. LUTHERIDEN-VEREINIGUNG, FAMILIENBLATT DER... [Genealogical bulletin of the Society of the Descendants of Luther]. Q. Lutheriden-Vereinigung e.V., Ahrensbökerstr. 47, Reinfeld (Holstein).

182. MÄHRISCH-SCHLESISCHE HEIMAT [Moravian-Silesian homeland]. Vierteljahresschrift für Kultur und Wirtschaft [Quarterly for culture and economy]. Q. Quellenverlag V. Diwisch, Steinheim (Main). DM 8

183. MAINFRÄNKISCHES JAHRBUCH FÜR GESCHICHTE UND KUNST [Main-Franconia yearbook for history and art]. A. Freunde Mainfränkischer Kunst und Geschichte e.V., Zwinger 5, Würzburg, for Historischer Verein für Unterfranken und Aschaffenburg, Gerbrunnerweg 11, Würzburg. pni

184. MAINZER ZEITSCHRIFT [Mainz journal]. Mittelrheinisches Jahrbuch für Archäologie, Kunst und Geschichte [Middle Rhine yearbook for archaeology, art and history]. A. Verlag des Mainzer Altertumsvereins, c/o Fritz Arens, In den Gärten 11, Mainz-Bretzenheim. pv (DM 12-27)

185. DER MANGFALLGAU [Mangfall region]. Heimatkundliches Jahrbuch für den Landkreis Bad Aibling [Local topographical yearbook for the district of Bad Aibling]. A. Historischer Verein für Bad Aibling und Umgebung, Rosenheim. pni

186. MÄNNER VOM MORGENSTERN, JAHRBUCH DER... [Yearbook of the "Men of the Morning Star"]. A. "Männer vom Morgenstern" Heimatbund an Elb- und Wesermündung, Moorreye 120, Hamburg-Langenhorn 1. (memb.) DM 8

187. MEMMINGER GESCHICHTSBLÄTTER [Memmingen historical bulletins]. Irr. Verlag der Heimatpflege Memmingen, c/o W. Braun, Marktplatz I/III, Memmingen. pni

188. MENNONITISCHE GESCHICHTSBLÄTTER [Mennonite historical bulletins]. Irr. Mennonitischer Geschichtsverein, c/o P. Schowalter, Weierhof bei Marnheim (Pfalz). (memb.) DM 3

189. MERCKSCHE FAMILIEN-ZEITSCHRIFT [Journal of the Merck family]. Irr. Pub. address: c/o Fritz Merck, Am Oberfeld 22, Darmstadt. free

190. MERKUR [Mercury]. Deutsche Zeitschrift für europäisches Denken [German review for European thought]. M. Deutsche Verlags-Anstalt, Stuttgart. DM 32

191. MINDENER HEIMATBLÄTTER [Minden local bulletins]. Heimatkundliches Organ für die Kreise Minden und Lübbecke [Journal for local studies of the districts Minden and Lübbecke]. M. Mindener Geschichts- und Museumsverein Stadtarchiv, Minden. memb. free

MITTEILUNGEN. For titles beginning with "Mitteilungen," followed by the name of the publishing or sponsoring institution or society, see the respective institution or society.

192. MITTEILUNGEN AUS DER LIPPISCHEN GESCHICHTE UND LANDESKUNDE [Communications pertaining to Lippe history and provincial studies]. A. Klasing-Verlag, Kassenstr. 3, Detmold, for Naturwissenschaftlicher und Historischer Verein für das Land Lippe. pni

193. MITTEILUNGEN FÜR DIE ARCHIVPFLEGE IN BAYERN [Communications on the keeping of archives in Bavaria]. Q (S-A). 1955 (1960: vol. 6). Generaldirektion der Staatlichen Archive Bayerns, Arcisstr. 12, München 2. Ed: Edgar Krausen, Bayerisches Hauptstaatsarchiv, München. Art. on the holdings and funds of Bavarian archives, archival theory and practice and the use of archives; biographies of Bavarian archivists and lists of their pub.; professional news and announcements; a special no. (Sonderheft 1) has also been pub., to be followed by another. DM 2.30

194. MITTEILUNGEN ZUR LANDESGESCHICHTE UND VOLKSKUNDE IN DEN REGIERUNGSBEZIRKEN TRIER UND KOBLENZ [Communications on provincial history and folklore in the government districts of Trier and Koblenz]. Q (Irr.). Arbeitsgemeinschaft für Landesgeschichte und Volkskunde des Trierer Raumes, Weberbachstr. 25, Trier.

195. MITTEILUNGSBLATT ZUR RHEINHESSISCHEN LANDESKUNDE [Information bulletin for Rheinhessen studies]. Q. Arbeitsgemeinschaft rheinhessischer Heimatforscher, Historisches Seminar der Universität Mainz, Mainz. DM 2.40

MITTEILUNGSBLÄTTER DES HISTORISCHEN VEREINS FÜR HESSEN see HISTORISCHER VEREIN FÜR HESSEN, MITTEILUNGSBLÄTTER DES...

196. MITTELDEUTSCHES JAHRBUCH [Central German yearbook]. A. Ed: W. Hoffmann, Ebenhausen bei München. pub. suspended. DM 12

197. DER MONAT [The month]. M. Pub. address: Schorlemer Allee 28, Berlin-Dahlem. DM 15

198. MONATSSCHRIFT FÜR EVANGELISCHE KIRCHENGESCHICHTE DES RHEINLANDES [Monthly for the history of the Evangelical Church in the Rhineland]. B-W. Verlag Kirche in der Zeit, Cecilienallee 13, Düsseldorf. DM 10

199. MONATSSCHRIFT FÜR PASTORALTHEOLOGIE [Monthly journal for pastoral theology]. Zur Vertiefung des gesamten pfarramtlichen Wirkens [For the deepening of the entire parochial activity]. M. Vandenhoeck and Ruprecht, Theaterstr. 13, Göttingen. DM 20.80

200. MULOTSCHER FAMILIENVERBAND ALS HUGENOTTEN UND WALDENSER NACHKOMMEN, ZEITSCHRIFT DES... (Zeitschrift des Mulotschen Familienverbandes als Hugenotten und Waldenser Nachkommen) [Journal of the Mulot Family Society as Descendants of the Huguenots and the Waldensians]. Irr. W. Mulot, Walluferstr. 10, Wiesbaden. (memb.) DM 5

NACHRICHTEN. For titles beginning with "Nachrichten," followed by the name of the publishing or sponsoring institution or society, see the respective institution or society.

NACHRICHTEN AUS NIEDERSACHSENS URGESCHICHTE see NIEDERSÄCHSISCHES JAHRBUCH FÜR LANDESGESCHICHTE

201. NACHRICHTENBLATT DER DENKMALPFLEGE IN BADEN-WÜRTTEMBERG [News bulletin for the preservation of monuments in Baden-Württemberg]. Q. Kultusministerium Baden-Württemberg, c/o R. Keller, Jacob-Burckhardtstr. 3, Freiburg i. Br. nfs

202. NASSAUISCHE ANNALEN [Nassau annals]. A. Verein für Nassauische Altertumskunde und Geschichtsforschung, c/o Nassauische Landesbibliothek, Rheinstr. 55-57, Wiesbaden. (memb.) DM 10 (including subscription for Nassauische Heimatblätter)

203. NASSAUISCHE HEIMATBLÄTTER [Nassau local bulletins]. S-A. Verein für Nassauische Altertumskunde und Geschichtsforschung, c/o Nassauische Landesbibliothek, Rheinstr. 55-57, Wiesbaden. Includes annual Fundbericht des Landesamtes für kulturgeschichtliche Bodenaltertümer. (memb.) DM 10 (including subscription for Nassauische Annalen)

204. DIE NATIONALITÄTENPOLITIK MOSKAUS. NATSIONALNA POLITIKA MOSKVI [Moscow's policy concerning nationalities]. A. Ukrainische Unabhängige Assoziation der Forscher der sowjetischen Theorie und Praxis bezüglich der nationalen Probleme, c/o J. Bojko, Ayingerstr. 19, München 8. Table of contents also in English and Ukrainian. pni

NATSIONALNA POLITIKA MOSKVI see DIE NATIONALITÄTENPOLITIK MOSKAUS

205. NEUBURGER KOLLEKTANEENBLATT [Collected papers of Neuburg]. A. Heimatverein (Historischer Verein), Weveldhaus, Amalienstr. A 19, Neuburg (Donau).

206. NEUE DEUTSCHE HEFTE [New German journal]. Beiträge zur europäischen Gegenwart [Contributions to the European present]. M. Sigbert Mohn Verlag, Gütersloh. p (1) DM 3

207. DIE NEUE RUNDSCHAU [The new review]. Q. S. Fischer Verlag, Zeil 65-69, Frankfurt (Main). DM 14

208. NEUES ABENDLAND [New Occident]. Neue Folge. Jahrbuch für Politik und Geschichte [New series. Yearbook for politics and history]. Q. 1946 (1958: vol. 13). Pub. address: Tizianstr. 90, München 19. Ed: Emil Franzel. Art. on political, cultural and literary hist., and on contemporary international relations and events, mostly with a conservative approach; bk. rev. Ceased pub. in 1958. p (1) DM 3

209. NEUES ARCHIV FÜR NIEDERSACHSEN [New archives for Lower Saxony]. Landeskunde, Statistik, Landesplanung [Topography, statistics, planning]. M. Walter Dorn Verlag, Bremen-Horn, for Wirtschaftswissenschaftliche Gesellschaft zum Studium Niedersachsens, Niedersächsischer Heimatbund and Institut für Landesplanung und für niedersächsische Landeskunde. DM 12

210. NEUES MAGAZIN FÜR HANAUISCHE GESCHICHTE [New magazine for the history of Hanau]. Irr. Waisenhaus-Druckerei Hanau, for Hanauischer Geschichtsverein.

211. NEUSSER JAHRBUCH FÜR KUNST, KULTURGESCHICHTE UND HEIMATKUNDE [Neuss yearbook for art, cultural history and local studies]. A. Clemes-Sels-Museum, Im Obertor, Neuss. DM 2.80

212. NIEDERLÄNDISCHE AHNENGEMEINSCHAFT E. V., MITTEILUNGEN DER... (Mitteilungen der Niederländischen Ahnengemeinschaft e.V.) [Communications of the Society of Mutual Ancestors from the Netherlands]. Irr. (S-A). Niederländische Ahnengemeinschaft e. V., Papenhuderstr. 36, Hamburg 22. p(1) DM 2

213. NIEDERRHEINISCHES JAHRBUCH [Lower Rhine yearbook]. A.(Irr.). A. Mack, Krefeld; for Verein Linker Niederrhein e.V. pv

214. NIEDERSACHSEN [Lower Saxony]. Zeitschrift für Heimat und Kultur [Journal for homeland and culture]. Q. Niedersächsischer Heimatbund e.V., Sophienstr. 2, Hannover. DM 4.80

215. NIEDERSÄCHSISCHES JAHRBUCH FÜR LANDESGESCHICHTE [Lower Saxon yearbook for local history]. Neue Folge der "Zeitschrift des Historischen Vereins für Niedersachsen" [New series of the "Journal of the Historical Society of Lower Saxony"]. A. Historische Kommission für Niedersachsen, Am Archiv 1 (Staatsarchiv), Hannover. An appendix of each vol. contains Nachrichten aus Niedersachsens Urgeschichte; systematic register for vol. 1-25 in vol. 25. pv (DM 18-20)

216. NORDDEUTSCHE FAMILIENKUNDE [North German genealogy]. Q. Arbeitsgemeinschaft genealogischer Verlage, Nürnbergerstr. 27-29, Neustadt a.d. Aisch, for Deutsche Arbeitsgemeinschaft genealogischer Verbände und Abteilung Genealogie und Heraldik im Gesamtverein der deutschen Geschichts- und Altertumsvereine. DM 10

217. NORDFRÄNKISCHE MONATSBLÄTTER [North Franconian monthly bulletins]. Beiträge zur Geschichte, Kultur und Wirtschaft zwischen Rennsteig und Main [Contributions to the history, culture and economy between Rennsteig and Main]. M. K. Ihl und Co., Postfach 683, Coburg.

218. NORDMÄHRISCHES HEIMATBUCH [Northern Moravian local book]. A. Quellenverlag Diwisch, Steinheim a.M., for Nordmährische Kulturstelle, c/o Albert Rotter, Wabern (Hessen).

219. NORDPFÄLZER GESCHICHTSVEREIN. BEITRÄGE ZUR HEIMATGESCHICHTE [Historical Society of the Northern Palatinate. Contributions to local history]. Q. Nordpfälzer Geschichtsverein e.V., Rockenhausen.

220. NORTHEIMER HEIMATBLÄTTER [Northeim local bulletin]. Zeitschrift für Heimatforschung und Heimatpflege [Journal for research on and conservation of the homeland]. 3xy. Hahnwald Verlag, Northeim (Hannover). DM 2

221. NUMISMATISCHES NACHRICHTENBLATT [Numismatic news bulletin]. 10xy. 1952 (1960: vol. 9). Hamburger Museumsverein e.V., Holstenwall 24, Hamburg 36, for Verband der westdeutschen Münzvereine and Numismatische Kommission der Länder in der Bundesrepublik Deutschland. Ed: P. Berghaus, Domplatz 10, Münster (Westf.). News from the German numismatic soc. and reports on new findings as well as on new coins; reports on new pub., with short descriptions of contents. DM 6

222. OBERBAYERISCHES ARCHIV FÜR VATERLÄNDISCHE GESCHICHTE [Upper Bavarian archives for the history of the fatherland]. A. Historischer Verein für Oberbayern, Winzererstr. 68, Stadtarchiv, München 13. pv (DM 10 - DM 16) (memb. DM 7)

223. DIE OBERPFALZ [Upper Palatinate]. Eine Heimatzeitschrift für den ehemaligen Bayerischen Nordgau: die Oberpfalz, die freie Reichsstadt Nürnberg, das Fürstbistum Eichstätt, Egerland und die angrenzenden Gebiete [A local journal for the former Bavarian northern province: Upper Palatinate, the free imperial city of Nuremberg, the princely episcopate of Eichstätt, the county of Eger and the adjacent territories]. M. M. Lassleben, Kallmünz über Regensburg. DM 10

224. OBERPFÄLZER HEIMAT [Upper Palatine homeland]. A. Heimatkundlicher Arbeitskreis im Oberpfälzer-Wald-Verein, Prechtlstr. 31, Weiden. DM 2.85

225. OBERPOSTDIREKTION SAARBRÜCKEN, POSTGESCHICHTLICHE BLÄTTER DER... [Postal history bulletins of the Postmaster-General's office Saarbrücken]. Irr. Bezirksgruppe Saarbrücken der Gesellschaft für deutsche Postgeschichte e.V., Oberpostdirektion, Saarbrücken. (memb.) DM 4.20

226. OBERRHEINISCHER GESCHICHTSVEREIN, MITTEILUNGEN DES... (Mitteilungen des Oberrheinischen Geschichtsvereins) [Communications of the Upper Rhine Historical Society]. A. Oberrheinischer Geschichtsverein, Universitätsbibliothek, Giessen. (memb.) DM 4

227. OFFA ZEITSCHRIFT [OFFA journal]. A. Karl Wachholtz Verlag, Neumünster, for Schleswig-Holsteinisches Landesmuseum für Vor- und Frühgeschichte in Schleswig and Institut für Ur- und Frühgeschichte, Universität Kiel, Kiel. DM 20

228. OLDENBURGER BALKENSCHILD [Oldenburg fesse escutcheon]. Kleine Hefte zur Volks und Heimatkunde [Little bulletins for folklore and local studies]. Irr. Niedersächsisches Staatsarchiv, Oldenburg, for Oldenburger Landesverein für Geschichte, Natur- und Heimatkunde.

229. OLDENBURGER JAHRBUCH [Oldenburg yearbook]. A. Oldenburger Landesverein für Geschichte, Natur- und Heimatkunde, Damm 40, Oldenburg. pv

230. ORIENS CHRISTIANUS. Hefte für die Kunde des christlichen Ostens [Bulletins for studies of the Christian East]. A. O. Harrassowitz, Taunusstr. 5, Wiesbaden. DM 20

231. ORIENS EXTREMUS. Zeitschrift für Sprache, Kunst und Kultur der Länder des Fernen Ostens [Journal for the language, art and culture of the countries of the Far East]. S-A. O. Harrassowitz, Taunusstr. 5, Wiesbaden, for Seminar für Sprache und Kultur Chinas, Bornplatz 1-3, Hamburg 13. DM 28

232. DIE ORTENAU. A. Verlag des Historischen Vereins für Mittelbaden e.V., Offenburg. DM 8

233. OSNABRÜCKER MITTEILUNGEN [Osnabrück communications]. A. Verlag Meinders und Elstermann, Osnabrück, for Verein für Geschichte und Landeskunde von Osnabrück, Grosse Str. 17, Osnabrück. DM 9 (memb. free)

234. OSTBAIRISCHE GRENZMARKEN [East Bavarian border counties]. Passauer Jahrbuch für Geschichte, Kunst und Volkskunde [Passau yearbook for history, art and folklore]. A. J. Oswald, Passau, for Institut für Ostbairische Heimatforschung, Michaeligasse 13, Passau. pni

235. OSTBRIEF [Eastern letter]. M. Ostdeutsche Akademie, Herderstr. 1-11, Lüneburg. DM 12

236. OSTDEUTSCHE FAMILIENKUNDE [East German genealogy]. Zeitschrift für Familiengeschichtsforschung im deutschen Osten [Journal for genealogical research in the German East]. Q. Arbeitsgemeinschaft genealogischer Verlage, Nürnbergerstr. 27-29, Neustadt a.d. Aisch, for Deutsche Arbeitsgemeinschaft genealogischer Verbände and Abteilung Genealogie und Heraldik im Gesamtverein der deutschen Geschichts- und Altertumsvereine. DM 5

237. OSTDEUTSCHE MONATSHEFTE [East German monthly bulletins]. Kulturzeitschrift für den Osten. Aus Vergangenheit und Gegenwart [Cultural journal for the East. From past and present]. M. H. Rauschenbruch Verlag, Stollhamm (Oldb.). DM 14

238. OSTDEUTSCHER LITERATUR-ANZEIGER [East German literary gazette]. B-M. Göttinger Arbeitskreis e.V., Sternstr. 2, Göttingen. Critical bk. rev. DM 2

239. OSTERODER ZEITUNG [Osterode newspaper]. Älteste Tageszeitung im Regierungsbezirk Allenstein [Oldest newspaper in the government district Allenstein]. S-A. W. Kowalski, Mainzerstr. 17, Bacharach (Rhein).

240. OSTEUROPA [Eastern Europe]. Zeitschrift für Gegenwartsfragen des Ostens [Journal for current problems of the East]. Q. 1925 (1960: new series, vol. 10). Deutsche Gesellschaft für Osteuropakunde e.V., Leonhardsplatz 28/IV, Stuttgart S. Ed: K. Mehnert. Art. on present and recent developments in the U.S.S.R., including its Asian parts, and other East European countries, and occasionally also on Asian states; sketches of East European statesmen; survey of current internal politics in East European states and of their

current relations with Germany; rev. of bk. and art.; reports on East European studies; short biblio. of selected art., mostly from European periodicals.
DM 25 (memb. DM 17.50)

241. OSTFRIESLAND [East Frisia]. Q. G. Rautenberg Verlag, Am Pferdemarkt, Leer (Ostfriesland). p(1) DM 4.50

242. OSTKIRCHLICHE STUDIEN [Eastern church studies]. Q. 1952 (1960: vol. 9). Augustinus-Verlag, Grabenberg 2, Würzburg, for Arbeitsgemeinschaft der deutschen Augustinerordensprovinz zum Studium der Ostkirche. Ed: H. M. Biedermann OESA, Steinbachtal 2a, Würzburg. Art. on the hist. of the Eastern churches (the early Byzantine Church, the Eastern Orthodox Church and the Eastern Rite of the Roman Catholic Church), with emphasis on the hist. development of ritualistic and doctrinal divergences between Orthodoxy and Catholicism, and on present ecumenical strivings; bk. rev.; rev. of Russian theological periodicals, with sum. of art.; biblio. of bk. and art., arranged by subject.
DM 20

243. PAIDEUMA. Mitteilungen zur Kulturkunde [Communications on cultural studies]. Irr. Frobenius-Institut an der Johann Wolfgang Goethe-Universität Frankfurt (Main), for Deutsche Gesellschaft für Kulturmorphologie e.V., Liebigstr. 41, Frankfurt (Main). (memb.) DM 20

244. PFÄLZER HEIMAT [Homeland Palatinate]. Zeitschrift für pfälzische Landeskunde, zugleich Mitteilungsblatt für Archivpflege, Bibliotheks- und Museumswesen in der Pfalz [Journal for the geography of the Palatinate, being also an information bulletin for archives, libraries and museums in the Palatinate]. Q. Jaegersche Buchdruckerei GmbH, Korngasse 28, Speyer a. Rh., for Pfälzische Gesellschaft zur Förderung der Wissenschaften. DM 6

245. PFÄLZISCHE FAMILIEN- UND WAPPENKUNDE [Genealogy and heraldry of the Palatinate]. Q. Arbeitsgemeinschaft für Pfälzische Familien- und Wappenkunde e.V., Oggersheimerstr. 10, Ludwigshafen (Rhein). DM 12

246. PFÄLZISCHE POSTGESCHICHTE [Postal history of the Palatinate]. Postgeschichtliche Blätter [Bulletins for postal history]. Irr. Gesellschaft für deutsche Postgeschichte e.V., Bezirksgruppe Neustadt (Weinstrasse).
(memb.) DM 4.20

247. DIE POLITISCHE MEINUNG [Political opinion]. Monatshefte für Fragen der Zeit [Monthly for current questions]. M. Verlag Staat und Gesellschaft GmbH, Meckenheimerstr. 62, Bonn. p(1) DM 1.50

248. POLITISCHE STUDIEN [Political studies]. M. Hochschule für Politische Wissenschaften, Von-der-Tann-Str. 2, München 22. DM 20

249. POSTGESCHICHTE AM NIEDERRHEIN [Postal history on the Lower Rhine]. Irr. Gesellschaft für deutsche Postgeschichte e.V., Bezirksgruppe Düsseldorf, Oberpostdirektion, Düsseldorf. (memb.) DM 4.80

250. POSTGESCHICHTLICHE BLÄTTER [Bulletins of postal history]. Irr. Gesellschaft für deutsche Postgeschichte e.V., Bezirksgruppe Karlsruhe, Oberpostdirektion, Karlsruhe. (memb.) DM 3.60

251. POSTGESCHICHTLICHE BLÄTTER [Bulletins of postal history]. Irr. Gesellschaft für deutsche Postgeschichte, Bezirksgruppe Koblenz, Postamt, Bad Kreuznach. (memb.) DM 3.60

252. POSTGESCHICHTLICHE BLÄTTER AUS TRIER [Postal history bulletins from Trier]. Irr. Verlag E. Wagner, Trier, for Bezirksgruppe Trier der Gesellschaft für deutsche Postgeschichte e.V. (memb.) DM 3.60

253. POSTGESCHICHTLICHE BLÄTTER AUS WÜRTTEMBERG [Postal history bulletins from Württemberg]. Irr. Gesellschaft für deutsche Postgeschichte e.V., Bezirksgruppen Stuttgart und Tübingen. memb. free

POSTGESCHICHTLICHE BLÄTTER DER GESELLSCHAFT FÜR DEUTSCHE POSTGESCHICHTE E. V., BEZIRKSGRUPPE DORTMUND see GESELLSCHAFT FÜR DEUTSCHE POSTGESCHICHTE E.V., BEZIRKSGRUPPE DORTMUND, POSTGESCHICHTLICHE BLÄTTER DER...

POSTGESCHICHTLICHE BLÄTTER DER OBERPOSTDIREKTION SAARBRÜCKEN see OBERPOSTDIREKTION SAARBRÜCKEN, POSTGESCHICHTLICHE BLÄTTER DER...

254. POSTGESCHICHTLICHE BLÄTTER HAMBURG [Hamburg bulletins of postal history]. Irr. Gesellschaft für deutsche Postgeschichte e.V., Bezirksgruppe Hamburg, Postmuseum am Stephansplatz 1, Hamburg 36. (memb.) DM 3.60

255. POSTGESCHICHTLICHE BLÄTTER "WESER-EMS" ["Weser-Ems" postal history bulletins]. Irr. Gesellschaft für deutsche Postgeschichte e.V., Bezirksgruppe Bremen, Lagerstr. 139, Bremen. (memb.) DM 3.60

PRACTICE IN GENEALOGICAL RESEARCH see PRAKTISCHE FORSCHUNGSHILFE

256. PRÄHISTORISCHE ZEITSCHRIFT [Prehistorical journal]. Irr. 1909 (1959: vol. 37). Walter de Gruyter und Co., Genthinerstr. 13, Berlin W 35. Ed: W. Unverzagt, Sybelstr. 41, Berlin-Charlottenburg. Art. on culture, art and archaeology in Europe from prehist. times to the early Middle Ages; bk. rev.; report on excavations and research; illus. DM 56

257. PRAKTISCHE FORSCHUNGSHILFE [Practical aid in research]. PRACTICE IN GENEALOGICAL RESEARCH. Archiv für Sippenforschung und alle verwandten Gebiete [Archives for genealogical research and all related fields]. Q. Verlag C.A. Starke, Limburg (Lahn). p (1) DM 1.50

258. PROBLEMES SOVIETIQUES [Soviet problems]. S-A. Inst. for the Study of the U.S.S.R., Mannhardtstr. 6, München 22. DM 8

259. PROBLEMS OF THE PEOPLES OF THE USSR. Q. League for the Liberation of the Peoples of the U.S.S.R. Ed. address: Beichstr. 8-9, München 23. p (1) DM 2 / $0.50

260. QUARTÄR [Quaternary]. **Jahrbuch für Erforschung des Eiszeitalters** und der Steinzeit. Annales pour l'Etude du Quaternaire et de l'Age de Pierre. Annals for the Story of the Pleistocene and Associated Stone Age Cultures. A. 1949 (1958: vol. 10). L. Röhrscheid Verlag, Bonn. Ed: L.F. Zotz. Art. on findings from the Stone Age and the Pleistocene and its culture; bk. rev.; reports on excavations; in German and occasionally in English or French. pv (DM 16 - 49.50)

QUELLEN UND FORSCHUNGEN AUS ITALIENISCHEN ARCHIVEN UND BIBLIOTHEKEN see section on Italy

261. QUELLEN UND FORSCHUNGEN ZUR OSTFRIESISCHEN FAMILIEN- UND WAPPENKUNDE [Sources and researches in East Frisian genealogy and heraldry]. Irr. (M). Ostfriesische Landschaft, Arbeitsgruppe Familienkunde und Heraldik, Aurich. p (1) DM 0.50

262. RAVENSBERGER BLÄTTER [Ravensberg bulletins]. A. Historischer Verein für die Grafschaft Ravensberg, Wertherstr. 3, Bielefeld.

RECORDER OF ORDER RESEARCHES see section on International Periodicals

263. DER REMTER [The refectory]. Zeitschrift für Kultur und Politik in Osteuropa [Journal for politics and culture in Eastern Europe]. B-M. Evangelisches Verlagswerk, Stuttgart. DM 12

264. RHEINISCH-WESTFÄLISCHE ZEITSCHRIFT FÜR VOLKSKUNDE [Rhenish-Westphalian journal for folklore]. Q (S-A) . Volkskundliche Abteilung des Instituts für geschichtliche Landeskunde der Rheinlande an der Universität Bonn, Poppelsdorfer Allee 25, Bonn, and Volkskundliche Kommission des Landschaftsverbandes Westfalen - Lippe, Münster (Westf.). DM 12

265. RHEINISCHE VIERTELJAHRSBLÄTTER [Rhenish quarterly bulletins]. Q. L. Röhrscheid Verlag, Am Hof 36, Bonn, for Institut für geschichtliche Landeskunde der Rheinlande, Poppelsdorfer Allee 25, Bonn. DM 20

266. RHEINISCHES JAHRBUCH FÜR VOLKSKUNDE [Rhineland yearbook for folklore]. A. Ferdinand Dümmlers Verlag, Kaiserstr. 33-37, Bonn, for Rheinische Vereinigung für Volkskunde, Bonn. DM 11.80

267. RHEINISCHES LANDESMUSEUM IN BONN UND DER VEREIN VON ALTERTUMSFREUNDEN IM RHEINLANDE, BONNER JAHRBÜCHER DES... (Bonner Jahrbücher des Rheinischen Landesmuseums in Bonn und des Vereins von Altertumsfreunden im Rheinlande) [Bonn yearbooks of the Rhineland Provincial Museum in Bonn and the Society of the Friends of Archaeology in the Rhineland]. A. Butzon und Bercker Verlag, Kevelaer (Rhld.), for Rheinisches Landesmuseum Colmantstr. 16, Bonn, and Verein von Altertumsfreunden im Rheinlande, Neustr. 11, Kevelaer (Rhld.). pv (c. DM 20 - 28)

268. ROMERIKE BERGE [Romerike mountains]. Zeitschrift für Heimatpflege, Volkskunde, Kunst, Museumswesen, Denkmalspflege und Naturschutz im Bergischen Land [Journal for homeland preservation, folklore, art, museums, preservation of monuments and nature in the Berg country]. Q. L. Reinmöller, Montanusstr. 8, Burscheid. DM 8

269. RÖMISCH-GERMANISCHES ZENTRALMUSEUM MAINZ, JAHRBUCH DES... (Jahrbuch des Römisch-Germanischen Zentralmuseums Mainz) [Yearbook of the Roman-Germanic Central Museum of Mainz]. A. Römisch-Germanisches Zentralmuseum, Kurfürstliches Schloss, Mainz. DM 30

270. RÖMISCHE QUARTALSSCHRIFT FÜR CHRISTLICHE ALTERTUMSKUNDE UND KIRCHENGESCHICHTE [Roman quarterly for christian antiquity and church history]. S-A. 1905 (1959: vol. 54). Herder Verlag, Hermann-Herder-Str. 4, Freiburg i.Br. Ed: A.Schucherdt, E.Kirschbaum, S.J., Via

della Sagrestia 17, Città del Vaticano. Art. on the hist. of the Roman Catholic Church from the earliest times to the present; bk. rev.; illus. DM 32

271. RUPERTO-CAROLA. Irr.(S-A). Gerhard Hinz, Alte Universität, Heidelberg, for Vereinigung der Freunde der Studentenschaft der Universität Heidelberg e.V., Heidelberg. Illus. DM 12

272. SAARBRÜCKER HEFTE [Saarbrücken pamphlets]. A. Minerva-Verlag, Futterstr. 25, Saarbrücken, for Kultur- und Schulamt der Stadt Saarbrücken. DM 6

273. SAECULUM. Jahrbuch für Universalgeschichte [Yearbook for universal history]. Q. 1950 (1960: vol. 11). Karl Alber Verlag, Johanniterstr. 4, Freiburg i. Br. Ed: O Köhler, Hermann-Herder-Str. 4, Freiburg i. Br. Art. on hist., historiography, philosophy of hist., mythology and world cultures. DM 28

SAMMELBLATT DES HISTORISCHEN VEREINS INGOLSTADT see HISTORISCHER VEREIN INGOLSTADT, SAMMELBLATT DES...

274. SAVIGNY-STIFTUNG FÜR RECHTSGESCHICHTE, ZEITSCHRIFT DER... [Journal of the Savigny Foundation for Legal History]. A. 1880 (1960: vol. 77). Verlag Hermann Böhlaus Nachfolger, Meyerstr. 50a, Weimar, D.D.R. Each vol. contains the following three separately-bound sections: a) Germanistische Abteilung [Section for German law]. Ed: Hans Thieme, Lugostr. 10, Freiburg i. Br. (for art.), Karl S. Bader, Geisingen (Baden) (for rev.). Art. on the hist. of Germanic law, with emphasis on the medieval and earlier periods; bk. rev.; list of dissertations with descriptions of contents, arranged by univ.; list of bk. received; professional and univ. news. b) Kanonistische Abteilung [Section for Canon Law]. Ed: Hans Erich Feine, Biesingerstr. 9, Tübingen (for Roman Catholic Canon Law), and Johannes Heckel, St. Paulsplatz 9, München 15 (for Protestant Church Law). Art. on the hist. of Church Law, both Roman Catholic and Protestant; bk. rev.; list of dissertations; list of bk. received; professional and univ. news. c) Romanistische Abteilung [Section for Roman law]. Ed: Wolfgang Kunkel, Bergstr. 79, Heidelberg (for art.), and Max Kaser, Prinz-Eugen-Str. 12, Münster (Westf.) (for rev.). Art. on the hist. of Roman, Greek and Egyptian law; bk. rev.; list of dissertations; list of bk. received; professional and univ. news. Each section contains a table of contents for all the three sections of the vol. pv

275. SCHAU-INS-LAND. A. Breisgau-Geschichtsverein Schau-ins-Land, Mozartstr. 30, Freiburg i. Br. (memb.) DM 5

276. SCHLESIEN [Silesia]. Niederschlesien - Oberschlesien - Sudetenschlesien. Kunst - Wissenschaft - Volkstum [Lower Silesia - Upper Silesia - Sudeten Silesia. Art - science - ethnological questions]. Q. Pub. address: Herrnstr. 1, Würzburg. DM 12

277. SCHLESISCHE FRIEDRICH-WILHELMS-UNIVERSITÄT ZU BRESLAU, JAHRBUCH DER... (Jahrbuch der Schlesischen Friedrich-Wilhelms-Universität zu Breslau) [Yearbook of the Silesian Frederick William University at Breslau]. A. Holzner Verlag, Würzburg, for Göttinger Arbeitskreis, Sternstr. 2, Göttingen.

278. SCHMOLLERS JAHRBUCH FÜR GESETZGEBUNG, VERWALTUNG UND VOLKSWIRTSCHAFT [Schmoller's yearbook for legislation, administration

and economics]. B-M. Duncker und Humblot Verlag, Geranienstr. 2, Berlin-Lichterfelde-West. DM 80

279. SCHOLASTIK [Scholasticism]. Vierteljahresschrift für Theologie und Philosophie [Quarterly for theology and philosophy]. Q. Verlag Herder, Hermann-Herder-Str. 4, Freiburg i. Br. DM 34

280. DAS SCHÖNE ALLGÄU [Beautiful Allgäu]. Q. Volkswirtschaftlicher Verlag GmbH, Postfach 221, Kempten (Allgäu). DM 6.40

281. SCHÖNERE HEIMAT [More beautiful homeland]. Erbe und Gegenwart [Inheritance and present]. Q. Bayerischer Verein für Heimatpflege e.V., Ludwigstr. 14, München 22. (memb.) DM 8

282. SCHÖNHENGSTER JAHRBUCH [Schönhengst yearbook]. A. Kulturstelle des Landschaftsrates Schönhengstgau, c/o Rudolf Pechhold, Göppingen (Württ.). DM 2.90

SCHRIFTEN DES VEREINS FÜR GESCHICHTE DES BODENSEES UND SEINER UMGEBUNG see VEREIN FÜR GESCHICHTE DES BODENSEES UND SEINER UMGEBUNG, SCHRIFTEN DES...

283. SCHRIFTTUMSBERICHTE ZUR GENEALOGIE UND IHREN NACHBARGEBIETEN [Reports on literature pertaining to genealogy and related disciplines]. Irr. 1951 (1951-1959: vol. 1, no. 1-12). Verlag Degener und Co., Neustadt a.d. Aisch, for Deutsche Arbeitsgemeinschaft genealogischer Verbände. Ed: H. Mitgau, Kirchweg 24, Göttingen. Biblio. on genealogy and related fields, each no. being devoted to one aspect. Distributed as supplement to local pub. in the field. pni

284. SCHWÄBISCHE BLÄTTER FÜR VOLKSBILDUNG UND HEIMATPFLEGE [Swabian bulletins for people's education and homeland preservation]. Q. Pub. address: Prinzregentenstr. 11, Augsburg. p(1) DM 0.70

285. DIE SIEBEN SCHWABEN [The seven Swabians]. Q. Volkswirtschaftlicher Verlag GmbH, Postfach 221, Kempten (Allgäu). DM 6.40

286. DER SIEBENSTERN [The starflower]. B-M. Fichtelgebirgsverein e.V., Altstadt 36, Hof. memb. free

287. SIEGERLAND [The Sieg country]. 3xy. Siegerländer Heimatverein, Oberes Schloss (Museum), Siegen. (memb.) DM 5

288. SOCIOLOGUS. Zeitschrift für empirische Soziologie, sozialpsychologische und ethnologische Forschung. Journal for Empirical Sociology, Social Psychology and Ethnic Researches. S-A. Verlag Duncker und Humblot, Geranienstr. 2, Berlin-Lichterfelde. English sum. DM 24

289. SOESTER ZEITSCHRIFT [Soest journal]. A. Westfälische Verlagsbuchhandlung Mocker und Jahn, Soest, for Verein für die Geschichte von Soest und Börde. (memb.) DM 5

290. SOWJETSTUDIEN [Soviet studies]. S-A. Inst. for the Study of the U.S.S.R., Mannhardtstr. 6, München 22. DM 8

291. SOZIALE WELT [Social world]. Zeitschrift für Wissenschaft und Praxis des sozialen Lebens [Journal for the science and practice of social life]. Q.. Otto Schwartz und Co., Annastr. 7, Göttingen, for Arbeitsgemeinschaft sozialwissenschaftlicher Institute. DM 28

292. SPESSART. Zeitschrift für Wandern, Heimatgeschichte und Naturwissen [Journal for hiking, local history and nature studies]. M. Pub. address: Pfaffengasse 11, Aschaffenburg. DM 4.80

STADEN JAHRBUCH see section on Brazil

293. STADER GESCHICHTS- UND HEIMATVEREIN, MITTEILUNGEN DES... (Mitteilungen des Stader Geschichts- und Heimatvereins) [Communications of the Stade Historical and Local Society]. Q. Stader Geschichts- und Heimatverein, Eisenbahnstr. 21, Stade (Niederelbe).

294. STADER JAHRBUCH [Stade yearbook]. A. Stader Geschichts- und Heimatverein, Eisenbahnstr. 21, Stade (Niederelbe). DM 5

295. DAS STEINKREUZ [The stone cross]. Mitteilungsblatt der Deutschen Steinkreuzforschung [Information bulletin of German stone cross research]. S-A. L. Wittmann, Denisstr. 30, Nürnberg. (memb.) DM 5

296. DIE STIMME FRANKENS [The voice of Franconia]. Zeitschrift für fränkische Kultur, Volkstum, Landeskunde und Volksbildung [Journal for Franconian culture, national characteristics, topographical studies and popular education]. B-M. Lorenz Spindler Verlag, Spitalgasse 2-6, Nürnberg. DM 5

297. STUDIEN UND MITTEILUNGEN ZUR GESCHICHTE DES BENEDIKTINER-ORDENS UND SEINER ZWEIGE [Studies and communications on the history of the Benedictine Order and its branches]. S-A. 1880 (1959: vol. 70). Bayerische Benediktiner Akademie, Abtei St. Bonifaz, Karlstr. 34, München 2. Ed: **P. R. Bauerreiss O.S.B.** Art. on the medieval hist. of Benedictine monastries, and on monasticism and the Church in Germany; bk. rev.; biblio. of bk. and art. pv

298. STUDIES ON THE SOVIET UNION. Q. Inst. for the Study of the U.S.S.R., Mannhardtstr. 6, München 22. Supersedes Caucasian Review, East Turkic Review, Ukrainian Review, Vestnik and Belorussian Review, pub. separately up to 1961. DM 25 / $6

299. STUDIUM GENERALE. Zeitschrift für die Einheit der Wissenschaften im Zusammenhang ihrer Begriffsbildungen und Forschungsmethoden [Journal for the unity of the sciences in the interrelation of their concept formation and research methods]. M. Springer Verlag, Heidelberger Platz 3, Berlin-Wilmersdorf. DM 78

300. SUDETENLAND. Böhmen - Mähren - Schlesien. Kunst - Literatur - Volkstum - Wissenschaft [Bohemia - Moravia - Silesia. Art - literature - ethnological questions - science]. Q. V. Aschenbrenner, Rückertstr. 6, Wiesbaden. DM 12

301. SUDHOFFS ARCHIV FÜR GESCHICHTE DER MEDIZIN UND DER NATURWISSENSCHAFTEN [Sudhoff's archives for the history of medicine and the natural sciences]. Q. 1908 (1960: vol. 44). Franz Steiner Verlag, Bahnhofstr. 39, Wiesbaden. Ed. board: Edith Heischkel, Hans Schimank, Johannes Steudel,

Rudolph Zaunick. Art. on the hist. of the natural sciences and medicine, and on museum holdings; bk. rev.; in German and occasionally in English; illus. Pub. suspended from 1945 to 1952. DM 48 / $11.43

302. SÜDOSTDEUTSCHE VIERTELJAHRESBLÄTTER [Southeast German quarterly]. Q. Südostdeutsches Kulturwerk, Güllstr. 7, München 15. DM 8

303. SÜDOSTDEUTSCHES ARCHIV [Southeast German archives]. A. 1958 (1959: vol. 2). R. Oldenbourg Verlag, Rosenheimerstr. 145, München, for Südostdeutsche Historische Kommission. Ed. board: H. Steinacker, B. Saria, Güllstr. 7, München 15. Art. on the political and cultural hist. of Germans in Southeast Europe from the earliest times to the present; bk. rev.; illus. DM 15

304. SÜDOSTFORSCHUNGEN [Southeastern researches]. Internationale Zeitschrift für Geschichte, Kultur und Landeskunde Südosteuropas [International journal for the history, culture and geography of Southeast Europe]. S-A. 1936 (1959: vol. 18). R. Oldenbourg Verlag, Rosenheimerstr. 145, München, for Südostinstitut, Güllstr. 7, München 15. Art. on the hist., culture and geography of Southeast Europe; rev. of bk. and periodicals, arranged by area; reports on research; in German, English or French; illus. DM 40

305. SÜDTIROL IN WORT UND BILD [South Tyrol in word and picture]. Q. Bergisel-Verlag, München, for Kulturwerk für Südtirol, Karlsplatz 11, München 2. DM 11 / L 1600

306. SÜDWESTDEUTSCHE BLÄTTER FÜR FAMILIEN- UND WAPPENKUNDE [Southwest German bulletins for genealogy and heraldry]. 3-4 x y. Aegis-Verlag, Gideon-Bacherstr. 3, Ulm. p (1) DM 1.75

307. DAS TOR [The gate]. Düsseldorfer Heimatblätter [Düsseldorf local bulletins]. M. "Düsseldorfer Jonges" e.V., Golzheimerstr. 124, Düsseldorf. DM 24

308. TRADITION. Zeitschrift für Firmengeschichte und Unternehmerbiographie [Journal for the history of firms and the biographies of entrepreneurs]. Q. 1956 (1960: vol. 5). August Lutzeyer GmbH, Lichtentalerstr. 61, Baden-Baden. Ed: Wilhelm Treue, Schildgraben 3, Göttingen. Art. on modern business and entrepreneurial hist., pertaining mostly to Germany; news and reports on business archives councils; illus. DM 24

309. TRIBUS. Irr. Württembergischer Verein für Handelsgeographie e.V., for Linden-Museum, Museum für Länder- und Völkerkunde, Hegelplatz 1, Stuttgart N. pni

310. TRIERER GESELLSCHAFT FÜR NÜTZLICHE FORSCHUNGEN, VIERTELJAHRESBLÄTTER DER... [Quarterly bulletins of the Trier Society for Useful Researches]. Q. Stadtbibliothek, Brotstr. 33, Trier. DM 6

311. TRIERER THEOLOGISCHE ZEITSCHRIFT [Trier theological journal]. B-M. Paulus-Verlag, Fleischstr. 64-65, Trier, for Katholisch-Theologische Fakultät, Trier. DM 15

312. TRIERER ZEITSCHRIFT FÜR GESCHICHTE UND KUNST DES TRIERER LANDES UND SEINER NACHBARGEBIETE [Trier journal for the history and art of the Trier country and its neighboring areas]. Irr.(S-A). Paulinus Verlag, Fleischstr. 64-65, Trier, for Rheinisches Landesmuseum Trier, Ostallee 44, Trier. pv

313. TRIERISCHES JAHRBUCH [Trier yearbook]. A. Paulinus-Verlag, Fleischstr. 64-65, Trier, for Stadtbibliothek Trier and Verein "Trierisch." pv (c. DM 3.60)

314. TÜBINGER BLÄTTER [Tübingen bulletins]. A. Schwäbisches Tageblatt, Tübingen, for Bürger- und Verkehrsverein Tübingen e.V. DM 2

315. TÜBINGER THEOLOGISCHE QUARTALSCHRIFT [Tübingen theological quarterly]. Q. Schwabenverlag, Landhausstr. 25, Stuttgart O, for Katholisch-Theologische Fakultät der Universität Tübingen, Tübingen. DM 12

316. TUTTLINGER HEIMATBLÄTTER [Tuttlingen local bulletins]. A. Heimatverlag Tuttlingen, Heimatmuseum, Donaustr. 50, Tuttlingen (Württ.).

317. UKRAINIAN REVIEW. A. Inst. for the Study of the U.S.S.R., Mannhardtstr. 6, München 22. Superseded in 1961 by Studies on the Soviet Union. DM 4

318. UKRAINSKY ZBIRNYK [Ukrainian review]. A. Inst. for the Study of the U.S.S.R., Mannhardtstr. 6, München 22. Ceased pub. in 1961. DM 3

319. ULM UND OBERSCHWABEN [Ulm and Upper Swabia]. Zeitschrift für Geschichte und Kunst [Journal for history and art]. A. Verein für Kunst und Altertum in Ulm and Oberschwaben, Neue Str. 92-96, Ulm (Donau). pv

UNGARISCHE JAHRBÜCHER see URAL-ALTAISCHE JAHRBÜCHER

320. UNIVERSITAS. Zeitschrift für Wissenschaft, Kunst und Literatur [Journal for science, art and literature]. M. Wissenschaftliche Verlagsgesellschaft mbH, Postfach 40, Stuttgart S. p (1) DM 2.50

321. UNIVERSITAS SARAVIENSIS, ANNALES... (Annales Universitatis Saraviensis). Q. Schriftleitung für wissenschaftliche Veröffentlichungen, Philosophische Fakultät, Universität des Saarlandes, Saarbrücken 15. DM 10

322. UNSERE DIÖZESE IN VERGANGENHEIT UND GEGENWART [Our diocese, past and present]. A. Verein für Heimatkunde im Bistum Hildesheim, Hildesheim. (memb.) DM 5

323. UNTERRICHTSHILFE FÜR DAS SCHWABACH-ROTHER LAND [Educational help for the country of Schwabach-Roth]. Irr. Pub. address: Zöllnerstr. 12/I, Schwabach. p (1) DM 0.70

324. URAL-ALTAISCHE JAHRBÜCHER [Ural-Altaic yearbooks]. Q(S-A). 1921 (1958: vol. 30). O. Harrassowitz, Taunusstr. 5, Wiesbaden, for Finnisch-ugrisches Seminar der Universität Göttingen, Prinzenstr. 21, Göttingen. Art. on the hist. of the languages and cultures of the Finno-Ugric nations; reports on the activities of the seminar; bk. rev.; biblio. of bk. and art. with short descriptions of contents, arranged by subject; in German, English or French; illus. Formerly pub. under the title: Ungarische Jahrbücher. DM 40

325. VEREIN FÜR GESCHICHTE DER STADT NÜRNBERG, MITTEILUNGEN DES... (Mitteilungen des Vereins für Geschichte der Stadt Nürnberg) [Communications of the Society for the History of the City of Nuremberg]. A. Verein für Geschichte der Stadt Nürnberg, Bärenschanzstr. 34, Nürnberg. DM 6

326. VEREIN FÜR GESCHICHTE DES BODENSEES UND SEINER UMGEBUNG, SCHRIFTEN DES... (Schriften des Vereins für Geschichte des Bodensees und seiner Umgebung) [Publications of the Society for the History of Lake Constance and its Environs]. A. Jan Thorbecke Verlag, Lindau, for Verein für Geschichte des Bodensees und seiner Umgebung. DM 11.50

327. VEREIN FÜR GESCHICHTE UND LANDESKUNDE ZU BAD HOMBURG V.D. HÖHE, MITTEILUNGEN DES... (Mitteilungen des Vereins für Geschichte und Landeskunde zu Bad Homburg v.d. Höhe) [Communications of the Society for History and Knowledge of the Country in Bad Homburg v.d. Höhe]. Irr. Verein für Geschichte und Landeskunde, Bad Homburg v.d. Höhe. nfs

328. VEREIN FÜR HAMBURGISCHE GESCHICHTE, ZEITSCHRIFT DES... (Zeitschrift des Vereins für Hamburgische Geschichte) [Journal of the Society for the History of Hamburg]. A. Hans Christians Verlag, Kleine Theaterstr. 10, Hamburg 36, for Verein für Hamburgische Geschichte, Staatsarchiv, Rathaus, Hamburg 1. pv (c. DM 9 - 22.50)

329. VEREIN FÜR HESSISCHE GESCHICHTE UND LANDESKUNDE, ZEITSCHRIFT DES... (Zeitschrift des Vereins für Hessische Geschichte und Landeskunde) [Journal of the Society of Hessian History and Geography]. A. Bärenreiter Verlag, Kassel-Wilhelmshöhe, for Verein für Hessische Geschichte und Landeskunde, Kassel. DM 15

330. VEREIN FÜR LÜBECKISCHE GESCHICHTE UND ALTERTUMSKUNDE, ZEITSCHRIFT DES... (Zeitschrift des Vereins für Lübeckische Geschichte und Altertumskunde) [Journal of the Society for the History and Archaeology of Lübeck]. Irr. Verlag M. Schmidt-Römhild, Mengstr. 16, Lübeck. DM 12

331. VEREIN FÜR ORTS- UND HEIMATKUNDE IN DER GRAFSCHAFT MARK, JAHRBUCH DES... (Jahrbuch des Vereins für Orts- und Heimatkunde in der Grafschaft Mark) [Yearbook of the Society for Rural and Local Studies in the Mark county]. A. Verein für Orts- und Heimatkunde in der Grafschaft Mark, Husemannstr. 12, Witten a.d. Ruhr. DM 7.50

VERHANDLUNGEN. For titles beginning with "Verhandlungen," followed by the name of the publishing or sponsoring institution or society, see the respective institution or society.

332. VESTISCHES JAHRBUCH [Vest yearbuch]. Zeitschrift der Vereine für Orts- und Heimatkunde in Vest Recklinghausen [Journal of the societies for rural and local studies in Vest Recklinghausen]. A. Verlagsdruckerei Bongers, Recklinghausen. DM 4

333. VESTNIK [Journal]. S-A. Inst. for the Study of the U.S.S.R., Mannhardtstr. 6, München 22. Superseded in 1961 by Studies on the Soviet Union. DM 8

VIERTELJAHRESBLÄTTER DER TRIERER GESELLSCHAFT FÜR NÜTZLICHE FORSCHUNGEN see TRIERER GESELLSCHAFT FÜR NÜTZLICHE FORSCHUNGEN, VIERTELJAHRESBLÄTTER DER...

334. VIERTELJAHRESHEFTE FÜR ZEITGESCHICHTE [Quarterly journal for contemporary history]. Q. 1953 (1960: vol. 8). Deutsche Verlags-Anstalt, Stuttgart, for Institut für Zeitgeschichte, Möhlstr. 26, München 27. Ed: Hans

Rothfels, Theodor Eschenburg, Helmut Krausnick (manag. ed.). Art. on German and European hist., pertaining mostly to the period 1918 - 1945, and occasionally also on world hist.; extensive doc. section; critical source studies; biblio. of bk. and art., classified by subject and area. DM 24

335. VIERTELJAHRSCHRIFT FÜR SOZIAL- UND WIRTSCHAFTSGESCHICHTE [Quarterly for social and economic history]. Q. 1903 (1959: vol. 45). F. Steiner Verlag, Bahnhofstr. 39, Wiesbaden. Ed: H. Aubin. Art. on social and economic hist. and the hist. of law, with emphasis on Germany; rev. art.; bk. rev. p (1) DM 12 / $2.86

336. WAFFEN- UND KOSTÜMKUNDE [Studies of weapons and costumes]. S-A. 1897 (1960: no vol. indic.). Deutscher Kunstverlag, München, for Gesellschaft für historische Waffen- und Kostümkunde. Ed: A. von Reitzenstein, Bayer. Nationalmuseum, Prinzregentenstr. 3, München; M. Braun-Ronsdorf, Zentralinstitut für Kunstgeschichte, Meiserstr. 10, München. Art. on weapons and costumes; reports on holdings of museums; illus. DM 20

337. WEHRKUNDE [Military science]. Zeitschrift für alle Wehrfragen [Journal for all military questions]. M. Gesellschaft für Wehrkunde, Marsstr. 12/II, München 2. p (1) DM 2

338. WEHRWISSENSCHAFTLICHE RUNDSCHAU [Survey of military science]. Zeitschrift für die europäische Sicherheit [Journal for European security]. M. 1951 (1959: vol. 9). Arbeitskreis für Wehrforschung, Feldbergstr. 49, Frankfurt (Main). Ed: A. Philippi, Postfach 1725, Karlsruhe. Art. on the hist. and contemporary problems of German military science and on foreign military affairs; bk. rev.; occasional supplements ("Beihefte"), containing monographs on military hist. and modern strategy.
DM 21.60 (supplements: pv: c. DM 3.60-6.75 each)

339. DIE WELT ALS GESCHICHTE [The world as history]. Eine Zeitschrift für Universalgeschichte [A journal for universal history]. Q. 1935 (1960: vol. 20). W. Kohlhammer, Urbanstr. 12-14, Stuttgart O. Ed: Hans Erich Stier, Domplatz 20, Münster (Westf.); Fritz Ernst, Heiligenbergstr. 19, Heidelberg. Art. on world hist. DM 10.80

DIE WELT DES ISLAMS see section on the Netherlands

340. DIE WELT DES ORIENTS [The world of the Orient]. Wissenschaftliche Beiträge zur Kunde des Morgenlandes [Academic contributions to Oriental studies]. Irr. Vandenhoeck und Ruprecht, Theaterstr. 13, Göttingen. DM 8

341. WERTHEIMER JAHRBUCH FÜR GESCHICHTE, VOLKS- UND HEIMATKUNDE DES MAIN-TAUBERLANDES [Wertheim yearbook for history, folklore and local studies of the Main-Tauber country]. A. Historischer Verein Wertheim e.V., Wertheim (Main).

342. WESTDEUTSCHE GESELLSCHAFT FÜR FAMILIENKUNDE E.V., MITTEILUNGEN DER...(Mitteilungen der Westdeutschen Gesellschaft für Familienkunde e.V.) [Communications of the West German Society for Genealogy]. Q. Westdeutsche Gesellschaft für Familienkunde e.V., Gereonskloster 12, Köln.
DM 12

343. WESTFALEN [Westphalia]. Hefte für Geschichte, Kunst und Volkskunde [Journal for history, art and folklore]. 3 x y. Aschendorffsche Verlags-

buchhandlung, Gallitzinstr. 13, Münster (Westf.), for Verein für Geschichte und Altertumskunde Westfalens, Landesmuseum für Kunst und Kulturgeschichte, and Landeskonservator von Westfalen-Lippe. pv (c. DM 15) (memb. free)

344. WESTFÄLISCHE FORSCHUNGEN [Westphalian researches]. Mitteilungen des Provinzial-Instituts für westfälische Landes- und Volkskunde [Communications of the Provincial Institute for Westphalian Geography and Ethnography]. A. Aschendorffsche Verlagsbuchhandlung, Gallitzinstr. 13, Münster (Westf.). pv

345. WESTFÄLISCHE ZEITSCHRIFT [Westphalian journal]. A. Verein für Geschichte und Altertumskunde Westfalens, Fürstenbergstr. 14, Münster (Westf.). DM 12 (memb. DM 9)

346. WETTERAUER GESCHICHTSBLÄTTER [Wetterau historical bulletins]. Beiträge zur Geschichte und Landeskunde [Contributions to history and geography]. A. C. Bindernagel Verlag, Postfach 145, Friedberg (Hessen), for Friedberger Geschichtsverein, Heimatverein Bad Nauheim, and Geschichtsverein für Butzbach und Umgebung. DM 5

347. DER WORMSGAU [The district of worms]. Zeitschrift der Kulturinstitute der Stadt Worms und des Altertumsvereins Worms [Journal of the cultural institutes of the city of Worms and the Worms Antiquity Association]. S-A. Städtische Kulturinstitute, Weckerlingplatz 7, Worms. (memb.) DM 12

348. WORT UND WAHRHEIT [Word and truth]. Monatsschrift für Religion und Kultur [Monthly for religion and culture]. 10 x y. Herder Verlag, Hermann-Herder-Str. 4, Freiburg i. Br. DM 24

349. WÜRTTEMBERGISCH FRANKEN [Württemberg's Franconia]. A. Historischer Verein für Württembergisch Franken, Untere Herrengasse 8-10, Schwäbisch-Hall.

WÜRTTEMBERGISCHE JAHRBÜCHER FÜR STATISTIK UND LANDESKUNDE see JAHRBÜCHER FÜR STATISTIK UND LANDESKUNDE VON BADEN-WÜRTTEMBERG

350. WÜRZBURGER DIÖZESAN-GESCHICHTSBLÄTTER [Historical bulletins of Würzburg diocese]. A. Bischöfliches Ordinariat Würzburg. memb. free

ZEITSCHRIFT. For titles beginning with "Zeitschrift," followed by the name of the publishing or sponsoring institution or society, see the respective institution or society.

351. ZEITSCHRIFT FÜR AGRARGESCHICHTE UND AGRARSOZIOLOGIE [Journal for agricultural history and agricultural sociology]. S-A. 1953 (1960: vol. 8). Deutsche Landwirtschafts-Gesellschaft-Verlags-GmbH, Zimmerweg 16, Frankfurt (Main). Ed: G. Franz, Schloss, Stuttgart-Hohenheim. Art. on the hist. of agriculture, agricultural movements and the sociology of rural populations confined mostly to Germany; bk. rev. DM 20

352. ZEITSCHRIFT FÜR ASSYRIOLOGIE UND VORDERASIATISCHE ARCHÄOLOGIE [Journal of assyriology and Near Eastern archaeology]. Irr. W. de Gruyter und Co., Genthinerstr. 13, Berlin W 35. DM 56

353. ZEITSCHRIFT FÜR AUSLÄNDISCHES ÖFFENTLICHES RECHT UND VÖLKERRECHT [Journal for foreign public law and international law]. Q. W. Kohlhammer Verlag, Urbanstr. 12-14, Stuttgart O, for Max-Planck-Institut für ausländisches Recht und Völkerrecht. DM 56

354. ZEITSCHRIFT FÜR BAYERISCHE KIRCHENGESCHICHTE [Journal for Bavarian church history]. S-A. Verein für bayerische Kirchengeschichte, Veilhofstr. 28, Nürnberg. DM 10

355. ZEITSCHRIFT FÜR BAYERISCHE LANDESGESCHICHTE [Journal for Bavarian provincial history]. 3 x y. C.H. Becksche Verlagsbuchhandlung, Wilhelmstr. 9, München 23, for Kommission für bayerische Landesgeschichte bei der Bayerischen Akademie der Wissenschaften, Arcisstr. 12, München 2, in collaboration with Gesellschaft für fränkische Geschichte. pv (c. DM 30)

356. ZEITSCHRIFT FÜR DEUTSCHES ALTERTUM UND DEUTSCHE LITERATUR [Journal of German antiquity and German literature]. Q. Franz Steiner, Bahnhofstr. 39, Wiesbaden. DM 48 / $11.43

357. ZEITSCHRIFT FÜR DIE GESCHICHTE DER SAARGEGEND [Journal for the history of the Saar area]. A. Historischer Verein für die Saargegend e.V., Saarbrücken.

358. ZEITSCHRIFT FÜR DIE GESCHICHTE DES OBERRHEINS [Journal for the history of the Upper Rhine]. S-A. Verlag Braun, Karl-Friedrich-Str. 14, Karlsruhe, for Kommission für die geschichtliche Landeskunde in Baden-Württemberg, Gutenbergstr. 109, Stuttgart. DM 20

359. ZEITSCHRIFT FÜR DIE GESCHICHTE UND ALTERTUMSKUNDE ERMLANDS [Journal for the history and archaeology of Ermland]. A. Historischer Verein für Ermland e.V., Münster (Westf.) and Institut für ostdeutsche Kultur- und Kirchengeschichte.

360. ZEITSCHRIFT FÜR ETHNOLOGIE [Journal for ethnology]. S-A. A. Limbach Verlag, Hutfiltern 8, Braunschweig, for Deutsche Gesellschaft für Völkerkunde. DM 26 (memb. DM 19.50)

361. ZEITSCHRIFT FÜR EVANGELISCHES KIRCHENRECHT [Journal for Evangelical church law]. Q. J.C.B. Mohr (Paul Siebeck) Verlag, Wilhelmstr. 18, Tübingen. DM 28.80

362. ZEITSCHRIFT FÜR HEERES- UND UNIFORMKUNDE [Journal for army and uniform studies]. B-M. Verlag H.G. Schulz, Gröningerstr. 22, Hamburg 11, for Deutsche Gesellschaft für Heereskunde e.V., Berlin. (memb.) DM 12

363. ZEITSCHRIFT FÜR KIRCHENGESCHICHTE [Journal for church history]. S-A. 1876/77 (1960: vol. 71). W. Kohlhammer Verlag, Urbanstr. 12-14, Stuttgart O. Ed. board: H. Büttner, H. Frhr. von Campenhausen, K.A. Fink, W. Schneemelcher, E. Wolf. Art. on the Christian Church throughout the world; studies on problems of scholarship; bk. rev., arranged by period; list of periodicals on church hist., with brief descriptions of contents. DM 36

364. ZEITSCHRIFT FÜR KUNSTGESCHICHTE [Journal for the history of art]. Q. Deutscher Kunstverlag, Rondell Neuwittelsbach 8, München. DM 50

365. ZEITSCHRIFT FÜR KUNSTWISSENSCHAFT [Journal for studies in art]. S-A. Deutscher Verein für Kunstwissenschaft e.V., Kunstbibliothek, Jebensstr. 2, Berlin-Charlottenburg. DM 20

366. ZEITSCHRIFT FÜR NIEDERSÄCHSISCHE FAMILIENKUNDE [Journal for Lower Saxon genealogy]. B-M. Verlag Zentralstelle für Niedersächsische Familienkunde e.V., c/o A. Clasen, Schlenkreye 19, Hamburg 13. (memb.) DM 12

367. ZEITSCHRIFT FÜR OSTFORSCHUNG [Journal for East European research]. Länder und Völker im östlichen Mitteleuropa [Lands and people of Eastern Central Europe]. Q. 1952 (1960: vol. 9). N.G. Elwert-Verlag, Marburg (Lahn), for Johann Gottfried Herder-Forschungsrat, Behringweg 7, Marburg (Lahn). Ed: Hermann Aubin, Erich Keyser, Herbert Schlenger. Art. on the hist. and geography of Eastern and East Central Europe; excerpts from research studies; reports on the present situation in Eastern European countries; doc.; rev. art.; rev. of bk. and periodicals; extensive classified biblio.; graph. DM 24

368. ZEITSCHRIFT FÜR POLITIK [Journal for politics]. Q. C. Heymens Verlag KG, Gutenbergstr. 3, Berlin-Charlottenburg, for Vereinigung für die Wissenschaft von der Politik. p (1) DM 4.50

369. ZEITSCHRIFT FÜR RELIGIONS- UND GEISTESGESCHICHTE [Journal for religious and intellectual history]. Q. 1949 (1960: vol. 12). E.J. Brill GmbH, Haus am Griesenplatz, Köln. Ed: E. Benz, Lahntor 3, Marburg; H.J. Schoeps, Kochstr. 4, Erlangen. Art. on religious and intellectual hist. and on philosophy, particularly the philosophy of religion; bk. rev.; in German and occasionally in English. DM 26

370. ZEITSCHRIFT FÜR STAATSSOZIOLOGIE [Journal for the sociology of the state]. Politik - Wirtschaft - Kultur - Erziehung [Politics - economy - culture - education]. Q. Themis-Verlag, Freiburg i. Br., for Forschungsinstitut für Staatssoziologie und Politik, Gehrensstr. 2, Freiburg. DM 7

371. ZEITSCHRIFT FÜR VOLKSKUNDE [Journal of folklore]. S-A. W. Kohlhammer Verlag, Urbanstr. 12-14, Stuttgart O, for Verband der Vereine für Volkskunde. DM 24 (memb. DM 18)

372. ZEITSCHRIFT FÜR WÜRTTEMBERGISCHE LANDESGESCHICHTE [Journal for Württemberg provincial history]. S-A. Kommission für geschichtliche Landeskunde in Baden-Württemberg, Gutenbergstr. 109, Stuttgart W. pv (c. DM 20)

ADDENDA

373. BALTISCHE STUDIEN [Baltic studies]. A. Gesellschaft für Pommersche Geschichte, Altertumskunde und Kunst e.V., Postfach 34, Hamburg-Harburg. DM 12

374. BAYERISCHE VORGESCHICHTSBLÄTTER [Bavarian journal for prehistory]. Irr. 1921 (1960: no. 25). C.H.Beck'sche Verlagsbuchhandlung, München, for Kommission für bayerische Landesgeschichte bei der Bayerischen Akademie der Wissenschaften and Bayerisches Landesamt für Denkmalpflege.

Art. on pre-hist. finds in Bavaria, descriptions of new finds, arranged by period; bk. rev.; classified biblio.; maps; illus. pv (c. DM 24)

375. BAYERLAND. Die illustrierte bayerische Monatsschrift [Illustrated Bavarian monthly]. M. Bayerland-Verlag e.V., Schellingstr. 39-41, München 22, for Verein Bayerland e.V. DM 6 (Q subscription)

376. BOHEMIA. Irr. Verlag Robert Lerche, München, for Collegium Carolinum, Forschungsstelle für die böhmischen Länder. DM 25

377. GUTENBERG-JAHRBUCH [Gutenberg yearbook]. A. Gutenberg Gesellschaft, Vereinigung für Geschichte und Gegenwart der Druckkunst in allen Ländern der Erde, Rheinallee 3, Mainz. DM 45

378. HARBURGER JAHRBUCH [Harburg yearbook]. A. (Irr.). Museums- und Heimatverein Harburg Stadt und Land e.V., Harburg. pni

379. HESSISCHES JAHRBUCH FÜR LANDESGESCHICHTE [Yearbook for Hessian history]. A. 1951 (1959: vol. 9). Arbeitsgemeinschaft der Historischen Kommissionen in Darmstadt, Frankfurt, Marburg und Wiesbaden. Ed. address: Kugelgasse 10, Marburg (Lahn). Art. on various aspects of the hist. of the region from the Middle Ages to the 19th cent.; critical evaluations of medieval doc. bk. rev.; classified biblio.; news and notes; maps; reproductions of doc.; illus. pni

380. SCHWÄBISCHE HEIMAT [Swabian homeland]. Zeitschrift zur Pflege von Landschaft, Volkstum, Kultur [Journal for the preservation of landscape, folklore, culture]. B-M. W. Kohlhammer, Urbanstr. 12-14, Stuttgart O, for Schwäbischer Heimatbund, Charlottenstr. 15, Stuttgart O. DM 7.50

381. ZEITSCHRIFT FÜR DIE GESAMTE STAATSWISSENSCHAFT [Journal for all fields of political science]. Irr. J.C.B. Mohr (Paul Siebeck), Wilhelmstr. 18, Tübingen. Ed. address: Universitätsstr. 14-16, Münster (Westf.). p (1) DM 18

382. DER ZWIEBELTURM [The bulbous dome]. Monatsschrift für das bayerische Volk und seine Freunde [Monthly for the Bavarian people and their friends]. M. Verlag Josef Habbel, Gutenbergstr. 17, Regensburg. DM 4.30 (Q subscription)

383. ZWISCHEN SEMPF UND ISEN [Between Sempf and Isen]. Heimatblätter des Erdinger Landkreises [Local bulletins of Erding county]. A. Kreisverein für Heimatschutz und Denkmalspflege, Schrannenplatz 2, Erding.

Great Britain

Prepared with the assistance of

John A. S. Grenville, University of Nottingham,

Miss Sylvia L. England, North Library, British Museum, London,

A. M. C. Field, Institute of Historical Research, University of London, and

Mrs. Veronica Roberts, London

1. AFRICA. Q. International African Inst., 10-11 Fetter Lane, London, E. C. 4. 35s

2. AFRICA DIGEST. B-M. Africa Bureau, 69 Great Peter St., London, S. W. 1. 25s

3. AFRICAN AFFAIRS. Q. Royal African Soc., 18 Northumberland Ave., London W. C. 2. In English and occasionally in French. 24s

4. THE AGRICULTURAL HISTORY REVIEW. S-A. 1953 (1959: vol. 7). British Agricultural Hist. Soc., c/o Department of Agriculture, Oxford Univ., Parks Rd., Oxford. Ed: H. P. R. Finberg, 34 Sheffield Terr., London, W. 8. Art. on agrarian hist. and related social and economic topics, with emphasis on Great Britain; bk. rev. and A. biblio. of bk. and art.; news about the activities of the soc.; professional news; cum. subject and author index for vol. 1-5. p(1) 12s 6d

5. ALCUIN CLUB. COLLECTIONS. Irr. Alcuin Club, c/o Canon Gate House, Chichester. (memb.) 21s

6. THE AMATEUR HISTORIAN. Q. 1952 (1956-58: vol. 3). Alden and Blackwell Ltd., Eton College, Windsor, Berkshire. Ed. address: Pestells, West Wickham, Cambridgeshire. Art. on the social and economic hist. of Great Britain, with emphasis on the modern period, and on methods of hist. and archaeological research, particularly in local hist., heraldry, genealogy and related fields; bk. rev. 15s

7. AMBIX. Irr. 1937 (1959: vol. 7). W. Heffer and Sons Ltd., Cambridge, for Soc. for the Study of Alchemy and Early Chemistry. Ed: D. Geoghegan, Higher Westerland, Nr. Paignton, Devon. Art. on all aspects of alchemy and early chemistry, including that of China, ancient Mesopotamia and medieval Europe; bk. rev.; illus. 52s 6d

8. ANATOLIAN STUDIES. A. 1951 (1959: vol. 9). British Inst. of Archaeology at Ankara, 56 Queen Anne St., London, W. 1. Ed: O. R. Gurney. Art. on Anatolian archaeology and allied subjects, and sum. of research conducted in Turkey during the preceding year by the inst.; A. report of the inst. 32s 6d

9. ANCIENT MONUMENTS SOCIETY, TRANSACTIONS OF THE. A. 1953 (1958: new series, vol. 6). Ancient Monuments Soc., Clifford's Inn, London, E. C. 4. Ed: R. B. Wood-Jones, School of Architecture, Univ. of Manchester,

Manchester 13. Papers on the hist. of architecture, and on non-architectural aspects of hist. monuments; occasional papers on aspects of repair and preservation of ancient monuments; each vol. includes A. report on the activities of the soc.; list of memb. of the soc. 21s

10. ANNALS OF SCIENCE. A Quarterly Review of the History of Science since the Renaissance. Q. 1936 (1957: vol. 13). Taylor and Francis., Red Lion Court, Fleet St., London, E. C. 4. Ed. board: Harcourt Brown, D. Mckie, H. W. Robinson, N. H. de V. Heathcote. Art. on the hist. of science, including medicine and technology, and on science teaching; biographical art.; bk. rev. Contains Bulletin of the British Society for the History of Science. 63s

ANNUAL. For titles beginning with "Annual," followed by the name of the publishing or sponsoring institution or society, see the respective institution or society.

11. ANNUAL BULLETIN OF HISTORICAL LITERATURE. A. Ed: Jean Lindsay, c/o Hist. Assoc., 59a Kennington Park, London. Digest of bk. on hist., classified by period; index. 3s 6d

ANNUAL REPORT OF THE INSTITUTE OF ARCHAEOLOGY see INSTITUTE OF ARCHAEOLOGY, BULLETIN OF THE

ANNUAL REPORT OF THE KEEPER OF PUBLIC RECORDS ON THE WORK OF THE PUBLIC RECORD OFFICE see PUBLIC RECORD OFFICE, ANNUAL REPORT OF THE KEEPER OF PUBLIC RECORDS ON THE WORK OF THE

12. THE ANTIQUARIES JOURNAL. Q. (2 double no. p.a.). 1921 (1959: vol. 39). Oxford Univ. Press, for Soc. of Antiquaries of London, Burlington House, London, W. 1. Ed: Philip Corder. Art. on prehist., Romano-British and Saxon archaeology and hist., and Greek and Roman antiquities; rev. art.; bk. rev.; biblio. of bk. and periodicals; professional news; proceedings of the soc.; A. subject index. 40s

13. THE ANTIQUE COLLECTOR. B-M. Ed: G. W. Whitman, 16 Strutton Ground, Victoria St., London, S. W. 1. 24s/$4

14. ANTIQUE DEALER AND COLLECTORS' GUIDE. M. Patina Press Ltd., 92 Fleet St., London, E. C. 4. Rev. of art.; occasional bk. rev. and sale price rev. 30s/ $6

15. ANTIQUITIES OF SUNDERLAND AND ITS VICINITY. Irr. Sunderland Antiquarian Soc., 5 Heatherlea Gardens, Sunderland, Durham. 20s/$6

16. ANTIQUITY. A Quarterly Review of Archaeology. Q. 1927 (1959: vol. 33). H. W. Edwards, Ashmore Green, Newbury, Berkshire. Ed: Glyn Daniel, St. John's College, Cambridge. Art. on archaeology, with emphasis on Europe, Africa and Asia from the Stone Age to the 6th cent.; doc.; bk. rev.; notes and news on recent finds, archaeological expeditions, conferences and congresses; vol. subject and author index. 30s

17. THE ARAB WORLD. Q. Anglo-Arab Assoc., 27 Eaton Pl., London, S. W. 1. 21s

18. ARCHAEOLOGIA. S-A. 1770 (1959: vol. 97; news series, vol. 47). Soc. of Antiquaries of London, Burlington House, London, W. 1. Art. on the archaeology and arts of ancient and medieval Britain; vol. subject index. pv (p (1) c. 73s)

19. ARCHAEOLOGIA AELIANA. Miscellaneous Tracts Relating to Antiquity. A. 1822 (1959: 4th series, vol. 37). Soc. of Antiquaries of Newcastle-upon-Tyne, Black Gate, Newcastle-upon-Tyne. Ed: C. H. Hunter Blair, 57 Highbury, Newcastle-upon-Tyne. Art. and reports on prehist. and Roman excavations, and general art. relating to the hist. of North England; bk. rev.; memoirs of the soc. (memb.) 40s

20. ARCHAEOLOGIA CAMBRENSIS [The archaeology of Wales]. A. 1846 (1958: vol. 107). William Lewis (Printers) Ltd., Penarth Rd., Cardiff, for Cambrian Archaeological Assoc. Ed: J. D. K. Lloyd, Bron Hafren, Garthmyl, Montgomery. Art. on the archaeology of Wales from prehist. to modern times; notes and reports about the assoc.; illus.; subject index in each vol. 25s

21. ARCHAEOLOGIA CANTIANA. A. Kent Archaeological Soc., The Museum, St. Faith's St., Maidstone, Kent. 20s

22. ARCHAEOLOGICAL JOURNAL. A. 1843 (1957: vol. 114). Royal Archaeological Inst., London Museum, Kensington Palace, London, W. 8. Ed: Mary Raldwin. Art. on archaeology and hist., mainly architectural, of Great Britain from prehist. to the Victorian period; bk. rev.; report on the A. meeting of the soc.; illus.; occasional supplements. 45s (memb. free)

23. THE ARCHAEOLOGICAL NEWS LETTER. Irr. 1948 (1959: vol. 6 no. 10). Pub. address: 60 Frederick St., Gray's Inn Rd., London, W. C. 1. Ed: D. Heighes Woodforde. Art. on archaeology, with emphasis on Great Britain, and on the work of British archaeological soc.; rev. art.; bk. rev.; professional news; illus. 18s

24. ARCHITECTURAL AND ARCHAEOLOGICAL SOCIETY OF DURHAM AND NORTHUMBERLAND, TRANSACTIONS OF THE. B. Architectural and Archaeological Soc. of Durham and Northumberland, c/o C. W. Gibby (secretary), Prebends Gate, Quarry Head, Durham. (memb.) 10s

25. ARCHIVES. S-A. 1949 (1957/8: vol. 3 or no. 17-20 [1 vol. for 2 years]). British Records Assoc., 1 Lancaster Pl., Strand, London, W. C. 2. Ed: Joan C. Lancaster, c/o Inst. of Hist. Research, Senate House, London, W. C. 1. Art. on archives and archival collections, with emphasis on Great Britain and local archives, and on techniques of research and pub.; reports on the activities of the British Record. Assoc. and similar inst.; notes of professional interest; bk. rev.; biblio. notes. 16s (memb.) 12s

26. ARCHIVISTS' REPORT. A. Lincolnshire Archives Committee, Lincolnshire Archives Office, Exchequer Gate, Lincoln. 2s 6d

27. ARMS AND ARMOUR SOCIETY, JOURNAL OF THE. Q. 1953 (1956-58: vol. 2). Arms and Armour Soc., c/o Hon. Secretary, 40 Great James St., Holborn, London, W. C. 1. Ed: C. Blair, "Stepping Stones," Woodlands Rd. Little Bookham, Leatherhead, Surrey. Art. on the hist. of arms and armor, and on famous collections of arms and armor, with emphasis on Great Britain; biblio. of recent pub. and art. from periodicals devoted to arms, armor and military subjects; illus. (memb.) 25s

28. THE ARMY QUARTERLY AND DEFENCE JOURNAL. Q. 1920 (1959: vol. 78, no. 2). William Clowes and Sons Ltd., Little New St., London, E. C. 4. Ed: Brigadier C. N. Barclay. Art. on the Fighting Services including strategy, tactics and allied matters, current and hist. 40s

29. ART AND LETTERS, INDIA, PAKISTAN AND CEYLON. S-A. Royal India, Pakistan and Ceylon Soc., 19 Temple Chambers, London, E. C. 4. 10s

30. ASIA MAJOR. A British Journal of Far Eastern Studies. S-A. 1923 (1959: vol. 7). Percy Lund, Humphries and Co. Ltd., London, for London School of Oriental and African Studies, Univ. of London, London, W. C. 1. Ed: B. Schindler, 12 Bedford Sq., London, W. C. 1. "Asia Major is devoted to the study of the languages, literatures, arts and civilizations of the Far East, South and South-East Asia, and Central Asia"; bk. rev.; biblio. of bk. received. 70s/$10

31. ASIAN ANNUAL. The "Eastern World" Handbook. A. "Eastern World," 58 Paddington St., London, W. 1. 20s

32. THE ASIAN REVIEW. Q. East and West Ltd., 191 Temple Chambers, Temple Ave., London, E. C. 4. Incorporates The Asiatic Review and The Journal of the East India Association. 20s

THE ASIATIC REVIEW see THE ASIAN REVIEW

33. ATLANTE. Q. Hispanic and Luso-Brazilian Councils, 2 Belgrave Sq., London, S. W. 1. English, Portuguese and Spanish hist. and hispanic literature. 15s

34. THE BAPTIST QUARTERLY. Q. 1908 (1959: vol. 18). Carey Kingsgate Press Ltd., 6 Southampton Row, London, W. C. 1, for Baptist Hist. Soc. Ed: W. M. S. West, 18 Gurney Court Rd., St. Albans, Herts. Art. on all aspects of Baptist hist. in Great Britain from the 19th cent. to the present, and occasionally on subjects relating to the principles and practices of the Baptist denomination in Great Britain; bk. rev.; vol. subject and author index. 21s

35. BATHAFARN. A. 1946 (1958: vol. 13). Hist. Soc. of the Methodist Church in Wales, Garth, 108 Wenallt Rd., Rhiwbina, Cardiff. Ed: A. H. Williams. Art. on the hist. of the Methodist Church in Wales; biographical art.; doc.; notes; A. report of the Methodist Church in Wales; in English and Welsh. 3s

36. BEDFORDSHIRE ARCHAEOLOGIST. Irr. South Bedfordshire Archaeological Soc., 45 Ashcroft Rd., Luton, Bedfordshire. 5s

37. BEDFORDSHIRE HISTORICAL RECORD SOCIETY. PUBLICATIONS. A. Bedfordshire Hist. Record Soc., c/o C. E. Freeman (secretary), Museum and Art Gallery, Wardown Park, Luton, Bedfordshire. 21s

38. BEDFORDSHIRE MAGAZINE. Q. Staddons, The Crescent Press, Crescent Rd., Luton. 4s 10d

39. BELLONA. Kwartalnik Wojskowo-Historyczny [Quarterly review of military history]. Q. 1945/6 (1957: vol. 39). Instytut Historyczny Im. Gen. Sikorskiego [General Sikorski Hist. Inst.], 20 Princes Gate, London, S. W. 7. Art. on Polish military science and hist. during the modern period, with emphasis

on the Second World War; rev. art.; bk. rev.; news and notes; in Polish; vol. subject index. p (1) 3s 6d

40. BERKSHIRE ARCHAEOLOGICAL JOURNAL. A. Berkshire Archaeological Soc., Claremont, Castle Ave., Datchet, Berkshire. 16s

BIOGRAPHICAL STUDIES see RECUSANT HISTORY

41. BIRMINGHAM ARCHAEOLOGICAL SOCIETY. TRANSACTIONS AND PROCEEDINGS. A. 1870 (1956 [1958]: vol. 74). Birmingham Archaeological Soc., Midland Inst., Paradise St., Birmingham 1. Ed: Paul Morgan, Univ. Library, Birmingham 15. Art. on archaeology from prehist. to modern times, with emphasis on the counties of Warwickshire and Staffordshire; professional notes of mainly local interest; A. report of the soc.; illus. (memb.) 30s

42. BOARD OF CELTIC STUDIES, BULLETIN OF THE. S-A. 1921 (1958/59: vol. 18). Univ. Board of Celtic Studies, Univ. Registry, Cathays Park, Cardiff. Ed: Henry Lewis, Glyn Roberts, H. N. Savory. Art. on the language, literature, hist., law, archaeology and art of Wales; illus. 10s

43. THE BODLEIAN LIBRARY RECORD. Irr. (at present S-A). 1914 (1959: vol. 6). Bodleian Library, Oxford. Ed: The Librarian. Art. on libraries and bk. collections and on manuscripts and bk. housed in the Bodleian; news of professional interest and on the personnel, holdings and activities of the library and of the soc. "Friends of the Bodleian." p (1) 3s 6d

44. THE BOOK COLLECTOR. Q. 1952 (1959: vol. 8). Shenval Press Ltd., 58 Frith St., London, W. 1. Ed. board: John Hayward, John Carter, Ian Fleming, P. H. Muir. Art. on bk. collections and libraries, and on the hist. of printing and bk. binding; art. on individual authors and biblio. notes and queries; bk. rev. 30s/$5

45. BRADFORD ANTIQUARY. B-A. Bradford Hist. and Antiquarian Soc., c/o Wilfrid Robertshaw (secretary), Cartwright Memorial Hall, Bradford. (memb.) 15s

46. BRADFORD HISTORICAL AND ANTIQUARIAN SOCIETY. LOCAL RECORD SERIES. Irr. Bradford Hist. and Antiquarian Soc., c/o Wilfrid Robertshaw (secretary), Cartwright Memorial Hall, Bradford.

47. BRISTOL AND GLOUCESTERSHIRE ARCHAEOLOGICAL SOCIETY. RECORDS BRANCH. Irr. Bristol and Gloucestershire Archaeological Soc.

48. BRISTOL AND GLOUCESTERSHIRE ARCHAEOLOGICAL SOCIETY, TRANSACTIONS OF THE. A. Bristol and Gloucestershire Archaeological Soc. Ed: J. Evans, Thousand Acres, Wotton-under-Edge, Gloucestershire, and Stewart Gracie, The Yew, Pinfarthings, Ambrley, Gloucestershire. 25s (memb. 21s)

49. BRISTOL RECORD SOCIETY. PUBLICATIONS. Irr. Ed: David Douglas, Univ. of Bristol, Bristol. (memb.) 21s

50. BRITAIN AND HOLLAND. Q. Anglo-Netherland Soc., 191 Temple Chambers, Temple Ave., London, E. C. 4. 10s

51. BRITISH ACADEMY, PROCEEDINGS OF THE. A. 1903 (1957: vol. 43). Oxford Univ. Press, Amen House, London, E. C. 4, for British Acad. Papers of the acad. on the humanities, including all areas and periods of hist.; news and notes on the activities of the acad. pv (c. 60s)

52. BRITISH ARCHAEOLOGICAL ASSOCIATION, JOURNAL OF THE. A. 1844 (1958: 3rd series, vol. 21). British Archaeological Assoc., 11 Chandos St., London, W. 1. Ed: Irene Scouloudi, 67 Victoria Rd., Kensington, London, W. 8. Art. on the archaeology and antiquities of Great Britain, with emphasis on the period from Roman Britain to the 16th cent.; rev. art.; bk. rev.; vol. subject index. 35s

53. BRITISH ASSOCIATION FOR AMERICAN STUDIES. BULLETIN. Irr. 1956 (1959 no. 9). Ed: George Shepperson, Department of Hist., Univ. of Edinburgh, Edinburgh 8. Art. on United States politics, hist. and literature; rev. of work done in British univ. in the field of American studies; bk. rev., occasional lists of manuscripts and other holdings pertaining to American studies available in British libraries; research in progress; notes and news of the assoc. (memb.) 21s

54. BRITISH JOURNAL OF EDUCATIONAL STUDIES. S-A. 1952 (1959: vol. 7). Faber and Faber Ltd., 24 Russell Sq., London, W. C. 1. Ed: A. C. F. Beales. Art. on education, educational philosophy and the hist. of education, particularly in the 19th and 20th cent.; bk. rev.; professional news. 16s 8d/$2.35

55. THE BRITISH JOURNAL OF SOCIOLOGY. Q. Routledge and Kegan Paul, 68-74 Carter Lane, London, E. C. 4, for London School of Economics and Political Science, Houghton St., Aldwych, London, W. C. 2. 40s

56. THE BRITISH MUSEUM QUARTERLY. Q. 1926 (1958: vol. 21). Trustees of the British Museum, British Museum, London, W. C. 1. Ed: Director and Principal Librarian. "A journal dealing with recent acquisitions and research concerning the Museum's collections"; illus. 20s

57. THE BRITISH NUMISMATIC JOURNAL. Including the Proceedings of the British Numismatic Society. A. 1903 (1955-57 [1958]: vol. 28). British Numismatic Soc., c/o C. S. S. Lyon (secretary), Chantry Way, Abbot Rd., Guildford, Surrey. Ed: C. E. Blunt, H. H. King. Art. and shorter communications on the coinage of Great Britain and its dependencies from the earliest times to the present day, and on the coinage of North America, token coinage and medals and badges of all descriptions; bk. rev.; news of the soc. (memb.) 63s

58. BRITISH RECORD SOCIETY LTD. INDEX LIBRARY. Irr. British Record Soc. Ltd., c/o H. K. Percy-Smith (hon. secretary), 120 Chancery Lane, London, W. C. 2.

59. BRITISH SCHOOL AT ATHENS, THE ANNUAL OF THE. A. 1894 (1957 [1959]: vol. 52). Managing Committee of the British School at Athens, 50 Bedford Sq., London, W. C. 1. Ed: L. H. Jeffery. Art. on classical archaeology and reports of recent excavations; vol. subject index and index of classical authors; illus. 63s

60. BRITISH SCHOOL AT ROME, PAPERS OF THE. A. 1902 (1958: vol. 26; new series, vol. 13). British School at Rome, (London address) 1 Lowther Gardens, Exhibition Rd., London S. W. 7. Ed: Director of the school.

Art. on the archaeology and ancient and medieval hist. of Italy and the Mediterranean; biblio.; in English, occasionally in Italian or French; illus. 50s

BRITISH SCHOOL OF ARCHAEOLOGY IN JERUSALEM, BULLETIN OF THE see PALESTINE EXPLORATION QUARTERLY

61. BRITISH SOCIETY FOR THE HISTORY OF SCIENCE, BULLETIN OF THE. Irr. 1949 (mri 1956: vol. 2, no. 14). Taylor and Francis Ltd., Red Lion Court, Fleet St., London, E. C. 4, for British Soc. for the Hist. of Science. Ed: N. H. de V. Heathcote, Univ. College, London. Occasional art. on the hist. of science; bk. rev.; news and notes on the activities of the soc. Appears as a supplement to Annals of Science.

62. BRITISH YEAR BOOK OF INTERNATIONAL LAW. A. Oxford Univ. Press, Amen House, Warwick Sq., London, E. C. 4. pv (c. 60s-80s)

63. BUCHAN CLUB, TRANSACTIONS OF THE. Irr. Ed: J. Fairweather Milne, Boddam, Peterhead. 10s

64. BUCKINGHAMSHIRE ARCHAEOLOGICAL SOCIETY. PUBLICATIONS. A. Buckinghamshire Archaeological Soc., The Museum, Church St., Aylesbury, Buckinghamshire. 10s

65. BUCKINGHAMSHIRE RECORD SOCIETY. PUBLICATIONS. Irr. Buckinghamshire Record Soc., c/o J. G. Jenkins (hon. secretary), Twitchells End, Jordans, Buckinghamshire. (memb.) 21s

BULLETIN. For titles beginning with "Bulletin," followed by the name of the publishing or sponsoring institution or society, see the respective institution or society.

66. BULLETIN OF HISPANIC STUDIES. Q. Liverpool Univ. Press, 123 Grove St., Liverpool 7. 30s/$4.50

67. THE BURLINGTON MAGAZINE. M. Pub. address: 12 Bedford Sq., London, W. C. 1. 100s/$16

68. BUSINESS HISTORY. S-A. 1958 (1958: vol. 1). Liverpool Univ. Press 123 Grove St., Liverpool 7. Ed. board: F. E. Hyde, S. B. Saul, J. R. Harris. Art. on business hist. in general and on the hist. of individual firms, with emphasis on the 19th cent. and Great Britain; information on the work of the Business Archives Council (London); bk. rev. 30s/ $5

69. CAERNARVONSHIRE HISTORICAL SOCIETY. TRANSACTIONS. CYMDEITHAS HANES SIR GAERNARFON. TRAFODION. A. Caernarvonshire Hist. Soc., County Offices, Caernarvon. In English or Welsh. 10s (memb. 7s 6d)

70. CAERNARVONSHIRE RECORD SERIES. Irr. Caernarvonshire Hist. Soc., County Offices, Caernarvon.

CAHIERS D'HISTOIRE see TEKI HISTORYCZNE

71. CAMBRIDGE ANTIQUARIAN SOCIETY, PROCEEDINGS OF THE. A. Cambridge Antiquarian Soc., c/o Museum of Archaeology and Ethnology,

Downing St., Cambridge. (memb.) 35s

72. CAMBRIDGE BIBLIOGRAPHICAL SOCIETY, TRANSACTIONS OF THE. A. 1949 (1958: vol. 2, part 5). Bowes and Bowes Pub. Ltd., 42 Great Russell St., London, W. C. 1. Ed: Bruce Dickins, A. N. L. Munby. Art. and biblio. on manuscripts and library collections dealing with the medieval and modern literature and hist. of Great Britain; news and notes on the activities of the soc. 25s

THE CAMBRIDGE HISTORICAL JOURNAL see THE HISTORICAL JOURNAL

73. CAMDEN SOCIETY TRANSACTIONS. Irr. Ecclesiological Soc., Walcot House, 139 Kennington Rd., Lambeth, London, S. E. 11. p (1) 7s 6d

74. CAMDEN THIRD SERIES. Formerly CAMDEN SOCIETY. Irr. Royal Hist. Soc., 96 Cheyne Walk, Chelsea, London, S. W. 10. (memb.) 84s

75. CANTERBURY AND YORK SOCIETY. PUBLICATIONS. A. Oxford Univ. Press, Amen House, Warwick Sq., London, E. C. 4. 30s

76. CARMARTHEN ANTIQUARY. A. Hon. Secretary, Museum, Carmarthen. 10s 6d

77. CELA ZĨMES [Milestones]. B-M. Soc. of Latvians in Great Britain, 37a Kensington High St., London, W. 8. 33s/$6.80

78. CENTRAL ASIAN REVIEW. A Quarterly Review of Current Developments in Soviet Central Asia and Kazakhstan. Q. 1953 (1958: vol. 6). Central Asian Research Centre (in collaboration with St. Anthony's College, Oxford), Soviet Affairs Study Group, 66 King's Rd., London, S. W. 3. Ed: Geoffrey Wheeler, David Footman. Art. on the hist., arts, linguistics, education and ethnography of the Republics of Azerbaydzhan, Uzbekistan, Tadzhikistan, Kirgizia, Turkmenistan and Kazakhstan, and on Soviet pub. on the adjacent countries of Persia, Afghanistan, the Indian sub-continent and the Sinkiang-Uygur Autonomous Region; bk. rev.; news digest. 42s

79. CEREDIGION. A. Cymdeithas Hynafleathwayr Sir Aberteifi [Cardiganshire Antiquarian Soc.], National Library of Wales, Aberystwyth. 10s

80. THE CHESHIRE HISTORIAN. A. Cheshire Community Council, 53 Watergate Row, Chester. 2s 6d

81. CHESTER AND NORTH WALES ARCHITECTURAL, ARCHAEOLOGICAL AND HISTORIC SOCIETY. A. Chester and North Wales Architectural, Archaeological and Hist. Soc., c/o Grosvenor Museum, Chester. 21s

82. CHURCH HISTORICAL SOCIETY. PUBLICATIONS. Church Hist. Soc., c/o Hon. Secretary, S. P. C. K., Holy Trinity Church, Marylebone Rd., London, N. W. 1. (memb.) 21s

83. THE CHURCH QUARTERLY REVIEW. Q. Soc. for Promoting Christian Knowledge, Holy Trinity Church, Marylebone Rd., London, N. W. 1. 20s

84. CLASSICAL ASSOCIATION, PROCEEDINGS OF THE. A. 1904 (1958: vol. 55). John Murray, 50 Albemarle St., London, W. 1, for Classical Assoc. Ed: L. J. D. Richardson, Univ. College of South Wales and Monmouthshire, Cathays Park, Cardiff. A. report of the assoc. and sum. of papers read at meetings; notes and reports of local branches and of allied assoc. 4s 6d

85. THE CLASSICAL QUARTERLY. Q (usually double no.). 1907 (1959: new series, vol. 9). Oxford Univ. Press, Amen House, Warwick Sq., London, E. C. 4, for Classical Assoc. Ed: D. W. Lucas, A. R. W. Harrison. Art. on Greek and Latin philology, literature, hist. and antiquities, with emphasis on the treatment of literary or linguistic evidence; vol. author index. 30s

86. COLLECTIONS FOR A HISTORY OF STAFFORDSHIRE. Irr. Staffordshire Record Soc. (formerly William Salt Archaeological Soc.), c/o William Salt Library, Stafford. (memb.) 21s

87. CONGREGATIONAL HISTORICAL SOCIETY. TRANSACTIONS. Irr. 1901 (1956-58: vol. 18). Congregational Hist. Soc., Memorial Hall, Farringdon St., London, E. C. 4. Ed: Geoffrey F. Nuttall, 2 Brim Hill, London, N. 2, John H. Taylor, 211 Alborough Rd., Seven Kings, Ilford, Essex. Art. on the hist. of the Congregational Church, with emphasis on Great Britain, and on theological subjects; bk. rev. p (1) 6s

88. CONTEMPORARY REVIEW. M. British Periodicals Ltd., 46-47 Chancery Lane, London, W. C. 2. 53s

89. COUNCIL FOR THE PRESERVATION OF BUSINESS ARCHIVES. PUBLICATIONS. Irr. Pub. address: c/o Secretary, Business Archives Council, Devereux Court, London, W. C. 2.

90. CUMBERLAND AND WEST MORELAND ANTIQUARIAN AND ARCHAEOLOGICAL SOCIETY. TRACT SERIES. Irr. Cumberland and West Moreland Antiquarian and Archaeological Soc. (memb.) 40s

91. CUMBERLAND AND WEST MORELAND ANTIQUARIAN AND ARCHAEOLOGICAL SOCIETY. TRANSACTIONS. B. Ed: Eric Birley, Department of Archaeology, Hatfield College, Durham, and Canon M. L. Bouch, Clifton Rectory, Penrith. 21s

CYLCHGRAWN. For titles beginning with "Cylchgrawn," followed by the name of the publishing or sponsoring institution or society, see the respective institution or society.

92. CYMDEITHAS HANES EGLWYS METHODISTIAID CALFINAI CYMRU, CYLCHGRAWN... (Cylchgrawn Cymdeithas Hanes Eglwys Methodistaid Calfinai Cymru). THE JOURNAL OF THE HISTORICAL SOCIETY OF THE METHODIST CHURCH OF WALES. 3 x y. Hist. Soc. of the Methodist Church of Wales, c/o Tom Benyon (secretary), Llwynarel, Penparcan, Aberystwyth. (memb. free)

CYMDEITHAS HANES SIR GAERNARFON. TRAFODION see CAERNARVONSHIRE HISTORICAL SOCIETY. TRANSACTIONS

93. DERBYSHIRE ARCHAEOLOGICAL AND NATURAL HISTORY SOCIETY JOURNAL OF THE. A. Derbyshire Archaeological and Natural Hist. Soc., St. Mary's Bridge Chapel House, Derby. Art. on the archaeology and hist. of Derbyshire; doc.; subject index for the years 1879-1952. 25s

94. DEVON AND CORNWALL NOTES AND QUERIES. A Quarterly Journal Devoted to the Local History, Archaeology, Biography and Antiquities of the Counties of Devon and Cornwall. Q. Ed: M. C. S. Cruwys, Cruwys Morchard House, Tiverton, Devonshire. 20s

95. DEVON AND CORNWALL RECORD SOCIETY. PUBLICATIONS. A. Univ. of Exeter, Bedford. (memb.) 21s

96. DEVON ARCHAEOLOGICAL EXPLORATION SOCIETY, PROCEEDINGS OF THE. A. (Irr.). Devon Archaeological Exploration Soc., Culmcott, Uffculme, Devon. 20s/20s

97. THE DEVONSHIRE ASSOCIATION FOR THE ADVANCEMENT OF SCIENCE, LITERATURE AND ART. REPORT AND TRANSACTIONS. A. Devonshire Assoc. for the Advancement of Science, Literature and Art, 7 The Close, Exeter, Devonshire. 21s/$ 3.75

98. DORSET NATURAL HISTORY AND ARCHAEOLOGICAL SOCIETY, PROCEEDINGS OF THE. A. Dorset Natural Hist. and Archaeological Soc., Dorset County Museum, High West St., Dorchester, Dorset. 42s

99. DUGDALE SOCIETY. PUBLICATIONS. Irr. Ed: Levi Fox, Shakespeare's Birthplace, Stratford-Upon-Avon. (memb.) 21s

100. DUMFRIESSHIRE AND GALLOWAY NATURAL HISTORY AND ANTIQUARIAN SOCIETY. TRANSACTIONS AND JOURNAL OF PROCEEDINGS. A. Dumfriesshire and Galloway Natural Hist. and Antiquarian Soc., Ewart Library, Dumfries. 21s

101. THE DURHAM UNIVERSITY JOURNAL. 3 x y. 1876 (1958/9: vol. 51). Univ. of Durham, 46 North Bailey, Durham. Ed: J. C. Maxwell, King's College, Newcastle-upon-Tyne 1. Art. on all subjects within the scope of the humanities, including literature, philology, philosophy, classics and all fields and periods of hist., with emphasis on Western Europe; bk. rev.; vol. subject index; supplement containing news of the univ. 6s 6d

102. EAST HERTFORDSHIRE ARCHAEOLOGICAL SOCIETY. TRANSACTIONS. T. Stephen Austin and Son, Printers, Hertford, for East Hertfordshire Archaeological Soc. pni

EAST INDIA ASSOCIATION, THE JOURNAL OF THE see THE ASIAN REVIEW

103. EAST LOTHIAN ANTIQUARIAN AND FIELD NATURALISTS' SOCIETY. TRANSACTIONS. Irr. George Murray, 24 Duddington Park, Portovello, Edinburgh. (memb.) 10s

104. EAST RIDING ANTIQUARIAN SOCIETY. TRANSACTIONS. B. East Riding Antiquarian Soc., 34 Salisbury St., Hull. p (1) 10s 6d

105. THE ECONOMIC HISTORY REVIEW. 3 x y. 1927 (1959/60: new series, vol. 12). Economic Hist. Soc., St. Catharine's College, Cambridge. Ed: H. J. Habakkuk, M. M. Postan, R. M. Hartwell. Art. on social and economic hist. in all its aspects, with emphasis on Great Britain; bk. rev.; special

sections on Italy, France, Germany, U.S.A., Scandinavia and the Low Countries; A. index. 20s

106. ECONOMIC JOURNAL. Q. Macmillan and Co. Ltd., St. Martin's St. London, W. C. 2, for Royal Economic Soc., 21 Bentinck St., London, W. 1. 41s

107. ECONOMICA. Q. London School of Economics and Political Science, Houghton St., Aldwych, London, W. C. 2. 30s

108. EDUCATIONAL REVIEW. 3 x y. Inst. of Education, Univ. of Birmingham, Edmund St., Birmingham 3. 15s

109. THE ENGLISH HISTORICAL REVIEW. Q. 1866 (1959: vol. 74). Longmans, Green and Co. Ltd., 6-7 Clifford St., London, W. 1. Ed: J. G. Edwards, Denys Hay, Hist. Department, Univ. of Edinburgh. Art. on the social, economic and political hist. of all periods, with emphasis on Britain and the British Commonwealth and Empire; doc.; rev. of bk. and art., notes of professional interest; vol. author index. 70s

110. ENGLISH PLACE-NAME SOCIETY. PUBLICATIONS. Irr. General Editor: A. H. Smith, Univ. College, Gower St., London, W. 1. (memb.) 25s

111. ESSEX ARCHAEOLOGICAL SOCIETY, TRANSACTIONS OF THE. A. Essex Archaeological Soc., The Museum, Colchester. 25s (memb. free)

112. ESSEX REVIEW. A. Benham and Co. Ltd., Colchester. Until January 1957 appeared Q. p (1) 5s

113. FLINTSHIRE HISTORICAL SOCIETY, PUBLICATIONS OF THE. A. (Irr.). Flintshire Hist. Soc., c/o Flintshire Record Office, Old Rectory, Harwarden, Chester. 15s

114. FOLKLORE. Q. 1878 (1959: vol. 70). Folklore Soc., Univ. College, Gower St., London, W. C. 1. Ed: Christina Hole. Art. on general and regional folklore, folk-custom and tradition of all peoples; rev. of bk. and art.; news of international congresses, and of British folklore museums; minutes and reports of the soc.; illus. 42s/$6.50

115. FRIENDS HISTORICAL SOCIETY, JOURNAL OF THE. S-A. Friends Hist. Soc., Friends House, Euston Rd., London, N. W. 1. Ed; John L. Nickalls. Art. on the hist. of the Quaker movement.

116. FRIENDS HISTORICAL SOCIETY. PUBLICATIONS. Irr. Friends Hist. Soc., Friends House, Euston Rd., London, N. W. 1.

117. THE GENEALOGICAL QUARTERLY. Notes and Queries Dealing with British and American Family and Clan History and Biography. Q. 1931 (1957/8: vol. 24). Research Pub. Co., 52 Lincoln's Inn Fields, London, W. C. 2. Ed: Christopher Telford. Art. on genealogical research, with emphasis on Great Britain and the United States, and on related subjects such as heraldry; bk. rev.; readers' notes and queries. Incorporates The Topographical Quarterly. 17s 6d/$5

118. THE GENEALOGISTS' MAGAZINE. Q. 1925 (1958: vol. 12). Soc. of Genealogists, 37 Harrington Gardens, London, W. W. 7. Ed: C. D. P. Nicholson, F. W. Bennett (secretary). Art. on genealogy, topography and

heraldry, with emphasis on Great Britain and North America; bk. rev.; notes of interest to the soc., and of general genealogical interest.
40s (memb. 20s)/$6 (memb. $ 3)

119. GEOGRAPHICAL JOURNAL. Q. Royal Geographical Soc., 1 Kensington Gore, London, S. W. 7. 43s/42s 6d

120. GERMAN LIFE AND LETTERS. Q. Ed: L. W. Forster, Univ. College, Gower St., London, W. C. 1. 35s

121. GLASGOW ARCHAEOLOGICAL SOCIETY. TRANSACTIONS. B. Titus Wilson and Son Ltd., 28 High Gate, Kendal, for Glasgow Archaeological Soc., 91 Mitchell St., Glasgow, C. 1. pv (p (1) c. 6 - 21s)

122. GOWER. A. Sidney Heath, Wind St., Swansea, for Gower Soc., Royal Inst., Swansea. (memb.) 10s

123. GREECE AND ROME. A Journal of Classical Literature, History and Art. S-A. 1931 (1959: 2nd series, vol. 6). Oxford Univ. Press, Amen House, Warwick Sq., London, E. C. 4, for Classical Assoc. Ed: G. T. W. Hooker, E. R. A. Sewter. Art. on classical literary and hist. subjects, of particular interest to the teaching profession; rev. art.; bk. rev.; illus. 20s/$ 3

124. GREENWICH AND LEWISHAM ANTIQUARIAN SOCIETY, TRANSACTIONS OF THE. A. Blackheath Press Ltd., Blackheath, London, S. E. 3.
15s

125. THE GUILDHALL MISCELLANY. A. (Irr.). 1952 (1958: no. 9). Library Committee of the Corporation of London, Guildhall, London, E. C. 2. Ed: The Librarian. "The object of this Miscellany is to record contributions of historical, antiquarian or literary interest based wholly, or in part, on material in the custody of the Library Committee of the Corporation of London"; illus.
p (1) 5s

126. GYPSY LORE SOCIETY, JOURNAL OF THE. Q. 1888 (1959: 3rd series, vol. 38). Gypsy Lore Soc., c/o H. J. Francis (hon. treasurer), 17 Stoneygate Rd., Leicester. Ed: D. E. Yates, Univ. Library, Liverpool. Art. on all aspects of gypsy life, past and present; bk. rev.; notes and queries.
35s

127. HAKLUYT SOCIETY. PUBLICATIONS. Irr. Hakluyt Soc., c/o British Museum, London, W. C. 1. (memb.) 42s

128. HAMPSHIRE FIELD CLUB AND ARCHAEOLOGICAL SOCIETY. PAPERS AND PROCEEDINGS. A. Hampshire Field Club and Archaeological Soc., c/o R. L. P. Jowitt (secretary), Gore Grange, New Milton, Hampshire.
(memb.) 21s

129. HARLEIAN SOCIETY. PUBLICATIONS. Irr. Harleian Soc., 79 Duke St., London, W. 1.

130. HAWICK ARCHAEOLOGICAL SOCIETY, TRANSACTIONS OF THE. A. R. E. Scott, 4 Dovecote St., Hawick. 5s

131. HENRY BRADWHAW SOCIETY, PUBLICATIONS. Irr. Henry Bradwhaw Soc., c/o A.J. Collins (secretary), 34 The Close, Salisbury, Wilts.
(memb.) 42s

132. THE HIBBERT JOURNAL. A Quarterly Review of Religion, Theology and Philosophy. Q. George Allen and Unwin Ltd., 40 Museum St., London, W. C. 1. 17s 6d/$4.50

133. THE HISTORICAL JOURNAL. S-A. 1958 (1959: vol. 2). Cambridge Univ. Press, Bentley House, 200 Euston Rd., London, N. W. 1, for Cambridge Hist. Soc. Ed: J. P. T. Bury, Corpus Christi College, Cambridge. Art. on the constitutional, economic and political hist. of Britain, from the Middle Ages to the present; doc.; rev. art.; bk. rev.; lists of bk. received. Replaces The Cambridge Historical Journal. 25s/$4.25

HISTORICAL PAPERS see TEKI HISTORYCZNE

134. **HISTORICAL SOCIETY OF LANCASHIRE AND CHESHIRE, TRANSACTIONS OF THE. A. Hist. Soc. of Lancashire and Cheshire, Royal Inst., Colquitt St., Liverpool 1. 30s**

135. **HISTORICAL SOCIETY OF THE CHURCH IN WALES, JOURNAL OF THE. A. 1947 (1959: vol. 9). Hist. Soc. of the Church in Wales, Llandaff House, Penarth, Glamorgan. Ed: Canon E. T. Davies, Llangibby Rectory, Usk, Monmouthshire. Art. on the hist. of the Church in Wales; biographical art.; in English and Welsh. 10s**

136. HISTORICAL SOCIETY OF THE CHURCH IN WALES. PUBLICATIONS. Irr. Hist. Soc. of the Church in Wales, Llandaff House, Penarth, Glamorgan.

HISTORICAL SOCIETY OF THE METHODIST CHURCH OF WALES, THE JOURNAL OF THE see CYMDEITHAS HANES EGLWYS METHODISTIAID CALFINAI CYMRU, CYLCHGRAWN...

137. HISTORY. 3 x y. 1916 (1959: vol. 44, no. 150-152). Routledge and Kegan Paul Ltd., for Hist. Assoc., 59a Kennington Park Rd., London, S. E. 11. Ed: Alfred Cobban, Univ. College, Gower St., London, W. C. 1. Art. on all aspects of hist., with emphasis on European hist., during the period from the 15th to the 20th cent., on the philosophy of hist., and hist. teaching; rev. art.; extensive bk. rev. section, classified by period and area; list of bk. received; A. index of bk. reviewed. 24s (memb. 22s 6d) /$3.50

138. HISTORY TODAY. M. 1951 (1959: vol. 9). Pub. address: 72 Coleman St., London, E. C. 2. Ed: Peter Quennell, Alan Hodge. Art. on hist., not confined to any area or period, but with some emphasis on Great Britain; bk. rev.; illus.; intended primarily for the general reader. 42s/$6

139. HONOURABLE SOCIETY OF CYMMRODORION, TRANSACTIONS OF THE. A. 1892 (1958: no vol. indic.). Honourable Soc. of Cymmrodorion, 20 Bedford Sq., London, W. C. 1. Ed: I. Li. Foster, Jesus College, Oxford. Art. on the hist. of Wales, with emphasis on social, cultural and economic hist. and on the modern period; biographical art.; bk. rev.; A. report of the soc.; in English and Welsh; illus. (memb.) 21s

140. HUDSON'S BAY RECORD SOCIETY. PUBLICATIONS. Irr. Hudson's Bay Record Soc., c/o Hon. Secretary, Beaver House, Great Trinity Lane, London, E. C. 4. (memb.) 21s

141. HUGUENOT SOCIETY OF LONDON, PROCEEDINGS OF THE. A. 1885 (1959: vol. 19, no. 6). Huguenot Soc. of London, c/o Barclays Bank Ltd., 1 Pall Mall East, London, S. W. 1. Art. on the hist. of the Huguenots and on the cultural and social life of the group, with emphasis on the Huguenots in Great Britain; genealogies of Huguenot families; news and notes; A. report of the soc. (memb.) 42s

142. HUGUENOT SOCIETY OF LONDON. PUBLICATIONS. Irr. Huguenot Soc. of London, c/o Irene Scouloudi (hon. secretary), 67 Victoria Rd., London, W. 8.

143. HUNTER ARCHAEOLOGICAL SOCIETY, TRANSACTIONS OF THE. Hunter Archaeological Soc., c/o D. N. Riley (hon. secretary), 3 Highway Close, Sheffield 11. 21s

INDEX LIBRARY see BRITISH RECORD SOCIETY LTD. INDEX LIBRARY

144. THE INDEXER. S-A. Soc. of Indexers, c/o L.E.C. Hughes, (gen. secretary), 15 Avenue House, Allitsen Rd., London, N.W. 8 10s 6d/$ 1.50

145. THE INNES REVIEW. Scottish Catholic Historical Studies. S-A. 1950 (1959: vol. 10). Scottish Catholic Hist. Committee, 195 Buccleuch St., Glasgow C. 3. Ed: Rev. David McRoberts, St. Peter's College, Cardross, Dumbarton. Art. on Scottish ecclesiastical hist., notably the hist. of the Roman Catholic Church; doc.; bk. rev.; biblio.; illus. 10s

INSTITUTE OF ARCHAEOLOGY, ANNUAL REPORT OF THE see INSTITUTE OF ARCHAEOLOGY, BULLETIN OF THE

146. INSTITUTE OF ARCHAEOLOGY, BULLETIN OF THE. A. 1938 (1959: new series, vol. 1). Inst. of Archaeology, Univ. of London, 31-34 Gordon Sq., London, W.C. 1. Ed: W. F. Grimes. Art. on archaeology, not confined to Great Britain, with emphasis on prehist. times; A. report on the activities of the inst.; illus. Until 1958 appeared under the title: Annual Report of the Institute of Archaeology. 10s

147. INSTITUTE OF CLASSICAL STUDIES, BULLETIN OF THE. A. 1954 (1958: no. 5). Inst. of Classical Studies, Univ. of London, 31-34 Gordon Sq., London, W. C. 1. Ed: E. G. Turner. Art. on classical philology, archaeology, epigraphy, hist., philosophy and Greek and Latin literature; proceedings of the London Classical Soc.; titles of theses submitted for advanced degrees in univ. in Great Britain and Ireland; illus. 10s

148. INSTITUTE OF HISTORICAL RESEARCH, BULLETIN OF THE. S-A. 1923 (1958: vol. 31, no. 83-84). Athlone Press, for Inst. of Hist. Research, Univ. of London, Gower St., London, W. C. 1. Ed: J. G. Edwards. Art. on medieval and modern hist., with emphasis on Great Britain; doc.; "Theses Supplement" including sum. of theses on hist. and list of theses on hist. completed or in progress in the United Kingdom; professional news; notes about hist. manuscripts. p (1) 7s 6d

149. INTERNATIONAL AFFAIRS. Q. Oxford Univ. Press, Press Rd., Neasden, London, N.W. 10, for Royal Inst. of International Affairs, Chatham House, St. James's Sq., London, S.W. 1. Extensive classified bk. rev. section. 27s 6d/$ 4.50

150. INTERNATIONAL AND COMPARATIVE LAW QUARTERLY. Q. Soc. of Comparative Legislation, Nuffield Lodge, Regent's Park, London, N.W. 1. 42s

151. INTERNATIONAL RELATIONS. S-A. David Davies Memorial Inst. of International Studies, Thorney House, Smith Sq., London. 10s

152. THE INTERNATIONAL REVIEW OF MISSIONS. Q. Oxford Univ. Press, for International Missionary Council, 2 Eaton Gate, Sloane Sq., London, S.W. 1, and 156 5th Ave., New York 10, N.Y. Bk. rev. and classified international missionary biblio. 15s 6d/$ 3.50

153. IRAQ. S-A. 1934 (1959: vol. 21). British School of Archaeology in Iraq, 5 New Sq., Lincoln's Inn, London, W. C. 2. Ed: M.E.L. Mallowan, Inst. of Archaeology, 31-34 Gordon Sq., London, W.C. 1. "... devoted to studies of the hist., art, archaeology, religion, and social life of Iraq, and to a lesser degree of the neighbouring countries (Iran, Armenia, Anatolia, Syria, and Arabia) from the earliest times down to about A.D. 1700"; rev. art.; notes and special features on current British excavations in Iraq; occasionally also in German or French. 31s

154. THE ISLAMIC QUARTERLY. A Review of Islamic Culture. Q. 1954 (1957: vol. 4). Islamic Cultural Centre, Regent's Lodge, 146 Park Rd., London, N.W. 8. Ed: Hammouda Ghoraba. Art. on Islamic culture, religion, philosophy and literature; bk. rev. 30s

155. THE ISLAMIC REVIEW. M. Woking Muslim Mission and Literary Trust, The Shah Jehan Mosque, Woking, Surrey. 30s/$ 5

156. THE JAPAN SOCIETY OF LONDON. BULLETIN. 3xy. Japan Soc. of London, c/o Lieutenant-Colonel J.W. Marsden, 42 Dry Hill Park Rd., Tonbridge, Kent. (memb.) 31s

157. JEWISH OBSERVER AND MIDDLE EAST REVIEW. W. Ed: Jon Kimche, 129 Salisbury Sq. House, Fleet St., London, E.C. 4. 26s

158. JOHN RYLANDS LIBRARY, MANCHESTER, BULLETIN OF THE. S-A. 1903 (1958/59: vol. 41). John Rylands Library, Deansgate, Manchester 3. Ed: The Librarian. Art. embodying the results of original investigation by British and foreign scholars in the fields of classical studies, theology, hist. (with emphasis on Great Britain), and other subjects pertaining to the humanities; doc.; notes and news of the library. 32s

JOURNAL. For titles beginning with "Journal," followed by the name of the publishing or sponsoring institution or society, see the respective institution or society.

159. THE JOURNAL OF AFRICAN HISTORY. S-A. 1960 (1960: vol. 1). Cambridge Univ. Press, Bentley House, 200 Euston Rd., London, N.W. 1. Ed: R.A. Oliver, J.D. Fage. "The Journal is addressed to the many people.. who are now trying to see African History as a whole extending back to the Stone Age, and not simply in terms of the European empires which were established there only during the last few centuries"; research contributions and bk. rev.; in English and French. 30s

160. THE JOURNAL OF ECCLESIASTICAL HISTORY. S-A. 1950 (1959: vol. 10). Faber and Faber Ltd., 24 Russell Sq., London, W. C. 1. Ed: C. W. Dugmore, c/o King's College, Univ. of London, Strand, London, W.C. 2. Art. on all aspects of ecclesiastical hist. from Biblical to modern times, with emphasis on Great Britain, and occasional biblio. art. on research in progress; bk. rev. and list of bk. received; vol. author index. 30s/$ 4.20

161. JOURNAL OF EGYPTIAN ARCHAEOLOGY. A. 1914 (1958: vol. 44). Egypt Exploration Soc., 2 Hinde St., London, W. 1. Ed: R.O. Faulkner, Flat 2, Bosworth House, Thoroughfare, Woodbridge, Suffolk. Art. on the archaeology, hist., religion, culture, literature and arts of ancient Egypt and the Sudan, mainly in connection with excavations conducted by the soc.; bk. rev. and biblio. of bk. and periodicals on Egyptian archaeology, with brief sum. of contents; professional news and notes. 50s

162. THE JOURNAL OF HELLENIC STUDIES. A. 1880 (1959: vol. 79). Council of the Soc. for the Promotion of Hellenic Studies, 31-34 Gordon Sq., London, W.C. 1. Ed: John Boardman, Department of Antiquities, Ashmolean Museum, Oxford. Art. on the ancient Greek Empire, including Greek literature, the arts and Greek mythology and numismatics; textual criticism; rev. of relevant international pub.; research reports; vol. subject index and index of Greek and Latin authors; in English or other European languages; illus. 60s/$ 6

163. THE JOURNAL OF JEWISH STUDIES. Q. 1948 (1958: vol. 9). Jewish Chronicle Pub., 37 Furnival St., London, E. C. 4, in assoc. with Soc. for Jewish Study and Inst. of Jewish Studies. Ed: A. Altmann, c/o Inst. of Jewish Studies, Stenecourt, Singleton Rd., Salford 7, Lancashire. Art. on Jewish learning, particularly such branches as ancient literature and religious thought, ancient and modern Jewish philosophy, and philology; rev. of current international literature; notes and reports of the pub. inst. 21s/$ 3.50

164. JOURNAL OF ROMAN STUDIES. A. 1911 (1958: vol. 48). Soc. for the Promotion of Roman Studies, 31-34 Gordon Sq., London, W.C. 1. Ed: Miss M.V. Taylor, Haverfield Library, Ashmolean Museum, Oxford. Art. on Roman antiquity, with emphasis on archaeological and epigraphic evidence; rev. art.; bk. rev.; doc. consisting of Romano-British inscriptions; biblio. of bk. and periodicals; news and notes on the proceedings of the soc.; special features on Roman Britain, excavations, etc.; vol. subject and author index. 60s

165. JOURNAL OF SEMITIC STUDIES. Q. 1956 (1958: vol. 3). Manchester Univ. Press, 316-324 Oxford Rd., Manchester 13. Ed: H.H. Rowley, Department of Semitic Studies, Manchester Univ., Manchester 13, and P.R. Weis. Art. on ancient Near and Middle East archaeology, hist., religion, linguistics and literature, with emphasis on Jewish studies; textual criticism; bk. rev.; biblio of art. 32s/$ 4.50

166. THE JOURNAL OF THEOLOGICAL STUDIES. S-A. 1899 (1957: vol. 8). Oxford Univ. Press, Amen House, Warwick Sq., London, E.C.4. Ed: H. Chadwick, Queen's College, Cambridge, and H.F.D. Sparks, Oriel College, Oxford. Art. on theology, Biblical research and Church hist., with emphasis on the early period; bk. rev.; in English and, occasionally, French or German. 40s

167. JOURNAL OF TRANSPORT HISTORY. S-A. 1953 (1958: vol. 4). Univ. College of Leicester, Univ. Rd., Leicester. Ed: Jack Simmons, R. M. Robbins. Art. on all aspects of transport hist., with emphasis on Great Britain and the 18th and 19th cent.; bk. rev.; biblio. of bk. and periodicals; news and notes (in the form of editorials); subject and author index for vol. 1. 18s

168. THE KENT AND SUSSEX JOURNAL. Q. English Counties Periodical Ltd., 6 Illington Ave., Leamington Spa, Warwickshire. 7s 6d

169. LANCASHIRE AND CHESHIRE ANTIQUARIAN SOCIETY, TRANSACTIONS OF THE. A. Lancashire and Cheshire Antiquarian Soc., c/o Central Reference Library, St. Peter's Sq., Manchester 2. 40s

170. LANCASHIRE PARISH REGISTER SOCIETY, PUBLICATIONS. Irr. Lancashire Parish Register Soc., c/o F. Taylor (hon. secretary), John Rylands Library, Deansgate, Manchester 3. 31s 6d

171. LAW QUARTERLY REVIEW. Q. Stevens and Sons, 119/120 Chancery Lane, London, W. C. 2. 42s

172. LEATHERHEAD AND DISTRICT LOCAL HISTORY SOCIETY, PROCEEDINGS OF THE. A. Leatherhead and District Local Hist. Soc., 53 Nutcroft Grove, Fetcham, Leatherhead, Surrey. (memb.) 5s

173. LEEDS PHILOSOPHICAL AND LITERARY SOCIETY, PROCEEDINGS OF THE. Literary and Historical Section. Irr. Leeds Philosophical and Literary Soc., City Museum, Leeds. pni

174. LEICESTERSHIRE ARCHAEOLOGICAL AND HISTORICAL SOCIETY, TRANSACTIONS OF THE. A. Leicestershire Archaeological and Hist. Soc., The Guildhall, Guildhall Lane, Leicester.

175. LINCOLN RECORD SOCIETY. PUBLICATIONS. Irr. Lincoln Record Soc., St. Swithun's Sq., Lincoln. (memb.) 21s

176. LINCOLNSHIRE ARCHIVES COMMITTEE. REPORT. A. Archives Office, Exchequer Gate, Lincoln.

177. THE LINCOLNSHIRE HISTORIAN. A. Lincolnshire Local Hist. Soc., 86 Newland, Lincoln. 15s

178. LIVERPOOL BULLETIN. 3xy. Liverpool Corporation Libraries, Museums and Art Committee, Municipal Offices, Liverpool. "A journal concerned with material belonging to or connected with the Liverpool Public Libraries, the Liverpool Public Museums and the Walker Art Gallery." p (1) 1s 6d

179. LLYFRGELL GENEDLAITHOL CYMRU, CYLCHGRAWN... (Cylchgrawn Llyfrgell Genedlaithol Cymru) [Journal of the National Library of Wales]. S-A. Council of the National Library of Wales, Aberystwyth, Cardiganshire. Ed: Thomas Parry. Art. representing, for the most part, research on collections of the library on all periods of Welsh hist.; doc.; news of the library; illus. Separately pub. supplements containing facsimiles and lists of manuscripts and incunabula. 10s

180. LONDON AND MIDDLESEX ARCHAEOLOGICAL SOCIETY. TRANSACTIONS. A. Pub. address: c/o Bishopsgate Inst., 230 Bishopsgate, London, E.C. 2. 42s

181. LONDON TOPOGRAPHICAL RECORD. London Topographical Soc., 120 Chancery Lane, London, W.C. 2. (memb.) 21s

182. MALAYAN BULLETIN. British Assoc. of Malaya, 18 Northumberland Ave., London, W.C. 2.

183. MAN. A Monthly Record of Anthropological Science. M. 1901 (1959: vol. 59). Royal Anthropological Inst., 21 Bedford Sq., London, W.C. 1. Ed: W. B. Fagg, c/o British Museum, London, W.C. 1. Art. on physical and cultural anthropology, prehist., hist. of domestication, social evolution, and related subjects; rev. of bk. and art. 30s

184. MANCHESTER LITERARY AND PHILOSOPHICAL SOCIETY, MEMOIRS AND PROCEEDINGS OF THE. A. Manchester Literary and Philosophical Soc., c/o Portico Library, 57 Mosley St., Manchester. Sum. of each art. 31s 6d

185. THE MANCHESTER SCHOOL OF ECONOMIC AND SOCIAL STUDIES. 3xy. 1930 (1959: vol. 27). Department of Economics, Univ. of Manchester, Manchester 13. Ed: W. A. Lewis. Art. on the economic and social hist. of Great Britain and British foreign trade since 1870, and on economic thought, mainly of the 18th and 19th cent.; rev. art. 20s

186. MANX MUSEUM, JOURNAL OF THE. A. Manx Museum and National Trust, Douglas, Isle of Man. 6s

187. MARINER'S MIRROR. Q. 1911 (1959: vol. 45). Cambridge Univ. Press, Bentley House, 200 Euston Rd., London, N.W. 1, for Soc. for Nautical Research. Ed: G.R.G. Worcester, Penny Cottage, Pound Lane, Windlesham, Surrey. Art. on naval hist., the hist. of shipbuilding, relating to seafaring, not confined to any country or period; doc.; bk. rev.; notes and section of questions and answers; vol. subject index. 60s

188. MEDICAL HISTORY. A Quarterly Journal Devoted to the History and Bibliography of Medicine and the Related Sciences. Q. 1957 (1959: vol. 3). William Dawson and Sons, Ltd., 16 West St., Farnham, Surrey. Ed: W.J. Bishop, 1 Queen Anne St., London, W. 1. Art. on the hist. of all branches of medicine; biographical art. on prominent scholars of medicine; doc.; bk. rev.; reports of the Cambridge Univ. Hist. of Medicine Soc., the Norwegian Soc. for the Hist. of Medicine, the Osler Club of London, the Royal Soc. of Medicine, and the Scottish Soc. of the Hist. of Medicine. 50s/$ 7.50

MEMOIRS. For titles beginning with "Memoirs," followed by the name of the publishing or sponsoring institution or society, see the respective institution or society.

189. MERIONETH HISTORICAL AND RECORD SOCIETY, JOURNAL OF THE. A. Merioneth Hist. and Record Soc., County Office, Dolgelly, Merionethshire. 10s

190. MILITARY HISTORICAL SOCIETY. BULLETIN. Q. Military Hist. Soc., Imperial War Museum, Lambeth Rd., London, S.E. 1

191. THE MODERN LANGUAGE REVIEW. Q. Cambridge Univ. Press, 200 Euston Rd., London, N. W. 1, for Modern Humanities Research Assoc. 60s

192. MODERN LAW REVIEW. B-M. Stevens and Sons, Ltd., 119/120 Chancery Lane, London, W.C. 2. 42s

193. THE MONTGOMERYSHIRE COLLECTIONS. A. Manchester Museum, Univ. of Manchester, Manchester 13, for Powys-land Club.

194. THE MONTH. M. Soc. of Jesus, 114 Mount St., London, W. 1 34s 6d/$ 6

195. MORGANNWG. Glamorgan Local Hist. Soc., Cardiff, Wales.

196. MUSEUMS JOURNAL. M. 1901 (1959: vol. 59). Museums Assoc., 33 Fitzroy St., London, W. 1. Ed: Michael Nightingale. Art. on museum holdings, acquisitions, conservation and administration; bk. rev.; illus. 44s (memb. free)

NATIONAL LIBRARY OF WALES JOURNAL see LLYGRGELL GENEDLAETHOL CYMRU, CYLCHGRAWN...

197. NATIONAL REGISTER OF ARCHIVES, BULLETIN OF THE. Irr. 1948 (1957: vol. 9). Hist. Manuscripts Commission, National Register of Archives, Public Record Office, Chancery Lane, London, W.C. 2. Notes about manuscript holdings in Great Britain, particularly those of local and ecclesiastical authorities and family and estate papers whose location has been reported to the National Register of Archives. nfs

198. NAVY RECORDS SOCIETY. PUBLICATIONS. Irr. Navy Records Soc., c/o Christopher C. Lloyd (hon. secretary), Royal Naval College, Greenwich, London, S.E. 10. (memb.) 42s

199. THE NEW INDEX. Irr. 1955 (1959: vol. 1, no. 11). Confederate Research Club, 33 Highclere Ave., Leigh Park, Havant, Hampshire. Ed: Patrick C. Courtney. "Devoted to the Naval, Military and Civil history of the Confederate States of America, 1861-1865, and the War between the States in general"; bk. rev.; illus. (memb.) 26s/$ 4

200. NEW WORLD ANTIQUITY. M. Marham House Press, 31 Kings Rd., London, S. W. 3. 21s/$ 3

201. NEWCOMEN SOCIETY FOR THE STUDY OF THE HISTORY OF ENGINEERING AND TECHNOLOGY, TRANSACTIONS OF THE. A. (Irr.). 1921 (1953-55 [1958]: vol. 29). Newcomen Soc. for the Study of the Hist. of Engineering and Technology, Science Museum, London, S.W. 7. Ed: S.B. Hamilton. Papers, read at meetings of the soc., on the hist. of engineering and technology, with emphasis on the British Isles and on the period from the 18th cent.; "Analytical Bibliography of the History of Engineering and Applied Sciences" A. report of the soc.; vol. subject and name index; illus. 50s/$ 7.15

202. THE NIGERIAN FIELD. Q. Arthurs Press Ltd., Woodchester, Stroud, Gloucestershire, for Nigerian Field Soc. 30s

203. NORFOLK ARCHAEOLOGY. Miscellaneous Tracts Relating to the Antiquities of the County of Norfolk. A. Norfolk and Norwick Archaeological Soc., Garsett House, St. Andrew's Hall Plain, Norwich. 25s

204. NORFOLK RECORD SOCIETY. PUBLICATIONS. Irr. Hon. Ed: Percy Millican, Sprowston Court East, Norwich. (memb.) 21s

205. THE NORSEMAN. B-M. Ed: H.K. Lehmkuhl, 25 Belgrave Sq., London, S. W. 1. Ceased pub. in December 1958. p(1) 2s 6d

206. NORTH STAFFORDSHIRE FIELD CLUB, TRANSACTIONS AND ANNUAL REPORT OF THE. A. North Staffordshire Field Club, c/o City Museum, Hanley, Stoke-on-Trent. 15s

207. NORTHAMPTONSHIRE PAST AND PRESENT. A. Northamptonshire Record Soc., Lamport Hall, Northampton. 2s 6d

208. NORTHAMPTONSHIRE RECORD SOCIETY. PUBLICATIONS. Irr. Northamptonshire Record Soc., c/o Joan Wake (hon. secretary), 11 Charlbury Rd., Oxford. (memb.) 21s

209. NOTES AND QUERIES. For Readers and Writers, Collectors and Librarians. M. 1849 (1959: new series, vol. 6). Oxford Univ. Press, Amen House, Warwick Sq., London, E.C. 4. Brief art. on literary subjects, the hist. of literature, and the general hist. of Great Britain, written for the general public; rev. of bk and art.; vol. subject index pub. separately. 48s

210. NOTES AND QUERIES FOR SOMERSET AND DORSET. 3 x y. Ed: T.J. Hunt, Orchard End, Cheddon Rd., Taunton, and P.N. Dawe, 13 Parchment St., Winchester. 10s

211. NOTTINGHAM MEDIAEVAL STUDIES. A. 1957 (1958: vol. 11). Univ. of Nottingham, Nottingham. Ed: Lewis Thorpe. Art., normally embodying the result of research work done at the univ., on medieval cultural, religious and political hist. and philology. 15s

THE NUMISMATIC CHRONICLE AND JOURNAL OF THE ROYAL NUMISMATIC SOCIETY see ROYAL NUMISMATIC SOCIETY, THE NUMISMATIC CHRONICLE AND JOURNAL OF THE

212. NUMISMATIC CIRCULAR. 11 x y. 1893 (1959: vol. 68). Messrs. Spink and Son Ltd., Art Dealers, 5 King St., London, S. W. 1. Ed: H. W. A. Linecar. Art. on numismatics; lists of coins and medals; bk. rev.; biblio.; in English and other languages; illus. 10s

213. OLD CORNWALL. Irr. (A. or S-A). Federation of Old Cornwall Soc., c/o R. Morton Nance Chylason (ed.), Carbis Bay, St. Ives, Cornwall. p (1) 2s

214. ORIENTAL AND CERAMIC SOCIETY. TRANSACTIONS. Irr. Oriental and Ceramic Soc., 48 Davies St., London, W. 1. pv

215. ORIENTAL ART. Q. Pub. address: 125 High Holborn, London, W. C. 1 23s / $7

216. OXFORD HISTORICAL SOCIETY. PUBLICATIONS. Irr. Clarendon Press, Oxford, for Oxford Hist. Soc., Oxford.

217. OXFORD SLAVONIC PAPERS. Irr. 1950 (1958: vol. 8). Oxford Univ. Press, Warwick Sq., Amen House, London, E. C. 4. Ed: S. Konovalov. Art. on Slav, mainly Russian hist., literature and languages; reproductions of original texts. 18s

OXFORDSHIRE ARCHAEOLOGICAL SOCIETY, REPORT OF THE see OXONIENSIA

218. OXFORDSHIRE RECORD SOCIETY. PUBLICATIONS. Irr. Oxfordshire Record Soc., c/o W. O. Hassall (hon. secretary), The Manor House, Wheatley, Oxford. (memb.) 21s

219. OXONIENSIA. A Journal Dealing with the Archaeology, History and Architecture of Oxford and its Neighbourhood. A. (irr.). Oxford Architectural and Hist. Soc., Ashmolean Museum, Oxford. Incorporates the Report of the Oxfordshire Archaeological Society. 27s 6d

PALESTINE EXPLORATION FUND, QUARTERLY STATEMENT OF THE see PALESTINE EXPLORATION QUARTERLY

220. PALESTINE EXPLORATION QUARTERLY. S-A. 1869 (1958: vol. 19). Palestine Exploration Fund, 2 Hinde St., Manchester Sq., London, W. 1. Ed: F. F. Bruce. Art. on the archaeology of Palestine and on the progress of excavations; bk. rev.; illus.; embodies the Quarterly Statement of the Palestine Exploration Fund and the Bulletin of the British School of Archaeology in Jerusalem 30s

221. THE PALL MALL QUARTERLY. Q. Liberal International, 123 Pall Mall, London, S. W. 1. Succeeds World Liberalism, pub. from 1951 to 1957. 16s/$3

PAPERS. For titles beginning with "Papers," followed by the name of the publishing or sponsoring institution or society, see the respective institution or society.

222. PARLIAMENTARY AFFAIRS. Q. 1947 (1958/59: vol. 12). Hansard Soc. for Parliamentary Government, 79/80 Petty France, London, S.W. 1. Ed: Ann Dewar. Art. on parliamentary government and its hist. throughout the world; bk. rev., including pub. on constitutional and administrative topics and political theory; A. subject index. 30s/$4.50

223. PAST AND PRESENT. A Journal of Historical Studies. S-A. 1952 (1959: no. 15/16). Past and Present, c/o Titus Wilson and Son Ltd., 28 Highgate, Kendal. Ed: John Morris, Univ. College, London. Hist. art. on all areas, with emphasis on social and economic hist. and on the modern period; rev. art.; notes of professional interest. 15s

224. PHILOSOPHY. Q. Macmillan and Co., St. Martin's St., London, W. C. 2, for Royal Inst. of Philosophy, Univ. Hall, 14a Gordon Sq., London, W. C. 1. 21s

225. PIPE ROLL SOCIETY. PUBLICATIONS. Irr. Pipe Roll Soc., c/o Lady Stenton (hon. secretary), Whitley Park Farm, Reading, Berkshire. (memb.) 42s

226. POLITICAL STUDIES. 3xy. 1953 (1958: vol. 6). Oxford Univ. Press, Amen House, Warwick Sq., London, E.C. 4, for Political Studies Assoc. of the United Kingdom. Art. on political science and constitutional and administrative hist., with emphasis on the modern period; bk. rev.; news of the assoc. 33s 6d/$ 5

227. POPULATION STUDIES. A Journal of Demography. 3xy. 1947 (1958/59: vol. 12). Population Investigation Committee, London School of Economics, Houghton St., Aldwych, London, W.C. 2. Ed: D.V. Glass, E. Grebenik. Art. on demography and related fields, with emphasis on the modern period; bk. rev.; sum. 42s/$ 6.75

228. PORUKA JUGOSLOVENSKOJ EMIGRACIJI, SRBIMA, HRVATIMA I SLOVENCIMA [Message to Yugoslav emigrants, Serbs, Croats and Slovenes]. B-M. Jugoslovenski Narodni Odbor [Yugoslav National Committee], 12 Egerton Gardens, London, S.W. 3. 1s 6d

229. PREHISTORIC SOCIETY, PROCEEDINGS OF THE. A. 1935 (1958: vol. 24). Prehist. Soc., c/o H.J. Case (hon. secretary), Department of Antiquities, Ashmolean Museum, Oxford. Ed: J.G.D. Clark, Univ. Museum of Archaeology and Ethnology, Downing St., Cambridge. Art. on prehist., predominantly European; notes on recent excavations and notes of general professional interest; bk. rev.; A. report of the soc.; list of memb. 42s/$ 6

230. PRESBYTERIAN HISTORICAL SOCIETY OF ENGLAND, JOURNAL OF THE. A. 1914 (1957: vol. 11). Presbyterian Hist. Soc. of England, 86 Tavistock Pl., London, W.C. 1. Ed: Lillian W. Kelly. Art. on Church hist. in England, with emphasis on the Presbyterian Church; A. report and transactions of the soc.; bk. rev. 6s

PROCEEDINGS. For titles beginning with "Proceedings," followed by the name of the publishing or sponsoring institution or society, see the respective institution or society.

231. PUBLIC ADMINISTRATION. Q. Royal Inst. of Public Administration, Haldane House, 76a New Cavendish St., London, W. 1. Art. on all aspects of contemporary national and local government adminstration, and on the hist. of public administration in the 19th and 20th cent., with emphasis on the United Kingdom; bk. rev.; biblio. of recent British government pub.; news and notes on the activities of the inst. 30s/$ 5

232. PUBLIC RECORD OFFICE, ANNUAL REPORT OF THE KEEPER OF PUBLIC RECORDS ON THE WORK OF THE. A. H.M. Stationery Office, York House, Kingsway, London, W.C. 2, for Public Record Office. Report on public records and regulations governing its use; lists transfers of records, deposits, loans and gifts to Public Record Office during the year.

233. PUBLIC RECORD OFFICE. TEXTS AND CALENDARS. Irr. H. M. Stationery Office, York House, Kingsway, London, W.C. 2, for Public Record Office. pv

PUBLICATIONS. For titles beginning with "Publications," followed by the name of the publishing or sponsoring institution or society, see the respective institution or society.

QUARTERLY STATEMENT OF THE PALESTINE EXPLORATION FUND see PALESTINE EXPLORATION QUARTERLY

234. RADNORSHIRE SOCIETY, TRANSACTIONS OF THE. A. Radnorshire Soc., c/o Library Department, County Hall, Llandrindod Wells, Radnorshire. Index for vol. 1-26 pub. in 1960. 12s 6d/$ 1.75

235. RAILWAY AND CANAL HISTORICAL SOCIETY, JOURNAL OF THE. B-M. 1954 (1959: vol. 5). Railway and Canal Hist. Soc., c/o Maurice Berrill (hon. secretary), 33 Top Rd., Calow, Chesterfield, Derbyshire. Ed: J. G. Spence, Tuborg Cottage, 34 Manor Ave., Caterham, Surrey. Art. on railway and canal hist. in Great Britain; biographical art.; biblio. of relevant pub.; letters to the ed. (memb.) 21s

236. RECUSANT HISTORY. A Journal of Research in Post-Reformation Catholic History in the British Isles. 3 xy. 1951 (1959: vol. 5). Arundel Press Sussex Rd., Bognor Regis, for Catholic Record Soc. Ed: A.F. Allison, British Museum, London, W.C. 1, and D.M. Roger, The Bodleian Library, Oxford. Formerly pub. under the title: Biographical Studies. 12s 6d/$ 2

237. REMAINS HISTORICAL AND LITERARY CONNECTED WITH THE PALATINE COUNTIES OF LANCASTER AND CHESTER. Irr. Chetham Soc., c/o Rev. J. Flitcroft (secretary), Hulme Hall, Victoria Park, Manchester 14. (memb.) 30s

238. RENAISSANCE AND MODERN STUDIES. A. 1957 (1958: vol. 2). Sisson and Parker, Wheeler Gate, Nottingham, for Univ. of Nottingham, Univ. Park, Nottingham. Ed: V. de Sola Pinto. Essays and studies by memb. of the univ. on literature, language, hist. (including the hist. of science), law, philosophy, theology, music and fine arts, with emphasis on Great Britain and the period from 1500 to the present; doc.; illus. 13s 3d/$ 1.85

REPORT AND TRANSACTIONS. SOCIETE GUERNESIAISE see SOCIETE GUERNESIAISE. REPORT AND TRANSACTIONS

REPORT OF THE OXFORDSHIRE ARCHAEOLOGICAL SOCIETY see OXONIENSIA

239. RICKMANSWORTH HISTORICAL SOCIETY. MAGAZINE. Irr. (2 or 3 xy). Rickmansworth Hist. Soc., 3 Repton Way, Croxley Green, Rickmansworth, Hertshire. 5s (for 4 no.)

240. ROLLS SERIES. Chronicles and Memorials of Great Britain and Ireland during the Middle Ages, Published under the Direction of the Master of the Rolls. Irr. H.M. Stationery Office, York House, Kingsway, London, W. C. 2 pv

241. ROXBURGHE CLUB. Irr. Roxburghe Club, c/o Eric George Millar (secretary), 28 Holland Park Rd., Kensington, London, W. 14. nfs

242. ROYAL ANTHROPOLOGICAL INSTITUTE OF GREAT BRITAIN AND IRELAND, JOURNAL OF THE. S-A. 1871 (mri 1956: vol. 86). Royal Anthropological Inst., 21 Bedford Sq., London, W.C. 1. Ed: G.W.B. Huntingford. Art. on general anthropological subjects, archaeology and cultural problems; news of A. meetings of the inst. 40s

243. ROYAL ASIATIC SOCIETY OF GREAT BRITAIN AND IRELAND, JOURNAL OF THE. S-A. 1844 (1958: parts 3 and 4). Royal Asiatic Soc. of Great Britain and Ireland, incorporating the Soc. of Biblical Archaeology, 56 Queen Anne St., London, W. 1. Art. on the archaeology, art, hist., language, literature, beliefs and customs of the East; doc.; bk. rev., classified by geographical area; A. report of the soc. and list of presentations and acquisitions to the library; A. name and subject index; illus. 60s (memb. 42s)

244. ROYAL CENTRAL ASIAN SOCIETY, JOURNAL OF THE. Q. Royal Central Asian Soc., 2 Hinde St., London, W. 1. 25s

245. ROYAL COMMISSION ON HISTORICAL MANUSCRIPTS. REPORTS AND CALENDARS. Irr. H.M. Stationery Office, York House, Kingsway, London, W.C. 2. pv

246. ROYAL INSTITUTION OF GREAT BRITAIN, PROCEEDINGS OF THE. A. Royal Inst. of Great Britain, 21 Albemarle St., London, W. 1. 12s 6d

247. ROYAL NUMISMATIC SOCIETY, THE NUMISMATIC CHRONICLE AND JOURNAL OF THE. A. 1836 (1958: no vol. indic.). Royal Numismatic Soc., c/o Department of Coins and Medals, British Museum, London, W.C. 2. Ed. board: John Walker, E.S.G. Robinson, C.H.V. Sutherland. Art. dealing with coinage of all periods; descriptions of coin hoards, mainly those found in the British Isles; rev. of bk. on all numismatic subjects and background material relevant to hist. and art. 80s

248. ROYAL UNITED SERVICE INSTITUTION, JOURNAL OF THE. Q. 1857 (1958: vol. 103). Royal United Service Inst., Whitehall, London, S.W. 1. Ed: P.K. Kemp. Art. on military strategy, the hist. of the British naval, military and air force, and on campaigns, with emphasis on the wars of the 19th and 20th cent.; "Navy Notes," "Army Notes" and "Air Notes"; bk. rev.; A. report of the inst. 30s

249. SAGA-BOOK. Irr. 1892 (1956/57: vol. 14, part 4). Viking Soc. for Northern Research, Univ. College, Gower St., London, W.C. 1. Ed. board: Ursula Brown, Somerville College, Oxford, P.G. Foote, Joan Turville-Petre. Art. on old Norse language, mythology and literature; bk. rev. 30s

250. SCHOOL OF ORIENTAL AND AFRICAN STUDIES, BULLETIN OF THE. 3xy. 1917 (1958: vol. 21). School of Oriental and African Studies, Univ. of London, London, W. C. 1. Ed: J. Brough. Art., shorter notes and communications on the hist., archaeology, philology and literature of Asia and Africa, with some emphasis on the ancient and medieval periods; bk. rev.; biblio. of bk. received. 90s

251. THE SCOTTISH GEOGRAPHICAL MAGAZINE. 3xy. Royal Scottish Geographical Soc., Synod Hall, Castle Terr., Edinburgh 1. Bk. rev. section, classified by area and subject. 15s

252. THE SCOTTISH HISTORICAL REVIEW. S-A. 1903 (1959: vol. 38, no. 125/126). Thomas Nelson and Sons, Parkside Works, Edinburgh 9. Ed: W. Croft Dickinson. Art. on Scottish hist. (mostly modern); rev. of bk. and doc.; short notes on periodical literature; A. subject index; illus. 21s

253. SCOTTISH RECORD OFFICE. TEXTS AND CALENDARS. Irr. Scottish Record Office, Edinburgh 2. (memb.) 21s

254. SEABY'S COIN AND MEDAL BULLETIN. M. 1945 (1959: vol. 11). B.A. Seaby Ltd., 65 Great Portland St., London, W. 1. Ed: P. J. Seaby. Art. on numismatics and allied subjects; bk. rev.; correspondence; reports of numismatic soc.; answers to questions; lists of coins and medals for sale; illus.; cum. table of contents every 10 years. 7s 6d

255. SELDEN SOCIETY. PUBLICATIONS. Irr. Selden Soc., 25 Russell Sq., London, W.C. 1. nfs

256. SHROPSHIRE ARCHAEOLOGICAL SOCIETY, TRANSACTIONS OF THE. A. (Irr.). Wilding and Son Ltd., Castle St., Shrewsbury, Shropshire, for Shropshire Archaeological Soc. 21s

257. SLAVONIC AND EAST EUROPEAN REVIEW. S-A. 1922 (1959: vol. 37, no. 89). School of Slavonic and East European Studies, Univ. of London, Senate House, London, W.C. 1. Ed: G.H. Bolsover. Art. on all aspects of Slavonic hist., life and literature; bk. rev.; doc.; vol. subject and author index. 40s

258. SOCIETE GUERNESIAISE [Society of Guernsey]. REPORT AND TRANSACTIONS. A. Guille Allès Library, Guernsey C. 1. pv (5s - 8s)

259. SOCIETE JERSIAISE [Society of Jersey]. ANNUAL BULLETIN. A. Société Jersiaise, Museum, 9 Pier Rd., St. Helier, Jersey. "For the study of the history, the geology, the natural history, and the antiquities of the island and their preservation; also the publication of historical documents." 8s 6d

260. SOCIETY FOR ARMY HISTORICAL RESEARCH, JOURNAL OF THE. Q. 1921 (1958: vol. 36, no. 145-148). Soc. for Army Hist. Research, c/o The Library, War Office, London, S.W. 1. Ed: T.H. McGuffie. Art. on the hist., customs and traditions of the British army, with emphasis on the period from the 17th cent. to 1900 and on campaigns, weapons and armor; notes; bk. rev. subject indices for vol. 1-12 and 13-28; a "Museum Supplement" containing art. on regimental and military museums appears with each no.; illus. 21s

261. SOCIETY OF ANTIQUARIES OF SCOTLAND, PROCEEDINGS OF THE. A. 1851 (1956/57 [1959]: vol. 90). Soc. of Antiquaries of Scotland, National Museum of Antiquities, Queen St., Edinburgh. Art. on the archaeology of Scotland during the prehist., Roman and medieval periods. (memb. free)

262. SOCIETY OF ARCHIVISTS, JOURNAL OF THE. S-A. 1955 (1958: vol. 1, no. 7/8). Soc. of Archivists, Guildhall Library, Basinghall St., London, E.C. 2. Ed: A.E.J. Hollaender. Art. on the hist., structure and holdings of British, Commonwealth and American archives, on archival techniques and the ad ministration of archives; rev. art. and bk. rev.; notes about the activities of the soc. 15s

263. SOMERSET RECORD SOCIETY. PUBLICATIONS. Irr. Somerset Record Soc., c/o Mrs. S.W. Rawlins (hon. secretary), Newton Surmaville, Yeovil, Somerset. (memb.) 21s

264. SOMERSETSHIRE ARCHAEOLOGICAL AND NATURAL HISTORY SOCIETY. PROCEEDINGS. A. (Irr.). Somersetshire Archaeological and Natural Hist. Soc., Taunton Castle, Taunton. 21s

265. SOUTH WALES AND MONMOUTH RECORD SOCIETY. PUBLICATIONS. Irr. South Wales and Monmouth Record Soc., 346 Cyncoed Rd., Cardiff. (memb.) 21s

266. SOUTHAMPTON RECORD SOCIETY. PUBLICATIONS. Irr. Southampton Record Soc., c/o H. Rothwell (ed.), Univ. of Southampton, Southampton.

267. SOVIET STUDIES. A Quarterly Review of the Social and Economic Institutions of the U.S.S.R. Q. Basil Blackwell, Broad St., Oxford, for the Department for the Study of the Social and Economic Inst. of the U.S.S.R., Univ. of Glasgow, Glasgow. 42s

SOVIET SURVEY see section on International Periodicals

268. STANFORD AND RUTLAND ARCHAEOLOGICAL AND NATURAL HISTORY SOCIETY. ANNUAL REPORT AND TRANSACTIONS. A. Stanford and Rutland Archaeological and Natural Hist. Soc., 15 Rutland Terr., Stanford, Lincolnshire.

STUDIES IN CONSERVATION see section on International Periodicals

269. STUDIES IN LEICESTERSHIRE AGRARIAN HISTORY. Irr. Leicestershire Archaeological and Hist. Soc., The Guildhall, Guildhall Lane, Leicester. Ed: W.G. Hoskins.

270. SUFFOLK INSTITUTE OF ARCHAEOLOGY, PROCEEDINGS OF THE. A. Suffolk Inst. of Archaeology, c/o School of Art, Bury St. Edmunds, Suffolk. 25s

271. SURREY ARCHAEOLOGICAL COLLECTIONS. Relating to the History and Antiquities of the County. Irr. Surrey Archaeological Soc., Castle Arch, Guildford, Surrey. pni

272. SURREY RECORD SOCIETY. PUBLICATIONS. Irr. Surrey Record Soc., c/o Castle Arch, Guildford, Surrey. (memb.) 20s

273. SURTEES SOCIETY. PUBLICATIONS. Irr. Surtees Soc., c/o H. S. Offler (secretary), 28 Old Elvet, Durham. (memb.) 42s

274. SUSSEX ARCHAEOLOGICAL COLLECTIONS. A. Sussex Archaeological Soc., Barbican House, Lewes, Sussex. (memb. free)

275. SUSSEX NOTES AND QUERIES. S-A. Sussex Archaeological Soc., Barbican House, Lewes, Sussex. 6s (memb. free)

276. SUSSEX RECORD SOCIETY. PUBLICATIONS. Irr. Sussex Record Soc., 53 The Avenue, Lewes, Sussex. (memb.) 21s

277. TEKI HISTORYCZNE. CAHIERS D'HISTOIRE. HISTORICAL PAPERS. A. 1947 (1958: vol. 9). Nakladem Instytutu Historycznego Imienia Generala Sikorskiego, London, for Polskie Towarzystwo Historyczne na Obczyznie [Polish Hist. Soc. in Exile], 20 Princes Gate, London, S. W. 7. Ed: Marian Kukiel. Art. mostly on Polish hist. and historiography; bk. rev.; professional news and short indications of contents of selected periodicals from Poland and other countries. pv

278. THORESBY SOCIETY. PUBLICATIONS. Irr. Thoresby Soc., 16 Queen's Square, Leeds 2. (memb.) 15s

279. THOROTON SOCIETY OF NOTTINGHAMSHIRE, TRANSACTIONS OF THE. A. Ed: R. Smith, M. Barley, Univ. of Nottingham, Univ. Park, Nottingham. (memb.) 31s 6d

280. THOROTON SOCIETY. RECORD SERIES. Irr. Thoroton Soc., c/o Univ. of Nottingham, Univ. Park, Nottingham.

281. TOP. OXON. A Bulletin of Oxfordshire Local History. S-A. Oxfordshire Archaeological Soc., Oxford.

THE TOPOGRAPHICAL QUARTERLY see THE GENEALOGICAL QUARTERLY

TRANSACTIONS. For titles beginning with "Transactions," followed by the name of the publishing or sponsoring institution or society, see the respective institution or society.

282. THE UKRAINIAN REVIEW. Q. Assoc. of Ukrainians in Great Britain, 49 Linden Gardens, London, W. 2. 20s

283. UNITARIAN HISTORICAL SOCIETY, TRANSACTIONS OF THE. A. 1917 (1959: vol. 12). Unitarian Hist. Soc., Unitarian College, Victoria Park, Manchester 14. Ed: Rev. C. Gordon Bolam, 13 Devonshire Rd., West Bridgford, Nottingham. Art. on the hist. of the Unitarian and kindred movements in the United Kingdom and elsewhere; doc.; rev. art.; bk. rev.; biblio. of bk. and periodicals; news and notes; vol. subject and author index. 7s 6d

284. UNIVERSITY OF BIRMINGHAM HISTORICAL JOURNAL. A. 1947 (1957/58: vol. 6). School of Hist., Univ. of Birmingham, Edmund St., Birmingham 3. Ed: Philip Styles. Art. on all periods of hist., including the classical, with emphasis on the political, social and economic hist. of Great Britain; doc. 12s 6d

285. UNIVERSITY OF BRISTOL SPELAEOLOGICAL SOCIETY, PROCEEDINGS OF THE. A. Univ. of Bristol Spelaeological Soc., U. B. S. S. Rooms, Bristol Univ., Bristol 8. 10s

286. WARBURG AND COURTAULD INSTITUTES, JOURNAL OF THE. S-A. 1937 (1958: vol. 21). Warburg and Cortauld Inst., Univ. of London, Imperial Inst. Bldgs., South Kensington, London, S. W. 1. Ed. board: E. H. Gombrich, J. B. Trapp, Frances A. Yates, Anthony Blunt, T. S. R. Boase,

Warburg Inst., Univ. of London, Woburn Sq., London, W. C. 1. Art. on the hist. of art and culture of all areas and periods, and on comparative religion. 63s

287. WARWICKSHIRE AND WORCESTERSHIRE MAGAZINE. M. English Counties Periodicals Ltd., 6 Lillington Ave., Leamington Spa., Warwickshire. 25s

288. WESLEY HISTORICAL SOCIETY, PROCEEDINGS OF THE. Q. 1897 (1959: vol. 32). Wesley Hist. Soc., 136 Cottingham Rd., Hull, Yorkshire. Ed: W.F. Swift, 45 Kingsway, Lytham St. Annes, Lancashire. Art. on the hist. of the Methodist Church, with emphasis on the 19th cent., and biographical art. dealing with John Wesley; bk. rev. and notes and queries; report on the activities of the soc.; index for vol. 1-16; illus. 7s 6d/$ 1

289. WIENER LIBRARY BULLETIN. Irr. Wiener Library, 18 Adam St., Strand, London, W.C. 2. Bk. rev. and biblio. 105s (individuals 42s)

290. WILTSHIRE ARCHAEOLOGICAL AND NATURAL HISTORY MAGAZINE. A. Wiltshire Archaeological and Natural Hist. Soc., 41 Long St., Devizes, Wiltshire. 32s 6d

291. WILTSHIRE ARCHAEOLOGICAL AND NATURAL HISTORY SOCIETY. RECORDS BRANCH. Irr. Wiltshire Archaeological and Natural Hist. Soc., 41 Long St., Devizes, Wiltshire.

292. WOODFORD AND DISTRICT HISTORICAL SOCIETY. PROCEEDINGS AND TRANSACTIONS. B-M. Kentish Independent Printing Works, Wellington St., Woolwich, London, S.E. 18, for Woodford and District Hist. Soc. 20s

293. WOOLWICH AND DISTRICT ANTIQUARIAN SOCIETY. ANNUAL REPORTS. A. Kentish Independent Printing Works, Wellington St., Woolwich, London, S.E. 18.

294. WORCESTERSHIRE ARCHAEOLOGICAL SOCIETY, TRANSACTIONS OF THE. A. Worcestershire Archaeological Soc. c/o Clifford Baylis (hon. secretary), Tintagel, Thornloe, Worcestershire. 20s

295. WORCESTERSHIRE HISTORICAL SOCIETY. PUBLICATIONS. Irr. Hon. General Ed: P.H. Sawyer, School of History, Univ. of Birmingham, Birmingham. (memb.) 21s

WORLD LIBERALISM see THE PALL MALL QUARTERLY

296. THE YORKSHIRE ARCHAEOLOGICAL JOURNAL. A. Yorkshire Archaeological Soc., 10 Park Pl., Leeds 1. (memb.) 20s

297. YORKSHIRE ARCHAEOLOGICAL SOCIETY. RECORD SERIES. Irr. Yorkshire Archaeological Soc., 10 Park Pl., Leeds 1. (memb.) 30s

298. YORKSHIRE BULLETIN OF ECONOMIC AND SOCIAL RESEARCH. S-A. Dept. of Economics, Univ. of Hull, Leeds and Sheffield. (Pub. address: c/o A.J. Brown (ed.), Dept. of Economics and Commerce, Univ. of Leeds, Leeds 2). 15s

ADDENDA

299. THE COAT OF ARMS. Q. 1950 (1959: vol. 5, no. 37-40). Heraldry Soc., 21 East Knoyle, Wiltshire. Ed: C.M. Egan. Art. on heraldry, with emphasis on Great Britain, and on related subjects, such as genealogy; bk. rev.; correspondence; reports on other British soc. of a similar nature. 12s / $ 2

300. ROYAL HISTORICAL SOCIETY, TRANSACTIONS OF THE. A. 1869-71 (1959: 5th series, vol. 9). Royal Hist. Soc., 96 Cheyne Walk, London, S.W. 10. Art. on all aspects of medieval and modern hist.; A. reports of the Council of the Royal Hist. Soc.

Greece

Prepared with the assistance of

Mrs. Catherine Koumarianoû, Neohellenic Research Center, Athens, and the

Gennadius Library, American School of Classical Studies, Athens

Note: The main titles of the periodicals are transcribed with the aim of approximating the pronunciation of Modern Greek. The acute and the circumflex accents indicate stress. On the other hand, the subtitles of the periodicals and the names of the publishing or sponsoring institutions or societies are consistently transliterated according to the system used in Webster's New International Dictionary (second edition). This reproduces the orthography of ancient, medieval and modern Greek but does not attempt to render the pronunciation of post-classical Greek.

1. AKADIMÍA ATHINÔN, PRAGMATEÎAI TÎS... (Pragmateîai tîs Akadimías Athinôn) [Papers of the Academy of Athens]. Irr. Akadimía Athinôn [Acad. of Athens], Athinai. In Greek and other languages. pv (c. Drs 30)

2. AKADIMÍA ATHINÔN, PRAKTIKÁ TÎS... (Praktiká tîs Akadimías Athinôn) [Proceedings of the Academy of Athens]. A. 1926 (1957: vol. 32). Akadimía Athinôn [Acad. of Athens], Athinai. Mainly the communications of the memb. of the acad. on philology, literature (ancient, Byzantine and modern), philosophy, archaeology, political science, law, mathematics, physics and chemistry; subject and author indices; proceedings of the meetings of the acad. pv (c. Drs 100)

3. ANDRIAKÁ CHRONIKÁ [Chronicles of Andros]. Q. Andriakós Ómilos [Soc. of Andros], Andros.

4. ARCHEÎON [Archives]. Triminiaîon periodikón Archeologías, Istorías, Laographías [Quarterly publication of archaeology, history, folklore]. Q. Mitrópolis Messinías [Diocese of Messinia], Kalamata. pv

5. ARCHEÎON EKLISIASTIKOÛ KÉ KANONIKOÛ DIKAÍOU [Archives of ecclesiastical and canon law]. Tetraminiaía nomokanonikí epitheóresis [Triannual review of canon law]. 4 x y. 1946 (1958: vol. 13). Pub. and ed: Panagiotis I, Panagiotakos, Odós Ionós 5, Athinai. Art. on the hist. and juridical status of the Greek Orthodox Church and the Ecumenical Patriarchate and on related subjects; biographical art.; biblio. Drs 75 / $ 8

6. ARCHEÎON EVVOIKÔN MELETÔN [Archives of Euboean studies]. Irr. 1935 (1958: vol. 5). Etaireía Evvoikôn Meletôn [Soc. of Euboean Studies], Tásos Záppas, Odós Aristotélous 135, Athinai. Ed. board: G.I. Fousáras, K.A. Alexandrís, I. Papadimitríou, D.S. Stefanídis, and the Metropolitan of Thavmakoû Chrysóstomos. Art. on all subjects relating to Euboea, with emphasis on medieval

and modern hist. and literature; rev. of bk. and studies on Euboean hist., literature, travel, theology, art, archaeology, folklore, politics, sociology, commerce, medicine, law and music; biblio. on Euboea (1473-1958), now pub. separately; biblio. of Euboean periodicals. p (1) Drs 50

7. ARCHEÎON OIKONOMIKÔN KÉ KOINONIKÔN EPISTIMÔN [Archives of economic and social sciences]. Q. Ioan. Kolláros, Odós Stadiou 38, Athinai. p (1) Drs 35 / 40s

8. ARCHEÎON PÓNTOU [Archives of Pontus]. A. 1928 (mri 1956: vol. 2). Epitropí Pontiakôn Meletôn [Committee of Studies of Pontus], Odós Thiséos 16, Athinai. Ed. board: Anthimos Papadópoulos (director), Odysséus Lampsídis, Stavros Kanonídis. Art. on the hist., topography, archaeology, and culture of the Greeks of Pontus, from antiquity to the present; bk. rev. Drs 50

9. ARCHEÎON SÁMOU [Archives of Samos]. Irr. Nikólaos I. Zafiríou, Odós Doïránis 158, Kalithéa, Athinai. pv

10. ARCHEÎON TÎS ISTORÍAS TOÛ ELLINIKOÛ DIKAÍOU, EPITIRÍS TOÛ... (Epetirís toû Archeíou tîs Istorías toû Ellinikoû Dikaíou) [Yearbook of the Archives of the History of Greek Law]. A. 1948 (1958: vol. 8). Archeîon tîs Istorías toû Ellinikoû Dikaíou, Akadimía Athinôn [Archives of the Hist. of Greek Law, Acad. of Athens], Athinai. Ed: J. Visvízis (director of the archives). Art. on Greek legal hist. from ancient times to the present and on related subjects. Drs 30 / $ 1

11. ARCHEÎON TÔN BYZANTINÔN MNIMÍON TÎS ELLÁDOS [Archives of the Byzantine monuments of Greece]. S-A. 1935 (mri 1955/56: vol. 8). Pub. and ed: Anastásios K. Orlándos, Odós Navarínou 6, Athinai. Art. on the Byzantine monuments of Greece; information on excavations carried on by the ed.; illus. Drs 75

12. ARCHEÎON TOÛ THRAKIKOÛ LAOGRAPHIKOÛ KÉ GLOSIKOÛ THISAVROÛ [Archives of the treasury of Thracian folklore and language]. Q. 1934 (1958: vol. 23). Ed: Polýdoros Papachristodoúlou, Odós Lefkádos 32, Athinai. Art. on the hist., archaeology, linguistics, folklore, and education of the Greeks of Thrace from ancient times to the present; bk. rev.; biblio.; subject index. Drs 10

13. ARCHEOLOGIKÍ EPHIMERÍS [Archaeological journal]. Irr. 1837 (1953/54 [1958]: vol. 92/93). I en Athínais Archeologikí Etaireía [Archaeological Soc. in Athens], Odós Venizélou (Panepistimiou) 22, Athinai. Art. on ancient Greek sculpture, architecture, painting and inscriptions, and on Byzantine hist. and art; occasional art. in French, German and English. pni

ARCHEOLOGIKÓN DELTÍON TOÛ YPOURGÎON TÔN EKLISIASTIKÔN KÉ TÎS DIMOSÍAS EKPEDÉFSEOS see YPOURGÎON TÔN EKLISIASTIKÔN KÉ TÎS DIMOSÍAS EKPEDÉFSEOS, ARCHEOLOGIKÓN DELTÍON...

14. ATHINÁ [Athena]. A. 1889 (1957: vol. 61). I en Athínais Epistimonikí Etaireía [Scientific Soc. in Athens], Odós Massalías 4, Athinai, and Odós Gytheiou 10, Athinai. Ed. board: N. Tomadákis (director), Stylianós Korrés, M.I. Manoúsakas, G. Spyridákis. Art. mainly on Greek literature and language from ancient times to the present, and also on Greek hist., culture, etymology, and philosophy; bk. rev. Drs 100

15. O BIBLIÓPHILOS [Bibliophile]. Q. "Angelos Zambákis," Odós Ippocrátous 5, Athinai. Art. on the hist. of bk. Drs 30 / $ 3

16. BULLETIN DE CORRESPONDANCE HELLENIQUE [Bulletin of Greek Communications]. Q. 1877 (1958: vol. 82). Ecole Française d'Athènes, Odós Sina 29-31, Athinai. Ed: Georges Daux. Art. on Greek archaeological explorations and excavations, and on Hellenic and Byzantine art. N. Fr. 80 / $ 10.50

DELTÍON TÎS ISTORIKÎS KÉ ETHNOLOGIKÎS ETAIREÍAS TÎS ELLÁDOS see ISTORIKÍ KÉ ETHNOLOGIKÍ ETAIREÍA TÎS ELLÁDOS, DELTÍON TÎS...

17. DODEKANISIAKÓN ARCHEÎON [Dodecanesian archives]. A. 1955 (1956/57: vol. 2). Dodekanisiakí Istorikí ké Laographikí Etaireía [Dodecanesian Hist. and Folklore Soc.], Athinai. Ed: Emm. G. Protopsáltis, General State Archives, Acad. of Athens, Athinai. Art. on the hist. and civilization of the Dodecanese Islands from antiquity to the present, and on archaeology, linguistics and folklore; doc on the modern hist. of the Islands; bk. rev.; biblio.; maps; illus. Drs 70

18. EKLISÍA [The Church]. B-W. 1923 (1958: vol. 35). Eklisía tîs Elládos [Church of Greece], Odós Philothéis 19, Athinai. Ed: Theodósios Sperántzas. Art. on religion and ecclesiastical hist.; news and notes; biblio.

19. ELLINIKÁ [Matters pertaining to Greece]. Philologikón, Istorikón ké Laographikón Sýngramma [Philological, historical and folkloric journal]. S-A (Irr.). 1928 (1959: vol. 16). Etaireía Makedonikôn Spoudôn [Soc. of Macedonian Studies], Odós Vasilíssis Sophias 2, Salonika. Ed. board: Stílpon P. Kyriakídis, Línos N. Polítis. Art. on Greek hist., literature and culture from antiquity to the present; doc.; bk. rev.; biblio.; news and notes; art. also in languages other than Greek. Drs 80 / $ 5

20. I EN ATHÍNAIS ARCHEOLOGIKÍ ETAIREÍA, PRAKTIKÁ... (Praktiká tîs en Athínais Archaiologikîs Etaireías) [Proceedings of the Archaeological Society in Athens]. A. 1837 (mri 1954: 4th series, vol. 110). I en Athínais Archeologikí Etaireía [Archaeological Soc. in Athens], Odós El. Venizélou (Panepistimiou) 22, Athinai. A. report of the soc.; reports on recent excavations by Greek archaeologists. pv (Drs 100-250)

21. O EN CHÍO SÝLOGOS ARGÉNTIS, PERIODIKÓN... (Periodikón toû en Chío Sylógou Argénti) [Publication of the Argenti's Association in Chios]. S-A. 1938 (mri 1956: vol. 5). Pub. and ed: Stéfanos D. Kavádas, for Chío Sylógou Argénti, Khíos. Art. on the hist., literature, linguistics, folklore, education, art, architecture, administration, and economy of the island of Chios; doc. of the period after 1453; combined subject and name index. Drs 100 / $ 5

EPETIRÍS. For titles beginning with "Epetirís," followed by the name of the publishing or sponsoring institution or society, see the respective institution or society.

EPISTIMONIKÍ EPETIRÍS TÎS PHILOSOPHIKÎS SCHOLÎS TOÛ PANEPISTIMÍOU ATHINÔN see PHILOSOPHIKÍ SCHOLÍ TOÛ PANEPISTIMÍOU ATHINÔN, EPISTIMONIKÍ EPETIRÍS TÎS...

EPISTIMONIKÍ EPETIRÍS TÎS PHILOSOPHIKÎS SCHOLÎS TOÛ PANEPISTIMÍOU THESSALONIKIS see PHILOSOPHIKÍ SCHOLÍ TOÛ PANEPISTIMÍOU THESSALONIKIS, EPISTIMONIKÍ EPETIRÍS TÎS...

22. EPITHEÓRISI TÉCHNIS [Art review]. Miniaîo Periodikó Gramáton ké Technôn [Monthly review of letters and arts]. M. Pub. and ed: Nícos Siapkídis, Odós Gambetta 6, Athinai. Drs 120 / $ 8

23. EPTANISIAKÁ PHÝLA [Heptanesian leaves]. Periodikí philologikí, laographikí ké istorikí ékdosi [Periodical literary, folklore and historical publication]. Irr. Pub. and ed: Dínos Konómos, Vivliothiki tîs Voulîs [Library of the Greek Parliament], Athinai. pni

24. ETAIREÍA BYZANTINÔN SPOUDÔN, EPETIRÍS...(Epetirís Etaireías Byzantinôn Spoudôn) [Yearbook of the Society of Byzantine Studies]. A. (Irr.). 1924 (1957: vol. 27). Etaireía Byzantinôn Spoudôn [Soc. of Byzantine Studies], Odós Massalías 4, Athinai. Ed: N. Tomadákis. Art. and doc. on Byzantine hist., literature, law and art and on Greek hist. and literature since 1453 and other related subjects; news and notes; reports on the activities of the soc.; French sum. available on exchange basis

25. ILIAKÁ [Matters pertaining to Elis]. Triminiaîo periodikó laographikîs, istorikîs, ké glosikîs spoudîs tîs Ilías [Quarterly journal of the folklore and historical and linguistic studies of Elis]. Q. Pub. and ed: Dinos Psichoyiós, Lechainá. Art. on the archaeology, hist., folklore, language and agriculture of Elis. Drs 20 / $ 2

26. IPIROTIKÍ ESTÍA [Epirotic hearth]. M. 1952 (1959: vol. 8). Pub. and ed: Michaél Mános, Demosthenes Kókinos, Odós 28is Octovríou 60, Yánnina, Epeiros. Art. on the hist., culture, folklore and literature of Epirus from antiquity to the present; biographical sketches; bk. rev.; news and notes. Drs 150 / $ 10

27. ISTORÍA KÉ ZOÍ [History and life]. Anthología ké Engyclopédia tîs Istorías [Anthology and encyclopedia of history]. M. 1956 (1957: vol. 4). Pub. and ed: Stéfanos I. Stefánou, Márkou Reniéri 4, Philothéi, Athinai, and Odós Kriezótou 4, Athinai. Art. on Greek hist. from antiquity to the present; occasional art. on European hist.; biblio. of new works in Greek, French and English. Pub. discontinued in 1957. Drs 90 / $ 6

28. ISTORIKÍ KÉ ETHNOLOGIKÍ ETAIREÍA TÎS ELLÁDOS, DELTÍON TÎS...(Deltíon tîs Istorikîs ké Ethnologikîs Etaireías tîs Elládos) [Bulletin of the Historical and Ethnological Society of Greece]. A. 1883 (1957/58: vol. 12). Istorikí ké Ethnologikí Etaireía tîs Elládos, Odós Amalias 38, Athinai. Ed. board: N. Tomadákis, G. Kólias, E. Photiádis. Art. on modern Greek hist. and literature; doc.; biblio. of new bk., especially on the Greek War of Independence (1821); news and notes; bk. rev.; biblio. of Greek hist. including related subjects such as pub. of doc., codices, biographies, law and administration, education, ecclesiastical hist., art; news on the activities of the soc.; tables of contents in Greek, French and English.

29. KAINOÚRIA EPOCHÍ [New epoch]. Pangósmia Epitheórisi Pneumatikîs Kaliérgias [World review of arts and letters]. Pub. and ed: Goudélis Yánnis, Odós Stadíou 33, Athinai. Drs 160 / $ 6

30. KERKIRAÏKÁ CHRONIKÁ [Chronicles of Corfu]. A. 1951 (1958: vol. 6). Pub. and ed: Kostas Daphnís, Kérkyra. Art. on the hist., literature, folklore and art of Corfu. pv (c. Drs 60)

31. KRITIKÁ CHRONIKÁ [Cretan chronicles]. 3 x y. 1947 (1957: vol. 11). Andréas Kalokairinós, Iráklion (Candia), Krete. Ed. board: N. Pláton, M.G. Parlamâs, K. Lasithiotákis, I. Papaïoánnou. Art. on the hist., literature, and art of the island of Crete; doc.; bk. rev.; news and notes; occasional art. in French and English; A. index of names, subjects and place names; supplements (monographs pub. separately) on the following topics: "O Kritikós argaleiós ké tá kritiká mesaioniká ké metamesaioniká roûcha" [The Cretan loom and Cretan medieval and post-medieval clothing], 1955, and "Paratirímata" [Superstitions], 1957. pv (Drs 45 - Drs 120)

32. KRITIKÍ ESTÍA [Cretan hearth]. M. Id. Papagrigorákis, Odós Tsouderôn 17, Canea, Krete. Drs 60 / $ 5

33. KYKLADIKÁ [Annals of Cyclades]. Grámata, Istoría, Téchni, Laographía, Archaiología, Tourismós [Letters, history, art, folklore, archaeology, tourism]. B-M. Pub. and ed: St. I. Vaphías, Sýros. Drs 75 / $ 5

34. LAOGRAPHÍA [Folklore]. S-A. 1909 (1958: vol. 17). Ellinikí Laographikí Etaireía [Greek Folklore Soc.], c/o G. Mégas, Odós G. Iakovídou 26, Athinai. Ed: G. Mégas. Art. on Greek folklore, popular art, and village and local architecture; biblio. of bk. and periodicals; table of contents by subject and by author; French sum. pv (c. Drs 115)

35. LAOGRAPHIKÓN ARCHEÎON, EPETIRÍS TOÛ... (Epetirís toû Laographikoû Archeíou) [Yearbook of the Folklore Archives]. A. Laographikón Archeîon, Akadimía Athinôn [Archives of Folklore, Acad. of Athens], Athinai. pv (Drs 50-80 / $ 2-3)

36. LESVIAKÁ [Matters pertaining to Lesbos]. A. Etaireía Lesviakôn Meletôn [Soc. for Studies of Lesbos], c/o D.G. Bernardakis, Odós Skrâ 27, Mytilini. pv (c. Drs 50)

37. LESVIAKÓN IMEROLÓGION [Almanac of Lesbos]. A. Pub. and ed: P.I. Samarâs, Mytilini. pv (c. Drs 70)

38. MAKEDONIKÁ [Matters pertaining to Macedonia]. Irr. 1940 (1957: vol. 4). Etaireía Makedonikôn Spoudôn [Soc. of Macedonian Studies], Vasilíssis Sophías 2, Salonika. Art. on the hist. of the Greek Church, archaeology, Byzantine and post-Byzantine art, and on the folklore, customs and linguistics of Macedonia; doc.; bk. rev.; reports on the activities of the soc. pv (c.Drs 200)

39. MAKEDONIKÓN IMEROLÓGION [Macedonian almanac]. A. Pub. and ed: Nikólaos A. Sfendónis, Odós Konstantinoupóleos 71, Salonika, and Odós Vasilísis Sophías, Salonika. pni

40. TO MÉLON TÎS ÝDRAS [The future of Hydra]. Miniaîon Periodikón tôn kalôn Ydraíon ké tôn Philydraíon [Monthly review of the good Hydriotes and of the friends of Hydra]. M. Pub. and ed: Antónios Maníkis, Odós Vas. Konstantínou ké Philellínon 24, Peiraieus. pni

41. MESAIONIKÓN ARCHEÎON, EPETIRÍS TOÛ... (Epetirís toû Mesaionikoû Archeíou) [Yearbook of the Medieval Archives]. A. 1939 (1958: vol. 7).

Mesaionikón Archeîon, Akadimía Athinôn [Medieval Archives, Acad. of Athens], Athinai. Ed: M.I. Manoúsakas. Art. on medieval Greek life, hist. and culture and on related subjects; hist. and legal doc.; news on the activities of the Mesaionikón Archeîon; combined author and subject index. Drs 50 / $ 1.70

42. MIKRASIATIKÁ CHRONIKÁ [Chronicles of Asia Minor]. Irr. 1938 (1957: vol. 7). Tmîma Mikrasiatikôn Meletôn tîs Enóseos Smyrnéon [Section of Asia Minor Studies of the Smyrniots Assoc.], Odós 3is Septemvríou 2, Athinai. Art. on the hist., culture, and literature of the Greeks of Asia Minor; bk. rev.; biblio. of bk. printed in Asia Minor up to 1922; biblio. of current bk. on Asia Minor; news and notes; indices; occasional art. also in English. Drs 100 / $ 5

43. NÉA ESTÍA [New hearth]. S-A. Pub. and ed: Pétros Háris, Odós Nikis 16, Athinai. Drs 300 / $ 17

44. NÉON ATHÍNAION [New Athenaeum]. S-A. 1955 (1957: vol. 2). Pub. and ed: N.A. Oikonomídis, Odós Spetsôn 93, Kypséli, Athinai. Art. on Greek hist., literature, language, education, archaeology, theology, folklore and law; doc. from the time of the Greek War of Independence; legal doc. Drs 80 / $ 4

45. PEDÍA KÉ ZOÍ [Education and life]. M. I. Zacharópoulos, Stoa Arsakíou, Athinai. Drs 75 / Drs 90

46. PELOPONISIAKÁ [Peloponnesian review]. A. 1956 (1957: vol. 2). Etaireía Peloponisiakôn Spoudôn [Soc. of Peloponnesian Studies], Odós Akadimias 54, Athinai. Ed: P.I. Zépos, D.A. Petrópoulos. Art. on the hist. and civilization of Peloponnesus from antiquity to the present; bk. rev.; biblio.; English sum. Drs 125

47. PELOPONISIAKÍ PROTOCHRONIÁ [Peloponnesian new year]. Istoría, Laographía, Téchni, Epistími [History, folklore, art, science]. A. 1957 (1958: vol. 2). Pub. and ed: Mímis Papachristophílou, Odós Ermoû 129, Athinai. Art. on the hist. of Peloponnesus, with emphasis on the period since 1453 and also on poetry, literature, folklore, mythology and costumes; doc. Drs 40

PERIODIKÓN TOÛ EN CHÍO SYLÓGOU ARGÉNTI see O EN CHÍO SÝLOGOS ARGÉNTIS, PERIODIKON...

48. PHILOLOGIKÍ PROTOCHRONIÁ [Literary new year]. Etísia Logotechnikí ké Kalitechnikí ékdosi [Annual literary and artistic review]. A. Pub. and ed: Ar. N. Mavrídis, Odós Themistokléous 11, Athinai. Drs 50

49. PHILOSOPHIKÍ SCHOLÍ TOÛ PANEPISTIMÍOU ATHINÔN, EPISTIMONIKÍ EPETIRÍS TÎS... (Epistimonikí Epetirís tîs Philosophikîs Scholîs toû Panepistimíou Athinôn) [Scientific yearbook of the Faculty of Philosophy of the University of Athens]. A. 1935 (1957/58: vol. 8). Philosophikí Scholí, Panepistimíou Athinôn, Athinai. Ed: G. Th. Zóras. Art. on Greek hist., literature, language, archaeology and art from ancient times to the present, critical and philological analyses of Greek and Latin texts; biblio.; art. also in French and English; news of the activities of the Faculty of Philosophy. pv

50. PHILOSOPHIKÍ SCHOLÍ TOÛ PANEPISTIMÍOU THESSALONIKÍS, EPISTIMONIKÍ EPETIRÍS TÎS... (Epistimonikí Epetirís tîs Philosophikîs Scholîs toû Panepistimíou Thessalonikís) [Scientific yearbook of the Faculty of Philosophy of the University of Thessalonike]. A. (1957: vol. 7). Philosophikí Scholí toû Panopistimíou Thessaloníkis, Thessaloníke. Art. on hist., literature, language and art. Drs 150

51. PHTHIÔTIS [Matters pertaining to Phthiotis]. Diminiaía epitheórisis tîs Roúmelis [Bi-monthly review of the Greek Mainland]. B-M. 1955 (1958: vol. 4). Nomarchía Phthiótidos [The Nomarchy of Phthiôtis], Periodikón "Phthiôtis," Lamía. Ed: Níkos K. Thános, Odós Mesologíou 25, Athinai. Art. on the hist., religion, archaeology, folklore, linguistics and architecture of Phthiôtis, from antiquity to the present, and on the present problems of the area such as tourism, commerce and public health; bk. rev.; literary and art news of Phthiôtis; news and notes on the activities of the civil service of the Greek Mainland. Drs 100 /$ 10

52. PLÁTON [Plato]. S-A. 1949 (1957: vol. 9). Etaireía Ellínon Philológon [Assoc. of Greek Philologists], c/o K.D. Georgoúlis, Odós Póntou 42, Athinai. Ed: K.D. Georgoúlis. Art. chiefly on the literature, hist , social life, civilization and culture of ancient Greece; bk. rev. A supplement dealing with the problems of education in Greece was pub. in 1958. Drs 50 / $ 8

53. POLÉMON. Pub. and ed: A. Payianópoulos-palaiós, "Polémon," Psychikon, Athinai. pni

54. PONTIAKÍ ESTÍA [Pontic hearth]. M. Pub. and ed: Ph. Ktenídis, Odós Tsimiski 54, Salonika. Drs 80 / $ 8

PRAGMATEÎAI TÎS AKADIMÍAS ATHINÔN see AKADIMÍA ATHINÔN, PRAGMATEÎAI TÎS...

PRAKTIKÁ TÎS AKADIMÍAS ATHINÔN see AKADIMÍA ATHINÔN, PRAKTIKÁ TÎS...

PRAKTIKÁ TÎS EN ATHÍNAIS ARCHEOLOGIKÎS ETAIREÎAS see I EN ATHÍNAIS ARCHEOLOGIKÍ ETAIREÍA, PRAKTIKÁ...

55. SERAÎKA CHRONIKÁ [Chronicles of Seres]. Irr. Pub. and ed: Istorikí ké Laographikí Etaireía Serôn-Meleníkou [Hist. and Folklore Soc. of Seres and Meleniko], Pétros Pénnas, Odós Dragatsaníou 4, Athinai. Hist., literature, archaeology and folklore of the cities of Seres and Meleniko in central Macedonia; doc. pv (c. Drs 60)

56. O SYLLÉKTIS [The collector]. Periodikón Istorías, Vivliologías, Kallitechnías ké pantós spaníou antikeiménou apoteloûntos stoicheîon syllogîs [Periodical of history, bibliology, art, and of every rare object which can be part of a collection]. Irr. 1947 (1952-58: vol. 2). Pub. and ed: Geórgios G. Ladâs, Odós Ippocrátous 4, Athinai. Art. on Greek life and culture, with emphasis on hist., literature and art, from Byzantine times to the present; doc. pv (c. Drs 100)
to the present; doc. pv (c. Drs 100)

57. TÁ ATHINAIKÁ [Matters pertaining to Athens]. Q (Irr.). Sylógou tôn Athinaion [The Assoc. of Athenians], Odós Kékropos 4, Athinai. pni

58. THEOLOGÍA [Theology]. Q. 1923 (1958: vol. 29). I Ierá Sýnodos tîs Eklisias tîs Elládos [Holy Synod of the Church of Greece], Odós Philothéis 19, Athinai. Ed. board: The Archbishop of Athens, Panayiótis Bratsiótis, Basílios Véllas, Ioánnis Karmíris. Art. on the hist. and doctrines of Christianity, chiefly Eastern, and on canon law and Byzantine and ecclesiastical literature; doc.; bk. rev.; biblio.; in Greek and occasionally in French and English; author and subject indices; index of foreign names. Drs 100

59. THRAKIKÁ [Annals of Thrace]. A. Thrakikón Kéntron [Thracian Center], Odós Koray 5, Athinai. pv (c. Drs 50)

60. YPOURGÎON TÔN EKLISIASTIKÔN KÉ TÎS DIMOSÍAS EKPEDÉFSEOS, ARCHEOLOGIKÓN DELTÍON... (Archeologikón deltíon toû Ypourgíou tôn Eklisiastikôn ké tîs dimosías Ekpedéfseos) [Archaeological bulletin of the Ministry for the Church and Public Education]. Irr. 1915 (mri 1933-35: vol. 15). Archeologikí Ypiresia toû Ypourgeíou Ethnikîs Paideías ké Thriskevmáton [Archaeological Service of the Ministry of National Education and Church Affairs], Athinai. Art. on the activities of the Greek Archaeological Service, with supplements in each vol. containing A. reports of memb. of the Greek Archaeological Service and of curators of museums; results of excavations carried on during the year; reports of the foreign archaeological schools in Greece; laws relating to the functioning of the Archaeological Service. Pub. suspended in 1935 but expected to be resumed soon again. available on exchange basis

ADDENDUM

61. BALKAN STUDIES. S-A. 1960 (1960: vol. 1). Ídryma Meletôn tîs Chersonísou toû Aímou [Inst. for Balkan Studies], Odós Vassilísis Sophías 2, Salonika. Ed. board: St. Kyriakidis (chief ed.), N.P. Andriotis, D. Delivanis, Ch. Fragistas, Basil Laourdas (manag. ed.). Art. on the political, economic social and literary hist. of the Balkans from early times to the present, with emphasis on the post-Ottoman era; in English and occasionally in German, French or Italian. $ 8

Hungary

Prepared with the assistance of

Margit Szekeres, Librarian, Országos Széchényi Könyvtár [National Széchényi Library], Budapest, and

Francis S. Wagner, Library of Congress, Washington, D.C.

ACTA ACADEMIAE PAEDAGOGICAE SZEGEDIENSIS see A SZEGEDI PEDAGÓGIAI FŐISKOLA ÉVKÖNYVE

1. ACTA ANTIQUA ACADEMIAE SCIENTIARUM HUNGARICAE. A. Akadémiai Kiadó, Alkotmány utca 21, Budapest 5, for Magyar Tudományos Akadémia [Hungarian Acad. of Sciences], Akadémia utca 2, Budapest 5. Art. on classical philology and ancient hist.; in English, French, German, Latin or Russian. Ft 110

2. ACTA ARCHAEOLOGICA ACADEMIAE SCIENTIARUM HUNGARICAE. Q. 1951 (1959: vol. 10). Akadémiai Kiadó, Alkotmány utca 21, Budapest 5, for Magyar Tudományos Akadémia [Hungarian Acad. of Sciences], Akadémia utca 2, Budapest 5. Ed. board: Gyula Moravcsik (chief ed.), A. Dobrovits, F. Fülep, J. Harmatta, M. Párducz. Art. on archaeology, with emphasis on Hungary and neighboring countries, including the Soviet Union; in English, French, German and Russian, with sum. in a language different from that of the art.; A. vol. index. Ft 160 / Ft 220

3. ACTA ETHNOGRAPHICA ACADEMIAE SCIENTIARUM HUNGARICAE. A. Akadémiai Kiadó, Alkotmány utca 21, Budapest 5, for Magyar Tudományos Akadémia [Hungarian Acad. of Sciences], Akadémia utca 2, Budapest 5. Art. on ethnography, with emphasis on Finno-Ugric ethnography; in German, English, French or Russian. Ft 110

4. ACTA HISTORIAE ARTIUM ACADEMIAE SCIENTIARUM HUNGARICAE. A. 1953 (1959: vol. 5). Akadémiai Kiadó, Alkotmány utca 21, Budapest 5. Ed. board: Lajos Fülep (chief ed.), Dezső Dercsényi, Lajos Vayer, Anna H. Zádor. Art. on the hist. of art (mostly fine arts) with emphasis on Hungary; bk. rev.; in English, French, German, Italian or Russian; sum. in a language different from that of the art.; illus. Ft 110

5. ACTA HISTORICA. Journal of the Hungarian Academy of Sciences (Subtitle also in French, Hungarian and German). Q. 1951 (1958: vol. 5). Magyar Tudományos Akadémia [Hungarian Acad. of Sciences], Akadémia utca 2, Budapest 5. Ed: E. Molnár (chief ed.), E. Pamlényi, Belgrád rakpart 5, Budapest 5. Art. mostly on modern Hungarian and related hist.; doc.; bk. rev.; reports on hist. inst. and chronicle of professional activities in Hungary; biblio. of bk. and art. which appeared in Hungary during the preceding six months, arranged by subject and period (from pre-hist. on); sum. in a language different from that of the art. Prior to 1958 pub. under the title: Acta Historica Academiae Scientiarum Hungaricae.

ACTA HISTORICA ACADEMIAE SCIENTIARUM HUNGARICAE see ACTA HISTORICA

6. ACTA LINGUISTICA ACADEMIAE SCIENTIARUM HUNGARICAE. A. Akadémiai Kiadó, Alkotmány utca 21, Budapest 5, for Magyar Tudományos Akadémia [Hungarian Acad. of Sciences], Akadémia utca 2, Budapest 5. Finno-Ugrian, Slavonic, Germanic, Oriental and Romance linguistics as well as linguistics in general; in English, French, German or Russian; sum. in a language different from that of the art. Ft 110

7. ACTA LITTERARIA ACADEMIAE SCIENTIARIUM HUNGARICAE. Irr. Akadémiai Kiadó, Alkotmány utca 21, Budapest 5, for Magyar Tudományos Akadémia [Hungarian Acad. of Sciences], Akadémia utca 2, Budapest 5. In French, German, English or Russian. Ft 80 / Ft 110

8. ACTA ORIENTALIA ACADEMIAE SCIENTIARUM HUNGARICAE. A. Akadémiai Kiadó, Alkotmány utca 21, Budapest 5, for Magyar Tudományos Akadémia [Hungarian Acad. of Sciences], Akadémia utca 2, Budapest 5. Art. on Oriental philology and culture; in English, French, German or Russian; Russian sum. Ft 80 / Ft 110

9. AGRÁRTÖRTÉNETI SZEMLE. HISTORIA RERUM RUSTICARUM [Review of agrarian history]. Irr. 1957 (1957: vol. 1). Agrártudományi Egyetem Központi Könyvtára [Central Library, Univ. of Agricultural Sciences], Gödöllő. Ed: Domokos Kosáry. Art., based on unpub. material, on the socio-economic aspects of the hist. of agricultural production in Hungary, pertaining mostly to the period 1500-1900; evaluative biographies of Hungary's outstanding agricultural experts (including economic historians); rev. of bk. and art.; annotated biblio. of Hungarian and foreign bk. and art., arranged by country; professional news; French and Russian sum. pni

10. ALFÖLD. Irodalmi és müvészeti folyóirat [Review of literature and art]. Irr. Debrecen megyei jogu Városi Tanács Végrehajtó Bizottsága [Executive Committee of the Council of the City of Debrecen], Debrecen. Ft 48

11. AZ ÁLLAM-ÉS JOGTUDOMÁNYI INTÉZET ÉRTESÍTŐJE [Bulletin of the Institute of Political and Legal Sciences]. Irr. Akadémiai Kiadó, Alkotmány utca 21, Budapest 5, for Magyar Tudományos Akadémia Állam-és Jogtudományi Intézete [Inst. of Political and Legal Sciences, Hungarian Acad. of Sciences], Akadémia utca 2, Budapest 5. French and Russian sum. Ft 60

ANNALES UNIVERSITATIS SCIENTIARUM BUDAPESTINENSIS DE ROLANDO EÖTVÖS NOMINATAE see UNIVERSITAS SCIENTIARUM BUDAPESTINENSIS DE ROLANDO EÖTVÖS NOMINATAE, ANNALES...

12. ANTHROPOLÓGIAI KÖZLEMÉNYEK [Anthropological publications]. Irr. Akadémiai Kiadó, Alkotmány utca 21, Budapest 5, for Magyar Biológiai Társaság Anthropológiai Szakosztálya [Section of Anthropology, Hungarian Biological Soc.]. Physical anthropology; English, French, German or Russian sum. Ft 40

13. ANTIK TANULMÁNYOK. STUDIA ANTIQUA [Studies on antiquities]. Q. 1954 (1959: vol. 5). Akadémiai Kiadó, Alkotmány utca 21, Budapest 5, for Magyar Tudományos Akadémia [Hungarian Acad. of Sciences], Akadémia utca 2, Budapest 5. Ed. board: Gyula Moravcsik (chief ed.), Aladár Dobrovits, János Harmatta, Imre Trencsényi-Waldapfel, Pesti Barnabás utca 1, Budapest 5. Art. on classical and Oriental antiquities; discussions; bk. rev.; professional news; in French and Hungarian; A. table of contents.

14. ARCHAEOLÓGIAI ÉRTESÍTŐ [Archaeological journal]. S-A. 1869 (1958: vol. 85). Magyar Régészeti, Művészettörténeti és Éremtani Társulat [Hungarian Soc. of Archaeology, Art Hist., and Numismatics], Múzeum körút 14-16 [Nemzeti Múzeum-Történeti Múzeum], Budapest 8. Ed. board: Éva B. Bónis, János Harmatta, Mihály Párducz. Art. on archaeology, art hist., and numismatics, with emphasis on Hungary and neighboring countries; rev. of bk. and periodicals; reports on research activities; professional news; English, French, German or Russian sum. Ft 40

15. BARANYAI MÜVELŐDÉS [Cultural life of Baranya]. Irr. Baranya megyei Tanács VB Müvelődésügyi osztálya [Cultural Section, Executive Committee of the Council of the County of Baranya], Pécs. p (1) Ft 8

16. BORSODI SZEMLE [Borsod review]. A Tudományos Ismeretterjesztő Társulat Borsod Megyei Szervezete, a megyei és városi Tanács folyóirata [Bulletin of the Borsod County Organization of the Scientific Educational Society and of the County and Municipal Council]. B-M. Tudományos Ismeretterjesztő Társulat, Széchenyi utca 16, Miskolc. Includes a literary supplement: Széphalom. p (1) Ft 6

BULLETIN DU MUSEE NATIONAL HONGROIS DES BEAUX-ARTS see MUSEE NATIONAL HONGROIS DES BEAUX-ARTS, BULLETIN DU...

17. CRANIA HUNGARICA. Irr. Magyar Nemzeti Muzeum Embertani Osztálya [Section of Anthropology, Hungarian National Museum], Bajza utca 39, Budapest 6. In French and German. nfs

18. DEMOGRÁFIA [Demography]. Népességtudományi folyóirat [Journal of the science of demography]. Q. 1958 (1959: vol. 2). Központi Statisztikai Hivatal [Central Statistical Office], Buday László utca 1, Budapest 2. Ed. board: György Péter (chief ed.), Egon Szabady (manag. ed.). Art. on demography and related subjects viewed in hist. perspective (dealing mostly with the period since 1900), with emphasis on Hungary and Central and Eastern Europe; bk. rev.; professional news; English and Russian sum.; table of contents also in English and Russian. Ft 48

DISSERTATIONES ARCHAEOLOGICAE EX INSTITUTO ARCHAEOLOGICO UNIVERSITATIS DE ROLANDO EÖTVÖS NOMINATAE see RÉGÉSZETI DOLGOZATOK AZ EÖTVÖS LÓRÁND TUDOMÁNYEGYETEM RÉGÉSZETI INTÉZETÉBŐL

19. EGYHÁZTÖRTÉNET [History of the church]. Egyházi történettudományi folyóirat [Review of church history]. Q. 1958. Magyarországi Református Egyház Egyetemes Konventje [General Convent of the Hungarian Reformed Churches], Abonyi utca 21, Budapest 14. Ed: Tamás Esze, Kálvin tér 8.1.10/c, Budapest 9. Art. on the hist. of the reformed Churches in Hungary and other countries; doc.; bk. rev. Ft 80 / Ft 100

20. ÉLET ÉS IRODALOM [Life and literature]. W. Lapkiadó Vállalat, Lenin körút 9-11, Budapest 7. Literary trends and cultural traditions in Hungary. Ft 36 (S-A subscription)

21. ÉLET ÉS MÜVELŐDÉS [Life and cultural education]. Hajdu-Bihar Megye és Debrecen megyei jogu város müvelődési kiadványa [Publication for the cultural education of the county of Hajdu-Bihar and the City of Debrecen]. Irr. Hajdu-Bihar megyei Tanács VB Müvelődésügyi Osztálya [Executive Committee of

the Cultural Section of the Council of the County of Hajdu-Bihar], Debrecen. p (1) Ft 5

22. ÉLET ÉS TUDOMÁNY [Life and science]. W. Tudományos Ismeretterjesztő Társulat [Scientific Educational Soc.], Rosenberg házaspár utca 15, Budapest 5. Also on social and hist. sciences (with the aim of educating readers in dialectical materialism) and on the hist. of natural and technical sciences. p (1) Ft 1.20

23. ÉPITÉS - ÉS KÖZLEKEDÉSTUDOMÁNYI KÖZLEMÉNYEK [Publications on architecture and communication]. A Magyar Tudományos Akadémia Műszaki Tudományok Osztályának keretében működő Épitéstudományi -Épitészettörténeti és Elméleti, Hidrológiai és Vizgazdálkodási, Közlekedéstudományi és Településtudományi Bizottságának Közlönye [Bulletin of the Committee for the Science of Building, History and Theory of Architecture, Hydrology, Science of Communication and Settlement of the Technical Section of the Hungarian Academy of Sciences]. Q. Akadémiai Kiadó, Alkotmány utca 21, Budapest 5, for Magyar Tudományos Akadémia, Akadémia utca 2, Budapest 5. Bk. rev.; professional news; graph, maps, illus. Ft 100

24. AZ ÉREM [Coin]. Közlemények az éremgyűjtés köréből [Publications in the field of coin collecting]. Irr. 1922 (1959: vol. 15). Magyar Régészeti, Művészettörténeti és Éremtani Társulat Éremtani Szakosztálya [Section of Numismatics, Hungarian Soc. of Archaeology, Art Hist., and Numismatics], Magyar Nemzeti Múzeum - Történeti Múzeum [Hungarian National Museum-Hist. Museum], 8, Múzeum körút 14-16, Budapest. Ed. board: Lajos Huszár, Mihály Kupa, Elemér Pávó. Art. on coins and coin collecting past and present, with emphasis on Hungary; professional news; illus.; cum. index for vol. 1-10. p (1) Ft 4

25. ETHNOGRAPHIA. Q. Magyar Néprajzi Társaság [Hungarian Ethnographical Soc.], Pesti Barnabás utca 1, Budapest 5. English, French, German or Russian sum.; illus. Ft 40

24. FILOLÓGIAI KÖZLÖNY [Philological journal]. A Magyar Tudományos Akadémia Irodalomtörténeti Intézetének világirodalmi folyóirata [Review of world literature of the Institute of Literary History of the Hungarian Academy of Sciences] Q. Akadémiai Kiadó, Alkotmány utca 21, Budapest 5, for Magyar Tudományos Akadémia Irodalomtörténeti Intézete, Budapest 5. English, French, German, Italian or Russian sum. Ft 40

27. A FÖLDRAJZ TANÍTÁSA [Teaching of geography]. B-M. Tankönyvkiadó Vállalat, Szalay utca 10-14, Budapest 5, for Müvelódésügyi Minisztérum [Ministry of Cultural Affairs]. Illus. Ft 14.40

28. FÖLDRAJZI ÉRTESÍTŐ [Geographical journal]. Q. Akadémiai Kiadó, Alkotmány utca 21, Budapest 5, for Magyar Tudományos Akadémia Földrajztudományi Kutatócsoportja [Geographical Research Group of the Hungarian Acad. of Sciences], Nádor utca 7, Budapest 5. English, French, German or Russian sum. Ft 40

29. FÖLDRAJZI KÖZLEMÉNYEK [Geographical review]. Q. Magyar Földrajzi Tärsaság [Hungarian Geographical Soc.], Nádor utca 7, Budapest 5. Hist., geography and anthropo-geography, with emphasis on Hungary and neighboring countries; English, French, German or Russian sum.; table of contents also in English, German and Russian. Ft 32

30. FÖLDTANI KÖZLÖNY [Journal of geology]. A Magyar Földtani Társulat folyóirata. Bulletin de la Société Géologique de Hongrie. Zeitschrift der Ungarischen Geologischen Gesellschaft [Bulletin of the Hungarian Geological Society]. Q. Akadémiai Kiadó, Alkotmány utca 21, Budapest 5, for Magyar Földtani Társulat. Bk. rev.; biblio. of bk. for the previous year; professional news; English, French, German or Russian sum.; illus. Ft 40

31. A HADTÖRTÉNELMI INTÉZET ÉRTESÍTŐJE [Bulletin of the Institute of Military History]. Irr. 1957 (1958: vol. 2). Hadtörténelmi Intézet [Inst. of Military Hist.], Kapisztrán tér 2, Budapest 1. Ed: József Balázs. Art. on military hist. and strategy; doc.; bk. rev.; news of the inst.; professional news. nfs

32. HADTÖRTÉNELMI KÖZLEMÉNYEK [Publications on military history]. Q (S-A with effect from 1959). 1954 (1958: vol. 5). Hadtörténelmi Intézet [Inst. of Military Hist.], Kapisztrán tér 2, Budapest 1. Ed: Miklós Horváth. Art. on military hist. (with emphasis on Hungary), pertaining mostly to the period 1848-1945; doc.; bk. rev. Ft 16

HISTORIA RERUM RUSTICARUM see AGRÁRTÖRTÉNETI SZEMLE

33. HUNGARIAN REVIEW. M. Lapkiadó Vállalat, Lenin körút 9/11, Budapest 7. Appears also in separate French, German and Russian editions. nfs

34. IRODALOMTÖRTÉNET [Literary history]. Q. Magyar Irodalomtörténeti Társaság [Hungarian Soc. of Literary hist.], Pesti Barnabás utca 1, Budapest 5. French, German or Russian sum. Ft 24

35. IRODALOMTÖRTÉNETI KÖZLEMÉNYEK [Communications in literary history]. Q. Magyar Tudományos Akadémia Irodalomtörténeti Intézete [Inst. of Literary Hist. of the Hungarian Acad. of Sciences], Ménesi út. 11-13, Budapest 11. Table of contents also in German and Russian. Ft 40

36. JÁSZKUNSÁG. Q. Tudományos Ismeretterjesztő Társulat Szolnok Megyei Szervezete [Szolnok County Branch of the Scientific Educational Soc.], Szolnok. Ft 20

KATOLIKUS SZEMLE see section on Italy

37. KISKUNSÁG [Little Cumania]. Irodalmi és művészeti folyóirat [Review of literature and art]. B-M. Bács-Kiskun megyei Tanács V.B. Művelődési Osztálya [Cultural Section of the Executive Committee of the Council of the County of Bács-Kiskun], Kecskemét. Ft 30

38. KÖNYVBARÁT [Bibliophile]. M. Lapkiadó Vállalat, Lenin körút 9-11, Budapest 7, for Művelődésügyi Minisztérium [Ministry of Cultural Affairs], Budapest. p (1) Ft 3

39. A KÖNYVTÁROS [Librarian]. M. Lapkiadó Vállalat, Lenin körút 9-11, Budapest 7, for Művelődésügyi Minisztérium [Ministry of Cultural Affairs], Budapest. Ft 48

40. KÖZNEVELÉS [Public education]. B-W. Tankönyvkiadó Vállalat, Szalay utca 10-14, Budapest 5, for Művelődésügyi Minisztérium [Ministry of Cultural Affairs]. Includes a supplement: Alsótagozati Oktatás-Nevelés [Educational instruction of the lower classes]. Ft 24

41. LEVÉLTÁRI HÍRADÓ [Archival review]. Q. 1951 (1959: vol. 8). Művelődésügyi Minisztérium Levéltári Osztálya (Levéltárak Országos Központja) [Section of Archives of the Ministry of Cultural Affairs (National Center of Archives)], Uri utca 54-56, Budapest 1. Manag. ed: Károly Vörös. Art. on the hist., theory and practical problems of archives; description of source material housed in Hungarian archives as well as of unpub. material relating to Hungary, stored in foreign archives; detailed description of inventories of Hungarian archives; translations from foreign archival periodicals; professional news; French, German and Russian sum. pni

42. LEVÉLTÁRI KÖZLEMÉNYEK [Archival publications]. A. 1923 (1958: vol. 28). Országos Levéltári Központ [National Archival Center], Bécsi Kaputér 4, Budapest 1, Vár. Ed: Győző Ember. Art. on archival holdings of East European countries, with emphasis on Hungarian archives and their hist., and on archival methods; rev. of Hungarian and foreign bk. and periodicals; professional news; Russian and French sum.; table of contents also in Russian and French. Pub. suspended from 1947 to 1953. Ft 60

43. MAGYAR FILOZÓFIAI SZEMLE [Hungarian philosophical review]. Q. Magyar Tudományos Akadémia Filozófiai Intézete [Inst. of Philosophy of the Hungarian Acad. of Sciences], Nádor utca 13.IV.435, Budapest 5. English, French, German or Russian sum. Ft 60

44. MAGYAR KÖNYVSZEMLE [Hungarian book review]. Q. Magyar Tudományos Akadémia Könyvtártudományi Főbizottsága [General Committee on Library Science, Hungarian Acad. of Sciences], Múzeum körút 14-16, Budapest 8. Ft 60

A MAGYAR NEMZETI MÚZEUM SZÉPMŰVÉSZETI MÚZEUM KÖZLEMÉNYEI see MUSEE NATIONAL HONGROIS DES BEAUX-ARTS, BULLETIN DU...

45. MAGYAR NYELV [Hungarian language]. Q. Magyar Nyelvtudományi Társaság [Hungarian Linguistic Soc.], Pesti Barnabás utca 1, Budapest 5. Ft 30

46. MAGYAR NYELVŐR [Hungarian language purist]. Q. Magyar Tudományos Akadémia Nyelvtudományi Intézete [Linguistic Inst. of the Hungarian Acad. of Sciences], Szalay utca 10-14.V.em, Budapest 5. Ft 18

47. MAGYAR TUDOMÁNY [Hungarian science]. M. Akadémiai Kiadó, Alkotmány utca 21, Budapest 5, for Magyar Tudományos Akadémia [Hungarian Acad. of Sciences], Akadémia utca 2, Budapest 5. Art. and news on all branches of science, including social and hist. sciences, with emphasis on Hungary; table of contents also in English, French, German and Russian. Ft 60

48. A MAGYAR TUDOMÁNYOS AKADÉMIA NYELV-ÉS IRODALOMTUDOMÁNYI OSZTÁLYÁNAK KÖZLEMÉNYEI [Publications of the Section on Linguistics and Literary Science, Hungarian Academy of Sciences]. Q. Magyar Tudományos Akadémia Nyelv- és Irodalomtudományi Osztálya, Széchenyi rakpart 3.,I. 145, Budapest 5. Ft 92

49. A MAGYAR TUDOMÁNYOS AKADÉMIA TÁRSADALMI-TÖRTÉNETI TUDOMÁNYOK OSZTÁLYÁNAK KÖZLEMÉNYEI [Publications of the Section of Social and Historical Sciences, Hungarian Academy of Sciences]. Q. 1951 (1959: vol. 9). Magyar Tudományos Akadémia Társadalmi-Történeti Tudományok Osztálya [Section of Social and Hist. Sciences, Hungarian Acad. of Sciences], Széchenyi rakpart 3, Budapest 5. Ed. board: Imre Szabó (chief ed.), Erik Molnár,

Imre Szabó. Art. on hist., philosophy, classical philology, archaeology, art, ethnography, pedagogy, law, economics, and geography; professional news; table of contents also in French, German and Russian. Ft 40 / Ft 60

MAGYAR TUDOMÁNYOS AKADÉMIA TÖRTÉNETTUDOMÁNYI INTÉZETÉNEK ÉRTESÍTŐJE see TÖRTÉNELMI SZEMLE

50. MEGYEI ÉS VÁROSI STATISZTIKAI ÉRTESÍTŐ [Statistical bulletin of countries and cities]. M. Központi Statisztikai Hivatal [Central Statistical Office], Keleti Károly utca 5-7, Budapest 2. Includes art. on Hungarian local hist. Ft 36

51. MŰEMLÉKVÉDELEM [Protection of historical monuments]. Műemlékvédelmi és építészettörténeti szemle [Journal for the protection of historical monuments and the history of architecture]. Q. 1957 (1959: vol. 3). Gondolat Könyv-, Lapkiadó és Terjesztő Vállalat, Bródy Sándor utca 16, Budapest 8, for Magyar Építőművészek Szövetsége Műemléki Bizottsága [Committee for Hist. Monuments of the Federation of Hungarian Architects]. Ed: László Gerő. Art. on the hist. of monuments, with emphasis on Hungary and its neighboring countries, and on methods of preserving hist. monuments; rev. of bk. and art.; professional news, including news of meetings in Hungary and neighboring countries; French sum.; illus. Ft 28

52. MUSEE NATIONAL HONGROIS DES BEAUX-ARTS, BULLETIN DU... A MAGYAR NEMZETI MÚZEUM SZÉPMŰVÉSZETI MÚZEUM KÖZLEMÉNYEI [Bulletin of the Museum of Fine Arts of the Hungarian National Museum]. A. Képzőművészeti Alap Kiadóvállalata, Budapest, for Magyar Nemzeti Múzeum - Szépművészeti Múzeum [Museum of Fine Arts of the Hungarian National Museum], Budapest. Art. on the hist. of the creative arts, with emphasis on the collections housed in the Museum of Fine Arts, Budapest; in French and Hungarian. pni

53. MŰTEREM [Art studio]. Művészeti folyóirat [Review of art]. M. Lapkiadó Vállalat, Lenin körút 9-11, Budapest 7. Table of contents also in French and Russian. Ft 120

54. MŰVÉSZETTÖRTÉNETI ÉRTESÍTŐ [Journal on the history of art]. Q. 1952 (1959: vol. 8). Akadémiai Kiadó, Alkotmány utca 21, Budapest 5, for Magyar Régészeti, Művészettörténeti és Éremtani Társulat [Hungarian Soc. of Archaeology, Art Hist. and Numismatics], Budapest. Ed: Lajos Fülep. Art. on archaeology, numismatics and the hist. of art, with emphasis on Hungary; bk. rev.; research reports; table of contents also in French and Russian; illus. A. author and subject index. Ft 100

55. MUZSIKA [Music]. M. Lapkiadó Vállalat, Lenin körút 9-11, Budapest 7. Ft 60

56. NAGYVILÁG [The wide world]. Világirodalmi folyóirat [Review of world literature]. M. Lapkiadó Vállalat, Lenin körút 9-11, Budapest 7. p (1) Ft 12

57. NÉPMŰVELÉS [People's education]. M. Lapkiadó Vállalat, Lenin körút 9-11. IV. em, Budapest 7, for Országos Népművelési Tanácas [National Council of People's Education], Budapest. p (1) Ft 3

58. NÉPRAJZI KÖZLEMÉNYEK [Ethnographical publications]. Q. Magyar Nemzeti Múzeum - Néprajzi Múzeum [Ethnographical Museum of the Hungarian National Museum], Budapest. German sum.; table of contents also in German. pni

59. NUMIZMATIKAI KÖZLÖNY [Journal of numismatics]. A. 1902 (1957/58: vol. 56/57). Magyar Régészeti, Művészettörténeti és Éremtani Társulat Éremtani Szakosztálya [Section of Numismatics, Hungarian Soc. of Archaeology, Hist. of Art and Numismatics], Magyar Nemzeti Múzeum - Történeti Múzeum [Hungarian National Museum - Hist. Museum], Múzeum körút 14-16, Budapest 8. Ed: Lajos Huszár. Art. on numismatics, with emphasis on ancient, medieval and new coins, medals and banknotes in Hungary, and on the hist. of Hungarian mints; doc.; bk. rev.; biblio.; professional news; French or Russian sum.; graph, illus. Ft 20

60. NYELVTUDOMÁNYI KÖZLEMÉNYEK [Bulletin of linguistic studies]. Magyar Tudományos Akadémia Nyelvtudományi Főbizottsága [General Committee for Linguistics, Hungarian Acad. of Sciences], Szalay utca 10-14. V. emelet, Budapest 5. Art. on Finno-Uric comparative philology and on ancient hist., with emphasis on Hungary and the Hungarian language. Ft 16

61. AZ ORSZÁGOS ORVOSTÖRTÉNETI KÖNYVTÁR KÖZLEMÉNYEI [Publications of the National Library of Medical History]. Communicationes ex Bibliotheca Historiae Medicae Hungarica. Irr. 1955 (1959: no. 14). Medicina Egészségügyi Könyvkiadó, Beloiannisz utca 8, Budapest 5, for Országos Oryostörténeti Könyvtár [National Library of Medical Hist.], Budapest. Ed: Ákos Palla, Török utca 12, Budapest 2. Art. on medical hist., with emphasis on Hungary, and on ancient and modern therapy and treatments; doc.; bk. rev.; biblio.; in Hungarian, German, English, Russian, Italian or Rumanian; illus. pni

62. ORVOSI HETILAP [Medical weekly]. W. Medicina Egészségügyi Könyvkiadó, Beloiannisz utca 8, Budapest 5, for Orvos-Egészségügyi Szakszervezet [Medical and Sanitary Trade Union]. Russian or German sum. Ft 120

63. PADAGÓGIAI SZEMLE [Pedagogical review]. M. Pedagógiai Tudományos Intézet [Scientific Pedagogic Inst.], Szalay utca 10-14, Budapest 5. Includes art. on the hist. of education; table of contents in French, German and Russian. Ft 48

64. PÁRTTÖRTÉNETI KÖZLEMÉNYEK [Publications of Party history]. Q. 1956 (1959: vol. 5). Magyar Szocialista Munkáspárt Központi Bizottsága Párttörténeti Intézet [Inst. of Party Hist. of the Central Committee of the Hungarian Socialist Workers' Party], Alkotmány utca 2, Budapest 6. Ed: Tibor Erényi. Art. on the hist. of the Communist and labor parties, with emphasis on Hungary and the people's democracies and on proletarian revolutions, peasants' revolts and labor movements; doc.; bk. rev.; biblio. of the Hungarian labor movement. p (1) Ft 8

65. RÉGÉSZETI DOLGOZATOK AZ EÖTVÖS LÓRÁND TUDOMÁNYEGYETEM RÉGÉSZETI INTÉZETÉBŐL. DISSERTATIONES ARCHAEOLOGICAE EX INSTITUTO ARCHAEOLOGICO UNIVERSITATIS DE ROLANDO EÖTVÖS NOMINATAE. Irr. 1958 (1958: no. 1). Eötvös Lóránd Tudományegyetem Régészeti Tanszéke [Chair of Archaeology, Eötvös Lóránd Univ.], Pesti Barnabás utca 1, Budapest 5. Ed. board: János Banner, Gyula László, Zoltán Oroszlán. Art. on archaeology, doctoral dissertations and abstr. of state examination papers; detailed biblio.; French, German and Russian sum.; illus. nfs

66. SOPRONI SZEMLE [The Sopron review]. Helytörténeti folyóirat [Bulletin of local history]. Q. Sopron Város Tanácsa [City Council of Sopron], Sopron. Ft 48

67. STATISZTIKAI SZEMLE [Statistical review]. M. Központi Statistikai Hivatal [Central Statistical Office], Keleti Károly utca 5, Budapest 2. Includes art. on hist. statistics, pertaining mostly to the period 1900-45, with emphasis on Hungary and its neighboring countries; A. index; supplement containing table of contents and sum. of art. in English and Russian. Ft 108

STUDIA ANTIQUA see ANTIK TANULMÁNYOK

68. STUDIA SLAVICA ACADEMIAE SCIENTIARUM HUNGARICAE. Irr. 1955 (1958: vol. 4). Akadémiai Kiadó, Alkotmány utca 21, Budapest 5, for Magyar Tudományos Akadémia Nyelv-és Irodalomtudományi Osztálya [Section of Linguistics and Literary Science, Hungarian Acad. of Sciences], Budapest. Ed. board: István Kniezsa (chief ed.), E. Balaczky, L. Hadrovics, J. Harmatta. Art. on Slavic studies (linguistics, hist., etc.), with emphasis on Hungary and its neighboring countries, including the Soviet Union; bk. rev.; biblio. of Hungarian pub.; professional news from Hungary; in Slavic languages, English, French and German; A. "Index vocabulorum et Nominum." Ft 120

69. SZÁZADOK [Centuries]. B-M. 1867 (1959: vol. 93). Akadémiai Kiadó, Budapest, for Magyar Történelmi Társulat [Hungarian Hist. Assoc.], Budapest. Ed: Erik Molnár (chairman), Belgrád rakpart 5, Budapest 5. Art. on Hungarian hist., mostly modern, and on European hist., with emphasis on the Habsburg Monarchy; doc.; bk. rev.; biblio.; discussions; chronicle; French and Russian sum.; table of contents in English, French, German and Russian. Ft 36

70. A SZEGEDI PEDAGÓGIAI FŐISKOLA ÉVKÖNYVE. ACTA ACADEMIAE PAEDAGOGICAE SZEGEDIENSIS. A. 1956 (1958). Szegedi Pedagógiai Főiskola [Szeged College of Pedagogy], Szeged. Ed: Károly Lerner. Well-documented art. by the teaching staff of the college on various aspects of pedagogy and the social sciences, including hist., with emphasis on Hungary, especially the Alföld Great Hungarian Plains; biblio.; German and Russian sum.; maps, illus. pni

71. SZOVJET MŰVÉSZETTÖRTÉNET [Soviet art history]. Irr. Magyar Nemzeti Múzeum - Szépművészeti Múzeum [Museum of Fine Arts of the Hungarian National Museum], Múzeum körút 14-16, Budapest 8. Translations of art. from Soviet periodicals on Russian and Soviet art. nfs

72. SZOVJET RÉGÉSZET [Soviet archaeology]. Irr. Magyar Nemzeti Múzeum - Történeti Múzeum [Hist. Museum of the Hungarian National Museum], Múzeum körút 14-16, Budapest 8. Translations of art. from Soviet periodicals on archaeology and numismatics, with emphasis on the Soviet Union; illus. nfs

73. TÁRSADALMI SZEMLE [Social review]. A Magyar Szocialista Munkáspárt elméleti és politikai folyóirata [Theoretical and political journal of the Hungarian Socialist Workers' Party]. M. Kossuth Könyv-és Lapkiadó Vállalat, Vörösmarty tér 4, Budapest 5, for Magyar Szocialista Munkáspárt, Budapest. Includes doc. on the hist. of the Communist Party of Hungary. Ft 32

74. THEOLOGIAI SZEMLE [Review of theology]. A magyarországi evangéliumi protestantizmus havi folyóirata [Monthly of the Hungarian Protestant Churches]. M. Magyarországi Egyházak Ökuménikus Tanácsa [Ecumenical Council of Hungarian Churches], Abonyi utca 21, Budapest 14. Ft 140

75. TISZATÁJ [Tisza districts]. Irodalmi, művészeti és társadalmi lap [Review of literature, art and sociology]. M. Csongrád Megyei Tanács és Szeged mj. Város Tanácsa [Councils of the County of Csongrád and the City of Szeged], Dugonics tér 13, Szeged. Ft 24

76. TÖRTÉNELEMTANÍTAS [Teaching of history]. A Művelődésügyi Minisztérium módszertani kiadványa [Methodological publication of the Ministry of Cultural Affairs]. B-M. 1956 (1960: vol. 5). Tankönyvkiadó, Szalay utca 10, Budapest, for Művelődésügyi Minisztérium [Ministry of Cultural Affairs], Budapest. Ed: János Almási. Art. on the theory and methods of teaching hist. fron the Marxist-Leninist viewpoint; rev. of periodicals. Ft 14.40

77. TÖRTÉNELMI SZEMLE [Historical review]. Q. 1958 (1959). Magyar Tudományos Akadémia Történettudományi Intézete [Hist. Inst. of the Hungarian Acad. of Sciences], Belgrad rakpart 5, Budapest 5. Ed: Éva H. Balázs, Miklós Lackó. Art. on hist., mostly modern, with emphasis on Hungary and its neighboring countries, including the U.S.S.R.; bk. rev.; professional news from Hungary and other countries (mainly people's democracies); list of foreign hist. periodicals with titles of art.; French, German and Russian sum.; table of contents also in English, French, German and Russian; graph. Supersedes A Magyar Tudományos Akadémia Történettudomanyi Intézetének Értesítője [Bulletin of the Hist. Inst. of the Hungarian Acad. of Sciences]. Ft 40

78. TÖRTENÉTI STATISZTIKAI KÖZLEMÉNYEK [Historical statistical publications]. Q. 1957 (1958: vol. 2). Központi Statisztikai Hivatal Könyvtára [Library of the Central Statistical Office], Keleti Károly utca 5-7, Budapest 2, and Levéltárak Országos Központja [National Center of Archives], Budapest. Ed: József Kovacsics. Art. on statistics pertaining to the Habsburg Empire, with special emphasis on Hungary, based mainly on unpub. sources; doc.; bk. rev.; English, German or Russian sum. nfs

79. ÚJ EMBER [New man]. W. Actio Catholica, Kossuth Lajos utca 11 lépcső, 1.em.1, Budapest 5. Art. on the hist. of the Roman Catholic Church. p (1) Ft 1

80. UNIVERSITAS SCIENTIARUM BUDAPESTINENSIS DE ROLANDO EÖTVÖS NOMINATAE, ANNALES... (Annales Universitatis Scientiarum Budapestinensis de Rolando Eötvös Nominate). Sectio Historica. A. 1957. Eötvös Lóránd Univ., Pesti Barnabás utca 1, Budapest 5. Art. on prehist. and on general, social and economic hist., mostly of Hungary, with emphasis on the Middle Ages and the 19th cent.; German, Russian, English or French sum.; illus.

81. VALÓSÁG [Reality]. A TIT társadalomtudományi közlönye [Sociological bulletin of the Scientific Educational Society]. B-M. Gondolat Könyv-, Lapkiadó és Terjesztő Vállalat, Bródy Sándor utca 16, Budapest 8, for Tudományos Ismeretterjesztő Társulat (TIT), Rosenberg házaspár utca 15, Budapest 5. Ft 72

82. VASI SZEMLE [The Vas County review]. Helyismereti évkönyv [Yearbook of local lore]. A. Vas megye és Szombathely város tanácsa [Council of the County of Vas and of the City of Szombathely], Szombathely. p (1) Ft 23

83. VESZPRÉMI SZEMLE [The Veszprém review]. Q. Hazafias Népfront Veszprém Megyei Bizottsága [Veszprém County Committee of the Patriotic People's Front], Veszprém. p (1) Ft 7

84. VILÁGIRODALMI FIGYELŐ [World literary observer]. A Magyar Tudományos Akadémia Irodalomtörténeti Intézetének dokumentációs és kritikai folyóirata [Documentary and critical journal of the Institute of Literary History, Hungarian Academy of Sciences]. Q. Magyar Tudományos Akadémia Irodalomtörténeti Intézete, Ménesi utca 11-13, Budapest 11. French and Russian sum. Ft 32

Iceland

Prepared with the assistance of

Rigsbibliotekarembedet [The Office of the National Librarian], Copenhagen

1. ANDVARI. A. (1959: vol. 84). Íslenzka Pjóovinafélags [Icelandic "Folk Friend" Soc.], Reykjavík. Art. mainly on Icelandic hist.; cum. index in vol. 83.

ÁRBÓK HINS ÍSLENZKA FORNLEIFAFÉLAGS see ÍSLENZKA FORNLEIFAFÉLAGS, ÁRBÓK HINS...

2. ISLENZKA FORNLEIFAFÉLAGS, ÁRBÓK HINS...[Yearbook of the Icelandic Archaeological Society]. A. 1886 (1957/58). Íslenzka Fornleifafélags, Reykjavík. Art. on Icelandic archaeology; English sum.; cum. indices pub. in 1904, 1929, and 1954.

3. SKÍRNIR. A. (1958: vol. 132). Íslenzka Bókmenntafélag [Icelandic Literary Soc.], Reykjavík. Art. on the humanities, including hist., not limited to Icelandic subjects.

Ireland

Prepared with the assistance of the
National Library of Ireland, Dublin

NORTHERN IRELAND

BULLETIN OF THE ULSTER PLACE-NAME SOCIETY see ULSTER PLACE-NAME SOCIETY, BULLETIN OF THE

HISTORICAL STUDIES see section on the Republic of Ireland

IRISH HISTORICAL STUDIES see section on the Republic of Ireland

1. IRISH UNIVERSITY HISTORY STUDENTS' CONGRESS. BULLETIN. A. 1956 (1959: no vol. indic.). Irish Univ. Hist. Students' Congress, Queen's Univ., Belfast. Ed: David Thornley, Owen Edwards. Papers, not confined to Irish hist., read at the conference. 1s

2. SEANCHAS ARDMHACHA [Armagh history]. A. Cumann Seanchas Ardmhacha [Armagh Diocesan Hist. Soc.], c/o The Secretary, 23 Abbey St., Armagh. Doc. section; in Irish or English. 20s

3. ULSTER JOURNAL OF ARCHAEOLOGY. S-A. 1853 (1958: 3rd series, vol. 21). Ulster Archaeological Soc., c/o A.H. George, 7 Sans Souci Park, Belfast. Ed: E.M. Jope, c/o Queen's Univ., Belfast. Art. on the archaeology and hist. of Ulster, with emphasis on the medieval and earlier periods; illus. 20s

4. ULSTER PLACE-NAME SOCIETY, BULLETIN OF THE. 3 x y. 1952 (1957: vol. 5). Ulster Place-Name Soc., c/o Dept. of Celtic, Queen's Univ., Belfast. Ed: J.B. Arthurs. Art. dealing with the origin and hist. of place names, with emphasis on Northern Ireland. pni

THE REPUBLIC OF IRELAND

1. **ARCHIVUM HIBERNICUM**. Irish Historical Records. A. 1912 (1958: vol. 21). Catholic Record Soc. of Ireland, St. Patrick's College, Maynooth, County Kildare. Ed: Rev. P.J. Corish. Art. and doc. pertaining to all periods of Irish hist.; in English or Latin. 25s (memb. 20s)

2. BEALOIDEAS [Folklore]. Irr. Irish Folklore Commission, 82 St. Stephen's Green, Dublin. In Irish and English. 20s (memb. 15s)

BULLETIN. For titles beginning with "Bulletin," followed by the name of the publishing or sponsoring institution or society, see the respective institution or society.

3. CARLOVIANA. A. Old Carlow Soc., c/o W.V. Hadden, "Four Winds," Carlow. 1s

4. CHRISTUS REX. An Irish Quarterly Journal of Sociology. Q. Christus Rex Pub., Naas, County Kildare. p (1) 2s 6d

5. CLOGHER RECORD. A. R. and S. Printers, Old Cross Sq., Monaghan, for Cumann Seanchais Chlochair [Hist. Soc. of the Diocese of Clogher]. Genealogical tables; maps; illus.; list of memb. of the soc. 10s

6. CLONMEL HISTORICAL AND ARCHAEOLOGICAL SOCIETY, JOURNAL OF THE. A. Clonmel Hist. and Archaeological Soc., 30 Ard na Greine, Clonmel, Tipperary. 2s 6d

7. COLLECTANEA HIBERNICA. A. 1958 (1958: vol. 1). Clonmore and Reynolds Ltd., 29 Kildare St., Dublin, for Franciscan House of Celtic Studies and Hist. Research. Ed: Benignus Millett, O.F.M., Dún Mhuire, Killiney, County Dublin. "Devoted exclusively to the publication of sources for Irish history and guides to such sources. It will publish editions of manuscripts dealing with various aspects of Irish history and catalogues of manuscript collections, in Ireland and elsewhere, containing Irish historical material." 12s 6d / $ 2

8. CORK HISTORICAL AND ARCHAEOLOGICAL SOCIETY, JOURNAL OF THE. S-A. Guy and Co., Ltd., Cork, for Cork Hist. and Archaeological Soc. Cum. index for the years 1892-1940; illus. 35s (memb. 30s)

9. AN COSANTÓIR [The defender]. The Irish Defence Journal. M. Castle Pub. Ltd., 38 Merrion Sq., Dublin, for Army General Headquarters, Red House, Infirmary Rd., Parkgate, Dublin. In English and occasionally in Irish. 14s / 15s

10. COUNTY KILDARE ARCHAEOLOGICAL SOCIETY, JOURNAL OF THE Leinster Leader Ltd., Naas, County Kildare. p (1) 10s

11. COUNTY LOUTH ARCHAEOLOGICAL SOCIETY, JOURNAL OF THE. Irr. Ed: Mrs. Bernard MacGuinness, Farndreg House, Dundalk, County Louth. 20s

12. THE DONEGAL ANNUAL. S-A. County Donegal Hist. Soc., c/o Rev. Patrick Gallagher, St. Tighearnach's Secondary School, Clones. pni

13. DUBLIN HISTORICAL RECORD. Q. Old Dublin Soc., City Assembly House, 58 South William St., Dublin. p (1) 2s 6d

14. ÉIGSE [Learning]. A Journal of Irish Studies. S-A. Colm O Lochlainn At the Sign of the Three Candles, Fleet St., Dublin. Texts of manuscripts in Old, Middle and Modern Irish and reproduction of material in Irish from oral narration; in Irish and English. p (1) 2s 6d

15. GALVIA. A. 1954 (1957: vol. 4). Galway Archaeological and Hist. Soc., Univ. College, Galway. Ed: Síle Ní Chinnéide, T.S.Ó. Máille. Art. on all periods of Irish hist. and on archaeology, with emphasis on Galway; doc.; in Irish; illus. 7s 6d / $ 1

16. HERMATHENA. S-A. 1873 (1958: no. 91-92). Hodges Figgis and Co. Ltd., 6 Dawson St., Dublin, for Trinity College, Dublin. Ed: W.B. Stanford.

Papers by memb. of the college on literary and general hist., with emphasis on Ireland, on classical studies, and on the hist. of the college; bk. rev. p(1) 10s

17. HISTORICAL STUDIES. A. 1958 (1959: vol. 2). Conference of Irish Historians, Univ. College, Dublin, and Queen's Univ., Belfast. Ed: Michael Roberts, Queen's Univ., Belfast, and T. Desmond Williams, Univ. College, Dublin. Papers on hist., hist. methodology and historiography, with emphasis on Irish hist., read before the A. Conference of Irish Historians. 10s 6d

18. IRISH CATHOLIC HISTORICAL COMMITTEE, PROCEEDINGS OF THE. A. 1955 (1957 [1958]: no. 3). M.H. Gill and Son, 50 Upper O'Connell St., Dublin, for Irish Catholic Hist. Committee, Dublin. 2s

19. IRISH COMMITTEE OF HISTORICAL SCIENCES, BULLETIN OF THE. Q. 1939 (1959: new series, vol. 7). Irish Committee of Hist. Sciences, Dept. of Hist., Univ. College, Dublin. Ed: H.F. Kearney. Sum. of papers on Irish hist. of all periods and occasionally on British, European or American hist., read before the Irish Hist. Soc., the Ulster Soc. for Irish Hist. Studies, the Dublin Hist. Assoc. and the Conference of Irish Historians; bk. rev.; notes on the activities of local hist. soc. memb. free

20. IRISH ECCLESIASTICAL RECORD. M. Browne and Nolan Ltd., Nassau St., Dublin. 40s / $ 7

21. IRISH GEOGRAPHY. A. Geographical Soc. of Ireland, 19 Dawson St., Dublin. (memb.) 15s for residents of Dublin and its vicinity, and 7s 6d for others

22. IRISH HISTORICAL STUDIES. S-A. 1938 (1958: vol. 11). Hodges, Figgis and Co. Ltd., 6 Dawson St., Dublin, for Irish Hist. Soc. and Ulster Soc. for Irish Hist. Studies. Ed: T.W. Moody, T. Desmond Williams. Art. on all periods of Irish hist., and occasionally on the hist. of other countries; bk. rev.; doc.; biblio.: "Writings on Irish History"; A. report of the Irish Committee of Hist. Sciences and news of the sponsoring soc. 20s

23. IRISH RAILWAY RECORD SOCIETY, JOURNAL OF THE. S-A (1 vol. for 3 years). 1947 (1958-60: vol. 5). Irish Railway Record Soc., 1 Beaumont Cres., Dublin. Ed: R.N. Clements, Killadoon, Celbridge, County Kildare. Art. on the hist. of Irish railways from 1830 to the present; notes and news on railways and railroad building; news about the soc.; illus.; vol. indices of papers, recent developments, miscellanea, matters concerning the soc. and illus. (memb.) 10s

24. THE IRISH SWORD. S-A (A. from 1949 to 1954). 1949/50 (1958: vol. 3). Military Hist. Soc. of Ireland, c/o The Secretary, 22 Calderwood Ave., Whitehall, Dublin. Ed: G.A. Hayes-McCoy, 4 Richview Villas, Clonskea, Dublin. Art. on Irish military hist. and on Irish military and naval men who served in foreign armed forces, with emphasis on the period after 1500; notes, statistics; illus. p (1) 15s (memb. 21s p.a.)

JOURNAL. For titles beginning with "Journal," followed by the name of the publishing or sponsoring institution or society, see the respective institution or society.

25. NORTH MUNSTER ANTIQUARIAN JOURNAL. Irr. Thomond Archaeological Soc., c/o D.F. Gleeson, Carnelly, Clarecastel, County Clare. 15s

26. OLD KILKENNY REVIEW. A. Kilkenny Archaeological Soc., St. Kieran's College, Kilkenny. 2s 6d

PROCEEDINGS OF THE IRISH CATHOLIC HISTORICAL COMMITTEE see IRISH CATHOLIC HISTORICAL COMMITTEE, PROCEEDINGS OF THE

27. REPORTORIUM NOVUM. Dublin Diocesan Historical Record. Irr. Browne and Nolan Ltd., Nassau St., Dublin. p (1) 20s

28. RÍOCHT NA MIDHE [Kingdom of Meath]. A. "Drogheda Independent," Drogheda, County Louth, for Meath Archaeological and Hist. Soc. 5s

29. ROYAL SOCIETY OF ANTIQUARIES OF IRELAND, THE JOURNAL OF THE. S-A. 1890/91 (1959: 7th series, vol. 89). Royal Soc. of Antiquaries of Ireland, 63 Merrion Sq., Dublin. Ed: Liam Price, 8 Herbert Park, Bellsbridge, Dublin. Art. on the prehist., medieval and, occasionally, modern hist. of Ireland; doc.; bk. rev.; proceedings of the soc.; index. 40s

30. STUDIES. An Irish Quarterly Review. Q. Talbot Press, 89 Talbot St., Dublin. 20s

31. VEXILLA REGIS [Standards of the king]. A. Assoc. of the Laymen of Maynooth, c/o Henry O'Mara (ed.), 20 Palmerston Park, Dublin. 5s

Italy

Prepared with the assistance of

Benvenuto Reghini, Vice Director, Biblioteca Nazionale Centrale, Florence, and

Miss Pamela H. Sutton, Rome

1. ACADEMIA SCIENTIARUM TAURINENSIS, ACTA... ATTI DELLA ACCADEMIA DELLE SCIENZE DI TORINO. Parte Seconda: Classe di Scienze Morali, Storiche e Filologiche [Second part: Section for Philosophy, History and Philology]. S-A. 1759 (1957: old series, vol. 115; new series, vol. 4). Libreria F. Casanova e C., Via C. Battisti 7, Torino, for Accademia delle Scienze, Via Accademia delle Scienze 6, and Via Maria Vittoria 3, Torino. Ed: Lionello Vincenti. Art. on the literature of ancient Greece, Rome and India, Italian literature, Greek philosophy, the early hist. of Christianity, and the hist. of northern Italy; news of the acad.; list of memb. pni

ACCADEMIA ARETINA DI SCIENZE, LETTERE ED ARTI, ATTI DELL'... see ACCADEMIA PETRARCA DI LETTERE, ARTI E SCIENZE. ATTI E MEMORIE

ACCADEMIA DEGLI AGIATI, ATTI DELL'... see ACCADEMIA ROVERETANA DEGLI AGIATI, ATTI DELL'...

2. ACCADEMIA DEGLI EUTELETI DELLE CITTÀ DI SAN MINIATO, BOLLETINO DELL'... [Bulletin of the "Euteleti" Academy of the City of San Miniato]. Q. Accademia degli Euteleti, Via A. Conti 8, San Miniato, Pisa. pni

ACCADEMIA DELLE SCIENZE DI TORINO, ATTI DELLA... see ACADEMIA SCIENTIARUM TAURINENSIS, ACTA...

3. ACCADEMIA DI AGRICOLTURA, SCIENZE E LETTERE DI VERONA, ATTI E MEMORIE DELLA... [Proceedings and memoirs of the Academy of Agriculture, Sciences and Letters of Verona]. A. Accademia di Agricoltura, Scienze e Lettere, Via Leoncino 6, Verona. Index for vol. 1-75 (1807-99), pub. under the title: Memorie dell' Accademia di Agricoltura, Lettere, Arti e Commercio. pni

4. ACCADEMIA DI ARCHEOLOGIA, LETTERE E BELLE ARTI, RENDICONTI DELLA... [Proceedings of the Academy of Archaeology, Letters and Arts]. A. (1957 [1958]: new series, vol. 32). Stabilimento "L'Arte Tipografica," San Biagio dei Librai, Napoli, for Società Nazionale di Scienze, Lettere ed Arti, Napoli. Ed: R. Filangieri. Art. on ancient literary works, Roman architectural monuments, papyri, and on old Italian literature; news of the activities and meetings of the acad. and of archaeological excavations. pni

5. ACCADEMIA DI SCIENZE DELL' ISTITUTO DI BOLOGNA, MEMORIE DELL'... [Memoirs of the Academy of Sciences of the Institute of Bologna]. Classe di Scienze Morali [Section for Philosophy]. S-A. Accademia delle Scienze dell' Istituto di Bologna, Via Zamboni 31, Bologna. pni

6. ACCADEMIA DI SCIENZE, LETTERE ED ARTI, AGRIGENTO. ATTI [Academy of Sciences, Letters and Arts, Agrigent. Transactions]. Irr. Accademia Agrigentina, Agrigento. pni

ACCADEMIA DI SCIENZE, LETTERE ED ARTI DEGLI AGIATI, ATTI DELL'... see ACCADEMIA ROVERETANA DEGLI AGIATI, ATTI DELL'...

7. ACCADEMIA DI SCIENZE, LETTERE ED ARTI DI MODENA. ATTI E MEMORIE [Academy of Sciences, Letters and Arts of Modena. Transactions and memoirs]. A. Società Tipografica Editrice Modenese, Modena, for Accademia di Scienze, Lettere ed Arti, Corso Vittorio Emanuele II 59, Modena. 1st series (1833-1922) pub. under the title Memorie della R. Accademia di Scienze, Lettere ed Arti di Modena. pni

8. ACCADEMIA DI SCIENZE, LETTERE E ARTI DI PALERMO, ATTI DELLA... [Transactions of the Academy of Sciences, Letters and Arts of Palermo]. A. Accademia di Scienze, Lettere ed Arti, ex. Palazzo Reale, Palermo. pni

9. ACCADEMIA DI SCIENZE, LETTERE E ARTI DI UDINE, ATTI DELL'... [Transactions of the Academy of Sciences, Letters and Arts of Udine]. 3xy. Arti Grafiche Friulane, Udine, for Accademia di Scienze, Lettere e Arti, Via Bartolini 3, Udine. Cum. index for the years 1910-1951. Formerly pub. under the title Atti dell' Accademia di Udine. pni

ACCADEMIA DI UDINE, ATTI DELL'... see ACCADEMIA DI SCIENZE, LETTERE E ARTI DI UDINE, ATTI DELL'...

10. ACCADEMIA ETRUSCA DI CORTONA, ANNUARIO DELL'... [Annual of the Etruscan Academy of Cortona]. A. (mri 1954/55 [1956]: new series, vol. 3). Tipografia Commerciale, for Accademia Etrusca, Cortona. Ed: B. Barbadoro. Art. on the religious orders and hist. personalities of Cortona, Etruscan archaeological excavations, Egyptian art treasures in the museum of Cortona, and on the literature, philosophy and art of the Middle Ages in the Cortona region; news and notes; vol. 3 contains a cum. index for the years 1934-1955. From 1927 to 1933 pub. under the title Bolletino dell' Accademia Etrusca di Cortona. pni

ACCADEMIA ETRUSCA DI CORTONA, BOLLETTINO DELL'... see ACCADEMIA ETRUSCA DI CORTONA, ANNUARIO DELL'...

ACCADEMIA FIORENTINA DI SCIENZE MORALI "LA COLOMBARIA," ATTI E MEMORIE DELL'... see ACCADEMIA TOSCANA DI SCIENZE E LETTERE "LA COLOMBARIA," ATTI E MEMORIE DELL'...

11. ACCADEMIA LIGURE DI SCIENZE E LETTERE, ATTI DELL'... [Transactions of the Ligurian Academy of Sciences and Letters]. A. Accademia Ligure di Scienze e Lettere, Palazzo Reale, Via Balbi 10, Genova. Illus. Supersedes Atti della Società Ligustica di Scienze Naturali e Geografiche, Atti della Società di Scienze e Lettere and Atti della Società di Scienze e Lettere di Genova, formerly pub. separately. L 6,000 / $ 10

12. ACCADEMIA LUCCHESE DI SCIENZE, LETTERE ED ARTI, ATTI DELL'... [Transactions of the Lucca Academy of Sciences, Letters and Arts]. A. Accademia Lucchese di Scienze, Lettere ed Arti, Via Battisti 17, Palazzo Lucchesini, Lucca. pni

13. ACCADEMIA LUNIGIANESE DI SCIENZE, LETTERE ED ARTI "GIOVANNI CAPPELLINI," MEMORIE DELL'... [Memoirs of the Lunigiana Academy of Sciences, Letters and Arts "Giovanni Cappellini"]. A. Accademia Lunigianese di Scienze, Lettere ed Arti "Giovanni Cappellini," La Spezia. Hist., ethnography and literature. pni

14. ACCADEMIA NAZIONALE DEI LINCEI, ATTI DELLA... [Transactions of the "Accademia Nazionale dei Lincei"]. Memorie della Classe di Scienze Morali, Storiche e Filologiche [Memoirs of the Section for Philosophy, History and Philology]. Irr. G. Bardi, Salita de' Crescenzi 16, Roma, for Accademia Nazionale dei Lincei, Via della Lungara 10, Roma. Illus. From 1847 to 1872 pub. under the title Acta Pontificiae Academiae Scientiarum. L 6,000 / L 7,000

15. ACCADEMIA NAZIONALE DEI LINCEI, ATTI DELLA... [Transactions of the "Accademia Nazionale dei Lincei"]. Notizie sugli Scavi di Antichita, Comunicate alla Accademia dal Ministero della Pubblica Istruzione [Reports on ancient excavations communicated to the Academy by the Ministry of Public Instruction]. S-A or A. 1873 (1957: 8th series, vol. 11). G. Bardi, Salita de' Crescenzi 16, Roma, for Comitato di Redazione delle "Notizie degli Scavi," Accademia Nazionale dei Lincei, Roma. Ed: Giuseppe Lugli. Art. on archaeological excavations in Italian towns; A. author, subject, epigraphical and topographical index; illus. L 8,000/ L 9,000

16. ACCADEMIA NAZIONALE DEI LINCEI, ATTI DELLA... [Transactions of the "Accademia Nazionale dei Lincei"]. Rendiconti della Classe di Scienze Morali, Storiche e Filologiche [Proceedings of the Section for Philosophy, History and Philology]. B-M (Irr.). 1873 (1958: 8th series, vol. 13). G. Bardi, Salita de' Crescenzi 16, Roma, for Accademia Nazionale dei Lincei, Via della Lungara 10, Roma. Ed: R. Morghen. Art. on old geographical works, old Arabic, Syrian and Italian literature, religious hist., with emphasis on the origins of Christianity, and on ancient Greek colonies in Southern Italy; reports of the meetings of the acad. L 7,000 / L 8,000

17. ACCADEMIA NAZIONALE DI SCIENZE MORALI E POLITICHE IN NAPOLI, ATTI DELL'... [Transactions of the National Academy of Philosophy and Political Science in Naples]. A. 1864 (1958 [1959]: vol. 69). Stabilimento Tipografico Guglielmo Genovese, Pallonetto S. Chiara 22, Napoli, for Società Nazionale di Scienze, Lettere ed Arti in Napoli, Università, Cortile del Salvatore, Napoli. Art. on church hist., Italian economic, social and literary hist., ancient Italian law, public law in Southern Italy, and on the origins of dialectical materialism and Communism; biographical art.; list of memb. of the soc. pni

18. ACCADEMIA PATAVINA DI SCIENZE, LETTERE ED ARTI, ATTI E MEMORIE DELL'... [Transactions and memoirs of the Paduan Academy of Sciences, Letters and Arts]. Classe di Scienze Morali, Lettere ed Arti [Section for Philosophy, Letters and Arts]. A. Accademia Patavina di Scienze, Lettere ed Arti, Via Accademia 13-15, Padova. pni

19. ACCADEMIA PELORITANA, ATTI DELLA... [Transactions of the Peloritana Academy]. Lettere, Filosofia, Belle Arti [Letters, philosophy and arts]. Irr. Accademia Peloritana dei Pericolanti, Palazzo dell'Università, Via T. Cannizzaro, Messina. Cum. index for vol. 1-16 (1878-1902) appeared in vol. 17. pni

20. ACCADEMIA PETRARCA DI LETTERE, ARTI E SCIENZE, ATTI E MEMORIE DELLA... [Transactions and memoirs of the "Accademia Petrarca"

of Letters, Arts and Sciences]. A. Accademia Petrarca di Lettere, Arti e Scienze, Via dell' Orto, Casa del Petrarca, Arezzo. 1st series pub. under the title Atti dell' Accademia Aretina di Scienze, Lettere ed Arti. pni

21. ACCADEMIA PONTANIANA, ATTI DELLA... [Transactions of the Pontaniana Academy]. Irr. Francesco Giannini e Figli Tipografia, Cisterna dell' Olio, Napoli, for Accademia Pontaniana, Napoli. Law, hist., literature, art and philosophy. L 4,000

22. ACCADEMIA ROVERETANA DEGLI AGIATI, ATTI DELLA... [Transactions of the "Accademia Roveretana degli Agiati"]. S-A. Accademia Roveretana degli Agiati, Corso Bettini, Rovereto. Art. on hist., literature, agriculture, and the culture of Rovereto; news and notes; biblio. Former titles: Atti della Accademia degli Agiati and Atti della Accademia di Scienze, Lettere ed Arti degli Agiati. pni

. 23. ACCADEMIA TOSCANA DI SCIENZE E LETTERE "LA COLOMBARIA," ATTI E MEMORIE DELLA... [Transactions and memoirs of the Tuscan Academy of Sciences and Letters "La Colombaria"]. Irr. Leo S. Olschki, for Accademia Toscana di Scienze e Lettere "La Colombaria," Via S. Egidio 21, Firenze. From 1837 to 1942 pub. under the title Atti della Società Colombaria di Firenze, and from 1943 to 1950 under the title Atti e Memorie della Accademia Fiorentina di Scienze Morali "La Colombaria." pni

24. ACCADEMIA TOSCANA DI SCIENZE E LETTERE "LA COLOMBARIA." STUDI BALTICI [Tuscan Academy of Sciences and Letters "La Colombaria." Baltic Studies]. Irr. 1931 (mri 1952: vol. 9; new series, vol. 1). Accademia Toscana di Scienze e Lettere "La Colombaria," Via S. Egidio 21, Firenze. Art. on Lithuanian philology, mythology and, occasionally, hist.; in English, German or Italian. Old series pub. by Istituto per l'Europa Orientale, Roma. pni

25. ACCADEMIA VIRGILIANA: MANTOVA. ATTI E MEMORIE [Vergil Academy of Mantua. Transactions and memoirs]. Irr. Accademia Virgiliana, Via Accademia 23, Mantova. pni

26. ACCADEMIE E BIBLIOTECHE D' ITALIA [Academies and libraries of Italy]. B-M. Fratelli Palombibi Editori, Roma, for Ministerio della Pubblica Istruzione, Direzione Generale delle Accademie e Biblioteche, Roma. Illus. L 5,600 / L 10,000

27. ACME [Acme]. Annali della Facoltà di Filosofia e Lettere dell' Università Statale di Milano [Annals of the Faculty of Philosophy and Letters of the State University of Milan]. 3xy. 1948 (1956 [1958]: vol. 9). Istituto Poligrafico dello Stato P.V., Roma, for Università degli Studi, Via Festa del Perdono 3, Biblioteca, Milano. Ed: Sergio Donadoni. Art. on the hist. of Western culture, Greek and Roman papyri, antiquities and doc.; biographical art.; bk. rev.; in Italian and, occasionally, German. nfs

ACTA ORDINIS FRATRUM MINORUM VEL AD ORDINEM QUOQUE MODO PERTINENTIA see ORDO FRATRUM MINORUM VEL AD ORDINEM QUOQUE MODO PERTINENTIA, ACTA...

28. AEGYPTUS. Rivista Italiana di Egittologia e di Papirologia [Italian review of Egyptology and the study of papyri]. Q. 1920 (1958: vol. 38). Società Editrice "Vita e Pensiero," Piazza S. Ambrogio 9, Milano, for Scuola di Papiro-

logia dell' Università Cattolica del Sacro Cuore, Milano. Ed: Aristide Calderini, Domenico Lofrese. Art. on Egyptology, the study of papyri, and on the early Christian period; reproductions of papyri and ancient doc.; bk. rev.; extensive biblio., classified by subject, and biblio. information on papyri and relevant texts; professional notes; in English, French, German or Italian; illus. L 2,000 /$6.50

29. AEVUM [Era]. Rassegna di Scienze Storiche, Linguistiche, Filologiche [Review of history, linguistics and philology]. B-M. 1927 (1958: vol. 32). Società Editirce "Vita e Pensiero," Piazza S. Ambrogio 9, Milano, for Facoltà di Lettere dell' Università Cattolica del Sacro Cuore, Milano. Ed. board: Ezio Framceschini, Aristide Calderini, Mario Apollonio, Domenico Lofrese. Art. on modern and classical philology, literature and the arts, and on hist.; bk. rev.; biblio.; in English, Italian or Spanish. L 2,000 / $ 6.50

AFFRICA see AFRICA

30. AFRICA. Rivista Bimestrale di Studi e Documentazione [Bi-monthly review of study and documentation]. B-M. 1946 (1959: vol. 14). Istituto di Propaganda Internazionale, Via Tadino 62, Milano, for Istituto Italiano per l'Africa, Via Aldrovandi 16, Roma. Art. and doc. on hist., economics and folklore; biblio.; illus. Vol. 1-11 (1946-1956) pub. under the title Affrica.
L 2,500 / L 4,000

31. ALTAMURA. Irr. Casa Editrice Cressati, Bari, for Archivio-Biblioteca-Museo Civico (A.B.M.C.). Illus. pni

32. L'ALTRA SPONDA [The other side]. M. Associazione Nazionale Venezia Giulia e Dalmazia, Comitato di Milano, Via Rugabella 9, Milano. Ed. address: Via A. Bazzini 20, Milano. Art. on the hist., literature, and art of Venetia Julia and Dalmatia; doc.; biblio.; illus. L 5,000

33. AMOR DI LIBRO [Friend of the book]. Rassegna di Bibliografia e di Erudizione [Review of bibliography and instruction]. Q. Sansoni Antiquariato, Via Ricasoli 44, Firenze. Illus. L 3,000 / L 4,500

ANALECTA. For titles beginning with "Analecta," followed by the name of the publishing or sponsoring institution or society, see the respective institution or society.

ANNALI. For titles beginning with "Annali," followed by the name of the publishing or sponsoring institution or society, see the respective institution or society.

34. ANNALI DI STORIA DEL DIRITTO [Annals of the history of law]. Rassegna Internazionale [International review]. A. Casa Editrice Giuffré, Via Solferino 19, Milano, for Istituto di Storia del Diritto Italiano and Scuola di Perfezionamento nella Storia del Diritto Medievale e Moderno, Università, Roma. Ed: Francesco Calasso. Art. on the hist. of law in Italy, Europe and South America from the Middle Ages to modern times, and on juridical historiography; short art. on inst. in medieval municipalities, canon law and on juridical and linguistic hist.; rev. of art.; news of the activities of assoc. for the hist. of law; A. author index; in French, German or Italian. L 3,000 / L 3,300

ANNUARIO. For titles beginning with "Annuario," followed by the name of the publishing or sponsoring institution or society, see the respective institution or society.

35. ANTIQUITAS. Q. 1946 (mri 1956: vol. 11). Ed: Riccardo Avallone, Via Indépendenza 92, Salerno. Art. on classical literature, art and archaeology. L 2,000 / L 4,000

36. AQUILEIA NOSTRA [Our Aquileia]. A. Museo Archeologico di Aquileia, Udine, for Associazione Nazionale per Aquileia. L 1,250 (memb. L 1,000)

37. ARCHEOGRAFO TRIESTINO [Trieste archaeographer]. A. Presso la Biblioteca Civica, Piazza Attilio Hortis 4, Trieste, for Società di Minerva. Art. and essays on the art, archaeology and political and social evolution of Trieste; cum. index for vol. 1-42 (1829-1929). L 2,000

38. ARCHEOLOGIA CLASSICA [Classical archaeology]. S-A. 1949 (1958: vol. 10). Facoltà di Lettere, Università di Roma, for Istituto di Archeologia e Storia dell' Arte Greca e Romana, and Istituto di Etruscologia e Antichità Italiche. Ed: Massimo Pallotino. Art. on the archaeology, art and culture of Etruscan, Greek and Roman times; rev. of art.; biblio.; news and notes; index; supplements; illus. L 7,000 / $ 13

39. ARCHIGINNASIO [The old gymnasium]. Q. 1906 (mri 1956: vol. 51). Biblioteca Comunale dell' Archiginnasio, Piazza Galvani 1, Bologna. Art. on hist. and literature; doc.; bk. rev.; biblio.; news and notes; cum. index for vol. 1-30 (1906-1935). pni

39. ARCHIVI [Archives]. Archivi d'Italia e Rassegna Internazionale degli Archivi [Archives of Italy and international review of archives]. Q. 1914 (1958: 2nd series, vol. 25). Biblioteca d'Arte Editrice, Palazzo Ricci, Via Giulia 147, Roma. Ed: Velia Giovannelli Recchi. Art. on the holdings of the archives and the social, economic and cultural hist. of Italy, concentrating on the period from the Middle Ages to modern times; official communications of the National Union of the Friends of Archives and Libraries; doc.; biblio.; news and notes; index; illus. From 1914 to 1921 (vol. 1-8) pub. under the title Gli Archivi Italiani and from 1933 to 1934 under the title Archivi d'Italia. L 7,000 / $ 15

ARCHIVI D' ITALIA see ARCHIVI

40. ARCHIVI DI STATO, RASSEGNA DEGLI... [Review of the State Archives]. 3xy. 1955 (1958: vol. 18). Ministero dell' Interno, Ufficio Centrale degli Archivi di Stato, c/o Libreria dello Stato, Piazza Verdi 10, Roma. Ed. board: Carlo de Nardo, Antonio Lombardo, Elio Lodolini. Art. on archival science and holdings, and on the hist. of archives; biographical art. on archivists; occasional art. on hist.; doc.; list of bk. and periodicals received.
L 1,030 / L 2,000

GLI ARCHIVI ITALIANI see ARCHIVI

ARCHIVIO DELLA DEPUTAZIONE ROMANA DI STORIA PATRIA see SOCIETÀ DI STORIA PATRIA, ARCHIVIO DELLA...

41. ARCHIVIO ECONOMICO DELL' UNIFICAZIONE ITALIANA [Economic archives of the Itali n Unification]. Ricerca Promossa dell' Istituto per la Ricostruzione Industriale "I.R.I." in Occasione del Ventennio di Fondazione [Research sponsored by the Institute for Industrial Reconstruction "I.R.I." on the occasion of the twentieth anniversary of its foundation]. Q. 1956 (1957: no. 7). "I.L.T.E." Industria Libreria Tipografica Editrice, C. Bramante 20, Torino, fo

Istituto per la Ricostruzione Industriale, Via Vittorio Veneto 89, Roma. Art. on the economic, cultural and hist. aspects of the Italian Unification.
L 3,000 / L 3,800

42. ARCHIVIO GLOTTOLOGICO ITALIANO [Glottological archives of Italy]. S-A. 1873 (1959: vol. 43). Casa Editrice F. Le Monnier, Via S. Gallo 33, Firenze, for Istituto di Glottologia dell' Università, Via Carlo Alberto 10, Torino. Art. on the hist. of the Italian language and dialects, on Indo-European, in particular Latin, Greek and Mediterranean, linguistics, and on methodology; bk. rev.; biblio. L 1,000 / L 1,500

43. ARCHIVIO PALEOGRAFICO ITALIANO, BULLETTINO DELL'... [Bulletin of the Italian Paleographic Archives]. Rivista Italiana di Paleografia, Diplomatica e Scienze Ausiliarie della Storia [Italian review of paleography, diplomatics and auxiliary historical disciplines]. A. 1908 (1957: new series, vol. 3). Leo Olschki, Casella Postale 295, Firenze, for Istituto di Paleografia dell' Università di Roma, Città Universitaria. Art. on paleography, diplomatics and auxiliary hist. disciplines; in English, French, German, Italian or Spanish; bk. rev.; biblio.; doc.; illus. pv (c. L 12,000 / $24)

44. ARCHIVIO PER L'ALTO ADIGE [Archives for Alto Adige (South Tyrol)]. A. 1906 (1958: vol. 52). Stabilimento Tipografico A. Francolini S.r.l., Via Magazzini 12, Firenze, for Istituto di Studi per l'Alto Adige, Firenze. Ed: Carlo Battisti. Art. on the hist. of South Tyrol from prehist. to modern times, supporting Italy's claims to the territory; doc.; etymology of personal and place names; subject and author index; illus. pni

45. ARCHIVIO STORICO (BANCO DI NAPOLI), BOLLETTINO DELL'... [Bulletin of the Historical Archives (Bank of Naples)]. S-A. 1950 (1959: no. 13). Libreria Aldo Lubrano, Via Enrico Pessina 12, Napoli. Ed. address: Via Salvator Rosa 353, Napoli. Art. on hist., literature, economics and finance; index. (biennial subscription) L 2,200 / L 3,600

46. ARCHIVIO STORICO DI BELLUNO, FELTRE E CADORE [Historical archives of Belluno, Feltre and Cadore]. Q. Feltre-Tipografia Castaldi, Via Veneto 10, Belluno, for Archivio Storico di Belluno, Feltre e Cadòre, Via Gregorio XVI 9, Belluno. Illus. L 700

47. ARCHIVIO STORICO DI TERRA DI LAVORO [Historical archives of Terra di Lavoro]. A. Società di Storia Patria di Terra di Lavoro, Palazzo Reale, Caserta. pni

48. ARCHIVIO STORICO ITALIANO [Italian historical archives]. Q. 1842 (1959: vol. 117). Leo S. Olschki, Via delle Caldaie 14, Firenze, for "Deputazione Toscana di Storia Patria," Firenze. Ed: Niccolò Rodolico. Art. on the hist. of Italy, with emphasis on the Middle Ages; doc.; bk. rev.; biblio.; professional news; in Italian and, occasionally, English, French or German; cum. 3-vol. general index for the first 100 vol. (1842-1941); illus.
L 3,500 / $8

49. ARCHIVIO STORICO LODIGIANO [Historical archives of Lodi]. S-A. Biblioteca Comunale Laudense, Corso Umberto 63, Lodi. From 1881 to 1935 (vol. 1-54) pub. under the title Archivio Storico per la Città e Comuni del Circondario (poi anche) e della Diocesi di Lodi, from 1936 to 1947 (vol. 55-66) under the title Archivio Storico per la Città e Comuni del Territorio Lodigiano e della Diocesi di Lodi, and from 1948 to 1957 (vol. 67-70) under the title Archivio Sto-

rico Lodigiano per la Città e i Comuni dell' ex Circondario e della Diocesi di Lodi. L 600 / L 1,000

ARCHIVIO STORICO LODIGIANO PER LA CITTÀ E I COMUNI DELL' EX CIRCONDARIO E DELLA DIOCESI DI LODI see ARCHIVIO STORICO LODIGIANO

50. ARCHIVIO STORICO LOMBARDO [Historical archives of Lombardy]. A. Società Storica Lombarda, Via Morone 1, Milano. Cum. index for vol. 1-60 (1874-1933). L 2,500 / L 3,000

51. ARCHIVIO STORICO MESSINESE [Historical archives of Messina]. A. Tipografia Ditta d'Amico, Messina, for Società Messinese di Storia Patria, Messina. Ed: Gaetano Vinci. From 1936 to 1938 (vol. 36-39) pub. under the title Bollettino Storico Messinese. pni

52. ARCHIVIO STORICO PER LA CALABRIA E LA LUCANIA [Historical archives of Calabria and Luciania]. Q. 1931 (1958: vol. 27). Collezione Meridionale Editrice, Via di Monte Giordano 36, Palazzo Taverna, Roma, for Archivio Storico per la Calabria e la Lucania. Ed: Umberto Zanotti-Bianco. Art. on all aspects of the prehist. and ancient hist. of Europe, with emphasis on Italy; biographical art.; doc.; bk. rev.; biblio.; notes and news; cum. index for vol. 1-10 (1931-40); illus. L 3,000 / L 3,500

ARCHIVIO STORICO PER LA CITTÀ E COMUNI DEL CIRCONDARIO [POI ANCHE] E DELLA DIOCESI DI LODI see ARCHIVIO STORICO LODIGIANO

ARCHIVIO STORICO PER LA CITTÀ E COMUNI DEL TERRITORIO LODIGIANO E DELLA DIOCESI DI LODI see ARCHIVIO STORICO LODIGIANO

ARCHIVIO STORICO PER LA SICILIA see ARCHIVIO STORICO SICILIANO

53. ARCHIVIO STORICO PER LA SICILIA ORIENTALE [Historical archives of Eastern Sicily]. 3 x y. Società di Storia Patria per la Sicilia Orientale, Piazza Stesicoro 29, Catania. Vol. 1-12 (1936-1947) pub. under the title Bollettino Storico Catanese. L 2,500 / L 3,000

54. ARCHIVIO STORICO PER LE PROVINCIE NAPOLETANE [Historical archives of the Province of Naples]. A. Stabilimento "L' Arte Tipografica," S. Biagio dei Librai, Napoli, for Società Napoletana di Storia Patria, Piazza Dante 3, Napoli. Cum. index for vol. 1-20 (1876-95). pni

55. ARCHIVIO STORICO PER LE PROVINCIE PARMENSI [Historical archives of the Province of Parma]. A. Deputazione di Storia Patria per le Provincie Parmensi, Via del Conservatorio, Parma. From 1863 to 1876 pub. under the title Atti e Memorie delle RR. Deputazioni di Storia Patria per le Provincie Modenese e Parmense, and from 1877 to 1882 under the title Atti e Memorie delle RR. Deputazioni di Storia Patria dell' Emilia. pni

56. ARCHIVIO STORICO PRATESE [Historical archives of Prato]. Q. Stabilimento Lito-Tipografico Giovanni Bechi, Prato, for Società Pratese di Storia Patria, Via S. Iacopo 19, Prato (Firenze). Illus. L 500 / $ 1

57. ARCHIVIO STORICO PUGLIESE [Historical archives of Apulia]. Q. Casa Editrice Cressati, Via Carlo Rosselli 15, Bari, for Società di Storia Patria per la Puglia, Palazzo dell' Ateneo, Bari. Ed: Pier Fausto Palumbo. Illus. L 3,000 / $ 10

58. ARCHIVIO STORICO SARDO [Historical archives of Sardinia]. A. CEDAM (Casa Editrice Dott. Andrea Milani), Padova, for Deputazione di Storia Patria per la Sardegna, Facoltà di Lettere, Università, Cagliari. L 5,000

59. ARCHIVIO STORICO SICILIANO [Historical archives of Sicily]. A. (1956 [1957]: 3rd series, vol. 8). Scuola Tipografica "Boccone del Povero," Via Pindemonte 3, Palermo, for Società Siciliana per la Storia Patria, Vico Gagini 1, Palermo. Ed: Antonio de Stefano. Art. on the hist. of Sicily; cum. index for vol. 1-25 (1873-1900). From 1935 to 1943 pub. under the title Archivio Storico per la Sicilia. L 3,500 / L 4,000

60. ARCHIVIO STORICO SIRACUSANO [Historical archives of Syracuse]. A. Azienda Autonoma del Turismo, Via della Maestranza 40, Siracusa, for Società Siracusana di Storia Patria. Index; illus. L 1,000 / $ 1,60

61. ARCHIVIO VENETO [Archives of Venice]. A. Premiate Officine Grafiche Carlo Ferrari, Venezia, for Deputazione Veneta di Storia Patria, S. Stefano, Palazzo Pisani, Venezia. Cum. index for vol. 1-65 (1871-1930). From 1891 to 1921 pub. under the title Nuovo Archivio Veneto and from 1922 to 1926 under the title Archivio Veneto-Trentino. L 1,500 (individuals L 3,000) / L 3,000

ARCHIVIO VENETO-TRENTINO see ARCHIVIO VENETO

62. ARCHIVUM FRANCISCANUM HISTORICUM. Q. 1908 (1959: vol. 52). Collegio di S. Bonaventura, Brozzi-Quaracchi, Firenze. Ed: Rev. Gerold Fussenegger. Art. on the hist. and overseas missionary activities of the Franciscan Order; bk. rev.; doc.; biblio.; news and notes; in Italian, Latin, English, French, German and Spanish; Latin sum.; cum. index for vol. 1-50 in preparation. L 2,500 / $ 5

63. ARCHIVUM FRATRUM PRAEDICATORUM. A. 1931 (1959: vol. 29). Istituto Storico Domenicano S. Sabina, Piazza Pietro di Illiria, Roma. Art. on the hist. of the Dominican Order; biblio. pni

ARCHIVUM HISTORICUM SOCIETATIS IESU see SOCIETAS IESU, ARCHIVUM HISTORICUM...

64. ARCHIVUM SCHOLARUM PIARUM. A. Pub. address: Piazza dei Massimi 4, Roma. pni

65. ARMI ANTICHE [Ancient armor]. Irr. Accademia di S. Marciano, Via Mazzini 27, Torino. Illus. pni

66. L'ARTE [Art]. Q. 1898 (1958: new series, vol. 23). Pub. address: Piazza Stuparich 2, Milano. Ed. address: Via Gaetano Previati 3, Milano. Art. on the hist. of medieval and modern art; bk. rev.; biblio. L 6,000 / L 9,000

67. ARTE ANTICA E MODERNA [Ancient and modern art]. Q. Casa Editrice Zanichelli, Bologna, for Istituto di Archeologia dell' Università, Via dei Musei 8, Bologna, and Istituto di Storia dell' Arte dell' Università, Via Zamboni 33, Bologna. Art. on archaeology and the hist. of ancient and modern art; bk. rev.; biblio. L 8,000 / L 10,000

68. ARTE CRISTIANA [Christian art]. Rivista Illustrata d'Arte Liturgica... [Illustrated review of liturgical art...]. M. 1913 (1959: vol. 47). Scuola Beato Angelico, Viale S. Gimignano 19, Milano. Art. on the hist. and criticism of Christian art, liturgy and symbolism; bk. rev.; biblio.; news and notes; illus. L 2,000 / L 3,500

69. ARTE FIGURATIVA ANTICA E MODERNA [Ancient and modern figurative art]. Rivista Bimestrale di Pittura, Scultura, Arredamento, Antiquariato [Bi-monthly review of painting, sculpture, furnishings and antiquities]. B-M. Pub. address: Via Pancaldo 7, Milano. L 3,500 / L 6,000

70. ARTE LOMBARDA [Art of Lombardy]. Rivista di Storia dell' Arte [Review of the history of art]. S-A. Edizioni La Rete, Via Statuto 8, Milano. Illus. L 8,000 / $ 16

71. ARTE VENETA [Venetian art]. Rivista di Storia dell' Arte [Review of the history of art]. Q. 1947 (1957 [1958]: vol. 11). Casa Editrice Arte Veneta, Alfieri Editore, S. Marco 746 A, Venezia. Art. and critical essays on hist. and philology; doc.; biblio.; news and notes; illus. L 9,500 / $ 18

72. ASSOCIAZIONE PER IMOLA STORICO-ARTISTICA, ATTI DELL'... [Transactions of the Association for the Art History of Imola]. Irr. Cooperazione Tipografica Editrice Paolo Galeati, Imola. Illus. L 600

73. ATENE E ROMA [Athens and Rome]. Q. 1951 (1958: new series, vol. 3). Casa Editrice G. d'Anna, Via Jacopo Nardi 6, Firenze, for Associazione Italiana di Cultura Classica, c/o Istituto di Filologia Classica, Università di Firenze, Piazza S. Marco 4, Firenze. Art. on classical hist., literature and mythology and on neo-humanism; bk. rev.; biblio. L 1,500 / L 2,800

74. ATENEO DI BRESCIA, COMMENTARI DELL'... [Commentaries of the Athenaeum of Brescia]. A. Tipografia Fratelli Geroldi, Brescia, for Ateneo di Brescia, Via Tosio 12, Brescia. Art. on the hist. and art of Brescia and surrounding provinces from ancient to modern times, and on recent economic problems; reports on the activities of regional scientific assoc. and the Athenaeum; illus. pni

75. ATENEO DI SCIENZE, LETTERE ED ARTI IN BERGAMO, ATTI DELL'... [Transactions of the Athenaeum of Sciences, Letters and Art in Bergamo]. A. Tipografia Editrice Secomandi, Bergamo, for Ateneo di Scienze, Lettere ed Arti, Via T. Tasso 4, Bergamo. Illus. pni

ATENEO DI TREVISO see ATENEO VENETO

76. ATENEO VENETO [Athenaeum of Venice]. Rivista di Scienze, Lettere ed Arti [Review of sciences, letters and art]. M. Pub. address: Campo S. Fantin 1897, Venezia. Illus.; cum. index for the years 1901-1936. From 1817 to 1834 pub. under the title Ateneodi Treviso, and from 1837 to 1880 under the title Atti dell' Ateneo Veneto. pni

ATENEO VENETO, ATTI DELL'... see ATENEO VENETO

77. ATHENAEUM. Studi Periodici di Letteratura e Storia dell' Antichità [Periodical studies in literature and the history of antiquity]. Q. 1913 (1958: new series, vol. 36). Università di Pavia, Pavia. Ed: P. Fraccaro, E. Malcovati. Art. on Greek and Roman literature and on various aspects of classical hist.; bk. rev.; in Italian and occasionally in other European languages with Italian sum.; A. author index; illus. L 2,000 / L 3,000

ATTI. For titles beginning with "Atti," followed by the name of the publishing or sponsoring institution or society, see the respective institution or society.

ATTI DELLA DEPUTAZIONE DI STORIA PATRIA PER LA LIGURIA see SOCIETÀ SAVONESE DI STORIA PATRIA

ATTI E MEMORIE DELLA DEPUTAZIONE DI STORIA PATRIA PER LE PROVINCIE MODENESI see DEPUTAZIONE DI STORIA PATRIA PER LE ANTICHE PROVINCIE MODENESI. ATTI E MEMORIE

ATTI E MEMORIE DELLE RR. DEPUTAZIONI DI STORIA PATRIA DELL' EMILIA see ARCHIVIO STORICO PER LE PROVINCIE PARMENSI

ATTI E MEMORIE DELLE RR. DEPUTAZIONI DI STORIA PATRIA PER LE PROVINCIE MODENESE E PARMENSE see ARCHIVIO STORICO PER LE PROVINCIE PARMENSI

ATTI E MEMORIE DI STORIA PATRIA PER LE PROVINCIE MODENESE E PARMENSI see DEPUTAZIONE DI STORIA PER LE ANTICHE PROVINCIE MODENESI, ATTI E MEMORIE DELLA...

78. AUREA PARMA [The golden Parma]. Rivista Trimestrale di Lettere, Arte e Storia [Quarterly review of sciences, art and history]. Q. Pub. address: Vicolo Leon d'Oro 8, Parma. Cum. index for vol. 1-25 (1912-1941). L 1,200 / L 2,400

79. BADIA GRECA DI GROTTAFERRATA, BOLLETTINO DELLA... [Bulletin of the Greek Abbey of Grottaferrata]. Q. 1947 (1958: new series, vol. 12). Monastero Esarchico di S. Maria di Grottaferrata, Grottaferrata (Roma), for Badia Greca di Grottaferrata. Ed: Teodoro Minisci. Art. on the hist. of the Greek Orthodox Church and of the monastery; Byzantine studies; doc.; rev. of bk. and periodicals; illus.; subject and author index for vol. 1-10 (1947-1956). L 800 / L 1,200

80. BENEDICTINA. Fascicoli Trimestrali di Studi Benedettini [Quarterly journal of Benedictine studies]. Q. Padri Benedettini di S. Paolo, Via Ostiense 186, Roma. L 1,500 / L 3,000

81. BERGOMUM. Q. Civica Biblioteca, Piazza Vecchia 15, Bergamo. Cum. index for vol. 1-20 (1907-1933). From 1907 to 1926 pub. under the title Bollettino della Biblioteca Civica di Bergamo. L 1,500 / L 2,500

82. LA BIBLIOFILIA [Bibliophilism]. Rivista di Storia del Libro e delle Arti Grafiche, di Bibliografia ed Erudizione... [Review of the history of books, the art of printing, of bibliography and education...]. Q. 1899 (1959: vol. 41).

Casa Editrice Leo S. Olschki, Via della Chiesa 16, Firenze. Ed: Roberto Ridolfi. Art. on the hist. of bk., the art of printing, and on incunabula holdings in various parts of the world; biblio.; rev. of bk. and art.; news and notes; in Italian, English and French; cum. index for the years 1899-1948; illus.
L 5,000 / $ 12

BIBLIOTECA CIVICA DI BERGAMO, BOLLETTINO DELLA... see BERGOMUM

BOLLETTINO. For titles beginning with "Bollettino," followed by the name of the publishing or sponsoring institution or society, see the respective institution or society.

83. IL BOLLETTINO FILATELICO [The philatelic bulletin]. M. Pub. address: Casella Postale 548, Firenze. Illus. L 750 / L 1,500

84. BOLLETTINO LIGUSTICO PER LA STORIA E LA CULTURA REGIONALE [Ligurian bulletin for regional history and culture]. Q (Irr.). Soc. Ligure di Storia Patria, Via Garibaldi 9, Genova. Illus.
L 1,000 / L 2,000

85. BOLLETTINO STORICO-BIBLIOGRAFICO SUBALPINO [Historical-bibliographical bulletin of the Subalpine region]. Q. (1958: 56th year). Deputazione Subalpina di Storia Patria, Palazzo Carignano, Torino. Ed: Francesco Cognasso. Art. on the hist. of Piedmont, with emphasis on the 17th and 18th cent.; professional news and reports on hist. meetings; bk. rev.; list of memb. of the "Deputazione"; cum. index for the years 1896-1952. L 3,000

BOLLETTINO STORICO CATANESE see ARCHIVIO STORICO PER LA SICILIA ORIENTALE

86. BOLLETTINO STORICO CREMONESE [Historical bulletin of Cremona]. Miscellanea di Scritti Originali [Miscellany of original writings]. Irr. Deputazione di Storia Patria per la Lombardia, Sezione di Cremona, Via Ugolani Dati 4, Cremona. L 1,500 / L 3,000

87. BOLLETTINO STORICO LIVORNESE [Historical bulletin of Livorno]. 3 x y (Irr.). Società Editrice Tirrena, Via Grande 60, Livorno. L 1,000

88. BOLLETTINO STORICO MANTOVANO [Historical bulletin of Mantua]. Q. Pub. address: Via Grioli 19 b, Mantova. L 1,500

BOLLETTINO STORICO MESSINESE see ARCHIVIO STORICO MESSINESE

BOLLETTINO STORICO PAVESE see SOCIETÀ PAVESE DI STORIA PATRIA, BOLLETTINO DELLA...

89. BOLLETTINO STORICO PER LA PROVINCIA DI NOVARA [Historical bulletin of the Province of Novara]. S-A. Società Storica Novarese, Broletto-Novara. Cum. index for vol. 1-46; illus. L 1,000

90. BOLLETTINO STORICO PIACENTINO [Historical bulletin of Piacenza]. 3 x y. Pub. address: Via Carducci 18, Piacenza. L 500 / L 1,000

91. BOLLETTINO STORICO PISANO [Historical bulletin of Pisa]. A.

Tipografia Umberto Giardini, Pisa, for Società Storica Pisana, Biblioteca Universitaria, Pisa. L 1,600 / L 2,100

BOLLETTINO STORICO VALTELLINESE see SOCIETÀ STORICA VALTELLINESE, BOLLETTINO DELLA...

92. BOZNER JAHRBUCH FÜR GESCHICHTE, KULTUR UND KUNST [Bolzano yearbook for history, culture and art]. Irr. Verlagsanstalt Athesia, Bolzano. Vol. 3-4 (1931-1936) pub. under the title Jahrbuch für Geschichte, Kultur und Kunst. pni

BULETINUL SOCIETĂTI ACADEMICE ROMÂNE see SOCIETATEA ACADEMICA ROMÂNA, BULETINUL...

BULLETTINO. For titles beginning with "Bullettino," followed by the name of the publishing or sponsoring institution or society, see the respective institution or society.

93. BULLETTINO DI PALETNOLOGIA ITALIANA [Bulletin of Italian paleethnology]. S-A. 1875 (1957 [1958]: new series, vol. 11). Museo Preistorico-Etnografico "L. Pigorini," Via del Collegio Romano 26, Roma. Ed: Ciro Drago. Art. on the prehist., early hist. and paleethnology of Italy; bk. rev.; professional notes; maps; illus. L 4,000 / L 5,000

94. BULLETTINO SENESE DI STORIA PATRIA [Bulletin for the local history of Siena]. A. Accademia Senese degli Intronati, Palazzo Patrizi-Piccolomini, Via di Città 75, Siena. L 1,500 / L 3,000

95. BULLETTINO STORICO EMPOLESE [Historical bulletin of Empoli]. S-A. Editrice Capparini, Empoli, for Associazione Turistica "Pro Empoli," Piazza Farinata 4, Empoli. Illus. L 1,000

96. BULLETTINO STORICO PISTOIESE [Historical bulletin of Pistoia]. S-A. Biblioteca Forteguerriana, Piazza della Sapienza 4, Pistoia, for Società Pistoiese di Storia Patria (Sezione della Deputazione di Storia Patria per la Toscana). Cum. index for vol. 1-51 (1899-1949). L 1,000

97. CAHIERS LIGURES DE PREHISTOIRE ET D'ARCHEOLOGIE [Ligurian journal for prehistory and archaeology]. A. 1952 (1958: no. 7). Section Française de l'Institut International d'Etudes Ligures, Musée Bicknell, Via Romana 17 bis, Bordighera. Art. on the prehist. and archaeology of Liguria; biblio.; illus. L 3,000

98. CALABRIA NOBILISSIMA [Noblest Calabria]. Periodico di Arte, Storia e Letteratura Calabrese [Journal of Calabrian art, history and literature]. Irr. (B-M). Pub. address: Via Guglielmo Tocci 6, Cosenza. Illus. L 2,000 / L 3,500

99. CALABRIA NOSTRA [Our Calabria]. B-M. Eredi Serafino, Via Caroprese, Celico (Cosenza). L 800 / L 1,600

100. CAPITOLIUM. M. Istituto Romano d'Arti Grafiche, Roma, for Comune di Roma, Via del Campidoglio 3, Roma. Statistics; illus. L 4,000 / L 8,000

101. CARMELUS. S-A. 1954 (1958: vol. 5). Società A.B.E.T.E., Via

Prenestina 68, Roma, for Institutum Carmelitanum, Via Sforza Pallavicini 10, Roma. Ed: Joachim Smet. Art. on theology (with emphasis on spiritual theology and Mariology) and on the hist. of the Carmelite Order; doc.; bk. rev.; list of bk. received; A. biblio. of Carmelitana, classified by subject; in English, Latin, French, German, Italian or Spanish. L 2,500 / $ 4

102. CASTALIA. Rivista di Storia della Medicina [Journal of the history of medicine]. Q. 1945 (1959: vol. 15). Pub. address: Via G. Strambio 25, Milano. Art. on the hist. of medicine; illus. L 2,000 / L 4,000

103. CE FASTU? [What do you do?]. B-M. Società Filologica Friulana, Piazza Marconi 9, Udine. Illus. L 1,000 / L 2,000

104. CIRCOLO NUMISMATICO NAPOLETANO, BOLLETTINO DEL... [Bulletin of the Numismatic Circle of Naples]. A. 1916 (1957: 42nd year). Circolo Numismatico Napoletano, Castello Angioino, Napoli. Ed: Luigi Giliberti. Art. on numismatics and related sciences; bk. rev.; news and notes; illus.

105. LA CIVILTÀ CATTOLICA [The Catholic civilization]. B-M. Pub. address: Via di Porta Pinciana 1, Roma. Art. on philosophy and theology; academic news; Catholic chronicle of Italy and other countries; bk. rev.; biblio.; cum. index for the years 1850-1940. L 5,000 / $ 10

106. CIVITAS. Rivista Mensile di Studi Politici [Monthly review of political studies]. M. Pub. address: Corso Rinascimento 113, CC. Postale 1/32669, Roma. French, English and German sum. L 3,000

107. COLLECTANEA FRANCISCANA. Q. 1931 (1959: vol. 29). Istituto Storico dei Frati Minori Cappuccini, Via Boncompagni 71, Roma (350). Ed: Padre Isidoro de Villapadierna. Art. on the hist. of the Capuchin and other Franciscan Orders, and on theology; doc.; rev. of bk. dealing with the general hist. of the Church; list of pub. received; A. index, classified by subject, name and place; in Latin, French, Italian, German or Spanish; bk. rev. in Latin. L 3,000 / $ 6.50

COMMENTARI. For titles beginning with "Commentari," followed by the name of the publishing or sponsoring institution or society, see the respective institution or society.

108. COMMENTARI [Commentaries]. Rivista di Critica e Storia dell' Arte [Review of criticism and the history of art]. Q. De Luca Editore, Via Gaeta 14, Roma. L 4,000 / L 6,000

109. COMMISSIONE ARCHEOLOGICA COMUNALE DI ROMA, BULLETTINO DELLA... [Bulletin of the Archaeological Commission of the Municipality of Rome]. Q. 1872 (mri 1953-55 [1956]: vol. 75). Casa Editrice "L'Erma," Via Cassiodoro 19, Roma, for Comune di Roma, 10 Ripartizione, Via della Tribuna di Campitelli 33, Roma. Ed: Antonio M. Colini. Art. on all aspects of the prehist., hist., and archaeology of Rome and the Roman Empire; rev. of bk. and art.; biblio.; news and notes; in Italian and French; cum. index for the years 1872-1920; illus. Appendix entitled Bullettino del Museo della Civiltà Romana. L 4,000 / $ 9

110. LA COMUNITÀ INTERNAZIONALE [The international community]. Q. CEDAM, Padova, for Società Italiana per l'Organizzazione Internazionale, Palazzetto di Venezia, Via S. Marco 3, Roma. L 3,500 / L 6,000

111. CONGREGATIO SANCTISSIMI REDEMPTORIS (CSSR), SPICILEGIUM HISTORICUM...(Spicilegium Historicum Congregationis Sanctissimi Redemptoris [CSSR]). S-A. 1953 (mri 1956: vol. 4). Institutum Historicum CSSR, Via Merulana 31, Roma. Art. on the foundation, hist. and work of the Congregation of the Most Holy Redeemer, and on the life and thought of its founder, St. Alphonsus de Liguori, and other outstanding memb.; doc.; bk. rev.; biblio.; in Latin, Italian, English, French, German or Spanish; Latin sum.; index every 5 years. pni

112. CONVIVIUM. B-M. 1929 (1959: new series, vol. 27). Società Editrice Internazionale, Corso Regina Margherita 176, Torino, for Università di Bologna. Ed: Giovanni Battista Pighi, Marco Boni, Via Belmeloro 3, Bologna. Art. on the hist. of ancient and modern culture and literature; bk. rev.; biblio.; news and notes. L 2,400 / L 3,600

113. CRITERIO [Criterion]. Mensile di Cultura, Società, Politica [Monthly for culture, society and politics]. M. Pub. address: Via Ricasoli 31, Firenze. L 3,000 / L 4,000

114. CRITICA D'ARTE NUOVA [Criticism of new art]. B-M. Case Editrice Vallecchi, Viale dei Mille 90, Firenze, for Studio Italiano di Storia dell' Arte, Via Ricasoli 31, Firenze. Illus. L 4,000 / L 7,000

115. CRONACHE MERIDIONALI [Southern chronicles]. M. Pub. address: Via Giosuè Carducci 57-59, Napoli. L 2,000

116. CRONACHE UMBRE [Chronicles of Umbria]. B-M. Pub. address: Piazza Repubblica 71, Perugia. L 1,000

CUADERNOS DE TRABAJOS DE LA ESCUELA ESPAÑOLA DE HISTORIA Y ARQUEOLOGÍA EN ROMA see ESCUELA ESPAÑOLA DE HISTORIA Y ARQUELOGÍA EN ROMA, CUADERNOS DE TRABAJOS DE LA...

117. CULTURA ATESINA. KULTUR DES ETSCHLANDES [Culture of Adige]. Q. Museo dell' Alto Adige, Bolzano. In Italian and German. L 2,500 / L 3,200

118. CUNEO "PROVINCIA GRANDA." 3 x y. Camera di Commercio, Industria e Agricoltura di Cuneo, Corso Nizza 28, Cuneo. Illus. L 1,000 / L 2,000

119. DELTA. Rivista di Critica e di Cultura [Review of criticism and culture]. Q. Pub. address: Viale Michelangiolo 16, Napoli. L 1,500 /$ 5

120. DEPUTAZIONE ABRUZZESE DI STORIA PATRIA, BULLETTINO DELLA... [Bulletin of the Local History Commission of the Abruzzi]. A. Deputazione Abruzzese di Storia Patria, L'Aquila. From 1889 to 1909 pub. under the title Bollettino della Società di Storia Patria Anton Ludovico Antinori negli Abruzzi. pv (L 2,000)

DEPUTAZIONE DI STORIA PATRIA PER L'EMILIA E LA ROMAGNA, ATTI E MEMORIE DELLA... see DEPUTAZIONE PROVINCIALE FERRARESE DI STORIA PATRIA. ATTI E MEMORIE

121. DEPUTAZIONE DI STORIA PATRIA PER L'UMBRIA, BOLLETTINO DELLA... [Bulletin of the Local History Commission of Umbria]. A. Biblioteca Comunale, Perugia, for Deputazione di Storia Patria per l'Umbria.

Cum. index for the years 1895-1901. From 1895 to 1896 pub. under the title Bollettino della Società Umbra di Storia Patria. pv (1957: L 3,000)

122. DEPUTAZIONE DI STORIA PATRIA PER LE ANTICHE PROVINCIE MODENESI. ATTI E MEMORIE [Local History Commission of the Old Province of Modena. Transactions and memoirs]. A. Pub. address: Aedes Muratoriana, Modena. Illus. From 1863 to 1876 (vol. 1-8) pub. under the title Atti e Memorie di Storia Patria per le Provincie Modenese e Parmensi, and from 1937 to 1948 under the title Atti e Memorie della Deputazione di Storia Patria per le Provincie Modenesi. pni

123. DEPUTAZIONE DI STORIA PATRIA PER LE MARCHE. ATTI E MEMORIE [Local History Commission of the Marches. Transactions and memoir A. Tipografia Sociale, Via Moriggia 12, Monza, for Deputazione di Storia Patria per le Marche, Piazza S. Francesco, Ancona. pni

124. DEPUTAZIONE DI STORIA PATRIA PER LE PROVINCIE DI ROMAGNA. ATTI E MEMORIE [Local History Commission of the Province of Romagna. Transactions and memoirs]. A. Deputazione di Storia Patria per la Provincie di Romagna, Via Zamboni 18, Bologna. Cum. index for the years 1862-1935. L 2,000

DEPUTAZIONE DI STORIA PATRIA PER LE PROVINCIE MODENESI see DEPUTAZIONE DI STORIA PATRIA PER LE ANTICHE PROVINCIE MODENESI. ATTI E MEMORIE

DEPUTAZIONE FERRARESE DI STORIA PATRIA, ATTI E MEMORIE DELLA... see DEPUTAZIONE PROVINCIALE FERRARESE DI STORIA PATRIA. ATTI E MEMORIE

125. DEPUTAZIONE PROVINCIALE FERRARESE DI STORIA PATRIA. ATTI E MEMORIE [Ferrara Provincial Commission of Local History. Transactions and memoirs]. A. Società Tipografica Editrice Rodigina, Rovigo, for Deputazione Provinciale Ferrarese di Storia Patria, Ferrara. Cum. index for vol. 1-30 (1886-1936). From 1886 to 1936 pub. under the title Atti e Memori della Deputazione Ferrarese di Storia Patria, and from 1942 to 1945 under the title Atti e Memorie della Deputazione di Storia Patria per l'Emilia e la Romagna. pni

126. IL DIALOGO [The dialogue]. Quaderni di Cultura Filosofica [Quarterly of the philosophy of culture]. Q. Pub. address: Via S. Igoia 67, Bologna. L 3,000

127. DIOCESI DI BRESCIA, MEMORIE STORICHE DELLA... [Historical memoirs of the Diocese of Brescia]. Q. Società Storica Diocesana, Via Grazie 13, Brescia. Forms part of Monografie di Storia Bresciana. pni

128. DIOCESI DI MILANO, MEMORIE STORICHE DELLA... [Historical memoirs of the Diocese of Milan]. A. Pub. address: Biblioteca Ambrosiana. L 1,500

129. IL DIRITTO ECCLESIASTICO [Ecclesiastical law]. M. A. Giuffrè, Via Solferino 19, Milano. L 3.000 / L 4.000

130. "DOMUS MAZZINIANA," BOLLETTINO DELLA... [Bulletin of the "Domus Mazziniana"]. S-A. Istituto "Domus Mazziniana," Via Mazzini 29, Pisa L 1,00

131. EAST AND WEST. Q. 1951 (1958 [1959]: new series, vol. 9). Istituto Italiano per il Medio ed Estremo Oriente, Via Merulana 248, Roma. Ed: Giuseppe Tucci. Art. on various aspects of the cultures of Asia, with some emphasis on religions, anthropology and literature; bk. rev.; reports on the activities of the inst. L 1,500 / $ 3.20

132. ECONOMIA E STORIA [Economy and history]. Rivista Italiana di Storia Economica e Sociale [Italian review of economic and social history]. Q. 1954 (1959: vol. 6). Fratelli Bocca Editori, Via Monte del Gallo 86, Roma. Ed: Amintore Fanfani. Art. on the economic and social hist. of Italy and on economic theory; doc.; abstr. of art.; bk. rev.; graph. L 1,800 / L 3,000

133. EMILIA PREROMANA. Irr. Centro Emiliano di Studi Preistorici, Via dei Musei 8, Bologna. L 1,800

134. EMPORIUM. Rivista Mensile d'Arte e di Cultura [Monthly review of art and culture]. M. Istituto Italiano d'Arti Grafiche, Bergamo.
L 3,000 / L 5,000

135. EPIGRAPHICA. Rivista Italiana di Epigrafia [Italian review of epigraphy]. Q. 1939 (1956 [1958]: vol. 18). Casa Editrice Ceschina, Via Castelmorrone 15, Milano. Ed: A. Calderini, Via Giustiniano 1, Milano. Art. on Greek and Roman epigraphy; bk. rev.; news and notes; illus.
L 2,500 / L 3,500

136. ESCUELA ESPAÑOLA DE HISTORIA Y ARQUEOLOGIA EN ROMA, CUADERNOS DE TRABAJOS DE LA... [Journal of the activities of the Spanish School of History and Archaeology in Rome]. Irr. 1912 (1958: vol. 10). Escuela Española de Historia y Arqueología, Via de Villa Albani 16, Roma. Ed: Francisco Iñiguez Almech. Art. and monographs on hist. and archaeology.
pv

137. EUROPA. B-M. Pub. address: Via Antonio Nibby 11, Roma. Ed: Carlo Curcio. L 3,000 / L 4,500

138. FAENZA. Rivista di Studi di Storia e di Tecnica dell'Arte Ceramica [Review of studies of the history and technique of the art of ceramics]. B-M. 1913 (1959: vol. 45). Museo Internazionale delle Ceramiche, Via Campidori 2, Faenza. Ed: Giuseppe Liverani. Art. on the hist. of pottery, particularly faiences, in Italy, and on the art of ceramics; doc.; news of interest in the field of ceramics, and about the activities of the museum; bk. rev.; A. tables of contents also in English and French; illus. L 1,500 / $ 2.40

139. FASTI ARCHAEOLOGICI [Archaeological records]. Annual bulletin of Classical Archaeology. A. 1946 (1956 [1959]: vol. 11). Ed: Sansoni, Firenze, for International Assoc. for Classical Archaeology. L 15,000 / $ 25

140. FEDE E ARTE [Faith and art]. Rivista internazionale di arte sacra [International review of religious art]. M. Pontifica Commissione Centrale per l'Arte Sacra in Italia, Piazza della Cancelleria 1, Roma. Illus. L 3,000 /$ 9

141. FELIX RAVENNA. Q. Pub. address: Basilica di S. Apollinare Nuovo, Ravenna. Illus.; cum. index for the years 1911-1929. pni

142. FOLKLORE. Rivista di Tradizioni Popolari [Review of popular tradition]. Q. 1947 (1957: vol. 11). Editori R. Pironti e Figli, Napoli. Ed: Raffaele

Corso, Via Mezzocannone 75, Napoli. Art. on Italian folklore; bk. rev.; biblio.
L 1,200 / L 2,400

143. FRATE FRANCESCO [Franciscan friar]. Rivista di Cultura Francescana [Review of Franciscan culture]. Q. 1923 (1959: new series, vol. 6). Pub. address: Via Merulana 124, Roma. Art. on the hist. of the Franciscan Order.
L 1,000 / L 1,500

GIORNALE. For titles beginning with "Giornale," followed by the name of the publishing or sponsoring institution or society, see the respective institution or society.

144. GIORNALE DEGLI ECONOMISTI E ANNALI DI ECONOMIA [Journal of economists and annals of economics]. M. CEDAM, Padova, for Università Commerciale Luigi Bocconi, Milano. L 3,000 / L 5,000

145. GIORNALE DI ARALDICA E GENEALOGIA [Journal of heraldry and genealogy]. Rivista Mensile di Scienze Storico-Politiche, Araldiche, Genealogiche e Cavalleresche [Monthly review of the sciences of history, politics, heraldry, genealogy and cavalry]. M. 1952 (1958: vol. 7). Pub. address: Via del Corso 26, Roma. Art. on heraldry, genealogy and hist.; biographical studies; biblio.; illus. L 2,000

146. GIORNALE STORICO DELLA LETTERATURA ITALIANA [Historical journal of Italian literature]. Q. 1883 (1958: vol. 135). Casa Editrice Loescher-Chiantore, Via Vittorio Amedeo 18, Torino. Art. on the hist. of Italian literature; biographies; doc. with annotations; bk. rev.; biblio.; cum. index for vol. 1-100 (1883-1932). L 3,000 / L 4,500

147. GIORNALE STORICO DELLA LUNIGIANA [Historical journal of Lunigiana]. Q. Biblioteca Civica, Via Cavour 39, La Spezia, for Istituto Internazionale di Studi Liguri, Sezione Lunense. Illus. L 1,600

148. HISTORIA. Mensile Illustrato di Storia [Illustrated monthly of history]. M. Cino Del Duca Editrice, Via Borgogna 3, Milano. Maps; illus.
L 1,000 / L 2,000

149. HISTORICA. Rivista Bimestrale di Cultura [Bi-monthly cultural review]. B-M. 1948 (1959: vol. 12). Pub. address: Via Domenico Muratori 25, Reggio Calabria. Ed: Domenico de Giorgio, Domenico Scoleri. Art. on the hist., mainly modern, of Italy, particularly Calabria, with emphasis on cultural aspects and the philosophy of hist.; doc.; bk. rev.; abstr. of art.
L 1,000 / L 1,500

150. HUMANITAS. Rivista Mensile di Cultura [Monthly cultural review]. M. Editrice "Morcelliana," Brescia. Ed. address: Via F. Crispi 2, Brescia.
L 3,000 / L 4,000

151. IDEA [Idea]. Mensile di Cultura Politica e Sociale, Letteratura, Arte, Scienze [Monthly of political and social culture, literature, art and science]. M. Società Editoriale "Idea," Via Francesco Crispi 82, Roma.
L 3,000 / $ 9.50

152. INEDITA. Rivista di Documenti Storici, Scientifici e Letterari mai Finora Pubblicati [Review of unpublished historical, scientific and literary documents]. M. Pub. address: Via Omero 6, Civitanova Marche (Macerata).
L 5,000 / L 10,000

153. INFORMAZIONI ARCHIVISTICHE E BIBLIOGRAFICHE SUL SALENTO [Archival and bibliographical information on Salento]. M. Pub. address: Via A. Imperatore 16, Lecce. Illus. L 2,000 / L 5,000

INSTITUT HISTORIQUE BELGE DE ROME, BULLETIN DE L'... see section on Belgium

154. ISTITUTO CENTRALE DEL RESTAURO, BOLLETTINO DELL'... [Bulletin of the Central Institute of the Restoration]. Q. 1950 (1958 [1959]: no. 34-35). Istituto Poligrafico dello Stato, Libreria dello Stato, Piazza Verdi 4, Roma, for Ministero della Pubblica Istruzione, Roma. Ed: Cesare Brandi, Piazza S. Francesco di Paola 9, Roma. Art. on the hist. and interpretations of the Restoration; bk. rev.; news and notes; English sum.; cum. index; illus. L 3,500 / L 6,000

155. ISTITUTO DI DIRITTO ROMANO "VITTORIO SCIALOJA," BULLETTINO DELL'... [Bulletin of the "Vittorio Scialoja" Institute for Roman Law]. Irr. Editore A. Giuffrè, Milano, for Istituto di Diritto Romano "Vittorio Scialoja," Roma. L 3,000 / L 4,000

156. ISTITUTO GIANGIACOMO FELTRINELLI, ANNALI DELL'... [Annals of the Giangiacomo Feltrinelli Institute]. A. 1958 (1958: vol. 1). Istituto Giangiacomo Feltrinelli, Via Scarlatti 26, Milano. Ed: Giangiacomo Feltrinelli, Via Andegari 6, Milano. Art. on the Marxist movement and on socialism in individual countries; biographical studies; doc.; bk. rev.; biblio. of the Communist International from the 1st to the 7th Congress; list of pub. received by the inst., with brief descriptions of contents, classified by country and subject; biblio. of selected periodical literature, classified by country and subject; in Italian, English or French; English and French sum. pv (c. L 4,000)

157. ISTITUTO ITALIANO DI NUMISMATICA, ANNALI DELL'... [Annals of the Italian Numismatic Institute]. A. 1954 (1957 [1958]: vol. 4). Istituto Italiano di Numismatica, Via IV Fontane, Palazzo Barberini, Roma. Art. on numismatics, with emphasis on Italy; doc.; reports on collections of coins; professional news; biblio.; list of pub. received by the inst. Supersedes Atti e Memorie dell' Istituto Italiano di Numismatica. L 3,000 / $7

ISTITUTO ITALIANO DI NUMISMATICA, ATTI E MEMORIE DELL' see ISTITUTO ITALIANO DI NUMISMATICA, ANNALI DELL'...

158. ISTITUTO NAZIONALE DI ARCHEOLOGIA E STORIA DELL' ARTE, RIVISTA DELL'... [Review of the National Institute of Archaeology and the History of Art]. A. 1929 (1959: new series, vol. 7). "L'Erma" di Bretschneider, Via Cassiodoro 19, Roma, for Istituto Nazionale di Archeologia e Storia dell' Arte, Roma. Art. on archaeology and the hist. of art; index. L 12,000

159. ISTITUTO STORICO ARTISTICO ORVIETANO, BOLLETTINO DELL' ...[Bulletin of the Orvieto Institute for History and Art]. A. 1925 (1957: 13th year). Tipografia degli Orfanelli, Orvieto, for Istituto Storico Artistico Orvietano, c/o Sottosezione di Archivio di Stato di Orvieto. Ed: Crispino Ferri. Art. on the hist. (of all periods), archaeology, linguistics, art, literature and numismatics of Orvieto and its environs; bk. rev.; news of the inst.; reports on the activities of local soc.; illus. pni

160. ISTITUTO STORICO E DI CULTURA DELL' ARMA DEL GENIO, BOLLETTINO DELL'... [Bulletin of the Historical and Cultural Institute of Mili-

tary Engineers]. Q. 1935 (1958: vol. 24). Istituto Storico e di Cultura dell' Arma del Genio, Lungotevere della Vittoria 31, Roma. Ed: Mario Tirelli, Corrado Picone. Art. on arms and fortifications, both ancient and modern; biographical studies; news of the inst.; professional notes; bk. rev. comprising general hist. literature; abstr. of art. from relevant periodicals; illus.
L 1,000 / $ 4

161. ISTITUTO STORICO ITALIANO PER IL MEDIO EVO E ARCHIVIO MURATORIANO, BULLETTINO DELL'... [Bulletin of the Italian Historical Institute for the Middle Ages and of the Muratori Archives]. A. 1886 (1958: no. 70). Istituto Storico Italiano per il Medio Evo, Palazzo Borromini, Roma. Art. on medieval hist.; doc.; bk. rev.; biblio.; news and notes. pv (L 8,000)

162. ISTITUTO STORICO ITALIANO PER L'ETÀ MODERNA E CONTEMPORANEA, ANNUARIO DELL'... [Annual of the Italian Historical Institute for the Modern and Contemporary Eras]. Q. 1935 (1957/58: vol. 9/10). Istituto Storico Italiano per l'Età Moderna e Contemporanea, Via Michelangiolo Caetani 32, Roma. Art. on modern and contemporary hist.; doc.; news and notes.
L 4,000

163. ISTITUTO UNIVERSITARIO ORIENTALE DI NAPOLI. ANNALI [Oriental Institute of the University of Naples. Annals]. A. Istituto Universitario Orientale, Piazza S. Giovanni Maggiore 30, Napoli. L 3,000

164. ISTITUTO VENETO DI SCIENZE, LETTERE ED ARTI. ATTI [Venetian Institute of Sciences, Letters and Art. Transactions]. Classe di Scienze Morali e Lettere [Section for Philosophy and Letters]. A. Istituto Veneto di Scienze, Lettere ed Arti, Palazzo Loredan, Venezia. pni

165. ISTITUTO VENETO DI SCIENZE, LETTERE ED ARTI, MEMORIE DELL'... [Memoirs of the Venetian Institute for Sciences, Letters and Arts]. Classe di Scienze Morali e Lettere [Section for Philosophy and Letters]. Irr. 1843 (1958: vol. 32). Istituto Veneto di Scienze, Lettere ed Arti, Palazzo Loredan (Campo F. Morosini), Venezia. Art. on the hist. and literature of Venetia and Dalmatia; maps. pni

166. L'ITALIA FRANCESCANA [Franciscan Italy]. Rivista di Cultura [Cultural review]. B-M. Centro Nazionale del Terz' Ordine Francescano, Piazza della Consolazione 84, Roma. L 1,000 / L 2,000

167. ITALIA MEDIOEVALE E UMANISTICA [Medieval and humanist Italy]. A. 1958 (1958: vol. 1). Editrice Antenore, Via Baldissera 7, Padova. Ed. board Giuseppe Billanovich, Augusto Campana, Carlo Dionisotti, Paolo Sambin. Art on various aspects of Italian hist. from the 6th to the 16th cent.; in Italian, French or English; index of names and places, and of the manuscripts and doc. of the archives; illus. L 5,000

168. ITALIA NUMISMATICA. M. 1950 (1958: 9th year). Ed: Oscar Rinaldi, Casteldario (Mantova). Art. on ancient and modern numismatics and on rarities; bk. rev.; biblio.; illus. L 1,030 / $ 2

169. ITINERARI [Itineraries]. Rivista Bimestrale di Storia, Letteratura e Società [Bi-monthly review of history, literature and society]. B-M. Pub. address: Corso Italia 12, Genova. L 2,000 / L 3,500

170. IURA. Rivista Internazionale di Diritto Romano Antico [International review of ancient Roman law]. S-A. 1950 (1958: 9th year). Editore Jovene, Via Mezzocannone 109, Napoli, for Istituto di Diritto Romano dell' Università di Catania e Palermo. Ed. address: Seminario Giuridico dell' Università di Catania. Art. on Roman and ancient law; bk. rev.; biblio.; news on the scientific activities of the inst. and the univ.; in several languages. L 5,000 / L 5,000

JAHRBUCH FÜR GESCHICHTE, KULTUR UND KUNST see BOZNER JAHRBUCH FÜR GESCHICHTE, KULTUR UND KUNST

171. JULIA DERTONA. S-A. Società per gli Studi di Storia, Economia ed Arte nel Tortonese, Palazzo Guidobono, Piazzetta Arzano, Tortona. L 1,000 / $ 2

172. KATOLIKUS SZEMLE [Catholic review]. Q. Külföldi Magyar Actio Catholica - Actio Catholica Hungarorum in Exteris, Via della Conciliazione 44, Roma. Art. on the Church in Hungary and on Hungary's literary, political and social life; English sum.; A. index. $ 0.50

KULTUR DES ETSCHLANDES see CULTURA ATESINA

173. LARES. Q. 1930 (1958: 24th year). Leo S. Olschki, Via della Chiesa 16, Firenze, for Società di Etnografia Italiana and Istituto di Storia delle Tradizioni Popolari dell' Università di Roma. Ed: Paolo Toschi, Via Tacito 50, Roma. Art. on the principal aspects of Italian popular tradition and methods of research and comparison, and on the holdings of the ethnographical and demological museums; biblio. L 2,000 / $ 5

174. LEVANTE. Q. Centro per le Relazioni Italo-Àrabe, Via di Villa Ruffo 6, Roma. In Italian and Arabic; statistics; illus. L 1,000 / L 1,400

175. LIGURIA. Rassegna Mensile dell' Attività Ligure [Monthly review of activities in Liguria]. M. Pub. address: Piazzale Brignole 2, Genova. Statistics; illus. L 2,000

176. MAIA. Rivista di Letterature Classiche [Review of classical literature]. Q. Casa Editrice Loescher-Chiantore, Via Vittorio Amedeo 18, Torino. Ed. address: Piazza d'Azeglio 6, Firenze. In Italian, French or German. L 2,000 / L 3,000

MEDEDELINGEN VAN HET NEDERLANDS INSTITUUT TE ROME see NEDERLANDS INSTITUUT TE ROME, MEDEDELINGEN VAN HET...

MEMORIE. For titles beginning with "Memorie," followed by the name of the publishing or sponsoring institution or society, see the respective institution or society.

MEMORIE DELLA R. DEPUTAZIONE DI STORIA PATRIA see SOCIETÀ "ARTE E STORIA," MEMORIE DELLA...

177. MEMORIE DOMENICANE [Dominican memoirs]. Rivista di Religione, Storia, Arte [Review of religion, history and art]. Q. 1884 (1959: new series, 35th year). Pub. and ed. address: Convento di Santa Maria Novella, Firenze. Art. on Dominican hist. and art; biblio.; statistics; illus. From 1884 to 1920 pub. under the title Il Rosario. Memorie Domenicane. L 800 / L 1,000

MEMORIE STORICHE CIVIDALESI see MEMORIE STORICHE FOROGIULIESI

178. MEMORIE STORICHE FOROGIULIESI [Historical memoirs of Friuli]. Irr. Deputazione di Storia Patria per il Friuli, Udine. From 1905 to 1906 pub. under the title Memorie Storiche Cividalesi. pni

179. MISCELLANEA FRANCESCANA. Rivista trimestrale di Scienze teologiche e di Studi francescani [Quarterly review of theological science and Franciscan studies]. Q. 1886 (1958: vol. 58). Pontificia Facoltà Teologica di San Bonaventura O.F.M. Conv., via S. Teodoro 42, Roma (357). Ed: Lorenzo di Fonzo, O.F.M. Art. on theology and Church hist., with emphasis on the Franciscan Order; biographical art.; doc.; bk. rev.; "Cronaca Generale"; notes of professional interest; biblio. notes; in Italian, French or Latin; Latin sum.; index for vol. 1-33 (1886-1930); statistics. L 2,000 / $ 5

180. MISCELLANEA STORICA DELLA VALDELSA [Historical miscellanies of Valdelsa]. B-W. Società Storica della Valdelsa, Via Tilli 27, Castelfiorentino (Firenze). Cum. index for the years 1903-1922. L 1,000 / L 2,000

181. MONDO CATTOLICO [Catholic world]. Rassegna di Civiltà Cristiana [Review of Christian civilization]. Q. Casa Editrice Org. Trans Video, Milano. Ed. address: Via Lepontina 5, Milano. Illus. L 5,000

MONOGRAFIE DI STORIA BRESCIANA see DIOCESI DI BRESCIA, MEMORIE STORICHE DELLA...

182. MONUMENTI ANTICHE [Ancient monuments]. A. 1889 (1958: vol. 44). G. Bardi, Tipografo dell' Accademia Nazionale dei Lincei, for Accademia Nazionale dei Lincei, Roma. Art. on new archaeological discoveries; illus. pv (vol. 44: L 2,000)

183. IL MOVIMENTO DI LIBERAZIONE IN ITALIA [The Liberation Movement in Italy]. Rassegna di Studi e Documenti [Review of studies and documents]. Q. 1949 (1959: no. 54-57). Istituto Nazionale per la Storia del Movimento di Liberazione in Italia, Piazza Duomo 14 (Palazzo ex Reale), Milano. Art. on the hist. of the Italian resistance movement (mostly during 1943-45), occasionally on resistance movements generally and on Fascism and National Socialism; doc; bk. rev.; news of the inst.; professional notes. L 1,500 / L 2,500

184. MOVIMENTO OPERAIO [Labor movement]. B-M. Biblioteca Feltrinelli, Via Scarlatti 26, Milano. Ceased pub. in 1959. pv (1956: p (1) L 400)

MOVIMENTO OPERAIO E CONTADINO IN LIGURIA see IL MOVIMENTO OPERAIO E SOCIALISTA IN LIGURIA

185. IL MOVIMENTO OPERAIO E SOCIALISTA IN LIGURIA [Labor and socialist movement in Liguria]. B-M. Centro per gli Studi sul Movimento Operaio e Socialista in Liguria, Via G. D'Annunzio 1, Genova. Till 1958 pub. under the title Movimento Operaio e Contadino in Liguria. L 1,000

186. IL MULINO [The mill]. Rivista Bimestrale di Cultura e di Politica [Bi-monthly review of culture and politics]. B-M. Pub. address: Via Gramsci 5, Bologna. L 2,000 / L 4,000

187. MUSEI E GALLERIE D' ITALIA [Museums and galleries of Italy]. S-A. "L'Erma" di Bretschneider, Via Cassiodoro 19, Roma, for Associazione Nazionale dei Musei Italiani, Piazza S. Marco 49, Roma. Reports on the activities and exhibitions of Italian museums; list of guides and catalogues; news and notes; illus. L 1,200

188. MUSEO CIVICO DI PADOVA, BOLLETTINO DEL... [Bulletin of the Civic Museum of Padua]. Rivista Padovana di Arte Antica e Moderna, di Numismatica, di Araldica, di Storia e di Letteratura [Padua review of ancient and modern art, numismatics, heraldry, history and literature]. A. Museo Civico, Piazza del Santo 10, Padova. L 2,500

189. MUSEO DEL RISORGIMENTO, BOLLETTINO DEL... [Bulletin of the Museum of the Risorgimento]. A. 1956 (1958: vol. 3). Tipografia Vighi e Rizzoli, Via Santa 6, Bologna, for Museo del Risorgimento, Via dei Musei 8, Bologna. Ed: Giovanni Maioli. Reprints of doc. and documented art. on the period of the Risorgimento, with emphasis on Bologna; rev. art.
L 1,000 / L 2,000

190. MUSEO PITRE, ANNALI DEL... [Annals of the Pitrè Museum]. A. (Irr.). G.B. Palumbo, Via Cavour 117, Palermo, for Museo Etnografico Siciliano (Museo Pitrè), Parco della Favorita, Palermo, and Istituto di Storia delle Tradizioni Popolari dell' Università di Palermo. L 1,500

191. MUSEO TRENTINO DEL RISORGIMENTO E DELLA LOTTA PER LA LIBERTÀ, BOLLETTINO DEL... [Bulletin of the Trent Museum of the Risorgimento and of the struggle for independence]. 3 x y. Museo Trentino del Risorgimento e della Lotta per la Libertà, Castello del Buonconsiglio, Trento. Illus. L 300

192. NEDERLANDS HISTORISCH INSTITUUT TE ROME, MEDEDELINGEN VAN HET... [Communications of the Dutch Historical Institute in Rome]. A. (Irr.). 1921 (1957: 3rd series, vol. 9). Ministeri voor Onderwijs, Kunsten en Wetenschappen [Ministry of Education, Arts and Sciences], 's-Gravenhage, for Istituto Storico Olandese, Via Omero 12, Valle Giulia, Roma. Art. on the hist. of art and archaeology and on general hist.; A. reports of scientific investigations, mainly on the hist. of art; A. reports of the inst. pni

193. NOVA HISTORIA. Rassegna di Cultura Storica [Review of the history of culture]. M. Scuola Superiore di Scienze Storiche "L. A. Muratori," Via Pallone 9, Verona. Illus. L 2,000 / L 3,800

194. NUMISMATICA. Rivista Bimestrale di Numismatica, Medaglistica, Glittica, Sfragistica [Bi-monthly review of numismatics, the science of medals, glyptics and sphragistics]. B-M. 1935 (mri 1953/54: 19th-20th year). P. e P. Santamaria Editori, Roma. Ed. address: Piazza di Spagna 35, Roma. Art. on numismatics, medals and sphragistics; illus. From 1935 to 1940 pub. under the title Numismatica e Scienze Affini. L 1,500 / L 2,000

NUMISMATICA E SCIENZE AFFINI see NUMISMATICA

195. NUOVA ANTOLOGIA DI LETTERE, ARTI E SCIENZE [New anthology of letters, the arts and science]. M. Pub. address: Via del Collegio Romano 10, Roma. Doc.; subject and name index for the years 1931-1950.
L 4,000 / L 6,000

196. NUOVA RIVISTA STORICA [New historical review]. B-M. 1917 (1958: vol. 42). Società Editrice Dante Alighieri (Albrighi, Segati e C.), Milano, Roma, Napoli, and Città di Castello. Ed. address: Lungo Tevere Prati 22, Roma. Art. on hist., art and religion with special reference to Italy; bk. rev.; biblio. L 1,800 / L 3,600

197. NUOVI ARGOMENTI [New discussions]. B-M. Pub. address: Via degli Orsini 34, Roma. Ed: Alberto Moravia, Alberto Carocci. L 3,000 / L 4,000

NUOVO ARCHIVIO VENETO see ARCHIVIO VENETO

198. NUOVO BOLLETTINO BIBLIOGRAFICO SARDO [New bibliographical bulletin of Sardinia]. B-M. Società Editoriale Italiana, Viale Regina Elena 12-14, Cagliari, for Regione Autonoma della Sardegna, Cagliari. Ed: Giuseppe Della Maria, c/o 49/R, Cagliari. Art. on the hist. of Sardinia; classified biblio. on Sardinia; illus. L 2,000 / L 4,000

199. OCCIDENTE [Occident]. Rassegna Mensile di Studi Politici [Monthly review of political studies]. M. Pub. address: Corso Porta Vittoria 28, Milano, and Nuffield College, Oxford. L 2,000 / $ 4

200. L' ORDINE NUOVO D' EUROPA [The New Order of Europe]. M. Pub. address: Corso Garibaldi 84, Foggia. L 600 / L 1,200

201. ORDO CARMELITARUM, ANALECTA... (Analecta Ordinis Carmelitarum). M. Istituto Carmelitano, Via Sforza Pallavicini 10, Roma. pni

202. ORDO CARMELITARUM DISCALCEATORUM, ANALECTA... (Analecta Ordinis Carmelitarum Discalceatorum). Q. Pub. address: Corso d'Italia 38, Roma. pni

203. ORDO FRATRUM MINORUM CAPUCCINORUM, ANALECTA... (Analecta Ordinis Fratrum Minorum Capuccinorum). B-M. 1884 (1959: vol. 75). Curia Generale dei Frati Minori Capuccini, Via Piemonte 70, Roma. Art. on the hist., liturgy and rules of the Capuchin Order; transactions and decrees and official doc. of the Order and reports of its missionary activities; biblio.; cum. index for vol. 1-70 (1884-1954). From 1884 to 1939 pub. under the title Analecta Ordinis Minorum Capuccinorum. pni

204. ORDO FRATRUM MINORUM VEL AD ORDINEM QUOQUE MODO PERTINENTIA, ACTA... (Acta Ordinis Fratrum Minorum vel ad Ordinem quoque modo pertinentia). B-M. 1882 (1959: 78th year). Tipografia del Collegio di S. Bonaventura, Firenze, for Collegio di S. Bonaventura, Quaracchi (Firenze). Ed: Augustinus Sépiuski. Transactions of the "Cunia Generale" of the Order; chronicle; statistics. pni

ORDO MINORUM CAPUCCINORUM, ANALECTA... (Analecta Ordinis Minorum Capuccinorum) see ORDO FRATRUM MINORUM CAPUCCINORUM, ANALECTA...

205. ORDRE SOUVERAIN MILITAIRE DE MALTE, REVUE DE L'... [Review of the Sovereign Military Order of Malta]. Q. L'Ordre Souverain Militaire de Malte, Via Boezio 92, Roma. Ed: M. Bocchino. L 4,000 / $ 7

206. ORIENTE MODERNO [The modern Orient]. Divulgazione Scientifica

sul Vicino Oriente [Scientific information on the Near East]. M. Istituto per l'Oriente, Via Davide Lubin 2, Roma. L 4,000 / $ 10

207. PAGINE ISTRIANE [Istrian pages]. Q. Associazione Istriana di Studi e di Storia Patria, Piazza S. Caterina 1, Trieste. L 1,500 / L 3,000

208. LA PAROLA DEL PASSATO [The word of the past]. Rivista di Studi Antichi [Review of classical studies]. B-M. 1946 (1958: vol. 13). Gaetano Macchiaroli, Via Michetti al Vomero 11, Napoli. Ed: G. Pugliese Cavatelli, Piazza San Marco 4, Firenze. Art. on classical philology, archaeology and hist.; doc.; bk. rev.; in Italian and other major European languages; 10-year author index and cum. table of contents (1946-1955). L 2,000 / $ 4

209. PASSATO E PRESENTE [Past and present]. Problemi della Società Moderna [Problems of modern society]. Pub. address: Via Venti Settembre 16, Torino. L 2,400 / L 4,000

210. IL PENSIERO MAZZINIANO [The thought of Mazzini]. M. Associazione Mazziniana Italiana, Via Morgari 23, Torino. L 500 / L 1,000

211. IL PENSIERO NAZIONALE [The thought of the nation]. Periodico di Critica e Azione Politica [Periodical of political criticism and action]. Quinquennail. Pub. address: Via Velletri 21, Roma. p (1) L 1,000 / p (1) L 2,000

PERIODICO DELLA SOCIETÀ STORICA COMENSE see SOCIETÀ STORICA COMENSE, PERIODICO DELLA...

212. PHOENIX. Rivista Trimestrale di Scienze, Lettere ed Arti [Quarterly review of science, letters and arts]. Q. Accademia di Studi Superiori "Minerva," Via Tresani 106, Bari. L 3,600 / $ 6

213. LA PIE [The parish]. Poesia, Arte, Storia, Costumi e Tradizioni Romagnoli [Poetry, art, history, customs and traditions of Romagna]. Pub. address: Via P. Ravaioli 8, Forli. L 1,500 / L 3,000

214. POLITICA E SOCIETÀ [Politics and society]. Studi e Ricerche [Studies and research]. Q. Pub. address: Via Viotti 4, Torino.

215. IL POLITICO [The politician]. Rivista di Scienze Politiche [Review of political science]. Q. 1928 (1958: vol. 23). Istituto di Scienze Politiche dell' Università degli Studi di Pavia, Pavia. Ed: Bruno Leoni. Art. on political science and hist., with emphasis on modern Italy; bk. rev.; notes on the activities of the inst.; in Italian, English or French; English, French and German sum. of Italian art. L 2,500 / L 3,000

216. IL PONTE [The bridge]. Rivista Mensile di Politica e Letteratura [Monthly review of politics and literature]. M. "La Nuova Italia" Editrice s.p.a., Piazza Indipendenza 29, Firenze. L 4,000 / L 4,500

PONTIFICIA ACADEMIA SCIENTIARUM, ACTA... see ACCADEMIA NAZIONALE DEI LINCEI, ATTI DELLA...

217. PROTESTANTESIMO [Protestantism]. Q. 1946 (1958: vol. 13). Facoltà Valdese di Teologia, Via Pietro Cossa 42, Roma. Ed: Vittorio Subilia. Art. on Christian theology and the hist. of the Church, with emphasis on Protestantism; rev. art.; bk. rev.; in Italian, French and German. L 1,500 / L 1,800

PUBBLICAZIONE. For titles beginning with "Pubblicazione," followed by the name of the publishing or sponsoring institution or society, see the respective institution or society.

218. QUATERNARIA. Quaternary Natural and Cultural History (sub-title also in Italian, French, German and Spanish). A. 1954 (1957 [1958]: vol. 4). Istituto Italiano di Paleontologia Umana, Via Giulio Caccini 1, Roma. Ed: A.C. Blanc. Art. on the paleontology and geology of the Quaternary; bk. rev.; list of pub. received by the inst.; in Italian, English, French or German; sum. in several languages; graph; illus. L 4,500 / $ 8.25

219. QUELLEN UND FORSCHUNGEN AUS ITALIENISCHEN ARCHIVEN UND BIBLIOTHEKEN [Sources and researches from Italian archives and libraries] A. 1898 (1959: vol. 39). Deutsches Historisches Institut in Rom, Corso Vittorio Emanuele 209, Roma. Ed: Walter Holtzmann. Art. on the hist. of German-Italian relations, from the Middle Ages to modern times, with emphasis on church hist., usually based on doc. in Italian archives and libraries; biblio.; reports of the inst.; in French, German or Italian. DM 40

RASSEGNA. For titles beginning with "Rassegna," followed by the name of the publishing or sponsoring institution or society, see the respective institution or society.

220. RASSEGNA DELLE LETTERE E ARTI D'ITALIA [Review of Italian art and literature]. M. Pub. address: Borgo Palazzo 37, Bergamo. L 5,000 / L 10,000

221. RASSEGNA DI FILOSOFIA [Review of philosophy]. Q. Casa Editrice Universale, Via Sistina 48, Roma, for Istituto di Filosofia della Università di Roma. L 1,500 / L 2,500

222. RASSEGNA DI STORIA E BIBLIOGRAFIA SCOLOPICA [Review of "Scolopi" history and bibliography]. S-A. Editiones Calasanctianae, Piazza dei Massimi 4, Roma. L 2,400 / L 2,400

223. RASSEGNA ITALIANA DI POLITICA E DI CULTURA [Italian review of politics and culture]. M. Centro Italiano di Studi per la Riconciliazione Internazionale, Viale David Lubin 2, Roma. L 2,500 / L 3,500

224. RASSEGNA STORICA DEL RISORGIMENTO [Historical review of the Risorgimento]. Q. 1914 (1958: vol. 45). Istituto per la Storia del Risorgimento Italiano, Vittoriano, Roma. Ed: Alberto M. Ghisalberti (ed.), Emilia Morelli (secretary). Art., including biographical art., pertaining to Italian hist. and political thought in the 18th and 19th cent., mostly on the Risorgimento; doc.; bk. rev.; comprehensive list of relevant Italian periodicals, classified by subject; notes on the inst. L 2,000 / L 3,500

225. RASSEGNA STORICA SALERNITANA [Historical review of Salerno]. S-A. Società Salernitana di Storia Patria, Via Francesco Cantarella 7, Salerno. L 2,000 / L 4,000

226. RASSEGNA VOLTERRANA [Volterra review]. Rivista d'Arte e di Cultura [Review of art and culture]. Accademia dei Sepolti, Volterra.

R. [REALE] ACCADEMIA DI SCIENZE, LETTERE E ARTI DI MODENA, MEMORIE DELLA... see ACCADEMIA DI SCIENZE, LETTERE E ARTI DI MODENA. ATTI E MEMORIE

RR. [REALI] DEPUTAZIONI DI STORIA PATRIA DELL' EMILIA see ARCHIVIO STORICO PER LE PROVINCIE PARMENSE

RR. [REALI] DEPUTAZIONI DI STORIA PATRIA PER LE PROVINCIE MODENESE E PARMENSE, ATTI E MEMORIE DELLE... see ARCHIVIO STORICO PER LE PROVINCIE PARMENSE

227. RELAZIONI INTERNAZIONALI [International relations]. Settimanale di Politica Estera [Foreign policy weekly]. W. Istituto per gli Studi Politica Internazionale, Via Clerici 5, Milano. L 7,000 / L 10,500

RENDICONTI. For titles beginning with "Rendiconti," followed by the name of the publishing or sponsoring institution or society, see the respective institution or society.

228. RICERCHE DI STORIA RELIGIOSA [Researches on religious history]. Rivista di Studi Storico-Religiosi [Review of historical-religious studies]. 3 x y. 1957 (1957: vol. 1). Edizioni dell' Ateneo, Roma. Ed: Carlo Cecchelli. Art. on ancient and medieval ecclesiastical and secúlar hist. and theology; bk. rev.; in English, French and Italian. L 4,500 / $ 9.50

229. RINASCIMENTO [Renaissance]. S-A. 1950 (1957: vol. 8). Editrice Sansoni, Viale Mazzini 46, Firenze, for Istituto Nazionale di Studi sul Rinascimento. Ed. board: Mario Salmi, Alberto Chiari, Alessandro Perosa, Pier Giorgio Ricci. Art. on the philosophy, art, literature and philology of the Renaissance; bk. rev.; biblio.; in Italian and other major European languages; illus. L 2,000 / L 2,600

230. RINASCITA ARTISTICA [Artistic rebirth]. Rivista Internazionale d'Arte e Turismo [International review of art and travel]. M. Pub. address: Via Cedronio 31, Napoli. L 2,000 / L 4,000

231. IL RISORGIMENTO [The Risorgimento]. 3 x y. 1949 (1957: vol. 9). Edizioni Amici del Museo del Risorgimento, Via Borgonuovo 23, Milano. Ed. board: Enrico Cabella, Frederico Curato, Leopold Marchetti, Franco Valsecchi. Art. on the hist. of the Risorgimento, on the European situation in the 19th cent. and its bearing on Italy, and biographical art.; bk. rev.; notes on the activities of the museum. L 1,000 / L 2,000

RIVISTA. For titles beginning with "Rivista," followed by the name of the publishing or sponsoring institution or society, see the respective institution or society.

232. RIVISTA ARALDICA [Heraldic review]. Storica Araldica [History of heraldry]. M. 1903 (1959: vol. 56). Collegio Araldico di Roma, Via S. Maria dell' Anima 16, Roma. Art. on Italian heraldry and hist. and on heraldry in general; bk. rev.; biblio.; index; illus. L 3,000

233. RIVISTA CRITICA DI STORIA DELLA FILOSOFIA [Critical review of the history of philosophy]. Q. 1946 (1958: vol. 13). La Nuova Italia Editrice, Piazza Indipendenza 29, Firenze. Ed. board: Mario Dal Pre, Eugenio Garin, Giulio Preti. Art. on philosophy and philosophers from ancient to modern times in Europe, Asia and America; rev. of bk. and art.; in Italian and French. L 2,000 / L 3,000

234. RIVISTA D'ARTE [Review of art]. A. Leo S. Olschki Editore, Via della Chiesa 16, Firenze. L 4,000 / $ 8

235. RIVISTA DEGLI STUDI ORIENTALI [Review of Oriental studies]. Irr. 1907 (1958: vol. 33). Istituto degli Studi Orientali, Città Universitaria, Roma. Ed: Giovanni Bardi, Salita de' Crescenzi 16, Roma. Art. on Assyriology, Hittitology, Egyptology, Israel, Ethiopia, Arabia, Islam, Syrian and Latin Christian philosophy, and Oriental law and linguistics; bk. rev.; in Italian, German, English and French; illus. L 6,000 / $ 10

236. RIVISTA DI ETNOGRAFIA [Review of ethnography]. A. Istituto Italiano di Etnografia, Via Cesare Rossaroll 200, Napoli. L 1,500 / L 2,500

237. RIVISTA DI FILOLOGIA E ISTRUZIONE CLASSICA [Review of philology and classical instruction]. Q. Casa Editrice Loescher-Chiantore, Via Vittorio Amedeo 18, Torino. Index. L 2,600

238. RIVISTA DI FILOSOFIA [Review of philosophy]. Q. Casa Editrice Taylor, Via Valeggio 26, Torino. In Italian and other European languages. L 2,300 / L 4,000

239. RIVISTA DI FILOSOFIA NEOSCOLASTICA [Review of neoscholastic philosophy]. B-M. Facoltà di Filosofia dell' Università Cattolica del Sacro Cuore, Piazza S. Ambrogio 9, Milano. L 1,800 / L 3,500

240. RIVISTA DI SCIENZE PREISTORICHE [Review of prehistorical sciences]. Q. 1946 (1957: vol. 12). Istituto Italiano di Preistoria e Protostoria, Via S. Egidio 21, Firenze. Ed: P. Graziosi, A. Micheli. Art. on prehist., X-ray research on prehist. material, craniological analyses of prehist. cemeteries and on prehist. art, cultural development and findings; news and reports on prehist. soc. and congresses; bk. rev.; biblio.; Italian, French and English sum.; index; illus. L 2,850

241. RIVISTA DI STORIA ARTE E ARCHEOLOGIA PER LE PROVINCIE DI ALESSANDRIA E ASTI [Review of history, art, archaeology for the provinces of Alessandria and Asti]. A. (mri 1954 [1955]: vol. 63). Pier Ciriaco Astori, Piazza Duomo 2, Alessandria, for Società di Storia Arte e Archeologia, Accademia degli Immobili, Alessandria. Art. on the ancient and modern hist., archaeology, art, and literature of the provinces of Alessandria and Asti; bk. rev.; news about literary doc. of the region; reports of the general assembly of the soc.; list of memb. of the soc. L 500 / L 1,500

242. RIVISTA DI STORIA DEL DIRITTO ITALIANO [Review of the history of Italian law]. A. (mri 1956: vol. 29). Vittorio Cavallari Editore, Via Spiga 32, Milano, for Fondazione Sergio Mochi Onory per la Storia del Diritto Italiano, Verona. Ed. board: Guido Astuti, Gian Piero Bognetti, Mario E. Viora. Art. on the hist. of Italian legal inst. from the Middle Ages to modern times, and on international law; bk. rev. L 2,200 / L 3,000

243. RIVISTA DI STORIA DELLA CHIESA IN ITALIA [Review of the history of the Church in Italy]. 3 x y. (1958: vol. 12). Istituto Grafico Tiberino, Via Gaeta 14, Roma. Ed: Michele Maccarrone. Art. on the lives of saints, inspection tours of the higher clergy to the dioceses in the past, and on the administrative and diplomatic activities of the Holy See in the Middle Ages; notes on appointments of ecclesiastical dignitaries; bk. rev.; biblio. L 2,000 / $ 8

244. RIVISTA DI STUDI CLASSICI [Review of classical studies]. 3 x y. 1953 (1959: vol. 7). Pub. and ed: Vittorio D'Agostino, Via S. Pio V 16, Torino

Art. on Latin and Greek literature and on ancient hist. and philosophy; news and notes; rev. of bk. and periodicals; biblio. L 1,500 / L 2,500

245. RIVISTA DI STUDI LIGURI [Review of Ligurian studies]. Irr. (Q or S-A). Presso il Museo Bicknell, for Istituto Internazionale di Studi Liguri, Via Romana 17, Bordighera. (Pub. address in France: c/o Maurice Louis, Vice-président Français de l'Institut International d'Etudes Ligures, 3 rue Granier, Montpellier). In Italian and French. L 3,000

246. RIVISTA DI STUDI POLITICI INTERNAZIONALI [Review of studies on international politics]. Q. 1934 (1958: vol. 25). Pub. address: Lungarno del Tempio 40, Firenze. Ed: Giuseppe Vedovato. Art. on international relations and diplomatic hist., with emphasis on modern hist. and on Italy; doc.; bk. rev. L 2,400 / L 4,000

247. RIVISTA INGAUNA E INTEMELIA [Review of Ingauna and Intemelia]. Q. Istituto Internazionale di Studi Liguri, Via Romana 17 bis, Bordighera. L 2,000 / L 2,000

248. RIVISTA INTERNAZIONALE DI SCIENZE SOCIALI E DISCIPLINE AUSILIARIE [International review of social sciences and auxiliary disciplines]. B-M. Pub. address: Piazza S. Ambrogio 9, Milano. L 1,500 / L 3,000

249. RIVISTA ITALIANA DI ECONOMIA, DEMOGRAFIA E STATISTICA [Italian review of economics, demography and statistics]. Q. Pub. address: Via C. Balbo 16, Roma. L 3,000 / L 6,000

250. RIVISTA ITALIANA DI NUMISMATICA E SCIENZE AFFINI [Italian review of numismatics and related sciences]. Irr. 1888 (1958: 6th series, vol. 6). Società Numismatica Italiana, Milano.

251. RIVISTA MILITARE [Military review]. M. Ministero Difesa-Esercito, Via di S. Marco 8, Roma. L 4,000 / L 6,000

252. RIVISTA STORICA DEL SOCIALISMO [Review of the history of socialism]. Q. 1958 (1959: vol. 2). Pub. address: Via Cerva 22, Milano. Ed: Luigi Cortesi, Stefano Merli, Via Gaetano Strambio 27, Milano. L 2,000 / L 4,000

253. RIVISTA STORICA ITALIANA [Italian historical review]. Q. 1884 (1959: vol. 71). Edizioni Scientifiche Italiane, Via Roma 406, Napoli, for Rivista Storica Italiana, Via Po 17, Torino. Ed: Delio Cantimori, Via Michelangelo Caetani 32, Roma. Art. on Italian and European hist., with emphasis on modern hist.; doc.; bk. rev.; biblio. notes. L 2,000 / L 3,500

IL ROSARIO. MEMORIE DOMENICANE see MEMORIE DOMENICANE

254. SACRO ORDO CISTERCIENSIS, ANALECTA... (Analecta Sacri Ordinis Cisterciensis). Q. 1945 (1958: vol. 14). Editiones Cistercienses, Piazza del Tempio di Diana 14, Roma (Aventino). Art. on spiritual and monastic life and on the general hist. of the Church; unpub. doc.; biographical studies; biblio.; in Latin, French, German, English and Italian. L 4,000 / L 4,000

255. SACRO ORDO FRATRUM PRAEDICATORUM, ANALECTA... (Ana-

lecta Sacri Ordinis Fratrum Praedicatorum). Q. Convento di S. Sabina, Aventino, Roma 8-48. Ed: Michael Browne. pni

256. SAMNIUM. Q. Archivio Storico Provinciale, Chiostro S. Sofia, Benevento. L 600 / L 600

257. DER SCHLERN. Illustrierte Monatsschrift für Heimat- und Volkskunde [Illustrated monthly for local studies and folklore]. M. 1920 (1958: vol. 32). Druck- und Verlagsanstalt Athesia, Museumstr. 42, Bozen (Bolzano). Ed: Anton Romen, Bozen. Art. on the hist. (including hist. of art) and folklore of South Tyrol; news and notes; bk. rev.; biblio. of bk. and art.; A. index. L 3,000

258. SCUOLA NORMALE SUPERIORE DI PISA, ANNALI DELLA... [Annals of the "Scuola Normale Superiore" of Pisa]. Lettere, Storia e Filosofia [Letters, history and philosophy]. Q. 1873 (1958: vol. 27). Scuola Normale Superiore di Pisa, Palazzo dei Cavalieri, Pisa. Ed: Tristano Bolelli. Art. on cultural and literary subjects, philosophy and philology, cultural and literary hist., and on general hist.; bk. rev.; professional notes; in Italian or other European languages. L 4,000 / $ 10

259. SELE ARTE [Selection of art]. B-M. Studio Italiano di Storia dell' Arte, Via Ricasoli 31, Firenze. English, French, German or Spanish sum.; index; illus. L 1,200 / L 2,400

260. SICULORUM GYMNASIUM. Rassegna Semestrale di Letteratura, Storia e Filosofia [Semi-annual review of literature, history and philosophy]. S-A. Facoltà di Lettere, Università de Catania, Catania. L 2,000 / L 4,000

261. SOCIETÀ [Society]. B-M. 1945 (1959: vol. 15). Parenti Editore, Via Borgonuovo 1, c/c postale n. 3/7504, Milano. Ed: Mario Spinella (ed.), Paola Ballardin (secretary). Art. on social hist. and the hist. of ideas, with emphasis on the 19th and 20th cent., and on philosophy, politics and literature; rev. of Italian and foreign bk., classified by subject; notes of hist. and literary interest. L 3,000 / L 4,500

262. SOCIETÀ "ARTE E STORIA," MEMORIE DELLA... [Memoirs of the Society "Art and History"]. A. Museo Civico, Legnano. Illus. From 1933 to 1934 pub. under the title <u>Memorie della R. Deputazione di Storia Patria.</u> pni

SOCIETÀ DI SCIENZE E LETTERE, ATTI DELLA... see ACCADEMIA LIGURE DI SCIENZE E LETTERE, ATTI DELL'...

SOCIETÀ DI SCIENZE E LETTERE DI GENOVA, ATTI DELLA... see ACCADEMIA LIGURE DI SCIENZE E LETTERE, ATTI DELL'...

SOCIETÀ DI STORIA PATRIA ANTON LUDOVICO ANTINORI NEGLI ABRUZZI, BOLLETTINO DELLA... see DEPUTAZIONE ABRUZZESE DI STORIA PATRIA, BULLETTINO DELLA...

SOCIETÀ DI STORIA VALDESE, BOLLETTINO DELLA... see SOCIETÀ DI STUDI VALDESI, BOLLETTINO DELLA...

263. SOCIETÀ DI STUDI VALDESI, BOLLETTINO DELLA... [Bulletin of the Society for Studies on Waldo]. Irr. (S-A). Tipografia Subalpina, Torre Pel-

lice, for Società di Studi Valdesi, Torre Pellice. From 1881 to 1933 pub. under the title Bulletin de la Société d'Histoire Vaudoise, and in 1934 and 1935 under the title Bollettino della Società di Storia Valdese. L 700 / $ 1.50

264. SOCIETÀ GEOGRAFICA ITALIANA, BOLLETTINO DELLA... [Bulletin of the Italian Geographical Society]. M. Società Geografica Italiana, Villa Celimontana, Roma. Index; illus. L 1,000 / L 1,500

265. SOCIETÀ ISTRIANA DI ARCHEOLOGIA E STORIA PATRIA, ATTI E MEMORIE DELLA... [Transactions and memoirs of the Istrian Society for Archaeology and Local History]. S-A. Società Istriana di Archaeologia e Storia Patria, Rialto 1, Palazzo dei Camerlenghi, Venezia. Illus.; cum. index for the years 1884-1902. pni

SOCIETÀ LIGUSTICA DI SCIENZE NATURALI E GEOGRAFICHE, ATTI DELLA... see ACCADEMIA LIGURE DI SCIENZE E LETTERE, ATTI DELL'...

266. SOCIETÀ PAVESE DI STORIA PATRIA, BOLLETTINO DELLA... [Bulletin of the Pavia Society for Local History]. S-A. Società Pavese di Storia Patria, Museo Civico, Piazza Petrarca 2, Pavia. Illus.; cum. index for the years 1902-1935. In 1893 and 1894, and from 1937 to 1945 pub. under the title Bollettino Storico Pavese. L 1,200

267. SOCIETÀ PER GLI STUDI STORICI, ARCHEOLOGICI ED ARTISTICI NELLA PROVINCIA DI CUNEO, BOLLETTINO DELLA... [Bulletin of the Society for Historical, Archaeological and Artistic Studies in the Province of Cuneo]. S-A. Biblioteca Civica, Palazzo Audifredi, Cuneo. L 1,000

268. SOCIETÀ PIEMONTESE DI ARCHEOLOGIA E DI BELLE ARTI, BOLLETTINO DELLA... [Bulletin of the Piedmont Society for Archaeology and Art]. A. Musei Civici, Palazzo Madama, Piazza Castello, Torino. Illus. L 2,000

269. SOCIETÀ ROMANA DI STORIA PATRIA, ARCHIVIO DELLA... [Archives of the Roman Society for Local History]. Q. 1878 (1956 [1958]: 3rd series, vol. 10). Società Romana di Storia Patria, c/o Biblioteca Vallicelliana, Roma. Art. on Roman hist.; descriptions and illus. of hist. doc. and monuments; biblio.; news and notes; cum. index for vol. 1-50. From 1935 to 1946 (vol. 58-69) pub. under the title Archivio della Deputazione Romana di Storia Patria. pni

270. SOCIETÀ SAVONESE DI STORIA PATRIA, ATTI DELLA... [Transactions of the Savona Society for Local History]. A. Tipografia Priamar, Savona, for Società Savonese di Storia Patria, Savona. From 1935 to 1939 pub. under the title Atti della Deputazione di Storia Patria per la Liguria. pni

271. SOCIETÀ STORICA COMENSE, PERIODICO DELLA... [Periodical of the Historical Society of Como]. A. Scuola Tipografica "Figli della Provvidenza," Lucino, for Società Storica Comense, Como. pni

272. SOCIETÀ STORICA VALTELLINESE: BOLLETTINO DELLA... [Bulletin of the Valtellin Historical Society]. A. Società Storica Valtellinese, Sondrio. From 1937 to 1944 pub. under the title Bollettino Storico Valtellinese. L 500

273. SOCIETÀ STORICA VARESINA, RIVISTA DELLA... [Review of the Historical Society of Varese]. A. Biblioteca Civica, Via Sacco 9, Varese. L 1,000

274. SOCIETÀ TIBURTINA DI STORIA E D'ARTE, ATTI E MEMORIE DELLA... [Transactions and memoirs of the Tiburtine Society for History and Art]. A. 1921 (1955/56 [1957]: vol. 28/29). Società Tiburtina di Storia e d'Arte Villa d'Este, Tivoli, Roma. Art. on all periods of the hist. of Tivoli, and on archaeology and art; biblio.; news and notes; illus. L 2,000 / L 2,000

SOCIETÀ UMBRA DI STORIA PATRIA, BOLLETTINO DELLA... see DEPUTAZIONE DI STORIA PATRIA PER L'UMBRIA, BOLLETTINO DELLA...

275. SOCIETAS IESU, ARCHIVUM HISTORICUM... (Archivum Historicum Societatis Iesu) [Historical Archives of the Society of Jesus]. S-A. 1932 (1959: vol. 28). Institutum Historicum Societatis Iesu, Via dei Penitenzieri 20, Roma. Ed: Michaël Batllori, S.J. Art. on the hist. of the Jesuit Order in particular and of the Church in general; unpub. doc.; bk. rev.; classified biblio. of the hist. of the Soc. of Jesus; notes on the activities and pub. of the inst. and of the Jesuit Order; list of pub. received; in Latin, German, French, English and Spanish; cum. index for vol. 1-20 (1932-1951). L 2,500 / $ 4.56

276. SOCIETATEA ACADEMICA ROMÂNA, BULETINUL... (Buletinul Societătii Academice Române) [Bulletin of the Rumanian Academic Society]. Irr. Societatea Academica Română, Passeggiata del Gianicolo 5, Roma.

SOCIETE D'HISTOIRE VAUDOISE, BULLETIN DE LA... see SOCIETÀ DI STUDI VALDESI, BOLLETTINO DELLA...

SOVRANO MILITARE ORDINE DI MALTA, RIVISTA DEL... see ORDRE SOUVERAIN ET MILITAIRE DE MALTE, REVUE DE L'...

SPICILEGIUM HISTORICUM CONGREGATIONIS SANCTISSIMI REDEMPTORIS (CSSR) see CONGREGATIO SANCTISSIMI REDEMPTORIS (CSSR), SPICILEGIUM HISTORICUM...

277. STORIA ILLUSTRATA [Illustrated history]. M. Mondadori, Via Bianca di Savoia 20, Milano. L 1,800 / L 2,500

STUDI BALTICI see ACCADEMIA TOSCANA DI SCIENZE E LETTERE "LA COLOMBARIA." STUDI BALTICI

278. STUDI E MATERIALI DI STORIA DELLE RELIGIONI [Studies and materials on the history of religions]. S-A. 1925 (1958: vol. 29). Cesare Marzioli Editore, Via Siracusa 4, Roma, for Istituto di Studi Storico-Religiosi, Università di Roma, Facoltà di Lettere e Filosofia, Roma. Ed. board: Alessandro Bausani, Angelo Brelich, Ernesto de Martino, Alberto Pincherle, Nicola Turchi. Art. on the hist. of religions, on primitive mythology and on theology; rev. of bk. and art.; biblio. news and notes. L 5,000 / $ 9.50

279. STUDI ETRUSCHI [Etruscan studies]. A. 1927 (1959: vol. 27). Leo S. Olschki, Via della Chiesa 16, Firenze, for Istituto di Studi Etruschi e Italici, Piazza SS. Annunziata 93, Firenze. Art. on the hist., archaeology and art of Italy with special reference to Etruria; index. L 10,000 / $ 15

280. STUDI FRANCESCANI [Franciscan studies]. Q. (1958: vol. 55).

Convento di S. Francesco, Via A. Giacomini 3, Firenze. Ed: Gaudenzio Melani, O.F.M. Art. on famous literary works of the early Franciscan age; doc. pertaining to the hist. of the Order, the life of St. Francis of Assisi, and the role played by Franciscan friars in hist. up to the 19th cent.; bk. rev. dealing with the missionary activities of the Order and the hist. of local Orders; biblio.; news on cultural activities of the Order. L 1,000 / $ 3

281. STUDI ITALIANI DI FILOLOGIA CLASSICA [Italian studies of classical philology]. A. Casa Editrice Felice Le Monnier, Via San Gallo 33, Firenze, for Istituto di Filologia Classica dell' Università, Piazza S. Marco 4, Firenze. Vol. index, arranged by author. L 2,500 / L 3,000

282. STUDI POLITICI [Political studies]. Q. Casa Editrice Sansoni, Viale Mazzini 46, Firenze. L 2,500 / L 3,500

283. STUDI ROMANI [Roman studies]. B-M. 1953 (1958: vol. 6). Istituto di Studi Romani, Piazza dei Cavalieri di Malta 2, Roma. Ed: Quinto Tosatti, Paolo Brezzi, Fernanda Roscetti. Art. on the hist. of ancient and modern Rome, with emphasis on literature and the arts, and on Vatican and Church hist.; biographical art.; bk. rev.; chronicle of cultural and religious life in Rome; professional notes; reports on the activities of the inst.; classified biblio.
L 2,000

284. STUDI SASSARESI [Studies of Sassari]. A. Istituto Giuridico dell' Università, Sassari. L1,000

285. STUDI STORICI [Historical studies]. Q. 1959 (1959/60: vol. 1). Istituto Gramsci Editore, Via Sicilia 136, Roma. Ed: Gastone Manacorda. Art. on ancient and recent hist., with emphasis on economics; bk. rev.; biblio.; list of bk. received by the inst.; index. L 2,500 / L 5,000

286. STUDI TRENTINI DI SCIENZE STORICHE [Trentine studies of historical sciences]. Q. Biblioteca Civica, Via Roma 51, Trento.
L 1,200 / L 1,600

287. STUDI URBINATI [Studies on Urbino]. Serie B. Storia, Filosofia, Letterarura [Series B. History, philosophy, literature]. Irr. Università degli Studi di Urbino, Via Saffi 2, Urbino. L 2,000 / L 2,500

288. STUDIA PICENA [Picenian studies]. A. Pontificio Seminario Marchigiano "Pio XI," Fano. Ed: Vittorio Bartoccetti, Piazza San Callisto 16, Roma. Illus. pni

289. TEMPI ITALIANI [Italian times]. 5 x y. Edizioni Cinque Lune, Via Muzio Clementi 18, Roma. L 800 / L 1,100

290. TEORESI [Theoretical matters]. Rivista di Cultura Filosofica [Review of philosophical culture]. Q. Pub. address: Via Concezione 8, Messina.
L 1,500 / L 3,000

291. TERTIO ORDO REGULARIS SANCTI FRANCISCI DE PAENTITENTIA, ANALECTA... (Analecta Tertii Ordinis Regularis Sancti Francisci de Paenitentia). Q. 1933 (1959: 27th year). Pub. address: Via dei Fori Imperiali 1, Roma. Art. on hist., law and missionary activities; transactions of the Order; illus. pni

292. IL TESAUR [Thesaurus]. Pub. address: Via Vittorio Veneto 20, Udine. L 500 / $ 2

293. TRADIZIONE MILITARE [Military tradition]. Pub. address: Viale Giulio Cesare 52, Roma.

294. ULISSE [Ulysses]. Rivista di Cultura Internazionale [Review of international culture]. 3 x y. Casa Editrice Sansoni, Viale Mazzini 46, Firenze. L 3,000 / L 3,500

295. UNIVERSITÀ CATTOLICA DEL SACRO CUORE. ANNUARIO [Catholic University of the Sacred Heart. Annals]. A. 1922 (1957: no vol. indic.). Società Editrice "Vita e Pensiero," Piazza S. Ambrogio 9, Milano, for Università Cattolica del Sacro Cuore, Milano. Art. on law, political and commercial sciences, philosophy and hist.; inaugural, commencement and commemorative lectures delivered at the univ.; reports on academic activities. pni

UNIVERSITÀ DEGLI STUDI DI PERUGIA, ANNALI DELL' ISTITUTO GIURIDICO... see UNIVERSITÀ DEGLI STUDI DI PERUGIA, ANNALI DELLA FACOLTÀ DI GIURISPRUDENZA DELL'...

296. UNIVERSITÀ DEGLI STUDI DI PERUGIA, ANNALI DELLA FACOLTÀ DI GIURISPRUDENZA DELL'... [Annals of the Faculty of Law of the "Università degli Studi" of Perugia]. Irr. "CEDAM," Padova, for Istituto Giuridico, Università degli Studi di Perugia, Piazza dell' Università 2, Perugia. From 1885 to 1888 pub. under the title Annali della Facoltà Giuridica dell' Università degli Studi di Perugia, from 1891 to 1902 under the title Pubblicazioni Periodiche della Facoltà di Giurisprudenza dell' Università degli Studi di Perugia, and from 1925 to 1929 under the title Annali dell' Istituto Giuridico della Università degli Studi di Perugia. pni

UNIVERSITÀ DEGLI STUDI DI PERUGIA, ANNALI DELLA FACOLTÀ GIURIDICA DELL'... see UNIVERSITÀ DEGLI STUDI DI PERUGIA, ANNALI DELLA FACOLTÀ DI GIURISPRUDENZA DELL'...

UNIVERSITÀ DEGLI STUDI DI PERUGIA, PUBBLICAZIONI PERIODICHE DELLA FACOLTÀ DI GIURISPRUDENZA DELL'... see UNIVERSITÀ DEGLI STUDI DI PERUGIA, ANNALI DELLA FACOLTÀ DI GIURISPRUDENZA DELL'...

297. UNIVERSITÀ DI BARI, ANNALI DELLA FACOLTÀ DI LETTERE E FILOSOFIA DELLA... [Annals of the Faculty of Letters and Philosophy of the University of Bari]. A. Università, Bari. pni

298. UNIVERSITÀ DI CAGLIARI, ANNALI DELLA FACOLTÀ DI LETTERE, FILOSOFIA E MAGISTERO DELL'... [Annals of the Faculty of Letters, Philosophy and Pedagogy of the University of Cagliari]. A. Università, Cagliari. pni

299. UNIVERSITÀ DI NAPOLI, ANNALI DELLA FACOLTÀ DI LETTERE E FILOSOFIA DELLA... [Annals of the Faculty of Letters and Philosophy of the University of Naples]. A. Istituto Editoriale del Mezzogiorno, Via Costantinopoli 3, Napoli, for Università, Napoli. pni

300. L'URBE [The city]. Rivista Romana di Storia, Arte, Lettere, Costumanze [Roman review of history, art, letters and customs]. B-M. Fratelli Pa-

lombi Editori, Via dei Gracchi 181-185, Roma. L 2,000 / L 4,000

301. VALBONA. Pub. address: Via Pelligario 4, Urbino. L 4,000 / L 6,000

302. VARI [Miscellaneous]. Digest Religioso [Religious digest]. Q. Officium Libri Catholici, Roma. A separate edition also appears in German. L 700

303. IL VASARI. Rivista d'Arte e di Studi Rinascimentali [Review of art and studies of the Renaissance]. Q. 1927 (1958: vol. 16). Pub. address: Casella Postale 15, Via Cavour 4, Arezzo. Ed: Alessandro del Vita. Art. on the hist. of art and art criticism, with emphasis on the Italian Renaissance and on the work of Vasari; cum. table of contents for the years 1927-1943 pub. in 1958. L 3,000

304. IL VELTRO [The greyhound]. Rassegna di Vita Italiana [Review of Italian life]. Società Nazionale "Dante Alighieri," Piazza Firenze 27, Roma. Includes art. on Italian life and hist. L 2,500 / $ 7

305. VITA E ARTE [Life and art]. M. Pub. address: Viale Mazzini 41, Roma. L 500 / L 1,000

306. VITA E PENSIERO [Life and thought]. Rassegna Italiana di Cultura [Italian review of culture]. M. Pub. address: Piazza S. Ambrogio 9, Milano. L 1,600 / L 3,500

ADDENDA

307. ANTONIANUM. Periodicum philosophico-theologicum trimestre [Quarterly journal of philosophy and theology]. Q. Pontifico Ateneo Antoniano, via Merulana 124, Roma. Art. on philosophy, theology and church hist., with emphasis on the Franciscan Order; bk. rev.; biblio.; notes and news. L 2,500 / $ 5

308. BRUTIUM. Rassegna di storia dell' Arte [Review of the history of art]. A. Società "Mattia Preti," Viale Amendola 29, Reggio Calabria. L 1,000 / L 2,000

COMPRENDRE see section on International Periodicals

309. ORIENTALIA. Q. 1932 (1959: new series, vol. 28). Pub. and ed: Pontificum Institutum Biblicum, Piazza Pilotta 35, Roma 204. Art. on various aspects of the hist. and archaeology of the Orient; reports on congresses of Oriental studies; research and findings; bk. rev.; biblio.; news and notes; illus., index; in English, French, German and Italian. L 7,900 / $ 14.50

310. ORIENTALIA CHRISTIANA ANALECTA. Irr. 1923 (1959: no. 153). Pontificum Institutum Orientalium, Piazza S. Maria Maggiore 7, Roma. Art. on archaeology and hist. L 3,000 / L 5,000

311. ORIENTALIA CHRISTIANA PERIODICA. Commentarii de Re Orientali Aetatis Christianae Sacra et Profana... S-A. 1935 (1958: vol. 24). Pontificum

Institutum Orientalium Studiorum, Piazza S. Maria Maggiore 7, Roma. Ed: Gioacchino Patti. Art. on Byzantine hist., liturgy, patrology and philosophy and on the art of the Eastern Church, with emphasis on the Balkan peninsula, Asia minor and Russia; bk. rev.; in English, French, German, Italian and Latin.
L 3,500 / L 3,800

312. PONTIFICIA ACCADEMIA ROMANA DI ARCHEOLOGIA, ATTI DELLA... [Papers of the Pontifical Roman Academy of Archaeology]. Irr. 1923 (1957: vol. 28). "L'Erma" di Bretschneider, via Cassiodoro 19, Roma, for Pontificia Accademia Romana di Archeologia, Palazzo della Cancelleria Apostolica, Piazza della Cancelleria, Roma. Ed: Pietro Romanelli. Art. on archaeological excavations, ancient monuments, inscriptions, and ancient Christian and Renaissance art; reports of the sessions of the acad.; list of memb. of the acad.; illus.

313. PONTIFICIA ACCADEMIA ROMANA DI ARCHEOLOGIA, RENDICONTI DELLA... [Proceedings of the Pontifical Roman Academy of Archaeology]. A. 1921 (1959). "L'Erma" di Bretschneider, via Cassiodoro 19, Roma, for Pontifica Accademia Romana di Archeologia, Palazzo della Cancelleria Apostolica, Piazza della Cancelleria, Roma. L 2,500

314. RIVISTA DI ARCHEOLOGIA CRISTIANA [Review of Christian archaeology]. Q. (mri 1956: vol. 23). Pontifica Commissione di Archeologia Cristiana, and Pontifico Istituto di Archeologia Cristiana, via Napoleone III 1, Roma. Ed: Luciano de Bruyne. Art. on ecclesiastical monuments, works of art, and inscriptions of the early Christian age; bk. rev.; biblio. of bk. and periodicals dealing with architecture, art, and inscriptions of the early Christian age; in English, French, German, Italian and Spanish; illus. L 3,000 / $6

315. STUDIA ET DOCUMENTA HISTORIAE ET IURIS. A. 1935 (1958: vol. 24). Pontificium Institutum Utriusque Iuris, and Pontificia Universitas Lateranensis, Piazza S. Giovanni in Laterano 4, Roma. Ed: Arcadius Larraona, Gabríus Lombardi. Art. and doc. on the hist. of law, with emphasis on Roman law; bk. rev.; professional news. L 6,000 / L 6,500

Liechtenstein

1. HISTORISCHER VEREIN FÜR DAS FÜRSTENTUM LIECHTENSTEIN, JAHRBUCH DES... (Jahrbuch des historische Vereins für das Fürstentum Liechtenstein) [Yearbook of the Historical Society for the Principality of Liechtenstein]. A. 1901 (1957: vol. 57). Historischer Verein für das Fürstentum Liechtenstein, Vaduz. Art. on the hist. (including literary hist.), philology, archaeology and folklore of Liechtenstein, not confined to any period; reports on excavations; A. report and list of memb. of the soc.; illus., maps.

Luxembourg

Prepared with the assistance of

Robert Schumacher, Bibliothèque Nationale, Luxembourg

ANNUAIRE DE LA SOCIETE DES AMIS DES MUSEES DANS LE GRAND DUCHE DE LUXEMBOURG see SOCIETE DES AMIS DES MUSEES DANS LE GRAND DUCHE DE LUXEMBOURG, ANNUAIRE DE LA...

ANNUAIRE DE LA SOCIETE HERALDIQUE LUXEMBOURGEOISE see SOCIETE HERALDIQUE LUXEMBOURGEOISE, ANNUAIRE DE LA...

1. DE BIERGMANN [The miner]. Unabhängiges Nachrichtenblatt für die Interessen des Kayltales und des gesamten Erzbassins [Independent journal for the interests of the Kayl-Valley and the whole Mining District]. B-W. Léon Berens, Rumelange, Luxembourg. Mostly in German; illus. Lfr 100

2. BULLETIN LINGUISTIQUE ET ETHNOLOGIQUE [Bulletin of linguistics and ethnology]. Irr. 1953 (mri 1955: no. 4-6). Section de linguistique, de Folklore et de Toponymie de l'institut Grand Ducal, 50 Grand'Rue, Luxembourg. Ed: Joseph Meyers, 16 rue Fresez, Luxembourg. Art. on the language, literature and literary hist. of Luxembourg; in German or French. Till 1950 pub. under the title: Revue trimestrielle d'études linguistiques, folkloriques et toponymiques.

3. LES CAHIERS LUXEMBOURGEOIS [Journal of Luxembourg]. Revue libre des lettres, des sciences et des arts [Independent review of letters, sciences and the arts]. B-M. 1923 (1959: vol. 31). Imprimerie Bourg-Bourger, 40 ave. de la Gare, Luxembourg. Ed: Raymond Mehlen, 52 ave. du 10 Septembre, Luxembourg. Art. on the hist. of Luxembourg, with emphasis on the 18th and 19t cent., on French, German and local literature, and on art and the hist. of art; doc.; news and notes on literary life in the Grand Duchy; in French and German; illus.; maps. Lfr 200

4. T'HEMECHT [The homeland]. Zeitschrift für Luxemburger Geschichte [Review of Luxembourg history]. Q. 1948 (1959: vol. 12). Verlag der Sankt-Paulus Druckerei, A.G. Luxemburg, 6-8 rue Jean Origer, Luxembourg. Ed: A. Steffen, 39 rue de la Faïencerie, Luxembourg. Art. on the hist. of Luxembourg, including the policies of the various European kings and emperors who rule Luxembourg, on folklore, religion and art, and on the hist. of Luxembourg cities; archival and other reports; bk. rev.; in French and German; illus., maps. Lfr 120

5. INSTITUT GRAND DUCAL DE LUXEMBOURG, PUBLICATIONS DE LA SECTION HISTORIQUE DE L'... [Publications of the Historical Section of the Grand Ducal Institute of Luxembourg]. Irr. 1845 (1958: vol. 76). Imprimerie de la Cour Joseph Beffort, Luxembourg, for Section des sciences historiques de l'institut Grand Ducal, 4 bd. Roosevelt, Luxembourg. Ed. board: Nic. Margue, A. Steffen, J. Meyers, J. Hess, J. Goedert. Art. and monographs, by memb. of the section, on the hist., art and archaeology of Luxembourg; in French or German; illus., maps. Lfr 140

6. D'LETZEBURGER DUEREF [The Luxembourg village]. M. Action Catholique Masculine Luxembourgeoise, 14 bd. Grande-Duchesse Charlotte, Luxembourg. Includes art. on Luxembourg local and parochial hist.; illus. Lfr 5

PUBLICATIONS DE LA SECTION HISTORIQUE DE L'INSTITUT GRAND DUCAL DE LUXEMBOURG see INSTITUT GRAND DUCAL DE LUXEMBOURG, PUBLICATIONS DE LA SECTION HISTORIQUE DE L'...

REVUE TRIMESTRIELLE D'ETUDES LINGUISTIQUES, FOLKLORIQUES ET TOPONYMIQUES see BULLETIN LINGUISTIQUE ET ETHNOLOGIQUE

7. SOCIETE DES AMIS DES MUSEES DANS LE GRAND DUCHE DE LUXEMBOURG, ANNUAIRE DE LA... [Yearbook of the Society of Friends of the Museums in the Grand Duchy of Luxembourg]. Irr. 1928 (mri 1949: vol. 5). Société des Amis des Musées dans le Grand Duché de Luxembourg, 7 bd. de Verdun, Luxembourg. Ed: Louis Wirion. Art. on the holdings of Luxembourg museum, on the hist. of towns, art and architecture, and on archaeology and paleontology; bk. rev.; news and notes on museums in the Grand Duchy; in French and occasionally in German.

8. SOCIETE HERALDIQUE LUXEMBOURGEOISE, ANNUAIRE DE LA... [Yearbook of the Heraldic Society of Luxembourg]. Irr. 1948 (mri 1953/54: vol. 6/7). Société Heraldique Luxembourgeoise, 22 Grand'Rue, Luxembourg. Ed. board: J. Harps, A. Sprunck, R. Matagne. Art. on the hist. of the coats of arms and ceremonial customs of Luxembourg, its rulers, nobles, towns and communes, and occasionally on genealogy and foreign coats of arms; bk. rev.; news and notes on the activities of the soc.; in French and German and occasionally in English.

Monographic series

and

bibliographical and abstracts publications

are not included in this book

Malta

Prepared with the assistance of
The Library of the Royal University of Malta, Valletta

1. THE CLASSICAL JOURNAL. Irr. 1949 (1952: vol. 5). Malta Univ. Branch of the Virgil Soc., c/o Royal Univ. of Malta, Valletta. Ed: Very Rev. E. Coleiro. Art. on Roman classics and hist. 2s 6d (Maltese) / 3s 6d

2. MELITA HISTORICA. A. 1948 (1959: vol. 11). Malta Hist. Soc., c/o Royal Univ. of Malta, Valletta. Ed: J. Cassar-Pullicino, c/o Dept. of Information, Valletta. Art. on the local hist. of Malta, including its churches, public monuments, trade, finances, and the Order of St. John; rev.; in English and Maltese. 2s 6d (Maltese) / 4s 6d

ORDRE SOUVERAIN MILITAIRE DE MALTE, REVUE DE L'... see section on Italy

3. SCIENTIA. Scientific Review. Q. 1935 (1959: vol. 25). St. Dominic Priory, Valletta. Ed: S.M. Zarb, O.P., c/o Royal Univ. of Malta, Valletta. Art. on the general and ecclesiastical hist. of Malta. 6s (Maltese) / 12s

---

The Netherlands

Prepared with the assistance of

A.W. Willemsen, wetenschappelijk ambtenaar,
Koninklijke Bibliotheek, The Hague

1. AKADEMIEDAGEN [Academy days]. A. N.V. Noordhollandse Uitgeversmaatschappij, Amsterdam, for Koninklijke Nederlandse Akademie van Wetenschappen [Royal Dutch Acad. of Sciences]. f 6

2. AMSTELODAMUM. Maandblad voor de Kennis van Amsterdam. Orgaan van het Genootschap "Amstelodamum" [Monthly for studies of Amsterdam. Organ of the Society "Amstelodamum"]. M. Genootschap "Amstelodamum" ["Amstelodamum Soc.], c/o J.H. de Bussy, Rokin 62, Amsterdam C. f 12

ANNUAIRE EUROPEEN see section on International Periodicals

3. ANTIQUITY AND SURVIVAL. An International Review of Traditional Art and Culture. B-M. 1955 (1957/58: vol. 2). N.V. Luctor et Emergo, Laakweg 26, 's-Gravenhage. Art. on archaeology, ethnology and primitive art; biblio.; bk. rev.; graph; in English, French or German; sum. in English, French, German, Italian and Spanish. f 20 / $ 5.50

4. ARABICA. Revue d'Etudes arabes [Review of Arab studies]. 3 x y. 1954 (1958: vol. 5). E.J. Brill, Leiden. Ed: R. Blachère, D. Sourdel, 13 rue du Four, Paris 6e. Art. on Arab hist., literature, philology, archaeology, art; doc.; bk. rev.; biblio. of bk. and art.; news of Arabic research; 5 year index; in French or occasionally English. f 26

5. ARCHIEF [Archives]. Vroegere en Latere Mededelingen, voornamelijk in Betrekking tot Zeeland [Announcements about earlier and later times, mainly in relation to Zeeland]. A. Zeeuwsch Genootschap der Wetenschappen [Zeeland Soc. of Sciences], Middelburg. nfs

ARCHIEF TEVENS ORGAAN VAN DE OUDHEIDKUNDIGE VERENIGING "DE GRAAFSCHAP" EN VAN DE MEESTER HENDRIK WILLEM HEUVEL STICHTING see OUDHEIDKUNDIGE VERENIGING "DE GRAAFSCHAP" EN VAN DE MEESTER HENDRIK WILLEM HEUVEL STICHTING

6. ARCHIEF VOOR DE GESCHIEDENIS VAN DE KATHOLIEKE KERK IN NEDERLAND [Archives of the history of the Catholic Church in the Netherlands]. 3 x y. 1959 (1959: vol. 1). Uitgeverij Het Spectrum N.V., Postbus 2073, Utrecht; Lamonièrestraat 153, Antwerpen. Ed: J.G. Louter (secretary), Theologicum, Warmond. Art. on all aspects of the hist. of the Roman Catholic Church in the Netherlands; doc. Supersedes Archief voor de Geschiedenis van het Aartsbisdom Utrecht [Archives of the history of the archbishopric of Utrecht] and Haarlemsche Bijdragen. Bouwstoffen voor de Geschiedenis van het Bisdom Haarlem [Haarlem contributions. Materials for the history of the bishopric of Haarlem].
f 15 / bfr 115

ARCHIEF VOOR DE GESCHIEDENIS VAN HET AARTSBISDOM UTRECHT see ARCHIEF VOOR DE GESCHIEDENIS VAN DE KATHOLIEKE KERK IN NEDERLAND

7. IT BEAKEN [The beacon]. B-M. Van Gorcum en comp N.V., Assen, for Fryske Akademy [Frisian Acad.], Coulonhûs Doelestrj. 8, Ljoûwert (Leeuwarden). f 4.50

8. BENEDICTIJNS TIJDSCHRIFT VOOR GEESTELIJK LEVEN EN GESCHIEDENIS [Benedictine review of spiritual life and history]. 5 x y. 1939 (1958: vol. 19). Sint Adelberts Abdij, Egmond Binnen. Art. on religion and religious hist., with emphasis on the Benedictine Order and Benedictine Abbey of Egmond; bk. rev. f 3

BERICHTEN. For titles beginning with "Berichten," followed by the name of the publishing or sponsoring institution or society, see the respective institution or society.

9. BIBLIOTHECA ORIENTALIS. International Reviewing and Bibliographical Bimonthly for Near Eastern and Mediterranean Studies. B-M. 1943 (1959: vol. 16). Nederlands Instituut voor het Nabije Ooosten [Netherlands' Inst. for the Near and Middle East], Noordeindsplein 4a, Leiden. Ed: A.A. Kampman. Art. on all fields of the study of the Near and Middle East from antiquity on, including archaeology, hist., hist. of art, philology, and Oriental and classical law; extensive bk. rev. section; reports on excavations and exhibitions; professional news ; illus., maps; in English, French or German; A. author index. f 45 / $ 12.50

BIJDRAGEN EN MEDEDELINGEN. For titles beginning with "Bijdragen en Mededelingen," followed by the name of the publishing or sponsoring institution or society, see the respective institution or society.

10. BIJDRAGEN EN MEDEDELINGEN GELRE [Gelder contributions and communications]. A. Vereeniging tot Beoefening van Geldersche Geschiedenis, Oudheidkunde en Recht [Soc. for the Study of Gelder Hist., Archaeology and Law], S. Gouda Quint, Bakkerstraat 17, Arnhem. Art. on the hist. of the province of Gelderland. f 15

11. BIJDRAGEN TOT DE GESCHIEDENIS DER GENEESKUNDE [Contributions to the history of medicine]. Irr. 1921 (mri 1952-54 [1955]: vol. 32-34). Erven F. Boon N.V., Haarlem. Reprints of art. on the hist. of medicine previously pub. in the Tijdschrift voor Geneeskunde [Journal of medicine]. pv

BIJDRAGEN TOT DE GESCHIEDENIS, INZONDERHEID VAN HET OUI HERTOGDOM BRABANT see section on Belgium

BIJDRAGEN TOT DE PRIJZENGESCHIEDENIS see CAHIERS D'HISTOIRE DES PRIX in the section on Belgium

12. BIJDRAGEN VOOR DE GESCHIEDENIS DER NEDERLANDEN [Contributions to the history of the Netherlands]. Q. 1946 (1960: vol. 15). Martinus Nijhoff, P.O.B. 269, 's-Gravenhage, and De Sikkel, Antwerpen. Ed: W. Jappe Alberts, Kromme Nieuwe Gracht 20, Utrecht (for the Netherlands); H. van Werveke, Nieuwstraat 12, Sint Denÿs-Westrem (for Belgium). Art. by Belgian, Dutch and South African historians on the hist. of the Netherlands, Belgium and South Africa; rev. of bk. and art. f 19 / $ 5.05

13. BIJDRAGEN VOOR DE GESCHIEDENIS VAN DE PROVINCIE DER MINDERBROEDERS IN DE NEDERLANDEN [Contributions to the history of the province of the Minorites in the Netherlands]. Irr. 1947 (1959: no. 29-30).

N.V. Grafische Kunstinrichting J. van Poll Suykerbuyk, Roosendaal. Ed. board: P. Cunibertus Sloots, Leunseweg 2, Venray; P. Bertilo de Boer, P. Albertus Fick. Art. on the religious hist. of the Netherlands, with emphasis on the Roman Catholic Church and the Franciscan Order in particular; doc.; bk. rev. and biblio. notes; illus.; French sum. p (1) f 4

14. HET BOEK [The book]. Q. 1912 (1958: 3rd series, vol. 33). Martinus Nijhoff N.V., P.O.B. 269, 's-Gravenhage. Ed. board: L. Brummel, H. de la Fontaine Verwey, F. Kossmann, M.E. Kronenberg, G.W. Ovink. Art. on biblio. (mainly 15th and 16th cent., but also modern), library hist., paleography, bk. collecting, typography; bk. rev.; survey of periodicals on biblio. and related subjects; mainly in Dutch, but also in English and French; English sum. of Dutch art. f 25

15. BOSSCHE BIJDRAGEN ['s-Hertogenbosch contributions]. Bouwstoffen voor de Geschiedenis van het Bisdom 's-Hertogenbosch [Materials for the history of the Diocese of 's-Hertogenbosch]. Irr. (no more than 3 x y). Drukkerij Instituut voor Doofstommen, St. Michielsgestel. Indices. f 10

16. BRABANTIA. M. Zuid-Nederlandsche Drukkerij N.V., St. Jorisstraat 37, 's-Hertogenbosch, for Provinciaal Genootschap van Kunsten en Wetenschappen in Noord-Brabant [Provincial Soc. of Arts and Sciences in North Brabant], and Stichting Brabantia Nostra [Brabantia Nostra Foundation], Bethaniestraat 4, 's-Hertogenbosch. f 7.50 / bfr 110

17. BRABANTS HEEM [Brabantine home]. Tweemaandelijks Tijdschrift voor Brabantse Heem- en Oudheidkunde [Bimonthly journal for Brabantine local studies and archaeology]. B-M. Stichting "Brabants Heem," ["Brabants Heem" Foundation], c/o P. Dorenbosch (secretary), Mgr. Wilmerstraat 10, Boxtel. f 3.50 / f 4

18. DE BRABANTSE LEEUW [The Brabantine lion]. M. 1952 (1958: vol. 7). N.V. Drukkerij van Gebr. Juten, Engelsestraat 19, Bergen op Zoom, for Sectie voor Geslacht-, Naam- en Wapenkunde van het Provinciaal Genootschap van Kunsten en Wetenschappen in Noord-Brabant [Section for Genealogy, Heraldry and Blazonry of the Provincial Soc. of Arts and Sciences in North Brabant]. A. index of names. f 4.75 / f 5

19. DE BRONK [Term of Limburg dialect for a sacramental procession -- ed.]. Limburgs Maandblad [Limburg monthly]. M. Pub. address: Lenculenstraat 33, Maastricht. f 7.50

BULLETIN VAN DE NEDERLANDSE OUDHEIDKUNDIGE BOND see KONINKLIJKE NEDERLANDSE OUDHEIDKUNDIGE BOND. NIEUWS-BULLETIN

20. CARMEL. Tijdschrift voor Geestelijk Leven [Journal of spiritual life]. Q. H. Gianotten, Bredaseweg 57, Tilburg. f 7.50 / bfr 100

21. CENTRAAL BUREAU VOOR GENEALOGIE, JAARBOEK VAN HET... [Yearbook of the Central Bureau for Genealogy]. A. 1947 (1957: vol. 11). Centraal Bureau voor Genealogie, Nassaulaan 18, 's-Gravenhage. Ed: F. Josselin de Jong. A. reports of the bureau; genealogies; A. alphabetical index of names. (memb.) f 5

22. CENTRAL ASIATIC JOURNAL. International Periodical for the Languages, Literature, History and Archaeology of Central Asia. Q. Mouton en Co., Kerklaan 74, Rijswijk, 's-Gravenhage. f 34

23. HET CHRISTELIJK OOSTEN EN HERENIGING [The Christian East and reunification]. Q. 1948 (1958/59: vol. 11). Instituut voor Byzantijnse Studies, Oecumenisch Instituut. Ed: E. van Montfort, P.N. Royackers, Sophiaweg 42, Nijmegen. Art. on the dogma, liturgy, nature and hist. of the Eastern Orthodox Church; extensive news section on the Orthodox Church, and related matters, classified by country; bk. rev. f 8.50

CITEAUX IN DE NEDERLANDEN see section on Belgium

24. COMMISSIE VOOR 'S RIJKS GESCHIEDKUNDIGE PUBLICATIËNS, JAARVERSLAG VAN DE... [Annual report of the Commission of the State Historical Publications]. B or T (2 or 3 A. reports together). Staatsdrukkerij en Uitgeversbedrijf, 's-Gravenhage, for Commissie voor 's Rijks Geschiedkundige Publicatiëns. pni

COMMISSION INTERNATIONALE DE NUMISMATIQUE COMPTE-RENDU see section on International Periodicals

25. COMMISSION POUR L'HISTOIRE DES EGLISES WALLONES, BULLETIN DE LA... [Bulletin of the Commission for the History of the Walloon Churches]. Irr. (once every 3-5 years). Bibliothèque Wallone, Pietorskerhof 40, Leiden. pni

COMPARATIVE STUDIES IN SOCIETY AND HISTORY see section on the United States of America

26. DÖRP EN STAD [Village and town]. M. Drukkerij-Uitgeversbedrijf J.D. van der Veen N.V., Winschoten, for Grunneger Genootschap [Groningen Soc.]. In Groningen (Saxon) dialect. f 5 (memb. f 3)

27. DRENTHE. Provinciaal Drents Maandblad [Monthly of the Province of Drenthe]. M. Van Gorcum en Co., Brink 10-12, Assen, for Drents Genootschap [Drenthe Soc.]. Occasionally in Saxon dialect. f 4.50

28. DE DRIE KWARTIEREN [The three quarters]. Tijdschrift voor Gelderland [Journal of Gelderland]. 10 x y. Drukkerij en Uitgeverij Linders, Janslangstraat 24, Arnhem, for the foundation "De Gelderse Bloem" [The flower of Gelderland]. f 7.50

29. DRIEMAANDELIJKSE BLADEN [Quarterly magazine]. Tijdschrift voor taal en volksleven in het Oosten van Nederland [Journal of the language and folkways in the eastern Netherlands]. Q. J.K. Hertz en Co., De Millystraat 5, Zuidlaren, for Nedersaksisch Instituut der Rijksuniversiteit te Groningen [Lower Saxon Inst. of the State Univ. in Groningen]. f 5.50

30. ECONOMISCH-HISTORISCH JAARBOEK [Economic-historical yearbook]. Bijdragen tot de economische Geschiedenis van Nederland [Contributions to the economic history of the Netherlands]. Irr. 1916 (1958: vol. 27). Martinus Nijhoff, P.O.B. 269, 's-Gravenhage, for Vereniging Het Nederlandsch economisch-historisch Archief [Archives of the Dutch Economic-Hist. Soc.], 's-Gravenhage. Ed. board: P.J. van Winter, J.G. van Dillen, W.S. Unger, I.J. Brugmans. Art. on the economic hist. of the Netherlands; A. reports of the soc. f 16

31. FORUM DER LETTEREN [Literary forum]. Q. 1960 (1960: no. 1). A.W. Sijthoff's Uitgeversmaatschappij N.V., Doezastraat 1, Leiden. "Articles on general subjects and theoretical problems in the fields of philology, litera-

ture and history"; bk. rev. Succeeds Museum. Tijdschrift voor Filologie en Geschiedenis, which was discontinued in 1959. f 15

32. FRANCISCAANS LEVEN [Franciscan life]. Tweemaandelijks Tijdschrift voor Franciscaanse Ascetiek, Geschiedenis en Kunst [Bimonthly for Franciscan asceticism, history and art]. B-M. 1917 (1959: vol. 42). B. van Eerd en Zn., Lange Nieuwstraat 237, Tilburg, for Provincialaat der P.P. Capucijnen, 's-Hertogenbosch. Ed:P. Optatus, O.F.M. Cap., Capucijnenklooster, Udenhout. Art. on all aspects of Franciscan life, with emphasis on the Netherlands; numerous short hist. biographies of saints and priests; notes; bk. rev. f 15 / bfr 70

FRANCISCANA see section on Belgium

33. FREE UNIVERSITY QUARTERLY. A Quarterly for Christian Knowledge and Life. Q. J.H. Kok N.V., Oudestraat 5, Kampen. f 10 / $2.75

34. FRIES GENOOTSCHAP VAN GESCHIED-, OUDHEID- EN TAALKUNDE EN FRIES MUSEUM, VERSLAGEN VAN HET... [Reports of the Frisian Society for History, Archaeology and Philology and of the Frisian Museum]. A. (1957: vol. 129). Fries Genootschap van Geschied, Oudheid- en Taalkunde, Koningsstraat 1, Leeuwarden. f 1

35. GAZETTE. International Journal of the Science of the Press. Internationale Zeitschrift für Zeitungswissenschaft. Revue internationale de Science de la Presse. Q. H.E. Stenfert Kroese N.V., Leiden, for Inst. of Journalism, Univ. of Amsterdam, Keizersgracht 604, Amsterdam. In English and, occasionally, French or German; English sum. of art. in French and German. .f 14.50 / f 15.50

36. GENOOTSCHAP AMSTELODAMUM, JAARBOEK VAN HET... [Yearbook of the Amstelodamum Society]. A. J.H. de Bussy, Rokin 62, Amsterdam C. General index vol: 1-33. nfs

37. GENOOTSCHAP VOOR NAPOLEONTISCHE STUDIEN, PUBLICATIES VAN HET... [Publications of the Society for Napoleonic Studies]. Irr. (1958: no. 11). A. Sijthoff N.V., 's-Gravenhage, for Genootschap voor Napoleontische Studien, 's-Gravenhage. Ed: K.J. Frederiks, Nassaulaan 11, 's-Gravenhage. Art. on various aspects of Napoleonic hist.; biblio. of bk. on Napoleon and his times. p (1) f 5

38. GENS NOSTRA. Ons Geslacht [Our ancestry]. M. 1946 (1958: vol. 13). Nederlandse Genealogische Vereniging [Dutch Genealogical Soc.], c/o J. Hagoort, Kloosterstraat 11, Naarden. Ed: W.D.H. Rosier, Postbus 976, Amsterdam. Art. and notes on Dutch genealogy, heraldry and topography; short bk. rev.; survey of art. in related Dutch and foreign periodicals; question column; A. alphabetical index. (memb.) f 10

39. GESCHIED- EN OUDHEIDKUNDIGE KRING VAN STAD EN LAND VAN BREDA "DE ORANJEBOOM," JAARBOEK VAN DE...[Yearbook of the Historical and Archaeological Circle of the Town and Country of Breda "The Orange Tree"]. A. Geschied- en Oudheidkundige Kring van Stad en Land van Breda "De Oranjeboom," c/o Gemeentearchief, Breda. (memb.) f 5

40. DE GEUZENPENNING [The beggars' medal]. Munt- en Penningkundig Nieuws [Numismatic news]. Q. 1951 (1959: vol. 9). Koninklijke Nederlandse Genootschap voor Munt- en Penningkunde [Royal Dutch Numismatic Soc.] and

Vereniging voor Penningkunst [Soc. for Numismatics], Keizersgracht 448, Amsterdam C. Ed. board: J.P. Guépin, H.H. Zwager, J. Vinkenborg, J. Schulman (ed. secretary). Art. and notes on numismatics; bk. rev.; news of local numismatic groups; index 1951-55; illus. f 3

41. 'S-GRAVENHAGE [The Hague]. Maandblad der Gemeente 's-Gravenhage [Monthly of the municipality of The Hague]. M. Afdeling Publiciteit der Gemeentesecretarie [Publicity Section of the Town Clerk's Office], Burgemeester-de Monchyplein 12, 's-Gravenhage. f 6

42. GRONINGEN. Cultureel Maandblad [Cultural monthly]. 10 x y. Dijkstra Drukkerij N.V., for Stichting Groningse Culturele Gemeenschap [Groningen Cultural Community Foundation], Groningen. Culture, folklore, hist. and current events of the province of Groningen. (memb.) f 12.50

43. GRONINGSE VOLKSALMANAK [Groningen people's almanac]. Jaarboekje voor Geschiedenis, Taal- en Oudheidkunde der Provincie Groningen [Yearbook for history, philology and archaeology of the Province of Groningen]. A. N.V. Erven B. van der Kamp, St. Jansstraat 1-3, Groningen. Indices for 10 vol. f 8

44. GROTIANA. Irr. 1928 (mri 1947: vol. 10). Drukkerij Humanitas, Laan van Meerdervoort 88, 's-Gravenhage, for Vereniging voor de Uitgave van Grotius [Soc. for the Pub. of Grotius]. Reports on proceedings of the soc.; art. on Grotius and his times; biblio. of Grotius' works and of works on Grotius; in Dutch, English, French and German. pv

HAARLEMSCHE BIJDRAGEN see ARCHIEF VOOR DE GESCHIEDENIS VAN DE KATHOLIEKE KERK IN NEDERLAND

45. HAERLEM. JAARBOEK [Haerlem. Yearbook]. A. De Erven F. Bohn N.V., Frankestraat 42, Haarlem, for Vereniging Haerlem [Soc. of Old Haarlem]. f 3.50 (memb. f 1.90)

46. DIE HAGHE [The Hague]. A. Drukkerij Trio, Nobelstraat 27, 's-Gravenhage, for Vereniging "Die Haghe" ["The Hague" Soc.]. Alphabetical index. (memb.) f 9

47. HEEMSCHUT [Preservation of local cultural and natural beauty]. B-M. 1924 (1959: vol. 36). N.V. Van Munster's Uitgeverij, Haarlemmerweg B 378, Amsterdam, for Bond Heemschut. Ed: Ton Koon, Geurt Brinkgreve, Singel 512, Amsterdam. Art. and notes on the preservation of monuments and hist. sites. (memb.) f 10

48. HERMENEUS. Maandblad voor de antieke cultuur [Monthly for ancient culture]. 10 x y. N.V. Uitgeversmij. W.E.J. Tjeenk Willink, Melkmarkt 2, Zwolle, for Nederlands Klassiek Verbond [Dutch Classical Soc.]. f 4.50

49. HISTORIA AGRICULTURAE. A. 1953 (1957 [1958]: vol. 4). J.B. Wolters N.V., Groningen, for Nederlands Agronomisch-Historisch Instituut [Dutch Inst. of Agricultural Hist.], Oude Boteringestraat 44, Groningen. Art. on agricultural hist.; report of the inst.; biblio. of bk. and art. on agricultural hist. pv (vol. 4 f 16.50)

50. HISTORISCH GENOOTSCHAP, BIJDRAGEN EN MEDEDELINGEN VAN HET... [Contributions and communications of the Historical Society]. A. 1895

(1958: vol. 72). J.B. Wolters, Groningen, for Historisch Genootschap, Rijksuniversiteit, Utrecht. Doc.; author index for vol. 1-60 pub. in vol. 61, and for vol. 61-72 pub. in vol. 72; notes on the soc. and list of the soc. memb. Pub. jointly with Verslag van de Algemene Vergadering van het Historisch Genootschap. memb. free

51. HISTORISCH GENOOTSCHAP, VERSLAG VAN DE ALGEMENE VERGADERING VAN HET... [Report of the general meeting of the Historical Society]. A. 1895 (1958: vol. 72). J.B. Wolters, Groningen, for Historisch Genootschap, Rijksuniversiteit, Utrecht. Report of the A. meeting of the soc.; lectures on Dutch hist., delivered at the meeting; author index for the years 1895-1957 pub. in vol. 72. Pub. jointly with Bijdragen en Mededelingen van het Historisch Genootschap. memb. free

52. HISTORISCHE KRING "HET LAND VAN HERLE," BULLETIN VAN DE... [Bulletin of the Historical Circle "The Country of Herle"]. B-M. Historische kring "Het Land van Herle," Gemeentearchief, Raadhuis, Heerlen. f 2

53. HISTORY AND THEORY. Studies in the Philosophy of History. Irr. 1960 (1960: no. 1). Mouton en Co., Kerklaan 74, Rijswijk, 's-Gravenhage. Ed: G.N. Nadel, P.O.B. 99, Cambridge 38, Mass., U.S.A. Art. on the philosophy and methodology of hist., and on historiography and related disciplines; bk. rev.; biblio.; notes. $ 5 per vol.

54. INDO-IRANIAN JOURNAL. Q. 1957 (1959: vol. 3). Mouton en Co., N.V. Uitgeverij, Herderstraat 5, 's-Gravenhage. Ed: F.B.J. Kuiper (ed. secretary), Haagweg 43, Leiden; J.W. de Jong. Art. mainly on philology and also on religion and hist.; biblio.; bk. rev.; in English and, occasionally, French or German. f 30 / f 30

55. INDONESIË [Indonesia]. Tweemaandelijks Tijdschrift gewijd aan Indonesië en verwant cultuurgebied [Bi-monthly review dedicated to Indonesia and related cultural areas]. B-M. N.V. Uitgeverij W. van Hoeve, Barentszstraat 20, 's-Gravenhage. Hist., ethnology, politics, economics, literature and art of the Indonesian archipelago; in Dutch or English. f 15.50 / f 16.50

56. INSTITUUT STAD EN LANDSCHAP VAN ZUID-HOLLAND. JAARVERSLAG [Institute for Urban and Rural South Holland. Annual report]. A. Instituut Stad en Landschap van Zuid-Holland, Delfsestraat 15 B, Rotterdam. pni

57. INTERNATIONAAL INSTITUUT VOOR SOCIALE GESCHIEDENIS. JAARVERSLAG [International Institute of Social History. Annual report]. A. Internationaal Instituut voor Sociale Geschiedenis, Keizersgracht 264, Amsterdam. Announcements concerning the inst. and its activities. pni

58. INTERNATIONAL JOURNAL OF SLAVIC LINGUISTICS AND POETICS. Irr. Mouton en Co. N.V., Kerklaan 74, Rijsvijk (Z.H.), 's-Gravenhage. In English, French, German or Slavic languages. f 15 / $ 4

59. INTERNATIONAL REVIEW OF SOCIAL HISTORY. 3 x y. 1956 (1958: vol. 3). N.V. Van Gorcum, Assen, for Internationaal Instituut voor Sociale Geschiedenis [International Inst. of Social Hist.], Keizersgracht 264, Amsterdam. Ed: F. Kool (secretary). Art. on social hist., with emphasis on modern social movements; extensive annotated and critical biblio. of bk. on social hist. and related subjects; in English, French or German; A. indices of names and of subjects and countries. f 23 / $ 6

60. INTERNATIONALE SPECTATOR [International spectator]. Tijdschrift voor Internationale Politiek [Journal of international politics]. B-M. Het Nederlandsch Genootschap voor Internationale Zaken [The Dutch Soc. for International Affairs], 's-Gravenhage. In Dutch and occasionally English, French or German; A. alphabetical index. f 15 / f 17.50

JAARBERICHT. For titles beginning with "Jaarbericht," followed by the name of the publishing or sponsoring institution or society, see the respective institution or society.

JAARBOEK. For titles beginning with "Jaarboek," followed by the name of the publishing or sponsoring institution or society, see the respective institution or society.

61. JAARBOEK VOOR MUNT- EN PENNINGKUNDE [Yearbook for numismatics]. A. 1914 (1957: vol. 44). Koninklijk Nederlands Genootschap voor Munt- en Penningkunde [Royal Dutch Soc. for Numismatics], Amsterdam, and Zeestraat 71 b, 's-Gravenhage. Ed. board: H. Enno van Gelder, A. Gorter, O.N. Keuzenkamp-Roovers, A.N. Zadoks-Josephus Jitta, N.E.H.J.J. Zon. Art. and notes on numismatics; bk. rev.; illus., mainly of coins; reports on the discoveries of coins; in Dutch and occasionally English, French or German; sum. in English or French; table of contents for the years 1914-42 pub. separately. f 15

62. JAARBOEKJE VAN "OUD-UTRECHT" [Yearbook of "Old Utrecht"]. A. Vereniging tot Beoefening en tot Verspreiding van de Kennis der Geschiedenis van Stad en Provincie Utrecht [Soc. for the Study and the Dissemination of Knowledge of the Hist. of the Town and Province of Utrecht], Vereniging Utrecht, Nieuwe Gracht 133, Utrecht. nfs

63. JAARBOEKJE VOOR GESCHIEDENIS EN OUDHEIDKUNDE VAN LEIDEN EN OMSTREKEN [Yearbook for the history and archaeology of Leiden and vicinity]. A. A.W. Sijthoff, Doezastraat 1, Leiden, for Vereniging "Oud Leiden" ["Old Leiden" Soc.]. General index for the years 1904-58 pub. in 1958. f 5.75

JAARVERSLAG, JAARVERSLAGEN. For titles beginning with "Jaarverslag" or "Jaarverslagen," followed by the name of the publishing or sponsoring institution or society, see the respective institution or society.

64. JOURNAL OF ECONOMIC AND SOCIAL HISTORY OF THE ORIENT. 3 x y (Irr.). 1957 (1959: vol. 2). E.J. Brill, Leiden. Ed: Claude Cahen (secretary), 31 av. de la Forêt Noire, Strasbourg, France. Art. on the economic and social hist. of the Orient; bk. rev. in English, French or German. f 30 / DM 33

65. KAMPER ALMANAK [Kampen almanac]. A. Frans Walkate Archief, Nutsspaarbank, Kampen. Includes as an appendix Bijdragen tot de Geschiedenis van Kampen [Contributions to the hist. of Kampen]. f 4

DE KATHOLIEK see STUDIA CATHOLICA

66. KEESINGS HISTORISCH ARCHIEF [Keesing's historical archives]. W. N.V. Internationale Uitgeverij en Handelmaatschappij "Systemen Keesing," Ruysdaelstraat 71-75, Amsterdam, and Algemene Uitgeverij "Systemen Keesing," Haantjeslei 38, Antwerpen. Sum. of the important news of the week; art. on current events. f 30

67. KLEIO. 3 x y. 1959 (1960: no. 3). Van Goor en Zonen, 's-Gravenhage, for Vereniging van Geschiedenis-leraren in Nederland [Soc. of Hist. Teachers in the Netherlands]. Ed: A.F. Manning, S.B.J. Zilverberg, R. Reinsma, Mispelstraat 18, 's-Gravenhage. Art. on hist. and on methods of teaching hist.; bk. rev.; professional news. (memb.) f 10

68. KONINKLIJK NEDERLANDSCH AARDRIJKSKUNDIG GENOOTSCHAP TE AMSTERDAM, TIJDSCHRIFT VAN HET... [Journal of the Royal Dutch Geographical Society in Amsterdem]. Q. E.J. Brill N.V., Leiden, for Koninklijk Nederlandsch Aardrijkskundig Genootschap te Amsterdam, Amsterdam. Sum. in English; general indices at regular intervals. f 26.25

69. KONINKLIJK OUDHEIDKUNDIG GENOOTSCHAP TE AMSTERDAM, JAARVERSLAG VAN HET... [Annual report of the Royal Antiquarian Society at Amsterdam]. B (2 A. reports together). Koninklijik Oudheidkundig Genootschap, c/o Rijksmuseum, Hobbemastraat 21, Amsterdam. A. reports of the soc. and some hist. contributions. for memb. only

70. KONINKLIJKE NEDERLANDSE AKADEMIE VAN WETENSCHAPPEN, AFDELING LETTERKUNDE, MEDEDELINGEN DER... [Communications of the Royal Dutch Academy of Sciences, Section of Letters]. Irr. (c. 15 x y). 1858 (1958: new series, vol. 21). N.V. Noordhollandse Uitgeversmaatschappij, Voorburgwal 68-70, for Afdeling Letterkunde, Koninklijke Nederlandse Akademie von Wetenschappen. Short monographs on linguistics, hist., literature, hist. of art, sociology, and related subjects; each no. contains 1 monograph; in Dutch, English, French or German. pv

71. KONINKLIJKE NEDERLANDSE AKADEMIE VAN WETENSCHAPPEN, AFDELING LETTERKUNDE, VERHANDELINGEN DER... [Transactions of the Royal Dutch Academy of Sciences, Section of Letters]. Irr. (2 or 3 x y). 1858 (1958: new series, vol. 65). N.V. Noordhollandse Uitgeversmij., Voorburgwal 68-70, Amsterdam C, for Afdeling Letterkunde, Koninklijke Nederlandse Akademie van Wetenschappen. Art. on various subjects within the domain of the Section of Letters; in Dutch, English, French or German. pv

72. KONINKLIJKE NEDERLANDSE OUDHEIDKUNDIGE BOND. BULLETIN [Royal Dutch Archaeological Society. Bulletin]. 5 x y. 1899 (mri 1954: 6th series, vol. 12). Koninklijke Nederlandse Oudheidkundige Bond. Ed: N.E.H.J.J. Zon (secretary), Rijswijkseweg 141, 's-Gravenhage. Art. on the archaeology and hist. of art of the Netherlands, with emphasis on the medieval period; sum. in English. Includes as supplement Koninklijke Nederlandse Oudheidkundige Bond. Nieuws-Bulletin [News bulletin of the Royal Dutch Archaeological Association]. f 25 (individuals f 15)

LIMBURGS GESCHIED- EN OUDHEIDKUNDIG GENOOTSCHAP, JAARBOEK VAN... see SOCIETE HISTORIQUE ET ARCHEOLOGIQUE DANS LE LIMBOURG, PUBLICATIONS DE LA...

73. DE LIMBURGSE LEEUW [The Limburg lion]. Orgaan tot bevordering van de studie der Genealogie en Heraldiek in Limburg [Organ for the promotion of the study of genealogy and heraldry in Limburg]. B-M. Ed: Alb. Corten (secretary), Valkenburgerweg 165, Heerlen. A. index of names. f 7.50

74. MAANDBLAD VAN "OUD-UTRECHT" [Monthly of "Old Utrecht"]. M. Vereniging tot beoefening en tot verspreiding van de kennis der geschiedenis van de stad en de provincie Utrecht [Soc. for the Study and for Dissemination of Know-

ledge of the Hist. of the City and the Province of Utrecht], c/o N.V. ten Bokkel Huinink, Nieuwe Gracht 113, Utrecht. A. index. f 3.50

75. DE MAASGOUW [The Maas district]. Tijdschrift voor Limburgse Geschiedenis en Oudheidkunde [Journal of history and archaeology of Limburg]. B-M. Limburgs Geschied- en Oudheidkundig Genootschap [Hist. and Archaeological Soc. of Limburg], Bonnefanten 4, Maastricht. Survey of bk. and periodicals concerning the Limburg district. (memb.) f 10

76. MAATSCHAPPIJ DER NEDERLANDSE LETTERKUNDE TE LEIDEN, JAARBOEK VAN DE... [Yearbook of the Society for Dutch Literature in Leiden]. B. E.J. Brill, Leiden. f 6.30

77. MARINEBLAD [Naval review]. 8 x y. Drukkerij en Uitgeverij v/h C. de Boer jr. N.V., Zeverijnstraat 4, Hilversum, for Vereniging van Marineofficieren [Soc. of Naval Officers]. f 15

78. DE MARS [The marsh]. Maandblad van en voor Overijssel [Monthly of and for Overijssel]. M. Drukkerij Smit N.V., Hengelo. Culture, folklore, hist. and current events of the province of Overijssel. f 7.10 / f 8

MEDEDELINGEN. For titles beginning with "Mededelingen," followed by the name of the publishing or sponsoring institution or society, see the respective institution or society.

MEDEDELINGENBLAD VAN DE SOCIAAL-HISTORISCHE STUDIEKRING see SOCIAAL-HISTORISCHE STUDIEKRING

79. MENS EN MAATSCHAPPIJ [Man and society]. B-M. N.V. Drukkerij 't Koggeschip, Nieuwe Achtergracht 102-104, Amsterdam C, for Nederlands Genootschap voor Anthropologie [Dutch Soc. of Anthropology], Nederlandse Sociologische Vereniging [Dutch Sociological Soc.] and Instituut voor Sociaal Onderzoek van het Nederlandse Volk [Inst. for Social Research on the Dutch people]. f 15 / $ 4

80. MENS EN MELODIE [Man and melody]. M. Uitgeverij Het Spectrum N.V., Maliebaan 10 a, Utrecht. A. indices. f 14

81. HET MISSIEWERK [The missionary work]. Nederlands Tijdschrift voor Missiewetenschap [Dutch review of missionary science]. Q. 1919 (1959: vol. 38). Missiologisch Instituut der R.K. Universiteit te Nijmegen, Nijmegen. Ed: Alph. Mulders, Sterreschansweg 45, Nijmegen. Art. on the theory and principles of missions, missionary methods and the hist. of missions; bk. rev.; news; A. biblio. of the world's missiological literature. f 4 (memb. f 3)

LE MONDE DE L'ISLAM see DIE WELT DES ISLAMS

82. MUSEUM. Tijschrift voor Filologie en Geschiedenis. Revue critique de philologie et d'histoire. Journal of Philology and History. Q. 1894 (1959: vol. 64). A.W. Sijthoff's Uitgeversmaatschappij N.V., Doezastraat 1, Leiden. Ed. board: S. Dresden, J.C. Kamerbeek, Th. J.G. Locher, C.F.P. Stutterheim, E.M. Uhlenbeck. Extensive section of bk. rev. comprising literature of general philological or hist. interest; in Dutch, English, French or German; listing of contents of important relevant periodicals. Superseded in 1960 by Forum der Letteren. f 18.50

83. MUSEUM BOYMANS. BULLETIN. Irr. Museum Boymans, Mathenesserlaan 18, Rotterdam. pni

84. NAAMKUNDE COMMISSIE VAN DE KONINKLIJKE NEDERLANDSE AKADEMIE VAN WETENSCHAPPEN TE AMSTERDAM, BIJDRAGEN EN MEDEDELINGEN DER... [Contributions and communications of the Onomastic Committee of the Royal Dutch Academy of Sciences in Amsterdam]. Irr. 1949 (1958: vol. 13). N.V. Noord-Hollandsche Uitgeversmij, N.Z. Voorburgmal 68-70, Amsterdam C, for Naamkunde Commissie, Koninklijke Nederlandse Akademie van Wetenschappen te Amsterdam. Papers on onomastic subjects read before the committee. pv

85. DE NAVORSCHER [The investigator]. Nederlands Archief voor Genealogie en Heraldiek, Heemkunde en Geschiedenis [Dutch archives of genealogy and heraldry, local studies and history]. B-M. 1851 (1959: vol. 98). Van Gorcum en Co. N.V., Aanden Brink 10-12, Assen. Ed: J.M. Reinboud. Art. mainly on genealogy, but also on heraldry, local studies and hist.; bk. rev.; A. index of names. f 10

86. NEDERLANDS ARCHIEF VOOR KERKGESCHIEDENIS [Dutch archives of church history]. Irr. 1884 (1957/58: new series, vol. 42). Martinus Nijhoff N.V., P.O.B. 269, 's-Gravenhage. Ed. board: J. Lindeboom, M. van Rhijn, J.N. Bakhuizen van den Brink, C.C. de Bruin, W.F. Dankbaar. Art. on ecclesiastical hist., with emphasis on the Netherlands and on the early modern period, and biographical art.; bk. rev. on general ecclesiastical hist.; report of the activities of the Kerkhistorisch Gezelschap [Church Hist. Soc.]. f 15.75

87. NEDERLANDS ARCHIEVENBLAD [Dutch archival journal]. Q. 1892 (1957/58: vol. 62). N.V. Erven B. van der Kamp, St. Jansstraat 1-3, Groningen, for Vereniging van Archivarissen in Nederland [Archivists Assoc. of the Netherlands]. Ed: W.J. Formsma. Art. on archival theory, practice and organization and on the auxiliary sciences of hist. f 10.50

NEDERLANDS HISTORISCH INSTITUUT TE ROME, MEDEDELINGEN VAN HET... see section on Italy

88. NEDERLANDS KUNSTHISTORISCH JAARBOEK [Dutch yearbook of art history]. A. 1947 (1959: vol. 10). Uitgeversmaatschappij C.A.J. van Dishoeck, Nw. 's-Gravel.weg 19, Bussum, for Stichting Nederlands Kunsthistorisch Jaarboek [Dutch Art Hist. Yearbook Foundation], 's-Gravenhage. Art. on general and Dutch art hist.; in Dutch, English, French or German; English sum. of non-English art.; illus.; subject index. f 25

89. NEDERLANDS PATRICIAAT [The Netherlands' patriciate]. A. 1910 (1959: vol. 45). Centraal Bureau voor Genealogie [Central Office of Genealogy], Nassaulaan 18, 's-Gravenhage. Ed: F. de Josselin de Jong. Genealogies; index of family names in vol. 1-45 pub. in 1959. f 16.50

90. DE NEDERLANDSCHE LEEUW [The Dutch lion]. M. 1883 (1959: vol. 76). Koninklijk Nederlandsch Genootschap van Geslacht- en Wapenkunde [Royal Dutch Soc. for Genealogy and Heraldry], 's-Gravenhage. Ed: W.W. van Valkenburg, "Nijenstede," Backershagenlaan 70, Wassenaar. Art. on genealogy and heraldry; announcements; queries; bk. rev.; lists of acquisitions of the library of the soc.; A. lexicographical index. f 20

91. NEERLANDS VOLKSLEVEN [Dutch folkways]. Q. 1950 (1959: vol. 9). Drukkerij-Uitgeverij "Neerlandia," Sluisgracht 5, Meppel, for Nederlands Volkskundig Genootschap [Dutch Soc. for Folklore]. Ed. board: K. ter Laan, W.D. Scheepers, H. Cats, R.C. Hekker, T.W.R. de Haan (secretary), Kerkstraat 64, Wassenaar. Art. on Dutch and Flemish folklore. f 4.50 / f 5.50

92. NEHALENNIA. Driemaandelijks Tijdschrift, gewijd aan de studie der Westerse Oudheid en de nawerking daarvan tot op heden [Quarterly devoted to the study of Western antiquity and its after-effects up to the present]. Q. 1956 (1959: vol. 4). Uitgeverij Thule, Emmastraat 58, Jilversum. Ed. board: L. Boer, F.C. Bursch, F. de Fremery, F.S. Sixma Baron van Heemstra, Henriette van Lennep, F. Wiersma-Verschaffelt. Art. on the cultural hist. of ancient Western Europe and its remnants in medieval and modern times, with emphasis on literature, customs, popular belief and folkways; illus. of archaeological finds. f 5.60

93. DE NIEUWE DRENTSCHE VOLKSALMANAK [The new Drenthe people's almanac]. A. Van Gorcum en comp. N.V., Brink 10-12, Assen, for Het Provinciaal Museum van Drenthe [The Provincial Museum of Drenthe], Het Drents Genootschap [The Drenthe Soc.], Vrienden van het Provinciaal Museum van Drenthe [Friends of the Provincial Museum of Drenthe], and De Drents Praehistorische Vereniging [The Drenthe Prehist. Soc.]. f 8.50

94. NIEUWE WESTINDISCHE GIDS [New West Indian guide]. Q. Martinus Nijhoff, P.O.B. 269, 's-Gravenhage. Hist., culture and economy of the Netherlands Antilles and Surinam. Supersedes West Indische Gids (pub. in Holland), Vox Guyanae (pub. in Surinam), and Christoffel (pub. in the Netherlands Antilles). f 12.50

NOVUM TESTAMENTUM see section on International Periodicals

95. NUMAGA. Tijdschrift gewijd aan heden en verleden van Nijmegen en omgeving [Journal dedicated to the present and past of Nijmegen and environs]. Q. Drukkerij Gebr. Janssen, Nijmegen, for Soc. "Numaga," Mariënburg 26, Nijmegen. (memb.) f 6.50

NUMEN see section on International Periodicals

96. ONS AMSTERDAM [Our Amsterdam]. M. Stadsdrukkerij, Amsterdam, for Gemeentelijke Commissie Heemkennis [Minicipal Commission for Local Studies], Willemsparkweg 125, Amsterdam. Local hist. of Amsterdam; bk. rev. f 3.50 / $4.60

ONS GEESTELIJK ERF see section on Belgium

97. ONS HEEM [Our home]. Tijdschrift ter Bevordering van Heemkundig Gericht onderwijs [Journal for the promotion of the teaching of local studies]. B-M. Committee for Local Studies of the "R.K.O.B." in the diocese of Roermond, Schouwberg 23, Maasniel. f 5

98. ORIENS. Milletlerasi sark tetkikleri cemiyeti mecmuasi. Journal of the International Society for Oriental Research. Journal de la Société Internationale d'Etudes Orientales. Zeitschrift der Internationalen Gesellschaft für Orientforschung. S-A (Irr.). E.J. Brill, Ouden Rijn 33a, Leiden, for International Soc. for Oriental Research. Art. on Oriental studies, including such subjects as hist., culture, language, literature and art; bk. rev.; biblio.; in English, French and German; illus.; index. f 20

99. OUD-HOLLAND [Ancient Holland]. Driemaandelijks Tijdschrift voor Nederlandse Kunstgeschiedenis [Quarterly for Dutch art history]. Q. J.H. de Bussy, Rokin 62, Amsterdam C. Sum. in English; vol. table of contents in Dutch and English; alphabetical index of names; index for the first 60 vol. pub. in 1946. f 50 / $ 14

100. OUDHEIDKUNDIG GENOOTSCHAP "NIFTARLAKE," JAARBOEKJE VAN HET... [Yearbook of the Archaeological "Niftarlake" Society]. A. Drukkerij H.J. Smits, Oudegracht 231, Utrecht, for Oudheidkundig Genootschap "Niftarlake." f 5

101. OUDHEIDKUNDIGE KRING "DE GHULDEN ROOS" ROOSENDAAL, JAARBOEK VAN DE... [Yearbook of "The Golden Rose" Archaeological Circle at Rosendaal]. A. N.V. Grafische Kunstinrichting J. van Poll Suykerbuyk, Roosendaal, for Oudheidkundige Kring "De Ghulden Roos" Roosendaal. f 3.50

102. OUDHEIDKUNDIGE KRING "DIE GOUDE." BIJDRAGEN ["Die Goude" Antiquarian Circle. Contributions]. Irr. Oudheidkundige Kring "Die Goude," Krugerlaan 153, Gouda. Local hist. of Gouda. nfs

OUDHEIDKUNDIGE MEDEDELINGEN UIT HET RIJKSMUSEUM VAN OUDHEDEN TE LEIDEN see RIJKSMUSEUM VAN OUDHEDEN TE LEIDEN

103. OUDHEIDKUNDIGE VERENIGING "DE GRAAFSCHAP" EN VAN DE MEESTER HENDRIK WILLEM HEUVELSTICHTING, ARCHIEF TEVENS ORGAAN VAN DE... [Archives as well as organ of the "De Graafschap" Antiquarian Society and of the Meester Hendrik Willem Heuvel Foundation]. A. (Irr.). Lochemse Handels- en Couranten drukkerij, Lochem, for Oudheidkundige Vereniging "De Graafschap", and Meester Hendrik Willem Heuvelstichting. In Dutch or East Netherlands (Saxon) dialect. p (1) f 5.15

104. OVERIJSSEL. Jaarboek voor Cultuur en Historie [Yearbook for culture and history]. A. N.V. De Erven J.J. Tijl, Melkmarkt 13-23, Zwolle. In Dutch or East Netherlands (Saxon) dialect. pv (1959: f 9.50)

105. PALAEOHISTORIA. Irr. 1951 (1959: vol. 5). J.B. Wolters N.V., Groningen, for Het Biologisch-Archaeologisch Instituut der Rijksuniversiteit Biologisch-Archaeologisch Instituut der Rijksuniversiteit [Biological-Archaeological Inst. of the State Univ. of Groningen]. Ed: H.T. Waterbolk, Groningen. Treaties mainly on Dutch prehist. and archaeology; in English or German; plans, diagrams; charts; illus. pv (vol. 5: f 15)

PUBLICATIES. For titles beginning with "Publicaties," followed by the name of the publishing or sponsoring institution or society, see the respective institution or society.

PUBLICATIONS. For titles beginning with "Publications," followed by the name of the publishing or sponsoring institution or society, see the respective institution or society.

REVUE D'HISTOIRE DU DROIT see TIJDSCHRIFT VOOR RECHTSGESCHIEDENIS

REVUE DU NORD see section on France

106. RIJKSDIENST VOOR HET OUDHEIDKUNDIG BODEMONDERZOEK, BERICHTEN VAN DE... [Proceedings of the State Service for Archaeological Investigations in the Netherlands]. A. 1950 (1957/58: vol. 8). Staatsdrukkerij- en uitgeversbedrijf, 's-Gravenhage, for Rijksdienst voor het oudheidkundig bodemonderzoek, Kleine Haag 2, Amersfoort. Art. on the archaeology of the Netherlands; bk. rev.; in Dutch, English or French; sum. in English; a cum. table of contents for the years 1950-60 will be pub. in vol. 10; alphabetical author index; illus.; graph. f 8

107. RIJKSMUSEUM. BULLETIN [State Museum. Bulletin]. Q. 1953 (1959: vol. 7). Staatsdrukkerij en Uitgeversbedrijf, 's-Gravenhage, for Rijksmuseum, Amsterdam. Art. on the collections and acquisitions of the museum; sum. in English; illus.; A. index of art. and of artists cited. f 4 / $ 0.50

108. RIJKSMUSEUM VAN OUDHEDEN TE LEIDEN, OUDHEIDKUNDIGE MEDEDELINGEN UIT HET... [Archaeological communications from the State Museum of Antiquities in Leiden]. A. 1907 (1957: 2nd series, vol. 38). Rijksmuseum van Oudheden, Leiden. Ed: W.D. van Wijngaarden. Art. on archaeology and ancient hist.; in Dutch, English, French or German. pv

109. ROTTERDAMS JAARBOEKJE [Rotterdam yearbook]. A. W.L. en J. Brusse's Uitgeversmij. N.V., Walenburgerweg 72-74, Rotterdam C, for Historisch Genootschap Roterodamum [Roterodamum Hist. Soc.], and Archief gebouw der Gemeente Rotterdam [Archives of the Municipality of Rotterdam]. f 6.75

110. SOCIAAL-HISTORISCHE STUDIEKRING, MEDEDELINGENBLAD VAN DE... [Communications of the Study Group for Social History]. Irr. 1953 (1958: no. 14). Sociaal-historische Studiekring, c/o K. van Boeschoten, Graaf Willem de Oudelaan 41, Naarden. Ed: P.J. Meertens, Prinsegracht 1101, Amsterdam. Notes and sum. of lectures on social hist.; short biographies of Dutch labor leaders, 1860-1918; biblio. notices. f 2

111. SOCIETE HISTORIQUE ET ARCHEOLOGIQUE DANS LE LIMBOURG, PUBLICATIONS DE LA... [Publications of the Historical and Archaeological Society in Limburg]. JAARBOEK VAN LIMBURGS GESCHIED- EN OUDHEIDKUNDIG GENOOTSCHAP [Yearbook of the Historical and Archaeological Society in Limburg]. A. (2 vol. pub. together B). Grafische Kunstinrichting "Ernest van Aelst," Witmakerstraat 35, Maastricht, for Limburgs Geschied- en Oudheidkundig Genootschap, Boonefanten 4, Maastricht. In Dutch; index of names; indices for vol. 1-75 (1864-1939) pub. in 1940. (memb.) f 10

112. SPIEGEL VAN LIMBURG [Mirror of Limburg]. Irr. Uitgeverij de Koepel, Vredestraat 8, Nijmegen. f 2.90

113. STUDIA CATHOLICA. Nieuwe reeks van "De Katholiek" [New series of "The Catholic"]. Q. Dekker en van de Vegt N.V., Oranjesingel 4, Nijmegen. f 12.50

TIJDSCHRIFT. For titles beginning with "Tijdschrift," followed by the name of the publishing or sponsoring institution or society, see the respective institution or society.

114. TIJDSCHRIFT VOOR GESCHIEDENIS [Journal of history]. 3 x y. 1886 (1958: vol. 71). P. Noordhoff, Oude Boteringestraat 12, Groningen. Ed: J.G. van Dillen, Ruysdaelkade 11, Amsterdam (secretary of the ed. board), Ch. Verlinden, Armand Huysmanslaan 44, Bruxelles (secretary for Belgium).

Art. on general hist. and the hist. of the Netherlands; news and notes; bk. rev.; biblio. of bk.; surveys of hist. periodicals. f 19

115. TIJDSCHRIFT VOOR RECHTSGESCHIEDENIS. REVUE D'HISTOIRE DU DROIT [Journal of the history of law]. Q. 1918 (1958: vol. 26). J.B. Wolters Uitgevers Maatschappij N.V., Groningen (for Holland); Etablissements Emile Bruylants S.A., Bruxelles (for Belgium and France); Martinus Nijhoff, P.O.B. 269, 's-Gravenhage (for other countries). Ed: R. Feenstra (secretary for Holland), van Slingelandtlaan 3, Leiden; L. Th. Maes (secretary for Belgium), Ridder Dessainlaan 57, Mechelen. Art. on the hist. of law, with emphasis on the Middle Ages and the period before the French Revolution; bk. rev.; survey of art. on the hist. of law; in Dutch, English, French or German; A. author index; general index of vol. 1-25 pub. in vol. 25 (1957). f 25 / Bfr 350

116. T'OUNG PAO [General review]. Archives concernant l'histoire, les langues, la géographie, l'ethnographie et les arts de l'Asie orientale [Archives concerning the history, languages, geography, ethnography and arts of the Far East]. Irr. 1890 (1958: vol. 44). E.J. Brill, Oude Rijn 33a, Leiden. Ed: Paul Demiéville, 234 bd. Raspail, Paris 14. Art. on the hist. (including modern hist.), languages, geography, ethnography and arts of the Far East; news and notes; in French and Chinese; general index for vol. 1-47 (1890-1944) pub. in 1953. f 40

117. VEREENIGING NEDERLANDSCH HISTORISCH SCHEEPVAART MUSEUM TE AMSTERDAM, JAARVERSLAG VAN DE... [Annual report of the Society of the Dutch Historical Maritime Museum at Amsterdam]. B or T (2 or 3 A. reports together). Vereeniging Nederlandsch Historisch Scheepvaart Museum, Cornelis Schuytstraat 57, Amsterdam. A. reports of the soc. and some contributions on maritime hist. for memb. only

118. VEREENIGING "ORANJE NASSAU MUSEUM," GEVESTIGD TE 'S-GRAVENHAGE, JAARVERSLAG DER... [Annual report of the Society "Oranje Nassau Museum," established at The Hague]. A. Vereeniging "Oranje Nassau Museum," Prinsegracht 3, 's-Gravenhage. A. reports of the soc. and some hist. contributions. for memb. only

119. VEREENIGING TOT BEOEFENING VAN OVERIJSSELSCH REGT EN GESCHIEDENIS, VERSLAGEN EN MEDEDELINGEN DER... [Reports and communications of the Society for the Study of the Law and History of Overijssel]. A. N.V. Deventer, Boek- en Steendrukkerij, vroeger firma J. de Lange, Deventer, for Vereeniging tot Beoefening van Overijsselsch Regt en Geschiedenis, c/o G.J. ter Kuile (secretary), Sassenpoort te Zwolle. In Dutch and occasionally German. f 8 / $ 2.10

120. VEREENIGING TOT BEVORDERING DER KENNIS VAN DE ANTIEKE BESCHAVING TE 'S-GRAVENHAGE, BULLETIN VAN DE... [Bulletin of the Society for the Promotion of Knowledge of Ancient Culture in The Hague]. A. Vereeniging tot Bevordering der Kennis van de Antieke Beschaving te 's-Gravenhage, c/o Archaeologisch Instituut, Rapenburg 20, Leiden. Art. on ancient art and archaeology; in English, French or German; bk. rev. (in Dutch). f 15

121. VEREENIGING TOT UITGAAF DER BRONNEN VAN HET OUD-VADERLANDSCHE RECHT, VERSLAGEN EN MEDEDELINGEN VAN DE... [Reports and communications of the Society for the Publication of the Sources of Old Dutch Law]. Irr. (1959: vol. 11). Kemink en Zoon N.V., Domplein 2, Utrecht, for Vereeniging tot Uitgaaf der Bronnen van het Oud-vaderlandsche Recht. (memb.) f 10

122. VEREENIGING VOOR NAAMKUNDE TE LEUVEN EN DE COMMISSIE VOOR NAAMKUNDE TE AMSTERDAM, MEDEDELINGEN VAN DE... [Communications of the Society for Onomastics in Leuven and the Commission for Onomastics in Amsterdam]. Q. 1925 (1959: vol. 35). Bureau voor Naamkunde, Koninklijke Nederlandse Akademie van Wetenschappen [Office of Onomastics, Royal Dutch Acad. of Sciences], Nieuwe Hoogstraat 17, Amsterdam, for Vereeniging voor Naamkunde te Leuven and Commissie voor Naamkunde te Amsterdam. Ed. board: (Flanders) H.J. van de Wijer, H. Draye, K. Roelandts; (Netherlands) M. Schönfeld, S.J. Fockema Andrae, P.J. Mertons. Art. on place and personal names and on onomastic activities, with emphasis on the Netherlands and Flanders; rev. of bk. and art. f 4

123. VEREENIGING VOOR TERPENONDERZOEK, JAARVERSLAG VAN DE... [Annual report of the Society for Terp Research]. A. J.B. Wolters' Uitgeversmij. N.V., Groningen. 2 supplementary vol. containing illus., maps and plans for the years 1948-53 appeared in 1955. pv (1955: f 40)

VERSLAGEN. For titles beginning with "Verslagen," followed by the name of the publishing or sponsoring institution or society, see the respective institution or society.

124. VERSLAGEN OMTRENT 'S RIJKS OUDE ARCHIEVEN [Reports concerning the old public record offices]. A. 1897 (1958: 2nd series, no. 30). Staatsdrukkerij- en Uitgeverijbedrijf, 's-Gravenhage. Reports on the public record offices. f 3

VETUS TESTAMENTUM see section on International Periodicals

125. VIGILIAE CHRISTIANAE. A Review of Early Christian Life and Language. Q. 1947 (1959: vol. 13). North-Holland Pub. Co., P.O.B. 103, Amsterdam C. Ed: J.H. Waszink (secretary), Witte Singel 91, Leiden. "Articles and short notices of a historical and cultural, linguistic or philological nature on Early Christian literature in the widest sense of the word, as well as on Christian epigraphy and archaeology. Church and dogmatic history will be dealt with if they bear directly on social history; Byzantine and Medieval literature only in so far as it exhibits continuity with the Early Christian period"; bk. rev.; in English, French or German. f 19 / $ 5

126. VOLKSKUNDE [Folklore]. Driemaandelijks Tijdschrift voor de Studie van het Volksleven [Quarterly for the study of folkways]. Q. Uitgeversmij. N.V. Standaard-Boekhandel, Singel 100, Amsterdam C, and Belgiëlei 151, Antwerpen, for Volkskunde-Commissie der Koninklijke Nederlandse Akademie van Wetenschappen [Folklore Committee of the Royal Dutch Acad. of Sciences]. In Dutch and occasionally French or German. f 12

127. VONDELJAARBOEK [The "Vondel" yearbook]. Irr. Vereniging "Het Vondelmuseum" [The Vondel-Museum Soc.], Singel 421, Amsterdam C. (memb.) f 3

128. VOORAZIATISCH-EGYPTISCH GENOOTSCHAP "EX ORIENTE LUX," JAARBERICHT VAN HET... [Annual report of the Near Eastern-Egyptian Society "Ex Oriente Lux"]. Annuaire de la société "Ex Oriente Lux." A. 1933 (1957/58 vol. 15). Vooraziatisch-Egyptisch Genootschap "Ex Oriente Lux," Noordeinsplein 4a, Leiden. Ed: F.M. Th. de Liagre Böhl, A. de Buck, Roodborststraat 16, Leiden. Art. on Oriental archaeology, literature, philology and hist.; illus.; in Dutch, English, French or German. pv

129. VOORAZIATISCH-EGYPTISCH GENOOTSCHAP "EX ORIENTE LUX," MEDEDELINGEN EN VERHANDELINGEN VAN HET... [Communications and transactions of the Near Eastern-Egyptian Society "Ex Oriente Lux"]. A. 1934 (1957: vol. 12). E.J. Brill, Oude Rijn 33a, Leiden. Monographs on Oriental archaeology, philology, literature and hist.; in Dutch, English or French. (memb.) f 7.50

130. DE VRIJE FRIES [The free Frisian]. Irr. Van Gorcum en comp. N.V., Assen, for Fries Genootschap van Geschied-, Oudheid- en Taalkunde [Frisian Soc. for Hist., Archaeology and Philology], and Fryske Akademy [Frisian Acad.]. In Dutch and occasionally Frisian or German. pv (c. f 10)

131. DIE WELT DES ISLAMS. THE WORLD OF ISLAM. LE MONDE DE L'ISLAM. Internationale Zeitschrift für die Entwicklungsgeschichte des Islams, besonders in der Gegenwart. International Journal for the Historical Development of Contemporary Islam. Revue internationale pour l'Evolution historique de l'Islam moderne. Q (Irr.). 1913 (1958: new series, vol. 5). E.J. Brill, Oude Rijn 33a, Leiden. Ed: G. Jäschke, Hüfferstr. 69, Münster / Westf., Germany. Art. on all aspects of the recent hist. of Islam; bk. rev.; in German, French or English; illus. f 25

132. WEST-FRIESLAND OUD EN NIEUW [West Frisia, old and new]. A. N.V. Drukkerij "West-Friesland," Hoorn, for Historisch Genootschap Oud West Friesland ["Old West Frisia" Hist. Soc.]. In Dutch and occasionally West Frisian dialect. pni

133. WEST-INDISCHE GIDS [West Indian guide]. Q. Martinus Nijhoff, P.O.B. 269, 's-Gravenhage. Art. on hist., culture and economy of the Netherlands, Antilles and Surinam; general index for vol. 1-25 (1919-43) pub. in 1946. Superseded by Nieuwe Westindische Gids. f 12.50

134. WESTERHEEM [Western home]. B-M. H.J. Verhagen, Morskade 12, Leiden, for Archaeologische werkgemeenschap voor Westelijk Nederland [Archaeological Study Group for the Western Netherlands]. pni

135. WETENSCHAPPELIJK GENOOTSCHAP VOOR GOEREE EN OVERFLAKKEE, JAARBOEK VAN HET... [Yearbook of the Scientific Society for Goeree and Overflakkee]. A. Flakkeesche Drukkerij J. en M. Boomsma, Voorstraat 15, Middelharnis, for Het Wetenschappelijk Genootschap voor Goeree en Overflakkee. f 5.50

THE WORLD OF ISLAM see DIE WELT DES ISLAMS

136. ZEEUWS TIJDSCHRIFT [The Zealand review]. B-M. "Zeeuws Tijdschrift" Foundation, c/o P.J. van der Koorde, Veerseweg 62, Middelburg. f 8.25 / Bfr 140

137. ZUID-HOLLAND [South Holland]. Tweemaandelijks orgaan van de Historische Vereniging voor Zuid-Holland onder de zinspreuk "Vigilate Deo Confidentes" [Bimonthly organ of the Historical Society for South Holland with the motto "Vigilate Deo Confidentes"]. Irr. Historische Vereniging voor Zuid-Holland, Laan van Swaenesteyn 28, Voorburg. nfs

138. ZUID-HOLLANDSE VERENIGING VOOR GENEALOGY "ONS VOORGESLACHT," JAARBOEK VAN DE... [Yearbook of the South Holland Genealogical Society "Our Ancestors"]. Irr. J. Lingbeek, Poortugaal. f 3.45

Norway

Prepared with the assistance of
Haakon Falck Myckland, Librarian,
and the staff of the
Royal University Library, Oslo

1. ÆTT OG HEIM [Family and home]. A. Rogaland historie-og ættesogelag [Hist. and Genealogical Soc. of Rogaland], P.O.B. 311, Stavanger. Supersedes Rogaland historielag. Årsskrift [Hist. Soc. of Rogaland. Yearbook], pub. from 1914 to 1947 and Rogaland ættesogelag. Årshefte [Genealogical Soc. of Rogaland. Yearbook], pub. from 1941 to 1947. Ncr 10

2. AGDER BISPEDØMME, ÅRBOK FOR... [Yearbook of the Diocese of Agder]. A. Agder bispedømmeråd [Council of the Diocese of Agder], Kristiansand S. Ncr 5 / $0.75

3. AGDER HISTORIELAG, ÅRSSKRIFT FOR... [Yearbook of the Agder Historical Society]. A. Agder historielag, Kristiansand S. Index for the years 1914 to 1949 in vol. 29 (1949). From 1914 to 1943 pub. under the title: Bidrag til Agders historie [Contributions to the hist. of Agder]. Ncr 6

ÅRBOK. For titles beginning with "Årbok," followed by the name of the publishing or sponsoring institution or society, see the respective institution or society.

ÅRBOK. AUST-AGDER-MUSEET, AUST-AGDER-ARKIVET see AUST-AGDER ARV

4. ÅRBOK FOR DEN NORSKE KIRKE [Yearbook of the Norwegian Church]. A. Forlaget Land og Kirke, Ö. Slottsgt. 25, Oslo. Statistics; illus. Ncr 12

ÅRBOK FOR DØLARINGEN see ÅRBOK FOR GUDBRANDSDALEN

5. ÅRBOK FOR GLÅMDALEN [Yearbook for Glamdalen]. A. Markvard Bækken, Elverum. Ncr 10

6. ÅRBOK FOR GUDBRANDSDALEN [Yearbook for Gudbrandsdalen]. A. Dølaringen historielag [Dølaringen Hist. Soc.], in collaboration with Gudbrandsdal historielag [Gudbrandsdalen Hist. Soc.], Lom. From 1930 to 1938 pub. under the title: Årbok for Dølaringen [Yearbook for Dølaringen]. Ncr 7

ÅRBOK FOR JÆREN see ÅRBOK FOR JÆREN OG DALANE

7. ÅRBOK FOR JÆREN OG DALANE [Yearbook for Jæren and Dalane]. A. Rogaland historie og ættesogelag [Hist. and Genealogical Soc. of Rogaland], Stavanger. In 1952 pub. under the title: Årbok for Jæren. Ncr 11

8. ÅRBOK FOR KARMSUND [Yearbook for Karmsund]. Irr. (about once every 5 years). Museums-og-historielaget for Haugesund og bygdene [Museum and Hist. Soc. for Haugesund and its environs], Haugesund. Illus. Super-

sedes Haugesund museum. Årshefte [Haugesund Museum. Annual journal], pub. from 1935 to 1950. Ncr 5 / $1

9. ÅRBOK FOR NORDFJORD [Yearbook for Nordfjord]. Eit skrift for folke og kulturminne, arbeidsliv og ungdomslagsarbeid [A review of folk and cultural history, the labor world and youth work]. A. (Irr.). Nordfjord sogelag [Nordfjord Hist. Soc.], Sandane. Ncr 6

10. ÅRBOK FOR TELEMARK [Yearbook for Telemark]. A. Telemark mållag [Telemark Language Soc.], Skien. Ncr 10

11. ÅRDAL SOGELAG, ÅRBOK FOR... [Yearbook for the Årdal Historical Society]. A. (Irr.). Årdal sogelag, Årdal, Sogn. Ncr 8

ARENDALS MUSEUM. ÅRBOK see AUST-AGDER ARV

ÅRSHEFTE. For titles beginning with "Årshefte," followed by the name of the publishing or sponsoring institution or society, see the respective institution or society.

ÅRSSKRIFT. For titles beginning with "Årsskrift," followed by the name of the publishing or sponsoring institution or society, see the respective institution or society.

12. ASKER OG BÆRUM HISTORIELAGS SKRIFT [Journal of the Asker and Bærum Historical Society]. A. Asker og Bærum historielag, Hvalstad, Asker. Includes A. report of the soc. Ncr 5

13. AUST-AGDER ARV [Heritage of Aust-Agder]. Irr. Aust-Agder-museet [Aust-Agder Museum], Aust-Agder-arkivet [Aust-Agder Archives], and Aust-Agder museumslag [Aust-Agder Museum Soc.], Arendal. From 1946 to 1955 pub. under the title: Arendals museum. Årbok, from 1956 to 1958 under the title: Aust-Agder-museet. Årbok and in 1959 under the title: Årbok. Aust-Agder-museet, Aust-Agder-arkivet.

AUST-AGDER-MUSEET. ÅRBOK see AUST-AGDER ARV

14. BERGENS HISTORISKE FORENINGS SKRIFTER [Publications of the Bergen Historical Society]. A. Bergens historiske forening, Bergen. Index for the years 1895-1918 pub. in vol. 25/26 (1919/20) and for the years 1919-43 in vol. 50 (1944). Ncr 22.25

15. BIBLIOTEK OG FORSKNING [Library and research]. A. Norsk bibliotekarlag og Norsk forskning bibliotekarers forening [Assoc. of Norwegian Public Librarians and Assoc. of Norwegian Research Librarians], c/o Universitetsbiblioteket, Oslo. English sum. Ncr 8

BIDRAG TIL AGDERS HISTORIE see AGDER HISTORIELAG, ÅRSSKRIFT FOR...

16. BJØRGVIN. A. Bjørgvin bispedømmeråd [Council of the Diocese of Bjørgvin], Bergen. Ncr 4

17. BY OG BYGD [Town and country]. A. Johan Grundt Tanum, Oslo, for Norsk folkemuseum [Norwegian Public Museum], Oslo.

18. BYMINNER [Reminiscences of the old town]. Q. Oslo bymuseum [Oslo City Museum], Frognerveien 67, Oslo. Ncr 10

19. DRAMMENS MUSEUM. ÅRBOK [Drammen Museum. Yearbook]. A. (Irr.). Drammens museum, Drammen. Ncr 8.50

20. EDDA. Nordisk tidsskrift for literaturforskning [Scandinavian journal of literary research]. Q. H. Aschehoug and Co., Sehestads plass 3, Oslo. In Norwegian and occasionally in other languages; cum. index every 10 years. Ncr 28

21. EIKER HISTORIELAG. ÅRBOK [Yearbook of the Eiker Historical Society]. A. (Irr.). Ragnar Holmen, for Eiker historielag, Mjøndalen. Ncr 7

22. FEDRANE KYRKJE I ROGALAND [The church of our forefathers in Rogaland]. A. Stavanger bispedømmeråd [Council of the Diocese of Stavanger], Stavanger. News of the diocese; illus. Ncr 6

23. FOLKEKUNST [Popular art]. Irr. (2-4 x y). Norsk bygdekunstlag [Norwegian Country Art Soc.], Thor Olsensgt. 5, Oslo. Ncr 5

24. FOLLO HISTORIE-OG MUSEUMSLAG, ÅRBOK FOR... [Yearbook of the Follo Historical and Museum Society]. A. (Irr.). Follo historie-og museumslag, Drøbak. Ncr 4

25. FORENINGEN "BERGENS SJØFARTSMUSEUM." ÅRSHEFTE [Yearbook of the society "Bergen's Museum of Maritime History"]. A. Bergens Sjøfartsmuseum, Bergen. c. Ncr 2

26. FORENINGEN TIL NORSKE FORTIDSMINNESMERKERS BEVARING. ÅRBOK [Yearbook of the Society for the Preservation of Norwegian Antiquities]. A. 1845 (1957 [1958]: vol. 112). Foreningen til norske fortidsminnesmerkers bevaring, Kirkegt. 14/16/18, Oslo. Ed. board: Gudolf Blakstad, Roar Hauglid, Arne Stenseng. Art. on the archaeological activities of the soc. and on Norwegian architects and craftsmen of pre-modern times; doc.; biblio. of bk. and art., arranged by place, with author index; Norwegian archaeological news; in Norwegian and occasionally in English; occasional English sum.; illus. Ncr 18

27. FOSEN HISTORIELAG. ÅRSSKRIFT [Yearbook of the Fosen Historical Society]. A. (Irr.). F. Bruns bokhandels forlag, Trondheim. Ncr 8.15

28. FOSSEGRIMEN [Water-sprite]. Irr. Torolv Solheim, Risør. Art. on social questions, hist. and literature. Ncr 15

29. FRÅ FJON TIL FUSA [From Fjon to Fusa]. A. Lunde and Co., Bergen, for Nord- og Midhordland sogelag [North and Middle Hordaland Hist. Soc.], Bergen. Ncr 7.75

30. FYLKESMUSEET FOR TELEMARK OG GRENLAND. ÅRSSKRIFT [The County Museum of Telemark and Grenland. Yearbook]. A. Fylkesmuseet for Telemark and Grenland, Skien.

31. GAMALT FRÅ HADELAND [The old culture in Hadeland]. 1-2 x y. Erik Mjønvolden, Mjønvald, Hadeland.

32. GAMLE BERGEN [Ancient Bergen]. A. Gamle Bergen, Bergen.
Ncr 4

33. GAULDALSMINNE [Reminiscences of Gauldal]. Tidsskrift for bygdehistorie og folkeminne [Journal of local history and folklore]. Irr. (10 no. constitute a vol.). Gauldal historielag [Gauldal Hist. Soc.], Melhus. Ncr 5

34. GRANNEN [Neighbor]. Samlingsblad til segn og soge for Flekkefjord og bygdene [Bulletin for the preservation and history of Flekkefjord and its environs]. Q. Mållaget i Flekkefjord [Language Soc. in Flekkefjord], Flekkefjord. Ncr 2

35. HÆRMUSEET. ÅRBOK [Army Museum. Yearbook]. Irr. 1946 (1956 [1958]: no vol. indic.). Hærmuseet, Akershus, Oslo. Descriptive catalogues, reference lists and illus. of banners, standards, weapons and pennants of the Norwegian Army, Peasant and Town Militia; English sum.; A. report of the activities of the museum. Ncr 16.35

36. HALØYGMINNE [Reminiscences of old Hålogaland]. Q. Hålogaland historielag [Hålogaland Hist. Soc.], Harstad. Index for the years 1920-44 pub. in vol. 25 (1944) and also separately in 1945. Ncr 8

37. HARDANGER. A. Hardanger historielag [Hardanger Hist. Soc.], Norheimsund. Cum. index for the years 1908-35 pub. in 1935 and for the years 1936-45 in 1946. Ncr 8

HAUGESUND MUSEUM. ÅRSHEFTE see ÅRBOK FOR KARMSUND

38. HEDMARK SLEKTSHISTORIELAGS TIDSSKRIFT [Journal of the Hedmark Genealogical Society]. Irr. (2-4 x y). M. Gravdahls bokhandel, Hamar, for Hedmark slekthistorielag, Hamar. Ncr 10 / $1.50

39. HEDMARKSMUSEET OG DOMKIRKEODDEN [Hedmark Museum and Cathedral steeples]. Irr. Hedmarksmuseet, Hamar. Illus.
Ncr 3.30

40. HEIMEN [Home]. Q (1 vol. every 3 years). 1922 (mri 1955-1958: vol. 10). Universitetsforlaget, Karl Johansgt. 47, Oslo, for Landslaget for bygde- og byhistorie [Federation for Local Hist.], Oslo. Ed: Lars Reinton, Universitetsbiblioteket, Drammensvegen 42, Oslo. Art. and dissertations on the urban and rural hist. of Norway, and on folklore, regional research work, and sources and methods for the study of local hist.; rev. art.; rev. of bk. and art.; biblio. of bk. and periodicals; news and notes on organizations devoted to the study of local and regional hist.; vol. index of personal and place names and vol. author index.
Ncr 10

41. HERØY SOGELAG, TIDSSKRIFT FOR... [Journal of the Herøy Historical Society]. Irr. Herøy sogelag, Herøy. Ncr 4

42. HISTORIELAGET FOR SOGN, TIDSSKRIFT UTGITT AV... [Journal of the Historical Society of Sogn]. S-A. Historielaget for Sogn, Amla i Sogn.
Ncr 5.50

43. HISTORIELAGET FOR TELEMARK OG GRENLAND. ÅRSSKRIFT [Historical Society of Telemark and Grenland. Yearbook]. Irr. Historielaget for Telemark og Grenland, Skien.

44. HISTORISK TIDSSKRIFT [Historical review]. Q. 1871 (1960: vol. 39). Universitetsforlaget, Karl Johansgt. 47, Oslo, for Norske historiske forening [Norwegian Hist. Soc.], Oslo. Ed: Dagfinn Mannsåker, Hans Øverlands vei 12, Høvik. Art. on Scandinavian political, diplomatic, economic, social and cultural hist., with emphasis on the modern period, and on the methodology of hist.; doc.; rev. art.; bk. rev.; A. installments of "Politiske Dagbøker og Minner" [Political diaries and memoirs] by Ludvig Daae, and "Norsk Historisk Bibliografi" [Norwegian hist. biblio.] by H. Falck Myckland; in Norwegian, Danish or Swedish; occasional English sum.; illus.; combined author, personal and geographical index in each vol.; cum. index for the years 1871-1936 pub. in 1937.
(memb.) Ncr 10 / (memb.) Ncr 14

45. HUMANIORA NORVEGICA. The Year's Work in Norwegian Humanities. A. Universitetsforlaget, Karl Johansgt. 47, Oslo. Critical rev. and abstr. of bk. and art.; in English. $ 5

46. IBSENFORBUNDET. ÅRBOK [Ibsen Society. Yearbook]. A. Ibsenforbundet, Herman Baggersgt. 6, Skien. Ncr 15

47. INTERNASJONAL POLITIKK [International politics]. M. Chr. Michelsens Institutt for Vitenskap og Åndsfrihet [Chr. Michelsens Inst. for Science and Intellectual Freedom], Kalvedalsvei 12, Bergen. Calendar of important political events. Ncr 12 / Ncr 15

48. KIRKE OG KULTUR [Church and culture]. 10 x y. Forlaget Land og kirke, Ø. Slottsgt. 25, Oslo. Index for the years 1894-1913 pub. in Kristiania in 1914. Supersedes Luthersk ugeskrift [Lutheran weekly], pub. from 1877 to 189[illegible]

49. DET KONGELIGE NORSKE VIDENSKABERS SELSKAB. MUSEET. ÅRBOK [The Museum of the Royal Norwegian Society of Sciences. Yearbook]. A. F. Bruns bokhandels forlag, Trondheim. Ncr 11.10

50. KUNST OG KULTUR [Art and culture]. Q. Gyldendal norsk forlag, Oslo. Ncr 30

51. KUNSTEN IDAG [Art today]. Q. Galleri Per, Kristian Augustsgt. 19, Oslo. In Norwegian and English; illus. Ncr 50 / $7.50

52. KUNSTINDUSTRIMUSEET I OSLO. ÅRBOK [Oslo Museum of Applied Art. Yearbook]. Irr. Kunstindustrimuseet, Oslo. c. Ncr 12

53. LAND OG HAV [Land and sea]. A. Lunde and Co., Bergen, for Hordaland landbruksmuseum [Hordaland Museum of Agriculture], Bergen.
Ncr 12.25

54. LARDAL HISTORIELAG. ÅRBOK [Lardal Historical Society. Yearbook]. A. Lardal historielag, Svarstad p.å. Ncr 2.50

LUTHERSK UGESKRIFT see KIRKE OG KULTUR

55. MAAL OG MINNE [Language and tradition]. Norske studier [Norwegian studies]. Q. H. Aschehoug and Co., Sehesteds plass 3, Oslo, for Bymaalslaget [Bymaal Soc.], Universitetsbiblioteket, Oslo. Cum. index pub. every 10 years. Ncr 10

56. MAIHAUGEN. A. (Irr.). 1931 (1953-56 [1957]: no vol. indic.). Sandvigske samlinger [Sandvig Collections], Lillehammer. Ed: Sigurd Grieg. Descriptive and hist. art. on objects in the Sandvig collections and museums covering the period from the Middle Ages to the early 20th cent.; news and notes on the activities of the soc. From 1931 to 1949 pub. under the title: De sandvigske samlinger. Årbok [The Sandvig Collections. Yearbook].

MELDING FRÅ NORDTRØNDELAG HISTORIELAG see NORDTRØNDELAG HISTORIELAG. ÅRBOK

57. MUSEUMSNYTT [Museum news]. Q. Norske museers landsforbund [Norwegian Assoc. of Museums], St. Olavsgt. 1, Oslo. Illus.; index for the years 1951-53 pub. in 1953. Ncr 8

58. NIDAROS BISPEDØMME, ÅRBOK FOR... [Yearbook of the Diocese of Nidaros]. A. F. Bruns bokhandels forlag, Trondheim. Ncr 3

59. NORDENFJELDSKE KUNST-INDUSTRIMUSEUM. ÅRBOK [North Norway Museum of Art Industry. Yearbook]. A. F. Bruns bokhandelsforlag, Trondheim. Ncr 12

60. NORDMANNS FORBUNDET [League of Norsemen]. M. Nordmanns forbundet, Raadhusgt. 23 B, Oslo. Art. on the hist. of Norwegian emigration and of Norwegians settled abroad. Ncr 20 / $3

61. NORDMØRE HISTORIELAG, ÅRSSKRIFT FOR... [Yearbook of the Nordmøre Historical Society]. A. Nordmøre historielag, Kristiansund N. Index for the years 1921-40 pub. in 1941-44. Ncr 9

62. NORDTRØNDELAG HISTORIELAG. ÅRBOK [Yearbook of the North Trøndelag Historical Society]. A. Nordtrøndelag historielag, Steinkjer. In 1921-22 pub. under the title: Melding frå Nordtrøndelag historielag [Report from the North Trøndelag Hist. Soc.]. Ncr 6

NORDTRØNDELAG HISTORIELAG, MELDING FRÅ... see NORDTRØNDELAG HISTORIELAG. ÅRBOK

63. NORSK FOLKEMINNELAG [Norwegian Folklore Society]. Irr. Universitetsbiblioteket, Oslo, for Norsk folkeminnelag, Oslo. Index for vol. 1-49 pub. in vol. 50 (1943). pv (p (1) c. Ncr 18) (memb. Ncr 10 p.a.)

64. NORSK GEOGRAFISK TIDSSKRIFT [Norwegian geographical journal]. Q. A.W. Bröggers boktrykkeri, Oslo, for Geografisk institutt [Geographical Inst.], Universitetet, Blindern, Oslo. Ncr 6

65. NORSK MILITÆRT TIDSSKRIFT [Norwegian military review]. M. 1831 (1958: vol. 117). August Hansens forlag, Tollbugt. 30, Oslo, for Oslo militære samfund [Oslo Military Soc.], Myntgaten 1, Oslo. Ed: J. Berg. Art. on Norwegian military affairs and hist., with emphasis on the 20th cent., and on military strategy and military developments in other countries; occasional reprints of art. from foreign newspapers and periodicals; rev. art.; rev. of bk. and art.; news of the soc. Ncr 12

66. NORSK MUSIKKGRANSKNING [Norwegian research in music]. A. (Irr.). J. Grundt Tanum forlag, Oslo, for Norsk samfund for musikkgranskning [Norwegian Soc. for Research in Music], Oslo. pv (c. Ncr 25)

67. **NORSK SLEKTSHISTORISK TIDSSKRIFT** [Norwegian journal of genealogy] S-A (1 vol. for 2 years). 1928 (1959: vol. 17). Cammermeyers bokhandel, Oslo, for Norsk slektshistorisk forening [Norwegian Genealogical Soc.], Oslo. Ed: Harald Gram. Art. on Norwegian genealogy; bk. rev.; biblio. of bk. and periodicals; news of the activities of the soc. Supersedes Norsk tidsskrift for genealog personalhistorie, biografi og literærhistorie [Norwegian journal of genealogy, personal hist., biography and literary hist.], pub. from 1910 to 1926. Ncr 15

68. NORSK TEOLOGISK TIDSSKRIFT [Norwegian theological review]. Q. 1900 (1958: vol. 59). Universitetsforlaget, Karl Johansgt. 47, Oslo. Ed: Johan B. Hygen, Jacob Aallsgt. 30, Oslo N.V. Art. on theological subjects and religious and church hist., with emphasis on Norway; rev. of bk. and periodicals; professional news; vol. 56 (1955) contains a special no. with art. in English, French or German; indices for the years 1900-24 pub. in 1924, and for the years 1925-49 in 1950. Ncr 15

NORSK TIDSSKRIFT FOR GENEALOGI, PERSONALHISTORIE, BIOGRAFI OG LITERÆRHISTORIE see NORSK SLEKTSHISTORISK TIDSSKRIFT

69. NORSK TIDSSKRIFT FOR MISJON [Norwegian review of missions]. Q. Egede-instituttet [Egede Inst.], Tullinsgt. 4, Oslo. Ncr 12.50

70. NORSK TIDSSKRIFT FOR SJØVESEN [Norwegian naval journal]. 10 x y Sjømilitære samfund [Naval Officers' Soc.], Horten. Ncr 17.50 / c. $ 2.50

71. NORSK TIDSSKRIFT FOR SPROGVIDENSKAP [Norwegian journal of linguistics]. Irr. H. Aschehoug and Co., Sehestads plass 3, Oslo. In Norwegian, English, French and German. Ncr 20

72. DET NORSKE TURISTFORENINGS ÅRBOK [The yearbook of the Norwegian Touring Club]. A. Norske turistforening, Stortingsgt. 28, Oslo. Index for the years 1868-1918 pub. in Kristiana in 1920 and for the years 1919-43 pub. in Oslo in 1943. Ncr 17

73. NORVEG [Norway]. Tidsskrift for folkelivsgransking. Journal of Norwegian ethnology. A. 1934 (1958 [1959]: new series, vol. 6). Aschehoug and Co., Sehestads plass 3, Oslo, for Instituttet for Folkelivsgransking [Inst. of Ethnology], Universitetsbiblioteket, Oslo. Ed. board: Arne Berg, Olav Bö, Svale Solheim, Hilmar Stigum. Art. on the ethnology, culture and folklore of Scandinavia, with emphasis on Norway; bk. rev. (in English); biblio. of bk., periodicals and art.; in Norwegian and occasionally in English; English and German sum. illus. Ncr 13.30

74. NORVEGIA SACRA. Årbok til kunnskap om den norske kirke i fortid og samtid [Yearbook of information about the Norwegian Church, past and present]. Irr. 1921 (1940 [1950]: vol. 20). Jacob Dybwad, Ø Vollgt. 15, Oslo. Manag. ed: Ingolf Kvamen. Art. on Norwegian church hist., missionary activities and theological problems; bishops' A. reports and reports of missions abroad; church statistics. pv (vol. 20: Ncr 16)

75. THE NORWAY YEARBOOK. Irr. J. Grundt Tanum forlag, Oslo. Vol. subject index. Ncr 27.20

76. ODAL. Irr. Sør-Odal historielag [South Odal Hist. Soc.], Skarnes. Ncr 4

77. OSLO KOMMUNES KUNSTSAMLINGER. ÅRBOK [Oslo Municipal Art Collections. Yearbook]. A. (Irr.). Cammermeyers bokhandel, Oslo, for Oslo kommunes kunstsamlinger, St. Olavsgt. 1, Oslo. Ncr 10

78. ØSTFOLD HISTORIELAG, TIDSSKRIFT UTGITT AV... [Journal of the Østfold Historical Society]. S-A. Østfold historielag, Sarpsborg. Ncr 7 / $1

79. ØSTFOLDARV [Heritage of Østfold]. Årbok for museer og historielag i Østfold [Yearbook of the museums and Historical Society in Østfeld]. Irr. Fylkeskonservatoren [County Conservator], Sarpsborg. Professional news; maps; illus. Ncr 5 / $1

80. RENNEBU HISTORIELAG. ÅRSSKRIFT [Rennebu Historical Society. Yearbook]. A. Rennebu historielag, Ingebrikt Ytterhus, Rennebu. Ncr 4.50

81. RINGERIKE. S-A. Ringerike ungdomslag [Ringerike Youth Soc.], and Ringerikes museum [Ringerike Museum], Hønefoss. Ncr 2.50

ROGALAND ÆTTESOGELAG. ÅRSHEFTE see ÆTT OG HEIM

ROGALAND HISTORIELAG. ÅRSSKRIFT see ÆTT OG HEIM

82. ROMERIKE ÆTTEHISTORIELAGS ÅRBOK [Yearbook of the Romerike Genealogical Society]. A. Eriksen Ganer, Vidarsgt. 10, Oslo, for Romerike Ættehistorielag. Ncr 12

83. ROMERIKE HISTORIELAG, ÅRBOK FOR... [Yearbook of the Romerike Historical Society]. A. Romerike historielag, Aksel Krogh, Hemnes i Høland. Ncr 13

84. ROMSDAL SOGELAG. ÅRSSKRIFT [Romsdal Historical Society. Yearbook]. A. Romsdal sogelag, Molde. Illus. Ncr 6

85. ROMSDALSMUSEET. ÅRBOK [Romsdal Museum. Yearbook]. A. Romsdalsmuseet, Molde. Ncr 2

86. ST. HALLVARD. B-M. Aschehoug and Co., Sehestads plass 3, Oslo, for Selskapet for Oslo byes vel [Soc. for the Welfare of the City of Oslo], Oslo. Cum. index for vol. 1-30 pub. in 1954. Ncr 16

SAMELIV see SAMI ÆLLIN

87. SAMI ÆLLIN. SAMELIV [Lapp life]. Sámi Særvi Jakkigir'ji. Samisk selskaps årbok [Yearbook of the Lappish Society]. A. (Irr.). Universitetsforlaget, Oslo, for Samisk selskap, etnografisk museum, Tullinlökka, Oslo. Art. on Lappish culture; periodical reports of the soc.; in Norwegian and occasionally in Lappish; graph; illus. Ncr 7.50

88. SAMTIDEN [Our time]. Tidsskrift for politikk, litteratur og samfunnsspørsmål [Review of politics, literature and social questions]. 10 x y. H. Aschehoug and Co., Sehestads plass 3, Oslo. Index for the years 1890-1910 pub. in 1910 and for the years 1911-42 in 1946. Ncr 20

89. SANDEFJORD BYMUSEUM. ÅRBOK [Sandefjord City Museum. Yearbook]. A. (Irr.). Sandefjord bymuseum, Sandefjord. A. report of the museum; graph; illus. nfs

DE SANDVIGSKE SAMLINGER. ÅRBOK see MAIHAUGEN

90. SOGNDAL. HEIMBYGDI VÅR [Sogndal. Our native country]. A. (Irr.). J.O. Skjeldestad bok- og papirhandel, Sogndal: Sogn, for Sogndal solelag [Sogndal Hist. Soc.], Sogndal i Sogn. Ncr 5

91. SOLUM HISTORIELAG. ÅRSSKRIFT [Solum Historical Society. Yearbook]. A. Solum historielag, Skotfoss. Ncr 6

92. STATSØKONOMISK TIDSSKRIFT [Journal of political economy]. B-M. Ed: Johan Vogt, Frederiksgt. 3, Oslo. Ncr 10

93. STAVANGER MUSEUM. ÅRBOK [Stavanger Museum. Yearbook]. A. 1890 (mri 1956: vol. 66). Stavanger museum, Stavanger. Ed: Jan Hendrich Lexov. Art. on Norwegian hist. and archaeology. Ncr 10

94. SUNNHORDLAND. A. Sunnhordland folkemuseum [Sunnhordland Public Museum], P.O.B. 51, Stord. A. report of the museum; illus. Ncr 5 / c. $ 0.75

95. SUNNMØRE HISTORISKELAG, TIDSSKRIFT FOR... [Journal of the Sunnmøre Historical Society]. A. Sunnmøre historiskelag, Ålesund. Ncr 8

96. SYN OG SEGN [Seeing and narrating]. Norsk tidsskrift [Norwegian journal]. 10 x y. Noregs boklag, Rosenkrantzgt. 8, Oslo. Cum. index for the years 1894-1919 pub. in 1920 and for the years 1920-44 in 1950; occasionally illus. Ncr 18

TIDSSKRIFT. For titles beginning with "Tidsskrift," followed by the name of the publishing or sponsoring institution or society, see the respective institution or society.

97. TIDSSKRIFT FOR DET NORSKE LANDBRUK [Review of Norwegian agriculture]. M. Selskapet for norges vel [Soc. for Norwegian Welfare], Rosenkrantzgt. 8, Oslo. Ncr 5

98. TIDSSKRIFT FOR RETTSVITENSKAP [Journal of jurisprudence]. 5 x y. H. Aschehoug and Co., Sehestads plass 3, Oslo. Cum. indices pub. every 10 years. Ncr 30

99. TIDSSKRIFT FOR TEOLOGI OG KIRKE [Journal of theology and the church]. Q. Lutherstiftelsen [Luther Foundation], Akersgt. 47, Oslo. Ncr 12

100. TOTN. Irr. Toten historielag [Toten Hist. Soc.], Steinberg, Bøverbru. Ncr 7

101. TRONDHJEMS SJØFARTSMUSEUM. ÅRSSKRIFT [Maritime Museum of **Trondheim. Yearbook]. Irr. Trondhjems sjøfartsmuseum, Trondheim.**

102. TRONDHJEMSKE SAMLINGER **[Trondheim collections].** Irr. Trondhjems historiske forening **[Trondheim Hist. Soc.], Trondheim.** Ncr 12.50

103. UNIVERSITETS OLDSAKSAMLING. ÅRBOK [University Museum of Antiquities. Yearbook]. S-A. 1927 (mri 1954/55 [1956]: no vol. indic.). Universitetets oldsaksamling, Frederiksgt. 2, Oslo. Ed: Bjørn Hougen. Art. on archaeological discoveries (pertaining to the prehist., ancient and medieval

periods) and excavations in progress in Scandinavia, and on archaeological techniques and acquisitions of the museum; rev. art.; bk. rev.; biblio. of bk. and periodicals; news and notes on the activities of the museum. Ncr 20 / $ 3

104. VALDRES HISTORIELAG, TIDSSKRIFT FOR... [Journal of the Valdres Historical Society]. A. Valdres historielag, Leira, Valdres. p (1) Ncr 5

105. VÅR HÆR [Our army]. M. Hærens fastlönte offiserers landsforening [Norwegian Regular Officers' National Assoc.], Kirkegt. 12, Oslo. Ncr 10

106. VÅR KIRKE I NORD [Our church in the North]. A. Hålogaland bispedømmeråd [Council of the Diocese of Hålogaland], Bøde. Ncr 3

107. VARDØHUS MUSEUM, ÅRBOK FOR... [Yearbook of the Vardøhus Museum]. A. (Irr.). Vardøhus museumsforening [Vardøhus Museum Soc.], Vardø. Ncr 3

108. VERDAL HISTORIELAG. ÅRBOK [Verdal Historical Society. Yearbook]. A. O. Suul, Søndregt. 5, Trondheim, for Verdal historielag, Trondheim. Ncr 5

109. VESTFOLDMINNE [Reminiscences of Vestfold]. A. Vestfold fylkesmuseum [Vestfold County Museum], Tønsberg. Ncr 12

110. VESTLANDSKE KUNSTINDUSTRIMUSEUM. ÅRBOK [Art Industry Museum of Western Norway. Yearbook]. A. Vestlandske kunstindustrimuseum, Bergen. Ncr 12.50

111. VIKING [Viking]. Tidsskrift for norrøn arkeologi [Review of Nordic archaeology]. A. 1937 (1957/58: vol. 21/22). Cammermeyers bokhandel, Oslo, for Norsk arkeologisk selskap [Norwegian Archaeological Soc.], Universitets Øldsaksamling, Frederiksgt. 2, Oslo. Ed: Bjørn Hougen. Art. on Nordic archaeology; A. biblio. of Scandinavian archaeology, arranged by author; English or French sum.; statistics; graph; illus. Ncr 25 / $3.50

112. VINDUET [Window]. Gyldendals tidsskrift for litteratur [Gyldendal journal of literature]. Q. Gyldendal norsk forlag, Oslo. Ncr 16

113. VOLDA SOGELAG, ÅRSSKRIFT FOR... [Yearbook of the Volda Historical Society]. A. (Irr.). Volda sogelag, Volda. Ncr 3

114. VOLUND. A. Norsk teknisk museum [Norwegian Museum of Technology], Vikingeskiphuset, Bygdøy, Oslo. Ncr 10

115. VOSSABYGDENE [Concerning Voss district]. Irr. Voss sogelag [Voss Hist. Soc.], Voss. Ncr 3.50

Poland

Prepared with the assistance of

Instytut Historii, Polska Akademia Nauk [Historical Institute, Polish Academy of Sciences], Cracow

1. ACTA POLONIAE HISTORICA. A. (1960: vol. 3). Instytut Historii, Polska Akademia Nauk [Hist. Inst., Polish Acad. of Sciences], Rynek Starego Miasta 31, Warszawa. Ed: Marian Małowist. Art. on Polish hist. and on subjects of interest to Polish and foreign historians; bk. rev.; chronicle of academic activities in Poland; in French, German or English. zł 57

• ANNALES D'HISTOIRE DU DROIT see CZASOPISMO PRAWNO-HISTORYCZNE

ANNALES D'HISTOIRE SOCIALE ET ECONOMIQUE see ROCZNIKI DZIEJÓW SPOŁECZNYCH I GOSPODARCZYCH

2. ARCHEION. Czasopismo naukowe poświęcone sprawom archiwalnym [Periodical devoted to archival questions]. A. 1928 (1960: vol. 33). Państwowe Wydawnictwo Naukowe, Warszawa, for Naczelna Dyrekcja Archiwów Państwowych, Miodova 8-10, Warszawa. Ed: Piotr Bańkowski. Art. on the hist. and holdings of Polish and foreign (mostly East European) archives and on archival science; news on Polish archives; reports on conferences and research; bk. rev.; rev. of foreign archival periodicals, with indications of contents; Russian, English and French sum. pv (vol. 27: zł 66; vol. 28: zł 53)

3. ARCHEOLOGIA. A. 1947 (1959: vol. 4). Instytut Historii Kultury Materialnej, Polska Akademia Nauk [Inst. of the Hist. of Material Culture of the Polish Acad. of Sciences], Warszawa. Ed: Kazimierz Majewski, Ordynacka 15, Warszawa. Art. on problems of the archaeology of the ancient world; rev. of archaeological holdings in the Polish collections; notices of bk. and periodicals; biblio.; professional news from Poland and abroad; Russian, English and French sum. pv (vol. 8: zł 95)

4. ARCHIWALNY BIULETYN INFORMACYJNY [Archival information bulletin]. Q. Naczelna Dyrekcja Archiwów Państwowych, ul. Wilcza 9a, Warszawa. In two series: 1) general remarks on the holdings of Polish district archives; 2) index of researchers and researches at Polish archives. zł 10

5. BIBLIOTEKA KÓRNICKA, PAMIĘTNIK... (Pamiętnik Biblioteki Kórnickiej) [Review of the Kórnik Library]. Irr. 1929 (1959: vol. 7). Biblioteka Kórnicka, Polska Akademia Nauk [Kórnik Library, Polish Acad. of Sciences], Kórnik. Ed: Stanisława Jasińska. Art. based on the archival collections of the library; doc.; news of the library; illus. p (1) zł 70

6. BIBLIOTEKA POLSKIEJ AKADEMII NAUK W KRAKOWIE, ROCZNIK... (Rocznik Biblioteki Polskiej Akademii Nauk w Krakowie) [Yearbook of the Library of the Polish Academy of Sciences at Cracow]. A. 1955 (1955 [1957]: vol. 1). Biblioteka Polskiej Akademii Nauk, Kraków. Ed: Jan Dąbrowski, Sławkowska 17, Kraków. Art. based on the collection of manuscripts in the library; descriptions of doc. zł 60

BIULETYN. For titles beginning with "Biuletyn," followed by the name of the publishing or sponsoring institution or society, see the respective institution or society.

7. BLETER FAR GESZICHTE [Historical papers]. Q. 1948 (1960: vol. 13). Żydowski Instytut Historyczny [Jewish Hist. Inst.], Al. Gen. K. Swierczewskiego 79 (Tłomackie 5), Warszawa. Ed: B. Mark. Art. on the modern hist. of the Jews, with emphasis on Eastern Europe; doc.; rev. art.; rev. of bk. and periodicals; lists of bk. and periodicals received; in Yiddish. p (1) zł 20

8. CZASOPISMO PRAWNO-HISTORYCZNE [Review of the history of law]. ANNALES D'HISTOIRE DU DROIT [Annals of the history of law]. A. 1948 (1960: vol. 12). Instytut Nauk Prawnych, Polska Akademie Nauk [Inst. of the Science of Law, Polish Acad. of Sciences], Warszawa. Ed: Michał Sczaniecki, Gwardii Ludowej 11 m. 10a, Poznań. Art. on the hist. of law, mainly in Poland; doc.; rev. art. and notices; discussions; professional news; biblio. of Polish pub. on historical-legal questions; French sum. zł 75

9. EKONOMISTA [The economist]. Czasopismo poświęcone nauce i potrzebom życia [A periodical devoted to science and the necessities of life]. B-M. 1901 (1960: vol. 60). Państwowe Wydawnictwo Naukowe, Miodowa 10, Warszawa, for Komitet Nauk Ekonomicznych Polskiej Akademii Nauk [Committee of Economic Sciences of the Polish Acad. of Sciences] and Polskie Towarzystwo Ekonomiczne [Polish Economic Soc.], Warszawa. Ed: Edward Lipiński (chief ed.), B. Minc (ed.), M. Pohorille (ed.), A. Łukaszewicz (secretary), Nowy Świat 49, Warszawa. Art. on economics and on economic hist.; bk. rev.; notes and comments; biblio. notes; Russian and English sum. zł 120

10. ETNOGRAFIA POLSKA [Polish ethnography]. A. 1958 (1959: vol. 2). Instytut Historii Kultury Materialnej Polska Akademia Nauk [Inst. for the Hist. of Material Culture, Polish Acad. of Sciences], ul. Nowy Świat 72, Warszawa. Ed: Witold Dynowski. Art. on Polish ethnography (including its methodology and hist.) and cultural hist.; research reports on ethnographic field studies, arranged by Polish areas; reports on conferences and congresses; index of names; Russian and English sum. p (1) zł 55

11. FILOMATA [Philomath]. 10 x y. Ed: Z. Gansiniec, Al. Słowackiego 56 m. 11, Kraków. Continuation of Filomata, pub. in Lwów during the interwar period. $ 2. 50

12. FONTES ARCHAEOLOGICI POZNANIENSES. A. 1950 (1959: vol. 10). Muzeum Archeologiczne [Museum of Archaeology], Lampego 27/28, Poznań. Ed: Józef Kostrzewski. Art. on archaeology; reports on excavations; French sum.; illus. Former title: Fontes Praehistorici. zł 160

FONTES PRAEHISTORICI see FONTES ARCHAEOLOGICI POZNANIENSES

HISTORIA I NAUKA O KONSTYTUCJI see WIADOMOŚCI HISTORYCZNE

13. KATOLICKIEGO UNIWERSYTETU LUBELSKIEGO, ZESZYTY NAUKOWE... (Zeszyty Naukowe Katolickiego Uniwersytetu Lubelskiego) [Scientific papers of the Lublin Catholic University]. Q. Towarzystwo Naukowe Katolickiego Uniwersytetu Lubelskiego [Scientific Soc. of the Lublin Catholic Univ.], Al. Racławickie 14, Lublin. English and French sum. zł 180/ $ 8

KOMUNIKATY DZIAŁU INFORMACJI NAUKOWEJ INSTYTUTU MAZURSKIEGO W OLSZTYNIE see KOMUNIKATY MAZURSKO-WARMINSKIE

14. KOMUNIKATY MAZURSKO-WARMIŃSKIE [Masurian and Warmian reports]. Q. 1957 (1958: vol. 2). Stacja Naukowa Polskiego Towarzystwa Historycznego [Scientific Station of the Polish Hist. Soc.], Stare Miasto 33, Olsztyn. Art. and source materials on the hist. of Warmia and Masuria; rev. of Polish and foreign pub. dealing with regional themes; scientific chronicle of Olsztyn; reports of the Polish Hist. Soc.; biblio. of pub. on Warmia and Masuria. Supersedes Komunikaty Działu Informacji Naukowej Instytutu Mazurskiego w Olsztynie [Reports of the Scientific Information Department of the Masurian Inst. at Olsztyn].
p (1) zł 10

15. KRONIKA MIASTA POZNANIA [Chronicle of the Town of Poznań]. Kwartalnik poświęcony problematyce współczesnego Poznania [A quarterly devoted to the problems of contemporary Poznań]. Q. Prezydium Rady Narodowej Miasta Poznania [Presiding Committee of the National Council of the Town of Poznań], Nowy Ratusz, Poznań. zł 60/ $ 2.50

16. KULTURA I SPOŁECZEŃSTWO [Culture and society]. Q. 1957 (1960: vol. 4). Państwowe Wydawnictwo Naukowe, Miodowa 10, Warszawa, for Zakład Socjologii i Historii Kultury, Polska Akademia Nauk [Dept. of Sociology and Hist. of Culture], Pałac Staszica, Nowy Świat 72, Warszawa. Ed: Jósef Chałasinski, H. Jarnuszkiewicz (secretary), Łódz Uniwersytet, ul. Narutowicza 59a, Łódz. Art. on sociology and social and cultural hist.; bk. rev.; academic news from home and abroad. zł 80

17. KWARTALNIK HISTORII KULTURY MATERIALNEJ [Quarterly of the history of material culture]. Q. 1953 (1960: vol. 8). Państwowe Wydawnictwo Naukowe, Miodowa 10, Warszawa, for Instytut Historii Kultury Materialnej, Polska Akademia Nauk [Inst. for the Hist. of Material Culture, Polish Acad. of Sciences], ul. Nowy Świat 72, Warszawa. Ed: Aleksander Gieysztor (chief ed.), J. Leskiewiczowa (ed.), K. Majewski (ed.), J. Sztetyłło (secretary), Rynek Starego Miasta 31, Warszawa. Art. on Polish economic, social and cultural hist., with emphasis on mining, metallurgy, production techniques used in crafts and building and on the hist. of agriculture, settlement and transport; reports on archaeological field work; discussions; rev. of bk. and periodicals; professional news from home and abroad; English, French or Russian sum.; supplements; illus. p (1) zł 35

18. KWARTALNIK HISTORII NAUKI I TECHNIKI [Quarterly of the history of science and technology]. Q. 1956 (1960: vol. 5). Komitet Historii Nauki, Polska Akademia Nauk [Committee for the Hist. of Sciences, Polish Acad. of Sciences], Pałac Kultury i Nauki, Warszawa. Ed: Bogdan Suchodolski (chief ed.), E. Olszewski (ed.), Freta 16, Warszawa. Art. on the hist. of science, scientific soc. and centers of higher education, dealing with the general problems of the hist. of science as well as its special disciplines, technical, biological, medical, mathematical-physical and social sciences; professional news; reports on the activities of the committee; Russian and English sum. p (1) zł 30

19. KWARTALNIK HISTORYCZNY [Historical quarterly]. Q. 1887 (1960: vol. 67). Instytut Historii, Polska Akademia Nauk [Inst. of Hist., Polish Acad. of Sciences], Rynek Starego Miasta, 29/31, Warszawa. Ed: Bogusław Leśnodorski. Art. on Polish and world hist.; doc.; bk. rev.; academic news from home and abroad; biblio. of art. on Poland pub. abroad during the preceding year, with short indications of contents; table of contents and sum. in Russian and French.
zł 120 / $ 7.50

20. LUD [The folk]. A. 1895 (1956[1958]: vol. 43). Polskie Towarzystwo Ludoznawcze [Polish Soc. of Ethnology], Wrocław. Ed: Józef Gajek, ul. Nankera 4, Wrocław. Art. on ethnography; rev. of the ethnographic sections of the Polish museums; professional news; biblio. of Polish ethnographic pub. zł 75

21. MAŁOPOLSKIE STUDIA HISTORYCZNE [Historical studies on Little Poland]. Q. 1958 (1958: vol. 1). Polskie Towarzystwo Historyczne [Polish Hist. Soc.], Kielce, Kraków, Nowy Sącz, Przemyśl, Rzeszów and Sandomierz. Ed: Zofia Budkowa, Straszewskiego 27, Kraków. Art. on the political, economic and cultural hist. of hist. Little Poland; doc. materials; rev. and reports on pub. dealing with the region; professional news, mainly concerning regional research. p (1) zł 30

22. MATERIAŁY WCZESNOŚREDNIOWIECZNE [Materials for the history of the early Middle Ages]. Irr. 1949 [1951](mri 1956: vol. 4). Państwowe Muzeum Archeologiczne [State Museum of Archaeology], Warszawa. Ed: Zdzisław Rajewski, Jerzy Antoniewicz, Jerzy Halicki, Długa 52, Arsenał, Warszawa. Art. and reports on excavations dealing with the early Middle Ages in different parts of Poland; Russian and English sum.; illus. zł 40.30

23. MEANDER [Meander]. M. Polish Philogical Soc., Krakowskie Przedmieście 26/28, Warszawa. Includes art. on the culture of the antique world, hist. (including hist. of the arts), archaeology and papyrology; translations from antique literature; Latin sum. $ 6

24. MÓWIĄ WIEKI [The centuries speak]. Magazyn Historyczny [Historical magazine]. M. 1958 (1960: vol. 3). Państwowe Zakłady Wydawnictw Szkolnych, Warszawa, in co-operation with Polskie Towarszystwo Historyczne [Polish Hist. Soc.], Warszawa. Ed: Maria Bogucka, Plac Dąbrowskiego 8, Warszawa. Art. of popular interest on the hist. of Poland and other countries; excerpts from hist. doc.; biographical sketches of hist. personalities; bk. rev.; "Calendarum": chronology of events of a given period. p (1) zł 4

25. NASZA PRZESZŁOŚĆ. NOTRE PASSE [Our past]. Studia z dziejów Kościoła i kultury katolickiej w Polsce. Etudes sur l'Histoire de l'Eglise et de la Culture Catholique en Pologne [Studies on the history of the Church and Catholic culture in Poland]. A. 1946 (1960: vol. 11). Instytut Teologiczny Księży Misjonarzy [Theological Inst. of the Missionaries], Kraków. Ed: Alfons Schletz, C.M., Stradom 4, Kraków. Art. on Polish religious hist.; doc.; rev. of bk. and art.; news on Catholic life in Poland; table of contents also in French; illus. pv (zł 50-100)

26. NAUKA POLSKA [Polish science]. Czasopismo poświęcone zagadnieniom rozwoju nauki w Polsce [A periodical devoted to the problems of the development of science in Poland]. Q. 1953 (1960: vol. 8). Państwowe Wydawnictwo Naukowe, Miodowa 10, Warszawa, for Polska Akademia Nauk [Polish Acad. of Sciences], Warszawa. Ed: Janusz Lech Jakubowski, Pałac Kultury i Nauki, Warszawa. Art. on the development and hist. of the natural sciences and humanities in Poland; biographies of memb. of the acad.; research reports and professional news; Russian and English sum. p (1) zł 20

NOTRE PASSE see NASZA PRZESZŁOŚĆ

NOVA POLONIA SACRA see POLONIA SACRA

27. NOWE DROGI [New ways]. Organ teoretyczny i polityczny Komitetu Centralnego Polskiej Zjednoczonej Partii Robotniczej [Theoretical and political organ of the Central Committee of the Polish United Workers' Party]. M. 1947 (1958: vol. 12). Komitet Centralnego Polskiej Zjednoczonej Partii Robotniczej, Górnośląska 18, Warszawa. Art. on Polish social, political and economic life, mostly on current affairs but sometimes of hist. interest, and on the hist. of labor movements and the Communist Party; rev. art.; rev. of Socialist and Marxist pub. zł 72 / $ 5.36

28. ODRODZENIE I REFORMACJA W POLSCE [Renaissance and Reformation in Poland]. A. 1956 (1959: vol. 4). Instytut Historii, Polska Akademia Nauk [Hist. Inst. of the Polish Acad. of Sciences], Warszawa. Ed: Kazimierz Lepsy, Sławkowska 17, Kraków. Art. on the intellectual, cultural and general hist. aspects of the Polish Renaissance, on its social and economic basis, and on the Reformation and its relation to other movements in the Renaissance; doc.; bk. rev. and notices; professional news; biblio.; English, Russian and French sum. zł 60

PAMIĘTNIK. For titles beginning with "Pamiętnik," followed by the name of the publishing or sponsoring institution or society, see the respective institution or society.

29. PAMIĘTNIK LITERACKI [Literary review]. Czasopismo kwartalne poświęcone historii i krytyce literatury polskiej [Quarterly devoted to the history and critical studies of Polish literature]. Q. 1902 (1960: vol. 51). Zakład Narodowy im. Ossolińskich, Warszawa-Wrocław, for Instytut Badań Literackich, Polska Akademia Nauk [Inst. of Literary Research, Polish Acad. of Sciences], Nowy Świat 72, Warszawa. Well-documented art. on the hist. of Polish literature, literary criticism and the arts; bk. rev.; survey of scientific pub.; news of the pub. soc. zł 120

30. PAŃSTWO I PRAWO [State and law]. M. Instytut Nauk Prawnych, Polska Akademia Nauk [Inst. of Legal Science, Polish Acad. of Sciences], ul. Wiejka 12, Warszawa. English, French and Russian sum., printed separately. zł 120

31. POLISH PERSPECTIVES. M. Pałac Kultury i Nauki [Palace of Culture and Science], 17th floor, Warszawa. In English. 24s

32. POLONIA SACRA. Kwartalnik Kanonistyczno-Historyczny. [Quarterly for the history of canon law]. Q. 1948 (1958: vol. 10). Akademia Teologii Katolickiej [Acad. of Catholic Theology], Warszawa. Ed: Marian Myrcha, ul. Gwiazdzista 81, Bielany, Warszawa. Doc. concerning the hist. of the Catholic Church; art. on canon law; bk. rev.. Continuation of Nova Polonia Sacra, founded in 1928. p (1) zł 20

33. PRZEGLĄD ARCHEOLOGICZNY [Archaeological review]. Czasopismo poświęcone Archeologii [A journal devoted to archaeology]. Revue Archéologique Polonaise [Polish archaeoligcal review]. A. 1919 (1954-56 [1958]: vol. 10). Zakład Narodowy im. Ossolińskich, Wrocław, for Polskie Towarzystwo Archeologiczne [Polish Archaeological Soc.], Jezuicka 6, Warszawa. Ed: Jósef Kostrzewski, Biskupińska 1, Poznań 15. Art. on archaeology and excavations relating to Poland and Slavic countries; bk. rev.; French sum.; illus. zł 110 / $ 5

34. PRZEGLĄD BIBLIOTECZNY [Library review]. Q. 1927 (1960: vol. 28). Stowarzyszenie Bibliotekarzy Polskich [Assoc. of Polish Librarians], Warszawa. Ed: Bogdan Horodyski, Biblioteka Narodowa, Rakowiecka 6, Warszawa.

Art. on library science and the hist. of bk.; rev. and reports on Polish and foreign pub.; reports on the activities of scientific libraries. p (1) zł 12

35. PRZEGLĄD GEOGRAFICYNY [Geographical review]. Q. Geographical Inst. of the Polska Akademia Nauk [Polish Acad. of Sciences], Krakowskie Przedmieście 30, pok. 123, Warszawa. Includes art. on the hist. of geography; in Polish, English, French or German; English, French and Russian sum. $ 5

36. PRZEGLĄD HISTORYCZNY [Historical review]. Q. 1905 (1960: vol. 51). Towarzystwo Miłośników Historii [Soc. of the Friends of Hist.], Warszawa. Ed: Stefan Kieniewicz (chief ed.), I. Bieżuńska-Matowist (ed.), A. Mączak (secretary), Instytut Historyczny, Krakowskie Przedmieście 26/28, Warszawa. Art. on political, social and economic hist., mostly of Poland; doc.; bk. rev.; professional news of the soc.; Russian and French sum. p (1) zł 25

37. PRZEGLĄD NAUK HISTORYCZNYCH I SPOŁECZNYCH [Review of historical and social sciences]. A. 1950 (1956 [1958]: vol. 7). Łódzkie Towarzystwo Naukowe [Scientific Soc. of Łódź], Sienkiewicza 29, Łódź. Ed: Józef Chałasiński, Natalia Gąsiorowska, Marian Serejski, Uniwersytecka 3/IV p, Łódź. Art. mainly on Polish hist. during the 19th and 20th cent., with emphasis on social problems; professional news; bk. rev. zł 80

38. PRZEGLĄD ORIENTALISTYCZNY [Review of Orientalia]. Q. 1948 (1960: no. 29-32). Państwowe Wydawnictwo Naukowe, ul. Miodowa 10, Warszawa, for Polskie Towarzystwo Orientalistyczne [Polish Oriental Soc.]. Ed: Jan Reychman, ul. Freta 16, Warszawa. Art. on Orientalia (hist., culture, literature and the arts); translations; rev. of bk. and art.; professional news; table of contents also in Russian and French; illus. p (1) zł 20

39. PRZEGLĄD SOCJOLOGICZNY. SOTSIOLOGICHESKII ZHURNAL. SOCIOLOGICAL REVIEW. A. 1930/31 (1959: vol. 13). Zakład Narodowy im. Ossolińskich, Wrocław, for Łódzkie Towarzystwo Naukowe [Scientific Soc. of Łódź], Łódź. Ed: Józef Chałasiński, Uniwersytecka 3, Łódź. Art. on sociology, the hist. of social thought and social hist.; professional news from Poland and other countries; bk. rev. and survey of periodicals; English sum. zł 60

40. PRZEGLĄD ZACHODNI [Western review]. B-M. 1945 (1960: vol. 16). Instytut Zachodni [Western Inst.], ul. Chełmońskiego 1, Poznań. Ed: K. Piwarski. Art. on the hist. of the Polish Western territories, Poland's relations with Germany, and on German affairs; doc.; professional news and reports; biblio. on "Germany under Imperialism," with emphasis on the period since World War I, consisting of short rev. of bk. and art.; letters to the ed.; English table of contents and sum., printed separately. zł 150 / zł 210

ROCZNIK. For titles beginning with "Rocznik," followed by the name of the publishing or sponsoring institution or society, see the respective institution or society

41. ROCZNIK GDAŃSKI [Yearbook of Gdańsk]. A. Gdańskie Towarzystwo Naukowe [Scientific Soc. of Gdańsk], Gdańsk. English and French sum. zł 90

42. ROCZNIK KRAKOWSKI [Yearbook of Kraków]. Irr. Towarzystwo Miłośników Historii Zabytków Krakowa [Soc. of the Friends of the Hist. and Monuments of Cracow], Kraków. pv

43. ROCZNIK ORIENTALISTYCZNY [Yearbook of Orientalia]. S-A. Państwowe Wydawnictwo Naukowe, Warszawa, for Komitet Orientalistyczny, Polska Akademia Nauk [Committee for Orientalia, Polish Acad. of Sciences], ul. Freta 16, Warszawa. pv (vol. 22, no. 1: zł 36; no. 2: zł 34)

44. ROCZNIK WROCŁAWSKI [Yearbook of Wrocław]. A. Towarzystwo Miłośników Wrocławia [Soc. of the Friends of Wrocław], Wrocław. zł 30

45. ROCZNIKI DZIEJÓW SPOŁECZNYCH I GOSPODARCZYCH. ANNALES D'HISTOIRE SOCIALE ET ECONOMIQUE [Yearbook of social and economic history]. A. 1931 (1959 [1960]: vol. 21). Państwowe Wydawnictwo Naukowe, Poznań for Poznańskie Towarzystwo Przyjaciół Nauk, Wydział Historii i Nauk Społecznych [Poznań Soc. of the Friends of Sciences, Section for Hist. and Social Sciences] ul. A. Lampego 27/29, Poznań. Ed: Władysław Rusiński, Czerwonej Armii 90, Poznań. Art. on Polish economic and social hist.; extensive section on rev. of bk. and art.; biblio. of social and economic hist., mostly of Europe, grouped by subject; French and Russian sum. pv (vol. 17: zł 35.45; vol. 18: zł 100)

46. ROCZNIKI HISTORYCZNE [Historical yearbooks]. A. 1925 (1959: vol. 25). Poznańskie Towarzystwo Przyjaciół Nauk, Wydział Historii i Nauk Społecznych [Poznań Soc. of the Friends of Sciences, Section for Hist. and Social Sciences] Ed: Kazimierz Tymieniecki, Gerard Labuda, Lampego 27/29, Poznań. Art. on the hist. of Great Poland and the West Slavic countries; bk. rev.; French sum. zł 99

47. ROCZNIKI HUMANISTYCZNE [Yearbooks of the humanities]. Irr. Towarzystwo Naukowe Katolickiego Uniwersytetu Lubelskiego [Scientific Soc. of the Catholic Univ. of Lublin], Lublin. Each no. devoted to different humanistic disciplines. pv

48. ŚLĄSKI KWARTALNIK HISTORYCZNY SOBÓTKA [Silesian historical quarterly "Bonfire"]. Q. 1946 (1960: vol. 15). Zakład Narodowy im. Ossolińskich, Wrocław, for Wrocławskie Towarzystwo Miłośników Historii [Wrocław Soc. of the Friends of Hist.], Wrocław. Ed: Józef Gierowski, Ewa Maleczyńska, Szewska 49, Wrocław. Art. on Silesian hist., mostly modern; doc.; descriptions of holdings of archives; rev. of bk. and art.; professional news; A. classified biblio. of bk. and art. on Silesia; German sum. Before 1957 appeared under the title Sobótka [Bonfire]. zł 80 / $ 3.35

49. SLAVIA ANTIQUA. Rocznik poświęcony starożytnościom słowiańskim [Yearbook devoted to Slavic antiquities]. Irr. 1948 (1957-59: vol. 6). Zakład im. Ossolińskich, Wrocław, for Katedra Archeologii Polskie Uniwersytetu im. Adama Mickiewicznaw Poznaniu [Dept. of Polish Archaeology at the Adam Mickiewicz Univ. at Poznań], ul. Czerwonej Armii 90, Poznań. Ed: Witold Hensel, Traugutta 28m. 5, Poznań. Art. on ancient and medieval Slavicism; professional news on Slavistic studies abroad; art. in the authors' languages; French sum. pv (vol. 5: zł 72.50)

50. SLAVIA ORIENTALIS. Q. 1958 (1960: vol. 9). Neo-Philological Committee of the Polska Akademia Nauk [Polish Acad. of Sciences], Foksal 10, Warszawa. Ed: Samuel Fiszman. Art., papers, texts of archival doc., rev. and scientific reports devoted to the hist. of literature, languages and culture of the Western Slavs of the Soviet Union; Russian sum. zł 120 / $ 4

SOBÓTKA see ŚLĄSKI KWARTALNIK HISTORYCZNY SOBÓTKA

SOCIOLOGICAL REVIEW see PRZEGLĄD SOCJOLOGICZNY

SOTSIOLOGICHESKII ZHURNAL see PRZEGLĄD SOCJOLOGICZNY

51. STUDIA FILOZOFICZNE [Philosophical studies]. B-M. Inst. of Philosophy and Sociology of the Polska Akademia Nauk [Polish Acad. of Sciences], Nowy Świat 49, Warszawa. Table of contents also in Russian and English. $ 6

52. STUDIA I MATERIAŁY DO DZIEJÓW WIELKOPOLSKI I POMORZA [Studies and materials on the history of Great Poland and Pomerania]. S-A. Polskie Towarzystwo Historyczne [Polish Hist. Soc.], Poznań. Ed: Zdzisław Kaczmarczyk, ul. Chełmońskiego 1 m. 9, Poznań. Art. on the hist. of Great Poland and Pomerania; doc.; bk. rev.; biblio. notes; professional news; German sum. p (1) zł 106.50

STUDIA MEDII AEVI see STUDIA WCZESNOŚREDNIOWIECZNE

53. STUDIA WCZESNOŚREDNIOWIECZNE [Studies on the early Middle Ages]. STUDIA MEDII AEVI. Irr. 1952 (1958: vol. 4). Instytut Historii Kultury Materialnej Polskiej Akademii Nauk [Inst. of the Hist. of Material Culture of the Polish Acad. of Sciences], Nowy Świat 70/72, Warszawa. Ed: Aleksander Gieysztor, Rynek Starego Miasta 31, Warszawa. Studies, doc. and reports on the hist. of the early Middle Ages in Poland, with emphasis on the origin of the Polish state; research reports, also on archaeology; English or Russian sum.; illus.; graph. pv (zł 55-80)

54. STUDIA ŹRÓDŁOZNAWCZE [Studies on the science of sources]. Irr. 1957 (1959: vol. 4). Instytut Historii, Polska Akademia Nauk [Inst. of Hist. of the Polish Acad. of Sciences], Warszawa. Ed: A. Gieysztor, G. Labuda, B. Kürbisówna, ul. Czerwonej Armii 90, or ul. Wilcza 8 m. 20, Warszawa. Art. on the auxiliary disciplines of hist. and the science of sources, with emphasis on Poland and the Middle Ages; rev. art.; Russian and French sum.; illus. p (1) zł 107

55. TEKI ARCHIWALNE [Archival portfolios]. Irr. 1953 (1959: vol. 6). Naczelna Dyrekcja Archiwów Państwowych [General Office of the State Archives], Wilcza 9a, Warszawa. Ed: Adam Stebelski. List of pub. source materials on Polish hist. pv

56. UNIVERSITAS MARIAE CURIE SKŁODOWSKA, ANNALES... (Annales Universitatis Mariae Curie Skłodowska). Sectio F. Nauki Filozoficzne i humanistyczne [Section on philosophical sciences and humanities]. Irr. 1946 (1956 [1960]: vol. 11). Uniwersytet im. Curie-Skłodowskiej [Curie-Skłodowska Univ.], pl. Litewski 5, Lublin. Ed: Grzegorz L. Seidler. Art. on the prehist. and hist. of Poland as well as on universal hist.; academic news; Russian and German sum. pni

57. WIADOMOŚCI ARCHEOLOGICZNE [Archaeological news]. Bulletin Archéologique Polonais [Polish archaeological bulletin]. A. 1873 (1959: vol. 26). Państwowe Muzeum Archeologiczne [State Museum of Archaeology], Warszawa. Ed: Zdzisław Rajewski, Długa 52, Arsenał, Warszawa. Art. on archaeology; reports on excavations and research in different parts of Poland; professional news; English and Russian sum. Former sub-title: Spostrzeżenia lat ostatnich w dziedzinie starożytności krajowych. Czasy Przedhistoryczne [Observations from recent years in the field of native antiquities. Prehistoric times]. zł 60

58. WIADOMOŚCI HISTORYCZNE [Historical news]. B-M. 1958 (1960: vol. 3). Państwowe Zakłady Wydawnictw Szkolnych, Plac Dąbrowskiego 8, Warszawa, for Ministerstwo Oświaty [Ministry of Education], Warszawa. Ed: Józef Garbacik, Wyższa Szkoła Pedagogiczna, ul. Straszewskiego 22, Kraków. Art. on hist., with emphasis on Poland, and on problems relating to the teaching of hist. in schools; rev. of bk. and periodicals; biblio.; professional news; letters to the ed. Supersedes Historia i Nauka o Konstytucji [History and knowledge about the constitution]. zł 4

59. WIADOMOŚCI NUMIZMATICZNE [Numismatic news]. Q. 1957 (1959: vol. 3). Polskie Towarzystwo Archeologiczne [Polish Archaeological Soc.], Jezuicka 6, Warszawa. Ed: Ryszard Kiersnowski. Art. on Polish numismatic finds and new coins and medals; rev. of bk. and periodicals; professional news and notes; English sum.; illus. zł 48 / $ 3.20

60. WOJSKOWY PRZEGLĄD HISTORYCZNY [Military historical review]. Q. 1956 (1960: vol. 5). Ed: Jerzy Bordziłowski, Rakowiecka 4, Warszawa. Art. on the hist. of military art and war operations; rev. of doc. and bk.; professional news; maps and charts. p (1) zł 25

61. Z OTCHŁANI WIEKÓW [From past centuries]. Dwumiesięcznik popularnonaukowy Polskiego Towarzystwa Archeologicznego. Scientific and Popular Review of the Polish Archaeological Society Published Every Other Month. B-M. 1926 (1960: vol. 26). Zakład Narodowy im. Ossolińskich, Rynek 9, Wrocław, for Polskie Towarzystwo Archeologiczne [Polish Archaeological Soc.], ul. Jezuick 6, Warszawa. Ed: Bogdan Kostrzewski, Lampego 27/29, Poznań. Art. on archaeology, mostly of Poland; reports on archaeological research and discoverie professional news of the soc., and from Poland and abroad; rev. of bk. and art.; English sum.; illus. zł 48 / $ 4.50

62. Z POLA WALKI [From the battlefield]. Kwartalnik poświęcony dziejom ruchu robotniczego [A quarterly devoted to the history of the workers' movement]. Q. 1958 (1960: no. 3 [11]). Książka i Wiedza, ul. Smolna 13, Warszawa, for Dept. of the Hist. of the Party, Central Committee of the Polish United Workers' Party, Warszawa. Ed: Feliks Tych, ul. Nowy Świat 6/12, Warszawa. Art. and source material on the hist. of the workers' movement till 1945, with emphasis on Poland; doc. and records; biographies and biblio. of leading party memb.; rev. art. and bk. rev.; professional news; table of contents also in Russian, French and English. zł 80 / $ 4

63. ZAPISKI HISTORYCZNE [Historical notes]. Kwartalnik poświęcony historii Pomorza [A quarterly devoted to the history of Pomerania]. Q. Section for Hist., Legal and Social Sciences of the Towarzystwo Naukowe w Toruniu [Scientific Soc. at Toruń], Toruń. Russian and English sum. Formerly pub. unde the title: Zapiski Towarzystwa Naukoweg w Toruniu [Notes of the Scientific Soc. at Toruń]. p (1) zł 78

ZAPISKI TOWARZYSTWA NAUKOWEG W TORUNIU see ZAPISKI HISTORYCZNE

ZESZYTY. For titles beginning with "Zeszyty," followed by the name of the publishing or sponsoring institution or society, see the respective institution or society

64. ŻYDOWSKI INSTYTUT HISTORYCZNY, BIULETYN... (Biuletyn Żydowskiego Instytutu Historycznego) [Bulletin of the Jewish Historical Institute].

Q. 1949 (1960: no. 33). Państwowe Wydaniwctwo Naukowe, Krakowskie Przedmieście 79, Warszawa, for Zydowski Instytut Historyczny, Al. Gen. Swierczewskiego 79 (Tłomackie 5), Warszawa. Ed. board: B. Mark (chief ed.), T. Berenstein, A. Eisenbach, A. Rutkowski (secretary). Art. on the hist. (mostly modern) of the Jews in Poland and on the hist. of Jews in general, with emphasis on social and economic problems; doc. on the extermination of the Jews during the Second World War; rev. of bk. and art.; English sum. p (1) zł 25 / $ 4

Portugal

Prepared with the assistance of the
Academia Portuguesa da História, Lisbon

1. ACADEMIA DAS CIÊNCIAS DE LISBOA, BOLETIM DA... [Bulletin of the Lisbon Academy of Sciences]. Irr. Academia das Ciências de Lisboa, Rua da Academia das Ciências, Lisboa 2. pv

2. ACADEMIA DAS CIÊNCIAS DE LISBOA, CLASSE DE LETRAS, MEMORIAS DA... [Records of the Lisbon Academy of Sciences, Section of Letters]. Irr. Academia das Ciências de Lisboa, Rua da Academia das Ciências, Lisboa 2 pv

3. ACADEMIA PORTUGUESA DA HISTORIA, ANAIS DA... [Annals of the Portuguese Academy of History]. Irr. 1st series: 1940 (1954: vol. 12); 2nd serie 1946 (1959: vol. 9). Academia Portuguesa da História, Rua da Escola Politécnica nº. 167-1º., Lisboa 2. Art. on the hist. and archaeology of Portugal, dealing with all periods. pv

4. AÇOREANA [Native of the Azores]. Revista de estudos Açoreanos [Review of studies on the Azores]. A. Sociedade Afonso Chaves, Ponta Delgada, S. Miguel, Açores. pni

ANAIS. For titles beginning with "Anais," followed by the name of the publishing or sponsoring institution or society, see the respective institution or society.

5. ANAIS DAS BIBLIOTECAS E ARQUIVOS [Annals of libraries and archives] Revista trimestral de bibliografia, biblioteconomia, bibliotecografia, arquivologia, etc. [Quarterly review of bibliography, library science, archival science, etc.]. Q. Inspecção das Bibliotecas e Arquivos, Ministério da Educação Nacional, Largo da Biblioteca Pública, Lisboa 2. Esc. 150 / $ 5.3(

6. ARQUEOLOGIA E HISTORIA [Archaeology and history]. A. 1865 (mri 1956: 8th series, vol. 7). Associação dos Arqueólogos Portugueses, Largo do Carmo, Lisboa 2. Art. on the archaeology and all periods of the hist. of Portugal, and of Portuguese overseas possessions, and occasionally on general hist. subjects. Esc. 60/Esc. 60

7. ARQUEOLOGO PORTUGUÊS [The Portuguese archaeologist]. Colecção ilustrada de materiais publicada pelo Museu Etnográfico Português [Illustrated collection of materials published by the Portuguese Ethnographic Museum]. 1895 (mri 1953: new series, vol. 2). Art. on Portuguese archaeology and on the work of the museum; indices.

8. ARQUIVO COMBRÃO [Coimbra archives]. A. Biblioteca Municipal de Coimbra, Coimbra. pni

9. ARQUIVO DE BEJA [Beja archives]. A. Câmara Municipal, Rua do Esquível, nº. 44A, Beja. pni

10. ARQUIVO DE BIBLIOGRAFIA PORTUGUESA [Archives of Portuguese bibliography]. Q. 1955 (1959: vol. 5). Atlântida Editora, Rua de Ferreira Borges, n°. 103-111, Coimbra. Ed: Manuel Lopes de Almeida. Art. on hist., with emphasis on the hist. of civilization, and on the sources for Portuguese hist., as well as on Portuguese libraries and archives; doc., biblio. of pub. on hist. in the archives and libraries of Portugal. Esc. 45

11. ARQUIVO DISTRITAL DE ANGRA DO HEROISMO, BOLETIM DO... [Bulletin of the District Archives of Angra do Heroismo]. Irr. Arquivo Distrital de Angra do Heroismo, Angra do Heroismo, Açores. pni

12. ARQUIVO DO ALTO MINHO [Alto Minho archives]. Repositório de estudos e documentos regionais [Repository of regional studies and documents]. A. Pub. address: Vila de Punhe, Minho II. Esc. 30/Esc. 30

13. ARQUIVO DO DISTRITO DE AVEIRO [Archives of the district of Aveiro]. Revista trimestral para publicação de documentos e estudos relativos ao distrito [Quarterly review for the publication of documents and studies concerning the district]. Q. Francisco Ferreira Neves, Estrada da Esgueira, Aveiro. Esc. 40

14. ARQUIVO HISTORICO DA MADEIRA [Madeira historical archives]. Q. Arquivo Distrital do Funchal, Funchal, ilha da Madeira. Illus. Esc. 25/Esc. 25

15. ARQUIVO HISTORICO DE GOIS [Gois historical archives]. Revista de história, etnografia e regionalismo do concelho de Gois [Review of the history, ethnography and folklore of the Gois region]. Irr. Ed: Mário Paredes Ramos, Rua do Conde de Tarouca, Torres Vedras. Esc. 50

16. ARQUIVO HISTORICO DE PORTUGAL [Historical archives of Portugal]. Q. 1932 (1958: 2nd series, vol. 1). Pub. and ed: António Machado de Faria, Avenida de João Crisóstomo, n°.51-r/c., Lisboa 1. Art. on the hist. of Portugal and Portuguese overseas territories and on genealogy and paleography; doc ; bk. rev.; biblio. of periodical literature concerned with Portuguese hist. ("Cultura Histórica Portuguesa: Artigos de Revistas Portuguesas"); indices of 1st series, vol. 1-5, pub. in 1st series, vol. 6. Esc. 200/$ 7

17. ARQUIVO HISTORICO MILITAR, BOLETIM DO... [Bulletin of the Archives of Military History]. A. 1930 (1958: no. 28). Arquivo Histórico Militar, Museu Militar, Largo do Museu de Artilharia, Lisboa 2. Catalogues of decrees of the former Conselho de Guerra; reports of the Comissão de Historia Militar and of the archives. Esc. 50/Esc.50

18. ATLANTIDA [Name of a legendary island in the Atlantic Ocean -- ed.]. Q. Seminário Episcopal, Angra do Heroismo, Ilha Terceira, Açores. Esc. 40/Esc. 50

19. BEIRA ALTA. Arquivo provincial. Revista trimestral para a publicação de documentos e estudos relativos às terras da Beira-Alta [Provincial archives. Quarterly review for the publication of documents and studies relating to the Beira Alta district]. Q. Junta de Província da Beira Alta, Viseu. Esc. 20/Esc. 20

20. BELAS ARTES [Fine arts]. Revista e boletim da Academia Nacional de Belas Artes [Review and bulletin of the National Academy of Fine Arts]. A.

Academia Nacional de Belas Artes, Largo da Biblioteca Pública, Lisboa 2. pv

21. BIBLIOTECA DA UNIVERSIDADE DE COIMBRA, BOLETIM DA... [Bulletin of the Coimbra University Library]. Irr. Biblioteca Geral Universidade de Coimbra, Coimbra. pni

22. BIBLOS. Irr. Biblioteca da Faculdade de Letras da Universidade de Coimbra, Coimbra. Esc. 60/Esc. 80

BOLETIM. For titles beginning with "Boletim," followed by the name of the publishing or sponsoring instiution or society, see the respective institution or society.

23. BOLETIM DE TRABALHOS HISTORICOS [Bulletin of historical papers]. A. Arquivo Municipal "Alfredo Pimenta," Guimarães. Esc. 10

24. BOLETIM GERAL DO ULTRAMAR [General overseas bulletin]. M. Agência Geral do Ultramar, Rua de S. Pedro de Alcântara, nº. 81, Lisboa 2. Esc. 72/Esc. 100

25. BRACARA AUGUSTA. Revista cultural da Câmara Municipal de Braga [Cultural review of the Municipal Council of Braga]. A. Câmara Municipal de Braga, Braga. pni

26. BRASILIA. Irr. Instituto de Estudos Brasileiros, Faculdade de Letras, Coimbra. pni

27. BROTERIA [The title is derived from the name of the Portuguese botanist Brotero, 1744-1828 -- ed.]. Revista contemporânea de cultura [Contemporary review of culture]. M. Ed: Gaspar Maria Leal Gomes Pereira Cabral, Caixa Postal, 2364, Lisboa 3. Esc. 100 / Esc. 120

28. BULLETIN DES ETUDES PORTUGAISES ET DE L'INSTITUT FRANÇAIS AU PORTUGAL [Bulletin of Portuguese studies and of the French Institute in Portugal]. 1930 (1958: vol. 21). Institut Français au Portugal, Rua de Santos o Velho 11, Lisboa 2. Art. on all periods of Portuguese hist., archaeology and literature and on the hist. of Portuguese-French relations; biblio. pni

29. CAMARA MUNICIPAL DO PORTO, BOLETIM CULTURAL DA... [Cultural bulletin of the Oporto Municipal Council]. A. Câmara Municipal do Porto, Gabinete de História da Cidade, Calçada de D. Pedro Pitões, Porto. Esc. 40/ Esc. 130

30. CENTRO DE ESTUDOS GEOGRAFICOS, BOLETIM DO... [Bulletin of the Center of Geographical Studies]. Irr. Centro de Estudos Geográficos, Faculdade de Letras, Coimbra. pni

31. A CIDADE DE EVORA [The city of Évora]. S-M. Comissão Municipal de Turismo, Câmara Municipal, Évora. Esc. 50/$ 2

32. CIDADE NOVA [New city]. B-M. Fernão Pacheco de Castro Bairro de S. José, nº. 22, Coimbra. Esc. 45/Esc. 60

33. COLOQUIO [Colloquium]. Revista de artes e letras [Review of arts and letters]. M. Fundação Calouste Gulbenkian, Avenida de Berne, Parque de Palhavã, Lisboa 1. Esc. 25/Esc. 30

34. COMISSÃO DE ARTE E ARQUEOLOGIA, BOLETIM DA... [Bulletin of the Commission of Art and Archaeology]. Irr. Câmara Municipal de Mafra, Mafra. pni

35. O CONCELHO DE SANTO TIRSO, BOLETIM CULTURAL [The municipality of Santo Tirso, Cultural bulletin]. Irr. Câmara Municipal, Santo Tirso. Esc. 15/Esc. 15

36. CONTRIBUIÇÕES PARA OS ESTUDO DA ANTROPOLOGIA PORTUGUESA [Contributions to the study of Portuguese anthropology]. Irr. (2 or 3 x y). 1936 (1959: vol. 27). Instituto de Antropologia, Coimbra. Ed: A. Xavier da Cunha. Art. on the paleoanthropology of Portugal; each no. contains 1 art.; English sum. nfs

37. DOURO LITORAL. Irr. Museu de Etnografia e História (Comissão Provincial de Etnografia e História), Largo de S. João Novo, n°. 11, Porto. pni

38. ESTREMADURA. 3 x y. Junta da Província da Estremadura, Rua Pascoal de Melo, n°. 25, Lisboa 1. pni

39. ESTUDOS ETNOGRAFICOS, FILOLOGICOS E HISTORICOS [Ethnographical, philological and historical studies]. A. Comissão de Etnografia e História, Junta de Província do Douro Litoral, Porto. pni

40. ETHNOS. Irr. 1935 (mri 1948: vol. 3). Instituto Português de Arqueologia, História e Etnografia, Museu Etnológico "Dr. Leite de Vasconcelos," Edifício dos Jerónimos, Belém, Lisboa 3. Art. on the archaeology, ethnography, folklore, and all periods of the hist. of Portugal; notes and news. pni

41. FACULDADE DE LETRAS, REVISTA DA... [Review of the Faculty of Arts]. Faculdade do Letras, Universidade de Lisboa, Cidade Universitária, Lisboa 4. Esc. 40 / Esc. 40

42. GABINETE DE ESTUDOS ULTRAMARINOS, REVISTA DO... [Review of the Cabinet of Overseas Studies]. Q. Centro Universitário de Lisboa da Mocidade Portuguesa, Rua de D. Estefânia, 14, Lisboa 1. Esc. 55/Esc. 75

43. GARCIA DE ORTA. Q. Junta das Missões Geográficas e de Investigações do Ultramar, Rua da Junqueira, n°. 86, Lisboa 3. Esc. 15/Esc. 15

44. GIL VICENTE. Revista de Portugalidade [Review of "Portugalism"]. M. Ed: Manuel Alves de Oliveira, Avenida de Duarte Pacheco, Guimarães. Esc. 40/Esc. 80

45. GRUPO ALCAIDES DE FARIA, BOLETIM DO... [Bulletin of the group "Alcaides de Faria"]. Irr. Frupo "Alcaides de Faria," Associação dos Arqueologos Portugueses, Campo da Feira, 57, Barcelos. pni

46. HUMANITAS. A. Instituto de Estudos Clássicos, Faculdade de Letras, Coimbra. pni

47. INDEPENDENCIA [Independence]. Revista de cultura Lusíada [Review of Portuguese culture]. A. 1940 (1959: no. 22). Sociedade Histórica Independência de Portugal, Palácio da Independência, Largo de S. Domingos, Lisboa 2.

Ed: D. José Pedro de Saldanha Oliveira e Sousa (Conde da Azinhaga). Art. on the hist. of Portugal and Portuguese possessions; news of the soc. Esc. 25

INSTITUT FRANÇAIS AU PORTUGAL, BULLETIN DE L'... see BULLETIN DES ETUDES PORTUGAISES ET DE L'INSTITUT FRANÇAIS AU PORTUGAL

48. O INSTITUTO [The Institute]. Irr. Instituto de Coimbra, Rua da Ilha, Coimbra. pni

49. INSTITUTO HISTORICO DA ILHA TERCEIRA, BOLETIM DO... [Bulletin of the Historical Institute of Ilha Terceira]. Irr. 1943 (1958: no. 6). Junta Geral do Distrito Autónomo de Angra do Heroismo, Angra do Heroismo, Açores. Art. on aspects of the hist. of the island of Terceira; transactions of the inst. pni

50. INSULANA [Insular]. S-M. Instituto Cultural, Ponta Delgada. pni

51. ITINERARIUM. Colectânea de Estudos [Collection of studies]. Q. Editorial Franciscana, Braga. Esc. 50

52. JUNTA DE INVESTIGAÇÕES DO ULTRAMAR, ANAIS DA... [Annals of the Council for Research on the Overseas Areas]. A. Junta das Missões Geográficas e de Investigações do Ultramar, Rua da Junqueira, nº. 86, Lisboa. pv

53. LUSIADA. Revista ilustrada de cultura, arte, literature, historia e critica [Illustrated review of culture, art, literature, history and criticism]. Q. Pub. address: Rua Miguel Bombarda, 467, Porto.

54. LUSITANIA SACRA [Sacred Portugal]. A. 1956 (1959: vol. 4). Livraria União Gráfica, Rua de Santa Marta, nº. 48, Lisboa 2, for Centro de Estudos de História Eclesiástica. Art. on the ecclesiastical hist. of Portugal and on church historiography; doc.; notes and news. Esc. 60/$ 2.20

MEMORIAS. For titles beginning with "Memorias," followed by the name of the publishing or sponsoring institution or society, see the respective institution or society.

55. MUSEU [Museum]. Arte, arqueologia, tradição [Art, archaeology, tradition]. Irr. 1949 (mri 1950: vol. 6). Museu Nacional Soares dos Reis, Rua de D. Manuel II, Palácio das Carrancas, Porto. Art. on Portuguese fine arts and numismatics. Esc. 40/Esc. 50

56. MUSEU-BIBLIOTECA "CONDE DE CASTRO GUIMARÃES," BOLETIM DO... [Bulletin of the "Count Castro Guimarães" Library Museum]. Museu-Biblioteca "Conde de Castro Guimarães," Cascais. pni

57. MUSEU NACIONAL DE ARTE ANTIGA, BOLETIM DO... [Bulletin of the National Museum of Ancient Art]. A. Museu Nacional de Arte Antiga, Rua das Janelas Verdes, Lisboa 2. Esc. 25/Esc. 25

58. NVMVS. Numismática, medalhística, arqueologia [Numismatics and archaeology]. A. 1952 (1958: vol. 5). Sociedade Portuguesa de Numismática, Rua de Santa Catarina, nº. 339-3º, Porto. Art. on numismatics with reference to Portugal and Portuguese possessions; biblio.; notes and news. p(1) Esc. 25/p(1) $ 1

59. OCIDENTE [Occident]. Revista Portuguesa mensal [Monthly Portuguese review]. M. Ed: António H. de Azevedo Pinto, Rua de S. Félix, nº.41-1º Dtº., Lisboa 2. Esc. 190/$ 10

60. OLISIPO. Q. Grupo "Amigos de Lisboa," Largo Trinidade Coelho, nº.9, 1º, Lisboa 2. Esc. 25/Esc. 25

61. PORTUCALE. Irr. Ed: Joaquim Moreira, Rua de Nogueira da Maia, Porto. Esc. 40/$ 2.50

62. PORTUGAL EM AFRICA [Portugal in Africa]. Revista de cultura missionária [Review of missionary culture]. B-M. Instituto Superior Missionário do Espirito Santo, Rua de Santo Amaro, à Estrela, nº. 47, Lisboa 2. Esc. 40/Esc. 50

REVISTA. For titles beginning with "Revista," followed by the name of the publishing or sponsoring institution or society, see the respective institution or society.

63. REVISTA DAS ARTES E DA HISTORIA DA MADEIRA [Review of the arts and history of Madeira]. Revista de cultura da Sociedade de Concertos da Madeira [Cultural review of the Madeira Concert Association]. Irr. Ed: Luís Peter Clode, Avenida de Arriaga, nº. 13, Funchal, Madeira. Local hist. Esc. 85/Esc. 110

64. REVISTA DE GUIMARÃES [Review of Guimarães]. S-A. Sociedade Martins Sarmento, Rua de Paio Galvao, Guimarães. Esc. 40

65. REVISTA PORTUGUESA DE HISTORIA [Portuguese review of history]. Irr. Faculdade de Letras da Universidade de Coimbra, Instituto de Estudos Históricos "Dr. António de Vasconcelos," Coimbra. pni

66. SEARA NOVA [New seed]. B-M. Empresa de Publicidade, Rua de Luciano Cordeiro, nº. 103-1º., Lisboa 1. Esc. 50/Esc. 100

67. SOCIEDADE DE GEOGRAFIA DE LISBOA, BOLETIM DA... [Bulletin of the Lisbon Geographical Society]. Q. Sociedade de Geografia de Lisboa, Rua das Portas de Santo Antão, nº. 100, Lisboa 2. Esc. 60/Esc. 100

68. STUDIA. S-A. 1958 (1960: no. 5-6). Centro de Estudos Históricos Ultramarinos, Calçada da Boa Hora, nº. 30 (Palácio da Ega), Lisboa 3. Art. on all periods of Portuguese overseas hist.; extensive doc. section; notes on relevant meetings; bk. rev.; sum. of art. on Portuguese overseas hist. (mainly from Portuguese and Brazilian periodicals); in Portuguese and occasionally in English or French. p(1) Esc. 60/p(1) Esc. 60

69. STUDIUM GENERALE. Q. Centro de Estudos Humanísticos, Museu de Maximiano Lemos, Faculdade de Medicina, Porto. pni

70. TRABALHOS DE ANTROPOLOGIA E ETNOLOGIA [Works on anthropology and ethnology]. Irr. (usually 1-2 no. p.a.) 1919 (1959: new series, vol. 17). Instituto de Antropologia, Faculdade de Ciências, Universidade do Porto, Porto, for Sociedade Portuguesa de Antropologia e Etnologia and Centro de Estudos de Etnologia Peninsular. Art. on anthropology, ethnology, archaeology, prehist., protohist. and occasionally on the hist. (mainly cultural hist.) of later

periods, with emphasis on Portugal, as well as on research and methodological problems in these fields; bk. rev.; general index of vol. 1-10, pub. in 1946. nfs

71. UNIVERSIDADE DE COIMBRA, REVISTA DA... [Review of the University of Coimbra]. A. Universidade de Coimbra, Coimbra. pni

72. VIRIATIS. Arte, arqueologia, museologia [Art, archaeology, museology]. Irr. Museu Grão Vasco, Paço dos Três Escalões, Viseu. Esc. 25/$ 1

Rumania

Prepared with the assistance of the

Biblioteca Academiei Republicii Populare Romîne, Bucharest, and

Eugen Stănescu, Chief Editor of Studii, Bucharest

ANALELE. For titles beginning with "Analele," followed by the name of the publishing or sponsoring institution or society, see the respective institution or society.

1. ANALELE ROMÂNO-SOVIETICE [Rumanian-Soviet annals]. Seria istorie [Historical series]. Q. 1949 (mri 1953: vol. 7). Institutul de Studii Romîno-Sovietic, Academia Republicii Populare Romîne, Bucureşti. Ed: Petre Constantinescu-Iaşi. Art. (mostly translations from Russian periodicals) on the modern hist. and culture of Rumania and the U.S.S.R.; rev. of bk. and periodicals; chronicle; discussion of events of academic interest in the U.S.S.R.; A. author index. p (1) Lei 5

ANALELE ŞTIINŢIFICE ALE UNIVERSITĂŢII "AL. I. CUZA" DIN IAŞI see UNIVERSITATEA "AL. I. CUZA" DIN IAŞI, ANALELE ŞTIINŢIFICE ALE...

2. BULETIN ŞTIINŢIFIC [Scientific bulletin]. Secţia de geologie şi geografie [Section of geology and geography]. Q. Editura Academiei R.P.R., Str. I.C. Frimu 22, Bucureşti. Russian and French sum. p (1) Lei 5

BULETINUL UNIVERSITĂŢILOR "V. BABEŞ" ŞI "BOLYAYI," CLUJ see UNIVERSITĂŢI "V. BABEŞ" ŞI "BOLYAYI," CLUJ, BULETINUL...

3. CĂLĂUZA BIBLIOTECARULUI [The librarian's guide]. Buletin lunar pentru îndrumarea bibliotecarilor [Monthly bulletin for the librarian's guidance]. M. 1947 (1958: vol. 12). Ministerul Invăţămîntului şi Culturii, bd. 6 Martie 29, Bucureşti. Art. on libraries in Rumania, the Soviet Union and other countries and on Rumanian hist. and culture; bk. rev.; A. index. p (1) Lei 2

4. CERCETĂRI FILOZOFICE [Philosophical studies]. B-M. 1954 (1958: vol. 5). Editura Academiei R.P.R., Str. I.C. Frimu 22, Bucureşti, for Institutul de Filozofie, Academia Republicii Populare Romîne, bd. Ilie Pintilie 6, Bucureşti. Art. and discussions on the hist. of ideas and culture in Rumania; Russian and French sum. A. index. p (1) Lei 6

5. CONTEMPORANUL [Contemporary times]. Săptămînal politic, social, cultural [Political, social and cultural weekly]. W. Ministerul Culturii, Piaţa Scînteii 1, Bucureşti. p (1) Lei 0.50

6. CONTRIBUŢII LA ISTORIA LIMBII ROMÎNE LITERARE ÎN SECOLUL XIX-LEA [Contributions to the history of the Rumanian literary language in the 19th century]. Irr. Editura Academiei R.P.R., Str. I.C. Frimu 22, Bucureşti. p (1) Lei 16

7. DACIA. Journal of Archaeology and Ancient History (sub-title also in Russian, French and German). A. 1924 (1957: new series, vol. 1). Editura Academiei R.P.R., Str. I.C. Frimu 22, Bucureşti, for Institutul de Arheologie, Academia Republicii Polulare Romîne, Str. I.C. Frimu 11, Bucureşti. Ed: Vladimir Dumitrescu. Art. on the archaeology, ancient hist. and civilization of Rumania; reports on archaeological excavations in Rumania; rev. of bk. and art.; in French, German, Russian and Italian; illus. p (1) Lei 33

DESTIN see section on Spain

8. INSTITUTUL DE ISTORIE A PARTIDULUI DE PE LÎNGĂ C.C. AL P.M.R., ANALELE... (Analele Institutului de Istorie a Partidului de pe Lîngă C.C. al P.M.R.) [Annals of the Institute of the History of the Party attached to the Central Committee of the Rumanian Workers' Party]. B-M. 1955 (1957: vol. 3). Editura politică, Casa Scînteii, Piaţa Scînteii 1, Bucureşti, for Institutul de Istorie a Partidului, Str. Ministerului 4, Bucureşti. Art., notes, doc. and biographical sketches relating to the hist. of the Rumanian Workers' Party; Russian, French and English sum. p (1) Lei 4

9. LIMBA ŞI LITERATURA [Language and literature]. A. Societatea de ştiinţe istorice şi filologice din R.P.R., bd. I.V. Stalin 1, Bucureşti. Hist. of Rumanian literature and language. p (1) Lei 10

10. MATERIALE ŞI CERCETĂRI ARHEOLOGICE [Archaeological documents and research]. A. 1953 (1959: vol. 5). Editura Academiei R.P.R., Str. I.C. Frimu 22, Bucureşti, for Institutul de arheologie, Academia R.P.R., Str. I.C. Frimu 11, Bucureşti. Ed: Em. Condurachi. Art. and reports on Rumanian archaeology and excavations; Russian and French sum.; illus. pv (Lei 25-75)

11. MONUMENTE ŞI MUZEE [Monuments and museums]. Buletinul Comisiei ştiinţifice a muzeelor şi monumentelor istorice şi artistice [Bulletin of the Scientific Commission of Historical and Artistic Museums and Monuments]. S-A. 1958 (1958: vol. 1). Editura Academiei R.P.R., Str. I.C. Frimu 22, Bucureşti, for Comisia ştiinţifică a muzeelor şi monumentelor istorice şi artistice, Academi[a] R.P.R., Calea Victoriei 125, Bucureşti. Art. on hist. and artistic monuments pertaining to Rumania; museum studies and rev.; Russian and French sum. p (1) Lei 21.50

12. NATURA [Nature]. B-M. 1949 (1958: vol. 10). Societatea de ştiinţe naturale şi geografie din R.P.R., Splaiul Independenţei 91-95, Bucureşti. Russian and English sum. p (1) Lei 3

PERSPECTIVE CREŞTINE see section on Spain

13. PRESA NOASTRĂ [Our press]. M. Uniunea Ziariştilor din R.P.R., Calea Victoriei 163, Bucureşti. Art. and studies on the Rumanian press and its hist.; Russian and English sum. p (1) Lei 3

14. PROBLEME DE ANTROPOLOGIE [Problems of anthropology]. Irr. 1954 (1957: vol. 3). Editura Academiei R.P.R., Str. I.C. Frimu 22, Bucureşti, for Centrul de cercetări antropologice, Academia R.P.R., Bf. Glisson Stalin 34, Bucureşti. Art. on general anthropology, paleo-anthropology, physical and cultural anthropology, and the anthropology of contemporary man; bk. rev.; Russian and French sum. pv (Lei 9.45 - 14.50)

15. PROBLEME DE GEOGRAFIE [Problems of geography]. A. Irr. Editura Academiei R.P.R., Str. I.C. Frimu 22, Bucureşti, for Institutul de Cerectări Geografice, Academia R.P.R., Bucureşti. Russian and French sum. p (1) Lei 22.50

16. REVISTA ARHIVELOR [Archival review]. S-A. 1924 (1958: new series, vol. 2). Direcţia Generală a Arhivelor Statului din R.P.R., Str. Arhivelor 2, Bucureşti. Ed: C. Timaru (chief ed.), Gh. Ungureanu, I. Gh. Vasile. Art. on Rumanian and foreign archives and their holdings, as well as on hist. and auxiliary sciences; rev. of bk. and periodicals; Russian and French sum. p (1) Lei 12

17. REVISTA DE FILOLOGIE ROMANICĂ ŞI GERMANICĂ [Review of Romance and Germanic philology]. Irr. 1957 (1957: vol. 1). Editura Academiei R.P.R., Str. I.C. Frimu 22, Bucureşti, for Subsecţia de limbă şi literatură, Academia R.P.R., Calea Victoriei 125, Bucureşti. Art. on the hist. of the language and culture of Rumania; Russian and French sum. p (1) Lei 12

18. REVISTA DE FOLCLOR [Review of folklore]. Q. 1956 (1958: vol. 3). Institutul de folclor, Str. Nikos Beloiannis 25, Bucureşti. Ed: Mihai Pop. Art., doc., notes and news on Rumanian folklore; Russian and English sum.; A. index. p (1) Lei 10

19. REVISTA DE PEDAGOGIE [Review of pedagogy]. M. 1952 (1958: vol. 7). Editura de Stat didactică şi pedagogică, Piaţa Scînteii 1, Bucureşti, for Institutul de ştiinţe pedagogice din R.P.R., Str. Sf. Apostoli 14, Bucureşti. Art. on pedagogy and its hist., and on methodology; biblio.; Russian and French sum.; A. index. p (1) Lei 3

20. REVISTA DE PSIHOLOGIE [Review of psychology]. Q. 1955 (1958: vol. 4). Editura Academiei R.P.R., Str. I.C. Frimu 22, Bucureşti, for Institutul de Psihologie, Academia R.P.R., bd. 6 Martie 64, Bucureşti. Art. on psychology and the hist. of psychology and culture; rev. of bk. and periodicals; Russian and French sum.; classified biblio. of Rumanian works on psychology for the years 1953-57, pub. in vol. 4, no. 1. p (1) Lei 6

21. REVUE DES SCIENCES SOCIALES [Review of the social sciences]. S-A. 1952 (1957: new series, vol. 2). Editura Academiei R.P.R., Str. I.C. Frimu 22, Bucureşti, for Secţia de filosofie, Academia R.P.R., Calea Victoriei 125, Bucureşti. Art. on philosophy, logic, economics, and the hist. of culture and ideas; in Russian, French, English or German. p (1) Lei 10

ROMÂNIA see section on the United States of America

ROMÂNIA MUNICITOARE see section on France

SOCIETATEA ACADEMICE ROMÂNE, BULETINUL... see section on Italy

22. STUDIA ET ACTA ORIENTALIA. Irr. 1958 (1958: vol. 1). Societatea de ştiinţe istorice şi filologice din R.P.R., bd. I.V. Stalin 1, Bucureşti. Art. and discussions on the hist., language, and civilization of the Oriental countries; in French, English or German; French sum. p (1) Lei 50

23. STUDII [Studies]. Revista de Istorie [Review of history]. B-M. 1948 (1959: vol. 12). Subsecţia de Ştiinţe Istorice şi Institutul de Istorie din Bucureşti,

Academia Republicii Populare Romîne, B-dul I.V. Stalin 1, Bucureşti. Ed: Eugen Stănescu (chief ed.), P. Constantinescu-Iaşi. Art. on Rumanian hist. (mostly modern) and occasionally on historiography; doc.; rev. of bk. and art. on European hist., with emphasis on Southeast Europe; chronicle; professional news (also on pub.); biblio. of art. in Rumanian periodicals, arranged by subject and author; sum. of main art. in Russian and French; table of contents also in Russian and French; separate subject and alphabetical index for the years 1948-57.
p (1) Lei 6

24. STUDII ŞI ARTICOLE DE ISTORIE [Historical studies and articles]. A. 1956 (1957: vol. 2). Editura Ştiinţifică, Piaţa Scînteii nr 1, Bucureşti, for Societatea de ştiinţe istorice şi filologice din R.P.R., bd. I.V. Stalin 1, Bucureşti Art. on Rumanian hist. p (1) Lei 20

25. STUDII ŞI CERCETĂRI DE BIBLIOLOGIE [Studies and research on bibliology]. Irr. 1955 (1957: vol. 2). Editura Academiei R.P.R., Str. I.C. Frimu 22, Bucureşti, for Biblioteca Academiei R.P.R., Calea Victoriei 125, Bucureşti. Art. on libraries, the hist. of writing, and on biblio. and documentation in Rumania; rev. of biblio.; biblio. notes; chronicles of the activities of Rumanian libraries; Russian and French sum. pv (Lei 18.45 - 24)

26. STUDII ŞI CERCETĂRI DE ISTORIA ARTEI [Studies and research on the history of art]. S-A. 1954 (1958: vol. 5). Editura Academiei R.P.R., Str. I.C. Frimu 22, Bucureşti. Russian and French sum. p (1) Lei 20

27. STUDII ŞI CERCETĂRI DE ISTORIE [Historical studies and research]. Q. 1950 (1957: vol. 8). Editura Academiei Republicii Populare Romîne, Str. I.C. Frimu 22, Bucureşti, for Academia R.P.R. Cluj, Str. Pavlov 27, Cluj. Art., notes, doc. and discussions on the hist. and culture of Transylvania and the Banat; Russian and French sum. Before 1956 pub. under the title: Studii şi cercetări ştiinţifice. Academia R.P.R. Filiale Cluj. p (1) Lei 8

28. STUDII ŞI CERCETĂRI DE ISTORIE LITERARĂ ŞI FOLCLOR [Studies and research on literary history and folklore]. Q. 1952 (1958: vol. 8). Editura Academiei R.P.R., Str. I.C. Frimu 22, Bucureşti, for Institutul de istorie literară şi folclor, Academia Republicii Populare Romîne, bd. Republicii 73, Bucureşti. Art. on Rumanian literary hist. and the influence of folklore on literature; biographical sketches; chronicles; Russian and French sum.
p (1) Lei 10

29. STUDII ŞI CERCETĂRI DE ISTORIE VECHE [Studies and research on ancient history]. S-A. 1950 (1958: vol. 9). Editura Academiei R.P.R., Str. I.C. Frimu 22, Bucureşti, for Institutul de arheologie, Academia R.P.R., Str. I.C. Frimu 11, Bucureşti. Art., notes and discussions on ancient Rumanian hist. and archaeology; Russian and French sum. Lei 24

30. STUDII ŞI CERCETĂRI DE NUMISMATICĂ [Studies and research on numismatics]. Irr. 1957 (1958: vol. 2). Editura Academiei R.P.R., Str. I.C. Frimu 22, Bucureşti, for Cabinetul Numismatic, Academia R.P.R., Calea Victoriei 125, Bucureşti. Art., notes and discussions on numismatics, sigillography, heraldry, and blazonry; Russian and French sum.; illus.
pv (Lei 31 - 38.40)

STUDII ŞI CERCETĂRI ŞTIINŢIFICE see STUDII ŞI CERCETĂRI ŞTIINŢIFICE. ISTORIE ŞI FILOLOGIE

STUDII ŞI CERCETĂRI ŞTIINŢIFICE. ACADEMIA R.P.R. FILIALA CLUJ see STUDII ŞI CERCETĂRI DE ISTORIE

STUDII ŞI CERCETĂRI ŞTIINŢIFICE. ISTORIE see STUDII ŞI CERCETĂRI ŞTIINŢIFICE. ISTORIE ŞI FILOLOGIE

31. STUDII ŞI CERCETĂRI ŞTIINŢIFICE. ISTORIE ŞI FILOLOGIE [Scientific studies and research. History and philology]. S-A. 1950 (mri 1956: vol. 7). Editura Academiei, R.P.R., Str. I.C. Frimu 22, Bucureşti, for Academia R.P.R., Filiala Iaşi, Str. Filimon Sirbu 7, Iaşi. Art., notes and doc. on the hist. and archaeology of Moldavia and on philology; Russian and French sum.; alphabetical and subject index for the years 1950-56. From 1950 to 1956 appeared under the title: Studii şi cercetări ştiinţifice and in 1956 and 1957 under the title Studii şi cercetări ştiinţifice. Istorie. p (1) Lei 3

32. STUDII ŞI MATERIALE DE ISTORIE CONTEMPORANĂ [Studies and documents on contemporary history]. Irr. 1956 (1958: vol. 2). Editura Academiei R.P.R., Str. I.C. Frimu 22, Bucureşti, for Institutul de istorie, Academia R.P.R., bd. I.V. Stalin 1, Bucureşti. Art. on recent Rumanian hist.; Russian and French sum. pv (Lei 20.25 - 25.50)

33. STUDII ŞI MATERIALE DE ISTORIE MEDIE [Studies and documents on medieval history]. Irr. 1956 (1957: vol. 2). Editura Academiei R.P.R., Str. I.C. Frimu 22, Bucureşti, for Institutul de istorie, Academia R.P.R., bd. I.V. Stalin 1, Bucureşti. Art. and doc. on medieval Rumanian hist. and auxiliary hist. disciplines; Russian and French sum. pv (Lei 21.10 - Lei 33)

34. STUDII ŞI MATERIALE DE ISTORIE MODERNĂ [Studies and documents on modern history]. Irr. 1957. Editura Academiei R.P.R., Str. I.C. Frimu 22, Bucureşti, for Institutul de istorie, Academia R.P.R., bd. I.V. Stalin 1, Bucureşti. Art. and doc. on modern Rumanian hist., pertaining mostly to the 19th and early 20th cent. Lei 26

35. UNIVERSITAŢEA "AL. I. CUZA" DIN IAŞI, ANALELE ŞTIINŢIFICE ALE...(Analele ştiinţifice ale Universităţii "Al. I. Cuza" din Iaşi) [Scientific annals of the "Al. I. Cuza" University of Iassy]. Secţiunea III (Ştiinţe sociale) [Section III (social sciences)]. S-A. Universitatea "Al. I. Cuza" din Iaşi, Calea 23, August 11, Iaşi. Russian and French sum. pni

36. UNIVERSITAŢEA "C. I. PARHON," ANALELE... (Analele Universităţii "C.I. Parhon") [Annals of the "C.I. Parhon" University]. Seria Acta Logica. S-A. Editura tehnică, Str. Alex. Beldiman 2, Bucureşti. In French and English. p (1) Lei 10

37. UNIVERSITAŢEA "C. I. PARHON," ANALELE... (Analele Universităţii "C.I. Parhon") [Annals of the "C.I. Parhon" University]. Seria ştiinţelor naturii [Natural science series]. S-A. Editura tehnică, Alex. Beldiman 2, Bucureşti. Russian and French sum. p (1) Lei 6

38. UNIVERSITAŢEA "C. I. PARHON," ANALELE... (Analele Universităţii "C.I. Parhon") [Annals of the "C.I. Parhon" University]. Seria ştiinţe sociale [Social science series]. S-A. 1954 (mri 1956: no. 5). Editura tehnică, Alex. Beldiman 2, Bucureşti, for Universitatea "C.I. Parhon," bd. 6 Martie 64, Bucureşti. Art. on the social sciences, including Rumanian hist.; bk. rev.; Russian and French sum. p (1) Lei 6

39. UNIVERSITAŢI "V. BABEŞ" ŞI "BOLYAI," CLUJ, BULETINUL... (Buletinul Universităţilor "V. Babeş" şi "Bolyai," Cluj) [Bulletin of the "V. Babes" and "Bolyai" Universities, Cluj]. Seria Ştiinţc Sociale [Social science series]. S-A. 1956 (1957: vol. 2). Universitatea Victor Babes, Str. Milail Kogălniceanu 1, Cluj. Art. and notes on the hist. of Rumania (especially Transylvania), and on philosophy, political economy, psychology, law and philology; Russian and French sum.; table of contents also in Russian and French. Pub. suspended in 1957. pni

---

Readers searching for a periodical are also advised to see

the ADDENDA sections

included at the end of some lists.

Spain

Prepared with the assistance of

Eloy Benito Ruano, Consejo Superior de Investigaciones Científicas, Escuela de Estudios Medievales, Madrid,

and the staff of

Indice Historico Español, Barcelona

1. ACADEMIA [Academy]. S-A. Real Academia de Bellas Artes de San Fernando, Madrid. 100 ptas / 150 ptas

2. ACADEMIA IBEROAMERICANA Y FILIPINA DE HISTORIA POSTAL, BOLETIN DE LA... [Bulletin of the Ibero-American and Philippine Academy of Postal History]. Q. 1945 (1959: vol. 14). Dirección General de Correos y Telecomunicación, Madrid. Ed: Ricardo Ortiz Vivas. Art. on postal hist. and the hist. of telecommunications in the Spanish world; biographical art.; doc.; illus. pni

3. ACADEMIA MALLORQUINA DE ESTUDIOS GENEALOGICOS. MEMORIAS [Mallorcan Academy of Genealogical Studies. Transactions]. Q. Academia Mallorquina de Estudios Genealógicos, Estanco 3, Palma de Mallorca. pni

ACTAS Y MEMORIAS DE LA SOCIEDAD ESPAÑOLA DE ANTROPOLOGIA, ETNOGRAFIA Y PREHISTORIA see SOCIEDAD ESPAÑOLA DE ANTROPOLOGIA, ETNOGRAFIA Y PREHISTORIA, ACTAS Y MEMORIAS DE LA...

4. AFRICA. M. Instituto de Estudios Africanos, Castellana 5, Madrid. Illus. 100 ptas

5. ALTAMIRA. 3xy. Centro de Estudios Montañeses, Diputación Provincial, Santander. Hist. of the province of Santander. 70 ptas / 90 ptas

6. AMPURIAS [Greek town on Catalan coast -- ed.]. Revista de Arqueología, Prehistoria y Etnología [Review of archaeology, prehistory and ethnology]. A. 1939 (mri 1956: vol. 18). Departamento de Barcelona del Instituto Rodrigo Caro, de Arqueología y Prehistoria (Consejo Superior de Investigaciones Científicas, Diputación Provincial de Barcelona), Barcelona. Ed: Martin Almagro, Museo Arqueológico, Parque de Montjuich, Barcelona. Art. on the prehist. and ancient hist. of Spain, with emphasis on Catalonia; archaeological reports and professional news of archaeological inst.; biblio. of bk. and periodicals, not confined to Spain. pv

7. ANALECTA MONTSERRATENSIA. A. 1917 (mri 1954/55: new series, vol. 8). Abadía de Montserrat, Barcelona. Art. on the hist. of the Benedictine Order in Aragon and its political and religious relations with other communities and with neighboring countries, from the establishment of the Order to the present; biblio.; in Catalan and other Romance languages. 200 ptas / $ 5

8. ANALECTA SACRA TARRACONENSIA. Revista de Ciencias Histórico-Eclesiásticas [Review of historical-ecclesiastical sciences]. S-A. 1925 (1958: vol. 31). Biblioteca Balmes, Durán y Bas 9-11, Barcelona. Ed: José Vives.

Art. on ecclesiastical and liturgical hist., the hist. of parishes in Spain, and on theology; comprehensive biblio. also pub. separately under the title: Bibliografía Hispánica de Ciencias Histórico-Eclesiasticas; list of bk. received; in Spanish and occasionally in French. 80 ptas / 120 ptas

ANALES. For titles beginning with "Anales," followed by the name of the publishing or sponsoring institution or society, see the respective institution or society.

9. ANALES CERVANTINOS [Cervantes annals]. A. Consejo Superior de Investigaciones Científicas, Instituto "Miguel de Cervantes," Medinaceli 4, Madrid. 160 ptas / 180 ptas

10. ANALES DE ECONOMIA [Economic annals]. Consejo Superior de Investigaciones Científicas, Instituto de Economía "Sancho de Moncada," Medinaceli 4, Madrid. pni

11. AL-ANDALUS. S-A. 1932 (1958: vol. 23). Escuela de Estudios Arabes de Madrid, San Vicente, 60, Madrid, and Escuela de Estudios Arabes de Granada. Ed: Emilio García Gómez. Art. on Arabic philology and the hist. of philosophy, art, literature, law and institutions in Moslem Spain; notes of professional interest; rev. of bk. and art.; biblio. classified by subject; in Spanish, Italian, French or English. 70 ptas

12. ANTROPOLOGIA Y ETNOGRAFIA [Anthropology and ethnography]. S-A. 1949 (1958: vol. 12). Consejo Superior de Investigaciones Científicas, Instituto "Bernardino de Sahagún," Paseo de Atocha 11, Madrid. Ed: José Pérez de Barradas. Art. on Spanish and general anthropology, ethnology and folklore; bk. rev.; biblio. 100 ptas

13. ANUARIO DE ESTUDIOS AMERICANOS [Yearbook of American studies] A. 1944 (1956 [1958]: vol. 13). Escuela de Estudios Hispano-Americanos, Universidad de Sevilla, Alfonso XII, Sevilla. Ed. board: Vicente Rodríguez Casado, Antonio Muro Orejón, José Antonio Calderon Quijano, Octavio Gil Munilla, Francisco Morales Padrón. Art. on the hist. of Latin America since the discoveries; doc.; bk. rev. and biblio. of relevant literature with abstr., classified by subject; illus.; 10-year table of contents (1944-53) pub. in vol. 10. 140 ptas / 180 ptas

14. ANUARIO DE ESTUDIOS ATLANTICOS [Yearbook of Atlantic studies]. A. 1955 (1958: vol. 4). Casa de Colón, Argensola 2, Madrid, and Casa de Colón, Las Palmas, Islas Canarias. Ed: Antonio Rumeu de Armas, Miguel Santiago Rodríguez. Art. on hist., philological and natural sciences pertaining to areas on the Atlantic, especially the Canary Islands; biblio. 150 ptas / 150 ptas

15. ANUARIO DE HISTORIA DEL DERECHO ESPAÑOL [Yearbook of Spanish legal history]. A. 1924 (1957/58: vol. 27/28). Instituto Nacional de Estudios Jurídicos, Medinaceli 6, Madrid. Ed: José Lopez Ortíz, Alfonso García Gallo, José Maldonado, Alvaro D'Ors, Juan García Gonzalez. Art. on Spanish legal, constitutional and general hist.; rev. art.; doc.; biblio. of bk. received; professional notes. 200 ptas / 240 ptas

16. ANUARIO MUSICAL [Musical yearbook]. A. Consejo Superior de Investigaciones Científicas, Instituto Espanol de Musicología, Barcelona. Includes art. on the hist. of music in Spain. 80 ptas / 90 ptas

17. ARBOR. Revista General de Investigación y Cultura [General review of research and culture]. M. Consejo Superior de Investigaciones Científicas, Serrano 117, Madrid. 160 ptas / 220 ptas

18. ARCHIVO AGUSTINIANO [Augustinian archives]. Revista de Investigacíon Histórica de los Padres Agustinos Españoles [Review of historical research of the Spanish Augustinian fathers]. 3 x y. PP. Agustinos, Goya 87, Madrid. pni

19. ARCHIVO DE ARTE VALENCIANO [Archives of Valencian art]. A. Real Academia de Bellas Artes de San Carlos, Calle de San Pío 5, Valencia. pni

20. ARCHIVO DE PREHISTORIA LEVANTINA [Archives of Levantine prehistory]. A. Consejo Superior de Investigaciones Científicas, Instituto "Alfonso el Magnánimo," Valencia. 80 ptas / 100 ptas

21. ARCHIVO ESPAÑOL DE ARQUEOLOGIA [Spanish archives of archaeology]. S-A. 1925 (1957: vol. 30, no. 95-96). Consejo Superior de Investigaciones Científicas, Instituto Español de Arqueología "Rodrigo Caro," Medinaceli 4, Madrid. Ed: Antonio García y Bellido, Universidad de Madrid, Madrid. Art. on the archaeology of the Mediterranean area from prehist. times to the Arab conquest of Spain; bk. rev.; A. archaeological biblio.; announcements of works to be pub.; notes on archaeological excavations and finds; in Spanish and occasionally in other major European languages. 120 ptas / 180 ptas

22. ARCHIVO ESPAÑOL DE ARTE [Spanish archives of art]. Q. 1925 (1959: vol. 22). Consejo Superior de Investigaciones Científicas, Instituto Diego Velázquez, Medinaceli 4, Madrid. Ed: Diego Angulo Iñiguez. . Art. on the hist. of Spanish art.; biblio.; illus. 120 ptas

23. ARCHIVO HISPALENSE [Sevillian archives]. Revista Histórica, Literaria y Artística [Historical, literary and art review]. B-M. Diputación Provincial, Patronato de Cultura, Plaza del Triunfo 3, Palacio Provincial, Aptdo. 25, Sevilla. 80 ptas / 90 ptas

24. ARCHIVO IBERO-AMERICANO [Ibero-American archives]. Revista de Estudios Históricos [Review of historical studies]. Q. 1914 (1958: vol. 18, no. 69-72). PP. Franciscanos Españoles, Joaquín Costa 36, Madrid 2. Art. on the hist. of religious orders, especially the Franciscan, with emphasis on their missionary work abroad, particularly in Latin America; biographies; bk. rev., including general religious literature. 75 ptas / $ 4

25. ARCHIVO IBERO-AMERICANO DE HISTORIA DE LA MEDICINA Y ANTROPOLOGIA MEDICA [Ibero-American archives of medicine and medical anthropology]. Q. 1949 (1958: vol. 10). Consejo Superior de Investigaciones Científicas, Instituto Arnaldo de Vilanova, Medinaceli 4, Madrid. Ed: P. Laín Entralgo, A. Ruiz Moreno. Art. on the hist. of medicine and physical anthropology; doc.; notes on the activities of the inst.; rev. of bk. and periodicals. 140 ptas / 200 ptas

26. ARCHIVOS DE PROTOCOLOS, ESTUDIOS HISTORICOS Y DOCUMENTOS DE LOS... [Historical studies and documents of the Archives of the Protocols]. Irr. 1948 (mri 1955). Colegio Notarial de Barcelona, Notariado 4, Barcelona. Art. on the hist. of Catalonia, based largely on doc. from the Archives of the Protocols, with emphasis on the Middle Ages; doc.

ARCHIVOS DEL INSTITUTO DE ESTUDIOS AFRICANOS see INSTITUTO DE ESTUDIOS AFRICANOS, ARCHIVOS DEL...

27. ARCHIVOS LEONESES [León archives]. S-A. Centro de Estudios e Investigación "San Isidoro," León. 50 ptas / $ 2

28. ARCHIVUM [Archives]. Q. 1951 (1958: vol. 8). Facultad de Filosofía y Letras, Universidad de Oviedo, Oviedo. Art. on the hist., mainly cultural, of Northern Spain from prehist. times to the present; biblio. of bk. and periodicals. 100 ptas / 300 ptas

29. ARGENSOLA. Q. Instituto de Estudios Oscences, Huesca. 60 ptas / 70 ptas

30. ASOCIACION ESPAÑOLA DE AMIGOS DE LOS CASTILLOS, BOLETIN DE LA... [Bulletin of the Spanish Association of Friends of the Castles]. Q. Asociación Española de Amigos de los Castillos, Madrid.

31. ATLANTICO [Atlantic]. Revista de Cultura Contemporánea [Review of contemporary culture]. Irr. Casa Americana, Madrid. free

32. AUSA. Q. Patronato de Estudios Ausonenses, Vich, Barcelona. pni

33. BERCEO [(Gonzalo de) Berceo]. Q. Consejo Superior de Investigaciones Científicas, Instituto de Estudios Riojanos, Hermanos Moroy 1, Longroño. 70 ptas / 90 ptas

34. BIBLIOTECA, ARCHIVO Y MUSEO, REVISTA DE LA... [Review of the Library, Archives and Museum]. S-A. Archivo Municipal, Plaza Mayor 27, Madrid, for Ayuntamiento de Madrid. 60 ptas

35. BIBLIOTECA MENENDEZ PELAYO, BOLETIN DE LA... [Bulletin of the Library of Menendez Pelayo]. Q. Biblioteca Menéndez Pelayo, Rubio 6, Santander. 65 ptas / 100 ptas

BOLETIN. For titles beginning with "Boletín," followed by the name of the publishing or sponsoring institution or society, see the respective institution or society.

36. BOLETIN AMERICANISTA [Americanist bulletin]. 3xy. 1959 (1959 [1960]: vol. 1). Facultad de Filosofía y Letras, Universidad de Barcelona, Barcelona. Ed: Jaime Delgado. Art. on the colonial hist. and pre-colonial ethnology of Latin America; bk. rev.; biblio.; news section containing news of congresses and description of the holdings of the Museum of Ethnology, Barcelona illus. 90 ptas

37. BOLETIN ARQUEOLOGICO [Archaeological bulletin]. Q. 1901 (1957: vol. 57). Real Sociedad Arqueológica Tarraconense (Sección de Arqueología e Historia Instituto de Estudios Tarraconenses "Ramón Berenguer IV"), Comisión Provincial de Monumentos Museo Arqueológico Provincial, Mayor 39, Tarragona. Ed: Pedro Batlle Huguet, Nuestra Señora del Claustro 5, Tarragona. Art. and information on archaeology, with emphasis on the province of Tarragona. memb. free

38. BOLETIN DE INFORMACION DOCUMENTAL [Bulletin of documental information]. Seccion de Letras [Section of letters]. Q. Dirección General

de Archivos y Bibliotecas y Biblioteca General del Consejo Superior de Investigaciones Científicas, Serrano 123, Madrid. 60 ptas

39. BURGENSE. Collectanea Scientifica. A. Seminario Metropolitano de Burgos. 125 ptas / $ 3

BUTLLETI DE LA SOCIETAT CATALANA D'ESTUDIS HISTORICS see SOCIETAT CATALANA D'ESTUDIS HISTORICS, BUTLLETI DE LA...

40. CAESARAUGUSTA. S-A. 1951 (1958: no. 11-12). Consejo Superior de Investigaciones Científicas, Institución "Fernando el Católico," Diputación Provincial, Palacio Provincial, Planta Baja, Plaza de España, Zaragoza, for Seminario de Arqueologia y Numismática Aragonesas. Ed: Antonio Beltrán Martínez. Art. on archaeology, numismatics and ethnology, with emphasis on the Aragon provinces; doc.; bk. rev., including general Spanish hist.; professional news; in Spanish and occasionally in French; illus. pv (c. 60-80 ptas)

41. CELTIBERIA. S-A. Centro de Estudios Sorianos Casa de la Cultura, Plaza General Franco 6, Soria. 45 ptas

42. CENTRO DE CULTURA VALENCIANA, ANALES DEL... [Annals of the Valencian Cultural Center]. S-A. 1928 (1959: 2nd series, vol. 20). Centro de Cultura Valenciana, Lonja de la Seda, Valencia. Art. on the literature, art and hist. of Valencia. 100 ptas / 150 ptas

43. LA CIENCIA TOMISTA [Thomistic studies]. Q. Dominicos Españoles, Convento de San Esteban, Salamanca.

44. LAS CIENCIAS [The sciences]. 3xy. Asociación Española para el Progreso de las Ciencias, Valverde 24, Madrid. Includes a section on hist. and philology. 70 ptas

45. LA CIUDAD DE DIOS [The City of God]. Revista Agustinia [Augustinian review]. Q. 1882 (1958: vol. 171). PP.Agustinos, Real Monasterio de El Escorial, El Escorial, Madrid. Art. on church hist., mainly Spanish, and on philosophy, theology and cultural hist.; doc. and texts; bk. rev. section covering theology, philosophy, hist., literature, education and the social sciences; list of bk. received. 90 ptas / $ 4

46. CLAVILEÑO [Name of a fantastic wooden horse in Don Quixote -- ed.]. B-M. Asociación Internacional de Hispanísmo, Velázquez 102, Madrid. Ceased pub. in 1957. 150 ptas

47. COMISARIA GENERAL DE EXCAVACIONES ARQUEOLOGICAS, INFORMES Y MEMORIAS DE LA... [Reports and transactions of the General Commissariat of Archaeological Excavations]. Irr. 1940 (mri 1956: vol. 32). Comisaría General de Excavaciones Arqueológicas, Medinaceli 4, Aptdo. 1039, Madrid. Ed: Julio Martínez Santa-Olalla, Serrano 41, Madrid. Memoirs concerning archaeological excavations in Spain. pv

48. COMISION PROVINCIAL DE MONUMENTOS HISTORICOS Y ARTISTICOS, BOLETIN DE LA... [Bulletin of the Commission for Historical and Artistic Monuments]. S-A. Comisión de Monumentos Históricos y Artísticos, Orense. pni

49. COMISION PROVINCIAL DE MONUMENTOS HISTORICOS Y ARTISTICOS DE LUGO, BOLETIN DE LA... [Bulletin of the District Commission of Historical and Artistic Monuments of Lugo]. S-A. Comisión Provincial de Monumentos Históricos y Artísticos, Plaza de la Soledad 6, Lugo. Includes doc. on the hist. of the province; biblio.; A. name and place indices. 20 ptas

50. COMPOSTELLANUM. Sección de Estudios Jacobeos [Section for studies of St. James]. Q. Consejo Superior de Investigaciones Científicas, Centro de Estudios Jacobeos, Trav. de Altamira 1-2ª, Santiago, for Archidiocesis de Santiago de Compostela. 100 ptas / 150 ptas

51. CUADERNOS AFRICANOS Y ORIENTALES [African and Oriental journal]. Q. Instituto de Estudios Políticos, Plaza de la Marina Española 8, Madrid. Ceased pub. in January 1958. 120 ptas / 120 ptas

52. CUADERNOS DE ESTUDIOS GALLEGOS [Journal of Galician studies]. 3 x y. Consejo Superior de Investigaciones Científicas, Instituto Padre Sarmiento, Medinaceli 4, Madrid. 110 ptas / 110 ptas

53. CUADERNOS DE ESTUDIOS MANCHEGOS [Journal of La Mancha studies]. A. Instituto Estudios Manchegos, Patronato José María Quadrado, Ciudad Real. 20 ptas / 25 ptas

54. CUADERNOS HISPANOAMERICANOS [Hispanic American journal]. Revista Mensual de Cultura Hispánica [Monthly review of Hispanic culture]. M. Instituto de Cultura Hispanica, Avenida de los Reyes Catolicos, Madrid. 200 ptas / 200 ptas

55. CUADERNOS DE HISTORIA DIPLOMATICA [Journal of diplomatic history]. A. 1954 (1957: vol. 4). Consejo Superior de Investigaciones Científicas, Institución "Fernando el Católico," and Seminario de Estudios Inernationales "Jordán de Asso," Universidad de Zaragoza, Zaragoza. Ed: Luis García Arias. Art., with doc., on diplomatic hist., mainly of Spain; rev. of bk. and periodicals, including non-Spanish pub.; biblio.; illus. 100 ptas / 100 ptas

56. CUADERNOS DE HISTORIA PRIMITIVA [Journal of primitive history]. S-A (Irr.). 1946 (mri 1953: vol. 8). Seminario de Historia Primitiva, Serrano 41, Madrid. Ed: Julio Martínez Santa-Olalla, Serrano 41, Madrid. Art. on ancient ethnology and archaeology; bk. rev.; information about excavations. 90 ptas / $1.75

57. DESTIN [Destiny]. Revistă de Cultură Românească [Review of Rumanian culture]. Irr. Ed: George Uscătescu, Melendez Valdes 59, Madrid. In Rumanian.

58. DIRECCION GENERAL DE ARCHIVOS Y BIBLIOTECAS. BOLETIN [General Directorate of Archives and Libraries. Bulletin]. Q. Dirección General de Archivos y Bibliotecas, c/o Biblioteca Nacional, Calvo Soleto 20, Madrid. 125 ptas / 250 ptas

59. EIDOS [Idea]. Revista de Investigación y Cultura [Review of research and culture]. S-A. Institución Teresiana, General Mola 84, Madrid. 70 ptas / 100 ptas

60. EMERITA. Revista de Lingüística y Filología Clásica [Review of linguistics and classical philology]. S-A. Consejo Superior de Investigaciones Científicas, Instituto "Antonio de Nebrija," Medinaceli 4, Madrid.
100 ptas / 130 ptas

61. ESPAÑA MISIONERA [Missionary Spain]. Q. 1944 (1958: vol. 14). Consejo Superior de Misiones, José Marañón 3, Madrid. Ed: Domingo Rodríguez Rancaño. Art. on the hist. of Spanish Catholic missions. Pub. suspended after no. 60 (1958). 60 ptas / 60 ptas

62. ESTUDIOS [Studies]. 3xy. PP. de la Orden de la Merced, Duque de Sexto 32, Madrid. 50 ptas

63. ESTUDIOS ABULENSES [Studies of Avila]. Instituto "Alonso de Madrigal," Avila. 125 ptas / 175 ptas

64. ESTUDIOS AMERICANOS [American studies]. Revista de Síntesis e Interpretación [Review of synthesis and interpretation]. M. 1948 (1959: vol. 17). Escuela de Estudios Hispanoamericanos, Alfonso XII 12, Sevilla. Chief ed: Octavio Gil Munilla. Art. on culture, politics, hist. and historiography, pertaining mainly to Latin America and occasionally to North America; rev. of art.; comments on current cultural and political affairs; news; illus. 150 ptas

65. ESTUDIOS BIBLICOS [Biblical studies]. Q. Consejo Superior de Investigaciones Científicas, Instituto "Francisco Suárez," Medinaceli 4, Madrid.
80 ptas / 120 ptas

66. ESTUDIOS CLASICOS [Classical studies]. 3xy. 1950. Consejo Superior de Investigaciones Científicas, Instituto San José de Calasanz, and Patronato Menéndez y Pelayo Serrano 127, Madrid. 50 ptas

67. ESTUDIOS DE DEUSTO [Deusto studies]. S-A. Universidad de Deusto, Bilbao. Art. on law and occasionally on the hist. of law. 100 ptas / $ 4

68. ESTUDIOS DE EDAD MEDIA DE LA CORONA DE ARAGON [Studies of the Kingdom of Aragon in the Middle Ages]. Irr. 1945 (mri 1956: vol. 6). Consejo Superior de Investigaciones Científicas, Escuela de Estudios Medievales, Universidad de Zaragoza, Zaragoza. Ed: José Maria Lacarra. Art. on the hist. of the Kingdom of Aragon during the Middle Ages; doc.; rev. art.; bk. rev.; professional news and notes. pv

69. ESTUDIOS DE HISTORIA MODERNA [Studies on modern history]. A. 1950 (mri 1956: vol. 5). Centro de Estudios Históricos Internacionales, Facultad de Filosofía y Letras, Universidad de Barcelona, Barcelona. Art. on all aspects of Spanish hist., pertaining mainly to the modern period; doc.; news of professional interest. pv (80-200 ptas)

ESTUDIOS DEL SEMINARIO DE HISTORIA DE LA MEDICINA DE LA UNIVERSIDAD DE SALAMANCA see SEMINARIO DE HISTORIA DE LA MEDICINA DE LA UNIVERSIDAD DE SALAMANCA, ESTUDIOS DEL...

70. ESTUDIOS ECLESIASTICOS [Ecclesiastical studies]. Revista Teológica de Investigación e Información [Theological review of research and information]. Q. Ediciones FAX, Zurbano 80, Aptdo. 8001, Madrid, for the theological faculties of the Univ. of Santander, Granada, Burgos and Barcelona.
140 ptas

71. ESTUDIOS FRANCISCANOS [Franciscan studies]. 3 x y. Convento de los PP. Capuchinos, Barcelona-Sarria. 50 ptas / 65 ptas

72. ESTUDIOS GEOGRAFICOS [Geographical studies]. Q. Consejo Superior de Investigaciones Científicas, Instituto "Juan Sebastián Elcano" de Geografía, Medinaceli 4, Madrid. 125 ptas / 170 ptas

ESTUDIOS HISTORICOS Y DOCUMENTOS DE LOS ARCHIVOS DE PROTOCOLOS see ARCHIVOS DE PROTOCOLOS, ESTUDIOS HISTORICOS Y DOCUMENTOS DE LOS...

73. ESTUDIOS LULIANOS [Studies on (Raymond) Lully]. Revista Cuatrimestral de Investigación Luliana y Medievalística [Tri-annual review of research on Lully and the Middle Ages]. 3 x y. Escuela Lulística, Palma de Mallorca. 100 ptas / 140 ptas

74. ESTUDIOS SEGOVIANOS [Segovian studies]. 3 x y. Consejo Superior de Investigaciones Científicas, Instituto "Diego de Colmenares," Capuchinos Alta, 4 y 6, Segovia. 100 ptas / 125 ptas

75. GOYA. Revista de Arte [Review of art]. B-M. 1953 (1959: vol. 6). Fundación Lázaro Galdiano, Serrano 122, Madrid. Ed: José Camón Aznar. Art. on art and the hist. of art; bk. rev.; biblio.; illus. 150 ptas / $ 6

76. HELMANTICA. Revista de Humanidades Clasicas de la Pontificia Universidad Eclesiástica [Review of classical letters of the Pontifical Ecclesiastical University]. Q. Universidad Pontificia, Salamanca. pni

77. HIDALGUIA [Nobility]. Revista de Genealogía, Nobleza y Armas [Review of genealogy, nobility and arms]. B-M. 1953 (1958: vol. 6). Ed: Vicente de Cadenas, calle de Atocha 91, Madrid. Art. on Spanish genealogy and heraldry; professional news on the activities of Spanish and foreign heraldic and genealogical soc.; biblio. 450 ptas / $ 11

78. HISPANIA. Revista Española de Historia [Spanish historical review]. Q. 1940 (1959: vol. 19). Consejo Superior de Investigaciones Científicas, Instituto "Jerónimo Zurita," Medinaceli 4, Madrid. Ed. board: Antonio de la Torre (chief ed.), Eloy Benito Ruano (secretary). Art. on hist., mainly of Spain, with emphasis on medieval and early modern court and political hist.; bk. rev., including general hist. literature. 150 ptas / 200 ptas

79. HISPANIA SACRA. Revista de Historia Eclesiástica [Review of ecclesiastical history]. S-A. 1948 (1958: vol. 11). Consejo Superior de Investigaciones Científicas, Instituto "P. Enrique Flórez," Serrano 123, Madrid. Ed: José Vives, Durán y Bas 9, Barcelona. Art. on the hist. of the Roman Catholic Church, mainly in Spain, and on Church-State relations; doc.; bk. rev. 100 ptas

80. HUMANIDADES [Humanities]. Revista de las Literaturas Clásicas Griega, Latina y Nacional [Review of the classical Greek, Latin and national literatures]. S-A. Universidad Pontificia Comillas, Santander. 70 ptas / $3

81. IBIZA. Irr. Instituto de Estudios Ibicencos, Ibiza, Baleares. p (1) 6 ptas

82. ILERDA. S-A. Consejo Superior de Investigaciones Científicas, Instituto de Estudios Ilerdenses de la Diputación Provincial, Lérida. 30 ptas

83. INDICE [Index]. De artes y letras [Of arts and letters]. M. Juan Fernández Figueroa, Juan Bravo 62, Madrid. 210 ptas / $ 8

INFORMES Y MEMORIAS DE LA COMISARIA GENERAL DE EXCAVACIONES ARQUEOLOGICAS see COMISARIA GENERAL DE EXCAVACIONES ARQUEOLOGICAS, INFORMES Y MEMORIAS DE LA...

84. INSTITUCION FERNAN GONSALEZ Y COMISION PROVINCIAL DE MONUMENTOS, BOLETIN DE LA... [Bulletin of the Fernán González Institution and of the District Monuments Commission]. Q. Institución Fernán González, Palacio de la Diputación, Sala Cidiana de la Excma, Diputación Provincial, Burgos 35 ptas / 65 ptas

85. INSTITUCION TELLO TELLEZ DE MENESES, PUBLICACIONES DE LA... [Publications of the Tello Tellez de Meneses Institution]. A. Institución Tello Tellez de Meneses, Diputación Provincial, Palencia. 40 ptas / 60 ptas

86. INSTITUTO BERNARDINO DE SAHAGUN, DE ANTROPOLOGIA Y ETNOLOGIA, TRABAJOS DEL... [Works of the Bernardino de Sahagún Institute of Anthropology and Ethnology]. Irr. Consejo Superior de Investigaciones Científicas, Instituto "Bernardino de Sahagún," Paseo de Atocha 11, Madrid. pv

87. INSTITUTO DE ESTUDIOS AFRICANOS, ARCHIVOS DEL... [Archives of the Institute of African Studies]. 3xy. Patronato "Diego Saavedra Fajardo," Instituto de Estudios Africanos, Castellana 5, Madrid. Ed: José Díaz de Villegas, Manuel Melis Clavería. Art. on Africa, with emphasis on Spanish territories; divided into sections on natural sciences and the humanities. 45 ptas / 60 ptas

88. INSTITUTO DE ESTUDIOS ASTURIANOS, BOLETIN DEL... [Bulletin of the Institute of Asturian studies]. 3xy. Instituto de Estudios Asturianos, Santa Susana 1, Oviedo. 60 ptas / 65 ptas

89. INSTITUTO DE ESTUDIOS GERUNDENSES, ANALES DEL... [Annals of the Institute for the Study of Gerona]. A. Consejo Superior de Investigaciones Científicas, Instituto de Estudios Gerundenses, Plaza del Aceite 7, Gerona. 60 ptas / 70 ptas

90. INSTITUTO DE ESTUDIOS GIENNENSES, BOLETIN DE LA... [Bulletin of the Institute of Jaén studies]. Q. Instituto de Estudios Giennenses, Palacio Provincial, Jaén. pni

91. INSTITUTO DE ESTUDIOS ISLAMICOS, REVISTA DEL... [Review of the Institute of Islamic Studies]. S-A. 1953 (1957: vol. 5). Instituto de Estudios Islámicos, Matías Montero 14, Madrid. Ed: Mahmoud Makki. Art. on Hispanic-Arabic studies, with emphasis on cultural hist. and the impact of Arabic culture, thought and religion on Spain; separate sections in Arabic and in European languages. Prior to 1958 pub. under the title: Revista del Instituto Egipcio de Estudios Islámicos. 120 ptas / $ 4.50

INSTITUTO EGIPCIO DE ESTUDIOS ISLAMICOS, REVISTA DEL... see preceding entry

92. JERONIMO ZURITA. Cuadernos de Historia [Journal of history]. Irr. 1951 (1954 [1958]: vol. 6/7). Consejo Superior de Investigaciones Científicas, Instituto "Fernando el Católico," Diputación Provincial, Zaragoza. Ed: Angel Canellas, José Navarro Latorre. Art. on the political and cultural hist. of Spain, with emphasis on the time of Ferdinand II of Aragon and the Kingdom of Aragon, and coccasionally on the hist. of other countries; historiographical material; doc.; bk. rev. and biblio. classified under "Generalia," "Europea," "Ibérica," "Aragonensia" and "Americana"; professional news; subject, name and place indices. pv (p (1) 35-50 ptas)

93. MISCELANEA COMILLAS. Colaboración Científica de los Profesores y Doctores de la Universidad [Scientific collaboration of the professors and doctors of the University]. S-A. 1942 (1959: vol. 31). Universidad Pontificia, Comillas, Santander. Ed: Camilo M. Abad, Quintín Aldea. Well-documented art. on the ecclesiastical and general hist. of Spain, with emphasis on the late medieval and early modern periods. pv

94. MISCELANEA DE ESTUDIOS ARABES Y HEBRAICOS [Miscellany of Arabic and Hebraic studies]. Anejo al Boletín de la Universidad de Granada [Annex to the "Bulletin of the University of Granada"]. S-A. 1952 (1958: vol. 7). Secretariado de Publicaciones de la Universidad de Granada, Granada. Ed: Luis Seco de Lucena Paredes, David Gonzalo Maeso, Darío Cabanelas, O.P.M. Art. on Hebrew philology, the Bible, Judaism, Islam, and Arabic studies; bk. rev. pni

95. MISSIONALIA HISPANICA. 3xy. 1944 (1958: vol. 15). Consejo Superior de Investigaciones Científicas, Departamento de Misionologia, Serrano 123, Madrid. Ed: Fidel de Lejarza, O.F.M., Manuel Merino, O.S.A. Art. on the hist. of Hispanic Catholic missions; biblio. 100 ptas / 130 ptas

96. MUNDO [World]. Revista de Política Exterion y Economía [Review of foreign policy and economics]. W. Vicente Gállego y Castro, c/o Quintana 15, Aptdo. 998, Madrid. 300 ptas

97. MURGETANA. Academia de Alfonso X, El Sabio, de Murcia, Murcia. pni

98. MUSEO CANARIO [Museum of the Canaries]. Irr. Museo Canario, Dr. Chil y Naranjo 33, Las Palmas, Islas Canarias. 45 ptas / 45 ptas

99. EL MUSEO DE PONTEVEDRA [The Museum of Pontevedra]. Q. Patronato del Museo de Pontevedra, Calle de la Pasantería, Pontevedra. 50 ptas

100. MUSEOS DE ARTE DE BARCELONA, ANALES Y BOLETIN DE LOS.... [Annals and bulletin of the Museums of Art in Barcelona]. A. Museos de Arte de Barcelona, Palacio de la Ciudadela (Parque), Barcelona. pv (c. 150 ptas)

101. NOTICIARIO ARQUEOLOGICO HISPANO [Spanish archaeological newsletter]. Irr. 1952 (1959: vol. 3). Comisaría General de Excavaciones Arqueológicas, Medinaceli 4, Aptdo. 1039, Madrid. Ed: Julio Martínez Santa-Olalla, Serrano 41, Madrid. Archaeological news; short reports on excavations; biblio. of Spanish archaeological work. 900 ptas / $ 15

102. NUESTRO TIEMPO [Our time]. Revista de Cuestiones Actuales [Review of current problems]. M. Sociedad Anónima de Revista, Periódicos y Ediciones, Gaztambide 11, Madrid. 100 ptas

103. NUMARIO HISPANICO [Spanish numismatics]. S-A. 1952 (1958: vol. 7). Consejo Superior de Investigaciones Científicas, Instituto "Antonio Agustin" de Numismatica, Serrano 13, Madrid. Ed: Joaquín Ma de Navascués y de Juan. Art. on the numismatic hist. of Spain, and on Greek and Roman numismatics; notes on recent discoveries of coins; news on international numismatic soc. and meetings; descriptions of museum collections of coins; bk. rev.; biblio. of numismatic journals, classified by country. 160 ptas / 215 ptas

104. NUMISMA [Coin]. Q. 1951 (1958: vol. 8). Sociedad Ibero-Americana de Estudios Numismáticos, Plaza de Colón 4, Madrid. Ed: F. Xavier Calicó. Art. on the hist. of coins, medals and minting; bk. rev.; biblio. 50 ptas

105. ORIENTE CRISTIANO [Christian Orient]. M. 1944. Centro de Estudios Orientales - Conde de Cartagena 47, Madrid. 20 ptas

106. ORIENTE EUROPEO [European Orient]. Q. 1951 (mri 1956: vol. 6). Centro de Estudios Orientales - Conde Cartagena 47, Madrid. 40 ptas / 50 ptas

107. PERSPECTIVE CREŞTINE [Christian perspectives]. Ed: Pater Alexandru Mircea, Calle Santa Amelia 45 (Sarriá), Barcelona. pv (c. $ 5)

108. PIRINEOS [Pyrenees]. Q. 1945 (1957: vol. 13). Consejo Superior de Investigaciones Científicas, Patronato "Diego Saavedra Fajardo," Instituto de Estudios Pirenaicos, calle de Costa 18, Zaragoza. Ed. board: José García Siñériz, Luis Solé Sabarís, José Manuel Casas Torres, Juan Antonio Cremades Royo. Art. on the cultural, economic and political hist. of the Pyrenees region of France and Spain, with emphasis on the period at the end of the Middle Ages, and on toponymy, linguistics, geography and natural sciences; biblio. with brief rev., classified by subject; in Spanish, Catalan or French; Spanish, French or German sum.; maps; illus. 150 ptas

109. POLITICA INTERNACIONAL [International politics]. B-M. Instituto de Estudios Políticos, Plaza de la Marina Española 8, Madrid. Biblio. of art., grouped by subject and country; doc. 100 ptas / 120-150 ptas

110. PRINCIPE DE VIANA [Prince of Viana]. Q. 1940 (1960: vol. 21). Consejo de Cultura de Navarra de la Excma, Diputación Foral, Institución "Príncipe de Viana," Pamplona. Art. on the hist., archaeology, art and literature of the ancient Kingdom of Navarre; bk. rev.; biblio. p (1) 30 ptas

PUBLICACIONES DE LA INSTITUCION TELLO TELLEZ DE MENESES see INSTITUCION TELLO TELLEZ DE MENESES, PUBLICACIONES DE LA...

111. PUNTA EUROPA [Promontory of Europe]. M. Vicente Marrero, Montalbán 14, Madrid. 150 ptas

112. RAZON Y FE [Reason and faith]. Revista Hispanoamericana de Cultura [Hispanic-American cultural review]. M. Ediciones FAX, Zurbano 80, Aptdo. 8001, Madrid. 140 ptas / $ 4

113. REAL ACADEMIA DE BUENAS LETRAS DE BARCELONA, BOLETIN DE LA... [Bulletin of the Royal Academy of Letters in Barcelona]. A. 1901 (1957/58: vol. 27). Real Academia de Buenas Letras, Obispo Cassador 3, Barcelona. Ed: Ramón de Abadal y Viñals (president), Obispo Cassador 3, Barcelona. Art. on the hist., art, philology and literature of Catalonia; in Spanish and Catalan. pni

114. REAL ACADEMIA DE CORDOBA, BOLETIN DE LA... [Bulletin of the Royal Academy of Córdoba]. S-A. Real Academia de Córdoba de Ciencias, Bellas Letras y Nobles Artes, Palacio de la Diputación, Córdoba. 100 ptas

115. REAL ACADEMIA DE LA HISTORIA, BOLETIN DE LA... [Bulletin of the Royal Academy of History]. Q. 1877 (1959: vol. 145). Real Academia de la Historia, León 21, Madrid. Ed: Francisco-Javier Sánchez Cantón, Alfonso XII, 52, Madrid. Art. on hist., archaeology and art, with emphasis on Spain. 200 ptas / 300 ptas

116. REAL ACADEMIA ESPAÑOLA, BOLETIN DE LA... [Bulletin of the Royal Academy of Spain]. 3xy. Real Academia Española, Felipe IV, 4, Madrid. 50 ptas

117. REAL ACADEMIA GALLEGA, BOLETIN DE LA... [Bulletin of the Royal Academy of Galicia]. B-M. Real Academia Gallega, La Coruña. pni

118. REAL SOCIEDAD GEOGRAPHICA, BOLETIN DE LA... [Bulletin of the Royal Geographical Society]. Q. Real Sociedad Geográfica, Valverde 18, Madrid. 60 ptas / 76 ptas

119. REAL SOCIEDAD VASCONGADA DE AMIGOS DEL PAIS, BOLETIN DE LA... [Bulletin of the Basque Society of the Friends of the Country]. Q. Real Sociedad Vascongada de Amigos del País, Museo de San Telmo, Plaza de Ignacio Zuloaga, San Sebastian. 60 ptas

120. RELIGION Y CULTURA [Religion and culture]. Q. Provincia Agustiniana del Santísimo Nombre de Jesús de España, Columela 12, Madrid. 100 ptas

REVISTA. For titles beginning with "Revista," followed by the name of the publishing or sponsoring institution or society, see the respective institution or society.

121. REVISTA DE ARCHIVOS, BIBLIOTECAS Y MUSEOS [Review of archives, libraries and museums]. S-A. 1871 (1958: vol. 64). Cuerpo de Archiveros, Bibliotecarios y Arqueólogos, Calvo Sotelo 20, Madrid. Ed: Director General, Archivos y Bibliotecas. Art. on Spanish hist., with emphasis on the humanites, archaeological studies, methodology of hist. research, library science and archival techniques; bk. rev., including reference works and biblio. from non-Hispanic countries; in Spanish and occasionally in English, French or German. 200 ptas / 300 ptas

122. REVISTA DE DIALECTOLOGIA Y TRADICIONES POPULARES [Review of dialectology and popular traditions]. Q. 1945. Consejo Superior de Investigaciones Científicas, Centro de Estudios de Etnología, Peninsular, Vitrubio 16, Madrid. Ed: Vicente García de Diego, Felipe IV, 4, Madrid. Art. on dialectology, ethnology and folklore; rev. of bk. and art.; A. biblio. of bk. received. 100 ptas

123. REVISTA DE ESTUDIOS EXTREMEÑOS [Review of studies of Extremadura]. 3xy. Institución de Servicios Culturales de la Diputación Provincial, Flechas Negras 1, Badajoz. 60 ptas / 70 ptas

124. REVISTA DE ESTUDIOS POLITICOS [Review of political studies]. B-M. 1941 (1958: no. 97-104). Instituto de Estudios Políticos, Plaza de la Marina Española 8, Madrid. Ed: Francisco Javier Conde García. Art. on political science, political thought, constitutional law, international relations, sociology, political hist., and on issues concerning the Spanish-speaking countries; bk. rev.; abstr. of art.; news on the activities of the inst. 100 ptas

125. REVISTA DE FILOLOGIA ESPAÑOLA [Review of Spanish philology]. Q. Consejo Superior de Investigaciones Científicas, Instituto "Miguel de Cervantes," Medinaceli 4, Madrid. 150 ptas / 200 ptas

REVISTA DE HISTORIA see next entry

126. REVISTA DE HISTORIA CANARIA [Review of the history of the Canaries]. Q (usually 2 double no. p.a.). 1924 (1958: vol. 24, no. 121-124). Universidad de la Laguna, Facultad de Filosofía y Letras, La Laguna de Tenerife, Islas Canarias. Ed: Elías Serra Ráfols. Art. on the hist., language and culture of the Canary Islands and Spain; doc.; bk. rev.; biblio. of periodical literature; professional news; genealogical tables. Prior to 1958 pub. under the title: Revista de Historia. 100 ptas

127. REVISTA DE HISTORIA MILITAR [Review of military history]. Q. 1956 (1959: vol. 4). Servicio Histórico Militar, Estado Mayor Central, Mártires de Alcalá 9, Madrid. Art. on the hist. of war and military organization; bk. rev.; biblio. 150 ptas

128. REVISTA DE IDEAS ESTETICAS [Review of aesthetic ideas]. Q. Consejo Superior de Investigaciones Científicas, Instituto "Diego Velázquez," Medinaceli 4, Madrid. 80 ptas / 110 ptas

129. REVISTA DE INDIAS [Review of the Indies]. Q. 1940 (1959: vol. 19). Consejo Superior de Investigaciones Científicas, Instituto "Gonzalo Fernández de Oviedo," Medinaceli 4, Madrid. Ed. board: Ciriaco Pérez Bustamente, Rodolfo Barón Castro, Manuel Ballesteros Gaibrois. Art. on the hist. of the Americas and the West Indies, with emphasis on the Spanish-speaking West Indies; doc.; rev. of bk. and art.; in Spanish, French and other European languages; A. indices; general index for vol. 1-12 (1940-53). 100 ptas / 150 ptas

130. REVISTA DE LITERATURA [Review of literature]. Q. Consejo Superior de Investigaciones Científicas, Medinaceli 4, Madrid. 100 ptas

131. REVISTA DE MENORCA [Review of Minorca]. M. Ateneo Científico Literário y Artístico de Mahón, Plaza de José Antonio 7, Mahón, Baleares. 60 ptas

132. REVISTA INTERNACIONAL DE SOCIOLOGIA [International review of sociology]. Q. 1942 (1959: vol. 17, no. 65-68). Consejo Internacional de Investigaciones Científicas, Instituto Balmes de Sociología, Medinaceli 4, Madrid. Art. on sociology, population problems, social thought and hist.; bk. rev.; notes. 75 ptas

133. SAITABI [Ancient name of Játiva (province of Valencia) -- ed.]. B. Institutos de Investigaciones Históricas "Roque Chabás" y "Juan Bautista Maña," Facultad de Filosofía y Letras; Universidad de Valencia, Valencia. p(1) 50 ptas

134. SALMANTICENSIS. Commentarius de Sacris Disciplinis Cura Facultatum Pontificiae Universitatis Editus. 3xy. Universidad Pontificia, Salamanca. 80 ptas / $ 4

135. SANTES CREUS. A. Archivo Bibliográfico de Santes Creus, Plaza de San Bernardo Calvó, Santes Creus, Tarragona. Doc. and texts on the hist. of the monastery; in Spanish and Catalan. 150 ptas

136. SCRINIUM. Irr. 1951 (1956-59 [1960]: no. 16-22). Archivo y Biblioteca Capitular de la S.I. Catedral de Barcelona, Barcelona. Information about the manuscript materials of the pub. institution, pertaining mainly to the medieval period; doc. pni

137. SEFARAD [Hebrew name for Spain -- ed.]. S-A. 1941 (1958: vol. 18). Consejo Superior de Investigaciones Científicas, Instituto Arias Montano de Estudios Hebraicos y Oriente Próximo, Serrano 117, Madrid. Ed: Francisco Cantera y Burgos, Viriato 46, Madrid; José María Millás Vallicrosa. Art. on Jewish hist., with emphasis on the cultural and religious hist. of Jewish communities in Spain; philological essays; bk. rev.; comprehensive biblio. of Spanish and non-Spanish periodicals, with table of contents and abstr.; list of pub. received; notes and news; in Spanish and occasionally in English; illus. 110 ptas / 120 ptas

138. SEMINARIO DE ARTE ARAGONES [Seminar of Aragon art]. A. Institución "Fernando el Católico," Plaza de España, Zaragoza. 75 ptas / 85 ptas

139. SEMINARIO DE ESTUDIOS DE ARTE Y ARQUEOLOGIA, BOLETIN DEL... [Bulletin of the Seminar for Studies of Art and Archaeology]. A. 1932 (1958: vol. 24). Universidad de Valladolid, Valladolíd. Ed: José María de Azcárate, Pedro de Palol. Art. on Spanish archaeology and art hist.; bk. rev. 125 ptas

140. SEMINARIO DE HISTORIA DE LA MEDICINA DE LA UNIVERSIDAD DE SALAMANCA, ESTUDIOS DEL... [Studies of the Seminar for the History of Medicine, University of Salamanca]. Irr. 1956/57 (1958/59: vol. 2). Seminari de Historia de la Medicina, Universidad de Salamanca. Ed: Luis Granjel. Art. and studies on the hist. of medicine; bk. rev.; biblio. pni

141. SOCIEDAD ARQUEOLOGICA LULIANA, BOLETIN DE LA... [Bulletin of the (Raymond) Lully Archaeological Society]. Q. Sociedad Arqueológica Luliana, Almudaina 8, Palma de Mallorca, Baleares. 60 ptas

142. SOCIEDAD CASTELLONENSE DE CULTURA, BOLETIN DE LA... [Bulletin of the Cultural Society of Castellon]. Q. Sociedad Castellonense de Cultura, c/o Biblioteca Municipal. Calle Mayor. 60 ptas

143. SOCIEDAD ESPAÑOLA DE ANTROPOLOGIA, ETNOGRAFIA Y PREHISTORIA, ACTAS Y MEMORIAS DE LA... [Proceedings and transactions of the Spanish Society of Anthropology, Ethnography and Prehistory]. A. (mri 1951: vol. 26). Sociedad Española de Antropología, Etnografía y Prehistoria,

Aptdo. 1014, Madrid. Ed: Julio Martínez Santa-Olalla, Serrano 41, Madrid. Art. on anthropology, ethnography and prehist.; bk. rev.; news of the activities of the soc. pv

144. SOCIEDAD ESPAÑOLA DE HISTORIA DE LA FARMACIA, BOLETIN DE LA... [Bulletin of the Spanish Society for the History of Pharmacy]. Ciencia, Literatura y Arte [Science, literature and arts]. Q. 1950 (1959: vol. 10). Sociedad de Historia de la Farmacia, Campoamor 18, Madrid. Ed: Rafael Roldan y Guerrero, Povedilla 13, Madrid. Art. on the hist. of pharmacy. 50 ptas (memb. free)

145. SOCIETAT CATALANA D'ESTUDIS HISTORICS, BUTLLETI DE LA... [Bulletin of the Catalan Society of Historical Studies]. A. Societat Catalana d'Estudis Històrics, P.O.B. 1146, Barcelona. Art. on the hist. of Catalonia and the areas comprising the medieval Kingdom of Aragon, from prehist. times to the modern period; biblio.; professional notes; sum. of the activities of the various sections of the soc.; in Catalan. pni

146. STUDIA MONASTICA. S-A. 1959 (1959: vol. 1). Abadía de Montserrat, Barcelona. Art. on monastic hist.; bk. rev.; chronicles; research news; in Catalan, Latin and modern European languages. 250 ptas / $ 6.25

147. TERUEL. S-A. Instituto de Estudios Turolenses, Plaza del Seminario, Teruel. 40 ptas

TRABAJOS DEL INSTITUTO BERNARDINO DE SAHAGUN, DE ANTROPOLOGIA Y ETNOLOGIA see INSTITUTO BERNARDINO DE SAHAGUN, DE ANTROPOLOGIA Y ETNOLOGIA, TRABAJOS DEL...

148. TRABAJOS Y CONFERENCIAS [Works and lectures]. Irr. 1952 (1959: vol. 3). Seminario de Estudios Americanistas, Facultad de Filosofía y Letras, Universidad de Madrid. Ed: Manuel Ballesteros-Gaibrois. Art. and reprints of lectures on ethnology, hist. and archaeology pertaining to America; accounts of theses and memoirs. p (1) 20 ptas / $ 0.50

149. UNIVERSIDAD [University]. Revista de Cultura y Vida Universitaria [Review of culture and university life]. S-A. Universidad de Zaragoza, Zaragoza. 175 ptas / 250 ptas

150. UNIVERSIDAD COMPOSTELANA, BOLETIN DE LA... [Bulletin of the Compostela University]. A. Secretariado Universitario de Publicaciones, Universidad de Santiago de Compostela, Santiago de Compostela. Includes art. on medieval and Galician hist. pni

151. UNIVERSIDAD DE GRANADA, BOLETIN DE LA... [Bulletin of the University of Granada]. Revista General [General review]. Irr. Universidad de Granada, Secretariado de Publicaciones, Granada. Includes as a S-A supplement: Miscelánea de Estudios Arabes y Hebraicos. pni

152. UNIVERSIDAD DE MADRID, REVISTA DE LA... [Review of the University of Madrid]. Q. 1870 (1958: vol. 7). Universidad de Madrid, San Bernardo 49, Madrid. Ed: Rector, Univ. of Madrid. Art. on subjects covering all fields of learning, with some emphasis on the humanities; sum. of doctorate theses submitted at the univ.; news from the univ.; illus.; individual no. devoted to special subjects. 100 ptas / 150 ptas

153. UNIVERSIDAD DE MURCIA, ANALES DE LA... [Annals of the University of Murcia]. Filosofía y Letras [Philsophy and letters]. Q. Universidad de Murcia, 1 Santo Cristo, Murcia. pni

154. UNIVERSIDAD DE VALENCIA, ANALES DE LA... [Annals of the University of Valencia]. A. Secretariado de Publicaciones, Universidad de Valencia. Art. pertaining to the respective fields of studies of each faculty of the univ. pni

155. UNIVERSIDAD HISPALENSE, ANALES DE LA... [Annals of the University of Seville]. A. 1938 (1959: vol. 20). Universidad de Sevilla, Sevilla. Art. pertaining to the respective fields of studies of each faculty of the univ. pni

156. VERDAD Y VIDA [Truth and life]. Revista de las Ciencias del Espíritu [Review of spiritual sciences]. Q. 1943 (1959: vol. 17). PP. Franciscanos de San Francisco el Grande, San Buenaventura 1, Madrid. Ed: Bernardo Aperribay. 100 ptas / 150 ptas

157. ZARAGOZA. S-A. Institución "Fernando el Católico," Diputación Provincial, Zaragoza. pni

158. ZEPHYRUS. 3xy. Seminario de Arqueología, Facultad de Filsofía y Letras, Universidad de Salamanca, Salamanca. 125 ptas / 200 ptas

---

Sweden

Prepared with the assistance of

Nils Palmborg, Librarian, Universitetsbiblioteket
[The University Library], Lund

1. ACADEMIA REGIA SCIENTIARUM UPSALIENSIS, ANNALES (Annales Academiae Regiae Scientiarum Upsaliensis). A. 1957 (1959: vol. 3). Almqvist och Wiksell, Gamla Brogatan 26, Stockholm C., for Kungl. Vetenskapssamhället i Uppsala [Royal Acad. of Arts and Sciences of Uppsala]. Research art. on all branches of learning, particularly those represented at the Univ. of Uppsala and the neighboring Agricultural College of Ultuna; in English, French or German; occasional sum. pv (Scr 18-20)

2. AKADEMISKA FÖRENINGENS ÅRSSKRIFT [Yearbook of the Academic Society]. A. 1955 (1959: no vol. indic.). Akademiska föreningen, Lund. Ed. board: Daniel Hjort, Sven Håkan Ohlsson, Ture Sjögren. Art. on the Univ. of Lund and the hist. of student life in Lund. pni

3. ÅKERBO HEMBYGDSFÖRENING. ÅRSBOK [Åkerbo Local Society. Yearbook]. A. Åkerbo hembygdsförening, Böda. Scr 4.50

4. AKTUELLT OCH HISTORISKT [Topical and historical subjects]. A. 1953 (1958: no vol. indic.). Hörsta förlag AB, for Försvarsstabens krigshistoriska avdelning [Dept. of War Hist. of the Defense Staff], Stockholm 80. Art. on Scandinavian military hist. from the 17th cent. to the present; English sum.; maps, illus. Scr 7.50 / $2

5. ÅNGERMANLAND. Irr. Ångermanlands hembygdsförbund [Local Soc. of Ångermanland], Härnösand. Scr 6

ANNALES ACADEMIAE REGIAE SCIENTIARUM UPSALIENSIS see ACADEMIA REGIA SCIENTIARUM UPSALIENSIS, ANNALES...

6. ARBETARNAS KULTURHISTORISKA SÄLLSKAP, NOTISER FRÅN... [Bulletin of the Workers' Society for the History of Culture]. B-M. 1926 (1957: no vol. indic.). Ivan Larsson, Johanneshov, Thunbergsgatan 25, for Arbetarnas kulturhistoriska sällskap. Ed: E.J. Lundqvist, Pontonjärgatan 28 I, Stockholm. Short art. on the hist. of professions and trades. pni

7. ARKIV FÖR NORRLÄNDSK HEMBYGDSFORSKNING [Archives of Norrland Local Research]. Irr. Kulturhistoriska föreningen Murberget [Soc. for Cultural Hist. "Murberget"], Härnösand. Scr 12

ÅRSBERÄTTELSE. For titles beginning with "Årsberättelse," followed by the name of the publishing or sponsoring institution or society, see the respective institution or society.

ÅRSBOK. For titles beginning with "Årsbok," followed by the name of the publishing or sponsoring institution or society, see the respective institution or society.

ÅRSSKRIFT. For titles beginning with "Årsskrift," followed by the name of the publishing or sponsoring institution or society, see the respective institution or society.

ÅRSTRYCK. For titles beginning with "Årstryck," followed by the name of the publishing or sponsoring institution or society, see the respective institution or society.

8. ARV [Heritage]. Tidskrift för nordisk folkminnesforskning. Journal of Scandinavian Folklore. A. 1945 (1957: vol. 13). Almqvist och Wiksells boktryckeri AB, Uppsala, for Kungl. Gustav Adolfs Akademien [Royal Gustavus Adolphus Acad.], Uppsala. Ed: Dag Strömbäck, Wahlenbergsvägen 13, Uppsala. Art. on Scandinavian and comparative folklore; rev. art.; bk. rev.; in Swedish, Danish, Norwegian, English, French or German; English sum. of art. in Scandinavian languages; illus. Scr 15 / $3

9. BIDRAG TILL SÖDERMANLANDS ÄLDRE KULTURHISTORIA [Contributions to Södermanland's earlier cultural history]. Irr. Södermanlands fornminnesförening [Södermanland Antiquarian Soc.], Strängnäs. pni

10. BLEKINGEBOKEN [Blekinge book]. A. Blekinge musei- och hembygdsförbund [Blekinge Museum and Local Soc.], Karlskrona. Scr 7

11. BONNIERS LITTERÄRA MAGASIN MED ALL VÄRLDENS BERÄTTARE [Bonnier's literary magazine with reports from the whole world]. 10 x y. Albert Bonniers förlag, Sveavägen 56, Stockholm C. Scr 25 / $4.82

12. BROMMA HEMBYGDSFÖRENINGS ÅRSSKRIFT [Yearbook of the Bromma Local Society]. A. Hugo Hamilton, Ålstensgatan 87, Bromma, for Bromma hembygdsförening, Bromma. Scr 7.50

BULLETIN. For titles beginning with "Bulletin," followed by the name of the publishing or sponsoring institution or society, see the respective institution or society.

13. BYGD OCH NATUR [Countryside and nature]. 5 x y. Samfundet för hembygdsvård [Soc. for the Preservation of Local Monuments], Mäster Samuelsgatan 3, Stockholm. pni

14. CARL JOHANS FÖRBUNDETS HANDLINGAR [Proceedings of the Carl Johan Society]. Quinquennial. 1852 (1948-52: no vol. indic.). Carl Johans förbundet, Uppsala. Ed: A. Liljenkrantz, Walleriusvägen 12, Uppsala. Art. on the life and times of Carl Johan (General Bernadotte), and on related subjects; report on the activities of the soc.; list of memb.; illus.; table of contents for the period 1848 to 1947 in the 1948-52 vol. Scr 5 / $1

15. CREDO. Katolsk tidskrift [Catholic review]. 5 x y. Pub. address: S:t Johannesgatan 5 b, Uppsala. Scr 20

16. DAEDALUS. A. Tekniska museet [Technical Museum], Stockholm Ö. Scr 20 / $5

17. DALARNAS HEMBYGDSBOK [Local book of Dalecarlia]. A. Dalarnas fornminnes- och hembygdsförbund [Antiquarian and Local Soc. of Dalecarlia], Falun. Scr 8 / $2

18. EKERÖ FÖRR OCH NU [Ekerö past and present]. Sockenhistorisk årsskrift [Parish history yearbook]. A. Pub. in Ekerö. Scr 3

19. EKONOMISK REVY [Economic review]. 10 x y. Swedish Banks Assoc., P.O.B. 16143, Stockholm 16. Scr 12

20. EKONOMISK TIDSKRIFT [Economic review]. Q. Almqvist och Wiksells boktryckeri AB, Uppsala. pni

21. ETHNOS. Q. Statens etnografiska museum [State Ethnographical Museum], Stockholm Ö. Scr 15 / $ 3

22. FALBYGDEN [Fal country]. A. Falbygdens hembygds- och fornminnesförening [Fal Local and Antiquarian Soc.], Falköping. Scr 7

23. FATABUREN [Store-house]. Nordiska museets och Skansens årsbok [Yearbook of the Nordic Museum and Skansen]. A. 1881 (mri 1953: no vol. indic.). Nordiska museet, Stockholm. Ed: Erik Andrén. Art. mostly on museum holdings, reflecting on all aspects of Swedish hist., including arts, applied arts, furniture and clothing; reports on new acquisitions of the museum; English sum. of all art., printed separately; illus. Scr 10

24. FOLK-LIV [Folk life]. Acta Ethnologica et Folkloristica Europaea. Irr. 1937 (1957: vol. 21). Generalstabens litografiska anstalts förlag, Drottninggaten 20, Stockholm C, for Kungl. Gustav Adolfs Akademien [Royal Gustavus Adolphus Acad.], Stockholm Ö. Ed: Sigurd Erixon, Ormängsgatan 63, Stockholm-Vällingby. Art. on European ethnology and folklore; bk. rev.; notes and news on professional congresses and meetings; in Swedish, German, English, French or Danish; English or German sum. of several Swedish-language art.; illus. pv

25. FÖRENINGEN GAMLA HALMSTADS ÅRSBOK [Yearbook of the Society for Old Halmstad]. A. Föreningen Gamla Halmstad, Halmstad. Scr 12

26. FÖRENINGEN ÖREBRO LÄNS MUSEUM. MEDDELANDEN [Örebro Country Museum Society. Communications]. Irr. Örebro Läns museum, Örebro. Scr 3

FÖRENINGEN SVERIGES SJÖFARTSMUSEUM I STOCKHOLM. ÅRSBOK see SJÖHISTORISK ÅRSBOK

27. FORNVÄNNEN [The friend of antiquity]. Tidskrift för Svensk antikvarisk forskning. Journal of Swedish Antiquarian Research. B-M. 1906 (mri 1956: vol. 51). Kungl. vitterhets-, historie- och antikvitetsakademien [Royal Acad. of Letters, Hist. and Antiquity], in collaboration with Svenska fornminnesföreningen [Swedish Archaeological Assoc.], Storgatan 41, Stockholm Ö. Ed. board: Bengt Thordeman, Erik Bohrn, Ulla Behr. Art. on the prehist., ancient and medieval archaeology and hist. of Scandinavia, with emphasis on Sweden, and on philology, religion, folklore, numismatics, and preservation of monuments; rev. art.; bk. rev.; biblio. of bk. and periodicals; notes on excavations in progress and news of Swedish archaeological museums and soc.; English, German or French sum.; illus.; subject and author index for the years 1906-55 in no. 6, 1955. Scr 20

28. FRÅN ÅDALAR OCH FJÄLL. HÄRNÖSANDS STIFTS JULBOK [From valleys and mountains. The Christmas book of the Härnösand diocese]. A. Gustaf Risberg, Skönsberg, for Härnösands stift. Scr 4.50

29. FRÅN BERGSLAG OCH BONDEBYGD [From mining district and farmer's country]. A. Örebro Läns museum [Örebro Country Museum], Örebro. Scr 15

30. FRÅN BORÅS OCH DE SJU HÄRADERNA [From Borås and the Seven Countries]. A. Borås museum, Borås. Scr 10 / $2.30

31. FRÅN BYGD OCH VILDMARK I VÄSTERBOTTEN OCH NORRBOTTEN LULEÅ STIFTS JULBOK [From settlements and wilderness in Västerbotten and Norrbotten. The Christmas book of the Luleå diocese]. A. Västerbottens tryckeri aktiebolag, Skellefteå. Scr 4

32. FRÅN GÄSTRIKLAND [From Gästrikland]. A. Gästriklands kulturhistoriska förening [Gästrikland Soc. for Cultural Hist.], Gävle museum, Gävle. Scr 10

33. FRÅN STAD OCH BYGD I MEDELPAD [From town and country in Medelpad]. Irr. Pub. in Sundsvall. Scr 15

34. GAMMAL HÄLSINGEKULTUR [The old culture of the people of Hälsinge Irr. Hälsinglands fornminnessällskap [Archaeological Soc. of Hälsingland], Hudiksvall. Scr 5

35. GÄRDS HÄRADS HEMBYGDSFÖRENINGS ÅRSBOK [Yearbook of the Local Society of the Gärd Country]. A. Gärds härads hembygdsförening, Djurröd. Scr 4

36. GEOGRAFISKA ANNALER [Geographical annals]. S-A. Generalstabens litografiska anstalt, Vasagatan 16, Stockholm, for Svenska sällskapet för antropologi och geografi [Swedish Soc. for Anthropology and Geography]. Scr 15

37. GÖINGE HEMBYGDSFÖRENINGS ÅRSBOK [Yearbook of the Göinge Local Society]. A. Göinge hembygdsförening, Broby. Scr 6

38. GÖTEBORGS ARKEOLOGISKA MUSEUM. ÅRSTRYCK [Archaeological Museum of Göteborg. Yearbook]. A.(Irr.). 1906. Göteborgs arkeologiska museum, Göteborg. Reports of the museum and art. on Swedish archaeology. Till 1952 formed part of Göteborgs museum. Årsredogörelse [Museum of Göteborg. Annual report]. pni

39. GÖTEBORGS ETNOGRAFISKA MUSEUM. ÅRSTRYCK [Ethnographical Museum of Göteborg. Yearbook]. A.(Irr.). 1906 (mri 1953-55: no vol. indic.) Göteborgs etnografiska museum, Göteborg. Reports of the museum and art. on Swedish ethnography. Till 1952 formed part of Göteborgs museum. Årsredogörelse [Museum of Göteborg. Annual report]. pni

40. GÖTEBORGS HISTORISKA MUSEUM. ÅRSTRYCK [Historical Museum of Göteborg. Yearbook]. A.(Irr.). 1906 (1957: no vol. indic.). Göteborgs historiska museum, Göteborg. Reports of the museum and art. on Swedish hist. Till 1952 formed part of Göteborgs museum. Årsredogörelse [Museum of Göteborg. Annual report]. Scr 5

41. GÖTEBORGS KONSTMUSEUM. ÅRSTRYCK [Göteborg Museum of Art. Yearbook]. A.(Irr.). 1906 (mri 1955/56: no vol. indic.). Göteborgs konstmuseum, Göteborg. Reports of the museum and art. on Swedish art

hist. Till 1952 formed part of Göteborgs museum. Årsredogörelse [Museum of Göteborg. Annual report]. pni

GÖTEBORGS MUSEUM. ÅRSREDOGÖRELSE see entries 38, 39, 40, 41 and 42

42. GÖTEBORGS NATURHISTORISKA MUSEUM. ÅRSTRYCK [Göteborg Museum of Natural History. Yearbook]. A.(Irr.). 1906 (mri 1956: no vol. indic.). Göteborgs naturhistoriska museum, Göteborg. Reports of the museum and art. on natural hist. Till 1952 formed part of Göteborgs museum. Årsredogörelse [Museum of Göteborg. Annual report]. pni

43. GÖTEBORGS- OCH BOHUSLÄNS FORNMINNESFÖRENINGS TIDSKRIFT [Journal of the Göteborg and Bohuslän Antiquarian Society]. Irr. Wettergren and Kerbers förlag, V. Hamngatan 22, Göteborg, for Göteborgs- och Bohusläns fornminnesförening. pni

44. GOTLÄNDSKT ARKIV [Gotland's archives]. A. Föreningen Gotlands fornvänner [Soc. of Gotland's Antiquity], Gotlands Fornsal, Visby. Scr 10/ $ 2

45. HALLAND, VÅR BYGD [Halland, our country]. A. Hallands hembygdsförbund [Local Soc. of Halland], Hallands museum, Halmstad. Scr 6

46. HANDLINGAR ANGÅENDE VILLANDS HÄRAD [Proceedings concerning Villand district]. A. Villands Härads hembygdsförening [Villand District Local Soc.], Kristianstad. Scr 2.50

47. HEMBYGDEN [Homeland]. A. A.B. Dalkrans, Karlstad, for Dalslands fornminnes- och hembygdsförbund [Antiquarian and Local Soc. of Dalecarlia], Vänersborgs museum, Vänersborg. Scr 6

48. HEMBYGDSFÖRENINGEN ARBOGA MINNE. ÅRSBOK [Regional History Society "Arboga Minne." Yearbook]. A. Hembygdsföreningen Arboga Minne, Arboga. Scr 5

49. HISTORIELÄRARNAS FÖRENINGS ÅRSSKRIFT [Yearbook of the Association of Teachers of History]. A. 1942 (1957/58: no vol. indic.). Historielärarnas förening, Holbergsgatan 124, Bromma. Ed: Ivar Seth, Tingvallagatan 1 C, Karlstad. Art. predominantly on the hist. of Sweden and on hist. teaching; reports on professional congresses; short rev. of bk., mostly Swedish, pub. during the preceding year; A. reports on the activities of the soc. and local branches; table of contents for the years 1942-1956/57 pub. in 1958. Scr 5 / $ 1

50. HISTORISK TIDSKRIFT [Historical review]. Q. 1881 (1958: 2nd series, vol. 21). Svenska historiska föreningen [Swedish Hist. Soc.], Storgatan 41, Stockholm Ö. Ed: Torvald T:son Höjer. Art. on all aspects and periods of Scandinavian hist., particularly Swedish (with some emphasis on political hist.), and on historiography and the philosophy of hist.; rev. art.; bk. rev.; doc.; biblio. of bk.; news and notes on the activities of Scandinavian hist. soc.; separate A. biblio., Svensk historisk bibliografi [Swedish hist. biblio.], with subject and author indices and a list of bk. rev. Scr 20

51. JÄMTEN [The man from Jämtland]. A. Heimbygdas förlag, Östersund. Scr 10

52. JÄMTLANDS LÄNS BIBLIOTEKS ÅRSSKRIFT [Yearbook of the Provincial Library of Jämtland]. A. Föreningen Jämtlands Läns biblioteks Vänner, Jämtlands Läns bibliotek, Östersund. Scr 5 / $ 1

53. JÖNKÖPINGS LÄNS HEMBYGDSFÖRBUND. MEDDELANDEN [Local Society of the Jönköping Country. Communications]. A. Jönköpings Läns hembygdsförbund, Jönköping. Scr 10

JOURNAL OF THE ROYAL ARMOURY see LIVRUSTKAMMAREN

54. JULBOK FÖR VÄSTERÅS STIFT [Christmas book of the Västerås diocese]. A. Falu nya boktryckeri AB, Falun. Scr 4

55. JULBOKEN TILL FÖRSAMLINGARNA I GÖTEBORGS STIFT [Christmas book to the parishes of the Göteborg diocese]. A. Stiftelsen Pro Caritates förlag, Norra Allégatan 5, Göteborg C. Scr 4

56. JULHÄLSNING TILL FÖRSAMLINGARNA I ÄRKESTIFTET [Christmas greeting to the parishes of the archdiocese]. A. Almqvist och Wiksells boktryckeri AB, Uppsala. Scr 4

57. JULHÄLSNINGAR TILL FÖRSAMLINGARNA FRÅN PRÄSTER I GÖTEBORGS STIFT [Christmas greetings to the parishes from the clergy of the Göteborg diocese]. A. Göteborgs Stifts tidnings förlag, Göteborg. Scr 4

58. JULHÄLSNINGAR TILL FÖRSAMLINGARNA I SKARA STIFT [Christmas greetings to the parishes of the Skara diocese]. A. Bengt Gierup, Skara. Scr 3.50

59. JULHÄLSNINGAR TILL FÖRSAMLINGARNA I VISBY STIFT [Christmas greetings to the parishes of the Visby diocese]. A. Visby stiftsråd, Visby. Scr 5

60. KALMAR LÄN [The province of Kalmar]. Årsbok för Kulturhistoria och Hembygdsvård [Yearbook for cultural history and preservation of local monuments]. A. Kalmar Läns fornminnesförening [Antiquarian Soc. of Kalmar Province], Kalmar. Scr 5

61. KARLSTADS STIFTS JULBOK [Christmas book of the Karlstad diocese]. A. Stiftsrådskansliet [Chancellery of the Diocesan Council], Karlstad. Scr 4

62. KAROLINSKA FÖRBUNDETS ÅRSBOK [Yearbook of the Carolinian Society]. A. 1910 (1958: no vol. indic.). Karolinska förbundet, Riddargatan 47, Stockholm Ö. Ed: Ingel Wadén. Art. on all aspects of the hist. of Sweden during the reigns of Charles X, Charles XI and Charles XII, with emphasis on politic and military hist.; rev. art.; A. reports of the soc. and lists of its memb.; illus. (memb.) Scr 15

63. KOLSVABYGD [Kolsva country]. A. Kolsva-ortens hembygdsförening [Kolsva Local Hist. Soc.], Kolsva. Scr 5

64. KONSTHISTORISK TIDSKRIFT [Review of the history of art]. Q (2 double no. p.a.). A. Bonniers förlag, Sveavägen 53, Stockholm, for Konsthistoriska sällskapet [Soc. for the Hist. of Art], Stockholm. Scr 20 / $ 4

65. KRONOBERGSBOKEN [Kronoberg book]. A. Kronobergs Läns hembygdsförbund [Local Soc. of Kronoberg Province], Smålands museum, Växjö, for Hyltén-Cavalliusföreningen [Hyltén-Cavallius Soc.]. Scr 7 / $1.40

66. KULLABYGD [Kulla country]. A. Kullens Hembygdsförening [Kullen Local Soc.], Höganäs. Scr 4

67. KULTUREN. A. Kulturhistoriska föreningen för Södra Sverige [Cultural Hist. Soc. of Southern Sweden], Lund, for Kulturhistoriska museet i Lund [Museum of Cultural Hist. in Lund]. Scr 10 / $2

68. KUNGL. ARMEMUSEUM, MEDDELANDE FRÅN... [Communications from the Royal Army Museum]. A. 1938 (1957: vol. 18). Föreningen armémusei Vänner [Soc. of the Friends of the Army Museum], Riddargatan 13, Stockholm 7. Ed: Heribert Seitz. Art. on old Swedish arms and army equipment, fortifications, uniforms, regimental colors and trophies taken by the Swedish army, pertaining to the period from the 16th cent. to the present; A. report on the activities of the soc.; illus.; cum. subject and author index for the first 10 vol. in vol. 11. Scr 8

69. KUNGL. HUMANISTISKA VETENSKAPS-SAMFUNDET I LUND. ÅRSBERÄTTELSE [Royal Society of Letters at Lund. Annual report]. BULLETIN DE LA SOCIETE ROYALE DES LETTRES DE LUND. A. 1918/19 (1956/57: no vol. indic.). C.W.K. Gleerup, Lund, for Kungl. humanistiska vetenskaps-samfundet i Lund. Art. on archaeology, antiquities, hist. (mostly cultural), philosophy, literature and linguistics; A. reports of the soc.; list of memb. of the soc.; in German, Swedish, English or French; German, English or French sum. of Swedish-language art. The vol. for 1956/57 contains a cum. chronological table of contents of all previous vol. and an index of the monograph series pub. by the soc. Included Meddelanden från Lunds universitets historiska museum (now pub. separately) from 1929/30 to 1956/57.

70. KUNGL. HUMANISTISKA VETENSKAPS-SAMFUNDET I UPPSALA. ÅRSBOK [Yearbook of the Royal Society for Humanities in Uppsala]. A. 1943 (1957: no vol. indic.). Almqvist och Wiksells boktryckeri AB, Uppsala, for Kungl. humanistiska vetenskaps-samfundet i Uppsala, Sune Lindqvist, S:t Larsgatan 6A, Uppsala. Ed: Secretary of the soc. Art. on the humanities, especially on philology, literature, and the hist. of Western civilization; report on the activities of the soc.; list of memb.; in Swedish and occasionally in German or Danish; occasional German sum.; illus. The 1951 vol. contains a cum. table of contents and an alphabetic author index for the years 1943 to 1951. pni

71. KUNGL. KRIGSVETENSKAPS AKADEMIENS HANDLINGAR OCH TIDSKRIFT [Proceedings and review of the Royal Military Science Academy]. 10 x y. 1780 (1957: vol. 161). AB Östgöta correspondenten, Linköping, for Kungl. krigsvetenskaps akademien, Östermalmsgatan 87, Stockholm. Ed: S.E. Allstrin. Art. on military strategy and military hist., mostly recent, and on the development of modern weapons; rev. art.; bk. rev.; A. reports on the activities of the acad.; list of memb.; in Swedish, Norwegian and Danish; illus. Scr 8.50 / $3

72. KUNGL. VETENSKAPS-SOCIETETENS ÅRSBOK [Yearbook of the Royal Society of Sciences]. A. Kungl. vetenskaps-societeten, S:t Larsgatan 1, Uppsala. Scr 5 / $1

73. KUNGL. VITTERHETS-, HISTORIE- OCH ANTIKVITETSAKADEMIENS ÅRSBOK [Yearbook of the Royal Academy of Letters, History and Antiquities].

A. 1926 (1957: no vol. indic.). Kungl. vitterhets-, historie- och antikvitetsakademien, Storgatan 41, Stockholm. Reports on the activities of the acad.; excerpts from the A. report of the King's Custodian of Antiquities, with English sum. Scr 3

74. KYRKOHISTORISK ÅRSSKRIFT [Yearbook of church history]. A. 1900 (1959: vol. 59). Almqvist och Wiksell, Gamla Brogatan 26, Stockholm, for Svenska kyrkohistoriska föreningen [Swedish Soc. of Church Hist.], Geijersgatan 18, Uppsala. Ed: Sven Göransson, Uppsala. Art. on Scandinavian and Baltic religious and cultural hist. from the 12th to the 19th cent.; doc.; rev. art.; bk. rev.; biblio. of bk. and periodicals; news on the activities of the soc.; in Swedish and occasionally in German; illus.; subject and author index for the years 1900-1909 pub. separately in 1910 and for the years 1910 to 1935 pub. separately in 1939; a similar index will be pub. for the years 1936 to 1960. Scr 18

75. LIDINGÖBOKEN [Lidingö book]. A.(Irr.). Lidingö hembygdsförening [Lidingö Local Soc.], Lidingö. Scr 4

76. LINKÖPINGS STIFTS JULBOK [Christmas book of the Linköping diocese]. A. Linköpings stiftsråds kansli [Chancellery of the Linköping Diocesan Council], Linköping. Scr 4

77. LIVRUSTKAMMAREN [The Royal Armory]. JOURNAL OF THE ROYAL ARMOURY. Q. 1937 (1955-57: vol. 7, no. 1-12). Kungl. Livrustkammaren, Stockholm Ö. Ed: Svante Svärdström. Art. on armor and weapons; in Swedish, English, German or Dutch; English, Swedish or French sum.; illus.; alphabetical index of authors printed separately for every vol. Scr 10

LUNDS STIFTS JULBOK see LUNDS STIFTSBOK

78. LUNDS STIFTSBOK [The Lund diocese book]. A. Sydsvenska dagbladet [South Swedish Daily Newspaper], Malmö. Before 1958 appeared under the title: Lunds stifts julbok [Christmas bk. of the Lund diocese]. Scr 4.50

79. LUNDS UNIVERSITETS HISTORISKA MUSEUM, MEDDELANDEN FRÅN... [Communications from the Historical Museum of Lund University]. MEMOIRES DE LA MUSEE HISTORIQUE DE LUND [Memoirs of the Historical Museum of Lund]. A. C.W.K. Gleerup, Vårfrug. 8, Lund, for Lunds universitets historiska museum. Formed part of Kungl. humanistiska vetenskaps-samfundet i Lund from 1929/30 to 1956/57. nfs

80. LYCHNOS [The lamp]. Lärdomshistoriska samfundets årsbok. Annual of the Swedish History of Science Society. Annuaire de la Société Suédoise d'Histoire des Sciences. Jahrbuch der Schwedischen Gesellschaft für Geschichte der Wissenschaften. A. 1936 (mri 1956: no vol. indic.). Almqvist och Wiksells-boktryckeri AB, Uppsala, for Lärdomshistoriska samfundet, N. Rudbecksgatan 14, Uppsala. Ed: Sten Lindroth, Vindhemsgatan 13, Uppsala. Art. on the hist. of science and on intellectual and cultural hist.; extensive bk. rev. section; biblio. of periodicals; professional notes and communications of the soc.; in Swedish, English, German or French; illus. Scr 20

81. MALMÖ FORNMINNESFÖRENINGS ÅRSSKRIFT [Yearbook of the Malmö Antiquarian Society]. A. Malmö fornminnesförening, Stadsarkivet, Stortorget 2A, Malmö C. Scr 10 / $ 2

82. MED HAMMARE OCH FACKLA! [With hammer and torch!]. A. 1928 (mri 1953/54: vol. 20) Sancte Örjans Gille [Guild of Sancte Örjan], Kungsträdgårdsgatan 6, Stockholm. Ed. board: Harald Carlborg, Torsten Althin (manag. ed.), Govert Indebetou, Sven Tunberg. Art. on mining and its hist. pni

MEDDELANDE(N). For titles beginning with "Meddelande(n)," followed by the name of the publishing or sponsoring institution or society, see the respective institution or society.

83. MEDICINHISTORISK ÅRSBOK [Yearbook of medical history]. A. 1953 (1958: no vol. indic.). Medicinhistoriska museet [Museum of Medical Hist.], Åsögatan 146, Stockholm Sö, for Föreningen Medicinhistoriska museets vänner [Assoc. of the Friends of the Museum of Medical Hist.], Stockholm. Art. on medical hist., mostly Swedish, from the 16th cent. to the present, with emphasis on the 18th cent. and on Carl Linnaeus; English sum.; illus. Scr 10

MEMOIRES DE LA MUSEE HISTORIQUE DE LUND see LUNDS UNIVERSITETS HISTORISKA MUSEUM, MEDDELANDEN FRÅN...

MUSEE HISTORIQUE DE LUND, MEMOIRES DE LA... see LUNDS UNIVERSITETS HISTORISKA MUSEUM, MEDDELANDEN FRÅN...

84. MUSEUM OF FAR EASTERN ANTIQUITIES, BULLETIN OF THE. A. 1929 (1957: vol. 29). Östasiatiska samlingarna [Museum of Far Eastern Antiquities], Storgatan 41, Stockholm Ö. Art. on antiquities, prehist., folklore, archaeology and other aspects of Far Eastern studies; in English and occasionally in French or German. pv (Scr 18-60)

85. NAMN OCH BYGD [Name and country]. Tidskrift för Nordisk ortsnamnsforskning [Journal for Scandinavian toponymy]. A. 1913 (1957: vol. 45). Kungl. Gustav Adolfs akademien [Royal Gustavus Adolphus Acad.], Odinslund 2, Uppsala. Ed: Jöran Sahlgren. Art. on Scandinavian toponymy; bk. rev.; biblio. of bk. and art.; index of place names at the end of every 2nd vol.; illus. Scr 15 / $3

86. NATIO SMOLANDICA. A. Smålands Nations kamratförening [Småland Undergraduates' Club], Uppsala. Author, biographical and subject indices for vol. 1-20 (1938-57), pub. in 1957. Scr 10 / $2

87. NAUTISK TIDSKRIFT [Nautical review]. Organ för Svensk sjöfart [Organ for Swedish navigation]. M. (1957: vol. 50). Sveriges fartygsbefälsförening [Assoc. of Swedish Marine Officers], Stockholm. Ed: H. Bååw. Art. on Swedish and international navigation, and on social and technical matters regarding marine personnel. Scr 12

NEW SOCIETY OF LETTERS AT LUND, YEARBOOK OF THE see VETENSKAPS-SOCIETETEN I LUND. ÅRSBOK

88. NIEDERDEUTSCHE MITTEILUNGEN [Low German communications]. A. Niederdeutsche Arbeitsgemeinschaft, Lund. In German, English, Swedish or Dutch. pni

89. NORDISK NUMISMATSK ÅRSSKRIFT [Scandinavian numismatic yearbook]. A. 1940 (mri 1954 [1956]: no vol. indic.). P.A. Norstedt och Söner, Stockholm, for Nordisk numismatisk union [Scandinavian Numismatic Union].

Art. on numismatic hist. from Roman times to the present, concentrating on Scandinavia in the 17th, 18th and 19th cent.; A. reports on national coin collections and mints in Denmark, Finland, Norway and Sweden; in the Scandinavian languages and occasionally in English; illus. pni

90. NORDISK TIDSKRIFT FÖR BOK- OCH BIBLIOTEKSVÄSEN [Scandinavian review of book and library science]. Q. 1914 (mri 1955: vol. 42). Almqvist och Wiksells boktryckeri AB, Stockholm and Uppsala. Ed. board: Tönnes Kleberg, Uppsala, Øyvind Anker, Oslo, Palle Birkelund, København, Paul Nyberg, Helsingfors. Art. on library science, and the hist. and holdings of libraries, pertaining mainly to Scandinavia; rev. art.; bk. rev.; news and reports from the field of library science, divided into an international, a Scandinavian and a Swedish section; biblio. news; in English, French, German or Scandinavian languages; English, French or German sum. of Scandinavian-language art.; illus.; Scandinavian biblio. and index of bk. on library science for 1951/52 in vol. 41. Scr 20

. 91. NORDISK TIDSKRIFT FÖR VETENSKAP, KONST OCH INDUSTRI [Scandinavian journal for science, art and industry]. 8 x y. Letterstedtska föreningen [Letterstedt Soc.] and Föreningen Norden [Scandinavian Soc.], Vasagatan 52, Stockholm. In Scandinavian languages. pni

92. NORRBOTTENS LÄNS HEMBYGDSFÖRENINGS ÅRSBOK [Yearbook of the Local Society of the Province of Norrbotten]. A. Norrbottens Läns hembygdsförening, Luleå. Scr 10 / $2

93. NORRKÖPINGS MUSEUM. BERÄTTELSE ÖVER VERKSAMHETEN JÄMTE BIFOGADE SKRIFTER [Norrköping Museum. Report on its activities with supplements]. A. Norrköpings museum, Norrköping. pni

NOTISER. For titles beginning with "Notiser," followed by the name of the publishing or sponsoring institution or society, see the respective institution or society.

94. NY KYRKLIG TIDSKRIFT [New church review]. B-M. 1932 (1958: vol. 27). Wretmans boktryckeri AB, Uppsala. Ed: R. Josefson, Y. Rudberg. Art. on theological subjects, especially on present tendencies in theology and church life; in Scandinavian languages. Scr 10

95. NY MILITÄR TIDSKRIFT [New military review]. M. 1927 (1958: vol. 31). Ed: B. Steckzén, Linnég 7, Stockholm Ö. Art. on military politics and on questions regarding the armed forces. Scr 15

96. ORD OCH BILD [Word and picture]. Kulturtidskrift för de nordiska länderna [Cultural review for the Scandinavian countries]. B-M. Pub. address: Johannesgatan 22 B 1, Stockholm C. Scr 32 / $ 6.19

97. ORIENTALIA SUECANA. A. Universitetsbiblioteket [The Univ. Library], Uppsala. In English, German or French. Scr 20

98. ORTNAMNSSÄLLSKAPET I UPPSALA. ÅRSSKRIFT [Society of Toponymy at Uppsala. Yearbook]. A. 1936 (mri 1956: no vol. indic.). Lundequistska bokhandeln, Uppsala, for Ortnamnssällskapet i Uppsala. Ed: H. Lindberg, Uppsala. Art. on Swedish toponymy. pni

99. ÖSTERGÖTLANDS- OCH LINKÖPINGS STADS MUSEUM. MEDDELANDEN [Östergötland and Linköping City Museum. Communications]. B-A. Östergötlands- och Linköpings Stads museum, Linköping. pni

100. PERSONHISTORISK TIDSKRIFT [Genealogical review]. Q (1 double and 2 single no. p.a.). 1899 (1958: vol. 56). Personhistoriska samfundet [Genealogical Soc.], Krigsarkivet, Stockholm 80. Ed: Bertil Broomé. Art. on the genealogy and biography of Scandinavians, based largely on diaries and journals, concentrating on Sweden and the period from the Middle Ages to the present; rev. art.; bk. rev.; in Swedish and occasionally in German; index of names in the last no. of each vol. Scr 18

101. POSTRYTTAREN [Post-rider]. A. Kungl. Generalpoststyrelsen [Royal General Post-Office Board], Stockholm, for Postmuseum [Postal Museum], Lilla Nygatan 6, Stockholm 2. Scr 5

102. RIDDARHUSET, MEDDELANDEN FRÅN... [Communications from the Swedish House of the Nobility]. A. 1947 (1957: vol. 11). Riddarhuset, P.O.B. 2022, Stockholm 2. Ed: Wilhelm Tham. Hist. and cultural essays concerning the Swedish nobility; bk. rev.; report on the activities of the Swedish House of the Nobility; family news about memb. of the Swedish nobility; illus. Scr 4

103. RIG. Q. 1918 (1958: vol. 41). Föreningen för svensk kulturhistoria [Assoc. for Swedish Cultural Hist.], in collaboration with Nordiska museet [Scandinavian Museum], Stockholm, and Folklivsarkivet [Archives of Folk Life], Lund. Ed. board: Gösta Berg, Mats Rehnberg, Sigfrid Svensson, Nordiska museet, Stockholm Ö. Art. on the cultural hist. of Scandinavia, with emphasis on Sweden; rev. art.; bk. rev.; A. report of the assoc.; English, German or French sum.; illus. Scr 10

104. RÖHSSKA KONSTSLÖJDMUSEETS ÅRSTRYCK [Yearbook of the Röhsska Museum of Applied Arts]. A. Röhsska konstslöjdmuseet, Göteborg. In Swedish, English or German.

105. SAGA OCH SED [Saga and custom]. A. 1932 (mri 1956: no vol. indic.). Kungl. Gustav Adolfs akademien [Royal Gustavus Adolphus Acad.], Uppsala. Ed: Jöran Sahlgren. Art. on Scandinavian folklore, ethnography, dialects and toponymy; in Scandinavian languages, English or German. Scr 10 / Scr 10

106. SALABYGDENS FORNMINNESFÖRENINGS ÅRSBOK [Yearbook of the Antiquarian Society of the Sala Country]. A. Salabygdens fornminnesförening, Sala. Scr 5

107. SAMFUNDET SANKT ERIKS ÅRSBOK [Yearbook of St. Erik's Society]. A. Samfundet St. Erik, Stockholms stadsmuseum, Götgatan 1, Stockholm Sö. Scr 15

108. SAMLAREN [The collector]. Tidskrift för svensk litteraturhistorisk forskning [Journal for research in Swedish literary history]. A. Svenska litteratursällskapet [Swedish Literary Soc.], Uppsala. Scr 15

109. SAMTID OCH FRAMTID [The present and the future]. Tidskrift för idépolitik och kultur [Journal of the politics of ideas and culture]. Q. Bokförlaget Natur och kultur, Torsgatan 31, Stockholm. Scr 12

110. SCANDIA. Tidskrift för historisk forskning [Journal of historical research]. Irr. (1 vol. with 2 no., pub. every 2 or 3 years). 1928 (1958: vol. 24). Bokförlaget Natur och kultur, Stockholm. Ed. board: Sture Bolin, Erik Lönnroth, Sven A. Nilsson, Jerker Rosén, Jörgen Weibull. Art. on all aspects and periods of Scandinavian hist., with emphasis on political and social hist.; in Swedish

and occasionally in Danish or Norwegian; illus.; index for the years 1928 to 1957, arranged by period, author and name, pub. separately in 1958. Scr 15

111. SCANDINAVIAN ECONOMIC HISTORY REVIEW. S-A. 1953 (1957: vol. 5). Scandinavian Soc. for Economic and Social Hist. and Hist. Geography, Ekonomisk-historiska institutet, Tegnerlund. 10, Stockholm Va. Ed: Ernst F. Söderlund. Art. on economic and social hist., mostly of Scandinavia, and hist. geography; bk. rev.; in English. Scr 15

112. SJÖHISTORISK ÅRSBOK [Yearbook of maritime history]. B (A. till 1950). 1927 (mri 1955/56: no vol. indic.). Föreningen Sveriges sjöfartsmuseum [Soc. of the Swedish Maritime Museum], c/o Statens sjöhistoriska museum [National Museum of Maritime Hist.], Djurgårdsbrunnsvägen, Stockholm. Ed: Gerhard Albe. Art. on Scandinavian maritime hist. from prehist. times to the present, with emphasis on Sweden since the 17th cent., and on museum holdings; report on the activities of the museum and the soc.; list of memb. of the soc.; occasional English sum.; illus.; cum. table of contents for the years 1940-53/54 pub. in 1955/56. Before 1946 appeared under the title Föreningen Sveriges sjöfartsmuseum i Stockholm. Årsbok [Soc. of the Swedish Maritime Museum. Yearbook]. Scr 18

113. SKANES HEMBYGDSFÖRBUNDS ÅRSBOK [Yearbook of the Skåne Local Society]. A. Skånes hembygdsförbund, Lund. Scr 8

114. SLÄKT OCH HÄVD [Family and tradition]. 3 x y. 1950 (1957: no vol. indic.) Genealogiska föreningen [Genealogical Soc.], c/o Riksförening för släktforskning [National Soc. for Genealogical Research], Försvarsstabens krigshist. avd., Stockholm 80. Ed. board: B. Furtenbach, Lennart Zielfelt, Birger Lindén, Pontus Möller. Art. on Swedish genealogy; rev. art.; bk. rev.; doc.; news of the soc.; A. index of names. (memb.) Scr 12

SOCIETE ROYALE DES LETTRES DE LUND, BULLETIN DE LA... see KUNGL. HUMANISTISKA VETENSKAPS-SAMFUNDET I LUND. ÅRSBERÄTTELSE

115. SÖRMLANDSBYGDEN [Sörmland country]. A. Södermanlands hembygdsförbund [Södermanland's Local Soc.], Nyköping. Scr 8

116. STATSVETENSKAPLIG TIDSKRIFT FÖR POLITIK, STATISTIK, EKONOMI [Political science journal of politics, statistics, economics]. Ny följd [New series]. 5 x y. 1897 (1958: vol. 61). C.W.K. Gleerup, Lund, for Fahlbeckska stiftelsen [Fahlbeck Foundation], Lund. Ed. board: Erik Fahlbeck, Carl Arvid Hessler, Gunnar Heckscher. Art. on political science, including current constitutional questions, and modern economic and political hist., mostly of Sweden; reports on current research; biblio. of art. from social science journals pub. in Scandinavia, Britain, France, Germany and the U.S.A.; statistics. Scr 15

117. STOCKHOLMS STADS ARKIVNÄMND OCH STADSARKIV. ÅRSBERÄTTELSE [The Board of the Records of Stockholm and the City Record-Office. Annual report]. A. Stadskollegiet, Kansliexpeditionen, Stadshuset, Stockholm, for Stockholms stads arkivnämnd och stadsarkiv, Stockholm. pni

118. STOCKHOLMS STIFTSBOK [Stockholm diocesan book]. A. Pub. address: Jakobsbergsgatan 19, Stockholm. Scr 5

119. STRANDA. A. C.E. Fritze, Stockholm, for Stranda härads hembygdsförening [Local Soc. of Stranda District]. Scr 10

120. SVENSK-FINLAND [Swedish Finland]. 5 x y. Föreningen Svensk-Finlands vänner [Assoc. of the Friends of Swedish Finland], Regeringsgatan 26, Stockholm. Scr 10

121. SVENSK JURISTTIDNING [Swedish legal review]. 10 x y. Pub. address: St. Nygatan 2A, Stockholm. Scr 25

122. SVENSK LITTERATURTIDSKRIFT [Swedish review of literature]. Q. C.W.K. Gleerup, Lund, for Samfundet De Nio [Soc. of "The Nine"]. Scr 12

123. SVENSK·TIDSKRIFT [Swedish review]. 10 x y. E.G.E. Anners, Uppsala. Scr 20

124. SVENSK TIDSKRIFT FÖR MUSIKFORSKNING [Swedish journal for research in music]. A. Svenska samfundet för musikforskning [Swedish Soc. for Research in Music], Stockholm, and Institutionen för Musikforskning vid Uppsala Universitet [Inst. for Research in Music, Uppsala Univ.], Övre Slottsgatan 12, Uppsala. Scr 18 / $ 3.50

125. SVENSKA LANDSMÅL OCH SVENSKT FOLKLIV [Swedish dialects and Swedish folk life]. Archives des Traditions Populaires Suédoises [Archives of Swedish popular traditions]. A. 1878 (1957: vol. 80). P.A. Norstedt och Söner, Stockholm, for Landsmåls- och folkminnesarkivet [Archives for Dialects and Folklore], Universitetsbiblioteket, Uppsala. Ed: Dag Strömbäck, Wahlenbergsvägen 13, Uppsala. Art. on the hist. and contemporary philological aspects of Scandinavian, especially Swedish, dialects, and on ethnography, folklore and toponymy; doc.; bk. rev.; biblio. of bk. and periodicals; news on research in Swedish provinces; professional news; in Swedish and occasionally in Norwegian; French sum.; illus.; supplements; indices (arranged by subject, place name and author) for the years 1878-1938 pub. separately in 1940, and for the years 1939-52 pub. as a supplement in 1955. Scr 12 / $2.50

126. SVENSKA LINNÉ-SÄLLSKAPETS ÅRSSKRIFT [Yearbook of the Swedish Linnaean Society]. A. 1918 (mri 1954/55: vol. 37/38]. Svenska Linné-sällskapet, P.O.B. 47, Uppsala. Art. on Carl von Linné and his contemporaries; table of contents also in English. Scr 25

127. SVENSKA RIKSARKIVET, MEDDELANDEN FRÅN... [Communications from the National Swedish Archives]. A. (sometimes B). 1875 (1957: no vol. indic.). P.A. Norstedt och Söner, Stockholm, for Svenska riksarkivet. Art. on holdings in Swedish archives, Swedish hist. and archival science; rev. art.; doc.; A. report of the Svenska riksarkivet and news of its activities. Scr 5

128. SVENSKA STADSFÖRBUNDETS TIDSKRIFT [Review of the Swedish Federation of Municipalities]. Organ för Sveriges Städer, Köpingar och Municipalsamhällen [Organ for the towns, villages and municipalities of Sweden]. 20 x y. Pub. address: Gustaf Adolfs Torg 14, Stockholm C. Scr 24

129. SVENSKA STATENS KONSTSAMLINGAR, ÅRSBOK FÖR... [Yearbook of the art galleries of the Swedish State]. A. Ehlin, Stockholm. English sum. pv (1957: Scr 18)

130. SVERIGES ALLMÄNNA KONSTFÖRENINGS PUBLIKATION [Publication of the Swedish General Art Society]. A. Sveriges allmänna konstförening, P.O.B. 7002, Stockholm 7. pni

131. SVERIGES FLOTTA [Swedish navy]. M. Förening för sjövärn och sjöfart (Maritime Soc.), Stockholm Ö. Scr 15

132. SVERIGES RIDDERSKAPS- OCH ADELSKALENDER [Calendar of Sweden's knighthood and aristocracy]. A. Riddarhus-Direktionen [Board of the House of the Nobility], Stockholm. Genealogies. Scr 48 / Scr 48

133. SVIO-ESTONICA. Irr. Ed: P. Wieselgren, Södergatan 14, Eslöv, for Svensk-Estniska samfundet [Swedish-Estonian Soc.]. Scr 7

134. SYDSVENSKA ORTSNAMNSSÄLLSKAPETS ÅRSSKRIFT [Yearbook of the South Sweden Society of Toponymy]. A. Sydsvenska ortsnamnssällskapets förlag, Lund. Scr 8

135. TÄLJEBYGDEN [Tälje country]. A. Östra Södermanlands kultur-historiska förening [East Södermanland Cultural Hist. Soc.], Södertälje. Scr 5

136. TIDEN [Time]. Tidskrift för socialistisk kritik och politik [Journal for socialistic critique and politics]. 10 x y. 1908 (1958: vol. 50). Sveriges socialdemokratiska arbetareparti [Swedish Social Democratic Workers' Party], Stockholm Ed: Olle Svensson, Sveav. 68, Stockholm Va. Art. on politics, economics, soc. and culture. Scr 15

137. TIDSKRIFT FÖR KONSTVETENSKAP [Journal of the science of art]. Irr. Allhems förlag, Malmö. Scr 14

138. TILL HEMBYGDEN [To the home district]. En julhälsning till församlingarna i Strängnäs stift från Stiftsrådet [A Christmas greeting to the parishes of the Strängnäs diocese from the Diocesan Council]. A. Domkapitlet [Cathedral Chapter], Strängnäs. Scr 4.50

139. TJUSTBYGDENS KULTURHISTORISKA FÖRENING. MEDDELANDE [Cultural History Society of Tjustbygden. Communications]. A. Tjustbygdens kulturhistoriska förening, Västervik. Scr 7

140. TOFTERYDSBYGDEN [Tofteryd country]. Irr. Tofteryds sockens hembygdsförening [Tofteryd Parish Local Soc.], Tofteryd. Scr 5

141. TOR. Irr. 1948 (1957: vol. 3). Appelbergs boktryckeri AB, Uppsala for Uppsala universitets museum för nordiska fornsaker [Uppsala Univ. Museum for Scandinavian Antiquities], Uppsala. Ed: Mårten Stenberger. Art. on archaeology and artifacts, especially of Sweden; German, English or French sum. in vol. 3; illus. pv

142. UNDA MARIS. A. Sjöfartsmuseet [Maritime Museum], Göteborg. Scr 12

143. UPPLAND. A. Upplands fornminnesförening [Uppland Antiquarian Soc.], Uppsala. Scr 10

144. UPPLANDS FORNMINNESFÖRENINGS TIDSKRIFT [Journal of the Antiquarian Society of Uppland]. Irr. Upplands fornminnesförening, Uppsala. Scr 8

145. VADSBOBYGDEN [Vadsbo country]. A. Vadsbo hembygds- och fornminnesförening [Vadsbo Local and Antiquarian Soc.], Torsö. pni

146. VÄNERSBORGS SÖNERS GILLE. ÅRSSKRIFT [Society of the Sons of Vänersborg. Yearbook]. A. Vänersborgs museum, Vänersborg, for Vänersborgs söners gille. Scr 4

147. VÅR HEMBYGD [Our homeland]. A. Huskvarna hembygdsförening [Huskvarna Local Soc.], Huskvarna. Scr 5

148. VÅR MARIN [Our navy]. Marinens årsbok [Yearbook of the navy]. A. Hörsta förlag, Stockholm. pni

149. VARBERGS MUSEUM. ÅRSBOK [Varberg Museum. Yearbook]. A. Varbergs museum, Varberg. Scr 6

150. VÄRENDSBYGDEN [Värends country]. A. Norra Allbo hembygdsförening [North Allbo Local Soc.], Alvesta. Scr 6

151. VÄRMDÖ SKEPPSLAGS FORNMINNESFÖRENINGS ÅRSBOK [Yearbook of the Antiquarian Society of the District of Värmdö]. A. Värmdö skeppslags fornminnesförening, Norrtälje. pni

152. VÄRMLAND FÖRR OCH NU [Värmland, past and present]. A. Värmlands fornminnes- och museiförening [Värmland Antiquarian and Museum Assoc.], Värmlands museum, Karlstad. Scr 10 / $2

153. VÅRT FÖRSVAR [Our defense]. Allmänna försvarsföreningens tidskrift [Journal of the General Federation for Defense]. Q. Allmänna försvarsföreningen, Storgatan 29, Stockholm. p (1) Scr 3

154. VÄSTERBOTTEN. A. Västerbottens läns hembygdsförening [Local Soc. of Västerbotten Province], Umeå. pni

155. VÄSTERGÖTLANDS FORNMINNESFÖRENINGS TIDSKRIFT [Journal of the Antiquarian Society of Västergötland]. Irr. Västergötlands fornminnesförening, Skara. pni

156. VÄSTERMANLANDS FORNMINNESFÖRENINGS ÅRSBOK [Yearbook of the Antiquarian Society of Västmanland]. Irr. Västmanlands fornminnesförening, Västerås. pni

157. VÄXJÖ STIFTS HEMBYGDSKALENDER [The local calendar of the Växjö diocese]. A. Ebba Eckerbom, Staglabergsgatan 9, Växjö. Scr 3.50

158. VETENSKAPS-SOCIETETEN I LUND. ÅRSBOK [Society of Science at Lund. Yearbook]. YEARBOOK OF THE NEW SOCIETY OF LETTERS AT LUND. A. 1920 (mri 1956: no vol. indic.). C.W.K. Gleerup, Lund, for Vetenskapssocieteten i Lund. Ed: Birger Sallnäs. Art. on medieval law, philology and cultural hist.; A. report of the soc.; list of memb.; in Swedish, English, French or German; occasional English, French or German sum. of Swedish-language art.; cum. index for the years 1920-45 pub. in 1946. Scr 18

YEARBOOK OF THE NEW SOCIETY OF LETTERS AT LUND see VETENSKAPS-SOCIETETEN I LUND. ÅRSBOK

159. YMER. Q. Generalstabens litografiska anstalt [Lithographical Inst. of the General Staff], Vasagatan 16, Stockholm, for Svenska sällskapet för antropologi och geografi [Swedish Soc. for Anthropology and Geography]. pni

ADDENDUM

160. EESTI TEADUSLIK SELTS ROOTSIS. AASTARAAMAT [Estonian Learned Society in Sweden. Annals]. Annales Societatis Litterarum Estonicae. Quinquennial. Eesti Teaduslik Selts Rootsis, c/o Stutens historiska museum, Storgatan 41, Stockholm. Humanities, including modern Estonian hist. and anthropology; in Estonian, German or English; sum. of some art. in German or English. pni

Switzerland

Prepared with the assistance of the
Schweizerische Landesbibliothek, Bern

1. AARAUER NEUJAHRSBLÄTTER [Aarau New Year's papers]. A. H.R. Sauerländer und Co., for Literarische und Lesegesellschaft Aarau. Sfr 2.90

ACTA MUSICOLOGICA see section on International Periodicals

ACTES. For titles beginning with "Actes," followed by the name of the publishing or sponsoring institution or society, see the respective institution or society.

ALMANACH GENEALOGIQUE SUISSE see SCHWEIZERISCHES GESCHLECHTERBUCH

2. ALPENHORN [Alpine horn]. Illustrierte Sonntagsbeilage zum Emmenthaler-Blatt [Illustrated Sunday supplement of the "Emmenthal Newspaper"]. W. Buchdruckerei Emmenthaler-Blatt A.G., Langnau, Bern. pni

ANNALES. For titles beginning with "Annales," followed by the name of the publishing or sponsoring institution or society, see the respective institution or society.

3. ANNALES FRIBOURGEOISES [Fribourg annals]. A. Imprimerie Fragnière Frères, Fribourg, for Société d'Histoire du Canton de Fribourg. Includes art. on the hist. of the canton of Fribourg. Sfr 10

4. ANNALES VALAISANNES [Valais annals]. Q. Société d'histoire de Valais Romand, Bibliothèque cantonale, Sion. Sfr 8

ANNUAIRE DE LA SOCIETE SUISSE DE PREHISTOIRE see SCHWEIZERISCHE GESELLSCHAFT FÜR URGESCHICHTE, JAHRBUCH DER...

ANNUARIO DELLA SOCIETA SVIZZERA DI PREISTORIA see SCHWEIZERISCHE GESELLSCHAFT FÜR URGESCHICHTE, JAHRBUCH DER...

5. ANTHROPOS. International Review of Ethnology and Linguistics [Subtitle also in French, Latin, Italian, Spanish and German]. B-M (3 double no. p.a.). 1906 (1958: vol. 53). Paulus Verlag, Fribourg, for Anthropos-Institut, Posieux (Fribourg). Ed: Rudolf Rahmann. Art. on ethnology, ethnography, physical anthropology, prehist., linguistics and related fields, and on their methodology; descriptions of studies available on microfilm; bk. rev.; in English, German or French; author, geographical, subject and illus. indices pub. separately for each vol. Sfr 60

6. ANTIQUARISCHE GESELLSCHAFT IN ZÜRICH, NEUJAHRSBLATT DER... (Neujahrsblatt der Antiquarischen Gesellschaft in Zürich) [New Year's bulletin of the Antiquarian Society in Zürich]. A. Antiquarische Gesellschaft in Zürich, Zürich. pv (Sfr 4-13)

7. APPENZELLISCHE GESCHICHTSBLÄTTER [Appenzell historical notes]. Chronik der Appenzell I. Rh. Liegenschaften von Jakob Signer [Chronicle of the Appenzell Inner Rhodes lands of Jakob Signer]. M. Genossenschaftsdruckerei, Appenzell. Sfr 12.50

8. APPENZELLISCHE JAHRBÜCHER [Appenzell yearbooks]. A. Feersche Buchhandlung, St. Gallen, for Appenzellische Gemeinnützige Gesellschaft. pv (Sfr 4.50-6)

ARCHIV. For titles beginning with "Archiv," followed by the name of the publishing or sponsoring institution or society, see the respective institution or society.

9. ARCHIV FÜR SCHWEIZERISCHE FAMILIENKUNDE. ARCHIVES SUISSES DE GENEALOGIE. ARCHIVIO SVIZZERO DI GENEALOGIA [Archives for Swiss genealogy]. Irr. J. P. Zwicky, Verlag für schweizerische Personen- und Familiengeschichte, Zürich, for Genealogisches Institut Zwicky, Zürich, Sihlstr.3 (per vol.) Sfr 95/$ 24

10. ARCHIVES HERALDIQUES SUISSES. SCHWEIZERISCHES ARCHIV FÜR HERALDIK. ARCHIVIO ARALDICO SVIZZERO [Swiss heraldic archives]. A. 1887 (1958: vol. 72). Imprimeries Réunies S. A., Avenue de la Gare 33, Lausann for Société Suisse d'héraldique, c/o Bibliothèque Cantonale, Fribourg. Ed: Olivier Clottu, Saint-Blaise (Neuchâtel), P. Rudolf Heuggeler. Art. on heraldry, mainly of Switzerland; A. report of the soc.; in French or German; illus. Sfr 20

11. ARCHIVES SUISSES D'ANTHROPOLOGIE GENERALE [Swiss archives of general anthropology]. Anthropologie, archéologie, ethnographie [Anthropology, archaeology, ethnography]. A. Institut d'Anthropologie, Université de Genève, 44 c rue des Maraîchers, Genève. Sfr 15/Sfr 20

ARCHIVES SUISSES DE GENEALOGIE see ARCHIV FÜR SCHWEIZERISCHE FAMILIENKUNDE

ARCHIVES SUISSES DES TRADITIONS POPULAIRES see SCHWEIZERISCHES ARCHIV FÜR VOLKSKUNDE

ARCHIVIO ARALDICO SVIZZERO see ARCHIVES HERALDIQUES SUISSES

ARCHIVIO SVIZZERO DI GENEALOGIA see ARCHIV FÜR SCHWEIZERISCHE FAMILIENKUNDE

12. ARCHIVUM HERALDICUM. Internationales Bulletin. Bulletin international. Bollettino internationale [International bulletin]. Q. 1887 (1958: vol. 72) Imprimeries Réunies S.A., Av. de la Gare 33, Lausanne, for Société Suisse d'héraldique, c/o Bibliothèque Cantonale, Fribourg. Ed: Olivier Clottu, Saint-Blaise (Neuchâtel), P. Rudolf Heuggeler. Art. and short notes on heraldry; bk. rev.; international news of professional interest and on the activities of heraldic soc.; in French or German; illus. Sfr 5

13. ARGOVIA. A. H. R. Sauerländer, Aargau, for Historische Gesellschaft des Kantons Aargau. pv (Sfr 10-29.50)

14. ARMES ANCIENNES [Old arms]. Revue consacrée à l'étude des armes anciennes [Review devoted to the study of old arms]. 1953 (1958: vol. 2). Pub. and ed: René Géroudet, 4 Place Claparède, Genève. Art. on the hist. of weapons, armor and weapon collections; news for amateurs and collectors concerning old weapons; bk. rev. Sfr 9/$ 2.25

15. ART-DOCUMENTS. Encyclopédie générale des beaux-arts aux XIXe et XXe siècles. Peintres, sculpteurs, graveurs, architectes, décorateurs, etc. [General encyclopedia of fine arts in the 19th and 20th centuries. Painters, sculptors, engravers, architects, decorators, etc.]. S-M. Editions Pierre Cailler, 12 Rue Alcide-Jentzer, Genève. Sfr 20

ARTIBUS ASIAE see section on U.S.A.

16. ASIATISCHE STUDIEN. ETUDES ASIATIQUES [Asian studies]. Q. 1947 (1957/58: vol. 11). Verlag A. Francke AG, Bern, for Schweizerische Gesellschaft für Asienkunde. Ed: E.H. von Tscharner, Constantin Regamey. Art. on the hist., literature, culture and philosophy of Asia; news of the soc.; bk. rev.; in French, German or English. Sfr 18

17. ASSOCIATION DU VIEUX MOUDON, BULLETIN DE...[Bulletin of the Association of Old Moudon]. Irr. Imprimerie "Echo de la Broye Moudon." Sfr 1.60

18. BADENER NEUJAHRSBLÄTTER [Baden New Year's notes]. A. Gesellschaft der Biedermeier und der Vereinigung für Heimatkunde des Bezirks Baden, Baden. Sfr 2.50

19. BASELBIETER HEIMATBLÄTTER [Baselland local notes]. Q. Landschäfter AG, Liestal, Basel-Land. Supplement to Landschäftler Sfr 2

20. BASELBIETER HEIMATBUCH [Book of the Baselland canton]. Irr. Drucksachen- und Materialzentrale Liestal, for Kommission zur Erhaltung von Altertümern des Kantons Basel-Landschaft. Sfr 8.70

21. BASLER JAHRBUCH [Basel yearbook]. A. Helbing und Lichtenhahn, Basel. Sfr 14.50

22. BASLER ZEITSCHRIFT FÜR GESCHICHTE UND ALTERTUMSKUNDE [Basel journal for history and classical studies]. A. Historische und Antiquarische Gesellschaft zu Basel, Universitätsbibliothek, Basel. Art. on the hist. and archaeology of Basel. Sfr 14

23. BEITRÄGE ZUR GESCHICHTE NIDWALDENS [Contributions to the history of Nidwalden]. Irr. J. von Matt, Stans, for Historischer Verein von Nidwalden. Sfr 3 (memb. Sfr 1.50)

24. BEITRÄGE ZUR HEIMATKUNDE [Contributions to local studies]. A. Fragnière Frères, Fribourg, for Verein für Heimatkunde des Sensebezirkes und der benachbarten interessierten Landschaften. Sfr 5

BERICHT. For titles beginning with "Bericht," followed by the name of the publishing or sponsoring institution or society, see the respective institution or society.

25. BERNER ZEITSCHRIFT FÜR GESCHICHTE UND HEIMATKUNDE [Bern journal of history and local studies]. Q. Verlag Paul Haupt, Bern, for Staatsarchiv des Kantons Bern, Falkenplatz 4, Bern. Sfr 5

26. BERNISCHES HISTORISCHES MUSEUM IN BERN, JAHRBUCH DES... (Jahrbuch des Bernischen Historischen Museums in Bern) [Yearbook of the Bernese Historical Museum in Bern]. Irr. 1895 (1955/56 [1957]: vol. 35/36). Bernisches Historisches Museum, Helvetiaplatz 5, Bern. Ed: M. Stettler. Art. on hist. and prehist., archaeology, art hist., numismatics and ethnography, mainly in reference to items in the museum; reports of the museum; illus. Sfr 8

27. BIBLIOTHEQUE D'HUMANISME ET RENAISSANCE [Library of humanism and renaissance]. 3 x y. 1941 (1959: vol. 21). Librairie E. Droz, Genève, for Assoc. "Humanisme et Renaissance." Ed: A. Renaudet, F. Desonay, E. Droz. Art. on the culture and particularly the literature of the Renaissance, and occasionally on the intellectual hist. and historiography of the Renaissance; bk. rev.; news and notes (Chronique) on important events in the field of Renaissance studies; in French or English, Italian or German. Sfr 25 / $ 6

BLÄTTER. For titles beginning with "Blätter," followed by the name of the publishing or sponsoring institution or society, see the respective institution or society.

28. BLÄTTER AUS DER WALLISER GESCHICHTE [Notes from the history of Valais]. A. Geschichtsforschender Verein von Oberwallis, Kollegium Spiritus Sanctus, Brig, Valais. Contains biblio. on the hist. of Upper Valais. Sfr 4/$ 1

29. BLÄTTER FÜR HEIMATKUNDE AUS DEM ENTLEBUCH [Notes for local studies from Entlebuch]. Irr. Buchdruckerei Schüpfheim AG., Schüpfheim. Supplement to Entlebucher Anzeiger. Sfr 4

30. BODENSEEGESCHICHTSVEREIN. HEIMATKUNDLICHE MITTEILUNGEN [Lake Constance Historical Society. Reports on local studies]. Irr. E. Leisi, Frauenfeld. pni

31. BRUGGER NEUJAHRSBLÄTTER [Brugg New Year's bulletin]. A. Effingerhof AG., Brugg, for Kulturgesellschaft des Bezirks Brugg. Sfr 2.50

BULLETIN. For titles beginning with "Bulletin," followed by the name of the publishing or sponsoring institution or society, see the respective institution or society.

32. BÜNDNER MONATSBLATT [Graubünden monthly paper]. Zeitschrift für bündnerische Geschichte, Heimat- und Volkskunde [Review of the history, local studies and folklore of Graubünden]. M. Buchdruckerei Gasser und Eggerlin Chur. Sfr 7.50

33. BURGDORFER JAHRBUCH [Burgdorf yearbook]. A. Langlois und Co., Burgdorf, for Casinogesellschaft Burgdorf, and Ortsgruppe Burgdorf, Bernischer Verein für Heimatschutz. Sfr 6

34. CAHIERS BENJAMIN CONSTANT [Benjamin Constant review]. B. Librairie Bonnard, Lausanne, for Assoc. des amis de Benjamin Constant. p(1) Sfr 2.50/fr. 200

35. CENOBIO [Cenacle]. Rivista mensile di cultura [Monthly cultural review]. M. Ed. address: Via Serafino Balestra 39, Lugano. Sfr 18.50/Sfr 30

36. CHRONIK DES AMTES FRAUBRUNNEN [Chronicle of the Fraubrunnen district]. B. Ökonomischer und gemeinnützziger Verein des Amtes Fraubrunnen, Jegenstorf. Sfr 4.50

COSTUMES ET COUTUMES see HEIMATLEBEN

37. DAVOSER REVUE [Davos review]. Zeitschrift für Freunde von Davos und Graubünden [Review for friends of Davos and Graubünden]. B-M. Jules Ferdmann, Davos-Platz. Sfr 7.50 / Sfr 8.50

38. ECUMENICAL REVIEW. Q. World Council of Churches, 17 Route de Malagnou, Genève. In English. Sfr 10/$ 3

ETUDES ASIATIQUES see ASIATISCHE STUDIEN

39. ETUDES DE LETTRES [Studies on letters]. 5 x y. Imprimerie Fawer und Favre S.A., Lausanne, for Société des études de lettres. Sfr 6/Sfr 8

ETUDES SUISSES D'HISTOIRE GENERALE see SCHWEIZER BEITRÄGE ZUR ALLGEMEINEN GESCHICHTE

40. FOLKLORE SUISSE [Swiss folklore]. Q. Schweizerische Gesellschaft für Volkskunde, Fischmarkt 1, Basel. A separate German edition appears under the title Schweizer Volkskunde. Sfr 7 (memb. free)

41. FREIBURGER GESCHICHTSBLÄTTER [Fribourg historical notes]. A. Deutscher Geschichtsforschender Verein des Kantons Freiburg, Kantons- und Universitätsbibliothek, Fribourg. Sfr 7 (memb. Sfr 5)

42. FREIBURGER ZEITSCHRIFT FÜR PHILOSOPHIE UND THEOLOGIE [Fribourg review of philosophy and theology]. Jahrbuch für Philosophie und spekulative Theologie [Yearbook for philosophy and speculative theology]. A. Paulus Verlag, Fribourg. Sfr 12 / Sfr 16

43. DIE FRIEDENS-WARTE [Vantage point for peace]. Blätter für internationale Verständigung und zwischenstaatliche Organisation [Journal for international understanding and inter-state organization]. Q. 1899 (1957/58: vol. 54). Verlag für Recht und Gesellschaft AG., Bundesstr. 15, Basel. Ed: Hans Wehberg, Avenue de la Grenade 1, Genève. Art. on international public and private law and international organization, peace movements, and on related topics; doc.; bk. rev. and list of bk. received; rev. of relevant current periodicals; in German or French. Sfr 24

GAZETTE NUMISMATIQUE SUISSE see SCHWEIZERISCHE MÜNZBLÄTTER

44. GEMEINDE-JAHRBUCH MÖRIKEN-WILDEGG [Möriken-Wildegg municipality yearbook]. B. Gemeindekanzlei Möriken. Sfr 2

45. GENAVA. Revue d'archéologie et d'histoire de l'art [Review of archaeology and the history of art]. Q. Musée d'art et d'histoire, Rue Charles-Galland, Genève. Sfr 14

LE GENEALOGISTE SUISSE see DER SCHWEIZER FAMILIENFORSCHER

46. GEOGRAPHICA HELVETICA. Schweizerische Zeitschrift für Länder- und Völkerkunde. Revue suisse de géographie et d'ethnographie. Rivista svizzera di geografia et d'etnografia [Swiss review of geography and ethnography]. Q. 1946 (1958: vol. 13). Kümmerly und Frey, Geographischer Verlag, Bern, for Geographisch-ethnographische Gesellschaft, Zähringerstr. 6, Zürich 1, Geographisch-ethnologische Gesellschaft Basel, Geographische Gesellschaft Bern, and Ostschweizerische Geographische Gesellschaft, St. Gallen. Art. on geography, ethnography, folklore, and on the hist. of geography and cartography; news and notes on Swiss soc.; lists of lectures and seminars on geography and ethnography at Swiss univ.; bk. rev.; in German and, occasionally, French and Italian; illus.; graph. Sfr 16 / Sfr 20

47. DER GESCHICHTSFREUND [The friend of history]. Irr. Gasser und Co., Rapperswil (St. Gallen). Free supplement to Die Linth und Rapperswiler Nachrichten.

48. DER GESCHICHTSFREUND [The friend of history]. A. J. von Matt, Stans, for Historischer Verein der fünf Orte Luzern, Uri, Schwyz, Unterwalden und Zug. pni

49. GESELLSCHAFT PRO VINDONISSA. JAHRESBERICHT [Pro Vindonissa Society. Annual Report]. A. Vindonissa-Museum, Brugg. (memb.) Sfr 7

50. GESNERUS. Q (usually double no.). 1943 (1958: vol. 15). H.R. Sauerländer und Co., Aarau, for Schweizerische Gesellschaft für Geschichte der Medizin und der Naturwissenschaften. Ed: Hans Fischer, Pharmakologisches Institut, Universität Zürich. Art. on the hist. of medicine and the sciences; bk. rev.; in German and French. Sfr 20

51. GUGGISBERG. Jahrbuch für die Bürger und Freunde des Schwarzenburgerlandes [Yearbook for the citizens and friends of the Schwarzenburg region]. Irr. GBS-Verlag, Schwarzenburg. pv (Sfr 4-8)

52. HEIMAT-KLÄNGE [Sounds of home]. Kulturelle Beilage zu den Zuger Nachrichten [Cultural supplement of the "Zug News"]. 20 x y. Zuger Nachrichten, Zug. p (1) Sfr 0.20

53. HEIMAT UND VOLK [Native land and people]. M. Dietschi und Co., Olten. Supplement to Oltner Tagblatt. Prior to 1958 appeared under the title Historische Mitteilungen. p (1) Sfr 0.30

54. HEIMATBUCH BAAR [Book of the Baar municipality]. A. Verkehrs- und Verschönerungsverein, Baar. Sfr 3.50

55. HEIMATBUCH DÜBENDORF [Book of the Dübendorf municipality]. A. Verkehrs- und Verschönerungsverein Dübendorf. Sfr 3.50

56. HEIMATCHRONIK FÜR WIL UND DIE UMLIEGENDEN LANDSCHAFTEN [Local chronicle for Wil and environs]. Q. Buchdruckerei Wiler Bote, Wil, St. Gallen. pni

57. HEIMATKUNDE AUS DEM SEETAL [Seetal local studies]. A. Verlag der Historischen Vereinigung Seetal, Seengen. Sfr 3

58. HEIMATKUNDE DES WIGGERTALS [Local studies of the Wiggertal]. A. Verlag der Heimatvereinigung des Wiggertales, Buchs. Sfr 3

59. HEIMATKUNDE VOM LINTHGEBIET [Local studies of the Linth area]. Q. (also pub. A. with same contents). Gebrüder Oberholzer, Uznach, for Verein für Heimatkunde vom Linthgebiet. Sfr 2

60. HEIMATLEBEN [Life in the native land]. Zeitschrift für Trachtenkunde und Volksbräuche [Review of costume studies and customs]. Q. Schweizerische Trachtenvereinigung, Postfach, Zürich 23. A separate French edition appears under the title Costumes et Coutumes. Sfr 5 / Sfr 6

61. HEIMATSCHUTZKOMMISSION GRÜNINGEN, NEUJAHRSBLATT DER... [New Year's bulletin of the Local Preservation Commission of Grüningen]. A. Heimatschutzkommission Grüningen. pni

62. HEIMATWERK [Local art and crafts]. Blätter für Volkskunst und Handwerk [Papers on popular art and handicrafts]. Q. Schweizer Heimatwerk "Heimathuus," Rudolf Brun-Brücke, Zürich. Sfr 5 / Sfr 6

63. HELVETIA FRANCISCANA. Studien und Beiträge zur Geschichte der schweizerischen Kapuzinerprovinz [Studies and contributions pertaining to the history of the Swiss Capuchin Province]. 3 x y. Provinzialiat der Schweizer Kapuziner, Luzern. for memb. only

64. HISTORISCH-ANTIQUARISCHE GESELLSCHAFT VON GRAUBÜNDEN, JAHRESBERICHT DER... (Jahresbericht der Historisch-Antiquarischen Gesellschaft von Graubünden) [Annual report of the Historical-Antiquarian Society of Graubünden]. A. Verlag der Historisch-Antiquarischen Gesellschaft, Chur. Sfr 7

HISTORISCHE MITTEILUNGEN see HEIMAT UND VOLK

65. HISTORISCHE VEREINIGUNG WYNENTAL, BERICHT DER... (Bericht der Historischen Vereinigung Wynental) [Report of the Wynental Historical Society]. Irr. E. und H.R. Tenger, Reinach. Sfr 1.50

66. HISTORISCHER VEREIN DES KANTONS BERN, ARCHIV DES... (Archiv des Historischen Vereins des Kantons Bern) [Archives of the Historical Society of the Canton Bern]. A.H. Lang und Co., Bern. Sfr 15

67. HISTORISCHER VEREIN DES KANTONS GLARUS, JAHRBUCH DES... (Jahrbuch des Historischen Vereins des Kantons Glarus) [Yearbook of the Historical Society of the Canton Glarus]. A.J. Baeschlin, Glarus. pv

68. HISTORISCHER VEREIN DES KANTONS SCHWYZ, MITTEILUNGEN DES... (Mitteilungen des Historischen Vereins des Kantons Schwyz) [Communications of the Historical Society of the Canton Schwyz]. B. Buchdruckerei Einsiedler Anzeiger AG., Einsiedeln. Sfr 6.25

69. HISTORISCHES NEUJAHRSBLATT [Historical New Year's paper]. A. Verein für Geschichte und Altertümer von Uri, Altdorf. pv (c. Sfr 10)

70. DER HOCHWÄCHTER [The mountain look-out]. Blätter für heimatliche Art und Kunst mit Beilage "Schaffendes Bern" [Papers for the local manner and art containing the supplement "Working Bern"]. M. Paul Haupt, Falkenplatz 14, Bern. Sfr 16 / $ 4

71. HÜLFSGESELLSCHAFT IN ZÜRICH, NEUJAHRSBLATT DER... [New Year's paper of the Hülfsgesellschaft in Zürich]. A. Komm. Beer und Co., Zürich. pv (c. Sfr 6)

72. INNERRHODER GESCHICHTSFREUND [The Inner Rhodes friend of history]. A. Historischer Verein Appenzell, Appenzell. Sfr 3.50

73. INNERSCHWEIZERISCHES JAHRBUCH FÜR HEIMATKUNDE [Local studies yearbook of the Swiss interior]. A. Diebold Schilling Verlag, Luzern. Sfr 29

74. INSTITUT NATIONAL GENEVOIS, BULLETIN DE... [Bulletin of the National Genevan Institute]. Irr. Institut national genevois, Palais du conseil général, Rue Jacques-Balmat 2, Genève. Sfr 5.75

75. LES INTERETS DU JURA [The interests of Jura]. M. R. Steiner, Delémont, for Association pour la défense des interêts du Jura, chambre d'économie et d'utilité publique du Jura Bernois. Sfr 8

JAHRBUCH. For titles beginning with "Jahrbuch," followed by the name of the publishing or sponsoring institution or society, see the respective institution or society.

76. JAHRBUCH DES STANDES AARGAU [Yearbook of the Canton Aargau]. A. Neue Aargauer Zeitung, Aarau. Sfr 8

77. JAHRBUCH FÜR SOLOTHURNISCHE GESCHICHTE [Yearbook for Solothurn history]. A. Buchdruckerei Gassmann AG., Solothurn, for Historischer Verein des Kantons Solothurn. Includes "Bibliographie der Solothurner Geschichtsliteratur." pv (c. Sfr 9)

78. JAHRBUCH VOM THUNER- UND BRIENZERSEE [Yearbook of Lakes Thun and Brienz]. A. Uferschutzverband Thuner- und Brienzersee, Interlaken. Sfr 4.50

79. JAHRBUCH VOM ZÜRICHSEE [Lake Zürich yearbook]. Zürichseebuch [Lake Zürich book]. B. Verband zum Schutze des Landschaftsbildes am Zürichsee. Th. Gut und Co., Zürich Stäfa. Sfr 19

JAHRESBERICHT. For titles beginning with "Jahresbericht," followed by the name of the publishing or sponsoring institution or society, see the respective institution or society.

JAHRESGABE. For titles beginning with "Jahresgabe," followed by the name of the publishing or sponsoring institution or society, see the respective institution or society.

JAHRHEFT. For titles beginning with "Jahrheft," followed by the name of the publishing or sponsoring institution or society, see the respective institution or society.

80. JUDAICA. Beiträge zum Verständnis des jüdischen Schicksals in Vergangenheit und Gegenwart [Contributions to the understanding of the fate of the Jews, past and present]. Q. Zwingli-Verlag, Cramerstr. 15/17, Zürich, for Schweizerische Evangelische Judenmission. Sfr 15

81. JURABLÄTTER [Jura notes]. Monatsschrift für Heimat- und Völkerkunde [Monthly journal for local studies and ethnography]. M. Buchdruckerei Habegger und Co., Derendingen, for Gesellschaft Raurachischer Geschichtsfreunde. Sfr 7.50

82. KANTONSBIBLIOTHEK URI. JAHRESGABE [Uri Cantonal Library. Annual presentation]. A. Kantonsbibliothek Uri, Altdorf. Sfr 2.50

83. KULTURELLE KOMMISSION ALBISRIEDEN, JAHRHEFT DER...(Jahrheft der Kulturellen Kommission Albisrieden) [Annual journal of the Cultural Commission of Albisrieden]. A. M. Winter-Keller, In der Ey 34, Albisrieden. Sfr 2.50

84. KYKLOS. International Review for Social Sciences (subtitle also in German and French). Q. Kyklos Verlag, Postfach 20 365, Basel 2. Sfr 26 / $ 6

85. LENZBURGER NEUJAHRSBLÄTTER [Lenzburg New Year's notes]. A. Wirz und Co., Aarau, for Vereinigung für Natur und Heimat von Lenzburg und Umgebung. Sfr 3

86. LESEGESELLSCHAFT WÄDENSWIL, NEUJAHRSBLATT DER...[New Year's bulletin of the Reading Society of Wädenswil]. A. Buchdruckerei A. Stutz und Co., Wädenswil, for Lesegesellschaft Wädenswil. Sfr 8

87. LIBRARIUM. 3 x y. Schweizerische bibliophile Gesellschaft, c/o Albert Bettex, Sonnenbergstr. 47, Thalwil (Zürich). (memb.) Sfr 30/(memb.) $ 10

MITTEILUNGEN. For titles beginning with "Mitteilungen," followed by the name of the publishing or sponsoring institution or society, see the respective institution or society.

88. MONATS-CHRONIK [Monthly chronicle]. M. E. Löpfe-Benz AG., Rorschach. Illus. supplement of Ostschweizerisches Tagblatt. Sfr 4.50

MUSEE GUTENBERG SUISSE see SCHWEIZERISCHES GUTENBERG-MUSEUM

89. MUSEE NEUCHATELOIS [Neuchâtel Museum]. B-M. Imprimerie Centrale, Neuchâtel, for Société d'histoire du canton de Neuchâtel. Sfr 12.50 (memb. Sfr 10) / Sfr 15 (memb. Sfr 12.50)

90. LES MUSEES DE GENEVE [The museums of Geneva]. 10 x y. Services des Musées et Collections, Hôtel Municipal, Genève. free

91. MUSEUM HELVETICUM. Schweizerische Zeitschrift für klassische Altertumswissenschaft. Revue suisse pour l'étude de l'antiquité classique. Rivista svizzera di filologia classica [Swiss journal for the study of classical antiquity]. Q. 1944 (1958: vol. 15). Verlag Benno Schwabe und Co., Basel. Ed: Olof Gigon, Gurtenweg 59, Muri bei Bern, and Fritz Wehrli, Keltenstr. 24, Zürich. Art. on all aspects of Greek and Roman antiquity, including culture, language, literature, art, law and general hist.; bk. rev.; in English, French or German. Sfr 16 / $ 3.70

92. MUSEUMSGESELLSCHAFT ARBON. ORTSGESCHICHTLICHES [Arbon Museum Society. Local historical matters]. Irr. Museumsgesellschaft Arbon, Arbon. pni

93. NEUE ZEITSCHRIFT FÜR MISSIONSWISSENSCHAFT. NOUVELLE REVUE DE SCIENCE MISSIONNAIRE [New review of missionary science]. Q. 1945 (1959: vol. 15). Seminar Schöneck, Beckenried. Ed: Joh. Beckmann S. M. B., Laurentius Kilger O. S. B., Pierre de Menasce O. P., and Walbert Bühlmann O. F. M. Art. on missionary problems and the hist. of Catholic missions and missionary orders throughout the world; bk. rev.; in German, French or, occasionally, English. Sfr 40/ $ 4

NEUJAHRSBLATT. For titles beginning with "Neujahrsblatt," followed by the name of the publishing or sponsoring institution or society, see the respective institution or society.

94. NEUJAHRSBLATT [New Year's paper]. A. Helbing und Lichtenhahn, Basel, for Gesellschaft zur Beförderung des Guten und Gemeinnützigen. Sfr 4.15

95. NEUJAHRSBLATT [New Year's paper]. A. Historischer Verein des Kantons St. Gallen, St. Gallen. Includes a biblio. of St. Gallen literature. pv (Sfr 6 - 10)

96. NEUJAHRSBLATT VON DIETIKON [New Year's paper of Dietikon]. A. Buchdruckerei Oscar Hummel, Dietikon, for Kommission für Heimatkunde, Dietikon. Sfr 2.50

NOUVELLE REVUE DE SCIENCE MISSIONNAIRE see NEUE ZEITSCHRIFT FÜR MISSIONSWISSENSCHAFT

97. NOVA ET VETERA. Q. L. Méroz, 12 Blvd. Georges Favon, Genève. Sfr 10 / Sfr 12

98. OBWALDNER GESCHICHTSBLÄTTER [Obwalden historical notes]. Irr. Buchdruckerei Louis Ehrli, Sarnen, for Historisch-antiquarischer Verein von Obwalden. Sfr 5.50

99. OLTNER NEUJAHRSBLÄTTER [Olten New Year's notes]. A. Q. Müller-Wilhelm, Olten, for Akademia Olten. pv (c. Sfr 6)

100. PAGES MONTHEYSANNES [Monthey pages]. Bulletin Annuel du "Vieux Monthey" [Annual bulletin of "Vieux Monthey"]. Irr. L. Borgeaud, Monthey. p (1) Sfr. 53

101. QUADERNI GRIGIONITALIANI [Journal of Italian Graubünden]. Rivista Trimestrale delle Valli Grigionitaliane [Quarterly review of the valleys of Italian Graubünden]. Q. T. Romolo, Engadinstr. 6, Chur, for "Pro Grigioni Italiano." Sfr 6 (memb. Sfr 5)

102. RANDENSCHAU [The Randen review]. Schaffhauser Heimatblätter [Schaffhausen local notes]. M. J.G. Stamms Erben, Schleitheim. Sfr 3

103. RAPPERSWIL DIE ROSENSTADT [Rapperswil, the city of roses]. Jahrbuch für Rapperswil und die Nachbarschaft [Yearbook for Rapperswil and environs]. A. Gasser und Co., Rapperswil, St. Gallen. Sfr 4

104. REVUE DE DROIT INTERNATIONAL, DE SCIENCES DIPLOMATIQUES ET POLITIQUES [Review of international law and diplomatic and political sciences]. Q. Antoine Sottile, Case Postale 178 Mt. Blanc, Genève. Sfr 59.50/Sfr 61.50

105. REVUE DE THEOLOGIE ET DE PHILOSOPHIE [Review of theology and philosophy]. Q. Imprimerie La Concorde, Lausanne, for Revue de théologie et de philosophie, 3 Rue Cité Devant, Lausanne. Sfr 14/Sfr 17

106. REVUE HISTORIQUE VAUDOISE [Review of Vaud history]. Q. Société vaudoise d'histoire et d'archéologie et de la commission des monuments historiques, Maupas 47, Lausanne. Sfr 14

107. REVUE JURASSIENNE [Jura review]. A. Imprimerie "Le Jura S. A." Delémont, "Pro Jura." Sfr 3

108. REVUE ROMANDE DES ARTS [French Swiss review of arts]. Irr. Club des arts, Rue de l'avenir 27, Genève. Sfr 12

REVUE SUISSE D'ART ET D'ARCHEOLOGIE see ZEITSCHRIFT FÜR SCHWEIZERISCHE ARCHÄOLOGIE UND KUNSTGESCHICHTE

REVUE SUISSE D'HISTOIRE see SCHWEIZERISCHE ZEITSCHRIFT FÜR GESCHICHTE

REVUE SUISSE DE NUMISMATIQUE see SCHWEIZERISCHE NUMISMATISCHE RUNDSCHAU

109. RHEINFELDER NEUJAHRSBLÄTTER [Rheinfelden New Year's notes]. A. Buchdruckerei A. Herzog, Rheinfelden. pv (Sfr 2.50-5.80)

110. RITTERHAUS-VEREINIGUNG ÜRIKON-STÄFA. JAHRESBERICHT MIT ABHANDLUNGEN [Ritterhaus-Vereinigung Ürikon-Stäfa. Annual report with essays]. A. Buchdruckerei Stäfa AG., Stäfa. pni

111. RITTERHAUSGESELLSCHAFT BUBIKON, JAHRHEFT DER...[Annual journal of the Bubikon Ritterhausgesellschaft]. A. Ritterhausgesellschaft, Bubikon. Sfr 1.50

112. RIVISTA PATRIZIALE TICINESE [Ticino patrician review]. B-M. Alleanza Patriziale Ticinese, Riva San Vitale. Sfr 5

RIVISTA STORICA SVIZZERA see SCHWEIZERISCHE ZEITSCHRIFT FÜR GESCHICHTE

RIVISTA SVIZZERA D'ARTE E D'ARCHEOLOGIA see ZEITSCHRIFT FÜR SCHWEIZERISCHE ARCHÄOLOGIE UND KUNSTGESCHICHTE

113. RORSCHACHER NEUJAHRSBLATT [Rorschach New Year's paper]. A. E. Löpfe-Benz AG., Rorschach. Sfr 5

114. SARGANSERLAND [The Sargans region]. Beiträge zu seiner Geschichte und Kultur [Contributions to its history and culture]. M. Sarganserländische Buchdruckerei AG., Mels. Sfr 4.50

115. SCHAFFHAUSER BEITRÄGE ZUR VATERLÄNDISCHEN GESCHICHTE [Schaffhausen contributions to the history of the fatherland]. A. K. Augustin, Thayngen, for Historischer Verein des Kantons Schaffhausen. Contains a biblio. of the hist. (including art hist.) of Schaffhausen. pv (Sfr 13-18)

116. DIE SCHWEIZ. LA SUISSE. LA SVIZZERA [Switzerland]. Ein nationales Jahrbuch. Annuaire national. Annuario nazionale [National yearbook]. A. Jahrbuch-Verlag der Neuen Helvetischen Gesellschaft, Bern. Sfr 10

117. SCHWEIZER BEITRÄGE ZUR ALLGEMEINEN GESCHICHTE. ETUDES SUISSES D'HISTOIRE GENERALE. STUDI SVIZZERI DI STORIA GENERALE [Swiss studies on general history]. A. 1943 (1958: vol. 16). Herbert Lang und Co., Bern. Ed: Werner Näf, Ernst Walder. Art. on general, cultural, social and religious hist. and on hist. methodology; reports on research; in English, French or German. Sfr 16.20

118. DER SCHWEIZER FAMILIENFORSCHER. LE GENEALOGISTE SUISSE [The Swiss genealogist]. Schweizerische Zeitschrift für Genealogie [Swiss journal of genealogy]. M (usually double no.). 1934 (1958: vol. 25). Werner Debrunner, Rietstr. 25, Erlenbach (Zürich), for Schweizerische Gesellschaft für Familienforschung. Ed: Alfred von Speyr, Hergiswil (Nidwalden). Art. on Swiss genealogy and related subjects; bk. rev., notes of professional interest. Sfr 10 (memb. free)

119. SCHWEIZER MONATSHEFTE [Swiss monthly journal]. M. Gesellschaft Schweizer Monatshefte, Arbenzstr. 20, Zürich 8. Sfr 20

120. SCHWEIZER THEATER-JAHRBUCH DER SCHWEIZERISCHEN GESELLSCHAFT FÜR THEATERKULTUR [Swiss theater yearbook of the Swiss Society for Theater Culture]. Irr. (A. or B). Theaterkultur-Verlag, Thalwil (Zürich), for Schweizerische Gesellschaft für Theaterkultur. pv

121. SCHWEIZER VOLKSKUNDE. FOLKLORE SUISSE [Swiss folklore]. B-M. Schweizerische Gesellschaft für Volkskunde, Fischmarkt 1, Basel. A separate French edition appears under the title Folklore suisse. Sfr 7 (memb. free)

122. SCHWEIZERISCHE GESELLSCHAFT FÜR URGESCHICHTE, JAHRBUCH DER... (Jahrbuch der Schweizerischen Gesellschaft für Urgeschichte) ANNUAIRE DE LA SOCIETE SUISSE DE PREHISTOIRE. ANNUARIO DELLA SO-

CIETA SVIZZERA DE PREISTORIA [Yearbook of the Swiss Society for Prehistory]. A. 1909 (1957 [1958]: vol. 46). Verlag Huber und Co.AG., Frauenfeld, for Schweizerische Gesellschaft für Urgeschichte, Rheinsprung 20, Basel. Ed: Rudolf Degen. Art. on prehist. and archaeology, with emphasis on Switzerland; archaeological reports; A. reports of the soc.; bk. rev.; list of memb. of the soc.; in French, German or Italian. Sfr 12 / Sfr 18

123. SCHWEIZERISCHE MÜNZBLÄTTER. GAZETTE NUMISMATIQUE SUISSE [Swiss coin gazette]. Q. 1950 (1958: vol. 32). Schweizerische Numismatische Gesellschaft, c/o Colin Martin (president), Place B.-Constant 2, Lausanne. Ed: Herbert Cahn, Rütimeyerstr. 12, Basel. Art. on coins and medals; reports of numismatic finds; rev. of numismatic pub.; professional news; in French or German. Sfr 10 (memb. free)

124. SCHWEIZERISCHE MUSIKZEITUNG. REVUE MUSICALE SUISSE [Swiss musical review]. M. 1861 (1959: vol. 99). Hug Co., Limmatquai 28, Zürich 1, for Schweizerischer Tonkünstlerverein and "Suisa," Schweizerische Gesellschaft der Urheber und Verleger. Ed: Willi Schuh, Zeisigweg 6, Zürich 38. Art. on the hist. of music, musical criticism and the theater; biographies and memoirs; doc.; in German or French. Sfr 14/ Sfr 16

125. SCHWEIZERISCHE NUMISMATISCHE RUNDSCHAU. REVUE SUISSE DE NUMISMATIQUE [Swiss numismatic review]. A. 1890 (1957: vol. 38). Schweizerische Numismatische Gesellschaft, Bern, c/o Colin Martin (president), Place B.-Constant 2, Lausanne. Ed: D. Schwarz, Schweizerisches Landesmuseum, Zürich 23. Art. on numismatics of all periods dealing also with the general hist. and economic background to numismatic subjects, with some emphasis on Switzerland; doc.; illus.; in German and French. Sfr 30

126. SCHWEIZERISCHE ZEITSCHRIFT FÜR GESCHICHTE. REVUE SUISSE D'HISTOIRE. RIVISTA STORICA SVIZZERA [Swiss journal of history]. Q. 1921 (1959: vol. 9). Allgemeine Geschichtsforschende Gesellschaft der Schweiz, and Vereinigung schweizerischer Archivare. Ed: Walter Schmid, Niederhofenrain 4, Zürich 8, and Jean-Charles Biaudet, 1 Rue Cité-Devant, Lausanne. Art. on the hist., mostly modern, of Switzerland and aspects of European hist. related to Switzerland; rev. art.; extensive bk. rev. section; professional notes; list of bk. and periodicals received; report on the activities of the soc.; in German, French or Italian. Sfr 25 (memb. Sfr 18)

SCHWEIZERISCHES ARCHIV FÜR HERALDIK see ARCHIVES HERALDIQUES SUISSES

127. SCHWEIZERISCHES ARCHIV FÜR VOLKSKUNDE. ARCHIVES SUISSES DES TRADITIONS POPULAIRES [Swiss archive of folklore]. Q. 1897 (1958: vol. 54). Schweizerische Gesellschaft für Volkskunde, Fischmarkt 1, Basel. Ed: Robert Wildhaber, Peter Ochs-Str. 87, Basel. Art. on Swiss folklore, hist., linguistics, toponymy and related subjects of all periods; rev. of bk. and art. of relevant European pub.; illus.; in German and, occasionally, French or Italian. Sfr 15 (memb. Sfr 10)

128. SCHWEIZERISCHES GESCHLECHTERBUCH. ALMANACH GENEALOGIQUE SUISSE [Swiss genealogical almanac]. Irr. 1905 (1958: vol. 11). Pub. and ed: J.P. Zwicky von Gauen, for Genealogisches Institut Zwicky, Zürich. Genealogies of important Swiss families. Sfr 48

129. SCHWEIZERISCHES GUTENBERGMUSEUM. MUSEE GUTENBERG SUISSE [Swiss Gutenberg Museum]. Zeitschrift für Buchdruckgeschichte, Graphik- und Zeitungskunde. Revue d'histoire de l'imprimerie, des arts graphiques et de la presse [Review of the history of printing, graphic arts and the press]. Q. Büchler Co., Marienstr. 8, Bern. Sfr 11 / Sfr 13

130. SINOLOGICA. Zeitschrift für chinesische Kultur und Wissenschaft. Revue des sciences et des arts en Chine. Review of Chinese culture and science. Irr. 1947/48 (1958: vol. 5). Verlag für Recht und Gesellschaft AG., Basel. Ed. board: Wolfram Eberhard, Berkeley; Walter Fuchs, München; Emile Gaspardone, Paris; Alfred Gigon, Basel; Alfred Steinmann, Zürich. Art. on the general, cultural, art and religious hist. and folklore of China; bk. rev.; in English, French or German. Sfr 30

131. SOCIETA RETORUMANTSCHA, ANNALES DE LA... [Yearbook of the Rhaeto-Romance Society]. A. Stampa romontscha, Mustér (Disentis), for Società retorumantscha. Sfr 5

132. SOCIETE D'HISTOIRE ET D'ARCHEOLOGIE DE GENEVE, BULLETIN DE LA... [Bulletin of the Historical and Archaeological Society of Geneva]. A. 1892 (1957 [1958]: vol. 11). Société d'histoire et d'archéologie de Genève, Bibliothèque publique et universitaire de Genève. (memb.) Sfr 20

133. SOCIETE JEAN-JACQUES ROUSSEAU, ANNALES DE LA... [Annals of the Jean-Jacques Rousseau Society]. T. A. Jullien, Genève, for Société Jean-Jacques Rousseau. pv (Sfr 25-35)

134. SOCIETE JURASSIENNE D'EMULATION, ACTES DE LA... [Records of the Jura Emulation Society]. A. Imprimerie Le Jura S. A., Porrentruy. Art. on the hist. of the Bernese Jura. Sfr 10

135. STADTBIBLIOTHEK WINTERTHUR, NEUJAHRSBLATT DER... [New Year's bulletin of the Winterthur town library]. A. Stadtbibliothek Winterthur. Sfr 8

STUDI SVIZZERI DI STORIA GENERALE see SCHWEIZER BEITRÄGE ZUR ALLGEMEINEN GESCHICHTE

LA SUISSE see DIE SCHWEIZ

LA SVIZZERA see DIE SCHWEIZ

136. SVIZZERA ITALIANA [Italian Switzerland]. Rivista bimestrale di cultura [Bimonthly cultural review]. B-M. Arti grafiche, Bellinzona. Sfr 15

137. THEOLOGISCHE ZEITSCHRIFT [Theological review]. B-M. Friedrich Reinhard AG., Missionsstr. 36, Basel 12, for Theologische Fakultät, Universität Basel. Sfr 23.50 / Sfr 28

138. THURGAUER JAHRBUCH [Thurgau yearbook]. A. Huber Co. AG., Frauenfeld. Sfr 4.50

139. THURGAUISCHE BEITRÄGE ZUR VATERLÄNDISCHEN GESCHICHTE [Thurgau studies on the history of the fatherland]. A. Historischer Verein des Kantons Thurgau, Frauenfeld. Contains biblio. of Thurgau hist. literature. pv (Sfr 8.50-12)

140. TOGGENBURGBLÄTTER FÜR HEIMATKUNDE [Toggenburg local notes]. Q. A. Mäder Söhne, Lichtensteig. Supplement of the Toggenburger Bote. Sfr 3

141. TOGGENBURGER CHRONIK [Toggenburg chronicle]. Irr. E. Kalberer, Bazenheid. Illus. supplement of Alttoggenburger und Toggenburger Volksblatt. p (1) Sfr 0.50

142. TOGGENBURGER HEIMAT-JAHRBUCH [Toggenburg local yearbook]. A. Thur-Verlag, E. Kalberer AG., Bazenheid. Sfr 2.90

143. UNSERE HEIMAT [Our native land]. A. Historische Gesellschaft Freiamt, Wohlen (Aargau). Sfr 5

144. UR-SCHWEIZ. LA SUISSE PRIMITIVE [Primitive Switzerland]. Mitteilungen zur Ur- und Frühgeschichte der Schweiz. Notices sur la préhistoire et l'archéologie suisses [Notes on Swiss prehistory and archaeology]. Q. 1937 (1958: vol. 22). Institut für Ur- und Frühgeschichte der Schweiz, Rheinsprung 20, Basel, for Schweizerische Gesellschaft für Urgeschichte. Ed: R. Laur-Belart, Basel, E. Pelichet, Nyon. Art. on the prehist., early hist., and archaeology of Switzerland and adjacent areas, with emphasis on the classical Roman period; in French or German; illus. Sfr 4 / Sfr 5

145. VALLESIA. A. Bibliothèque cantonale, Sion, for the cantonal library and archives of Valais and the museums of Valère and Majorie. In French or German. pv (Sfr 12-15)

146. VEREINIGUNG PRO SIHLTAL, BLÄTTER DER... [Notes of the Pro Sihltal Society]. A. Vereinigung Pro Sihltal, Klosbachstr. 72, Zürich 7/32. Sfr 1.50

147. VERKEHRSVEREIN RÜTI-TANN. JAHRHEFT [Rüti-Tann Tourist Association. Annual journal]. A. Buchdruckerei A. Köhler, Rüti, Zürich. Sfr 3

148. VOLKSHOCHSCHULE [Adult education]. 10 x y. Verein zur Förderung der Volkshochschule des Kantons Zürich. Fraumünsterstr. 27, Zürich 1. Sfr 8

149. VOM JURA ZUM SCHWARZWALD [From the Jura to the Black Forest]. Blätter für Heimatkunde und Heimatschutz [Notes for local studies and country preservation]. A. Buch- und Kunstdruck A. Fricker, Frick, for Fricktalisch-Badische Vereinigung für Heimatkunde. Sfr 4

150. VON EUSERER WALDER HEIMET [About your Wald home]. Q. Kommission des Heimatmuseums, Wald. Supplement of Volksblatt vom Bachtel. Sfr 1

151. VOX ROMANICA. Annales helvetici explorandis linguis romanicis destinati. S-A. 1936 (1958: vol. 17). Verlag A. Francke AG., Bern. Ed: A. Steiger, Herzogstr. 7, Zürich 44. Art. on the philology and hist. of the Romance languages, and on the hist. of the literatures of the Romance-language countries; textual criticism; bk. rev. and biblio. of relevant Swiss dissertations and periodicals; in French, German or Italian. Sfr 44

152. WEINFELDER HEIMATBLÄTTER [Weinfelden local notes]. Q. W. Schläpfer und Söhne, Weinfelden. Supplement of Thurgauer Tagblatt. Sfr 2

153. WINTERTHURER JAHRBUCH [Winterthur yearbook]. A. Buchdrukkerei Winterthur AG., Winterthur. pv (c. Sfr 8)

154. ZEITSCHRIFT FÜR SCHWEIZERISCHE ARCHÄOLOGIE UND KUNSTGESCHICHTE. REVUE SUISSE D'ART ET D'ARCHEOLOGIE. RIVISTA SVIZZERA D'ARTE E D'ARCHEOLOGIA [Journal of Swiss archaeology and history of art]. Q. 1939 (1958: vol. 12). Birkhäuser Verlag, Basel, for Direktion des Schweizerischen Landesmuseums in Zürich, Zürich. Ed: D. Schwarz. Art. on archaeology, hist. of art and architecture, with emphasis on Switzerland; bk. rev.; news on architectural repairs and restoration with brief hist. description of the monuments; organ of the Verband der Schweizerischen Altertumssammlungen, Gesellschaft für Schweizerische Kunstgeschichte and Gesellschaft für das Schweizerische Landesmuseum; illus. Sfr 14.80 / Sfr 18

155. ZEITSCHRIFT FÜR SCHWEIZERISCHE KIRCHENGESCHICHTE. REVUE D'HISTOIRE ECCLESIASTIQUE SUISSE [Journal of Swiss ecclesiastical history]. Q. 1907 (1959: vol. 53). Paulus-Verlag, for Vereinigung Katholischer Historiker der Schweiz, Fribourg. Ed: Oskar Vasella, Fribourg. Art. on the hist. of the Christian Church, mainly in Switzerland, and on general and cultural hist.; professional news; in French or German. Sfr 10 / Sfr 11

156. ZOFINGER NEUJAHRSBLATT [Zofingen New Year's paper]. A. F. Schoder, Zofingen, for Freunde der Heimat. Sfr 3

157. ZUGER NEUJAHRSBLATT [Zug New Year's paper]. A. Graphische Werkstätte Eberhard Kalt-Zehnder, Zug, for Gemeinnützige Gesellschaft des Kantons Zug. Sfr 7

158. ZÜRCHER CHRONIK [Zürich chronicle]. Zeitschrift für zürcherische Geschichte und Heimatkunde [Journal for Zürich history and local studies]. Q. E. Jäggli und Co., Bühlhofweg 1-3, Seen-Winterthur. Sfr 10.40 / Sfr 14.60

159. ZÜRCHER TASCHENBUCH [Zürich pocketbook]. A. Buchdruckerei a/d Sihl AG., Zürich. Biblio. of the hist., geography and folklore of the city and canton of Zürich. Sfr 10

160. ZÜRCHER UNTERLANDER MUSEUMSVEREIN, JAHRHEFT DES... (Jahrheft des Zürcher Unterlander Museumsvereins) [Annual journal of the Zürich Lowlands Museum Society]. A. M. Müller, Ruhtalstr. 20, Winterthur. Sfr 2

161. ZWINGLIANA. Beiträge zur Geschichte Zwinglis, der Reformation und des Protestantismus in der Schweiz [Studies on the history of Zwingli, the Reformation and Protestantism in Switzerland]. S-A. 1897 (1958: vol. 10). Zwingliverein, Zentralbibliothek, Zürich. Ed: L. v. Muralt, Wybüelstr. 20, Zollikon. Art. on the Swiss Reformation and the hist. of Swiss Protestantism, and biographical art. on Zwingli and his contemporaries.
Sfr 30 (individuals Sfr 8)

ADDENDA

ACTUALITES EUROPEENNES see section on International Periodicals

BULLETIN ECÓNOMIQUE POUR L'EUROPE see section on International Periodicals

CAHIERS D'HISTOIRE MONDIALE see section on International Periodicals

CENTRE EUROPEEN DE LA CULTURE, BULLETIN DU... see section on International Periodicals

ECONOMIQUE BULLETIN FOR LATIN AMERICA see section on International Periodicals

Vatican City

Prepared with the assistance of

P. Michael Lacko, S.J., Pontificium Institutum
Orientalium Studiorum, Rome

ACTA APOSTOLICAE SEDIS see APOSTOLICA SEDES, ACTA...

ACTA SANCTAE SEDIS see APOSTOLICA SEDES, ACTA...

1. APOSTOLICA SEDES, ACTA... (Acta Apostolicae Sedis) [Transactions of the Apostolic See]. B-M. 1909 (1958: vol. 50). Libreria Editrice Vaticana, Città del Vaticano. From 1865 to 1908 (vol. 1-41) pub. under the title: Acta Sanctae Sedis. L 1,500 / L 2,300

2. ARCHIVA ECCLESIAE [Archives of the Church]. A. 1958 (1958: vol.1) Associazione Archivistica Ecclesiastica, Città del Vaticano. Proceedings of the First Congress of Church Archivists, Rome (5-8 November 1957); reports on the activities of the assoc. and of ecclesiastical archives in the Vatican and in Italy, including descriptions of archival holdings. L 800 (memb. L 500)/ L 1,000

RÖMISCHE QUARTALSSCHRIFT FÜR CHRISTLICHE ALTERTUMSKUNDE UND KIRCHENGESCHICHTE see section on the Federal Republic of Germany

Yugoslavia

Prepared with the assistance of the

Bibliografski institut FNRJ [Bibliographical Institute of the Federal People's Republic of Yugoslavia], Belgrade, and the

Istoriski institut Srpske akademije nauka [Historical Institute of the Serbian Academy of Sciences], Belgrade

Note: The periodicals in this list appear in the Serbo-Croatian language (Roman script), except where stated otherwise. Notation is made if a periodical appears in the Cyrillic script or in another language.

1. ACADEMIE SERBE DES SCIENCES, BULLETIN DE LA... (Bulletin de l'académie serbe des sciences) [Bulletin of the Serbian Academy of Sciences]. Section des sciences sociales [Section for the social sciences]. Irr. 1933 (1959: vol. 24 or social science (new) series no. 7). Srpska akademija nauka [Serbian Acad. of Sciences], Knez Mihailova 35, Beograd. Ed: Dušan Nedeljković. Sum. of papers presented to the acad. in the field of the social sciences (with strong emphasis on hist., archaeology and related fields) pertaining mostly to Yugoslavia; in French, English or German; illus. pni

ANALI. For titles beginning with "Anali," followed by the name of the publishing or sponsoring institution or society, see the respective institution or society.

ANNUAIRE DE LA SOCIETE HISTORIQUE DE BOSNIE ET HERZEGOVINE see ISTORISKO DRUŠTVO BOSNE I HERCEGOVINE, GODIŠNJAK...

2. ARCHAEOLOGIA JUGOSLAVICA. A. (Irr.). 1954 (1959: vol. 3). Arheološko društvo Jugoslavije [Archaeological Soc. of Yugoslavia], Knez Mihailova 35, Beograd. Ed. board: Milutin Garašanin, Stipe Gunjača, Duje Rendić-Miočevič. Art. on prehist., Greek, Roman, Byzantine and Slavic archaeology and architecture and on ancient and Christian plastic arts; in German, French or English; illus. $5.35

3. ARHEOLOŠKI MUZEJ. ZBORNIK [Archaeological Museum. Review]. Irr. Arheološki muzej, Skopje. In Macedonian (Cyrillic script). Din 2,000

4. ARHEOLOŠKI VESTNIK [Archaeological bulletin]. Acta archaeologica. Q. 1950 (1959: vol. 9/10). Arheološka sekcija, Slovenska akademija znanosti in umetnosti [Archaeological Section, Serbian Acad. of Sciences and Arts], Poštni predal 323, Ljubljana. Ed. board: Srečko Brodar (manag. ed.), Josip Korošec, France Stelè, Božo Skerlj. Art. on archaeology and cultural anthropology, mostly of Slovenia and other parts of Yugoslavia, pertaining to the pre-Slavic and Slavic periods; in Slovenian; a few art. also in Serbo-Croatian; table of contents in Slovenian, English and German; German, English or French sum.; illus. pni / $6.95

5. ARHIVIST [Archivist]. Q. 1951 (1960: vol. 10). Savez društava arhivskih radnika Jugoslavije [Archivists' Assoc. of Yugoslavia], Birčaninova 1/IV, Beograd. Ed. board: Franjo Biljan (manag. ed.), Olga Jelisavetov, Mirko Androi Fabijan Trgo. Art. on the hist., organization and administration of archives and on Yugoslav archival holdings; bk. rev.; biblio.; reports on the activities of archival soc.; appendix: information on Yugoslav archives; French sum.
Din 1,000 / $5.35

6. ARHIVSKI ALMANAH [Almanac of archives]. A. 1958 (1960: vol. 2/3). Društvo arhivskih radnika N.R. Srbije [Federal Soc. of Archivists of the People's Republic of Serbia]. Karnedžieva 2, Beograd. Ed: Edib Hasanagić, Smiljka Durić. Art. on general problems concerning archives; reports on the present and past work of the soc.; rev. of art. Replaces Arhivski pregled [Archival review], which ceased pub. in 1957. Din 500 / $2.15

ARHIVSKI PREGLED see ARHIVSKI ALMANAH

7. ARHIVŠKI VJESNIK [Archival review]. Irr. 1958 (1959: vol. 2). Državni arhiv N.R. Hrvatske [State Archives of the Croatian People's Republic], Marulićev trg 21, Zagreb. Ed: Bernard Stulli. Art. on hist. sources in Yugoslav and some foreign archives, pertaining to all periods, with emphasis on the 19th and 20th cent.; bk. rev.; reports on the activities of Yugoslav and foreign archival soc.; German, French or English sum. $2

8. BALKANOLOŠKI INSTITUT, NAUČNO DRUŠTVO N.R. BOSNE I HERCEGOVINE. GODIŠNJAK [Institute of Balkan Studies, Scientific Society of the People's Republic of Bosnia and Herzegovina. Yearbook]. Balkanološki institut, Naučno društvo N.R. Bosne i Hercegovine, Obala Vojvode Stepe 41, Sarajevo. In Serbo-Croatian (Cyrillic and Roman scripts), Macedonian, French or German; French sum. of art. in Serbo-Croatian and Macedonian. Din 500

9. BIBLIOTEKAR [Librarian]. Q. Društvo bibliotekara N.R. Srbije [Librarians' Soc. of the People's Republic of Serbia], Bulevar Revolucije 71, Beograd In Serbo-Croatian (Cyrillic script). p (1) Din 500 / $3.20 p.a.

BULLETIN. For titles beginning with "Bulletin," followed by the name of the publishing or sponsoring institution or society, see the respective institution or society.

BULLETIN D'ARCHEOLOGIE ET D'HISTOIRE DALMATE see VJESNIK ZA ARHEOLOGIJU I HISTORIJU DALMATINSKU

10. CELJSKI ZBORNIK [Celje review]. Irr. Svet za prosveto in kulturo okraja Celje [Council of Education and Culture of the District of Celje], Celje. Hist. of the town of Celje and surrounding districts from ancient times to the present; in Slovenian. pni

11. ČLANCI I GRADJA ZA KULTURNU ISTORIJU ISTOČNE BOSNE [Artic and source material on the cultural history of Eastern Bosnia]. Irr. Zavičajni muzej [Local Museum], Tuzla. German, French or English sum. pni

12. DRUŠTVO MUZEJSKO- KONZERVATORSKIH RADNIKA N.R. HRVATSKE, VIJESTI... (Vijesti Društva muzejsko-konzervatorskih radnika N.R. Hrvatske) [Bulletin of the Society of Museum Curators of the People's Republic of Croatia]. B-M. Društvo muzejsko-konzervatorskih radnika N.R. Hrvatske, Opatička 20, Zagreb. p (1) Din 250 / p (1) $1.50

13. ETNOGRAFSKI INSTITUT, GLASNIK... (Glasnik Etnografskog instituta). BULLETIN DE L'INSTITUT ETHNOGRAPHIQUE [Bulletin of the Ethnographical Institute]. A. (Irr.). Etnografski institut Srpske akademije nauka [Ethnographical Inst. of the Serbian Acad. of Sciences], Knez Mihailova 35, Beograd. In Serbo-Croatian (Cyrillic script); English or French sum. $1.87

14. ETNOGRAFSKI MUZEJ, GLASNIK... (Glasnik Etnografskog muzeja). BULLETIN DU MUSEE ETHNOGRAPHIQUE DE BEOGRAD [Bulletin of the Ethnographical Museum]. A. (Irr.). Etnografski muzej, Studentski trg 13, Beograd. Biblio.; in Serbo-Croatian (Cyrillic script); English, French, German, Russian or Italian sum.; illus. Din 700 / $ 1.90

15. FILOZOFSKA FAKULTETA, ZBORNIK... (Zbornik Filozofske fakultete) [Review of the Philosophical Faculty]. Irr. Prirodoslovno-matematičko-filozofska fakultete [Faculties of Natural Sciences, Mathematics and Philosophy], trg Revolucije 11, Ljubljana. In Slovenian; French and English sum. pni

16. FILOZOFSKI FAKULTET, ODSJEK ZA POVIJEST, RADOVI... (Radovi Filozofskog fakulteta. Odsjek za povijest) [Works of the Philosophical Faculty, Department of History]. Irr. 1959 (1959: vol. 2). Odsjek za povijest, Filozofski fakultet Sveučilišta u Zagrebu [Dept. of Hist., Philosophical Faculty of the Univ. of Zagreb], Dalmatinska 8, Zagreb. Ed: Jaroslav Šidak. Art. on all periods of the hist. of Yugoslavia, with emphasis on Croatia; French or German sum. pni

17. FILOZOFSKI FAKULTET U NOVOM SADU, GODIŠNJAK... (Godišnjak Filozofskog fakulteta u Novom Sadu) [Yearbook of the Philosophical Faculty of Novi Sad]. A. Filozofski fakultet u Novom Sadu, Njegoševa 1, Novi Sad. In Serbo-Croatian (Cyrillic or Roman script); French, English or German sum. Din 820

18. FILOZOFSKI FAKULTET, ZBORNIK... (Zbornik Filozofskog fakulteta) [Review of the Philosophical Faculty]. A. 1948 (1959: vol. 4, part 2). Filozofski fakultet univerziteta u Beogradu [Faculty of Philosophy of the Univ. in Belgrade], Studentski trg 1, Beograd. Art. on literature, philology and cultural hist.; in Serbo-Croatian (Cyrillic script); French, English or German sum. pni

GLAS, GLASNIK. For titles beginning with "Glas" or "Glasnik," followed by the name of the publishing or sponsoring institution or society, see the respective institution or society.

19. GODIŠEN ZBORNIK [Yearbook]. Annuaire. A. 1948 (1959: vol. 10/11). Istorisko-filološki oddel, Filosofski fakultet na universitetot Skopje [Hist.-Philological Section, Faculty of Philosophy of the Univ. of Skoplje], Braće Miladinov 26, Skopje. Art. on literature, pertaining to all periods, and on hist. and philology; in Serbo-Croatian (Cyrillic and Roman scripts) or Macedonian (Cyrillic script); Russian, French or English sum. Din 600

GODIŠNJAK, GODIŠNIK. For titles beginning with "Godišnjak" or "Godišnik," followed by the name of the publishing or sponsoring institution or society, see the respective institution or society.

20. GODIŠNJAK GRADA BEOGRADA [Yearbook of the town of Belgrade]. A. Narodni odbor grada Beograda [People's Committee of the Town of Belgrade], Uzun Mirkova 1, Beograd. Archaeology, hist. and art of Belgrade, pertaining to all periods; French or German sum. Prior to 1959 appeared under the title: Godišnjak muzeja grada Beograda [Yearbook of the Museum of Belgrade]. $8.55

GODIŠNJAK MUZEJA GRADA BEOGRADA see GODIŠNJAK GRADA BEOGRADA

21. GRADJA ZA POVIJEST KNJIŽENOSTI HRVATSKE [Sources on the history of Croatian literature]. Irr. 1897 (mri 1956: vol. 27). Jugoslavenska akademija znanosti i umjetnosti [Yugoslav Acad. of Sciences and Arts], Opatička 18, Zagreb. p (1) Din 400

22. GRADJA ZA PROUČAVANJE SPOMENIKA KULTURE VOJVODINE [Sources for the study of the cultural monuments of Vojvodina]. A. (Irr.). 1957 (1958: vol. 2). Zavod za zaštitu i naučno proučavanje spomenika kulture Autonomne Pokrajine Vojvodine [Inst. for the Preservation of and Scientific Research on the Cultural Monuments in the Autonomous Province of Vojvodina], Petrovaradinska tvrdjava, Novi Sad. English sum. pni

23. HISTORIJSKI ARHIV, RIJEKA. VJESNIK [Historical Archives, Rieka. Bulletin]. A. 1953 (1959: vol. 5). Historijski arhiv, Park VI Nazora broj 2, Rijeka. Ed: Mirko Zjačić. Art. on economic, political, juridical and hist. relations between Rijeka and Venice and neighboring cities, from the 14th to the 19th cent., with emphasis on the Middle Ages; sources; biblio. footnotes; index of doc.; inventory of archives in Rieka; English or French sum.; illus. pni

24. HISTORIJSKI INSTITUT JUGOSLAVENSKE AKADEMIJE, ZBORNIK... (Zbornik historijskog instituta Jugoslavenske akademije) [Review of the Historical Institute of the Yugoslav Academy]. A. 1954 (1959: vol. 2). Jugoslavenska akademija znanosti i umjetnosti [Yugoslav Acad. of Sciences and Arts], Strossmayerov trg 2, Zagreb. Ed. board: Marko Kostrenčić, Grga Novak, Vaso Bogdanov. Art. on the earlier and modern hist. of the Croatian and Yugoslav people archival news; German, French, English or Italian sum. $2.15

25. HISTORIJSKI INSTITUT U DUBROVNIKU, ANALI... (Anali Historijskog instituta u Dubrovniku) [Annals of the Historical Institute in Dubrovnik]. A. 1952 (1957-59: vol. 6/7). Historijski institut Jugoslavenske akademije znanosti i umjetnosti [Hist. Inst. of the Yugoslav Acad. of Sciences and Arts], Dubrovnik. Ed: Cvito Fisković. Art. on the hist. of Dubrovnik and surrounding districts; English, French, German or Italian sum. Din 1,500

26. HISTORIJSKI PREGLED [Historical survey]. Q. 1954 (1959: vol. 5). "Školska knjiga" ["School books"], Ilica 28, Zagreb, for Savez historijskih društava FNRJ [Union of Hist. Soc. of the Federated People's Republic of Yugoslavia]. Ed: Juraj Kolaković, Matoševa 12, Zagreb. Art. on the hist. of the people of Yugoslavia; biblio.; in Serbo-Croatian (Roman or Cyrillic script). $2.70

27. HISTORIJSKI ZBORNIK [Historical review]. A. 1948 (1959: vol. 12). Povijesno društvo Hrvatske [Hist. Soc. of Croatia], Matoševa 12, Zagreb. Ed. board: Oleg Mandić, Jakša Ravlić, Jaroslav Šidak (manag. ed.). Art. on the hist. of the peoples of Yugoslavia from the Middle Ages to the 20th cent., and on sources for the political and economic hist. of Croatia; rev. of Yugoslav, German and Russian bk. and of Yugoslav periodicals; biblio. footnotes; reports on the work of the soc. and of other learned inst.; English, French, German or Italian sum.; index of pub. exchanged with Yugoslav assoc. and foreign countries. $2.15

INSTITUT ETHNOGRAPHIQUE, BULLETIN DE L'... see ETNOGRAFSKI INSTITUT, GLASNIK...

28. INSTITUT JUGOSLAVENSKE AKADEMIJE ZNANOSTI I UMJETNOSTI U ZADRU, RADOVI... (Radovi Instituta Jugoslavenske akademije znanosti i umjetnosti u Zadru) [Works of the Institute of the Yugoslav Academy of Sciences and Arts in Zadar]. Irr. 1954 (1958/59: vol. 4/5). Jugoslavenska akademija znanosti i umjetnosti, Braće Kavurića 1, Zagreb, for Institut Jugoslavenske akademije znanosti i umjetnosti u Zadru, Zadar. Ed: Grga Novak, Vjekoslav Maštrovic. Art. on the hist. of countries in the Adriatic region; English or French sum. pv

29. INSTITUT ZA HISTORIJSKE NAUKE U ZADRU, ZBORNIK... (Zbornik instituta za historijske nauke u Zadru) [Review of the Institute of Historical Sciences in Zadar]. A. 1955 (1956/57: vol. 2). Institut za historijske nauke, Filozofski fakulteti u Zagrebu i Zadru [Inst. of Hist. Sciences, Faculties of Philosophy in Zagreb and Zadar]. Ed: Mirko Deanović, Hercegovačka 36, Zagreb. Art. on the hist. of Yugoslavia and its relations with neighboring countries from ancient times to the present; French, German or Italian sum. Din 800

30. INSTITUT ZA NACIONALNA ISTORIJA, GLASNIK... (Glasnik na Institutot za nacionalnu istoriju) [Bulletin of the Institute of National History]. S-A. 1957 (1958: vol. 2). Institut za nacionalnu istoriju, "11 oktobri" 37, Skopje. Ed: Ljuben Lape. Art. on the hist. of Macedonia; bk. rev.; biblio.; in Macedonian (Cyrillic script); French sum. Din 700

31. ISTORIJA XX VEKA [History of the twentieth century]. Zbornik radova [Collected works]. Irr. 1959 (1959: vol. 1). Odeljenje za istoriske nauke, Istitut društvenih nauka [Dept. of Hist. Sciences, Inst. of Social Sciences], Narodnog fronta 45, Beograd. Ed: Dragoslav Janković. Art. on the hist. of the Yugoslav peoples in the 20th cent.; French, Russian or German sum. pv

32. ISTORISKI ČASOPIS [Historical review]. A. 1948 (1959: vol. 9/10). Istoriski institut, Srpska akademija nauka [Hist. Inst., Serbian Acad. of Sciences], Knez Mihailova 35, Beograd. Ed: Mita Kostić (director of the inst.). Art. on all periods of Serbian hist. and on hist. geography; rev. of bk. and periodicals; biblio.; in Serbo-Croatian (Cyrillic script); English, French or German sum.; index. $5.35

33. ISTORISKI GLASNIK [Historical bulletin]. Q (2 double no. p.a.). 1948 (1959). Društvo istoričara N.R. Srbije [Hist. Soc. of the People's Republic of Serbia], Filozofski fakultet [Philosophical Faculty], Studentski trg br. 1, Beograd. Ed: Dušan Perović. Art. on Balkan hist., with emphasis on Serbia and Montenegro; rev. of bk. and periodicals; biblio.; notes and news on soc. and inst.; in Serbo-Croatian (Cyrillic script); English, French or German sum. Din 800 / $3.20

ISTORISKI PREGLED see HISTORIJSKI PREGLED

34. ISTORISKI ZAPISI [Historical chronicle]. Q. 1948 (1960: vol. 17). Istoriski institut N.R. Crne Gore [Hist. Inst. of the People's Republic of Montenegro], and Istorisko društvo N.R. Crne Gore [Hist. Assoc. of the People's Republic of Montenegro], Post. Fah 101, Titograd. Ed. board: Dimo Vujović, Slavko Mijušković, Niko C. Martinović, Mirceta Durović (manag. ed.). Art. on all periods of the hist. of Montenegro, based on Yugoslav and foreign sources; bk. rev.; report on the activities of the sponsoring assoc.; in Serbo-Croatian (Cyrillic script). Din 900 / $2.40

35. ISTORISKO DRUŠTVO BOSNE I HERCEGOVINE, GODIŠNJAK... (Godišnjak istoriskog društva Bosne i Hercegovine). ANNUAIRE DE LA SOCIETE

HISTORIQUE DE BOSNIE ET HERZEGOVINE [Yearbook of the Historical Society of Bosnia and Herzegovina]. A. 1949 (1959: vol. 10). Istorisko društvo Bosne i Hercegovine, Sarajevo. Ed. board: Branislav Djurdjev, Milorad Ekmečić, Hamdija Kapidžić (manag. ed.), Esad Pašalić. Art. mostly on the cultural and political hist. of Bosnia and Herzegovina, pertaining to all periods, with emphasis on the 19th and 20th cent.; bk. rev.; report on the activities of the soc.; table of contents in Serbo-Croatian and French; German sum. Din 500 / $3.20

36. JADRANSKI INSTITUT, ANALI... (Anali Jadranskog instituta) [Annals of the Adriatic Institute]. Irr. 1956 (1958: vol. 3). Jadranski institut Jugoslovenske akademije znanosti i umjetnosti [Adriatic Inst. of the Yugoslav Acad. of Sciences and Arts], Opatička 18, Zagreb. Ed: Ivo Krbok, Jabukovac 22, Zagreb. Art. on the hist., economy, and other questions of the Yugoslav districts on the Adriatic coast; English sum. Din 650

37. JADRANSKI ZBORNIK [Adriatic review]. Prilozi za povijest Istre, Rijeke i Hrvatskog Primorja [Contributions on the history of Istria, Rieka and the Croatian littoral]. A. 1956 (1959: vol. 2). Povijesno društvo Hrvatske Podružnica u Rijeci i Puli [Hist. Soc. of Croatia. Sections in Rieka and Pola]. Ed: Vjekoslav Bratulić, Frana Supila 11, Rijeka. French, German, Italian or English sum. Din 700

38. JUGOSLAVENSKA AKADEMIJA ZNANOSTI I UMJETNOSTI, ODJEL ZA LIKOVNE UMJETNOSTI, BULLETIN... (Bulletin Odjela za likovne umjetnosti Jugoslovenske akademije znanosti i umjetnosti) [Bulletin of the Section of Plastic Art of the Yugoslav Academy of Sciences and Arts]. S-M (Irr.). Odjel za likovne umjetnosti Jugoslovenske akademije znanosti i umjetnosti, ul. Braće Kavurića 1, Zagreb. pni

39. JUGOSLAVENSKA AKADEMIJA ZNANOSTI I UMJETNOSTI, RAD... (Rad Jugoslavenske akademije znanosti i umjetnosti) [Transactions of the Yugoslav Academy of Sciences and Arts]. Odjel za filozofiju i društvene nauke [Section of philosophy and social sciences]. 1867 (1959: no. 38; new series, no. 8). Jugoslavenska akademija znanosti i umjetnosti [Yugoslav Acad. of Sciences and Arts], Zrinski trg 11, Zagreb. Ed: Grga Novak. Art. on the social sciences, including Yugoslav hist., not confined to any period.

40. JUGOSLOVENSKI RADNIČKI POKRET [Yugoslav labor movement]. Irr. 1952 (1958: no vol. indic.). Izdavačko produzeće "Rad," Beograd. Studies of the Yugoslav labor movement. pni

41. JUŽNOSLOVENSKI FILOLOG [The Yugoslav philologist]. B-M (Irr.). 1913 (1958: vol. 23). Institut za srpski jezik S.A.N. [Inst. for the Serbian Language of the Serbian Acad. of Sciences], Knez Mihailova 35, Beograd. Art. on philology and the hist. of Serbian literature and language; French or Russian sum. $4

42. KAMNIŠKI ZBORNIK [Kamnik review]. A. Ed: Zvone Verstovšek, Kamnik, L.R.Slovenija. Din 320

43. KOVČEŽIĆ [Treasure chest]. Prilozi i gradja o Dositeju i Vuku [Contributions and sources concerning Dositej and Vuk]. Irr. 1958 (1959: vol. 2). Vukov i Dositejev muzej [Museum of Vuk and Dositej], Gospodar Jevremova 21, Beograd. Ed: Đ. Gavela. Art. and sources on the writers Vuk (Karadžić) and Dositej (Obradović) and on literary hist., mostly of the 18th and 19th cent.; in Serbo-Croatian (Cyrillic script). pni

44. KRONIKA [Chronicle]. Časopis za slovensko krajevno zgodovino [Bulletin of Slovenian regional history]. 3xy. Zgodovinsko društvo za Slovenijo [Hist. Soc. of Slovenia], Mestni trg 27/II, Ljubljana. Art. on Slovenian hist.; bk. rev.; biblio.; in Slovenian; illus. Din 400

LETOPIS MUZEJA NARODNE OSVOBODITVE LRS V LJUBLJANI see MUSEJ NARODNE OSVOBODITVE LRS V LJUBLJANI, LETOPIS...

45. LIHNID. Godišen zbornik na Narodniot muzej vo Ohrid [Yearbook of the National Museum in Ohrid]. A. Narodni muzej, Ohrid. In Macedonian (Cyrillic script); English and French sum.; illus. pni

46. LOŠKI RAZGLEDI [Škofja Loka review]. Irr. Muzejsko društvo [Museum Soc.], Škofja Loka. In Slovenian. pni

47. MATICA SRPSKA, ZBORNIK... ZA KNJIŽEVNOST I JEZIK (Zbornik Matice srpske za književnost i jezik) [Journal of "Matica srpska" for literature and language]. A. Matica srpska, ulica Matice srpske 1, Novi Sad. Hist. of Serbian literature and philology; in Serbo-Croatian (Cyrillic script). pni

48. MONUMENTA TURCICA HISTORIAM SLAVORUM MERIDIONALIUM. Irr. Orijentalni institut [Oriental Inst.], Sarajevo. Illus.

MUSEE DES ARTS DECORATIFS. RECUEIL DE TRAVAUX see MUZEJ PRIMENJENE UMETNOSTI. ZBORNIK

MUSEE ETHNOGRAPHIQUE DE BEOGRAD, BULLETIN DU... see ETNOGRAFSKI MUZEJ, GLASNIK...

49. MUSEJ NARODNE OSVOBODITVE LRS V LJUBLJANI, LETOPIS... (Letopis muzeja narodne osvoboditve LRS v Ljubljani) [Annals of the Museum of National Liberation of the People's Republic of Slovenia in Ljubljana]. A. 1957 (1958: vol. 2). Muzej narodne osvoboditve LRS, Celovska 23, Ljubljana. Art. on the war of national liberation in Slovenia (during World War II); in Slovenian; English and Russian sum. pni

MUZEJ GRADA BEOGRADA, GODIŠNJAK... see GODIŠNJAK GRADA BEOGRADA

50. MUZEJ KOSOVA I METOHIJE, GLASNIK... (Glasnik Muzeja Kosova i Metohije) [Bulletin of the Museum of Kosovo and Metohija]. A.(Irr.). Muzej Autonomne Kosovsko-Metohiske Oblasti [Museum of the Autonomous District of Kosovo-Metohija], Priština. Albanian and, occasionally, English or French sum. $2.70

51. MUZEJ PRIMENJENE UMETNOSTI. ZBORNIK. MUSEE DES ARTS DECORATIFS. RECUEIL DE TRAVAUX [Museum for Decorative Arts. Collections of works]. A. Muzej primenjene umetnosti, Vuka Karadžića 18, Beograd. Includes hist. art.; English or French sum. Din 650

52. MUZEJI [Museums]. A.(Irr.). Savez muzejsko-konzervatoriskih radnika FNRJ [Union of Museum Curators of the People's Republic of Yugoslavia], trg Maršala Tita 10, Zagreb. English, French or German sum. Din 1,300

53. NARODNI MUZEJ, ZBORNIK RADOVA... (Zbornik radova Narodnog muzeja) [Collection of studies of the National Museum]. A. 1956 (1959: vol. 2).

Narodni muzej, trg Republike 3, Beograd. Ed. board: Draga Garašanin, Djordje Mano-Zisi, Momčilo Stefanović, Mirjana Ćorović-Ljubinković. Art. on archaeological excavations, art collections, numismatics, medieval icons, and cultural anthropology from Greco-Illyric, Roman, and early Slavic times to the 18th cent.; reports on the activities of the museum; statutes of the museum; in Serbo-Croatian (Cyrillic script); French or German sum.; tables, maps, illus. Din 2,000

54. NAŠE STARINE [Our antiquities]. A.(Irr.). 1953 (1958: vol. 5). Zavod za zaštitu spomenika kulture i prirodnih rijetkosti N.R. Bosne i Hercegovine [Inst. for the Preservation of Cultural Monuments and Natural Rarities of the People's Republic of Bosnia and Herzegovina], Vojvode Putnika 7, Sarajevo. French or German sum. Din 450

55. NAUČNO DRUŠTVO NR BOSNE I HERCEGOVINE. RADOVI [Scientific Society of the People's Republic of Bosnia and Herzegovina. Works]. Odjeljene istorisko-filoloških nauka [Section of historical and philological sciences]. Irr. 1954 (1958: vol. 4). Naučno društvo NR Bosne i Hercegovine, Obala Vojvode Stepe 41, Sarajevo. Ed: Anto Babić. Art. on hist. and philology, pertaining mostly to Bosnia and Herzegovina; English, French, German or Russian sum. pv

56. NUMIZMATIČKE VIJESTI [Numismatic news]. Irr. Numizmatičko društvo [Numismatic Soc.], Gundulićeva ulica 14, Zagreb. $0.80

57. NUMIZMATIČNI VESTNIK [Numismatic review]. Irr. Numizmatično društvo Slovenije [Numismatic Soc. of Slovenia], Pražakova 8, Ljubljana. In Slovenian; German sum. Din 50 / $0.90

58. OGLEDI [Essays]. Zbornik radova [Collection of studies]. Irr. "Rad," Moše Pijade 14, Beograd. Literature, art and criticism; English, French, German or Russian sum. pni

59. OPUSCULA ARCHEOLOGICA. Irr. Arheološki institut Sveučilišta [Archaeological Inst. of the Univ.], Zrinjevac 19, Zagreb. Archaeological research and finds in Croatia; German sum. pni

60. OSJEČKI ZBORNIK [Osijek review]. A.(Irr.). (1958: vol. 6). Muzej Slavonije [Museum of Slavonia], Partizanski trg 6, Osijek. Ed. board: Emil Spajić, Marija Malbaša, Danica Pinterović (manag. ed.). Art. on archaeology numismatics, ethnography, folklore and art; reports and news; English, French or German sum.; maps; graph; illus. pni

61. POMORSKI MUZEJ U KOTORU, GODIŠNJAK... (Godišnjak Pomorskog muzeja u Kotoru) [Yearbook of the Marine Museum in Kotor]. A. Pomorski muzej, Kotor. Maritime hist. of Boka Kotorska and the surrounding area and its foreign relations; English sum. Din 700

62. POSAVJE. Irr. Svet za prosveto in kulturo občine Celje [Council of Education and Culture of the Community of Celje], Celje. pni

63. PRAVNI FAKULTET U SARAJEVU, GODIŠNJAK... (Godišnjak Pravnog fakulteta u Sarajevu) [Yearbook of the Faculty of Law in Sarajevo]. A. Pravni fakultet univerziteta, Obala Vojvode Stepe 7, Sarajevo. French sum. Din 450

64. PRAVNI FAKULTET VO SKOPJE, GODIŠNIK... (Godišnik na pravniot fakultet vo Skopje) [Yearbook of the Faculty of Law in Skoplje]. A. Pravni fakultet, Skopje. Economic hist. of Macedonia; in Macedonian (Cyrillic script); English or French sum. pni

65. PREGLED [Review]. Časopis za društvena pitanja [Bulletin for social problems]. M. Novinsko preduzeće "Oslobodjenje," Maršala Tita br. 9a, Sarajevo. Current social, political and economic questions and international affairs; some hist. art.; rev. and biblio. of **Yugoslav bk.**; **illus.**
Din 1,000/ $5.35

66. PRILOZI ZA KNJIŽEVNOST, JEZIK, ISTORIJU I FOLKLOR [Contributions on literature, language, history and folklore]. Q (2 double no. p.a.). 1921 (1959: vol. 25). "Rad," Moše Pijade 14/IV, Beograd, for Katedra za istoriju jugoslovenskih književnosti filozofskog fakulteta u Beogradu [Chair for the Hist. of Yugoslav Literature of the Philosophical Faculty in Belgrade], with the collaboration of Katedra za žive jesike i književnosti filozofskog fakulteta u Beogradu [Chair for Modern Languages and Literature of the Philosophical Faculty in Belgrade], Beograd. Ed. board: Nikola Banašević, Dragoljub Pavlović, Vido Latković (manag. ed.), Ljubostinjska 3, Beograd. Art. on literature and social and cultural hist., mostly of Yugoslavia, pertaining to the medieval and modern periods, with emphasis on the 19th cent.; bk. rev.; biblio.; in Serbo-Croatian (Cyrillic script). p (1) Din 400

67. PRILOZI ZA ORIJENTALNU FILOLOGIJU I ISTORIJU JUGOSLOVENSKIH NARODA POD TURSKOM VLADAVINOM. REVUE DE PHILOLOGIE ORIENTALE ET D'HISTOIRE DES PEUPLES YUGOSLAVES SOUS LA DOMINATION TURQUE [Contributions on oriental philology and the history of the people of Yugoslavia under Turkish rule]. A.(Irr.). 1950 (1956/57: vol. 6/7). Orijentalni institut, Vojvode Putnika 7, Sarajevo. Ed. board: Branislav Djurdjev, Nedim Filipović (ed.), Hamid Hadzibegić, Saćir Sikirić. Art. on hist., archaeology, politics and philology since the 14th cent.; rev. of bk. and periodicals; English, French or German sum.; illus. Din 1,500

68. PTT ARHIV [PTT archives]. Irr. PTT muzej [PTT Museum], Palmotićeva 2, Beograd. French sum. pni

RAD, RADOVI. For titles beginning with "Rad" or "Radovi," followed by the name of the publishing or sponsoring institution or society, see the respective institution or society.

69. RAD VOJVOĐANSKIH MUZEJA. TRAVAUX DES MUSEES DE VOIVODINA [Works of the museums of Voivodina]. A. 1952 (1958: vol. 7). Pub. address: Narodnih heroja 11/I, Novi Sad. Ed: Rajko Nikolić. Art. on archaeology, ethnology, hist., auxiliary hist. disciplines, and natural sciences; in Serbo-Croatian; English, French or German sum. pni

RAZPRAVE SLOVENSKE AKADEMIJA ZNANOSTI IN UMETNOSTI see SLOVENSKA AKADEMIJA ZNANOSTI IN UMETNOSTI, RAZPRAVE...

RECUEIL DES TRAVAUX SUR LA PROTECTION DES MONUMENTS HISTORIQUES see ZBORNIK ZAŠTITE SPOMENIKA KULTURE

REVUE DE PHILOLOGIE ORIENTALE ET D'HISTOIRE DES PEUPLES YUGOSLAVES SOUS LA DOMINATION TURQUE see PRILOZI ZA ORIJENTALNU FILOLOGIJU I ISTORIJU JUGOSLOVENSKIH NARODA POD TURSKOM VLADAVINOM

70. SLAVISTIČNA REVIJA [Slavonic review]. A.(Irr.). Slavistično društvo v Ljubljani, Institut za slovenski jezik pri Slovenski akademiji [Slavonic Soc. in Ljubljana, Inst. of Slovenian language at the Slovenian Acad.], Murnikova 24, Ljubljana. In Slovenian; Russian sum. $4.30

71. SLOVENSKA AKADEMIJA ZNANOSTI IN UMETNOSTI, RAZPRAVE... (Razprave Slovenske akademija znanosti in umetnosti) [Transactions of the Slovenian Academy of Sciences and Arts]. Razred za zgodovinske in družbene vede [Section on historical and social sciences]. Irr. 1950 (1958: vol. 4). Slovenska akademija znanosti in umetnosti, Novi trg 3, Ljubljana. Ed: France Stelè. Art. on Slovene hist., archaeology and other social sciences, covering all periods; in Slovenian; English, French or German sum. pni

72. SLOVO [Word]. Irr. Staroslavenski institut [Old Slovenian Inst.], Demetrova 11, Zagreb. Old Slovenian language and literature; in Serbo-Croatian and foreign languages; English, French or German sum. of art. in Serbo-Croatian. $0.55

SOCIETE HISTORIQUE DE BOSNIE ET HERZEGOVINE, ANNUAIRE DE LA... see ISTORISKO DRUŠTVO BOSNE I HERCEGOVINE, GODIŠNJAK...

73. SPOMENIK [Memorial]. Irr. 1890; new series, 1950 (1960: vol. 109). Odeljenje društvenih nauka, Srpska akademija nauka [Section for Social Sciences, Serbian Acad. of Sciences], Knez Mihailova 35, Beograd. Ed: Georg Ostrogorsky (secretary of the section). Art. and source material on Serbian hist.; in Serbo-Croatian (Cyrillic script); English, French, German, Italian or Russian sum. pv

74. SRPSKA AKADEMIJA NAUKA, ETNOGRAFSKI INSTITUT. ZBORNIK RADOVA [Serbian Academy of Sciences, Ethnographical Institute. Collection of studies]. Irr. Etnografski institut Srpske akademije nauka, Knez Mihailova 35, Beograd. In Serbo-Croatian (Cyrillic script); English, French or German sum. pni

75. SRPSKA AKADEMIJA NAUKA, GLAS... (Glas Srpske akademije nauka) [Transactions of the Serbian Academy of Sciences]. Odeljenje društvenih nauka [Section for social sciences]. Irr. 1887 (1960: vol. 239; new series, no. 8). Odeljenje društvenih nauka, Srpske akademije nauka, Knez Mihailova 35, Beograd. Ed: Dušan Nedeljković. Art. on hist. and other social sciences, covering all periods; in Serbo-Croatian (Cyrillic script); English, French, German or Russian sum. The numbering of the new series is consecutive for the section on social sciences, but the vol. no. are used for all series. pv

76. SRPSKA AKADEMIJA NAUKA, GLAS... (Glas Srpske akademije nauka) [Transactions of the Serbian Academy of Sciences]. Odeljenje literature i jezika [Section of literature and language]. Irr. 1887; new series: 1951 (1960: vol. 270 or no. 5). Odeljenje literature i jezika, Srpska akademija nauka, Knez Mihailova 35, Beograd. Ed: Petar Kolendić (secretary of the section). Art. on classical, medieval, and early modern literature, and on the hist. of literature; in Serbo-Croatian (Cyrillic script); Latin, French, German or Russian sum.; illus. pv

77. SRPSKA AKADEMIJA NAUKA, GLASNIK... (Glasnik Srpske adademije nauka) [Bulletin of the Serbian Academy of Sciences]. Q. 1949 (1958: vol. 11). Srpska akademija nauka, Knez Mihailova 35, Beograd. Ed: V.V.Mišković.

Reports on the meetings and work of the acad.; sum. of research in natural and social sciences and hist.; biblio. of pub. of the acad.; in Serbo-Croatian (Cyrillic script). pv

78. SRPSKA AKADEMIJA NAUKA, VIZANTOLOŠKI INSTITUT. ZBORNIK RADOVA [Serbian Academy of Sciences. Byzantine Institute. Collection of studies]. Irr. 1952 (1960: vol. 6). Vizantološki institut Srpske akademije nauka, Knez Mihailova 35, Beograd. Ed: Georg Ostrogorsky (director of the inst.). Studies on Byzantine and medieval Serbian hist.; in Serbo-Croatian (Cyrillic script); English, French, German, Italian or Russian sum. pni

79. STARINAR [Antiquarian]. A. 1884; new series: 1950 (1958/59: vol. 9/10). Arheološki institut Srpske akademije nauka [Archaeological Inst. of the Serbian Acad. of Sciences], Knez Mihailova 35, Beograd. Ed. board: Aleksandar Deroko, Milutin Garašanin, Miodrag Grbić, Vojislav Korać, Đurađe Bošković (manag. ed.). Art. on archaeology, cultural anthropology, and paleoanthropology; reports on new research and findings; rev. of foreign bk.; biblio. of bk. on archaeology, art and cultural hist. pub. in Yugoslavia; in Serbian (Cyrillic script);English, French, German, Italian or Russian sum.; illus. $15.47

80. STARINE [Antiquities]. A. 1869 (1959: vol. 49). Odjel za filozofiju i društvene nauke, Jugoslovenska akademija znanosti i umjetnosti [Section of Philosophy and Social Sciences, Yugoslav Acad. of Sciences and Arts], Braće Kavurića 1, Zagreb. Ed: Grgo Novak, Kršnjavoga 25, Zagreb. Art. on Croatian and South Slavonic hist. pni

81. STAROHRVATSKA PROSVJETA [Ancient Croatian culture]. Irr. 1895 (1958: series 3, vol. 6). Muzej Hrvatskih starina Jugoslavenske akademije znanosti i umjetnosti [Museum of Croatian Antiquity of the Yugoslav Acad. of Sciences and Arts], Zagreb. Ed. board: Stipe Gunjača (manag. ed.), Marko Kostrenčić, Grga Novak. Art. on Croatian archaeology, monuments, new excavations, and cultural anthropology, pertaining mostly to the Roman period and occasionally to the Slavic era; report on the activities of the museum; French, English, German or Italian sum.; maps, illus. Din 1,100

82. STAROSLAVENSKI INSTITUT, RADOVI... (Radovi Staroslovenskog instituta) [Works of the Old Slavic Institute]. Irr. 1952 (1958: vol. 3). Staroslovenski institut, Demetrova 11, Zagreb. French or German sum. pni

83. SVEUČILIŠTA U ZAGREBU, FILOZOFSKI FAKULTET. ZBORNIK RADOVA [University of Zagreb, Philosophical Faculty. Collection of studies]. Irr. Filozofski fakultet Sveučilišta u Zagrebu [Faculty of Philosophy of the Univ. of Zagreb], trg Maršala Tita 14, Zagreb. French, German, English or Italian sum. pni

VESNIK VOJNOG MUZEJA JUGOSLOVENSKA NARODNE ARMIJE see VOJNI MUZEJ JUGOSLOVENSKE NARODNE ARMIJE, VESNIK...

VIJESTI DRUŠTVA MUZEJSKO-KONZERVATORSKIH RADNIKA N.R. HRVATSKE see DRUŠTVO MUZEJSKO-KONZERVATORSKIH RADNIKA N.R. HRVATSKE, VIJESTI...

84. VJESNIK BIBLIOTEKARA HRVATSKE [Bulletin of the Croatian librarians]. Q (Irr.). Društvo bibliotekara Hrvatske [Soc. of Croatian Librarians], Marulićev trg 21, Zagreb. French, English or German sum. $2.15

85. VJESNIK ZA ARHEOLOGIJU I HISTORIJU DALMATINSKU. BULLETIN D'ARCHEOLOGIE ET D'HISTOIRE DALMATE [Bulletin of Dalmatian archaeology and history]. A. (Irr.). 1878 (1954-57: vol. 56-59). Arheološki muzej, Split. Ed. board: Duje Rendić-Miočević, Mate Suić, Mladen Nikolanci. Art. on Dalmatian archaeology, pertaining to all periods: Roman, pre-Slavic and Slavic; German, English or French sum.; illus. $4.80

86. VOJNI ISTORISKI GLASNIK [Journal of military history]. B-M. 1950 (1960: vol. 11). Istoriski institut JNA [Hist. Inst. of the Yugoslav People's Army], Kneza Miloša 41, Beograd. Ed: Danilo Jauković. Art. on the military and political hist. of Yugoslavia, pertaining to all periods, with emphasis on the war of national liberation (1941-45); bk. rev.; in Serbo-Croatian (Cyrillic and Roman scripts); French and Russian sum. Din 420

87. VOJNI MUZEJ JUGOSLOVENSKE NARODNE ARMIJE, VESNIK... (Vesnik Vojnog muzeja Jugoslovenske narodne armije) [Bulletin of the Military Museum of the Yugoslav People's Army]. A. Vojni muzej JNA., Kalemegdan, Beograd. French and, occasionally, German sum. Din 600

88. ZADARSKA REVIJA [Review of Zadar]. Q. Pododbor Matice Hrvatske [Subcommittee of the Croatian Matrix (Soc.)], Zagrebačka 1, Zadar. Din 600

89. ZADRUŽNI ARHIV [Archives of cooperatives]. Irr. Zadružni arhiv Vojvodine, Jovana Djordjevića 9, Novi Sad. pv

ZBORNIK. ZBORNIK RADOVA. For titles beginning with "Zbornik" or "Zbornik radova," followed by the name of the publishing or sponsoring institution or society, see the respective institution or society.

90. ZBORNIK ZA DRUŠTVENE NAUKE [Review of social sciences]. 3 x y. 1950 (1959: vol. 24). Matica srpska, ulica Matice srpske 1, Novi Sad. Ed: Rajko Nikolić. Art. on all aspects of the hist. and folklore of Serbia, with some stress on local hist. and biography, predominantly of the Voivodina and its various ethnic groups, pertaining to all periods but mostly the 19th and 20th cent.; shorter contributions also on folklore, cultural anthropology, archaeology and church hist.; bk. rev.; in Serbo-Croatian (Cyrillic script); French or German sum. pni

91. ZBORNIK ZA NARODNI ŽIVOT I OBIČAJE JUŽNIH SLOVENA [Collection on South Slavic folklore]. Irr. Jugoslavenska akademija znanosti i umjetnosti [Yugoslav Acad. of Sciences and Arts], Braće Kavurića 1, Zagreb. French, German or English sum. pni

92. ZBORNIK ZA UMETNOSNO ZGODOVINO [Collection on the history of art]. Irr. Državna založba Slovenije [State Pub. of Slovenia], Stritarjeva 3/II, Ljubljana, for Umetnosno zgodovinsko društvo [Soc. for the Hist. of Art], Ljubljana. In Slovenian; German or French sum. pni

93. ZBORNIK ZAŠTITE SPOMENIKA KULTURE [Journal on the preservation of cultural monuments]. RECUEIL DES TRAVAUX SUR LA PROTECTION DES MONUMENTS HISTORIQUES [Collection of works on the protection of historical monuments]. A. Savezni institut za zaštitu spomenika kulture [Federal Inst. for the Preservation of Cultural Monuments], Gospodara Vučića 50, Beograd. Methods of preservation of hist. monuments; in Serbo-Croatian (Cyrillic and Roman scripts); French sum. Din 600

94. ZBORNIK ZNANSTVENIH RADOVA [Collection of scientific works]. A. Pravni odelek, Pravno-ekonomska fakulteta v Ljubljani [Law Section, Faculty of Law and Economics in Ljubljana], trg Revolucije 11, Ljubljana. In Slovenian; French or German sum. pni

95. ZEMALJSKI MUZEJ U SARAJEVU, GLASNIK... (Glasnik Zemaljskog muzeja u Sarajevu) [Bulletin of the Regional Museum in Sarajevo]. Istorija, etnografija - arheologija [History, ethnography - archaeology]. A. 1889 (1959: new series, vol. 14). Zemaljski muzej u Sarajevu, V. Putnika 7, Sarajevo. Ed: Alojz Benac. Art. on hist., ethnography and archaeology, pertaining to all periods; bk. rev.; biblio.; English, French or German sum. $4.30

96. ZGODOVINSKI ČASOPIS [Historical review]. A. 1947 (1956/57: vol. 10/11). Zgodovinsko društvo za Slovenijo [Hist. Soc. for Slovenia], Stari trg 26, Ljubljana. Ed: Bogo Grafenauer. Art. on all periods of Slovenian hist.; reports on meetings and on the work of the soc. and other hist. inst.; rev. of bk. and periodicals; biblio.; in Slovenian; English, French, Russian or German sum. $2.70

97. ŽIVA ANTIKA [Living antiquity]. S-A (Irr.). 1950 (1959: vol. 9). Seminar za klasičnu filologiju [Seminar of Classical Philology], "13 novembri" 10, Skopje. Ed: Mihailo D. Petruševski. Art. on classical philology and ancient hist.; in English, French, German or Serbo-Croatian; English, French or German sum. of Serbo-Croatian art. $8

LATIN AMERICA AND THE WEST INDIES

Argentina

Prepared with the assistance of

Oswald F.A. Menghin, Centro Argentino de Estudios Prehistóricos, Buenos Aires, and

Guillermo Céspedes del Castillo, University of Seville

1. ACADEMIA AMERICANA DE LA HISTORIA, REVISTA DE LA... [Review of the American Academy of History]. Irr. Academia Americana de la Historia, Reconquista 567, Buenos Aires. pni

2. ACADEMIA ARGENTINA DE LETRAS, BOLETIN DE LA... [Bulletin of the Argentine Academy of Letters]. 3 x y. Academia Argentina de Letras, Sánchez de Bustamente 2663, Buenos Aires. pv

3. ACADEMIA NACIONAL DE LA HISTORIA, BOLETIN DE LA... [Bulletin of the National Academy of History]. A. 1924 (1957: vol. 28). Academia Nacional de la Historia, San Martín 336, Buenos Aires. Art. on all periods of the hist. of South America. pv

4. ACTA PRAEHISTORICA. A. 1957 (1957: vol. 1). Centro Argentino de Estudios Prehistóricos, Moreno 350, Buenos Aires. Ed: Oswald F.A. Menghin. Art. on the pre-hist. of Argentina. pv (c. $ 5)

ANALES. For titles beginning with "Anales," followed by the name of the publishing or sponsoring institution or society, see the respective institution or society.

5. ANALES DE ARQUEOLOGIA Y ETNOLOGIA [Annals of archaeology and ethnology]. A. 1940 (1957 [1959]: vol. 13). Instituto de Arqueología y Etnología, Universidad Nacional de Cuyo, Rivadavia 544, Mendoza. Ed: Juan Schobinger. Art. on the anthropology, archaeology, ethnology, prehist. and folklore of Argentina; bk. rev.; illus. pni (available on exchange basis)

6. ANALES DE HISTORIA ANTIGUA Y MEDIEVAL [Annals of ancient and medieval history]. A. 1948 (mri 1956: vol. 7). Instituto de Historia Antigua y Medieval, Reconquista 694, Buenos Aires. Ed: Alberto Freixas. Art. on ancient and medieval hist., with some emphasis on the origins of Western civilization; doc.; biblio. pni

7. ARCHIVUM. Irr. 1943 (1959: vol. 3). Ediciones Theoría, Casilla de correo 5096, Buenos Aires, for Junta de Historia Eclesiástica Argentina. Ed: P. Guillermo Furlong, S.J. Art., notes and doc. on the ecclesiastical hist. of Argentina; biblio. of bk. and art.; index. pni

8. ARGENTINA AUSTRAL [Southern Argentina]. M. Sociedad Anónima Importadora y Exportadora de la Patagonia, Av. Pres. Roque Sáenz Peña 547, Buenos Aires. Includes art. on the hist. and ethnology of Patagonia; illus. pni

9. ARS. Revista de Arte [Review of art]. J. Schlagmann, Rodriguez Peña 335, Buenos Aires. Hist. of art; illus.

10. BIBLIOTECA NACIONAL, REVISTA DE LA... [Review of the National Library]. Q. Biblioteca Nacional, Ministerio de Educación, Dirección General de Cultura, México 566, Buenos Aires. pni

BOLETIN. For titles beginning with "Boletín," followed by the name of the publishing or sponsoring institution or society, see the respective institution or society.

11. BOLETIN [Bulletin]. Q. Ministerio de Relaciones Exteriores y Culto, División Publicaciones, Avenales 761, Buenos Aires. free

12. BOLETIN DE ESTUDIOS GERMANICOS [Bulletin of Germanic studies]. Irr. Instituto de Lenguas y Literaturas Modernas, Sección Lengua y Literatura Alemana, Universidad Nacional de Cuyo, Mendoza. pni

13. COMENTARIO [Comment]. Q. Instituto Judio Argentino de Cultura e Información, Tucumán 2137, Buenos Aires. M$N 55/M$N 75

14. CUADERNOS DE HISTORIA DE ESPAÑA [Papers on the history of Spain]. S-A. 1944 (1958: no. 28). Instituto de Historia de España, Viamonte 414, Buenos Aires. Ed: Claudio Sánchez Albornoz. Well-documented art. on all periods of the hist. of Spain; doc.; bk. rev. pni

15. CURSOS Y CONFERENCIAS [Courses and conferences]. Q. Colegio Libre de Estudios Superiores, Callao 468, 1° piso, Oficina 7A, Buenos Aires. M$N 60/$ 5

16. ESCUELA DE ESTUDIOS POLITICOS Y SOCIALES, BOLETIN DE LA... [Bulletin of the School of Political and Social Studies]. A. 1950 (1957: vol. 8). Escuela de Estudios Políticos y Sociales, Universidad Nacional de Cuyo, Mendoza Ed: Facundo Suárez Civil. Art. on social and cultural hist., with emphasis on the 19th and 20th cent.; biblio. of bk. and periodicals, classified by subject. pn

17. ESTUDIOS [Studies]. Revista Argentina de Cultura, Información y Documentación [Argentine review of culture, information and documentation]. 10 x y. 1911 (1960). Universidad del Salvador, Callao 542, Buenos Aires. Ed: Héctor N. Grandinetti, Ismael Quiles. Art. on politics, culture, religion, sociology and hist., with emphasis on Argentina; biblio.; sum. M$N 200/$ 3

18. FACULTAD DE FILOSOFIA Y HUMANIDADES, REVISTA DE LA... [Review of the Faculty of Philosophy and Humanities]. 3 x y (A.). 1949 (mri 1954: vol. 6). Facultad de Filosofía y Humanidades, Universidad Nacional de Córdoba, Córdoba. Ed: Carlos Luque Colombres. Art. on regional hist., anthropology and prehist. pni

19. GENEALOGIA [Genealogy]. Irr. 1940 (1957: vol. 12). Instituto Argentina de Ciencias Genealógicas, Moreno 790, 5° piso, Buenos Aires. Ed: Raul A. Molina. Art. on genealogy. pni

20. HISPANIA. M. Asociación Patriótica Española, Hipólito Irigoyen 672, Buenos Aires. pni

21. HISTONIUM. Carlos della Peña, Paraná 464, Buenos Aires. Hist of art; illus.

22. HISTORIA [History]. Revista trimestral de historia argentina, americana y española [Quarterly review of Argentine, American and Spanish history]. Q. 1955 (1959: vol. 5). Pub. address: Lavalle 1226, 2° piso, Buenos Aires. Ed: Raul A. Molina. Art. on Argentine, American and Spanish hist., with emphasis on the colonial period; archival notes; bk. rev.; biblio. of bk. and periodicals; illus. M$N 240/$ 8

23. HUMANITAS. 3 x y. Facultad de Filosofía y Letras, Universidad Nacional de Tucumán, San Miguel de Tucumán. pni

24. IMAGO MUNDI. Revista de historia de la cultura [Review of cultural history]. Q. 1954 (mri 1956: no. 11/12). Av. Pres. Roque Sáenz Peña 832, Buenos Aires. Art. on the cultural hist. of the Western world and on current issues seen in hist. perspective; rev. art.; bk. rev. Ceased pub. M$N 50/$ 4

25. INSTITUTO AMERICANO DE ESTUDIOS VASCOS, BOLETIN DEL... [Bulletin of the American Institute of Basque Studies]. Q. Editorial Vasca Ekin, S.R.L., Perú 175, Oficina 11, Buenos Aires, for Instituto Americano de Estudios Vascos. M$N 60/M$N 65

26. INSTITUTO DE ANTROPOLOGIA, REVISTA DEL... [Review of the Institute of Anthropology]. Irr. 1934 (1957: vol. 7). Instituto de Etnología, Universidad Nacional de Tucumán, Calle Buenos Aires 260, San Miguel de Tucumán. Ed: Branimiro Males. Art. on anthropology, ethnology and prehist.; illus. pni

27. INSTITUTO DE ARTE AMERICAN E INVESTIGACIONES ESTETICAS, ANALES DEL... [Annals of the Institute of American Arts and Aesthetic Researches]. A. Facultad de Arquitectura, Instituto de Arte American e Investigaciones Estéticas, Casilla 3790, Buenos Aires. pni

28. INSTITUTO DE HISTORIA ARGENTINA "DOCTOR EMILIO RAVIGNANI," BOLETIN DEL...[Bulletin of the "Doctor Emilio Ravignani" Institute for Argentine History]. Q. 1956 (1957: vol. 2). Instituto de Historia Argentina "Doctor Emilio Ravignani," Facultad de Filosofía y Letras, Universidad de Buenos Aires, Buenos Aires. Art. on the hist. of America, particularly South America, and linguistics; doc.; notes of professional interest; biographical notes. Formerly pub. under the title: Boletín del Instituto de Investigaciones Históricas. pni

29. INSTITUTO DE HISTORIA Y DISCIPLINAS AUXILIARES, ANALES DEL... [Annals of the Institute of History and Auxiliary Disciplines]. Irr. 1943 (mri 1950: vol. 5). Instituto de Historia y Disciplinas Auxiliares, Universidad Nacional de Cuyo, Mendoza. Collection of doc. on South American hist.; index for each vol. pni

INSTITUTO DE INVESTIGACIONES HISTORICAS, BOLETIN DEL... See INSTITUTO DE HISTORIA ARGENTINA "DOCTOR EMILIO RAVIGNANI," BOLETIN DEL...

30. INSTITUTO DE SAN FELIPE Y SANTIAGO DE ESTUDIOS HISTORICOS DE SALTA, BOLETIN DEL... [Bulletin of the San Felipe y Santiago Institute of Historical Studies of Salta]. A. Instituto de San Felipe y Santiago de Estudios Históricos de Salta, Salta. pni

31. MUSEO DE HISTORIA NATURAL DE MENDOZA, REVISTA DEL... [Review of the Natural History Museum of Mendoza]. A. Museo de Historia Natural de Mendoza, Plaza Independencia, Mendoza. Art. on prehist. and archaeology; illus. pni

32. MUSEO DE LA PLATA, ANALES DEL... [Annals of the Museum of La Plata]. Sección antropología [Anthropological section]. Irr. 1950 (mri 1953: no. 3). Museo de Ciencias Naturales de La Plata, La Plata. Art. on anthropology, ethnology and prehist.; illus. pni

33. MUSEO DE LA PLATA, REVISTA DEL... [Review of the Museum of La Plata]. Sección antropología [Anthropological section]. Irr. 1890 (1958: new series, vol. 5). Museo de Ciencias Naturales de La Plata, La Plata. Art. on anthropology, ethnology, prehist., folklore, and archaeology, with emphasis on South America; biblio.; illus. pni

34. MUSEO MITRE, REVISTA DEL... [Review of the Mitre Museum]. Irr. 1948 (mri 1956: vol. 8). Dirección de Cultura, Comisión Nacional de Museos y Monumentos Históricos, San Martín 336, Buenos Aires, for Museo Mitre. Art. on the hist. of Argentina; illus. pni

35. MUSEO MUNICIPAL DE CIENCIAS NATURALES Y TRADICIONAL DE MAR DEL PLATA, REVISTA DEL... [Review of the Municipal Museum for the Natural History and Traditions of Mar del Plata]. Irr. Museo Municipal de Ciencias Naturales y Tradicional de Mar del Plata, Palacio Municipal, Mar del Plata. pni (available on exchange basis)

36. NORTE [North]. Revista Argentina de cultura [Argentine review of culture]. Irr. Comisión Provincial de Cultura, Gobierno de Tucumán, San Miguel de Tucumán. p (1) M$N 8

37. NUEVO MUNDO [New world]. M. Pub. address: Casilla No. 1, Suc. 31, Buenos Aires. p (1) M$N 1.50

PUBLICACIONES DE LA SOCIEDAD GOETHEANA ARGENTINA see SOCIEDAD GOETHEANA ARGENTINA, PUBLICACIONES DE LA...

REVISTA. For titles beginning with "Revista," followed by the name of the publishing or sponsoring institution or society, see the respective institution or society.

38. REVISTA CATAMARQUEÑA DE CULTURA [Catamarcan review of culture]. 3 x y. San Martín 669, Catamarca. pni

39. REVISTA DE EDUCACION [Review of education]. M. Ministerio de Educación, La Plata. Art. and abstr. on hist. and other disciplines; bk. rev. illus. pni (available on exchange basis)

40. REVISTA DE HISTORIA [Review of history]. Q. 1956 (1958: no. 3). Av. Corrientes 1389, Buenos Aires. Ed: Enrique M. Barba. Art. on general hist., with emphasis on Argentina (post-colonial period); doc.; biblio.; illus. M$N 40/$ 5

41. REVISTA DE HISTORIA AMERICANA Y ARGENTINA [Review of American and Argentine history]. A. 1956/57 (1956/57: vol. 1). Instituto de Historia, Sección de Historia Americana y Argentina, Universidad Nacional de Cuyo, 9 de

julio 786, Mendoza. Ed. board: Edverto Oscar Acevedo, Martha S. Páramo de Isleño, Lube Roitman, Esteban J. Fontana. Art. on American and Argentine hist.; doc.; biblio.; bk. rev. pni

42. REVISTA DE LA UNIVERSIDAD [Review of the university]. Q. Universidad Nacional de La Plata, Plaza Rocha 137, La Plata. pni (available on exchange basis)

43. RUNA [Rune]. Archivo para las ciencias del hombre [Archives for the human sciences]. Irr. 1948 (1956/57: vol. 8). Instituto de Antropologia de la Facultad de Filosofía y Letras, Universidad de Buenos Aires, Moreno 350, Buenos Aires. Art. on anthropology, ethnology, prehist., folklore and linguistics; bk. rev.; biblio.; illus. pni

44. SAN MARTIN. M. Instituto Nacional Sanmartiniano, Plaza Grand-Bourg, Buenos Aires. pni

45. SOCIEDAD GOETHEANA ARGENTINA, PUBLICACIONES DE LA... [Publications of the Argentine Goethe Society]. Sección Mendoza [Mendoza section]. Irr. Godoy Cruz, Mendoza, for Sección Mendoza, Sociedad Goetheana Argentina. pni

46. STORNIA. Revista de Historia, Etnologia y Folklore [Review of history, ethnology and folklore]. Irr. (B). Julio S. Storni, Tucumán. pni

47. TRABAJOS Y COMUNICACIONES [Works and communications]. Irr. 1949 (1958: vol. 7). Dept. de Historia, Facultad de Humanidades y Ciencias de la Educación, Universidad Nacional de La Plata, Calle 2, No. 662, La Plata. Ed: Ricardo R. Caillet-Bois. Art. on colonial and post-colonial Argentine hist. pni

48. UCRANIA LIBRE [Free Ukraine]. Revista informativo-cultural [Informative-cultural review]. Q. Instituto Informativo Editorial Ucránio, Soler 5039, Buenos Aires. Art. (some hist.) on Ukraine and neighboring areas; doc. p(1) M$N 5

49. UNIVERSIDAD [University]. S-A. Universidad Nacional del Litoral, Bulevar Pellegrini 2750, Santa Fe. M$N 200

50. UNIVERSIDAD DE BUENOS AIRES, REVISTA DE LA... [Review of the University of Buenos Aires]. Q. Universidad de Buenos Aires, Lavalle 465, Buenos Aires. pni

51. UNIVERSIDAD NACIONAL DE CORDOBA, REVISTA DE LA... [Review of the National University of Córdoba]. 5 x y (Irr.). Universidad Nacional de Córdoba, Córdoba.

Bermuda

1. BERMUDA HISTORICAL QUARTERLY. Q. Bermuda Hist. Soc., Hamilton. 30 s/35 s

Bolivia

Prepared with the assistance of
Guillermo Céspedes del Castillo, University of Seville

1. ANALES DE LA ARQUEOLOGIA DE BOLIVIA [Annals of Archaeology of Bolivia]. A. (Irr.). Sociedad Arqueológica de Bolivia, Av. Chacaltaya 500, Casilla 1487, La Paz. pni

BOLETIN. For titles beginning with "Boletín," followed by the name of the publishing or sponsoring institution or society, see the respective institution or society.

2. KHANA. Revista Municipal de Artes y Letras [Municipal review of arts and letters]. Q (Irr.). 1953 (1956/57: vol. 4). Dirección de Cultura de la Honorable Municipalidad, Alcáldia Municipal, La Paz. Ed: Jacobo Liberman Z. Art. on hist., archaeology, folklore, arts and letters. pni

3. SOCIEDAD DE ESTUDIOS GEOGRAFICOS E HISTORICOS, BOLETIN DE LA... [Bulletin of the Society of Geographical and Historical Studies]. S-A (A.). 1904 (mri 1953: new series, vol. 4). Sociedad de Estudios Geográficos e Históricos, Calle Bolívar 211, Santa Cruz de la Sierra. Art. on the hist. and anthropology of Bolivia; doc.; illus. pni

4. SOCIEDAD GEOGRAFICA "SUCRE," BOLETIN DE LA... [Bulletin of the Geographical Society of Sucre]. Irr. 1889 (mri 1955: no. 442). Sociedad Geográfica de Sucre, Plaza 25 de Mayo, Aptdo. 101, Sucre. Ed: Jorge Urioste Arana, Plaza Principal, Sucre. Art. on Bolivian hist. from the 16th cent., and on archaeology and geography. pni

5. SOCIEDAD GEOGRAFICA Y DE HISTORIA "POTOSI," BOLETIN DE LA... [Bulletin of the Geographical and Historical Society of Potosi]. M. 1913 (mri 1953: no. 12). Sociedad Geográfica y de Historia "Potosi," Casa Nacional de Moneda, Casilla 39, Potosi. Art. on the hist. and geography of Bolivia; biblio.; news of the soc. pni

Brazil

Prepared with the assistance of

José Honorio Rodrigues, Director, Arquivo Nacional, Rio de Janeiro,

Instituto Brasileiro de Bibliografia e Documentação, Rio de Janeiro, and

Guillermo Céspedes del Castillo, University of Seville

ANAES. ANAIS. For titles beginning with "Anaes" or "Anais," followed by the name of the publishing or sponsoring institution or society, see the respective institution or society.

1. ANHEMBI. M. Redatorial Anhembí Ltda., Rua Marconi 53, 9° andar, São Paulo. Cr $ 660 / $ 10

ANUARIO DO MUSEO IMPERIAL see MUSEO IMPERIAL, ANUARIO DO...

2. ANUARIO GENEALOGICO LATINO [Latin genealogical yearbook]. A. 1949 (1957: vol. 9). Instituto Genealógico Brasileiro, Rua Dr. Zuquim 1525, São Paulo. Ed: Salvador de Moya. Art. on genealogy and heraldry. Cr $100/ $1

3. ARQUIVO PUBLICO DA BAHIA, ANAES DO... [Annals of Bahia Public Archives]. Irr. Arquivo Público da Bahia, Cidade de Salvador, Bahia. pni

ARQUIVOS DO MUSEO NACIONAL see MUSEO NACIONAL, ARQUIVOS DO...

4. BIBLIOTECA E ARCHIVO PUBLICO DO PARA, ANAIS DA... [Annals of the Library and Public Archives of Pará]. Irr. Biblioteca e Archivo Público do Pará, Rua Campos Sales, Belém, PA. pni

5. BIBLIOTECA NACIONAL, ANAIS DA... [Annals of the National Library]. Irr. 1876 (mri 1954: vol. 73). Divisão de Obras Raras e Publicações da Biblioteca Nacional, Av. Rio Branco 219/239, Rio de Janeiro, DF. Doc., biblio. catalogues, indices and inventories of manuscripts on Brazilian hist. pni

BOLETIM. For titles beginning with "Boletím," followed by the name of the publishing or sponsoring institution or society, see the respective institution or society.

6. BOLETIM GEOGRAFICO [Geographical bulletin]. 6 x y. Instituto Brasileiro de Geográfia e Estatística, Av. Rio Branco 453, Rio de Janeiro. Cr $30

7. DEPARTAMENTO DO ARQUIVO DO ESTADO DE SÃO PAULO, BOLETIM DO... [Bulletin of the São Paulo State Archives Department]. Irr. Departamento do Arquivo do Estado de São Paulo, Largo General Osório 116, São Paulo, SP. pni

8. INSTITUTO ARQUEOLOGICO E GEOGRAFICO PERNAMBUCANO, REVISTA DO... [Review of the Pernambuco Archaeological and Geographical Institute]. Irr. 1863 (mri 1955: vol. 43). Instituto Arqueológico, Histórico e geográfico Pernambucano, Rua do Hospicio 130, Recife, PE. Art. on local and national hist., source material and folklore. pni

9. INSTITUTO DO CEARA, REVISTA DO... [Review of the Ceará Institute]. A. 1887 (mri 1956: vol. 70). Instituto do Ceará, Av. Visconde de Cauipe 2431, Fortaleza, CE. Art. on local and national hist. free

10. INSTITUTO GEOGRAFICO E HISTORICO DA BAHIA, REVISTA DO... [Review of the Bahia Historical and Geographical Institute]. A. 1894 (mri 1956: vol. 67). Instituto Geográfico e Histórico do Bahia, Av. Sete de Setembro 94-A, Salvador, BA. Art. on local and national hist.; doc.; biblio.; illus. pni

11. INSTITUTO HISTORICO E GEOGRAFICO BRASILEIRO, REVISTA DO... [Review of the Brazilian Historical and Geographical Institute]. Q. 1838 (1959: vol. 24). Instituto Histórico e Geográfico Brasileiro, Av. Augusto Severo 4, Rio de Janeiro. Art. on local and national hist. and on historiography; doc.; bk. rev.; biblio.; illus. pni

12. INSTITUTO HISTORICO E GEOGRAFICO DE SÃO PAULO, REVISTA DO... [Review of the Historical and Geographical Institute of São Paulo]. A. 1895 (1957: vol. 54). Instituto Histórico e Geográfico de São Paulo, Rua Benjamin Constant 152, São Paulo, SP. Art. on local and national hist.; biblio. pni

13. INSTITUTO HISTORICO E GEOGRAFICO DE SERGIPE, REVISTA DO.. [Review of the Historical and Geographical Institute of Sergipe]. Irr. Instituto Histórico e Geográfico de Sergipe, Rua Itabaianinha 41, Aracaju, SE. pni

14. INSTITUTO HISTORICO E GEOGRAFICO DO PARA, REVISTA DO... [Review of the Historical and Geographical Institute of Pará]. Irr. Instituto Histórico e Geográfico do Pará, Pça. D. Pedro II 35, Belém, PA. pni

15. INSTITUTO HISTORICO E GEOGRAFICO DO RIO GRANDE DO SUL, REVISTA DO... [Review of the Historical and Geographical Institute of Rio Grand do Sul]. Q. 1921 (mri 1950: vol. 29). Instituto Histórico e Geográfico do Rio Grande do Sul, Rua Riachuelo 1305, Pôrto Alegre, RS. Ed: Armando Dias de Azevedo, Othelo Rosa, Lowrenço M. Prunes. Art. on local and national hist. colonial and post-colonial; doc.; biblio. pni

16. INSTITUTO HISTORICO E GEOGRAFICO PARAIBANO, REVISTA DO... [Review of the Paraiba Historical and Geographical Institute]. Irr. Instituto Histórico e Geográfico Paraibano, C.P. 37, João Pessoa, PB. pni

17. MUSEU HISTORICO NACIONAL, ANAIS DO... [Annals of the National Historical Museum]. A. 1940 (1957: vol. 8). Museu Histórico Nacional, Pça. Marechal Ancora, Rio de Janeiro, DF. Art. on cultural hist., arts and sciences; news of the activities of the museum. pni

18. MUSEU IMPERIAL, ANUARIO DO... [Yearbook of the Imperial Museum Irr. 1940 (mri 1954: vol. 15). Museu Imperial, Av. 7 de Setembro 220, Petrópolis, RJ. Art. on hist. and genealogy pertaining to Brazil, with emphasis on the imperial period. pni

19. MUSEU NACIONAL, ARQUIVOS DO... [Archives of the National Museum]. Irr. Museu Nacional, Quinta de Bõa Vista, São Cristovão, Rio de Janeiro. pni

20. MUSEU PAULISTA, ANAIS DO... [Annals of the São Paulo Museum]. A. Seção de História do Museu Paulista, C.P. 32-B, São Paulo, SP. pni

21. MUSEU PAULISTA, BOLETIM DO... [Bulletin of the São Paulo Museum]. Irr. Museu Paulista, Alto de Ipiranga, C.P. 8032, Ipiranga, São Paulo. pni

22. PESQUISAS [Researches]. A. Instituto Anchietano de Pesquisas, Rua Duque de Cazias 1247, C.P. 358, Pôrto Alegre, RS. pni

REVISTA. For titles beginning with "Revista," followed by the name of the publishing or sponsoring institution or society, see the respective institution or society.

23. REVISTA DE ANTROPOLOGIA [Review of anthropology]. S-A. C.P. 5459, São Paulo, Cr $ 60

24. REVISTA DE HISTORIA [Historical review]. Q. 1950 (1958: vol. 17). Faculdade de Filosofia, Ciencias e Letras, Univ. de São Paulo, Rua Maria Antonia 294, C.P. 8105, São Paulo. Ed: Simões de Paula. Art. on pre- and post-colonial Brazil, on general hist. and related fields; doc.; bk. rev.; biblio. Cr $ 200 / $ 6

25. REVISTA DO LIVRO [Review of the book]. Q. Instituto Nacional do Livro, Ministério da Educação e Cultura, Av. Rio Branco 219/139, 4° andar, Rio de Janeiro. Cr $ 120 / $ 1

26. REVISTA GENEALOGICA LATINA [Latin genealogical review]. S-A (A). 1949 (1958: vol. 9-10). Instituto Genealógico Brasileiro, Rua Dr. Zuquim 1525, São Paulo, SP. Ed: Salvador de Moya. Art. on genealogy. Cr $ 100/ $ 1

27. SERVICO DO PATRIMONIO HISTORICO E ARTISTICO NACIONAL, REVISTA DO... [Review of the Service of the National Historical and Artistic Patrimony]. A. 1937 (mri 1955: no. 12). Diretoria do Patrimõnio Histórico e Artístico Nacional, Ministério da Educação e Cultura, Rua da Imprensa 16, 8° andar, Rio de Janeiro, DF. Ed: Rodrigo M.F. Andrade. Art. on Brazilian art hist.; doc.; illus. pni

28. STADEN JAHRBUCH [Staden yearbook]. Beiträge zur Brasilkunde [Contributions to Brazilian studies]. A. 1953(mri 1955: vol. 3). Instituto Hans Staden, Rua Conselheiro Crispiniano 53, 12° andar, São Paulo. Ed: Egon Schaden, C.P. 5459, São Paulo. Art. on the social, cultural, and economic hist. of Brazil, with emphasis on ethnological studies and on relations between Germany and Brazil; bk. rev. and German-Brazilian biblio. of bk. and periodicals; in German. pv (Cr $ 60 - Cr $ 80)

British Guiana

1. TIMEHRI. Irr. 1882 (1957: no. 36). Royal Agricultural and Commercial Soc. of British Guiana. Ed: Vincent Roth. Art. on hist., anthropology and natural sciences with reference to British Guiana; illus. Pub. suspended in 1903 and resumed in 1911. $ 1

Chile

Prepared with the assistance of

Ricardo Donoso, Director, Sociedad Chilena de Historia y Geografía, Santiago,

Oswald F.A. Menghin, Centro Argentino de Estudios Prehistoricos, Buenos Aires, and

Guillermo Céspedes del Castillo, University of Seville

1. ACADEMIA CHILENA DE LA HISTORIA, BOLETIN DE LA... [Bulletin of the Chilean Academy of History]. S-A. 1933 (1957: vol. 24). Academia Chilena de la Historia, Casilla 2437, Santiago de Chile. Ed: Jaime Eyzaguirre. Art. on all periods of the hist. of Chile and, to a lesser extent, other South American countries with emphasis on the 18th and 19th cent.; doc.; bk. rev.; notes on the activities of the acad. Pesos 3,000

ANALES DE LA UNIVERSIDAD DE CHILE see UNIVERSIDAD DE CHILE, ANALES DE LA...

BOLETIN DE LA ACADEMIA CHILENA DE LA HISTORIA see ACADEMIA CHILENA DE LA HISTORIA, BOLETIN DE LA...

BOLETIN DEL MUSEO NACIONAL DE HISTORIA NATURAL see MUSEO NACIONAL DE HISTORIA NATURAL, BOLETIN DEL...

2. CENTRO DE ESTUDIOS ANTROPOLOGICOS, NOTAS DEL... [Notes of the Center of Anthropological Studies]. Irr. Centro de Estudios Antropológicos, Calle Ejército 233, Santiago de Chile. pni

3. CENTRO DE ESTUDIOS ANTROPOLOGICOS. PUBLICACIONES [Center of Anthropological Studies. Publications]. Irr. Centro de Estudios Antropológicos, Calle Ejército 233, Santiago de Chile. Illus. pv

4. FINIS TERRAE. Q. Departámento de Extensión Cultural de la Universidad Católica de Chile, Avda. Bernardo O'Higgins 340, Santiago de Chile. Pesos 2,000

5. MUSEO ARQUEOLOGICO DE LA SERENA, LAS NOTAS DEL... [Notes of the Archaeological Museum of La Serena]. Irr. Museo Arqueológica de La Serena, Casilla 117, La Serena. p (1) $ 0.20

6. MUSEO NACIONAL DE HISTORIA NATURAL, BOLETIN DEL... [Bulletin of the National Museum of Natural History]. Irr. Museo Nacional de Historia Natural, Casilla 787, Santiago de Chile. Includes art. on archaeology; illus. pv

7. MUSEO NACIONAL DE HISTORIA NATURAL. NOTICIARIO MENSUAL [National Museum of Natural History. Monthly communications]. M. Museo Nacional de Historia Natural, Casilla 787, Santiago de Chile. Art. of popular interest on archaeology and ethnology; illus. pni

NOTAS DEL CENTRO DE ESTUDIOS ANTROPOLOGICOS see CENTRO DE ESTUDIOS ANTROPOLOGICOS, NOTAS DEL...

LAS NOTAS DEL MUSEO ARQUEOLOGICA DE LA SERENA see MUSEO ARQUEOLOGICA DE LA SERENA, LAS NOTAS DEL...

8. REVISTA CHILENA DE HISTORIA Y GEOGRAFIA [Chilean review of history and geography]. A. (B). 1911 (1959: no. 125). Sociedad Chilena de Historia y Geografía, Casilla 1386, Santiago de Chile. Ed: Ricardo Donoso. Art. on hist. and geography, mainly of Chile; doc. (with biographical emphasis); bk. rev. (also from non-American countries). pni

9. REVISTA DE ESTUDIOS HISTORICOS [Review of historical studies]. A. 1949 (mri 1954/55: vol. 4/5). Instituto Chileno de Investigaciónes Genealógicas, Amunategui 447, Santiago de Chile. Ed: Fernando Guarda Geywitz. Art. on hist., genealogy, and heraldry, primarily of Chile; biblio. pni

10. REVISTA UNIVERSITARIA [University review]. Irr. Universidad Católica de Chile, Casilla 114, Santiago de Chile. pni

11. UNIVERSIDAD DE CHILE, ANALES DE LA... [Annals of the University of Chile]. Q. 1931 (1958: 3rd series, vol. 116). Universidad de Chile, Departamento de Publicaciones, Casilla 10 D, Santiago de Chile. Ed: G. Feliú Cruz. Art. on the humanities and social sciences, with some emphasis on biography, literature, philosophy, and literary and political hist.; biblio. art. and bk. rev.; notes and doc.; illus. Pesos 2,800/ $3.60

Colombia

Prepared with the assistance of

Luis Martinez Delgado, Director, Sección de Coordinación de Estudios Históricos, Ministerio de Educación Nacional, República de Colombia, Bogota, and

Guillermo Céspedes del Castillo, University of Seville

1. ACADEMIA COLOMBIANA, BOLETIN DE LA... [Bulletin of the Colombian Academy]. Q. Academia Colombiana, Edificio de la Biblioteca Nacional, Calle 24, No. 5-60, Oficina 113, Aptdo. 815, Bogotá. Pesos 4

2. ACADEMIA DE HISTORIA DEL VALLE DEL CAUCA, BOLETIN DE LA... [Bulletin of the Academy of History of the Cauca Valley]. S-A (occasionally 3 x y). Academia de Historia del Valle del Cauca, Calle 15, No. 5-22, Aptdo. 409, Cali. pni

3. ARCHIVO NACIONAL DE COLOMBIA, REVISTA DEL... [Review of the National Archives]. M. 1936 (1957: no. 75). Archivo Nacional de Colombia, Biblioteca Nacional, 4° piso, Aptdo. 2587, Bogotá. Ed: Enrique Ortega Ricaurte. Hist. doc. of archives. Pub. temporarily suspended in 1957. pni

BOLETIN. For titles beginning with "Boletín," followed by the name of the publishing or sponsoring institution or society, see the respective institution or society.

4. BOLETIN DE HISTORIA Y ANTIGUIDADES [Bulletin of history and antiquities]. Q. 1903 (1958: vol. 45). Academia Colombiana de Historia, Calle 10, No. 8-95, Bogotá. Ed. board: Mario-Germán Romero (chief ed.), Alberto Miramon, Roberto Lievano. Art. on the hist. of Colombia and its corresponding colonial area, with strong biographical emphasis; news of the acad.; illus. Pesos 18/ $5

5. BOLETIN HISTORIAL [Historical bulletin]. Irr. 1915 (1957: no. 128). Academia de la Historia de Cartagena de Indias, Palacio de la Inquisición, Cartagena. Art. on local and national hist.; biographies; news of the acad. pni

6. ESTUDIO [Study]. Irr. Academia de Historia de Santander, Bucaramanga. free

7. HACARITAMA. M. Centro de Historia de Ocaña, Norte de Santander. pni

8. HISTORIA [History]. Q. 1955 (mri 1956: vol. 2). Instituto Colombiano de Estudios Históricos, Aptdo. 8743, Bogotá. Ed. board: Joaquin Perez Villa, Victor Alba. Art. on colonial and post-colonial South American hist., and on philosophy and the hist. of ideas; doc. and textual criticism; bk. rev.; biblio. of bk. and periodicals; professional notes; news on the activities of the inst. pni

9. HOJAS DE CULTURA POPULAR COLOMBIANA [Pamphlets on popular Colombian culture]. M. Dirección de Información y Propaganda, Bogotá. free

10. POPAYAN. Irr. Centro Departamental de Historia, Universidad del Cauca, Aptdo. 113, Popayan. pni

11. PROMETEO [Prometheus]. Una revista para los gentes que piensan [A review for people who think]. M. Av. Jimenez de Quesada 8-56, Oficina 406, Bogotá. Pesos 12

12. REPERTORIO BOYACENSE [Boyacá repertory]. Q (Irr.). Academia Boyacense de Historia, Carrera 6a, No. 6-91, Tunja, Boyacá. pni

13. REVISTA BOLIVAR [Bolivar review]. 10 x y (Irr.). Ministerio de Educación Nacional, Sección de Publicaciones, Calle 24, No. 7-59, Aptdo. 486, Bogotá. pni

14. REVISTA COLOMBIANA DE ANTROPOLOGIA [Colombian review of anthropology]. A. Instituto Colombiano de Antropología, Bogotá. pni

15. REVISTA DE HISTORIA [Review of history]. 4 x y. Academia Nariñense de Historia, Carrera 22, No. 19-10, Pasto. pni

REVISTA DE LA UNIVERSIDAD NACIONAL DE COLOMBIA see UNIVERSIDAD NACIONAL DE COLOMBIA, REVISTA DE LA...

REVISTA DEL ARCHIVO NACIONAL DE COLOMBIA see ARCHIVO NACIONAL DE COLOMBIA, REVISTA DEL...

16. STUDIUM. 3 x y. 1957 (1957: vol. 1). Universidad Nacional de Colombia, Facultad de Filsofia y Letras, Bogotá. Ed: Antonio Antelo Iglesias. Art. on the hist. of Spanish America, principally Colombia, and on historiography, philology, philosophy, political science, arts and letters. pni

17. THESAURUS. 3 x y. Instituto Caro y Cuervo, Aptdo. 2950, Bogotá. Pesos 20 / $ 6

18. UNIVERSIDAD DE ANTIOQUIA [University of Antioquia]. Q. Universidad de Antioquia, Calle 49, No. 42 A-39, Aptdo. 217, Medellin. pni

19. UNIVERSIDAD NACIONAL DE COLOMBIA, REVISTA DE LA... [Review of the National University of Colombia]. Revista trimestral de cultura moderna [Quarterly review of modern culture]. Q. Universidad Nacional de Colombia, Bogotá. pni

20. UNIVERSITAS [University]. S-A. Facultad de Ciencias Económicas y Juridicas, Pontificia Universidad Católica Javeriana, Carrera 7a, No. 40-62, Bogotá. Pesos 12/ $ 3

21. VIRTUD Y LETRAS [Virtue and letters]. Q. Facultades Eclesiasticas Claretianas de Colombia, Aptdo. 51, Manizales.

Costa Rica

Prepared with the assistance of
Guillermo Céspedes del Castillo, University of Seville

1. ACADEMIA COSTARRICENSE DE CIENCIAS GENEALOGICAS, REVISTA DE LA... [Review of the Costa Rican Academy of Genealogical Sciences]. Irr. 1954 (1957: no. 4). Academia Costarricense de Ciencias Genealógicas, Aptdo. 1261, San José. Ed: Jorge A. Lines, Aptdo. 101, San José. Art. on Costa Rican genealogy. Formerly pub. under the title: Memoria de la Academia de Geografía e Historia de Costa Rica. pni

2. ACADEMIA COSTARRICENSE DE LA HISTORIA, REVISTA DE LA... [Review of the Costa Rican Academy of History]. Irr. 1949 (1957: no. 20). Academia Costarricense de la Historia, Aptdo. 4499, San José. Art. on all periods of Costa Rican hist. pni

3. ARCHIVOS NACIONALES DE COSTA RICA, REVISTA DE LOS... [Review of the National Archives of Costa Rica]. S-A. 1936 (1957: vol. 21). Archivos Nacionales, Aptdo. 2148, San José. Ed: José Luis Coto Conde. Art. on the colonial and independence period of Central American hist., with emphasis on the political hist. of Costa Rica; doc. and lists of doc. from the archives; illus. pni

4. COMBATE [Combat]. B-M. Instituto Internacional de Estudios Político-Sociales, Aptdo. 4292, San José. Colon 10 / $ 1.50

MEMORIA DE LA ACADEMIA DE GEOGRAFIA E HISTORIA DE COSTA RICA see ACADEMIA COSTARRICENSE DE CIENCIAS GENEALOGICAS, REVISTA DE LA...

REVISTA. For titles beginning with "Revista," followed by the name of the publishing or sponsoring institution or society, see the respective institution or society.

5. UNIVERSIDAD DE COSTA RICA, REVISTA DE LA... [Review of the University of Costa Rica]. A. (Irr.). Biblioteca Central de la Universidad de Costa Rica, San José. free

Cuba

Prepared with the assistance of
Guillermo Céspedes del Castillo, University of Seville

1. ACADEMIA DE LA HISTORIA, ANALES DE LA... [Annals of the Academy of History]. B-M (Irr.). 1919 (mri 1948 [1950]: vol. 30). Academia de la Historia, Edificio Barraque, 7° piso, Cuba y Amargura, La Habana. Art. and doc. on the hist. of Cuba, with emphasis on literary hist.; biographies. pni

2. ACADEMIA NACIONAL DE ARTES Y LETRAS, ANALES DE LA... [Annals of the National Academy of Arts and Letters]. Q(Irr.) Academia Nacional de Artes y Letras, Antiguo Colegio de Belén, Acosta y Compostela, La Habana. pni

ANALES DE LA ACADEMIA DE LA HISTORIA see ACADEMIA DE LA HISTORIA, ANALES DE LA...

ANALES DE LA ACADEMIA NACIONAL DE ARTES Y LETRAS see ACADEMIA NACIONAL DE ARTES Y LETRAS, ANALES DE LA...

3. ARCHIVO JOSE MARTI [José Martí archive]. S-A (Irr.). Dirección de Cultura, Ministério de Educación, La Habana. pni

4. ARCHIVO NACIONAL, BOLETIN DEL...[Bulletin of the National Archives]. A. 1902 (1957: vol. 56). Archivo Nacional, Compostela y San Isidro, La Habana. Ed: Jorge Quintana. Art. and doc. on the social and economic hist. of Cuba; catalogue of archives. free

5. ARCHIVOS DEL FOLKLORE CUBANO [Archives of Cuban folklore]. Q. Sociedad del Folklore Cubano, Calle 27, No. 160, Vedado, La Habana.
M$N 5/$4

6. BIBLIOTECA NACIONAL, REVISTA DE LA... [Review of the National Library]. Q. 1909 (1957: vol. 8). Biblioteca Nacional, Castillo de la Fuerza, La Habana. Ed: Lilia Castro de Morales. Art. on hist. and genealogy; doc.; notes on library science and on the activities of the library; bk. rev. pni

BOLETIN DEL ARCHIVO NACIONAL see ARCHIVO NACIONAL, BOLETIN DEL...

BOLETIN DEL COMITE DE ARCHIVOS see COMITE DE ARCHIVOS, BOLETIN DEL...

7. BOLETIN HISTORICO DEL MUNICIPIO DE HOLGUIN [Historical bulletin of the City of Holguin]. M. Histŏriador Municipal, Agramonte 114, Holguín, Provincia de Oriente. pni

8. COMITE DE ARCHIVOS, BOLETIN DEL... [Bulletin of the Committee on Archives]. Q. 1958 (1958: vol. 1). Comisión de Historia del Instituto Panamericano de Geografía e Historia, La Habana, for Comité de Archivos, Edificio

del Archivo Nacional, Compostela y Velazco, La Habana. Art. on archival science and genealogy; biblio. pni

CUADERNOS DEL INSTITUTO INTERAMERICANO DE HISTORIA MUNICIPAL E INSTITUTIONAL see INSTITUTO INTERAMERICANO DE HISTORIA MUNICIPAL E INSTITUTIONAL, CUADERNOS DEL...

9. INSTITUTO INTERAMERICANO DE HISTORIA MUNICIPAL E INSTITUTIONAL, CUADERNOS DEL... [Papers of the Inter-American Institute of Municipal and Institutional History]. Irr. Instituto Interamericano de Historia Municipal e Institutional, Leonor Perez 251, La Habana. pni

10. REVISTA BIMESTRE CUBANA [Bi-monthly Cuban review]. B-M. Sociedad Económica de Amigos del Pais, Carlos III, 710, Aptdo. 214, La Habana.
M$N 5

REVISTA DE LA BIBLIOTECA NACIONAL see BIBLIOTECA NACIONAL, REVISTA DE LA...

11. UNIVERSIDAD DE LA HABANA [University of Havana]. Irr. Departamento de Intercambio Universitario, Universidad de la Habana, La Habana.
M$N 2.50

Dominican Republic

Prepared with the assistance of

Vetilio Alfau Durán, Director of the Library of the University of Santo Domingo, Ciudad Trujillo, and

Guillermo Céspedes del Castillo, University of Seville

ANALES DE LA UNIVERSIDAD DE SANTO DOMINGO see UNIVERSIDAD DE SANTO DOMINGO, ANALES DE LA...

1. ARCHIVO GENERAL DE LA NACION, BOLETIN DEL... [Bulletin of the National General Archives]. Q. 1938 (1958: vol. 20). Archivo General de la Nación, Editora Montalvo, Ciudad Trujillo. Ed: Emilio Rodriguez Demorizi. Doc. from the archives on the hist. of the Dominican Republic, Latin America generally, and also on auxiliary fields such as genealogy; archival inventories and catalogues; index of doc. on foreign relations. pni

BOLETIN DEL ARCHIVO GENERAL DE LA NACION see ARCHIVO GENERAL DE LA NACION, BOLETIN DEL...

2. CLIO. Q. 1933 (1959: vol. 27). Comisión de Publicaciones, Academia Dominicana de la Historia, Plaza de Tirso de Molina, Ciudad Trujillo. Ed. board: Vetilio Alfau Duran, Emilio Rodriguez Demorizi, Fray Cipriano de Utrera. Art. on the hist. of the Dominican Republic; doc. pni

3. EL FARO A COLON [The beacon to Columbus]. 3 x y. 1950 (1959: vol. 10). Comité Ejecutivo Permanente del Faro de Colon, Ciudad Trujillo. Ed: Fernando A. Garrido. Art. on the hist. of Santo Domingo, with emphasis on matters pertaining to Christopher Columbus in both the New and Old World; doc. for later periods. free

4. REVISTA DE TRABAJO [Labor review]. Q (Irr.). Secretaria de Estado de Justicia y Trabajo, Departamento de Trabajo, Ciudad Trujillo. pni

5. REVISTA DOMINICANA DE CULTURA [Dominican review of culture]. M. Ministerio de Relaciones Exteriores, Ciudad Trujillo. Alphabetical index in each vol. pni

6. UNIVERSIDAD DE SANTO DOMINGO, ANALES DE LA... [Annals of the University of Santo Domingo]. Irr. Universidad de Santo Domingo, Ciudad Trujillo. pni

Ecuador

Prepared with the assistance of
Guillermo Céspedes del Castillo, University of Seville

1. ACADEMIA NACIONAL DE HISTORIA, BOLETIN DE LA... [Bulletin of the National Academy of History]. S-A. 1912 (1959: vol. 39). Academia Naciona de Historia, Carrera Mejia 734, Quito. Ed: Isaac J. Barrera. Art. on the hist. and geography of Ecuador; biographies of leading Ecuadorean figures; doc., bk. rev.; official communications of the acad. pv (p(1) c. Sucres 6-10)

2. ANALES [Annals]. S-A (?). Universidad Central del Ecuador, Aptdo. 166, Quito. pni

3. ARCHIVO NACIONAL DE HISTORIA, BOLETIN DEL... [Bulletin of the National Archives of History]. S-A (Irr.). 1950 (mri 1956: vol. 4). Archivo Nacional de Historia, Casa de la Cultura Ecuatoriana, Quito. Ed: Alfredo Chaves, P.O.B. 67, Quito. Art. on the hist. of Ecuador and the activities of the archives; doc. and index of doc. Sucres 20 / $2

BOLETIN. For titles beginning with "Boletín," followed by the name of the publishing or sponsoring institution or society, see the respective institution or society.

4. BOLETIN DE INFORMACIONES CIENTIFICAS NACIONALES [National scientific information bulletin]. Irr. (2-6 x y). Secciones Científicas de la Casa de la Cultura Ecuatoriana, Apartado postal 67, Quito. pni

5. BOLETIN DE INFORMACIONES Y DE ESTUDIOS SOCIALES Y ECONOMICOS [Bulletin of social and economic reports and studies]. Q. Instituto Nacional de Previsión, Departamento de Investigación Social y Propaganda, Calle Bogotá 123, Quito. pni

6. CASA DE LA CULTURA ECUATORIANA. REVISTA [Ecuadorian House of Culture. Review]. Irr. (A. or S-A). Casa de la Cultura Ecuatoriana, Apartado postal 67, Quito. Anthropology, ethnology, literary criticism, hist. and international politics pertaining to Ecuador and Latin America; illus. p (1) Sucres 5

7. CENTRO DE INVESTIGACIONES HISTORICAS, BOLETIN DEL... [Bulletin of the Center for Historical Investigations]. A. 1931 (mri 1955: vol. 10). Centro de Investigaciones Históricas, Aptdo. 75, Guayaquil. Ed. board: Carlos A. Rolando, Pedro Robles Chambers. Art. on the hist. of Ecuador and the local hist. of Guayaquil; occasional art. on the hist. of other countries, not limited to South America; genealogy; illus. pni

8. EL CHIMBORAZO. Revista mensual independiente [Independent monthly review]. M. Empresa de Publicaciones "Ecuatoriana," Apartado postal 594 (calle Flores, 737), Quito. Politics, culture and hist. pertaining to Ecuador and Latin America; sum.; illus. p (1) Sucres 2

9. COLEGIO NACIONAL "VICENTE ROCAFUERTE," REVISTA DEL... [Review of the Vicente Rocafuerte National College]. A. Biblioteca "Angel Andres Garcia," Colegio Nacional "Vicente Rocafuerte," Velez 2203, Aptdo. 330, Guayaquil. pni

10. CUADERNOS DE HISTORIA Y ARQUEOLOGIA [Papers on history and archaeology]. S-A. 1951 (mri 1955: vol. 5). Casa de la Cultura Ecuatoriana, Núcleo del Guayas, Pedro Moncayo y 9 de Octubre, Casilla 3542, Guayaquil. Ed: C. Zevallos Menéndez. Art. on the hist. of Ecuador and the archaeology of South America; biblio. Sucres 45 /$ 2.80

11. INSTITUTO NACIONAL "MEJIA," BOLETIN DEL... [Bulletin of the Mejia National Institute]. Irr. Instituto Nacional "Mejia," Quito. Pedagogy, language, literature, sociology, national hist.; biblio.; sum. pni

12. EL LIBERTADOR [The liberator]. Irr. Sociedad Bolivariana del Ecuador, Ma Luisa Calle, Quito. pni

13. MUSEO HISTORICO [Historical museum]. Q (Irr.). 1949 (1958: vol. 10). Departamento Municipal de Educación y Cultura Popular, Quito, for Museo de Historia. Ed: Jorge A. Garcés G., Aptdo. 3054, Quito. Art. on Ecuadorean hist. and its sources, on archaeology and folklore; doc.; illus. pni

14. NUCLEO DEL AZUAY DE LA CASA DE LA CULTURA ECUATORIANA, REVISTA DEL... [Review of the Azuay Center of the House of Ecuadorean Culture]. Irr. Casa de la Cultura Ecuatoriana, Aptdo. 4907, Cuenca. pni

REVISTA DEL COLEGIO NACIONAL "VICENTE ROCAFUERTE" see COLEGIO NACIONAL "VICENTE ROCAFUERTE," REVISTA DEL...

REVISTA DEL NUCLEO DEL AZUAY DE LA CASA DE LA CULTURA ECUATORIANA see NUCLEO DEL AZUAY DE LA CASA DE LA CULTURA ECUATORIANA, REVISTA DEL...

El Salvador

Prepared with the assistance of

Guillermo Céspedes del Castillo, University of Seville

ANALES DEL MUSEO NACIONAL "DAVID J. GUZMAN" see MUSEO NACIONAL "DAVID J. GUZMAN," ANALES DEL...

1. ANAQUELES [Shelves]. Irr. Biblioteca Nacional, 8A Av. Norte, no. 16 San Salvador. Culture, literature and hist.; hist. doc.; sum. pni

2. ATENEO [Athenaeum]. Q. · Ateneo de El Salvador, San Salvador. pni

3. E C A. ESTUDIOS CENTRO AMERICANOS [Central American studies]. Revista de orientación y cultura [Review of orientation and culture]. M. Colegio Externado San Jose for the PP. Jesuitas de C.A., Aptdo. 668, San Salvador. pni

4. MUSEO NACIONAL "DAVID J. GUZMAN," ANALES DEL... [Annals of the National Museum "David J. Guzman"]. Irr. Museo Nacional "David J. Guzman," Cuzcatlan, San Salvador. pni

5. SINTESIS [Synthesis]. Revista cultural de El Salvador [Cultural review of El Salvador]. M. Secretaría de Información de la Presidencia de la República San Salvador. Sum. pni

The Federation of the West Indies

1. BARBADOS MUSEUM AND HISTORICAL SOCIETY. JOURNAL. Q. Barbados Museum and Hist. Soc., St. Ann's Garrison, Bridgetown. $1.25

2. THE CARIBBEAN HISTORICAL REVIEW. A. Hist. Soc. of Trinidad and Tobago, c/o Caribbean Commission, Kent House, Port-of-Spain. $ 1

3. CARIBBEAN QUARTERLY. Q. 1949 (1958: vol. 5). Univ. College of the West Indies, Extra Mural Dept., Port-of-Spain. Art. on the hist. of the British West Indies and, to a lesser extent, other areas, pertaining mainly to cultural hist. and folklore; illus. 8s 4d/ $2

4. JAMAICA HISTORICAL REVIEW. Irr. Jamaica Hist. Soc., 14-16 Eas St., Kingston. pni

5. SOCIAL AND ECONOMIC STUDIES. Q. Inst. of Social and Economic Research, Univ. College of the West Indies, Mona. 30 s/$4.25

Guatemala

Prepared with the assistance of
Guillermo Céspedes del Castillo, University of Seville

ANALES DE LA SOCIEDAD DE GEOGRAFIA E HISTORIA DE GUATEMALA see SOCIEDAD DE GEOGRAFIA E HISTORIA DE GUATEMALA, ANALES DE LA...

1. ANTROPOLOGIA E HISTORIA DE GUATEMALA [Anthropology and history of Guatemala]. S-A. 1949 (1957: vol. 9). Instituto de Antropología e Historia de Guatemala, Edificio No. 5 de "La Aurora," Ciudad de Guatemala. Ed. board: Adolfo Molina Orantes, Antonio Tejeda F., David Vela, Carlos Samayoa Chinchilla. Art. on anthropology and the political and social hist. of Guatemala, with some emphasis on colonial hist. $2.50

2. HUMANIDADES [Humanities]. Irr. Facultad de Humanidades, Universidad de San Carlos, 2a Avenida, no. 12-40, Ciudad de Guatemala. Pedagogy, literary criticism, philosophy and hist.; sum. pni

3. SOCIEDAD DE GEOGRAFIA E HISTORIA DE GUATEMALA, ANALES DE LA... [Annals of the Geographical and Historical Society of Guatemala]. A. 1924 (mri 1956: vol. 29). Sociedad de Geografía e Historia de Guatemala, 3a Avenida Sur 1, Ciudad de Guatemala. Ed: Ricardo Castañeda Paganini. Art. on the hist. of Guatemala, with emphasis on the hist. of individual provinces; biographical art.; news of the soc.; illus. Q 2

4. UNIVERSIDAD DE SAN CARLOS [University of San Carlos]. Q. Universidad de San Carlos, 2a Avenida, no. 12-40, Ciudad de Guatemala. pni

Haiti

Prepared with the assistance of

Guillermo Céspedes del Castillo, University of Seville

BULLETIN DE LA SOCIETE D'ETUDES OCEANIENNES see SOCIETE D'ETUDES OCEANIENNES, BULLETIN DE LA...

BULLETIN DU BUREAU D'ETHNOLOGIE see BUREAU D'ETHNOLOGIE BULLETIN DU...

1. BUREAU D'ETHNOLOGIE, BULLETIN DU... [Bulletin of the Bureau of Ethnology]. S-A. Bureau d'ethnologie, Cité de l'Exposition, Port-au-Prince. pn

REVUE DE LA SOCIETE HAÏTIENNE D'HISTOIRE, DE GEOGRAPHIE ET DE GEOLOGIE see SOCIETE HAÏTIENNE D'HISTOIRE, DE GEOGRAPHIE ET DE GEOLOGIE, REVUE DE LA...

2. SOCIETE D'ETUDES OCEANIENNES, BULLETIN DE LA... [Bulletin of the Society of Oceanic Studies]. Q. 1917 (1958: vol. 10). Société d'Etudes Océaniennes, Papeete. Art. on the hist., anthropology, ethnology, philology, folklore, and natural sciences of the Caribbean area. F. 200 / $4

3. SOCIETE HAÏTIENNE D'HISTOIRE, DE GEOGRAPHIE ET DE GEOLOGIE, REVUE DE LA... [Review of the Haitian Society of History, Geography and Geology]. Q. 1930 (mri 1954/55; vol. 25/26). Société Haïtienne d'Histoire, de Géographie et de Géologie, Angle Nord-Est des Rues Rigaud et Faubert, Pétion-Ville. Ed: Jean Price Mars. Art. on the hist. of Haiti and contemporary problems; biblio. pni

Honduras

Prepared with the assistance of
Guillermo Céspedes del Castillo, University
of Seville

1. ARCHIVO Y BIBLIOTECA NACIONALES, REVISTA DEL... [Review of the National Archives and Library]. M. 1904 (mri 1954/55: vol. 33). Sociedad de Geografía e Historia de Honduras, Tegucigalpa, D. C. Ed: Esteban Guardiola. Art. on the hist., geography and archaeology of Honduras and Central America, biblio. pni

2. CULTURA [Culture]. B-M. Instituto Central, Tegucigalpa, D. C. pni

REVISTA DE LA SOCIEDAD GEOGRAFICA E HISTORICA DE HONDURAS see SOCIEDAD GEOGRAFICA E HISTORICA DE HONDURAS, REVISTA DE LA...

REVISTA DEL ARCHIVO Y BIBLIOTECA NACIONALES see ARCHIVO Y BIBLIOTECA NACIONALES, REVISTA DEL...

3. SOCIEDAD GEOGRAFICA E HISTORICA DE HONDURAS, REVISTA DE LA... [Review of the Geographical and Historical Society of Honduras]. M (4 triple no. p.a.). 1926 (1959: vol. 38). Sociedad Geográfica e Histórica de Honduras, Avenida Cervantes 49, Tegucigalpa, D. C. Ed: José Reina Valenzuela. Art. on the hist., geography, archaeology, folklore, art and literature of Honduras, doc.; biblio.; sum. pni

Martinique

1. ANNALES DES ANTILLES [Annals of the Antilles]. Q. Société d'Histoire de la Martinique, Fort-de-France. pni

Mexico

Prepared with the assistance of

Señora Carmen Cook de Leonard, Editor, El Mexico Antiguo, Mexico, D. F., and

Guillermo Céspedes del Castillo, University of Seville

1. ABSIDE [Apse]. Revista de cultura mejicana [Review of Mexican culture]. Q. Plateros 76, México 19, D.F. Pesos 20/ $3

2. ACADEMIA MEXICANA DE GENEALOGIA Y HERALDICA. BOLETIN [Mexican Academy of Genealogy and Heraldry]. Irr. Academia Mexicana de Genealogia y Heraldica, Gante 7, México, D.F. $6

3. ACADEMIA MEXICANA DE LA HISTORIA, MEMORIAS DE LA... [Memoirs of the Mexican Academy of History]. Correspondiente de la Real de Madrid [Correspondent of the Royal (Academy of History) of Madrid]. Q. 1942 (1959: vol. 18). Academia Mexicana de la Historia, Plaza Carlos Pacheco 21, México 1, D.F. Ed: Manuel Carrera Stampa. Art. on all periods of Spanish-American hist.; extensive biblio.; doc.; bk. rev. Pesos 32/ $3

4. ACADEMIA NACIONAL DE HISTORIA Y GEOGRAFIA, MEMORIA DE LA...[Memoirs of the National Academy of History and Geography]. 10 x y. Secretaria de las Relaciones Exteriores, Av. Juárez 109, México 1, D.F., for Academia Nacional de Historia y Geografía. pni

5. AMERICA INDIGENA [Indian America]. Q. Instituto Indigenista Interamericano, Niños Héroes 139, México 7, D.F. Includes supplement entitled: Boletín indigenista. Pesos 32/ $4

6. ANALES [Annals]. Q. Provincia Franciscana del Santo Evangelio de México, Editorial Franciscana, Madero 7, Coyeacan, México, D.F. pni

ANALES DEL INSTITUTO DE INVESTIGACIONES ESTETICAS see INSTITUTO DE INVESTIGACIONES ESTETICAS, ANALES DEL...

ANALES DEL INSTITUTO NACIONAL DE ANTROPOLOGIA E HISTORIA see INSTITUTO NACIONAL DE ANTROPOLOGIA E HISTORIA, ANALES DEL...

ANUARIO DE LA SOCIEDAD FOLKLORICA DE MEXICO see SOCIEDAD FOLKLORICA DE MEXICO, ANUARIO DE LA...

7. ARCHIVO GENERAL DE LA NACION, BOLETIN DEL... [Bulletin of the General National Archives]. Q. Archivo General de la Nación y Universidad Nacional Autónoma, Universidad Nacional Autónoma de México, Justo Sierra 16, México, D.F. Hist. doc. with commentary; catalogue of archives. pni

8. BIBLIOTECA NACIONAL, BOLETIN DE LA... [Bulletin of the National Library]. Q. Universidad Nacional Autónoma de México, Ciudad Universitaria de México, San Angel, Aptdo. 12131, México 1, D.F., for Biblioteca Nacional. free

BOLETIN. For titles beginning with "Boletín," followed by the name of the publishing or sponsoring institution or society see the respective institution or society.

9. BOLETIN [Bulletin]. M. Sociedad Chihuahuense de Estudios Históricos, Aptdo. 21, Chihuahua, Chih. pni

10. B.B.A.A. Boletín bibliográfico de antropología americana. Boletím bibliographico de antropologia americana. Bibliographical Bulletin of American Anthropology. Bulletin bibliographique d'anthropologie americaine. A. 1937 (mri 1954 [1955]: vol. 17). Instituto Panamericano de Geografía e Historia, Ex-Arzobispado 29, Tacubaya, México 18, D.F. Ed. board: Eusebio Davalos Hurtado (chief ed.), E. Ortega, J. Pardo, J. Zavala. Art. on the anthropology, ethnology, hist., and folklore of the Americas; bk. rev. listed by country of pub.; biblio. $5

BOLETIN BIBLIOGRAFICO DE LA SECRETARIA DE HACIENDA Y CREDITO PUBLICO see SECRETARIA DE HACIENDA Y CREDITO PUBLICO, BOLETIN BIBLIOGRAFICO DE LA...

11. BOLETIN BIBLIOGRAFICO MEXICANO [Mexican bibliographical bulletin]. B-M. Libreria de Porrua Hermanos y Co., Aptdo. 7990, México 1, D.F. free

BOLETIN INDIGENISTA see AMERICA INDIGENA

12. CENTRO DE INVESTIGACIONES ANTROPOLOGICAS DE MEXICO, BOLETIN DEL... [Bulletin of the Center for Anthropological Research of Mexico]. Irr. 1956 (1958: no. 5). Centro de Investigaciones Antropológicas de México, Aptdo. 2242, México, D.F. Ed: Carmen Cook de Leonard. Preliminary information on anthropological discoveries and research; art. on archaeology, hist. and art; translation of material not easily accessible; biblio.; some art. in English. free to subscribers to Yan

13. COLEGIO NACIONAL, MEMORIA DEL... [Memoirs of the National College]. A. El Colegio Nacional, Calle Luis González Obregón 23, México 1, D.F. pni (available on exchange basis)

14. CUADERNOS AMERICANOS [American papers]. La revista del nuevo mundo [Review of the New World]. B-M. 1942 (1958: vol. 17). Pub. address: Av. Rep. de Guatemala 42, Aptdo. 965, México, D.F. Ed. board: Jesús Silva Herzog, Rafael Loera y Chavez. Art. and essays on the humanities and cultural affairs throughout the world, including hist. (mostly intellectual) and historiography, with some emphasis on Latin America; bk. rev.; illus.; table of contents for the years 1942-52 pub. separately. Pesos 60 /$6.50

15. CUADERNOS DE ESTUDIOS YUCATECOS [Papers on Yucatan studies]. Irr. Calle 58, No. 530, letra C, Merida, Yucatán. Pesos 12 /$2

16. ESTUDIOS HISTORICOS [Historical studies]. Q. 1955 (1960: vol. 2). Instituto Jaliscense de Cultura Hispánica, Aptdo. 1029, Guadalajara, Jalisco. Ed: Salvador Reinoso. Art. on Mexican hist., with emphasis on the colonial period; occasional short biblio. Pesos 15 / $2

17. HISTORIA MEXICANA. Q. 1951 (mri 1956: vol. 6). El Cólegio de México, Aptdo. 2123, México 1, D.F. Ed. board: Arturo Arnaiz y Freg, Daniel Cosio, Silvio Zavala. Art. and doc. on hist. and anthropology; bk. rev. Pesos 20 /$ 4

18. INSTITUTO DE INVESTIGACIONES ESTETICAS, ANALES DEL...[Annals of the Institute of Aesthetical Research]. S-A. Instituto de Investigaciones Estéticas, Universidad Nacional Autónoma de México, Torre de Humanidades, 6° piso, Ciudad Universitaria, México 20, D.F. Pesos 10 / p (1) $1

19. INSTITUTO NACIONAL DE ANTROPOLOGIA E HISTORIA, ANALES DEL... [Annals of the National Institute of Anthropology and History]. A. (Irr.). 1939 (1957: no. 38). Instituto Nacional de Antropología e Historia, Secretaria de Educación Pública, Córdoba 73, Aptdo. 15265, México, D.F. Ed: Eusebio Dávalos Hurtado. Art. on the archaeology, ethnography, anthropology and hist. of Mexico; doc. pv

20. INSTITUTO NACIONAL INDIGENISTA. MEMORIAS [National Indian Institute. Memoirs]. Irr. Instituto Nacional Indigenista, Paseo de la Reforma 336-3, México 5, D.F. pni

21. JUAN DIEGO. Revista guadalupana [Guadalupan review]. M. Aptdo. 63, Cuernavaca, Morelos. Illus. Pesos 15 /$2

22. LECTURA [Reading]. Revista crítica de ideas y libros [Critical review of ideas and books]. S-M. Pub. address: Aptdo. 545, Bolívar 23-4, México, D.F. Sum. Pesos 20

MEMORIA. MEMORIAS. For titles beginning with "Memoria" or "Memorias," followed by the name of the publishing or sponsoring institution or society, see the respective institution or society.

23. EL MEXICO ANTIGUO [Ancient Mexico]. Revista internacional de arqueología, etnología, folklore, prehistoria, historia antigua y lingüística mexicanas [International review of the archaeology, ethnology, folklore, prehistory, ancient history and linguistics of Mexico]. Irr. 1919 (1959: vol. 9). Sociedad Alemana Mexicanista, Aptdo. 318, México, D.F. Ed: Carmen Cook de Leonard. Art. within the range listed in the subtitle; mostly in Spanish, English and German and occasionally in French; sum. of each art. in two other languages. Pesos 45/ $ 5

24. MEXICO EN EL ARTE [Mexico in the arts]. M. Instituto Nacional de Bellas Artes Y Letras, Palacio de Bellas Artes, México, D.F. pni

25. MIRADOR [Spectator]. Revista de información bibliográfica [Review of bibliographical information]. Editorial Grijalbo, S.A., Aptdo. 28568, México 17, D.F. $ 3

26. MONUMENTOS COLONIALES [Colonial monuments]. B-M. Departamento de Monumentos Coloniales, Córdoba 47, México, D.F. Short art. on Mexican art and archaeology, with emphasis on the colonial period; illus. free

27. REVISTA DE HISTORIA DE AMERICA [Review of the history of America]. S-A. 1938 (1958: no. 46). Comisión de Historia, Instituto Panamericano de Geografía e Historia, Ex-Arzobispado 29, Tacubaya, México 18, D.F. Ed: Silvio Zavala. Art. principally on the hist. of Latin America; bk. rev.; ex-

tensive biblio. of bk. and periodicals pub. in Western languages on hist. and related fields, with notes or abstr., sometimes evaluative, classified by subject and country; notes on professional meetings; acad. news; list of pub. of the inst.; art. in Spanish, Portuguese, English or French. $6

REVISTA DE LA UNIVERSIDAD DE MEXICO see UNIVERSIDAD DE MEXICO, REVISTA DE LA...

REVISTA DE LA UNIVERSIDAD VERACRUZANA see UNIVERSIDAD VERACRUZANA, REVISTA DE LA...

28. REVISTA IBEROAMERICANA [Spanish-American review]. S-A (Irr.). Julio Jimina Rueda, Puebla 394, México, D.F. Pesos 4

29. REVISTA INTERNACIONAL Y DIPLOMATICA [International and diplomatic review]. Al servicio de la solidaridad americana [In the service of American solidarity]. M. Ed: Francisco Agüera Cenarro, Av. Independencia 72, 7° piso, México 1, D.F. Pesos 36

30. REVISTA MEXICANA DE ESTUDIOS ANTROPOLOGICOS [Mexican review of anthropological studies]. Irr. 1927 (1956/57: vol. 14). Sociedad Mexicana de Antropologia, Córdoba 45, México, D.F. Ed: Ignacio Bernal. Art. on anthropology and hist.; in Spanish and, occasionally, English, French and German. (memb.) Pesos 30 / $3

31. REVISTA MEXICANA DE SOCIOLOGIA [Mexican review of sociology]. 3 x y. Instituto de Investigaciones Sociales de la Universidad Nacional Autónoma de México, Torre de Humanidades, Ciudad Universitaria, México 20, D.F. Pesos 20/$1.50

32. SECRETARIA DE HACIENDA Y CREDITO PUBLICO, BOLETIN BIBLIOGRAFICO DE LA... [Bibliographical bulletin of the Secretariat of Public Finance and Credit]. S-M. 1954 (1959: no. 154). Biblioteca de la Secretária de Hacienda y Credito Público, Corre Mayor 31, México, D.F. Ed: Jesús Castanón Rodriguez. Art. on hist., archaeology, ethnology, linguistics and literature; biblio. Pesos 12 / $1

33. SOCIEDAD FOLKLORICA DE MEXICO, ANUARIO DE LA... [Yearbook of the Folklore Society of Mexico]. A. (Irr.). Sociedad Folklorica de México, Niños Héroes, 196-D, depto. 4, México, D.F. Pesos 10 / $1

34. SOCIEDAD MEXICANA DE GEOGRAFIA Y ESTADISTICA, BOLETIN DE LA... [Bulletin of the Mexican Society of Geography and Statistics]. B-M. Sociedad Mexicana de Geografía y Estadística, Calle del Maestro Justo Sierra 19, Aptdo. 10739, México, D.F. Pesos 20

35. TLATOANI [The speaker]. Q (Irr.). Luis G. León, Sociedad de Alumnos de la Escuela Nacional de Antropología e Historia, Moneda 13, México 1, D.F., for Instituto Nacional de Antropología e Historia. Pesos 15 / $2

36. UNIVERSIDAD DE MEXICO, REVISTA DE LA... [Review of the University of Mexico]. M. Universidad Nacional Autónoma de México, Edificio de la Rectoria, Ciudad Universitaria, México 20, D.F. Pesos 20 / $4

37. UNIVERSIDAD VERACRUZANA, REVISTA DE LA... [Review of the University of Veracruz]. Q. Universidad Veracruzana, Jalapa, Ver. pni

38. UNIVERSIDADES [Universities]. Q. Unión de Universidades de América Latina, Aptdo. 29802, México 18, D.F. Pesos 40 / $4

UNIVERSIDADES DE LATINOAMERICA see UNIVERSIDADES

39. YAN [Life]. Ciencias antropológicas [Anthropological sciences]. Irr. Centro de Investigaciones Antropológicas de México, Aptdo. 2242, México 1, D.F. Pesos 20 / p (1) $2

Nicaragua

Prepared with the assistance of

Guillermo Céspedes del Castillo, University of Seville

1. ACADEMIA DE GEOGRAFIA E HISTORIA DE NICARAGUA, REVISTA DE LA... [Review of the Academy of Geography and History of Nicaragua]. Irr. 1936 (mri 1952: vol. 11). Academia de Geografía e Historia de Nicaragua, Managua. Art. on Nicaraguan hist., principally in the 19th cent. and, to a lesser extent, on the earlier period of discovery and exploration, and on Central American geography; doc. pni

2. EDUCACION [Education]. Revista cultural [Cultural review]. Q. 1957 (1959: vol. 3). Ministerio de Educación Pública, Managua. Art. on cultural hist., contemporary culture, and education; biblio. pni

REVISTA DE LA ACADEMIA DE GEOGRAFIA E HISTORIA DE NICARAGUA see ACADEMIA DE GEOGRAFIA E HISTORIA DE NICARAGUA, REVISTA DE LA...

Panama

Prepared with the assistance of
Guillermo Céspedes del Castillo, University of Seville

1. ACADEMIA PANAMEÑA DE LA HISTORIA, BOLETIN DE LA... [Bulletin of the Panamanian Academy of History]. Q (Irr.). 1933 (mri 1954: 2nd series, vol. 11). Academía Panameña de la Historia, Aptdo. 973, Panamá. Art. on Panamanian hist. from the first European expeditions, and on the earlier native culture; news of the acad.; sum. pni

BOLETIN DE LA ACADEMIA PANAMEÑA DE LA HISTORIA see ACADEMÍA PANAMEÑA DE LA HISTORIA, BOLETIN DE LA...

2. UNIVERSIDAD [University]. Irr. Universidad de Panamá, Panamá. pni

Paraguay

Prepared with the assistance of
Guillermo Céspedes del Castillo, University of Seville

1. HISTORIA PARAGUAYA [Paraguayan history]. A. 1956 (1957: vol. 2). Instituto Paraguayo de Investigaciones Históricas, Asunción. Ed: Julio César Chaves, Estrella 151, Asunción. Art. on the hist. of Paraguay and papers read before the soc.; doc.; bk. rev.; news from hist. soc. in Spain and Latin America; index; illus. pni

Peru

Prepared with the assistance of

Guillermo Céspedes del Castillo, University of Seville

1. ARCHIVO HISTORICO DEL CUZCO, REVISTA DEL... [Review of the Historical Archives of Cuzco]. A. 1950 (1957: vol. 8). Universidad Nacional del Cuzco, Casilla 37, Cuzco, for Archivo Histórico del Cuzco. Ed: Jorge Cornejo Bouroncle. Art. on the hist. of Peru and of the arts; doc. and inventory of doc. in archives. pni

2. ARCHIVO NACIONAL DEL PERU, REVISTA DEL... [Review of the National Archives of Peru]. S-A. 1920 (1958: vol. 22). Archivo Nacional del Perú, Aptdo.1802, Lima. Ed: Oscar Malca Olguín. Art. on Peruvian hist. from the 16th to the 19th cent.; doc.; A. report of the director of the archives; illus.; index for vols. 1-18 (1920-46) in vol. 19. pni

3. ARCHIVOS PERUANOS DE FOLKLORE [Peruvian archives of folklore]. A. 1955 (mri 1956: vol. 2). Sociedad Peruana de Folklore, c/o Universidad Nacional del Cuzco, Casilla 361, Cuzco. Ed: Efrain Morote Best. Art. on the folklore, archaeology, ethnology and pre-Spanish hist. of Peru; news of the soc. p (1) Soles 10

4. BIBLIOTECA NACIONAL, BOLETIN DE LA ... [Bulletin of the National Library]. A. Biblioteca Nacional, Aptdo. 2335, Lima. pni

BOLETIN. For titles beginning with "Boletín," followed by the name of the publishing or sponsoring institution or society, see the respective institution or society.

5. BOLETIN BIBLIOGRAFICO [Bibliographical bulletin]. Q. Biblioteca Central, Universidad Nacional Mayor de San Marcos, Parque Universitario, Aptdo. 454, Lima. pni

6. CENTRO DE ESTUDIOS HISTORICO-MILITARES, REVISTA DEL... [Review of the Center for Historical-Military Studies]. Irr. 1948(mri 1954/55: vol. 8). Centro de Estudios Histórico-Militares, Cotabambas 494, Aptdo. 1785, Lima. Ed: Manuel Belaunde Guinassi. Art. on military and general hist.; biblio.; notes on the activities of the Center; professional news. pni

7. CHIMOR. A. 1953 (mri 1956: vol. 4). Museo de Arqueologia, Universidad Nacional de Trujillo, Trujillo. Art. on anthropology, archaeology and ethnology, principally of Peru; news of the museum; illus. pni

8. CUADERNOS DE INFORMACION BIBLIOGRAFICA [Papers on bibliographical information]. Irr. Seminario de Historia del Instituto Riva-Aguero, Pontificia Universidad Catolica del Perú, Aptdo. 1761, Lima. pni

9. CULTURA [Culture]. Q. Dirección de Cultura, Arqueología e Historia, Edificio del Ministerio de Educación, 13° piso, Lima. pni

10. CULTURA PERUANA [Peruvian culture]. M. Empresa Editora "La Crónica" y "Variedades," S.A., Casilla 2060, Lima. Illus. Soles 48/$ 6

11. DOCUMENTA. Irr. 1948 (1951-55 [1957]: vol. 3). Sociedad Peruana de Historia, Aptdo. 17, Miraflores, Lima. Art, including biblio. art., on South American hist., principally Peru, with emphasis on biographies; doc. pni

12. FACULTAD DE CIENCIAS ECONOMICAS Y COMERCIALES, REVISTA DE LA... [Review of the Faculty of Economic and Commercial Sciences]. S-A. Facultad de Ciencias Económicas y Comerciales, Universidad Mayor de San Marcos, Casilla 2031, Lima. Soles 15

13. FENIX [Phoenix]. Irr. Biblioteca Nacional, Departamento de Revistas y Periódicos, Aptdo. 2335, Lima. pni

14. FOLKLORE AMERICANO [American folklore]. Irr. 1953 (1957: no. 5). Comité Interamericano de Folklore, Av. Alfonso Ugarte 650, Casilla 3048, Lima. Ed: Luis E. Valcárcel. Art. on the folklore of the Western hemisphere and comparative studies of European folklore; biblio. pni

15. INSTITUTO AMERICANO DE ARTE, REVISTA DEL... [Review of the American Institute of Arts]. A. Instituto Americano de Arte, Av. Santa Clara 521, Casilla 281, Cuzco. Soles 25

16. INSTITUTO RIVA AGÜERO, BOLETIN DEL... [Bulletin of the Riva Aguero Institute]. Irr. 1951/52 (mri 1953/55: vol. 2). Pontificia Universidad Católica del Perú, Aptdo. 1761, Lima, for Instituto Riva Agüero. Ed: Victor Andrés Belaunde. Art. on philosophy and the hist. of ideas and literature. pni

17. LETRAS [Letters]. S-A. Facultad de Letras, Universidad Nacional Mayor de San Marcos, Aptdo. 7405, Lima. pni

18. MERCURIO PERUANO [Peruvian Mercury]. Revista mensual de ciencias sociales y letras [Monthly review of social sciences and letters]. M. Pub. address: Aptdo. 1000, Lima. Soles 80

19. MUSEO E INSTITUTO ARQUEOLOGICO, REVISTA DEL... [Review of the Museum and Institute of Archaeology]. Irr. 1948 (1959: no. 18). Universidad Nacional del Cuzco, Calle Tigre 8, Cuzco, for Museo e Instituto Arqueologíco. Art. on archaeology, toponymy, geology and hist. of Peru, pertaining to the pre-Spanish period; illus. pni

20. MUSEO NACIONAL, REVISTA DEL... [Review of the National Museum]. A. 1932 (1957: vol. 26). Biblioteca del Museo Nacional de Historia, Aptdo. 3048, Lima. Art. on the hist., archaeology, ethnology, and linguistics of Latin America, principally Peru; biblio. pni

21. MUSEO NACIONAL DE ANTROPOLOGIA Y ARQUEOLOGIA, REVISTA DEL... [Review of the National Museum of Anthropology and Archaeology]. Irr. Museo Nacional de Antropología e Historia, Magdalena Vieja, Lima. pni

22. PERU INDIGENA [Indian Peru]. 2 x y. 1948 (mri 1956: vol. 17). Instituto Indigenista Peruano, Ministerio del Trabajo y Asuntos Indígenas, 4° piso,

Av. Salaverry, Lima. Ed: Manuel D. Velazco. Art. on the anthropology, ethnology, hist., folklore, and philology of Peru; biblio. Soles 100/$4

REVISTA. For titles beginning with "Revista," followed by the name of the publishing or sponsoring institution or society, see the respective institution or society.

23. REVISTA DE DERECHO Y CIENCIAS POLITICAS [Review of law and political science]. S-A. Facultad de Derecho, Universidad Nacional Mayor de San Marcos, Aptdo. 524, Lima. $2.50

24. REVISTA HISTORICA [Historical review]. A. 1905 (mri 1955/56: vol. 22). Instituto Histórico del Perú, Giron Ucayali 478, Lima. Ed: Manuel Moreyra Paz Soldán, Santa Luisa 295, San Isidro, Lima. Art. on all periods of the hist. of Peru and South America; doc.; news of the inst.; occasional bk. rev. pni

25. REVISTA MILITAR DEL PERU [Military review of Peru]. B-M. 1937 (1958: no. 649). Ministerio de Guerra, Jiron Ancash 676, Aptdo. 2483, Lima. Ed: Mayor Abel Carrera Naranjo. Art. on the military hist. of Peru and, to a lesser extent, South America and Europe; doc.; illus. Soles 36/Soles 50

26. REVISTA PERUANA DE CIENCIAS JURIDICAS Y SOCIALES [Peruvian review of juridical and social sciences]. Q. Carabaya 1126, Oficinas 104-105, Lima. p (1) Soles 30

27. REVISTA UNIVERSITARIA [University review]. S-A. Universidad Nacional del Cuzco, Dept. de Extensión Cultural, Plaza de Armas, Casilla 167, Cuzco. pni

28. REVISTA UNIVERSITARIA [University review]. S-A. Universidad Nacional de Trujillo, Aptdo. 315, Trujillo. pni

29. SOCIEDAD GEOGRAFICA DE LIMA, BOLETIN DE LA... [Bulletin of the Geographical Society of Lima]. Q (Irr). Sociedad Geográfica de Lima, Calle Padre Jerónimo 456, altos, Aptdo. 1176, Lima. Maps, illus. pni

30. TRADICION [Tradition]. Revista peruano de cultura [Peruvian review of culture]. Irr. Grupo Tradición del Perú, Aptdo. 361, Cuzco. pni

Puerto Rico

Prepared with the assistance of
Guillermo Céspedes del Castillo, University of Seville

1. ASOMANTE [A coined word used in the sense of "ascendant" -- ed.]. Q. Asociación de Graduadas de la Universidad de Puerto Rico, Aptdo. 1142, San Juan. $ 4/$ 4.50

2. HISTORIA [History]. S-A. 1951 (mri 1956: vol. 6). Universidad de Puerto Rico, Rio Piedras, for Sociedad Nacional Honoraria de Historia, Phi Alpha Theta, Capitulo Beta Delta. Ed: Luis M. Diaz Saler, Enrique Lugo Silva. Art. on hist. and social sciences, with special reference to Puerto Rico, the United States, and modern Europe; bk. rev.; news of the soc.; in English and Spanish. p (1) $ 0.60

3. INSTITUTO DE CULTURA PUERTORRIQUEÑA, REVISTA DEL... [Review of the Institute of Puerto Rican Culture]. Q. Instituto de Cultura Puertorriqueña, San Juan. pni

4. REVISTA DE CIENCIAS SOCIALES [Review of social sciences]. Q. Colegio de Ciencias Sociales de la Universidad de Puerto Rico, Rio Piedras. Ed: Raul Serrano Geyls. Art. on philosophy, sociology, social hist. and politics, with special reference to Puerto Rico; biblio.; English sum. $ 3

REVISTA DEL INSTITUTO DE CULTURA PUERTORRIQUEÑA see INSTITUTO DE CULTURA PUERTORRIQUEÑA, REVISTA DEL...

5. REVISTA JURIDICA DE LA UNIVERSIDAD DE PUERTO RICO [Legal review of the University of Puerto Rico]. B-M (Irr). Colegio de Derecho, Universidad de Puerto Rico, Rio Piedras. $ 5

6. LA TORRE [The tower]. Q. Universidad de Puerto Rico, Rio Piedras. $ 1.50

UNIVERSIDAD DE PUERTO RICO, REVISTA JURIDICA DE LA see REVISTA JURIDICA DE LA UNIVERSIDAD DE PUERTO RICO

Uruguay

Prepared with the assistance of

Armando D. Pirotto, President of the Comité Uruguay de Ciencias Históricas, Montevideo,
and
Guillermo Céspedes del Castillo, University of Seville

ANALES DE LA UNIVERSIDAD see UNIVERSIDAD, ANALES DE LA..

1. ARCHIVO GENERAL ADMINISTRATIVO, REVISTA DEL... [Review of the General Administrative Archives]. Colección de Documentos para Servir al Estudio de la Historia de la República Oriental del Uruguay [Collection of documents serving the study of the history of the Republic of Uruguay]. Irr. 1887 (mri 1953: vol. 18). Archivo General de la Nación, Convención No. 1474, Montevideo. Doc. on Uruguayan hist.; biblio. pv

2. BOLETIN HISTORICO [Historical bulletin]. S-A. 1928 (1959: no. 80). Estado Mayor General del Ejército, Soriano 1090, Montevideo. Ed: Luis E. Tolosa. Art. on military hist.; doc.; bk. rev. pni

3. ESTUARIO [Estuary]. 3 x y. 1958 (1959: no. 4). Sociedad Geográfica del Uruguay, 18 de Julio 1828, Montevideo. Art. on the hist. and geography of Uruguay. p (1) $0.20

4. FACULTAD DE HUMANIDADES Y CIENCIAS, REVISTA DE LA... [Review of the Faculty of Humanities and Sciences]. A. 1948 (1959: no. 11). Facultad de Humanidades y Ciencias, Cerrito 75, Montevideo. Art. on hist., philology, literature and sciences; bk. rev.; illus. $0.50

5. INSTITUTO HISTORICO Y GEOGRAFICO DEL URUGUAY, REVISTA DEL... [Review of the Institute of History and Geography of Uruguay]. A. 1916 (1959: no. 38). Instituto Histórico y Geográfico del Uruguay, 18 de Julio 1195, Montevideo. Ed: Ariosto D. González. Art. on hist., with emphasis on Uruguay; biblio.; news of the inst. p (1) $1.20

REVISTA. For titles beginning with "Revista," followed by the name of the publishing or sponsoring institution or society, see the respective institution or society.

6. REVISTA DE ARQUEOLOGIA [Review of archaeology]. Irr. 1927 (195 vol. 16). Sociedad de Amigos de la Arqueología, 18 de Julio 1195, Montevideo. Art. on Uruguayan prehist., early hist., and paleo-anthropology; bk. rev.; illus. p (1)$1

REVISTA HISTORICA see REVISTA HISTORICA DE LA UNIVERSIDAD

7. REVISTA HISTORICA DE LA UNIVERSIDAD [Historical review of the University]. S-A. 1907 (1959: no. 85). Instituto de Investigaciones Históricas de la Facultad de Humanidades y Ciencias, Universidad de Montevideo, Juan Lindolfo Cuestas 15-25, Montevideo. Art. on the hist. of Uruguay; doc.; bk. re

illus. Pub. for some time by the Archivo y Museo Histórico Nacional, Rincón 429, Montevideo, under the title: Revista Histórica. p (1) $0.50

8. REVISTA NACIONAL [National review]. Literatura - Arte - Ciencia [Literature - arts - science]. M. 1938 (1959: no. 198). Ministério de Instrucción Pública, 25 de Mayo 350, Montevideo. Art. on hist., literature, art and philosophy. p (1) $0.20

9. SOCIEDAD DE AMIGOS DE LA ARQUEOLOGIA, REVISTA DE LA... [Review of the Society of Friends of Archaeology]. A. Sociedad de Amigos de la Arqueología, 18 de Julio 1195, Montevideo. Ed. board: Juan Giuría, Horacio Arredondo, Simón Lucuix. Art. on the archaeology and numismatics of Uruguay; cultural notes; news of the soc. pni

10. UNIVERSIDAD, ANALES DE LA... [Annals of the University]. Irr. 1889 (1958: vol. 42). Universidad de Montevideo, 18 de Julio 1828, Montevideo. Art. on hist. and its auxiliary disciplines, and on philosophy, literature and the sciences; bk. rev.; professional and univ. news; illus. p (1) $1

Venezuela

Prepared with the assistance of

Guillermo Céspedes del Castillo, University of Seville

1. ACADEMIA NACIONAL DE LA HISTORIA, BOLETIN DE LA... [Bulletin of the National Academy of History]. Q. 1912 (1958: vol. 41). Imprenta Nacional, Caracas, for Academia Nacional de la Historia. Ed. board: José Nucete-Sardi, Héctor García Chuecos, Héctor Parra Márquez. Art. on the hist. of Latin American countries; lectures; biographies; biblio., dealing predominantly with the hist. of Latin America; news and notes of the acad.; illus. pni

2. ACTA VENEZOLANA [Venezuelan records]. Q. Grupo de Caracas de la Sociedad Interamericana de Antropología y Geografía. pni

ANALES DE LA UNIVERSIDAD CENTRAL DE VENEZUELA see UNIVERSIDAD CENTRAL DE VENEZUELA, ANALES DE LA...

3. ANTROPOLOGICA. Irr. Sociedad de Ciencias Naturales La Salle, Colegio La Salle, Aptdo. 681, Caracas. Illus. Short monographs pub. separately as supplements. pni

4. ARCHIVO GENERAL DE LA NACION, BOLETIN DEL... [Bulletin of the General Archives of the Nation]. Q. 1923 (1958: vol. 45). Imprenta Nacional Santa Capilla a Carmelitas, Caracas, for Archivo General de la Nación, Ministerio de Justicia. Ed: Héctor García Chuecos. Doc. and indices of doc. on Venezuelan hist.; biographical notes (indexed); list of pub. received (mainly from the Latin American countries and the U.S.). pni

5. ARCHIVOS VENEZOLANOS DE FOLKLORE [Venezuelan archives of Folklore]. A.(B). Instituto de Antropología e Historia, Facultad de Humanidades y Educación, Universidad Central de Venezuela, Caracas. p (1) Bs 3

BOLETIN DE LA ACADEMIA NACIONAL DE LA HISTORIA see ACADEMIA NACIONAL DE LA HISTORIA, BOLETIN DE LA...

BOLETIN DEL ARCHIVO GENERAL DE LA NACION see ARCHIVO GENERAL DE LA NACION, BOLETIN DEL...

6. CRONICA DE CARACAS [Chronicles of Caracas]. Q. Consejo Municipal del Distrito Federal, Caracas. Local hist., current events, arts and letters; short biblio. comments; illus. pni

7. CULTURA UNIVERSITARIA [University culture]. B-M. Dirección de Cultura, Universidad Central de Venezuela, Caracas. pni

8. EDUCACION [Education]. Revista para el magisterio [Review for the teacher]. B-M (Irr.). Ministerio de Educación Nacional, Dirección de Cultura y Bellas Artes, Caracas. free

9. EL FAROL [The lantern]. B-M. Creole Petroleum Corporación, Aptdo. 889, Caracas. Culture, art, and national and Latin American hist. free

10. GACETA INDIGENISTA [Indian gazette]. M. Edificio Lincoln, Sabana Grande, Caracas. pni

11. LA RAZA [Race]. 10 x y (Irr.). Maximiliano von Lowenthal, Avenida José Félix Rivas, Quinta "Clarita," La Castellana, Caracas. Politics, society, culture, and Venezuelan and Latin American hist.; illus.

REVISTA. **For titles beginning with "Revista," followed by the name of the publishing or sponsoring institution or society, see the respective institution or society.**

12. REVISTA NACIONAL DE CULTURA [National review of culture]. B-M. Ministerio de Educación Nacional, Dirección de Cultura y Bellas Artes, Caracas. pni

13. REVISTA SHELL [Shell review]. Q. Companía Shell de Venezuela, Aptdo. 809, Caracas. free

14. SOCIEDAD BOLIVARIANA DE VENEZUELA, REVISTA DE LA ... [Review of the Bolivar Society of Venezuela]. Q. 1939 (1959: vol. 18). Sociedad Bolivariana de Venezuela, Cují a Salvador de Leon 6, Caracas. Ed. board: Cristóbal L. Mendoza, J. A. Escalona, Lino Iribarren. Art. on the life, activities, influence and epoch of Simón Bolívar; doc.; biblio.; news of the soc.; illus. pni

15. SOCIEDAD VENEZOLANA DE HISTORIA DE MEDICINA, REVISTA DE LA... [Review of the Venezuelan Society of the History of Medicine]. Irr. (3 x y). 1953 (1958: vol. 6). Sociedad Venezolana de Historia de Medicina, Caracas. Art. on the hist. of medicine in Venezuela; some general art.; occasionally pub. as a monograph with biblio. and index; illus. pni

16. UNIVERSIDAD CENTRAL DE VENEZUELA, ANALES DE LA... [Annals of the Central University of Venezuela]. Irr. Universidad Central de Venezuela, Caracas. pni

17. UNIVERSIDAD DEL ZULIA, REVISTA DE LA... [Review of the University of Zulia]. Q. Universidad del Zulia, Maracaibo. pni

18. VIEJO Y RARO [Old and rare]. M. Aptdo. 4654, Este, Caracas. p (1) Bs 2/ $2.25 (quarterly subscription)

NEAR AND MIDDLE EAST

Afghanistan

1. AFGHANISTAN. Q. Anjumane Tareekh [Hist. Soc.], Afghan Acad., Kabul. Director: Ahmed Ali Kohzad. Art. on the hist. of Afghanistan; in English and French.

2. ARYANA [Pertaining to the Aryans]. M. Anjumane Tareekh [Hist. Soc.], Afghan Acad., Kabul. Director: Ahmed Ali Kohzad. Art. on the hist. of Afghanistan; in Persian.

3. LITERATURE QUARTERLY. Q. Faculty of Literature, Univ. of Kabul, Kabul. Ed: Abdul Ahad.

4. POLITICAL SCIENCE AND LAW QUARTERLY. Q. Faculty of Law, Univ. of Kabul, Kabul. Ed: F.R. Farid.

Iran

Prepared with the assistance of the
National Library, Tehran

Note: Persian words in this list have been transliterated according to the system used by the National Library, Tehran.

1. AMOUZECH VA PARVARESH [Teaching and education]. M. Pub. Dept., Ministry of Education, Tehran. Rls 100

2. ANDISHEH VA HONAR [Art and craftsmanship]. M. Djavad Pour Vakili, Khiaban Ferdowsi, Kouche Club, Tehran. Rls 180

3. ARMAGHAN [Gift]. M. Nasime Dastgherdi, Kiaban Iran, Tehran. Rls 200 / $ 5

4. ATTELAAT MAHANEH [Monthly information]. M. Massudi, Tehran. p (1) Rls 20

5. BANK SAKHTEMANI, MAJALLEH... [Journal of the Bank of Construction]. M. Nasser Badii, Khiaban Ramsar, Tehran, for Bank Sakhtemani. Rls 250

6. DANESHKADEH ADABIYAT TABRIZ, MAJALLEH... [Journal of the Faculty of Letters of the University of Tabriz]. Q. Daneshkadeh Adabiyat Tabriz, Tabriz. Rls 70

7. DANESHKADEH ADABIYAT TEHRAN, MAJALLEH... [Journal of the Faculty of Letters of the University of Tehran]. Q. Daneshkadeh Adabiyat Tehran, Tehran. Rls 70

8. FARHANGE-IRAN ZAMIN [Iranian review]. Q. Iradj Afshar, P.O.B. 1021, Tehran. Rls 250 / $ 4

MAJALLEH. For titles beginning with "Majalleh," followed by the name of the publishing or sponsoring institution or society, see the respective institution or society.

9. MAJALLEH MOUALEM [Teachers' journal]. M. Organization of the B.A. of Teachers' College, Khiaban Ghavam-Saltaneh, Tehran. Rls 150

10. MARDOM SHENASI [Anthropology]. Q. Institute d'Anthropologie, Tehran. Rls 300

11. MOUSIGHI [Music]. M. Faculty of Art, Khiaban Daneshkadeh, Tehran. Rls 120

12. MOUZIC IRAN [Iranian music]. M. Bahman Heerbud, Khiaban Khayam, Tehran. Rls 180

13. NAGHSHE NEGHAR [Painting and decoration]. Q. Fine Arts Dept., Office of Pub. and Art Relations, Tehran. Rls 100 / $ 1.5

14. NAMAYESH [Theater]. Q. General Administration of Fine Arts, Baharestan, Tehran. Rls 80 / $ 1

15. PAYAME NOVIN [New message]. M. Mehdi Bayani, for Anjuman Ravabete Iran ba Chouravi [Iranian-Soviet Relations Soc.], Khiaban Vassal, Tehran. Rls 150

16. SADAF [Shell]. M. Ahmad Azeemi Zavarehi, Khiaban Ekbatan, Tehran. Rls 150

17. SEPEIDEH FARDA [The dawn of tomorrow]. M. Teachers' College, Tehran. Rls 220

18. SOKHAN [Tale]. M. Anjuman Doustdaran Sokhan, Khiaban Hafez, Chaharah College, Tehran. Rls 200

19. TOOSHEH [Provisions]. M. Edward Joseph and Mahin Afshar Ghasemlou, Shah-Reza, Tehran. Rls 160

20. VEZARAT GOMROKAT VA INHESARAT, MAJALLEH... [Journal of the Ministry of Customs and Monopolies]. M. Vezarat Gomrokat va Inhesarat, Tehran. p (1) Rls 20

21. YAGHMA [Plunder]. M. Habib-i-Yaghma-i, Shah-Abad, Tehran. Rls 200

Iraq

Prepared with the assistance of the
Ministry of Guidance, Republic of Iraq, Baghdad

1. AL-ADIB AL-IRAQI [Iraqi littérateur]. M. Al-Makhzumi, c/o Itihad al-Udabaa al-Iraqiyin, Baghdad.

2. AL-FIKR [Thought]. B-M. M. Jawad Gadban, c/o Al-Fikr, Baghdad.

3. AL-GHARI. A.R.S. al-Iraqayn, Najaf.

4. AL-HUQOOQ [Law]. W. Saleh Naji, c/o Al-Huqooq, Baghdad.

5. AL-MAARIF [Knowledge]. M.H. al-Talkani, c/o Al-Maarif, Najaf.

MAJALLAT AL-MAJMAʿ AL-ʿILMI AL-ʿIRAQI see MAJMAʿ AL-ʿILMI AL-ʿIRAQI, MAJALLAT AL-...

6. MAJMAʿ AL-ʿILMI AL-ʿIRAQI, MAJALLAT AL-... [Bulletin of the Iraqi Academy]. Irr. Majmaʿ al-ʿIlmi al-ʿIraqi, Baghdad. pni

7. AL-MUTHAQAF [The intellectual]. B-M. Mahdi Murtada, c/o Al-Muthaqaf, Baghdad.

8. AL-NAJAF. H. Fayadh, c/o Al-Najaf, Najaf.

9. SUMER. A Journal of Archaeology in Iraq. Majallah ʿIlmiyah Tabḥath fi āthar al-ʿIraq al-Qadimah. S-A. 1945 (1958: vol. 14). Directorate-General of Antiquities, Baghdad. Ed: Sadiq Hadi El-Hasani. · Reports and art. mainly on excavations and archaeological finds in Iraq and on museum holdings, with special reference to the activities of the Directorate-General; mainly in English and Arabic, but occasionally also in French and German. ID 1 / $ 4.50

10. AL-TATAWOR [Evolution]. W. Amer Abdullah, c/o Al-Tatawor, Baghdad.

11. AL-TAWABEA' [Stamps]. Q. Stamps Soc., Baghdad.

12. AL-THAQAFA AL-ISLAMIA [Islamic culture]. A.J. Ahdami, c/o Al-Thaqafa al-Islamia, Baghdad.

13. AL-THAQAFA ALJADIDA [Modern culture]. B-M. Salah Khalis, c/o Al-Thaqafa Aljadida, Baghdad.

Israel

Prepared with the assistance of

E. Pfeffermann, Jewish National and University Library, Jerusalem

1. ASUPOTH [Collections]. A Publication Devoted to the History of the Labour Movement. Irr. 1945 (1957: vol. 5). Archives and Museum of the Jewish Labour Movement, P.O.B. 303, Tel-Aviv. Art. on the Jewish labor movement; doc. and photographs from the archives of the General Federation of Jewish Labour in Israel; table of contents also in English. pni

2. 'ATIQOT [Antiquities]. Irr. 1955 (mri 1955: vol. 1). Dept. of Antiquities, Ministry of Education and Culture, Govt. of Israel, P.O.B. 586, Jerusalem. Reports on the archaeological activities of the dept. in Israel. Appears in two separate editions, one in English (containing also art. in French) and the other in Hebrew. IL 4 / $3

3. BETH MIKRA [The house of scriptures]. Q. Israel Soc. for Biblical Research, P.O.B. 7024, Jerusalem. pni

BITRÀZON see section on the United States of America

4. ERETZ-ISRAEL [The land of Israel]. Archaeological, Historical and Geographical Studies. A. (Irr.). 1951 (1958: vol. 5). Israel Exploration Soc., P.O.B. 7041, Jerusalem. Ed: M. Avi-Yonah, H.Z. Hirschberg, Y. Yadin, H. Tadmor. Art. on the archaeology and hist. of Palestine in Biblical and post-Biblical times; reports on recent archaeological discoveries in Israel; separate Hebrew and English sections; Hebrew sum. of English art. and English sum. of Hebrew art.; illus. pv (vol. 1-4: IL 11 each / $ 10 each; vol. 5: IL 15 / $ 12)

5. HAMIZRAḤ HEḤADASH [The new East]. Israel Oriental Soc., c/o Hebrew Univ., Jerusalem. English sum.; table of contents also in English. IL 5 / $ 6

6. HEAWAR [The past]. A Quarterly Devoted to the History of the Russian Jews. Irr. 1952/53 (1957: vol. 5). "Althira," Assoc. for the Study of Russia and the Ukraine, P.O.B. 118, Tel-Aviv. Ed: Benzion Katz, Baruch Caron. Art. on the hist. of the Russian Jews; doc.; biblio.; table of contents also in English. pni

7. ISRAEL EXPLORATION JOURNAL. Q. 1950/51 (1958: vol. 8). Israel Exploration Soc., P.O.B. 7041, Jerusalem. Ed. board: M. Avi-Yonah (chief ed.), A. Malamat, U. Ben-Horin, Hebrew Univ. of Jerusalem. Art. on the hist. and archaeology of Biblical and later periods, and on geography, geology, soil science and natural hist. pertaining to Israel and the Near East; rev. of bk. and art.; reports on excavations and explorations; professional news; letters to the ed.; in English or French; illus. IL 7 / $ 6

8. KOROTH [Chronicles]. A Quarterly Journal Devoted to the History of Medicine and Science. S-A. 1952 (1959: vol. 2). Israel Soc. of the Hist. of Medicine and Science, 54 St. of the Prophets, Jerusalem. Ed: Süssmann Muntner.

Art. on medical and scientific hist.; proceedings of the soc. and professional news; bk. rev.; English sum.; author index (in Hebrew and English) and subject index. IL 6 / $ 3

MEASSEF see ZION

9. SCRIPTA HIEROSOLYMITANA. Irr. 1954 (1959: vol. 5). Magnes Press, Hebrew Univ., P.O.B. 503, Jerusalem. In English. All art. in a vol. are devoted to a particular field in the humanities (previous vol. devoted to law, classics, Jewish Hellenism, medieval and modern thought and literature). pni

10. SINAI. A Monthly for Torah, Science and Literature. M. Inst. of Rabbi Kook, P.O.B. 642, Jerusalem. IL 5 / $ 5

11. SURA. Israeli-American Annual for Study and Research in Problems Relating to Israel and the World in the Past and Present. A. Sura Inst. for Research and Pub., P.O.B. 739, Jerusalem, and Yeshiva Univ., Amsterdam Ave. and 186th St., New York 33, N.Y. Table of contents in Hebrew and English. pni

12. TARBIZ [Academy]. A Quarterly for Jewish Studies. Q. Magnes Press, Hebrew Univ., P.O.B. 503, Jerusalem. English sum. IL 8 / $ 6

13. YAD-WASHEM STUDIES ON THE EUROPEAN JEWISH CATASTROPHE AND RESISTANCE. Irr. 1957 (1959: vol. 3). Pub. Dept., Jewish Agency, P.O.B. 7044, Jerusalem, for Yad-Washem Remembrance Authority. Ed. board: Benzion Dinur, Joseph Melkman, Shaul Esh, Joseph Kermish. Art. on the destruction of European Jewry during the Second World War; doc. Appears in separate English and Hebrew editions. pni

14. YEDIOT HA-HEBRA LE-HAKIRAT EREZ YISRAEL WE-ATIKOTEHA [Bulletin of the Israel Exploration Society]. Q (2 double no. p.a.). 1933/34 (1958: vol. 22). Israel Exploration Soc., P.O.B. 7041, Jerusalem. Ed: B. Mazar, A. Malamat, Hebrew Univ., Jerusalem. Art. on the archaeology and hist. of Palestine in Biblical and post-Biblical times; reports on the activities of the soc.; English sum.; table of contents in Hebrew and English; illus. pni

15. ZION. Rivon le-ḥeḳer toledot Yisrael [A quarterly for research in Jewish history]. Q. 1935/36 (1958: vol. 23). Hist. Soc. of Israel, P.O.B. 1062 Jerusalem. Ed. board: I.F. Baer, D. Dinur, I. Halpern, 9 Shlomzion Hamalka St., Jerusalem. Art. on the archaeology of Palestine and on Jewish hist., not confined to any period or area; doc.; professional news and reports of the soc. and the Jewish Hist. General Archives; English sum.; table of contents also in English; cum. indices of authors, subjects and areas, in Hebrew and English, for vol. 1-20 pub. separately in 1955. Supersedes Meassef, pub. irr. from 1925 to 1934. IL 5 (memb.) / $5

Jordan

Prepared with the assistance of the

Ministry of Education of the Hashemite Kingdom of Jordan, Amman

1. PROCHE-ORIENT CHRETIEN [The Christian Near East]. Q. Direction des Professeurs du Séminaire Sainte-Anne, B.P. 79, Jerusalem (Arab Zone). In French. DJ 1/ $ 3.50

2. STUDII BIBLICI FRANCISCANI. LIBER ANNUS [Franciscan Biblical studies. Yearbook]. A. 1950/51 (1956/57: vol. 7). Apud Aedem Flagellationis, Jerusalem (Old City, Arab Zone), for Studium Biblicum Franciscanum, Jerusalem (Old City, Arab Zone). Art. on all aspects of Biblical and ecclesiastical hist. and Biblical archaeology; in Latin, French, Italian and English. pni

3. TIERRA SANTA [Holy Land]. M. 1921 (1959: vol. 34). Convento de San Salvador, P.O.B. 4136, Jerusalem (Old City), for Custodia de Tierra Santa. Ed: P.F. Andres. Art. mainly on the Christian Church in the Holy Land; notices; in Spanish; charts, illus.

Lebanon

Prepared with the assistance of

Members of the Arab Studies Program of the American University of Beirut

Note: Arabic words in this list have been transliterated according to the system used by the American University of Beirut and the Journal of the Royal Asiatic Society of Great Britain and Ireland, London.

1. AL-ABHĀTH [Studies]. Q. American Univ. of Beirut, Beirut. LL 9

2. AWRĀQ LUBNĀNIYYAH [Lebanese papers]. M. Yousef I. Yazbek, Hadeth, Beirut. pni

3. AL-DIRĀSĀT AL ADABIYYAH [Literary studies]. Fi al-thagafatayn al-ʻarabiyyah wa al-fānisiyyah wa-tafāʻulihima [Dealing with the Arab and Persian cultures and their mutual influence on each other]. Q. 1959 (1960: vol. 2). Al-Jāmiʻah al-Lubnāniyyah Qism al-lughag al-fārisiyyah wa-ādābiha [Lebanese Univ., Dept. of Persian Language and Literature], Beirut. Art. on Arab and Persian hist. and literature; rev. of Arab and Persian bk. in the field; in Arabic and Persian.

4. AL-ʻIRFĀN [Knowledge]. M. Shaykh Aḥmad ʻĀrif al-Zayn, Sidon. LL 10

5. AL-MASARRAH [Goodwill]. M. St. Paul's Mission, Ḥarīṣa. LL 8 / $5

6. AL-MASHRIQ [The Levant]. B-M. Ed: ʻAbduh Khalifa, S.J., Université St. Joseph, Beirut. LL 25

MELANGES DE L'UNIVERSITE SAINT JOSEPH see UNIVERSITE SAINT JOSEPH, MELANGES DE L'...

7. MIDDLE EAST FORUM. 10xy. Alumni Assoc. of the American Univ. of Beirut, P.O.B. 751, Beirut. LL 15 / $5

8. MUḤĀḌARĀT AL-NADWAH [Conferences of the Cenacle]. Q. Michel Asmar, Cénacle Libanais, Beirut. In Arabic and French. LL 15

9. UNIVERSITE SAINT JOSEPH, MELANGES DE L ... [Miscellany of the University of St. Joseph]. A. (1957 : vol. 34). Imprimerie Catholique, Beirut. Art. on Arab hist., philology and philosophy, particularly on its relations with classical (Greek and Roman) culture, and on archaeology; doc.; biblio.; rev. of bk. and periodicals, classified by subject; biblio.; illus.; graph. pv (LL 18-LL 35)

Turkey

Prepared with the assistance of the
Milli Kütüphane, Bibliyografya Enstitüsü
[National Library, Bibliographical Institute], Ankara

1. ANATOLIA. Revue annuelle d'archéologie [Annual review of archaeology]. A. 1956. Ankara Üniversitesi, Dil ve Tarih-Coğrafya Fakültesi, Arkeoloji Enstitüsü [Faculty of Languages, Hist. and Geography, Archaeological Inst., Ankara Univ.], Ankara. . Art. on archaeology, hist. (including the hist. of art) and philology with special reference to Turkey; biblio. notes and rev.; reports; in Turkish, French, German or English. TL 4

2. ANKARA ÜNİVERSİTESİ DİL VE TARİH-COĞRAFYA FAKÜLTESİ DERGİSİ [Review of the Faculty of Languages, History and Geography, University of Ankara]. Q. 1942 (1958: vol. 15). Ankara Üniversitesi Dil ve Tarih-Coğrafya Fakültesi, Ankara. Art. on hist., not confined to any country or period, paleontology, geography, philosophy, religion and literature; bk. rev.; biblio.; in Turkish and a Western language. pni

ANNALES DE L'UNIVERSITE D'ANKARA see UNIVERSITE D'ANKARA, ANNALES DE L'...

3. AZERBAYCAN [Azerbaijan]. Monthly Cultural Review. M. Azerbaycan Kültür Derneği [Cultural Soc. of Azerbaijan], Vakıf İş Hanı No. 324, Anafartalar. Art. on the hist. and culture of Azerbaijan. TL 6 / TL 12

4. BELLETEN [Bulletin]. Q. 1937 (1958: vol. 22). Türk Tarih Kurumu [Turkish Hist. Soc.], Ankara. Ed: Uluğ Iğdemir. Art. on the culture and hist., including prehist., of the Turkish people; doc.; bk. rev.; news on the activities of the soc.; lists of bk. and periodicals received; in Turkish and, occasionally, English or another Western language; table of contents in Turkish and French; illus.; graph. TL 144 / $ 16

5. HARP TARİHİ VESİKALARİ DERGİSİ [Review of the documents of the history of war]. Q. 1952 (1958: no vol. indic.). Erkâni Harbiyei Umumiye Reisliği Harb Tarihi Dairesi Beşkanlığı [Office of the Chief, General Staff, Directorate of the War Hist. Department], Ankara. Rev. of doc. relating to Turkish hist., with emphasis on Turkey's war of independence; reproductions of original doc. Pub. as a supplement to the Ordu Dergisi [Army review]. p (1) T Kr 150

HISTORICAL RESEARCHES see TARİH ARAŞTIRMALARI

6. İLÂHİYAT FAKÜLTESİ DERGİSİ [Review of the Faculty of Theology]. Q (sometimes combined no.). 1952. Ankara Üniversitesi İlâhiyat Fakültesi Dekanlıgı [Dean of the Faculty of Theology, Univ. of Ankara], Ankara. Art. on the hist. of Turkey, Islam and Islamic art; bk. rev.; biblio. pni

7. İSLÂM TETKİKLERİ ENSTİTÜSÜ DERGİSİ [Review of the Islamic Research Institute]. Irr. 1953 (1957: vol. 2). İstanbul Üniversitesi Edebiyat Fakültesi [Faculty of Literature, Univ. of Istanbul], İstanbul. Art. on Islamic hist. and art and on related subjects; bk. rev.; title page also in English. pni

8. İSTANBUL ENSTİTÜSÜ DERGİSİ [Review of the Istanbul Institute]. A. 1955 (1958: no vol. indic.). İstanbul Enstitüsü [Istanbul Inst.], İstanbul. Art. on the hist., geography, archaeology, art, language, literature and folklore of Istanbul; bk. rev.; doc.; in Turkish and foreign languages; A. author index. p (1) TL 12.50

9. İSTANBUL ÜNİVERSİTESİ EDEBİYAT FAKÜLTESİ TARİH DERGİSİ [Historical review of the Faculty of Literature, University of Istanbul]. A. 1949. İstanbul Üniversitesi Edebiyat Fakültesi, Bayezit-İstanbul. Ed: M. Cavit Baysun, Cemal Tukin, M. Münir Aktepe. Art. on the hist. of Turkey and other countries, covering all periods but with emphasis on the modern period; bk. rev.; biblio. pni

10. ORDU DERGİSİ [Army review]. Q. Erkânı Harbiyei Umumiye Reisliği Egitim Dairesi Baskanlığı [Directorate of the Training Department, Office of the Chief of the General Staff], Ankara. Art. and doc. about the hist. of war. pni

11. ŞARKİYAT MECMUASI [Oriental review]. A. İstanbul Üniversitesi Şarkiyat Enstitüsü, Üniversite İstanbul [Oriental Inst., Univ. of Istanbul], İstanbul. pni

12. SEBİLÜRREŞAD. M. Eşref Edip, 87 Ankara Caddesi, İstanbul. Art. on Islam and Turkish hist. p (1) T Kr 50

13. TARİH ARAŞTIRMALARI. HISTORICAL RESEARCHES. A. 1957 (1957: no vol. indic.). Faculty of Languages, Hist. and Geography, Univ. of Ankara, Ankara. Ed: Akdes Nimet Kurat. Art. on hist., anthropology, archaeology and ethnology, not confined to any country or period; in English, French and German. Ceased pub. after first no. pni

14. TARİH VESİKALARI [Historical documents]. Irr. 1941 (mri 1955: new series, vol. 1). Maarif Vekâleti Türk Kültür Eserleri Bürosu [Bureau of Turkish Cultural Works, Ministry of Education], Ankara. Art. and doc. on Turkish hist.; bk. rev. Pub. suspended after 1944 and resumed in 1955. pv (1955: TL

15. TÜRK YURDU [The land of the Turks]. Publishes the Ideas of the Turkish Public Clubs. M. Abdülhak Şinasi Hisar, Türkocağı Merkezi Aksaray, Teceddüt Sokaği 29, İstanbul. Turkish hist., sociology, pedagogy, literature, art. Pub. suspended in 1942 and resumed in 1954. TL 12 / $ 5

16. TÜRKIYAT MECMUASI [Review of Turkology]. Irr. 1925. İstanbul Üniversitesi Türkoloji Enstitüsü [Turkology Inst., Istanbul Univ.], İstanbul. Ed: Cavid Baysun. Art. on Turkish hist., literature, folklore, art and science; bk. rev.; in Turkish; index for each fascicle. pni

17. UNIVERSITE D'ANKARA, ANNALES DE L'... [Annals of the University of Ankara]. A. Ankara Üniversitesi [Univ. of Ankara], Ankara.

18. YENİ TARIH DERGİSİ [New review of history]. M. 1957 (1959: no vol. indic.). İskit Yayznevi, Cağaloğlu, Himayeietfal Sokak 4, İstanbul. Ed: Server A. İskit. Art. on hist., with emphasis on Turkey; chronology of Ottoman hist.; A. index; illus. Supersedes Resimli Tarih Mecmuasi [Illustrated review of history], which first appeared in 1950. TL 42 / $ 4.66

United Arab Republic

EGYPT

Prepared with the assistance of

Josef M. A. Janssen, Editor, Annual Bibliography of the International Association of Egyptologists, Leiden

ANNALES DU SERVICE DES ANTIQUITES DE L'EGYPTE see SERVICE DES ANTIQUITES DE L'EGYPTE, ANNALES DU...

BULLETIN DE L'INSTITUT D'EGYPTE see INSTITUT D'EGYPTE, BULLETIN DE L'...

BULLETIN OF THE FACULTY OF ARTS, UNIVERSITY OF ALEXANDRIA see FACULTY OF ARTS, UNIVERSITY OF ALEXANDRIA, BULLETIN OF THE

1. LES CAHIERS COPTES [Coptic papers]. Q(Irr.). 1952 (1957: no. 13-15). Institut Copte, 4, rue Soliman Pacha, Cairo. Art. on Coptic religion and religious art as well as on Coptic doc. discovered in the Near East; in French and occasionally in English or German; illus. Pub. suspended. PT 100/$2.89

2. CAHIERS D'HISTOIRE EGYPTIENNE [Egyptian history papers]. Histoire - Ethnographie - Documents [History - ethnography - documents]. Irr. 1949 (mri 1955: vol. 7). Pub. address: 18, Avenue du Baron Empain, Héliopolis. Ed: Mme. Jacques Tagher (secretary-gen.). Art. on the hist. of Egypt, with emphasis on the 18th and 19th cent.; doc.; biblio.; rev. of bk. and art.; political chronicle; reports on cultural events in Egypt; in French and occasionally in English; illus. PT 100 / PT 120

EGYPTIAN HISTORY PAPERS see CAHIERS D'HISTOIRE EGYPTIENNE

3. FACULTY OF ARTS, UNIVERSITY OF ALEXANDRIA, BULLETIN OF THE. Irr. Faculty of Arts, Univ. of Alexandria, Alexandria. In Arabic, English and French.

4. INSTITUT D'EGYPTE, BULLETIN DE L'... [Bulletin of the Egyptian Institute]. S-A. (1954/55 [1956]: vol. 37). Institut d'Egypte, 13 Sharia Cheikh Rihane, Cairo. Art. on old Egyptian religion, culture and art as well as on museum holdings; in French and occasionally in English; illus. pv

5. SERVICE DES ANTIQUITES DE L'EGYPTE, ANNALES DU... [Annals of the Department of Antiquities of Egypt]. S-A. 1900 (1959: vol. 56). Service des Antiquités de l'Egypte, St. Mariette Pacha, Kasr el-Nil, Cairo. Ed: Louis A. Christophe, M. Hasan abd el-Rehman. Art. on ancient Egyptian hist., archaeology, numismatics and museum holdings; reports of excavations in Egypt; in English, French, German or Italian; maps, graph, illus. PT 400

6. SOCIETE ARCHEOLOGIQUE D'ALEXANDRIE. BULLETIN. [Archaeological Society of Alexandria. Bulletin]. Irr. 1898 (mri 1956: no. 41). Société Archéologique d'Alexandrie, 6 Sharia Gerbel, Alexandria. Ed: Max Debanne. Art. on Egyptian archaeology and Egyptian, especially Alexandrian, museum holdings; reports of the soc.; in English, French and Italian; list of memb. of the soc.; illus. PT 200

SYRIA

Prepared with the assistance of

Joseph G. Zakhour, Director,
Damascus University Library

ACADEMIE ARABE DE DAMAS, REVUE DE L'... see MAJMAʿ AL-ʿILMĪ AL-ʿARABĪ BI DIMASHQ, MAJALLAT AL-...

1. LES ANNALES ARCHEOLOGIQUES DE SYRIE [Archaeological annals of Syria]. Revue d'Archéologie et d'Histoire Syriennes [Review of Syrian archaeology and history]. A. 1951 (1957: vol. 7). Direction Générale des Antiquités de la Province Syrienne, République Arabe Unie, Damascus. Art. on museum holdings, recent excavations, new archaeological discoveries and epigraphy, pertaining to Syria; in Arabic or French and occasionally in English or German; illus. graph. LS 20 / $10

2. BULLETIN D'ETUDES ORIENTALES [Bulletin of Oriental studies]. Irr. Institut Français de Damas, Damascus.

3. AL-DHĀD [The fifteenth letter of the Arabic alphabet -- ed.]. M. Ed: Abdallah Yorki Hallak, c/o Al-Dhād, Alep. LS 7

4. ETUDE MENSUELLE SUR L'ECONOMIE ET LES FINANCES DE LA SYRIE ET DES PAYS ARABES [Monthly study on the economy and finances of Syria and the Arab countries]. M. Centre d'Etudes et de Documentations Economiques, Financières et Sociales, 27, rue Georges Haddad (Raouda), Damascus. LS 200 / $60

5. AL-HADITH [Talk]. M. Ed: Sami al-Kayyali, Majallat al-Hadith, Alep. LS 25

6. AL-IMAN [The belief]. M. Pub. in Damascus. p(1) LS 0,75

7. AL-JUNOLI [The soldier]. W. Office Culturel de l'Etat Major, Damascus. LS 50

8. AL-MAJALLAT AL-ASKARYIA [Military review]. M. Etat Major, Damascus. LS 25

MAJALLAT AL-MAJMAʿ AL-ʿILMĪ AL-ʿARABĪ BI DIMASHQ see MAJMAʿ AL-ʿILMĪ AL-ʿARABĪ BI DIMASHQ, MAJALLAT AL-...

9. MAJALLAT AL-TAMADDUN AL-ISLÂMI [Review of the Muslim civilization]. Q. Ed: Ahmad Mazhar al-Azmah, c/o Majallat al-Tamaddun al-Islâmi, Damascus. LS 8

10. MAJMAʿ AL-ʿILMĪ AL-ʿARABĪ BI DIMASHQ, MAJALLAT AL-... REVUE DE L'ACADEMIE ARABE DE DAMAS [Review of the Arab Academy at Damascus]. M. Académie Arabe de Damas, Damascus. LS 12 / $4

11. AL-MU'ALLEM AL-ʿARABĪ [The Arab school teacher]. M. Ministry of National Education, Damascus.

12. AL-MUSLIMUN [The Moslems]. B-M. Pub. in Damascus. LS 10

13. AL-NI'MA [Grace]. M. Patriarchat Grec Orthodoxe, Damascus. LS 5

14. AL-QANOUN [The law]. M. Ministry of Justice, Damascus.

15. RECUEIL DES LOIS ET DE LA LEGISLATION FINANCIERE DE LA REPUBLIQUE ARABE UNIE: PROVINCE DE SYRIE [Collection of laws and the financial legislation of the United Arab Republic: Province of Syria]. M. Ed: V. Syriani, P.O.B. 539, Damascus. LS 100 / $27,77

REVUE DE L'ACADEMIE ARABE DE DAMAS see MAJMAʿ AL-ʿILMĪ AL-ʿARABĪ BI DIMASHQ, MAJALLAT AL-...

16. AL-THĀQAFAT [Culture]. M. Ed: M. Akkach, c/o Al-Thāqafat, Damascus. LS 30

NORTH AMERICA

(For Mexico see the section on Latin America and the West Indies.)

Canada

Prepared with the assistance of
The National Library of Canada, Ottawa, and
The Public Archives of Canada, Ottawa

1. ALBERTA HISTORICAL REVIEW. Q. 1953 (1959: vol. 7). Alberta Hist. Soc., c/o E. S. George, Treasurer, 9817 107th St., Edmonton, Alta. Ed: Hugh A. Dempsey, 95 Holmwood Ave., Calgary, Alta. Art. on the hist. of Western Canada from the first white settlements; bk. rev. C $ 2

2. ANNALS OF THE FORTY. A. Grimsby Hist. Soc., c/o Miss C. Freshwater, Box 241, Grimsby, Ont. C $ 1.50

3. ARCTIC. Q. Arctic Inst. of North America, 3485 University St., Montreal 2, P.Q. C $ 5

4. ATLANTIC GUARDIAN. The Magazine of Newfoundland. M. Guardian, Ltd., 96 Water St., St. John's, Nfld. C $ 2

5. THE BEAVER. Magazine of the North. Q. 1920 (1959/60: "Outfit" 270, Summer). Hudson's Bay Company, Hudson's Bay House, Winnipeg 1, Man. Ed: Malvina Bolus. "The interests of The Beaver cover the territory with which the Company has been or is now associated, historically and currently"; art. mostly on social and cultural hist.; bk. rev. C $ 2 / C $ 1.55

6. BEHIND THE HEADLINES. B-M. Canadian Inst. of International Affairs, 230 Bloor St. West, Toronto 5, Ont. Pamphlets on current problems, each on one topic. C $ 1 / C $ 1.15

7. BRITISH COLUMBIA HISTORICAL QUARTERLY. Q. 1937 (mri 1956: vol. 20). Archives of British Columbia, in cooperation with the British Columbia Hist. Assoc., Provincial Archives, Parliament Bldgs., Victoria, B.C. Ed: William E. Ireland. Art. on the hist. of British Columbia; bk. rev.; "Notes and Comments" on the activities of the hist. inst. C $ 2

8. THE BULLETIN. Records and Proceedings of the Committee on Archives of the United Church of Canada. A. 1948 (1959: no. 12). United Church of Canada, Committee on Archives, The Archives, Victoria Univ., Queen's Park, Toronto 5, Ont. Ed: Rev. George Byle. Reports of the work of the Central Archives and of the Conference and Presbytery Committees; analyses of collections of the Church's archives; art. of hist. interest, particularly those based on material in the archives; art. on Canadian church hist. free

9. BULLETIN DES RECHERCHES HISTORIQUES [Bulletin of historical research]. Q. 1895 (1959: vol. 64). Pub. address: 2050 St.-Cyrille Ouest, Quebec, P.Q. Ed: Antoine Roy. Art. on hist., auxiliary disciplines, and archaeology, with some emphasis on biography and social and cultural hist., mostly of French North America and the Province of Quebec; doc.; bk. rev.; questions and answers on research. C $ 3 / C $ 3.50

BULLETIN OF THE ROYAL ONTARIO MUSEUM OF ARCHAEOLOGY see ROYAL ONTARIO MUSEUM OF ARCHAEOLOGY, BULLETIN OF THE

CAHIERS D'HISTOIRE DE LA SOCIETE HISTORIQUE DE QUEBEC see SOCIETE HISTORIQUE DE QUEBEC, CAHIERS D'HISTOIRE DE LA...

10. LES CAHIERS DES DIX [The journal of the Ten]. A. Librairie Ducharme, 455 St.-Sulpice, Montreal, P.Q. C $ 3

11. CANADIAN ARMY JOURNAL. Q. Directory of Military Training, c/o Supervisor of Govt. Pub., Dept. of Public Printing and Stationery, Ottawa, Ont. C $ 2

12. THE CANADIAN BANKER. 3xy. Canadian Bankers' Assoc., Federation Bldg., 275 St. James St. West, Montreal, P.Q. C $ 1.50

13. CANADIAN GEOGRAPHICAL JOURNAL. M. 1930 (1959: vol. 57/58). Royal Canadian Geographical Soc., 54 Park Ave., Ottawa 4, Ont. Ed: Gordon M. Dallyn. Art. on geography, anthropology and hist. of regions, not limited to Canada; bk. rev. C $ 5

14. THE CANADIAN HISTORICAL ASSOCIATION. REPORT OF THE ANNUAL MEETING. A. 1922 (1959: no vol. indic.) Canadian Hist. Assoc., c/o Public Archives of Canada, Ottawa, Ont. Ed: David Shadd. Art. (papers read at the A. meeting) on all periods, with some emphasis on modern hist. and on North America; reports of officers of the assoc.; personal notes; list of memb.; in English or French; cum. index for the years 1922-51. C $ 4

15. THE CANADIAN HISTORICAL REVIEW. Q. 1920 (1959: vol. 40). Univ. of Toronto Press, Toronto 5, Ont. Ed: J. T. Saywell. Art. on Canadian hist., with emphasis on political hist. and imperial and foreign relations; rev. art. and bk. rev.; biblio.; "Recent Publications Relating to Canada": art. with short notations, and bk., mostly pub. in Canada, grouped by topic and province; professional news, including reports of meetings; A. list of graduate theses in Canadian hist. pub. in the British Commonwealth and U.S.A. C $ 4

16. CANADIAN HOME ECONOMICS JOURNAL. Q. Canadian Home Economics Assoc., Box LV, 290 Vaughan St., Winnipeg, Man. C $ 1.50

17. CANADIAN JEWISH ARCHIVES. A.(Irr.). 1951 (1959: vol. 1, no.5). Canadian Jewish Congress, 493 Sherbrooke St. West, Montreal, P.Q. Ed: Louis Rosenberg. Doc. on the hist. and activities of Jews in Canada, with emphasis on the earliest period (1763 to 1809). free / C $ 1

18. THE CANADIAN JOURNAL OF ECONOMICS AND POLITICAL SCIENCE. Q. 1935 (1958: vol. 24). Univ. of Toronto Press, Toronto 5, Ont., for the Canadian Political Science Assoc. Ed: J.H.Dales, 273 Bloor St. West, Toronto 5, Ont. Art. on economics and political science, including economic and political hist., especially of Canada and the Commonwealth countries, primarily of the 19th and 20th cent.; rev. art.; bk. rev.; notes on economic trends and news of congresses; personal news; biblio. (arranged alphabetically by author) of literature received; charts, statistical tables. C $ 6 / C $ 7

19. THE CANADIAN NUMISMATIC JOURNAL. M. 1956 (1959: vol. 4). Canadian Numismatic Assoc., c/o Mrs. L. Graham, Secretary, 23 Hollywood Ave., Willowdale, Ont. Ed: A.E.H.Petrie, Public Archives of Canada, Ottawa,

Ont. Art. on Canadian numismatics; biblio.; list of new memb.; reports of the assoc. chapters; statistics. C $ 5 / C $ 5.25

20. CULTURE [Culture]. Sciences Réligieuses et Profanes au Canada [Religious and secular sciences in Canada]. Q. L'Association de Recherches sur les Sciences Réligieuses et Profanes au Canada, 733, rue de l'Alverne, Quebec, P.Q. C $ 3

21. DALHOUSIE REVIEW. Q. Dalhousie Univ., Halifax, N.S. C $ 4

22. ETUDES SLAVES ET EST-EUROPEENNES. SLAVIC AND EAST EUROPEAN STUDIES. Q. 1956 (1958/59: vol. 3). Dept. of Slavic Studies, Univ. of Montreal, Montreal, P.Q. Ed: Théodore F. Domaradzki. Art. on Slavic hist. and culture; bk. rev.; news of professional interest; in French and English. C $ 4 / $ 4.20

23. EXTERNAL AFFAIRS. M. Dept. of External Affairs, Govt. of Canada, Ottawa, Ont. C $ 1

24. GEOGRAPHICAL BULLETIN. S-A. Geographical Branch, Dept. of Mines and Technical Surveys, 601 Booth St., Ottawa, Ont. C $ 1

25. HISTORIC KINGSTON. A. Kingston Hist. Soc., Royal Military College, Kingston, Ont. C $ 1

26. HISTORICAL AND SCIENTIFIC SOCIETY OF MANITOBA, PAPERS READ BEFORE THE. A. Hist. and Scientific Soc. of Manitoba, 255 Legislative Bldg., Winnipeg 1, Man. Mostly on the hist. of Manitoba. C $ 3

27. HISTORICAL SOCIETY OF OTTAWA. ANNUAL REPORT. Irr. Hist. Soc. of Ottawa, c/o Mable M. Stewart, Secretary, 465 Tweedsmuir Ave., Ottawa, Ont. Since 1956/57 printed in combination with Annual Report of the Women's Canadian Historical Society of Ottawa. pni

28. INTERNATIONAL JOURNAL. Q. Canadian Inst. of International Affairs, 230 Bloor St. West, Toronto 5, Ont. C $ 3

29. JOURNAL OF AUSTRONESIAN STUDIES. Irr. 1953 (1958: vol. 1, part 3; part 1 pub. in 1953, part 2 in 1956). Ed: Peter A. Lanyon-Orgill, 1701 Beach Drive, Victoria, B.C. Art. on "all aspects of Austronesian studies, including philology, ethnology, anthropology, history, archaeology, sociology, exploration and discovery, folklore and customs, and kindred subjects, as well as comparative studies of the Austronesian and other fields, such as the Austro-Asiatio (Mon-Khmer), Sino-Tibetan, American, Papuan and Australian, and so on"; bk. rev.; illus. 90s (for 3 parts) or 35s (per part)

MEMOIRES DE LA SOCIETE ROYALE DU CANADA see SOCIETE ROYALE DU CANADA, MEMOIRES DE LA...

30. THE NEWFOUNDLAND QUARTERLY. Opening New Doorways of Knowledge about Newfoundland. Q. 1901 (1959: vol. 58). P.O.B. E-5419, St. John's, Nfld. Ed: L.W.Janes. Art. on the political and cultural hist. of Newfoundland, and biographical art., with emphasis on the period after the discovery; biblio.; illus. C $ 1 / C $ 1.25

31. NOVA SCOTIA HISTORICAL SOCIETY. COLLECTIONS. Irr. 1878 (1959: vol. 32). Nova Scotia Hist. Soc., Province Bldg., Halifax, N.S. Papers, read before the soc., on Nova Scotia hist. from the first white settlements to the present. pni

32. OKANAGAN HISTORICAL SOCIETY. REPORT. A. Okanagan Hist. Soc., c/o Vera Bennett, Secretary, Box 2278, R.R.1, Penticton, B.C.

33. ONTARIO HISTORY. Q. 1899 (1959: vol. 51). Ontario Hist. Soc., c/o Edna Ash, Secretary-Treasurer, 27 Surrey Place, Toronto 5, Ont. Ed: Morris Zaslow, Dept. of Hist., Univ. of Toronto, Toronto, Ont. Art. on all periods of the hist. of Ontario and Upper Canada; bk. rev.; news of the soc.

PAPERS READ BEFORE THE HISTORICAL AND SCIENTIFIC SOCIETY OF MANITOBA see HISTORICAL AND SCIENTIFIC SOCIETY OF MANITOBA, PAPERS READ BEFORE THE

34. THE PHOENIX. Q. 1946 (1960: vol. 14). Univ. of Toronto Press, Toronto, Ont., for Classical Assoc. of Canada. Ed: Mary E. White, Trinity College, Toronto, Ont. Art. on ancient hist. and the classics, and, to a lesser degree, on medieval Europe; bk. rev., list of bk. received; illus.
(memb.) C $6 /(memb.) C $6.25

35. QUEEN'S QUARTERLY. Q. Queen's Univ., Kingston, Ont. "Politics, Foreign Affairs, Science, Arts and Letters." C $4

36. REVUE D'HISTOIRE DE L'AMERIQUE FRANÇAISE [Review of the history of French America]. Q. 1947 (1959/60: vol. 13). Institut d'Histoire de l'Amérique Française, 261 Avenue Bloomfield, Montreal, Ont. Ed: Lionel Groulx. Art. on the hist. of French settlement and culture in the Americas, with emphasis on Canada; bk. rev. and occasional abstr. of art.; biblio.: "Bibliographie de la Société de Notre-Dame de Montréal (1639-1663)" since vol. 5; news of the inst.; index of the first 10 vol. pub. separately (C $5). C $5

37. ROYAL ONTARIO MUSEUM OF ARCHAEOLOGY, BULLETIN OF THE. Irr. 1923 (1958: vol. 27). Univ. of Toronto, 100 Queen's Park, Toronto 5, Ont. Art. on North American archaeology; illus. (memb.) C $10

ROYAL SOCIETY OF CANADA, TRANSACTIONS OF THE see SOCIETE ROYALE DU CANADA, MEMOIRES DE LA...

38. SAGUENAYENSIA. B-M. Société Historique du Saguenay, Séminaire de Chicoutimi, Chicoutimi, P.Q. C $2

39. SASKATCHEWAN HISTORY. 3xy. Saskatchewan Archives Office, Univ. of Saskatchewan, Saskatoon, Sask. C $1 / C $1.05

SLAVIC AND EAST-EUROPEAN STUDIES see ETUDES SLAVES ET EST-EUROPEENNES

40. LA SOCIETE CANADIENNE D'HISTOIRE DE L'EGLISE CATHOLIQUE. RAPPORT [Canadian Society for the History of the Catholic Church. Report]. A. 1933/34 (1958: vol. 25). Société Canadienne d'Histoire de l'Eglise Catholique, Université d'Ottawa, Ottawa, Ont. Art. on the hist. of the Roman Catholic Church, principally in French Canada, from the first settlements to the present.
C $3

41. SOCIETE GENEALOGIQUE CANADIENNE-FRANÇAISE. MEMOIRES [French Canadian Genealogical Society. Memoirs]. Q. 1944/45 (1959: vol. 10) Pub. address: C. P. 335, Place d'Armes, Montreal 1, Que. Ed: Irénée Daigle, 6275, 36e avenue, Rosemont, Montreal 36, Que. Art. on genealogy of individuals and groups; doc.; tables; list of memb.; index of names for each vol. C $ 5

42. SOCIETE HISTORIQUE DE LA VALLEE DU RICHELIEU, CAHIERS DE LA... [Journal of the Historical Society of the Valley of Richelieu]. Irr. Editions du Richelieu, 170, rue Saint-Jacques, Saint-Jean, P.Q.

43. SOCIETE HISTORIQUE DE QUEBEC, CAHIERS D'HISTOIRE DE LA... [Journal of history of the Historical Society of Quebec]. A. Société historique de Québec, Univ. Laval, Quebec, P.Q. C $ 2

44. SOCIETE ROYALE DU CANADA, MEMOIRES DE LA... TRANSACTIONS OF THE ROYAL SOCIETY OF CANADA. A. 1882/83 (1959: 3rd series, vol. 53). Royal Soc. of Canada, National Research Bldg., Sussex Dr., Ottawa, Ont. Art. on "literature, history, archaeology, sociology, political economy, and allied subjects," mostly on 18th-20th cent. Canada; section I in French and section II in English, bound together. C $ 3 (sections I and II combined)

TRANSACTIONS OF THE ROYAL SOCIETY OF CANADA see SOCIETE ROYALE DU CANADA, MEMOIRES DE LA...

45. UNIVERSITY OF TORONTO QUARTERLY. Q. Univ. of Toronto, Toronto, Ont. C $ 4

46. VANCOUVER ART GALLERY BULLETIN. M. Vancouver Art Gallery, 1145 W. Georgia St., Vancouver, B.C. nfs

47. VANCOUVER HISTORICAL JOURNAL. A. 1958 (1959: no. 2). Archives Soc. of Vancouver, 750 Burrard St., Vancouver 1, B.C. Ed: J.S. Matthews. Art. on the hist. of Vancouver and vicinity, based on doc. in the Vancouver City Archives; doc.; graph; illus. (memb.) C $ 2.50

48. WENTWORTH BYGONES. A. Head-of-the-Lake Hist. Soc., c/o Mrs. R. S. Charlton, 59 Amelia St., Hamilton, Ont. Pub. suspended after first vol. (1958). C $ 1

49. WESTERN ONTARIO HISTORICAL NOTES. Q. Lawson Memorial Library, Univ. of Western Ontario, London, Ont. free

50. WESTERN ONTARIO HISTORICAL NUGGETS. Q. Lawson Memorial Library, Univ. of Western Ontario, London, Ont. free

WOMEN'S CANADIAN HISTORICAL SOCIETY OF OTTAWA. TRANSACTIONS see HISTORICAL SOCIETY OF OTTAWA. ANNUAL REPORT

United States of America

Prepared with the assistance of
Mrs. Marilyn M. Houston, Washington, D.C.,
the staffs of the
Serial Division and the General Reference and Bibliography Division of the Library of Congress, Washington, D.C., and of the
Executive Director, National Historical Publications Commission, Bethesda, Md.

1. ADMINISTRATIVE SCIENCE QUARTERLY. Q. Graduate School of Business and Public Administration, Cornell Univ., Ithaca, N.Y. $ 7.50

2. AGRICULTURAL HISTORY. Q. 1927 (1960: vol. 34). Garrard Press, 510-522 North Hickory St., Champaign, Ill., for Agricultural Hist. Soc. Ed: C. Clyde Jones, 214 David Kinley Hall, Univ. of Illinois, Urbana, Ill. (New ed. from 1961: Frederick W. Kohlmeyer, Dept. of Economics, Univ. of Ill., Urbana, Ill.). Art. and doc. pertaining to the hist. of agriculture not confined to any country; source materials; bk. rev.; biblio. of art.; professional news and notes. $ 5

3. AIR POWER HISTORIAN. Q. Air Force Hist. Foundation, 830 Maxwell Air Force Base, Montgomery, Ala. $ 3

4. ALABAMA ACADEMY OF SCIENCE. JOURNAL. Q. Alabama College Montevallo, Ala. memb. free

5. ALABAMA GENEALOGICAL REGISTER. Q. Pub. address: P.O.B. 284, Tuscaloosa, Ala. $ 5

6. THE ALABAMA HISTORICAL QUARTERLY. Q. State Dept. of Archives and Hist., Montgomery, Ala. pni

7. ALABAMA REVIEW. A Journal of Alabama History. Q. Alabama Hist Assoc., University, Ala. $ 3

8. ALBANY INSTITUTE OF HISTORY AND ART. BULLETIN. Q. 125 Washington Ave., Albany 10, N.Y. pni

9. ALLEN MEMORIAL ART MUSEUM. BULLETIN. 3 x y. Allen Art Museum, Oberlin College, Oberlin, O. Short art. on art dealing with all per: ods, with emphasis on the collections of the museum; news of the museum; catalogue of recent additions; index for vol. 1-10; maps; illus. $ 3.50

10. AMERICAN ACADEMY OF POLITICAL AND SOCIAL SCIENCE, THE ANNALS OF THE. B-M. 1890 (1958: vol. 316). American Acad. of Political and Social Science, 3937 Chestnut St., Philadelphia 4, Penn. Ed: Thorsten Selli Art. on problems in social and political science, with appropriate hist. backgrou both U.S. and international; extensive bk. rev. arranged according to discipline; index in each issue. (memb.) $ 6

11. AMERICAN ANTHROPOLOGICAL ASSOCIATION. BULLETIN. 5 x y. W.S. Godfrey, Logan Museum, Beloit College, Beloit, Wis. memb. free

12. AMERICAN ANTHROPOLOGIST. B-M. American Anthropological Assoc., c/o Betty J. Meggers, Executive Secretary, Smithsonian Inst., Washington 25, D.C. A. index. $ 12 (individuals $ 8.50) / $ 12 (individuals $ 8.50)

13. AMERICAN ANTIQUARIAN SOCIETY. PROCEEDINGS. S-A. 1812 (1958: vol. 68). American Antiquarian Soc., Worcester, Mass. Ed: Frederick Lewis Weis, Walter Muir Whitehill, Clifford K. Shipton. Papers read before the soc. (often with annotated biblio.), and relevant doc. on American hist., with some emphasis on social and literary hist. of the 18th and 19th cent.; news of the soc. and list of memb.; A. subject index. Partial index for the years 1812-1880; cum. table of contents for the years 1880-1903. $ 4

14. AMERICAN ANTIQUITY. Q. 1935 (1959: vol. 24). Soc. for American Archaeology, Logan Museum, Beloit College, Beloit, Wis. Ed: Raymond H. Thompson, Dept. of Anthropology, Univ. of Arizona, Tucson, Ariz. Art. on archaeology, mainly North American but other areas and related fields are also represented; bk. rev.; "News and Notes." memb. free

15. AMERICAN ARCHIVIST. Q. 1938 (1960: vol. 23). Soc. of American Archivists, 324 Third St., S.E., Cedar Rapids, Ia. Ed: Ken Munden. Art. on the problems of archival theory and practice (sorting, classification, inventory, etc.), on the activities of archive centers in the United States, on archival techniques, archival organization and legislation in the United States and abroad, and on hist. sources and their use; bk. rev.; A. biblio. of pub. concerning archives, administrative doc. and hist. manuscripts; news on the activities of American and foreign archives. $ 7

16. AMERICAN ASSOCIATION FOR STATE AND LOCAL HISTORY. BULLETIN. Irr. American Assoc. for State and Local Hist., 816 State St., Madison 6, Wis. $ 0.75

17. AMERICAN BAR ASSOCIATION. JOURNAL. M. American Bar Assoc., 1155 E. 60th St., Chicago 37, Ill. $ 5

18. AMERICAN CATHOLIC HISTORICAL SOCIETY OF PHILADELPHIA, RECORDS OF THE. Q (S-A). 1886 (1958: vol. 69). American Catholic Hist. Soc. of Philadelphia, 715 Spruce St., Philadelphia 6, Penn. Ed: Hugh J. Nolan. Art. on the hist. of Roman Catholicism in the U.S.A. and occasionally on general U.S. hist.; doc.; continuing feature (since 1954): "Catholic Serials in the 19th Century in the United States: A Bibliographical Survey and a Union List"; notes and comments; cum. index for vol. 1-31 (1886-1920) and vol. 32-41 (1921-1930). memb. free

19. AMERICAN ECONOMIC REVIEW. 5 x y. (mri 1954: vol. 44). American Economic Assoc., 450 Ahnaip St., Menasha, Wis. Ed: Bernard F. Haley, Stanford Univ., Stanford, Calif. Art. on economics; rev. art.; bk. rev.; communications; notes; titles of doctoral dissertations. memb. free

20. AMERICAN GENEALOGIST. Q. 1932 (1959: vol. 35). Pub. address: P.O.B. 3032, Westville Station, New Haven 15, Conn. Ed: Donald L. Jacobus. Art. on genealogy; bk. rev.; genealogical tables. $ 6

21. AMERICAN HERITAGE. The Magazine of History. B-M. 1954 (1958: vol. 9). James Parton, American Heritage Pub. Co., 551 Fifth Ave., New York 17, N.Y., for American Assoc. for State and Local Hist. and the Soc. of American Historians. Ed: Bruce Catton. Art. of popular interest on American cultural hist.; excerpts from bk.; illus. $ 12.50 / $ 13.50

22. THE AMERICAN HISTORICAL REVIEW. Q. 1895 (1958/59: vol. 64). Macmillan Co., 60 Fifth Ave., New York, N.Y., for American Hist. Assoc., 400 A St., S.E., Washington 3, D.C. Ed: Boyd C. Shafer. Art. on world hist. (mostly political and diplomatic) and historiography, with emphasis on the U.S.A. and on the 19th and 20th cent.; bk. rev. arranged by period and area, with additional extensive lists of recently pub. bk., art. and doc.; list of bk. received; new of the assoc.; international hist. activities and other professional and personal news, mostly U.S.; letters to the ed.; A. index of authors, art., rev., names and subjects. Cum. index for vol. 1-40 (1895-1935) pub. separately in 4 vol. (memb.) $ 7.50

23. THE AMERICAN INDIAN. Q. Assoc. on American Indian Affairs, Inc., 48 E. 86th St., New York 28, N.Y. $ 3

24. AMERICAN JEWISH ARCHIVES. Irr. 1948 (1959: vol. 11). Hebrew Union College, Jewish Inst. of Religion, Clifton Ave., Cincinnati 20, O. Ed: Jacob Rader Marcus. Art. on Jews and Jewish communities in the U.S.A. from colonial times; bk. rev. pni

25. AMERICAN JEWISH HISTORICAL SOCIETY. PUBLICATION. Q. 1893 (1958/59: vol. 48). American Jewish Hist. Soc., 224 N. 15th St., Philadelphia 2, Penn. Ed: Isidore S. Meyer, 3080 Broadway, New York 27, N.Y. Art. on the hist. of the Jews in North and, to a lesser extent, South America, the influence of Jewish philosophy on the hist. of Jewish civilization, and on resources on American Jewish hist. in American libraries and archives; doc.; bk. rev.; index of names and subjects; cum. index of vol. 1-20 pub. in 1914. $ 8

26. AMERICAN JOURNAL OF ARCHAEOLOGY. Q. 1885 (1958: vol. 62). Archaeological Inst. of America, 5 Washington Sq., New York 3, N.Y. Ed: Richard Stillwell, 233 McCormick Hall, Princeton Univ., Princeton, N.J. Art. on archaeology, world-wide in scope; bk. rev. $ 10

27. AMERICAN JOURNAL OF INTERNATIONAL LAW. Q. 1826 Jefferso Pl., N.W., Washington 6, D.C. Official doc. on international relations; A. subject index. pni

28. THE AMERICAN JOURNAL OF LEGAL HISTORY. Q. 1957 (1959: vol. 3). Temple Univ. School of Law, 1715 North Broad St., Philadelphia 22, Penn., for American Soc. for Legal Hist. Ed: Erwin C. Surrency. Art. on legal hist., occasionally followed by biblio.; biblio. of current literature; occasional biblio. on particular topics; bk. rev. $ 7.50 (individuals $ 2)

29. AMERICAN JOURNAL OF PHILOLOGY. Q. Johns Hopkins Press, Baltimore 18, Md. $ 6 / $ 6.50

30. AMERICAN JOURNAL OF PHYSICAL ANTHROPOLOGY. Q. Pub. address: Woodland Ave., and 36th St., Philadelphia 4, Penn. $ 7.50

31. AMERICAN LITERATURE. A Journal of Literary History, Criticism, and Bibliography. Q. Duke Univ. Press, College Station, Durham, N.C. $ 5 / $ 5.60

32. AMERICAN MUSEUM OF NATURAL HISTORY. ANTHROPOLOGICAL PAPERS. Irr. American Museum of Natural Hist., Central Park West and 79th St., New York, N.Y. pv

33. THE AMERICAN NEPTUNE. A Quarterly Journal of Maritime History. Q. 1941 (1959: vol. 19). Pub. address: Peabody Museum, Salem, Mass. Ed: Ernest S. Dodge. Art. on maritime hist., mostly of the U. S. A., including inland waters and, occasionally, naval hist.; extensive A. world-wide biblio. ("Recent Writings in Maritime History") of bk. and art.; illus., graph; cum. indices pub. in 1945, 1950 and 1955. $ 10

34. AMERICAN NUMISMATIC SOCIETY. MUSEUM NOTES. Irr. American Numismatic Soc., Broadway between 155th and 156th St., New York 32, N.Y.

35. AMERICAN ORIENTAL SOCIETY. JOURNAL. Q. American Oriental Soc., 329 Sterling Memorial Library, Yale Station, New Haven, Conn. $ 8

36. THE AMERICAN PHILATELIST. M. American Philatelic Soc., 390 West End Ave., Apt. 3 D, New York 24, N.Y. (memb.) $ 5

37. AMERICAN PHILOSOPHICAL SOCIETY. PROCEEDINGS. B-M. 1838 (1958: vol. 102). American Philosophical Soc., 104 South Fifth St., Philadelphia 6, Penn. Ed: Luther P. Eisenhart. Papers, read before the soc. and other papers accepted for pub. by the Committee on Pub., on the natural sciences, classical literature, hist. and other fields of scholarship. $ 5 / $ 5

38. AMERICAN PHILOSOPHICAL SOCIETY. YEARBOOK. A. American Philosophical Soc., 104 South Fifth St., Philadelphia 6, Penn. Index. $ 1.50 / $ 1.50

39. THE AMERICAN POLITICAL SCIENCE REVIEW. Q. 1906 (1959: vol. 53). American Political Science Assoc., 1726 Massachusetts Ave., N.W., Washington 6, D.C. Ed: Harvey C. Mansfield, 100 Univ. Hall, Ohio State Univ., Columbus 10, O. Art. on political science, including political and constitutional hist.; bk. rev.; biblio. of art., grouped by subject and area; professional news; index; cum. index for vol. 1-20 (1906-26). $ 10 / $ 11

40. AMERICAN QUARTERLY. 5xy. 1948 (1958: vol. 10). Univ. of Pennsylvania, P.O.B. 46, College Hall, Philadelphia 4, Penn. Ed: Hennig Cohen. Art. on the cultural hist. of the U. S. A., with emphasis on literary hist.; bk. rev.; notes of professional interest in a section entitled: "American Calendar." $ 4

41. THE AMERICAN SCANDINAVIAN REVIEW. Q. American Scandinavian Foundation, 127 East 73rd St., New York 21, N.Y. $ 4

42. THE AMERICAN SCHOLAR. Q. United Chapters of Phi Beta Kappa, 1811 Q St., N.W., Washington 9, D.C. Current affairs, humanities, literature and the arts. $ 4 / $ 4.50

43. AMERICAN SCHOOLS OF ORIENTAL RESEARCH. BULLETIN. Q. Drawer 93 A, Yale Station, New Haven 11, Conn. pni

44. AMERICAN SCIENTIST. Q. Soc. of the Sigma Xi, 54 Hillhouse Ave., New Haven 11, Conn. $ 2 / $ 2.50

45. THE AMERICAN SLAVIC AND EAST EUROPEAN REVIEW. Q. 1942 (1958: vol. 17). Columbia Univ. Press, 2960 Broadway, New York, 27, N.Y., for American Assoc. for the Advancement of Slavic Studies. Ed: John N. Hazard, 431 West 117th St., New York 27, N.Y. Art. on Russian and East European hist., pertaining mostly to the 19th and 20th cent., and on current affairs, with some emphasis on the Socialist and Communist movements; bk. rev.; news section: "Institutional Activities," "Appointments and Staff Changes," and "Awards and Announcements." $ 6 / $ 6.30

46. AMERICAN SOCIOLOGICAL REVIEW. B-M. New York Univ., Washington Sq., New York 3, N.Y. $ 8

47. AMERICAN SPEECH. Q. Columbia Univ. Press, 2960 Broadway, New York 27, N.Y. $ 6 / $ 6.30

48. THE AMERICAN-SWEDISH INSTITUTE. BULLETIN. 2600 Park Ave Minneapolis 7, Minn. pni

49. THE AMERICAS. A Quarterly Review of Inter-American Cultural History. Q. 1944 (1958/59: vol. 15). Acad. of American Franciscan Hist., Washington, D.C. Ed: Mathias C. Kiemen, O.F.M., 5401 W. Cedar Lane, Washington 14, D.C. Art. on Latin American and occasionally North American cultural hist. since the 16th cent.; doc.; bk. rev.; biblio.; news on pub. and conferences; index. $ 6 / $ 4

50. AMONG FRIENDS. Q. Friends of the Detroit Public Library, 5201 Woodward Ave., Detroit 2, Mich. pni

51. ANGLICAN THEOLOGICAL REVIEW. Q. Pub. address: 600 Haven St Evanston, Ill. $ 3.50

ANNALS. For titles beginning with "Annals," followed by the name of the publishing or sponsoring institution or society, see the respective institution or society.

52. ANNALS OF IOWA. Q. Iowa State Dept. of Hist. and Archives, Hist. Bldg., Des Moines 19, Ia. $ 1 / $ 1.25

53. ANNALS OF WYOMING. S-A. Wyoming State Archives and Hist. Dept., State Office Bldg., Cheyenne, Wyo. $ 2

ANNUAIRE DE LA COMMISSION DU DROIT INTERNATIONAL see section on International Periodicals

ANNUAIRE JURIDIQUE INTERAMERICAIN see section on International Periodicals

ANNUAL OF THE NEW CANAAN HISTORICAL SOCIETY see NEW CANAAN HISTORICAL SOCIETY. ANNUAL

ANTHROPOLOGICAL PAPERS. AMERICAN MUSEUM OF NATURAL HISTORY see AMERICAN MUSEUM OF NATURAL HISTORY. ANTHROPOLOGICAL PAPERS

54. ANTHROPOLOGICAL QUARTERLY. Q. Catholic Univ. of America Press, Washington 17, D.C. $3

55. THE ANTIOCH REVIEW. Q. Antioch Press, Antioch College, Yellow Springs, O. $3 / $4

56. ANTIQUARIAN BOOKMAN. W. Specialist Bk. Trade Weekly, P.O.B. 1100, Newark 1, N.J. $8 / $9

57. THE ANTIQUE AUTOMOBILE. B-M. Antique Automobile Club of America, Museum Park, Huntingdon, Penn. $5 (memb. $4.50)

58. ANTIQUES. M. 601 Fifth Ave., New York 17, N.Y. Illus. $8.50 / $10

59. THE ANTIQUES JOURNAL. M. Guide Pub. Co., Westfield, N.Y. $4 / $4.50

ANUARIO JURIDICO INTERAMERICANO see section on International Periodicals

60. APPALACHIA. 12 x y. Appalachian Mountain Club, 5 Joy St., Boston, Mass. $4

61. THE ARCHAEOLOG. Irr. Sussex Soc. of Archaeology and Hist., Lewes, Del. pni

62. ARCHAEOLOGICAL NEWSLETTER. 3 x y. Upper Ohio Valley Archaeological Survey, Section of Man, Carnegie Museum, Pittsburgh 13, Penn. p (1) $0.25

63. ARCHAEOLOGICAL SOCIETY OF CENTRAL NEW YORK. BULLETIN. M. Cayuga Museum of Hist. and Art, Auburn, N.Y. pni

64. ARCHAEOLOGICAL SOCIETY OF NEW JERSEY. BULLETIN. S-A. Archaeological Soc. of New Jersey, New Jersey State Museum, State House Annex, Trenton 25, N.J. $1 / $1.50

65. ARCHAEOLOGICAL SOCIETY OF NEW JERSEY. NEWSLETTER. Q. Archaeological Soc. of New Jersey, New Jersey State Museum, State House Annex, Trenton 25, N.J. pni

66. ARCHAEOLOGY. A Magazine Dealing with the Antiquity of the World. Q. 1948 (1958: vol. 11). Archaeological Inst., 5 Washington Sq., N., New York 3, N.Y. Ed: Gladys Davidson Weinberg. Art. on archaeological surveys and discoveries, not confined to any country, and on the background of the cultures involved; bk. rev.; professional news. $5

67. ARCHAEOLOGY IN MONTANA. Q. Archaeology Soc. of Montana, Bozeman, Mont. pni

68. ARIZONA AND THE WEST. Q. Univ. of Arizona, Tucson, Ariz. $ 5

69. THE ARIZONA QUARTERLY. Q. Univ. of Arizona, Tucson, Ariz. Mostly literature and humanities. $ 2

70. ARKANSAS FOLKLORE. Irr. Arkansas Folklore Soc., c/o English Dept., Univ. of Arkansas, Fayetteville, Ark., and Univ. Folklore Research Project, Univ. of Arkansas, Fayetteville, Ark. pni

71. ARKANSAS HISTORICAL QUARTERLY. Q. Arkansas Hist. Assoc., Fayetteville, Ark. $ 3

72. THE ARLINGTON HISTORICAL MAGAZINE. A. Arlington Hist. Soc., 3119 Eighth St., N., Arlington 1, Va. pni

73. ARMENIAN REVIEW. Q. Hairenik Assoc., Inc., 212 Stuart St., Boston 16, Mass. $ 6

74. ARS ORIENTALIS. Irr. Freer Gallery of Art, Smithsonian Inst., Washington 25, D.C. pni

75. ART IN AMERICA. Q. Pub. address: 635 Madison Ave., New York, N.Y. $ 5 / $ 5.50

76. ART INSTITUTE OF CHICAGO. QUARTERLY. Q. Art Inst. of Chicago, Michigan at Adams St., Chicago 3, Ill. $ 1

ARTIBUS ASIAE see entry 541 below

77. ASSOCIATES IN FINE ARTS AT YALE UNIVERSITY. BULLETIN. Irr. Yale Univ. Art Gallery, New Haven, Conn. memb. free

78. THE ATLANTA HISTORICAL BULLETIN. Irr. Atlanta Hist. Soc., Inc., 1753 Peachtree St., NE, Atlanta 9, Ga. pv (memb. free)

79. ATLANTIC. M. Atlantic Monthly Corporation, 8 Arlington St., Boston 16, Mass. $ 7.50

80. AYDELOTT FAMILY ASSOCIATION. BULLETIN. Irr. Aydelott Family Assoc., RCA Bldg., New York 20, N.Y. pni

81. THE BALTIC REVIEW. Q. 1953 (1958: no. 13-16). Committees for a Free Estonia, Latvia and Lithuania, 70 Fifth Ave., New York 11, N.Y. Ed. board: Antanas Trimakas (chief ed.), Alfreds Berzins, Johannes Klesment. Art. on the recent hist. of the Baltic States, with emphasis on their current status pni

82. BIBLICAL ARCHAEOLOGIST. Q. 1938 (1959: vol. 22). American Schools of Oriental Research, Drawer 93a, Yale Station, New Haven, Conn. Ed: G. Ernest Wright, Frank M. Cross, Jr., Floyd V. Filson, 45 Francis Ave., Cambridge 38, Mass. Art. on archaeological discoveries relating to Biblical times. $ 1

83. BIBLIOGRAPHICAL SOCIETY OF AMERICA. PAPERS. Q. P.O.B. 397, Grand Central Station, New York 17, N.Y. $ 7

84. BITZARON [Stronghold]. The Hebrew Monthly of America. M. Managing ed: Maurice E. Chernowitz, 1141 Broadway, New York, N.Y. $ 7 / $ 8

85. BLAISDELL PAPERS. Irr. Blaisdell Family Assoc., c/o Lizzie Blasdel Westmoreland (president), P.O.B. 772, Eagle Lake, Tex. Illus.; index. $ 2

86. THE BOSTON PUBLIC LIBRARY. QUARTERLY. Q. Trustees of the Public Library of the City of Boston, P.O.B. 286, Boston 17, Mass. $ 2

87. BRANDING IRON. Q. The Westerners, Los Angeles Corral, 640 Terraine Ave., Long Beach 14, Calif. memb. free

88. BROOKLYN MUSEUM. BULLETIN. Q. Brooklyn Museum, Eastern Parkway, Brooklyn 38, N.Y. $ 1

BULLETIN. For titles beginning with "Bulletin," followed by the name of the publishing or sponsoring institution or society, see the respective institution or society.

89. BULLETIN OF THE HISTORY OF MEDICINE. B-M. Johns Hopkins Press, Homewood, Baltimore 18, Md., for American Assoc. for the Hist. of Medicine and the Johns Hopkins Inst. of the Hist. of Medicine. $ 6 / $ 6.50

90. THE BUSINESS HISTORY REVIEW. Q. 1926 (1959: vol. 33). Harvard Graduate School of Business Administration, 214-216 Baker Library, Soldiers Field, Boston 63, Mass. Ed: George S. Gibb. Art. on the hist. of business, management and labor, industrial development, and related topics, with emphasis on the U.S.A.; readers' contributions; rev. art.; bk. rev.; A. subject index; cum. indices for vol. 1-15 and vol. 16-22. $ 10

91. CALIFORNIA ACADEMY OF SCIENCE. PROCEEDINGS. Irr. California Acad. of Science, San Francisco, Calif. pni

CALIFORNIA HISTORICAL QUARTERLY see WESTERN FOLKLORE

92. CALIFORNIA HISTORICAL SOCIETY. QUARTERLY. Q. California Hist. Soc., 456 McAllister St., San Francisco 2, Calif. memb. free

93. CALUMET. Q. Marquette League for Catholic Indian Missions, 289 Fourth Ave., New York 10, N.Y. pni

94. THE CATHOLIC EDUCATIONAL REVIEW. Q. Catholic Education Press, Catholic Univ. of America, Washington 17, D.C. $ 5

95. THE CATHOLIC HISTORICAL REVIEW. Q. 1915 (1959: vol. 45). Catholic Univ. of America Press, Catholic Univ. of America, Washington 17, D.C. Ed: Martin R.P. McGuire, Alfred C. Rush, John Tracy Ellis. Art. on the hist. of Roman Catholicism, with emphasis on the U.S.; extensive bk. rev. section, not confined to Catholic hist.; biblio. of bk. and art.; "Miscellany," including reports of the A. meeting of the American Catholic Hist. Assoc.; "Notes and Comments." $ 6

96. THE CATTLEMAN. M. Texas and Southwestern Cattle Raisers Assoc., 410 East Weatherford St., Fort Worth 2, Tex. $ 3 / $ 6

97. THE CENTENNIAL REVIEW OF ARTS AND SCIENCES. Q. College of Science and Arts, Michigan State Univ., East Lansing, Mich. pni

98. CENTRAL ASIAN COLLECTANEA. Irr. Pub. address: 1417 N St., N.W., Washington 5, D.C. pni

99. CENTRAL STATES ARCHAEOLOGICAL JOURNAL. Q. Pub. address: 2016 Jersey St., Quincy, Ill. Illus. memb. free

100. CENTRAL TEXAS GENEALOGICAL SOCIETY. BULLETIN. M. Central Texas Genealogical Soc., Waco, Tex. pni

101. CESARE BARBIERI COURIER. Irr. Cesare Barbieri Center of Italian Studies, Trinity College, Hartford, Conn. pni

102. THE CHEMUNG HISTORICAL JOURNAL. Q. Chemung County Hist. Soc., Inc., 425 E. Market St., Elmira, N.Y. pni

103. CHICAGO HISTORY. Q. Chicago Hist. Soc., Lincoln Park at North Ave., Chicago 14, Ill. pni

104. CHRISTIANITY AND CRISIS. B-W. Pub. address: 537 W. 121st St., New York 27, N.Y. $ 5

105. CHRONICLE. A Baptist Historical Quarterly. Q. Pub. address: 610 Walnut Ave., Scottdale, Penn. $ 1

106. THE CHRONICLES OF OKLAHOMA. Q. Oklahoma Hist. Soc., Hist. Bldg., Oklahoma City, Okla. $ 3

107. CHURCH HISTORY. Q. 1932 (1959: vol. 28). American Soc. of Church Hist., c/o Guy S. Klett (treasurer), 520 Witherspoon Bldg., Philadelphia 7, Penn. Ed: J.H. Nichols, F.A. Norwood, 306 Swift Hall, Univ. of Chicago, Chicago 37, Ill. Art. on the hist. and theology of the Christian Churches, mostly in Europe and America, with emphasis on Protestantism; bk. rev.; abstr. of related doctoral dissertations submitted at U.S. univ. $ 5 / $ 5.25

108. CINCINNATI ART MUSEUM. BULLETIN. Q. Cincinnati Art Museum, Cincinnati, O. pni

109. CITY ART MUSEUM OF ST. LOUIS. BULLETIN. Q. City Art Museum of St. Louis, Forest Park, St. Louis 5, Mo. $ 2

110. CIVIL WAR HISTORY. Q. 1955 (1958: vol. 4). State Univ. of Iowa, Iowa City, Ia. Ed: Clyde C. Walton, Illinois State Hist. Library, Springfield, Ill. Art. dealing primarily with the American Civil War, Slavery and Reconstruction; rev. art.; bk. rev.; doc.; biblio. news: "For Collectors Only"; readers' column: "Notes and Queries"; news column on current pub. on the Civil War: "The Continuing War"; illus. $ 5 / $ 5.75

111. CIVIL WAR ROUND TABLE OF LEXINGTON, KENTUCKY. BULLETIN. Irr. Civil War Round Table of Lexington, P.O.B. 631, Lexington, Ky. pni

112. CIVIL WAR TIMES. 10 x y. Hist. Times, Inc., Gettysburg, Penn. Ed: Robert H. Fowler, P.O.B. 1861, Mechanicsburg, Penn. "A non-partisan, illustrated magazine devoted to America's most exciting and crucial period." $ 4.95

113. THE CLASSICAL BULLETIN. M (November-April). 1925 (1959: vol. 35). Dept. of Classical Languages, St. Louis Univ., 221 North Grand Blvd., St. Louis 3, Mo. Ed: William Charles Korfmacher. Art. on classical studies; poems; news of interest to classicists; bk. rev.; list of bk. received; A. index. $ 2

114. CLASSICAL JOURNAL. 8 x y. Classical Assoc. of the Middle West and South, Dept. of Classics, Indiana Univ., Bloomington, Ind. $ 3.75 / $ 4

115. CLASSICAL OUTLOOK. M. American Classical League, Miami Univ., Oxford, O. $ 1

116. CLASSICAL PHILOLOGY. Q. Univ. of Chicago Press, 5750 Ellis Ave., Chicago 37, Ill. Languages, literatures and hist. of classical antiquity. $ 6 / $ 7

117. CLASSICAL WEEKLY. W. Classical Assoc. of the Atlantic States, Fordham Univ., 441 E. Fordham Rd., New York 58, N.Y. $ 3.75 / $ 4.25

118. CLEVELAND MUSEUM OF ART. BULLETIN. 10 x y. Cleveland Museum of Art, 11 150 East Blvd., Cleveland 6, O. $ 3

119. COLLECTOR. A Magazine for Autograph and Historical Collectors. 8 x y. 18 E. 77th St., New York 21, N.Y. $ 2

120. THE COLLECTORS CLUB PHILATELIST. B-M. Collectors Club, 22 E. 35th St., New York 16, N.Y. $ 10

121. THE COLORADO COLLEGE STUDIES. Colorado College, Colorado Springs, Col. pni

122. COLORADO GENEALOGIST. Q. Colorado Genealogical Soc., c/o Samuel P. Sheperd, P.O.B. 3322, Alcott Station, Denver 12, Col. (memb.) $ 2

123. COLORADO MAGAZINE. Q. State Hist. Soc. of Colorado, State Museum, E. 14th Ave. and Sherman St., Denver 3, Col. $ 4

124. COLORADO QUARTERLY. Q. Hellems 103 West, Univ. of Colorado, Boulder, Col. Literature, humanities and social sciences. $ 3 / $ 3.50

125. COLORADO-WYOMING ACADEMY OF SCIENCE. JOURNAL. A. Colorado College, Colorado Springs, Col. pni

126. COLUMBIA HISTORICAL SOCIETY, RECORDS OF THE. A. Columbia Hist. Soc., 1307 New Hampshire Ave., N.W., Washington, D.C. (memb.) $ 7.50

127. COMMENTARY. M. American Jewish Committee, 34 W. 33rd St., New York 1, N.Y. $ 5 / $ 6

COMMISSION DU DROIT INTERNATIONAL, ANNUAIRE DE LA... see section on International Periodicals

128. COMPARATIVE STUDIES IN SOCIETY AND HISTORY. An International Quarterly. Q. 1958 (1958/59: vol. 1). Mouton and Co., The Hague, Netherlands, for Chicago, California, Columbia, Pennsylvania, Princeton,

Roosevelt and Rutgers Univ. Ed: Sylvia L. Thrupp, Faculty Exchange, Univ. of Chicago, Chicago 37, Ill. Art. on comparative studies in soc. and hist., "with particular reference to the explanation of stability and of change in social organization or in ways of thought and expression"; news of interest to scholars. $ 6

129. CONCORDIA HISTORICAL INSTITUTE. QUARTERLY. Q. Concordia Hist. Inst., 801 De Mun Ave., St. Louis 5, Mo. $ 3

130. CONFLUENCE. Q. Pub. address: Weld Hall, Cambridge 38, Mass. **Ceased pub. in 1958.** $ 3.50

131. CONNECTICUT ACADEMY OF ARTS AND SCIENCES. TRANSACTIONS. Irr. New Haven, Conn. pni

132. CONNECTICUT ANTIQUARIAN. S-A. Antiquarian and Landmarks Soc., c/o O.P. Kilbourn (president), P.O.B. 2, Hartford, Conn. memb. free

133. CONNECTICUT HISTORICAL SOCIETY. BULLETIN. Q. 1 Elizabeth St., Hartford 5, Conn. memb. free

134. CORTLAND COUNTY HISTORICAL SOCIETY. BULLETIN. M. Court House, Cortland, N.Y. memb. free

135. THE COTTON HISTORY REVIEW. Q. 1960 (1960: vol. 1). Cotton Hist. Group, Auburn Univ., Auburn, Ala. Ed: Richard W. Griffin, c/o Hist. Dept., Auburn Univ., Auburn, Ala. Art. on the hist. of the cotton industry of the U.S. and its role in the national hist., economy and politics; bk. rev. p (1) $ 1.50 (memb. free)

136. COVERED BRIDGE TOPICS. Q. National Soc. for the Preservation of Covered Bridges, 31 Federal St., Beverly, Mass. $ 1

137. CRESAP SOCIETY. BULLETIN. M. Pub. address: P.O.B. 252, Canton, Miss. memb. free

138. CURRENT HISTORY. M. Events Pub. Co., 108-110 Walnut St., Philadelphia 6, Penn. $ 7

139. DAEDALUS. Q. American Acad. of Arts and Sciences and Wesleyan Univ. Press, 356 Washington St., Middletown, Conn. $ 4.50 / $ 5

140. DAUGHTERS OF THE AMERICAN REVOLUTION. MAGAZINE. M. National Soc. of the Daughters of the American Revolution, 1776 D St., N.W., Washington 6, D.C. $ 2

141. DAVIDSON JOURNAL OF ANTHROPOLOGY. S-A. 1955 (1957: vol. 3). Dept. of Anthropology, Univ. of Washington, Seattle 5, W. Ed: James Garmen, Maxine Robbins, Malcolm Farmer. Art. on anthropology, mainly of the western U.S.; biblio.; charts, maps. $ 1.75

142. THE DECORATOR. S-A. Hist. Soc. of Early American Decoration, P.O.B. 894, Darien, Conn. $ 2.20

143. DELAWARE HISTORY. S-A. Hist. Soc. of Delaware, Old Town Hall, 6th and Market St., Wilmington, Del. (memb.) $ 5

144. DENVER ART MUSEUM. QUARTERLY. Q. Denver Art Museum, Denver, Col. pni

145. DEPARTMENT OF STATE. BULLETIN. W. Dept. of State, Washington 25, D.C. $ 8.50 / $ 12.25

146. THE DESERT MAGAZINE. M. Desert Magazine, Inc., Palm Desert, Calif. $ 4 / $ 4.50

147. DETROIT HISTORICAL SOCIETY. BULLETIN. M. Detroit Hist. Soc. and Museum, 5401 Woodward at Kirby, Detroit 2, Mich. pni

148. DETROIT INSTITUTE OF ARTS. BULLETIN. Q. Detroit Inst. of Arts, 5200 Woodward Ave., Detroit, Mich. $ 0.80

149. THE DETROIT SOCIETY FOR GENEALOGICAL RESEARCH. MAGAZINE. Q. Detroit Soc. for Genealogical Research, c/o Burton Hist. Collections, Detroit Public Library, Detroit 2, Mich. (memb.) $ 2

DIOGENES see section on International Periodicals

150. DUQUESNE REVIEW. A Journal of the Social Sciences. S-A. Dept. of Economics, Hist., Political Science, and Sociology, Duquesne Univ., Pittsburgh, Penn. $ 2.25

151. EAST EUROPE. A Monthly Review of East European Affairs. M. Free Europe Press, Free Europe Committee, 2 Park Ave., New York 16, N.Y. $ 3

ECONOMIC BULLETIN FOR ASIA AND THE FAR EAST see section on International Periodicals

152. ECONOMIC DEVELOPMENT AND CULTURAL CHANGE. Q. Univ. of Chicago, 1126 E. 59th St., Chicago 37, Ill. $ 3

153. ECONOMIC GEOGRAPHY. Q. Clark Univ., Worcester, Mass. $ 6

154. E L H. A Journal of English Literary History. Tudor and Stuart Club, Johns Hopkins Univ., Baltimore, Md. $ 4 / $ 4.40

155. ENCOUNTER. Q. Christian Theological Seminary, Indianapolis 7, Ind. $ 3

156. THE ESSAY-PROOF JOURNAL. Q. Essay-Proof Soc., c/o David Lidman, 6 Sixth St., Park Ridge, N.J. $ 10

157. ESSEX INSTITUTE. HISTORICAL COLLECTIONS. Q. Essex Inst., c/o Benjamin W. Labaree, 132-134 Essex St., Salem, Mass. $ 5

158. ETHICS. An International Journal of Social, Political and Legal Philosophy. Q. Univ. of Chicago Press, 5750 Ellis Ave., Chicago 37, Ill. $ 6 / $ 7

159. ETHNOHISTORY. Q. 1954(1959: vol. 6). Indiana Univ., and the American Indian Ethnohist. Conference. Ed: Erminie Wheeler-Voegelin, Rayl House, Indiana Univ., Bloomington, Ind. Art. on the hist. of the culture and

movements of primitive peoples (chiefly in the Americas), and related subjects, from the era of colonial expansion to the present day; news and notes; doc.; bk. rev. $ 3.50

160. EVOLUTION. International Journal of Organic Evolution. Q. Soc. for the Study of Evolution, Prince and Lemon St., Lancaster, Penn. $ 7

161. EXPEDITION. Q. Museum of the Univ. of Pennsylvania, 33rd and Spruce St., Philadelphia, Penn. Archaeology, exploration, art; illus. $ 3.50

162. EXPLORATIONS IN ENTREPRENEURIAL HISTORY. Q. 1949 (1957/58: vol. 10). Research Center in Entrepreneurial Hist., Harvard Univ., Cambridge 38, Mass. Ed: Jane W. Jack, 23 Holyoke House, Cambridge 38, Mass. Art. on business and entrepreneurial hist., and on social and economic hist., with emphasis on the industrially developed countries; bk. rev.; biblio., e.g., a list of autobiographies of businessmen pub. from 1950 to 1958. Discontinued in April 1958. $ 1

163. FAR EASTERN CERAMIC BULLETIN. S-A. Far Eastern Ceramic Group, c/o Robert Paul Dart (treasurer), Museum of Fine Arts, Boston, Mass. $ 10

164. FAR EASTERN SURVEY. M. American Inst. of Pacific Relations, 333 Sixth Ave., New York 14, N.Y. $ 6

165. FILM QUARTERLY. Q. Univ. of California Press, Berkeley, Calif. $ 4

166. FILSON CLUB. HISTORY QUARTERLY. Q. Filson Club, 118 W. Breckinridge St., Louisville 3, Ky. Bk. rev.; biblio.; illus.; cum. index. $ 6

167. THE FLORIDA ANTHROPOLOGIST. Q. Florida Anthropological Soc., Dept. of Anthropology, Florida State Univ., Tallahassee, Fla. Bk. rev.; biblio.; illus. (memb.) $ 3

168. FLORIDA HISTORICAL QUARTERLY. Q. Florida Hist. Soc., St. Augustine, Fla. Bk. rev.; illus.; cum. index. (memb.) $ 5

169. THE FOLKLORE AND FOLK MUSIC ARCHIVIST. Q. Indiana Univ. Research Center in Anthropology, Folklore, and Linguistics, Bloomington, Ind. free

170. FOREIGN AFFAIRS. Q. Council on Foreign Relations, 58 E. 68th St., New York 21, N.Y. $ 6

171. FORT TICONDEROGA MUSEUM. BULLETIN. A. Fort Ticonderoga Museum, Ticonderoga, N.Y. pni

172. FRENCH HISTORICAL STUDIES. A. (soon to become S-A). 1958 (1960: vol. 3). Soc. for French Hist. Studies, 112 Winston Hall, North Carolina State College, Raleigh, N.C. Ed: Marvin L. Brown. Art. on the hist. of France and its relations with the United States, and on the study of French hist. in the United States; rev. art.; doc.; classified biblio.; professional news; in English or French. $ 2.50

173. FRIENDS HISTORICAL ASSOCIATION. BULLETIN. S-A. 1906 (1958: vol. 47). Friends Hist. Assoc., c/o Swarthmore College, Swarthmore, Penn. Ed: Frederick B. Tolles, Friends Hist. Library of Swarthmore College, Swarthmore, Penn. Art. on Quaker hist. and biographical art. on prominent memb. of the assoc.; bk. rev. and "Brief Notices" on literature dealing with the Society of Friends; news and doc. concerning the assoc.
libraries: $ 1. 50 (memb. $ 3)

174. FRONTIER TIMES. Devoted to Frontier History, Border Tragedy, and Pioneer Achievement. Q. 1923 (1959: vol. 33, new series no. 7). Western Pub., P.O.B. 5008, 709 West 19th St., Austin 31, Tex. Ed: Norman B. Wiltsey. Dramatized hist. art., letters, diaries and reminiscences pertaining to the American West; bk. rev.; cum. index. $ 3

175. GALLEON. Irr. 1953. Soc. of Colonial Hist., 5 Washington Ave., Schenectady 5, N.Y. Ed: John H. Vrooman. Art. on American colonial hist.; news of the soc. p (1) $ 0. 50

176. GALLERY NOTES. S-A. Albright Art Gallery, 1285 Elmwood Ave., Buffalo 22, N.Y. List of acquisitions and reports on the activities of the Gallery. $ 2

177. GENEALOGICAL FORUM OF PORTLAND, OREGON. 10 x y. Pub. address: c/o Mrs. C.W. Carey, and Mrs. E.E. Brackett, Rt. 1, P.O.B. 47 B, Estacada, Ore. $ 2. 50 (individuals $ 3)

178. GENEALOGICAL HELPER. Q. Pub. address: 518 N. Main St., Logan, Ut. $ 2

179. THE GENEALOGICAL MAGAZINE OF NEW JERSEY. Q. Genealogical Soc. of New Jersey, P.O B. 208, Newark 1, N.J. A. index of names.
$ 3

180. GENEALOGICAL REGISTER. B-M. Pub. address: P.O.B. 335, Baton Rouge, La. $ 3

181. GENEALOGICAL SOCIETY BULLETIN. Irr. Fort Worth Genealogical Soc., c/o Mrs. E.P. Deckler, 3008 McPherson St., Fort Worth 9, Tex.
pni

182. GENEALOGY AND HISTORY. Q. Pub. address: Adrian Ely Mount, P.O.B. 1717, Washington 13, D.C. $ 2

183. GENEALOGY EXCHANGE. M. B. Robins, 2330 Delta, Long Beach, Calif. pni

184. GENERAL MAGAZINE AND HISTORICAL CHRONICLE. Q. General Alumnae Soc., Univ. of Pennsylvania, 3401 Spruce St., Philadelphia 4, Penn.
p (1) $ 0. 50

185. GENESEE COUNTRY SCRAPBOOK. A. Rochester Hist. Soc., Rochester, N.Y. pni

186. GEOGRAPHICAL REVIEW. Q. American Geographical Soc., Broadway at 156th St., New York 32, N.Y. $ 7. 50

187. GEORGIA ACADEMY OF SCIENCE. BULLETIN. Q. Pub. address: P.O.B. 534, Emory University, Ga. memb. free

188. GEORGIA HISTORICAL QUARTERLY. Q. Georgia Hist. Soc., 501 Whitaker St., Savannah, Ga. Cum. index. $ 5

189. GEORGIA REVIEW. Q. Univ. of Georgia Press, for Univ. of Georgia, Athens, Ga. $ 3

190. THE GERMANIC REVIEW. Q. Columbia Univ. Press, 2960 Broadway, New York 27, N.Y. $ 6 / $ 6.30

191. GERMANTOWN CRIER. Q. Germantown Hist. Soc., 5214 Germantown Ave., Philadelphia 44, Penn. $ 1

192. GREEK ORTHODOX THEOLOGICAL REVIEW. S-A. Holy Cross Greek Orthodox Theological School Press, 50 Goddard Ave., Brookline 46, Mass. $ 3.50

193. GREEK, ROMAN AND BYZANTINE STUDIES. Q. 1958 (1959: vol. 2). Pub. and ed: John J. Bilitz, P.O.B. 184, Elizabeth, N.J. Art. on the Greek, Roman and Byzantine empires with emphasis on art hist. and archaeology. $ 7

194. THE GUN REPORT. M. World-Wide Gun Report, Inc., P.O.B. 111, Aledo, Ill. Art. of interest to antique gun and cartridge collectors; bk. rev.; news of the Gun Club; program of meetings of interest to gun collectors; biblio.; maps, illus. $ 5 / $ 6

195. GUNS MAGAZINE. M. Pub. address: 8150 N. Central Park Ave., Skokie, Ill. $ 5

196. HALVE MAEN [The half moon]. Q. Holland Soc. of New York, 15 William St., New York 5, N.Y. memb. free

197. HARPER'S MAGAZINE. M. Harper and Bros., 49 E. 33rd St., New York 16, N.Y. $ 6 / $ 7.50

198. HARVARD EAST ASIAN STUDIES. Irr. Harvard Univ. Press, Cambridge, Mass. pni

199. HARVARD JOURNAL OF ASIATIC STUDIES. 1936 (1957: vol. 20). Harvard-Yenching Inst., Harvard Univ., Cambridge, Mass. Ed: John L. Bishop, 2 Divinity Ave., Cambridge 38, Mass. Art. on Asian hist., mostly cultural, with emphasis on language and literature; lengthy bk. rev.; list of bk. and periodicals received; in English and occasionally in other Western languages. $ 5

200. HARVARD LIBRARY BULLETIN. 3 x y. 1947 (1959: vol. 13). Harvard Univ. Library, Cambridge 38, Mass. Ed: George William Cottrell, Jr. Art. on social and cultural hist., with emphasis on literature and the arts, and on library holdings (Harvard and elsewhere); library news. $ 4

201. HAWAIIAN HISTORICAL SOCIETY. ANNUAL REPORTS. A. 1893 (1958: no. 66). Hawaiian Hist. Soc., P.O.B. 2596, Honolulu 3, Hawaii. Art. on the hist., culture and folklore of Hawaii; A. report of the soc. pv (memb. free)

202. HEBREW UNION COLLEGE - JEWISH INSTITUTE OF RELIGION. BULLETIN. 5 x y. Pub. address: 40 West 68th St., New York 23, N.Y. pni

203. HESPERIA. Q. 1932 (1959: vol. 28). Pub. at 20 Hopkins Pl., Baltimore, Md., for American School of Classical Studies at Athens, 54 Souidias St., Athens. Ed: Lucy T. Shoe, American School of Classical Studies at Athens, c/o Inst. for Advanced Study, Princeton, N.J. Art. on Athenian law, ancient Greek art, archaeology, ethnology and classical culture; maps, graph.; A. epigraphic index; illus. $ 7.50 / $ 8.50

204. HISPANIA. Q. American Assoc. of Teachers of Spanish and Portuguese, S. Memorial Drive, Appleton, Wis. (memb.) $ 4

205. THE HISPANIC AMERICAN HISTORICAL REVIEW. Q. 1918 (1958: vol. 38). Duke Univ. Press, P.O.B. 6697, College Station, Durham, N.C. Ed: Lewis Hanke, P.O.B. 7691, Univ. Station, Austin 12, Tex. Art. on Latin American hist., mostly from the 17th to the 19th cent.; bk. rev. classed by period; professional news and notes on conferences and grants; biblio.; list of doctoral dissertations on Latin American topics accepted by U.S. univ.; A. index of authors, reviewers, names and subjects. $ 6 / $ 6.60

206. HISPANIC AMERICAN REPORT. M. Hispanic American Studies, Stanford Univ., Stanford, Calif. $ 10 (individuals $ 6)

207. HISPANIC REVIEW. Q. Univ. of Pennsylvania, Philadelphia, Penn. $ 7.50

208. HISTORIA JUDAICA. A Journal of Studies in Jewish History, Especially in the Legal and Social History of the Jews. S-A. 1938 (1959: vol. 21, part 2). Pub. address: 40 W. 68th St., New York 23, N.Y. Ed: Guido Kisch. "Research in mediaeval and modern history of Jews with special emphasis on their legal and social relations to the surrounding world"; bk. rev. $ 5 / $ 6

209. DE HISTORIA MEDICINAE. Q. 1956/57 (1959: vol. 4). Alabama Soc. of Medical Hist., 1919 - 7th Ave., South Birmingham 3, Ala. Ed: Eleanor B. Lanier, Medical Library, Univ. of Alabama Medical Center, Birmingham 3, Ala. Art. on medical hist.; bk. rev.; graph, illus. $ 2 / $ 2.50

210. THE HISTORIAN. A Journal of History. Q. 1938 (1958: vol. 21). Phi Alpha Theta, National Honor Soc. in Hist., 2812 Livingston St., Allentown, Penn. Ed: Lynn W. Turner, Otterbein College, Westerville, O. Art. mostly on the hist. of the United States and Europe in the modern period; biographical art.; bk. rev.; news of the soc. $ 4

211. HISTORIC NANTUCKET. Q. Nantucket Hist. Assoc., P.O.B. 1016, Nantucket, Mass. p (1) $ 0.50 (memb. free)

212. HISTORIC PRESERVATION. Q. National Trust for Hist. Preservation, 2000 K St., N.W., Washington 6, D.C. $ 2 (individuals $ 5)

213. HISTORICAL AND PHILOSOPHICAL SOCIETY OF OHIO. BULLETIN. Q. Pub. address: Room 205, Library, Univ. of Cincinnati, Cincinnati 21, O. Cum. index for vol. 1-8 pub. in 1957. $ 5

214. HISTORICAL BULLETIN FOR TEACHERS AND STUDENTS OF HISTORY. Q. 1937 (mri 1956: no vol. indic.). Dept. of Hist., St. Louis Univ.,

St. Louis 3, Mo. Ed: Edward R. Vollmar. Art. on all periods of world hist.; bk. rev.; biblio. arranged by period. $ 2

HISTORICAL COLLECTIONS see ESSEX INSTITUTE. HISTORICAL COLLECTIONS

215. HISTORICAL MAGAZINE OF THE PROTESTANT EPISCOPAL CHURCH. Q. 1932 (1958: vol. 27). Pub. address: 5 Paterson St., New Brunswick, N.Y. Ed: Walter H. Stowe. Art. on church hist., with emphasis on the Protestant Episcopal Church and the Anglican Church, on theology and ecumenical problems and the activities of the Church; doc.; A. bk. rev. section consisting of "American Church History and Biography," "English and General Church History" and "Theology and Philosophy." $ 5

216. HISTORICAL NEW HAMPSHIRE. Irr. New Hampshire Hist. Soc., Concord, N.H. pni

217. HISTORICAL REVIEW OF BERKS COUNTY. Q. Hist. Soc. of Berks County, 940 Centre Ave., Reading, Penn. $ 3

218. THE HISTORICAL SOCIETY NEWS. M. Western Reserve Hist. Soc., 10,825-10,915 E. Blvd., Cleveland 6, O. pni

219. HISTORICAL SOCIETY OF MONTGOMERY COUNTY. BULLETIN. S-A. Pub. address: 1654 DeKalb St., Norristown, Penn. $ 1

220. HISTORICAL WYOMING. Q. County of Wyoming Board of Supervisors Warsaw, N.Y. free

221. THE HISTORIOGRAPHER OF THE EPISCOPAL DIOCESE OF CONNECTICUT. Q. Archivist and Historiographer of the Diocese, P.O.B. 1080, Hartford 1, Conn. $ 3

222. HISTORY OF EDUCATION JOURNAL. Q. (1957/58: vol. 9). Hist. of Education Section, National Soc. of College Teachers of Education. Ed: Claude Eggertsen, School of Education, Univ. of Michigan, Ann Arbor, Mich. Art. on the hist. of education, with emphasis on the United States and Europe, and on general educational subjects; bk. rev. $ 3.50 (memb. $ 3)

HISTORY QUARTERLY see FILSON CLUB. HISTORY QUARTERLY

223. HOBBIES. M. Lightner Pub. Corp., 1006 S. Michigan Ave., Chicago 5, Ill. $ 3.50 / $ 4.50

224. HOBBIES. 5 x y. Buffalo Museum of Science, Humboldt Park, Buffalo N.Y. $ 0.60

225. HORIZON. A Magazine of the Arts. B-M. Pub. address: 551 Fifth Ave., New York 17, N.Y. $ 18

226. THE HORSELESS CARRIAGE GAZETTE. B-M. Horseless Carriage Club of America, 7730 S. Western Ave., Los Angeles, Calif. $ 5 (memb. $ 7)

227. HUMAN BIOLOGY. Record of Research. Q. Wayne Univ. Press, Detroit 1, Mich. $ 5

228. HUMAN ORGANIZATION. Q. Soc. for Applied Anthropology, 150 E. 35th St., New York 16, N.Y. (memb.) $ 6

229. THE HUNTINGTON LIBRARY QUARTERLY. A Journal for the History and Interpretation of English and American Civilization. Q. 1937 (1959: vol. 22). Henry E. Huntington Library and Art Gallery, San Marino, Calif. Ed: Robert R. Wark, Nancy C. English. Art. on English and American literature, hist. and the fine arts, mostly from the 17th cent. on ; "Notes and Documents"; "Acquisitions" of the sponsoring library. $ 5

230. HYDE PARK HISTORIAN. Q. Pub. address: Hyde Park, N.Y. pni

IIC NEWSLETTER see section on International Periodicals

IIC NOTES D'ACTUALITE see section on International Periodicals

231. THE ILLINOIS FOLKLORE SOCIETY. NEWSLETTER. Irr. Illinois Folklore Soc., c/o William E. Simeone, Dept. of English, Southern Illinois Univ., Carbondale, Ill. $ 1

232. ILLINOIS LIBRARIES. 10 x y. Pub. Unit, Illinois State Library, Springfield, Ill. free

233. ILLINOIS STATE ARCHAEOLOGICAL SOCIETY. JOURNAL. Q. C.C. Burford, 907 S. Orchard St., Urbana, Ill., for Illinois State Archaeological Soc. Illus.; index. pni

234. ILLINOIS STATE HISTORICAL SOCIETY. JOURNAL. Q. Illinois State Hist. Soc., Centennial Bldg., Springfield, Ill. Illus.; cum. index. $ 3

235. INDIANA HISTORY BULLETIN. M. Indiana Hist. Bureau, 408 State Library and Hist. Bldg., Indianapolis, Ind. $ 0.50 / $ 1

236. THE INDIANA MAGAZINE OF HISTORY. Q. Indiana Univ. and Indiana Hist. Soc., c/o Hist. Dept., Indiana Univ., Bloomington, Ind. $ 5

INFORMACIONES ECONOMICAS see section on International Periodicals

237. INLAND SEAS. Q. Great Lakes Hist. Soc., 320 Republic Bldg., Cleveland 15, O. $ 6

238. INTER-AMERICAN ECONOMIC AFFAIRS. Q. Pub. address: P.O.B. 181, Benjamin Franklin Station, Washington 4, D.C. pni

INTER-AMERICAN JURIDICAL YEARBOOK see section on International Periodicals

239. INTER-AMERICAN REVIEW OF BIBLIOGRAPHY. REVISTA INTERAMERICANA DE BIBLIOGRAFIA ["RIB"]. Q. 1951 (1958: vol. 8). Inter-American Committee on Biblio., Division of Philosophy, Letters and Sciences, Dept. of Cultural Affairs, Pan American Union, Washington 6, D.C. Ed: Javier Malagón, José E. Vargas. Art. of biblio. interest, with emphasis on the literature of the Americas and on the biography of famous bibliophiles; bk. rev.; biblio: "Recent Books and Pamphlets" classified by subject and also comprising pub. of non-

American countries; "News and Notes"; in Spanish or English; bk. rev. occasionally in French. $ 3 / $ 3.50

240. INTERNATIONAL ANTHROPOLOGICAL AND LINGUISTIC REVIEW. Irr. A.H. Kelso de Montigny, P.O.B. 4791, Miami 29, Fla. $ 4

241. INTERNATIONAL CONCILIATION. 5 x y. Carnegie Endowment for International Peace, United Nations Plaza at 46th St., New York 17, N.Y. "The purpose of International Conciliation is to present to its readers factual statements and analyses of problems in the field of international organization." $ 1

242. INTERNATIONAL JOURNAL OF AMERICAN LINGUISTS. Q. Waverly Press, Mt. Royal and Guilford Ave., Baltimore 2, Md. $ 5

243. INTERNATIONAL ORGANIZATION. Q. World Peace Foundation, 40 Mt. Vernon St., Boston 8, Mass. $ 5 (individuals $ 1.50)

244. IOWA JOURNAL OF HISTORY. Q. State Hist. Soc. of Iowa, Iowa City, Ia. $ 2.50

245. ISIS. An International Review Devoted to the History of Science and its Cultural Influence. Q. 1912 (mri 1956: vol. 47). Widener Library 189, Harvard Univ., Cambridge 38, Mass. Ed: I. Bernard Cohen. Art. on the hist. of science, including medicine and technology, and on related social and cultural subjects; biographical art.; "Critical Bibliography of the History of Science and its Cultural Influences" (81st installment pub. in vol. 47) with topical and chronological classification, including bk. and art.; name index to biblio.; illus. pni

246. JEWISH QUARTERLY REVIEW. Q. Dropsie College, Broad and York St., Philadelphia 32, Penn. $ 6

247. JEWISH SOCIAL STUDIES. Q. 1939 (1958: vol. 20). Conference on Jewish Social Studies, 1841 Broadway, New York 23, N.Y. Ed: Salo W. Baron, Abraham G. Duker, Koppel S. Pinson, Meir Ben-Horin (manag. ed.). "Devoted to Contemporary and Historical Aspects of Jewsih Life"; bk. rev. $ 6 / $ 7

JOURNAL. For titles beginning with "Journal," followed by the name of the publishing or sponsoring institution or society, see the respective institution or society.

248. JOURNAL OF AMERICAN FOLKLORE. Q. 1888 (1959: vol. 72). American Folklore Soc., 110 Bennett Hall, Univ. of Pennsylvania, Philadelphia 4, Penn. Ed: Richard M. Dorson, Indiana Univ., Bloomington, Ind. Art. on U.S. cultural groups and their customs and legends. $ 6

249. THE JOURNAL OF ASIAN STUDIES. Review of Eastern and Southern Asia and the Adjacent Pacific Islands. 5 x y. 1941 (1958/59: vol. 18). Assoc. for Asian Studies, P.O.B. 2067, Ann Arbor, Mich. Ed: Roger F. Hackett, Northwestern Univ., 1808 Chicago Ave., Evanston, Ill. Art. on the hist. and culture of Asia and on the current problems of the Asian nations; rev. art.; bk. rev., arranged by country, and thereunder by subject; professional news; biblio. of Asian studies pub. A. as no. 5 (Ed: Howard P. Linton, East Asiatic Library, Columbia Univ., New York 27, N.Y.), arranged by area and country and thereunder by subject; vol. indices. $ 10 / $ 10

250. JOURNAL OF CENTRAL EUROPEAN AFFAIRS. Q. 1941 (1958/59: vol. 18). Univ. of Colorado, Boulder, Col. Ed: S. Harrison Thomson. Art. on the hist. (mostly diplomatic, and of the 19th and 20th cent.) and recent developments of Central and Eastern Europe and Russia; doc.; bk. rev.; biblio. of recent periodical literature; news; list of bk. received. $ 5

251. THE JOURNAL OF CONFLICT RESOLUTION. A Quarterly for Research Related to War and Peace. Q. Univ. of Chicago Press, for Dept. of Journalism, Univ. of Michigan, Ann Arbor, Mich. $ 5.50

252. JOURNAL OF CUNEIFORM STUDIES. Irr. American Schools of Oriental Research, Drawer 93-A, Yale Station, New Haven, Conn. $ 6

253. JOURNAL OF ECONOMIC HISTORY. Q. 1941 (1959: vol. 19). New York Univ. Press, Washington Sq., New York 3, N.Y. Ed: George Rogers Taylor. Art. on the hist. of business, industry, labor, transportation and trade, since the Industrial Revolution, not confined to any country; rev. art.; bk. rev. $ 6 / $ 6.25

254. JOURNAL OF INTER-AMERICAN STUDIES. Q. School of Inter-American Studies, P.O.B. 3625, Univ. Station, Gainesville, Fla. $ 2

255. JOURNAL OF INTERNATIONAL AFFAIRS. S-A. School of International Affairs, Columbia Univ., 429 West 117 St., New York 27, N.Y. $ 5 (triennial subscription)

256. JOURNAL OF LAW AND ECONOMICS. Q. Univ. of Chicago Law School, Chicago 37, Ill. $ 2.50

257. THE JOURNAL OF MISSISSIPPI HISTORY. Q. Mississippi Hist. Soc., P.O.B. 571, Jackson, Miss. (memb.) $ 4

258. THE JOURNAL OF MODERN HISTORY. Q. 1929 (1958: vol. 30). Univ. of Chicago Press, 5750 Ellis Ave., Chicago 37, Ill. Ed: Charles Loch Mowat, 1126 East 59th St., Chicago 37, Ill. Art. on world hist. (excluding the U.S.A. and Latin America), mostly political and diplomatic, since 1500, with emphasis on European hist.; biblio. art.; doc.; bk. rev.; biblio. of bk., arranged alphabethically by country; announcements of fellowships, activities of hist. soc. and of new periodical pub. $ 7.50 / $ 8.50

259. JOURNAL OF NEAR EASTERN STUDIES. Q. 1942 (1959: vol. 18). Dept. of Oriental Languages and Literatures, Univ. of Chicago, 5750 Ellis Ave., Chicago 37, Ill. Ed: Keith C. Seele. Art. on the hist., cultures and languages of the Near East; bk. rev.; maps, charts, illus. $ 6 / $ 7

260. THE JOURNAL OF NEGRO EDUCATION. Q. Howard Univ. Press, Howard Univ., Washington 1, D.C. $ 4 / $ 5

261. THE JOURNAL OF NEGRO HISTORY. Q. 1916 (1958: vol. 43). Assoc. for the Study of Negro Life and Hist., 1538 Ninth St., N.W., Washington, D.C. Ed: William M. Brewer. Art. on Negro hist., mostly in the U.S.A., in the 19th and 20th cent.; bk. rev.; world-wide biblio. of bk. and art., classed by area; reports of the assoc.; news; A. subject index. $ 5 / $ 5.50

262. THE JOURNAL OF POLITICAL ECONOMY. B-M. 1892 (1959: vol. 67). Univ. of Chicago Press, 5750 Ellis Ave., Chicago 37, Ill. Ed: Albert Rees, 1126 E. 59th St., Chicago 37, Ill. Art. on economics and economic hist.; bk. rev.; list of bk. received. $6 / $7

263. THE JOURNAL OF POLITICS. Q. 204 Peabody Hall, Univ. of Florida, Gainesville, Fla. $5 / $5.50

264. JOURNAL OF RELIGION. Q. Univ. of Chicago Press, 5750 Ellis Ave., Chicago 37, Ill. $6 / $7

265. JOURNAL OF SOUTHERN HISTORY. Q. 1935 (1960: vol. 26). Southern Hist. Assoc., Rice Inst., Houston, Tex. Ed: William H. Masterson. Art. on the hist. of the Southern U.S.A., pertaining mostly to the 19th cent.; bk. rev.; news; biblio. of U.S. pub. classed under 1) art. and 2) doc. and compilations, and under 1) the Lower South, 2) the Upper South, and "General" and "Regional." (memb.) $4

266. JOURNAL OF THE HISTORY OF IDEAS. A Quarterly Devoted to Cultural and Intellectual History. Q. 1940 (1959: vol. 20). City College, New York 31, N.Y. Ed: Philip P. Wiener (executive ed.), Aaron Noland (manag. ed.). Art., emphasizing "the inter-relations of several fields of historical study - the history of philosophy, of literature and the arts, of the natural and social sciences, of religion, and of political and social movements"; bk. rev.; list of bk. received. $6

267. THE JOURNAL OF THE HISTORY OF MEDICINE AND ALLIED SCIENCES. Q. 1946 (1958: vol. 13). Dept. of the Hist. of Medicine, Yale Univ., New Haven, Conn. Ed: John F. Fulton. Art. on "all aspects of the history of medicine, public health, dentistry, nursing, pharmacy, veterinary medicine, and the various sciences that impinge on medicine"; notes of professional interest; bk. rev.; illus. $7.50

268. JOURNALISM QUARTERLY. Devoted to Research in Journalism and Mass Communications. Q. Assoc. for Education in Journalism, Economy Advertising Bldg., Iowa City, Ia. "A Selected Bibliography from Foreign Journals": short abstr. from more than 30 periodicals pub. throughout the world, classified by subject; extensive professional section. $6 / $6.40

269. JUNIOR HISTORIAN. B-M. Texas State Hist. Assoc., P.O.B. 8011, Univ. Station, Austin 12, Tex. $2

270. KANSAS HISTORICAL QUARTERLY. Q. Kansas State Hist. Soc., Topeka, Kan. $3

271. KENTUCKY FOLKLORE RECORD. Q. Kentucky Folklore Soc., Western Kentucky State College, Bowling Green, Ky. Bk. rev.; news and notes. Mimeographed. $2

272. KENTUCKY GENEALOGIST. Q. Martha Porter Miller, P.O.B. 4894, Washington 8, D.C. $5

273. KEYSTONE FOLKLORE QUARTERLY. Irr. (2-4 x y). Pennsylvania Folklore Soc., Bucknell Univ., Lewisburg, Penn. p (1) $0.50

274. THE KIVA. Q. Arizona Archaeological and Hist. Soc., Arizona State Museum, Univ. of Arizona, Tucson, Ariz. $1

275. THE KROEBER ANTHROPOLOGICAL SOCIETY. PAPERS. S-A. Kroeber Anthropological Soc., c/o Dept. of Anthropology, Univ. of California, Berkeley 4, Calif. $ 3

276. LABOR HISTORY. 3 x y. 1960 (1960: vol. 1). Tamiment Inst., 7 East 15th St., New York 3, N.Y. Ed: Norman Jacobs. Art. on U.S. labor hist., labor problems, and trade unions; bk. rev.; A. index. $ 4 / $ 4.25

277. LANCASTER COUNTY HISTORICAL SOCIETY. JOURNAL. Q. Willson Memorial Bldg., 230 N. President Ave., Lancaster, Penn. $ 5

278. LANCASTER COUNTY HISTORICAL SOCIETY. PAPERS. 7 x y. 307 N. Duke St., Lancaster, Penn. p (1) $ 0.50

279. LAND ECONOMICS. A Quarterly Journal of Planning, Housing and Public Utilities. Q. Sterling Hall, Univ. of Wisconsin, Madison 6, Wis. $ 6

280. LANGUAGE. Q. Linguistic Soc. of America, P.O.B. 7790, Univ. Station, Austin 12, Tex. Includes occasional supplements (language dissertations and monographs). $ 8

281. THE LIBRARY CHRONICLE. Irr. Library of the Univ. of Texas, Austin 12, Tex. pni

282. LIBRARY OF CONGRESS. QUARTERLY JOURNAL OF CURRENT ACQUISITIONS. Q. 1943 (1959: vol. 16). Library of Congress, Washington 25, D.C. Art. on Library of Congress acquisitions: papers, manuscripts and rare bk. Pub. as a supplement of the Annual Report of the Librarian of Congress. $ 2 / $ 2.50

283. THE LIBRARY QUARTERLY. Q. Univ. of Chicago Press, for Graduate Library School, 5750 Ellis Ave., Chicago 37, Ill. $ 6 / $ 7

284. LINCOLN HERALD. Q. 1889 (1958: vol. 60). Lincoln Memorial Univ. Press, Harrogate, Tenn. Ed: Wayne C. Temple. "A magazine devoted to historical research in the field of Lincolniana and the Civil War, and to the promotion of Lincoln Ideas in American Education"; professional news including that of meetings of the Civil War Round Tables; "In the Literary Field. Book News Digest," and bk. rev. $ 4

285. LINCOLN LORE. M. Lincoln National Life Insurance Co., for Lincoln National Life Foundation, Fort Wayne, Ind. free

286. LITERATURE EAST AND WEST. Q. New York Univ., New York 53, N.Y. $ 1 / $ 1

287. LITUANUS. Lithuanian Collegiate Quarterly. Q. Lithuanian Student Assoc., 916 Willoughby Ave., Brooklyn 21, N.Y. $ 2

288. LOG CHIPS. The Publication of Recent Maritime History. Irr. Pub. address: c/o John Lyman, 7801 Gateway Blvd., Washington 28, D.C. $ 2

289. LOG OF MYSTIC SEAPORT. Q. Marine Hist. Assoc., Inc., Mystic, Conn. pv (c. $ 10) (memb. free)

290. LONG ISLAND FORUM. M. Pub. address: c/o Paul Bailey, Amityville, Long Island, N.Y. $ 2

291. LOS ANGELES COUNTY MUSEUM. BULLETIN OF THE ART DIVISION. Q. Art Division, Los Angeles County Museum, Los Angeles 7, Calif. (memb. free)

292. LOS ANGELES COUNTY MUSEUM. QUARTERLY. Q. Los Angeles County Museum of Hist., Science and Art, Los Angeles, Calif.

293. THE LOUISIANA HISTORICAL QUARTERLY. Q. (1957: vol. 40). Louisiana Hist. Soc., 521 Carondelet Bldg., New Orleans, La. Ed: Joseph G. Tregle, Jr., Dept. of Hist., Loyola Univ., New Orleans, La. Art. on the constitutional, political and cultural hist. of Louisiana and neighboring states, concentrating on the 19th cent.; edited doc.; bk. rev. Ceased pub.: replaced by Louisiana History. (memb.) $ 3

294. LOUISIANA HISTORY. Q. 1960 (1960: vol. 1). Louisiana Hist. Soc., in co-operation with Louisiana State Univ., Baton Rouge, La. Replaces The Louisiana Historical Quarterly. $ 5

295. LURE OF THE LITCHFIELD HILLS. S-A. Litchfield Hills Federation, 56 Broad St., East Hartford 8, Conn. "Dealing with the history of old mills, bridges, shops, homes, noted persons and places." $ 0.70

296. LUTHERAN QUARTERLY. Q. Ed: Council of Lutheran Theological Seminaries, 18 Carlisle St., Gettysburg, Penn. $ 2.75

MAGAZINE. For titles beginning with "Magazine," followed by the name of the publishing or sponsoring institution or society, see the respective institution or society.

297. MAIN CURRENTS IN MODERN THOUGHT. 5 x y. Foundation for Integrated Education, 246 East 46th St., New York 17, N.Y. $ 3 / $ 3.50

298. MANUSCRIPTA. 3 x y. St. Louis Univ. Bk. Store, 202 N. Grand, St. Louis 3, Mo. $ 4

299. MANUSCRIPTS. Q. Manuscript Library, 285 Madison Ave., New York 17, N.Y. $ 5

300. MARK TWAIN JOURNAL. S-A. Pub. address: Kirkwood 22, Mo. $ 2

301. MARYLAND HISTORICAL MAGAZINE. Q. Maryland Hist. Soc., 201 W. Monument St., Baltimore 1, Md. $ 4

302. MARYLAND HISTORY NOTES. Q. Maryland Hist. Soc., 201 W. Monument St., Baltimore 1, Md. (memb.) $ 8

303. MASSACHUSETTS ARCHAEOLOGICAL SOCIETY. BULLETIN. Q. Bronson Museum, 8 N. Main St., Attleboro, Mass. $ 3

304. M. H. S. MISCELLANY. Irr. Massachusetts Hist. Soc., 1154 Boylston St., Boston 15, Mass. pni

MASSACHUSETTS HISTORICAL SOCIETY. MISCELLANY see M. H. S. MISCELLANY

305. MASSACHUSETTS HISTORICAL SOCIETY. PROCEEDINGS. Irr. (3 vol. in the last 10 years). 1879 (1950-53 [1957]: vol. 70). Massachusetts Hist. Soc., 1154 Boylston St., Boston 15, Mass. Ed: Malcolm Freiberg. Art. mainly on American hist., but also on other countries; reports of meetings; list of holdings of the soc. and of current accessions; illus.; vol. index of authors, persons, places and subjects. $ 7.50 / $ 7.50

306. THE MASTERKEY. B-M. Southwest Museum, Highland Park, Los Angeles 42, Calif. (memb.) $ 7.50

307. THE MEDAL COLLECTOR. B-M. Orders and Medals Soc. of America, c/o Lottie Crawford, P.O.B. 772, San Diego, Calif. $ 5

308. THE MEDITERRANEAN AND EURAFRICA. B-M. Mediterranean and Levant Press of N.Y., Inc., 108 E. 81st St., New York 28, N.Y. $ 10 / $ 12

309. MENNONITE HISTORICAL BULLETIN. Q. (1959: vol. 20). Hist. Committee of Mennonite General Conference, Scottdale, Penn., for Mennonite Hist. Assoc. Ed: Irvin B. Horst, Eastern Mennonite College, Harrisonburg, Va. Art. on all aspects of the hist. of the Mennonites and their churches, with some emphasis on social and cultural hist., biography and genealogy; bk. rev.; professional news; index to vol. 11-20 (1950-1959) pub. as no. 4 of vol. 20. (memb.) $ 1.50

310. MENNONITE LIFE. Q. 1946 (1959: vol. 14). Bethel College, North Newton, Kan. Ed: Cornelius Krahn. Art. on the hist., culture and religious thought of the Anabaptists and Mennonites throughout the world; bk. rev.; notes on research in progress; A. biblio.(in April no.); in English and occasionally in German; illus. $ 3

311. MENNONITE QUARTERLY REVIEW. Q. Mennonite Hist. Soc., Goshen College, Goshen, Ind. $ 4 / $ 4.50

312. THE MENORAH JOURNAL. S-A. Menorah Assoc., Inc., 20 E. 69th St., New York 21, N.Y. (memb.) $ 10

313. THE METROPOLITAN MUSEUM OF ART. BULLETIN. 10 x y. Metropolitan Museum of Art, 5th Ave. at 82nd St., New York 28, N.Y. $ 5

314. MICHIGAN ALUMNUS. QUARTERLY REVIEW. Q. Alumni Assoc. of the Univ. of Michigan, Univ. of Michigan, Ann Arbor, Mich. $ 2

315. MICHIGAN HISTORY. Q. Michigan Hist. Commission, Cass Bldg., Lansing, Mich. $ 5

316. MID-AMERICA. An Historical Review. Q. 1918 (1959: vol. 41). Loyola Univ., 6525 Sheridan Rd., Chicago 26, Ill. Ed: Jerome V. Jacobsen. Art. on American hist., especially Middlewestern America, from the beginning of white settlements; bk. rev.; "Notes and Comments." $ 2

317. THE MIDDLE EAST JOURNAL. Q. Middle East Inst., 1761 N. St., N.W., Washington 6, D.C. Index. $ 6

318. MIDDLE EASTERN AFFAIRS. M. Council for Middle Eastern Affairs, 432 4th Ave., New York 16, N.Y. $ 5

319. MIDWEST FOLKLORE. Q. 1950 (1959: vol. 9). Indiana Univ., Bloomington, Ind. Ed: W. Edson Richmond, c/o Library, Room 41, Indiana Univ., Bloomington, Ind. Art. on folklore, with some emphasis on the American Midwest; rev. art.; bk. rev. $ 3

320. MIDWEST JOURNAL OF POLITICAL SCIENCE. Q. 1957 (1958: vol. 2). Wayne State Univ. Press, for Midwest Conference of Political Scientists, Drake Univ., Des Moines, Ia. Ed: David Fellman, Univ. of Wisconsin, Madison 6, Wis., and Charles W. Shull (manag. ed.), Wayne State Univ., Detroit 2, Mich. Art. on political science subjects not confined to any country, and on political hist. with emphasis on U.S. govt. and parties; bk. rev.; program of the meetings of the assoc. $ 6 (memb. $ 7.50) / $ 6.35

321. MILITARY AFFAIRS. Q. 1937 (1959: vol. 22). American Military Inst., 511 11th St., N.W., Washington 4, D.C. Ed: Victor Gondos, Jr. Art. on military hist., world-wide in scope; bk. rev.; biblio., "Notes and Documents"; "Headquarters Gazette" (news of the inst.). $ 5

322. MILITARY COLLECTOR AND HISTORIAN. Q. 1949 (1959: vol. 11). Company of Military Collectors and Historians, 77 Barnes St., Providence 6, R.I. Ed: Henry I. Shaw, Jr., 17 Tuckennan St., N.W., Washington 11, D.C. Art. on U.S. military hist., with emphasis on weapons and military uniforms; illus. $ 6.50

323. MILITARY REVIEW. M. Pub. address: U.S.A. CGSC, Fort Leavenworth, Kan. Separate editions appear also in Spanish and Portuguese. $ 3.50 / $ 4.50

324. THE MINNEAPOLIS INSTITUTE OF ARTS. BULLETIN. Q. Minneapolis Inst. of Arts, 201 East 24th St., Minneapolis 27, Minn. Short explanatory notes on the collections and new acquisitions of the inst.; illus. $ 2

325. MINNESOTA HISTORY. Q. Minnesota Hist. Soc., Central Ave. and Cedar St., St. Paul 1, Minn. Illus.; cum. index. $ 3 (memb. $ 4)

326. MISSISSIPPI GENEALOGICAL EXCHANGE. A Quarterly Devoted to Early Mississippi Families and Records. Q. Pub. address: 214 Massachusetts Ave., N.E., Washington 2, D.C. $ 3

327. THE MISSISSIPPI VALLEY HISTORICAL REVIEW. A Journal of American History. Q. 1914 (1958/59: vol. 45). Mississippi Valley Hist. Assoc., 1500 R St., Lincoln, Nebr. Ed: William C. Binkley, Tulane Univ. of Louisiana, New Orleans 18, La. Art. on American hist., mostly domestic, in the 19th and 20th cent.; bk. rev.; "Historical News and Comments"; A. index of authors, reviews, titles, names and subjects; cum. tables of contents for the years 1914-1919 and 1929-1939, pub. separately. (memb.) $ 5

328. THE MISSOURI ARCHAEOLOGIST. Q. Missouri Archaeological Soc., 15 Switzler Hall, Univ. of Missouri, Columbia, Mo. $ 2

329. MISSOURI HISTORICAL REVIEW. Q. State Hist. Soc. of Missouri, Columbia, Mo. Biblio.; index. $ 1

330. MISSOURI HISTORICAL SOCIETY. BULLETIN. Q. Missouri Hist. Soc., Jefferson Memorial Bldg., St. Louis 12, Mo. $ 5

331. MODERN DRAMA. Q. Dept. of English, Univ. of Kansas, Lawrence, Kan. $ 2

332. MONTANA. The Magazine of Western History. Q. 1951 (1960: vol. 10). Hist. Soc. of Montana, Roberts at 6th Ave., Helena, Mont. Ed: Michael Kennedy, 622 Harrison Ave., Helena, Mont. Art. on the hist. of the western U.S. $ 4

333. THE MONTH AT GOODSPEED'S. 9 x y. Goodspeed's Bk. Shop, 18 Beacon St., Boston 8, Mass. pni

334. MORAVIAN HISTORICAL SOCIETY. TRANSACTIONS. A. Moravian Hist. Soc., Nazareth, Penn. pni

335. MOST [Bridge]. Štvrťročník pre slovenskú kultúru [A quarterly for Slovak culture]. Q. Rev. J.J. Lach, for Slovak Writers and Artists Assoc., Slovak Inst., 2900 E. Blvd., Cleveland 4, O. $ 5

MUSEUM see section on International Periodicals

336. MUSEUM ECHOES. M. Ohio Hist. Soc., Ohio State Museum, High St. and 15th Ave., Columbus 10, O. pni

337. MUSEUM GRAPHIC. Q. Pub. address: St. Joseph Museum, St. Joseph, Mo. $ 1

MUSEUM NOTES. AMERICAN NUMISMATIC SOCIETY see AMERICAN NUMISMATIC SOCIETY. MUSEUM NOTES

338. MUSEUM OF FINE ARTS. BULLETIN. Q. Museum of Fine Arts, Boston 15, Mass. $ 1

339. MUSEUM SERVICE. 10 x y. Rochester Museum Assoc., 657 E. Ave., Rochester 7, N.Y. $ 5

340. THE MUSLIM WORLD. A Quarterly Journal of Islamic Study and of Christian Interpretation among Muslims. Q. Hartford Seminary Foundation, 55 Elizabeth St., Hartford 5, Conn. $ 3

341. NAMES. Q. American Name Soc., 2413 Dwinelle Hall, Univ. of California, Berkeley 4, Calif. Art. on personal, geographic, scientific, commercial and popular names; bk. rev.; biblio. $ 5

342. THE NASSAU COUNTY HISTORICAL JOURNAL. Q. Nassau County Hist. and Genealogical Soc., c/o Myron H. Luke, Hofstra College, Hempstead, N.Y. (memb.) $ 7.50

343. NATIONAL ARCHIVES ACCESSIONS. A. National Archives, Washington 25, D.C. pni

344. NATIONAL ASSOCIATION OF WATCH AND CLOCK COLLECTORS. BULLETIN. B-M. Pub. address: P.O.B. 33, 335 N. 3rd St., Columbia, Penn. (memb.) $ 8

345. THE NATIONAL BUTTON BULLETIN. B-M. National Button Soc., c/o Mrs. Robert McCreight, Jr., 7940 Montgomery Ave., Elkins Park, Philadelphia 17, Penn. $ 3.50

346. NATIONAL GENEALOGICAL SOCIETY. QUARTERLY. Q. 1912 (1958: vol. 46). National Genealogical Soc., 1921 Sunderland Pl., N.W., Washington 6, D.C. Ed: Milton Rubincam, 6303 20th Ave., Green Meadows, W. Hyattsville, Md. "It presents previously unpublished American source materials, including abstracts of pension applications, and publishes articles of genealogical interest and reviews of genealogical publications. An effort is made to secure data from as wide a range of territory as possible and to include data particularly from earlier settled areas"; bk. rev.; news of the soc.; separately paged supplement:"Index of Revolutionary War Pension Applications"; A. index pub. separately. $ 6

347. NATIONAL GEOGRAPHIC MAGAZINE. M. National Geographic Soc., 16th and M St., N.W., Washington 6, D.C. $ 8

348. NATIONAL RAILWAY HISTORICAL SOCIETY. BULLETIN. Q. National Railway Hist. Soc., c/o Charles W. Houser, 734 St. John St., Allentown, Penn. (memb.) $ 3.50.

349. NAVY. The Magazine of Sea Power. M. Navy League of the United States, The Mills Bldg., Washington 6, D.C. $ 2.50

350. NEBRASKA HISTORY. Q. Nebraska State Hist. Soc., 1500 R St., Lincoln 8, Nebr. $ 2

351. THE NEGRO HISTORY BULLETIN. 8 x y. Assoc. for the Study of Negro Life and Hist., Inc., 1538 9th St., N.W., Washington, D.C. "To inculcate an appreciation of the past of the Negro and to promote an understanding of his present status." $ 2

352. NEVADA HISTORICAL SOCIETY. QUARTERLY. Q. Nevada Hist. Soc., State Bldg., Reno, Nev. $ 5

353. NEW CANAAN HISTORICAL SOCIETY. ANNUAL. A. New Canaan Hist. Soc., 10 Cherry St., New Canaan, Conn. $ 2

354. NEW ENGLAND GALAXY. Q. Friends of Old Sturbridge Village, Sturbridge, Mass. $ 3

355. NEW ENGLAND HISTORICAL AND GENEALOGICAL REGISTER. Q. New England Hist. Genealogical Soc., 9 Ashburton Pl., Boston, Mass. Biblio.; illus.; cum. index. $ 7.50

356. THE NEW ENGLAND QUARTERLY. A Historical Review of New England Life and Letters. Q. 1928 (1958: vol. 31). Pub. address: Hubbard Hall, Brunswick, Me. Ed: Herbert Brown. Art. on the hist. of New England, with emphasis on literary hist.; doc.; bk. rev.; index of authors and bk. rev.; A. biblio. on New England. $ 5

357. NEW ENGLAND SOCIAL STUDIES BULLETIN. Q. Univ. of New Hampshire, Durham, N.H. $ 2

358. NEW HAMPSHIRE PROFILES. M. New Hampshire Profiles Corp., P.O.B. 900, Portsmouth, N.H. $ 4.50

359. NEW HAVEN COLONY HISTORICAL SOCIETY. JOURNAL. Q. Pub. address: 114 Whitney Ave., New Haven, Conn. pni

360. NEW JERSEY HISTORICAL SOCIETY. PROCEEDINGS. Q. New Jersey Hist. Soc., 230 Broadway, Newark 4, N.J. Cum. index. (memb.) $ 3.50

361. NEW JERSEY MESSENGER. 3 x y. Pub. address: 230 Broadway, Newark 4, N.J. pni

362. NEW LONDON COUNTY HISTORICAL SOCIETY. QUARTERLY BULLETIN. Q. Pub. address: Shaw Mansion, 11 Blinman St., New London, Conn. pni

363. NEW MEXICO HISTORICAL REVIEW. Q. Hist. Soc. of New Mexico, P.O.B. 1727, Santa Fe, N.M. Cum. index. $ 3

364. THE NEW YORK ACADEMY OF SCIENCES. TRANSACTIONS. 8 x y. Pub. address: 2 E. 63rd St., New York 21, N.Y. memb. free

365. NEW YORK FOLKLORE QUARTERLY. Q. New York Folklore Soc., c/o Farmers' Museum, Cooperstown, N.Y. $ 4

366. NEW YORK GENEALOGICAL AND BIOGRAPHICAL RECORD. Q. New York Genealogical and Biographical Soc., 122 E. 58th St., New York 22, N.Y. $ 6

367. NEW YORK HISTORICAL SOCIETY. QUARTERLY. Q. New York Hist. Soc., 170 Central Park West, New York 24, N.Y. $ 3

368. NEW YORK HISTORY. Q. New York State Hist. Assoc., Cooperstown, N.Y. $ 5

369. NEW YORK PUBLIC LIBRARY. BULLETIN. M. New York Public Library, 5th Ave. and 42nd St., New York 18, N.Y. $ 3

370. THE NEWBERRY LIBRARY BULLETIN. 3 x y. Newberry Library, 60 W. Walton St., Chicago 10, Ill. free

NEWSLETTER. For titles beginning with "Newsletter," followed by the name of the publishing or sponsoring institution or society, see the respective institution or society.

371. NIAGARA FRONTIER. Q. Buffalo Hist. Soc., Delaware Park, Buffalo 7, N.Y. $ 2

372. NINETEENTH CENTURY FICTION. Q. Univ. of California Press, Berkeley 4, Calif. $ 4

373. NORTH CAROLINA FOLKLORE. S-A. Univ. of North Carolina, P.O.B. 523, Chapel Hill, N.C. $ 2

374. THE NORTH CAROLINA HISTORICAL REVIEW. Q. State Dept. of Archives and Hist., Corner of Edenton and Salisbury St., Raleigh, N.C. $ 3

375. THE NORTH CAROLINIAN. A Quarterly Journal of Genealogy and History. Q. Pub. address: c/o Wm. Perry Johnson, P.O.B. 531, Raleigh, N.C. $ 5

376. NORTH DAKOTA HISTORY. Q. State Hist. Soc. of North Dakota, Bismarck, N.D. (memb.) $ 3

377. THE NORTH DAKOTA QUARTERLY. Q. Univ. of North Dakota Press, Grand Forks, N.D. $ 3.50

378. NORTHEAST FOLKLORE. Q. 1958 (1959: vol. 2). Northeast Folklore Soc., under the auspices of the Dept. of English, Univ. of Maine. Ed: Edward D. Ives, Basil F. Kirtley, 220 Stevens Hall, Univ. of Maine, Orono, Me. Studies of the folklore of New England and the Maritime Provinces; bk. rev.; biblio. (memb.) $ 7, including Journal of American Folklore

379. NORTHWEST OHIO QUARTERLY. A Journal of History and Civilization. Q. Hist. Soc. of Northwestern Ohio, Toledo, O. (memb.) $ 0.75

380. NOTES. Q. Music Library Assoc., Music Division, Library of Congress, Washington 25, D.C. $ 5

381. NOVYI ZHURNAL [The new review]. Irr. Pub. address: 506 W. 113th St., New York, N.Y. pni

382. NOW AND THEN. A Quarterly Magazine of History, Biography, and Genealogy. Q. Muncy Hist. Soc., P.O.B. 11, Muncy, Penn. $ 3 / $ 4

383. LA NUEVA DEMOCRACIA [The new democracy]. Q. Comité de Cooperación en la América Latina, 156 5th Ave., New York 10, N.Y. $ 2

384. THE NUMISMATIC SCRAPBOOK MAGAZINE. A Monthly Magazine for the Collector of Coins, Tokens, Medals and Paper Money. M. Hewitt Bros., 7320 Milwaukee Ave., Chicago 48, Ill. Advertisements, news and a few art. $ 4 / $ 4.50

385. THE NUMISMATIST. M. American Numismatic Assoc., c/o Lewis M. Reagan, P.O.B. 577, Wichita, Kan. $ 6

386. OHIO ARCHAEOLOGIST. Q. Archaeological Soc. of Ohio, 65 N. Foster St., Norwalk, O. Illus. (memb.) $ 3

387. OHIO HISTORICAL QUARTERLY. Q. Ohio Hist. Soc., Ohio State Museum, Columbus 10, O. Bk. rev.; cum. index. $ 6

388. OHIOANA. Of Ohio and Ohioans. Q. Martha Kinney Cooper, Ohioana Library Assoc., 1109 Ohio Dept. Bldg., Columbus 15, O. $ 2.50 (memb. $ 3)

389. THE OLD PRINT SHOP PORTFOLIO. M. Old Print Shop, 150 Lexington Ave., New York, N.Y. pni

390. OLD-TIME NEW ENGLAND. **Q.** Soc. for the Preservation of New England Antiquities, Harrison Gray Otis House, 141 Cambridge St., Boston 14, Mass. "Devoted to the ancient buildings, household furnishing, domestic arts, manners and customs, and minor antiquities of the New England people"; illus.; cum. index. $ 3

391. ORBIS. A Quarterly Journal of World Affairs. Q. Univ. of Pennsylvania Press, 3436 Walnut St., Philadelphia 4, Penn., for Foreign Policy Research Inst., Univ. of Pennsylvania. $ 5

392. OREGON HISTORICAL QUARTERLY. Q. Oregon Hist. Soc., 235 S.W. Market St., Portland 1, Oreg. $ 3

393. PACIFIC AFFAIRS. An International Review of the Far East. Q. Inst. of Pacific Relations, 333 6th Ave., New York, N.Y. $ 5

394. PACIFIC HISTORIAN. Q. 1956 (1959: vol. 3). College of the Pacific, Stockton 4, Calif. Ed: Reginald R. Stuart, Grace D. Stuart, Glenn W. Price. Art. and doc. on the hist. of the American West, particularly the West Coast and California. $ 3 (beginning with vol. 4)

395. PACIFIC HISTORICAL REVIEW. Q. 1932 (1959: vol. 28). Univ. of California Press, Berkeley 4, Calif. Ed: John W. **Caughey**, Univ. of California at Los Angeles. Art. on Western America, Spanish America, and countries of the Pacific, pertaining mainly to the 19th cent., but not including Spanish explorations; bk. rev.; "Historical News"; report of the Pacific Coast Branch of the American Hist. Assoc. $ 4 / $ 4.50

396. PACIFIC NORTHWEST QUARTERLY. Q. 1906 (1959: vol. 50). Univ. of Washington, Seattle 5, W. Ed: Charles M. Gates, Robert E. Burke. Art. on the Pacific Northwest of the U.S.A. and Canada from the time of the earliest settlements; bk. rev.; Washington State Hist. Soc. notes. $ 3.50

397. PACIFIC SOCIOLOGICAL REVIEW. S-A. Pacific Sociological Soc., 209 Commonwealth Hall, Univ. of Oregon, Eugene, Oreg. $ 3

398. EL PALACIO [The palace]. B-M. Archaeological Soc. of New Mexico and the School of American Research, Museum of New Mexico, Santa Fe, N.M. (memb.) $ 5

399. PALIMPSEST. M. State Hist. Soc. of Iowa, Iowa City, Ia. $ 2.50 (memb. $ 3)

PAPERS. For titles beginning with "Papers," followed by the name of the publishing or sponsoring institution or society, see the respective institution or society.

400. PASSAIC COUNTY HISTORICAL SOCIETY. BULLETIN. Irr. (2-4 x y). Passaic County Hist. Soc., Lambert Castle, Paterson 3, N.J. $ 2

401. PASSWORD. **Q.** El Paso Hist. Soc., El Paso, Tex. memb. free

402. PENNSYLVANIA ARCHAEOLOGIST. Q. Soc. for Pennsylvania Archaeology, V.R. Mruzoski, 407 Phillips St., Aliquippa, Penn. memb. free

403. PENNSYLVANIA FOLKLIFE. Q. Pennsylvania Dutch Folklore Center, Inc., 8 West King St., Lancaster, Penn. $ 3 / $ 3.50

404. THE PENNSYLVANIA GENEALOGICAL MAGAZINE. A. Genealogical Soc. of Pennsylvania, 1300 Locust St., Philadelphia 7, Penn. memb. free

405. PENNSYLVANIA HISTORY. Q. Pennsylvania Hist. Assoc., Pennsylvania State Univ., University Park, Penn. $ 5

406. PENNSYLVANIA MAGAZINE OF HISTORY AND BIOGRAPHY. Q. Hist. Soc. of Pennsylvania, 1300 Locust St., Philadelphia 7, Penn. $ 5

407. PHARMACY IN HISTORY. Q. American Inst. of the Hist. of Pharmacy, 356 Chemistry Bldg., Madison 6, Wis. One issue each year devoted to the report of the A. meeting of the inst.; illus. (memb.) $ 5

408. PHILADELPHIA MUSEUM BULLETIN. Q. Philadelphia Museum of Art, Parkway at 26th St., Philadelphia 1, Penn. $ 2

409. PHILOLOGICAL QUARTERLY. Q. Univ. of Iowa, Iowa City, Ia. $ 5

410. PHILOSOPHICAL REVIEW. Q. 231 Goldwin Smith Hall, Cornell Univ., Ithaca, N.Y. $ 6 (individuals $ 3)

411. THE PHYLON QUARTERLY. A Review of Race and Culture. Q. Atlanta Univ., Atlanta 14, Ga. $ 3 / $ 3.50

412. PICKET POST. A Record of Patriotism. Q. Valley Forge Hist. Soc., Valley Forge, Penn. $ 1.50

413. PILGRIM SOCIETY NOTES. Irr. Pilgrim Soc., Plymouth, Mass. pni

414. PLATEAU. Q. Northern Arizona Soc. of Science and Art, Museum of Northern Arizona, Flagstaff, Ariz. (memb.) $ 5

415. PMLA. 5 x y. Modern Language Assoc. of America, 6 Washington Sq. North, New York 3, N.Y. $ 7 / $ 10

416. POLISH AMERICAN STUDIES. A Journal Devoted to Polish American Life and History. S-A. Polish American Hist. Assoc., c/o Polish Inst. of Arts and Sciences in America, St. Mary's College, Orchard Lake, Mich. Bk. rev.; biblio. $ 2

417. POLISH FOLKLORE. Q. Alliance College, Cambridge Springs, Penn. Occasionally illus. $ 2

418. POLISH MEDICAL HISTORY AND SCIENCE BULLETIN. S-A. Polish Medical Alliance, 2424 Kedzie Blvd., Chicago 47, Ill. $ 5

419. THE POLISH REVIEW. Q. 1956 (1958: vol. 3). Polish Inst. of Arts and Sciences in America, 145 East 53rd St., New York 22, N.Y. Ed: Ludwik Krzyzanowski. Art. on Polish cultural life, particularly literature, and politics, mostly recent and contemporary, including hist., primarily of the 20th cent.; bk. rev.; chronicle of current Polish events; letters to the ed. $ 5

420. POLITICAL SCIENCE QUARTERLY. Q. Acad. of Political Science, Columbia Univ., New York 27, N.Y. (memb.) $6

421. PONY EXPRESS. Stories of Pioneers and Old Trails. M. Pub. address: P.O.B. 326, Sonora, Calif. $2.50

422. PRESBYTERIAN HISTORICAL SOCIETY, JOURNAL OF THE. Q. 1901 (1958: vol. 36). Dept. of Hist. of the United Presbyterian Church in the U.S.A. Ed: Charles A. Anderson, 520 Witherspoon Bldg., Philadelphia 7, Penn. Art. on the hist. of the Presbyterian Church in the U.S.A., pertaining mostly to the 18th and 19th cent., with some biographic emphasis, and on contemporary church life and views; occasional bk. rev.; index. $3 (memb. $5)

423. THE PRINCETON UNIVERSITY LIBRARY CHRONICLE. Q. Princeton Univ. Library, Princeton, N.J. $4

424. PRINT. America's Graphic Design Magazine. B-M. 535 Fifth Ave., New York 17, N.Y. $9 / $10

425. PROBLEMS OF COMMUNISM. B-M. United States Information Agency, 1728 L St., N.W., Washington 25, D.C. $1.50 / $2

PROCEEDINGS. For titles beginning with "Proceedings," followed by the name of the publishing or sponsoring institution or society, see the respective institution or society.

426. PROLOGUE. Q. Prologue Research and Pub. Assoc., Inc., 875 West End Ave., New York 25, N.Y. Mostly Ukrainian hist. and politics. $3

427. PUBLIC OPINION QUARTERLY. Q. Princeton Univ., P.O.B. 486, Princeton, N.J. $6 / $6.25

PUBLICATIONS. For titles beginning with "Publications," followed by the name of the publishing or sponsoring institution or society, see the respective institution or society.

QUARTERLY. For titles beginning with "Quarterly," followed by the name of the publishing or sponsoring institution or society, see the respective institution or society.

QUARTERLY BULLETIN OF THE NEW LONDON COUNTY HISTORICAL SOCIETY see NEW LONDON COUNTY HISTORICAL SOCIETY. QUARTERLY BULLETIN

428. THE QUARTERLY JOURNAL OF SPEECH. Q. Speech Assoc. of America, Louisiana State University, Baton Rouge 3, La. $5.50

QUARTERLY REVIEW. MICHIGAN ALUMNUS see MICHIGAN ALUMNUS. QUARTERLY REVIEW

429. THE QUARTERLY REVIEW OF HIGHER EDUCATION AMONG NEGROES. Q. Johnson C. Smith Univ., Charlotte, N.C. $2

430. RAILWAY AND LOCOMOTIVE HISTORICAL SOCIETY. BULLETIN. Irr. 1921 (1959: no. 100). Baker Library, Harvard Business School, Boston,

Mass. Ed: Charles E. Fisher. Art. on the hist. of railroading, almost exclusively of the U.S.; bk. rev.; biblio. of bk. and art.; illus. $ 3 (memb. free)

RECORDS. For titles beginning with "Records," followed by the name of the publishing or sponsoring institution or society, see the respective institution or society.

431. REGISTER. Q. Kentucky Hist. Soc., Frankfort, Ky. $ 5

432. THE REVIEW OF METAPHYSICS. A Philosophical Quarterly. Q. Philosophy Education Soc., 202 Linsly Hall, Yale Univ., New Haven, Conn. Cum. index for the years 1947-57. $ 6

433. THE REVIEW OF POLITICS. Q. 1939 (1959: vol. 21). Univ. of Notre Dame, Notre Dame, Ind. Ed: M.A. Fitzsimons. Art. on politics and related subjects; bk. rev.; A. cum. index. $ 5 / $ 5.40

434. REVISTA HISPANICA MODERNA [Modern Hispanic review]. Q. 1934 (1957: vol. 13). Hispanic Inst., Columbia Univ., 435 W. 117th St., New York 27, N.Y. Ed. board: Angel del Río, Eugenio Florit, Andrés Iduarte. Art. on literary hist., mostly of Spain, Portugal and the Latin American countries; list of pub. of the inst. in Spanish and English; bk. rev.; "Bibliografía Hispanoamericana": biblio. of bk. and periodicals, pub. recently in the U.S.A., Latin America, Spain and other European countries, classified by subject (general [including hist.] language, literature, folklore and Spanish relations), and thereunder by country. $ 4

435. REVISTA IBEROAMERICANA [Spanish-American review]. S-A. Pub. address: 31 E. 10th St., New York 3, N.Y. $ 4

REVISTA INTERAMERICANA DE BIBLIOGRAFIA see INTER-AMERICAN REVIEW OF BIBLIOGRAPHY

436. RHODE ISLAND HISTORY. Q. Rhode Island Hist. Soc., 52 Power St., Providence 6, R.I. $ 4

437. RHODE ISLAND JEWISH HISTORICAL NOTES. S-A. Rhode Island Jewish Hist. Assoc., 52 Power St., Providence 6, R.I. $ 5

438. ROCHESTER HISTORY. Q. City Historian, Rochester Public Library, 115 South Ave., Rochester 4, N.Y. $ 0.25

439. ROMÂNIA [Rumania]. M. Rumanian National Committee, 157 W. 57th St., New York 19, N.Y. pni

440. THE ROMANIC REVIEW. Q. Columbia Univ. Press, 2960 Broadway New York 27, N.Y., for Dept. of Romance Languages, Columbia Univ. Mostly literature. $ 6 / $ 6.30

441. THE RUSSIAN REVIEW. An American Quarterly Devoted to Russia, Past and Present. Q. 1941 (1959: vol. 18). Pub. address: 235 Baker Library, Hanover, N.H. Ed: Dimitri von Mohrenschildt. "The purpose of the RUSSIAN REVIEW is to interpret the real aims and aspirations of the Russian people, as distinguished from and opposed to Soviet Communism, and to advance general knowledge of Russian culture, history and civilization"; bk. rev. $ 5 / $ 6

442. RUTGERS UNIVERSITY LIBRARY. JOURNAL. S-A. Friends of the Library of Rutgers Univ., New Brunswick, N.J. $ 2

443. SAN DIEGO HISTORICAL SOCIETY. QUARTERLY. Q. San Diego Hist. Soc., Junipero Serra Museum, 2727 Presidio Drive, San Diego 3, Calif. (memb.) $ 2

444. SCANDINAVIAN STUDIES. Q. Soc. for the Advancement of Scandinavian Studies, George Banta Co., Inc., 450 Ahnaip St., Menasha, Wis. $ 3

445. SCIENCE. W. American Assoc. for the Advancement of Science, 1515 Massachusetts Ave., N.W., Washington 5, D.C. $ 8.50 / $ 10

446. SCIENÇE AND SOCIETY. Q. Pub. address: 30 E. 20th St., New York 3, N.Y. $ 3 / $ 3.50

447. SCIENTIFIC AMERICAN. M. Scientific American, Inc., 2 W. 45th St., New York, N.Y. $ 5 / $ 8

448. SCRIPTA MATHEMATICA. Q. Yeshiva Univ., Amsterdam Ave. and 186th St., New York 33, N.Y. $ 5

449. THE SHAWNEE COUNTY HISTORICAL SOCIETY. BULLETIN. Irr. Shawnee County Hist. Soc., Topeka, Kan. pni

450. SLAVIC AND EAST EUROPEAN JOURNAL. Q. American Assoc. of Teachers of Slavic and East European Languages, c/o J.T. Shaw, Indiana Univ., Bloomington, Ind. $ 5

451. SLOVAKIA. Q. Slovak League of America, P.O.B. 150, Middletown, Penn. $ 1 / $ 2

452. SOCIAL EDUCATION. 8 x y. National Council for Social Studies, 1201 16th St., N.W., Washington 6, D.C. $ 5

453. SOCIAL FORCES. Q. Univ. of North Carolina Press, Chapel Hill, N.C. $ 6

454. SOCIAL SCIENCE. Q. Social Science Pub. Co., 1414 E. 4th Ave., Winfield, Kan. $ 2

455. THE SOCIAL STUDIES. A Periodical for Teachers and Administrators. M. McKinley Pub. Co., 809-11 N. 19th St., Philadelphia 30, Penn. $ 3.50

456. SOCIAL WORK. Q. Pub. address: 374 Broadway, Albany 7, N.Y. $ 6

457. SOCIETY OF ARCHITECTURAL HISTORIANS. JOURNAL. Q. 1941 (1959: vol. 18). Soc. of Architectural Historians, Dept. of Art, Univ. of Mass., Amherst, Mass. Ed: Paul F. Norton. Art. on the buildings and architecture of all hist. cultures; bk. rev.; "American Notes" (news of architects, programs, works in progress, preservation, etc., in the U.S.); news of the soc.; illus., graph; A. index of subjects, authors and titles; cum. index for vol. 4-7 (1944-48). (memb.) $ 7.50

458. SONS OF THE AMERICAN REVOLUTION. MAGAZINE. Q. National Soc. of the Sons of the American Revolution, 1227 16th St., N.W., Washington 6, D.C. $ 2

459. SOUTH ATLANTIC QUARTERLY. Q. 1902 (1959: vol. 57). Duke Univ. Press, P.O.B. 6697, College Station, Durham, N.C. Manag. ed: W.B. Hamilton, Duke Univ., Durham, N.C. Art. on hist., economics, politics and the arts; bk. rev.; A. cum. index. $ 4

460. SOUTH CAROLINA HISTORICAL MAGAZINE. Q. South Carolina Hist. Soc., Charleston 5, S.C. Illus.; index. $ 6

461. SOUTHERN ECONOMIC JOURNAL. Q. Univ. of North Carolina, Chapel Hill, N.C. $ 6

462. SOUTHERN FOLKLORE QUARTERLY. Q. 1937 (1958: vol. 22). Univ. of Florida, Gainesville, Fla., and South Atlantic Modern Language Assoc. Ed: Alton C. Morris. Art. "devoted to the historical and descriptive study of folklore and to the discussion of folk material as a living tradition," mostly on the Southern U.S.; bk. rev.; comprehensive A. classified biblio. of art. (from 25 periodicals pub. in various countries) and bk., with annotations or abstr., on the folklore of the Western hemisphere. $ 3.50

463. SOUTHERN INDIAN STUDIES. A. Archaeological Soc. of North Carolina, Univ. of North Carolina, Chapel Hill, N.C. $ 1

464. SOUTHERN JEWISH HISTORICAL SOCIETY. JOURNAL. Irr. Mrs. Maurice L. Hutzler, 1411 Wentbridge Rd., Richmond 27, Va. $ 2

465. THE SOUTHWESTERN HISTORICAL QUARTERLY. Q. Texas State Hist. Assoc., Univ. Station, Austin 12, Tex. $ 5

466. SOUTHWESTERN JOURNAL OF ANTHROPOLOGY. Q. Univ. of New Mexico, Albuquerque, N.M. $ 4 / 20s

467. SOUTHWESTERN LORE. Q. Colorado Archaeological Soc., Univ. of Colorado, Boulder, Col. (memb.) $ 2.50

468. SOUTHWESTERN LOUISIANA JOURNAL. Q. Southwestern Louisiana Inst., Stephens Memorial Library, Lafayette, La. $ 2

469. SOUTHWESTERN SOCIAL SCIENCE QUARTERLY. Q. Southwestern Social Science Assoc., c/o James M. Owen, Louisiana State Univ., Baton Rouge 3, La. $ 5

470. SPECIAL LIBRARIES. 10 x y. Special Libraries Assoc., 31 E. 10th St., New York 3, N.Y. $ 7 / $ 7.50

471. SPECULUM. A Journal of Mediaeval Studies. Q. 1926 (1958: vol. 33) Mediaeval Acad. of America, 1430 Massachusetts Ave., Cambridge 38, Mass. Ed: Charles R.D. Miller. Art. on medieval Europe including literature, philology and the arts; extensive bk. rev.; biblio. of periodical literature; list of pub. of the acad.; proceedings of the acad.; professional news. $ 8

472. SPEECH MONOGRAPHS. Q. Speech Assoc. of America, Louisiana State Univ., Baton Rouge 3, La. $ 6

473. SPINNING WHEEL. A National Magazine About Antiques. M. Spinning Wheel Pub., Inc., Taneytown, Md. $ 3

474. SPUR. Life in Virginia. M. Holly Hill Press, Fredericksburg, Va. Illus. $ 2

475. STATEN ISLAND HISTORIAN. Q. Staten Island Hist. Soc., Richmondtown, Staten Island 6, N.Y. $ 2 (memb. $ 5)

476. STEAMBOAT BILL. Q. Steamship Hist. Soc. of America, Inc., West Barrington, R.I. libraries: $ 2 (memb. $ 4) / $ 2

477. STEWART CLAN MAGAZINE. Genealogical Records of Stewart-Stuart Families. M. Pub. address: c/o George Edson, 811 E. Park St., Olathe, Kan. $ 3

478. STUDIES IN BIBLIOGRAPHY AND BOOKLORE. S-A. Library of Hebrew Union College, Jewish Inst. of Religion, Cincinnati, O. $ 4 (biennial subscription)

479. STUDIES IN PHILOLOGY. Q. Southern Methodist Univ. Press, Dallas, Tex. $ 3

480. STUDIES IN THE RENAISSANCE. A. 1954 (1958: vol. 5). Renaissance Soc. of America, 1161 Amsterdam Ave., New York 27, N.Y. Ed: M.A. Shaaber, Univ. of Pennsylvania, Philadelphia 4, Penn. Art. on all aspects of the Renaissance in Europe. pni

481. SUSQUEHANNA UNIVERSITY STUDIES. Q. Susquehanna Univ. Press, Selinsgrove, Penn. p (1) $ 0.25

482. THE SWEDISH PIONEER. Historical Quarterly. Q. 1950 (1958: vol. 9). Augustana Bk. Concern, 639 38th St., Rock Island, Ill., for Swedish Pioneer Hist. Soc., 3225 Foster Ave., Chicago 25, Ill. Ed: E. Gustav Johnson. Art. on Swedes in America and relations between Sweden and America from the first Viking explorations to the present; bk. rev. covering a wide scope of Scandinavian and Scandinavian-American hist.; reports and announcements of the soc.; A. index. $ 3

483. TABLELAND TRAILS. Q. Pub. address: Rt. No. 1, "Mendeli," Oakland, Md. $ 5

484. TECHNOLOGY AND CULTURE. The International Quarterly of the Society for the History of Technology, Devoted to the Study of the Development of Technology and its Relations with Society and Culture. Q. 1960 (1960: vol. 1). Wayne State Univ. Press, Detroit 2, Mich., for Soc. for the Hist. of Technology, Room 311, Main Bldg., Case Inst. of Technology, Cleveland 6, O. Ed: Melvin Kranzberg. Art. on the hist. of all branches of technology, on cultural and social aspects of technological development, and on the hist. of ideas; bk. rev.; biblio.; notes about the soc. (memb.) $ 8

485. TENNESSEE ARCHAEOLOGIST. S-A. Tennessee Archaeological Soc., 6 Biology Bldg., Univ. of Tennessee, Knoxville, Tenn. Illus. (memb.) $ 3

486. TENNESSEE FOLKLORE SOCIETY. BULLETIN. Q. Tennessee Folklore Soc., c/o William J. Griffin, George Peabody College for Teachers, Nashville, Tenn. (memb.) $ 2

487. TENNESSEE HISTORICAL QUARTERLY. Q. Tennessee Hist. Soc. and Tennessee Hist. Commission, State Library and Archives Bldg., Nashville, Tenn. Illus.; index. $ 3

488. TEXAS GULF COAST HISTORICAL ASSOCIATION. PUBLICATIONS. S-A. Texas Gulf Coast Hist. Assoc., c/o James A. Tinsley, Dept. of Hist., Univ. of Houston, Houston, Tex. $ 3

489. THEOLOGY TODAY. Q. Pub. address: P.O.B. 29, Princeton, N.J. $ 3

490. THOUGHT. A Review of Culture and Idea. Q. Graduate School, Fordham Univ., New York, N.Y. 58. Bk. rev.; index. $ 5

491. TRADING POST. B-M. American Soc. of Military Insignia Collectors, c/o Ira L. Duncan, 744 Warfield Ave., Oakland 10, Calif. Data relating to the military insignia of American armed units; illus. (memb.) $ 5

492. TRADITION. The Monthly Magazine of America's Picturesque Past. M. 1958 (1959: vol. 2). American Tradition Corporation, 16, 854 Hamilton Ave. Detroit 3, Mich. Ed: L.W. Mueller. Art. on United States hist.; illus. Ceased pub. in 1959. $ 5

493. TRAINS. The Magazine of Railroading. M. Kalmbach Pub. Co., 1027 N. 7th St., Milwaukee 3, Wis. $ 6

TRANSACTIONS. For titles beginning with "Transactions," followed by the name of the publishing or sponsoring institution or society, see the respective institution or society.

494. TREE-RING BULLETIN. A. Tree-Ring Soc., Univ. of Arizona, Tucson, Ariz. $ 2

495. THE TWAINIAN. B-M. Mark Twain Research Foundation, Inc., Perry, Mo. (memb.) $ 5

496. ÚJ MAGYAR ÚT [New Hungarian way]. M. Magyar Szellemi Munkaközösség [Hungarian Study Group], P.O.B. 265, Silver Spring, Md. English sum.; author index. pni

497. UKRAINIAN ACADEMY OF ARTS AND SCIENCES IN THE U.S., ANNALS OF THE. S-A (plus one special issue). 11 1/2 West 26th St., New York 10, N.Y. $ 6

498. THE UKRAINIAN QUARTERLY. Q. Ukrainian Congress Committee of America, 302 W. 13th St., New York 14, N.Y. $ 5

499. UNDER TEXAS SKIES. M. Pub. address: Capital National Bank Bldg., Austin, Tex. Illus. $ 3

500. UNITED DAUGHTERS OF THE CONFEDERACY. MAGAZINE. M. Pub. address: P.O.B. 431, Covington, Ga. $ 1.50

501. UNITED STATES NAVAL INSTITUTE. PROCEEDINGS. For the Advancement of Professional, Literary, and Scientific Knowledge in the Navy. M. 1874 (1958: vol. 84). U.S. Naval Inst., Annapolis, Md. Ed: R.N. Adrian. Art. on the hist. of the U.S. navy; proceedings of the inst.; professional notes and news; bk. rev.; illus. $ 5 / $ 6

502. UNIVERSITY ARCHAEOLOGICAL SOCIETY. NEWSLETTER. 8xy. Brigham Young Univ., Provo, Ut. $ 3

503. UTAH HISTORICAL QUARTERLY. Q. Utah State Hist. Soc., 603 E. South Temple St., Salt Lake City 2, Ut. $ 3

504. VENTURA COUNTY HISTORICAL SOCIETY. QUARTERLY. Q. Ventura County Hist. Soc., Pioneer Museum, 77 North California St., Ventura, Calif. (memb.) $ 5

505. VERMONT HISTORY. Q. Vermont Hist. Soc., State Library Bldg., Montpelier, Vt. p (1) $ 1

506. VICTORIAN STUDIES. A Quarterly Journal of the Humanities, Arts and Sciences. Q. 1957 (1959: vol. 2). Indiana Univ., 128 North College Ave., Indianapolis 2, Ind. Ed: P. Appleman, W.A. Madden, M. Wolff, Indiana Univ., Bloomington, Ind. Art. on various aspects of Victorian England; bk. rev. $ 5

507. VINELAND HISTORICAL MAGAZINE. Q. Vineland Hist. Soc., 108 S. 7th St., Vineland, N.J. $ 3

508. VIRGINIA CAVALCADE. Q. Virginia State Library, Richmond 19, Va. $ 2

509. THE VIRGINIA GENEALOGIST. Q. Pub. address: P.O.B. 4883, Washington 8, D.C. $ 5

510. THE VIRGINIA MAGAZINE OF HISTORY AND BIOGRAPHY. Q. Virginia Hist. Soc., North Blvd. and Kensington Ave., Richmond 20, Va. $ 5

511. THE VIRGINIA QUARTERLY REVIEW. A National Journal of Literature and Discussion. Q. Univ. of Virginia, Charlottesville, Va. $ 4

512. THE VOICE OF FREE GEORGIA. Periodical Information Bulletin. Q. Ed: Alexander Tsomaia, 1335 Madison Ave., New York, N.Y. pni

513. WALT WHITMAN BIRTHPLACE BULLETIN. Q. Walt Whitman Birthplace Assoc., 264 Walt Whitman Rd., Huntington Station, N.Y. $ 1.50

514. WALTERS ART GALLERY. BULLETIN. 8xy. Pub. address: Charles and Center St., Baltimore 1, Md. $ 1

515. WASHTENAW IMPRESSIONS. Irr. Washtenaw Hist. Soc., 160 Rackham Bldg., Ann Arbor, Mich. (memb. free)

516. WEST TENNESSEE HISTORICAL SOCIETY. PAPERS. A. West Tennessee Hist. Soc., Memphis, Tenn. $ 4

517. WEST VIRGINIA ARCHAEOLOGIST. Irr. West Virginia Archaeological Soc., 315 7th St., Moundsville, W. Va. $ 2

518. WEST VIRGINIA HISTORICAL SOCIETY. PUBLICATIONS. Irr. West Virginia Hist. Soc., Parkersburg, W. Va. pni

519. WEST VIRGINIA HISTORY. Q. State Dept. of Archives and Hist., Charleston, W. Va. $ 3

520. WESTCHESTER HISTORIAN. Q. Westchester County Hist. Soc., County Office Bldg., White Plains, N.Y. Index; illus. $ 5

521. WESTERN FOLKLORE. Q. 1942 (1958: vol. 17). Univ. of California Press, Berkeley 4, Calif., for California Folklore Soc. Ed: Wayland D. Hand, Univ. of California, Los Angeles 24, Calif. Art. on folklore, with emphasis on the U.S.A. and the American West; bk. rev.; professional news; A. index, including an index of folk tales, classified by "motif-index numbers." Replaced California Historical Quarterly in 1947. (memb.) $ 4

522. WESTERN HUMANITIES REVIEW. Q. Inst. of American Studies, Univ. of Utah, 325 Spencer Hall, Salt Lake City 12, Ut. $ 3

523. WESTERN PENNSYLVANIA HISTORICAL MAGAZINE. Q. Hist. Soc. of Western Pennsylvania, 4338 Bigelow Blvd., Pittsburgh 13, Penn. $ 5

524. WESTERN POLITICAL QUARTERLY. Q. Inst. of Government, Univ. of Utah, Salt Lake City 1, Ut. $ 5 / $ 6

525. THE WESTERN RAILROADER. M. Ed: Francis A. Guido, P.O.B. 668, San Mateo, Calif. $ 1 / $ 2.64

526. THE WESTERNERS BRAND BOOK. M. Pub. address: 522 Willow Rd., Winnetka, Ill. pni

527. WESTWAYS. M. Pub. address: 8833 Olympic Blvd., Beverly Hills, Calif. $ 1.50

528. THE WILLIAM AND MARY QUARTERLY. A Magazine of Early American History. Q. 1892 (1958: 3rd series, vol. 15). Inst. of Early American Hist. and Culture, Williamsburg, Va. Ed: Lawrence W. Towner, P.O.B. 1298, Williamsburg, Va. Art. on American hist., from the colonial period to the early 19th cent.; doc.; "Trivia" (selections from diaries, newspapers and letters from the period); bk. rev.; announcements of the inst.; A. index of authors reviewers, names, and subjects; cum. indices for vol. 1-27 (1892-1919) and for 2nd series, vol. 1-23 (1921-1943); index of genealogical data for vol. 1-16 (1892-1908); illus. $ 4

529. THE WISCONSIN ARCHAEOLOGIST. Q. Wisconsin Archaeology Soc., Public Museum, Milwaukee, Wis. "For the purpose of advancing the study and preservation of Wisconsin Indian Antiquities." (memb.) $ 2

530. WISCONSIN MAGAZINE OF HISTORY. Q. State Hist. Soc. of Wisconsin, 816 State St., Madison 6, Wis. Index; illus. (memb.) $ 5

531. WISDOM. The Magazine of Knowledge for all America. M. Pub. address: 8800 Wilshire Blvd., Beverly Hills, Calif. $ 10 / $ 15

532. WORLD AFFARIS. Q. American Peace Soc., 1612 1st St., Washington, D.C. $ 2 / $ 2.50

WORLD AFFAIRS INTERPRETER see WORLD AFFAIRS QUARTERLY

533. WORLD AFFAIRS QUARTERLY. Q. 1930 (1958/59: vol. 29). School of International Relations, Univ. of Southern California, Univ. Park, Los Angeles 7, Calif. Ed: Richard W. Van Alstyne. Art. on world hist. and politics during the 19th and 20th cent.; bk. rev. Replaced World Affairs Interpreter in 1955. Ceased pub. in 1959. $ 3 / $ 3

534. WORLD POLITICS. A Quarterly Journal of International Relations. Q. Princeton Univ. Press, Princeton, N.J. $ 6

535. YALE REVIEW. A National Quarterly. Q. Yale Univ. Press, New Haven, Conn. $ 4

536. YALE UNIVERSITY LIBRARY GAZETTE. Q. Yale Univ. Library, New Haven, Conn. $ 3

YEARBOOK OF THE AMERICAN PHILOSOPHICAL SOCIETY see AMERICAN PHILOSOPHICAL SOCIETY. YEARBOOK

537. YIVO ANNUAL OF JEWISH SOCIAL SCIENCE. A.(Irr.). 1946 (1959: vol. 12). Yivo Inst. for Jewish Research, 1048 5th Ave., New York 28, N.Y. Ed: L. L. Lehrer, S. Noble. Art. on Jewish hist. and culture. $ 4

538. YIVO-BLETER. Irr. Yivo Inst. for Jewish Research, 1048 5th Ave., New York 28, N.Y. pni

539. YORKER. B-M. New York State Hist. Soc., 38 Pioneer St., Cooperstown, N.Y. $ 1.50

540. YOUR ANCESTORS. A National Magazine of Genealogy and Family History. Q. Pub. address: P.O.B. 27, Station C, Buffalo 9, N.Y. $ 3

ADDENDA

541. ARTIBUS ASIAE. Quarterly of Asian Art and Archaeology for Scholars and Connoisseurs. Q. 1925 (1958: vol. 21). Artibus Asiae Press, Ascona, for Inst. of Fine Arts, New York Univ., New York, N.Y. Ed. board: Richard N. Fyre, Stella Kramrisch, Alexander Griswold, Alexander Soper. Art. on the art and archaeology of the Near and Middle East, India, China and East Asia, with emphasis on the ancient period; bk. rev.; in English or French; illus. Sfr 50 / $ 12

542. ESTONIAN LEARNED SOCIETY IN AMERICA. YEARBOOK. A.(Irr.). Estonian Learned Soc. in America, Estonian House, 243 East 34th St., New York, N.Y. Natural and social sciences and the humanities, including modern Estonian and European hist. pni

PACIFIC AREA

Australia

Prepared with the assistance of the
Commonwealth National Library, Canberra

1. ARCHIVES AND MANUSCRIPTS. Irr. 1955 (1958: vol. 1). Archives Section of the Library Assoc. of Australia, c/o Public Library of New South Wales, Macquarie St., Sydney, N.S.W. Ed: H.J. Gibbney, c/o Archives Division, Commonwealth National Library, Canberra, A.C.T. Art. on archives and particular groups of records, with emphasis on material relating to Australia; rev. of material of interest to archivists and workers with manuscripts; notes and news. c. 20s (memb.free)

2. AUSTRALASIAN JOURNAL OF PHILOSOPHY. 3xy. Australasian Assoc. of Philosophy, P.O.B. 3822, Sydney, N.S.W. Occasional art. on the philosophy and methodology of hist. 27s 6d / $3.25

3. THE AUSTRALASIAN METHODIST HISTORICAL SOCIETY. JOURNAL AND PROCEEDINGS. S-A. Methodist Hist. Library and Museum, Room 27, 2nd Floor, Lyceum House, 214 Pitt St., Sydney, N.S.W. 5s (memb. free)

4. THE AUSTRALIAN GENEALOGIST. Q. 1933 (1958: vol. 9). Soc. of Australian Genealogists, P.O.B. 860, G.P.O. Sydney, N.S.W. Ed: O.B.McCarthy. Art. on genealogy and biography; doc. (copies of early church registers); subject indices included in some vol. p (1) 3s 6d

5. AUSTRALIAN GEOGRAPHER. S-A. Geographical Soc. of New South Wales, Science House, Gloucester St., Sydney, N.S.W. p (1) 7s 6d

6. AUSTRALIAN JEWISH HISTORICAL SOCIETY, JOURNAL AND PROCEEDINGS OF THE. S-A. Australian Jewish Hist. Soc., c/o Sydney B. Glass (hon.secretary), 2 Castlereagh St., Sydney, N.S.W. 10s (memb. free)

7. AUSTRALIAN JOURNAL OF POLITICS AND HISTORY. S-A. 1955 (1959: vol. 5). Univ. of Queensland Press, George St., Brisbane, Queensland. Ed: Gordon Greenwood, Univ. of Queensland, St. Lucia, Brisbane, Queensland. Art. on "political theory and institutions, Australian history and politics, and international affairs of particular interest to Australia"; Australian political chronicle; bk. rev. 21s / $2.75

8. AUSTRALIAN LIBRARY JOURNAL. Q (Irr.). Library Assoc. of Australia, c/o Public Library of New South Wales, Macquarie St., Sydney, N.S.W. 20s

9. AUSTRALIAN NUMISMATIC JOURNAL. Q. 1950 (1958: vol. 9). Numismatic Soc. of South Australia, c/o National Gallery, North Terr., Adelaide, S.A. Ed: J. Hunt Deacon. Art. on coins, tokens, paper money and medals, particularly the issues of Australia; notes on the acitivities and memb. of the soc. (memb.) 30s

10. THE AUSTRALIAN NUMISMATIC SOCIETY. MONTHLY REPORT. M. Australian Numismatic Soc., P.O.B. 3644, Sydney, N.S.W. pni (memb. free)

11. AUSTRALIAN OUTLOOK. Q. Australian Inst. of International Affairs, 177 Collins St., Melbourne, Victoria. 20s / $2.25

12. A.P.S.A.NEWS. Q. Australian Political Studies Assoc., c/o Dept. of Govt., Univ. of Sydney, Newtown, N.S.W. Devoted largely to current politics. pni

13. THE AUSTRALIAN QUARTERLY. Q. Australian Inst. of Political Science, 34 Elizabeth St., Sydney, N.S.W. Cum. index for the years 1929-53. p (1) 4s

14. THE AUSTRALIAN RAILWAY HISTORICAL SOCIETY. BULLETIN. M. Australian Railway Hist. Soc., c/o R.S.Fookes, 46 Austral Ave., Westmead, 1W, N.S.W. p (1) 2s 6d

15. BIBLIONEWS. M. Bk. Collectors' Soc. of Australia, c/o Walter Stone, 64 Young St., Cremorne, N.S.W. 10s 6d (memb. free)

16. BUSINESS ARCHIVES COUNCIL OF AUSTRALIA, BULLETIN OF THE. S-A. 1956 (1959: vol. 1). Business Archives Council of Australia (New South Wales Branch), c/o Faculty of Economics, Univ. of Sydney, Sydney, N.S.W. Ed: Alan Birch. Art. on Australian economic and business hist. and business archives and on related theoretical problems; reports of the work of the council's branches; rev. of hist. and archival pub.; lists of pub. received. 10s / $ 2

17. EARLY DAYS. Irr. 1927 (1957: vol. 5). Western Australian Hist. Soc. Inc., P.O.B. K 774, G.P.O. Perth. Ed: Ronald P. Wright. Art. on early Western Australian hist., including biography, early exploration, discoveries and later progress; lists of reference works; proceedings of the soc. 4s 6d

18. THE ECONOMIC RECORD. S-A. Melbourne Univ. Press, The Univ., Carlton, N. 3, Melbourne, Victoria, for Economic Soc. of Australia and New Zealand. 25s (memb. free)

19. GUIDE TO THE PUBLIC RECORDS OF TASMANIA. Irr. Tasmanian State Archives, Hobart, Tasmania. Descriptions, with introductions, of early official records of Tasmania. pni

20. HERITAGE. Irr. Methodist Hist. Soc. of Victoria, c/o N. Dobson (hon. secretary), 12 Holyrood St., Camberwell E. 6, Victoria. 7s 6d (memb. free)

21. HISTORICAL SOCIETY OF QUEENSLAND. BULLETIN. M. Hist. Soc. of Queensland, P.O.B. 1811 W, G.P.O., Brisbane. News of the soc. 4s

22. HISTORICAL SOCIETY OF QUEENSLAND: JOURNAL. A. Hist. Soc. of Queensland, P.O.B. 1811W, G.P.O., Brisbane. Hist. and biographical art., relating largely to Queensland. 8s

23. HISTORICAL STUDIES. Australia and New Zealand. S-A. 1940 (1959: vol. 8). Melbourne Univ. Press, Carlton, N. 3, Victoria. Ed: A.G.Serle. Art. on the political, economic and social hist. of Australia, New Zealand and some of the neighboring islands, from their discovery to the present; bk. rev.; accession lists of manuscripts in Australian and New Zealand libraries; professional and personal news from Australian and New Zealand univ. 21s / $2.50

JOURNAL. For titles beginning with "Journal," followed by the name of the publishing or sponsoring institution or society, see the respective institution or society.

24. MANKIND. Official Journal of the Anthropological Societies of Australia. S-A. 1931 (1959: vol. 5). Anthropological Soc. of New South Wales, c/o Australian Museum, College St., Sydney, N.S.W. Ed: F.L.S.Bell, Librarian, City of Sydney Public Library, Queen Victoria Bldg., Market St., Sydney, N.S.W. Art. on all branches of anthropology, ethnology and archaeology; bk. rev.; illus. 15s

MONTHLY JOURNAL OF THE NEWCASTLE AND HUNTER DISTRICT HISTORICAL SOCIETY see NEWCASTLE AND HUNTER DISTRICT HISTORICAL SOCIETY, MONTHLY JOURNAL OF THE

25. NEWCASTLE AND HUNTER DISTRICT HISTORICAL SOCIETY, MONTHLY JOURNAL OF THE. M. Newcastle and Hunter District Hist. Soc., 75 Barton St., Mayfield, N.S.W. pni

PROCEEDINGS. For titles beginning with "Proceedings," followed by the name of the publishing or sponsoring institution or society, see the respective institution or society.

26. QUEENSLAND GEOGRAPHICAL JOURNAL. Irr. Royal Geographical Soc. of Australasia, Gregory Court, 177-179 Ann St., Brisbane, Queensland. (memb.) 21s

27. ROYAL AUSTRALIAN HISTORICAL SOCIETY. JOURNAL AND PROCEEDINGS. Irr. 1901 (1959: vol. 44). Royal Australian Hist. Soc., History House, 8 Young St., Sydney, N.S.W. Art. on hist. and biographical art., relating mainly to New South Wales; bk. rev.; biblio.; vol. subject indices; cum. index for vol. 1-20 (1901-34). (memb.) 63s

28. ROYAL GEOGRAPHICAL SOCIETY OF AUSTRALASIA, SOUTH AUSTRALIAN BRANCH (INCORPORATED). PROCEEDINGS. A. 1885 (1956/57: vol. 58). Royal Geographical Soc. of Australasia, South Australian Branch Inc., Inst. Bldg., North Terr., Adelaide, S.A. Ed. board: H.J.Finnis, Warren Bonython, Grenfell Price, K. Thomson (hon. ed.). Art. on the geography, early exploration, later development, and political hist. of Australia, New Zealand and the Pacific Islands; A. reports of the soc.; illus. 12s 6d

29. TASMANIAN HISTORICAL RESEARCH ASSOCIATION. PAPERS AND PROCEEDINGS. Q. 1951 (1958: vol. 7). Tasmanian Hist. Research Assoc., c/o State Archives, Public Bldgs., Macquarie St., Hobart, Tasmania. Ed: P.R. Eldershaw. Art. on hist., with emphasis on Australia; bk. rev.; A. reports and minutes of meetings of the soc. 10s

30. VICTORIAN HISTORICAL MAGAZINE. Irr. Royal Hist. Soc. of Victoria, c/o Public Library of Victoria, Swanston St., Melbourne, Victoria. Hist. and geography of Victoria; includes proceedings of the soc.; table of contents of vol. 1-25 pub. in vol. 25, no. 4. p (1) 7s 6d

French Oceania

BULLETIN DE LA SOCIETE D'ETUDES OCEANIENNES - POLYNESIE ORIENTALE see entry below

1. SOCIETE D'ETUDES OCEANIENNES, BULLETIN DE LA... - POLYNESIE ORIENTALE (Bulletin de la Société d'Etudes Oceaniennes - Polynesie Orientale) [Bulletin of the Society of Oceanian Studies - East Polynesia]. Q. Bibliothécaire du Musée, B.P. 110, Papeete, Tahiti, for Société d'Etudes Oceaniennes. $4

New Zealand

Prepared with the assistance of

A. G. Bagnall, Librarian, National Library Centre, National Library Service, Wellington, and the New Zealand High Commissioner's Office, London

1. HISTORICAL REVIEW. Q. Whakatane and District Hist. Soc. Inc., P.O.B. 3, Whakatane. Art. on the hist. of the eastern Bay of Plenty. free

JOURNAL OF THE NELSON HISTORICAL SOCIETY INCORPORATED see NELSON HISTORICAL SOCIETY INCORPORATED, JOURNAL OF THE

JOURNAL OF THE POLYNESIAN SOCIETY see POLYNESIAN SOCIETY, JOURNAL OF THE

2. NELSON HISTORICAL SOCIETY INCORPORATED, JOURNAL OF THE. Irr. Lucas and Son, P.O.B. 12, Nelson, for Nelson Hist. Soc., Hardy St., Nelson. 3s

3. NEW ZEALAND LIBRARIES. M. New Zealand Library Assoc., Inc., c/o W. J. McEldowney (hon. secretary), National Library Service, Wellington. Includes art. on the hist. of New Zealand libraries. memb. free

4. NEW ZEALAND NUMISMATIC JOURNAL. S-A. (Irr.). 1931 (1956-59: vol. 9, no. 25-29). Royal Numismatic Soc. of New Zealand (Incorporated), P.O.B. 23, Wellington, C. 1. Ed. board: G. T. Stagg, J. C. M. Cresswell, Allan Sutherland. Art. on all aspects of numismatics (coins, medals, tokens, seals, paper money, native currencies) and related hist. subjects, with emphasis on New Zealand and Polynesia; bk. rev.; notes of meetings of the soc. and its branches; cum. index for vol. 1-3 (1931-1947); illus.; tables of New Zealand coinage and medal issues. memb. free

5. POLITICAL SCIENCE. S-A. 1948 (1959: vol. 10). Dept. of Political Science and School of Public Administration, Victoria Univ. of Wellington, P.O.B. 196, Wellington. Ed: R.S. Milne. Art. on political theory and inst., past and present, with emphasis on New Zealand; bk. rev. p(1) 2s 6d

6. POLYNESIAN SOCIETY, JOURNAL OF THE. A Quarterly Study of the Native Peoples of the Pacific Area. Q. 1891 (1958-59: vol. 67). Polynesian Soc., P.O.B. 5195, Wellington. Ed: Jack Golson, Dept. of Anthropology, Univ. of Auckland, Auckland, and Bruce Palmer, Teacher Training College, Wellington. "Articles on all aspects of the past and present cultural life and physical anthropology of the native peoples of the Pacific Ocean area, with preference for articles dealing with the Maori of New Zealand and other Polynesian peoples and the peoples of Melanesia and Micronesia"; bk. rev.; illus. 30s

7. TAURANGA HISTORICAL SOCIETY JOURNAL. Irr. Tauranga Hist. Soc., 39 Christopher St., Tauranga. memb. free

8. WESLEY HISTORICAL SOCIETY (NEW ZEALAND). PROCEEDINGS. Irr. 1943 (1958: vol. 16). Wesley Hist. Soc. (New Zealand), 12. Poronui St., Mt. Eden, Auckland, S. 1. Ed: Rev. L.R.M. Gilmore. Art. on the hist. of the Methodist Church of New Zealand. 7s 6d (memb. free)

The Philippines

Prepared with the assistance of

Maxima M. Ferrer, Library Coordinator, Inter-Departmental Reference Service, Institute of Public Administration, University of the Philippines, Manila

1. ASSOCIATION OF SPECIAL LIBRARIES OF THE PHILIPPINES, BULLETIN OF THE. Q. Assoc. of Special Libraries of the Philippines, c/o Inst. of Public Administration, Library, Padre Faura, Manila. P 5 / $ 3

BULETIN NG KAPISANANG PANGKASAYSAYAN NG PILIPINAS see HISTORICAL BULLETIN

BULETIN NG SAMAHANG PANGKASAYSAYAN NG PILIPINAS see HISTORICAL BULLETIN

BULLETIN OF THE ASSOCIATION OF SPECIAL LIBRARIES OF THE PHILIPPINES see ASSOCIATION OF SPECIAL LIBRARIES OF THE PHILIPPINES, BULLETIN OF THE

BULLETIN OF THE PHILIPPINE HISTORICAL ASSOCIATION see HISTORICAL BULLETIN

2. COMMERCE. Voice of Philippine Business. M. Board of Directors, Chamber of Commerce of the Philippines, Manila. P 8 / $ 8

3. DILIMAN REVIEW. Q. College of Liberal Arts, Univ. of the Philippines, Diliman, Quezon City. Vol. index. P 6 / $ 6

4. ECONOMIC RESEARCH JOURNAL. Q. Graduate School, Univ. of the East, Manila. P 4 / $ 6

5. EDUCATION QUARTERLY. Q. College of Education, Univ. of the Philippines, Diliman, Quezon City. P 8

6. FIL-SINO JOURNAL. Q. Filipino and Chinese Soc., Guevarra, Sta. Cruz, Manila. In English, Chinese and Spanish. P 4

7. FILIPINAS [The Philippines]. B-W. Ed: George J. Willmann, S. J. In Tagalog. P. 2.50 / $ 2.50

8. FOOKIEN TIMES, YEARBOOK OF THE. A. Go Puan Seng, for Fookien Times, Soler corner Alvarado, Manila. In English and Chinese. pni

9. HISTORICAL BULLETIN. Q. 1957 (1959: vol. 3). Kapisanang Pangkasaysayan ng Pilipinas [Philippine Hist. Assoc.], Room 304, Free Press Bldg., 708 Rizal Ave., Manila. Art. on modern Philippine hist., mostly political; doc.; bk. rev.; news of the assoc. and of the Philippine Assembly; in English and occasionally in Spanish or Tagalog. Formerly (before vol. 3) entitled Buletin ng Samahang Pangkasaysayan ng Pilipinas or Buletin ng Kapisanang Pangkasaysayan ng Pilipinas ["Bulletin of the Philippine Hist. Assoc."] P 8 / $ 6

10. IN THE GRADE SCHOOL. 10 x y (M except April and May). Ed: Patria A. C. Beltran, 539 P. Paterno, Quiapo, Manila. P 9 / $ 5

11. INDUSTRIAL PHILIPPINES. Exponent of Philippine Industrial Progress. M. Philippine Chamber of Industries, Manila Hotel, Manila. P 5 / $ 5

12. JOURNAL OF EAST ASIATIC STUDIES. Q. 1951. Graduate School, Univ. of Manila, 105 Alejandro VI, Sampaloc, Manila. Ed: Charles O. Houston, Jr. Art. on the archaeology, ethnology, hist. and economic development of the Philippines and East Asia; bk. rev.; biblio.; reprints from rare prewar Philippine periodicals. P 12 / $ 10

13. THE JOURNAL OF HISTORY. Q. 1941 (1959: vol. 6). Philippine National Hist. Soc., Suite 202, Maria Dolores Bldg., 1679 Azcarraga, Manila. Ed: Eufronio M. Alip. Art. on hist. with special reference to the Philippines; doc.; bk. rev.; news of the soc.; illus.; formerly (before vol. 3) entitled Journal of the Philippine Historical Society. P 6 / $ 5

JOURNAL OF THE PHILIPPINE HISTORICAL SOCIETY see THE JOURNAL OF HISTORY

KAPISANANG PANGKASAYSAYAN NG PILIPINAS, BULETIN NG... see HISTORICAL BULLETIN

14. PHILIPPINE EDUCATOR. The Voice of 120,000 Teachers. 10 x y (M except April and May). Philippine Public School Teachers' Assoc., 27 Banawe St., Quezon City. P 8 / $ 8

15. PHILIPPINE FREE PRESS. W. Pub. address: 708 Rizal Ave., Manila. P 12 / P 18

PHILIPPINE HISTORICAL ASSOCIATION, BULLETIN OF THE see HISTORICAL BULLETIN

PHILIPPINE HISTORICAL SOCIETY, JOURNAL OF THE see THE JOURNAL OF HISTORY

16. PHILIPPINE JOURNAL OF EDUCATION. 10 x y (M except April and May). Ed: Mrs. Francisco Benitez, 161, 15th Ave., Quezon City. P 9 / $ 5.75

PHILIPPINE SOCIAL SCIENCE REVIEW see PHILIPPINE SOCIAL SCIENCES AND HUMANITIES REVIEW

17. PHILIPPINE SOCIAL SCIENCES AND HUMANITIES REVIEW. Q. 1929 (1958: vol. 23). Pub. address: Liberal Arts Bldg., Univ. of the Philippines, Quezon City. Ed: Nicolas Zafra, Dept. of Hist., Univ. of the Philippines. Art. on hist., economics, political science, international relations, anthropology, archaeology, folklore, sociology and literature with special reference to the Philippines; doc.; bk. rev.; some issues devoted to a single topic. Formerly (before vol. 14) entitled Philippine Social Science Review. P 6 / $ 3

18. PHILIPPINE STUDIES. Q. Soc. of Jesus, Ateneo de Manila, Loyola Heights, Quezon City (P.O.B. 145, Manila). A. cum. index; statistics; graph; illus. P 8 / $ 5

19. PHILIPPINES TODAY. Irr. National Media Production Center, Corner Solana-Sta. Potenciana, Intramuros, Manila. In English and Tagalog. free

20. PHILIPPINES TRADE REVIEW. An Independent Business Magazine. M. Rizal F. Gatica, 413 Samanillo Bldg., Escolta, Manila. Pub. suspended temporarily. P 5/$ 5

21. RIZAL CENTENNIAL BULLETIN. A. Jose Rizal National Centennial Commission, Canonigo, Paco, Manila. In English and Spanish.
p (1) P 0.30

SAMAHANG PANGKASAYSAYAN NG PILIPINAS, BULETIN NG... see HISTORICAL BULLETIN

22. SILLIMAN JOURNAL. A Quarterly of Investigation and Discussion in the Humanities and in the Sciences. Q. Silliman Univ., Dumaguete City
P 8/$ 5

23. UNITAS. Revista de cultura y vida universitaria [Review of culture and university life]. Q. Facultad de la Universidade de Santo Tomas, Manila. Extracts of theses; reports of meetings of learned soc.; contents of periodicals received; chronicle of the Philippines; papers delivered in radio program: "Univ. of the Air"; in English and Spanish; graph; statistics; illus. P 10/$ 5

YEARBOOK OF THE FOOKIEN TIMES see FOOKIEN TIMES, YEARBOOK OF THE

SOUTH AND SOUTHEAST ASIA

Burma

Prepared with the assistance of
The Sarpay Beikman Institute, Rangoon,
The Burma Historical Commission, Rangoon,
Frank N. Trager, Center for International Affairs and Development, New York University,
J.D. Pearson, Librarian, School of Oriental and African Studies, University of London, and
D. Matthews, India Office Library, London

1. BURMA. Q. 1950 (1959: vol. 9). Ministry of Information, Govt. of the Union of Burma, Rangoon. Ed: Director of Information, 22-24 Phayre St., Rangoon. Reports and art. on the activities of the various governmental agencies in Burma including the Dept. of Education, Culture and Archaeology; in English and Burmese. No. 2 of each vol., appearing in January, is the independence anniversary issue. K 3.50

2. BURMA RESEARCH SOCIETY, JOURNAL OF THE. S-A. 1911 (1959: vol. 41). Burma Research Soc., Univ. Estate, Rangoon. Ed: Than Tun. Art. on Burmese hist., the economic, social and cultural life of Burma, and on scientific researches with reference to Burma; bk. rev.; biblio.; in English and Burmese; charts, maps, illus. K 5 (memb. free)/ K 10

3. BURMA WEEKLY BULLETIN. W. Ministry of Information, Govt. of the Union of Burma, 22-24 Phayre St., Rangoon. free

4. BURMA YEARBOOK AND DIRECTORY. A. Student Press, 49 Natmauk Lane (Park Lane), Rangoon. K 30 / $ 6.30

5. THE GUARDIAN. Burma's National Magazine. M. Pub. address: 392 Merchant St., Rangoon. Burmese politics, hist., soc., culture and economics. K 12

JOURNAL OF THE BURMA RESEARCH SOCIETY see BURMA RESEARCH SOCIETY, JOURNAL OF THE

6. MYAWADDY MAGGAZINN [Myawaddy·magazine]. M. Defence Service Inst., Sule Pagoda Rd., Rangoon. K 24

7. NEW BURMA WEEKLY. W. U Pe Sein, 74 Kokine Rd., Rangoon. Appeared from May 1958 to February 1959.

8. SHUMAWA YOKE-SONE MAGGAZINN [Shumawa illustrated magazine]. M. Shumawa Co., 146 Bogyoke Aung San Market, Rangoon. K 24

9. SIT PYINNYA JURNE [Sit Pyinnya journal]. Q. 1956 (1960: vol. 5). Burma Defence Services Hist. Inst., Stewart Rd., Rangoon. Ed: Than Kywe. Art. on military science, military hist. and military geography; illus. p (1) K 3

10. SOCIALIST ASIA. M. Asian Socialist Conference, 4 Windebar Rd., Rangoon. K 6 (surface mail); K 12 (air mail)/ $1.26 (surface mail); $4.20 (air mail)

11. YIN-KYE-HMU SARSAUNG [Cultural review]. M. 1956 (1959: vol. 3). Council for the Promotion of Union Culture, Ministry of Culture, Govt. of the Union of Burma, Rangoon. Ed: U Aung Thein. Art. on Burmese hist. and culture. K 12

Cambodia

Prepared with the assistance of

Cecil Hobbs, Head of the South Asia Section,
Library of Congress, Washington, D.C.

1. BULLETIN ECONOMIQUE ET STATISTIQUE DU CAMBODGE [Economic and statistical bulletin of Cambodia]. M. Ministère de l'Economie Nationale, Phnom Penh.

2. LES CAHIERS DU SANG KUM [The journal of Sang Kum]. Ministère de l'Information, Phnom Penh.

3. CAMBODGE [Cambodia]. Revue illustrée Khmère [Illustrated Khmère review]. L'Association Samdach Sutharot, Phnom Penh.

4. CAMBODIA TODAY. M. Ministère d'Education, Phnom Penh. In English and French.

5. JOURNAL OFFICIEL DU CAMBODGE [Official journal of Cambodia]. Pub. in Phnom Penh.

Ceylon

Prepared with the assistance of the
Office of the Registrar of Books and Newspapers,
Nuwara Eliya

Note: The Geiger system has been used below for the transliteration of Sinhalese words.

1. ĀRTHIKA ITIHĀSAYA [Economic history]. S-A. 1959(1959: vol. 1). Pub. and ed: P.B. Ekanayake, Univ. of Ceylon, Peradeniya. Art. on all aspects and periods of economic hist., with emphasis on Ceylon; in Sinhalese. p (1) Rs 1

2. CEYLON HISTORICAL JOURNAL. A. 1951 (1959: vol. 7). Pub. and ed: S.D. Saparamadu, 129 Dutugemunu St., Dehiwala. Art. on all periods and disciplines of hist. with emphasis on Ceylon and India; illus. Rs 10 / $ 2.75

3. THE CEYLON JOURNAL OF HISTORICAL AND SOCIAL STUDIES. S-A. 1958 (1959: vol. 2). Ceylon Hist. and Social Studies Pub. Board, the Library, Univ. Park, Peradeniya, Ceylon. Ed. board: R. Pieris, S. Arasaratnam, H.A.I. Goonetileke (manag. ed). Art. on the hist. of Ceylon, not confined to any period; graph; bk. rev.; A. index number. Rs 6 / $ 2

4. CEYLON TODAY. M. Dept. of Information, Govt. of Ceylon, Colombo. Rs 0.50

5. CEYLON UNIVERSITY MAGAZINE. Irr. Union Soc., Univ. of Ceylon, Peradeniya. pni

6. DINAMIṆA VESAK KALĀPAYA [Dinamina journal in commemoration of the Buddha's birth ("Dinamiṇa" is a proper name borne by a Ceylonese newspaper --ed.)]. A. **Associated Newspapers of Ceylon Ltd., Lake House, Colombo.** Supplement to the newspaper Dinamina; in Sinhalese; illus. Rs 3

7. DUTCH BURGHER UNION OF CEYLON, JOURNAL OF THE. Q. 1908 (1958: vol. 68). Dutch Burgher Union of Ceylon, Colombo. Ed: R.L. Brohier. Art. on all aspects of the hist. and culture of the Burghers in Ceylon; genealogical list. Rs 10

8. GUNASĒNA VESAK KALĀPAYA [Guṇasēna journal commemorating the Buddha's birth]. A. M.D. Gunasena and Co. Ltd., Norris Rd., Colombo. Ed: Lionel Lokuliyana, Govt. Central College, Kuliyapitiya. In Sinhalese; illus. Rs 3

9. ITIHĀSA [History]. Q. 1959 (1960: vol. 2). Harrischandra de Silva, Govt. Archives Dept., Nuwara Eliya. Ed: Karunaratne Wijetunga, Univ. of Ceylon, Peradeniya; Harrischandra de Silva. Art. on hist. and related subjects, with emphasis on Ceylon; bk. rev.; in Sinhalese. Rs 3

10. ITIHĀSA SANGARĀVA [Historical magazine]. Irr. 1960 (1960: vol. 1) Vidyodaya Univ., Maligakanda Rd., Colombo. Ed: Rev. Kahangamą Medhankara Thero. Art. on hist. and related subjects, with emphasis on Ceylon; bk. rev. in Sinhalese. p (1) Rs 2

JOURNAL OF THE CEYLON BRANCH OF THE ROYAL ASIATIC SOCIETY see ROYAL ASIATIC SOCIETY, JOURNAL OF THE CEYLON BRANCH OF THE

JOURNAL OF THE DUTCH BURGHER UNION OF CEYLON see DUTCH BURGHER UNION OF CEYLON, JOURNAL OF THE

11. NAVALŌKAYA [New world]. Pragatiwadi Masika Sangarawa [Progressive Sinhalese monthly]. M. Ceylon Peace Council, Udugampola, Gampaha. In Sinhalese. Rs 3.50

12. RASAVĀHINĪ [Good taste]. M. Times of Ceylon Ltd., Colombo 1. In Sinhalese; illus. Rs 9 / 20s

13. ROYAL ASIATIC SOCIETY, JOURNAL OF THE CEYLON BRANCH OF THE. A. 1845 (1958: vol. 5). Ceylon Branch, Royal Asiatic Soc., Thurston Rd., Colombo 3. Ed: A.R. Tampoe, Mrs. E. Rankine. Studies on the hist., religions, languages, literature, arts, sciences and social conditions of the present and past inhabitants of Ceylon and culturally related countries; biblio.; indices. Rs 4

14. SĀHITYAYA [Literature]. Q. Official Language Dept., Govt. of Ceylon, Colombo. In Sinhalese. Rs 1

15. SAṂSKṚTI [Culture]. Q. Saṃskṛti Pub., 19 Sunetra Devi Rd., Nugegoda. In Siṅhalese and English. Rs 3.50 / Rs 10

16. SIṂHALA BAUDDHAYĀ VESAK KALAPĀYẠ [Simhala Bauddhaya journal commemorating the Buddha's birth ("Siṃhala Bauddhaya" is a proper name borne by a Ceylonese newspaper -- ed.)]. A. Mahabodhi Soc. of Ceylon, (P.O.B. 250), 130 Maligakanda Rd., Colombo 10. Supplement to the newspaper Siṃhala Bauddhaya; in Sinhalese; illus. Rs 2.50

17. SPOLIA ZEYLANICA. Geology, Zoology, Anthropology. A. National Museums of Ceylon, Colombo 7. Maps, graph, statistics; general index; illus. Rs 4

18. ŚRĪ LAṄKĀ [Ceylon]. M. Dept. of Information, Govt. of Ceylon, Colombo. In Sinhalese and Tamil. Rs 3

19. UNIVERSITY OF CEYLON REVIEW. Q. 1942 (1958: vol. 16). Univ. of Ceylon, Peradeniya. Ed. board: K. Kanapathipillai, N.A. Jayawickrama, K.N. Jayatilake. Art. on hist., archaeology, religion, literature and philology; index. Rs 2

India

Prepared with the assistance of

Girja Kumar, Librarian, Indian Council of World Affairs Library, New Delhi;

The National Library, Calcutta, and

The National Information Service, Poona

ADYAR LIBRARY BULLETIN see BRAHMAVIDYA

1. AGRA UNIVERSITY JOURNAL OF RESEARCH. S-A. Registrar, Agra Univ., Agra. Alternate issues on natural science and letters. Rs 8 / Rs 12

2. ALL INDIA ORIENTAL CONFERENCE, PROCEEDINGS (AND TRANSACTIONS) OF THE. B. 1921 (1959: vol. 19). Bhandarkar Oriental Research Inst., Poona 4. Proceedings of, and papers read at, the conference; addresses of sectional presidents; in English and Sanskrit, and occasionally in an Indian regional language; author and subject indices of papers submitted at the first 17 sessions of the conference, with sum., pub. in 2 vol. pv

3. ANCIENT INDIA. A. 1946 (1958: no. 14). Archaeological Dept., Govt. of India, Janpath, New Delhi. Ed: A. Ghosh, Director General of Archaeology in India. Art. on the archaeology of India and adjacent countries; official report on archaeological excavations carried out in India; illus.; graph. Rs 4.50 / 7s

4. ANDHRA HISTORICAL RESEARCH SOCIETY, JOURNAL OF THE. A. 1929 (1956-58: vol. 24). Andhra Hist. Research Soc., 4th Ward, No. 90-91, Godavari Bund Rd., Rajahmundry, Andhra Pradesh. Ed: R. Subba Rao. Art. on the hist. and culture of Andhra; bk. rev.; A. report of the soc.; in English and Sanskrit. (memb.) Rs 6 (institutions Rs 9) / 12s

5. ANDHRA SAHITYA PARISHAT PATRIKA [Journal of the Andhra Literary Society]. M. Andhra Sahitya Parishat, Kakinad, Andhra. Rs 2

ANNALS. For titles beginning with "Annals," followed by the name of the publishing or sponsoring institution or society, see the respective institution or society.

6. ANNALS OF ORIENTAL RESEARCH. S-A. 1936/37 (1958/59: vol. 15). Univ. of Madras, Madras 5. Ed: M. Mariappa Bhat. Art. on Indological studies; bk. rev.; in Arabic, English, Hindi, Kannada, Malayalam, Persian, Sanskrit, Tamil, Telugu and Urdu. Rs 4

7. ANNAMALAI UNIVERSITY, JOURNAL OF THE. A. Univ. of Annamalai, Annamalainagar. Ed: R. Ramanujachari. In English, Tamil and Sanskrit; A. index. Rs 7.50 / 10s

8. ANNUAL REPORT ON INDIAN EPIGRAPHY. A. 1946. Manager of Pub., Govt. of India, Delhi. Ed: N. Lakshmi Narayan Rao, Govt. Epigraphist for India, Ootacamund. Reports of old inscriptions and coins, relating largely to ancient and medieval Indian hist., examined by the Office of the Govt. Epigraphist for India.

9. ANTHROPOLOGICAL SOCIETY OF BOMBAY, THE JOURNAL OF THE. S-A (Irr.). Anthropological Soc. of Bombay, 209, Dr. Dadabhai Naoroji Rd., Fort, Bombay. p (1) Rs 3

10. ANTHROPOLOGIST. S-A. Dept. of Anthropology, Univ. of Delhi, Delhi 8. Rs 6 / 12s

11. ARCHAEOLOGICAL SURVEY OF INDIA, MEMOIRS OF THE. Irr. 1919 (mri 1955: no. 73). Pub. and ed: Director-General of Archaeology in India, Dept. of Archaeology, Govt. of India, New Delhi. Monographs on Indology and Indian archaeology; plates; illus. pv

12. ART IN INDUSTRY. Q. Indian Inst. of Art in Industry, Artistry House, 15 Park St., Calcutta 16. Illus. p (1) Rs 2.50

13. ARTHA VIJÑĀNA [The science of economics]. Q. Gokhale Inst. of Politics and Economics, Poona 4. In English and Indian languages; English and Hindi sum. Rs 15 / $5.50

14. THE ARYAN PATH. M. Indian Inst. of World Culture, 6 North Public Square Rd., Basavangudi, Bangalore. Art. on literature, philosophy, hist. and the arts; bk. rev.; indices of art. and authors. Rs 6 / $3

15. ASIAN RECORDER. W. Mrs. D.B. Samuel, National Printing Works, 10 Daryaganj, Delhi 7. Sum. of outstanding Asian events; A. cum. index. Rs 75 / Rs 80

16. ASIATIC SOCIETY, JOURNAL OF THE. Q. 1832 (1958: vol. 24). Asiatic Soc., 1 Park St., Calcutta 16. Ed: J.M. Banerjee. Art. on antiquities, hist., linguistics and religion, with special reference to India; bk. rev.; biblio.; yearbk.; cum. index; illus. Rs 30 / $5

17. ASIATIC SOCIETY OF BOMBAY, JOURNAL OF THE. S-A. 1925 (1956/57: vol. 31/32). Asiatic Soc. of Bombay, Town Hall, Bombay 1. Ed. board: P.V. Kane, J.M. Unvala, H.D. Velankar, George M. Moraes, G.C. Jhala. Art. on Indology; bk. rev.; quotations from Sanskrit texts; illus. Rs 20

18. ASSAM RESEARCH SOCIETY, JOURNAL OF THE. A. Assam Research Soc., Kamarupa Anusandhan Samiti, Gauhati, Assam. Rs 4

AWAKENED INDIA see PRABUDDHA BHĀRATA

19. BANARAS HINDU UNIVERSITY, JOURNAL OF THE. A. Banaras Hindu Univ., Banaras. In English and Hindi.

20. BENGAL PAST AND PRESENT. A. 1907 (mri 1955: vol. 75). Calcutta Hist. Soc., 12/1 Old Post Office St., Calcutta. Ed: N.K. Sinha, 47 A Ekdalia Rd., Calcutta 19. Art. on the political and economic hist. of Bengal and India. Rs 20

21. BHANDARKAR ORIENTAL RESEARCH INSTITUTE, ANNALS OF THE. Q. 1919 (1958: vol. 39). Bhandarkar Oriental Research Inst., Poona 4. Ed: R.N. Dandekar, H.D. Velankar. Art. on the cultural hist. of ancient and medieval India and on Indian languages and literature; bk. rev.; in English and Sanskrit; author and subject indices for the first 36 vol. Rs 10

22. BHĀRATA ITIHĀSA SAṀSHODHAKA MAṆḌALA TRAIMĀSIKA [Quarterly journal of the Indian Historical Research Institute]. Q. 1921 (1958: vol. 38). Bhārata Itihāsa Saṁshodhaka Maṇḍala, 1321 Saḍashiva, Poona 2. Ed: G.H. Khare. Doc. and occasionally art. on Indian hist., with emphasis on the ancient and medieval periods; in Marathi and occasionally English; English sum.; index for vol. 1-8; illus. Rs 3.50 / Rs 3.50

23. BHĀRATĪYA VIDYĀ [Indian studies]. A Quarterly Research Organ of the Bhavan on All Subjects Connected with Indian Culture. Q. 1939 (1957: vol. 17). S. Ramakrishnan, for Bhāratīya Vidyā Bhavan [Inst. of Indian Studies], Chowpatty Rd., Bombay 7. Ed. board: Jayantkrishna H. Dave, H. D. Velankar, Asoka K. Majumdar, H. C. Bhayani. Art. mainly on Indian social and cultural hist. and Indian literature; bk. rev.; illus. Rs 6

24. BIHAR RESEARCH SOCIETY, THE JOURNAL OF THE. Q. 1915 (1957: vol. 43). Bihar Research Soc., Museum Buildings, Patna. Ed: K.K. Datta. Art. on the archaeology, numismatics and political and religious hist. of Bihar from the earliest times to the present; genealogy of the rulers of Bihar; bk. rev.; biblio.; A. report of the soc.; quotations from Sanskrit texts; in English and occasionally in Hindi; illus.; index. Rs 20

25. BIHAR UNIVERSITY JOURNAL. S-A. Registrar, Bihar Univ., Patna 4. 2 no., one dealing with the humanities and social sciences and the other with physical sciences; in English, Hindi and Sanskrit. Rs 10 / $2.50

26. BRAHMAVIDYA [Spiritual learning]. ADYAR LIBRARY BULLETIN. S-A. Director, Adyar Library and Research Centre, Adyar, Madras 20. In English. Rs 8

BULLETIN. For titles beginning with "Bulletin," followed by the name of the publishing or sponsoring institution or society, see the respective institution or society.

27. CALCUTTA REVIEW. M. 1844 (1958: vol. 149). Sibendranath Kanjilal, Calcutta Univ. Press, 48 Hazra Rd., Calcutta 19. Ed. board: Pramathanath Banerjee, Chapala Kanta, Bhattacharya, Satishchandra Ghosh, Jitendraprasad Niyogi, A. Verstraeten. Includes art. on recent Indian hist.; bk. rev.; index. Rs. 7.50 / 14s

28. THE CLERGY MONTHLY. M. St. Mary's Theological College, Darjeeling District. Theological and hist. art.; rev. of current Roman Catholic literature; doc. of the Holy See; biblio.; Q supplement dealing with the Indian mission field. Rs 7.50 / $2.50

29. EDUCATION. M. T.C.E. Journals and Pub., P.O.B. 63, Lucknow. In English and Hindi. Rs 10 / $2.50

30. EDUCATION AND PSYCHOLOGY. Q. Ed. address: 32 Faiz Bazar Rd., Delhi 7. Rs 10 / $4

31. ENQUIRY. Forum of Research and Discussion. Irr. Bipan Chandra, 15-c University Rd., Delhi 8. p (1) Rs 2

32. EPIGRAPHIA INDICA. Q. 1892 (1958: vol. 31). Manager of Pub., Govt. of India, Delhi, for Archaeological Survey of India, New Delhi. Ed: D.C. Sircar. Art. on the archaeology of ancient and medieval India; extensive

quotations from inscriptions in several Indian languages; detailed alphabetical index; illus.; separate Arabic and Persian supplement in continuation of the series "Epigraphia Indo-Moslemica." p (1) Rs 10 / p (1) 16s

33. FOREIGN AFFAIRS RECORD. M. External Publicity Division, Ministry of External Affairs, Govt. of India, New Delhi. free

34. FOREIGN AFFAIRS REPORTS. M. Indian Council of World Affairs, Sapru House, Barakhamba Rd., New Delhi 1. Rs 6 / 15s

35. GANGANATHA JHA RESEARCH INSTITUTE, JOURNAL OF THE. Q. 1943/44 (mri 1956: vol. 13). Ganganatha Jha Research Inst., Allahabad. Ed. board: B.C. Law, R.D. Ranade, A. Siddiqi, Ishwari Prasad, Umesha Mishra (manag. ed.). Art. on Indological studies; bk. rev. and supplements; in English and Sanskrit. Rs 12

36. GREATER INDIA SOCIETY, JOURNAL OF THE. S-A. 1934 (mri 1956: vol. 15). Greater India Soc., 9, Panchanan Ghose Lane, Calcutta 9. Ed: Nalinksha Dutt. Art. on Indian culture in "Greater India," i.e., Serindia, India Minor, Indo-China and Insulinde as well as in China, Korea, Japan and other countries of Asia and the Pacific area. pni

37. GUJARAT RESEARCH SOCIETY, JOURNAL OF THE. GUJARĀTA SAṀŚODHANA MAṆḌALANU TRAIMĀSIKA. Q. Gujarat Research Soc., 46-48, Esplanade Mansion, Mahatma Gandhi Rd., Bombay 1. In English and Gujarati; illus. Rs 6

38. GUJARAT UNIVERSITY BULLETIN. Q. Gujarat Univ., Navrangpura, Ahmedabad 9. Rs 4

GUJARĀTA SAṀŚODHANA MAṆḌALANU TRAIMĀSIKA see GUJARAT RESEARCH SOCIETY, JOURNAL OF THE

THE HALF-YEARLY JOURNAL OF THE MYSORE UNIVERSITY see MYSORE UNIVERSITY, THE HALF-YEARLY JOURNAL OF THE

39. HENRY MARTYN SCHOOL OF ISLAMIC STUDIES, BULLETIN OF THE. Q. 1941 (1958: no vol. indic.). Pub. and ed: Principal, Henry Martyn School of Islamic Studies, Aligarh, U.P. Art. on Islam, comparative studies of Islamic and Christian doctrines and on Christian literature written particularly for Moslems; biographies of converts from Islam to Christianity. Rs 2 / 3s

40. INDIA QUARTERLY. A Journal of International Affairs. Q. Asia Pub. House, Bombay, for Indian Council of World Affairs, Sapru House, Barakhamba Rd., New Delhi 1. A. cum. index. Rs 10 / 20s

41. INDIAN ACADEMY OF SCIENCES, PROCEEDINGS OF THE. M. Indian Acad. of Sciences, Hebbal Post, Bangalore. In English and occasionally in other European languages. Rs 36 / $9

42. INDIAN AFFAIRS RECORD. M. Diwan Chand Indian Information Centre, New Delhi. A. cum. index. Rs 12 / $4

43. INDIAN ARCHAEOLOGY. A. 1954 (1958: vol. 5). Pub. and ed: A. Ghosh, Director-General of Archaeology in India, Govt. of India, New Delhi. Survey of work done in India in the field of archaeology; chapters on archaeolo-

gical, epigraphical and numismatic discoveries; report on museums; list of Indian pub. bearing on the field of archaeology; illus. Rs 7.50 / 12s

44. THE INDIAN ARCHIVES. S-A. 1947 (1956 [1958]: vol. 10). National Archives of India, Janpath, New Delhi 2. Ed. board: K.D. Bhargava (chief ed.), G.L. Chopra, J.N. Mukherjee, S.R. Ranganathan, S.N. Sen. Art. on repositories of Indian records, on records relating to India's hist. kept in foreign countries, on archival theory and techniques, and on the hist. of archives in India (with emphasis on the British period) and other countries; bk. rev.; news of archives. Rs 4 / 6s

INDIAN CULTURE see THAQĀFATU'L-HIND

45. INDIAN ECONOMIC JOURNAL. Q. Dept. of Economics, Univ. of Bombay, Bombay 1. Cum. index. Rs 15 / $ 4

46. THE INDIAN ECONOMIC REVIEW. S-A. Delhi School of Economics, Univ. of Delhi, Delhi 8. Rs 10 / 15s

47. INDIAN GEOGRAPHER. S-A. Assoc. of Indian Geographers, P.O.B. 644, New Delhi. Rs 4 / $ 2

48. INDIAN HISTORICAL QUARTERLY. Q. 1925 (1959: vol. 35). J.C. Sarkhel, 9 Panchanan Ghosh Lane, Calcutta 9. Ed: Narendra Nath Law. Art. on Indian hist.; abstr. from Oriental journals; bk. rev.; biblio.; illus. Rs 12

49. INDIAN HISTORY CONGRESS, PROCEEDINGS OF THE. Irr. Indian Hist. Congress Assoc., Univ. of Allahabad, Allahabad. Art. on all periods of Indian hist.; illus.

50. THE INDIAN JOURNAL OF AGRICULTURAL ECONOMICS. Q. Indian Soc. of Agricultural Economics, 46-48 Esplanade Mansions, Mahatma Gandhi Rd., Fort, Bombay 1. Rs 12

51. INDIAN JOURNAL OF EDUCATION. Q. All India Federation of Educational Assoc., P.O. Bally, West Bengal. Rs 5

52. THE INDIAN JOURNAL OF POLITICAL SCIENCE. Q. 1938 (1958: vol. 20). Indian Political Science Assoc., c/o S.C. Dash, Ravenshaw College, Cuttack 3. Ed: A.L. Loomba, Model House, Lucknow. Art. on politics and related fields, with emphasis on India; bk. rev.; digest of cases of constitutional and administrative importance; list of Indian Union and U.P. State statutes. Rs 15 / $ 4.50

53. INDIAN JOURNAL OF PUBLIC ADMINISTRATION. Q. Indian Inst. of Public Administration, Indraprastha Estate, Ring Rd., New Delhi 1. Index. Rs 10

54. THE INDIAN JOURNAL OF SOCIAL WORK. A Quarterly Devoted to the Promotion of Professional Social Work, Scientific Interpretation of Social Problems and Advancement of Social Research. Q. Dept. of Pub., Tata Inst. of Social Sciences, Sion-Trombay Rd., Colaba, Bombay 38. Rs 10 / Rs 11

55. THE INDIAN JOURNAL OF THEOLOGY. Q. Pub. and ed: Rev. A. C. M. Hargreaves, Bishop's College, 224 Lower Circular Rd., Calcutta 17. Rs 5 / $ 2.50

56. INDIAN P.E.N. M. P.E.N. All-India Centre, 40 New Marine Lines, Bombay 1. Rs 5 / $ 2

57. THE INDIAN REVIEW. M. Manian Natesan, for G.A. Natesan and Co., Esplanade, Madras 1. Rs 6 / $4

58. INDIAN SOCIETY OF ORIENTAL ART, JOURNAL OF THE. A.(Irr.). Indian Soc. of Oriental Art, 15 Park St., Calcutta 16. Illus. Rs 16

59. THE INDIAN YEARBOOK OF INTERNATIONAL AFFAIRS. A. Indian Study Group of International Affairs, Univ. of Madras, Chepauk, Madras 5.

60. THE INDO-ASIAN CULTURE. Q. 1952 (1957/58: vol. 6). Indian Council for Cultural Relations, Pataudi House, New Delhi 1. Ed: A.C. Sen. Art. on Indian and Asian religions, philosophy, literature, hist., arts and the relationship with non-Asian countries; notes and news on congresses and inst.; indices of authors and art.; illus. Rs 6 / 10s

61. INDO-IRANICA. Q. Iran Soc., 159-B Dharamtala St., Calcutta 13. Rs 15 / 25s

62. INTERNATIONAL STUDIES. Q. 1959 (1960/61: vol. 2). Asia Pub. House, Contractor Bldg., Ballard Estate, Bombay 1, for Indian School of International Studies, Sapru House, Barakhamba Rd., New Delhi 1. Ed. board: A. Appadorai (chief ed.), S. Mookerjee, M.S. Venkataramani. Art., contributed by memb. of the school's faculty, on international relations and area studies; rev. art.; A. biblio. on India's foreign relations; index. Rs 22 / $ 6.60

63. THE IRAN LEAGUE QUARTERLY. Q. K.A. Fitter, for Iran League, Navasari Bldg., Hornby Rd., Bombay 1. In English, Gujarati and Persian. Rs 6 / 10s

64. ISLAMIC CULTURE. Q. 1927 (1959: vol. 33). Islamic Culture Board, B.P. 171, A-/19/644, Bait-al-Masarrat, Adikmet, Hyderabad-Deccan. Ed: G. Yazdani. Art. on Arabic literature and the religious, political and legal aspects of the hist. of Islam; bk. rev.; biblio. of selected art. from learned journals; illus. Rs 15 / $ 5

65. ITIHAS [History]. Q. 1950/51 (1957/58: vol. 8). Bengali Hist. Soc. 47 A Ekdalia Rd., Calcutta 19. Ed: N.K. Sinha. Art. on hist. (including the philosophy of hist.), with special reference to India; in Bengali.

66. JAIN SIDDHANT BHASKAR [Jain antiquary]. Q. 1934 (mri 1953: vol. 19). Central Jain Oriental Library, Jain Siddhant Bhavan, Arrah, Bihar. Ed. board: Hira Lal, A.N. Upadhyaya, Kamta Prasad, K. Bhujbali Shastri. Art. on early and medieval Indian hist. and culture, with special reference to Jainism; in Hindi and occasionally in English; illus. Rs 4

JOURNAL. For titles beginning with "Journal," followed by the name of the publishing or sponsoring institution or society, see the respective institution or society.

67. JOURNAL OF EDUCATION AND PSYCHOLOGY. Q. Faculty of Education and Psychology, Univ. of Baroda, Baroda. Rs 6 / 10s

68. JOURNAL OF INDIAN HISTORY. 3xy. 1920 (1959: vol. 37). Univ. of Kerala, Trivandrum, Kerala. Ed: P.S. Raghavan. Art. on the hist., archaeology, and religions of India, with emphasis on the ancient and medieval periods; bk. rev.; biblio. of selected art. Rs 10 / 16s

69. JOURNAL OF INDIAN MUSEUMS. A. 1945 (mri 1952: vol. 8). Museums Assoc. of India, Prince of Wales Museum, Bombay. Ed. board: Moti Chandra (manag. ed.), H. Goetz, V. S. Agarwala, R. G. Gyani. Art. and notes on Indian museums and on new archaeological discoveries; text of manuscripts; report of the assoc.; illus. pni

70. JOURNAL OF INDIAN TEXTILE HISTORY. A. Calico Museum of Textiles, Ahmedabad. Illus. Rs 8 / 10s 6d

71. JOURNAL OF ORIENTAL RESEARCH. Q. 1927 (1959: vol. 28). Kuppuswami Sastri Research Inst., Mylapore, Madras. Ed: V. Raghavan. Art. on Indology; bk. rev. and supplements; notes; sum.; illus. Rs 8 / 14s

72. JOURNAL OF SOCIAL RESEARCH. S-A. Council of Social and Cultural Research (Bihar), Dept. of Anthropology, Bihar Univ., Ranchi College, Ranchi. Rs 7 / $ 3

73. KARNATAK UNIVERSITY, JOURNAL OF THE. Humanities Number. S-A. 1956 (1958: vol. 1). Registrar, Karnatak Univ., Dharwar. Ed. board: Aramando Menzen (chief ed.), S. C. Nandimath, C. C. Pattanshetty, N. R. Kulkarani, R. C. Hiremath, B. A. Saletore. Research papers on hist., economics, politics, literature, religion and philosophy with special reference to India, contributed by teachers and research students of the univ.; rev. art.; notes. Rs 5 / Rs 5

74. KARNATAKA HISTORICAL REVIEW. S-A. 1932 (mri 1956: vol. 7). Secretary, Karnatak Hist. Research Soc., College Rd., Dharwar, Karnatak. Ed: R. S. Panchamukhi. Art. on ancient and medieval Indian hist., religion culture and linguistics, with special reference to Karnatak; notes; illus. Rs 5 / 15s

75. KERALA UNIVERSITY ORIENTAL MANUSCRIPTS LIBRARY, JOURNAL OF THE. Q. 1945 (1959: vol. 10). Curator, Kerala Univ. Oriental Manuscripts Library, Trivandrum. Ed: K. Raghavan Pillai. Reprints of rare works in Sanskrit from ancient manuscripts; news about manuscripts and source materials, with critical notes, relating to Indology. Rs 4 / 7s

76. LALIT KALĀ [Fine arts]. A Journal of Oriental Art, Chiefly Indian. S-A. Lalit Kalā Akadami [Acad. of Fine Arts], Jaipur House, New Delhi. Illus.; plates. pv (c. Rs 10).

77. MAHABODHI. A Monthly Journal of International Buddhist Brotherhood... M. Mahabodhi Bk. Agency, 4 A Bankim Chatterjee St., Calcutta, for Mahabodhi Soc. of India. Index; plates; illus. Rs 5 / $ 3

78. MAHARAJA SAYAJIRAO UNIVERSITY OF BARODA, JOURNAL OF THE. S-A. Faculty of Arts, Maharaja Sayajirao Univ. of Baroda, Baroda. Rs 10 / $ 3

79. MAN IN INDIA. A Quarterly Anthropological Journal. Q. Ed: Nirmal Kumar Bose, 18 Church Rd., Ranchi. Rs 15 / 25s

80. MARCH OF INDIA. M. Pub. Division, Ministry of Information and Broadcasting, Govt. of India, Old Secretariat, Delhi 8. Illus. Rs 10 / $2.75

81. MARG [Path]. A Magazine of the Arts. Q. Mulk Raj Anand, Marg Pub., 34-38 Bank St., Bombay. Illus. Rs 20 / 40s

82. MEDIEVAL INDIA QUARTERLY. Q. 1956 (1957: vol.2). Dept. of Hist., Muslim Univ., Aligarh. Ed: Shaikh Abdur Rashid. Art. on medieval Indian hist. and culture; biblio. Rs 16

MEMOIRS. For titles beginning with "Memoirs," followed by the name of the publishing or sponsoring institution or society, see the respective institution or society.

83. MODERN REVIEW. M (2 vol. p.a.). Ed: Kedar Nath Chatterji, 120-2, Upper Circular Rd., Calcutta. Excerpts from Indian and foreign periodicals; index. Rs 15 / Rs 24

84. MUSEUM AND PICTURE GALLERY, BARODA, BULLETIN OF THE. A. (Irr.). 1943 (1955/56 [1957]: vol. 12). Museum and Picture Gallery, Baroda Ed: V.L. Devkar. Art. on ancient and medieval archaeology, arts and manuscripts, with special reference to the region of Gujarat and mainly concerning the acquisitions of the museum; report of the museum; list of bk. added to the library; illus. Rs 7.50

85. MYSORE UNIVERSITY, THE HALF-YEARLY JOURNAL OF THE. S-A. Univ. of Mysore, Mysore. Rs 4

86. MYTHIC SOCIETY, QUARTERLY JOURNAL OF THE. Q. Mythic Soc., Daly Memorial Hall, Cenotaph Rd., Bangalore 2. Sanskrit verses; illus. Rs 10 / 20s

87. NAGPUR UNIVERSITY HISTORICAL SOCIETY, ANNUAL BULLETIN OF THE. A. (Irr.). V.R. Deoras, for Hist. Soc., Nagpur Univ., Nagpur. Rs 5 / 7s 6d

88. NAGPUR UNIVERSITY JOURNAL. A.(Irr.). Univ. of Nagpur, Nagpur Rs 3 / 5s

89. NAGPUR UNIVERSITY POLITICAL SCIENCE ASSOCIATION, BULLETIN OF THE. A.(Irr.). Univ. of Nagpur, Nagpur. free

90. NATIONAL CHRISTIAN COUNCIL REVIEW. M. National Christian Council of India, Christian Council Lodge, Nagpur 1. Rs 4 / $1.50

91. NEW AGE. M. Communist Pary of India, New Age Printing Press, 5 Jhandewallan Estate, Rani Jhansi Rd., New Delhi. Index. Rs 12

92. NOTES ON ISLAM. A Quarterly Bulletin of Information about Islam with Special Reference to India and Pakistan. Q. 1946 (1959: vol. 12). Islamic Section, Oriental Inst., 30 Park St., Calcutta 16. Ed: V. Courtois, S.J. Art. on Islamic hist. and theology and comparative studies on Islam and other religions and movements, with special reference to India and Pakistan; Moslem news digest; survey of relevant periodicals; bk. rev.; A. cum. index. Rs 5 / Rs 6.50

93. NUMISMATIC SOCIETY OF INDIA, JOURNAL OF THE. S-A. 1939 (mri 1956: vol. 18). Numismatic Soc. of India, Prince of Wales Museum, Bombay 1. Ed: V.S.Aggrawala. Art. on Indian coins and medieval Indian hist.; news and notes; illus. Rs 10

94. ORIENTAL INSTITUTE, M.S.UNIVERSITY OF BARODA, JOURNAL OF THE. Q (Irr.). 1951/52 (1957/58: vol. 7). Oriental Inst., M.S.Univ., Baroda. Ed: B.J.Sandesara. Art. on Indology, with emphasis on studies of the Ramayana; bk. rev.; news of manuscripts; survey of rare bk. in the Maharaja Sayajirao Univ. Oriental Series and of contemporary Oriental journals; quotations from Sanskrit texts; illus. Rs 15 / $ 3.50

95. ORIENTAL THOUGHT. A Sanskrit-English Quarterly Devoted to Research Work in All Fields of Oriental Literature. Q. G.V.Devasthali, Raste Krishna Mandir, Panchavati, Nasik, Bombay State. Rs 8 / 16s

96. ORISSA HISTORICAL RESEARCH JOURNAL. Q. B.V.Nath, New Capital, Bhubaneswar, Orissa. Rs 10

97. PHILOSOPHICAL QUARTERLY. Q. Indian Inst. of Philosophy, Amalner, East Khandesh. Rs 6 / $ 2.50

98. POONA ORIENTALIST. A Quarterly Journal Devoted to Oriental Studies. Q. 1936 (1958: vol. 23). Oriental Bk. Agency, 15, Shukrawar Peth, Poona 2. Ed: M.M.Patkar. Art. on Indology; bk. rev.; biblio.; in English and Sanskrit. Rs 10 / 20s

99. POPULATION REVIEW. Bi-Annual Journal of Asian Demography. S-A. Indian Inst. for Population Studies, Gandhinagar, Madras 20. Extracts from newspaper comments. Rs 10 / $ 4

100. PRABUDDHA BHĀRATA. AWAKENED INDIA. M. 1896 (1959: vol. 64). Swami Advayananda, 4 Wellington Lane, Calcutta 13, for Advaita Ashrama, P.O. Mayavati, District Almora, U.P. Ed: Swami Gambhirananda. Art. on philosophy, religion and hist., with special reference to India; poems; bk. rev.; in English; A. cum. index in each December issue; illus. Rs 5 / $ 4

101. PRĀCYAVĀṆĪ [Oriental learning]. A. Prācyavāṇī Mandira ["Inst. of Oriental Learning"], 3 Federation St., Calcutta 9. Index. Rs 6

102. PRINCE OF WALES MUSEUM OF WESTERN INDIA, BULLETIN OF THE. Irr. 1952 (1955-57: no. 5). Prince of Wales Museum of Western India, Bombay 1. Ed: Pramod Chandra. Art. on the hist. of Indian art and archaeology, with special reference to the collections of the musuem; illus. with color and half-tone plates; sum.; indices. pv

PROCEEDINGS. For titles beginning with "Proceedings," followed by the name of the publishing or sponsoring institution or society, see the respective institution or society.

103. PUNJAB UNIVERSITY, RESEARCH BULLETIN OF THE. Irr. Univ. of the Punjab, Hoshiarpur. pv

QUARTERLY JOURNAL OF THE MYTHIC SOCIETY see MYTHIC SOCIETY, QUARTERLY JOURNAL OF THE

104. QUEST. A Quarterly of Inquiry, Criticism and Ideas. Q. Sheela Singh, for Indian Committee for Cultural Freedom, Army and Navy Bldg., 148 Mahatma Gandhi Rd., Bombay 1. Rs 5 / $ 3

105. RAMAKRISHNA MISSION INSTITUTE OF CULTURE, BULLETIN OF THE. M. 1950 (1959: vol. 10). Ramakrishna Mission Inst. of Culture, 111 Pussa Rd., Calcutta 26. Ed: Swami Nityaswarupananda. Lectures and addresses delivered at the inst. on religion, philosophy, hist., culture and comparative literature, with special reference to Hinduism; bk. rev. and comments. Rs 4 / $ 2

RESEARCH BULLETIN OF THE PUNJAB UNIVERSITY see PUNJAB UNIVERSITY, RESEARCH BULLETIN OF THE

106. ROOPA-LEKHĀ [Fine arts]. An Illustrated Bi-Annual Art Journal. S-A. All-India Fine Arts and Crafts Soc., Old Mill Rd., New Delhi. Illus. Rs 7.50

107. SANGEET NATAK AKADAMI BULLETIN [Bulletin of the Academy of Music and Drama]. Q. Sangeet Natak Akadami, 4-A Mathura Rd., Jangpura, New Delhi 14. Illus. Rs 4

108. SCIENCE AND CULTURE. A Monthly Journal of Natural and Cultural Sciences. M. H.N.Saha, for Indian Science News Assoc., 92 Upper Circular Rd., Calcutta 9. Illus. Rs 15

SCIṆDIA ORIENTAL INSTIṬUTE, JOURNAL OF THE see SINDIAYĀ PRĀCYAVIDYĀ NIKETANA PATRIKĀ

109. SILPI [Artisan]. M. D.Sambasiva Rao, 10 Narasingapuram St., Mount Rd., Madras 2. Illus. Rs 10 / 36s

110. SINDIAYĀ PRĀCYAVIDYĀ NIKETANA PATRIKĀ. JOURNAL OF THE SCINDIA ORIENTAL INSTITUTE. Q (Irr.). 1955 (1956 [1959]: vol. 2). Scindia Oriental Inst., Ujjain, Madhya Bharat. Ed: Sadashiv Lakshmi Dhar Katrai. Art. on early Indian culture; reprints of ancient Sanskrit works; in Sanskrit, Hindi and English. Rs 8

111. SINO-INDIAN STUDIES. CHUNG-EN YAN CHIU. Q. 1947 (mri 1955: vol. 5). Visvabharati, Santiniketan, West Bengal, for Sino-Indian Cultural Soc. in India. Ed: Kshitis Roy. Art. on ancient Sino-Indian relations; in English; translations of ancient Indian texts from Chinese; illus. Rs 12 / 18s

112. SOCIOLOGICAL BULLETIN. S-A. K.M.Kapadia, for Indian Sociological Soc., Rajsi Mansion, 2nd Floor, near 3rd Pasta Lane, Colaba, Bombay 5. Rs 10 / $ 2.31

113. SRI VENKATESWARA ORIENTAL INSTITUTE, JOURNAL OF THE. S-A. Sri Venkateswara Oriental Inst., Tirupathi, Andhra. In English, Kannada, Sanskrit, Tamil and Telugu. Rs 10 / $ 6

114. T̲H̲AQĀFATU'L-HIND. INDIAN CULTURE. Q (Irr.). 1950 (1959: vol. 10). Indian Council for Cultural Relations, Pataudi House, New Delhi. Ed: Mohammad Ajmal Khan. Art. on Indian culture, literature, medicine and religion; bk. rev.; cultural news; in Persian; table of contents also in English. Rs 10 / 20s

115. THE THEOSOPHIST. M. K.S. Krishnamurti, for Theosophical Soc., Adyar, Madras 20. Includes supplement containing notices of activities of theosophists the world over. Rs 10 / $ 4

TRANSACTIONS. For titles beginning with "Transactions," followed by the name of the publishing or sponsoring institution or society, see the respective institution or society.

116. UNITED ASIA. International Magazine of Afro-Asian Affairs. B-M. United Asia Pub., 12 Rampart Row, Bombay 1. Rs 10 / $ 3

117. UNITED SERVICE INSTITUTION OF INDIA, JOURNAL OF THE. Q. United Service Inst. of India, Kashmir House, New Delhi 11. Rs 12

118. UNIVERSITY OF ALLAHABAD STUDIES. Irr. Univ. of Allahabad, Allahabad. nfs

119. UNIVERSITY OF BOMBAY, JOURNAL OF THE. 5xy. Univ. of Bombay, Fort, Bombay 1. No. 1 and 4 devoted to hist., economics and sociology, no. 2 to arts, and no. 3 and 5 to physical and biological sciences. Abstr. of theses. Rs 12 (Rs 5 for no. 1 and 4)

120. UNIVERSITY OF MADRAS, JOURNAL OF THE. S-A. Univ. of Madras, Triplicane, Madras 5. Contains 2 sections, one dealing with the humanities and the other with the natural sciences. Rs 4 (both sections together)

121. UNIVERSITY OF POONA, JOURNAL OF THE. Humanities Section. A. Registrar, Univ. of Poona, Ganeshkhind, Poona 7. Synopses of doctoral theses; in English, Sanskrit and Marathi. Rs 3

122. UTTAR PRADESH HISTORICAL SOCIETY, JOURNAL OF THE. S-A. U.P. Hist. Soc., Dept. of Hist., Univ. of Lucknow, Lucknow. Illus. Rs 6

123. VANYAJĀTI [Tribal people]. Q. D. Rangaiya, for Bharatiya Adimjati Sevak Sangh ["Soc. of Servants of Primitive Tribes in India"], Kingsway, Delhi 9. In English and Hindi; graph; statistics; A. cum. index; illus. Rs 3

124. VIKRAM [Valor]. Q. Vikram Univ., Ujjain. Illus. Rs 8

125. VISVABHARATI QUARTERLY. Q. Bidyut Ranjan Basu, for Visvabharati Univ., Santiniketan, Birbhum, West Bengal. A. cum. index; illus. Rs 8 / $ 3

Indonesia

Prepared with the assistance of the

Madjelis Ilmu Pengetahuan Indonesia
(Council for Sciences of Indonesia), Djakarta

1. AMERTA [Life-giving water]. Warna Warta Kepurbakalaan [Archaeological miscellany]. Irr. 1952 (1955: vol. 3). Dinas Purbakala Republik Indonesia [Archaeological Service of the Republic of Indonesia], Dj. Kimia 12, Djakarta. Ed: R. Soekmono. Art. on Indonesian archaeology, with emphasis on Hindu and Buddhist temples; plates and maps. nfs

BERITA DINAS PURBAKALA see DINAS PURBAKALA, BERITA...

2. DINAS PURBAKALA, BERITA... [Bulletin of the Archaeological Service] Irr. 1955 (1958: vol. 4). Dinas Purbakala Republik Indonesia [Archaeological Service of the Republic of Indonesia], Dj. Kimia 12, Djakarta. Ed: R. Soekmono. Art. on Indonesian archaeology; in English; sum.; plates and maps.
available on exchange basis

3. DINAS PURBAKALA REPUBLIK INDONESIA, LAPORAN TAHUNAN... [Annual report of activities of the Archaeological Service of the Republic of Indonesia]. A. Dinas Purbakala Republic Indonesia, Dj. Kimia 12, Djakarta. In English and Indonesian. Supersedes Oudheidkundig Verslag [Archaeological report]. free

LAPORAN TAHUNAN DINAS PURBAKALA REPUBLIK INDONESIA see DINAS PURBAKALA REPUBLIK INDONESIA, LAPORAN TAHUNAN...

4. MADJALAH UNTUK ILMU BAHASA, ILMU BUMI DAN KEBUDA JAAN [Journal for linguistics, social geography and culture]. Irr. Lembagu Kebudajaan Indonesia [Inst. for Indonesian Culture], Dj. Medan Merdeka Barat 12, Djakarta. Art. on Indonesian epigraphy, literature, folklore and general hist.; cum. table of contents; in English and Indonesian. Up to 1957 appeared in Dutch and Indonesian under the title Tijdschrift voor Indische Taal-, Land- en Volkenkunde [Journal for Indonesian linguistics, geography and culture]. Temporarily suspended. Rps 40

OUDHEIDKUNDIG VERSLAG see DINAS PURBAKALA REPUBLIK INDONESIA, LAPORAN TAHUNAN...

5. PRASASTI INDONESIA [Inscriptions of Indonesia]. Irr. 1950 (mri 1956: no. 2). Dinas Purbakala Republik Indonesia [Archaeological Service of the Republic of Indonesia], Dj. Kimia 12, Djakarta. Ed: R. Soekmono. Art. on epigraphic remains, belonging to different cent., discovered in Indonesia; biblio.; in English; texts of inscriptions quoted in original languages (Old Malay, Old Javanese and Sanskrit); index of words discussed in the texts and notes.
available on exchange basis

TIJDSCHRIFT VOOR INDISCHE TAAL-, LAND- EN VOLKENKUNDE see MADJALAH UNTUK ILMU BAHASA, ILMU BUMI DAN KEBUDA JAAN

Laos

Prepared with the assistance of

Cecil Hobbs, Head of the South Asia Section,
Library of Congress, Washington, D.C.

1. BULLETIN D'INFORMATION [Information bulletin]. Ministère de l'Information Nationale, Vientiane.

2. LA VOIX DU PEUPLE [The voice of the people]. Ministère de l'Information Nationale, Vientiane.

Malaya and Singapore

Prepared with the assistance of

Paul Wheatley, University of California, Berkeley, California,

Wang Gungwa, University of Malaya, Kuala Lumpur, and

Antony Croghan, Colonial Office Library, London

Note: The Wade-Giles system has been used below for the transliteration of Chinese words.

ANNUAL OF THE CHINA SOCIETY, SINGAPORE see CHINA SOCIETY, SINGAPORE, ANNUAL OF THE

BULLETIN OF THE INSTITUTE OF SOUTHEAST ASIA see NAN-YANG YEN-CHIU

1. CHINA SOCIETY, SINGAPORE, ANNUAL OF THE. A. China Soc., 47 Hill St., Singapore 6.

2. DEWAN BAHASA [Council of language]. M. Dewan Bahasa dan Pustaka [Language and Literature Council], Ministry of Education, Federation of Malaya, Peti Surat 803, Kuala Lumpur. M$ 6

FEDERATED MALAY STATES MUSEUM, THE JOURNAL OF THE see FEDERATION MUSEUMS JOURNAL

3. FEDERATION MUSEUMS JOURNAL. Irr. Museums Dept., Federation of Malaya, Kuala Lumpur. Ethnology, anthropology and archaeology. Before vol. 3, 1957, entitled: The Journal of the Federated Malay States Museum. pv (c. M$ 9)

4. THE HISTORICAL ANNUAL. A. 1953 (1958: no. 4). Univ. of Malaya Hist. Soc., Singapore. Ed: N. Rajendra, College Green, Singapore 11. Art. on hist., with emphasis on South and Southeast Asia; report on the acitivities of the soc.; maps; illus. M$2/$0.65

INSTITUTE OF SOUTHEAST ASIA, BULLETIN OF THE see NAN-YANG YEN-CHIU

THE JOURNAL OF THE FEDERATED MALAY STATES MUSEUM see FEDERATION MUSEUMS JOURNAL

JOURNAL OF THE MALAYAN BRANCH OF THE ROYAL ASIATIC SOCIETY see ROYAL ASIATIC SOCIETY, JOURNAL OF THE MALAYAN BRANCH OF THE

JOURNAL OF THE SOUTH SEAS SOCIETY see NAN-YANG HSÜEH-PAO

5. THE JOURNAL OF TROPICAL GEOGRAPHY. Irr. 1953 (1959: vol. 12). Dept. of Geography, Univ. of Malaya, Singapore 10, and Univ. of Malaya, Kuala Lumpur. Ed: W.L. Dale, Univ. of Malaya, Kuala Lumpur. Art. on geography and related fields (economics, hist. of all periods, archaeology, etc.), pertaining mostly to Africa, Southeast Asia, Australia and other tropical areas; graph, illus. Vol. 1-10 appeared under the title: Malayan Journal of Tropical Geography. p (1) M$5/p (1)$2.50

6. MALAYA IN HISTORY. S-A. 1954 (1959: vol. 5). Malayan Hist. Soc., c/o Muzium Negara, Damansara Rd., Kuala Lumpur. Ed: Mubin Sheppard. Art. on Malayan hist. (including local hist.), with emphasis on social and cultural hist., and archaeology; illus. Formerly (up to vol. 3, no. 1) entitled: Malayan Historical Journal. p (1) M$2

MALAYAN BULLETIN see section on Great Britain

7. MALAYAN ECONOMIC REVIEW. S-A. Malayan Economic Soc., P.O.B. 2900, Singapore. M$6

MALAYAN HISTORICAL JOURNAL see MALAYA IN HISTORY

MALAYAN JOURNAL OF TROPICAL GEOGRAPHY see THE JOURNAL OF TROPICAL GEOGRAPHY

MONUMENTA ORIENTALIA see TUNG-FANG HSÜEH-PAO

8. NAN-YANG HSÜEH-PAO [Southeast Asian journal]. JOURNAL OF THE SOUTH SEAS SOCIETY. S-A. 1940 (1959: vol. 15). South Seas Soc., P.O.B. 709, Singapore. Ed: Wang Gungwu, Univ. of Malaya, Kuala Lumpur. Art. on the hist. (mostly modern), literature and archaeology of Southeast Asia; rev. art. and bk. rev.; in Chinese or English. M$ 6

9. NAN-YANG YEN-CHIU [Nan-Yang studies]. BULLETIN OF THE INSTITUTE OF SOUTHEAST ASIA. A. 1959 (1959: vol. 1). Inst. of Southeast Asia, Nan-Yang Univ., Singapore. Ed: Hsü Yün-Ts'iao. Art. on the natural and social sciences and the humanities, including all periods of hist.; bk. rev.; biblio.; in Chinese and occasionally in English; table of contents in Chinese and English. M$ 6

10. ROYAL ASIATIC SOCIETY, JOURNAL OF THE MALAYAN BRANCH OF THE. Covering the Territories of the Federation of Malaya, the Colonies of Singapore, Sarawak and North Borneo, and the State of Brunei. Q (Irr.). 1923 (1957: vol. 30). Council of the Malayan Branch, Royal Asiatic Soc., c/o Raffles Museum, Singapore 6. Ed: C.A.Gibson-Hill. Art. on hist., archaeology, ethnology, linguistics, literature and art, dealing primarily with Malaya, Singapore and British Borneo, but occasionally also with adjacent areas of Indonesia and Southeast Asia. Hist. art. deal with all periods with special emphasis on European penetration and colonization in the last 400 years. Many issues reserved for monographs or symposiums on specific subjects; bk. rev.; A. report including list of memb.; cum. index for first 20 vol. pub. in vol. XXI, part 3 (1948); maps, graph, doc.; illus. p (1) M $5 (memb. $3.50) / p (1) $1.67

SOUTH SEAS SOCIETY, JOURNAL OF THE see NAN-YANG HSÜEH-PAO

11. THE STRAITS TIMES ANNUAL. A. Straits Times, Singapore. Illus. M $3.75

12. TUNG-FANG HSÜEH-PAO [Oriental studies]. MONUMENTA ORIENTALIA. Irr. 1957 (1958: vol. 1, no. 2). Tung-fang Hsüeh-hui ["Oriental Soc."], Singapore. Ed: Ho Kuang-chung (K.C.Ho), Chinese Dept., Univ. of Malaya, Singapore 10. Art. on Chinese literature, philology, philosophy, religion, hist., biography and archaeology of all periods; doc.; in Chinese and occasionally English. M $5

Nepal

Prepared with the assistance of

Leo E. Rose, Indian Press Digests, Center for South Asia Studies, Institute of International Studies, University of California, Berkeley, California,

Hugh B. Wood, Professor of Education, University of Oregon, Eugene, Oregon, and

Trailokya Nath Upraity, Principal, College of Education, and Deputy Secretary of Education, Kathmandu

1. COMMERCE. B-W. Nepal Chamber of Commerce, Kathmandu. Contemporary economic problems, including discussions of Nepalese economic hist.; in Nepali.

2. DHARMODAYA [Rise of religion]. M. Dharmodaya Sabha [Soc. for the Rise of Religion], Kathmandu. Buddhist religion and culture; in Newari.

3. EDUCATION. Q. College of Education, Kathmandu. Nepalese educational problems, including a treatment of their hist. background.

4. ITIHAS PRAKAS [Lights on history]. Irr. Itihas Prakas Mandala ["Itihas Prakas" Soc.], Kathmandu. Hist. of Nepal.

5. ITIHAS SAMSODHAN [Corrections of history]. Irr. 1952. Pub. in Kathmandu. Art., based on doc., manuscripts and inscriptions, criticizing various points made in existing pub. works on Nepalese hist.; in Nepali; about 40 issues have appeared so far.

6. KARMAVIR [Brave in action]. W. Prakash Press, Kathmandu, for Karmavir Mahamandal ["Karmavir" Assoc.], Kathmandu. Nepalese political affairs and interpretations of Nepalese hist.; in Nepali.

7. NAVIN SIKSHYA [New education]. M. College of Education, Kathmandu. Nepalese educational problems, including a treatment of their hist. background; in Nepali.

8. NEPAL ECONOMIST. B-W. Jagadudar Press, Kathmandu. Contemporary economic problems and discussions on Nepalese economic hist.; in English and Nepali.

9. THE NEPAL GUARDIAN. Irr. Ed: Baron Shamsher, Kathmandu. Hist. and current events of Nepal.

10. PRAGATI [Progress]. B-M. 1953. Pragati Prakashan, Patan. A literary journal, containing occasional hist. art.; in Nepali.

11. SANSKRIT SANDESH [Sanskrit message]. M. 1953. Dir Library, Kathmandu. Ed: Yogi Naraharinath, Buddigajar Parajuli. Texts, occasionally with a translation into Nepali, of ancient Sanskrit inscriptions and manuscripts; in Sanskrit and Nepali.

12. SHARADA [Another name for Saraswati, the Hindu Goddess of Learning -- ed.]. Irr. Jorganesh Press, Kathmandu. A literary journal, containing occasional hist. art.; in Nepali.

13. UNITED NATIONS ASSOCIATION JOURNAL. A. United Nations Assoc. of Nepal, Kathmandu.

Readers searching for a periodical are also advised to see the ADDENDA sections included at the end of some lists.

Pakistan

Prepared with the assistance of

A. Halim, Professor of History, University of Dacca,

Abdul Hamid, Professor of History, Government College, Lahore, and

M. Shuja-ud-Din, Professor of History, Dyal Singh College, Lahore

Note: Urdu words in this list have been transliterated according to the systems used in Rien's Catalogue of Persian Manuscripts and Storey's Persian Literature.

1. ASIATIC SOCIETY OF PAKISTAN, JOURNAL OF THE. B (A. before 1959). 1957 (1959: vol. 3). Asiatic Soc. of Pakistan, Ramna, Dacca 2, East Pakistan. Ed: S.S. Hasan. Art. mainly on hist., sociology and anthropology with special reference to Pakistan; appendix to vol. 2 (1958) containing translations of the scattered and extant inscriptions of Bengal during the pre-Mughal period. p (1) P Rs 7/8/- / $ 2.10 (appendix to vol. 2 : P Rs 5 / $ 1.05)

2. COMMERCE AND INDUSTRY. M. Pub. and ed: A.Z. Hami, Chandnighat Rd., Dacca, East Pakistan. Art. on the commerce, industry, agriculture and economic hist. of East Pakistan. P Rs -/8/- / c. $ 0.11

3. CULTURE AND PROGRESS. M. Ed: K. Khurshid Ali, Nazimuddin Hall, Dinajpur, East Pakistan. p (1) P Rs -/6/3 / p (1) c. $0.08

4. THE DACCA UNIVERSITY STUDIES. A. Ed. address: c/o Librarian, Univ. of Dacca, Ramna, Dacca 2, East Pakistan. available on exchange basis

5. DHAKA VISHVA-VIDYALAY BARSHIKI [Annual journal of Dacca University]. A. Ed. address: c/o Dacca Univ. Central Students' Union, Ramna, Dacca 2, East Pakistan. In Bengali. available on exchange basis

6. HILAL [Crescent]. Q. Ed: H. Hussain Imdad, P.O.B. 701, Karachi. A pub. of the Govt. of Pakistan; in Urdu.

7. THE ISLAMIC LITERATURE. M. Muhammad Ashraf, Kashmiri Bazar, Lahore, West Pakistan. Art. on Islamic literature, hist., jurisprudence and philosophy; bk. rev.; biblio. P Rs 10 / $3

JOURNAL. For titles beginning with "Journal," followed by the name of the publishing or sponsoring institution or society, see the respective institution or society.

8. MASHIK MOHAMMADI [Monthly "Mohammadi"]. M. Abdul Hakim Khan, Azad Press, Ramna, Dacca 2, East Pakistan. Literary, biographical and cultural art.; in Urdu. P Rs 7/8/- / $1.58

9. MEHRAN. Q. Ed: Muhammad Ibrahim Joyo, c/o "Mehran," Hyderabad, West Pakistan. Sindhi hist. and culture.

10. THE MIDDLE EAST. M. Pub. and ed: Mumtaz Tariq, Central Hotel Bldg., Khuhro Rd., P.O.B. 7208, Karachi, West Pakistan.

11. THE MUSEUMS JOURNAL. B. 1946 (1958: vol. 12). Allied Press, The Mall, Lahore, West Pakistan, for Museums Assoc. of Pakistan. Ed: Malik Shams. Art. on museums, archives and numismatics with reference to Pakistan and India. (memb.) P Rs 12 / (memb.) $ 2.52

12. THE NEW VALUES. B. Ed: S. Murshid, 67/A Azimpur Estate, Ramna, Dacca, East Pakistan. Art, philosophy, literary hist. and politics. p (1) P Rs 2 / c. $ 0.42

13. ORIENTAL COLLEGE MAGAZINE. Q. 1925 (1960: vol. 36). Oriental College, Univ. of the Panjab, Lahore, West Pakistan. Ed: S.M. Abdullah. Research art. on the literary and political hist. of Arabs, Persians and Indian Moslems; bk. rev.; in Urdu, English, Persian or Arabic; cum. table of contents for the years 1925-41 and 1942-58 pub. separately. P Rs 4

14. THE ORIENTAL GEOGRAPHER. B. Nafis Ahmad, c/o Dept. of Geography, Univ. of Dacca, Ramna. Dacca, East Pakistan, for East Pakistan Geographical Soc. p (1) P Rs 4 / $ 2

15. PAKISTAN ECONOMIC JOURNAL. Q. Economic Assoc. of Pakistan, c/o Dept. of Economics, Univ. of Dacca, Dacca 2, East Pakistan. P Rs 12 / $ 2.52

16. PAKISTAN HISTORICAL SOCIETY, JOURNAL OF THE. Q. 1953 (1960: vol. 8). Pakistan Hist. Soc., 30 New Karachi Co-operative Housing Soc., Karachi 5, West Pakistan. Art. on the hist. of Islam in general and of Pakistan and India in particular; bk. rev.; titles of research projects undertaken currently in the univ. of Pakistan and India. P Rs 10 / c. $ 2.10

17. PAKISTAN HISTORY CONFERENCE, THE PROCEEDINGS OF THE. A. 1951 (mri 1956). Pakistan Hist. Soc., 30 New Karachi Co-operative Housing Soc., Karachi 5, West Pakistan. Ed: S. Moinul Haq. Papers read at the A. conferences; contents divided into two parts: 1) Islamic hist., culture and art, and 2) various aspects and periods of the hist. of Pakistan and India; in English and Urdu. P Rs 7/8/3 /c. 1.60

18. PAKISTAN HORIZON. M. K. Sarwar Hasan, for Pakistan Inst. of International Affairs, Strachan Rd., Karachi 1, West Pakistan. International relations with special reference to Pakistan's foreign relations. P Rs 8 / 20s

19. PAKISTAN QUARTERLY. Q. Ed: S. Amjad Ali, P.O.B. 183, Karachi, West Pakistan. A pub. of the Govt. of Pakistan; illus. p (1) P Rs 2 / $ 0.42

20. PANJAB UNIVERSITY HISTORICAL SOCIETY, JOURNAL OF THE. S-A. 1932 (1960: vol. 11). Panjab Univ. Hist. Soc., Dept. of Hist., Panjab Univ., Lahore, West Pakistan. Ed. board: H. Montgomery Hyde, Zafar-ul-Islam, Agha Nasir Ahmad, Sh. Abdur Rashid. Art. on recent Moslem hist.

in Pakistan and India; titles of research projects completed in the Dept. of Hist., Panjab Univ., since 1935. Pub. suspended in 1947 and resumed in 1960.
P Rs 6 / 15s

THE PROCEEDINGS OF THE PAKISTAN HISTORY CONFERENCE see PAKISTAN HISTORY CONFERENCE, THE PROCEEDINGS OF THE

21. RANGPUR SAHITYA PARISAT PATRIKA [Journal of the Rangpur Literary Society]. Q. Panchanan Sarkar, for Rangpur Sahitya Parisat, Rangpur, East Pakistan. Local inscriptions, literary biographies, folklore, folk songs, ikons and manuscripts. P Rs 3 / $ 0.63

22. SAMAKAL [Contemporary times]. M. Sikandar Abu Ja'far, 13 Abhoy Das Lane, Dacca, East Pakistan. In Bengali. P Rs 6 / $ 1.26

23. TARAJIMUL HADIS [Translations of the Traditions]. Q. Ed: Abdullah Al-Kafi Quraishy, c/o Office of the East Pakistan Jama't-i Ahl-i Hadis, al-Hadis Printing Works, Qazi Alauddin Rd., Dacca, East Pakistan.
P Rs 6/8/- / $ 1.37

24. TARIKH-O-TAHQIQ [History and research]. B. Dept. of Hist., Dyal Singh College, Lahore, West Pakistan. Ed: M. Shuja-ud-Din. In Urdu and English.

25. UNIVERSITY OF THE PANJAB ARABIC AND PERSIAN SOCIETY, JOURNAL OF THE. Q. Muhammad Baqir, c/o Univ. of the Panjab Arabic and Persian Soc., Oriental College, Lahore, West Pakistan. In English or Urdu; illus. P Rs 2

26. VOICE OF ISLAM. Q. 1951. Jamiayat-ul Falah [Soc. for Human Progress], Karachi, West Pakistan. Ed: Manager, Voice of Islam, Karachi 3. Art. on the hist. of Islam. p (1) P Rs 2

27. WEST PAKISTAN. Q. Govt. of West Pakistan, Lahore.
p (1) P Rs 1

28. YOUNG PAKISTAN. M. Aziz Ahmad Bilyameeni, Sawghat Press, 66 Lyall St., Dacca, East Pakistan, for Pakistan Press Syndicate.
P Rs -/8/- / c. $ 0.11

Sarawak

1. THE SARAWAK MUSEUM JOURNAL. S-A. 1911 (1958: vol. 8). Sarawak Museum, Kuching. Ed: Tom Harrisson (curator of the museum). Documented art. on the hist., geography, ethnology, sociology, folklore, art, archaeology and numismatics of Borneo; biblio.; maps, charts, statistics; illus. M $6

Thailand

Prepared with the assistance of
The Fine Arts Department, Bangkok

THE JOURNAL OF THE SIAM SOCIETY see SIAM SOCIETY, JOURNAL OF THE

1. NAVIKASASTR [Navigation]. M. Navy Assoc., Dhonburi. p(1) Bahts 5 / p(1) $ 0.25

2. SARANUKROM THAI [Thai encyclopedia]. M (1 vol. with 20 no.). 1955 (1958: vol. 2). Royal Inst. of Thailand, Na Phra That Rd., Bangkok. Ed: Phya Anuman Rajadhon. Art. on various subjects, including those of hist. interest, arranged alphabetically, beginning with the first letter of the Thai alphabet. Bahts 50 per vol. / $ 2.50 per vol.

3. SIAM SOCIETY, THE JOURNAL OF THE. S-A. 1905 (1959: vol. 47). Siam Soc., 60 Asoka Rd., Bangkapi, Bangkok (P.O.B. 65, Bangkok). Ed: Cecil L. Sanford. Art. on the hist., archaeology, art and literature of Thailand and neighboring countries; bk. rev.; doc.; in English and French. Bahts 100/$5

4. SILPAKORN [Fine arts]. B-M (formerly M). 1947 (1959: vol. 3). Fine Arts Dept., Bangkok. Ed: Bunnak Pyakadej. Art. on the hist., archaeology, arts and literature of Thailand; news and notes on the activities of the soc. and on excavations; doc.; in English. Bahts 40 / $ 2

5. TAMRUAJ [Police]. M. Finance Division, Dept. of Police, Pathumwan, Bangkok. p(1) Bahts 3 / p(1) $0.15

6. VIDHYACHARN [Knowledge for teachers]. M. Guru Sabha [Teachers' Assoc.], Bangkok. p (1) Bahts 3 / p (1) $0.15

7. YUDHAKOS [Strategy]. M. Yudhakos Office, near Chang-rong-si Bridge, Bangkok. p (1) Bahts 3 / p (1) $0.15

REPUBLIC OF VIETNAM
(SOUTH VIETNAM)

Prepared with the assistance of
Truồng Bủu Lâm, Director, Institut National
des Recherches Historiques, Département de
l'Education Nationale, Republic du Viêt-Nam, Saigon

1. ASIAN CULTURE. Q. Vietnamese Assoc. for Asian Culture, 201, Lê văn Duyệt, Saigon. In English and French. p (1) VN $50 / $4

2. BÁCH KHOA [Encyclopedia]. S-M. Huỳnh Văn Lang, 160 Phan Đình Phùng, Saigon. p (1) VN $10

BULLETIN DE L'INSTITUT DE RECHERCHES HISTORIQUES see VIỆT NAM KHẢO-CỔ TẬP-SAN

BULLETIN DE LA SOCIETE DES ETUDES INDOCHINOISES see SOCIETE DES ETUDES INDOCHINOISES, BULLETIN DE LA...

3. ĐẠI HỌC [University]. M. Univ. of Huế, 3, rue Lê Lồi, Huê. General and cultural hist., philosophy and linguistics. VN $120

4. ĐẠI-HỌC VĂN-KHOA [Faculty of Letters]. Faculty of Letters, Univ. of Saigon. Art. on literature and general and cultural hist.; in Vietnamese, English and French; English or French sum. of Vietnamese-language art.

5. FRANCE-ASIE [France-Asia]. Revue mensuelle de culture et de synthèse franco-asiatique [Monthly review of culture and Franco-Asiatic synthesis]. M. René de Berval, 93, rue Nguyen van Thinh, Saigon. VN $450 / $10

6. GIÁO-DỤC PHỔ-THÔNG [Popularization of education]. S-M. Ed: Pham Quang Lộc, 8 Ngô đú'c Kế, Saigon. p (1) VN $10

HISTORICAL RESEARCH INSTITUTE, TRANSACTIONS OF THE see VIỆT NAM KHẢO-CỔ TẬP-SAN

INSTITUT DE RECHERCHES HISTORIQUES, BULLETIN DE L'... see VIỆT NAM KHẢO-CỔ TẬP-SAN

7. SOCIETE DES ETUDES INDOCHINOISES, BULLETIN DE LA... [Bulletin of the Indochinese Studies Society]. Q. 1883 (1959: new series, vol. 33). Societé des Etudes Indochinoises, Musée National du Viêt-Nam, Saigon. Ed: J. Bocquet. Art. on the anthropology, geography, prehist. art, and the linguistic, general and cultural hist. of Indochina and the countries of South-east Asia; news of the soc.; professional news; biblio. of bk. and periodicals; doc.; illus. VN $500 / fr. 5000

TRANSACTIONS OF THE HISTORICAL RESEARCH INSTITUTE see VIỆT NAM KHẢO-CỔ TẬP-SAN

8. VĂN-HOÁ Á-CHÂU [Asian culture]. M. Hội Việt-Nam nghiên-cứu liên-lạc văn-hoá Á-châu [Vietnamese Assoc. for Asian Cultural Relations], 201 Lê văn Duyệt, Saigon. General and cultural hist. of Asia, cultural relations among the countries of Asia, philosophy and sociology. VN $ 320

9. VĂN-HOÁ NGUYỆT-SAN [Monthly cultural review]. Cơ quan nghiên-cứu và phổ-thông [Organ of researches and popularization]. M. Direction of Cultural Affairs, Dept. of National Education, 266 rue Công-lý, Saigon. VN $ 240

10. VIỆT NAM KHẢO-CỔ TẬP-SAN [Vietnamese bulletin of historical research]. BULLETIN DE L'INSTITUT DE RECHERCHES HISTORIQUES. TRANSACTIONS OF THE HISTORICAL RESEARCH INSTITUTE. Irr. 1959 (1959: vol. 1). Institut de Recherches Historiques, Nguyễn Bỉnh Khiêm 7, Saigon. Ed: Trương Bửu Lâm. Art. on all periods and aspects of the hist. of Asian countries, with emphasis on Vietnam and South-east Asia; bk. rev.; biblio.; in Vietnamese, French and English; French and English sum. of Vietnamese-language art.; maps, charts; illus. VN $ 50 / $ 1

UNION OF SOVIET SOCIALIST REPUPLICS

Union of Soviet Socialist Republics

Prepared with the assistance of

Francis S. Wagner, Library of Congress, Washington, D.C.,

A.A. Zvorykin, Editor, Bol'shaia Sovetskaia Entsiklopediia [Great Soviet Encyclopedia], Moscow, and the

Institute for the Study of the U.S.S.R., Munich

Note: a) Words in Russian and other languages using the Cyrillic script have been transliterated below according to the system used by the Library of Congress, Washington, D.C.

b) The Russian word "Izdatel'stvo," which is often cited with the name of the sponsoring institution of a periodical, refers to the publishing house of the institution concerned.

c) Certain standard Russian abbreviations have been used in this list (such as TsKKP, to designate the Central Committee of the Communist Party), but a full translation into English is given wherever necessary.

ARMENIAN S.S.R.

1. AKADEMIIA NAUK ARMIANSKOI SSR, DOKLADY... (Doklady Akademii Nauk Armianskoi SSR) [Bulletins of the Academy of Sciences of the Armenian S.S.R.]. 10 x y. Izdatel'stvo Akademii Nauk Armianskoi SSR, Erevan. In Armenian or Russian. p (1) 0.20 rub.

2. AKADEMIIA NAUK ARMIANSKOI SSR, IZVESTIIA... (Izvestiia Akademii Nauk Armianskoi SSR) [Communications of the Academy of Sciences of the Armenian S.S.R.]. Seriia obshchestvennykh nauk [Social science series]. M. Akademiia Nauk Armianskoi SSR, Erevan. In Armenian or Russian. DM 20

DOKLADY AKADEMII NAUK ARMIANSKOI SSR see AKADEMIIA NAUK ARMIANSKOI SSR, DOKLADY...

3. ISTORIKO-FILOLOGICHESKII ZHURNAL. PATMA-BANASIRAKAN ANDES [Historical-philological journal]. Q. Akademiia Nauk ASSR [Acad. of Sciences of the Armenian S.S.R.], Erevan. In Armenian or Russian. p (1) 0.80 rub.

IZVESTIIA AKADEMII NAUK ARMIANSKOI SSR see AKADEMIIA NAUK ARMIANSKOI SSR, IZVESTIIA...

PATMA-BANASIRAKAN ANDES see ISTORIKO-FILOLOGICHESKII ZHURNAL

4. VESTNIK MATENADARANA [Matenadaran review]. Irr. Khranilishche Drevnikh Rukopisei pri Sovete Ministrov Armianskoi SSR [Depository for Old Manuscripts attached to the Council of Ministers of the Armenian S.S.R.], Erevan. In Armenian. p (1) DM 4.30

AZERBAIDZHAN S.S.R.

5. AKADEMIIA NAUK AZERBAIDZHANSKOI SSR, DOKLADY... (Doklady Akademii Nauk Azerbaidzhanskoi SSR) [Bulletins of the Academy of Sciences of the Azerbaidzhan S.S.R.]. M. Izdatel'stvo Akademii Nauk Azerbaidzhanskoi SSR, Baku. In Azerbaidzhani or Russian, with sum. in one of the two languages. p (1) 0.40 rub.

6. AKADEMIIA NAUK AZERBAIDZHANSKOI SSR, IZVESTIIA... (Izvestiia Akademii Nauk Azerbaidzhanskoi SSR) [Communications of the Academy of Sciences of the Azerbaidzhan S.S.R.]. Seriia obshchestvennykh nauk [Social science series]. M. Akademiia Nauk Azerbaidzhanskoi SSR, Baku. p (1) 0.80 rub.

DOKLADY AKADEMII NAUK AZERBAIDZHANSKOI SSR see AKADEMIIA NAUK AZERBAIDZHANSKOI SSR, DOKLADY...

IZVESTIIA AKADEMII NAUK AZERBAIDZHANSKOI SSR see AKADEMIIA NAUK AZERBAIDZHANSKOI SSR, IZVESTIIA...

BELORUSSIAN S.S.R.

7. AKADEMIIA NAUK BELORUSSKOI SSR, DOKLADY... (Doklady Akademii Nauk Belorusskoi SSR) [Bulletins of the Academy of Sciences of the Belorussian S.S.R.]. M. Izdatel'stvo Akademii Nauk Belorusskoi SSR, Minsk. p (1) 0.20 rub.

AKADEMIIA NAUK BELORUSSKOI SSR, IZVESTIIA... see AKADEMIIA NAVUK BSSR, VESTSI...

8. AKADEMIIA NAVUK BSSR, VESTSI... (Vestsi Akademii Navuk BSSR). IZVESTIIA AKADEMII NAUK BELORUSSKOI SSR [Communications of the Academy of Sciences of the Belorussian S.S.R.]. Seriia gramadskikh navuk. Seriia obshchestvennykh nauk [Social science series]. Q. Akademiia Navuk BSSR, Minsk. In Belorussian; Russian sum. DM 14

BIELARUSKI ZBORNIK see section on the Federal Republic of Germany

DOKLADY AKADEMII NAUK BELORUSSKOI SSR see AKADEMIIA NAUK BELORUSSKOI SSR, DOKLADY...

IZVESTIIA AKADEMII NAUK BELORUSSKOI SSR see AKADEMIIA NAVUK BSSR, VESTSI...

KOMMUNIST BELARUSI see KOMMUNIST BELORUSSII

9. KOMMUNIST BELORUSSII [Belorussian Communist]. M. Izdatel'stvo TsK KPB [Pub. House of the Central Committee of the Belorussian Communist Party], Minsk. A separate edition appears in Belorussian under the title: Kommunist Belarusi. p (1) 0.20 rub.

VESTSI AKADEMII NAVUK BSSR see AKADEMIIA NAVUK BSSR, VESTSI...

ESTONIAN S.S.R.

AKADEMIIA NAUK ESTONSKOI SSR, IZVESTIIA... see EESTI NSV TEADUSTE AKADEEMIA. TOIMETISED

ANNALES SOCIETATIS LITTERARUM ESTONICAE see EESTI TEADUSLIK SELTS ROOTSIS. AASTARAAMAT in the section on Sweden

EESTI KOMMUNIST see KOMMUNIST ESTONII

10. EESTI NSV TEADUSTE AKADEEMIA. TOIMETISED. IZVESTIIA AKADEMII NAUK ESTONSKOI SSR [Communications of the Academy of Sciences of the Estonian S.S.R.]. Ühiskonnateaduste seeria. Seriia obshchestvennykh nauk [Social science series]. Q. 1956 (1959: new series, vol. 8). Akademiia Nauk Estonskoi SSR, Tallin. Ed: G. Naan (chairman of the acad.), M. Pesti (vice-chairman), Sakala 35, Tallin. Art., mainly on the Baltic countries and the U.S.S.R., divided into three categories: (1) hist., mostly modern, and archaeology: this section includes reports of research projects completed or in progress on modern Estonian hist., pertaining mostly to social and economic aspects; (2) economics, and (3) language and literature; bk. rev.; professional news; news of the acad.; biographies of outstanding Estonian scholars; in Estonian or Russian; sum. in Russian or Estonian and in German, English or French; table of contents in Estonian, Russian, German, French and English; maps, illus. The social science series started with vol. 5 (1956). 1.20 rub.

EESTI TEADUSLIK SELTS ROOTSIS. AASTARAAMAT see section on Sweden

IZVESTIIA AKADEMII NAUK ESTONSKOI SSR see EESTI NSV TEADUSTE AKADEEMIA. TOIMETISED

11. KOMMUNIST ESTONII [Estonian Communist]. M. Izdatel'stvo TsK KP ESSR [Pub. House of the Central Committee of the Communist Party of the Estonian S.S.R.], Tallin. A separate edition appears in Estonian under the title: Eesti Kommunist. p (1) 0.20 rub.

12. SKANDINAVSKII SBORNIK [Scandinavian review]. Irr. 1956 (1957: vol. 2). Estonskoe Gosudarstvennoe Izdatel'stvo, for Tartuskii Gosudarstvennyi Universitet [National Univ. of Tartu], Piarnu maante 10, Tallin. Ed: V.V. Pokhlebkin, L.K. Roots. Art. on Scandinavia, with emphasis on social and cultural hist. and on Scandinavian-U.S.S.R. relations; bk. rev.; news; in Russian; Estonian, Swedish and occasionally Finnish sum. pv(c. 1.26 - 1.55 rub.)

SOCIETAS LITTERARUM ESTONICAE, ANNALES... see EESTI TEADUSLIK SELTS ROOTSIS, AASTARAAMAT in the section on Sweden

SVIO ESTONICA see section on Sweden

GEORGIAN S.S.R.

13. AKADEMIIA NAUK GRUZINSKOI SSR, SOOBSHCHENIIA... (Soobshcheniia Akademii Nauk Gruzinskoi SSR) [Reports of the Academy of Sciences of the Georgian S.S.R.]. M. Izdatel'stvo Akademii Nauk Gruzinskoi SSR, ul. Dzerzhinskogo 8, Tbilisi. Contains a section each on archaeology and hist. Appears in two editions, one in Russian and the other in Georgian. p (1) 0.50 rub.

14. ISTORICHESKII VESTNIK [Historical review]. Arkhivnoe upravlenie MVD Gruzinskoi SSR [Archival directory of the Ministry of the Interior of the Georgian S.S.R.]. Irr. MVD Gruzinskoi SSR, Tbilisi. In Georgian or Russian. 2 rub.

SOOBSHCHENIIA AKADEMII NAUK GRUZINSKOI SSR see AKADEMIIA NAUK GRUZINSKOI SSR, SOOBSHCHENIIA...

KAZAKH S.S.R.

15. AKADEMIIA NAUK KAZAKHSKOI SSR, VESTNIK... (Vestnik Akademii Nauk Kazakhskoi SSR) [Bulletin of the Academy of Sciences of the Kazakh S.S.R.]. M. Akademiia Nauk Kazakhskoi SSR, Alma-Ata. In Russian. p (1) 0.60 rub.

16. KAZAKHSTAN KOMMUNISI [Kazakhstan Communist]. M. TsK KP Kazakhstana [Central Committee of the Communist Party of Kazakhstan], Alma-Ata. In Kazakhstani. A separate edition appears in Russian under the title: Kommunist.Kazakhstana. p (1) 0.12 rub. / DM 5 p.a.

VESTNIK AKADEMII NAUK KAZAKHSKOI SSR see AKADEMIIA NAUK KAZAKHSKOI SSR, VESTNIK...

KIRGIZ S.S.R.

17. KOMMUNIST [Communist]. M. TsK KP Kirgiziia [Central Committee of the Communist Party of Kirgizia], ul. Kirova 59, Frunze. Appears in two separate editions, one in Russian and the other in Kirgiz. DM 5

LATVIAN S.S.R.

AKADEMIIA NAUK LATVIISKOI SSR, IZVESTIIA... see LATVIJAS PSR ZINĀTŅU AKADĒMIJAS VĒSTIS

IZVESTIIA AKADEMII NAUK LATVIISKOI SSR see LATVIJAS PSR ZINĀTŅU AKADĒMIJAS VĒSTIS

18. KOMMUNIST SOVETSKOI LATVII [Communist of Soviet Latvia]. Obshchestvenno-politicheskii zhurnal TsK Kommunisticheskoi Partii Latvii [Social and political science journal of the Central Committee of the Communist Party of Latvia]. M. TsK Kommunisticheskoi Partii Latvii, Riga. Appears in two separate editions, one in Russian and the other in Latvian.
p (1) 0.20 rub. / DM 5 p.a.

19. LATVIJAS PSR ZINĀTŅU AKADĒMIJAS VĒSTIS. IZVESTIIA AKADEMII NAUK LATVIISKOI SSR [Communications of the Academy of Sciences of the Latvian S.S.R.]. M. 1947 (1959: no. 1 [138] - 12 [149]). Latvijas PSR Zinātņu Akadēmija, Smilshu iela 1, Riga. Manag. ed: K. Graudiņš. Art. on the sciences, arts and humanities, the first part of the periodical being devoted to the modern hist. of Latvia and the Soviet Union; bk. rev.; biblio.; professional news; news of the acad.; in Latvian or Russian; sum.; A. author index; supplements.
7.20 rub.

LITHUANIAN S.S.R.

AKADEMIIA NAUK LITOVSKOI SSR, TRUDY... see LIETUVOS TSR MOKSLŲ AKADEMIJA. DARBAI

20. KOMMUNIST [Communist]. M. Izdatel'stvo TsK KP Litvy [Pub. House of the Central Committee of the Communist Party of Lithuania], Vil'nius. In Russian. A separate edition appears in Lithuanian under the title: Komunistas.
DM 5

KOMUNISTAS see KOMMUNIST

21. LIETUVOS TSR MOKSLŲ AKADEMIJA. DARBAI. TRUDY AKADEMII NAUK LITOVSKOI SSR [Works of the Academy of Sciences of the Lithuanian S.S.R.]. Serija A. Seriia A [Series A]. S-A. 1955 (1960: vol. 8). Valstybinė Politinės ir Mokslinės Literatūros Leidykla [State Press of Political and Scientific Literature], for Lietuvos TSR Mokslų Akademija, Vil'nius. Ed: J. Matulis, Stalino pr. 3, Vil'nius. Art. on economics, hist., archaeology, philology and literature, pertaining to Lithuania; hist. art. deal mainly with modern and current hist., with emphasis on Lithuania's relations with Poland, Russia and Germany; in Lithuanian; Russian sum.; table of contents in Lithuanian and Russian.
0.20 rub.

22. LIETUVOS TSR MOKSLŲ AKADEMIJA. ZINYNAS [Academy of Sciences of the Lithuanian S.S.R. Transactions]. Irr. 1947 (mri 1952: vol. 9). Lietuvos TSR Mokslų Akademija, Vil'nius. Ed: J. Ziugzda. Art. on the natural and social sciences and the humanities, including modern Lithuanian hist.; bk. rev.; news of the acad.; in Lithuanian and Russian; Russian sum.; A. author index.
2.60 rub.

TRUDY AKADEMII NAUK LITOVSKOI SSR see LIETUVOS TSR MOKSLŲ AKADEMIJA. DARBAI

MOLDAVIAN S.S.R.

KOMMUNIST MOLDAVII see KOMUNISTUL MOLDOVEJ

23. KOMUNISTUL MOLDOVEJ [Moldavian Communist]. M. TsK KP MSSR [Central Committee of the Communist Party of the Moldavian S.S.R.], Kishinev. In Moldavian. A separate edition appears in Russian under the title: Kommunist Moldavii. DM 5

RUSSIAN S.F.S.R.

24. AKADEMIIA NAUK SSSR, INSTITUT ISTORII, DOKLADY I SOOBSHCHENIIA... (Doklady i soobshcheniia Instituta Istorii Akademii Nauk SSSR) [Bulletins and reports of the Historical Institute of the Academy of Sciences of the U.S.S.R.]. Irr. 1954 (1957: no. 12). Institut Istorii Akademii Nauk SSSR, Volkhonka 14, Moskva. Ed: L.S. Gaponenko. Art. primarily on Russian hist. with emphasis on the modern period; news and notes on the activities of hist. and related inst. p (1) 0.67

25. AKADEMIIA NAUK SSSR, INSTITUT SLAVIANOVEDENIIA, UCHENYE ZAPISKI... (Uchenye zapiski Instituta Slavianovedeniia Akademii Nauk SSSR) [Learned papers of the Institute of Slavic Studies of the Academy of Sciences of the U.S.S.R.]. 2-3 x y. 1949 (1958: vol. 16). Izdatel'stvo Akademii Nauk SSSR, Podsosenskii per. 21, Moskva B-34, for Institut Slavianovedeniia Akademii Nauk SSSR. Ed: P.N. Tret'iakov. Art. on Slavic studies in the U.S.S.R. and other Slavic countries and on the hist. (mostly modern) of Western and Southern Slavs, with special reference to revolutionary movements, the creation and development of post-World War II "people's democracy" and the reflection of major hist. movements in national literature and ideological struggles; academic news. pv (c. 2 rub.)

26. AKADEMIIA NAUK SSSR, ISTORICHESKIE ZAPISKI... (Istoricheskie zapiski Akademii Nauk SSSR) [Historical writings of the Academy of Sciences of the U.S.S.R.]. S-A (Irr.). 1937 (1960: no. 66). Institut Istorii Akademii Nauk SSSR [Hist. Inst. of the Acad. of Sciences of the U.S.S.R.], Moskva. Ed: A.L. Sidorov, Volkhonka 14, Moskva. Art. on Russian hist., pertaining mostly to the modern and recent periods; occasional biblio. and news about hist. meetings. p (1) 1.87 rub.

27. AKADEMIIA NAUK SSSR, OTDELENIE LITERATURY I IAZYKA, IZVESTIIA... (Izvestiia Akademii Nauk SSSR, Otdelenie Literatury i Iazyka) [Communications of the Academy of Sciences of the U.S.S.R., Department of Literature and Language]. B-M. Akademiia Nauk SSSR, Otdelenie Literatury i Iazyka, Volkhonka, Moskva. DM 30

28. AKADEMIIA NAUK SSSR, SIBIRSKOE OTDELENIE, IZVESTIIA... (Izvestiia Sibirskogo Otdeleniia Akademii Nauk SSSR) [Communications of the Siberian Department of the Academy of Sciences of the U.S.S.R.]. M. Novosibirskoe Knizhnoe Izdatel'stvo [Novosibirsk Bk. Pub. House], Krasnyi Prospekt 18, Novosibirsk, for Sibirskoe Otdelenie Akademii Nauk SSSR. p (1) 0.70 rub.

29. AKADEMIIA NAUK SSSR, VESTNIK... (Vestnik Akademii Nauk SSSR) [Bulletin of the Academy of Sciences of the U.S.S.R.]. M. Akademiia Nauk SSSR, Moskva. p (1) 0.80 rub.

BULLETIN ECONOMIQUE POUR L'EUROPE see section on International Periodicals

LE COURRIER DE L'UNESCO see UNESCO, LE COURRIER DE L'... in the section on International Periodicals

DOKLADY I SOOBSHCHENIIA INSTITUTA ISTORII AKADEMII NAUK SSSR see AKADEMIIA NAUK SSSR, INSTITUT ISTORII, DOKLADY I SOOBSHCHENIIA...

EKONOMICHESKOE POLOZHENIE KAPITALISTICHESKIKH STRAN see MIROVAIA EKONOMIKA I MEZHDUNARODNYE OTNOSHENIIA

30. GOSUDARSTVENNAIA BIBLIOTEKA SSSR IM. V. I. LENINA, OTDEL RUKOPISEI, ZAPISKI... (Zapiski Otdela Rukopisei Gosudarstvennoi Biblioteki SSSR) [Papers of the Manuscript Section of the V. I. Lenin State Library of the U.S.S.R.]. Irr. Otdel Rukopisei Gosudarstvennoi Biblioteki SSSR, Moskva. Descriptions of the holdings of the library; list of new acquisitions; printed doc. (with a translation into Russian if in another language); index of names and titles. pv

INSTITUTE FOR THE STUDY OF THE U.S.S.R. VESTNIK see VESTNIK in the section on the Federal Republic of Germany

INTERNATIONAL AFFAIRS see MEZHDUNARODNAIA ZHIZN'

ISTORICHESKIE ZAPISKI AKADEMII NAUK SSSR see AKADEMIIA NAUK SSSR, ISTORICHESKIE ZAPISKI...

31. ISTORICHESKII ARKHIV [Historical archives]. B-M. 1955 (1959: no vol. indic.). Institut Istorii Akademii Nauk SSSR [Hist. Inst. of the Acad. of Sciences of the U.S.S.R.], in collaboration with Institut Marksizma-Leninizma pri TsK KPSS [Inst. of Marxism-Leninism attached to the Central Committee of the Communist Party of the Soviet Union] and Glavnoe Arkhivnoe Upravlenie pri Sovete Ministrov SSSR [General Directorate of Archives attached to the Council of Ministers of the U.S.S.R.], Moskva. Ed: V.I. Shunkov, Volkhonka 14, Moskva. Source materials, with introductory comments, mostly on the modern and recent hist. of the U.S.S.R.; art. on archival science, with emphasis on source pub.; reports on archival holdings; rev. art.; rev. of bk. and periodicals; professional news and notes on Soviet archives; illus. 9 rub. / DM 51

32. ISTORIIA SSSR [History of the U.S.S.R.]. B-M. 1957 (1960: no vol. indic.). Institut Istorii Akademii Nauk SSSR, Kuznetskii most 19, Moskva. Ed: M.P. Kim. Art. on the hist. of the Russian Empire and the Soviet Union, with emphasis on the latter, and on Russia's relations with other countries; doc.; section on auxiliary hist. disciplines (including source materials); rev. art. and bk. rev., particularly on the treatment of Soviet hist. abroad; news of interest to scholars; table of contents also in English. 7.20 rub. / DM 41

IZVESTIIA AKADEMII NAUK SSSR, OTDELENIE LITERATURY I IAZYKA see AKADEMIIA NAUK SSSR, OTDELENIE LITERATURY I IAZYKA, IZVESTIIA...

IZVESTIIA SIBIRSKOGO OTDELENIIA AKADEMII NAUK SSSR see AKADEMIIA NAUK SSSR, SIBIRSKOE OTDELENIE, IZVESTIIA...

33. KHAKASS NAUCHNO-ISSLEDOVATEL SKII INSTITUT IAZYKA, LITERATURY I ISTORII, ZAPISKI... (Zapiski Khakasskogo Nauchno-Issledovatel'skogo Instituta Iazyka, Literatury i Istorii) [Papers of the Khakass Scientific Research Institute for Language, Literature and History]. Irr. Khakass Nauchno- Issledovatel'skii Institut Iazyka, Literatury i Istorii, Abakan. 0.45 rub.

34. KOMMUNIST [Communist]. Teoreticheskii i politicheskii zhurnal Tsentral'nogo Komiteta Kommunisticheskoi Partii Sovetskogo Soiuza [Theoretical and political journal of the Central Committee of the Communist Party of the Soviet Union]. 18 x y. Izdatel'stvo "Pravda" [Pub. House "Truth"], Moskva, for TsK KPSS, Moskva. 3.24 rub.

35. LENINGRADSKII UNIVERSITET, VESTNIK... (Vestnik Leningradskogo Universiteta) [Review of the University of Leningrad]. Seriia ekonomika, filosofiia i pravo [Series on economics, philosophy and law]. Q. Leningradskii Universitet, Leningrad. p (1) 1 rub.

36. LENINGRADSKII UNIVERSITET, VESTNIK... (Vestnik Leningradskogo Universiteta) [Review of the University of Leningrad]. Seriia istorii, iazyka i literatury [Series on history, language and literature]. Q. 1946 (1960: vol. 15). Leningradskii Universitet, Leningrad. Ed: V.V. Mavrodin. Art. on hist., predominantly Russian, with emphasis on the modern period, and on linguistics and literature; doc.; bk. rev.; professional news; English sum.; table of contents also in English. One of 6 series pub. by Leningrad Univ., all numbered continuously. Vol. 13 contains a list of art. in all series. p (1) 1 rub.

37. LITERATURA SLAVIANSKIKH NARODOV [Literature of the Slavic peoples]. Sbornik statei [Collection of essays]. Irr. Izdatel stvo Akademii Nauk SSSR, Moskva, for Institut Slavianovedeniia Akademii Nauk SSSR [Inst. of Slavic Studies of the Acad. of Sciences of the U.S.S.R.], Podsosenskii per. 21, Moskva. p (1) 0.97 rub.

38. MEZHDUNARODNAIA ZHIZN' [International life]. M. Izdatel'stvo "Znanie" [Pub. House "Knowledge"], Gorokhovskii pereulok 14, Moskva. Current international affairs and their hist. background; doc. A separate edition appears in English under the title: International Affairs. 6 rub.

39. MIROVAIA EKONOMIKA I MEZHDUNARODNYE OTNOSHENIIA [World economics and international relations]. M. Institut Mirovoi Ekonomiki i Mezhdunarodnykh Otnoshenii Akademii Nauk SSSR [Inst. of World Economics and International Relations of the Acad. of Sciences of the U.S.S.R.], Kitaiskii Proezd 7, Moskva. Includes a Q. supplement: Ekonomicheskoe polozhenie Kapitalisticheskikh Stran [Economic situation of the capitalist countries]. 6.60 rub.

40. MOSKOVSKAIA PATRIARKHIIA, ZHURNAL... (Zhurnal Moskovskoi Patriarkhii) [Journal of the Moscow Patriarchate]. M. Moskovskaia Patriarkhiia, Pirogovskaia 42, Moskva 48. pni

41. MOSKOVSKII UNIVERSITET, VESTNIK... (Vestnik Moskovskogo Universiteta) [Review of the University of Moscow]. Istoriko-filologicheskaia seriia [Historical-philological series]. B-M. 1946 (1959: vol. 14). Izdatel'stvo Moskovskogo Universiteta, Leninskie Gory, Moskva. Ed: A.V. Artsikhovskii. Art. on political and economic hist. from the Middle Ages to the present, with

emphasis on the 19th and 20th cent. and on philology and world literature, particularly Russian; bk. rev.; Moscow Univ. news; table of contents also in English. This series and Seriia ekonomiki, filosofii, prava (see next entry) replaced Seriia obshchestvennykh nauk [Social science series] in mid-1956. 4.80 rub.

42. MOSKOVSKII UNIVERSITET, VESTNIK... (Vestnik Moskovskogo Universiteta) [Review of the University of Moscow]. Seriia ekonomiki, filosofii, prava [Series on economics, philosophy, law]. B-M (Q prior to 1961). Moskovskii Universitet, Leninskie Gory, MGV, 9/904, Moskva. This series and Istoriko-filologicheskaia seriia (see preceding entry) replaced Seriia obshchestvennykh nauk [Social science series] in mid-1956. 4.80 rub.

43. NAUCHNO-ISSLEDOVATEL'SKII INSTITUT PRI SOVETE MINISTROV MORDOVSKOI SSR, ZAPISKI... (Zapiski Nauchno-Issledovatel'skogo Institut pri Sovete Ministrov Mordovskoi SSR) [Papers of the Scientific Research Institute attached to the Council of Ministers of the Mordovian S.S.R.]. Irr. Nauchno-Issledovatel'skii Institut pri Sovete Ministrov Mordovskoi SSR, Saransk. 7.30 rub.

44. NAUCHNYE DOKLADY VYSSHEI SHKOLY [Learned papers of higher schools]. Istoricheskie nauki [Historical sciences]. Q. 1958 (1959: no vol. indic.). Gosudarstvennoe Izdatel'stvo "Sovetskaia Nauka" [State Pub. House "Soviet Science"], Moskva, for Ministerstvo Vysshego Obrazovaniia SSR [Ministry of Higher Education of the U.S.S.R.], Moskva. Ed. board: P.P. Erifanov, I.S. Kashkin, K.M. Kolobova, P.A. Zaionchkovskii (manag. ed.), ul. Gertsena 6, Moskva K-9. Art. on the hist. of Russia and the U.S.S.R. and on general hist., contributed by Soviet professors, other academic personnel, and students of higher educational inst. p (1) 1 rub. / DM 23 p.a.

45. NOVAIA I NOVEISHAIA ISTORIIA [Modern and recent history]. B-M. 1957 (1960: no vol. indic.). Institut Istorii Akademii Nauk SSSR [Hist. Inst. of the Acad. of Sciences of the U.S.S.R.], Kuznetskii most, d. 19, Moskva K-31. Ed: A.A. Guber. Art. on modern and recent world hist. (except that of Russia) and on historiography; doc.; bk. rev.; abstr. ("Annotatsii") of new bk.; biblio. of bk., art. and doc. pub. in the U.S.S.R.; academic news from all over the world; table of contents also in English; illus. 6 rub. / DM 34

46. NOVYI MIR [New world]. M. Soiuz Pisatelei SSSR [Writers' Union of the U.S.S.R.], Moskva. Literature, criticism and political science; bk. rev.; diaries. DM 22

47. PALESTINSKII SBORNIK [Palestinian review]. Irr. 1881 (1959: vol. 4 [67]). Leningradskoe Otdelenie Izdatel'stvo Akademii Nauk SSSR [Leningrad Branch of the Pub. House of the Acad. of Sciences of the U.S.S.R.], B-164, Mendeleevskaia liniia., d.1., Leningrad, for Rossiiskoe Palestinskoe Obshchestvo [Russian Palestinian Soc. of the Acad. of Sciences of the U.S.S.R.]. Ed: N.V. Pigulevskaia. Art. on Palestinian and Middle Eastern studies, with emphasis on Soviet Russian research in the field; bk. rev.; table of contents also in English. Pub. suspended in 1917 and resumed in 1954. pv (p (1) 0.58 rub. - 1.50 rub.)

48. PREPODAVANIE ISTORII V SHKOLE [Teaching of history in schools]. B-M. 1946 (1961: vol. 16). Ministerstvo Prosveshcheniia RSFSR [Ministry of Education of the R.F.S.S.R.], Moskva. Ed: A.S. Kara-Murza, 3 proezd Mar'inoi voshchi 41, Moskva. Art. on hist. and hist. teaching, with emphasis on methods of instruction; one leading art. in each issue; rev. art.; bk. rev.; biblio.; answers to teachers' queries; professional news; chronicle of events of interest to hist. teachers; illus. 3 rub.

49. PROBLEMY ISTOCHNIKOVEDENIIA [Problems of source studies]. Irr. 1933 (1959: vol. 7). Institut Istorii Akademii Nauk SSSR [Hist. Inst. of the Acad. of Sciences of the U.S.S.R.], Podsosenskii per. d. 21, Moskva B-34. Ed: A.A. Novosel' skii. Art. on the general problems of the study of doc., collections and other source materials for hist. and its auxiliary disciplines, with special reference to the study of the hist. of the Soviet Union; hist. maps; illus. pv (1.57 rub. -2.40 rub.)

REVUE D'HISTOIRE DE LA CIVILISATION MONDIALE see VESTNIK ISTORII MIROVOI KUL'TURY

50. SOVETSKAIA ARKHEOLOGIIA [Soviet archaeology]. Q. 1936 (1960: no vol. indic.). Institut Arkheologii Akademii Nauk SSSR [Archaeological Inst. of the Acad. of Sciences of the U.S.S.R.], Moskva. Ed: A.V. Artsikhovskii. Art. on Soviet archaeology, ethnography, numismatics and sphragistics; reports on excavations in the U.S.S.R. and other countries; bk. rev.; table of contents also in French; graph, illus. 10 rub.

51. SOVETSKAIA ETNOGRAFIIA [Soviet ethnography]. B-M. 1931 (1960: no vol. indic.). Institut Etnografii im. N.N. Miklukho-Maklaia, Akademiia Nauk SSSR [N.N. Miklukho-Maklai Inst. of Ethnography, Acad. of Sciences of the U.S.S.R.], Moskva. Ed: S. P. Tolstov, ul. Frunze 10, Moskva G-19. Art. on ethnography (mostly hist.), including ethnogeny, and on folklore and linguistics, with emphasis on the peoples of the U.S.S.R. and Asia; news and reports of research; rev. of bk. and art. on ethnography, not confined to the study of the peoples of any area; English sum. of research art.; occasional French sum.; table of contents in Russian and French; cum. index for the years 1946-55; maps, illus. 108 rub.

52. SOVETSKOE GOSUDARSTVO I PRAVO [Soviet state and law]. M. Institut Gosudarstva i Prava Akademii Nauk SSSR [Inst. of State and Law of the Acad. of Sciences of the U.S.S.R.], Moskva. 14.40 rub.

53. SOVETSKOE KITAEVEDENIE [Soviet Sinology]. Q. 1958 (1959: no vol. indic.). Izdatel'stvo Vostochnoi Literatury [Pub. House for Oriental Literature], Kisel'nyi per. 4, Moskva B, for Institut Kitaevedeniia Akademii Nauk SSSR [Inst. of Sinology of the Acad. of Sciences of the U.S.S.R.], Moskva. Ed. board: G.V. Astaf'ev, L.I. Duman, N.I. Konrad, E.F. Kovalev (chief ed.), Kitaiskii proezd 7, Komn. 152, Moskva. Art. on Sinology, not confined to any period; bk. rev.; reports of research in the field of Sinology, carried on the the U.S.S.R. and other countries (particularly China); Chinese and English sum.; table of contents in Russian, Chinese, English, French and German. p (1) 1.20 rub.

54. SOVETSKOE VOSTOKOVEDENIE [Soviet Oriental studies]. B-M. Institut Vostokovedeniia Akademii Nauk SSSR [Inst. of Oriental Studies of the Acad. of Sciences of the U.S.S.R.], Armianskii per. 2, Moskva. Table of contents in Russian, English and Chinese. 7.20 rub.

55. SOVREMENNYI VOSTOK [Contemporary Orient]. M. Institut Vostokovedeniia, Akademiia Nauk SSSR [Inst. for the Study of the Contemporary Orient, Acad. of Sciences of the U.S.S.R.], Moskva. Illus. Title changed in 1961 to Azia i Afrika sevodnya [Asia and Africa today]. 3.60 rub.

UCHENYE ZAPISKI INSTITUTA SLAVIANOVEDENIIA AKADEMII NAUK SSSR see AKADEMIIA NAUK SSSR, INSTITUT SLAVIANOVEDENNIIA, UCHENYE ZAPISKI...

56. UCHENYE ZAPISKI PO NOVOI I NOVEISHEI ISTORII [Learned papers on modern and recent history]. A. 1955 (1958: vol. 4). Institut Istorii Akademii Nauk SSSR [Hist. Inst. of the Acad. of Sciences of the U.S.S.R.], Podsosenskii per. d. 21, Moskva B-34. Ed: A.N. Filippov. Art. on the hist. of labor, revolutionary and Communist movements in countries throughout the world, and on the social and political hist. of the underprivileged and minorities, primarily in the 19th and 20th cent. pv (c. 1.67 rub.)

UNESCO, LE COURRIER DE L'... see section on International Periodicals

VESTNIK. For titles beginning with "Vestnik," followed by the name of the publishing or sponsoring institution or society, see the respective institution or society.

57. VESTNIK DREVNEI ISTORII [Review of ancient history]. Q. 1937 (1959: no. 67-70). Institut Istorii Akademii Nauk SSSR [Hist. Inst. of the Acad. of Sciences of the U.S.S.R.], Volkhonka 14, Moskva. Ed: S.V. Kiselev. Art. on ancient hist., including the pre-Greek civilization; doc.; rev. art.; bk. rev.; biblio.; academic news and notes (including reports of conferences) from Russia and other countries; table of contents also in French; graph, illus. 9.60 rub.

58. VESTNIK ISTORII MIROVOI KUL'TURY. REVUE D'HISTOIRE DE LA CIVILISATION MONDIALE [Review of the history of world culture]. B-M. 1957 (1959: no. 13-18). Gosudarstvennoe Nauchnoe Izdatel'stvo "Bol'shaia Sovetskaia Entsiklopediia" [State Pub. House of the "Great Soviet Encyclopedia"], Moskva, for Otdelenie Istoricheskikh Nauk Akademii Nauk SSSR [Dept. of Hist. Sciences of the Acad. of Sciences of the U.S.S.R.], Moskva. Ed: A.A. Zvorykin, Pokrovskii Bul'var 8, Moskva Zh-28. Art. on the social, intellectual and cultural hist. of the world; reports on research in foreign countries; rev. of bk. and periodicals, divided into those pub. in the U.S.S.R. and those pub. in other countries; comments on the 6-vol. world hist. pub. under the sponsorship of the UNESCO; running biblio. of newly pub. bk. and periodicals in the U.S.S.R., arranged by republic; English, French or German sum.; table of contents in Russian, English and French. 9 rub.

59. VOKRUG SVETA [A round of the world]. M. TsK Vsesoiuznyi Leninskii Kommunisticheskii Soiuz Molodezhi [Central Committee of the Leninist Young Communist League of the Soviet Union], Moskva. DM 19

60. VOPROSY ARKHIVOVEDENIIA [Problems of archival science]. Nauchno-informatsionnyi biulleten' [Bulletin of scientific information]. Q. 1959 (1960: no. 6). Glavnoe Arkhivnoe Upravlenie pri Sovete Ministrov SSSR [General Directorate of Archives attached to the Council of Ministers of the U.S.S.R.], Moskva. Ed: L.I. Iakovlev. Art. on the hist., organization, activities and holdings of Soviet and foreign archives; bk. rev. p (1) 0.40 rub.

61. VOPROSY EKONOMIKI [Problems of economics]. M. Institut Ekonomiki Akademii Nauk SSSR [Inst. of Economics of the Acad. of Sciences of the U.S.S.R.], Moskva. p (1) 0.50 rub.

62. VOPROSY FILOSOFII [Problems of philosophy]. M. Institut Filosofii Akademii Nauk SSSR [Inst. of Philosophy of the Acad. of Sciences of the U.S.S.R.], Moskva. English sum.; table of contents in Russian, English, French, German and Spanish. p (1) 0.70 rub.

63. VOPROSY IAZYKOZNANIIA [Problems of linguistics]. B-M. Institut Iazykoznaniia Akademii Nauk SSSR [Inst. of Linguistics of the Acad. of Sciences of the U.S.S.R.], Moskva. Table of contents also in English and French.
p (1) 1.20 rub.

64. VOPROSY ISTORII [Problems of history]. M. 1945 (1961: no vol. indic.). Izdatel'stvo "Pravda" [Pub. House "Truth"], M. Putinkovskii per., 1/2, Moskva K-6, for Institut Istorii Akademii Nauk SSSR [Hist. Inst. of the Acad. of Sciences of the U.S.S.R.], Moskva. Ed: W.G. Trukhanovskii. Art. on hist. and historiography, with emphasis on recent Russian hist.; doc.; rev. art.; bk. rev.; news and notes of interest to historians; letters to the ed.; English sum. of major art.; table of contents also in Chinese, English, French and German.
8.40 rub. / DM 47

65. VOPROSY ISTORII KPSS [Problems of the history of the Communist Party of the Soviet Union]. B-M. 1957 (1961: vol. 5). Izdatel'stvo "Pravda," [Pub. House "Truth"], M. Putinkovskii per. 1/2, Moskva K-6, for Institut Marksizma-Leninizma pri TsK KPSS [Inst. for Marxism-Leninism attached to the Central Committee of the Communist Party of the Soviet Union], Sel'skokhoziaistvennyi proezd 4, Moskva. Ed: E.I. Bugaev. Art. on the hist. of the Communist Party in the U.S.S.R. and other countries and on labor movements; doc. and memoirs; editorials or communiques on decisions or meetings of the Central Committee and other organs of the Party; bk. rev.; biblio. of periodicals; professional news; table of contents also in Chinese, English, French and German.
4.80 rub. / DM 27

66. VOPROSY ISTORII RELIGII I ATEIZMA [Problems of the history of religion and atheism]. Irr. 1950 (mri 1956: vol. 4). Institut Istorii Akademii Nauk SSSR [Hist. Inst. of the Acad. of Sciences of the U.S.S.R.], Podsosenskii per. 21, Moskva. Art. on the hist. of the struggle against religious influences, with emphasis on the 20th cent.; doc. pv (p (1) c. DM 7.90)

67. VOPROSY SLAVIANSKOGO IAZYKOZNANIIA [Problems of Slavic linguistics]. Irr. Institut Slavianovedeniia Akademii Nauk SSSR [Inst. of Slavic Studies of the Acad. of Sciences of the U.S.S.R.], ul. Kropotkina 12, Moskva.
p (1) 0.91 rub.

ZAPISKI. For titles beginning with "Zapiski," followed by the name of the publishing or sponsoring institution or society, see the respective institution or society.

ZHURNAL MOSKOVSKOI PATRIARKHII see MOSKOVSKAIA PATRIARKHIIA, ZHURNAL...

TADZHIK S.S.R.

68. AKADEMIIA NAUK TADZHIKSKOI SSR, OTDELENIE OBSHCHESTVENNYKH NAUK, IZVESTIIA... (Izvestiia Otdeleniia Obshchestvennykh Nauk Akademii Nauk Tadzhikskoi SSR) [Communications of the Department of Social Sciences of the Academy of Sciences of the Tadzhik S.S.R.]. Irr. Izdatel'stvo Akademii Nauk Tadzhikskoi SSR, Stalinabad. pv (p (1) c. 1.09 rub.)

IZVESTIIA OTDELENIIA OBSHCHESTVENNYKH NAUK AKADEMII NAUK TADZHIKSKOI SSR see AKADEMIIA NAUK TADZHIKSKOI SSR, OTDELENIE OBSHCHESTVENNYKH NAUK, IZVESTIIA...

69. KOMMUNISTI TOCHIKISTON [Tadzhik Communist]. M. TsK KP Tadzhikistana [Central Committee of the Communist Party of Tadzhikistan], Stalinabad. In Tadzhik. DM 5

TURKMEN S.S.R.

70. AKADEMIIA NAUK TURKMENSKOI SSR, IZVESTIIA... (Izvestiia Akademii Nauk Turkmenskoi SSR) [Communications of the Academy of Sciences of the Turkmen S.S.R.]. Seriia obshchestvennykh nauk [Social science series]. B-M. Akademiia Nauk Turkmenskoi SSR, Ashkhabad. In Russian. p (1) 0.50 rub.

IZVESTIIA AKADEMII NAUK TURKMENSKOI SSR see AKADEMIIA NAUK TURKMENSKOI SSR, IZVESTIIA...

71. TURKMENISTAN KOMMUNISTI [Communist of Turkmenistan]. M. TsK KP Turkmenistana [Central Committee of the Communist Party of Turkmenistan], ul. Karla Marksa 22, Ashkhabad. In Turkmen. p (1) 0.20 rub. / DM 5 p.a.

UKRAINIAN S.S.R.

72. AKADEMIIA NAUK UKRAINS'KOI RSR, DOPOVIDI... (Dopovidi Akademii Nauk Ukrains'koi RSR) [Bulletins of the Academy of Sciences of the Ukrainian S.S.R.]. M. Vydavnytstvo Akademii Nauk Ukrains'koi RSR [Pub. House of the Acad. of Sciences of the Ukrainian S.S.R.], Vul. Lenina 42, Kiev. In Ukrainian; Russian sum. p (1) 0.50 rub.

73. AKADEMIIA NAUK UKRAINS'KOI RADIANS'KOI SOTSIALISTYCHNOI RESPUBLIKY, VISNYK... (Visnyk Akademii Nauk Ukrains'koi Radians'koi Sotsialistychnoi Respubliky) [Journal of the Academy of Sciences of the Ukrainian Soviet Socialist Republic]. M. Vydavnytstvo Akademii Nauk Ukrains'koi RSR [Pub. House of the Acad. of Sciences of the Ukrainian S.S.R.], Vul. Repina 3, Kiev. Natural and social sciences and the humanities; in Ukrainian. 4.80 rub.

DOPOVIDI AKADEMII NAUK UKRAINS'KOI RSR see AKADEMIIA NAUK UKRAINS'KOI RSR, DOPOVIDI...

74. INSTYTUT ISTORII, NAUKOVI ZAPYSKY... (Naukovi Zapysky Instytutu Istorii) [Learned papers of the Institute of History]. A. 1943. Instytut Istorii Akademii Nauk Ukrains'koi RSR [Inst. of Hist. of the Acad. of Sciences of the Ukrainian S.S.R.], Kiev. Art. on Ukrainian hist.; bk. rev.; news of the inst.; in Ukrainian. pv

75. KIEVSKII GOS. UNIVERSITET IM. T. G. SHEVCHENKO, ISTORIKO-FILOSOFSKII FAKUL'TET. NAUCHNYE ZAPISKI [**T.G.Shevchenko State University of Kiev, Historical-Philosophical Faculty. Learned papers]. Irr.**

Istoriko-Filosofskii Fakul'tet, Kievskii Gos. Universitet im. T. G. Shevchenko, Kiev. In Ukrainian or Russian. pv

76. KOMMUNIST UKRAINY [Communist of the Ukraine]. M. Izdatel'stvo "Radians'ka Ukraina" [Pub. House "The Soviet Ukraine"], Kiev, for TsK KP Ukrainy [Central Committee of the Communist Party of the Ukraine], ul. Lenina 19, Kiev. Appears in two separate editions, one in Russian and the other in Ukrainian. DM 5

77. LUTSKII GOS. PEDAGOGICHESKII INSTITUT IM. LESI UKRAINKY. NAUCHNYE ZAPISKI [Lesia Ukrainka State Pedagogical Institute of Lutsk. Learned papers]. Istoriko-filologicheskaia seriia [Historical-philological series]. Irr. Lutskii Gos. Pedagogicheskii Institut im. Lesi Ukrainky, Lutsk. In Ukrainian.

78. NARODNA TVORCHIST' TA ETNOGRAFIIA [People's art and ethnography]. Q. Vydavnytstvo Akademii Nauk Ukrains'koi RSR [Pub. House of the Acad. of Sciences of the Ukrainian S.S.R.], Byl. Lenina 42, Kiev, for Instytut Mystetstvoznavstva, Fol'kloru ta Etnografii Akademii Nauk Ukrains'koi RSR [Inst. of Art, Folklore and Ethnography of the Acad. of Sciences of the Ukrainian S.S.R.], Kiev. In Ukrainian. 2.40 rub.

NAUCHNYE ZAPISKI. For titles beginning with "Nauchnye zapiski," followed by the name of the publishing or sponsoring institution or society, see the respective institution or society.

NAUKOVI ZAPYSKY INSTYTUTU ISTORII see INSTYTUT ISTORII, NAUKOVI ZAPYSKY...

UKRAINSKY ZBIRNYK see section on the Federal Republic of Germany

79. UKRAINS'KYI ISTORYCHNYI ZHURNAL [Ukrainian historical journal]. B-M. 1957 (1960: no vol. indic.). Vydavnytstvo Akademii Nauk Ukrains'koi RSR [Pub. House of the Acad. of Sciences of the Ukrainian S.S.R.], Kiev, for Instytut Istorii Akademii Nauk Ukrains'koi RSR [Hist. Inst. of the Acad. of Sciences of the Ukrainian S.S.R.], Instytut Istorii Partii TsK KP Ukrainy [Inst. of Party Hist. of the Central Committee of the Communist Party of the Ukraine], and Filial Instytutu Marksyzmu-Leniniszmy pri TsK KPRS [Branch of the Inst. of Marxism-Leninism attached to the Central Committee of the Communist Party of the Soviet Union]. Ed: F.P. Shevchenko. Art. on Ukrainian hist., mostly modern, with emphasis on the period since the Russian Revolution; discussions on didactical and methodological problems of teaching hist.; doc.; rev. art.; bk. rev.; biblio.; news and notes, chiefly on the research work of Ukrainian inst.; in Ukrainian; table of contents in Ukrainian and Russian. p (1) 0.60 rub.

VISNYK AKADEMII NAUK UKRAINS'KOI RADIANS'KOI SOTSIALISTYCHNOI RESPUBLIKY see AKADEMIIA NAUK UKRAINS'KOI RADIANS'KOI SOTSIALISTYCHNOI RESPUBLIKY, VISNYK...

UZBEK S.S.R.

80. AKADEMIIA NAUK UZBEKSKOI SSR, DOKLADY... (Doklady Akademii Nauk Uzbekskoi SSR) [Bulletins of the Academy of Sciences of the Uzbek S.S.R.]. M. Izdatel'stvo Akademii Nauk Uzbekskoi SSR, Kuibysheva 15, Tashkent. p (1) 0.30 rub.

81. AKADEMIIA NAUK UZBEKSKOI SSR, IZVESTIIA... (Izvestiia Akademii Nauk Uzbekskoi SSR) [Communications of the Academy of Sciences of the Uzbek S.S.R.]. Obshchestvennye nauki v Uzbekistane [Social sciences of Uzbekistan]. M (B-M prior to 1961). Akademiia Nauk Uzbekskoi SSR, Tashkent. In Russian. Subtitle prior to 1961: Seriia obshchestvennykh nauk [Social science series].
p (1) 0.40 rub.

DOKLADY AKADEMII NAUK UZBEKSKOI SSR see AKADEMIIA NAUK UZBEKSKOI SSR, DOKLADY...

IZVESTIIA AKADEMII NAUK UZBEKSKOI SSR see AKADEMIIA NAUK UZBEKSKOI SSR, IZVESTIIA...

INDEX OF PERIODICALS

INDEX OF PERIODICALS

Numbers cited after titles refer to pages.

B

C

D

E

F

G

H

I

J

K

L

M

N

Q

R

S

T

U

V

W

Y

Z

Readers searching for a periodical are also advised to see
the ADDENDA sections
included at the end of some lists.

List of Countries

A separate section on International Periodicals appears on page 3.